Lecture Notes in Computer Science

Lecture Notes in Artificial Intelligence 14740

Founding Editor

Jörg Siekmann

Series Editors

Randy Goebel, *University of Alberta, Edmonton, Canada*
Wolfgang Wahlster, *DFKI, Berlin, Germany*
Zhi-Hua Zhou, *Nanjing University, Nanjing, China*

The series Lecture Notes in Artificial Intelligence (LNAI) was established in 1988 as a topical subseries of LNCS devoted to artificial intelligence.

The series publishes state-of-the-art research results at a high level. As with the LNCS mother series, the mission of the series is to serve the international R & D community by providing an invaluable service, mainly focused on the publication of conference and workshop proceedings and postproceedings.

Christoph Benzmüller · Marijn J. H. Heule ·
Renate A. Schmidt
Editors

Automated Reasoning

12th International Joint Conference, IJCAR 2024
Nancy, France, July 3–6, 2024
Proceedings, Part II

Springer

Editors
Christoph Benzmüller
Otto-Friedrich-Universität Bamberg
Bamberg, Germany

Marijn J. H. Heule
Computer Science Department
Carnegie Mellon University
Pittsburgh, PA, USA

Renate A. Schmidt
University of Manchester
Manchester, UK

ISSN 0302-9743 ISSN 1611-3349 (electronic)
Lecture Notes in Artificial Intelligence
ISBN 978-3-031-63500-7 ISBN 978-3-031-63501-4 (eBook)
https://doi.org/10.1007/978-3-031-63501-4

LNCS Sublibrary: SL7 – Artificial Intelligence

This Springer imprint is published by the registered company Springer Nature Switzerland AG
The registered company address is: Gewerbestrasse 11, 6330 Cham, Switzerland

Preface

This volume contains the papers of the 12th International Joint Conference on Automated Reasoning (IJCAR) held in Nancy, France, during July 3–6, 2024. IJCAR is the premier international joint conference on all aspects of automated reasoning, including foundations, implementations, and applications, comprising several leading conferences and workshops. IJCAR 2024 brought together the Conference on Automated Deduction (CADE), the International Symposium on Frontiers of Combining Systems (FroCoS), and the International Conference on Automated Reasoning with Analytic Tableaux and Related Methods (TABLEAUX).

Previous IJCAR conferences were held in Siena, Italy (2001), Cork, Ireland (2004), Seattle, USA (2006), Sydney, Australia (2008), Edinburgh, UK (2010), Manchester, UK (2012), Vienna, Austria (2014), Coimbra, Portugal (2016), Oxford, UK (2018), Paris, France (2020, virtual), and Haifa, Israel (2022).

IJCAR 2024 received 115 submissions (130 abstracts) out of which 45 papers were accepted (with an overall acceptance rate of 39%): 39 regular papers (out of 96 regular papers submitted, resulting in a regular paper acceptance rate of 41%) and 6 short papers (out of 19 short papers submitted, resulting in a short paper acceptance rate of 31%). Each submission was assigned to at least three Program Committee members and was reviewed in single-blind mode. All submissions were evaluated according to the following criteria: relevance, originality, significance, correctness, and readability. The review process included a feedback/rebuttal period, during which authors had the option to respond to reviewer comments.

In addition to the accepted papers, the IJCAR 2024 program included three invited talks:

- Jeremy Avigad (Carnegie Mellon University, USA) on "Automated Reasoning for Mathematics",
- Laura Kovács (TU Wien, Austria) on "Induction in Saturation", and
- Geoff Sutcliffe (University of Miami, USA) on "Stepping Stones in the TPTP World".

This year marks the 30th anniversary of the CADE ATP System Competition (CASC), which was conceived in 1994 after CADE-12 in Nancy, France, when Christian Suttner and Geoff Sutcliffe were sitting on a bench under a tree in Parc de la Pépinière. In the 28 competitions since then, CASC has been a catalyst for research and development, providing an inspiring environment for personal interaction between ATP researchers and users. A special event took place to celebrate this anniversary.

In addition to the main programme, IJCAR 2024 hosted ten workshops, which took place on July 1–2, and two systems competitions (CASC and Termination). The SAT/SMT/AR 2024 Summer School was held in Nancy the week prior to IJCAR 2024.

The Best Paper Award of IJCAR 2024 went to Hugo Férée, Iris van der Giessen, Sam van Gool, and Ian Shillito for the paper "Mechanised Uniform Interpolation for

Modal Logics K, GL, and iSL". The Best Student Paper Award went to Johannes Niederhauser (with Chad E. Brown and Cezary Kaliszyk) for the paper entitled "Tableaux for Automated Reasoning in Dependently-Typed Higher-Order Logic".

Another highlight of the conference was the presentation of the 2024 Herbrand Award for Distinguished Contributions to Automated Reasoning to Armin Biere (Albert-Ludwigs-University Freiburg, Germany) in recognition of "his outstanding contributions to satisfiability solving, including innovative applications, methods for formula pre- and in-processing and proof generation, and a series of award-winning solvers, with deep impact on model checking and verification."

The 2024 Bill McCune PhD Award was given to Katherine Kosaian for the PhD thesis "Formally Verifying Algorithms for Real Quantifier Elimination", completed at Carnegie Mellon University, USA, in 2023.

The main institutions supporting IJCAR 2024 were the University of Lorraine and the Inria research center at the University of Lorraine. We also thank as sponsors: the research laboratory for computer science in Nancy (LORIA), a joint research unit of the University of Lorraine, CNRS, and Inria, its Formal Methods Department, and Métropole du Grand Nancy. For hosting the conference, we thank IDMC Nancy.

We would also like to acknowledge the generous sponsorship of Springer and Imandra Inc., and the support by EasyChair. Finally, we are indebted to the entire IJCAR 2024 Organizing Team for their assistance with the local organization and general management of the conference, especially Didier Galmiche, Stephan Merz, Christophe Ringeissen (Conference Co-Chairs), Sophie Tourret (Workshop, Tutorial and Competition Chair), Peter Lammich (Publicity Chair) and Anne-Lise Charbonnier and Sabrina Lemaire (main administrative support).

May 2024

Christoph Benzmüller
Marijn J. H. Heule
Renate A. Schmidt

Organization

Conference Chairs

Didier Galmiche	University of Lorraine, France
Stephan Merz	Inria, University of Lorraine, France
Christophe Ringeissen	Inria, University of Lorraine, France

Program Committee Chairs

Christoph Benzmüller	Otto-Friedrich-Universität Bamberg and FU Berlin, Germany
Marijn J. H. Heule	Carnegie Mellon University, USA
Renate A. Schmidt	University of Manchester, UK

Workshop, Tutorial and Competition Chair

Sophie Tourret	Inria, France and Max Planck Institute for Informatics, Germany

Publicity Chair

Peter Lammich	University of Twente, The Netherlands

Local Arrangements

Anne-Lise Charbonnier	Inria, France
Sabrina Lemaire	Inria, France

Steering Committee

Arnon Avron	Tel-Aviv University, Israel
Franz Baader	TU Dresden, Germany
Jürgen Giesl	RWTH Aachen University, Germany
Marijn J. H. Heule	Carnegie Mellon University, USA

Lawrence Paulson	University of Cambridge, UK
Elaine Pimentel	University College London, UK
Christophe Ringeissen	Inria, University of Lorraine, France
Renate A. Schmidt	University of Manchester, UK

Program Committee

Franz Baader	TU Dresden, Germany
Haniel Barbosa	Universidade Federal de Minas Gerais, Brazil
Christoph Benzmüller	Otto-Friedrich-Universität Bamberg and FU Berlin, Germany
Armin Biere	University of Freiburg, Germany
Nikolaj Bjørner	Microsoft, USA
Jasmin Blanchette	Ludwig-Maximilians-Universität München, Germany
Maria Paola Bonacina	Università degli Studi di Verona, Italy
Florent Capelli	Université d'Artois, France
Agata Ciabattoni	TU Wien, Austria
Clare Dixon	University of Manchester, UK
Pascal Fontaine	Université de Liège, Belgium
Carsten Fuhs	Birkbeck, University of London, UK
Didier Galmiche	University of Lorraine, France
Silvio Ghilardi	Università degli Studi di Milano, Italy
Jürgen Giesl	RWTH Aachen University, Germany
Arie Gurfinkel	University of Waterloo, Canada
Marijn J. H. Heule	Carnegie Mellon University, USA
Andrzej Indrzejczak	University of Lodz, Poland
Moa Johansson	Chalmers University of Technology, Sweden
Daniela Kaufmann	TU Wien, Austria
Patrick Koopmann	Vrije Universiteit Amsterdam, The Netherlands
Konstantin Korovin	University of Manchester, UK
Peter Lammich	University of Twente, The Netherlands
Martin Lange	University of Kassel, Germany
Tim Lyon	Technische Universität Dresden, Germany
Kuldeep S. Meel	University of Toronto, Canada
Stephan Merz	Inria, University of Lorraine, France
Cláudia Nalon	University of Brasília, Brazil
Aina Niemetz	Stanford University, USA
Albert Oliveras	Universitat Politècnica de Catalunya, Spain
Xavier Parent	TU Wien, Austria
Nicolas Peltier	CNRS, Laboratory of Informatics of Grenoble, France

Rafael Peñaloza	University of Milano-Bicocca, Italy
Elaine Pimentel	University College London, UK
André Platzer	Karlsruhe Institute of Technology, Germany
Andrei Popescu	University of Sheffield, UK
Florian Rabe	FAU Erlangen-Nürnberg, Germany
Giles Reger	Amazon Web Services, USA and University of Manchester, UK
Giselle Reis	Carnegie Mellon University, Qatar
Andrew Reynolds	University of Iowa, USA
Christophe Ringeissen	Inria, University of Lorraine, France
Philipp Rümmer	University of Regensburg, Germany
Uli Sattler	University of Manchester, UK
Tanja Schindler	University of Basel, Switzerland
Renate A. Schmidt	University of Manchester. UK
Claudia Schon	Hochschule Trier, Germany
Stephan Schulz	DHBW Stuttgart, Germany
Roberto Sebastiani	University of Trento, Italy
Martina Seidl	Johannes Kepler University Linz, Austria
Viorica Sofronie-Stokkermans	University of Koblenz, Germany
Alexander Steen	University of Greifswald, Germany
Martin Suda	Czech Technical University in Prague, Czech Republic
Yong Kiam Tan	Institute for Infocomm Research, A*STAR, Singapore
Sophie Tourret	Inria, France and Max Planck Institute for Informatics, Germany
Josef Urban	Czech Technical University in Prague, Czech Republic
Uwe Waldmann	Max Planck Institute for Informatics, Germany
Christoph Weidenbach	Max Planck Institute for Informatics, Germany
Sarah Winkler	Free University of Bozen-Bolzano, Italy
Yoni Zohar	Bar-Ilan University, Israel

Additional Reviewers

Noah Abou El Wafa
Takahito Aoto
Martin Avanzini
Philippe Balbiani
Lasse Blaauwbroek
Frédéric Blanqui
Thierry Boy de La Tour
Marvin Brieger
Martin Bromberger
James Brotherston
Chad E. Brown
Florian Bruse
Filip Bártek
Julie Cailler

Cameron Calk
Christophe Chareton
Jiaoyan Chen
Karel Chvalovský
Tiziano Dalmonte
Anupam Das
Martin Desharnais
Paulius Dilkas
Marie Duflot
Yotam Dvir
Chelsea Edmonds
Sólrún Halla Einarsdóttir
Clemens Eisenhofer
Zafer Esen
Camillo Fiorentini
Mathias Fleury
Stef Frijters
Florian Frohn
Nikolaos Galatos
Alessandro Gianola
Matt Griffin
Alberto Griggio
Liye Guo
Raúl Gutiérrez
Xavier Généreux
Hans-Dieter Hiep
Jochen Hoenicke
Jonathan Huerta y Munive
Ullrich Hustadt
Cezary Kaliszyk
Jan-Christoph Kassing
Michael Kinyon
Lydia Kondylidou
Boris Konev
George Kourtis
Francesco Kriegel
Falko Kötter
Timo Lang
Jonathan Laurent
Daniel Le Berre
Jannis Limperg
Xinghan Liu
Anela Lolic
Etienne Lozes
Salvador Lucas
Andreas Lööw
Kenji Maillard
Sérgio Marcelino
Andrew M. Marshall
Gabriele Masina
Marcel Moosbrugger
Barbara Morawska
Johannes Oetsch
Eugenio Orlandelli
Jens Otten
Adam Pease
Bartosz Piotrowski
Enguerrand Prebet
Siddharth Priya
Long Qian
Jakob Rath
Colin Rothgang
Reuben Rowe
Jan Frederik Schaefer
Johannes Schoisswohl
Marcel Schütz
Florian Sextl
Ian Shillito
Nicholas Smallbone
Giuseppe Spallitta
Sergei Stepanenko
Georg Struth
Matteo Tesi
Guilherme Toledo
Patrick Trentin
Hari Govind Vediramana Krishnan
Laurent Vigneron
Renaud Vilmart
Dominik Wehr
Tobias Winkler
Frank Wolter
Akihisa Yamada
Michal Zawidzki

Contents – Part II

Contents – Part I

Invited Contributions

Theorem Proving and Tools

Intuitionistic Logics and Modal Logics

Model Construction for Modal Clauses

Ullrich Hustadt[2(✉)], Fabio Papacchini[3], Cláudia Nalon[1], and Clare Dixon[4]

[1] Department of Computer Science, University of Brasília, Brasília, Brazil
nalon@unb.br

[2] Department of Computer Science, University of Liverpool, Liverpool, UK
U.Hustadt@liverpool.ac.uk

[3] School of Computing and Communications, Lancaster University in Leipzig, Leipzig, Germany
f.papacchini@lancaster.ac.uk

[4] Department of Computer Science, University of Manchester, Manchester, UK
clare.dixon@manchester.ac.uk

Abstract. We present deterministic model construction algorithms for sets of modal clauses saturated with respect to three refinements of the modal-layered resolution calculus implemented in the prover K_SP. The model construction algorithms are inspired by the Bachmair-Ganzinger method for constructing a model for a set of ground first-order clauses saturated with respect to ordered resolution with selection. The challenge is that the inference rules of the modal-layered resolution calculus for modal operators are more restrictive than an adaptation of ordered resolution with selection for these would be. While these model construction algorithms provide an alternative means to proving completeness of the calculus, our main interest is the provision of a 'certificate' for satisfiable modal formulae that can be independently checked to assure a user that the result of K_SP is correct. This complements the existing provision of proofs for unsatisfiable modal formulae.

1 Introduction

Propositional modal logics can be applied to formalise and reason about a wide range of applications, including programming languages [22], knowledge representation and reasoning [4,9,23], verification of distributed systems [8,10,11] and terminological reasoning [26]. For such applications, it is expected that the underlying reasoning tool may be able to provide *certification* for their answer with respect to a particular problem. While at least one kind of certificate is expected to be produced, either in the form of a *proof* or a *model*, the production of both not only helps with the task related to the particular application (e.g. the generation of counter-examples in verification problems) but also assures the user that a reasoning tool has produced the right result as those certificates can be independently and automatically checked. Given the complexity of reasoning tools, with most of them implementing sophisticated optimization procedures which are very difficult to check for correctness, it is not surprising that the

C. Benzmüller et al. (Eds.): IJCAR 2024, LNAI 14740, pp. 3–23, 2024.
https://doi.org/10.1007/978-3-031-63501-4_1

community in automated reasoning has been encouraging the extraction of both kind of certificates: some tracks in the SAT competition[1] require both proofs and models; the same approach is argued for QBF reasoning tools [29]; and this is also required in some tracks of the CASC competition [32,33], with standards being currently under discussion[2].

There are several implemented tools for basic propositional modal logic K_n, the logic considered in this paper. However, and somehow surprisingly, most of state-of-the-art tools do not produce any kind of certificate (e.g. CEGARBOX [6]); produce only partial information on models (e.g. Spartacus [7], InKreSAT [12]; see also discussion in [14]); or, as in our case, produce only proofs ($\mathrm{K_SP}$ [17]). There are fully certified tools that do produce models and proofs (e.g. [34]), but their performance is usually not comparable to state-of-the-art provers.

In this paper we present the needed theoretical results that will allow us to implement certification for satisfiable problems in $\mathrm{K_SP}$ [19]. Our prover implements both the resolution calculi presented in [16] as well as the modal layered calculus MLR presented in [17]. Refinements, such as negative, positive, and ordered resolution are also implemented. As with other resolution-based systems, proofs produced by $\mathrm{K_SP}$ are easily readable and verifiable. However, as mentioned, model extraction has never been implemented. One of the reasons is that although the completeness proofs for the calculi in [16,17] are constructive they do not yield efficient procedures. Very briefly, those proofs are similar to canonical constructions for axiomatic proof systems and rely on the construction of some structures over the subsets of consistent formulae of an input formula (in clausal form), and even in the best case require exponential time and space.

Here we present novel model construction algorithms from saturated sets of clauses produced by the positive, negative or order resolution refinements of MLR. These refinements require different normal forms: SNF^-_{ml}, SNF^+_{ml}, and SNF^{++}_{ml}, respectively. We first show how to obtain models from sets of SNF^{++}_{ml} clauses saturated with respect to ordered resolution refinement of MLR (Sect. 3). This results in a deterministic procedure inspired by the Bachmair-Ganzinger model construction for ground first-order clauses [2]. For positive resolution, we adapt the procedure for SNF^{++}_{ml} clauses by constructing separate orderings for each world in a model (Sect. 4). We then obtain a procedure for negative resolution by flipping the polarity of literals in SNF^+_{ml} clauses and reusing the procedure for positive resolution (Sect. 5). From these procedures we obtain alternative completeness proofs for ordered and negative resolution; and provide the first completeness proof for positive resolution. Moreover, all procedures are deterministic and suitable for implementation.

The paper is structured as follows. In Sect. 2 we give details of the logic, resolution rules and resolution refinements. Sections 3, 4 and 5 provide the model construction algorithms for each refinement. We discuss our approach in relation to the Bachmair-Ganzinger method and consider complexity in Sect. 6. Section 7 presents how to perform model construction for extensions of basic modal logic. Finally, we draw conclusions and discuss future work in Sect. 8.

[1] https://satcompetition.github.io/2022/rules.html.
[2] https://www.tptp.org/TPTP/Proposals/InterpretationsModels.shtml.

2 Preliminaries

Let P be a denumerable set of *propositional symbols*. Let $A_n = \{1, \ldots, n\}$, with $n \in \mathbb{N}$, be a finite, fixed set of *agents*. The set of modal formulae over P and A_n is then the least set containing the two propositional constants **true** and **false**, all elements of P, and the formulae $\neg\varphi$, $(\varphi \wedge \psi)$, $(\varphi \vee \psi)$, $(\varphi \to \psi)$, $[a]\varphi$, and $\langle a\rangle\varphi$ provided φ and ψ are modal formulae and $a \in A_n$. The set of literals over P is $L_P = \{p, \neg p \mid p \in P\}$. For $p \in P$, a literal p is a *positive literal* and a literal $\neg p$ is a *negative literal*. A *modal literal* is $[a]l$ or $\langle a\rangle l$, for $a \in A_n$ and $l \in L_P$.

The semantics of modal formulae is provided by Kripke structures. A *Kripke structure* M over P and A_n is a tuple $\langle W, \{R_a\}_{a\in A_n}, V\rangle$ where W is a non-empty set of *worlds*, each *accessibility relation* R_a, $a \in A_n$, is a binary relation on W, and the *valuation* V is a function mapping each propositional symbol in P to a subset $V(p)$ of W. If $(w, w') \in R_a$, written wR_aw', we say w' is an *a-successor* of w; we may omit the index a when there is no need to distinguish the relation R_a and just say w' is a successor world of w.

Satisfaction (or truth) of a formula at a world w of a Kripke structure $M = \langle W, \{R_a\}_{a\in A_n}, V\rangle$ is inductively defined by:

$$
\begin{array}{ll}
\langle M, w\rangle \models \mathbf{true}; & \langle M, w\rangle \not\models \mathbf{false}; \\
\langle M, w\rangle \models p & \text{iff } w \in V(p), \text{ where } p \in P; \\
\langle M, w\rangle \models \neg\varphi & \text{iff } \langle M, w\rangle \not\models \varphi; \\
\langle M, w\rangle \models (\varphi \wedge \psi) & \text{iff } \langle M, w\rangle \models \varphi \text{ and } \langle M, w\rangle \models \psi; \\
\langle M, w\rangle \models (\varphi \vee \psi) & \text{iff } \langle M, w\rangle \models \varphi \text{ or } \langle M, w\rangle \models \psi; \\
\langle M, w\rangle \models (\varphi \to \psi) & \text{iff } \langle M, w\rangle \models \neg\varphi \text{ or } \langle M, w\rangle \models \psi; \\
\langle M, w\rangle \models [a]\varphi & \text{iff for every } v,\ wR_av \text{ implies } \langle M, v\rangle \models \varphi; \\
\langle M, w\rangle \models \langle a\rangle\varphi & \text{iff there is } v,\ wR_av \text{ and } \langle M, v\rangle \models \varphi.
\end{array}
$$

If $\langle M, w\rangle \models \varphi$ holds then M is a *model* of φ, φ is *true at* w *in* M and M *satisfies* φ. A modal formula φ is *(locally) satisfiable* iff there exists a Kripke structure M and a world w in M such that $\langle M, w\rangle \models \varphi$.

A *tree Kripke structure* M is an ordered pair $\langle\langle W, \{R_a\}_{a\in A_n}, V\rangle, w_0\rangle$ where $w_0 \in W$ and $\bigcup_{a\in A_n} R_a$ is a tree, that is, a directed acyclic connected graph where each node has at most one predecessor, with *root* w_0. Finally, M is a *tree Kripke model* of a modal formula φ iff $\langle\langle W, \{R_a\}_{a\in A_n}, V\rangle, w_0\rangle \models \varphi$. To simplify notation, in the following we write $\langle W, \{R_a\}_{a\in A_n}, V, w_0\rangle$ instead of $\langle\langle W, \{R_a\}_{a\in A_n}, V\rangle, w_0\rangle$. In a tree Kripke structure with root w_0 for every world $w_k \in W$ there is exactly one path $\boldsymbol{w}$ connecting w_0 and w_k; the *modal level of* w_k *(in* M*), denoted by* $\mathsf{ml}_M(w_k)$, is given by $\mathsf{len}(\boldsymbol{w})$. By $M[ml]$ we denote the set of worlds that are at a modal level ml in M, that is, $M[ml] = \{w \in W \mid \mathsf{ml}_M(w) = ml\}$.

In [18], we have introduced the *Separated Normal Form with Modal Levels*, SNF_{ml}, for modal formulae. For the local satisfiability problem, clauses in SNF_{ml} are in one of the following forms:

- Literal clause $\quad ml : \bigvee_{b=1}^{r} l_b$

- Positive a-clause $\quad ml : l' \rightarrow [a]l$
- Negative a-clause $\quad ml : l' \rightarrow \langle a \rangle l$

where $ml \in \mathbb{N}$ and l, l', $l_b \in L_P$, $1 \leq b \leq r$, $r \in \mathbb{N}$. We denote by ml : **false** an *empty clause*, that is, a literal clause with $r = 0$. Positive and negative a-clauses are together known as *modal a-clauses*. By a positive (negative) modal clause we mean a positive (negative) a-clause for an arbitrary agent $a \in A_n$. We also use $ml : l' \rightarrow (a)l$ to denote a modal a-clause that can either be a positive or a negative a-clause.

A tree Kripke structure M satisfies a clause $ml : \psi$ in SNF_{ml}, written $M \models ml : \psi$ iff for every $w \in M[ml]$, $\langle M, w \rangle \models \psi$. M satisfies a finite set Φ of clauses in SNF_{ml} iff for every $ml : \psi$ in Φ, M satisfies $ml : \psi$. We then call M a Kripke model of Φ. Finally, a set Φ of clauses in SNF_{ml} is satisfiable if there exists a tree Kripke structure M that satisfies Φ.

Theorem 1 ([17,18]). *Let φ be a modal formula. Then there exists a finite set Φ of clauses in SNF_{ml} such that φ is satisfiable iff Φ is satisfiable and if a tree Kripke structure M is a Kripke model of Φ then M is also a Kripke model of φ.*

The transformation of a modal formula φ into an equi-satisfiable set Φ of clauses in SNF_{ml} proceeds by replacing complex subformulae by new *surrogate propositional symbols* and including into Φ clauses defining those new symbols.

Given a finite set Φ of SNF_{ml} clauses, by P_Φ and L_P^Φ we denote the set of propositional symbols occurring in Φ and the set of propositional literals over P_Φ, respectively. For $ml \in \mathbb{N}$, by $\Phi[ml]$ we denote $\{ml : \psi \mid ml : \psi \in \Phi\}$. Then by $\Phi^{lit}[ml]$, $\Phi^{pos}[ml]$, and $\Phi^{neg}[ml]$ we denote the set of all literal clauses, all positive modal clauses, and all negative modal clauses in $\Phi[ml]$, respectively. The *maximal modal level* $\max_{ML}(\Phi)$ of Φ is $\max(\{ml + 1 \mid ml : \psi \in \Phi$ and $ml : \psi$ is a modal clause$\})$ and we assume $\max(\emptyset) = 0$.

In [18] we have also introduced a resolution calculus to reason with SNF_{ml}, the modal-layered resolution (MLR) calculus. Table 1 shows the inference rules of this calculus restricted to the labels occurring in the normal form defined above. We require that clauses are kept in simplified form, that is, if $ml \in \mathbb{N}$ and D is a (possibly empty) disjunction of literals, and $l \in L_P$, then: $ml : D \vee l \vee l$ simplifies to $ml : D \vee l$; $ml : D \vee$ **false** simplifies to $ml : D$; and $ml : D \vee l \vee \neg l$ and $ml : D \vee$ **true** simplify to ml : **true**.

Let C and D be disjunctions of propositional literals. A clause $ml : C$ *subsumes* a clause $ml : D$ if and only if D is of the form $C \vee C'$ where C' is a possibly empty disjunction of propositional literals.

Let Φ be a set of clauses in SNF_{ml}. A *derivation* by MLR from Φ is a sequence of sets $\Phi = \Phi_0, \Phi_1, \ldots$ where for each $i > 0$, either (i) $\Phi_{i+1} = \Phi_i \cup \{ml : \psi\}$ where $ml : \psi$ is the resolvent obtained by an application of one of the rules in Table 1 to premises in Φ_i, $ml : \psi$ is in simplified form, $ml : \psi$ is not subsumed by a clause in Φ_i, and $ml : \psi$ is not a tautology, or (ii) $\Phi_{i+1} = \Phi_i - \{ml : \psi\}$ where $ml : \psi$ is subsumed by a clause in $\Phi_i - \{ml : \psi\}$.

A set of clauses Φ in SNF_{ml} is *saturated with respect to MLR* if any further application of the inference rules LRES, MRES, GEN1, GEN2 and GEN3 generates

Table 1. Inference rules of the Modal Layered Resolution (MLR) calculus

$$\mathsf{LRES}: \frac{\begin{array}{c} ml : D \vee l \\ ml : D' \vee \neg l \end{array}}{ml : D \vee D'} \qquad \mathsf{MRES}: \frac{\begin{array}{c} ml : l_1 \to [a]l \\ ml : l_2 \to \langle a \rangle \neg l \end{array}}{ml : \neg l_1 \vee \neg l_2} \qquad \mathsf{GEN2}: \frac{\begin{array}{c} ml : l'_1 \to [a]l_1 \\ ml : l'_2 \to [a]\neg l_1 \\ ml : l'_3 \to \langle a \rangle l_2 \end{array}}{ml : \neg l'_1 \vee \neg l'_2 \vee \neg l'_3}$$

$$\mathsf{GEN1}: \frac{\begin{array}{c} ml : l'_1 \to [a]\neg l_1 \\ \vdots \\ ml : l'_m \to [a]\neg l_m \\ ml : l' \to \langle a \rangle \neg l \\ ml+1 : l_1 \vee \ldots \vee l_m \vee l \end{array}}{ml : \neg l'_1 \vee \ldots \vee \neg l'_m \vee \neg l'} \qquad \mathsf{GEN3}: \frac{\begin{array}{c} ml : l'_1 \to [a]\neg l_1 \\ \vdots \\ ml : l'_m \to [a]\neg l_m \\ ml : l' \to \langle a \rangle l \\ ml+1 : l_1 \vee \ldots \vee l_m \end{array}}{ml : \neg l'_1 \vee \ldots \vee \neg l'_m \vee \neg l'}$$

a clause already in Φ or subsumed by a clause in Φ. A set of clauses Φ' in SNF_{ml} is the *saturation* of Φ with respect to MLR if there is a derivation $\Phi = \Phi_0, \ldots, \Phi_n = \Phi'$ by MLR from Φ such that Φ' is saturated with respect to MLR.

Just as for propositional clausal logic, to improve the efficiency of the MLR calculus it is important to restrict applications of the LRES rule, that is, to use a *refinement* of this rule. However, when doing so it is not enough to ensure that from a set of literal clauses that logically implies a clause of the form ml : **false** we can derive that clause. Instead we have to make sure that all literal clauses that could be used as premises for GEN1 and GEN3 can still be derived. A sufficient, though not necessary, condition for that is to ensure that the refinement of LRES is consequence complete.

In [17] we have considered three refinements of propositional resolution as a basis for refinements of LRES:

- **Negative Resolution** [24] is a special case of semantic resolution [30], which restricts clause selection by using an interpretation as a guide. For the classical case, given an interpretation I, the (binary) *semantic resolution rule* allows to derive $D \vee D'$ from $D \vee l$ and $D' \vee \neg l$ provided one of the clauses in the premises is an *electron, that is, a clause which evaluates to false under* I. By taking $I(p) = true$, for all propositional symbols p, semantic resolution corresponds to *negative* resolution, that is, the electron is a clause containing only negative literals. Semantic resolution is complete irrespective of the interpretation chosen to guide the search for a proof [30]. Moreover, semantic resolution is also *consequence complete* [31]. The following theorem, which follows directly from the consequence completeness of semantic resolution, holds:

Theorem 2 ([31, Theorem 8]). *If a clause C is a prime consequence of a finite set Φ of clauses and contains no negative (positive) literals, then there is a positive (negative) resolution derivation of C from Φ.*

Theorem 2 ensures that all clauses containing only negative literals and which are consequences of a set of clauses are generated by applications of negative resolution to the clause set.

Our calculus for SNF_{ml} can be restricted to negative resolution with a small change in the normal form by allowing only positive literals in the scope of modal operators. Given a set Φ of clauses in SNF_{ml}, we exhaustively apply the following transformations to Φ (where $ml \in \mathbb{N}$, $t \in L_P$, $p \in P$, and t' is a new propositional symbol):

$$\Phi' \cup \{ml : \neg p \to (a)t\} \Rightarrow \Phi' \cup \{ml : t' \to (a)t, ml : t' \vee p\}$$
$$\Phi' \cup \{ml : t \to (a)\neg p\} \Rightarrow \Phi' \cup \{ml : t \to (a)t', ml + 1 : \neg t' \vee \neg p\}$$

Note that the transformation rules are not mutually exclusive. The first transformation ensures that resolvents of the modal inference rules are negative literal clauses. The second transformation rule ensures that only positive literals are in the scope of modal operators. It can be shown that the resulting set of clauses is satisfiable if, and only if, the original set of clauses is satisfiable. We call the resulting normal form, where there are no negative literals below modal operators, SNF^+_{ml}.

- **Positive Resolution** is then the analogous special case of semantic resolution for an interpretation in which all propositional symbols are false. Electrons then must be clauses in which all literals are positive.
  SNF_{ml} can be restricted to positive resolution if we only allow negative literals in the scope of modal operators. Given a set Φ of clauses in SNF_{ml}, we exhaustively apply the following transformation to Φ (where $ml \in \mathbb{N}$, $t \in L_P$, $p \in P$, and t' is a new propositional symbol):

  $$\Phi' \cup \{ml : p \to (a)t\} \Rightarrow \Phi' \cup \{ml : \neg p \vee \neg t', ml : \neg t' \to (a)t\}$$
  $$\Phi' \cup \{ml : t \to (a)p\} \Rightarrow \Phi' \cup \{ml : t \to (a)\neg t', ml + 1 : t' \vee p\}$$

  These transformation rules are analogous to those for SNF^+_{ml}. It can be shown that the resulting set of clauses is satisfiable if, and only if, the original set of clauses is satisfiable. We call the resulting normal form SNF^-_{ml}.
- **Ordered Resolution** is a refinement of resolution where inferences are restricted to maximal literals in a clause, with respect to a well-founded ordering on literals. Formally, let $\prec$ be a well-founded and total ordering on P_Φ. This ordering can be extended to literals L_P^Φ occurring in Φ by setting $p \prec \neg p$ and $\neg q \prec p$ whenever $q \prec p$, for all $p, q \in P_\Phi$. A literal l is said to be *maximal* with respect to a clause $C \vee l$ if, and only if, there is no l' occurring in C such that $l \prec l'$. In the case of classical binary resolution, the ordering refinement restricts the application to clauses $C \vee l$ and $D \vee \neg l$ where l is maximal with respect to C and $\neg l$ is maximal with respect to D.

  The key idea for achieving completeness when restricting LRES to ordered resolution is to introduce new literals in the scope of the modal operators

```
Function isTrue(V,w,l)
    if (l is negative and w ∉ V(|l|)) then
        return true ;                              /* l is negative and true at w */
    else if (l is positive and w ∈ V(l)) then
        return true ;                              /* l is positive and true at w */
    else
        return false ;                                       /* l is false at w */
Function isProductive(V,w,C,l)
    D ← C − {l};
    for (each literal l′ in D) do
        if (isTrue(V,w,l′)) then
            return false ;                      /* l′ is true at w and so is C */
    /* none of the literals in D is true at w                                  */
    return true
```

Fig. 1. Auxiliary functions isTrue and isProductive used in Fig. 2 and Fig. 4

and set their ordering to be "low enough" so that the relevant literal clauses needed for the modal hyper-resolution rules (i.e., the GEN rules) are generated. Given a set of clauses Φ in SNF_{ml} and a well-founded and total ordering $\prec$ on P_Φ, we exhaustively apply the following transformations to Φ (where $ml \in \mathbb{N}$, $t, l \in L_P^\Phi$ and t' is a new propositional symbol):

$$\Phi' \cup \{ml : t \to [a]l\} \Rightarrow \Phi' \cup \{ml : t \to [a]t', ml + 1 : \neg t' \vee l\}$$
$$\Phi' \cup \{ml : t \to \langle a \rangle l\} \Rightarrow \Phi' \cup \{ml : t \to \langle a \rangle t', ml + 1 : \neg t' \vee l\}$$

and extend the given ordering by setting $t' \prec p$, for all p occurring in Φ. Recall that Φ already includes surrogate propositional symbols from the transformation of a modal formula φ to SNF_{ml}. We call the resulting normal form SNF_{ml}^{++}. Note that we only need to apply the rewriting rule to the clauses in Φ, but not to the generated clauses in SNF_{ml}^{++}. Thus, the rewriting procedure is terminating. Two characteristics of SNF_{ml}^{++} that we will use in our proofs is that (i) the only positive occurrence of a symbol t' introduced by the transformation is below a modal operator, all other occurrences of t' are negative; and (ii) there are no two modal clauses with the same propositional symbol below a modal operator.

Theorem 3. *Let φ be a satisfiable modal formula, let Φ be the corresponding finite set of clauses in SNF_{ml}, SNF_{ml}^{-}, SNF_{ml}^{+}, or SNF_{ml}^{++}. If M is a Kripke model of Φ then M is a Kripke model of φ.*

Proof. Follows from the proofs of Lemmata 3.6 and 3.9 to 3.13 in [17].

Theorem 4. *Let Φ be a finite set of clauses in SNF_{ml}, SNF_{ml}^{-}, SNF_{ml}^{+}, or SNF_{ml}^{++}. Let Φ' be the saturation of Φ with respect to MLR or one of its refinements. If M is a Kripke model of Φ' then M is a Kripke model of Φ.*

3 Deterministic Model Construction for SNF^{++}_{ml} Clauses

We first describe a model construction algorithm for a set of SNF^{++}_{ml} clauses. Let Φ' be a satisfiable set of SNF^{++}_{ml} clauses. Let $\prec$ be a total ordering on the propositional symbols in $P_{\Phi'}$ compliant with the conditions set out in Sect. 2. Let Φ be the saturation of Φ' wrt the ordered resolution refinement of MLR with ordering $\prec$. Let $\max_{lit}$ be the function that maps a propositional clause C to the $\prec$-maximal literal in C.

For our model construction procedure we need to extend $\prec$ to a well-founded total ordering on SNF^{++}_{ml} clauses that we will also denote by $\prec$. Recall that $p \prec \neg p$ for every $p \in P_\Phi$ and $\neg p \prec q$ iff $p \prec q$ for every $p, q \in P_\Phi$. We now extend $\prec$ to propositional clauses (sets of propositional literals) such that $C_1 \prec C_2$ iff (i) $C_1 \neq C_2$, and (ii) whenever $l_1 \in C_1$ but $l_1 \notin C_2$ then there exists l_2 with $l_1 \prec l_2$, $l_2 \in C_2$, $l_2 \notin C_1$. Finally, on SNF^{++}_{ml} clauses we allow any well-founded total ordering such that $ml_1 : \psi_1 \prec ml_2 : \psi_2$ if (i) $ml_1 < ml_2$ or (ii) $ml_1 = ml_2$, ψ_1 and ψ_2 are propositional clauses, and $\psi_1 \prec \psi_2$. Strictly, the procedure itself only relies on the ordering on literal clauses but the correctness proof also requires an ordering between literal and modal clauses.

Figure 2 shows our deterministic model construction procedure for saturated sets of SNF^{++}_{ml} clauses. The procedure uses auxiliary functions isTrue and $\mathsf{isProductive}$ that are shown in Fig. 1. The procedure constructs a Kripke structure starting at modal level 0 with a root world and proceeds in much the same way as a classic tableau procedure [13]. The main difference is that the valuation for each world is constructed deterministically using the Bachmair-Ganzinger model construction (Lines 9–12). Once the valuation for a world w at modal level ml has been constructed, first each modal clause $ml : l' \to \langle a \rangle l$ is considered (Lines 14–19). If the literal l' is true at w, then a new successor world w' is created, using an auxiliary function $\mathsf{new}_{ml,a,l}(w)$, and a pair (w, w') added to the accessibility relation R_a for agent a. If the literal l is positive, then it will be added to the valuation for world w' After all those negative modal clauses have been considered, all successor worlds of w' necessary for a model have been created and each positive modal clause $ml : l' \to [a]l$ is considered (Lines 20–22). If the literal l' is true at w and the literal l is positive, then l is added to the valuation of each successor world w' of w for R_a. Crucially, for both positive and negative modal clauses in SNF^{++}_{ml}, the literal l below the modal operator is always positive. Since a world is never removed from the valuation V, later modifications of V will not result in a situation where l becomes false at a successor world w'.

Theorem 5. *Let φ be a satisfiable modal formula and let Φ' be the corresponding finite set of SNF^{++}_{ml} clauses. Let Φ be the saturation of Φ' wrt the ordered refinement of* MLR *with an ordering $\prec$. Let M be the Kripke structure constructed by the algorithm in Fig. 2 for Φ. Then M is a model of Φ', Φ, and φ.*

Example 1. Consider the satisfiable set Φ_1 of SNF_{ml} clauses consisting of the three clauses $0 : q$, $0 : q \to \langle a \rangle \neg r$ and $1 : q \vee r$. The transformation to SNF^{++}_{ml}

Algorithm: Local Model Construction for SNF^{++}_{ml}
Function `modelSNF++`(Φ,$\prec$)
  $V \leftarrow \emptyset$;
  $W_0 \leftarrow \{w_0\}$;
  for (*each agent* $a \in A_n$) **do**
    $R_a \leftarrow \emptyset$;
  for (*each modal level* ml, $0 \leq ml \leq \max_{ML}(\Phi)$) **do**
    for (*each world* $w \in W_{ml}$) **do**
      for (*each literal clause* $ml : C \in \Phi^{lit}[ml]$ *in* $\prec$*-order*) **do**
        $l \leftarrow \max_{lit}(C)$;
        if (l *is positive and* `isProductive`(V,w,C,l)) **then**
          $V(l) \leftarrow V(l) \cup \{w\}$;
      $W_{ml+1} \leftarrow \emptyset$;
      for (*each modal clause* $ml : l' \to \langle a \rangle l \in \Phi^{neg}[ml]$) **do**
        if (`isTrue`(V,w,l')) **then**
          $w' \leftarrow \mathsf{new}_{ml,a,l}(w)$;
          $W_{ml+1} \leftarrow W_{ml+1} \cup \{w'\}$;
          $R_a \leftarrow R_a \cup \{(w, w')\}$;
          /* In SNF^{++}_{ml} l is always positive */
          $V(l) \leftarrow V(l) \cup \{w'\}$;
      for (*each modal clause* $ml : l' \to [a]l \in \Phi^{pos}[ml]$) **do**
        if (`isTrue`(V,w,l')) **then**
          /* In SNF^{++}_{ml} l is always positive */
          $V(l) \leftarrow V(l) \cup \{w' \mid wR_aw'\}$;
  $W \leftarrow \bigcup_{ml=0}^{ml_{max}(\Phi)} W_{ml}$;
  return $\langle W, \{R_a\}_{a \in A_n}, V, w_0 \rangle$;

Fig. 2. Local Model Construction for SNF^{++}_{ml}

introduces an additional propositional symbol $t_{\neg r}$ and the resulting set Φ_1^{++} of SNF^{++}_{ml} clauses consists of

(1) $0 : q$ (2) $0 : q \to \langle a \rangle t_{\neg r}$ (3) $1 : q \vee r$
(4) $1 : \neg t_{\neg r} \vee \neg r$

In the ordering on propositional symbol on $P_{\Phi_1^{++}}$, $t_{\neg r}$ must be smaller than q and r. We assume $t_{\neg r} \prec q \prec r$. Saturation only derives one additional clause

(5) $1 : q \vee \neg t_{\neg r}$

by application of LRES to Clauses (3) and (4). The order between the three literal clauses at level 1 is $1 : q \vee \neg t_{\neg r} \prec 1 : q \vee r \prec 1 : \neg t_{\neg r} \vee \neg r$. The model construction process then proceeds as follows.

	Clause C	Kripke Structure M			Consideration of C
		W	R_a	V	
w_0	$0 : q$	$\{w_0\}$	$\emptyset$	$\emptyset$	*Because* $\langle M, w_1\rangle \not\models C$ *and* q *is maximal:* $V(q) = V(q) \cup \{w_0\}$
w_0	$0 : q \rightarrow \langle a\rangle t_{\neg r}$	$\{w_0\}$	$\emptyset$	$\{(q, \{w_0\})\}$	*Because* $w_0 \in V(q)$*:* $W = W \cup \{w_1\}$ $R_a = R_a \cup \{(w_0, w_1)\}$ $V(t_{\neg r}) = V(t_{\neg r}) \cup \{w_1\}$
w_1	$1 : q \vee \neg t_{\neg r}$	$\{w_0, w_1\}$	$\{(w_0, w_1)\}$	$\{(q, \{w_0\}),$ $(t_{\neg r}, \{w_1\})\}$	*Because* $\langle M, w_1\rangle \not\models C$ *and* q *is maximal:* $V(q) = V(q) \cup \{w_1\}$
w_1	$1 : q \vee r$	$\{w_0, w_1\}$	$\{(w_0, w_1)\}$	$\{(q, \{w_0, w_1\}),$ $(t_{\neg r}, \{w_1\})\}$	*Because* $\langle M, w_1\rangle \models C$*: no change*
w_1	$\neg t_{\neg r} \vee \neg r$	$\{w_0, w_1\}$	$\{(w_0, w_1)\}$	$\{(q, \{w_0, w_1\}),$ $(t_{\neg r}, \{w_1\})\}$	*Because* C *is negative: no change*

The constructed Kripke structure is

$$W = \{w_0, w_1\} \quad R_a = \{(w_0, w_1)\} \quad V(q) = \{w_0, w_1\} \quad V(r) = \emptyset \quad V(t_{\neg r}) = \{w_1\}$$

which is a model of both Φ_1^{++} and Φ_1.

4 Deterministic Model Construction for SNF^{-}_{ml} Clauses

The model construction for sets of SNF^{++}_{ml} clauses saturated with respect to the ordered refinement of MLR used the same ordering $\prec$ as was used by the calculus. However, the positive resolution refinement of MLR is not based on an ordering and therefore there is no pre-existing ordering that can be used in the model construction for sets of SNF^{-}_{ml} clauses saturated with respect to the positive resolution refinement of MLR. So, to adapt the procedure presented in Sect. 3 to sets of SNF^{-}_{ml} clauses, we need to construct an ordering. The fact that below operators we now only have negative propositional literals further complicates things as we have to make sure that we do not unnecessarily produce corresponding positive literals from literal clauses.

Suppose we have a world w at modal level ml and we have determined that $\langle a\rangle\neg p_1, \ldots, \langle a\rangle\neg p_m$, $[a]\neg q_1, \ldots, [a]\neg q_n$, $0 < m$, $0 \leq n$ are all the modal literals that have to be true at w. For each $\langle a\rangle\neg p_i$, $1 \leq i \leq m$, we have to create a successor world w_i of w at modal level $ml + 1$. Then we have to make sure that $p_i, q_1, \ldots, q_n$ are smaller than all other propositional symbols for w_i, $1 \leq i \leq m$, in order to ensure that literal clauses $ml + 1 : \psi$ do not unnecessarily produce p_i or one of the q_j, $1 \leq j \leq n$, when considered for the world w_i. For this purpose,

```
Function constructOrdering(P)
    ≺ ← ∅;
    D ← ∅;
    for (each propositional symbol p ∈ P) do
        D ← D ∪ {p};
        for (each propositional symbol p' ∈ P_Φ − D) do
            ≺ ← ≺ ∪ {(p, p')};
    for (each propositional symbol p ∈ P_Φ − P) do
        D ← D ∪ {p};
        for (each propositional symbol p' ∈ P_Φ − D) do
            ≺ ← ≺ ∪ {(p, p')};
    return ≺
```

Fig. 3. Auxiliary function constructOrdering used in Fig. 4

first we use a function-valued variable PS that for each successor world w_i keeps track of the propositional symbols p_i, q_1, …, q_n. Second we use a function `constructOrdering` (Fig. 3) that, given $PS(w_i)$ for some world w_i, constructs an ordering $\prec_{w_i}$ on propositional symbols specifically for w_i that has the desired property.

This ordering is then extended to literals and to literal clauses with the same modal level as in Sect. 3. This is sufficient for the model construction procedure in Fig. 4. Except for the function-valued variable PS and the function `constructOrdering` the only other difference to the model construction procedure for SNF^{++}_{ml} in Fig. 2 is that literals below modal operators are always negative and therefore never change the valuation.

However, for our correctness proof we need to combine and extend these orderings into a total ordering. This total ordering will not be on the clauses themselves but on ordered pairs $\langle w, ml : \psi\rangle$ consisting of a world w at modal level ml in a Kripke structure M and a clause $ml : \psi \in \Phi$. We use $H(\Phi, M)$ to denote the set of all such ordered pairs.

Let W be the set of worlds in a Kripke structure M produced by the algorithm in Fig. 4. We can use the order in which the worlds in W were generated to impose a total ordering $\prec_W$ on W. Note that $\mathsf{ml}_M(w_1) < \mathsf{ml}_M(w_2)$ implies $w_1 \prec_w w_2$. Then on $H(\Phi, M)$ we allow any well-founded total ordering $\prec_{H(\Phi,M)}$ such that $\langle w_1, ml_1 : \psi_1\rangle \prec \langle w_2, ml_2 : \psi_2\rangle$ if (i) $ml_1 < ml_2$ or (ii) $ml_1 = ml_2$ and $w_1 \prec_w w_2$, or (iii) $ml_1 = ml_2$, $w_1 = w_2$, ψ_1 and ψ_2 are propositional clauses, and $\psi_1 \prec_{w_1} \psi_2$.

Theorem 6. *Let φ be a satisfiable modal formula and let Φ' be the corresponding finite set of SNF^{-}_{ml} clauses. Let Φ be the saturation of Φ' wrt the positive resolution refinement of* MLR. *Let M be the Kripke structure constructed by the algorithm in Fig. 4 for Φ. Then M is a model of Φ', Φ, and φ.*

```
Algorithm: Local Model Construction for SNF^-_ml
Function modelSNF-(Φ)
    V ← ∅;
    PS ← {(w_0, ∅)};
    W_0 ← {w_0};
    for (each agent a ∈ A_n) do
        R_a ← ∅;
    for (each modal level ml, 0 ≤ ml ≤ max_ML(Φ)) do
        for (each world w ∈ W_ml) do
            ≺_w ← constructOrdering(PS(w));
            for (each literal clause ml : C ∈ Φ^lit[ml] in ≺_w-order) do
                l ← max_lit(C);
                if (l is positive and isProductive(V,w,C,l)) then
                    V(l) ← V(l) ∪ {w};
            for (each modal clause ml : l' → ⟨a⟩l ∈ Φ^neg[ml]) do
                if (isTrue(V,w,l')) then
                    w' ← new_{ml,a,l}(w);
                    W_{ml+1} ← W_{ml+1} ∪ {w'};
                    R_a ← R_a ∪ {(w, w')};
                    /* In SNF^-_ml l is always negative, V unchanged    */
                    PS ← PS ∪ {(w', {|l|})};
            for (each modal clause ml : l' → [a]l ∈ Φ^pos[ml]) do
                if (isTrue(V,w,l')) then
                    /* In SNF^-_ml l is always negative, V unchanged    */
                    for (each w' ∈ {w' | w R_a w'}) do
                        PS(w') ← PS(w') ∪ {|l|};
    W ← ⋃_{ml=0}^{ml_max} W_ml;
    return ⟨W, {R_a}_{a∈A_n}, V, w_0⟩
```

Fig. 4. Local Model Construction for SNF^-_{ml}

Example 2. Consider the satisfiable set of clauses Φ_2^- in SNF^-_{ml}:

(6)	$0 : q$	(7)	$0 : \neg q \to \langle a \rangle \neg q$	(9)	$0 : \neg p \to [a]\neg t_1$
		(8)	$0 : \neg p \to \langle a \rangle \neg r$	(10)	$1 : t_1 \vee q \vee r$

where $\neg t_1$ is a surrogate introduced for $(q \vee r)$. This set of clauses is saturated with respect to the positive resolution refinement of MLR. The model construction for Φ_2^- proceeds as before:

	Clause C	Kripke Structure M			Consideration of C
		W	R_a	V	
w_0	$0 : q$	$\{w_0\}$	$\emptyset$	$\emptyset$	*Because* $\langle M, w_1\rangle \not\models C$ *and* q *is maximal in* C*:* $V(q) = V(q) \cup \{w_0\}$
w_0	$0 : \neg q \to \langle a\rangle\neg q$	$\{w_0\}$	$\emptyset$	$\{(q, \{w_0\})\}$	*Because* $w_0 \in V(q)$*: no change*
w_0	$0 : \neg p \to \langle a\rangle\neg r$	$\{w_0\}$	$\emptyset$	$\{(q, \{w_0\})\}$	*Because* $w_0 \notin V(p)$*:* $W = W \cup \{w_1\}$ $R_a = R_a \cup \{(w_0, w_1)\}$
w_0	$0 : \neg p \to [a]\neg t_1$	$\{w_0, w_1\}$	$\{(w_0, w_1)\}$	$\{(q, \{w_0\})\}$	*Because* $w_0 \notin V(p)$ *but* $\neg t_1$ *is negative: no change*

Before the model construction proceeds to w_1, we now determine the ordering $\prec_{w_1}$. The literals $\neg r$ and $\neg t_1$ 'contribute' to the construction of w_1, so r and t_1 must be smaller in $\prec_{w_1}$ than the other propositional symbols p and q. Let us assume $t_1 \prec_{w_1} r \prec_{w_1} p \prec_{w_1} q$. So, when we proceed to w_1 and the clause $1 : t_1 \vee q \vee r$, it will be q that will be made true not r:

	Clause C	Kripke Structure M			Consideration of C
		W	R_a	V	
w_1	$1 : t_1 \vee q \vee r$	$\{w_0, w_1\}$	$\{(w_0, w_1)\}$	$\{(q, \{w_0\})\}$	*Because* $\langle M, w_1\rangle \not\models C$ *and* q *is maximal in* C*:* $V(q) = V(q) \cup \{w_1\}$

The constructed Kripke structure M_2 is

$$\begin{array}{llll} W = \{w_0, w_1\} & V(p) = \emptyset & V(q) = \{w_0, w_1\} & V(r) = \emptyset \\ R_a = \{(w_0, w_1)\} & & & \end{array}$$

which is a model of Φ_2^-.

5 Deterministic Model Construction for SNF_{ml}^{+} Clauses

Our model construction for a set Φ of SNF_{ml}^{++} clauses saturated wrt the ordered resolution refinement of MLR started with a valuation in which every propositional symbol is false at every world and successively makes propositional symbols true at certain worlds in order to ensure all clauses of Φ are true in the constructed model.

For propositional clauses, negative resolution corresponds to semantic resolution wrt the valuation $V_\top$ in which all propositional symbols are true. A model construction for a set Φ of SNF^+_{ml} clauses saturated wrt the negative resolution refinement of MLR would therefore naturally start with a valuation in which every propositional symbol is true at every world and successively make propositional symbols false at certain worlds to obtain a model of Φ.

However, instead of devising a new model construction procedure that does so, we take advantage of the fact that we can simply reverse the polarity of all literals in Φ, to again start with a valuation in which every propositional symbol is false at every world.

More formally, let ι^- be a function on propositional literals such that for every propositional symbol $p \in P$, $\iota^-(p) = \neg p$ and $\iota^-(\neg p) = p$. The function ι^- can be homomorphically extended to clauses and set of clauses as follows:

$$\begin{aligned}
\iota^-(ml : l_1 \vee \cdots \vee l_m) &= ml : \iota^-(l_1) \vee \cdots \vee \iota^-(l_m) \\
\iota^-(ml : l' \rightarrow [a]l) &= ml : \iota^-(l') \rightarrow [a]\iota^-(l) \\
\iota^-(ml : l' \rightarrow \langle a\rangle l) &= ml : \iota^-(l') \rightarrow \langle a\rangle\iota^-(l)
\end{aligned}$$

and $\iota^-(\Phi) = \{\iota^-(ml : \psi) \mid ml : \psi \in \Phi\}$. Let I^+ be a function on Kripke structures such that for $M = \langle W, \{R_a\}_{a\in A_n}, V\rangle$, $I^+(M) = \langle W, \{R_a\}_{a\in A_n}, V^+\rangle$, such that $V^+(p) = W - V(p)$ for every $p \in P$.

Lemma 1. *Let Φ be a set of clauses in SNF_{ml}. Let M^f be a tree Kripke model of $\Phi^f = \iota^-(\Phi)$. Then $I^+(M^f)$ is a tree Kripke model of Φ.*

Lemma 2. *Let Φ^+ be a set of clauses in SNF^+_{ml} that is saturated with respect to the negative resolution refinement of* MLR. *Then $\Phi^f = \iota^-(\Phi^+)$ is (i) a set of clauses in SNF^-_{ml} and (ii) saturated with respect to the positive resolution refinement of* MLR.

Theorem 7. *Let φ be a satisfiable modal formula, let Φ' be the corresponding finite set of clauses in SNF^+_{ml}, and let Φ be the saturation of Φ' wrt the negative resolution refinement of* MLR. *Let $\Phi^f = \iota^-(\Phi)$, let M^f be the Kripke structure constructed by the algorithm in Fig. 4 for Φ^f, and let $M = I^+(M^f)$. Then M is a model of Φ', Φ, and φ.*

Example 3. Consider the satisfiable SNF^+_{ml} clause set $\Phi^+_3 = \{0 : p, 0 : p \rightarrow \langle a\rangle r, 0 : q \rightarrow [a]q, 1 : q \vee \neg r\}$. Reversing the polarity of all literals in Φ^+_3 gives us the SNF^-_{ml} clause set Φ^f_3

(11) $0 : \neg p$	(12) $0 : \neg p \rightarrow \langle a\rangle\neg r$	(14) $1 : \neg q \vee r$
	(13) $0 : \neg q \rightarrow [a]\neg q$	

which is saturated with respect to the positive resolution refinement of calculus MLR.

	Clause C	Kripke Structure M			Consideration of C
		W	R_a	V	
w_0	$0 : \neg p$	$\{w_0\}$	$\emptyset$	$\emptyset$	*Because* $\langle M_C, w_0\rangle \models \neg p$: *no change*
w_0	$0 : \neg p \to \langle a\rangle\neg r$	$\{w_0\}$	$\emptyset$	$\emptyset$	*Because* $\langle M_C, w_0\rangle \models \neg p$: $W = W \cup \{w_1\}$ $R_a = R_a \cup \{(w_0, w_1)\}$
w_0	$0 : \neg q \to [a]\neg q$	$\{w_0, w_1\}$	$\{(w_0, w_1)\}$	$\emptyset$	*Because* $\langle M_C, w_0\rangle \models \neg q$: *no change*

Before the model construction proceeds to w_1, we now fix the ordering $\prec_{w_1}$. The literals $\neg q$ and $\neg r$ 'contributed' to the construction of w_1, so q and r must both be smaller in $\prec_{w_1}$ than the only other propositional symbol p, while we can impose an arbitrary order between q and r, e.g., $q \prec_{w_1} r \prec_{w_1} p$.

	Clause C	Kripke Structure M			Consideration of C
		W	R_a	V	
w_1	$1 : \neg q \vee r$	$\{w_0, w_1\}$	$\{(w_0, w_1)\}$	$\emptyset$	*Because* $\langle M_C, w_1\rangle \models C$: *no change*

The resulting Kripke structure M_3^f is

$$W = \{w_0, w_1\} \quad R_a = \{(w_0, w_1)\} \quad V(p) = V(q) = V(r) = \emptyset$$

which is a model of Φ_3^f. We obtain M_3^+ by reversing the valuation in M_3^f:

$$\begin{aligned} W &= \{w_0, w_1\} \qquad\qquad V(p) = V(q) = V(r) = W - \emptyset = \{w_0, w_1\} \\ R_a &= \{(w_0, w_1)\} \end{aligned}$$

It is straightforward to check that M_3^+ is a model of $\Phi_3^+ = \{0 : p, 0 : p \to \langle a\rangle r, 0 : q \to [a]q, 1 : q \vee \neg r\}$.

6 Discussion

The model construction procedures presented in this paper are inspired by and closely related to the Bachmair-Ganzinger model construction procedure [2,15]. The primary purpose of this model construction procedure is to prove the completeness of resolution and superposition calculi, in particular, ordered resolution with selection for first-order clausal logic. But it can also be used to construct a Herbrand model of a specific saturated set of propositional or ground first-order clauses.

Commonalities and differences between the two approaches are best illustrated by an example. Consider the following set of clauses in SNF_{ml}^{++}.

(15) $0 : p_0$ (16) $0 : p_0 \rightarrow [a]q_1$ (18) $1 : \neg q_2 \vee \neg q_1 \vee q_0$
(17) $0 : p_0 \rightarrow \langle a \rangle q_2$

The corresponding set of first-order clauses, using the relational translation and ignoring the specific modal levels at which each SNF_{ml}^{++} clause is meant to hold, is as follows.

(19) $p_0(w_0)$ (20) $\neg p_0(x) \vee \neg r(x, y) \vee q_1(y)$ (23) $\neg q_2(x) \vee \neg q_1(x) \vee q_0(x)$
(21) $\neg p_0(x) \vee q_2(f(x))$
(22) $\neg p_0(x) \vee r(x, f(x))$

Following [28] on resolution-based decision procedures for the relational translation of basic modal logic, we choose an ordering that ensures that $\neg r(x, y)$, $q_2(f(x))$ and $r(x, f(x))$ are maximal in Clauses (20), (21) and (22), respectively. We are free to impose an arbitrary order on unary literals and we choose an ordering such that $p_0(x) \prec q_0(x) \prec q_1(x) \prec q_2(x)$. We can then derive the following additional clauses:

[ORes,20(2),22(2)] (24) $\neg p_0(x) \vee \neg p_0(x) \vee q_1(f(x))$
[ORes,21(2),23(1)] (25) $\neg p_0(x) \vee \neg q_1(f(x)) \vee q_0(f(x))$
[ORes,24(3),25(2)] (26) $\neg p_0(x) \vee \neg p_0(x) \vee \neg p_0(x) \vee q_0(f(x))$

Here 'ORes' denotes an inference by ordered resolution, followed by the identifying numbers of the clauses that are the premises of the inference. The number in parentheses identifies the literal in each premise on which we resolve. The Bachmair-Ganzinger model construction operates on ground clauses, in particular, all ground instances of the first-order clauses here, and it views clauses as multisets of literals. However, the Herbrand universe for this set of clauses is infinite. Given that a Kripke model for the set of SNF_{ml}^{++} clauses has at most depth 1, we can restrict ourselves to the terms w_0 and $f(w_0)$.

The constructed model consists of $p(w_0)$, $r(w_0, f(w_0))$, $q_0(f(w_0))$, $q_1(f(w_0))$ and $q_2(f(w_0))$. In particular, $q_0(f(w_0))$ is produced by an instance of Clause (26).

For this particular example, our own procedure will arrive at the same model, but the way it does so differs in a number of ways. First, we are more constrained regarding the order we can use. Regarding the propositional symbols q_0, q_1 and q_2 we have to ensure that the propositional symbols q_1 and q_2 that appear below modal operators are smaller than the other propositional symbols. So, the ordering $p_0 \prec q_0 \prec q_1 \prec q_2$ corresponding to the one we used in the first-order setting is not admissible. Instead we have to use, for example, $q_1 \prec q_2 \prec p_0 \prec q_0$.

Second, irrespective of the ordering, no inferences by MLR are possible on Clauses (15) to (18). This also means no equivalent of Clause (26) will be derived. Consequently, our model construction procedure has fewer clauses available and less explicit information about which propositional symbols have to be true.

Third, the order in which clauses are considered by the Bachmair-Ganzinger procedure for ground first-order clauses is solely down to the ordering. In contrast our model construction procedure considers literal clauses according to the ordering, but negative and positive modal clauses are handled separately.

This design choice is mainly down to the fact that the effects of existential and universal quantifiers are dealt with at different times. In the first-order setting, existential quantifiers are dealt with by the use of Skolem functions in first-order clauses while universal quantifiers are dealt with by instantiation when ground clauses are computed. In the modal setting, $\langle a \rangle$- and $[a]$-operators are only dealt with by the model construction procedure.

Regarding the complexity of our approach we can observe the following.

Theorem 8. *Let φ be a satisfiable modal formula, let Φ' be the corresponding finite set of clauses in one of the three normal forms SNF^{++}_{ml}, SNF^{+}_{ml} or SNF^{-}_{ml}, let Φ be the saturation of Φ' wrt to the corresponding refinement of MLR, and let M be model generated by the corresponding model construction procedure. Then*

a. the computation of Φ' from φ requires linear time in the size of φ and the number of clauses in Φ' as well as the size of Φ' is linear in the size of φ;
b. the computation of Φ from Φ' requires at most exponential time in the size of Φ and the number of literal clauses in Φ is at most exponential in the number of propositional symbols in Φ';
c. the generation of M requires at most exponential time in the size of Φ and the size of M is also at most exponential in the size of Φ'.

Theorem 8a follows from the fact that the normal form transformation introduces at most two clauses for each occurrence of a logical operator in φ. Regarding Theorem 8b, the resolution procedure for propositional clauses runs in deterministic exponential time in the number of literals occurring in the clause set [25]. The refinements we use and the additional modal inference rules in MLR do not change the overall complexity, in particular, no new modal clauses are generated by any of the inference rules. For Theorem 8c, the number of worlds in a tree Kripke model of φ is at most exponential in the size of φ [9]. For each of the worlds in the model we have to consider exponentially many literal clauses to determine the valuation of the model. The consideration of each clause takes at most linear time in the number of propositional symbols in Φ'.

It is worth pointing out that the Bachmair-Ganzinger procedure only takes time $O(|\Phi| l \log(|\Phi|))$ for a set of ground clauses Φ [15]. In the context of the translation of modal formulae to first-order clausal logic, the size of the set N' of non-ground clauses obtained from the translation of φ is linear in the size of φ. But the size of the set N of ground clauses obtained by instantiation can be exponential in the size of N' and therefore in the size of φ. So, while the construction of a Herbrand model then only requires polynomial time in the size of N, it takes exponential time in the size of N' and of φ. This then aligns with Theorem 8.

7 Extension to the Modal Cube

A multitude of extensions of the basic modal logic K_n can be formed by adding one or more axioms to the axiomatisation of K_n itself. The most extensively

```
Algorithm: Modal Logic L Model Construction
Function model(φ,L)
    Φ ← SNF2SNF++(ρ_L^sml(simplifiedNNF(φ)));
    ≺ ← constructOrderSNF++(Φ);
    ⟨W, R, V, w_0⟩ ← modelSNF++(Φ, ≺);
    R^L ← closure(R,L);
    return ⟨W, R^L, V, w_0⟩;
```

Fig. 5. Model Construction for modal logic L

studied axioms are $\psi \rightarrow [a]\langle a\rangle\psi$ (B), $[a]\psi \rightarrow \langle a\rangle\psi$ (D), $[a]\psi \rightarrow \psi$ (T), $[a]\psi \rightarrow [a][a]\psi$ (4), and $\langle a\rangle\psi \rightarrow [a]\langle a\rangle\psi$ (5). Model-theoretically, these additional axioms correspond to properties of the accessibility relation R_a for the agent $a \in A_n$. For the above axioms, the properties are symmetry, seriality, reflexivity, transitivity and Euclideaness, respectively.

In [20] we have presented reductions $\rho_L^{sml}(\varphi)$ for logics L that are extensions of the mono-modal logic K with these axioms and their combinations. We have shown that a formula φ in simplified negation normal form is L-satisfiable iff the set $\rho_L^{sml}(\varphi)$ of clauses in SNF_{ml} is satisfiable. In particular, we have shown that given a tree Kripke structure $M = \langle W, R, V, w_0\rangle$ that satisfies $\rho_L^{sml}(\varphi)$ we can obtain a Kripke structure $M^L = \langle W, R^L, V, w_0\rangle$ that satisfies φ where R^L is obtained by computing the closure of R corresponding to the additional axioms in L.

Putting these ingredients together gives us the algorithm in Fig. 5 where we are using ordered resolution refinement of MLR together with our model construction algorithm for sets of clauses in SNF_{ml}^{++}. Here, `simplifiedNNF` is a function that computes the simplified negation normal form of a modal formula, `SNF2SNF++` is a function that transforms a set of clauses in SNF_{ml} into a set of clauses in SNF_{ml} using additional renaming steps as described in Sect. 2, `constructOrderSNF++` constructs an ordering on the propositional symbols in a set of clauses in SNF_{ml}^{++} compliant with the conditions set out in Sect. 2, and `closure` is a function that computes the closure of a binary relation R with respect to the relation properties corresponding to the additional axioms in a modal logic L.

The Kripke structure returned by the algorithm in Fig. 5 is then an L-model of the formula φ.

8 Conclusion and Future Work

In this paper we have presented deterministic model construction algorithms for satisfiable sets of modal clauses saturated with respect to three refinements of the modal-layered resolution calculus. These algorithms are meant to complement the provision of refutations for unsatisfiable sets of modal clauses that is a standard byproduct of resolution-based calculi.

In future work we intend to implement these algorithms in the prover K_SP and to evaluate their effectiveness. For this it will be necessary to define a format in which Kripke models will be provided. Such a format was presented in [14]. Regarding an evaluation, a challenge will be to find other solvers for basic modal logic that can produce models. While there are range of solvers for basic modal logic available, few output models. As found in [14], even where a solver claims to output models, those might be incomplete. The main cause appears to be the use of simplification during pre-processing and reasoning (pure literal elimination, tautology elimination, simplification to true) that may remove propositional symbols without the produced model then indicating a valuation for these symbols even where that valuation is not arbitrary. This kind of interaction between simplification and model generation is also an issue that we will need to pay close attention to when implementing our algorithms.

A potential improvement of the algorithms is to reuse existing worlds during the model construction. In tableau decision procedures this technique is known as blocking [1,3,5,21,27]. What complicates its application in our context is that each SNF_{ml} clause only holds at a certain modal level instead of universally.

Acknowledgments. C. Dixon was partially supported by the EPSRC funded Prosperity Partnership, CRADLE, EP/X02489X/1.

Disclosure of Interests. The authors have no competing interests to declare that are relevant to the content of this article.

References

1. Baader, F., Buchheit, M., Hollunder, B.: Cardinality restrictions on concepts. Artif. Intell. **88**, 195–213 (1996)
2. Bachmair, L., Ganzinger, H., McAllester, D., Lynch, C.: Resolution theorem proving. In: Robinson, A., Voronkov, A. (eds.) Handbook of Automated Reasoning, chap. 2, pp. 19–99. North-Holland, Amsterdam (2001)
3. Baumgartner, P., Schmidt, R.A.: Blocking and other enhancements for bottom-up model generation methods. J. Autom. Reason. **64**(2), 197–251 (2020). https://doi.org/10.1007/s10817-019-09515-1
4. Fagin, R., Halpern, J.Y., Moses, Y., Vardi, M.Y.: Reasoning About Knowledge. MIT Press, Cambridge (1995)
5. Glimm, B., Horrocks, I., Motik, B.: Optimized description logic reasoning via core blocking. In: Giesl, J., Hähnle, R. (eds.) IJCAR 2010. LNCS (LNAI), vol. 6173, pp. 457–471. Springer, Heidelberg (2010). https://doi.org/10.1007/978-3-642-14203-1_39
6. Goré, R., Kikkert, C.: CEGAR-tableaux: improved modal satisfiability via modal clause-learning and SAT. In: Das, A., Negri, S. (eds.) TABLEAUX 2021. LNCS (LNAI), vol. 12842, pp. 74–91. Springer, Cham (2021). https://doi.org/10.1007/978-3-030-86059-2_5
7. Götzmann, D., Kaminski, M., Smolka, G.: Spartacus: a tableau prover for hybrid logic. Electron. Notes Theor. Comput. Sci. **262**, 127–139 (2010)

8. Hailpern, B.T.: Verifying Concurrent Processes Using Temporal Logic. LNCS, vol. 129. Springer, Berlin/New York (1982). https://doi.org/10.1007/3-540-11205-7
9. Halpern, J.Y., Moses, Y.: A guide to completeness and complexity for modal logics of knowledge and belief. Artif. Intell. **54**(3), 319–379 (1992)
10. Halpern, J.Y.: Using reasoning about knowledge to analyze distributed systems. Annu. Rev. Comput. Sci. **2**, 37–68 (1987)
11. Halpern, J., Manna, Z., Moszkowski, B.: A hardware semantics based on temporal intervals. In: Diaz, J. (ed.) ICALP 1983. LNCS, vol. 154, pp. 278–291. Springer, Heidelberg (1983). https://doi.org/10.1007/BFb0036915
12. Kaminski, M., Tebbi, T.: InKreSAT: modal reasoning via incremental reduction to SAT. In: Bonacina, M.P. (ed.) CADE 2013. LNCS (LNAI), vol. 7898, pp. 436–442. Springer, Heidelberg (2013). https://doi.org/10.1007/978-3-642-38574-2_31
13. Kripke, S.A.: Semantical analysis of modal logic I: normal modal propositional calculi. Zeitschr. f. math. Logik und Grundlagen d. Math. **9**, 67–96 (1963)
14. Lagniez, J.M., Berre, D.L., de Lima, T., Montmirail, V.: On checking Kripke models for modal logic K. In: PAAR 2016, pp. 69–81. No. 1635 in CEUR Workshop Proceedings (2016)
15. Lynch, C.: Constructing Bachmair-Ganzinger models. In: Voronkov, A., Weidenbach, C. (eds.) Programming Logics. LNCS, vol. 7797, pp. 285–301. Springer, Heidelberg (2013). https://doi.org/10.1007/978-3-642-37651-1_12
16. Nalon, C., Dixon, C.: Clausal resolution for normal modal logics. J. Algorithms **62**, 117–134 (2007)
17. Nalon, C., Dixon, C., Hustadt, U.: Modal resolution: proofs, layers, and refinements. ACM Trans. Comput. Log. **20**(4), 23:1–23:38 (2019)
18. Nalon, C., Hustadt, U., Dixon, C.: A modal-layered resolution calculus for K. In: De Nivelle, H. (ed.) TABLEAUX 2015. LNCS (LNAI), vol. 9323, pp. 185–200. Springer, Cham (2015). https://doi.org/10.1007/978-3-319-24312-2_13
19. Nalon, C., Hustadt, U., Dixon, C.: KSP: architecture, refinements, strategies and experiments. J. Autom. Reason. **64**(3), 461–484 (2020)
20. Nalon, C., Hustadt, U., Papacchini, F., Dixon, C.: Buy one get 14 free: evaluating local reductions for modal logic. In: Pientka, B., Tinelli, C. (eds.) CADE 2023. LNCS (LNAI), vol. 14132, pp. 382–400. Springer, Cham (2023). https://doi.org/10.1007/978-3-031-38499-8_22
21. Papacchini, F., Schmidt, R.A.: Terminating minimal model generation procedures for propositional modal logics. In: Demri, S., Kapur, D., Weidenbach, C. (eds.) IJCAR 2014. LNCS (LNAI), vol. 8562, pp. 381–395. Springer, Cham (2014). https://doi.org/10.1007/978-3-319-08587-6_30
22. Pratt, V.R.: Application of modal logic to programming. Stud. Logica. **39**(2/3), 257–274 (1980)
23. Rao, A.S., Georgeff, M.P.: Modeling rational agents within a BDI-architecture. In: Fikes, R., Sandewall, E. (eds.) KR 1991, pp. 473–484. Morgan Kaufmann, Burlington (1991)
24. Robinson, J.A.: Automatic deduction with hyper-resolution. Int. J. Comput. Math. **1**, 227–234 (1965)
25. Robinson, J.A.: A machine-oriented logic based on the resolution principle. J. ACM **12**(1), 23–41 (1965)
26. Schild, K.: A correspondence theory for terminological logics. In: Mylopoulos, J., Reiter, R. (eds.) IJCAI 1991, pp. 466–471. Morgan Kaufmann, Burlington (1991)

27. Schmidt, R.A., Tishkovsky, D.: Using tableau to decide description logics with full role negation and identity. ACM Trans. Comput. Log. **15**(7), 1–31 (2014). https://doi.org/10.1145/2559947
28. Schmidt, R.A., Hustadt, U.: First-order resolution methods for modal logics. In: Voronkov, A., Weidenbach, C. (eds.) Programming Logics. LNCS, vol. 7797, pp. 345–391. Springer, Heidelberg (2013). https://doi.org/10.1007/978-3-642-37651-1_15
29. Seidl, M.: Never trust your solver: certification for SAT and QBF. In: Dubois, C., Kerber, M. (eds.) CICM 2023. LNCS (LNAI), vol. 14101, pp. 16–33. Springer, Cham (2023). https://doi.org/10.1007/978-3-031-42753-4_2
30. Slagle, J.R.: Automatic theorem proving with renamable and semantic resolution. J. ACM **14**(4), 687–697 (1967)
31. Slagle, J.R., Chang, C.L., Lee, R.C.T.: Completeness theorems for semantic resolution in consequence-finding. In: Walker, D.E., Norton, L.M. (eds.) IJCAI 1969, pp. 281–286. William Kaufmann, New York (1969)
32. Sutcliffe, G.: The CADE ATP system competition - CASC. AI Mag. **37**(2), 99–101 (2016)
33. Sutcliffe, G., Desharnais, M.: The 11th IJCAR automated theorem proving system competition - CASC-J11. AI Commun. **36**(2), 73–91 (2023)
34. Wu, M., Goré, R.: Verified decision procedures for modal logics. In: Harrison, J., O'Leary, J., Tolmach, A. (eds.) ITP 2019. Leibniz International Proceedings in Informatics (LIPIcs), vol. 141, pp. 31:1–31:19. Schloss Dagstuhl – Leibniz-Zentrum für Informatik, Dagstuhl, Germany (2019). https://doi.org/10.4230/LIPIcs.ITP.2019.31

A Terminating Sequent Calculus for Intuitionistic Strong Löb Logic with the Subformula Property

Camillo Fiorentini[1](✉) and Mauro Ferrari[2]

[1] Department of Computer Science, Università degli Studi di Milano, Milan, Italy
fiorentini@di.unimi.it

[2] Department of Theoretical and Applied Sciences, Università degli Studi dell'Insubria, Varese, Italy
mauro.ferrari@uninsubria.it

Abstract. Intuitionistic Strong Löb logic iSL is an intuitionistic modal logic with a provability interpretation. We introduce $\mathsf{GbuSL}_\Box$, a terminating sequent calculus for iSL with the subformula property. $\mathsf{GbuSL}_\Box$ modifies the sequent calculus $\mathsf{G3iSL}_\Box$ for iSL based on G3i, by annotating the sequents to distinguish rule applications into an unblocked phase, where any rule can be backward applied, and a blocked phase where only right rules can be used. We prove that, if proof search for a sequent σ in $\mathsf{GbuSL}_\Box$ fails, then a Kripke countermodel for σ can be constructed.

1 Introduction

Intuitionistic Strong Löb Logic iSL is the intuitionistic modal logic obtained by adding both the Gödel-Löb axiom $\Box(\Box\varphi \to \varphi) \to \Box\varphi$ and the completeness axiom $\varphi \to \Box\varphi$ to $\mathbf{K}_\Box$, the $\Box$-fragment of Intuitionistic Modal Logic. Equivalently, iSL is the extension of $\mathbf{K}_\Box$ with the Strong Löb axiom $(\Box\varphi \to \varphi) \to \varphi$. Logic iSL has prominent relevance in the study of provability of Heyting Arithmetic HA. It is well known that the Gödel-Löb Logic, obtained by extending classical modal logic with Gödel-Löb axiom, is the provability logic of Peano Arithmetic [11]. However, it is an open problem what the provability logic of HA should be; a solution to this problem is claimed in a preprint paper [8]. In [16], it is shown that iSL is the provability logic of an extension of HA with respect to slow provability. Moreover, iSL plays an important role in the Σ_1-provability logic of HA [1]. We stress that iSL, as well as other related logics (such as the logics iGL, mHC and KM investigated in [13,14]), only treats the $\Box$-modality, connected with the provability interpretation; it is not clear what interpretation $\Diamond$ should have and which laws it should obey.

In this paper we investigate proof search for iSL. Recently, in [13,15] some sequent calculi for iSL have been introduced, obtained by enhancing the sequent calculus G3i [12] for IPL (Intuitionistic Propositional Logic) with the rule $R\Box$ to treat right $\Box$ (actually, four variants of such a rule are proposed). We start

C. Benzmüller et al. (Eds.): IJCAR 2024, LNAI 14740, pp. 24–42, 2024.
https://doi.org/10.1007/978-3-031-63501-4_2

by presenting the sequent calculus $\mathsf{G3iSL}^+_\Box$ (see Fig. 1), a polished version of the calculus $\mathsf{G3iSL}_\Box$ [13,15] where rule $R\Box$ avoids some redundant duplications of formulas. The calculus $\mathsf{G3iSL}^+_\Box$ has the *subformula property*, namely: every formula occurring in a $\mathsf{G3iSL}^+_\Box$-tree is a subformula of a formula in the root sequent. However, $\mathsf{G3iSL}^+_\Box$ is not well-suited for proof search. This is mainly due to the rule $L\rightarrow$ for left implication, which has applications where the sequent $\alpha \rightarrow \beta, \Gamma \Rightarrow \alpha$ is both the conclusion and the left premise, and this yields loops in backward proof search. We are interested in a sequent calculus $\mathcal{C}$ where backward proof search always terminates, that is: given a sequent of $\mathcal{C}$ and repeatedly applying the rules of $\mathcal{C}$ upwards, proof search eventually halts, no matter which strategy is used. A calculus of this kind is called *(strongly) terminating* and can be characterized as follows: there exists a well-founded relation $\prec$ on sequents of $\mathcal{C}$ such that, for every application ρ of a rule of $\mathcal{C}$, if the sequent σ is the conclusion of ρ and σ' is any of the premises, then $\sigma' \prec \sigma$. Clearly, any calculus containing rule $L\rightarrow$ is not terminating; in this case, to get a terminating proof search procedure for $\mathcal{C}$ some machinery must be introduced (for instance, loop-checking). A calculus $\mathcal{C}$ is *weakly terminating* if it admits a terminating proof search strategy. The calculus $\mathsf{G3i}$ is weakly terminating. A well-known terminating calculus for IPL is $\mathsf{G4i}$ [2]; this is obtained from $\mathsf{G3i}$ by replacing the looping rule $L\rightarrow$ with more specialized rules: basically, the left rule with main formula $\alpha \rightarrow \beta$ is defined according to the structure of α. The same approach is used in [13,15], where the G4-variants of the G3-calculi for iSL are introduced. The obtained calculi are weakly (but not strongly) terminating and the proof search procedure yields a countermodel in case of failure. This means that, if proof search for a sequent $\sigma = \Gamma \Rightarrow \delta$ fails, one gets a Kripke model for σ (as defined in [1,7]) certifying that δ is not an iSL-consequence of Γ. These results have been definitely improved in [10], where the G4-style (strongly) terminating calculus $\mathsf{G4iSLt}$ for iSL is presented. Notably, the proofs of termination and completeness (via cut-admissibility) have been formalized in the Coq Proof Assistant.

So far, it seems that the only way to design a (weakly or strongly) terminating calculus for iSL is to throw rule $L\rightarrow$ away and to comply with G4-style. As a side effect, the obtained calculi lack the subformula property. Now, an intriguing question is: is it possible to get a terminating variant of $\mathsf{G3iSL}^+_\Box$ still preserving the subformula property? To address this issue, we follow the approach discussed in [4,5], where (strongly) terminating variants of the intuitionistic calculus $\mathsf{G3i}$ are introduced: the crucial expedient is to decorate the sequents with one of the labels b (blocked) and u (unblocked). In backward proof search, if a sequent has label b, the (backward) application of left rules is blocked, so that only right rules can be applied. Accordingly, bottom-up proof search alternates between an unblocked phase, where both left and right rules can be applied, and a blocked phase, where the focus is on the right formula (the application of left rules is forbidden). We call the obtained calculus $\mathsf{GbuSL}_\Box$ (see Fig. 2). The subformula property for $\mathsf{GbuSL}_\Box$ can be easily checked; to ascertain that $\mathsf{GbuSL}_\Box$ is terminating, we introduce the well-founded relation $\prec_{\mathrm{bu}}$ on labelled sequents (Definition 2). We show that a $\mathsf{GbuSL}_\Box$-derivation can be translated into a $\mathsf{G3iSL}_\Box^+$-derivation; as a corollary, the calculus $\mathsf{G3iSL}_\Box^+$ is weakly terminating. To prove the completeness of $\mathsf{GbuSL}_\Box$, we show that, if proof search for a sequent σ with label u fails, then a countermodel for σ can be built. An implementation of the proof search procedure, based on the Java framework JTabWb [6], is available at https://github.com/ferram/jtabwb_provers/tree/master/isl_gbuSL; the repository also contains the online appendix we refer to henceforth.

2 The Logic iSL

Formulas, denoted by lowercase Greek letters, are built from an enumerable set of propositional variables $\mathcal{V}$, the constant $\bot$ and the connectives $\wedge$, $\vee$, $\to$ and $\Box$; $\neg\alpha$ is an abbreviation for $\alpha \to \bot$. Let α be a formula and Γ a multiset of formulas. By $\Box\Gamma$ we denote the multiset $\{\Box\alpha \mid \alpha \in \Gamma\}$. By $\mathrm{Sf}(\alpha)$ we denote the set of the subformulas of α, including α itself; $\mathrm{Sf}(\Gamma)$ is the union of the sets $\mathrm{Sf}(\alpha)$, for every α in Γ. The size of α, denoted by $|\alpha|$, is the number of symbols in α; the size of Γ, denoted by $|\Gamma|$, is the sum of the sizes of formulas α in Γ, taking into account their multiplicity. A relation R is *well-founded* iff there is no infinite descending chain $\dots Rx_2Rx_1Rx_0$; R is *converse well-founded* if the converse relation R^{-1} is well-founded.

An iSL-*(Kripke) model* $\mathcal{K}$ is a tuple $\langle W, \leq, R, r, V\rangle$ where W is a non-empty set (worlds), $\leq$ (the intuitionistic relation) and R (the modal relation) are subsets of $W \times W$, r (the root) is the minimum element of W w.r.t. $\leq$, V (the valuation function) is a map from W to $2^{\mathcal{V}}$ such that:

(M1) $\leq$ is reflexive and transitive;
(M2) R is transitive and converse well-founded;
(M3) R is a subset of $\leq$;
(M4) if $w_0 \leq w_1$ and $w_1 R w_2$, then $w_0 R w_2$;
(M5) V is persistent, namely: $w_0 \leq w_1$ implies $V(w_0) \subseteq V(w_1)$.

Given an iSL-model $\mathcal{K}$, the forcing relation $\Vdash$ between worlds of $\mathcal{K}$ and formulas is defined as follows:

$\mathcal{K}, w \Vdash p$ iff $p \in V(w)$, $\forall p \in \mathcal{V}$ $\qquad$ $\mathcal{K}, w \nVdash \bot$

$\mathcal{K}, w \Vdash \alpha \wedge \beta$ iff $\mathcal{K}, w \Vdash \alpha$ and $\mathcal{K}, w \Vdash \beta$ $\qquad$ $\mathcal{K}, w \Vdash \alpha \vee \beta$ iff $\mathcal{K}, w \Vdash \alpha$ or $\mathcal{K}, w \Vdash \beta$

$\mathcal{K}, w \Vdash \alpha \to \beta$ iff $\forall w' \geq w$, if $\mathcal{K}, w' \Vdash \alpha$ then $\mathcal{K}, w' \Vdash \beta$

$\mathcal{K}, w \Vdash \Box\alpha$ iff $\forall w' \in W$, if wRw' then $\mathcal{K}, w' \Vdash \alpha$.

We write $w \Vdash \varphi$ instead of $\mathcal{K}, w \Vdash \varphi$ when the model $\mathcal{K}$ at hand is clear from the context. One can easily prove that forcing is persistent, i.e.: if $w \Vdash \varphi$ and $w \leq w'$, then $w' \Vdash \varphi$. Let Γ be a (multi)set of formulas. By $w \Vdash \Gamma$ we mean that $w \Vdash \varphi$, for every φ in Γ. The iSL-consequence relation $\models_{\mathsf{iSL}}$ is defined as follows:

$$\Gamma \models_{\mathsf{iSL}} \varphi \quad \text{iff} \quad \forall \mathcal{K}\, \forall w\ (\mathcal{K}, w \Vdash \Gamma \implies \mathcal{K}, w \Vdash \varphi).$$

$$\frac{}{p, \Gamma \Rightarrow p}\ \mathrm{Id} \qquad \frac{}{\bot, \Gamma \Rightarrow \delta}\ L\bot \qquad \frac{\alpha, \beta, \Gamma \Rightarrow \delta}{\alpha \wedge \beta, \Gamma \Rightarrow \delta}\ L\wedge$$

$$\frac{\Gamma \Rightarrow \alpha \qquad \Gamma \Rightarrow \beta}{\Gamma \Rightarrow \alpha \wedge \beta}\ R\wedge \qquad \frac{\alpha, \Gamma \Rightarrow \delta \qquad \beta, \Gamma \Rightarrow \delta}{\alpha \vee \beta, \Gamma \Rightarrow \delta}\ L\vee \qquad \frac{\Gamma \Rightarrow \alpha_k}{\Gamma \Rightarrow \alpha_0 \vee \alpha_1}\ R\vee_k$$

$$\frac{\alpha \to \beta, \Gamma \Rightarrow \alpha \qquad \beta, \Gamma \Rightarrow \delta}{\alpha \to \beta, \Gamma \Rightarrow \delta}\ L\to \qquad \frac{\alpha, \Gamma \Rightarrow \beta}{\Gamma \Rightarrow \alpha \to \beta}\ R\to \qquad \frac{\Box\alpha, \Gamma, \Delta \Rightarrow \alpha}{\Gamma, \Box\Delta \Rightarrow \Box\alpha}\ R\Box$$

Fig. 1. The calculus $\mathsf{G3iSL}^+_\Box$ ($p \in \mathcal{V}$, $k \in \{0,1\}$).

The logic iSL is the set of formulas φ such that $\emptyset \models_{\mathsf{iSL}} \varphi$. Accordingly, if $\varphi \notin \mathsf{iSL}$, there exists an iSL-model $\mathcal{K}$ such that $r \nVdash \varphi$, with r the root of $\mathcal{K}$; we call $\mathcal{K}$ a *countermodel* for φ. We stress that iSL satisfies the finite model property [16]; thus, we can assume that iSL-models are finite and condition (M2) can be rephrased as "R is transitive and irreflexive".

Example 1. Figure 5 defines a formula ψ and a countermodel $\mathcal{K}$ for ψ. The worlds of $\mathcal{K}$ are w_2 (the root), w_7, w_{12}, w_{15}, w_{19}, w_{24}. The relations $\leq$ and R of $\mathcal{K}$ can be inferred by the displayed arrows, as accounted for in the figure. For instance $w_2 \leq w_{19}$, since there is a path from w_2 and w_{19} (actually, a unique path); $w_2 \leq w_{15}$ and $w_2 R w_{15}$, since the path from w_2 and w_{15} ends with the solid arrow $\rightarrow$. However, it is not the case that $w_2 R w_{19}$, since the path from w_2 to w_{19} ends with the dashed arrow $\dashrightarrow$. In each world w_k, the first line displays the value of $V(w_k)$, the remaining lines report (separated by commas) some of the formulas forced and not forced in w_k. Since $w_2 \nVdash \psi$, $\mathcal{K}$ is a countermodel for ψ.

We remark that, if we replace a dashed arrow with a solid arrow, or vice-versa, we get $w_2 \Vdash \psi$, thus $\mathcal{K}$ is no longer a countermodel for ψ. For instance, let us set $w_2 \rightarrow w_7$. Then, $w_2 R w_7$ and, since $w_7 \nVdash s$, we get $w_2 \nVdash \Box s$, hence $w_2 \nVdash \alpha$. Since $w_7 \Vdash \gamma$ and $w_{12} \Vdash \beta$, it follows that $w_2 \Vdash \psi$. Similarly, assume $w_{15} \rightarrow w_{19}$, which implies $w_{15} R w_{19}$. Then $w_{15} \nVdash \Box\neg p$ (indeed, $w_{15} R w_{19}$ and $w_{19} \nVdash \neg p$) and, by the fact that $w_2 R w_{15}$, we get $w_2 \nVdash \Box\Box\neg p$, thus $w_2 \nVdash \alpha$; as in the previous case, we conclude $w_2 \Vdash \psi$. Let us set $w_2 \rightarrow w_{12}$. Since $w_{12} \nVdash \Box\neg p$ and $w_2 R w_{12}$, we get $w_2 \nVdash \Box\Box\neg p$; this implies that $w_2 \Vdash \psi$. $\Diamond$

In the paper we introduce some sequent calculi for iSL. For the notation and the terminology about a generic calculus $\mathcal{C}$ (e.g., the notions of $\mathcal{C}$-tree, $\mathcal{C}$-derivation, branch, depth of a $\mathcal{C}$-tree), we refer to [12]. By $\vdash_{\mathcal{C}} \sigma$ we mean that the sequent σ is derivable in the calculus $\mathcal{C}$. Let $\mathcal{C}$ be a calculus and let $\prec$ be a relation on the sequents of $\mathcal{C}$. A rule $\mathcal{R}$ of $\mathcal{C}$ is *decreasing w.r.t.* $\prec$ iff, for every application ρ of $\mathcal{R}$, if σ is the conclusion of ρ and σ' is any of the premises of ρ, then $\sigma' \prec \sigma$. A calculus $\mathcal{C}$ is *terminating* iff there exists a well-founded relation $\prec$ such that every rule of $\mathcal{C}$ is decreasing w.r.t. $\prec$.

The calculus $\mathsf{G3iSL}^+_\Box$ in Fig. 1 is obtained by adding the rule $R\Box$ to the intuitionistic calculus G3i [12]. Sequents of $\mathsf{G3iSL}^+_\Box$ have the form $\Gamma \Rightarrow \delta$, where Γ is a finite multiset of formulas and δ is a formula. The calculus is very close to the variant $\mathsf{G3iSL}^a_\Box$ of the calculus $\mathsf{G3iSL}_\Box$ for iSL presented in [13,15]. The notable difference is in the presentation of rule $R\Box$: given the conclusion $\Gamma, \Box\Delta \Rightarrow \Box\alpha$, in $\mathsf{G3iSL}^a_\Box$ the premise is $\Box\alpha, \Gamma, \Box\Delta, \Delta \Rightarrow \alpha$, in $\mathsf{G3iSL}^+_\Box$ the redundant multiset $\Box\Delta$ is omitted. The calculus $\mathsf{G3iSL}^+_\Box$ is sound and complete for iSL:

Theorem 1. $\vdash_{\mathsf{G3iSL}^+_\Box} \Gamma \Rightarrow \delta$ *iff* $\Gamma \models_{\mathsf{iSL}} \delta$.

The soundness of $\mathsf{G3iSL}^+_\Box$ (the only-if side of Theorem 1) immediately follows from the soundness of $\mathsf{G3iSL}^a_\Box$ (for a semantic proof, see the online appendix); the completeness is discussed in Sect. 4.[1] It is easy to check that $\mathsf{G3iSL}^+_\Box$ enjoys the subformula property; however, as discussed in the Introduction, $\mathsf{G3iSL}^+_\Box$ is not terminating, due to the presence of rule $L{\rightarrow}$.

3 The Sequent Calculus $\mathsf{GbuSL}_\Box$

The sequent calculus $\mathsf{GbuSL}_\Box$ is obtained from $\mathsf{G3iSL}^+_\Box$ by refining the sequent definition: we decorate sequents by a label l, where l can be b (blocked) or u (unblocked). Thus, a $\mathsf{GbuSL}_\Box$-sequent σ has the form $\Gamma \overset{l}{\Rightarrow} \delta$, with $l \in \{\mathrm{b}, \mathrm{u}\}$; Γ and δ are referred to as the lhs and the rhs (left/right hand side) of σ respectively. We call l-sequent a sequent with label l; $\mathrm{Sf}(\Gamma \overset{l}{\Rightarrow} \delta)$ denotes the set $\mathrm{Sf}(\Gamma \cup \{\delta\})$. To define the calculus, we introduce the following evaluation relation.

Definition 1 (Evaluation). *Let Γ be a multiset of formulas and φ a formula. We say that Γ evaluates φ, written $\Gamma \rhd \varphi$, iff φ matches the following BNF:*

$$\varphi := \gamma \mid \varphi \wedge \varphi \mid \varphi \vee \alpha \mid \alpha \vee \varphi \mid \alpha \rightarrow \varphi \mid \Box\varphi \qquad \text{with } \gamma \in \Gamma \text{ and } \alpha \text{ any formula.}$$

By $\Gamma \rhd \Delta$ we mean that $\Gamma \rhd \delta$, for every $\delta \in \Delta$. We state some properties of evaluation.

Lemma 1.

(i) If $\Gamma \rhd \varphi$ and $\Gamma \subseteq \Gamma'$, then $\Gamma' \rhd \varphi$.
(ii) If $\Gamma \cup \Delta \rhd \varphi$ and $\Gamma' \rhd \Delta$, then $\Gamma \cup \Gamma' \rhd \varphi$.
(iii) If $\Gamma \rhd \varphi$, then $\Gamma \cap \mathrm{Sf}(\varphi) \rhd \varphi$.
(iv) If $\Gamma \rhd \varphi$, then $\vdash_{\mathsf{G3iSL}^+_\Box} \Gamma \Rightarrow \varphi$.
(v) If $\Gamma \rhd \varphi$ and $\mathcal{K}, w \Vdash \Gamma$, then $\mathcal{K}, w \Vdash \varphi$.

Proof. All the assertions are proved by induction on the structure of φ.
(i). Let $\Gamma \rhd \varphi$ and $\Gamma \subseteq \Gamma'$; we prove $\Gamma' \rhd \varphi$. If $\varphi \in \Gamma$, then $\varphi \in \Gamma'$, hence $\Gamma' \rhd \varphi$. Let us assume $\varphi \notin \Gamma$. If $\varphi = \alpha \wedge \beta$, then $\Gamma \rhd \alpha$ and $\Gamma \rhd \beta$. By the induction hypothesis, we get $\Gamma' \rhd \alpha$ and $\Gamma' \rhd \beta$, hence $\Gamma' \rhd \alpha \wedge \beta$. The other cases are similar.
(ii). Let $\Gamma \cup \Delta \rhd \varphi$ and $\Gamma' \rhd \Delta$; we prove $\Gamma \cup \Gamma' \rhd \varphi$. Let us assume $\varphi \in \Gamma \cup \Delta$. If $\varphi \in \Gamma$, then $\Gamma \cup \Gamma' \rhd \varphi$. Otherwise, it holds that $\varphi \in \Delta$. Since $\Gamma' \rhd \Delta$, we

[1] We stress that the completeness of $\mathsf{G3iSL}^+_\Box$ is not a consequence of the one of $\mathsf{G3iSL}^a_\Box$, since rule $R\Box$ of $\mathsf{G3iSL}^+_\Box$ is a restriction of rule $R\Box$ of $\mathsf{G3iSL}^a_\Box$.

get $\Gamma' \rhd \varphi$; by point (i), we conclude $\Gamma \cup \Gamma' \rhd \varphi$. Let us assume $\varphi \notin \Gamma \cup \Delta$. If $\varphi = \alpha \wedge \beta$, then $\Gamma \cup \Delta \rhd \alpha$ and $\Gamma \cup \Delta \rhd \beta$. By the induction hypothesis we get $\Gamma \cup \Gamma' \rhd \alpha$ and $\Gamma \cup \Gamma' \rhd \beta$, hence $\Gamma \cup \Gamma' \rhd \alpha \wedge \beta$. The other cases are similar.
(iii). Let $\Gamma \rhd \varphi$: we prove $\Gamma \cap \mathrm{Sf}(\varphi) \rhd \varphi$. If $\varphi \in \Gamma$, then $\varphi \in \Gamma \cap \mathrm{Sf}(\varphi)$, which implies $\Gamma \cap \mathrm{Sf}(\varphi) \rhd \varphi$. Let $\varphi \notin \Gamma$. If $\varphi = \alpha \wedge \beta$, then $\Gamma \rhd \alpha$ and $\Gamma \rhd \beta$. By the induction hypothesis, we get $\Gamma \cap \mathrm{Sf}(\alpha) \rhd \alpha$ and $\Gamma \cap \mathrm{Sf}(\beta) \rhd \beta$. Since $\mathrm{Sf}(\alpha) \subseteq \mathrm{Sf}(\alpha \wedge \beta)$ and $\mathrm{Sf}(\beta) \subseteq \mathrm{Sf}(\alpha \wedge \beta)$, by point (i) we get $\Gamma \cap \mathrm{Sf}(\alpha \wedge \beta) \rhd \alpha$ and $\Gamma \cap \mathrm{Sf}(\alpha \wedge \beta) \rhd \beta$; we conclude $\Gamma \cap \mathrm{Sf}(\alpha \wedge \beta) \rhd \alpha \wedge \beta$. The other cases are similar.
(iv). We prove the assertion by outlining an effective procedure to build a G3iSL$^+_\Box$-derivation of the sequent $\Gamma \Rightarrow \varphi$. We start by showing that:

(*) $\vdash_{\mathsf{G3iSL}^+_\Box} \varphi, \Gamma \Rightarrow \varphi$, for every formula φ and every multiset of formulas Γ.

We prove (*) by induction on the structure of φ. If $\varphi \in \mathcal{V} \cup \{\bot\}$, a G3iSL$^+_\Box$-derivation of $\varphi, \Gamma \Rightarrow \varphi$ is obtained by applying rule Id or rule $L\bot$. Otherwise, a G3iSL$^+_\Box$-derivation of $\varphi, \Gamma \Rightarrow \varphi$ can be built as follows, according to the form of φ, where the omitted G3iSL$^+_\Box$-derivations are given by the induction hypothesis:

$$\dfrac{\dfrac{\overset{\vdots}{\alpha, \beta, \Gamma \Rightarrow \alpha}}{\alpha \wedge \beta, \Gamma \Rightarrow \alpha}\,L\wedge \qquad \dfrac{\overset{\vdots}{\alpha, \beta, \Gamma \Rightarrow \beta}}{\alpha \wedge \beta, \Gamma \Rightarrow \beta}\,L\wedge}{\alpha \wedge \beta, \Gamma \Rightarrow \alpha \wedge \beta}\,R\wedge \qquad \dfrac{\dfrac{\overset{\vdots}{\alpha, \Gamma \Rightarrow \alpha}}{\alpha, \Gamma \Rightarrow \alpha \vee \beta}\,R\vee_0 \qquad \dfrac{\overset{\vdots}{\beta, \Gamma \Rightarrow \beta}}{\beta, \Gamma \Rightarrow \alpha \vee \beta}\,R\vee_1}{\alpha \vee \beta, \Gamma \Rightarrow \alpha \vee \beta}\,L\vee$$

$$\dfrac{\dfrac{\overset{\vdots}{\alpha, \alpha \to \beta, \Gamma \Rightarrow \alpha} \qquad \overset{\vdots}{\alpha, \beta, \Gamma \Rightarrow \beta}}{\alpha, \alpha \to \beta, \Gamma \Rightarrow \beta}\,L\to}{\alpha \to \beta, \Gamma \Rightarrow \alpha \to \beta}\,R\to \qquad \dfrac{\overset{\vdots}{\Box\alpha, \alpha, \Gamma \Rightarrow \alpha}}{\Box\alpha, \Gamma \Rightarrow \Box\alpha}\,R\Box$$

Let $\Gamma \rhd \varphi$; we show that $\Gamma \Rightarrow \varphi$ is provable in G3iSL$^+_\Box$. If $\varphi \in \Gamma$, the assertion follows by (*). Let us assume $\varphi \notin \Gamma$. According to the shape of φ, a G3iSL$^+_\Box$-derivation of $\Gamma \Rightarrow \varphi$ can be built as follows:

$$\dfrac{\overset{\vdots}{\Gamma \Rightarrow \alpha} \qquad \overset{\vdots}{\Gamma \Rightarrow \beta}}{\Gamma \Rightarrow \alpha \wedge \beta}\,R\wedge \qquad \dfrac{\overset{\vdots}{\Gamma \Rightarrow \alpha_k}}{\Gamma \Rightarrow \alpha_0 \vee \alpha_1}\,R\vee_k \qquad \dfrac{\overset{\vdots}{\alpha, \Gamma \Rightarrow \beta}}{\Gamma \Rightarrow \alpha \to \beta}\,R\to \qquad \dfrac{\overset{\vdots}{\Box\alpha, \Gamma \Rightarrow \alpha}}{\Gamma \Rightarrow \Box\alpha}\,R\Box$$

The omitted G3iSL$^+_\Box$-derivations exist by the induction hypothesis; for instance, if $\varphi = \alpha \wedge \beta$, then $\Gamma \rhd \alpha$ and $\Gamma \rhd \beta$, hence both $\Gamma \Rightarrow \alpha$ and $\Gamma \Rightarrow \beta$ are provable in G3iSL$^+_\Box$. In the cases $\varphi = \alpha \to \beta$ and $\varphi = \Box\alpha$, we also have to use point (i). For instance, let $\varphi = \alpha \to \beta$; then, $\Gamma \rhd \beta$ and, by point (i), we get $\Gamma \cup \{\alpha\} \rhd \beta$, hence the G3iSL$^+_\Box$-derivation of $\alpha, \Gamma \Rightarrow \beta$ exists by the induction hypothesis.
(v). Let $\Gamma \rhd \varphi$ and $w \Vdash \Gamma$ (in $\mathcal{K}$); we prove that $w \Vdash \varphi$. The case $\varphi \in \Gamma$ is trivial. Let $\varphi \notin \Gamma$. If $\varphi = \alpha \wedge \beta$, then $\Gamma \rhd \alpha$ and $\Gamma \rhd \beta$. By the induction hypothesis, we get $w \Vdash \alpha$ and $w \Vdash \beta$, hence $w \Vdash \alpha \wedge \beta$. The other cases are similar. ∎

$$\dfrac{}{\Gamma \overset{l}{\Rightarrow} \alpha}\,\mathrm{Ax}^{\rhd} \quad \text{if } \Gamma \rhd \alpha \qquad\qquad \dfrac{}{\bot, \Gamma \overset{\mathrm{u}}{\Rightarrow} \delta}\,L\bot$$

$$\dfrac{\alpha, \beta, \Gamma \overset{\mathrm{u}}{\Rightarrow} \delta}{\alpha \wedge \beta, \Gamma \overset{\mathrm{u}}{\Rightarrow} \delta}\,L\wedge \qquad\qquad \dfrac{\Gamma \overset{l}{\Rightarrow} \alpha \qquad \Gamma \overset{l}{\Rightarrow} \beta}{\Gamma \overset{l}{\Rightarrow} \alpha \wedge \beta}\,R\wedge$$

$$\dfrac{\alpha, \Gamma \overset{\mathrm{u}}{\Rightarrow} \delta \qquad \beta, \Gamma \overset{\mathrm{u}}{\Rightarrow} \delta}{\alpha \vee \beta, \Gamma \overset{\mathrm{u}}{\Rightarrow} \delta}\,L\vee \qquad\qquad \dfrac{\Gamma \overset{\mathrm{b}}{\Rightarrow} \alpha_k}{\Gamma \overset{l}{\Rightarrow} \alpha_0 \vee \alpha_1}\,R\vee_k$$

$$\dfrac{\alpha \to \beta, \Gamma \overset{\mathrm{b}}{\Rightarrow} \alpha \qquad \beta, \Gamma \overset{\mathrm{u}}{\Rightarrow} \delta}{\alpha \to \beta, \Gamma \overset{\mathrm{u}}{\Rightarrow} \delta}\,L\to$$

$$\dfrac{\Gamma \overset{l}{\Rightarrow} \beta}{\Gamma \overset{l}{\Rightarrow} \alpha \to \beta}\,R^{\rhd}_{\to} \quad \text{if } \Gamma \rhd \alpha \qquad\qquad \dfrac{\alpha, \Gamma \overset{\mathrm{u}}{\Rightarrow} \beta}{\Gamma \overset{l}{\Rightarrow} \alpha \to \beta}\,R^{\not\rhd}_{\to} \quad \text{if } \Gamma \not\rhd \alpha$$

$$\dfrac{\Gamma, \Delta \overset{\mathrm{u}}{\Rightarrow} \alpha}{\Gamma, \Box\Delta \overset{\mathrm{u}}{\Rightarrow} \Box\alpha}\,R^{\Box}_{\mathrm{u}} \qquad\qquad \dfrac{\Box\alpha, \Gamma, \Delta \overset{\mathrm{u}}{\Rightarrow} \alpha}{\Gamma, \Box\Delta \overset{\mathrm{b}}{\Rightarrow} \Box\alpha}\,R^{\Box}_{\mathrm{b}} \quad \text{if } \Gamma \cup \Box\Delta \not\rhd \Box\alpha$$

Fig. 2. The calculus $\mathsf{GbuSL}_{\Box}$ ($l \in \{\mathrm{b}, \mathrm{u}\}$, $k \in \{0, 1\}$).

The calculus $\mathsf{GbuSL}_{\Box}$ (see Fig. 2) consists of the axiom rules $\mathrm{Ax}^{\rhd}$ and $L\bot$, together with left/right rules for each logical operator. The calculus is oriented to backward proof search, where rules are applied bottom-up. If the conclusion of a rule has label b, the (bottom-up) application of left rules is blocked. There are two rules for right implication, namely $R^{\rhd}_{\to}$ and $R^{\not\rhd}_{\to}$; the choice between them is settled by the evaluation relation $\rhd$. Right $\Box$-formulas are handled by rules $R^{\Box}_{\mathrm{u}}$ and $R^{\Box}_{\mathrm{b}}$; here the choice is determined by the label of the conclusion. We remark that if $\sigma = \Gamma, \Box\Delta \overset{\mathrm{b}}{\Rightarrow} \Box\alpha$ and $\Gamma \cup \Box\Delta \rhd \Box\alpha$, then σ is an axiom sequent (see rule $\mathrm{Ax}^{\rhd}$) and an application of rule $R^{\Box}_{\mathrm{b}}$ to σ is prevented by the side condition of $R^{\Box}_{\mathrm{b}}$. Rule $R^{\Box}_{\mathrm{b}}$ is similar to rule $R\Box$ of $\mathsf{G3iSL}^{+}_{\Box}$: both rules introduce in the lhs of the premise a copy of the main formula $\Box\alpha$ (also called *diagonal formula*); in rule $R^{\Box}_{\mathrm{u}}$ such a duplication is not required. In backward proof search, a b-sequent starts the construction of a branch only containing b-sequents, where only right rules are applied. This phase ends either when an axiom sequent is obtained or when no rule can be applied or when one of the rules turning a label b into u is applied (namely, rules $R^{\not\rhd}_{\to}$ and $R^{\Box}_{\mathrm{b}}$).

Example 2. We show a $\mathsf{GbuSL}_{\Box}$-derivation of the u-sequent $\sigma_0 = \overset{\mathrm{u}}{\Rightarrow} \neg\neg\Box p$.

$$\dfrac{\dfrac{\dfrac{\dfrac{}{\Box p, \neg\Box p \overset{\mathrm{b}}{\Rightarrow} \Box p\ _{(4)}}\,\mathrm{Ax}^{\rhd} \qquad \dfrac{}{\Box p, \bot \overset{\mathrm{u}}{\Rightarrow} p\ _{(5)}}\,L\bot}{\Box p, \neg\Box p \overset{\mathrm{u}}{\Rightarrow} p\ _{(3)}}\,L\to}{\neg\Box p \overset{\mathrm{b}}{\Rightarrow} \Box p\ _{(2)}}\,R^{\Box}_{\mathrm{b}} \qquad \dfrac{}{\bot \overset{\mathrm{u}}{\Rightarrow} \bot\ _{(6)}}\,L\bot}{\dfrac{\neg\Box p \overset{\mathrm{u}}{\Rightarrow} \bot\ _{(1)}}{\overset{\mathrm{u}}{\Rightarrow} \neg\neg\Box p\ _{(0)}}\,R^{\not\rhd}_{\to}}\,L\to$$

In the derivations each sequent is marked with an index (n) so that we can refer to it as σ_n. The above derivation highlights some of the peculiarities of $\mathsf{GbuSL}_\Box$. In backward proof search, σ_2 is obtained by a (backward) application of rule $L\to$ to σ_1; the label b in σ_2 is crucial to block the application of rule $L\to$, which would generate an infinite branch. The sequent σ_3 is obtained by the application of rule $R^{\Box}_{\mathrm{b}}$ to σ_2. In this case, the key feature is the presence of the diagonal formula $\Box p$; without it, the sequent σ_3 would be $\neg\Box p \stackrel{\mathrm{u}}{\Rightarrow} p$ and, after the application of $L\to$ (the only applicable rule), the left premise would be $\sigma_4 = \neg\Box p \stackrel{\mathrm{b}}{\Rightarrow} \Box p$, which yields a loop ($\sigma_4 = \sigma_2$). $\Diamond$

We state the main properties of $\mathsf{GbuSL}_\Box$.

Theorem 2.

(i) $\mathsf{GbuSL}_\Box$ *has the subformula property.*
(ii) $\mathsf{GbuSL}_\Box$ *is terminating.*
(iii) $\vdash_{\mathsf{GbuSL}_\Box} \Gamma \stackrel{l}{\Rightarrow} \delta$ *implies* $\Gamma \models_{\mathsf{iSL}} \delta$ *(Soundness).*
(iv) $\Gamma \models_{\mathsf{iSL}} \delta$ *implies* $\vdash_{\mathsf{GbuSL}_\Box} \Gamma \stackrel{\mathrm{u}}{\Rightarrow} \delta$ *(Completeness).*

We remark that in soundness l is any label; instead, in completeness the label is set to u. For instance, since $p \vee q \models_{\mathsf{iSL}} q \vee p$, completeness guarantees that the u-sequent $\sigma^{\mathrm{u}} = p \vee q \stackrel{\mathrm{u}}{\Rightarrow} q \vee p$ is provable in $\mathsf{GbuSL}_\Box$. A $\mathsf{GbuSL}_\Box$-derivation of σ^{u} is obtained by first (upwards) applying rule $L\vee$ to σ^{u} and then one of the rules $R\vee_0$ or $R\vee_1$; if we first apply a right rule, we are stuck (e.g., if we apply $R\vee_0$ to σ^{u}, we get the unprovable sequent $p \vee q \stackrel{\mathrm{u}}{\Rightarrow} q$). On the contrary, the b-sequent $p \vee q \stackrel{\mathrm{b}}{\Rightarrow} q \vee p$ is not provable in $\mathsf{GbuSL}_\Box$, since the label b inhibits the application of rule $L\vee$ and forces the application of a right rule.

The subformula property of $\mathsf{GbuSL}_\Box$ can be easily checked by inspecting the rules; termination is discussed below and completeness in the next section. Soundness can be proved in different ways. One can exploit semantics, relying on the fact that rules preserve the consequence relation $\models_{\mathsf{iSL}}$ (see the online appendix). Here we prove the soundness of $\mathsf{GbuSL}_\Box$ by showing that $\mathsf{GbuSL}_\Box$-derivations can be mapped to $\mathsf{G3iSL}^{+}_{\Box}$-derivations.

Proposition 1. *If* $\mathsf{GbuSL}_\Box \vdash \Gamma \stackrel{l}{\Rightarrow} \delta$, *then* $\mathsf{G3iSL}^{+}_{\Box} \vdash \Gamma \Rightarrow \delta$.

Proof. Let $\mathcal{T}$ be a $\mathsf{GbuSL}_\Box$-tree with root sequent $\sigma = \Gamma \stackrel{l}{\Rightarrow} \delta$; $\mathcal{T}$ can be translated into a $\mathsf{G3iSL}^{+}_{\Box}$-tree $\tilde{\mathcal{T}}$ having root sequent $\tilde{\sigma} = \Gamma \Rightarrow \delta$ by erasing the labels and weakening the lhs of sequents when rules $R\stackrel{\rhd}{\to}$ and $R^{\Box}_{\mathrm{u}}$ are applied. Assume now that the $\mathsf{GbuSL}_\Box$-tree $\mathcal{T}$ is a $\mathsf{GbuSL}_\Box$-derivation of σ and let $\sigma^\star = \Delta \Rightarrow \varphi$ be a leaf of $\tilde{\mathcal{T}}$ which is not an axiom of $\mathsf{G3iSL}^{+}_{\Box}$. Note that $\Delta \rhd \varphi$, hence by Lemma 1(iv) we can build a $\mathsf{G3iSL}^{+}_{\Box}$-derivation $\mathcal{D}^\star$ of $\sigma^\star$. By replacing in $\tilde{\mathcal{T}}$ every leaf $\sigma^\star$ with the corresponding derivation $\mathcal{D}^\star$, we eventually get a $\mathsf{G3iSL}^{+}_{\Box}$-derivation of $\tilde{\sigma}$. ■

To prove the termination of $\mathsf{GbuSL}_\Box$ we have to introduce a proper well-founded relation $\prec_{\mathrm{bu}}$ on labelled sequents. As mentioned in the Introduction, the main problem stems from rule $L\to$. Let σ and σ' be the conclusion and the left premise of an application of rule $L\to$; we stipulate that $\sigma' \prec_{\mathrm{bu}} \sigma$ since σ' has label b and σ has label u; thus, we establish that b weighs less than u. Now, we need a way out to accommodate rules $R_{\to}^{\not\triangleright}$ and $R_{\mathrm{b}}^{\Box}$ that, read bottom-up, switch b with u. In both cases, we observe that the lhs of the premise evaluates a new formula; e.g., in the application of rule $R_{\to}^{\not\triangleright}$ having premise $\alpha, \Gamma \overset{\mathrm{u}}{\Rightarrow} \beta$ and conclusion $\Gamma \overset{l}{\Rightarrow} \alpha \to \beta$, it holds that $\Gamma \not\triangleright \alpha$ (side condition) and $\Gamma \cup \{\alpha\} \triangleright \alpha$ (definition of $\triangleright$); this suggests that here we can exploit the evaluation relation. Let Ev be defined as follows:

$$\mathrm{Ev}(\Gamma \overset{l}{\Rightarrow} \delta) \;=\; \{\varphi \mid \varphi \in \mathrm{Sf}(\Gamma \cup \{\delta\}) \text{ and } \Gamma \triangleright \varphi\}$$

Note that $\mathrm{Ev}(\sigma) \subseteq \mathrm{Sf}(\sigma)$. We also have to take into account the size of a sequents, where $|\Gamma \overset{l}{\Rightarrow} \delta| = |\Gamma| + |\delta|$. This leads to the definition of $\prec_{\mathrm{bu}}$:

Definition 2 ($\prec_{\mathrm{bu}}$). *$\sigma' \prec_{\mathrm{bu}} \sigma$ iff one of the following conditions holds:*

(a) $\mathrm{Sf}(\sigma') \subset \mathrm{Sf}(\sigma)$;
(b) $\mathrm{Sf}(\sigma') = \mathrm{Sf}(\sigma)$ *and* $\mathrm{Ev}(\sigma') \supset \mathrm{Ev}(\sigma)$;
(c) $\mathrm{Sf}(\sigma') = \mathrm{Sf}(\sigma)$ *and* $\mathrm{Ev}(\sigma') = \mathrm{Ev}(\sigma)$ *and* $\mathrm{label}(\sigma') = \mathrm{b}$ *and* $\mathrm{label}(\sigma) = \mathrm{u}$;
(d) $\mathrm{Sf}(\sigma') = \mathrm{Sf}(\sigma)$ *and* $\mathrm{Ev}(\sigma') = \mathrm{Ev}(\sigma)$ *and* $\mathrm{label}(\sigma') = \mathrm{label}(\sigma)$ *and* $|\sigma'| < |\sigma|$.

Proposition 2. *The relation $\prec_{\mathrm{bu}}$ is well-founded.*

Proof. Assume, by contradiction, that there is an infinite descending chain of the kind $\ldots \prec_{\mathrm{bu}} \sigma_1 \prec_{\mathrm{bu}} \sigma_0$. Since $\mathrm{Sf}(\sigma_0) \supseteq \mathrm{Sf}(\sigma_1) \supseteq \ldots$ and $\mathrm{Sf}(\sigma_0)$ is finite, the sets $\mathrm{Sf}(\sigma_j)$ eventually stabilize, namely: there is $k \geq 0$ such that $\mathrm{Sf}(\sigma_j) = \mathrm{Sf}(\sigma_k)$ for every $j \geq k$. Since $\mathrm{Ev}(\sigma_j) \subseteq \mathrm{Sf}(\sigma_j)$, we get $\mathrm{Ev}(\sigma_k) \subseteq \mathrm{Ev}(\sigma_{k+1}) \subseteq \ldots \subseteq \mathrm{Sf}(\sigma_k)$. Since $\mathrm{Sf}(\sigma_k)$ is finite, there is $m \geq k$ such that $\mathrm{Ev}(\sigma_j) = \mathrm{Ev}(\sigma_m)$ for every $j \geq m$. This implies that there exists $n \geq m$ such that all the sequents $\sigma_n, \sigma_{n+1}, \ldots$ have the same label; accordingly $|\sigma_n| > |\sigma_{n+1}| > |\sigma_{n+2}| > \ldots \geq 0$, a contradiction. We conclude that $\prec_{\mathrm{bu}}$ is well-founded. ∎

To prove that the rules of $\mathsf{GbuSL}_{\Box}$ are decreasing w.r.t.$\prec_{\mathrm{bu}}$, we need the following property.

Lemma 2. *Let ρ be an application of a rule of $\mathsf{GbuSL}_{\Box}$, let σ be the conclusion of ρ and σ' any of the premises. For every formula φ, if $\mathrm{lhs}(\sigma) \triangleright \varphi$ then $\mathrm{lhs}(\sigma') \triangleright \varphi$.*

Proof. The assertion can be proved by applying Lemma 1. For instance, let $\sigma = \Gamma, \Box\Delta \overset{\mathrm{u}}{\Rightarrow} \Box\alpha$ and $\sigma' = \Gamma, \Delta \overset{\mathrm{u}}{\Rightarrow} \alpha$ be the conclusion and the premise of rule $R_{\mathrm{u}}^{\Box}$; assume that $\Gamma \cup \Box\Delta \triangleright \varphi$. Since $\Delta \triangleright \Box\Delta$, by Lemma 1(ii) get $\Gamma \cup \Delta \triangleright \varphi$. ∎

Proposition 3. *Every rule of the calculus $\mathsf{GbuSL}_{\Box}$ is decreasing w.r.t. $\prec_{\mathrm{bu}}$.*

Proof. Let σ and σ' be the conclusion and one of the premises of an application of a rule of $\mathsf{GbuSL}_{\Box}$. Note that $\mathrm{Sf}(\sigma') \subseteq \mathrm{Sf}(\sigma)$; moreover, if $\mathrm{Sf}(\sigma') = \mathrm{Sf}(\sigma)$, by Lemma 2 we get $\mathrm{Ev}(\sigma') \supseteq \mathrm{Ev}(\sigma)$. We can prove $\sigma' \prec_{\mathrm{bu}} \sigma$ by a case analysis; we only detail two significant cases.

Γ^{at} is a multiset of propositional variables, $\Gamma^{\rightarrow}$ is a multiset of $\rightarrow$-formulas

$$\frac{}{\sigma}\ \mathrm{Irr}\quad \text{if } \sigma \text{ is irreducible} \qquad \frac{\alpha, \beta, \Gamma \overset{\mathrm{u}}{\not\Rightarrow} \delta}{\alpha \wedge \beta, \Gamma \overset{\mathrm{u}}{\not\Rightarrow} \delta}\ L\wedge \qquad \frac{\Gamma \overset{l}{\not\Rightarrow} \alpha_k}{\Gamma \overset{l}{\not\Rightarrow} \alpha_0 \wedge \alpha_1}\ R\wedge_k$$

$$\frac{\alpha_k, \Gamma \overset{\mathrm{u}}{\not\Rightarrow} \delta}{\alpha_0 \vee \alpha_1, \Gamma \overset{\mathrm{u}}{\not\Rightarrow} \delta}\ L\vee_k \qquad \frac{\Gamma \overset{\mathrm{b}}{\not\Rightarrow} \alpha \qquad \Gamma \overset{\mathrm{b}}{\not\Rightarrow} \beta}{\Gamma \overset{\mathrm{b}}{\not\Rightarrow} \alpha \vee \beta}\ R\vee \qquad \frac{\beta, \Gamma \overset{\mathrm{u}}{\not\Rightarrow} \delta}{\alpha \rightarrow \beta, \Gamma \overset{\mathrm{u}}{\not\Rightarrow} \delta}\ L\rightarrow$$

$$\frac{\Gamma \overset{l}{\not\Rightarrow} \beta}{\Gamma \overset{l}{\not\Rightarrow} \alpha \rightarrow \beta}\ R\overset{\rhd}{\rightarrow}\ \ \Gamma \rhd \alpha \qquad \frac{\alpha, \Gamma \overset{\mathrm{u}}{\not\Rightarrow} \beta}{\Gamma \overset{l}{\not\Rightarrow} \alpha \rightarrow \beta}\ R\overset{\not\rhd}{\rightarrow}\ \ \Gamma \not\rhd \alpha$$

$$\frac{\Box\alpha, \Gamma^{\mathrm{at}}, \Gamma^{\rightarrow}, \Delta \overset{\mathrm{u}}{\not\Rightarrow} \alpha}{\underbrace{\Gamma^{\mathrm{at}}, \Gamma^{\rightarrow}, \Box\Delta}_{\Gamma} \overset{\mathrm{b}}{\not\Rightarrow} \Box\alpha}\ R^{\Box}_{\mathrm{b}}\ \ \Gamma \not\rhd \Box\alpha \qquad \frac{\{\Gamma \overset{\mathrm{b}}{\not\Rightarrow} \alpha\}_{\alpha\rightarrow\beta\in\Gamma^{\rightarrow}}}{\Gamma^{\mathrm{at}}, \Gamma^{\rightarrow}, \Box\Delta \overset{\mathrm{u}}{\not\Rightarrow} \delta}\ \mathrm{S}^{\mathrm{At}}_{\mathrm{u}}\ \ \begin{array}{l}\Gamma^{\rightarrow} \neq \emptyset \\ \delta \in (\mathcal{V} \cup \{\bot\}) \setminus \Gamma^{\mathrm{at}}\end{array}$$

$$\frac{\{\Gamma \overset{\mathrm{b}}{\not\Rightarrow} \alpha\}_{\alpha\rightarrow\beta\in\Gamma^{\rightarrow}} \quad \Gamma \overset{\mathrm{b}}{\not\Rightarrow} \delta_0 \quad \Gamma \overset{\mathrm{b}}{\not\Rightarrow} \delta_1}{\Gamma^{\mathrm{at}}, \Gamma^{\rightarrow}, \Box\Delta \overset{\mathrm{u}}{\not\Rightarrow} \delta_0 \vee \delta_1}\ \mathrm{S}^{\vee}_{\mathrm{u}} \qquad \frac{\{\Gamma \overset{\mathrm{b}}{\not\Rightarrow} \alpha\}_{\alpha\rightarrow\beta\in\Gamma^{\rightarrow}} \quad \Gamma^{\mathrm{at}}, \Gamma^{\rightarrow}, \Delta \overset{\mathrm{u}}{\not\Rightarrow} \delta}{\Gamma^{\mathrm{at}}, \Gamma^{\rightarrow}, \Box\Delta \overset{\mathrm{u}}{\not\Rightarrow} \Box\delta}\ \mathrm{S}^{\Box}_{\mathrm{u}}$$

Fig. 3. The refutation calculus $\mathsf{RbuSL}_{\Box}$ ($l \in \{\mathrm{b}, \mathrm{u}\}$, $k \in \{0, 1\}$).

$$\frac{\sigma' \ =\ \alpha \rightarrow \beta, \Gamma \overset{\mathrm{b}}{\Rightarrow} \alpha \qquad \beta, \Gamma \overset{\mathrm{u}}{\Rightarrow} \delta}{\sigma\ =\ \alpha \rightarrow \beta, \Gamma \overset{\mathrm{u}}{\Rightarrow} \delta}\ L\rightarrow$$

If $\mathrm{Sf}(\sigma') \subset \mathrm{Sf}(\sigma)$, then $\sigma' \prec_{\mathrm{bu}} \sigma$ by point (a) of the definition. Otherwise, it holds that $\mathrm{Sf}(\sigma') = \mathrm{Sf}(\sigma)$ and $\mathrm{Ev}(\sigma') \supseteq \mathrm{Ev}(\sigma)$. If $\mathrm{Ev}(\sigma') \supset \mathrm{Ev}(\sigma)$, then $\sigma' \prec_{\mathrm{bu}} \sigma$ by point (b); otherwise, $\sigma' \prec_{\mathrm{bu}} \sigma$ follows by point (c).

$$\frac{\sigma' \ =\ \Box\alpha, \Gamma, \Delta \overset{\mathrm{u}}{\Rightarrow} \alpha}{\sigma\ =\ \Gamma, \Box\Delta \overset{l}{\Rightarrow} \Box\alpha}\ R^{\Box}_{\mathrm{b}} \qquad \Gamma \cup \Box\Delta \not\rhd \Box\alpha$$

If $\mathrm{Sf}(\sigma') \subset \mathrm{Sf}(\sigma)$, then $\sigma' \prec_{\mathrm{bu}} \sigma$ by point (a). Otherwise, $\mathrm{Sf}(\sigma') = \mathrm{Sf}(\sigma)$ and $\mathrm{Ev}(\sigma') \supseteq \mathrm{Ev}(\sigma)$. Note that $\Box\alpha \in \mathrm{Ev}(\sigma')$ and, by the side condition, $\Box\alpha \notin \mathrm{Ev}(\sigma)$. This implies that $\mathrm{Ev}(\sigma') \supset \mathrm{Ev}(\sigma)$, hence $\sigma' \prec_{\mathrm{bu}} \sigma$ by point (b). ■

By Proposition 2 and 3, we conclude that the calculus $\mathsf{GbuSL}_{\Box}$ is terminating.

4 The Refutation Calculus $\mathsf{RbuSL}_{\Box}$

A common technique to prove the completeness of a sequent calculus $\mathcal{C}$ consists in showing that, whenever a sequent σ is not provable in $\mathcal{C}$, then a counter-model for σ can be built (see, e.g., the proof of completeness of $\mathsf{G4iSL}_{\Box}$ discussed in [13,15]); we prove the completeness of $\mathsf{GbuSL}_{\Box}$ according with this plan. Following the ideas in [3–5,9], we formalize the notion of "non-provability in $\mathsf{GbuSL}_{\Box}$" by introducing the refutation calculus $\mathsf{RbuSL}_{\Box}$, a dual calculus to $\mathsf{GbuSL}_{\Box}$. Sequents of $\mathsf{RbuSL}_{\Box}$, called *antisequents*, have the form $\Gamma \overset{l}{\not\Rightarrow} \delta$. Intuitively, a derivation in $\mathsf{RbuSL}_{\Box}$ of $\Gamma \overset{l}{\not\Rightarrow} \delta$ witnesses that the sequent $\Gamma \overset{l}{\Rightarrow} \delta$ is refutable, that is, not provable, in $\mathsf{GbuSL}_\Box$. Henceforth, Γ^{at} denotes a finite multiset of propositional variables, $\Gamma^{\rightarrow}$ denotes a finite multiset of $\rightarrow$-formulas (i.e., formulas of the kind $\alpha \rightarrow \beta$). The axioms of $\mathsf{RbuSL}_\Box$ are the *irreducible antisequents*, namely the antisequents $\Gamma \stackrel{l}{\not\Rightarrow} \delta$ such that the corresponding dual sequents $\Gamma \stackrel{l}{\Rightarrow} \delta$ are not the conclusion of any of the rules of $\mathsf{GbuSL}_\Box$. Irreducible antisequents are characterized as follows:

Definition 3. *An antisequent σ is* irreducible *iff $\sigma = \Gamma^{\mathrm{at}}, \Gamma^{\rightarrow}, \Box\Delta \stackrel{l}{\not\Rightarrow} \delta$ and both (i) $\delta \in (\mathcal{V} \cup \{\bot\}) \setminus \Gamma^{\mathrm{at}}$ and (ii) $l = \mathrm{b}$ or $\Gamma^{\rightarrow} = \emptyset$.*

The rules of $\mathsf{RbuSL}_\Box$ are displayed in Fig. 3. In rules $\mathrm{S}_{\mathrm{u}}^{\mathrm{At}}$, $\mathrm{S}_{\mathrm{u}}^{\vee}$ and $\mathrm{S}_{\mathrm{u}}^{\Box}$ (we call *Succ rules*) the notation $\{\Gamma \stackrel{\mathrm{b}}{\not\Rightarrow} \alpha\}_{\alpha\rightarrow\beta\in\Gamma^{\rightarrow}}$ means that, for every $\alpha \rightarrow \beta \in \Gamma^{\rightarrow}$, the b-antisequent $\Gamma \stackrel{\mathrm{b}}{\not\Rightarrow} \alpha$ is a premise of the rule. Note that all of the Succ rules have at least one premise (in rule $\mathrm{S}_{\mathrm{u}}^{\mathrm{At}}$ this is imposed by the condition $\Gamma^{\rightarrow} \neq \emptyset$). The next theorem, proved below, states the soundness of $\mathsf{RbuSL}_\Box$:

Theorem 3 (Soundness of $\mathsf{RbuSL}_\Box$). *If $\vdash_{\mathsf{RbuSL}_\Box} \Gamma \stackrel{\mathrm{u}}{\not\Rightarrow} \delta$, then $\Gamma \not\models_{\mathsf{iSL}} \delta$.*

Example 3. Figure 4 displays the $\mathsf{RbuSL}_\Box$-derivation $\mathcal{D}$ of $\sigma_0 = \stackrel{\mathrm{u}}{\not\Rightarrow} \psi$. The (backward) application of rule $\mathrm{S}_{\mathrm{u}}^{\vee}$ to σ_2 has three premises, the left-most one is related to the formula $p \rightarrow q$ in Θ. The application of rule $\mathrm{S}_{\mathrm{u}}^{\mathrm{At}}$ to σ_7 has only the premise σ_8, generated by the formula $\neg s$ in Λ. To σ_{13} we must apply $R_{\rightarrow}^{\rhd}$, since $\Sigma \rhd q$. The application of rule $\mathrm{S}_{\mathrm{u}}^{\mathrm{At}}$ to σ_{24} gives rise to two premises, corresponding to the formulas $\neg\neg q$ and $\neg p$ in Ω. By Theorem 3, we get $\not\models_{\mathsf{IPL}} \psi$, namely $\psi \notin \mathsf{iSL}$. ◊

Countermodel Extraction. An iSL-model $\mathcal{K}$ with root r is a *countermodel for* $\sigma = \Gamma \stackrel{\mathrm{u}}{\not\Rightarrow} \delta$ iff $r \Vdash \Gamma$ and $r \nVdash \delta$; thus $\mathcal{K}$ certifies that $\Gamma \not\models_{\mathsf{iSL}} \delta$. Let $\mathcal{D}$ be an $\mathsf{RbuSL}_\Box$-derivation of a u-antisequent σ_0^{u}; we show that from $\mathcal{D}$ we can extract a countermodel $\mathrm{Mod}(\mathcal{D})$ for σ_0^{u}. A u-antisequent σ of $\mathcal{D}$ is *prime* iff σ is the conclusion of rule Irr or of a Succ rule. We introduce the relations $\preceq$, $\prec$ and $\prec_{\mathrm{R}}$ between antisequents occurring in $\mathcal{D}$:

- $\sigma_1 \prec \sigma_2$ iff σ_1 and σ_2 belong to the same branch of $\mathcal{D}$ and σ_1 is below σ_2;
- $\sigma_1 \preceq \sigma_2$ iff either $\sigma_1 = \sigma_2$ or $\sigma_1 \prec \sigma_2$;
- $\sigma_1 \prec_{\mathrm{R}} \sigma_2$ iff there exists a u-antisequent σ' such that $\sigma_1 \prec \sigma' \preceq \sigma_2$ and σ' is either the premise of rule $R_{\mathrm{b}}^{\Box}$ or the rightmost premise of $\mathrm{S}_{\mathrm{u}}^{\Box}$.

We define $\mathrm{Mod}(\mathcal{D})$ as the structure $\langle W, \leq, R, \sigma_r^{\mathrm{u}}, V\rangle$ where:

- W is the set of the prime antisequents of $\mathcal{D}$;
- $\leq$ and R are the restrictions of $\preceq$ and $\prec_{\mathrm{R}}$ to W respectively;
- σ_r^{u} is the $\leq$-minimum prime antisequent of $\mathcal{D}$;
- $V(\Gamma \stackrel{\mathrm{u}}{\not\Rightarrow} \delta) = \Gamma \cap \mathcal{V}$.

It is easy to check that $\mathrm{Mod}(\mathcal{D})$ is an iSL-model; in particular, σ_r^{u} exists since the antisequent at the root of $\mathcal{D}$ has label u. We introduce a *canonical map* Ψ between the u-antisequents of $\mathcal{D}$ and the worlds of $\mathrm{Mod}(\mathcal{D})$:

$\psi = \alpha \to (\beta \vee (\gamma \vee q))$ $\quad \alpha = (p \to q) \wedge \Box s \wedge \Box\Box\neg p \wedge \Box\Box\Box\neg q$

$\beta = \neg(p \wedge \neg s)$ $\quad \gamma = \neg\neg q \to \Box\delta$ $\quad \delta = \neg p \vee \Box\neg\neg p$

$\Theta = p \to q,\ \Box s,\ \Box\Box\neg p,\ \Box\Box\Box\neg q$ $\quad \Lambda = p,\ q,\ \neg s,\ \Box s,\ \Box\Box\neg p,\ \Box\Box\Box\neg q$

$\Sigma = q,\ \neg\neg q,\ \Box s,\ \Box\Box\neg p,\ \Box\Box\Box\neg q$ $\quad \Upsilon = q,\ s,\ \neg\neg q,\ \Box\neg p,\ \Box\Box\neg q$

$\Omega = q,\ s,\ \neg\neg q,\ \neg p,\ \Box\neg\neg p,\ \Box\neg q$ $\quad$ antisequents marked by $\star$ are prime

In $L\to$ application (†) the main formula is $p \to q$ (thus, $p \to q$ is replaced with q)

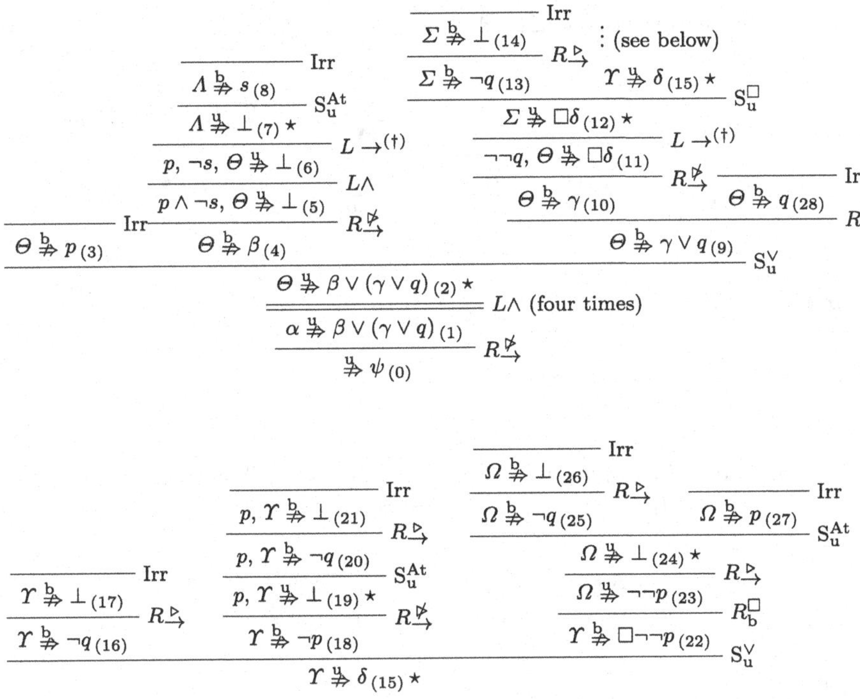

Fig. 4. The $\mathsf{RbuSL}_\Box$-derivation $\mathcal{D}$ of $\sigma_0 = \overset{\mathrm{u}}{\not\Rightarrow} \psi$ (see Example 3).

– $\Psi(\sigma^{\mathrm{u}}) = \sigma_p^{\mathrm{u}}$ iff σ_p^{u} is the $\preceq$-minimum prime antisequent σ such that $\sigma^{\mathrm{u}} \preceq \sigma$.

One can easily check that Ψ is well-defined and $\Psi(\sigma_p) = \sigma_p$, for every prime σ_p. We state the main properties of $\mathrm{Mod}(\mathcal{D})$.

Theorem 4. *Let $\mathcal{D}$ be an $\mathsf{RbuSL}_\Box$-derivation of a* u*-antisequent σ_0^{u}.*

(i) For every u*-antisequent $\sigma^{\mathrm{u}} = \Gamma \overset{\mathrm{u}}{\not\Rightarrow} \delta$ in $\mathcal{D}$, $\Psi(\sigma^{\mathrm{u}}) \Vdash \Gamma$ and $\Psi(\sigma^{\mathrm{u}}) \nVdash \delta$.*
(ii) $\mathrm{Mod}(\mathcal{D})$ *is a countermodel for σ_0^{u}.*

Point (ii) follows from (i) and the fact that $\Psi(\sigma_0^{\mathrm{u}})$ is the root of $\mathrm{Mod}(\mathcal{D})$. The proof of (i) is deferred below. We remark that point (ii) of Theorem 4 immediately implies the soundness of $\mathsf{RbuSL}_\Box$ (Theorem 3).

Example 4. At the top of Fig. 5 we represent the structure of the $\mathsf{RbuSL}_\Box$-derivation $\mathcal{D}$ of Fig. 4, displaying the information relevant to the definition of $\mathrm{Mod}(\mathcal{D})$. The countermodel $\mathrm{Mod}(\mathcal{D})$ for σ_0 coincides with the iSL-model in the figure and described in Example 1; the figure also reports the canonical map Ψ. $\Diamond$

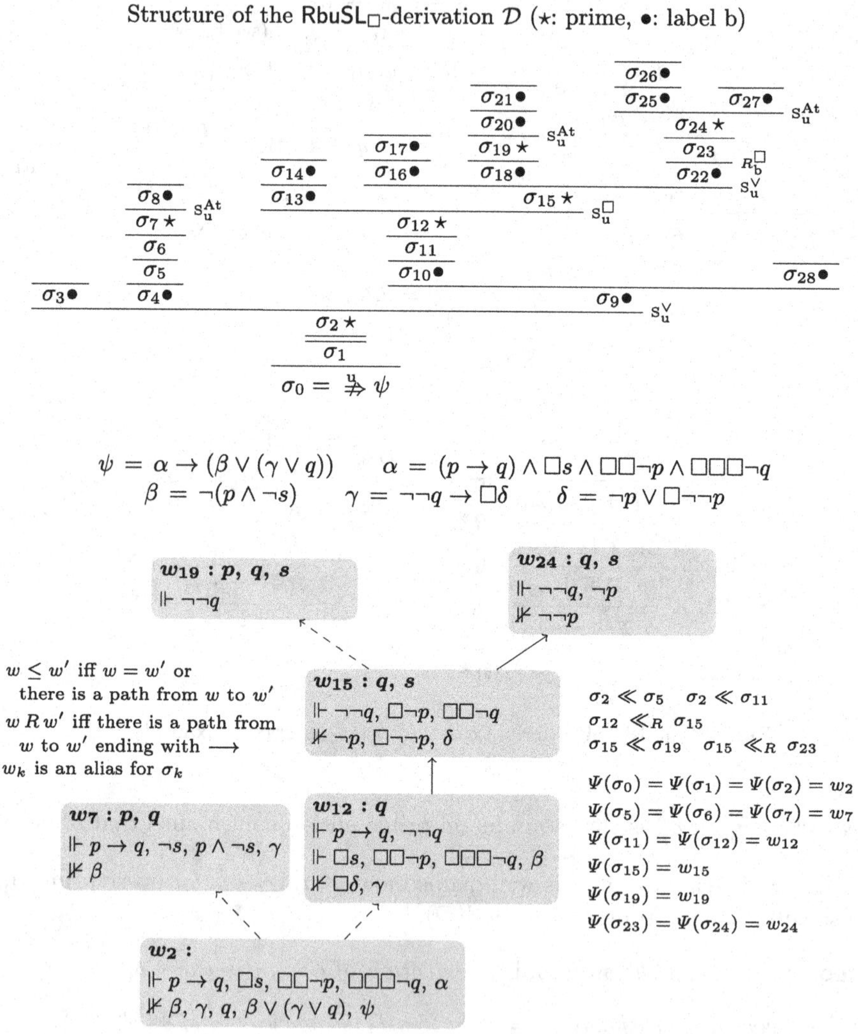

Fig. 5. The countermodel $\mathrm{Mod}(\mathcal{D})$ for ψ (see Examples 1, 4).

Proof Search. We investigate more deeply the duality between $\mathsf{GbuSL}_\Box$ and $\mathsf{RbuSL}_\Box$. A sequent $\sigma = \Gamma \stackrel{l}{\Rightarrow} \delta$ is *regular* iff $l = \mathrm{u}$ or $\Gamma = \Gamma^{\mathrm{at}}, \Gamma^{\rightarrow}, \Box\Delta$; by $\overline{\sigma}$ we denote the antisequent $\Gamma \overset{l}{\not\Rightarrow} \delta$. Let σ be a regular sequent; in the next proposition we show that either σ is provable in $\mathsf{GbuSL}_\Box$ or $\overline{\sigma}$ is provable in $\mathsf{RbuSL}_\Box$. The proof conveys a proof search strategy to build the proper derivation, based on backward application of the rules of $\mathsf{GbuSL}_\Box$. We give priority to the *invertible rules* of $\mathsf{GbuSL}_\Box$, namely: $L\wedge$, $R\wedge$, $L\vee$, $R\overset{\triangleright}{\to}$, $R\overset{\not\triangleright}{\to}$, $R^\Box_{\mathrm{b}}$; as discussed in the proof of Proposition 4, the application of such rules does not require backtracking. If the search for a $\mathsf{GbuSL}_\Box$-derivation of σ fails, we get an $\mathsf{RbuSL}_\Box$-derivation of $\overline{\sigma}$. The proof search procedure is detailed in the online appendix.

Proposition 4. *Let σ be a regular sequent. One can build either a $\mathsf{GbuSL}_\Box$-derivation of σ or an $\mathsf{RbuSL}_\Box$-derivation of $\overline{\sigma}$.*

Proof. Since $\prec_{\mathrm{bu}}$ is well-founded (Proposition 2), we can inductively assume that the assertion holds for every regular sequent σ' such that $\sigma' \prec_{\mathrm{bu}} \sigma$ (IH). If σ or $\overline{\sigma}$ is an axiom (in the respective calculus), the assertion immediately follows. If an invertible rule ρ of $\mathsf{GbuSL}_\Box$ is (backward) applicable to σ, we can build the proper derivation by applying ρ or its dual image in $\mathsf{RbuSL}_\Box$. For instance, let us assume that rule $L\vee$ of $\mathsf{GbuSL}_\Box$ is applicable with conclusion $\sigma = \alpha_0 \vee \alpha_1, \Gamma \overset{\mathrm{u}}{\Rightarrow} \delta$ and premises $\sigma_k = \alpha_k, \Gamma \overset{\mathrm{u}}{\Rightarrow} \delta$. Let $k \in \{0,1\}$; since $\sigma_k \prec_{\mathrm{bu}} \sigma$ (see Proposition 3), by (IH) there exists either a $\mathsf{GbuSL}_\Box$-derivation $\mathcal{D}_k$ of σ_k or an $\mathsf{RbuSL}_\Box$-derivation $\mathcal{E}_k$ of $\overline{\sigma_k}$. According to the case, we can build one of the following derivations:

$$\dfrac{\begin{array}{cc}\mathcal{D}_0 & \mathcal{D}_1\\ \alpha_0, \Gamma \overset{\mathrm{u}}{\Rightarrow} \delta & \alpha_1, \Gamma \overset{\mathrm{u}}{\Rightarrow} \delta\end{array}}{\alpha_0 \vee \alpha_1, \Gamma \overset{\mathrm{u}}{\Rightarrow} \delta}\, L\vee \qquad \dfrac{\begin{array}{c}\mathcal{E}_0\\ \alpha_0, \Gamma \overset{\mathrm{u}}{\not\Rightarrow} \delta\end{array}}{\alpha_0 \vee \alpha_1, \Gamma \overset{\mathrm{u}}{\not\Rightarrow} \delta}\, L\vee_0 \qquad \dfrac{\begin{array}{c}\mathcal{E}_1\\ \alpha_1, \Gamma \overset{\mathrm{u}}{\not\Rightarrow} \delta\end{array}}{\alpha_0 \vee \alpha_1, \Gamma \overset{\mathrm{u}}{\not\Rightarrow} \delta}\, L\vee_1$$

Let us assume that no invertible rule can be applied to σ; then:

- $\sigma = \Gamma \overset{\mathrm{u}}{\Rightarrow} \delta$ with $\Gamma = \Gamma^{\mathrm{at}}, \Gamma^{\to}, \Box\Delta$ and $\delta \in \mathcal{V} \cup \{\, \bot,\ \delta_0 \vee \delta_1,\ \Box\delta_0 \,\}$.

We only discuss the case $\delta = \Box\delta_0$. Let $\sigma_0 = \Gamma^{\mathrm{at}}, \Gamma^{\to}, \Delta \overset{\mathrm{u}}{\Rightarrow} \delta_0$ be the premise of the application of rule $R^\Box_{\mathrm{u}}$ of $\mathsf{GbuSL}_\Box$ to σ; for every $\alpha \to \beta \in \Gamma^{\to}$, let $\sigma_\alpha = \Gamma \overset{\mathrm{b}}{\Rightarrow} \alpha$ and $\sigma_\beta = \Gamma \setminus \{\alpha \to \beta\}, \beta \overset{\mathrm{u}}{\Rightarrow} \delta$ be the two premises of an application of rule $L\to$ of $\mathsf{GbuSL}_\Box$ to σ with main formula $\alpha \to \beta$. By the (IH):

- we can build either a $\mathsf{GbuSL}_\Box$-der. $\mathcal{D}_0$ of σ_0 or an $\mathsf{RbuSL}_\Box$-der. $\mathcal{E}_0$ of $\overline{\sigma_0}$.
- for every $\alpha \to \beta \in \Gamma^{\to}$ and for every $\omega \in \{\alpha, \beta\}$, we can build either a $\mathsf{GbuSL}_\Box$-derivation $\mathcal{D}_\omega$ of σ_ω or an $\mathsf{RbuSL}_\Box$-derivation $\mathcal{E}_\omega$ of $\overline{\sigma_\omega}$.

One of the following four cases holds:

(A) We get $\mathcal{D}_0$.
(B) There is $\alpha \to \beta \in \Gamma^{\to}$ such that we get both $\mathcal{D}_\alpha$ and $\mathcal{D}_\beta$.
(C) There is $\alpha \to \beta \in \Gamma^{\to}$ such that we get $\mathcal{E}_\beta$.
(D) We get $\mathcal{E}_0$ and, for every $\alpha \to \beta \in \Gamma^{\to}$, $\mathcal{E}_\alpha$.

According to the case, we can build one of the following derivations:

$$\text{(A)}\ \dfrac{\begin{array}{c}\mathcal{D}_0\\ \sigma_0\end{array}}{\sigma}\, R^\Box_{\mathrm{u}} \qquad \text{(B)}\ \dfrac{\begin{array}{cc}\mathcal{D}_\alpha & \mathcal{D}_\beta\\ \sigma_\alpha & \sigma_\beta\end{array}}{\sigma}\, L\!\to \qquad \text{(C)}\ \dfrac{\begin{array}{c}\mathcal{E}_\beta\\ \overline{\sigma_\beta}\end{array}}{\overline{\sigma}}\, L\!\to \qquad \text{(D)}\ \dfrac{\begin{array}{cc}\mathcal{E}_\alpha & \mathcal{E}_0\\ \ldots\ \overline{\sigma_\alpha}\ \ldots & \overline{\sigma_0}\end{array}}{\overline{\sigma}}\, \mathrm{S}^\Box_{\mathrm{u}}$$

In the proof search strategy, this corresponds to a backtrack point, since we cannot predict which case holds. ■

Let us assume $\Gamma \models_{\mathsf{iSL}} \delta$ and let $\sigma = \Gamma \overset{\mathrm{u}}{\Rightarrow} \delta$. By Soundness of $\mathsf{RbuSL}_\Box$ (Theorem 3) $\overline{\sigma}$ is not provable in $\mathsf{RbuSL}_\Box$, hence, by Proposition 4, σ is provable in $\mathsf{GbuSL}_\Box$; this proves the Completeness of $\mathsf{GbuSL}_\Box$ (Theorem 2(iv)). By Proposition 1 it follows that $\mathsf{G3iSL}^+_\Box$ is complete as well.

Properties of $\mathsf{RbuSL}_\Box$. It remains to prove point (i) of Theorem 4. By $\mathrm{Sf}^-(\alpha)$ we denote the set $\mathrm{Sf}(\alpha) \setminus \{\alpha\}$; $w < w'$ means that $w \leq w'$ and $w \neq w'$.

Lemma 3. *Let $\mathcal{T}^{\mathrm{b}}$ be an $\mathsf{RbuSL}_\Box$-tree only containing* b*-antisequents having root $\Gamma^{\mathrm{at}}, \Gamma^{\rightarrow}, \Box\Delta \overset{\mathrm{b}}{\not\Rightarrow} \delta$; let $\mathcal{K} = \langle W, \leq, R, r, V\rangle$ and $w \in W$ such that:*

(I1) $w \nVdash \delta'$, for every leaf $\Gamma^{\mathrm{at}}, \Gamma^{\rightarrow}, \Box\Delta \overset{\mathrm{b}}{\not\Rightarrow} \delta'$ of $\mathcal{T}^{\mathrm{b}}$;
(I2) $w \Vdash (\Gamma^{\rightarrow} \cap \mathrm{Sf}^-(\delta)) \cup \Box\Delta$;
(I3) $V(w) = \Gamma^{\mathrm{at}}$.

Then, $w \nVdash \delta$.

Proof. By induction on $\mathrm{depth}(\mathcal{T}^{\mathrm{b}})$. The case $\mathrm{depth}(\mathcal{T}^{\mathrm{b}}) = 0$ is trivial, since the root of $\mathcal{T}^{\mathrm{b}}$ is also a leaf. Let $\mathrm{depth}(\mathcal{T}^{\mathrm{b}}) > 0$; we only discuss the case where

$$\mathcal{T}^{\mathrm{b}} \;=\; \cfrac{\begin{matrix}\mathcal{T}_0^{\mathrm{b}}\\ \sigma_0^{\mathrm{b}} = \Gamma \overset{\mathrm{b}}{\not\Rightarrow} \beta\end{matrix}}{\Gamma \overset{\mathrm{b}}{\not\Rightarrow} \alpha \to \beta}\; R^{\rhd}_{\rightarrow} \qquad \begin{matrix}\Gamma = \Gamma^{\mathrm{at}}, \Gamma^{\rightarrow}, \Box\Delta\\ \Gamma \rhd \alpha\end{matrix}$$

By applying the induction hypothesis to the $\mathsf{RbuSL}_\Box$-tree $\mathcal{T}_0^{\mathrm{b}}$, having root σ_0^{b} and the same leaves as $\mathcal{T}^{\mathrm{b}}$, we get $w \nVdash \beta$. Let $\Gamma_\alpha = \Gamma \cap \mathrm{Sf}(\alpha)$; by Lemma 1(iii), $\Gamma_\alpha \rhd \alpha$. Since $\mathrm{Sf}(\alpha) \subseteq \mathrm{Sf}^-(\alpha \to \beta)$, by hypotheses (I2)– (I3) we get $w \Vdash \Gamma_\alpha$, which implies $w \Vdash \alpha$ (Lemma 1(v)). This proves $w \nVdash \alpha \to \beta$. ■

Let $\mathcal{D}$ be an $\mathsf{RbuSL}_\Box$-derivation having a Succ rule at the root. To display $\mathcal{D}$, we introduce the schema (1) below; at the same time, we define the relations $\ll$ and $\ll_R$ between u-antisequents in $\mathcal{D}$ (for exemplifications, see Fig. 5).

$$\mathcal{D} = \cfrac{\cdots \quad \begin{matrix}\mathcal{D}_\chi\\ \sigma_\chi^{\mathrm{b}} = \Gamma^{\mathrm{at}}, \Gamma^{\rightarrow}, \Box\Delta \overset{\mathrm{b}}{\not\Rightarrow} \chi\end{matrix} \quad \cdots \qquad \begin{matrix}\vdots\\ \sigma_\psi^{\mathrm{u}} = \Gamma^{\mathrm{at}}, \Gamma^{\rightarrow}, \Delta \overset{\mathrm{u}}{\not\Rightarrow} \psi\end{matrix}}{\sigma^{\mathrm{u}} = \Gamma^{\mathrm{at}}, \Gamma^{\rightarrow}, \Box\Delta \overset{\mathrm{u}}{\not\Rightarrow} \delta}\;\mathrm{Succ} \qquad (1)$$

- σ_χ^{b} is any of the premises of Succ having label b.
- σ_ψ^{u} is only defined if Succ is $\mathrm{S}^\Box_{\mathrm{u}}$ (thus $\delta = \Box\psi$); in this case we set $\sigma^{\mathrm{u}} \ll_R \sigma_\psi^{\mathrm{u}}$.

- The $\mathsf{RbuSL}_\square$-derivation $\mathcal{D}_\chi$ of σ^{b}_χ has the form

$$\dfrac{\dfrac{\dfrac{\vdots}{\sigma^{\mathrm{u}}_1}}{\sigma^{\mathrm{b}}_1}\rho_1 \quad \cdots \quad \dfrac{\dfrac{\vdots}{\sigma^{\mathrm{u}}_m}}{\sigma^{\mathrm{b}}_m}\rho_n \quad \dfrac{}{\tau^{\mathrm{b}}_1}\,\mathrm{Irr} \quad \cdots \quad \dfrac{}{\tau^{\mathrm{b}}_n}\,\mathrm{Irr}}{\mathcal{T}^{\mathrm{b}}_\chi \qquad \sigma^{\mathrm{b}}_\chi \;=\; \Gamma \overset{\mathrm{b}}{\not\Rightarrow} \chi} \qquad \begin{array}{l} m+n \geq 0 \\ \mathcal{T}^{\mathrm{b}}_\chi \text{ only contains} \\ \text{b-antisequents} \\ \Gamma = \Gamma^{\mathrm{at}}, \Gamma^{\rightarrow}, \square\Delta \end{array}$$

  - The $\mathsf{RbuSL}_\square$-tree $\mathcal{T}^{\mathrm{b}}_\chi$ has root σ^{b}_χ and leaves $\sigma^{\mathrm{b}}_1, \dots, \sigma^{\mathrm{b}}_m, \tau^{\mathrm{b}}_1, \dots, \tau^{\mathrm{b}}_n$.
  - For every $i \in \{1, \dots, m\}$, either (A) $\rho_i = R^{\not\Rightarrow}_{\rightarrow}$ or (B) $\rho_i = R^{\square}_{\mathrm{b}}$, namely:

$$(\mathrm{A})\ \dfrac{\sigma^{\mathrm{u}}_i \;=\; \alpha, \Gamma \overset{\mathrm{u}}{\not\Rightarrow} \beta}{\sigma^{\mathrm{b}}_i \;=\; \Gamma \overset{\mathrm{b}}{\not\Rightarrow} \alpha \rightarrow \beta}\, R^{\not\Rightarrow}_{\rightarrow} \qquad \text{or}$$

$$(\mathrm{B})\ \dfrac{\sigma^{\mathrm{u}}_i \;=\; \square\alpha, \Gamma^{\mathrm{at}}, \Gamma^{\rightarrow}, \Delta \overset{\mathrm{u}}{\not\Rightarrow} \alpha}{\sigma^{\mathrm{b}}_i \;=\; \Gamma \overset{\mathrm{b}}{\not\Rightarrow} \square\alpha}\, R^{\square}_{\mathrm{b}}$$

In case (A) we set $\sigma^{\mathrm{u}} \ll \sigma^{\mathrm{u}}_i$, in case (B) we set $\sigma^{\mathrm{u}} \ll_R \sigma^{\mathrm{u}}_i$.

Lemma 4. *Let $\mathcal{D}$ be an $\mathsf{RbuSL}_\square$-derivation of $\sigma^{\mathrm{u}} = \Gamma \overset{\mathrm{u}}{\not\Rightarrow} \delta$ having form (1) where $\Gamma = \Gamma^{\mathrm{at}}, \Gamma^{\rightarrow}, \square\Delta$; let $\mathcal{K} = \langle W, \leq, R, r, V\rangle$ and $w \in W$ such that:*

(J1) for every $w' \in W$ such that $w < w'$, it holds that $w' \Vdash \Gamma^{\rightarrow}$.
(J2) For every $w' \in W$ such that wRw', it holds that $w' \Vdash \Delta$.
(J3) For every $\sigma' = \alpha, \Gamma \overset{\mathrm{u}}{\not\Rightarrow} \beta$ such that $\sigma^{\mathrm{u}} \ll \sigma'$, there exists $w' \in W$ such that $w \leq w'$ and $w' \Vdash \alpha$ and $w' \nVdash \beta$.
(J4) For every $\sigma' = \square\alpha, \Gamma^{\mathrm{at}}, \Gamma^{\rightarrow}, \Delta \overset{\mathrm{u}}{\not\Rightarrow} \alpha$ such that $\sigma^{\mathrm{u}} \ll_R \sigma'$, there exists $w' \in W$ such that wRw' and $w' \nVdash \alpha$.
(J5) $V(w) = \Gamma^{\mathrm{at}}$.

Then, $w \Vdash \Gamma$ and $w \nVdash \delta$.

Proof. We show that:

(P1) $w \nVdash \chi$, for every premise $\sigma^{\mathrm{b}}_\chi = \Gamma \overset{\mathrm{b}}{\not\Rightarrow} \chi$ of Succ;
(P2) $w \Vdash \alpha \rightarrow \beta$, for every $\alpha \rightarrow \beta \in \Gamma^{\rightarrow}$.

We introduce the following induction hypothesis:

(IH1) to prove Point (P1) for a formula χ, we inductively assume that Point (P2) holds for every formula $\alpha \rightarrow \beta$ such that $|\alpha \rightarrow \beta| < |\chi|$;
(IH2) to prove Point (P2) for a formula $\alpha \rightarrow \beta$, we inductively assume that Point (P1) holds for every formula χ such that $|\chi| < |\alpha \rightarrow \beta|$.

We prove Point (P1). Let σ^{b}_χ be the premise of Succ displayed in schema (1). We show that the $\mathsf{RbuSL}_\square$-tree $\mathcal{T}^{\mathrm{b}}_\chi$ and w match the hypotheses (I1)–(I3) of Lemma 3, so that we can apply the lemma to infer $w \nVdash \chi$.

We prove (I1). Assume $m \geq 1$ and let $i \in \{1, \dots, m\}$; then either (A) $\sigma^{\mathrm{b}}_i = \Gamma \overset{\mathrm{b}}{\not\Rightarrow} \alpha \rightarrow \beta$ or (B) $\sigma^{\mathrm{b}}_i = \square\alpha, \Gamma^{\mathrm{at}}, \Gamma^{\rightarrow}, \Delta \overset{\mathrm{b}}{\not\Rightarrow} \square\alpha$. In case (A) we have $\sigma^{\mathrm{u}}_i = \alpha, \Gamma \overset{\mathrm{u}}{\not\Rightarrow} \beta$ and $\sigma^{\mathrm{u}} \ll \sigma^{\mathrm{u}}_i$; by hypothesis (J3), there is $w' \in W$ such that $w \leq$

w' and $w' \Vdash \alpha$ and $w' \nVdash \beta$, hence $w \nVdash \alpha \to \beta$. In case (B), we have $\sigma_i^{\mathrm{u}} = \Box\alpha, \Gamma^{\mathrm{at}}, \Gamma^{\to}, \Delta \overset{\mathrm{u}}{\nRightarrow} \alpha$ and $\sigma^{\mathrm{u}} \ll_R \sigma_i^{\mathrm{u}}$; by hypothesis (J4), there is w' such that wRw' and $w' \nVdash \alpha$, hence $w \nVdash \Box\alpha$. Assume $n \geq 1$, let $j \in \{1, \dots, n\}$ and $\tau_j^{\mathrm{b}} = \Gamma \overset{\mathrm{b}}{\nRightarrow} \delta_j$. Since τ_j^{b} is irreducible and $V(w) = \Gamma^{\mathrm{at}}$ (hypothesis (J5)), we get $w \nVdash \delta_j$. This proves that hypothesis (I1) holds.

We prove (I2). Let $\gamma \in \Gamma^{\to} \cap \mathrm{Sf}^{-}(\chi)$; since $|\gamma| < |\chi|$, by (IH1) we get $w \Vdash \gamma$. Moreover, $w \Vdash \Box\Delta$ by (J2), thus (I2) holds. Finally, (I3) coincides with (J5). We can apply Lemma 3 and conclude $w \nVdash \chi$, and this proves Point (P1).

We prove Point (P2). Let $\alpha \to \beta \in \Gamma^{\to}$, let $w' \in W$ be such that $w \leq w'$ and $w' \Vdash \alpha$; we show that $w' \Vdash \beta$. Note that $\sigma_\alpha^{\mathrm{b}} = \Gamma \overset{\mathrm{b}}{\nRightarrow} \alpha$ is a premise of Succ; since $|\alpha| < |\alpha \to \beta|$, by (IH2) we get $w \nVdash \alpha$. This implies that $w < w'$. By hypothesis (J1), $w' \Vdash \alpha \to \beta$, hence $w' \Vdash \beta$; this proves (P2).

We prove the assertion of the lemma. By (P2) and hypotheses (J2) and (J5), we get $w \Vdash \Gamma$. The proof that $w \nVdash \delta$ depends on the specific rule Succ at hand and follows from Point (P1) and hypothesis (J5). ■

Proof (Theorem 4(i)*)*. By induction on the depth of the sequent $\sigma^{\mathrm{u}} = \Gamma \overset{\mathrm{u}}{\Rightarrow} \delta$ in $\mathcal{D}$. Let ρ be the rule of $\mathsf{RbuSL}_\Box$ having conclusion σ^{u}. We proceed by a case analysis, only detailing some significant cases.

If $\rho = \mathrm{Irr}$, then $\Gamma = \Gamma^{\mathrm{at}}, \Box\Delta$ and $\delta \in (\mathcal{V} \cup \{\bot\}) \setminus \Gamma^{\mathrm{at}}$ and $\Psi(\sigma^{\mathrm{u}}) = \sigma^{\mathrm{u}}$. Since $V(\sigma^{\mathrm{u}}) = \Gamma^{\mathrm{at}}$ and σ^{u} is R-maximal, it follows that $\Psi(\sigma^{\mathrm{u}}) \Vdash \Gamma$ and $\Psi(\sigma^{\mathrm{u}}) \nVdash \delta$.

Let us assume that $\rho = R\overset{\triangleright}{\to}$. Then, $\sigma^{\mathrm{u}} = \Gamma \overset{\mathrm{u}}{\nRightarrow} \alpha \to \beta$, where $\Gamma \triangleright \alpha$, and the premise of ρ is $\sigma_1^{\mathrm{u}} = \Gamma \overset{\mathrm{u}}{\nRightarrow} \beta$. By the induction hypothesis, $\Psi(\sigma_1^{\mathrm{u}}) \Vdash \Gamma$ and $\Psi(\sigma_1^{\mathrm{u}}) \nVdash \beta$. By Lemma 1(v) we get $\Psi(\sigma_1^{\mathrm{u}}) \Vdash \alpha$, which implies $\Psi(\sigma_1^{\mathrm{u}}) \nVdash \alpha \to \beta$. Since $\Psi(\sigma^{\mathrm{u}}) = \Psi(\sigma_1^{\mathrm{u}})$, we conclude $\Psi(\sigma^{\mathrm{u}}) \Vdash \Gamma$ and $\Psi(\sigma^{\mathrm{u}}) \nVdash \alpha \to \beta$.

Let us assume $\rho = \mathrm{S}_{\mathrm{u}}^{\Box}$. We have $\sigma^{\mathrm{u}} = \Gamma \overset{\mathrm{u}}{\nRightarrow} \Box\delta$, where $\Gamma = \Gamma^{\mathrm{at}}, \Gamma^{\to}, \Box\Delta$, and $\Psi(\sigma^{\mathrm{u}}) = \sigma^{\mathrm{u}}$. Let $\mathcal{D}^{\mathrm{u}}$ be the subderivation of $\mathcal{D}$ having root sequent σ^{u}; we apply Lemma 4 setting $\mathcal{D} = \mathcal{D}^{\mathrm{u}}$, $\mathcal{K} = \mathrm{Mod}(\mathcal{D})$ and $w = \sigma^{\mathrm{u}}$. We check that hypotheses (J1)–(J5) hold.

Let w' be a world of $\mathrm{Mod}(\mathcal{D})$ such that $\sigma^{\mathrm{u}} < w'$. There exists an u-sequent $\sigma' = \Gamma' \overset{\mathrm{u}}{\Rightarrow} \delta'$ such that $\sigma^{\mathrm{u}} \prec \sigma' \preceq w'$ and $\Gamma^{\to} \subseteq \Gamma'$. Since $\mathrm{depth}(\sigma') < \mathrm{depth}(\sigma^{\mathrm{u}})$, by the induction hypothesis we get $\Psi(\sigma') \Vdash \Gamma'$, hence $\Psi(\sigma') \Vdash \Gamma^{\to}$. Since $\Psi(\sigma') \leq w'$, we conclude $w' \Vdash \Gamma^{\to}$, and this proves hypothesis (J1).

Let w' be a world of $\mathrm{Mod}(\mathcal{D})$ such that $\sigma^{\mathrm{u}} R w'$. There exists an u-sequent $\sigma' = \Gamma' \overset{\mathrm{u}}{\Rightarrow} \delta'$ such that $\sigma^{\mathrm{u}} \prec \sigma' \preceq w'$ and $\Delta \subseteq \Gamma'$. Reasoning as in the previous case, we get $w' \Vdash \Delta$, and this proves hypothesis (J2).

Let $\sigma^{\mathrm{u}} \ll \sigma' = \alpha, \Gamma \overset{\mathrm{u}}{\nRightarrow} \beta$. By the induction hypothesis, $\Psi(\sigma') \Vdash \alpha$ and $\Psi(\sigma') \nVdash \beta$. Since $\sigma^{\mathrm{u}} = \Psi(\sigma^{\mathrm{u}}) \leq \Psi(\sigma')$, hypothesis (J3) holds. The proof for hypothesis (J4) is similar. Hypothesis (J5) holds by the definition of V. By applying Lemma 4, we conclude that $\sigma^{\mathrm{u}} \Vdash \Gamma$ and $\sigma^{\mathrm{u}} \nVdash \delta$. ■

Conclusions. In this paper we have presented a terminating sequent calculus $\mathsf{GbuSL}_\Box$ for iSL enjoying the subformula property; iSL is obtained by adding labels to $\mathsf{G3iSL}_\Box^{+}$, a variant of the calculus $\mathsf{G3iSL}_\Box$ [13,15]. If a sequent σ is not derivable in $\mathsf{GbuSL}_\Box$, then σ is derivable in the dual calculus $\mathsf{RbuSL}_\Box$, and from

	Lineage	Termination	Subf. property	Other features
$\mathsf{GbuSL}_\Box$	G3i	Strong	✓	Count
$\mathsf{G3iSL}^+_\Box$	G3i	Weak	✓	
G4iSLt [10]	G4i	Strong	✗	Cut
$\mathsf{G3iSL}_\Box$ [13,15]	G3i	Weak	✓	Cut
$\mathsf{G4iSL}_\Box$ [13,15]	G4i	Weak	✗	Count

Fig. 6. Overview of the main sequent calculi for iSL. `Cut`: syntactic proof of cut-admissibility; `Count`: proof search procedure with countermodel generation.

the $\mathsf{RbuSL}_\Box$-derivation we can extract a countermodel for σ. In Fig. 6 we compare the known sequent calculi for iSL. We leave as future work the investigation of cut-admissibility for $\mathsf{GbuSL}_\Box$; this is a rather tricky task since labels impose strict constraints on the shape of derivations. We also aim to extend our approach to other provability logics related with iSL, such as the logics iGL, mHC and KM (for an overview, see e.g. [13]).

Acknowledgments. We thank the reviewers for their valuable and constructive comments. Camillo Fiorentini is member of the Gruppo Nazionale Calcolo Scientifico-Istituto Nazionale di Alta Matematica (GNCS-INdAM).

References

1. Ardeshir, M., Mojtahedi, S.M.: The Σ_1-provability logic of HA. Ann. Pure Appl. Log. **169**(10), 997–1043 (2018). https://doi.org/10.1016/J.APAL.2018.05.001
2. Dyckhoff, R.: Contraction-free sequent calculi for intuitionistic logic. J. Symbol. Logic **57**(3), 795–807 (1992). https://doi.org/10.2307/2275431
3. Ferrari, M., Fiorentini, C., Fiorino, G.: Contraction-free linear depth sequent calculi for intuitionistic propositional logic with the subformula property and minimal depth counter-models. J. Autom. Reason. **51**(2), 129–149 (2013). https://doi.org/10.1007/s10817-012-9252-7
4. Ferrari, M., Fiorentini, C., Fiorino, G.: A terminating evaluation-driven variant of G3i. In: Galmiche, D., Larchey-Wendling, D. (eds.) TABLEAUX 2013. LNCS (LNAI), vol. 8123, pp. 104–118. Springer, Heidelberg (2013). https://doi.org/10.1007/978-3-642-40537-2_11
5. Ferrari, M., Fiorentini, C., Fiorino, G.: An evaluation-driven decision procedure for G3i. ACM Trans. Comput. Log. **16**(1), 8:1–8:37 (2015). https://doi.org/10.1145/2660770
6. Ferrari, M., Fiorentini, C., Fiorino, G.: JTabWb: a Java framework for implementing terminating sequent and tableau calculi. Fundam. Informaticae **150**(1), 119–142 (2017). https://doi.org/10.3233/FI-2017-1462
7. Litak, T.: Constructive modalities with provability smack. In: Bezhanishvili, G. (ed.) Leo Esakia on Duality in Modal and Intuitionistic Logics. OCL, vol. 4, pp. 187–216. Springer, Dordrecht (2014). https://doi.org/10.1007/978-94-017-8860-1_8

8. Mojtahedi, M.: On provability logic of HA (2022). https://doi.org/10.48550/arXiv.2206.00445
9. Pinto, L., Dyckhoff, R.: Loop-free construction of counter-models for intuitionistic propositional logic. In: Behara, M., Fritsch, R., Lintz, R. (eds.) Symposia Gaussiana, Conference A, pp. 225–232. Walter de Gruyter, Berlin (1995)
10. Shillito, I., van der Giessen, I., Goré, R., Iemhoff, R.: A new calculus for intuitionistic strong Löb logic: strong termination and cut-elimination, formalised. In: Ramanayake, R., Urban, J. (eds.) TABLEAUX 2023. LNCS, vol. 14278, pp. 73–93. Springer, Cham (2023). https://doi.org/10.1007/978-3-031-43513-3_5
11. Solovay, R.M.: Provability interpretations of modal logic. Israel J. Math. **25**, 287–304 (1976). https://doi.org/10.1007/BF02757006
12. Troelstra, A.S., Schwichtenberg, H.: Basic Proof Theory. Cambridge Tracts in Theoretical Computer Science, 2nd edn, vol. 43. Cambridge University Press, Cambridge (2000). https://doi.org/10.1017/CBO9781139168717
13. van der Giessen, I.: Uniform interpolation and admissible rules: proof-theoretic investigations into (intuitionistic) modal logics. Ph.D. thesis, Utrecht University (2022). https://dspace.library.uu.nl/handle/1874/423244
14. van der Giessen, I.: Admissible rules for six intuitionistic modal logics. Ann. Pure Appl. Log. **174**(4), 103233 (2023). https://doi.org/10.1016/J.APAL.2022.103233
15. van der Giessen, I., Iemhoff, R.: Proof theory for intuitionistic strong Löb logic. In: Special Volume of the Workshop Proofs! held in Paris in 2017 (2020)
16. Visser, A., Zoethout, J.: Provability logic and the completeness principle. Ann. Pure Appl. Log. **170**(6), 718–753 (2019). https://doi.org/10.1016/J.APAL.2019.02.001

Mechanised Uniform Interpolation for Modal Logics K, GL, and iSL

Hugo Férée[1], Iris van der Giessen[2], Sam van Gool[1](✉), and Ian Shillito[3]

[1] Université Paris Cité, CNRS, IRIF, 75013 Paris, France
vangool@irif.fr
[2] University of Birmingham, Birmingham, UK
[3] Australian National University, Canberra, Australia

Abstract. The uniform interpolation property in a given logic can be understood as the definability of propositional quantifiers. We mechanise the computation of these quantifiers and prove correctness in the Coq proof assistant for three modal logics, namely: (1) the modal logic K, for which a pen-and-paper proof exists; (2) Gödel-Löb logic GL, for which our formalisation clarifies an important point in an existing, but incomplete, sequent-style proof; and (3) intuitionistic strong Löb logic iSL, for which this is the first proof-theoretic construction of uniform interpolants. Our work also yields verified programs that allow one to compute the propositional quantifiers on any formula in this logic.

Keywords: provability logic · uniform interpolation · propositional quantifiers · formal verification · proof theory

1 Introduction

Uniform interpolation is a strong form of interpolation, which says that propositional quantifiers can be defined inside the logic. More precisely, a left uniform interpolant of a formula φ with respect to a variable p is a p-free formula, denoted $\forall p\varphi$, which entails φ, and is a consequence of any p-free formula that entails φ. The dual notion is that of a right uniform interpolant, denoted $\exists p\varphi$, and a logic is said to have uniform interpolation if both left and right uniform interpolants exist for any formula. Said otherwise, uniform interpolation means that for any φ and p, the logic has a strongest formula without p that implies φ, and a weakest formula without p that is implied by φ.

The uniform interpolation property was first established for intuitionistic propositional logic IL by Pitts [23], and then for a number of modal logics, including basic modal logic K and Gödel-Löb provability logic GL [10,25,27]. Since then, uniform interpolation has been shown to hold in various modal fixpoint logics [1,22] and substructural logics [2], and connections have been developed with description logic [11], proof theory [12,18], model theory [10,19], and universal algebra [16,20].

C. Benzmüller et al. (Eds.): IJCAR 2024, LNAI 14740, pp. 43–60, 2024.
https://doi.org/10.1007/978-3-031-63501-4_3

Existing proof methods for uniform interpolation can be divided, roughly, into two strands: one is syntactic and relies on the existence of a well-behaved sequent calculus for the logic (see e.g. [18]), the other is semantic and uses Kripke models to establish definability of bisimulation quantifiers (see e.g. [10]). An advantage of the syntactic method over the semantic one is that, at least in theory, it provides better bounds on the complexity of computing uniform interpolants. In practice, however, it is not feasible to compute uniform interpolants by hand, as the calculations quickly become complex even on small examples. The algorithms for computing uniform interpolants are often intricate, and it is a non-trivial task to implement them correctly. The first- and third-named author recently developed the first verified implementation of Pitts' algorithm for computing uniform interpolants in the case of IL, using The Coq Proof Assistant in order to formally prove the correctness of the implementation [9].

In this article, we provide mechanised proofs of the uniform interpolation property for the classical modal logics K and GL and for an intuitionistic version of strong Löb logic, iSL. Of these three contributions, we discuss the first one in Sect. 3, which serves as a warm-up for what follows. The formalisation of uniform interpolation for GL starts from a sequent-style proof of this theorem [5]. During our work on formalising this proof in Coq, we uncovered an incompleteness in it, and our formalisation contains a corrected version of the construction of [5], as we will explain further in Sect. 4. Finally, the uniform interpolation result for iSL is new to this paper, and resolves an open question of [13]. (T. Litak and A. Visser have shared a draft paper with us in which they obtain a different, semantic, proof of the same result, available in preprint [28].) The proof we give extends the syntactic method of Pitts, while taking advantage both of the robustness of the earlier Coq formalisation for the case of IL, and of a recently developed sequent calculus for iSL [26].

All definitions and proofs that we describe in this paper are implemented in the constructive setting of the Coq proof assistant; the code is available online at https://github.com/hferee/UIML. In particular, this means that the definitions of the uniform interpolants for the three logics at hand here are effective, which allows us to extract from the Coq implementation an OCaml program that can generate interpolants from input formulas. Throughout the paper, links to an online-readable version of the Coq proofs are given by a clickable symbol. Finally, a demonstration webpage is available at https://hferee.github.io/UIML/demo.html where the uniform interpolants for each logic can be computed.

2 Sequent Calculi and Uniform Interpolation

In this section, we recall some standard notions that we need in this paper, pertaining to the classical modal logics K and GL, and intuitionistic modal logic iSL. We mostly follow the same notations as in [12, Ch. 1], and we refer the reader to that chapter for more details.

It will be convenient to use a more economical language for the classical setting than for the intuitionistic setting, so we define the precise syntax in some detail now. Both languages contain *boolean constant* $\bot$, *connective* $\to$, *modality* $\Box$ and a set $\mathcal{V}$ of countably many *(propositional) variables*, denoted $p, q, \dots$.

In the *classical modal language* we use the following standard classical constructors, $\neg$, $\vee$, $\wedge$, and $\Diamond$, which should be read as abbreviations: $\neg\varphi := \varphi \to \bot$, $\varphi \vee \psi := (\varphi \to \bot) \to \psi$, $\varphi \wedge \psi := (\varphi \to (\psi \to \bot)) \to \bot$, and $\Diamond\varphi := \Box(\varphi \to \bot) \to \bot$. The *intuitionistic modal language*, instead contains the *connectives* $\wedge$, $\vee$ (no $\Diamond$) ; only $\neg$ and $\top$ are abbreviations: $\neg\varphi := \varphi \to \bot$, $\top := \neg\bot$. In both the classical and intuitionistic setting, we denote modal formulas by lowercase Greek letters $\varphi, \psi, \dots$ and we write $\text{Vars}(\varphi)$ to denote the set of all propositional variables occurring as subformulas in the formula φ.

We briefly recall the axiomatisation of logics K, GL, and iSL. The logics K and GL are defined over the considered classical modal language and iSL over the intuitionistic modal language. To do so, we recall three axioms:

- the *normal axiom* (k) $\Box(p \to q) \to \Box p \to \Box q$,
- the *Gödel-Löb axiom* (gl) $\Box(\Box p \to p) \to \Box p$, and
- the *strong Löb axiom* (sl) $(\Box p \to p) \to p$.

Also recall the rules *modus ponens* (from φ and $\varphi \to \psi$ infer ψ), *necessitation* (from φ infer $\Box\varphi$), and *substitution* (from φ infer $\sigma\varphi$, for any uniform substitution σ). Now, logic K is defined by the classical propositional tautologies, axiom k, and the rules modus ponens, necessitation, and substitution. The logic GL is the extension of K by the axiom gl. Furthermore, intuitionistic propositional logic IL is defined by the intuitionistic tautologies, and the rules modus ponens, necessitation, and substitution; intuitionistic modal logic iSL is the extension of IL with axioms k and sl.

2.1 Sequent Calculi

A *sequent* is a pair of finite multisets of formulas Γ and Δ, which we denote by $\Gamma \Rightarrow \Delta$. In the intuitionistic case, Δ will necessarily be a singleton. A sequent $\Gamma \Rightarrow \Delta$ is *empty*, if Γ and Δ are empty multisets. Given two multisets Γ and Δ, we write Γ, Δ for the multiset addition of Γ and Δ, and, when φ is a formula, we write Γ, φ as notation for $\Gamma, \{\varphi\}$. Analogously to formulas, we write $\text{Vars}(\Gamma)$ to denote the set of all propositional variables occurring as subformulas in formulas in Γ. For $p \in \mathcal{V}$, we define $\Gamma_p := \Gamma \setminus \{p\}$ for any multiset Γ.

In the intuitionistic setting we use the following notation $\Box^{-1}$ on formulas:

$$\Box^{-1}\psi := \begin{cases} \varphi & \text{if } \psi = \Box\varphi \text{ for some formula } \varphi, \\ \psi & \text{otherwise.} \end{cases}$$

This notation is naturally overloaded to also apply to (multi)sets of formulas: $\Box^{-1}\Gamma := \{\Box^{-1}\varphi \mid \varphi \in \Gamma\}$.

Now we define the sequent calculi that we use throughout the paper. The sequent calculus KS consists of two *initial* rules (IdP) and ($\bot$L), left and right implication rules ($\to$ R) and ($\to$ L), and the modal rule (KR); all are displayed

$$\frac{}{p, \Gamma \Rightarrow \Delta, p} \text{(IdP)} \qquad \frac{}{\bot, \Gamma \Rightarrow \Delta} (\bot\text{L})$$

$$\frac{\Gamma \Rightarrow \Delta, \varphi \quad \psi, \Gamma \Rightarrow \Delta}{\varphi \to \psi, \Gamma \Rightarrow \Delta} (\to\text{L}) \qquad \frac{\varphi, \Gamma \Rightarrow \Delta, \psi}{\Gamma \Rightarrow \Delta, \varphi \to \psi} (\to\text{R})$$

$$\frac{\Gamma \Rightarrow \psi}{\Phi, \Box\Gamma \Rightarrow \Box\psi, \Delta} \text{(KR)} \qquad \frac{\Gamma, \Box\Gamma, \Box\psi \Rightarrow \psi}{\Phi, \Box\Gamma \Rightarrow \Box\psi, \Delta} \text{(GLR)}$$

Fig. 1. Classical sequent rules. Here, Φ does not contain boxed formulae.

in Fig. 1. The sequent calculus GLS is the variant of the calculus KS in which the rule (KR) is replaced by the rule (GLR) in Fig. 1. The sequent calculus KS is well-known to be sound and complete for K, and GLS is sound and complete for GL [24]. In the rule (GLR), the formula $\Box\psi$ is called the *diagonal* formula. We denote by KP(s) the multiset of all possible (KR)-premises for a given sequent s, and by GP(s) the multiset of all (GLR)-premises for s.

For iSL, we work with the calculus G4iSLt from [26], which was specifically designed with the aim to prove uniform interpolation for iSL. The calculus is an extension of the calculus G4iP for IL [7]. We show the calculus G4iSLt in Fig. 2, using the $\Box^{-1}$ operator to rephrase its definition slightly compared to [26].

For every sequent calculus S, we denote by $\vdash_{\mathsf{S}}$ the set of sequents that are derivable using the rules in S. For a sequent $\Gamma \Rightarrow \Delta$, we then write $\vdash_{\mathsf{S}} \Gamma \Rightarrow \Delta$ to mean that $\Gamma \Rightarrow \Delta$ is an element of the set $\vdash_{\mathsf{S}}$.

The crucial fact for proving uniform interpolation is that each of the three calculi KS, GLS, and G4iSLt has a *complete* and *terminating* backward proof search strategy, which may only depend on a *local* loop-check. *Completeness* means that the strategy finds a proof for any sequent provable in the calculus. *Termination* means that the strategy always ends in a finite proof search tree. By a *local* loop-check we mean: the criterion for deciding whether or not to stop the proof search for a given sequent only depends on the sequent itself, and does not depend on other sequents, encountered earlier by the proof search strategy. Termination for KS, GLS, and G4iSLt is discussed in detail in Sects. 3.1, 4.1 and 5.1 respectively.

2.2 Uniform Interpolation

Definition 1. *A logic L has the* uniform interpolation property *if, for every L-formula φ and variable p, there exist L-formulas, denoted by $\forall p\varphi$ and $\exists p\varphi$, satisfying the following three properties:*

1. p-freeness: *$Vars(\exists p\varphi) \subseteq Vars(\varphi) \setminus \{p\}$ and $Vars(\forall p\varphi) \subseteq Vars(\varphi) \setminus \{p\}$,*
2. implication: *$\vdash_L \varphi \to \exists p\varphi$ and $\vdash_L \forall p\varphi \to \varphi$, and*
3. uniformity: *for each formula ψ with $p \notin Vars(\psi)$:*

$$\vdash_L \varphi \to \psi \quad \textit{implies} \quad \vdash_L \exists p\varphi \to \psi,$$
$$\vdash_L \psi \to \varphi \quad \textit{implies} \quad \vdash_L \psi \to \forall p\varphi.$$

$$\frac{}{\bot, \Gamma \Rightarrow \chi}\ (\bot L) \qquad \frac{}{\Gamma, p \Rightarrow p}\ (\mathrm{IdP}) \qquad \frac{\Gamma, \varphi, \psi \Rightarrow \chi}{\Gamma, \varphi \wedge \psi \Rightarrow \chi}\ (\wedge L) \qquad \frac{\Gamma \Rightarrow \varphi \quad \Gamma \Rightarrow \psi}{\Gamma \Rightarrow \varphi \wedge \psi}\ (\wedge \mathrm{R})$$

$$\frac{\Gamma, \varphi \Rightarrow \chi \quad \Gamma, \psi \Rightarrow \chi}{\Gamma, \varphi \vee \psi \Rightarrow \chi}\ (\vee \mathrm{L}) \qquad \frac{\Gamma \Rightarrow \varphi_i}{\Gamma \Rightarrow \varphi_1 \vee \varphi_2}\ (\vee R_i)(i \in \{1,2\}) \qquad \frac{\Gamma, \varphi \Rightarrow \psi}{\Gamma \Rightarrow \varphi \to \psi}\ (\to \mathrm{R})$$

$$\frac{\Gamma, \varphi \to (\psi \to \chi) \Rightarrow \delta}{\Gamma, (\varphi \wedge \psi) \to \chi \Rightarrow \delta}\ (\wedge \to \mathrm{L}) \qquad \frac{\Gamma, \varphi \to \chi, \psi \to \chi \Rightarrow \delta}{\Gamma, (\varphi \vee \psi) \to \chi \Rightarrow \delta}\ (\vee \to \mathrm{L})$$

$$\frac{\Gamma, p, \varphi \Rightarrow \chi}{\Gamma, p, p \to \varphi \Rightarrow \chi}\ (p \to \mathrm{L}) \qquad \frac{\Gamma, \psi \to \chi \Rightarrow \varphi \to \psi \quad \Gamma, \chi \Rightarrow \delta}{\Gamma, (\varphi \to \psi) \to \chi \Rightarrow \delta}\ (\to\to \mathrm{L})$$

$$\frac{\Box^{-1}\Gamma, \Box\varphi \Rightarrow \varphi}{\Gamma \Rightarrow \Box\varphi}\ (\Box \mathrm{R}) \qquad \frac{\Box^{-1}\Gamma, \Box\varphi, \psi \Rightarrow \varphi \quad \Gamma, \psi \Rightarrow \chi}{\Gamma, \Box\varphi \to \psi \Rightarrow \chi}\ (\Box \to \mathrm{L})$$

Fig. 2. The sequent calculus G4iSLt. The sequent calculus G4iP is the restriction of G4iSLt obtained by omitting the two rules involving $\Box$.

Lemma 1. *Both classically and intuitionistically, the formulas $\forall p(\varphi \to \psi)$ and $\exists p(\varphi) \to \forall p(\varphi \to \psi)$ are equivalent.*

Proof. The left-to-right direction is clear. For the right-to-left direction, note that the formula $\exists p\varphi \to \forall p(\varphi \to \psi)$ is p-free by definition. Moreover, one easily obtains that $\exists p\varphi \to \forall p(\varphi \to \psi)$ implies $\varphi \to \psi$, using the implication rules and the implication properties of $\exists p$ and $\forall p$. Now uniformity ensures that $\exists p\varphi \to \forall p(\varphi \to \psi)$ implies $\forall p(\varphi \to \psi)$. $\Box$

To show uniform interpolation of the logics in the paper, we employ a standard proof-theoretic approach via the sequent calculi. The following definition merges the well-known definitions for intuitionistic logic from [23] and classical modal logic from [3].

Definition 2. *A set of provable sequents, denoted* $\vdash$, *has the* uniform interpolation property *if, for any sequent $\Gamma \Rightarrow \Delta$ and variable p, there exist modal formulas $\mathsf{E}_p(\Gamma)$ and $\mathsf{A}_p(\Gamma \Rightarrow \Delta)$ such that the following three properties hold:*

1. p-freeness: *(a) $Vars(\mathsf{E}_p(\Gamma)) \subseteq Vars(\Gamma) \setminus \{p\}$ and (b) $Vars(\mathsf{A}_p(\Gamma \Rightarrow \Delta)) \subseteq Vars(\Gamma, \Delta) \setminus \{p\}$,*
2. implication: *(a) $\vdash \Gamma \Rightarrow \mathsf{E}_p(\Gamma)$ and (b) $\vdash \Gamma, \mathsf{A}_p(\Gamma \Rightarrow \Delta) \Rightarrow \Delta$, and*
3. uniformity: *for any finite multisets of formulas Π and Σ such that $p \notin Vars(\Pi, \Sigma)$, if it holds that $\vdash \Pi, \Gamma \Rightarrow \Delta, \Sigma$, then it also holds that:*

$$(a) \vdash \Pi, \mathsf{E}_p(\Gamma) \Rightarrow \Delta, \Sigma \text{ if } p \notin Vars(\Delta), \text{ and}$$
$$(b) \vdash \Pi, \mathsf{E}_p(\Gamma) \Rightarrow \mathsf{A}_p(\Gamma \Rightarrow \Delta), \Sigma.$$

In the intuitionistic setting, we require Δ to be a singleton and Σ to be empty.

In this paper, we say that a sequent calculus S *has* uniform interpolation *if* $\vdash_{\mathsf{S}}$ *has the uniform interpolation property.*

We provide some observations and facts in the following remarks.

Remark 1. When proving uniform interpolation in the classical setting, we prove a stronger statement in clause (b) of uniformity:

$$\text{(b)} \vdash \Pi \Rightarrow \mathsf{A}_p(\Gamma \Rightarrow \Delta), \Sigma$$

where we omit the occurrence of $\mathsf{E}_p(\Gamma)$ on the left-hand side of the sequent. In fact, now we can take $\mathsf{E}_p(\Gamma) := \neg \mathsf{A}_p(\Gamma \Rightarrow \emptyset)$ and we only have to consider clauses (b) in every property of Definition 2 as in [3]. This will be the route taken in this paper for KS and GLS.

Remark 2. It is well-known that the uniform interpolation property for a sequent calculus results in the uniform interpolation property for its corresponding logic [4,23]. Both classically and intuitionistically, we can define $\forall p \varphi := \mathsf{A}_p(\emptyset \Rightarrow \varphi)$. In classical modal logic, we can define $\exists p \varphi$ as its dual, i.e., $\exists p \varphi := \neg \forall p (\neg \varphi)$. For intuitionistic modal logic, we define $\exists p \varphi := \mathsf{E}_p(\{\varphi\})$. One may then show that, for these definitions of $\forall p$ and $\exists p$, the three properties from Definition 1 follow from those in Definition 2, where, in the intuitionistic case, one needs to use the fact that $\mathsf{E}_p(\emptyset) = \top$.

Remark 3. In the sequel of the paper we explicitly construct operators $\mathsf{A}_p(\cdot)$ (and also $\mathsf{E}_p(\cdot)$ in the intuitionistic case) using the terminating sequent calculi for the logics. These operators have the following properties which could be viewed as Remark 2 applied to sequents instead of formulas. In both the classical and intuitionistic setting, $\mathsf{E}_p(\Gamma)$ serves as the formula $\exists p(\bigwedge \Gamma)$. In the classical case, the formula $\mathsf{A}_p(\Gamma \Rightarrow \Delta)$ will be equivalent to $\forall p(\bigwedge \Gamma \rightarrow \bigvee \Delta)$. However, intuitionistically, $\mathsf{A}_p(\Gamma \Rightarrow \varphi)$ is not equivalent to $\forall p(\bigwedge \Gamma \rightarrow \varphi)$, but it is computed as $\mathsf{E}_p(\Gamma) \rightarrow \mathsf{A}_p(\Gamma \Rightarrow \varphi)$. The latter does not contradict Remark 2 by Lemma 1. See also Remark 5 in [23].

3 Basic Modal Logic K

We start our investigations on uniform interpolation for provability logics by showcasing a simple example: the modal logic K. We follow the strategy in [3] using calculus KS and provide a formalisation in Coq.

3.1 Termination of the Sequent Calculus KS

To compute the uniform interpolants for sequent calculus KS, we provide a complete and terminating proof search strategy for it. For this, we define some useful notions for sequents $\Gamma \Rightarrow \Delta$. The *size* of $\Gamma \Rightarrow \Delta$ is the total number of symbols in the multiset Γ, Δ. We call a sequent *critical* if there is no formula of the form $\varphi \to \psi$ in Γ, Δ, and we call a critical sequent *initial* if either $\bot \in \Gamma$ or $\Gamma \cap \Delta \cap \mathcal{V} \neq \emptyset$, that is, if the sequent $\Gamma \Rightarrow \Delta$ can be proved with an initial rule.

A complete and terminating strategy for proof search in KS can easily be defined in three steps, as follows. Given a sequent, we first saturate it by maximally iterating applications of the rules ($\to$ L) and ($\to$ R). This step computes a finite multiset Can(s) of critical sequents, called the *canopy* of s. Note that, if s is not critical, then all sequents in Can(s) have strictly smaller size than s. Second, we try to apply the rules (IdP) and ($\bot$L), and close any branches where we have an initial sequent. Third, we try to apply the rule (KR) on any remaining sequents which are not initial. Since the size of sequents decreases during the execution of this strategy as long as sequents are not initial, this strategy clearly terminates.

3.2 Uniform Interpolation for KS

Definition 3 (). *Let $p \in \mathcal{V}$ be a variable and $s = (\Gamma, \Box\Gamma' \Rightarrow \Delta)$ a sequent, where no $\varphi \in \Gamma$ is a boxed formula. We define $\mathsf{A}^{\mathsf{K}}_p(s)$ recursively, as follows:*

if ...		... then $\mathsf{A}^{\mathsf{K}}_p(s)$ equals:
($\mathsf{A}^{\mathsf{K}}_p$1)	s is empty	$\bot$
($\mathsf{A}^{\mathsf{K}}_p$2)	s is not critical	$\bigwedge_{s' \in Can(s)} \mathsf{A}^{\mathsf{K}}_p(s')$
($\mathsf{A}^{\mathsf{K}}_p$3)	s is initial	$\top$
($\mathsf{A}^{\mathsf{K}}_p$4)	none of the above	$\bigvee_{q \in \Delta_p} q \vee \bigvee_{r \in \Gamma_p} \neg r \vee \bigvee_{s' \in KP(s)} \Box \mathsf{A}^{\mathsf{K}}_p(s') \vee \Diamond \mathsf{A}^{\mathsf{K}}_p(\Gamma' \Rightarrow)$

Termination of this function is proved by an induction on the size of sequents. This definition mirrors the termination of the proof search strategy for KS. The first case corresponds to a default where the sequent bares no content. The remaining cases obviously correspond to steps of the strategy: ($\mathsf{A}^{\mathsf{K}}_p$2) postpones the computation of the interpolant to the sequents in the canopy via recursive calls; ($\mathsf{A}^{\mathsf{K}}_p$3) checks for initiality; ($\mathsf{A}^{\mathsf{K}}_p$4) is the case where we apply (KR). As this last case is the most complex, we motivate that definition in more detail now.

Because an application of the (KR) rule on a sequent s deletes the non-boxed formulas in s, we need to first record all these formulas in $\mathsf{A}^{\mathsf{K}}_p(s)$: this is the role of the first two disjuncts, $\bigvee_{q \in \Delta_p} q$ and $\bigvee_{r \in \Gamma_p} \neg r$, which notably discard all occurrences of variable p. The third disjunct, $\bigvee_{s' \in \mathrm{KP}(s)} \Box \mathsf{A}^{\mathsf{K}}_p(s')$, contains recursive calls on all (KR)-premises of s, and prefixes them with a $\Box$ to reflect the logical strength of the rule. The last disjunct $\Diamond \mathsf{A}^{\mathsf{K}}_p(\Gamma' \Rightarrow)$ is needed to obtain the uniformity from Definition 2. It considers the possibility that our sequent $s = (\Gamma, \Box\Gamma' \Rightarrow \Delta)$ becomes provable once the context is extended, i.e., that a sequent of the form $\Phi, \Box\Phi', \Gamma, \Box\Gamma' \Rightarrow \Delta, \Delta'$ is provable. In a proof of the latter, suppose that the last rule applied was (KR), triggered by a formula $\Box\varphi$ in Δ'. In the premise $\Phi', \Gamma' \Rightarrow \varphi$ of that application, what remains of our sequent $\Gamma, \Box\Gamma' \Rightarrow \Delta$ is the sequent $\Gamma' \Rightarrow$, on which we then perform the recursive call $\mathsf{A}^{\mathsf{K}}_p(\Gamma' \Rightarrow)$. So, the last disjunct uses a $\Diamond$ to record the possibility for a "step aside" of the proof search tree, by considering a recursive call on what remains of s through a (KR) application in an extended context.

The complexity of the function $\mathsf{A}^{\mathsf{K}}_p$ lies in its recursive calls on *multisets* of sequents, and in the use of the canopy function which contains similar recursive calls. Since only computable functions can be defined in Coq, termination needs to be proved whenever Coq cannot automatically derive it. In order to formalise our two functions in Coq, we synchronously need to define them and convince Coq that all recursive calls are justified, by exhibiting a quantity which decreases along a well-founded order. Because of the complex recursive calls of our two functions, the traditional pen-and-paper definition of such an order is rather intricate to formalise, involving a well-founded order on multi-sets, cf. [9, Section 3]. To circumvent this difficulty in our formalisation of Definition 3, we use the Braga method [21] of Larchey-Wendling and Monin, which separates the definition of the function from the termination proof. More precisely, using this method we can first define a function as a relation which captures the *computational graph* of the function, and then prove that this relation is indeed functional and terminates. While this method was initially designed to capture partial functions in Coq, we here apply this method to the definition of $\mathsf{A}^{\mathsf{K}}_p$ and the canopy. This allows us to separate the concerns of defining these functions and proving that the definition terminates.

Given that $\mathsf{A}^{\mathsf{K}}_p$ is connected to the proof search tree, and its definition tailored to satisfy the three correctness properties for uniform interpolants, we can now prove the correctness of the definition, and formalise it in Coq.

Theorem 1. *The sequent calculus* KS *has the uniform interpolation property.*

Proof. We have formalised in the Coq proof assistant the proof from [3] with no major changes. We have to check the three properties from Definition 2, i.e., p-freeness, implication, and uniformity. It is evident that $\mathsf{A}_p(s)$ is p-free for every sequent s, as the computations in $\mathsf{A}^{\mathsf{K}}_p$ all make sure to discard p whenever propositional variables are recorded. Second, as $\mathsf{A}^{\mathsf{K}}_p(\Gamma \Rightarrow \Delta)$ follows closely the proof search tree of $\Gamma \Rightarrow \Delta$, we obtain rather straightforwardly that $\mathsf{A}^{\mathsf{K}}_p(\Gamma \Rightarrow \Delta), \Gamma \Rightarrow \Delta$ is provable, hence proving the implication property. Finally, we make a crucial use of the disjunct $\Diamond\mathsf{A}^{\mathsf{K}}_p(\Gamma \Rightarrow)$ of the case $(\mathsf{A}^{\mathsf{K}}_p 4)$ in the proof of uniformity. $\Box$

4 Classical Provability Logic GL

We now shift our focus to the logic GL. We will first provide a complete and terminating strategy for GLS. Then, in order to construct uniform interpolants for GL, we take inspiration from [5], but we modify the definition given there in order to fix an incompleteness in the correctness proof.

4.1 Terminating Strategy for Sequent Calculus GLS

In the rule (GLR), the multiset $\Box\Gamma$ on the left of the premise is preserved, while the diagonal formula $\Box\psi$ moves diagonally from the left to the right when moving from premise to conclusion. These features are known to be an obstacle to the termination of a strategy for GLS, which can be overcome by a local loop-check. Consider the following rule, labelled (IdB) for 'Identity Box'.

$$\frac{}{\Box\varphi, \Gamma \Rightarrow \Delta, \Box\varphi}\,(\mathrm{IdB})$$

Our proof search strategy for GLS extends the one for KS: first apply $(\rightarrow \mathrm{L})$ and $(\rightarrow \mathrm{R})$, then the initial rules (IdP), $(\bot\mathrm{L})$ and (IdB), and finally the rule (GLR). When following this strategy, any application of the rule (GLR) is such that its conclusion is critical but not initial, where our definition of *initial* sequent now also includes sequents that allow for an application of (IdB). Note a subtlety of our strategy: while (IdB) is not a rule of GLS its presence in our strategy is justified by its *admissibility* [17], ensuring the completeness of this strategy.

To show termination, we define a measure on sequents which decreases, in a well-founded order, as we move upwards by applying rules according to the proof strategy. Given a sequent $\Gamma \Rightarrow \Delta$, its measure $\Theta(\Gamma \Rightarrow \Delta)$ is a pair of natural numbers $(imp(\Gamma \Rightarrow \Delta), \beta(\Gamma \Rightarrow \Delta))$, where the first component is the number of occurrences of the symbol $\rightarrow$ in $\Gamma \Rightarrow \Delta$ and the second component is what we call the *number of usable boxes*, $\beta(\Gamma \Rightarrow \Delta)$, defined as the cardinal of the set $\{\Box\varphi \mid \Box\varphi \in \mathrm{Sub}(\Gamma \cup \Delta)\} \setminus \{\Box\varphi \mid \Box\varphi \in \Gamma\}$. The idea is that β counts the number of boxed formulas of a sequent $\Gamma \Rightarrow \Delta$ which might later become the diagonal formula of an instance of (GLR) in a derivation of this sequent, when following the proof search strategy. To show termination of our strategy via Θ, we use the lexicographic order $\ll$ on pairs of natural numbers, noting that, for any GLS rule with conclusion s and any premise s' of that rule, we have $\Theta(s') \ll \Theta(s)$.

4.2 Computing Uniform Interpolants for GLS

We now replicate the argument for K for GL, using the sequent calculus GLS and the terminating and complete proof search strategy for it. A first try would be to use the modified notion of initiality, and to change the function $\mathsf{A}_p^{\mathsf{K}}$ into a function $\mathsf{A}_p^{\mathsf{GL}}$ by exchanging the rule $(\mathsf{A}_p^{\mathsf{K}}4)$ for a similar rule that follows the rule (GLR) instead of (KR). However, this approach leads to a termination problem in the fourth case of the definition of the function, as was noticed in [3], and as we briefly explain now. In this case $\Gamma, \Box\Gamma' \Rightarrow \Delta$ is critical, not empty and not initial, so we would require a recursive call of the function on $\Gamma' \Box \Gamma' \Rightarrow$ in the last disjunct. However, this recursive call could fail to terminate, as we do not have in general that $\Theta(\Gamma', \Box\Gamma' \Rightarrow) \ll \Theta(\Gamma, \Box\Gamma' \Rightarrow \Delta)$. To address this problem, [3] used an auxiliary function N in the definition of $\mathsf{A}_p^{\mathsf{GL}}$ for GL.

We recall the definition of the function N as given in [5] in Fig. 3; in Definition 4 below, we will modify this table to obtain a mutually recursive definition of the function $\mathsf{A}_p^{\mathsf{GL}}$. Given the function N, the idea is, then, to replace the rule

	if ...	... then $\mathsf{N}_p(s,t)$ equals
(N1)	t is initial	$\top$
(N2)	t is not initial and $\beta(t) < \beta(s)$	$\mathsf{A}_p^{\mathsf{GL}}(t)$
(N3)	otherwise	$\bigvee_{q \in \Pi_p} q \vee \bigvee_{r \in \Sigma_p} \neg r \vee \bigvee_{t' \in \mathrm{GP}(t)} \Box \mathsf{A}_p^{\mathsf{GL}}(t')$

Fig. 3. Definition of function $\mathsf{N}_p(\cdot,\cdot)$ from [3], where $t = (\Sigma \Rightarrow \Pi)$.

($\mathsf{A}_p^{\mathsf{K}}4$) in Definition 3 by a rule which says that, if $s = (\Gamma, \Box\Gamma' \Rightarrow \Delta)$ and s is critical, not empty, and not initial, then $\mathsf{A}_p^{\mathsf{GL}}(s)$ equals

$$\bigvee_{q \in \Delta_p} q \vee \bigvee_{r \in \Gamma_p} \neg r \vee \bigvee_{s' \in \mathrm{GP}(s)} \Box \mathsf{A}_p^{\mathsf{GL}}(s') \vee \Diamond \bigwedge_{t \in \mathrm{Can}(\Gamma', \Box\Gamma' \Rightarrow)} \mathsf{N}_p(s,t) . \qquad (\mathsf{A}_p^{\mathsf{GL}}4)$$

Here, in the last disjunct of ($\mathsf{A}_p^{\mathsf{GL}}4$), we apply the function N to all elements of the canopy of the sequent $\Gamma', \Box\Gamma' \Rightarrow$, which is exactly what remains of the sequent s after applying (GLR) upwards. The purpose of the function N is to attempt another unfolding of $\mathsf{A}_p^{\mathsf{GL}}$ in the canopy of $\Gamma', \Box\Gamma' \Rightarrow$. Indeed, the definition of N first checks whether any recursive call is necessary via the initiality check in (N1), and then proceeds in (N2) to recursively call $\mathsf{A}_p^{\mathsf{GL}}$ if we are ensured that Θ decreases via the first component, or goes to (N3) if there is no such decrease. Notice that, in this last case, the definition of N is a truncation of ($\mathsf{A}_p^{\mathsf{GL}}4$), which omits the problematic last disjunct, as it cannot be guaranteed to decrease in the recursion. The termination of $\mathsf{A}_p^{\mathsf{GL}}$ is obviously ensured by definition. However, the correctness is no longer obvious, due to the truncation in the rule (N3). The key insight for proving the correctness is the following *fixed point* equivalence [5] which is valid in GL:

$$\Diamond \left(\bigwedge_i \left[\alpha_i \vee \Diamond \left(\bigwedge_i \alpha_i \wedge \beta \right) \right] \wedge \beta \right) \quad \leftrightarrow \quad \Diamond \left(\bigwedge_i \alpha_i \wedge \beta \right) .$$

This equivalence can be used to prove that the diamond disjunct from the rule ($\mathsf{A}_p^{\mathsf{GL}}4$) may be omitted in the rule (N3). In order to make this work formally, one needs the following equivalence to be derivable in GLS:

$$\Diamond \bigwedge_{s' \in \mathrm{Can}(\Gamma', \Box\Gamma' \Rightarrow)} \mathsf{N}_p(s,s') \quad \leftrightarrow \quad \Diamond \mathsf{A}_p^{\mathsf{GL}}(\Gamma', \Box\Gamma' \Rightarrow) . \qquad (1)$$

Assuming this equivalence, one can show that the uniform interpolation property holds for GLS. To justify (1), [5] relies on another equivalence between two formulas $\mathsf{N}_p(s,t_1)$ and $\mathsf{N}_p(s,t_2)$, where $t_i = \Gamma_i, \Box\Gamma_i \Rightarrow$ for $i = 1,2$, where the multisets Γ_1 and Γ_2 are known to be equal only when considered *as sets*, i.e., not counting multiplicities. This equivalence is not formally proved, but only "observe[d]" [5, p. 17]. Since the sequents t_1 and t_2 are *identical modulo contraction*, and contraction is an admissible rule in GLS, this sounds reasonable, but we were unable to formally derive this equivalence, even after consulting with the author of [5].

The difficulty in formally proving the observation primarily lies in the fact that the function N includes computations of the canopy of our two sequents t_1 and t_2. However, the canopies of two sequents can vastly differ, even if they are identical modulo contraction. We give a minimal example of such a situation in Fig. 4, where the sequents $q \Rightarrow p$ on the right find no counterparts on the left. This mismatch in canopies, then, makes it hard to prove that any call to $\mathsf{A}_p^{\mathsf{GL}}$ in one canopy has a counterpart in the other canopy.

$$\frac{\Rightarrow p \qquad q \Rightarrow}{p \to q \Rightarrow}\ (\to\mathrm{L}) \qquad\qquad \frac{\dfrac{\Rightarrow p, p \qquad q \Rightarrow p}{p \to q \Rightarrow p}\ (\to\mathrm{L}) \qquad \dfrac{q \Rightarrow p \qquad q, q \Rightarrow}{p \to q, q \Rightarrow}\ (\to\mathrm{L})}{p \to q, p \to q \Rightarrow}\ (\to\mathrm{L})$$

Fig. 4. Two sequents that are equivalent up to contraction, but the canopies are not.

In order to overcome this problem, we propose to modify the mutually recursive definition of $\mathsf{A}_p^{\mathsf{GL}}$ and N with respect to the one given in [5]: in strategic places, we *fully contract* sequents, notably before computing canopies. We denote by $\overline{s}$ the fully contracted version of the sequent s; that is, when $s = (\Gamma \Rightarrow \Delta)$, $\overline{s}$ denotes the sequent $(\Gamma' \Rightarrow \Delta')$, where Γ' and Δ' are the multisets obtained from Γ and Δ, respectively, by removing duplicates.

Definition 4 ( ). *Let $p \in \mathcal{V}$ be a variable. We define $\mathsf{A}_p^{\mathsf{GL}}$ and N_p by a mutual recursion, as follows. Let $s = (\Gamma, \Box\Gamma' \Rightarrow \Delta)$ be a sequent, where no $\varphi \in \Gamma$ is a boxed formula. If s is empty or initial, then $\mathsf{A}_p^{\mathsf{GL}}(s)$ equals $\mathsf{A}_p^{\mathsf{K}}(s)$, and*

	if ...	... then $\mathsf{A}_p^{\mathsf{GL}}(s)$ equals
$(\mathsf{A}_p^{\mathsf{GL}}2)$	s is not critical	$\bigwedge_{s' \in Can(\overline{s})} \mathsf{A}_p^{\mathsf{GL}}(s')$
$(\mathsf{A}_p^{\mathsf{GL}}4)$	otherwise	$\bigvee_{q \in \Delta_p} q \vee \bigvee_{r \in \Gamma_p} \neg r \vee \bigvee_{s' \in GP(\overline{s})} \Box\mathsf{A}_p^{\mathsf{GL}}(s')$ $\vee \Diamond \bigwedge_{t \in Can(\overline{\Gamma, \Box\Gamma \Rightarrow})} \mathsf{N}_p(s,t)$

Let $t = (\Sigma \Rightarrow \Pi)$ be a sequent. We also define ( ) the formula $\mathsf{N}_p(s,t)$ as in Fig. 3, but replacing the formula in the last row of the table with:

$$\bigvee_{q \in \Pi_p} q \vee \bigvee_{r \in \Sigma_p} \neg r \vee \bigvee_{t' \in GP(\overline{t})} \Box\mathsf{A}_p^{\mathsf{GL}}(t'),$$

where we note that the last disjunction is indexed by $GP(\overline{t})$ instead of $GP(t)$.

With this new definition, we obtain a proof of correctness of the equivalence (1), as we always fully contract sequents before computing their canopies. In our formalisation of Definition 4, we again made use of the Braga method already described in Sect. 3.

4.3 Syntactic Correctness Proof

Theorem 2. *The sequent calculus* GLS *has the uniform interpolation property.*

Proof. We refer to the formalised proofs of the first (🐓), second (🐓) and third (🐓) property. □

5 Intuitionistic Strong Löb iSL

The aim of this section is to give a sequent-based proof of the uniform interpolation property for intuitionistic strong Löb logic, iSL. We will simultaneously explain the proof method of this new result, and report on our mechanisation of the definition of the propositional quantifiers in Coq. The work in this section builds on an earlier formalisation [9] of Pitts' theorem [23] that uniform interpolation holds for IL. In order to make the explanation below for iSL understandable, we first briefly review some important points of that work. We subsequently explain how to extend that definition to deal with the modality of the logic iSL, and how the correctness proof can be extended to work for that logic.

As for the classical modal logics considered above, the definitions of the propositional quantifiers $\mathsf{A}_p(\cdot)$ and $\mathsf{E}_p(\cdot)$ for IL are guided by the terminating sequent calculus, G4iP (see Fig. 2). In [9,23], $\mathsf{A}_p(\cdot)$ and $\mathsf{E}_p(\cdot)$ are defined for G4iP as follows. Based on the rows ($\mathsf{E}^{\mathsf{IL}}_{\mathsf{p}}0$)-($\mathsf{E}^{\mathsf{IL}}_{\mathsf{p}}8$) and ($\mathsf{A}^{\mathsf{IL}}_{\mathsf{p}}1$)-($\mathsf{A}^{\mathsf{IL}}_{\mathsf{p}}13$) in Fig. 5, the sets $\mathcal{A}_{\mathsf{p}}(\Gamma \Rightarrow \varphi)$ and $\mathcal{E}_{\mathsf{p}}(\Gamma)$ are defined by pattern matching. Based on this we define,

$$\mathsf{A}^{\mathsf{IL}}_{\mathsf{p}}(\Gamma \Rightarrow \varphi) := \bigvee \mathcal{A}_{\mathsf{p}}(\Gamma \Rightarrow \varphi) \quad \text{and} \quad \mathsf{E}^{\mathsf{IL}}_{\mathsf{p}}(\Gamma) := \bigwedge \mathcal{E}_{\mathsf{p}}(\Gamma). \tag{2}$$

Theorem 3. *The sequent calculus for* IL *has the uniform interpolation property.*

5.1 Termination of Sequent Calculus G4iSLt

The calculus G4iSLt has already been shown to be terminating [26], but we find it convenient to provide a different termination ordering here, which is closer to, and compatible with, the termination ordering used by Pitts in the context of the sequent calculus G4iP, also see [7,8]. In particular, this lets us re-use some earlier Coq engineering work [9, Thm. 3.3] that was needed to be able to apply the theorem of Dershowitz and Manna [6] that the natural order on the set of multisets of well-founded order is again well-founded. The *weight* of a formula is inductively defined, by adding a given weight for each symbol: $\bot, \Box, \to$ and variables count for 1, $\wedge$ for 2 and $\vee$ for 3. This naturally defines a well-founded strict preorder on the set of formulas: $\varphi \prec_f \psi$ iff $\mathtt{weight}(\varphi) < \mathtt{weight}(\psi)$.

	Γ matches	$\mathcal{E}_p(\Gamma)$ contains
$(\mathsf{E}_p^{\mathsf{IL}}0)$	$\Gamma', \bot$	$\bot$
$(\mathsf{E}_p^{\mathsf{IL}}1)$	Γ', q	$\mathsf{E}_p(\Gamma') \wedge q$
$(\mathsf{E}_p^{\mathsf{IL}}2)$	$\Gamma', \psi_1 \wedge \psi_2$	$\mathsf{E}_p(\Gamma', \psi_1, \psi_2)$
$(\mathsf{E}_p^{\mathsf{IL}}3)$	$\Gamma', \psi_1 \vee \psi_2$	$\mathsf{E}_p(\Gamma', \psi_1) \vee \mathsf{E}_p(\Gamma', \psi_2)$
$(\mathsf{E}_p^{\mathsf{IL}}4)$	$\Gamma', (q \to \psi)$	$q \to \mathsf{E}_p(\Gamma', \psi)$
$(\mathsf{E}_p^{\mathsf{IL}}5)$	$\Gamma', p, (p \to \psi)$	$\mathsf{E}_p(\Gamma', p, \psi)$
$(\mathsf{E}_p^{\mathsf{IL}}6)$	$\Gamma', (\delta_1 \wedge \delta_2) \to \delta_3)$	$\mathsf{E}_p(\Gamma', (\delta_1 \to (\delta_2 \to \delta_3)))$
$(\mathsf{E}_p^{\mathsf{IL}}7)$	$\Gamma', (\delta_1 \vee \delta_2) \to \delta_3)$	$\mathsf{E}_p(\Gamma', (\delta_1 \to \delta_3), (\delta_2 \to \delta_3)))$
$(\mathsf{E}_p^{\mathsf{IL}}8)$	$\Gamma', (\delta_1 \to \delta_2) \to \delta_3)$	$[\mathsf{E}_p(\Gamma', (\delta_2 \to \delta_3)) \to \mathsf{A}_p(\Gamma', (\delta_2 \to \delta_3) \Rightarrow \delta_1 \to \delta_2)] \to \mathsf{E}_p(\Gamma', \delta_3)$
$(\mathsf{E}_p^{\mathsf{iSL}}9)$	$\Gamma', \Box\delta$	$\Box\mathsf{E}_p(\Box^{-1}\Gamma', \delta)$
$(\mathsf{E}_p^{\mathsf{iSL}}10)$	$\Gamma', (\Box\delta_1 \to \delta_2)$	$\Box[\mathsf{E}_p(\Box\Gamma', \delta_2, \Box\delta_1) \to \mathsf{A}_p(\Box\Gamma', \delta_2, \Box\delta_1 \Rightarrow \delta_1)] \to \mathsf{E}_p(\Gamma', \delta_2)$

	s matches	$\mathcal{A}_p(s)$ contains
$(\mathsf{A}_p^{\mathsf{IL}}1)$	$\Gamma, q \Rightarrow \varphi$	$\mathsf{A}_p(\Gamma \Rightarrow \varphi)$
$(\mathsf{A}_p^{\mathsf{IL}}2)$	$\Gamma, \psi_1 \wedge \psi_2 \Rightarrow \varphi$	$\mathsf{A}_p(\Gamma, \psi_1, \psi_2 \Rightarrow \varphi)$
$(\mathsf{A}_p^{\mathsf{IL}}3)$	$\Gamma, \psi_1 \vee \psi_2 \Rightarrow \varphi$	$[\mathsf{E}_p(\Gamma, \psi_1) \to \mathsf{A}_p(\Gamma, \psi_1 \Rightarrow \varphi)] \wedge [\mathsf{E}_p(\Gamma, \psi_2) \to \mathsf{A}_p(\Gamma, \psi_2 \Rightarrow \varphi)]$
$(\mathsf{A}_p^{\mathsf{IL}}4)$	$\Gamma, (q \to \psi) \Rightarrow \varphi$	$q \wedge \mathsf{A}_p(\Gamma, \psi \Rightarrow \varphi)$
$(\mathsf{A}_p^{\mathsf{IL}}5)$	$\Gamma, p, (p \to \psi) \Rightarrow \varphi$	$\mathsf{A}_p(\Gamma, \psi \Rightarrow \varphi)$
$(\mathsf{A}_p^{\mathsf{IL}}6)$	$\Gamma, (\delta_1 \wedge \delta_2) \to \delta_3) \Rightarrow \varphi$	$\mathsf{A}_p(\Gamma, (\delta_1 \to (\delta_2 \to \delta_3)) \Rightarrow \varphi)$
$(\mathsf{A}_p^{\mathsf{IL}}7)$	$\Gamma, (\delta_1 \vee \delta_2) \to \delta_3) \Rightarrow \varphi$	$\mathsf{A}_p(\Gamma, (\delta_1 \to \delta_3), (\delta_2 \to \delta_3)) \Rightarrow \varphi)$
$(\mathsf{A}_p^{\mathsf{IL}}8)$	$\Gamma, (\delta_1 \to \delta_2) \to \delta_3) \Rightarrow \varphi$	$[\mathsf{E}_p(\Gamma, (\delta_2 \to \delta_3)) \to \mathsf{A}_p(\Gamma, (\delta_2 \to \delta_3) \Rightarrow \delta_1 \to \delta_2)] \wedge \mathsf{A}_p(\Gamma, \delta_3 \Rightarrow \varphi)$
$(\mathsf{A}_p^{\mathsf{IL}}9)$	$\Gamma \Rightarrow q$	q
$(\mathsf{A}_p^{\mathsf{IL}}10)$	$\Gamma, p \Rightarrow p$	$\top$
$(\mathsf{A}_p^{\mathsf{IL}}11)$	$\Gamma \Rightarrow \varphi_1 \wedge \varphi_2$	$\mathsf{A}_p(\Gamma \Rightarrow \varphi_1) \wedge \mathsf{A}_p(\Gamma \Rightarrow \varphi_2)$
$(\mathsf{A}_p^{\mathsf{IL}}12)$	$\Gamma \Rightarrow \varphi_1 \vee \varphi_2$	$\mathsf{A}_p(\Gamma \Rightarrow \varphi_1) \vee \mathsf{A}_p(\Gamma \Rightarrow \varphi_2)$
$(\mathsf{A}_p^{\mathsf{IL}}13)$	$\Gamma \Rightarrow \varphi_1 \to \varphi_2$	$\mathsf{E}_p(\Gamma, \varphi_1) \to \mathsf{A}_p(\Gamma, \varphi_1 \Rightarrow \varphi_2)$
$(\mathsf{A}_p^{\mathsf{iSL}}14)$	$\Gamma \Rightarrow \Box\delta$	$\Box(\mathsf{E}_p(\Box\Gamma, \Box\delta) \to \mathsf{A}_p(\Box\Gamma, \Box\delta \Rightarrow \delta))$.
$(\mathsf{A}_p^{\mathsf{iSL}}15)$	$\Gamma, \Box\delta_1 \to \delta_2 \Rightarrow \varphi$	$\Box[\mathsf{E}_p(\Box\Gamma, \delta_2, \Box\delta_1) \to \mathsf{A}_p(\Box\Gamma, \delta_2, \Box\delta_1 \Rightarrow \delta_1)] \wedge \mathsf{A}_p(\Gamma, \delta_2 \Rightarrow \varphi)$

Fig. 5. The top part of each table, i.e., $(\mathsf{E}_p^{\mathsf{IL}}0)$-$(\mathsf{E}_p^{\mathsf{IL}}8)$ and $(\mathsf{A}_p^{\mathsf{IL}}1)$-$(\mathsf{A}_p^{\mathsf{IL}}13)$ define $\mathsf{E}_p(\Gamma)$ and $\mathsf{A}_p(\Gamma \Rightarrow \varphi)$ for IL as defined in [23]. The complete table provides definitions for $\mathsf{E}_p(\Gamma)$ and $\mathsf{A}_p(\Gamma \Rightarrow \varphi)$ for iSL. In all clauses, $q \neq p$.

In [7], the preorder on sequents used to prove the termination of G4iP is the *Dershowitz-Manna* ordering on multisets induced by this ordering on formulas: $\Gamma \Rightarrow \varphi \prec \Delta \Rightarrow \psi$ if the multiset Γ, φ is smaller than the multiset Δ, ψ. However, the $\Box_R$-rule of G4iSLt is not always compatible with this ordering. Indeed, with $\Gamma = \emptyset$ and $\varphi = \bot$, note that $\{\Box\bot, \bot\} \not\prec \{\Box\bot\}$. The reason is that this rule both replaces a boxed formula on the right hand side with its unboxed version, which is a strict subformula, but also moves the boxed formula to the left-hand side.

We fix this issue by counting twice the right-hand side of the sequent in the multiset, accounting for the fact that a formula on the right-hand side of a sequent might be duplicated using a $\Box_R$ rule.

Definition 5 (Sequent ordering). *$\Gamma \Rightarrow \varphi \prec \Delta \Rightarrow \psi$ whenever Γ, φ, φ is smaller than Δ, ψ, ψ for the multiset ordering induced by $\prec_f$.*

The ordering is again well-founded, as follows from an application of the Dershowitz-Manna theorem to the fact that the weight ordering on formulas is well-founded. Also, any hypothesis of an G4iSLt rule is smaller than its conclusion. This ensures the termination of proof search for G4iSLt, but we will also use this ordering to construct the uniform interpolants.

Note that, although this order does not strictly speaking contain the original order, it is the case that, if two sequents were comparable for the original one in Pitts proof, then they still are for this modified order. This means that changing the definition of the ordering does not break the proof structure for the existing cases with no modality involved. This allows us to adapt the existing Coq formalisation for G4iP at minimal cost.

5.2 Computing Uniform Interpolants for G4iSLt

Following the same proof scheme as Pitts' for IL, we now define $\mathsf{E}_p^{\mathsf{iSL}}(\Gamma)$ and $\mathsf{A}_p^{\mathsf{iSL}}(\Gamma \Rightarrow \varphi)$.

Definition 6. *The formulas $\mathsf{E}_p^{\mathsf{iSL}}(\Gamma)$ and $\mathsf{A}_p^{\mathsf{iSL}}(\Gamma \Rightarrow \varphi)$ are defined by mutual induction on the $\prec$ ordering, respectively as a conjunction of a multiset of formulas $\mathcal{E}_{\mathsf{p}}(\Gamma)$ and as a disjunction of a multiset of formulas $\mathcal{A}_{\mathsf{p}}(\Gamma \Rightarrow \varphi)$, both defined by the rules from Fig. 5.*

Remark 4. Our adaptation of Pitts' construction for IL to iSL adds formulas to the sets $\mathcal{E}_p$ and $\mathcal{A}_p$ only in the cases where some formula in Δ, θ contains a boxed subformula. As a consequence, $\mathsf{A}_p^{\mathsf{iSL}}(\Gamma \Rightarrow \varphi) = \mathsf{A}_{\mathsf{p}}^{\mathsf{IL}}(\Gamma \Rightarrow \varphi)$ and $\mathsf{E}_p^{\mathsf{iSL}}(\Gamma) = \mathsf{E}_{\mathsf{p}}^{\mathsf{IL}}(\Gamma)$ whenever Γ and φ do not contain the $\Box$ modality.

Remark 5. Rule ($\mathsf{E}_p^{\mathsf{iSL}}9$) can be read as adding $\Box\mathsf{E}_p^{\mathsf{iSL}}(\Box^{-1}\Gamma)$ to the set $\mathcal{E}_{\mathsf{p}}(\Gamma)$ whenever Γ contains at least one boxed formula (otherwise, $\Box^{-1}\Gamma = \Gamma$ and this definition would not be well-founded). An efficient implementation of this rule should then take care not to add multiple copies of $\Box\mathsf{E}_p^{\mathsf{iSL}}(\Box^{-1}\Gamma)$, i.e. for each boxed formula in Γ.

In order to prove the *implication* and *uniformity* properties of uniform interpolation (Definition 2) we will first require some admissibility lemmas for G4iSLt, in particular weakening and contraction. Note that, as for Pitts' proof for IL, the admissibility of cut is not necessary here and indeed, we do not use nor prove it in our Coq mechanisation. However, since cut is in fact admissible in G4iSLt [26], we allow ourselves to use this fact in our 'paper' explanations below. In addition, iSL satisfies the strongness property.

Lemma 2 (Strongness). *For any formula* φ, $\vdash_{\mathsf{iSL}} \varphi \Rightarrow \Box\varphi$.

However, we will actually use the following stronger, dual lemma instead, provable by induction on the proof derivation of $\vdash_{\mathsf{iSL}} \Delta, \varphi \Rightarrow \varphi$.

Lemma 3. *If* $\vdash_{\mathsf{iSL}} \Delta, \varphi \Rightarrow \psi$ *then* $\vdash_{\mathsf{iSL}} \Delta, \Box^{-1}\varphi \Rightarrow \psi$.

The following lemma highlights how the interpolant interacts with the $\Box$ modality and its dual $\Box^{-1}$.

Lemma 4. *For any multiset of formulas* Δ, $\vdash_{\mathsf{iSL}} \mathsf{E}_p^{\mathsf{iSL}}(\Delta) \Rightarrow \Box\mathsf{E}_p^{\mathsf{iSL}}(\Box^{-1}\Delta)$.

Proof. If Δ contains no boxed formulas, then $\Box^{-1}\Delta = \Delta$ and Lemma 2 lets us conclude. Otherwise, Δ is multiset-equivalent to $\Delta', \Box\delta$ for some Δ' and δ. Then, by rule ($\mathsf{E}_p^{\mathsf{iSL}}9$), $\mathsf{E}_p^{\mathsf{iSL}}(\Delta)$ is a conjunction containing $\Box(\mathsf{E}_p^{\mathsf{iSL}}(\Box^{-1}\Delta', \delta))$ which is equivalent to $\Box(\mathsf{E}_p^{\mathsf{iSL}}(\Box^{-1}\Delta))$ since the definition of $\mathsf{E}_p^{\mathsf{iSL}}(\cdot)$ is invariant under multiset-equivalence. $\Box$

Theorem 4. *The sequent calculus* G4iSLt *has uniform interpolation.*

Proof. The *p-freeness* property is easily proved ( ). The *implication* property is proved ( ) by well-founded induction of $\prec$ on the sequent $\Delta \Rightarrow \varphi$ and mostly relies on weakening. The proof of *uniformity* ( ) is by structural induction on the derivation of $\vdash_{\mathsf{iSL}} \Gamma, \Delta \Rightarrow \varphi$. If the last rule is an IL rule, then Pitts' proof of uniform interpolation for IL still applies. The cases for the modal rules are handled similarly, with a critical use of Lemmas 3 and 4. We postpone a detailed pen-and-paper version to a forthcoming journal publication. $\Box$

6 Conclusion and Future Work

We have provided formalised sequent-style proofs of three uniform interpolation results, one well-known (K), a second subtle (GL), and a third new (iSL). One recent application of the verified implementation of uniform interpolation of IL [9] was to prove non-definability results in intuitionistic logic [19]. We hope that the implementations given in this paper and the accompanying online demo can be similarly useful in the future.

As explained in detail in Sect. 4, our effort made in formalising the argument of [5] in Coq exposed an incompleteness in the paper proof, which we were eventually able to correct. This incompleteness would not have been discovered (nor corrected) as quickly without the formalisation effort. The work in that section thus provides a further example of the usefulness of such efforts when subtle correctness proofs of algorithms in logic are concerned.

We leave to future work a more modular formal development of uniform interpolation proofs. In particular, one could formalise the theoretical results of [18] in order to obtain a general algorithm which, given as input a sufficiently well-behaved sequent calculus, produces a verified calculation of uniform interpolants for the corresponding logic. A further piece of evidence that such a general development might be possible is that the generalisation from the known result for the logic IL to the new result for the logic iSL was relatively frictionless. This shows another strength of the formalisation endeavour, allowing for an easy experimentation with the boundaries of the formalised results.

A concrete logic that we would like to capture with our work is the intuitionistic version of GL, often referred to as iGL, for which it is an open problem whether or not uniform interpolation holds [12].

A final problem that we leave to future work is the formalisation of the semantic approach to uniform interpolation, via the definability of bisimulation quantifiers, as e.g. in [10,14,15,27]. This would allow for a comparison of the two approaches, both in terms of algorithmic complexity and ease of formalisation.

Acknowledgments. We thank Marta Bílková, Dominique Larchey-Wendling, and Tadeusz Litak for fruitful discussions. This research received funding from the Agence Nationale de la Recherche, project ANR-23-CE48-0012. This work was partially supported by a UKRI Future Leaders Fellowship, 'Structure vs Invariant in Proofs', project reference MR/S035540/1.

References

1. D'Agostino, G., Hollenberg, M.: Logical questions concerning the μ-calculus: interpolation. Lyndon and Łoś-Tarski. J. Symbolic Logic **65**(1), 310–332 (2000). https://doi.org/10.2307/2586539
2. Alizadeh, M., Derakhshan, F., Ono, H.: Uniform interpolation in substructural logics. Rev. Symbol. Logic **7**(3), 455–483 (2014). https://doi.org/10.1017/S175502031400015X
3. Bílková, M.: Interpolation in modal logics. Ph.D. thesis, Univerzita Karlova, Prague (2006)
4. Bílková, M.: Uniform interpolation and propositional quantifiers in modal logics. Studia Logica: Int. J. Symbol. Logic **85**(1), 1–31 (2007). http://www.jstor.org/stable/40210757
5. Bílková, M.: Uniform interpolation in provability logics (2022). https://arxiv.org/pdf/2211.02591.pdf
6. Dershowitz, N., Manna, Z.: Proving termination with multiset orderings. Commun. ACM **22**(8), 465–476 (1979). https://doi.org/10.1145/359138.359142
7. Dyckhoff, R.: Contraction-free sequent calculi for intuitionistic logic. J. Symbol. Logic **57**(3), 795–807 (1992). https://doi.org/10.2307/2275431
8. Dyckhoff, R., Negri, S.: Admissibility of structural rules for contraction-free systems of intuitionistic logic. J. Symbol. Logic **65**(4), 1499–1518 (2000). https://doi.org/10.2307/2695061
9. Férée, H., van Gool, S.: Formalizing and computing propositional quantifiers. In: Proceedings of the 12th ACM SIGPLAN International Conference on Certified Programs and Proofs. CPP 2023, pp. 148–158. Association for Computing Machinery (2023). https://doi.org/10.1145/3573105.3575668
10. Ghilardi, S., Zawadowski, M.: Sheaves, Games, and Model Completions, A Categorical Approach to Nonclassical Propositional Logics, vol. 14. Springer, Dordrecht (2002). https://doi.org/10.1007/978-94-015-9936-8

11. Ghilardi, S., Lutz, C., Wolter, F.: Did I damage my ontology? A case for conservative extensions in description logics. In: Doherty, P., Mylopoulos, J., Welty, C.A. (eds.) Proceedings, Tenth International Conference on Principles of Knowledge Representation and Reasoning, Lake District of the United Kingdom, 2–5 June 2006, pp. 187–197. AAAI Press (2006). http://www.aaai.org/Library/KR/2006/kr06-021.php
12. van der Giessen, I.: Uniform interpolation and admissible rules. Proof-theoretic investigations into (intuitionistic) modal logics. Ph.D. thesis, Utrecht University (2022). https://dspace.library.uu.nl/bitstream/handle/1874/423244/proefschrift%20-%206343c2623d6ab.pdf
13. van der Giessen, I., Iemhoff, R.: Proof theory for intuitionistic strong Löb logic. In: Accepted for publication in Special Volume of the Workshop Proofs! held in Paris in 2017 (2020). https://doi.org/10.48550/arXiv.2011.10383, preprint arXiv:2011.10383v2
14. van der Giessen, I., Jalali, R., Kuznets, R.: Uniform interpolation via nested sequents. In: Silva, A., Wassermann, R., de Queiroz, R. (eds.) WoLLIC 2021. LNCS, vol. 13038, pp. 337–354. Springer, Cham (2021). https://doi.org/10.1007/978-3-030-88853-4_21
15. van der Giessen, I., Jalali, R., Kuznets, R.: Extensions of K5: proof theory and uniform Lyndon interpolation. In: Ramanayake, R., Urban, J. (eds.) Automated Reasoning with Analytic Tableaux and Related Methods. TABLEAUX 2023, pp. 263–282. Springer, Cham (2023). https://doi.org/10.1007/978-3-031-43513-3_15
16. van Gool, S., Metcalfe, G., Tsinakis, C.: Uniform interpolation and compact congruences. Ann. Pure Appl. Logic **168**(10), 1927–1948 (2017). https://doi.org/10.1016/j.apal.2017.05.001
17. Goré, R., Ramanayake, R., Shillito, I.: Cut-elimination for provability logic by terminating proof-search: formalised and deconstructed using Coq. In: Das, A., Negri, S. (eds.) TABLEAUX 2021. LNCS (LNAI), vol. 12842, pp. 299–313. Springer, Cham (2021). https://doi.org/10.1007/978-3-030-86059-2_18
18. Iemhoff, R.: Uniform interpolation and sequent calculi in modal logic. Arch. Math. Logic **58**(1–2), 155–181 (2019)
19. Kocsis, Z.A.: Proof-theoretic methods in quantifier-free definability (2023). https://doi.org/10.48550/arXiv.2310.03640, preprint arXiv:2310.03640
20. Kowalski, T., Metcalfe, G.: Uniform interpolation and coherence. Ann. Pure Appl. Logic **170**(7), 825–841 (2019). https://doi.org/10.1016/j.apal.2019.02.004
21. Larchey-Wendling, D., Monin, J.F.: The Braga method: extracting certified algorithms from complex recursive schemes in Coq, Chapter 8, pp. 305–386. World Scientific, Singapore (2021). https://doi.org/10.1142/9789811236488_0008
22. Marti, J., Seifan, F., Venema, Y.: Uniform interpolation for coalgebraic fixpoint logic. In: Moss, L.S., Sobocinski, P. (eds.) 6th Conference on Algebra and Coalgebra in Computer Science (CALCO 2015). Leibniz International Proceedings in Informatics (LIPIcs), vol. 35, pp. 238–252. Schloss Dagstuhl – Leibniz-Zentrum für Informatik, Dagstuhl, Germany (2015). https://doi.org/10.4230/LIPIcs.CALCO.2015.238
23. Pitts, A.M.: On an interpretation of second order quantification in first order intuitionistic propositional logic. J. Symbol. Log. **57**(1), 33–52 (1992). https://doi.org/10.2307/2275175
24. Sambin, G., Valentini, S.: The modal logic of provability. The sequential approach. J. Philos. Logic **11**(3), 311–342 (1982). http://www.jstor.org/stable/30226252

25. Shavrukov, V.Y.: Subalgebras of diagonalizable algebras of theories containing arithmetic. Dissertationes Mathematicae **323** (1993). http://matwbn.icm.edu.pl/ksiazki/rm/rm323/rm32301.pdf
26. Shillito, I., van der Giessen, I., Goré, R., Iemhoff, R.: A new calculus for intuitionistic strong Löb logic: strong termination and cut-elimination, formalised. In: Ramanayake, R., Urban, J. (eds.) Automated Reasoning with Analytic Tableaux and Related Methods. TABLEAUX 2023, pp. 73–93. Springer, Cham (2023). https://doi.org/10.1007/978-3-031-43513-3_5
27. Visser, A.: Uniform interpolation and layered bisimulation. In: Hájek, P. (ed.) Gödel '96 proceedings. LNL, vol. 6, pp. 139–164. Springer, Heidelberg (1996). http://projecteuclid.org/download/pdf_1/euclid.lnl/1235417019
28. Visser, A., Litak, T.: Lewis and Brouwer meet Strong Löb (2024). https://arxiv.org/abs/2404.11969, preprint arXiv:2404.11969

Skolemisation for Intuitionistic Linear Logic

Alessandro Bruni[1], Eike Ritter[2(✉)], and Carsten Schürmann[1]

[1] Department of Computer Science, IT University of Copenhagen, Copenhagen, Denmark
{brun,carsten}@itu.dk

[2] School of Computer Science, University of Birmingham, Birmingham, UK
E.Ritter@bham.ac.uk

Abstract. Focusing is a known technique for reducing the number of proofs while preserving derivability. Skolemisation is another technique designed to improve proof search, which reduces the number of back-tracking steps by representing dependencies on the term level and instantiate witness terms during unification at the axioms or fail with an occurs-check otherwise. Skolemisation for classical logic is well understood, but a practical skolemisation procedure for focused intuitionistic linear logic has been elusive so far. In this paper we present a focused variant of first-order intuitionistic linear logic together with a sound and complete skolemisation procedure.

1 Introduction

Modern proof search paradigms are built on variants of focused logics first introduced by Andreoli [1]. Focused logics eliminate sources of non-determinism while preserving derivability. In this paper we consider the focused logic LJF [2]. By categorising the logical connectives according to the invertibility of its left or right rules, we obtain a so-called polarised logic [2]. For example, the $\forall$-right rule is invertible, making $\forall$ a negative (or asynchronous) connective, and the $\exists$-left rule is invertible, making $\exists$ a positive (or synchronous) connective.

But even a focused proof system does not eliminate all non-determinism. There is still residual non-determinism in-between focusing steps. It is well known that we can control this non-determinism using different search strategies, such as forcing backward-chaining and forward-chaining using the atom polarity. Another remaining source of non-determinism comes from the order of quantifier openings, as choosing the wrong order may lead to additional back-tracking.

For example, consider the following judgment in multiplicative linear logic:

$$\forall x.A(x) \multimap B(x), \forall y.\exists u.A(u) \vdash \exists z.B(z)$$

Variables u introduced by the well-known rules $\exists L^u$ and $\forall R^u$ (and written next to the rule name) are fresh and called Eigen-variables, which we can use to construct witness terms for the universal variables on the left or the existential

C. Benzmüller et al. (Eds.): IJCAR 2024, LNAI 14740, pp. 61–77, 2024.
https://doi.org/10.1007/978-3-031-63501-4_4

variables on the right. Because quantifier rules do not permute freely with other rules, one needs to resolve quantifiers in a particular order, or otherwise risk an exponential blow-up in the proof search. This fact has already been observed by Shankar [8] for LJ, who proposed to capture the necessary dependencies using Skolem functions to encode the permutation properties of LJ inference rules, guaranteeing reconstruction of LJ proofs from their skolemised counterparts.

However, naïve Skolemisation is unsound in linear logic. As first noted by Lincoln [3], the sequent

$$\forall x.A \otimes B(x) \vdash A \otimes \forall u.B(u)$$

does not admit a derivation in linear logic, but its naïve skolemisation does: $A \otimes B(x) \vdash A \otimes B(u())$, where x denotes an existential and $u()$ a universal variable that must not depend on x. Introducing replication creates a similar problem, where the following sequent does not admit a derivation:

$$\forall x.!A(x) \vdash !\forall u.A(u)$$

however again its naïve skolemisation loses the relative order between quantifier openings and replication, thus admitting a proof: $!A(x) \vdash !A(u())$.

In this paper we show that the ideas of skolemisation for classical logic and intuitionistic logic for LJ [8] carry over quite naturally to focused intuitionistic linear logics (LJF) [2]. We propose a quantifier-free version of LJF that encodes the necessary constraints called skolemised intuitionistic linear logic (SLJF). Our main contribution is to define a *skolemisation* procedure from LJF to SLJF that we show to be both sound and complete: any derivation in LJF is provable in SLJF after skolemisation and, vice versa, any derivation in SLJF of a skolemised formula allows to reconstruct a proof of the original formula. Hence we eliminate back-tracking points introduced by first-order quantifiers. We do not eliminate any back-tracking points introduced by propositional formulae.

The paper proceeds as follows: Sect. 2 introduces focused intuitionistic linear logic (LJF), Sect. 3 presents skolemised focused intuitionistic linear logic (SLJF), Sect. 4 presents a novel skolemisation procedure, Sect. 5 presents soundness and completeness results, and Sect. 6 presents our conclusion and related work.

Contributions: This work is to our knowledge the first work that successfully defines skolemisation for a variant of linear logic. The benefit is that during proof search any back-tracking caused by resolving quantifiers in the wrong order is eliminated and replaced by an admissibility check on the axioms.

2 Focused Intuitionistic Linear Logic

We consider the focused and polarised formulation of linear logic LJF [2] that we now present. The syntactic categories are defined as usual: we write u, v for Eigen-variables and x, y for existential variables that may be instantiated by other terms, finally N for negative formulas and P for positive formulas. We also distinguish between negative and positive atoms, written as A^- and A^+. We write $\uparrow$ to embed a positive formula into a negative, and $\downarrow$ for the inverse. The rest of the connectives should be self-explanatory.

Atom	$A, B ::= q(t_1 \dots t_n)$
Negative formula	$N ::= A^- \mid P \multimap N \mid \forall x.N \mid \uparrow P$
Positive formula	$P ::= A^+ \mid P_1 \otimes P_2 \mid !N \mid \exists x.P \mid \downarrow N$

We use the standard two-zone notation for judgments with unrestricted context Γ and linear context Δ: we write $\Gamma; \Delta \vdash N$ for the judgment, where at most one formula $[N] \in \Delta$ or $N = [P]$ can be in focus. All formulas in Γ are negative and all other formulas in Δ are positive. When $[N] \in \Delta$ we say that we focus on the left, whereas when $N = [P]$ we focus on the right, and we are in an inversion phase when no formula is in focus. To improve readability, we omit the leading $\cdot$; when the unrestricted context is empty. The rules defining LJF [2] are depicted in Fig. 1. We comment on a few interesting aspects of this logic. There are two axiom rules ax^- and ax^+ where, intuitively, ax^- triggers backwards-chaining, and ax^+ forward-chaining [6]. Hence we can assign polarities to atoms to select a particular proof search strategy. Once we focus on a formula, the focus is preserved until a formula with opposite polarity is encountered, in which case the focus is lost or blurred. After blurring, we enter a maximal inversion phase, where all rules without focus are applied bottom-up until no more invertible rules are applicable. The next focusing phase then commences.

Focusing is both sound and complete. i.e. every derivation (written as $\Gamma; \Delta \vdash_{\text{ILL}} F$) can be focused and every focused derivation can be embedded into plain linear logic [2]. In particular, in our own proofs in Sect. 5, we make use of the soundness of focusing.

Theorem 1 (Focusing). *If $\Gamma; \Delta \vdash_{\text{ILL}} F$ and Γ', Δ' and F' are the result of polarising Γ, Δ and F respectively by inserting $\uparrow$ and $\downarrow$ appropriately, then $\Gamma'; \Delta' \vdash F'$ in focused linear logic [2].*

We now present three examples of possible derivations of sequents in LJF. We will use these examples to illustrate key aspects of our proposed skolemisation.

Example 1. Consider the motivating formula from the introduction that we would like to derive in LJF, assuming that the term algebra has a term t_0.

$$\downarrow (\forall x.(\downarrow A(x)^-) \multimap B(x)^-), \downarrow (\forall x. \uparrow \exists u. \downarrow A(u)^-) \vdash \uparrow (\exists x. \downarrow B(x)^-)$$

All formulas are embedded formulas, which means that there is a non-deterministic choice to be made, namely on which formula to focus next. As this example shows, it is quite important to pick the correct formula, otherwise proof search will get stuck and back-tracking is required. This observation also holds if we determine the instantiation of universal quantifiers on the left and existential quantifiers on the right by unification instead of choosing suitable terms when applying the $\forall L$ or $\exists R$ rule.

$$\frac{}{\Gamma; [A^-] \vdash A^-}\ ax^- \qquad \frac{}{\Gamma; A^+ \vdash [A^+]}\ ax^+$$

$$\frac{\Gamma; \Delta, [N\{^t/_x\}] \vdash N'}{\Gamma; \Delta, [\forall\, x.\ N] \vdash N'}\ \forall L \qquad \frac{\Gamma; \Delta \vdash N\{^u/_u\}}{\Gamma; \Delta \vdash \forall\, u.\ N}\ \forall R^u$$

$$\frac{\Gamma; \Delta, P\{^u/_u\} \vdash N'}{\Gamma; \Delta, \exists\, u.\ P \vdash N'}\ \exists L^u \qquad \frac{\Gamma; \Delta \vdash [P\{^t/_x\}]}{\Gamma; \Delta \vdash [\exists\, x.\ P]}\ \exists R$$

$$\frac{\Gamma; \Delta_1 \vdash [P] \quad \Gamma; \Delta_2, [N] \vdash N'}{\Gamma; \Delta_1, \Delta_2, [P \multimap N] \vdash N'}\ \multimap L \qquad \frac{\Gamma; \Delta, P \vdash N}{\Gamma; \Delta \vdash P \multimap N}\ \multimap R$$

$$\frac{\Gamma; \Delta, P_1, P_2 \vdash N'}{\Gamma; \Delta, P_1 \otimes P_2 \vdash N'}\ \otimes L \qquad \frac{\Gamma; \Delta_1 \vdash [P_1] \quad \Gamma; \Delta_2 \vdash [P_2]}{\Gamma; \Delta_1, \Delta_2, \vdash [P_1 \otimes P_2]}\ \otimes R$$

$$\frac{\Gamma, N; \Delta \vdash N'}{\Gamma; \Delta, !\,N \vdash N'}\ !\,L \qquad \frac{\Gamma; \cdot \vdash N}{\Gamma; \cdot \vdash [!\,N]}\ !\,R \qquad \frac{\Gamma, N; \Delta, [N] \vdash N'}{\Gamma, N; \Delta \vdash N'}\ \mathit{copy}$$

$$\frac{\Gamma; \Delta, [N] \vdash N'}{\Gamma; \Delta, \downarrow N \vdash N'}\ \text{focus}L^* \qquad \frac{\Gamma; \Delta \vdash [P]}{\Gamma; \Delta \vdash \uparrow P}\ \text{focus}R^*$$

$$\frac{\Gamma; \Delta, P \vdash N'}{\Gamma; \Delta, [\uparrow P] \vdash N'}\ \text{blur}L \qquad \frac{\Gamma; \Delta \vdash N}{\Gamma; \Delta \vdash [\downarrow N]}\ \text{blur}R$$

Fig. 1. Focused intuitionistic linear logic (LJF)

Focusing on the first assumption before the second will not yield a proof. The Eigen-variable that eventually is introduced by the nested existential quantifier inside the second assumption is needed to instantiate the universal quantifier in the first assumption. If we start by focusing on the first assumption then none of the subsequent proof states is provable, as the following two proof states $(\downarrow A(t_0)^-) \multimap B(t_0)^-, A(t_1)^- \vdash B(t_0)^-$ and $(\downarrow A(t_0)^-) \multimap B(t_0)^-, A(t_1)^- \vdash B(t_1)^-$ demonstrate. Back-tracking becomes inevitable.

To construct a valid proof we must hence focus on the second assumption before considering the first. The result is a unique and complete proof tree that is depicted in Fig. 2. □

Example 2. Consider the sequent $\downarrow (\forall x.\ \uparrow (\downarrow A^- \otimes \downarrow B^-(x))) \vdash \uparrow (\downarrow A^- \otimes \downarrow \forall u.B^-(u))$. This sequent is not derivable in LJF: note that $\forall L$ needs to be above the $\forall R$ rule, but this step requires that $\otimes R$ is applied first. However, to apply $\otimes R$, we would need to have applied $\otimes L$ first, which requires that $\forall L$ is applied first. This cyclic dependency cannot be resolved. □

Example 3. Consider the sequent $\downarrow \forall x.\ \uparrow !A^-(x) \vdash \uparrow !\forall u.A^-(u)$. This sequent is not derivable in LJF either: note that the $\forall L$-rule needs to be above the $\forall R$ rule, but this step requires the $!R$ rule to be applied first. However, to apply the $!R$ rule we would need to apply the $\forall L$ rule first to ensure that the linear context is empty when we apply the $!R$ rule. This is another cyclic dependency. □

$$
\dfrac{\dfrac{\dfrac{\dfrac{}{[A(u_0)^-] \vdash A(u_0)^-}\,\mathrm{ax}^-}{\downarrow A(u_0)^- \vdash A(u_0)^-}\,\mathrm{focus}L^*}{\downarrow A(u_0)^- \vdash [\downarrow A(u_0)^-]}\,\mathrm{blur}R \qquad \dfrac{}{[B(u_0)^-] \vdash B(u_0)^-}\,\mathrm{ax}^-}{[(\downarrow A(u_0)^-) \multimap B(u_0)^-)], \downarrow A(u_0)^- \vdash B(u_0)^-}\,\multimap L
$$

$$\vdots$$

$$\downarrow (\forall x.(\downarrow A(x)^-) \multimap B(x)^-), \downarrow A(u_0)^- \vdash B(u_0)^-$$

$$\vdots$$

$$\downarrow (\forall x.(\downarrow A(x)^-) \multimap B(x)^-), \downarrow A(u_0)^- \vdash \uparrow (\exists x. \downarrow B(x)^-)$$

$$\vdots$$

$$\downarrow (\forall x.(\downarrow A(x)^-) \multimap B(x)^-), \downarrow (\forall x. \uparrow \exists u. \downarrow A(u)^-) \vdash \uparrow (\exists x. \downarrow B(x)^-)$$

Fig. 2. Example 1, unique and complete proof

Focusing removes sources of non-determinism from the propositional layer, but not from quantifier instantiation. In the next section we present a quantifier-free skolemised logic, SLJF, where quantifier dependencies are represented through skolemised terms. This way, proof search no longer needs to back-track on first-order variables, as the constraints capture all dependencies. Instead, unification at the axioms will check if the proof is admissible.

3 Skolemised Focused Intuitionistic Linear Logic

We begin now with the definition of a skolemised, focused, and polarised intuitionistic linear logic (SLJF), with the following syntactic categories:

Atom	$A, B ::= q(t_1 \dots t_n)$
Negative formula	$N ::= A^-_\Phi \mid P \multimap N \mid \uparrow P$
Positive formula	$P ::= A^+_\Phi \mid P \otimes P \mid !_{(a;\Phi;\sigma)} N \mid \downarrow N$
Variable	$v ::= x \mid u \mid a$
Term	$t ::= v \mid f(t) \mid (t, \dots, t)$
Variable context	$\Phi ::= \cdot \mid \Phi, v$
Modal context	$\Gamma ::= \cdot \mid \Gamma, (a; \Phi; \sigma) : N$
Linear context	$\Delta ::= \cdot \mid \Delta, P$
Parallel substitution	$\sigma ::= \cdot \mid \sigma, t/x \mid \sigma, u(t)/u \mid \sigma, t/a$

Following the definition of LJF, we distinguish between positive and negative formulas and atoms. Backward and forward-chaining strategies are supported in SLJF, as well.

SLJF does not define any quantifiers as they are removed by skolemisation (see Sect. 4). Yet, dependencies need to be captured in some way. Quantifier

$$\frac{}{\cdot : \Phi \rightarrow \cdot}\ s/\cdot \qquad \frac{\Phi \vdash t \quad \sigma : \Phi \rightarrow \Phi'}{\sigma, t/x : \Phi \rightarrow \Phi', x}\ \text{s/existential}$$

$$\frac{\Phi \vdash \vec{t} \quad \sigma : \Phi \rightarrow \Phi'}{\sigma, u(\vec{t})/u : \Phi \rightarrow \Phi', u}\ \text{s/Eigen} \qquad \frac{\Phi \vdash t \quad \sigma : \Phi \rightarrow \Phi'}{\sigma, t/a : \Phi \rightarrow \Phi', a}\ \text{s/special}$$

Fig. 3. Typing rules for substitutions

rules for $\forall R^u$ and $\exists L^u$ introduce Eigen-variables written as u. Quantifier rules for $\forall L$ and $\exists R$ introduce existential variables, which we denote with x. And finally other rules, such as $\otimes R$, $\multimap L$, and $!R$ are annotated with *special variables* a capturing the dependencies between rules that do not freely commute. These special variables are crucial during unification at the axiom level to check that the current derivation is admissible.

The semantics of the bang connective ! in SLJF is more involved than in LJF because we have to keep track of the variables capturing dependencies and form closures: One way to define the judgmental reconstruction of the exponential fragment of SLJF is to introduce a validity judgment $(a; \Phi; \sigma) : N$, read as N is valid in world $(a; \Phi; \sigma)$, which leads to a generalised, modal Γ that no longer simply contains negative formulas N, but also closures of additional judgmental information. The special variable a is the "name" of the world in which $N\sigma$ is valid, where all possible dependencies are summarised by Φ. Φ consists of variables, where we assume tacit variable renaming to ensure that no variable name occurs twice. We write $\llcorner \Phi \lrcorner$ for all existential and special variables declared in Φ. In contrast to LJF, atomic propositions A^-_Φ and A^+_Φ are indexed by Φ capturing all potential dependencies, which we will inspect in detail in Definition 2 where we define *admissibility*, the central definition of this paper, resolving the non-determinism related to the order in which quantifier rules are applied. The linear context remains unchanged.

Terms t are constructed from variables (existential, universal, and special) and function symbols f that are declared in a global signature $\Sigma ::= \cdot \mid \Sigma, f$. Well-built terms are characterised by the judgment $\Phi \vdash t$. Substitutions constructed by unification and communicated through proof search capture the constraints on the order of application of proof rules, which guarantee that a proof in SLJF gives rise to a proof in LJF. Their definition is straightforward, and the typing rules for substitutions are depicted in Fig. 3. For a substitution σ such that $\sigma : \Phi \rightarrow \Phi'$, we define the domain of σ to be Φ and the co-domain of σ to be Φ'. For any context Φ and substitution σ with co-domain Ψ we write $\sigma_{\uparrow\Phi}$ for the substitution σ restricted to $\Phi \cap \Psi$, i.e. $v\sigma_{\uparrow\Phi}$ is defined iff $v \in \Phi \cap \Psi$, and $v\sigma_{\uparrow\Phi} = v\sigma$ in this case. We write $\sigma \setminus \Phi$ for the substitution σ restricted to $\Psi \setminus \Phi$, i.e. $v\sigma \setminus \Phi$ is defined iff $v \in \Psi \setminus \Phi$, and $v\sigma \setminus \Phi = v\sigma$ in this case. For any substitution σ we define the substitution σ^n by induction over n to be $\sigma^1 = \sigma$, and $v\sigma^{n+1} = (v\sigma^n)\sigma$.

Definition 1 (Free Variables). *We define the free variables of a skolemised formula K, written $FV(K)$ by induction over the structure of formulae by*

$$\begin{aligned} FV(A_\Phi^-) &= FV(A_\Phi^+) = \Phi \\ FV(P_1 \otimes P_2) &= FV(P_1) \cup FV(P_2) \\ FV(P \multimap N) &= FV(P) \cup FV(N) \\ FV(!_{(a;\Phi;\sigma)} N) &= \Phi \end{aligned}$$

Now we turn to the definition of admissibility, which checks whether the constraints on the order of $\forall L$-and $\exists R$-rules (which instantiate quantifiers) and application of non-invertible propositional rules can be satisfied when reconstructing a LJF-derivation from an SLJF-derivation.

Definition 2 (Admissibility). *We say σ is* admissible *for Φ if firstly for all existential and special variables v and for all n, v does not occur in $v\sigma^n$, and secondly for all special variables a_L and a_R respectively and for all n, if $x\sigma^n$ contains a variable a_L or a_R for any x in the co-domain of σ, then the variable a_R or a_L respectively does not occur in Φ.*

The first condition in the definition of admissibility ensures that there are no cycles in the dependencies of $\forall L$-and $\exists R$-rules and non-invertible propositional rules. The second condition ensures that for each rule with two premises any Eigen-variable which is introduced in one branch is not used in the other branch. Examples of how this definition captures dependency constraints are given below.

Next, we define derivability in SLJF. The derivability judgment uses a substitution which captures the dependencies between $\forall L$-and $\exists R$-rules and non-invertible propositional rules.

Definition 3 (Proof Theory). *Let Φ be a context of variables, Γ the modal context (which refined the notion of unrestricted context from earlier in this paper), Δ the linear context, P a positive and N a negative formula, and σ a substitution. We define two mutually dependent judgments $\Gamma; \Delta \vdash N; \sigma$ and $\Gamma; \Delta \vdash [P]; \sigma$ to characterise derivability in SLJF. The rules defining these judgments are depicted in Fig. 4.*

The $!R$-rule introduces additional substitutions which capture the dependency of the $!R$-rule on the $\forall L$-and $\exists R$-rules which instantiate the free variables in the judgment. An example of this rule is given below. The copy-rule performs a renaming of all the bound variables in N.

Example 4. We give a derivation of the translation of the judgment of Example 1 in skolemised intuitionistic linear logic. We omit the modal context $\Gamma = \cdot$. Furthermore, let the goal of proof search be the following judgment:

$$\cdot; \uparrow (\downarrow A(x_1)^-_{(x_1,a_L)}) \multimap B(x_1)^-_{(x_1,a_R)}, \uparrow A(u)^-_{(x_2,u)} \vdash B(x_3)^-_{(x_3)}; \sigma$$

where σ must contain the substitution $u(x_2)/u$, which arises from skolemisation.

$$\frac{A^-\sigma = B^-\sigma \quad \sigma \text{ admissible for } \Phi_1, \Phi_2}{\Gamma; [A^-_{\Phi_1}] \vdash B^-_{\Phi_2}; \sigma}\, ax^-$$

$$\frac{A^+\sigma = B^+\sigma \quad \sigma \text{ admissible for } \Phi_1, \Phi_2}{\Gamma; A^+_{\Phi_1} \vdash [B^+_{\Phi_2}]; \sigma}\, ax^+$$

$$\frac{\Gamma; \Delta_1 \vdash [P]; \sigma \quad \Gamma; \Delta_2, [N] \vdash N'; \sigma}{\Gamma; \Delta_1, \Delta_2, [P \multimap N] \vdash N'; \sigma}\, \multimap L$$

$$\frac{\Gamma; \Delta_1 \vdash [P_1]; \sigma \quad \Gamma; \Delta_2 \vdash [P_2]; \sigma}{\Gamma; \Delta_1, \Delta_2 \vdash [P_1 \otimes P_2]; \sigma}\, \otimes R$$

$$\frac{\Gamma; \Delta, P \vdash N; \sigma}{\Gamma; \Delta \vdash P \multimap N; \sigma}\, \multimap R \qquad \frac{\Gamma; \Delta, P_1, P_2 \vdash N; \sigma}{\Gamma; \Delta, P_1 \otimes P_2 \vdash N; \sigma}\, \otimes L$$

$$\frac{\Gamma, (a; \Phi; \sigma') \colon N; \Delta \vdash N'; \sigma}{\Gamma; \Delta, !_{(a;\Phi;\sigma')}\, N \vdash N'; \sigma}\, !L$$

$$\frac{(a_i; \Phi_i; \sigma_i) \colon N_i; \cdot \vdash N; \sigma, \sigma', (\Phi_1, \ldots, \Phi_n)/a, (\Phi)/a_1, \ldots, (\Phi)/a_n}{(a_i; \Phi_i; \sigma_i) \colon N_i; \cdot \vdash [!_{(a,\Phi;\sigma')}\, N]; \sigma}\, !R$$

$$\frac{\Gamma, (a; \Phi; \sigma') \colon N; \Delta, [N\{\vec{v}'/\vec{v}\}] \vdash N'; \sigma, \sigma'\{\vec{v}'/\vec{v}\} \text{ where } \vec{v} = FV(N) \setminus \Phi}{\Gamma, (a; \Phi; \sigma') \colon N; \Delta \vdash N'; \sigma}\, copy$$

$$\frac{\Gamma; \Delta, [N] \vdash N'; \sigma}{\Gamma; \Delta, \downarrow N \vdash N'; \sigma}\, \text{focus}L^* \qquad \frac{\Gamma; \Delta \vdash [P]; \sigma}{\Gamma; \Delta \vdash \uparrow P; \sigma}\, \text{focus}R^*$$

$$\frac{\Gamma; \Delta, P \vdash N'; \sigma}{\Gamma; \Delta, [\uparrow P] \vdash N'; \sigma}\, \text{blur}L \qquad \frac{\Gamma; \Delta \vdash N; \sigma}{\Gamma; \Delta \vdash [\downarrow N]; \sigma}\, \text{blur}R$$

Fig. 4. Skolemised intuitionistic linear logic

We observe that only focusing rules are applicable. Focusing on A will not succeed, since A was assumed to be a negative connective, so we focus on the right. Recall, that we will not be able to remove the non-determinism introduced on the propositional level. We obtain the derivation in Fig. 5, where $\sigma = \cdot, u/x_1, x_1/x_3, u(x_2)/u$. This derivation holds because σ is admissible for x_1, a_L, x_2 and x_1, a_R, x_3. The constraint that the variable x_2 can be instantiated only after the $\forall R$-rule for u has been applied is captured by the substitution $u(x_2)/u$.

Example 5. Next, consider the sequent $\downarrow (\forall x. \uparrow (\downarrow A^- \otimes \downarrow B^- x)) \vdash \uparrow (\downarrow A^- \otimes \downarrow \forall u. B^-(u))$ from Example 2. To learn if this sequent is provable, we translate it into $\downarrow A^-_x \otimes \downarrow B(x)^-_x \vdash \uparrow (\downarrow A_{a_L} \otimes \downarrow B(u)^-_{a_R;u})$. The only possible proof yields an axiom derivation $[B^-_x] \vdash B^-_{a_R;u}; \cdot, u(a_R)/x$, which is not valid, as $\cdot, u/x, u(a_R)/u$ is not admissible for x, a_L. More precisely, the second condition of admissibility is violated. □

$$\dfrac{\dfrac{\dfrac{[A(u)^-_{(x_2,u)}] \vdash A(x_1)_{(x_1,a_L)};\sigma}{\downarrow A(u)^-_{(x_2,u)} \vdash [\downarrow A(x_1)^-_{(x_1,a_L)}];\sigma} \quad [B(x_1)^-_{(x_1,a_R)}] \vdash B(x_3)^-_{(x_3)};\sigma}{[(\downarrow A(x_1)^-_{(x_1,a_L)}) \multimap B(x_1)^-_{(x_1,a_R)}], \downarrow A(u)^-_{(x_2,u)} \vdash B(x_3)^-_{(x_3)};\sigma}}{\downarrow (\downarrow A(x_1)^-_{(x_1,a_L)}) \multimap B(x_1)^-_{(x_1,a_R)}, \downarrow A(u)^-_{(x_2,u)} \vdash B(x_3)^-_{(x_3)};\sigma}$$

Fig. 5. Example 4, unique complete proof

$$\begin{aligned} pos(A^-) &= \downarrow A^- \\ pos(P \multimap N) &= \downarrow (P \multimap N) \\ pos(\uparrow P) &= P \\ pos(A^+) &= A^+ \\ pos(\downarrow N) &= \downarrow N \\ pos(!_{(a;\Phi;\sigma)}\, N) &= !_{(a;\Phi;\sigma)}\, N \end{aligned} \qquad \begin{aligned} neg(A^-) &= A^- \\ neg(P \multimap N) &= P \multimap N \\ neg(\uparrow P) &= \uparrow P \\ neg(A^+) &= \uparrow A^+ \\ neg(P_1 \otimes P_2) &= \uparrow (P_1 \otimes P_2) \\ neg(\downarrow N) &= N \\ neg(!_{(a;\Phi;\sigma)}\, N) &= \uparrow !_{(a;\Phi;\sigma)}\, N \end{aligned}$$

Fig. 6. Polarity adjustments

Example 6. Now, consider the sequent $\downarrow \forall x.\ \uparrow !A^-(x) \vdash \uparrow !\forall u.A^-(u)$ from Example 3. The skolemised sequent is $!_{(a;x;\cdot)}A_{a,x}{}^- \vdash \uparrow !_{(b;u;u(b)/u)}A^-(u)_{u,b})$. The only possible derivation produces the substitution $\cdot, u/x, x/b, u(b)/u$, which is not admissible for $\cdot, x, u, b, a$. More precisely, the first condition of admissibility is violated for the variable b. This expresses the fact that in any possible LJF-derivation the instantiation of x has to happen before the $!R$-rule and the $!R$ -rule has to be applied before the instantiation of x, which is impossible.

4 Skolemisation

To skolemise first-order formulas in classical logic, we usually compute prenex normal forms of all formulas that occur in a sequent, where we replace all quantifiers that bind "existential" variables by Skolem constants. This idea can also be extended to intuitionistic logic [8]. This paper is to our knowledge the first to demonstrate that skolemisation can also be defined for focused, polarised, intuitionistic, first-order linear logic, as well. In this section, we show how.

Skolemisation transforms an LJF formula F (positive or negative) closed under Φ into an SLJF formula K and a substitution, which collects all variables introduced during skolemisation. Formally, we define two mutual judgments: $sk_L(\Phi, F) = (K;\sigma)$ and $sk_R(\Phi, F) = (K;\sigma)$. K is agnostic to polarity information, hence we prepend appropriate $\uparrow$ and $\downarrow$ connectives to convert K to the appropriate polarity by the conversion operations $pos(\cdot)$ and $neg(\cdot)$, depicted in Fig. 6. Alternatively, we could have chosen to distinguish positive and negative Ks syntactically, but this would have unnecessarily cluttered the presentation and left unnecessary backtrack points because of spurious $\uparrow\downarrow$ and $\downarrow\uparrow$ conversions.

We return to the definition of skolemisation, depicted in Fig. 7. The main idea behind skolemisation is to record dependencies of quantifier rules as explicit substitutions. More precisely, if an Eigen-variable u depends on an existential variable x, a substitution $u(x)/u$ is added during skolemisation. We do not extend the scope of an Eigen-variable beyond the !-operator as we have to distinguish between an Eigen-variable for which a new instance must be created by the copy-rule and one where the same instance may be retained.

Explicit substitutions model constraints on the order of quantifiers. The satisfiability of the constraints is checked during unification at the leaves via the admissibility condition (see Definition 2) which the substitution has to satisfy. Potential back-track points are marked by special variables a, which are associated with the ! connective. These annotations need to store enough information so that the set of constraints can be appropriately updated when copying a formula from the modal context into the linear context.

In our representation, any proof of the skolemised formula in SLJF captures an equivalence class of proofs under different quantifier orderings in LJF. Only those derivations where substitutions are admissible, i.e. do not give rise to cycles like $u(x)/x$ or introduce undue dependencies between the left and right branches of a $\otimes$ or $\multimap$, imply the existence of a proof in LJF.

The judgments can be easily extended to the case of contexts Γ and Δ for which we write $sk_L(\Phi;\Gamma)$ and $sk_L(\Phi;\Delta)$. Note that tacit variable renaming is in order, to make sure that no spurious cycles are accidentally introduced in the partial order defined by the constraints.

Example 7. We return to Example 1 and simply present the skolemisation of the three formulas that define the judgment:

$$\downarrow(\forall x.(\downarrow A(x))\multimap B(x)), \downarrow(\forall x. \uparrow \exists u. \downarrow A(u)) \vdash \uparrow(\exists x. \downarrow B(x))$$

First, we skolemise each of the formulas individually.

$$\begin{aligned} \mathrm{sk}_L(\cdot; \downarrow(\forall x.(\downarrow A(x))\multimap B(x))) &= (\downarrow A(x)_{(x,a_L)})\multimap B(x)_{(x,a_R)}; \cdot \\ \mathrm{sk}_L(\cdot; \downarrow(\forall x. \uparrow \exists u. \downarrow A(u))) &= A(u)_{(x,u)}; u(x)/u \\ \mathrm{sk}_R(\cdot; \uparrow(\exists x. \downarrow B(x))) &= B(x)_{(x)}; \cdot \end{aligned}$$

Second, we assemble the results into a judgment in SLJF, which then looks as follows. To this end, we α-convert the variables,

$$(\downarrow A(x_1)_{(x_1,a_L)})\multimap B(x_1)_{(x_1,a_R)}, A(u)_{(x_2,u)} \vdash B(x_3)_{(x_3)}; u(x_2)/u$$

The attentive reader might have noticed that we already gave a proof of this judgment in the previous section in Example 1, after turning the first two formulas positive, because they constitute the linear context.

5 Meta Theory

We begin now with the presentation of the soundness result (see Sect. 5.1) and the completeness result (see Sect. 5.2). Together they imply that skolemisation preserves provability. These theorems also imply that proof search in SLJF will be more efficient than in LJF since it avoids quantifier level back-tracking. Proof search in skolemised form will not miss any solutions.

$\mathsf{sk}_L(\Phi; A) = pos(A_\Phi); \cdot$

$\mathsf{sk}_L(\Phi; \forall x.F) = K; \sigma$
 where $\mathsf{sk}_L(x, \Phi; F) = K; \sigma$

$\mathsf{sk}_L(\Phi; \exists u.F) = K; \sigma, u(\llcorner\Phi\lrcorner)/u$
 where $\mathsf{sk}_L(u, \Phi; F) = K; \sigma$

$\mathsf{sk}_L(\Phi; F_1 \otimes F_2) = pos(K_1) \otimes pos(K_2); \sigma_1, \sigma_2$
 where $\mathsf{sk}_L(\Phi; F_1) = K_1; \sigma_1$
 $\mathsf{sk}_L(\Phi; F_2) = K_2; \sigma_2$

$\mathsf{sk}_L(\Phi; F_1 \multimap F_2) = pos(K_1) \multimap neg(K_2); \sigma_1, \sigma_2$
 where $\mathsf{sk}_R(\Phi, a_L; F_1) = K_1; \sigma_1$
 $\mathsf{sk}_L(\Phi, a_R; F_2) = K_2; \sigma_2$

$\mathsf{sk}_L(\Phi; !\,F) = !_{(a;\Phi;\sigma\backslash\Phi)}\, neg(K); \sigma_{\uparrow\Phi}$
 where $\mathsf{sk}_L(\Phi, a; F) = K; \sigma$

$\mathsf{sk}_L(\Phi; \downarrow F) = neg(K); \sigma$
 where $\mathsf{sk}_L(\Phi; F) = K; \sigma$

$\mathsf{sk}_L(\Phi; \uparrow F) = pos(K); \sigma$
 where $\mathsf{sk}_L(\Phi; F) = K; \sigma$

$\mathsf{sk}_R(\Phi; A) = neg(A_\Phi); \cdot$

$\mathsf{sk}_R(\Phi; \exists x.F) = K; \sigma$
 where $\mathsf{sk}_R(x, \Phi; F) = K; \sigma$

$\mathsf{sk}_R(\Phi; \forall u.F) = K; \sigma, u(\llcorner\Phi\lrcorner)/u$
 where $\mathsf{sk}_R(u, \Phi; F) = K; \sigma$

$\mathsf{sk}_R(\Phi; F_1 \otimes F_2) = pos(K_1) \otimes pos(K_2); \sigma_1, \sigma_2$
 where $\mathsf{sk}_R(\Phi, a_L; F_1) = K_1; \sigma_1$
 $\mathsf{sk}_R(\Phi, a_R; F_2) = K_2; \sigma_2$

$\mathsf{sk}_R(\Phi; F_1 \multimap F_2) = pos(K_1) \multimap neg(K_2); \sigma_1, \sigma_2$
 where $\mathsf{sk}_L(\Phi; F_1) = K_1; \sigma_1$
 $\mathsf{sk}_R(\Phi; F_2) = K_2; \sigma_2$

$\mathsf{sk}_R(\Phi; !\,F) = !_{(a,\Phi;\sigma\backslash\Phi)}\, neg(K); \sigma_{\uparrow\Phi}$
 where $\mathsf{sk}_R(\Phi, a; F) = K; \sigma$

$\mathsf{sk}_R(\Phi; \downarrow F) = neg(K); \sigma$
 where $\mathsf{sk}_R(\Phi; F) = K; \sigma$

$\mathsf{sk}_R(\Phi; \uparrow F) = pos(K); \sigma$
 where $\mathsf{sk}_R(\Phi; F) = K; \sigma$

Fig. 7. Skolemisation

5.1 Soundness

For the soundness direction, we show that any valid derivation in LJF can be translated into a valid derivation in SLJF after skolemisation.

Lemma 1 (Weakening).

(i) *Assume* $\Gamma; \Delta \vdash K; \sigma$ *Then also* $\Gamma, (a; \Phi; \sigma') \colon N; \Delta \vdash K; \sigma$.
(ii) *Assume* $\Gamma; \Delta \vdash [K]; \sigma$ *Then also* $\Gamma, (a; \Phi; \sigma') \colon N; \Delta \vdash [K]; \sigma$.
(iii) *Assume* $\Gamma; \Delta, [K'] \vdash K; \sigma$ *Then also* $\Gamma, (a; \Phi; \sigma') \colon N; \Delta, [K'] \vdash K; \sigma$.

Proof. The proof is a simple induction over derivation in all three cases.

Next, we prove three admissibility properties for $\otimes$R, $\multimap$L, and *copy*, respectively, that we will invoke from within the proof of the soundness theorem. In the interest of space, we provide a proof only for the first of the three lemmas.

Lemma 2 (Admissibility of $\otimes$R). *Assume* $\Gamma; \Delta_1 \vdash neg(K_1); \sigma$ *and* $\Gamma; \Delta_2 \vdash neg(K_2); \sigma$ *with proofs of height at most* n *such that the first application of the focus-rule is the focus R-rule. Then also* $\Gamma; \Delta_1, \Delta_2 \vdash neg(pos(K_1) \otimes pos(K_2)); \sigma$.

Proof. We prove this property by induction over n. There are several cases. Firstly, assume that there is any positive formula in Δ_1 or Δ_2 which is not an atom. Again, there are several cases. We start by assuming $\Delta_1 = K_1' \otimes K_2', \Delta_1'$ and the derivation is

$$\frac{\Gamma; K_1', K_2', \Delta_1' \vdash neg(K_1); \sigma}{\Gamma; K_1' \otimes K_2', \Delta_1' \vdash neg(K_1); \sigma}$$

Hence by induction hypothesis we have $\Gamma; K_1', K_2', \Delta_1', \Delta_2 \vdash neg(pos(K_1) \otimes pos(K_2)); \sigma$ and hence also $\Gamma; K_1' \otimes K_2', \Delta_1', \Delta_2 \vdash neg(pos(K_1) \otimes pos(K_2)); \sigma$. Now assume that $\Delta_1 = !_{(a;\Phi;\sigma')} N, \Delta_1'$ and the derivation is

$$\frac{\Gamma, (a; \Phi; \sigma') \colon N; \Delta_1' \vdash neg(K_1); \sigma}{\Gamma; !_{(a;\Phi;\sigma')} N, \Delta_1' \vdash neg(K_1); \sigma}$$

By Lemma 1, we also have $\Gamma, (a; \Phi; \sigma') \colon N; \Delta_2 \vdash neg(K_2); \sigma$. By induction hypothesis we have $\Gamma, (a; \Phi; \sigma') \colon N; \Delta_1', \Delta_2 \vdash neg(pos(K_1) \otimes pos(K_2)); \sigma$ and hence also $\Gamma; !_{(a;\Phi;\sigma')} N, \Delta_1', \Delta_2 \vdash neg(pos(K_1) \otimes pos(K_2)); \sigma$.

Secondly, assume that $K_1 = N_1$, where N_1 is a negative formula and $K_2 = P_2$, where P_2 is a positive formula. By assumption there is a derivation

$$\frac{\Gamma, \Delta_2 \vdash [P_2]\sigma}{\Gamma; \Delta_2 \vdash\uparrow P_2; \sigma}$$

There is also a derivation

$$\frac{\Gamma; \Delta_1 \vdash N_1; \sigma}{\Gamma; \Delta_1 \vdash [\downarrow N_1]; \sigma}$$

Hence we also have the following derivation:

$$\frac{\dfrac{\dfrac{\Gamma; \Delta_1 \vdash N_1; \sigma}{\Gamma; \Delta_1 \vdash [\downarrow N_1]; \sigma} \quad \Gamma; \Delta_2 \vdash [P_2]; \sigma}{\Gamma; \Delta_1, \Delta_2 \vdash [\downarrow N_1 \otimes P_2]; \sigma}}{\Gamma; \Delta_1, \Delta_2 \vdash\uparrow (\downarrow N_1 \otimes P_2); \sigma}$$

By assumption we obtain $\Gamma; \Delta_1, \Delta_2 \vdash\uparrow (\downarrow N_1 \otimes P_2); \sigma$. All other cases of K_1 and K_2 being positive or negative are similar.

Lemma 3 (Admissibility of $\multimap$L). *Assume*

$$\Gamma; \Delta_1 \vdash neg(K_1); \sigma \;\; \textit{and} \;\; \Gamma; \Delta_2, pos(K_2) \vdash K; \sigma$$

with proofs of height at most n such that the first application of the focus-rule is the focus L-rule for K_1. and the focus R-rule for K_2. Then also

$$\Gamma; \Delta_1, \Delta_2, neg(pos(K_1) \multimap pos(K_2)) \vdash K; \sigma$$

Proof. Similar to the proof of Lemma 2. □

Lemma 4 (Admissibility of *copy*). *Assume*

$$\Gamma, (a; \Phi; \sigma') \colon N; pos(N\{\vec{v}'/\vec{v}\}), \Delta \vdash neg(K); \sigma, \sigma'\{\vec{v}'/\vec{v}\}$$

with a proof of height at most n *such that the first application of the focus-rule is the focus L-rule applied to* $pos(N\{\vec{v}'/\vec{v}\})$. *Then also* $\Gamma, (a; \Phi; \sigma') \colon N; \Delta \vdash neg(K); \sigma$.

Proof. Similar to the proof of Lemma 2. □

Theorem 2 (Soundness). *Let* Φ *be a context which contains all the free variables of* Γ, Δ *and* F. *Let* $\sigma \colon \Phi \rightarrow \Phi$ *be a substitution. Assume* $\Gamma\sigma_{\uparrow\llcorner\Phi\lrcorner}; \Delta\sigma_{\uparrow\llcorner\Phi\lrcorner} \vdash F\sigma_{\uparrow\llcorner\Phi\lrcorner}$ *in focused intuitionistic linear logic. Let* $sk_L(\Phi; \Gamma) = \Gamma'; \sigma_{\Gamma'}$, $sk_L(\Phi; \Delta) = \Delta'; \sigma_{\Delta'}$ *and* $sk_R(\Phi; F) = K; \sigma_K$. *Let* $\tau = \sigma_{\Gamma'}, \sigma_{\Delta'}, \sigma_K$. *Let* $\Phi' = (FV(\Gamma') \cup FV(\Delta') \cup FV(\Phi_F)) \setminus \Phi$. *Assume that* σ *does not contain any bound variables of* Γ, Γ', Δ, Δ', F *or* K. *Moreover, assume whenever* Φ *contains a variable* a_L *or* a_R, *then the corresponding variable* a_R *or* a_L *respectively does not occur in* Φ. *Then there exists a substitution* $\sigma' \colon \Phi, \Phi' \rightarrow \Phi'$ *such that*

$$neg(\Gamma'); \Delta' \vdash K; \sigma, \tau, \sigma' \ .$$

Proof. Induction over the derivation of $\Gamma\sigma_{\uparrow\llcorner\Phi\lrcorner}; \Delta\sigma_{\uparrow\llcorner\Phi\lrcorner} \vdash F\sigma_{\uparrow\llcorner\Phi\lrcorner}$. The axiom case follows from the definition of admissibility, $\otimes$R follows from Lemma 2, and $\multimap$L from Lemma 3. Now we consider the case of $\forall$L. By definition, $\mathrm{sk}_L(\Phi; \forall x.F) = \mathrm{sk}_L((x, \Phi); F)$. Moreover, t contains only variables in Φ. Hence we can apply the induction hypothesis with replacing Φ by Φ, x. The next case is $\forall$R. Consider any formula $\forall u.F$. Skolemisation introduces another Eigenvariable u. Hence we can apply the induction hypothesis with replacing Φ by Φ, u. The case for *copy* is a direct consequence of Lemma 4. All other cases are immediate. □

5.2 Completeness

We now prove the completeness direction of skolemisation, which means that we can turn a proof in SLJF directly into a proof in LJF, by inserting at appropriate places quantifier rules, as captured by the constraints. We introduce an order relation to capture constraints on the order of rules in the proof.

Definition 4. *For any substitution* σ, *define an order* $<$ *by* $x < u$ *or* $x < a$ *if* a *or* u *occur in* $x\sigma$, *and* $u < x$ *or* $u < a$ *if the variable* x *or* a *occurs in* $u(z_1, \ldots, z_n)$.

Lemma 5 (Strengthening).

(i) Assume $\Gamma, (a'; \Phi; \sigma') : K; \Delta_1 \vdash K'; \sigma$ *and there exists a free variable* x *in* K *such that* a_R *occurs in* $x\sigma$. *Moreover assume that* a_L *occurs in every axiom of* K'. *Then also* $\Gamma; \Delta_1 \vdash K'\sigma$.

(ii) Assume $\Gamma, (a'; \Phi; \sigma') : K; \Delta_2 \vdash K'; \sigma$ *and there exists a free variable* x *in* K *such that* a_L *occurs in* $x\sigma$*. Then also* $\Gamma; \Delta_2 \vdash K'; \sigma$.

Proof. (i) If the copy-rule for K is applied during the derivation, the linear context contains the free variable x such that a_R occurs in $x\sigma$. As a_L occurs in all atoms of K', the variable x must not occur in any of the linear formulae in the axioms in the derivation of $\Gamma, (a'; \Phi; \sigma') : K; \Delta_1 \vdash K'; \sigma$ because of the admissibility condition. Hence no subformula of K can occur in the linear formulae in the axioms in this derivation either. Hence there is also a derivation of $\Gamma; \Delta_1 \vdash K'; \sigma$, which does not involve K. (ii) A similar argument applies. □

Lemma 6. *Assume* $\Gamma; \Delta_1, \Delta_2 \vdash\uparrow (K_1 \otimes K_2); \sigma$*. Furthermore assume that each formula* K *in* Δ_1 *and* Δ_2 *is either a formula* $\downarrow K'$*, or there exists a free existential variable* x *in* K *such that* a_L *or* a_R *occurs in* $x\sigma$*, where* a_L *and* a_R *are the special variables introduced by the skolemisation of* $K_1 \otimes K_2$*. Moreover assume that the first focusing rule applied is the focus R-rule. Then* $\Gamma; \Delta_1 \vdash K_1; \sigma$ *and* $\Gamma; \Delta_2 \vdash K_2; \sigma$*.*

Proof. We use an induction over the structure of Δ_1 and Δ_2. Firstly, consider the case $\Gamma; K_1' \otimes K_2', \Delta_1, \Delta_2 \vdash\uparrow (K_1 \otimes K_2); \sigma$. We have a derivation

$$\frac{\Gamma; K_1', K_2', \Delta_1, \Delta_2 \vdash\uparrow (K_1 \otimes K_2)'\sigma}{\Gamma; K_1' \otimes K_2', \Delta_1, \Delta_2 \vdash\uparrow (K_1 \otimes K_2); \sigma}$$

By induction hypothesis we have $\Gamma; \Delta_1'; \vdash K_1; \sigma$ and $\Gamma; \Delta_2' \vdash K_2; \sigma$. Assume a_L occurs in $x\sigma$. Because σ is admissible for $\Gamma; \Delta_2'$, K_1' and K_2' must be part of Δ_1'. Hence $\Delta_1' = K_1', K_2', \Delta_1$ and $\Delta_2' = \Delta_2$. An application of the $\otimes L$-rule now produces $\Gamma; K_1' \otimes K_2', \Delta_1; \vdash K_1; \sigma$.

Next we consider the case $\Gamma; !_{(a'\Phi;\sigma')}K, \Delta_1, \Delta_2 \vdash\uparrow (K_1 \otimes K_2); \sigma$. Assume without loss of generality a_R occurs in $x\sigma$. We have a derivation

$$\frac{\Gamma, (a'; \Phi; \sigma') : K; \Delta_1, \Delta_2 \vdash\uparrow (K_1 \otimes K_2); \sigma}{\Gamma; !_{(a';\Phi;\sigma')}K, \Delta_1, \Delta_2 \vdash\uparrow (K_1 \otimes K_2); \sigma}$$

By induction hypothesis we have $\Gamma, (a'; \Phi; \sigma') : K; \Delta_1; \vdash K_1; \sigma$ and $\Gamma, (a'; \Phi; \sigma') : K; \Delta_2 \vdash K_2; \sigma$. An application of the $!L$-rule yields $\Gamma; !_{(a';\Phi;\sigma')}K, \Delta_1; \vdash K_1; \sigma$ and Lemma 5 yields $\Gamma; \Delta_2 \vdash K_2; \sigma$. □

Lemma 7. *Assume* $\Gamma; \Delta_1, \Delta_2, \downarrow (K_1 \multimap K_2) \vdash K; \sigma$*. Furthermore assume that each formula* K' *in* Δ_1*,* Δ_2 *and* K *is either a formula* $\downarrow K''$*, or there exists a free existential variable* x *in* K' *such that* a_L *or* a_R *occurs in* $x\sigma$*. Moreover assume that the first focusing rule applied is the focus L-rule for* $K_1 \multimap K_2$*. Then* $\Gamma; \Delta_1 \vdash K_1; \sigma$ *and* $\Gamma; \Delta_2, K_2 \vdash K; \sigma$*.*

Proof. Similar to the proof of Lemma 6. □

Lemma 8. *Assume* $\Gamma; \Delta \vdash\downarrow !_{(a,\phi;\sigma')}K; \sigma$ *and the first occurrence of the focus-rule is the focus R-rule followed by* $!R$ *with* Γ' *containing the side formulae. Let* x *be a free variable* x *of* Γ*,* Δ *or* $!_{(a,\phi;\sigma')}K$*.*

(i) If the variable u occurs in $x\sigma$, then u is a free variable of Γ' or $!_{(a,\phi;\sigma')}K$.
(ii) The variable a does not occur in $x\sigma$.

Proof. (i) By induction over the number of steps before application of the focus R-rule. Assume that the first rule applied is the focus R-rule. There are several cases. Firstly, assume u occurs bound in Γ. We consider here only the case that u occurs in $(a_1, \Phi_1, \sigma_1) : N_1$, which is part of Γ; all other cases are similar. By assumption we have $u < a_1$ and $x < u$. The $!R$-rule implies $a_1 < a$. If x occurs freely in Γ, we also have $a < x$ via the $!R$-rule, which is a contradiction. If x occurs freely in K, then we also have $a_1 < x$ via the $!R$-rule, which is a contradiction. Secondly, assume u occurs bound in K. Hence x cannot be a free variable of K. In this case we have $u < a$ and $x < u$ by assumption, together with $a < x$ by the $!R$-rule, which is a contradiction. The step case is true because there are fewer free variables in the conclusion of a rule than in the premises.

(ii) Assume $x < a$. Then there must exist a u such that $x < u$ and $u < a$. The latter implies u is a bound variable in K, which is a contradiction to (i).

Theorem 3 (Completeness). *Let Φ be a set of Eigen-, special, and existential variables which contains all the free variables of Γ, Δ and F. Let $\sigma\colon \Phi \to \Phi$ be a substitution. Let $sk_L(\Phi;\Gamma) = (\Gamma';\sigma_{\Gamma'})$, $sk_L(\Phi;\Delta) = (\Delta';\sigma_{\Delta'})$ and $sk_R(\Phi;F) = (K;\sigma_K)$. Let $\Phi' = (FV(\Gamma') \cup FV(\Delta') \cup FV(K)) \setminus \Phi$ and $\tau = \sigma_{\Gamma'}, \sigma_{\Delta'}, \sigma_K$. Let $\sigma'\colon \Phi, \Phi' \to \Phi'$ be a substitution.*

(i) If $neg(\Gamma'); \Delta' \vdash K; \sigma, \tau, \sigma'$ then $\Gamma\sigma_{\uparrow\llcorner\Phi\lrcorner}; \Delta\sigma_{\uparrow\llcorner\Phi\lrcorner} \vdash F\sigma_{\uparrow\llcorner\Phi\lrcorner}$ in focused intuitionistic linear logic.
(ii) If $\Delta' = \Delta'', \downarrow K'$ and $neg(\Gamma'); \Delta'', [K'] \vdash K; \sigma, \tau, \sigma'$ then $\Gamma\sigma_{\uparrow\llcorner\Phi\lrcorner}; \Delta\sigma_{\uparrow\llcorner\Phi\lrcorner} \vdash F\sigma_{\uparrow\llcorner\Phi\lrcorner}$ in focused intuitionistic linear logic.
(iii) If $neg(\Gamma'); \Delta' \vdash [K]; \sigma, \tau, \sigma'$ then $\Gamma\sigma_{\uparrow\llcorner\Phi\lrcorner}; \Delta\sigma_{\uparrow\llcorner\Phi\lrcorner} \vdash F\sigma_{\uparrow\llcorner\Phi\lrcorner}$ in focused intuitionistic linear logic.

Proof. We use firstly an induction over the derivation of $neg(\Gamma'); \Delta' \vdash K; \sigma, \tau, \sigma'$ and secondly an induction over the structure of Δ, F. Let $\Delta = F_1, \ldots, F_n$ and $\Delta' = K_1, \ldots, K_n$. Let $V = \{x_1, \ldots, x_k, u_1, \ldots, u_m\}$ be the set of outermost bound variables of Δ', K (including names). There are several cases. Firstly, if there exists a i such that $1 \leq i \leq n$ and F_i is a tensor product or a formula $!N$, or F is a linear implication, we apply the corresponding inference rule and then the induction hypothesis.

Secondly, assume there exists an Eigen-variable $u \in V$. Assume $F = \forall u.F'$. Hence by induction hypothesis we have $\Gamma\sigma_{\uparrow\llcorner\Phi\lrcorner}; \Delta\sigma_{\uparrow\llcorner\Phi\lrcorner} \vdash F'\sigma_{\uparrow\llcorner\Phi\lrcorner}$. By assumption, u does not occur in $x\sigma$ for any variable x in the co-domain of σ. Now the $\forall R$-rule yields the claim. Now assume $F = \exists u.F'$. This case is similar to $\forall R$.

Thirdly, assume there exists an existential variable in V. Let x be an existential variable which is maximal in V. Assume $F = \exists x.F'$. We show that every Eigen-variable u of $x\sigma'$ is a free variable of Δ, F. By definition, we have $x < u$. Assume u is a bound variable in Δ, F. If u is a bound variable of F, we would have $u < x$, which is a contradiction. Hence u is a bound variable of Δ. Because u is not an outermost bound variable, there exists a bound existential variable

y such that $u < y$. Hence x is not a maximal bound variable. By induction hypothesis we have $\Gamma\sigma_{\uparrow\llcorner\Phi\lrcorner}; \Delta\sigma_{\uparrow\llcorner\Phi\lrcorner} \vdash F'\sigma_{\uparrow\llcorner\Phi\lrcorner}$, and now we apply the $\exists R$-rule. Now assume $F_1 = \forall x.F_1'$. Similar to the $\exists R$-case.

Next, assume there are no maximal first-order variables in V. By definition, the special variables corresponding to the last rule applied to the skolemised version where the principal formula is asynchronous are now the only maximal elements in V. $\otimes R$ and $\multimap L$ are direct consequences of Lemma 6 and Lemma 7, respectively. For $!R$, let x be any outermost bound variable in Γ, Δ or K which is not maximal in V. Because $x \not< a$, there exists a variable y or u in V such that $x < y$ or $x < u$, which is a contradiction. Hence we can use the $!R$-rule of the skolemised calculus and the induction hypothesis. Finally, the axiom rule in the skolemised calculus implies $n = 1$, and hence $\Gamma\sigma_{\uparrow\llcorner\Phi\lrcorner}; F_1\sigma_{\uparrow\llcorner\Phi\lrcorner} \vdash F\sigma_{\uparrow\llcorner\Phi\lrcorner}$. $\square$

6 Conclusion

In this paper, we revisit the technique of skolemisation and adopt it for proof search in first-order focused and polarised intuitionistic linear logic (LJF). The central idea is to encode quantifier dependencies by constraints, and the global partial order in which quantifier rules have to be applied by a substitution. We propose a domain specific logic called SLJF, which avoids back-tracking during proof search when variable instantiations are derived by unification.

Related Work: Shankar [8] first propose an adaptation of skolemisation to LJ. Our paper can be seen as a generalisation of this work to focused and polarised linear logic. Reis and Paleo [7] propose a technique called epsilonisation to characterise the permutability of rules in LJ. Their approach is elegant but impractical, because it trades an exponential growth in the search space with an exponential growth in the size of the proof terms. McLaughlin and Pfenning [4] propose an effective proof search technique based on the inverse method for focused and polarised intuitionistic logic. To our knowledge, the resulting theorem prover Imogen [5] would benefit from the presentation of skolemisation in our paper, since it requires backtracking to resolve the first-order non-determinism during proof search.

Applications: There are ample of applications for skolemisation. To our knowledge, proof search algorithms for intuitionistic or substructural logic are good at removing non-determinism from the propositional level, but don't solve the problem at the first-order level. Skolemisation can also be applied to improve intuitionistic theorem provers further, such as Imogen. With the results in this paper we believe that we are able to achieve such results without much of a performance penalty.

References

1. Andreoli, J.-M.: Logic programming with focusing proofs in linear logic. J. Log. Comput. **2**(3), 297–347 (1992)
2. Liang, C., Miller, D.: Focusing and polarization in linear, intuitionistic, and classical logics. Theor. Comput. Sci. **410**(46), 4747–4768 (2009)
3. Lincoln, P.D.: Deciding Provability of Linear Logic Formulas. London Mathematical Society Lecture Note Series, pp. 109–122 (1995)
4. McLaughlin, S., Pfenning, F.: Imogen: focusing the polarized inverse method for intuitionistic propositional logic. In: Cervesato, I., Veith, H., Voronkov, A. (eds.) LPAR 2008. LNCS (LNAI), vol. 5330, pp. 174–181. Springer, Heidelberg (2008). https://doi.org/10.1007/978-3-540-89439-1_12
5. McLaughlin, S., Pfenning, F.: Efficient intuitionistic theorem proving with the polarized inverse method. In: Schmidt, R.A. (ed.) CADE 2009. LNCS (LNAI), vol. 5663, pp. 230–244. Springer, Heidelberg (2009). https://doi.org/10.1007/978-3-642-02959-2_19
6. Pfenning, F.: Lecture notes on focusing, lectures 1–4, June 2010
7. Giselle Reis and Bruno Woltzenlogel Paleo: Epsilon terms in intuitionistic sequent calculus. IFCoLog J. Logic Appl. **4**(2), 402–427 (2017)
8. Shankar, N.: Proof search in the intuitionistic sequent calculus. In: Kapur, D. (ed.) CADE 1992. LNCS, vol. 607, pp. 522–536. Springer, Heidelberg (1992). https://doi.org/10.1007/3-540-55602-8_189

Local Intuitionistic Modal Logics and Their Calculi

Philippe Balbiani[1], Han Gao[2(✉)], Çiğdem Gencer[1], and Nicola Olivetti[2]

[1] CNRS-INPT-UT3, IRIT, Toulouse, France
{philippe.balbiani,cigdem.gencer}@irit.fr
[2] Aix-Marseille University, CNRS, LIS, Marseille, France
{gao.han,nicola.olivetti}@lis-lab.fr

Abstract. We investigate intuitionistic modal logics with locally interpreted $\Box$ and $\Diamond$. The basic logic **LIK** is stronger than constructive modal logic **WK** and incomparable with intuitionistic modal logic **IK**. We propose an axiomatization of **LIK** and some of its extensions. Additionally, we present bi-nested calculi for **LIK** and these extensions, providing both a decision procedure and a procedure of finite countermodel extraction.

Keywords: Intuitionistic Modal Logic · Axiomatization · Sequent Calculus · Decidability

1 Introduction

Intuitionistic modal logic (**IML**) has a long history, starting from the pioneering work by Fitch [10] and Prawitz [16]. Along the time, two traditions have emerged. The first tradition, called *intuitionistic modal logics* [7–9,15,17], aims to define modalities justified by an intuitionistic meta-theory. In this tradition, the fundamental logic is **IK**, considered as the intuitionistic counterpart of the minimal normal modal logic **K**. The second tradition, known as *constructive modal logics*, is mainly motivated by computer science applications like Curry-Howard correspondence, verification and contextual reasoning, etc. In this tradition, the basic logics are **CCDL** [19] and **CK** [3].

However, there are other intuitionistic modal logics with natural interpretations of modalities that have received little interest and deserve to be studied. One approach can be to study intuitionistic modal logic on a common semantic ground in terms of a bi-relational model $(W, \leq, R, V)$ combining an intuitionistic pre-order $\leq$ on states/worlds and an accessibility relation R for modalities. The present work aims to study several intuitionistic modal logics where, in a bi-relational model, the modal operators are classically interpreted:

(1) $x \Vdash \Box A$ iff for all y such that Rxy it holds $y \Vdash A$;
(2) $x \Vdash \Diamond A$ iff there exists y such that Rxy and $y \Vdash A$.

C. Benzmüller et al. (Eds.): IJCAR 2024, LNAI 14740, pp. 78–96, 2024.
https://doi.org/10.1007/978-3-031-63501-4_5

We call these forcing conditions "local" as they do not involve worlds $\leq$-greater or $\leq$-smaller than x. Meanwhile, we require that all the intuitionistic axioms remain valid in the full logic. This is conveyed by the *hereditary property* (HP), which says for any formula A, if A is forced by a world x, it will also be forced by any upper world of x. In order to ensure (HP), we need to postulate two frame conditions which relate $\leq$ and R in a bi-relational model: the conditions of *downward confluence* (DC) and *forward confluence* (FC) [1,4,9,17]. We call the basic **K**-style logic **LIK** by *local* **IK**.

In the literature, Božić and Došen [4] studied separately the $\Box$-fragment and the $\Diamond$-fragment of **LIK** and also considered a logic combining $\Box$ and $\Diamond$. However, the logic they obtained is stronger than **LIK**, since they considered a restricted class of frames. Moreover, in their setting, $\Diamond$ becomes definable in terms of $\Box$, which is inappropriate from an intuitionistic point of view. In other respect, Božić and Došen did not tackle the decidability issue. Besides, a logic related to **LIK** has been considered in [5] in the context of substructural logics. More recently, the S4-extension of **LIK** has been shown to be decidable [1].

In this paper, we consider **LIK** and some of its extensions with axioms characterizing seriality, reflexivity and transitivity of the accessibility relation R in a bi-relational model. We provide complete axiomatizations for them with respect to appropriate classes of models. The basic logic **LIK** is stronger than Wijesekera's **CCDL** as well as another intuitionistic modal logic **FIK** which only assumes forward confluence on models [2]. But **LIK** is incomparable with **IK**. It is noteworthy that **LIK** fails to satisfy the disjunction property. However, unexpectedly, its extension with axioms characterizing either seriality or reflexivity of the accessibility relation possesses this property.

Turning to proof theory, we propose bi-nested sequent calculi for **LIK** and its extensions. A bi-nested calculus uses two kinds of nestings in the syntax: the first one is used for $\geq$-upper worlds proposed by Fitting in [11]. Recently a nested sequent calculus using Fitting's nesting to capture an extension of **CCDL** has been presented in [6]. The second one is for R-successors, which is used in several nested sequent calculi for other **IML**s [12,14,18]. A calculus for **IK** intended to combine the two nestings was also preliminarily considered in [13]. A bi-nested sequent calculus with the same bi-nested structure is proposed for the logic **FIK** in [2] where the frame condition of forward confluence is captured by a suitable "interaction" rule. A calculus for **LIK** can be obtained from the calculus for **FIK** by adopting a "local" $\Box$, or by adding another "interaction" rule capturing the downward confluence frame condition. Calculi for the extensions of **LIK** are defined by adding suitable modal rules.

We prove that these calculi provide a decision procedure for the logic **LIK** and some of its extensions. Moreover, we show the semantic completeness of these calculi: from a single failed derivation under a suitable strategy, it is possible to extract a *finite* countermodel for the given sequent at the root. In addition, for the extensions of **LIK** with (**D**) or (**T**), a syntactic proof of the disjunction property via the calculi is provided. These results demonstrate that bi-nested sequent calculus is a powerful and flexible tool which constitutes an alternative to other formalisms like labelled sequent calculus and is capable to treat uniformly various **IMLs**.[1]

2 Local Intuitionistic Modal Logic

Let **At** be a set (with members called *atoms* and denoted p, q, etc.).

Definition 1 (Formulas). *Let $\mathcal{L}$ be the set (with members called* formulas *and denoted A, B, etc.) of finite words over* $\mathbf{At} \cup \{\supset, \top, \bot, \vee, \wedge, \Box, \Diamond, (,)\}$ *defined by*

$$A \ ::= \ p \mid (A \supset A) \mid \top \mid \bot \mid (A \vee A) \mid (A \wedge A) \mid \Box A \mid \Diamond A$$

where p ranges over **At**. *We follow the standard rules for omission of the parentheses. For all $A \in \mathcal{L}$, we write $\neg A$ as $A \supset \bot$.*

For all sets Γ of formulas, let $\Box\Gamma = \{A \in \mathcal{L} : \ \Box A \in \Gamma\}$ and $\Diamond\Gamma = \{\Diamond A \in \mathcal{L} : A \in \Gamma\}$.

Definition 2 (Frames). *A* frame *is a relational structure $(W, \leq, R)$ where W is a nonempty set of* worlds, *$\leq$ is a preorder on W and R is a binary relation on W. A frame $(W, \leq, R)$ is* forward (resp. downward) confluent *if $\geq \circ R \subseteq R \circ \geq$ (resp. $\leq \circ R \subseteq R \circ \leq$). For all $X \subseteq \{\mathbf{D}, \mathbf{T}, \mathbf{4}\}$, an X-frame is a frame $(W, \leq, R)$ such that R is serial if $\mathbf{D} \in X$, R is reflexive if $\mathbf{T} \in X$ and R is transitive if $\mathbf{4} \in X$. Let $\mathcal{C}^X_{\mathbf{fdc}}$ be the class of forward and downward confluent X-frames. We write "$\mathcal{C}_{\mathbf{fdc}}$" instead of "$\mathcal{C}^{\emptyset}_{\mathbf{fdc}}$".*

We can see that $\mathcal{C}^{\mathbf{ref}}_{\mathbf{fdc}} \subseteq \mathcal{C}^{\mathbf{ser}}_{\mathbf{fdc}} \subseteq \mathcal{C}_{\mathbf{fdc}}$.

Definition 3 (Valuations, Models and Truth Conditions). *For all frames $(W, \leq, R)$, a subset U of W is* $\leq$-closed *if for all $s, t \in W$, if $s \in U$ and $s \leq t$ then $t \in U$. A* valuation *on $(W, \leq, R)$ is a function $V : \mathbf{At} \longrightarrow \wp(W)$ such that for all $p \in \mathbf{At}$, $V(p)$ is $\leq$-closed. A* model *based on $(W, \leq, R)$ is a model of the form $(W, \leq, R, V)$. In a model $\mathcal{M} = (W, \leq, R, V)$, for all $x \in W$ and for all $A \in \mathcal{L}$, the* satisfiability of Aat $x$in $\mathcal{M}$ *(in symbols $\mathcal{M}, x \Vdash A$) is defined as usual when A's main connective is either $\top$, $\bot$, $\vee$ or $\wedge$ and as follows otherwise:*

- *$\mathcal{M}, x \Vdash p$ if and only if $x \in V(p)$,*
- *$\mathcal{M}, x \Vdash A \supset B$ if and only if for all $x' \in W$ with $x \leq x'$, if $\mathcal{M}, x' \Vdash A$ then $\mathcal{M}, x' \Vdash B$,*
- *$\mathcal{M}, x \Vdash \Box A$ if and only if for all $y \in W$ such that Rxy, $\mathcal{M}, y \Vdash A$,*
- *$\mathcal{M}, x \Vdash \Diamond A$ if and only if there exists $y \in W$ such that Rxy and $\mathcal{M}, y \Vdash A$.*

When $\mathcal{M}$ is clear from the context, we simply write $x \Vdash A$. The notions of truth and validity are defined as usual.

Lemma 1 (Hereditary Property). *Let $(W, \leq, R, V)$ be a forward and downward confluent model. For all $A \in \mathcal{L}$ and $x, x' \in W$, if $x \Vdash A$ and $x \leq x'$ then $x' \Vdash A$.*

[1] The full version with proofs is available on ArXiv: https://arxiv.org/abs/2403.06772.

Note that our definition of $\Vdash$ differs from the definitions proposed by Fischer Servi [9] and Wijesekera [19]. In both settings,

> $x \Vdash \Box A$ iff for all $x' \in W$ with $x \leq x'$ and for all $y \in W$ with $Rx'y$, it holds $y \Vdash A$;

whereas in [19],

> $x \Vdash \Diamond A$ iff for all $x' \in W$ with $x \leq x'$, there exists $y \in W$ such that $Rx'y$ and $y \Vdash A$.

However, these satisfiability relations collapse on forward and downward confluent frames.

Proposition 1. *In $\mathcal{C}_{\mathbf{fdc}}$, our definition of $\Vdash$ determines the same satisfiability relation as the relations determined by definitions in [9] and [19].*

From now on in this section, when we write frame (resp. model), we mean forward and downward confluent frame (resp. model).

Obviously, validity in $\mathcal{C}_{\mathbf{fdc}}$ is closed under the following inference rules:

$$\frac{A \supset B \quad A}{B}\ (\mathbf{MP}) \qquad \frac{A}{\Box A}\ (\mathbf{NEC})$$

Moreover, the following axiom schemes are valid in $\mathcal{C}_{\mathbf{fdc}}$:

$(\mathbf{K}_\Box)$ $\Box(A \supset B) \supset (\Box A \supset \Box B)$ $\quad$ $(\mathbf{K}_\Diamond)$ $\Box(A \supset B) \supset (\Diamond A \supset \Diamond B)$
$(\mathbf{DP})$ $\Diamond(A \vee B) \supset \Diamond A \vee \Diamond B$ $\quad$ $(\mathbf{RV})$ $\Box(A \vee B) \supset \Diamond A \vee \Box B$
$(\mathbf{N})$ $\neg\Diamond\bot$

In $\mathcal{C}^{\mathbf{D}}_{\mathbf{fdc}}$ (resp. $\mathcal{C}^{\mathbf{T}}_{\mathbf{fdc}}$, $\mathcal{C}^{\mathbf{4}}_{\mathbf{fdc}}$), modal axiom $\mathbf{D}$ (resp. $\mathbf{T}$, $\mathbf{4}$) is valid:

$$(\mathbf{D})\ \Diamond\top \quad (\mathbf{T})\ (\Box A \supset A) \wedge (A \supset \Diamond A) \quad (\mathbf{4})\ (\Box A \supset \Box\Box A) \wedge (\Diamond\Diamond A \supset \Diamond A)$$

Axiom $(\mathbf{RV})$ is also considered in [1] where it is called $(\mathbf{CD})$ for *constant domain*, since it is related with the first-order formula $\forall x.(P(x) \vee Q(x)) \supset \exists x.P(x) \vee \forall x.Q(x)$ which is intuitionistically valid when models with constant domains are considered.

Definition 4 (Axiom System). *For all $X \subseteq \{\mathbf{D}, \mathbf{T}, \mathbf{4}\}$, let **LIKX** be the axiomatic system consisting of all standard axioms of **IPL**, the inference rules $(\mathbf{MP})$ and $(\mathbf{NEC})$, the axioms $\mathbf{K}_\Box$, $\mathbf{K}_\Diamond$, $\mathbf{N}$, $\mathbf{DP}$ and $\mathbf{RV}$ and containing in addition the axioms from X. We write **LIK** for **LIK**$\emptyset$. Derivations are defined as usual. We write $\vdash_{\mathbf{LIK}X} A$ when A is **LIKX**-derivable. The set of all **LIKX**-derivable formulas is also denoted as **LIKX**.*

From now on in this section, let $X \subseteq \{\mathbf{D}, \mathbf{T}, \mathbf{4}\}$.

Lemma 2. *If $\mathbf{D} \in X$ or $\mathbf{T} \in X$ then $\Box p \supset \Diamond p$ and $\neg\Box\bot$ are in **LIKX**.*

Theorem 1 (Soundness). *$\mathbf{LIK}X$-derivable formulas are $\mathcal{C}^X_{\mathbf{fdc}}$-validities.*

Next we prove completeness, which is the converse of soundness, saying that every formula valid in $\mathcal{C}^X_{\mathbf{fdc}}$ is $\mathbf{LIK}X$-derivable. At the heart of our completeness proof lies the concept of theory. Let $\mathbf{L} = \mathbf{LIK}X$.

Definition 5 (Theories). *A theory is a set of formulas containing $\mathbf{L}$ and closed with respect to $\mathbf{MP}$. A theory Γ is proper if $\bot \notin \Gamma$. A proper theory Γ is prime if for all formulas A, B, if $A \vee B \in \Gamma$ then either $A \in \Gamma$, or $B \in \Gamma$.*

Lemma 3. *If $\mathbf{D} \in X$ or $\mathbf{T} \in X$ then for all theories Γ, we have $\Diamond\Box\Gamma \subseteq \Gamma$.*

Definition 6 (Canonical Model). *The* canonical model $(W_\mathbf{L}, \leq_\mathbf{L}, R_\mathbf{L}, V_\mathbf{L})$ *is a tuple where*

- *$W_\mathbf{L}$ is the nonempty set of all prime theories,*
- *$\leq_\mathbf{L}$ is the partial order on $W_\mathbf{L}$ defined by: $\Gamma \leq_\mathbf{L} \Delta$ iff $\Gamma \subseteq \Delta$,*
- *$R_\mathbf{L}$ is the binary relation on $W_\mathbf{L}$ defined by: $R_\mathbf{L}\Gamma\Delta$ iff $\Box\Gamma \subseteq \Delta$ and $\Diamond\Delta \subseteq \Gamma$,*
- *$V_\mathbf{L}$ is the valuation on $W_\mathbf{L}$ defined by: $V_\mathbf{L}(p) = \{\Gamma \in W_\mathbf{L} : p \in \Gamma\}$.*

Lemma 4. *1. $(W_\mathbf{L}, \leq_\mathbf{L}, R_\mathbf{L}, V_\mathbf{L})$ is forward confluent,*
2. $(W_\mathbf{L}, \leq_\mathbf{L}, R_\mathbf{L}, V_\mathbf{L})$ is downward confluent,
3. if $\mathbf{D} \in X$ (resp. $\mathbf{T} \in X$, $\mathbf{4} \in X$) then $(W_\mathbf{L}, \leq_\mathbf{L}, R_\mathbf{L}, V_\mathbf{L})$ is serial (resp. reflexive, transitive).

The proof of the completeness is based on the following lemmas.

Lemma 5 (Existence Lemma). *Let Γ be a prime theory.*

1. *If $B \supset C \notin \Gamma$ then there exists a prime theory Δ such that $\Gamma \subseteq \Delta$, $B \in \Delta$ and $C \notin \Delta$,*
2. *if $\Box B \notin \Gamma$ then there exists a prime theory Δ such that $R_\mathbf{L}\Gamma\Delta$ and $B \notin \Delta$,*
3. *if $\Diamond B \in \Gamma$ then there exists a prime theory Δ such that $R_\mathbf{L}\Gamma\Delta$ and $B \in \Delta$.*

Lemma 6 (Truth Lemma). *For all formulas A and all $\Gamma \in W_\mathbf{L}$, we have $A \in \Gamma$ if and only if $(W_\mathbf{L}, \leq_\mathbf{L}, R_\mathbf{L}, V_\mathbf{L}), \Gamma \Vdash A$.*

From Lemma 6, we conclude

Theorem 2 (Completeness). *All $\mathcal{C}^X_{\mathbf{fdc}}$-validities are $\mathbf{LIK}X$-derivable.*

In [17, Chapter 3], Simpson discusses the formal features that might be expected for an intuitionistic modal logic $\mathbf{L}$:

- $\mathbf{L}$ is conservative over Intuitionistic Propositional Logic,
- $\mathbf{L}$ contains all substitution instances of axioms of Intuitionistic Propositional Logic and is closed under modus ponens,
- $\mathbf{L}$ has the disjunction property: for each formula $A \vee B$, if $A \vee B$ is in $\mathbf{L}$ then either A is in $\mathbf{L}$, or B is in $\mathbf{L}$,
- by adding the law of excluded middle to $\mathbf{L}$ it yields modal logic $\mathbf{K}$,
- $\Box$ and $\Diamond$ are independent in $\mathbf{L}$.

Now, we show that **LIK**X possesses the formal features that might be expected of an intuitionistic modal logic.

Proposition 2. *1. **LIK**X is conservative over* **IPL**,
2. ***LIK**X contains all substitution instances of* **IPL** *and is closed with respect to modus ponens,*
3. ***LIK**X has the disjunction property if and only if* **D**$\in X$ *or* **T**$\in X$,
4. *the addition of the law of excluded middle to **LIK**X yields modal logic* **K**,
5. $\Box$ *and* $\Diamond$ *are independent in **LIK**X.*

3 Bi-nested Sequent Calculi

In this section we present bi-nested calculi for **LIK** and its extensions **LIKD** and **LIKT**. These calculi are called *bi-nested* in the sense that they make use of two kinds of nesting representing $\leq$-upper worlds and R-successors in the semantics, similar to the calculus for **FIK** presented in [2]. In a basic system for **LIK**, two rules encoding forward and downward confluence are contained. We will show that the latter rule called (inter$_\downarrow$) is admissible in a smaller system without it, thus by dropping out this rule we still have a complete calculus for **LIK**. However, as we will see, the (inter$_\downarrow$) rule is required to prove the semantic completeness of the calculus and further allows us to obtain counter-model extraction. We also prove the disjunction property for **LIKD** and **LIKT** using the calculi.

In order to define the calculi we first give some preliminary notions.

Definition 7 (Bi-Nested Sequent). *A bi-nested sequent S is defined as:*

- *The empty sequent $\Rightarrow$ is a bi-nested sequent;*
- $\Gamma \Rightarrow \Delta, \langle T_1\rangle, \dots, \langle T_n\rangle, [S_1], \dots, [S_m]$ *is a bi-nested sequent if both Γ and Δ are multisets of formulas, all the $S_1, \dots, S_m, T_1, \dots, T_n$ are bi-nested sequents where $m, n \geq 0$.*

We use S and T to denote a bi-nested sequent and simply call it "sequent" in the rest of this paper. The antecedent and consequent of a sequent S are denoted by $Ant(S)$ and $Con(S)$. Syntactic objects of the shape $\langle S\rangle$ and $[T]$ are called implication and modal blocks respectively.

The notion of modal degree can be extended from a formula to a sequent.

Definition 8 (Modal Degree). *Modal degree $md(F)$ for a formula F is defined as usual. Let Γ be a finite (multi)set of formulas, define $md(\Gamma) = md(\bigwedge\Gamma)$. For a sequent $S = \Gamma \Rightarrow \Delta, \langle T_1\rangle, \dots, \langle T_n\rangle, [S_1], \dots, [S_m]$, we define* $md(S) = \max\{md(\Gamma), md(\Delta), md(T_1), \dots, md(T_n), md(S_1)+1, \dots, md(S_m)+1\}$.

Context is defined as usual in standard nested calculi which can be regarded as a placeholder to be filled by a sequent.

Definition 9 (Context). *A context $G\{\ \}$ is inductively defined as follows:*

- *The empty context $\{\ \}$ is a context.*

– *if* $\Gamma \Rightarrow \Delta$ *is a sequent and* $G'\{\ \}$ *is a context, then both* $\Gamma \Rightarrow \Delta, \langle G'\{\ \}\rangle$ *and* $\Gamma \Rightarrow \Delta, [G'\{\ \}]$ *are contexts.*

Example 1. Given a context $G\{\ \} = p \wedge q, \Box r \Rightarrow \Diamond p, \langle \Box p \Rightarrow [\Rightarrow q]\rangle, [\{\ \}]$ and a sequent $S = p \Rightarrow q \vee r, [r \Rightarrow s]$, we have $G\{S\} = p \wedge q, \Box r \Rightarrow \Diamond p, \langle \Box p \Rightarrow [\Rightarrow q]\rangle, [p \Rightarrow q \vee r, [r \Rightarrow s]]$.

Definition 10 ($\in^{\langle\cdot\rangle}, \in^{[\cdot]}, \in^{+}$**-Relation).** *Let* $\Gamma_1 \Rightarrow \Delta_1, \Gamma_2 \Rightarrow \Delta_2$ *be two sequents. We denote* $\Gamma_1 \Rightarrow \Delta_1 \in_0^{\langle\cdot\rangle} \Gamma_2 \Rightarrow \Delta_2$ *if* $\langle \Gamma_1 \Rightarrow \Delta_1\rangle \in \Delta_2$ *and let* $\in^{\langle\cdot\rangle}$ *be the transitive closure of* $\in_0^{\langle\cdot\rangle}$. *Relations* $\in_0^{[\cdot]}$ *and* $\in^{[\cdot]}$ *for modal blocks are defined similarly. Besides, let* $\in_0^{+} = \in_0^{\langle\cdot\rangle} \cup \in_0^{[\cdot]}$ *and finally let* $\in^{+}$ *be the reflexive-transitive closure of* $\in_0^{+}$.

When we say $S' \in^{+} S$, it is equivalent to say that $S = G\{S'\}$ for some context G.

As we will see, some rules in the calculi propagate formulas in the antecedent ("positive part") or the consequent ("negative part") of sequents into a modal block. The two operators in the following definition single out these formulas of a sequent.

Definition 11 (♭-Operator and ♯-Operator). *Let* $\Lambda \Rightarrow \Theta$ *be a sequent and* $Fm(\Theta)$ *the multiset of formulas directly belonging to* Θ.

Let $\Theta^{\flat} = \emptyset$ *if* Θ *is* $[\cdot]$*-free;* $\Theta^{\flat} = [\Phi_1 \Rightarrow \Psi_1^{\flat}], \dots, [\Phi_k \Rightarrow \Psi_k^{\flat}]$, *if* $\Theta = \Theta_0, [\Phi_1 \Rightarrow \Psi_1], \dots, [\Phi_k \Rightarrow \Psi_k]$ *and* Θ_0 *is* $[\cdot]$*-free.*

Dually let $\Rightarrow \Theta^{\sharp} = \Rightarrow Fm(\Theta)$ *if* Θ *is* $[\cdot]$*-free;* $\Rightarrow \Theta^{\sharp} = \Rightarrow Fm(\Theta_0), [\Rightarrow \Psi_1^{\sharp}], \dots, [\Rightarrow \Psi_k^{\sharp}]$ *if* $\Theta = \Theta_0, [\Phi_1 \Rightarrow \Psi_1], \dots, [\Phi_k \Rightarrow \Psi_k]$ *and* Θ_0 *is* $[\cdot]$*-free.*

Example 2. Consider the sequent $G\{S\} = p \wedge q, \Box r \Rightarrow \Diamond p, \langle \Box p \Rightarrow [\Rightarrow q]\rangle, [p \Rightarrow q \vee r, [r \Rightarrow s]]$ of Example 1, denote $Ant(G\{S\})$ and $Suc(G\{S\})$ by Λ and Θ respectively, we can see by definition, $\Lambda \Rightarrow \Theta^{\flat} = p \wedge q, \Box r \Rightarrow [p \Rightarrow [r \Rightarrow]]$ while $\Rightarrow \Theta^{\sharp} = \Rightarrow \Diamond p, [\Rightarrow q \vee r, [\Rightarrow s]]$.

Definition 12. *Rules for the basic logic* ***LIK*** *and its modal extensions are given in Fig. 1, which consists of the basic calculus* $\mathbf{C_{LIK}}$ *and modal rules corresponding to axioms* (**D**), ($\mathbf{T}_\Diamond$) *and* ($\mathbf{T}_\Box$). *We define* $\mathbf{C_{LIKD}} = \mathbf{C_{LIK}} + (\mathbf{D})$ *and* $\mathbf{C_{LIKT}} = \mathbf{C_{LIK}} + (\mathbf{T}_\Box) + (\mathbf{T}_\Diamond)$.

The notions of *derivation* and *proof* in a calculus are defined as usual. We say a formula A is *provable* if the sequent $\Rightarrow A$ has a proof in the calculus.

Here are some remarks on the rules. First, the rule (id) which only concerns atoms can be easily generalized to arbitrary formulas. Reading the rule upwards, the rule ($\supset_R$) introduces an implication block $\langle\cdot\rangle$ while the rules ($\Diamond_L$) and ($\Box_R$) introduce a modal block $[\cdot]$. Observe that the ($\Box_R$) rule corresponds to the "local" interpretation of $\Box$. The rule (inter$_\rightarrow$) is intended to capture Forward Confluence, whereas the rule (inter$_\downarrow$) Downward Confluence. Finally the (trans) rule captures the Hereditary Property. All the rules of $\mathbf{C_{LIK}}$, except ($\Box_R$) and (inter$_\downarrow$) belong to the calculus $\mathbf{C_{FIK}}$ for the logic **FIK** [2], we will discuss the relation between the two calculi later in the section.

$$\frac{}{G\{\Gamma, \bot \Rightarrow \Delta\}}\ (\bot_L) \qquad \frac{}{G\{\Gamma \Rightarrow \top, \Delta\}}\ (\top_R) \qquad \frac{}{G\{\Gamma, p \Rightarrow \Delta, p\}}\ (\mathrm{id})$$

$$\frac{G\{A, B, \Gamma \Rightarrow \Delta\}}{G\{A \wedge B, \Gamma \Rightarrow \Delta\}}\ (\wedge_L) \qquad \frac{G\{\Gamma \Rightarrow \Delta, A\} \qquad G\{\Gamma \Rightarrow \Delta, B\}}{G\{\Gamma \Rightarrow \Delta, A \wedge B\}}\ (\wedge_R)$$

$$\frac{G\{\Gamma, A \Rightarrow \Delta\} \qquad G\{\Gamma, B \Rightarrow \Delta\}}{G\{\Gamma, A \vee B \Rightarrow \Delta\}}\ (\vee_L) \qquad \frac{G\{\Gamma \Rightarrow \Delta, A, B\}}{G\{\Gamma \Rightarrow \Delta, A \vee B\}}\ (\vee_R)$$

$$\frac{G\{\Gamma, A \supset B \Rightarrow A, \Delta\} \qquad G\{\Gamma, B \Rightarrow \Delta\}}{G\{\Gamma, A \supset B \Rightarrow \Delta\}}\ (\supset_L) \qquad \frac{G\{\Gamma \Rightarrow \Delta, \langle A \Rightarrow B\rangle\}}{G\{\Gamma \Rightarrow \Delta, A \supset B\}}\ (\supset_R)$$

$$\frac{G\{\Gamma, \Box A \Rightarrow \Delta, [\Sigma, A \Rightarrow \Pi]\}}{G\{\Gamma, \Box A \Rightarrow \Delta, [\Sigma \Rightarrow \Pi]\}}\ (\Box_L) \qquad \frac{G\{\Gamma \Rightarrow \Delta, [\Rightarrow A]\}}{G\{\Gamma \Rightarrow \Delta, \Box A\}}\ (\Box_R)$$

$$\frac{G\{\Gamma \Rightarrow \Delta, [A \Rightarrow]\}}{G\{\Gamma, \Diamond A \Rightarrow \Delta\}}\ (\Diamond_L) \qquad \frac{G\{\Gamma \Rightarrow \Delta, \Diamond A, [\Sigma \Rightarrow \Pi, A]\}}{G\{\Gamma \Rightarrow \Delta, \Diamond A, [\Sigma \Rightarrow \Pi]\}}\ (\Diamond_R)$$

$$\frac{G\{\Gamma, \Gamma' \Rightarrow \Delta, \langle \Gamma', \Sigma \Rightarrow \Pi\rangle\}}{G\{\Gamma, \Gamma' \Rightarrow \Delta, \langle \Sigma \Rightarrow \Pi\rangle\}}\ (\mathrm{trans})$$

$$\frac{G\{\Gamma \Rightarrow \Delta, \langle \Sigma \Rightarrow \Pi, [\Lambda \Rightarrow \Theta^{\flat}]\rangle, [\Lambda \Rightarrow \Theta]\}}{G\{\Gamma \Rightarrow \Delta, \langle \Sigma \Rightarrow \Pi\rangle, [\Lambda \Rightarrow \Theta]\}}\ (\mathrm{inter}_{\rightarrow})$$

$$\frac{G\{\Gamma \Rightarrow \Delta, \langle \Sigma \Rightarrow \Pi, [\Lambda \Rightarrow \Theta]\rangle, [\Rightarrow \Theta^{\sharp}]\}}{G\{\Gamma \Rightarrow \Delta, \langle \Sigma \Rightarrow \Pi, [\Lambda \Rightarrow \Theta]\rangle\}}\ (\mathrm{inter}_{\downarrow})$$

$$\frac{G\{\Gamma \Rightarrow \Delta, [\Rightarrow]\}}{G\{\Gamma \Rightarrow \Delta\}}\ (\mathbf{D}) \qquad \frac{G\{\Gamma, \Box A, A \Rightarrow \Delta\}}{G\{\Gamma, \Box A \Rightarrow \Delta\}}\ (\mathbf{T}_{\Box}) \qquad \frac{G\{\Gamma \Rightarrow \Delta, \Diamond A, A\}}{G\{\Gamma \Rightarrow \Delta, \Diamond A\}}\ (\mathbf{T}_{\Diamond})$$

Fig. 1. Bi-nested rules for local intuitionistic modal logics

We can verify that each axiom of **LIK** in Sect. 2 is provable in $\mathbf{C_{LIK}}$. An example of axiom (**RV**) is given below.

Example 3. We show $\Box(p \vee q) \Rightarrow \Diamond p \vee \Box q$ is provable.

$$\frac{\dfrac{\dfrac{\dfrac{\dfrac{\dfrac{}{\Box(p \vee q) \Rightarrow \Diamond p, [p \Rightarrow q, p]}\ (\mathrm{id}) \qquad \dfrac{}{\Box(p \vee q) \Rightarrow \Diamond p, [q \Rightarrow q, p]}\ (\mathrm{id})}{\Box(p \vee q) \Rightarrow \Diamond p, [p \vee q \Rightarrow q, p]}\ (\vee_L)}{\Box(p \vee q) \Rightarrow \Diamond p, [\Rightarrow q, p]}\ (\Box_L)}{\Box(p \vee q) \Rightarrow \Diamond p, [\Rightarrow q]}\ (\Diamond_R)}{\Box(p \vee q) \Rightarrow \Diamond p, \Box q}\ (\Box_R)}{\Box(p \vee q) \Rightarrow \Diamond p \vee \Box q}\ (\vee_R)$$

We now show that $\mathbf{C_{LIK}}$ is sound with respect to the semantics. The first step is to extend the forcing relation $\Vdash$ to sequents and blocks therein.

Definition 13. *Let $\mathcal{M} = (W, \leq, R, V)$ be a bi-relational model and $x \in W$. The satisfiability relation $\Vdash$ is extended to sequents as follows:*

- $\mathcal{M}, x \not\Vdash \emptyset$
- $\mathcal{M}, x \Vdash [T]$ *if for every* y *with* Rxy, $\mathcal{M}, y \Vdash T$
- $\mathcal{M}, x \Vdash \langle T \rangle$ *if for every* x' *with* $x \leq x'$, $\mathcal{M}, x' \Vdash T$
- $\mathcal{M}, x \Vdash \Gamma \Rightarrow \Delta$ *if either* $\mathcal{M}, x \not\Vdash A$ *for some* $A \in \Gamma$ *or* $\mathcal{M}, x \Vdash \mathcal{O}$ *for some* $\mathcal{O} \in \Delta$, *where* $\mathcal{O}$ *is a formula or a block.*

We say S *is* valid *in* $\mathcal{M}$ *iff* $\forall w \in W$, *we have* $\mathcal{M}, w \Vdash S$. *We say* S *is* valid *iff it is valid in every model.*

Definition 14. *For a rule (r) of the form* $\frac{G\{S_1\} \quad G\{S_2\}}{G\{S\}}$ *or* $\frac{G\{S_1\}}{G\{S\}}$, *we say (r) is valid if the following holds: if for each* i, $x \Vdash G\{S_i\}$, *then it follows* $x \Vdash G\{S\}$.

We can easily verify the validity of each rule and then obtain the soundness of $\mathbf{C_{LIK}}$ by a standard induction on a derivation. The soundness of $\mathbf{C_{LIKD}}$ and $\mathbf{C_{LIKT}}$ can be proven similarly.

Theorem 3 (Soundness of $\mathbf{C_{LIK}}$). *If a formula* A *is provable in* $\mathbf{C_{LIK}}$, *then it is valid in* **LIK**.

Next, we show that the rule (inter$_\downarrow$) is admissible in the calculus $\mathbf{C_{LIK^-}} = \mathbf{C_{LIK}} \setminus \{(\text{inter}_\downarrow)\}$. The proof can be easily extended to the modal extensions as well. In order to prove this, we need some preliminary facts. First, weakening and contraction rules $(w_L)(w_R)(c_L)(c_L)$ defined as usual are *height-preserving* (hp) admissible in $\mathbf{C_{LIK^-}}$, not only applied to formulas but also blocks. Moreover, extended weakening rules $\frac{S}{G\{S\}}$, $\frac{G\{\Gamma \Rightarrow \Delta^\flat\}}{G\{\Gamma \Rightarrow \Delta\}}$, $\frac{G\{\Gamma \Rightarrow \Delta^\sharp\}}{G\{\Gamma \Rightarrow \Delta\}}$ are hp-admissible as well.

Proposition 3. *The (inter$_\downarrow$) rule is admissible in* $\mathbf{C_{LIK^-}}$. *Consequently, a sequent* S *is provable in* $\mathbf{C_{LIK}}$ *if and only if* S *is provable in* $\mathbf{C_{LIK^-}}$.

As mentioned above, all the rules in $\mathbf{C_{LIK}}$, except $(\Box_R)$ and (inter$_\downarrow$), belong to the calculus $\mathbf{C_{FIK}}$ for the logic **FIK** [2]. As a difference with **LIK**, the logic **FIK** adopts the "global" forcing condition for $\Box$ as in [9,17,19] and only forward confluence on the frame. The $(\Box_R)$ rule in $\mathbf{C_{FIK}}$ is $\frac{G\{\Gamma \Rightarrow \Delta, \langle \Rightarrow [\Rightarrow A] \rangle\}}{G\{\Gamma \Rightarrow \Delta, \Box A\}}$. It can be proved that this rule is admissible in $\mathbf{C_{LIK^-}}$ and on the opposite direction, the "local" $(\Box_R)$ rule in $\mathbf{C_{LIK}}$ is admissible in $\mathbf{C_{FIK}}+$ (inter$_\downarrow$). Thus $\mathbf{C_{FIK}}+$ (inter$_\downarrow$) can be regarded as another equivalent variant of $\mathbf{C_{LIK}}$, which is obtained in *a modular way* from the one for **FIK**.

We end this section by considering the disjunction property. For simplicity, we only work in $\mathbf{C_{LIK^-}}$ and its extensions. Let $\mathbf{C_{LIKD^-}} = \mathbf{C_{LIK^-}} + (\mathbf{D})$ and $\mathbf{C_{LIKT^-}} = \mathbf{C_{LIK^-}} + (\mathbf{T}_\Box) + (\mathbf{T}_\Diamond)$. Consider the formula $\Box\bot \vee \Diamond\top$ which is provable in $\mathbf{C_{LIK^-}}$, but it is easy to see neither $\Box\bot$ nor $\Diamond\top$ are provable.[2] However, this counterexample does not hold in **LIKD** or **LIKT** since $\Diamond\top$ is provable in both calculi. We show that the disjunction property indeed holds for both $\mathbf{C_{LIKD^-}}$ and $\mathbf{C_{LIKT^-}}$. The key fact is expressed by the following lemma:

[2] We thank Tiziano Dalmonte for suggesting this counterexample.

Lemma 7. *Suppose $S = \Rightarrow A_1, \ldots, A_m, \langle G_1 \rangle, \ldots, \langle G_n \rangle, [H_1], \ldots, [H_l]$ is provable in $\mathbf{C_{LIKD^-}}$ (resp. $\mathbf{C_{LIKT^-}}$), where A_i's are formulas, G_j and H_k's are sequents. Further assume that each H_k is of the form $\Rightarrow \Theta_k$ and for each sequent $T \in^{[\cdot]} H_k$, T has an empty antecedent. Then either $\Rightarrow A_i$ or $\Rightarrow \langle G_j \rangle$ or $\Rightarrow [H_k]$ is provable in $\mathbf{C_{LIKD^-}}$ (resp. $\mathbf{C_{LIKT^-}}$) for some $i \leq m, j \leq n, k \leq l$.*

We obtain the disjunction property by an obvious application of the lemma.

Proposition 4 (Disjunction Property for $\mathbf{C_{LIKD^-}}$ and $\mathbf{C_{LIKT^-}}$). *For any formulas A, B, if $\Rightarrow A \vee B$ is provable in $\mathbf{C_{LIKD^-}}$ (resp. $\mathbf{C_{LIKT^-}}$), then either $\Rightarrow A$ or $\Rightarrow B$ is provable $\mathbf{C_{LIKD^-}}$ (resp. $\mathbf{C_{LIKT^-}}$).*

4 Termination

In this section we define decision procedure for **LIK** as well as its extensions **LIKD** and **LIKT** based on the calculi in Sect. 3. We treat first **LIK**, then at the end of the section we will briefly describe how to adopt the the procedure to the extensions. The terminating proof-search procedure is essential for the semantic completeness of the calculi, as well as for countermodel construction, as we will demonstrate in the following section.

We have introduced two calculi for **LIK**, namely $\mathbf{C_{LIK}}$ and $\mathbf{C_{LIK^-}}$. For $\mathbf{C_{LIK^-}}$, we can obtain a terminating proof-search procedure by adapting the one in [2] for the calculus of **FIK**. Actually, the decision procedure for $\mathbf{C_{LIK^-}}$ is remarkably simpler than that for **FIK**, as "blocking" is not needed to prevent loops. For $\mathbf{C_{LIK}}$, however, some extra work needs to be done. Despite the equivalence of $\mathbf{C_{LIK}}$ and $\mathbf{C_{LIK^-}}$ in terms of provability, constructing a countermodel from a failed proof in $\mathbf{C_{LIK^-}}$ poses a challenge due to the absence of a rule capturing downward confluence. Therefore, we need to explore a terminating proof-search procedure for $\mathbf{C_{LIK}}$ to further advance our goal of proving semantic completeness.

Recall our ultimate aim is to build a countermodel from a failed derivation, in which the main ingredient is the pre-order relation $\leq$ in the model construction. This relation is specified by the following notion of *structural inclusion* between sequents, which is also used in defining the saturation conditions required for termination.

Definition 15 (Structural Inclusion $\subseteq^{\mathbf{S}}$). *Let $S_1 = \Gamma_1 \Rightarrow \Delta_1, S_2 = \Gamma_2 \Rightarrow \Delta_2$ be two sequents. We say that S_1 is structurally included in S_2, denoted by $S_1 \subseteq^{\mathbf{S}} S_2$, when all the following holds:*

- *$\Gamma_1 \subseteq \Gamma_2$;*
- *for each $[\Lambda_1 \Rightarrow \Theta_1] \in \Delta_1$, there exists $[\Lambda_2 \Rightarrow \Theta_2] \in \Delta_2$ such that $\Lambda_1 \Rightarrow \Theta_1 \subseteq^{\mathbf{S}} \Lambda_2 \Rightarrow \Theta_2$;*
- *for each $[\Lambda_2 \Rightarrow \Theta_2] \in \Delta_2$, there exists $[\Lambda_1 \Rightarrow \Theta_1] \in \Delta_1$ such that $\Lambda_1 \Rightarrow \Theta_1 \subseteq^{\mathbf{S}} \Lambda_2 \Rightarrow \Theta_2$.*

It is easy to see $\subseteq^{\mathbf{S}}$ is both reflexive and transitive.

We now define an equivalent variant $\mathbf{CC_{LIK}}$ of $\mathbf{C_{LIK}}$ which adopts a cumulative version of the rules along with some bookkeeping. Moreover the $(\supset_R)$ rule is modified in order to prevent loops. This calculus will be used as a base for the following decision procedure and then semantic completeness. At first we reformulate the $\sharp$-operator as below, annotating the generated $\sharp$-sequents by the full sequent where it comes from.

Definition 16. *Let $Fm(\Theta)$ be the multiset of formulas directly belonging to Θ. We define the $\sharp$-operator with annotation as follows:*

- $\Rightarrow_{\Lambda\Rightarrow\Theta} \Theta^\sharp = \Rightarrow Fm(\Theta)$ *if* Θ *is* $[\cdot]$*-free;*
- $\Rightarrow_{\Lambda\Rightarrow\Theta} \Theta^\sharp = \Rightarrow Fm(\Theta_0), [\Rightarrow_{\Phi_1\Rightarrow\Psi_1} \Psi_1^\sharp], \dots, [\Rightarrow_{\Phi_k\Rightarrow\Psi_k} \Psi_k^\sharp]$ *if* $\Theta = \Theta_0, [\Phi_1 \Rightarrow \Psi_1], \dots, [\Phi_k \Rightarrow \Psi_k]$ *and* Θ_0 *is* $[\cdot]$*-free.*

The $\sharp$-sequents are generated only by applications of $(\text{inter}_\downarrow)$, and we use the annotation (the subscript of $\Rightarrow$) to "track" the implication block from which a $\sharp$-sequent is generated. The annotation can be omitted and we simply write $\Rightarrow \Theta^\sharp$ whenever we do not need to track an $(\text{inter}_\downarrow)$ application.

Definition 17 (The $\sharp$-Annotated Cumulative Calculus $\mathbf{CC_{LIK}}$). *The cumulative calculus $\mathbf{CC_{LIK}}$ operates on set-based sequents, where a set-based sequent $S = \Gamma \Rightarrow \Delta$ is defined as in definition 7, with the distinction that Γ is a* set *of formulas and Δ is a* set *of formulas and/or blocks (containing set-based sequents). The rules are as follows:*

- $(\bot_L)$, $(\top_R)$, *(id)*, $(\Box_L)$, $(\Diamond_R)$, *(trans) and* $(\text{inter}_\rightarrow)$ *as in* $\mathbf{C_{LIK}}$.
- $(\supset_R)$ *is replaced by two rules for* $A \in \Gamma$ *or* $A \notin \Gamma$*:*

$$\frac{G\{\Gamma \Rightarrow \Delta, A \supset B, B\}}{G\{\Gamma \Rightarrow \Delta, A \supset B\}}\ (A \in \Gamma) \qquad \frac{G\{\Gamma \Rightarrow \Delta, A \supset B, \langle A \Rightarrow B\rangle\}}{G\{\Gamma \Rightarrow \Delta, A \supset B\}}\ (A \notin \Gamma)$$

- $(\text{inter}_\downarrow)$ *is replaced by the following annotated rule:*

$$\frac{G\{\Gamma \Rightarrow \Delta, \langle \Sigma \Rightarrow \Pi, [\Lambda \Rightarrow \Theta]\rangle, [\Rightarrow_{\Lambda\Rightarrow\Theta} \Theta^\sharp]\}}{G\{\Gamma \Rightarrow \Delta, \langle \Sigma \Rightarrow \Pi, [\Lambda \Rightarrow \Theta]\rangle\}}\ (\text{inter}_\downarrow)$$

- *The other rules in $\mathbf{C_{LIK}}$ are modified by keeping the principal formula in the premises. For example, the cumulative versions of* $(\wedge_L)$, $(\Box_R)$ *are:*

$$\frac{G\{A, B, A \wedge B, \Gamma \Rightarrow \Delta\}}{G\{A \wedge B, \Gamma \Rightarrow \Delta\}}\ (\wedge_L) \qquad \frac{G\{\Gamma \Rightarrow \Delta, \Box A, [\Rightarrow A]\}}{G\{\Gamma \Rightarrow \Delta, \Box A\}}\ (\Box_R)$$

Given the admissibility of weakening and contraction in $\mathbf{C_{LIK}}$, the following proposition is a direct consequence.

Proposition 5. *A sequent S is provable in $\mathbf{C_{LIK}}$ iff S is provable in $\mathbf{CC_{LIK}}$.*

Next, we introduce saturation conditions for each rule in $\mathbf{CC_{LIK}}$. They are needed for both termination and counter-model extraction.

Definition 18 (Saturation Conditions). *Let $S = \Gamma \Rightarrow \Delta$ be a sequent. We say S satisfies the saturation condition on the top level with respect to*

$(\supset_R)$: *If $A \supset B \in \Delta$, then either $A \in \Gamma$ and $B \in \Delta$, or there is $\langle \Sigma \Rightarrow \Pi \rangle \in \Delta$ with $A \in \Sigma$ and $B \in \Pi$.*
$(\Diamond_R)$: *If $\Diamond A \in \Delta$ and $[\Sigma \Rightarrow \Pi] \in \Delta$, then $A \in \Pi$.*
$(\Diamond_L)$: *If $\Diamond A \in \Gamma$, then there is $[\Sigma \Rightarrow \Pi] \in \Delta$ with $A \in \Sigma$.*
$(\Box_R)$: *If $\Box A \in \Delta$, then there is $[\Lambda \Rightarrow \Theta] \in \Delta$ with $A \in \Theta$.*
$(\Box_L)$: *If $\Box A \in \Gamma$ and $[\Sigma \Rightarrow \Pi] \in \Delta$, then $A \in \Sigma$.*
$(inter_\downarrow)$: *If $\langle \Sigma \Rightarrow \Pi, [\Lambda \Rightarrow \Theta] \rangle \in \Delta$, then there is $[\Phi \Rightarrow \Psi] \in \Delta$ s.t. $\Phi \Rightarrow \Psi \subseteq^{\mathbf{S}} \Lambda \Rightarrow \Theta$.*
$(inter_\rightarrow)$: *If $\langle \Sigma \Rightarrow \Pi \rangle, [\Lambda \Rightarrow \Theta] \in \Delta$, then there is $[\Phi \Rightarrow \Psi] \in \Pi$ s.t. $\Lambda \Rightarrow \Theta \subseteq^{\mathbf{S}} \Phi \Rightarrow \Psi$.*
$(trans)$: *If $\langle \Sigma \Rightarrow \Pi \rangle \in \Delta$, then $\Gamma \subseteq \Sigma$.*

Saturation conditions for the other propositional rules are defined as usual.

We say a sequent is saturated with a rule (r) if it satisfies the saturation condition associated with (r). We say a backward application of a rule (r) to a sequent S is *redundant* if S already satisfies the corresponding saturation condition associated with (r).

Proposition 6. *Let $S = \Gamma \Rightarrow \Delta$ be a sequent. If S is saturated with $(trans)$, $(inter_\rightarrow)$ and $(inter_\downarrow)$, then for $\langle \Sigma \Rightarrow \Pi \rangle \in \Delta$, we have $\Gamma \Rightarrow \Delta \subseteq^{\mathbf{S}} \Sigma \Rightarrow \Pi$.*

In order to define a terminating proof-search strategy based on $\mathbf{CC_{LIK}}$, we first impose the following constraints:

(i) *No rule is applied to an axiom* and (ii) *No rule is applied redundantly.*

However there is a problem: backward proof search only respecting these basic constraints does not necessarily ensure that *any* leaf of a derivation, to which no rule can be applied non-redundantly, satisfies *all* the saturation conditions of rules in $\mathbf{CC_{LIK}}$. This is a significant difference from the calculus of **FIK** in [2]. The problematic case is the saturation condition for the (inter$_\downarrow$) rule.

Example 4. Let us consider the sequent $\Box(p \vee q) \Rightarrow \Box r \supset \Box s$. After some preliminary steps, we obtain two sequents:

(i). $\Box(p \vee q) \Rightarrow \Box r \supset \Box s, \langle \Box(p \vee q), \Box r \Rightarrow \Box s, [p \vee q, p, r \Rightarrow s] \rangle$
(ii). $\Box(p \vee q) \Rightarrow \Box r \supset \Box s, \langle \Box(p \vee q), \Box r \Rightarrow \Box s, [p \vee q, q, r \Rightarrow s] \rangle$

Suppose we select (i) and then apply (inter$_\downarrow$) obtaining (i'): $\Box(p \vee q) \Rightarrow \Box r \supset \Box s, \langle \Box(p \vee q), \Box r \Rightarrow \Box s, [p \vee q, p, r \Rightarrow s] \rangle, [\Rightarrow s]$. After applying $(\Box_L)$, $(\vee_L)$ and (inter$_\rightarrow$), we further obtain:

(iii). $\Box(p \vee q) \Rightarrow \Box r \supset \Box s, \langle \Box(p \vee q), \Box r \Rightarrow \Box s, [p \vee q, p, r \Rightarrow s] \rangle, [p \vee q, p \Rightarrow s]$
(iv). $\Box(p \vee q) \Rightarrow \Box r \supset \Box s, \langle \Box(p \vee q), \Box r \Rightarrow \Box s, [p \vee q, p, r \Rightarrow s], [p \vee q, q \Rightarrow] \rangle,$
$[p \vee q, q \Rightarrow s]$

We can see that (iii) satisfies the saturation condition for (inter$_\downarrow$), as $p \vee q, p \Rightarrow s \subseteq^{\mathbf{S}} p \vee q, p, r \Rightarrow s$ but (iv) does not, since there is no $[\Phi \Rightarrow \Psi]$ s.t. $\Phi \Rightarrow \Psi \subseteq^{\mathbf{S}} p \vee q, p, r \Rightarrow s$. Sequent (iv) would not give in itself a model satisfying (DC) and it is not obvious how to extend it in order to satisfy (DC).[3] This example also

[3] Observe that a disallowed *redundant* application of (inter$_\downarrow$) to the block $[p \vee q, q \Rightarrow]$ would not help, as it would reproduce the branching.

shows the inadequacy of $\mathbf{C_{LIK^-}}$ for semantic completeness, as sequent expansion in $\mathbf{C_{LIK^-}}$ terminates with (i) and (ii), from which we do not know how to define a model satisfying (DC).

This means that certain branches in a derivation may lead to unprovable sequents from which we do not know how to build a "correct" counter-model directly. Hence, to obtain a "correct" counter-model, we require a mechanism that chooses the suitable branch which ensures the saturation condition for (inter$_\downarrow$). This is provided by the tracking mechanism and realization procedure defined below.

Definition 19 (Tracking Record Based on $\in^{[\cdot]}$). *Let S be a set-based sequent which is saturated with respect to all the left rules in $\mathbf{CC_{LIK}}$. Take an arbitrary set of formulas, denoted as Γ. Let $\Omega = \{T \mid T = S \text{ or } T \in^{[\cdot]} S\}$. For each $T \in \Omega$, we define $\mathfrak{G}_S(T, \Gamma)$, the $\in^{[\cdot]}$-based tracking record of Γ in S, which is a subset of $Ant(T)$ as follows:*

- $\mathfrak{G}_S(S, \Gamma) = \Gamma \cap Ant(S)$;
- *If $T \in_0^{[\cdot]} T'$ for some $T' \in \Omega$, let $\mathfrak{G}_S(T, \Gamma)$ be the minimal set such that*
  - *if $\Box A \in \mathfrak{G}_S(T', \Gamma)$, then $A \in \mathfrak{G}_S(T, \Gamma)$;*
  - *if $\Diamond A \in \mathfrak{G}_S(T', \Gamma)$ and $A \in Ant(T)$, then $A \in \mathfrak{G}_S(T, \Gamma)$;*
  - *if $A \wedge B \in \mathfrak{G}_S(T, \Gamma)$, then $A, B \in \mathfrak{G}_S(T, \Gamma)$;*
  - *if $A \vee B \in \mathfrak{G}_S(T, \Gamma)$ and $A \in Ant(T)$, then $A \in \mathfrak{G}_S(T, \Gamma)$;*
  - *if $A \supset B \in \mathfrak{G}_S(T, \Gamma)$ and $B \in Ant(T)$, then $B \in \mathfrak{G}_S(T, \Gamma)$.*

Tracking record is used to control rule applications to and within a block created by (inter$_\downarrow$), preserving the saturation condition associated to it.

Definition 20 (Realization). *Let $S = \Gamma \Rightarrow \Delta, \langle S_1 \rangle, [S_2]$, where $S_1 = \Sigma \Rightarrow \Pi, [\Lambda \Rightarrow \Theta]$, $S_2 = \Rightarrow_{\Lambda \Rightarrow \Theta} \Theta^\sharp$ and $\Gamma \subseteq \Sigma$. Moreover, we assume that S_1 is saturated with respect to all the left rules in $\mathbf{CC_{LIK}}$. Using the $\in^{[\cdot]}$-based tracking record of Γ in S_1, we define the realization of the block $[S_2]$ in S as follows:*

(i). First for each $T \in^+ S_2$, define the realization function $f_{S_1}(T)$.
By definition, T is of the form $\Rightarrow_{\Phi \Rightarrow \Psi} \Psi^\sharp$ for some $\Phi \Rightarrow \Psi \in^+ \Lambda \Rightarrow \Theta$. $f_{S_1}(T)$ is defined inductively on the structure of $\Psi^\sharp$ as follows:
- *if $\Psi^\sharp$ is block-free, then $f_{S_1}(T) = \mathfrak{G}(\Phi \Rightarrow \Psi, \Gamma) \Rightarrow \Psi^\sharp$.*
- *otherwise $\Psi^\sharp = \Psi_0, [T_1], \ldots, [T_k]$ where Ψ_0 is a set of formulas, then $f_{S_1}(T) = \mathfrak{G}(\Phi \Rightarrow \Psi, \Gamma) \Rightarrow \Psi_0, [f_{S_1}(T_1)], \ldots, [f_{S_1}(T_k)]$.*

(ii). With $f_{S_1}(S_2)$, the realization of $[S_2]$ in S is $\Gamma \Rightarrow \Delta, \langle S_1 \rangle, [f_{S_1}(S_2)]$.

As the next proposition shows the expansion produced by a realization procedure is not an additional logical step; rather, it can be obtained by applying the rules of the calculus while selecting the appropriate branch.

Proposition 7. *Let $S = \Gamma \Rightarrow \Delta, \langle S_1 \rangle, [S_2]$, where $S_1 = \Sigma \Rightarrow \Pi, [\Lambda \Rightarrow \Theta]$ and $S_2 = \Rightarrow_{\Lambda \Rightarrow \Theta} \Theta^\sharp$ and $\Gamma \subseteq \Sigma$. If S_1 is saturated with respect to all the left rules in $\mathbf{CC_{LIK}}$, then for the sequent $S' = \Gamma \Rightarrow \Delta, \langle S_1 \rangle, [f_{S_1}(S_2)]$ which is obtained by the realization procedure in Definition 20, we have*

(i). S' is saturated with respect to all the left rules applied to or within $[f_{S_1}(S_2)]$;
(ii). $f_{S_1}(S_2) \subseteq^{\mathbf{S}} \Lambda \Rightarrow \Theta$;
(iii). S' can be obtained by applying left rules of $\mathbf{CC_{LIK}}$ to $[S_2]$ in S.

Example 5. We go back to sequent (i') in Example 4. Let

$$\begin{aligned} S\ &= \Box(p \vee q) \Rightarrow \Box r \supset \Box s, \langle \Box(p \vee q), \Box r \Rightarrow \Box s, [p \vee q, p, r \Rightarrow s]\rangle, [\Rightarrow s] \\ S_1 &= \Box(p \vee q), \Box r \Rightarrow \Box s, [p \vee q, p, r \Rightarrow s] \\ S_2 &= \ \Rightarrow s,\ T = p \vee q, p, r \Rightarrow s \end{aligned}$$

Since $[S_2]$ is produced by (inter$_\downarrow$) from T, we have $S_2 = \Rightarrow_T s$. We are intended to realize the block $[S_2]$ in S by the tracking record of $Ant(S)$ in S_1. By definition, we have

$$\begin{aligned} \mathfrak{G}_{S_1}(S_1, Ant(S)) &= Ant(S) = \{\Box(p \vee q)\} \\ \mathfrak{G}_{S_1}(T, Ant(S)) &= \{p \vee q, p\} \end{aligned}$$

According to realization, by applying $f_{S_1}(\cdot)$ to S_2, we get $f_{S_1}(\Rightarrow_T s) = p \vee q, p \Rightarrow s$. Thus, the entire output sequent is

$$\Box(p \vee q) \Rightarrow \Box r \supset \Box s, \langle \Box(p \vee q), \Box r \Rightarrow \Box s, [p \vee q, p, r \Rightarrow s]\rangle, [p \vee q, p \Rightarrow s]$$

And this is just (iii) in Example 4, which is the right expansion of (i').

In order to define the proof-search procedure, we first divide all the rules of $\mathbf{CC_{LIK}}$ into four groups as (R1): all propositional and modal rules except $(\supset_R)$; (R2): (trans) and (inter$_\rightarrow$); (R3): $(\supset_R)$; and (R4): (inter$_\downarrow$).

Let $S = \Gamma \Rightarrow \Delta$, we denote by $\bar{\Delta}$ the sequent obtained by removing all the (nested) occurrences of $\langle\cdot\rangle$-blocks in Δ.[4]

Definition 21 (Saturation). *Let $S = \Gamma \Rightarrow \Delta$ be a sequent and not an axiom. S is called:*

- R1-saturated *if $\Gamma \Rightarrow \bar{\Delta}$ satisfies all the saturation conditions of R1 rules;*
- R2-saturated *if S is R1-saturated and S satisfies saturation conditions of R2 rules for blocks $\langle S_1\rangle, [S_2]$ s.t. $S_1 \in_0^{\langle\cdot\rangle} S$ and $S_2 \in_0^{[\cdot]} S$;*
- R3-saturated *if S is R2-saturated and S satisfies saturation conditions of R3 rules for formulas $A \supset B \in \Delta$;*
- R4-saturated *S is R3-saturated and S satisfies saturation conditions of R4 rule for each implication block $\langle \Sigma \Rightarrow \Pi, [S_1]\rangle$ s.t. $\Sigma \Rightarrow \Pi, [S_1] \in_0^{\langle\cdot\rangle} S$.*

Definition 22 (Global Saturation). *Let S be a sequent and not an axiom. S is called* global-Ri-saturated *if for each $T \in^+ S$, T is Ri-saturated where $i \in \{1, 2, 3\}$;* global-saturated *if for each $T \in^+ S$, T is R4-saturated.*

In order to specify the proof-search procedure, we make use of the following four macro-steps that extend a given derivation $\mathcal{D}$ by expanding a leaf S. Each procedure applies rules *non-redundantly* to some $T = \Gamma \Rightarrow \Delta \in^+ S$.

[4] For example, let $\Delta = B, \langle \Sigma \Rightarrow \Pi\rangle, [\Lambda \Rightarrow [D \Rightarrow E, \langle P \Rightarrow Q\rangle]]$, then $\bar{\Delta} = B, [\Lambda \Rightarrow [D \Rightarrow E]]$.

Algorithm 1: PROC$_0(S_0)$

Input: S_0

initialization $\mathcal{D} = \Rightarrow S_0$;
repeat
  if *all the leaves of* $\mathcal{D}$ *are axiomatic* **then**
    return "PROVABLE" and $\mathcal{D}$
  else if *there is a non-axiomatic leaf of* $\mathcal{D}$ *which is global-R3-saturated* **then**
    return $\mathcal{D}$
  else
    select one non-axiomatic leaf S of $\mathcal{D}$
    if S *is global-R2-saturated* **then**
      for all non-R3-saturated $T \in^+ S$, let $\mathcal{D} =$ **EXP3**$(\mathcal{D}, S, T)$
    else if S *is global-R1-saturated* **then**
      for all non-R2-saturated $T \in^+ S$, let $\mathcal{D} =$ **EXP2**$(\mathcal{D}, S, T)$
    else
      for all non-R1-saturated $T \in^+ S$, let $\mathcal{D} =$ **EXP1**$(\mathcal{D}, S, T)$
until *FALSE*;

- **EXP1**$(\mathcal{D}, S, T) = \mathcal{D}'$ where $\mathcal{D}'$ is the extension of $\mathcal{D}$ obtained by applying R1-rules to every formula in $\Gamma \Rightarrow \bar{\Delta}$.
- **EXP2**$(\mathcal{D}, S, T) = \mathcal{D}'$ where $\mathcal{D}'$ is the extension of $\mathcal{D}$ obtained by applying R2-rules to blocks $\langle T_i \rangle, [T_j] \in \Delta$.
- **EXP3**$(\mathcal{D}, S, T) = \mathcal{D}'$ where $\mathcal{D}'$ is the extension of $\mathcal{D}$ obtained by applying R3-rules to formulas $A \supset B \in \Delta$.
- **EXP4**$(\mathcal{D}, S) = \mathcal{D}'$ where $\mathcal{D}'$ is the extension of $\mathcal{D}$ obtained by applying (i) R4-rule to each implication block $T' \in^+ S$ and (ii) realization procedures to modal blocks produced in (i). This step extends $\mathcal{D}$ by a *single* branch whose leaf is denoted by S'.

It can be proved that each of these four macro-steps terminates. The claim is almost obvious except for **EXP1** (see [2, Proposition 46]).

Proposition 8. *Given a finite derivation $\mathcal{D}$, a finite leaf S of $\mathcal{D}$ and $T \in^+ S$, then for $i \in \{1, 2, 3, 4\}$, each **EXPi**$(\mathcal{D}, S, T)$ terminates by producing a finite expansion of $\mathcal{D}$ where all sequents are finite.*

Now we define the procedure. We first demonstrate the preliminary procedure PROC$_0(S_0)$ (see Algorithm 1)which builds a derivation with root S_0 and only uses the macro-steps **EXP1**$(\cdot)$ to **EXP3**$(\cdot)$, thus only the rules in $\mathbf{C_{LIK}}$-are applied. It follows that PROC$_0(A)$ decides whether a formula A is valid in **LIK**. Additionally, the procedure PROC$_0(\cdot)$ is then used as a subroutine in the full procedure PROC$(\Rightarrow A)$ to obtain either a proof of A or a global-saturated sequent, see Algorithm 2.

Proposition 9. *Given a sequent S_0,* PROC$_0(S_0)$ *produces a finite derivation with all the leaves axiomatic or at least one global-R3-saturated leaf.*

Algorithm 2: PROC(A)

Input: A

initialization $\mathcal{D} = \text{PROC}_0(\Rightarrow A)$;
if *all the leaves of* $\mathcal{D}$ *are axiomatic* **then**
  return "PROVABLE" and $\mathcal{D}$
else
  while *(No global saturated leaf of* $\mathcal{D}$ *is found)* **do**
    select one global-R3-saturated leaf S of $\mathcal{D}$
    let $\mathcal{D} = \mathbf{EXP4}(\mathcal{D}, S)$
    let S' be the leaf of the unique branch of $\mathcal{D}$ expanded by $\mathbf{EXP4}(\mathcal{D}, S)$
     extend $\mathcal{D}$ by applying $\text{PROC}_0(S')$
  return "UNPROVABLE" and $\mathcal{D}$

Lastly, we show that PROC(A) terminates.

Theorem 4 (Termination for $\mathbf{CC_{LIK}}$). *Proof-search for a formula A in $\mathbf{CC_{LIK}}$ terminates with a finite derivation in which either all the leaves are axiomatic or there is at least one global-saturated leaf.*

We can also obtain decision procedures for $\mathbf{C_{LIKD}}$ and $\mathbf{C_{LIKT}}$ in a similar way. Consider a cumulative version $\mathbf{CC_{LIKD}}$ and $\mathbf{CC_{LIKT}}$ of the respective calculi and define suitable saturation conditions associated the extra modal rules, for a sequent $S = \Gamma \Rightarrow \Delta$:
(**D**): if $\Gamma^{\Box} \cup \Delta^{\Diamond}$ is non-empty. then Δ is not $[\cdot]$-free.
($\mathbf{T}_{\Box}/\mathbf{T}_{\Diamond}$): if $\Box A \in \Gamma$ (resp. $\Diamond A \in \Delta$), then $A \in \Gamma$ (resp. $A \in \Delta$).

The saturation condition for (**D**) prevents a useless generation of infinitely nested empty blocks of the form $[\Rightarrow [\ldots \Rightarrow [\Rightarrow] \ldots]]$, which can be created by the backward application of the (**D**)-rule. The procedure $\text{PROC}_0(\cdot)$ integrates the rules for (**D**) or (**T**)'s accordingly: the rule (**D**) is applied immediately after each round of **EXP2**($\cdot$) while the two (**T**) rules are integrated in **EXP1**($\cdot$). As a result, we can obtain:

Theorem 5 (Termination for $\mathbf{CC_{LIKD}}$ and $\mathbf{CC_{LIKT}}$). *Proof-search for a formula A in $\mathbf{CC_{LIKD}}$ and $\mathbf{CC_{LIKT}}$ terminates with a finite derivation in which either all the leaves are axiomatic or there is at least one global-saturated leaf.*

5 Completeness

Using the decision procedure from the previous section, we show how to build a countermodel for an unprovable formula, which entails the completeness of $\mathbf{CC_{LIK}}$. Subsequently, we adapt this construction to $\mathbf{CC_{LIKD}}$ and $\mathbf{CC_{LIKT}}$ as well.

Given a global-saturated sequent S in $\mathbf{CC_{LIK}}$, we define a model $\mathcal{M}_S$ for it as below.

Definition 23. *The model* $\mathcal{M}_S = (W_S, \leq_S, R_S, V_S)$ *is a quadruple where*
- $W_S = \{x_{\Phi\Rightarrow\Psi} \mid \Phi \Rightarrow \Psi \in^+ S\}$;
- $x_{S_1} \leq_S x_{S_2}$ *if* $S_1 \subseteq^{\mathbf{S}} S_2$;
- $R_S x_{S_1} x_{S_2}$ *if* $S_2 \in_0^{[\cdot]} S_1$;
- *for each* $p \in \mathbf{At}$, *let* $V_S(p) = \{x_{\Phi\Rightarrow\Psi} \mid p \in \Phi\}$.

Proposition 10. $\mathcal{M}_S$ *satisfies (FC) and (DC).*

Lemma 8 (Truth Lemma for $\mathbf{CC_{LIK}}$). *Let S be a global-saturated sequent in $\mathbf{CC_{LIK}}$ and $\mathcal{M}_S = (W_S, \leq_S, R_S, V_S)$ defined as above. (a). If $A \in \Phi$, then $\mathcal{M}_S, x_{\Phi\Rightarrow\Psi} \Vdash A$; (b). If $A \in \Psi$, then $M_S, x_{\Phi\Rightarrow\Psi} \nVdash A$.*

By the truth lemma we obtain as usual the completeness of $\mathbf{CC_{LIK}}$.

Theorem 6 (Completeness of $\mathbf{CC_{LIK}}$). *If A is valid in* **LIK**, *then A is provable in* $\mathbf{C_{LIK}}$.

Example 6. We show how to build a countermodel for the formula $(\Diamond p \supset \Box q) \supset \Box(p \supset q)$ which is not provable in $\mathbf{CC_{LIK}}$. Ignoring the first step, we initialize the derivation with $\Diamond p \supset \Box q \Rightarrow \Box(p \supset q)$. By backward application of rules, one branch of the derivation ends up with the following saturated sequent

$$S_0 = \Diamond p \supset \Box q \Rightarrow \Box(p \supset q), \Diamond p, [\Rightarrow p \supset q, p, \langle p \Rightarrow q\rangle]$$

and we further let $S_1 = \Rightarrow p \supset q, p, \langle p \Rightarrow q\rangle$ while $S_2 = p \Rightarrow q$. We then get the model $M_{S_0} = (W, \leq, R, V)$ where

- $W = \{x_{S_0}, x_{S_1}, x_{S_2}\}$;
- $x_{S_1} \leq x_{S_2}, x_{S_0} \leq x_{S_0}, x_{S_1} \leq x_{S_1}, x_{S_2} \leq x_{S_2}$;
- $R x_{S_0} x_{S_1}$;
- $V(p) = \{x_{S_2}\}$ and $V(q) = \varnothing$.

It is easy to see that $x_{S_0} \nVdash (\Diamond p \supset \Box q) \supset \Box(p \supset q)$.

Next, we consider the completeness of $\mathbf{CC_{LIKD}}$ and $\mathbf{CC_{LIKT}}$. We consider the model $\mathcal{M}_S = (W_S, \leq_S, R_S, V_S)$ for a global-saturated sequent S in either calculi, where $W_S, \leq_S$ and V_S as in Definition 23, R_S modified as follows:

- For $\mathbf{CC_{LIKD}}$: $R_S x_{S_1} x_{S_2}$ if $S_2 \in_0^{[\cdot]} S_1$ or $Suc(S_1)$ is $[\cdot]$-free and $x_{S_1} = x_{S_2}$;
- For $\mathbf{CC_{LIKT}}$: $R_S x_{S_1} x_{S_2}$ if $S_2 \in_0^{[\cdot]} S_1$ or $x_{S_1} = x_{S_2}$.

Trivially the relation R_S is serial or reflexive according to $\mathbf{C_{LIKD}}$ or $\mathbf{C_{LIKT}}$, moreover models for $\mathbf{CC_{LIKD}}$ and $\mathbf{CC_{LIKT}}$ still satisfy (FC) and (DC). Finally,

Theorem 7 (Completeness of $\mathbf{CC_{LIKD}}$ and $\mathbf{CC_{LIKT}}$). *If A is valid in* **LIKD** *(resp.* **LIKT***), then A is provable in* $\mathbf{CC_{LIKD}}$ *(resp.* $\mathbf{CC_{LIKT}}$*).*

6 Conclusion

We studied **LIK**, the basic intuitionistic modal logic with locally defined modalities as well as some of its extensions. In further research, we intend to investigate both axiomatizations and calculi of extensions to the whole modal cube. For instance, we would like to provide a (terminating) calculus for the **S4** extension of **LIK** (the logic is studied in [1]). Since **LIK** is incomparable with **IK**, we may also wonder what the "super" intuitionistic modal logic obtained by combining both is. Our broader goal is to establish a framework of axiomatization and uniform calculi for a wide range of **IMLs**, including other natural variants that have been little studied or remain entirely unexplored so far.

References

1. Balbiani, P., Diéguez, M., Fernández-Duque, D.: Some constructive variants of S4 with the finite model property. In: 36th Annual ACM/IEEE Symposium on Logic in Computer Science, LICS, pp. 1–13. IEEE (2021). https://doi.org/10.1109/LICS52264.2021.9470643
2. Balbiani, P., Gao, H., Gencer, c., Olivetti, N.: A natural intuitionistic modal logic: axiomatization and bi-nested calculus. In: 32nd EACSL Annual Conference on Computer Science Logic (CSL 2024). Leibniz International Proceedings in Informatics (LIPIcs), vol. 288, pp. 13:1–13:21 (2024). https://doi.org/10.4230/LIPIcs.CSL.2024.13
3. Bellin, G., De Paiva, V., Ritter, E.: Extended Curry-Howard correspondence for a basic constructive modal logic. In: Proceedings of Methods for Modalities, vol. 2 (2001)
4. Božić, M., Došen, K.: Models for normal intuitionistic modal logics. Stud. Logica. **43**, 217–245 (1984)
5. D'agostino, M., Gabbay, D.M., Russo, A.: Grafting modalities onto substructural implication systems. Stud. Logic. **59**, 65–102 (1997)
6. Das, A., Marin, S.: On intuitionistic diamonds (and lack thereof). In: Ramanayake, R., Urban, J. (eds.) TABLEAUX 2023. LNCS, vol. 14278, pp. 283–301. Springer, Cham (2023). https://doi.org/10.1007/978-3-031-43513-3_16
7. Fischer-Servi, G.: On modal logic with an intuitionistic base. Stud. Logic. **36**(3), 141–149 (1977). https://doi.org/10.1007/BF02121259
8. Fischer-Servi, G.: Semantics for a Class of Intuitionistic Modal Calculi, pp. 59–72. Springer, Dordrecht (1981).https://doi.org/10.1007/978-94-009-8937-5_5
9. Fischer-Servi, G.: Axiomatizations for some intuitionistic modal logics. Rendiconti del Seminario Matematico Università e Politecnico di Torino **42** (1984). https://cir.nii.ac.jp/crid/1371132818982119684
10. Fitch, F.B.: Intuitionistic modal logic with quantifiers. Portugaliae mathematica **7**(2), 113–118 (1948). http://eudml.org/doc/114664
11. Fitting, M.: Nested sequents for intuitionistic logics. Notre Dame J. Formal Log. **55**(1), 41–61 (2014).https://doi.org/10.1215/00294527-2377869
12. Galmiche, D., Salhi, Y.: Label-free natural deduction systems for intuitionistic and classical modal logics. J. Appl. Non-Classical Logics **20**(4), 373–421 (2010). https://doi.org/10.3166/jancl.20.373-421
13. Marin, S., Morales, M.: Fully structured proof theory for intuitionistic modal logics. In: AiML 2020 - Advances in Modal Logic (2020). https://hal.science/hal-03048959

14. Marin, S., Straßburger, L.: Label-free modular systems for classical and intuitionistic modal logics. In: Advances in Modal Logic, vol. 10 (2014)
15. Plotkin, G., Stirling, C.: A framework for intuitionistic modal logics. In: Proceedings of the 1st Conference on Theoretical Aspects of Reasoning about Knowledge (TARK), pp. 399–406 (1986). https://doi.org/10.5555/1029786.1029823
16. Prawitz, D.: Natural Deduction: A Proof-Theoretical Study. Dover Publications, Mineola (1965). https://doi.org/10.2307/2271676
17. Simpson, A.K.: The proof theory and semantics of intuitionistic modal logic. Ph.D. Thesis, University of Edinburgh (1994). https://api.semanticscholar.org/CorpusID:2309858
18. Straßburger, L.: Cut elimination in nested sequents for intuitionistic modal logics. In: Pfenning, F. (ed.) FoSSaCS 2013. LNCS, vol. 7794, pp. 209–224. Springer, Heidelberg (2013). https://doi.org/10.1007/978-3-642-37075-5_14
19. Wijesekera, D.: Constructive modal logics I. Ann. Pure Appl. Log. **50**(3), 271–301 (1990). https://doi.org/10.1016/0168-0072(90)90059-B

Non-iterative Modal Resolution Calculi

Dirk Pattinson[1(✉)] and Cláudia Nalon[2]

[1] School of Computing, The Australian National University, Canberra, Australia
dirk.pattinson@anu.edu.au

[2] Department of Computer Science, University of Brasília, Brasília, Brazil
nalon@unb.br

Abstract. Non-monotonic modal logics are typically interpreted over neighbourhood frames. For unary operators, this is just a set of worlds, together with an endofunction on predicates (subsets of worlds). It is known that all systems of not necessarily monotonic modal logics that are axiomatised by formulae of modal rank at most one (non-iterative modal logics) are Kripke-complete over neighbourhood semantics. In this paper, we give a uniform construction to obtain complete resolution calculi for all non-iterative logics. We show completeness for generative calculi (where new clauses with new literals are added to the clause set) by means of a canonical model construction. We then define absorptive calculi (where new clauses are generated by generalised resolution rules) and establish completeness by translating between generative and absorptive calculi. Instances of our construction re-prove completeness for already known calculi, but also give rise to a number of previously unknown complete calculi.

Keywords: Modal Logics · Automated Reasoning · Resolution

1 Introduction

There are two standard ways to define modal logics. The *syntactic* approach specifies a logic by means of its axioms and proof rules. One way of defining the modal logic K is as the least set of formulae that contains all instances of propositional tautologies and the K-axioms, and is closed under modus ponens and necessitation. Alternatively, we can take a *semantic* approach, and define a logic as the set of formulae that is valid over a given class of frames. For the modal logic K, this is typically the class of formulae valid over all Kripke frames, but we can alternatively define K as the class of all formulae that are valid in all neighbourhood frames where neighbourhoods are closed under finite intersections. More often than not, the frame class under consideration is also described using logical formulae as axioms.

No matter whether we take a syntactic or semantic approach, the questions remain the same: can we define a proof calculus that allows us to derive all formulae of the logic? Can we decide whether a formula is in the logic?

In this paper, we answer these questions uniformly for the class of all *non-iterative* modal logics and *resolution calculi*. Non-iterative logics are defined

C. Benzmüller et al. (Eds.): IJCAR 2024, LNAI 14740, pp. 97–113, 2024.
https://doi.org/10.1007/978-3-031-63501-4_6

(either syntactically or semantically) by axioms without nesting of modal operators. While this excludes e.g. logics with (generalised) transitivity axioms, it still covers a large class of specimens. Examples include various classical modal logics of Chellas [8], all standard conditional logics treated in [19], extensions of the modal logic K with reflexivity, seriality and functionality [6], graded and probabilistic modal logic [13,14], Pauly's coalition logic [22], a variety of deontic logics [24] and logics of agency [11]. For all these logics, we construct a complete resolution system that can be turned into a decision procedure. From a syntactic viewpoint, we cannot restrict ourselves to normal modal logics. That is, our basic modal systems will only include modal congruence (from $\phi \leftrightarrow \psi$ infer $\Box\phi \leftrightarrow \Box\psi$, or its multi-argument, multi-modal generalisation). Consequently on the semantic side, we adopt neighbourhood semantics as the most general semantic framework. For this semantics, Lewis [16] has already shown that non-iterative logics are complete with respect to the class of neighbourhood frames that are defined by their axioms. Here, completeness is understood with respect to a Hilbert-style system, where deduction is defined as the closure of propositional tautologies and axioms under substitution, modus ponens, and modal congruence. Here, we use the same classes of frames (that are defined by modal axioms), and show that our resolution systems are complete with respect to these frames. Considering the same semantics, this builds a bridge between syntactically defined logics, and the resolution systems that we introduce.

Our technical contribution is the definition, and analysis, of two different types of resolution calculi for each non-iterative logic. The first system that we call *generative* extends propositional resolution with modal rules that produce new clauses with possibly new modal literals. For example, the modal congruence rule above introduces the clause $\neg\Box p \vee \Box q$, i.e. $\Box p \rightarrow \Box q$, in contrast to more standard calculi that are based on resolving conflicting literals. In these calculi that we call *absorptive*, the modal congruence rule would identify $\Box p$ and $\neg\Box q$ as conflicting, and – assuming that p and q are equivalent – adds the clause $D \vee E$ if $D \vee \neg\Box p$ and $E \vee \Box q$ are already derived. The reason for introducing both calculi is technical: generative calculi are much more suited to a canonical model construction that we use to prove completeness. In particular, maximally consistent sets behave in the expected way (they contain every literal or its negation). On the other hand, absorptive calculi are the calculi *de rigeur*, and transforming generative proofs to absorptive proofs, we obtain completeness for absorptive calculi by translation.

Methodologically, we make an interesting, but not entirely unexpected discovery. While in propositional logic, we can derive completeness of resolution directly from completeness of a cut-free sequent calculus (e.g. [10]), this method *fails* for modal logic: for example, the set $\Phi = \{p, \neg p \vee q, \Box p, \neg\Box q\}$ is evidently satisfiable (at a world, in a neighbourhood or Kripke model), but $\Phi \vdash \bot$ in a sequent calculus for classical (or normal) modal logic where $\Delta \in \Phi$ are treated as additional axioms or initial sequents. Because the additional initial sequents Φ play the role of *global assumptions*, $\Phi \vdash \Gamma$ means that Γ is valid in all models where all $\Delta \in \Phi$ are true globally (at *all* worlds). Hence $\Phi \vdash \bot$ as there is no model where all $\phi \in \Phi$ are globally true. Despite the fact that we do not obtain a resolution calculus *directly* from a sequent calculus (by forgetting the propositional rules), both calculi are still closely related. To ensure *completeness* of the resolution systems, we employ the same technical condition that guarantees *cut elimination* in sequent calculi: in both cases, we require that modal rules are *cut-closed*, i.e. two applications of modal rules, followed by a resolution step between their conclusions, can be replaced by a single modal rule (whose premisses are derivable from the premisses of the original rule). In cut-elimination proofs, this is what allows us to propagate cut towards the leaves of a proof tree. For resolution calculi, this property ensures that a consistent set remains consistent if we extend the language: an inconsistency in the larger system would involve new variables, and cut-closure allows us to eliminate them. We discuss this phenomenon more in the conclusion.

Related Work. As far as we are aware, our paper is the first to study the construction of resolution calculi from a more general perspective, i.e. focusing on properties such as non-iterative axioms rather than on concretely given logical systems. There is a large body of work on resolution calculi on normal modal logics [1–3,7,9,12,17,18] but [20] appears to be the only paper on modal resolution for non-normal calculi. All of the above approaches focus on concretely given calculi in contrast to this paper that uniformly applies to all calculi with non-iterative axioms. The notion of cut-closure has been used to construct cut-free sequent calculi in [21]. Indeed, the results of *op.cit.* will give complete, cut-free sequent calculi that have precisely the same modal rules as our generative systems. Of course, we are not the first to observe this deep relationship between sequent calculi and resolution, although our paper appears to be the first that follows a semantic route to directly express completeness of resolution. Avron [4] has discussed the relationship between resolution and sequent calculi for propositional and first order logic, and Mints [17] has considered modal calculi; both from the perspective of syntactical translation. To our knowledge, there is no work that relates sequent calculi and resolution for non-normal modal logics, or on methods that apply to a range of logics in a uniform way.

2 Preliminaries

Definition 1. Let V be a set of propositional variables that we fix throughout. The language $\mathcal{L}$ of modal logic is given by the grammar

$$\mathcal{L} \ni \phi ::= p \mid \neg\phi \mid \phi \vee \phi \mid \Box\phi$$

where $p \in \mathsf{V}$. A *substitution* is a mapping $\sigma : \mathsf{V} \to \mathcal{L}$, and we denote the result of uniformly substituting each $p \in \mathsf{V}$ with $\sigma(p)$ in a formula ϕ by $\phi\sigma$. A *global formula* is of the form $\mathsf{G}(\phi)$ where ϕ is a formula. Propositional and modal literals are given by $\mathsf{PL}(\mathsf{V}) = \bigcup\{p, \neg p \mid p \in \mathsf{V}\}$ and $\mathsf{ML}(\mathsf{V}) = \bigcup\{\Box p, \neg\Box p \mid p \in \mathsf{V}\}$, respectively. We denote the set of literals over V by $\mathsf{Lit}(\mathsf{V}) = \mathsf{PL}(\mathsf{V}) \cup \mathsf{ML}(\mathsf{V})$. Two literals are *disparate* if the variables that occur in them are different.

A *clause* is a finite disjunction of (propositional or modal) literals. We identify a clause with the set of its literals, and sometimes say that a literal is an element of a clause, or write $D_0 \subseteq D_1$ to indicate that clause D_0 is a subclause of D_1. In particular, we consider two clauses as equal if they have the same literals. A clause is *propositional* if all literals are propositional. We distinguish local clauses, written $l_1 \vee \cdots \vee l_n$, and *global clauses*, written $\mathsf{G}(l_1 \vee \cdots \vee l_n)$. We sometimes refer to formulae and clauses as *local formulae* or *local* clauses to emphasise the distinction to their global counterparts. We write $\mathsf{Cl}(\mathsf{V}) = \{l_1 \vee \cdots \vee l_n \mid l_1, \ldots, l_n \in \mathsf{Lit}(\mathsf{V})\}$ for the set of clauses with literals in $\mathsf{Lit}(\mathsf{V})$.

The following notion of truth distinguishes local and global clauses.

Definition 2. A *neighbourhood frame* is a pair (W, N) where W is a set (of worlds) and $N : W \to \mathcal{PP}(W)$ is a (neighbourhood) function where $\mathcal{P}(X)$ denotes the powerset of a set X. A *neighbourhood model* is a triple (W, N, θ) where (W, N) is a neighbourhood frame, and $\theta : \mathsf{V} \to \mathcal{P}(W)$ is a (valuation) function. We say that the model (W, N, θ) is *based* on the frame (W, N). Truth $w \models \phi$ of a formula ϕ at a world $w \in W$ is given by

$$w \models p \text{ iff } w \in \theta(p) \qquad\qquad w \models \neg\phi \text{ iff } w \not\models \phi$$
$$w \models \phi \vee \psi \text{ iff } w \models \phi \text{ or } w \models \psi \qquad\qquad w \models \Box\phi \text{ iff } [\![\phi]\!] \in N(w)$$

where $[\![\phi]\!] = \{w \in W \mid w \models \phi\}$ is the truth set of $\phi \in \mathcal{L}$. We occasionally write $M, w \models \phi$ or even $(M, N, \theta), w \models \phi$ if we want to emphasise the (carrier of) the model. This defines the interpretation of local formulae and clauses. For global formulae and clauses, we have $w \models \mathsf{G}(\phi)$ iff $w' \models \phi$ for all $w' \in W$. We use standard terminology, and write $(W, N, \theta) \models \phi$ if $(W, N, \theta), w \models \phi$ for all $w \in W$, and $(W, N) \models \phi$ if $(W, N, \theta) \models \phi$ for all $\theta : \mathsf{V} \to \mathcal{P}(W)$. If F is a class of neighbourhood frames, we write $\mathsf{F} \models \phi$ if $F \models \phi$ for all frames $F \in \mathsf{F}$. A formula ϕ is *satisfiable* in a class F of neighbourhood frames if there is a neighbourhood model (W, N, θ) with $(W, N) \in \mathsf{F}$, and $w \in W$ such that $(W, N, \theta), w \models \phi$; otherwise, ϕ is *unsatisfiable* in F. The notion of (un)satisfiability is extended as usual to sets of formulae.

It is standard that every formula can be converted to an equi-satisfiable set of global and local clauses in linear time.

Proposition 3 (Normal Form [20]**).** *Every (local or global) formula can be converted to an equisatisfiable set of (global and local) clauses.*

Proof. Let $\phi \in \mathcal{L}$ be a formula and $p \in \mathsf{V}$ be a fresh propositional variable (that does not occur in ϕ). We write $R(p \equiv \phi)$ for $R(p)(\phi)$ where the function $R : \mathsf{V} \to \mathcal{L} \to \mathsf{Cl}(\mathsf{V})$ is given by

$$\begin{aligned}
R(p \equiv \phi_1 \wedge \phi_2) &= R(p_1 \equiv \phi_1) \cup R(p_2 \equiv \phi_2) \cup \{\neg p \vee p_1, \neg p \vee p_2, \neg p_1 \vee \neg p_2 \vee p\} \\
R(p \equiv \phi_1 \vee \phi_2) &= R(p_1 \equiv \phi_1) \cup R(p_2 \equiv \phi_2) \cup \{\neg p \vee p_1 \vee p_2, \neg p_1 \vee p, \neg p_2 \vee p\} \\
R(p \equiv \Box\phi) &= R(q \equiv \phi) \cup \{\neg p \vee \Box q, \neg\Box q \vee p\} \\
R(p \equiv \neg\phi) &= R(q \equiv \phi) \cup \{\neg p \vee q, \neg q \vee p\}
\end{aligned}$$

where, in each of the clauses, p_1, p_2 and q are fresh. It is a routine induction to show that ϕ and $\{p\} \cup \{\mathsf{G}(D) \mid D \in R(p \equiv \phi)\}$ are equi-satisfiable when p does not occur in ϕ. The same holds for $\mathsf{G}(\phi)$ and $\{\mathsf{G}(p)\} \cup \{\mathsf{G}(D) \mid D \in R(p \equiv \phi)\}$. □

3 Non-iterative Logics and Their Calculi

Definition 4. A formula $\phi \in \mathcal{L}$ is *non-iterative* if, for every subformula $\Box\psi$ of ϕ, the formula ψ is purely propositional, i.e. does not contain a modal operator. If Ax is a set of (not necessarily non-iterative) formulae, then $\mathsf{Frm}(\mathsf{Ax})$ is the class of neighbourhood frames (W, N) so that $(W, N) \models \phi$ for all $\phi \in \mathsf{Ax}$.

A *rule* is an $n+1$-tuple $(\phi_1, \ldots, \phi_n, \phi_0)$, written as $\phi_1 \ldots \phi_n / \phi_0$ where the ϕ_i are formulae, and $\phi_1, \ldots, \phi_n$ are the premisses, and ϕ_0 is the *conclusion*. It is *non-iterative* if all the premisses are propositional clauses, and the conclusion is a (not necessarily propositional) clause. If Rl is a set of (not necessarily non-iterative) rules, then the class of $\mathsf{Frm}(\mathsf{Rl})$ is the class (W, N) of neighbourhood frames such that $(W, N, \theta) \models \phi_0$ whenever $(W, N, \theta) \models \phi_i$ (all $i = 1, \ldots, n$), for all $\theta : \mathsf{V} \to \mathcal{P}(W)$.

A set Ax of formulae (thought of as axioms) and a set Rl of rules are *equivalent* if they define the same frames, i.e. $\mathsf{Frm}(\mathsf{Ax}) = \mathsf{Frm}(\mathsf{Rl})$.

It is easy to convert between non-iterative rules and axioms [23].

Definition 5. We write $\mathsf{cnf}(\phi)$ for a (chosen) conjunctive normal form of a formula ϕ. The rules *induced* by the non-iterative axiom ϕ are the rules induced by the (non-iterative) clauses $\gamma_1, \ldots, \gamma_n$ that constitute the conjunctive normal form of ϕ, that is, $\mathsf{cnf}(\phi) = \gamma_1 \wedge \cdots \wedge \gamma_n$.

A non-iterative clause $\gamma = l_1 \vee \ldots \vee l_n \vee \heartsuit\phi_1 \vee \cdots \vee \heartsuit\phi_n$ induces the rule $\iota(\gamma) = \delta_1 \ldots \delta_k / l_1 \vee \cdots \vee l_n \vee \heartsuit p_1 \vee \cdots \vee \heartsuit p_n$ where $p_1, \ldots, p_n$ are pairwise distinct, fresh, propositional variables, $\heartsuit \in \{\Box, \neg\Box\}$ and $\delta_1 \wedge \cdots \wedge \delta_k$ is a conjunctive normal form of $(p_1 \leftrightarrow \phi_1) \wedge \cdots \wedge (p_n \leftrightarrow \phi_n)$.

If on the contrary, $\rho = \gamma_1 \ldots \gamma_n / \gamma_0$ is a non-iterative rule, the *axiom* induced by ρ is $\iota(\rho) = \gamma_0\sigma$ where σ is the most general unifier of $\gamma_1 \wedge \cdots \wedge \gamma_n$.

The above construction ensures that induced axioms and rules are equivalent in the sense of Definition 4.

Proposition 6. *Every set* Ax *of axioms is equivalent to the set of* $\bigcup\{\iota(\alpha) \mid \alpha \in \mathsf{Ax}\}$ *of induced rules, and every set* Rl *of non-iterative rules is equivalent to the set* $\{\iota(\rho) \mid \rho \in \mathsf{Rl}\}$ *of induced axioms.*

In examples, the situation is as follows.

Example 7. The classical modal logic E is defined by the empty set of (extra) axioms that induce an empty set of rules. The K-axiom $\Box(p \to q) \to (\Box p \to \Box q)$ induces the rule $\neg r \vee \neg p \vee q, p \vee r, \neg q \vee r / \neg\Box r \vee \neg\Box p \vee \Box q$. In the presence of the congruence rule, necessitation can be replaced by the axiom $\Box\top$ which gives the rule $p/\Box p$. One can show that the (simplified) set of rules $N = \{\neg p \vee \neg q \vee$

$r/\neg\Box p \vee \neg\Box q \vee \Box r; p/\Box p\}$, as well as the set $S = \{\neg p_1 \vee \cdots \vee \neg p_n \vee p_0/\neg\Box p_1 \vee \cdots \vee \neg\Box p_n \vee \Box p_0 \mid n \geq 0\}$ are equivalent to the K-axiom and $\Box\top$. We call N and S the *non-standard* and *standard* rules for K. As we are demonstrating in Example 19 the non-standard rules will not give us completeness as they are not cut-closed (Definition 20).

As our calculi apply to *all* non-iterative logics, we are parametric in a set of (non-iterative) rules. For a set Rl of rules, we define an *generative* calculus that adds new clauses with possibly new literals, and an *absorptive* variant, where clauses are combined and conflicting literals are removed.

Definition 8. Let Rl be a set of non-iterative rules. The rules

$$\frac{D \vee l \quad D' \vee \neg l}{D \vee D'} \qquad \frac{\mathsf{G}(D)}{D} \qquad \frac{\mathsf{G}(D \vee l) \quad \mathsf{G}(D' \vee \neg l)}{\mathsf{G}(D \vee D')} \qquad \frac{\neg p \vee q \quad p \vee \neg q}{\neg\Box p \vee \Box q}$$

are called *local resolution* (LR), the *global-local rule* (GL), *global resolution* (GR), and the *modal congruence rule* (MC), respectively. We write $\mathsf{Rl}^{\mathsf{C}} = \mathsf{Rl} \cup \{(\mathsf{MC})\}$ for the extension of Rl with the modal congruence rule.
The *generative calculus* given by Rl has the rules (GR), (GL), (LR) and all rules

$$\frac{\mathsf{G}(D_1^s) \quad \ldots \quad \mathsf{G}(D_n^s)}{\mathsf{G}(D_0)}$$

for which $D_1 \ldots D_n/D_0 \in \mathsf{Rl}^{\mathsf{C}}$ and $D_1^s, \ldots, D_n^s$ are subclauses of $D_1, \ldots, D_n$. The *absorptive calculus* defined by Rl has the rules (GR), (GL), (LR) and the rules

$$\frac{\mathsf{G}(D_1^s) \quad \ldots \quad \mathsf{G}(D_n^s) \quad \mathsf{G}(E_1 \vee \neg l_1) \quad \ldots \quad \mathsf{G}(E_k \vee \neg l_k)}{\mathsf{G}(E_1 \vee \cdots \vee E_k)}$$

$$\frac{\mathsf{G}(D_1^s) \quad \ldots \quad \mathsf{G}(D_n^s) \quad E_1 \vee \neg l_1 \quad \ldots \quad E_k \vee \neg l_k}{E_1 \vee \cdots \vee E_k}$$

where $D_1 \ldots D_n/D_0 \in \mathsf{Rl}^{\mathsf{C}}$ and $D_i^s \subseteq D_i$ is a subclause of D_i, for all $i = 1, \ldots, n$.
If Γ is a set of local and global clauses, we write $\Gamma \vdash_G$ (resp. $\Gamma \vdash_A$) for the least set of (local and global) clauses that contains Γ and is closed under all instances of the rules of generative (resp. absorptive) rules defined by Rl. We write $\Gamma \vdash_* \gamma$ if $\gamma \in \Gamma \vdash_*$ for $* = G, A$.

Generative and absorptive calculi serve a different purpose: we are going to prove semantic completeness for generative calculi, and then show that derivation in absorptive calculi can be translated to generative calculi, thus establishing completeness for absorptive calculi as well. In particular, we only consider notions like maximal consistency for generative calculi.

Example 9. The modal logic E just has the congruence rule. The generative and absorptive local version of the congruence rule are

$$(\mathsf{GC})\frac{\mathsf{G}(D_0) \quad \mathsf{G}(D_1)}{\mathsf{G}(\neg\Box p \vee \Box q)} \qquad (\mathsf{ACL})\frac{\mathsf{G}(D_0) \quad \mathsf{G}(D_1) \quad C_1 \vee \Box p \quad C_2 \vee \neg\Box q}{C_1 \vee C_2}$$

where $D_0 \subseteq \neg p \vee q$ and $D_1 \subseteq \neg q \vee p$ are subclauses. In the global version (ACG) of the absorptive rule, all clauses of the rightmost rule are under a global modality. For the standard rule set of modal K, the generative version looks like the sequent rule on the left

$$\frac{\mathsf{G}(D)}{\mathsf{G}(\neg\Box p_1 \vee \cdots \vee \neg\Box p_n \vee \Box p_0)} \qquad \frac{\mathsf{G}(D) \quad D_1 \vee \Box p_1 \quad \ldots \quad D_n \vee \Box p_n \quad D_0 \vee \neg\Box p_0}{D_1 \vee \cdots \vee D_n \vee D_0}$$

with the local absorptive rule on the right. Again $D \subseteq \neg p_1 \vee \cdots \vee p_n \vee p_0$ is a subclause, and all clauses are under a global modality in the global absorptive variant of the rule.

It is easy to see that both the generative and the absorptive calculus are sound.

Proposition 10 (Soundness). *Let* Rl *be a set of non-iterative rules. Then* $\Gamma \vdash_* \epsilon$ *for both* $* = G, A$ *only if* Γ *is unsatisfiable in the class* $\mathsf{Frm}(\mathsf{Rl})$ *of* Rl*-frames.*

Proof. We show that γ is satisfiable whenever Γ is by induction on $\Gamma \vdash_* \gamma$. □

In particular, if Rl is equivalent to a set Ax of non-iterative axioms, the calculus $\vdash_{\mathsf{Rl}}$ is sound with respect to $\mathsf{Frm}(\mathsf{Ax})$. We collect some elementary results on the calculi just introduced. The most important one is the trichotomy theorem for generative calculi:

Theorem 11 (Trichotomy). *Let* l *be a modal or propositional literal, and let* Φ *be a set of local and global clauses, and* D *a local clause with* $\Phi \cup \{l\} \vdash_G D$. *Then (1)* $D = l$ *or (2)* $\Phi \vdash_G D$ *or (3)* $\Phi \cup \{\neg l\} \vdash_G D$.

Proof. By induction on the proof of $\Phi \cup \{l\} \vdash_G D$. Note that the format of the rules guarantees us that $\Phi \vdash_G \mathsf{G}(D)$ whenever $\Phi \cup \{l\} \vdash_G \mathsf{G}(D)$, as rules with global conclusions only have global premisses. □

Remark 12. The trichotomy fails for absorptive calculi. Over the empty set of rules $\mathsf{Rl} = \emptyset$, i.e. for the modal logic E, consider $\Phi = \{\mathsf{G}(\neg p \vee q), \mathsf{G}(\neg q \vee p), \neg\Box q\}$. Then $\Phi \cup \{\Box p\} \vdash_A \epsilon$ but neither $\epsilon = \Box p$ nor $\Phi \vdash_A \epsilon$ or $\Phi \vdash_A \neg\Box p$ hold.

The trichotomy property is a stepping stone to prove negation completeness for maximally consistent sets. As trichotomy fails for absorptive calculi, negation completeness only holds for generative calculi, too.

Definition 13. Let G be a set of global clauses over a (finite or infinite) set V of variables, and let Φ be a set of local clauses over the same set of variables. Then Φ is G-*inconsistent* if $\mathsf{G} \cup \Phi \vdash_G \epsilon$, and G-*consistent*, otherwise. The set Φ is G-*maximally consistent* if Φ is G-consistent, and for every clause $D \in \mathsf{Cl}(\mathsf{V})$ with $D \notin \Phi$, we have that $\Phi \cup \{D\}$ is G-inconsistent.

Technically speaking, it would be more appropriate to speak of generatively (maximally) consistent sets, but we elide the qualifier 'generative' as we never consider these notions for absorptive calculi.

Lemma 14. *Let M be* G*-maximally consistent and l be a (propositional or modal) literal. Then $l \in M$ or $\neg l \in M$.*

Proof. If neither $l \in M$ nor $\neg l \in M$, then $M \cup \{l\} \vdash_G \epsilon$ and $M \cup \{\neg l\} \vdash_G \epsilon$. Using the trichotomy lemma, this entails that $M \vdash_G \epsilon$, contradiction to M being consistent. □

Moreover, this gives a characterisation of maximally consistent sets as given by a set of singleton clauses.

Lemma 15. *Let* G *be a set of global clauses over a set* V_0 *of propositional variables. Let $L \subset \mathsf{V}_0 \cup \{\Box p \mid p \in \mathsf{V}\}$ be a set of positive literals, and $L^{\neg} = L \cup \{\neg l \mid l \in \mathsf{Lit}(V_0) \setminus L\}$. Then there is a 1-1 correspondence*

$$\{M \mid M \text{ G-}\textit{maximally consistent}\} \xrightarrow{f} \{L \subseteq \mathsf{V}_0 \mid L^{\neg} \text{ G-}\textit{consistent}\}$$

given by $f(M) = M \cap \mathsf{Lit}(\mathsf{V}_0)$ from left to right, and $f^{-1}(L) = \{D \vee l \mid D \in \mathsf{Cl}(\mathsf{V}_0), l \in L^{\neg}\}$. Moreover, $\bigwedge M$ and $\bigwedge(f(M))$ are logically equivalent.

The trichotomy law also allows us to show a limited form of deductive completeness for propositional resolution which is known in the literature, consequence completeness [15], although our proof appears to be new. We state the theorem for the generative calculi of Definition 8. It evidently remains true for propositional resolution.

Lemma 16. *Let Φ be a set of local clauses, and let D be a local clause with pairwise disparate literals such that $\bigwedge \Phi \to D$ is a propositional tautology. Then there is a subclause $D_0 \subseteq D$ of D such that $\Phi \vdash_G D_0$.*

Proof. We use completeness of propositional resolution (which is the only rule applicable) and assume that $D = l_1 \vee \cdots \vee l_n$ with the l_i pairwise disparate. If $\bigwedge \Phi \to D$ is a tautology, then $\Phi \cup \{\neg l_1, \ldots, \neg l_n\}$ is unsatisfiable. By completeness of propositional resolution, $\Phi \cup \{\neg l_1, \ldots, \neg l_n\} \vdash_G \epsilon$. Repeated application of the trichotomy lemma yields a subclause $D_0 \subseteq D$ such that $\Phi \vdash_G D_0$. □

Remark 17. The above theorem fails without the assumption that the literals that occur in D are pairwise disparate. Take for example $\Phi = \emptyset$ and $D = q \vee \neg q$. Then clearly $\bigwedge \Phi \to q \vee \neg q$ is a tautology, but $\Phi \vdash_G q \vee \neg q$ is false. The reason is that repeated application of the trichotomy lemma fails: we have $\Phi \cup \{q\} \cup \{\neg q\} \vdash_G \bot$. Hence by trichotomy, either $\Phi \cup \{q\} \vdash_G \bot$, or $\Phi \cup \{q\} \vdash_G q$ as $\neg q = \epsilon$ is impossible. In the first case, we can apply trichotomy again. In the second, another application leaves the evident possibility that $q = q$.

4 Completeness

Throughout the section, we fix a set Rl of non-iterative rules. Our first goal is to show completeness for the generative calculus. That is, if Φ is a finite and consistent set of local and global clauses, then Φ is satisfiable in $\mathsf{Frm}(\mathsf{Rl})$.

As Φ is finite, only a finite number of variables will appear in (clauses in) Φ. Our construction has two stages. We start with a finite set V_0 of propositional variables. This allows us to consider maximally consistent sets of clauses over V_0. We then extend the language with new variables V_1. The purpose of these new variables is to give names to collections of maximally consistent sets. For example, for every maximally consistent set M, we will have a variable p_M such that $p_M = \bigwedge M$, and for a set S of maximally consistent sets, we add a variable with the interpretation $p_S = \bigvee_{M \in S} \bigwedge M$.

Definition 18. Let V_0 be a finite set of variables, and G_0 be a finite set of global clauses over variables in V_0. The *extension* of V_0 and G_0 are the sets V_1 of variables, and G_1 of global clauses where the set V_1 extends V_0 with

- a variable p_D for every clause D over V_0
- a variable p_M for every set M of clauses over V_0
- a variable p_S for every set of clause sets over V_0.

The set G_1 extends G_0 with the clauses $\mathsf{G}(E)$ where E is in one of the following:

- $\{\neg p_S \vee \bigvee_{M \in S} p_M\} \cup \{\neg p_M \vee p_S \mid M \in S\}$, to express that $p_S \leftrightarrow \bigvee_{M \in S} p_M$;
- $\{\bigvee_{D \in M} \neg p_D \vee p_M\} \cup \{\neg p_M \vee p_D \mid D \in M\}$, to express $p_M \leftrightarrow \bigwedge_{D \in M} p_D$;
- $\{\neg p_D \vee p_M\} \cup \{\neg l \vee p_D \mid l \in D\}$, to express that $p_D \leftrightarrow D$.

We let $W_i = \{M \subseteq \mathsf{Cl}(\mathsf{V}_i) \mid M\ \mathsf{G}_0\text{-maximally consistent}\}$, defining two sets of maximally consistent sets of clauses: W_0 are clauses over the original variables V_0 and W_1 are maximally consistent sets over the extended language.

To define the structure of the canonical model, we would like to extend every G_0-maximally consistent set M to a G_1-maximally consistent set $\hat{M}$, and define $N_0(M) = \{S \subseteq W_0 \mid \Box p_S \in \hat{M}\}$. While this will allow us to establish that the frame conditions (defined by the rules of the calculus) hold, it is not true that every G_0-consistent set is G_1-consistent.

Example 19. Let $\mathsf{V}_0 = \{p, q, r, s\}$ and consider generative rules corresponding to the nonstandard rules for K from Example 7, that is

$$\frac{\mathsf{G}(D)}{\mathsf{G}(\neg\Box p \vee \neg\Box q \vee \Box r)}(D \subseteq \neg p \vee \neg q \vee r) \qquad \frac{\mathsf{G}(D)}{\mathsf{G}(\Box p)}(D \subseteq p)$$

Consider the set $\mathsf{G}_0 = \{\neg p \vee \neg q \vee \neg r \vee s\}$ and let $H = \{\Box p, \Box q, \Box r, \neg\Box s\}$. Then H is G_0-consistent (no resolution rule can be applied), but it is not G_1-consistent. If $S = \{M \in W_0 \mid \{p, q\} \subseteq M\}$, then p_S is equivalent to $p \wedge q$ under G_1. Hence we have that $\mathsf{G}_1 \vdash_G \mathsf{G}(\neg p \vee \neg q \vee p_S)$, and also $\mathsf{G}_1 \vdash_G \mathsf{G}(\neg p_S \vee \neg r \vee\ s)$. Applying the K-rule to both, we obtain $\mathsf{G}(\neg\Box p \vee \neg\Box q \vee \Box p_S)$ and $\mathsf{G}(\neg\Box p_S \vee \neg\Box r \vee \Box s)$. Applying resolution, and converting to a local clause, we have that $\mathsf{G}_1 \vdash_G \neg\Box p \vee \neg\Box q \vee \neg\Box r \vee \Box s$ so that H is clearly G_1-inconsistent.

The key here is that in G_1 we have more propositional variables and defining axioms that allow us to make more modal deductions. The crucial point in the above example is that we could apply the modal rule in two different ways, and the apply cut to the rule conclusions. Had we chosen the standard rules for K, i.e. $\neg p_1 \vee \cdots \vee \neg p_n \vee p_0 / \neg\Box p_1 \vee \cdots \vee \neg\Box p_n \vee \Box p_0$ for all $n \geq 0$, the above set H would not have been G_0-consistent. The requirement of *cut-closure* addresses this problem, and also ensures that G_0-consistency implies G_1-consistency.

Definition 20. Let Rl be a set of non-iterative rules. Then Rl is *cut-closed* if, for any two instances on the left

$$\frac{D_1 \vee \cdots \vee D_n}{l \vee D_0} \quad \frac{E_1 \vee \cdots \vee E_m}{\neg l \vee E_0} \qquad \rightsquigarrow \qquad \frac{F_1 \vee \cdots \vee F_k}{D_0 \vee E_0}$$

there exists a rule instance in Rl (on the right) such that $\{D_1,\ldots,D_n,E_1,\ldots,E_m\} \vdash F_i$ in propositional resolution for all $i = 1, \ldots, k$.

Clearly, the paradigmatic example is the rule set of K.

Example 21. The nonstandard set of rules for K from Example 7 is not cut-closed: a cut between two instances of the binary K-rule gives a conclusion of the form $\neg\Box p \vee \neg\Box q \vee \neg\Box r \vee \neg\Box t$ which is clearly not an instance of any of the rules. We therefore need to generalise the rule to $\neg p_1 \vee \cdots \vee \neg p_n \vee p_0 / \neg\Box p_1 \vee \cdots \vee \neg\Box p_n \vee \Box p_0$, i.e. the standard set of rules is cut-closed.

Crucially, cut-closed sets guarantee preservation of consistency.

Lemma 22. *Let* Rl *be a cut-closed set of non-iterative rules, and let* G_0 *and* G_1 *be as in Definition 18. Then every* G_0*-consistent set is* G_1*-consistent.*

Proof. We use the fact that resolution is confluent, i.e. that we can change the order of resolution steps *ad libitum*. That is, given clauses $D \vee l_1 \vee l_2$, $\neg l_1 \vee E_1$ and $\neg l_2 \vee E_2$, we can resolve with $\neg l_1 \vee E_1$ first (to obtain $D \vee E_1 \vee l_2$) and then resolve with $\neg l_2 \vee E_2$ to get $D \vee E_1 \vee E_2$, which we also obtain if we change the order of resolution steps.

Now assume that H is G_0-consistent, but G_1-inconsistent. Then the derivation of ϵ from $\mathsf{G}_1 \cup H$ needs to contain a modal rule, as the extension G_1 of G_0 is purely definitional.

Using the confluence property of resolution, we may permute resolution steps so that cuts between conclusions of modal rules are performed first. Using cut-closure, we can replace modal rules, and the cuts between their conclusions, by a single modal rule. We now claim that the ensuing proof is already a proof in G_0. This follows, as we can establish by induction that every proof that uses at least one G_1-axiom (with variables in $\mathsf{V}_1 \backslash \mathsf{V}_0$) has a clause with at least one variable in $\mathsf{V}_0 \backslash \mathsf{V}_1$ as a conclusion. □

Definition 23 (Canonical Model). In the terminology of the previous definition and now assuming that Rl is cut-closed, for $M \in W_0$, let $\hat{M} \in W_1$ be a maximally consistent extension of M, that is, we require that $M \subseteq \hat{M}$.

The *canonical model* over the set G_0 of global clauses and V_0 of variables is $\mathbb{M} = (W_0, N_0, \theta_0)$ where $\theta_0(p) = \{M \in W_0 \mid p \in M\}$ and $N_0(M) = \{S \subseteq W_0 \mid \Box p_S \in \hat{M}\}$.

In the sequel, we fix V_0 and G_0 and speak of *the* canonical model. Maximally consistent sets are closed under resolution:

Lemma 24. *Let* G *be a set of global clauses, and let* M *be a* G*-maximally consistent set. Then* $D \in M \iff M \vdash_G D$ *and* $D_1 \vee D_2 \in M$ *whenever both* $D_1 \vee \neg l$ *and* $D_2 \vee l \in M$.

Proof. The second item is immediate from the first. Assume for a contradiction that $M \vdash_G D$ but $D \notin M$. If $D = l_1 \vee \cdots \vee l_n$, then $\neg l_1, \ldots, \neg l_n \in M$. But then $M \vdash_G \epsilon$, contradicting the consistency of M. □

The truth lemma requires us to establish the premisses of the modal rules. This is split into two lemmas.

Lemma 25. *Let* $q \in \mathsf{V}_0$ *and let* $S = [\![q]\!] = \{M \in W_0 \mid q \in M\}$. *Then* $\mathsf{G}_1 \vdash_G \mathsf{G}(\neg p_S \vee q)$.

Proof. We have that $\mathsf{G}_1 \vdash_G \mathsf{G}(\neg p_M \vee p_q)$ for all $M \in S$ by definition of S. We also have $\mathsf{G}_1 \vdash_G \mathsf{G}(\neg p_S \vee \bigvee_{M \in S} p_M)$. By propositional resolution, we have $\mathsf{G}_1 \vdash_G \mathsf{G}(\neg p_S \vee p_q)$. As we also have $\mathsf{G}(\neg p_q \vee q) \in \mathsf{G}_1$ by construction, we apply resolution again to obtain $\mathsf{G}_1 \vdash_G \mathsf{G}(\neg p_S \vee q)$. □

The reverse implication is more difficult, and we need the following which essentially capitalises on the fact that all our rules with global conclusions have global premisses only.

Lemma and Definition 26. *Let* G *be a set of global clauses. The* global closure *of* G *is the set* $\mathsf{G}^G = \{\mathsf{G}(D) \mid \mathsf{G} \vdash_G \mathsf{G}(D)\}$ *of global clauses that are derivable from* D. *The* boundary *of* G *is the set* $\mathsf{G}^B = \{D \mid \mathsf{G}(D) \in \mathsf{G}^G\}$ *of local clauses that are derived from their global counterpart. With this terminology,* $\mathsf{G}^B = \{D \mid \mathsf{G} \vdash_G D\}$.

Proof. This is immediate from the shape of the rules, as there are no rules with local premisses and global conclusions. It can be proved straightforwardly using induction on the derivation of $\mathsf{G} \vdash_G D$. □

Lemma 27. *Let* G *be a set of global clauses, and suppose that* $\mathsf{G} \vdash_G D$, *for a local clause* D. *Then also* $\mathsf{G} \vdash_G \mathsf{G}(D)$.

Proof. By induction on the derivation of D. More precisely, we show that if $\mathsf{G} \vdash_G C$, for a local or global clause C, then $\mathsf{G} \vdash_G C_0$, where $C_0 = C$ if C is global, and $C_0 = \mathsf{G}(C)$, if C is local. The key here is that all rules that only deal with local clauses (propositional resolution) have a global counterpart. □

The following is the companion to Lemma 25.

Lemma 28. *Let* $q \in \mathsf{V}_0$ *and let* $S = [\![q]\!] = \{M \in W_0 \mid q \in M\}$. *Then* $\mathsf{G}_1 \vdash_G \mathsf{G}(D)$, *for a subclause* $D \subseteq \neg q \vee p_S$.

Proof. The formula $q \to \bigvee\{\bigwedge L^{\neg} \mid q \in L \subseteq \mathsf{V}_0\}$ is a tautology. As any G_1-inconsistent set is inconsistent with G_1^B, the same applies to $q \wedge \mathsf{G}_1^B \to \bigvee\{\bigwedge L^{\neg} \mid q \in L \subseteq \mathsf{V}_0 \mathsf{G}_1\text{-consistent}\}$. By Lemma 15 we get that $q \wedge \mathsf{G}_1^B \to \bigvee\{\bigwedge M \mid q \in M \in W_0\}$. As p_S is equivalent to the last disjunction under G_1^B, we finally obtain that $q \wedge \mathsf{G}_1^B \to p_S$ is a tautology. Lemma 26 then yields the claim. □

This gives us enough ammunition to establish the truth lemma:

Lemma 29 (Truth Lemma). *In the canonical model, we have $D \in M \iff M \models D$, for all $M \in W_1$ and all local clauses D over V_0.*

Proof. By Lemma 14 we just need to show the claim for singleton clauses. For propositional literals, this is immediate from the definition of the valuation θ: we have $M \models p$ iff $M \in \theta(p)$ iff $p \in M$. For the modal case, we have to show that $\Box q \in M$ iff $\Box p_S \in \hat{M}$ where $S = [\![q]\!] = \{M \in W_0 \mid q \in M\}$.

By Lemma 25 and Lemma 28, we have that $\mathsf{G}_1 \vdash_G \mathsf{G}(D_0)$ and $\mathsf{G}_1 \vdash_G \mathsf{G}(D_1)$, where D_0 is a subclause of $\neg p_S \vee q$ and D_1 is a subclause of $\neg q \vee p_S$. The modal rule allows us to conclude that $\mathsf{G}_1 \vdash_G \mathsf{G}(\neg\Box p_s \vee \Box q)$ as well as $\mathsf{G}(\neg\Box q \vee \Box p_s)$.

We can now argue that $\Box q \in M$ iff $\Box q \in \hat{M}$ (as M is G_0-maximally consistent and $M \subseteq \hat{M}$) iff $\Box p_S \in \hat{M}$ (by resolving with the derivable clauses $\neg\Box p_s \vee \Box q$ and $\neg\Box q \vee \Box p_s$). □

For completeness, we still need to establish that the canonical model satisfies all axioms in A. We use Lemma 15.

Lemma 30. *Let (W_0, N_0) be the frame of the canonical modal, and let $\theta : \mathsf{V} \to \mathcal{P}(W_0)$ be* any *valuation. Moreover, let D be a local propositional clause such that $(W_0, N_0, \theta) \models D$. Then there is a subclause $D_0 \subseteq D$ of D such that $\mathsf{G}_1 \vdash_G \mathsf{G}(D_0\sigma)$ where $\sigma(q) = p_{\theta(q)}$.*

Proof. This is similar in spirit to the proof of Lemma 28. We know that $\top \to \bigvee\{\bigwedge L^{\neg} \mid L \subseteq \mathsf{V}_0\}$ is a tautology. As every G_0-inconsistent set is inconsistent with the boundary G_1^B, we obtain that $\mathsf{G}_1^B \to \{\bigwedge L^{\neg} \mid q \in L \subseteq \mathsf{V}_0\ \mathsf{G}_0\text{-inconsistent}\}$. Using Lemma 15, we may replace $L^{\neg}$ with maximally consistent sets, i.e. $\mathsf{G}_1^B \to \bigvee\{\bigwedge M \mid M \in W_0\}$ is a tautology. As $(W_0, N_0, \theta) \models D$, any maximally consistent $M \in W_0$ is either an element of $\theta(q)$ for $q \in D$, or an element of $W_0 \setminus \theta(q)$, for $\neg q \in D$. As p_S is equivalent to $\bigvee\{M \mid M \in S\}$ under G_1^B, we obtain that $\{\mathsf{G}_1^B \to \bigvee p_{\theta(q)} \mid q \in D\} \vee \bigvee\{\neg p_{\theta(q)} \mid \neg q \in D\}$ are tautologies, which entails the claim as in Lemma 28. □

The previous lemma has shown that we can derive the substituted premiss of a rule in A. The next lemma shows that derivability of the substituted conclusion turns into semantic validity in the canonical model.

Lemma 31. *In the canonical model, for $M \in W_0$ and $S \subseteq W_0$, we have that $p_S \in \hat{M} \iff M \in S$ and $\Box p_S \in \hat{M} \iff S \in N_0(M)$.*

This allows us to show that the canonical model is in the right frame class.

Lemma 32. *Let* Ax *be a set of non-iterative axioms and* Rl *an equivalent set of rules. Then* $\mathbb{M} \in \mathsf{Frm}(A)$ *for the canonical model* $\mathbb{M}$ *given by* Rl.

Proof. Let θ be *any* valuation, and let π/γ be a rule in Rl such that $(W_0, N_0, \theta) \models \pi$. We show that $(W_0, N_0, \theta) \models \gamma$, and the result follows from Lemma 15. Assuming that $\pi = D_1 \dots D_n$, the previous lemma gives us subclauses $D_i^s \subseteq D_i$ such that $\mathsf{G}_1 \vdash_G \mathsf{G}(D_i^s \sigma)$ where $\sigma(q) = p_{\theta(q)}$. Applying the rule $\pi/\gamma \in A$, this gives $\mathsf{G}_1 \vdash_G \mathsf{G}(D_0 \sigma)$ where $D_0 = \gamma$ is the conclusion of the rule π/γ. Let $M \in W_0$, and showing that $(W_0, N_0, \theta), M \models D_0$ implies the claim. As $\hat{M}$ is maximally consistent, there is a literal $l \in D_0 \sigma$ with $l \in \hat{M}$. It follows from Lemma 31 that $(W_0, N_0, \theta) \models l$, hence $(W_0, N_0, \theta) \models D_0$. As $D_0 = \gamma$ was the conclusion of the rule π/γ, this is all we had to show. □

Finally:

Theorem 33 (Generative Completeness). *Let* Φ *be a set of local and global clauses, and let* Rl *be a set of non-iterative, cut-closed rules. If* Φ *is unsatisfiable in* $\mathsf{Frm}(\mathsf{Rl})$, *then* $\Phi \vdash_G \epsilon$.

Proof. As usual, by contraposition: Let G_0 denote the global clauses of Φ, and let M be a maximally G-consistent set that contains all the local clauses of Φ. In the canonical model, we have that $M \models \phi$ for all $\phi \in \Phi$, so Φ is satisfiable. By the last lemma, we have $\mathbb{M} \in \mathsf{Frm}(A)$ so that Φ is satisfiable in $\mathsf{Frm}(A)$. □

The criticism of generative calculi is that they are not very "resolution-like". In particular, the "spirit" of resolution is the removal of conflicting literals, i.e. the absorptive calculi. We now show that both are equivalent.

Lemma 34. *Suppose that* Φ *is a set of local or global clauses, and assume that* $\Phi \vdash_G \epsilon$. *Then* $\Phi \vdash_A \epsilon$ *whenever* $\vdash_G$ *and* $\vdash_A$ *are induced by a cut-closed set of rules.*

Proof. We demonstrate how to successively replace a generative instance of a rule in Rl^C by an absorptive one. If the derivation $\Phi \vdash_G \epsilon$ contains an instance of a modal rule (or the congruence rule), assume that there is no other modal rule further below. As the derivation ends in ϵ, every literal must either be resolved against the conclusion of a modal rule (in which case, we can use cut-closure to replace the two rule instances with a new one), or it must be resolved against a clause that is not. Successively applying cut-closure, we are left with just the second case, i.e. with a proof tree of the following form if the last clause is local:

$$\cfrac{\cfrac{\cfrac{\cfrac{\cfrac{\mathsf{G}(D_1^s) \quad \dots \quad \mathsf{G}(D_n^s)}{\mathsf{G}(l_1 \vee \dots \vee l_n)}}{l_1 \vee \dots \vee l_n} \qquad \neg l_1 \vee E_1}{E_1 \vee l_2 \dots \vee l_n} \qquad \neg l_2 \vee E_2}{\ddots}}{E_1 \vee \dots \vee E_n}$$

This proof tree can be replaced by its absorptive variant, i.e. the rule instance

$$\frac{\mathsf{G}(D_1^s) \quad \dots \quad \mathsf{G}(D_n^s) \quad \neg l_1 \vee E_1 \quad \dots \quad \neg l_n \vee E_n}{E_1 \vee \dots \vee E_n}$$

thus reducing the number of applications of generative rules by one. If the conclusion of the cascade of cuts is global, we use the global variant of the absorptive rule instead. □

This gives us completeness for the absorptive calculus, too.

Theorem 35 (Absorptive Completeness). *Let Φ be a set of local and global clauses, and let* Rl *be a set of cut-closed, non-iterative rules. If Φ is unsatisfiable in* $\mathsf{Frm}(A)$, *then $\Phi \vdash_A \epsilon$.*

Using Lewis' theorem, i.e. completeness of a Hilbert system for non-iterative axioms over the class of neighbourhood frames defined by the axioms, we can now also close the loop between syntactically defined logics, and their resolution systems.

Theorem 36. *Let* Ax *be a set of non-iterative axioms, and let* Rl *be a cut-closed, equivalent set of rules. If $\vdash_H \phi$ is the provability predicate in the Hilbert system given by* Ax, *and Φ is the result of translating ϕ into an equisatisfiable set of clauses, then $\vdash_H \phi \to \bot$ iff $\Phi \vdash_A \epsilon$ iff $\Phi \vdash_G \epsilon$ iff ϕ is unsatisfiable in* $\mathsf{Frm}(\mathsf{Ax})$.

Proof. Lewis [16] shows completeness of $\vdash_H$ with respect to $\mathsf{Frm}(\mathsf{Ax})$, and we apply Theorem 35 and Theorem 33. □

The task of finding a complete resolution calculus then boils down to exhibiting a cut-closed set of rules for a given modal logic. We demonstrate this using the example of functional roles in description logic, and role inclusions [5].

Example 37. We consider a modal logic with two normal operators, □ and ■. In description logic parlance, they correspond to two different roles. We assume that the role corresponding to ■ is functional ($R(i,j) \wedge R(i,k) \to j = k$). Axiomatically, this means that ■ is a K-modality and additionally satisfies $\blacklozenge p \wedge \blacklozenge q \to \blacklozenge(p \wedge q)$. The second modality, □, just satisfies the K-axioms. A role inclusion is expressed using a transfer axiom $\Box p \to \blacksquare p$. While the natural semantics here are Kripke frames (with two relations, the first functional, and a subset of the second), the semantics in terms of neighbourhood frames (with two neighbourhood functions) is equivalent (for weak completeness).

1. The axiom of functionality is equivalent to the rule

$$\frac{\neg p \vee q \vee r}{\neg \blacksquare p \vee \blacksquare q \vee \blacksquare r} \qquad \frac{\neg p_0 \vee p_1 \vee \dots \vee p_n}{\neg \blacksquare p_0 \vee \blacksquare p_1 \vee \dots \vee \blacksquare p_n}$$

which readily generalises to the rule scheme (for $n \geq 1$) above. Note that the rule $p/\blacklozenge p$ is not an instance of functionality. Cuts between the conclusion of the K-rule and the above scheme yield the rule

$$(\dagger_1)\frac{\neg a_1 \vee \dots \vee \neg a_n \vee b_1 \vee \dots \vee b_k}{\neg \blacksquare a_1 \vee \dots \vee \neg \blacksquare a_n \vee \blacksquare b_1 \vee \dots \vee \blacksquare b_k}$$

where $n \geq 0$ and $k \geq 1$. It is easy to see that this set is cut-closed.

2. The rule for the K-modality $\Box$ in Example 19, that is

$$(\dagger_2)\frac{\neg a_1 \vee \cdots \vee \neg a_n \vee a_0}{\neg\Box a_1 \vee \cdots \vee \neg\Box a_n \vee \Box a_0}$$

is already cut-closed.

3. To incorporate the role inclusion axiom $\Box p \to \blacksquare p$, we need to modify the above rules by resolving their conclusions with the axiom $\neg\Box p \vee \blacksquare p$. This changes the above rules to

$$(\dagger_3)\frac{\neg a_1 \vee \cdots \vee \neg a_n \vee b_1 \vee \cdots \vee b_k}{\neg \bigcirc a_1 \vee \cdots \vee \neg \bigcirc a_n \vee \blacksquare b_1 \vee \cdots \vee \blacksquare b_k}$$

where n, k are as above and $\bigcirc \in \{\Box, \blacksquare\}$, and

$$(\dagger_4)\frac{\neg a_1 \vee \cdots \vee \neg a_n \vee a_0}{\neg\Box a_1 \vee \cdots \vee \neg\Box a_n \vee \bigcirc a_0}$$

where $\bigcirc \in \{\Box, \blacksquare\}$. To this, we add the axiom as a rule without premiss, viz

$$(\dagger_5)\frac{}{\neg\Box p \vee \blacksquare q}$$

4. One now checks that the rules $(\dagger_3)$, $(\dagger_4)$ and $(\dagger_5)$ together are cut-closed and equivalent to the respective axioms. This means that we can apply Theorem 36 to obtain a complete resolution calculus.

5 Conclusion and Further Work

We have given a general method to construct complete resolution calculi for the class of all non-iterative modal logics. In doing so, we have defined, for each logic, a generative and an absorptive calculus that can be translated into one another. Conceptually, the generative calculus can be seen as a stripped-down sequent calculus that only consists of the modal rule and the cut rules, and we have proved completeness for this calculus, under the same condition, *cut-closure*, that would also give rise to cut elimination in a sequent calculus. The naive method to convert a sequent calculus to resolution (elide all propositional rules and just keep cut and the modal rules) is bound to fail. For example, consider the clauses (viewed as sequents) $\Phi = \{p, \Box p, \neg\Box q, \neg p \vee q\}$. With sequents in Φ as additional axioms in the sequent calculus for the modal logic E, we can derive the empty sequent (clause) using just cut, weakening and the congruence rule. However, Φ is evidently satisfiable in the class of neighbourhood frames: we need a world that validates both p and q, where p and q have different truth sets in the model, and stipulate the truth set of p to be the only neighbourhood. The reason is that proving $\bot$ in a sequent calculus with additional assumptions Φ, means that $\bot$ is valid in all models that satisfy Φ *globally* whereas the notion of consistency of interest in modal logic is *local*. *A fortiori*, this is the reason why we needed to distinguish between local and global clauses in the calculus we have given. This points to a deeper question on the relationship between sequent calculi and resolution systems. Can we just take *any* cut-free sequent calculus and turn it into a resolution system (with a suitable notion of global clause)? Can we use more liberal notions of cut-closure? Is there a purely syntactic way to translate between sequent calculi and resolution systems? Can we use this to lift the restriction to non-iterative axioms? Can we employ a more general notion of cut-closure, e.g. as in [21] which would immediately give resolution calculi for several conditional logics? We plan on discussing these questions in further work.

Acknowledgments. This research was partially supported by a gift from Northrop Grumman Corporation.

Disclosure of Interests. The authors have no competing interests to declare that are relevant to the content of this article.

References

1. Abadi, M., Manna, Z.: Modal theorem proving. In: Siekmann, J.H. (ed.) CADE 1986. LNCS, vol. 230, pp. 172–189. Springer, Heidelberg (1986). https://doi.org/10.1007/3-540-16780-3_89
2. Areces, C., de Nivelle, H., de Rijke, M.: Prefixed resolution: a resolution method for modal and description logics. In: CADE 1999. LNCS (LNAI), vol. 1632, pp. 187–201. Springer, Heidelberg (1999). https://doi.org/10.1007/3-540-48660-7_13
3. Auffray, Y.: Linear strategy for propositional modal resolution. Inf. Process. Lett. **28**(2), 87–92 (1988)
4. Avron, A.: Gentzen-type systems, resolution and tableaux. J. Autom. Reason. **10**(2), 265–281 (1993)
5. Baader, F., Calvanese, D., McGuinness, D., Nardi, D., Patel-Schneider, P. (eds.): The Description Logic Handbook: Theory, Implementation, and Applications. Cambridge University Press, Cambridge (2003)
6. Blackburn, P., de Rijke, M., Venema, Y.: Modal Logic. Cambridge University Press, Cambridge (2001)
7. Chan, M.-C.: The recursive resolution method for modal logic. N. Gener. Comput. **5**, 155–183 (1987)
8. Chellas, B.: Modal Logic. Cambridge (1980)
9. del Cerro, L.F.: A simple deduction method for modal logic. Inf. Process. Lett. **14**(2), 49–51 (1982)
10. Dowek, G.: Axioms vs. rewrite rules: from completeness to cut elimination. In: Kirchner, H., Ringeissen, C. (eds.) FroCoS 2000. LNCS (LNAI), vol. 1794, pp. 62–72. Springer, Heidelberg (2000). https://doi.org/10.1007/10720084_5
11. Elgesem, D.: The modal logic of agency. Nord. J. Philos. Log. **2**, 1–46 (1997)
12. Enjalbert, P., del Cerro, L.F.: Modal resolution in clausal form. Theoret. Comput. Sci. **65**, 1–33 (1989)
13. Fine, K.: In so many possible worlds. Notre Dame J. Formal Logic **13**(4), 516–520 (1972)
14. Heifetz, A., Mongin, P.: Probabilistic logic for type spaces. Games Econom. Behav. **35**, 31–53 (2001)

15. Lee, R.C.T.: A completeness theorem and computer program for finding theorems derivable from given axioms. Ph.D. thesis, Berkeley (1967)
16. Lewis, D.: Intensional logics without interative axioms. J. Philos. Log. **3**(4), 457–466 (1974)
17. Mints, G.: Gentzen-type systems and resolution rules part I propositional logic. In: Martin-Löf, P., Mints, G. (eds.) COLOG 1988. LNCS, vol. 417, pp. 198–231. Springer, Heidelberg (1990). https://doi.org/10.1007/3-540-52335-9_55
18. Nalon, C., Dixon, C.: Clausal resolution for normal modal logics. J. Algorithms **62**, 117–134 (2007)
19. Olivetti, N., Pozzato, G.L., Schwind, C.B.: A sequent calculus and a theorem prover for standard conditional logics. ACM Trans. Comput. Logic **8**(4) (2007)
20. Pattinson, D., Olivetti, N., Nalon, C.: Resolution calculi for non-normal modal logics. In: Ramanayake, R., Urban, J. (eds.) TABLEAUX 2023. LNCS, vol. 14278, pp. 322–341. Springer, Cham (2023). https://doi.org/10.1007/978-3-031-43513-3_18
21. Pattinson, D., Schröder, L.: Generic modal cut elimination applied to conditional logics. In: Giese, M., Waaler, A. (eds.) TABLEAUX 2009. LNCS (LNAI), vol. 5607, pp. 280–294. Springer, Heidelberg (2009). https://doi.org/10.1007/978-3-642-02716-1_21
22. Pauly, M.: A modal logic for coalitional power in games. J. Logic Comput. **12**(1), 149–166 (2002)
23. Schröder, L.: A finite model construction for coalgebraic modal logic. In: Aceto, L., Ingólfsdóttir, A. (eds.) FoSSaCS 2006. LNCS, vol. 3921, pp. 157–171. Springer, Heidelberg (2006). https://doi.org/10.1007/11690634_11
24. Straßer, C.: A deontic logic framework allowing for factual detachment. J. Appl. Log. **9**, 61–80 (2011)

A Logic for Repair and State Recovery in Byzantine Fault-Tolerant Multi-agent Systems

Hans van Ditmarsch[1], Krisztina Fruzsa[2], Roman Kuznets[2](✉), and Ulrich Schmid[2]

[1] CNRS, University of Toulouse, IRIT, Toulouse, France
[2] Embedded Computing Systems Group, TU Wien, Vienna, Austria
krisztina.fruzsa@tuwien.ac.at, {rkuznets,s}@ecs.tuwien.ac.at

Abstract. We provide novel epistemic logical language and semantics for modeling and analysis of byzantine fault-tolerant multi-agent systems, with the intent of not only facilitating reasoning about the agents' fault status but also supporting model updates for repair and state recovery. Besides the standard knowledge modalities, our logic provides additional agent-specific hope modalities capable of expressing that an agent is not faulty, and also dynamic modalities enabling change to the agents' correctness status. These dynamic modalities are interpreted as model updates that come in three flavors: fully public, more private, and/or involving factual change. Tailored examples demonstrate the utility and flexibility of our logic for modeling a wide range of fault-detection, isolation, and recovery (FDIR) approaches in mission-critical distributed systems. By providing complete axiomatizations for all variants of our logic, we also create a foundation for building future verification tools for this important class of fault-tolerant applications.

Keywords: byzantine fault-tolerant distributed systems · FDIR · multi-agent systems · modal logic

1 Introduction and Overview

State of the Art. A few years ago, the standard epistemic analysis of distributed systems via the runs-and-systems framework [13,18,28] was finally extended [22–24] to fault-tolerant systems with (fully) *byzantine* agents [25]. Byzantine agents constitute the worst-case scenario in terms of fault-tolerance: not only can they arbitrarily deviate from their respective protocols, but the perception of their own actions and observed events can be corrupted, possibly unbeknownst to them, resulting in false memories. Whether byzantine agents are actually present

K. Fruzsa—Was a PhD student in the FWF doctoral program LogiCS (W1255) and also supported by the FWF project DMAC [10.55776/P32431].
R. Kuznets—Funded by the FWF ByzDEL project [10.55776/P33600].

C. Benzmüller et al. (Eds.): IJCAR 2024, LNAI 14740, pp. 114–134, 2024.
https://doi.org/10.1007/978-3-031-63501-4_7

in a system, the very possibility of their presence has drastic and debilitating effects on the epistemic state of all agents, including the correct (i.e., non-faulty) ones, due to the inability to rule out so-called *brain-in-a-vat* scenarios [29]: a brain-in-a-vat agent is a faulty agent with completely corrupted perceptions that provide no reliable information about the system [23]. In such a system, *no* agent can ever know certain elementary facts, such as their own or some other agent's correctness, no matter whether the system is asynchronous [23] or synchronous [34]. Agents can, however, sometimes know their own faultiness or obtain belief in some other agents' faultiness [33].

In light of knowledge $K_i\varphi$ often being unachievable in systems with byzantine agents, [23] also introduced a weaker epistemic notion called *hope*. It was initially defined as $H_i\varphi := correct_i \to K_i(correct_i \to \varphi)$, where the designated atom $correct_i$ represents agent i's correctness. In this setting, one can define belief as $B_i\varphi := K_i(correct_i \to \varphi)$ [33]. Hope was successfully used in [15] to analyze the *Firing Rebels with Relay* (FRR) problem, which is the core of the well-known *consistent broadcasting* primitive [36]. Consistent broadcasting has been used as a pivotal building block in fault-tolerant distributed algorithms, e.g., for byzantine fault-tolerant clock synchronization [10,16,31,36,39], synchronous consensus [37], and as a general reduction of distributed task solvability in systems with byzantine failures to solvability in systems with crash failures [26].

The hope modality was first axiomatized in [14] using $correct_i$ as designated atoms. Whereas the resulting logic turned out to be well-suited for modeling and analyzing problems in byzantine fault-tolerant distributed computing systems like FRR [15], it is unfortunately not normal. Our long-term goal of also creating the foundations for *automated* verification of such applications hence suggested to look for an alternative axiomatization. In [6], we presented a normal modal logic that combines $\mathsf{KB4}_n$ hope modalities with $\mathsf{S5}_n$ knowledge modalities, which is based on defining $correct_i := \neg H_i\bot$ via frame-characterizable axioms. This logic indeed unlocks powerful techniques developed for normal modal logics both in model checkers like DEMO [11] or MCK [17] and, in particular, in epistemic theorem proving environments such as LWB [20].

Still, both versions [6,14] of the logic of hope target byzantine fault-tolerant distributed systems only where, once faulty, agents remain faulty and cannot be "repaired" to become correct again. Indeed, solutions for problems like FRR employ *fault-masking techniques* based on replication [35], which prevent the adverse effects of the faulty agents from contaminating the behavior of the correct agents but do not attempt to change the behavior of the faulty agents. Unfortunately, fault masking is only feasible if no more than a certain fraction f of the overall n agents in the system may become faulty (e.g., $n \geq 3f + 1$ in the case of FRR). Should it ever happen that more than f agents become faulty in a run, no properties can typically be guaranteed anymore, which would be devastating in mission-critical applications.

Fault-detection, isolation, and recovery (FDIR) is an alternative fault-tolerance technique, which attempts to discover and repair agents that became faulty in order to subsequently re-integrate them into the system. The primary target here are permanent faults, which do not go away "by themselves" after some time but rather require explicit corrective actions. Pioneering fault-tolerant systems implementations like MAFT [21] and GUARDS [30] combined fault-masking techniques like byzantine agreement [25] and FDIR approaches to harvest the best of both worlds.

Various paradigms have been proposed for implementing the steps in FDIR: Fault-detection can be done by a central FDIR unit, which is implemented in some very reliable technology and oversees the whole distributed system. Alternatively, distributed FDIR employs distributed diagnosis [38], e.g., based on evidence [1], and is typically combined with byzantine consensus [25] to ensure agreement among the replicated FDIR units. Agents diagnosed as faulty are subsequently forced to reset and execute built-in self tests, possibly followed by repair actions like hardware reconfiguration. Viewed at a very abstract level, the FDI steps of FDIR thus cause a faulty agent to become correct again. Becoming correct again is, however, not enough to enable the agent to also participate in the (on-going) execution of the remaining system. The latter also requires a successful *state recovery* step R, which makes the local state of the agent consistent with the current global system state. Various recovery techniques have been proposed for this purpose, ranging from pro-active recovery [32], where the local state of *every* agent is periodically replaced by a majority-voted version, to techniques based on checkpointing & rollback or message-logging & replay, see [12] for a survey. The common aspect of all these techniques is that the local state of the recovering agent is changed based on information originating from other agents.

Our Contribution. In this paper,[1] we provide the first logic that not only enables one to reason about the fault status of agents, but also provides mechanisms for updating the model so as to change the fault status of agents, as well as their local states. Instead of handling such dynamics in the byzantine extension of the runs-and-systems framework [22–24], i.e., in a temporal epistemic setting, we do it in a dynamic epistemic setting: we restrict our attention to the instants where the ultimate goal of (i) the FDI steps (successfully repairing a faulty processor) and (ii) the R step (recovering the repaired processor's local state) is reached, and investigate the dynamics of the agents' correctness/faultiness and its interaction with knowledge at these instants.

Our approach enables us to separate the issue of (1) verifying the correctness of the specification of an FDIR mechanism from the problem of (2) guaranteeing the correctness of its protocol implementation, and to focus on (1). Indeed, verifying the correctness of the implementation of some specification is the standard problem in formal verification, and powerful tools exist that can be used for this purpose. However, even a fully verified FDIR protocol would be completely useless if the FDIR specification was erroneous from the outset, in the sense that it does not correctly identify and hence repair faulty agents in some cases.

[1] An extended version of the paper, which also provides the proofs and additional details that had to be dropped here, can be found in [7].

Our novel logics and the underlying model update procedures provide, to the best of our knowledge, the first suitable foundations for (1), as they allow to formally specify (1.a) *when* a model update shall happen, and (1.b) the result of the model update. While we cannot claim that no better approach exists, our various examples at least reveal that we can model many crucial situations arising in FDIR schemes.

In order to introduce the core features of our logic and its update mechanisms, we use a simple example: Consider two agents a and b, each knowing their own local states, where global state ij, with $i, j \in \{0, 1\}$, means that a's local state is i and b's local state is j. To describe agent a's local state i we use an atomic proposition p_a, where p_a is true if $i = 1$ in global state ij and p_a is false if $i = 0$, and similarly for b's local state j and atomic proposition p_b.

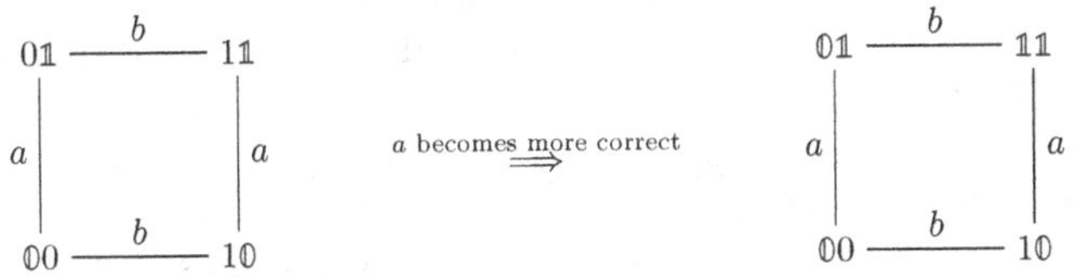

Knowledge and hope of the agents is represented in a Kripke model M for our system consisting of four states (worlds), shown in the left part of the figure above. Knowledge K_i is interpreted by a knowledge relation $\mathcal{K}_i$ and hope H_i is interpreted by a hope relation $\mathcal{H}_i$. Worlds that are $\mathcal{K}_i$-indistinguishable, in the sense that agent i cannot distinguish which of the worlds is the actual one, are connected by an i-labeled link, where we assume reflexivity, symmetry, and transitivity. Worlds ij that are in the non-empty part of the $\mathcal{H}_i$ relation, where agent i is correct, have i outlined as $\mathbb{0}$ or $\mathbb{1}$. For example, in the world depicted as $0\mathbb{1}$ above, agent a is faulty and agent b is correct.

Now assume that we want agent a to become correct in states 01 and 11 where p_b is true. For example, this could be dictated by an FDIR mechanism that caused b to diagnose a as faulty. Changing the fault status of a accordingly (while not changing the correctness of b) results in the updated model on the right in the above figure. Note that a was correct in state 00 in the left model, but did not know this, whereas agent a knows that she is correct in state 00 after the update. Such a model update will be specified in our approach by a suitable *hope update formula* for every agent, which, in the above example, is $\neg H_a\bot \vee p_b$ for agent a and $\neg H_b\bot$ for agent b. Note carefully that every hope update formula implicitly specifies both (a) the situation in the original model in which a change of the hope relation is applied, namely, some agent i's correctness/faultiness status encoded as $\neg H_i\bot / H_i\bot$, and (b) the result of the respective update of the hope relation.

Clearly, different FDIR approaches will require very different hope update formulas for describing their effects. In our logic, we provide two basic hope update mechanisms that can be used here: *public* updates, in which the agents are certain about the exact hope updates occurring at other agents, and *private* updates (strictly speaking, semi-private updates [5]), in which the agents may be uncertain about the particular hope updates occurring at other agents. The former is suitable for FDIR approaches where a central FDIR unit in the system triggers and coordinates all FDIR activities, the latter is needed for some distributed FDIR schemes.

Moreover, whereas the agents' local states do not necessarily have to be changed when becoming correct, FDIR usually requires to erase traces of erroneous behavior before recovery from the history in the R step. Our logic hence provides an additional *factual change* mechanism for accomplishing this as well. For example, simultaneously with or after becoming correct, agents may also need to change their local state by making false the atomic proposition that records that step 134 of the protocol was (erroneously) executed. Analogous to hope update formulas, suitable *factual change formulas* are used to encode when and how atomic propositions will change. Besides syntax and semantics, we provide complete axiomatizations of all variants of our logic, and demonstrate its utility and flexibility for modeling a wide range of FDIR mechanisms by means of many application examples. In order to focus on the essentials, we use only 2-agent examples for highlighting particular challenges arising in FDIR. We note, however, that it is usually straightforward to generalize those for more than two agents, and to even combine them for modeling more realistic FDIR scenarios.

Summary of the Utility of Our Logic. Besides contributing novel model update mechanisms to the state-of-the-art in dynamic epistemic logic, the main utility of our logic is that it enables epistemic reasoning and verification of FDIR mechanism *specifications*. Indeed, even a fully verified protocol implementation of some FDIR mechanism would be meaningless if its specification allowed unintended effects. Our hope update/factual change formulas formally and exhaustively specify what the respective model update accomplishes, i.e., encode both the preconditions for changing some agent's fault status/atomic propositions and the actual change. Given an initial model and these update formulas, our logic thus enables one to check (even automatically) whether the updated model has all the properties intended by the designer, whether certain state invariants are preserved by the update, etc. Needless to say, there are many reasons why a chosen specification might be wrong in this respect: the initial model might not provide all the required information, undesired fault status changes could be triggered in some worlds, or supporting information required for an agent to recover its local state might not be available. The ability to (automatically) verify the absence of such undesired effects of the specification of an FDIR mechanism is hence important in the design of mission-critical distributed systems.

Paper Organization. Section 2 recalls the syntax and semantics of the logic for knowledge and hope [6]. Section 3 expands this language with dynamic modalities for publicly changing hope. Section 4 generalizes the language to private updates. In Sect. 5, we add factual change to our setting. Some conclusions in Sect. 6 complete our paper.

2 A Logic of Hope and Knowledge

We succinctly present the logic of hope and knowledge [6]. Throughout our presentation, let $\mathcal{A} := \{1, \dots, n\}$ be a finite set of agents and let Prop be a non-empty countable set of atomic propositions.

Syntax. The language $\mathcal{L}_{KH}$ is defined as

$$\varphi ::= p \mid \neg\varphi \mid (\varphi \wedge \varphi) \mid K_i\varphi \mid H_i\varphi, \tag{1}$$

where $p \in \mathsf{Prop}$ and $i \in \mathcal{A}$. We take $\top$ to be the abbreviation for some fixed propositional tautology and $\bot$ for $\neg\top$. We also use standard abbreviations for the remaining boolean connectives, $\widehat{K}_i\varphi$ for the dual modality $\neg K_i \neg\varphi$ for 'agent a considers φ possible', $\widehat{H}_i\varphi$ for $\neg H_i\neg\varphi$, and $E_G\varphi$ for mutual knowledge $\bigwedge_{i\in G} K_i\varphi$ in a group $G \subseteq \mathcal{A}$. Finally, we define belief $B_i\varphi$ as $K_i(\neg H_i\bot \rightarrow \varphi)$; we recall that $\neg H_i\bot$ means that i is correct.

Structures. A *Kripke model* is a tuple $M = (W, \pi, \mathcal{K}, \mathcal{H})$ where W is a non-empty set of *worlds* (or *states*), $\pi\colon \mathsf{Prop} \rightarrow \mathcal{P}(W)$ is a *valuation function* mapping each atomic proposition to the set of worlds where it is true, and $\mathcal{K} : \mathcal{A} \rightarrow \mathcal{P}(W \times W)$ and $\mathcal{H} : \mathcal{A} \rightarrow \mathcal{P}(W \times W)$ are functions that assign to each agent i a *knowledge relation* $\mathcal{K}_i \subseteq W \times W$ respectively a *hope relation* $\mathcal{H}_i \subseteq W \times W$, where we have written $\mathcal{K}_i$ resp. $\mathcal{H}_i$ for $\mathcal{K}(i)$ and $\mathcal{H}(i)$. We write $\mathcal{H}_i(w)$ for $\{v \mid (w,v) \in \mathcal{H}_i\}$ and $w\mathcal{H}_i v$ for $(w,v) \in \mathcal{H}_i$, and similarly for $\mathcal{K}_i$. We require knowledge relations $\mathcal{K}_i$ to be equivalence relations and hope relations $\mathcal{H}_i$ to be shift-serial (that is, if $w\mathcal{H}_i v$, then there exists a $z \in W$ such that $v\mathcal{H}_i z$). In addition, the following conditions should also be satisfied:

$$\begin{array}{ll} \mathcal{H}\text{in}\mathcal{K}: & \mathcal{H}_i \subseteq \mathcal{K}_i, \\ \text{one}\mathcal{H}: & (\forall w, v \in W)(\mathcal{H}_i(w) \neq \varnothing \wedge \mathcal{H}_i(v) \neq \varnothing \wedge w\mathcal{K}_i v \Longrightarrow w\mathcal{H}_i v). \end{array}$$

It can be shown that all $\mathcal{H}_i$ relations are so-called *partial equivalence relations*: they are transitive and symmetric binary relations [27].

The class of Kripke models $(W, \pi, \mathcal{K}, \mathcal{H})$ (given $\mathcal{A}$ and Prop) is named $\mathcal{KH}$.

Semantics. We define truth for formulas $\varphi \in \mathcal{L}_{KH}$ at a world w of a model $M = (W, \pi, \mathcal{K}, \mathcal{H}) \in \mathcal{KH}$ in the standard way: in particular, $M, w \models p$ iff $w \in \pi(p)$ where $p \in \mathsf{Prop}$; boolean connectives are classical; $M, w \models K_i\varphi$ iff $M, v \models \varphi$ for all v such that $w\mathcal{K}_i v$; and $M, w \models H_i\varphi$ iff $M, v \models \varphi$ for all v such that $w\mathcal{H}_i v$. A formula φ is *valid in model* M, denoted $M \models \varphi$, iff $M, w \models \varphi$ for all $w \in W$, and it is *valid*, notation $\models \varphi$ (or $\mathcal{KH} \models \varphi$) iff it is valid in all models $M \in \mathcal{KH}$. The axiom system $\mathscr{KH}$ for knowledge and hope is given below.

P	all propositional tautologies	T^K	$K_i\varphi \rightarrow \varphi$
$H^\dagger$	$H_i\neg H_i\bot$	KH	$H_i\varphi \leftrightarrow (\neg H_i\bot \rightarrow K_i(\neg H_i\bot \rightarrow \varphi))$
K^K	$K_i(\varphi \rightarrow \psi) \wedge K_i\varphi \rightarrow K_i\psi$	MP	from φ and $\varphi \rightarrow \psi$, infer ψ
4^K	$K_i\varphi \rightarrow K_iK_i\varphi$	Nec^K	from φ, infer $K_i\varphi$
5^K	$\neg K_i\varphi \rightarrow K_i\neg K_i\varphi$		

Theorem 1 ([6]). *$\mathscr{KH}$ is sound and complete with respect to $\mathcal{KH}$.*

3 Public Hope Update

3.1 Syntax and Semantics

Definition 2 (Logical language). *Language* $\mathcal{L}_{KH}^{pub}$ *is obtained by adding the construct* $[\underbrace{\varphi, \dots, \varphi}_{n}]\varphi$ *to BNF* (1).

We read a formula of the shape $[\varphi_1, \dots, \varphi_n]\psi$, often abbreviated as $[\vec{\varphi}]\psi$ as follows: after revising or updating hope for agent i with respect to φ_i for all agents $i \in \mathcal{A}$ simultaneously, ψ (is true). We call the formula φ_i the *hope update formula for agent i*.

Definition 3 (Semantics of public hope update). *Let a tuple* $\vec{\varphi} \in (\mathcal{L}_{KH}^{pub})^n$, *a model* $M = (W, \pi, \mathcal{K}, \mathcal{H}) \in \mathcal{KH}$, *and a world* $w \in W$ *be given. Then*

$$M, w \models [\vec{\varphi}]\psi \quad \textit{iff} \quad M^{\vec{\varphi}}, w \models \psi,$$

where $M^{\vec{\varphi}} := (W, \pi, \mathcal{K}, \mathcal{H}^{\vec{\varphi}})$ *such that for each agent* $i \in \mathcal{A}$:

$$w\mathcal{H}_i^{\chi}v \qquad \textit{iff} \qquad w\mathcal{K}_i v, \quad M, w \models \chi, \quad \textit{and} \quad M, v \models \chi$$

and where we write $\mathcal{H}_i^{\chi}$ *for* $(\mathcal{H}^{\vec{\varphi}})_i$ *if the i-th formula in* $\vec{\varphi}$ *is* χ.

If $M, w \not\models \chi$, then $\mathcal{H}_i^{\chi}(w) = \varnothing$: agent i is faulty in state w after the update, i.e., $H_i\bot$ is true. Whereas if $M, w \models \chi$, then $\mathcal{H}_i^{\chi}(w) \neq \varnothing$: agent i is correct in state w after the update, i.e., $\neg H_i\bot$ is true. If the hope update formula for agent i is $\neg H_i\bot$, then $\neg H_i\bot$ is true in the same states before and after the update. Therefore, $\mathcal{H}_i^{\neg H_i\bot} = \mathcal{H}_i$: the hope relation for i does not change. On the other hand, if the hope update formula for agent i is $H_i\bot$, then $\mathcal{H}_i^{H_i\bot}(w) = \varnothing$ iff $\mathcal{H}_i(w) \neq \varnothing$: the correctness of agent i flips in every state. If we wish to model that agent i becomes *more correct* (in the model), then the hope update formula for agent i should have the shape $\neg H_i\bot \vee \varphi$: the left disjunct $\neg H_i\bot$ guarantees that in all states where i already was correct, she remains correct. We write

$$[\varphi]_i\psi \quad \text{for} \quad [\neg H_1\bot, \dots, \neg H_{i-1}\bot,\ \varphi,\ \neg H_{i+1}\bot, \dots, \neg H_n\bot]\psi$$

Similarly, we write $[\varphi]_G\psi$ if the hope update formulas for all agents $i \in G$ is φ and other agents j have the trivial hope update formula $\neg H_j\bot$.

Proposition 4. *If* $\vec{\varphi} \in (\mathcal{L}_{KH}^{pub})^n$ *and* $M = (W, \pi, \mathcal{K}, \mathcal{H}) \in \mathcal{KH}$ *then* $M^{\vec{\varphi}} \in \mathcal{KH}$.

Proof. Let $i \in \mathcal{A}$ and χ be the ith formula in $\vec{\varphi}$. We need to show that relation $\mathcal{H}_i^{\chi}$ is shift-serial and that it satisfies properties $\mathcal{H}$in$\mathcal{K}$ and one$\mathcal{H}$.

- [shift-serial]: Let $w \in W$. Assume $v \in \mathcal{H}_i^{\chi}(w)$, that is, $w\mathcal{K}_i v$, and $M, w \models \chi$ and $M, v \models \chi$. Now $v\mathcal{K}_i w$ follows by symmetry of $\mathcal{K}_i$. Therefore, $\mathcal{H}_i^{\chi}(v) \neq \varnothing$ since $w \in \mathcal{H}_i^{\chi}(v)$.
- [$\mathcal{H}$in$\mathcal{K}$]: This follows by definition.

- [one$\mathcal{H}$]: Let $w, v \in W$. Assume that $\mathcal{H}_i^\chi(w) \neq \varnothing$, that $\mathcal{H}_i^\chi(v) \neq \varnothing$, and that $w\mathcal{K}_i v$. It follows that there exists some $w' \in \mathcal{H}_i^\chi(w)$, implying that $M, w \models \chi$, and $v' \in \mathcal{H}_i^\chi(v)$, implying that $M, v \models \chi$. Now $w\mathcal{H}_i^\chi v$ follows immediately. □

The hope update φ for an agent a is reminiscent of the refinement semantics of public announcement φ [4]. However, unlike a public announcement, the hope update installs an entirely novel hope relation and discards the old one.

3.2 Applications

In this section, we apply the logical semantics just introduced to represent some typical scenarios that occur in FDIR applications. We provide several simple two-agent examples.

Example 5 (Correction based on agent b having diagnosed a as faulty). To correct agent a based on $K_b H_a \bot$, we update agent a's hope relation based on formula $\neg H_a \bot \vee K_b H_a \bot$ (and agent b's hope relation based on formula $\neg H_b \bot$). We recall that the disjunct $\neg H_a \bot$ guarantees that agent a will stay correct if he already was. The resulting model transformation is:

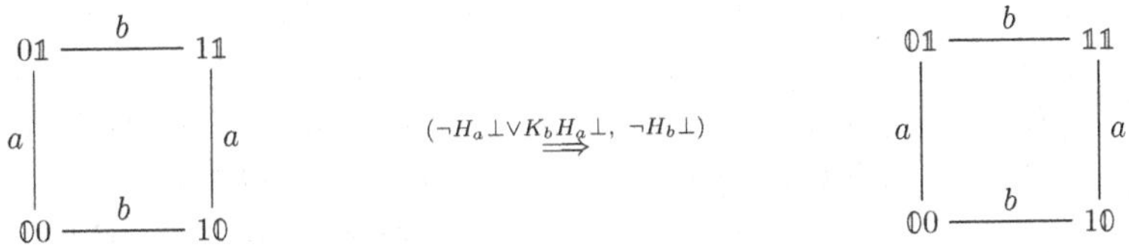

After the update, in states 00 where a was correct and 10 where a was faulty:

$M, 00 \models [\neg H_a \bot \vee K_b H_a \bot]_a \neg H_a \bot$ — a is still correct
$M, 00 \models [\neg H_a \bot \vee K_b H_a \bot]_a K_a \neg H_a \bot$ — a now knows he is correct
$M, 10 \models [\neg H_a \bot \vee K_b H_a \bot]_a H_a \bot$ — a is still faulty
$M, 10 \models [\neg H_a \bot \vee K_b H_a \bot]_a \widehat{K}_a \neg H_a \bot$ — a now considers possible he is correct
$M, 10 \models [\neg H_a \bot \vee K_b H_a \bot]_a K_b \widehat{K}_a \neg H_a \bot$ ... b now knows that

A straightforward generalization of this hope update is correction based on distributed fault detection, where all agents in some sufficiently large group G need to diagnose agent a as faulty. If G is fixed, $\neg H_a \bot \vee E_G H_a \bot$ achieves this goal. If any group G of at least $k > 1$ agents is eligible, then $\neg H_a \bot \vee \bigvee_{G \subseteq \mathcal{A}}^{|G|=k} E_G H_a \bot$ is the formula of choice.

Unfortunately, Example 5 cannot be applied in byzantine settings in general, since *knowledge* of other agents' faults is usually not attainable [23]. Hence, one has to either resort to a weaker belief-based alternative or else to an important special case of Example 5, namely, *self-correction*, where $G = \{a\}$, i.e., agent a diagnoses itself as faulty. This remains feasible in the byzantine setting because one's own fault is among the few things an agent can know in such systems [23]. We illustrate this in Example 6.

Example 6 (Self-correction under constraints). Self-correction of agent a without constraints is carried out on the condition that a knows he is faulty ($K_a H_a \bot$). The hope update formula for self-correction of agent a with an optional additional constraint φ is

$$\neg H_a \bot \vee (\varphi \wedge K_a H_a \bot)$$

where the $\neg H_a \bot$ part corresponds to the worlds where agent a is already correct and the $\varphi \wedge K_a H_a \bot$ part says that, if he knows that he is faulty ($K_a H_a \bot$), then he attempts to self-correct and succeeds if, additionally, a (possibly external) condition φ holds. Very similarly to Example 5 we now add an additional constraint $\varphi = p_b$. Notice that the update is indeed slightly different than in Example 5, as a no longer becomes correct in world 01.

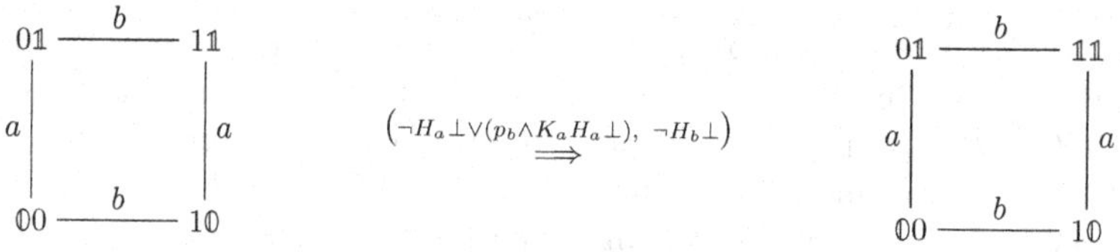

After the update, we get in states 00 and 10 (where a was correct resp. faulty):

$M, 00 \models [\neg H_a \bot \vee (p_b \wedge K_a H_a \bot)]_a \neg H_a \bot$	a is still correct
$M, 00 \models [\neg H_a \bot \vee (p_b \wedge K_a H_a \bot)]_a \widehat{K}_a H_a \bot$	a still cons. poss. he is faulty
$M, 10 \models [\neg H_a \bot \vee (p_b \wedge K_a H_a \bot)]_a H_a \bot$	a is still faulty
$M, 10 \models [\neg H_a \bot \vee (p_b \wedge K_a H_a \bot)]_a \widehat{K}_a \neg H_a \bot$	a now cons. poss. he is correct
$M, 10 \models [\neg H_a \bot \vee (p_b \wedge K_a H_a \bot)]_a K_b \widehat{K}_a \neg H_a \bot$	... b now knows that

Byzantine Agents. We now turn our attention to a different problem that needs to be solved in fault-tolerant distributed systems like MAFT [21] and GUARDS [30] that combine fault-masking approaches with FDIR. What is needed here is to monitor whether there are at most f faulty agents among the n agents in the system, and take countermeasures when the formula

$$Byz_f := \bigvee_{\substack{G \subseteq \mathcal{A} \\ |G| = n-f}} \bigwedge_{i \in G} \neg H_i \bot$$

is in danger of getting violated or even is violated already. The most basic way to enforce the global condition Byz_f in a hope update is by a constraint on the hope update formulas, rather than by their actual shape. All that is needed here is to ensure, given hope update formulas $\vec{\varphi} = (\varphi_1, \dots, \varphi_n)$, that at least $n - f$ of those are true, which can be expressed by the formula

$$\vec{\varphi}^{\,n-f} := \bigvee_{\substack{G \subseteq \mathcal{A} \\ |G| = n-f}} \bigwedge_{i \in G} \varphi_i.$$

We now have the validity

$$\models \vec{\varphi}^{n-f} \to [\vec{\varphi}]Byz_f.$$

In particular, we also have the weaker $\models Byz_f \wedge \vec{\varphi}^{n-f} \to [\vec{\varphi}]Byz_f$. In other words, $M, w \models Byz_f \wedge \vec{\varphi}^{n-f}$ implies $M^{\vec{\varphi}}, w \models Byz_f$. We could also consider generalized schemas such as: $M \models Byz_f \wedge \vec{\varphi}^{n-f}$ implies $M^{\vec{\varphi}} \models Byz_f$. In all these cases, the initial assumption Byz_f is superfluous.

Such a condition is, of course, too abstract for practical purposes. What would be needed here are concrete hope update formulas by which we can update a model when Byz_f might become false resp. is false already, in which case it must cause the correction of sufficiently many agents to guarantee that Byz_f is still true resp. becomes true again after the update. Recall that belief $B_i\psi$ is defined as $K_i(\neg H_i\bot \to \psi)$. If we define

$$B_{\geq f}\psi := \bigvee_{\substack{G\subseteq \mathcal{A}\\ |G|=f}} \bigwedge_{i\in G} B_i\psi,$$

it easy to see by the pigeonhole principle that $\models Byz_f \wedge B_{\geq f+1}\psi \to \psi$. Using $\psi = H_a\bot$ will hence result in one fewer faulty agent. To the formula $B_{\geq f+1}H_a\bot$ we add a disjunct $\neg H_a\bot$ to ensure correct agents remain correct.

$$\models Byz_f \wedge B_{\geq f+1}H_a\bot \to [\neg H_a\bot \vee B_{\geq f+1}H_a\bot]_a Byz_{f-1}.$$

3.3 Axiomatization

Axiomatization $\mathscr{KH}^{pub}$ of the logical semantics for $\mathcal{L}_{KH}^{pub}$ extends axiom system $\mathscr{KH}$ with axioms describing the interaction between hope updates and other logical connectives. The axiomatization is a straightforward reduction system, where the interesting interaction happens in hope update binding hope.

Definition 7 (Axiomatization $\mathscr{KH}^{pub}$). *$\mathscr{KH}^{pub}$ extends $\mathscr{KH}$ with*

$$\begin{array}{llll}
[\vec{\varphi}]p & \leftrightarrow p & [\vec{\varphi}]K_i\psi & \leftrightarrow K_i[\vec{\varphi}]\psi \\
[\vec{\varphi}]\neg\psi & \leftrightarrow \neg[\vec{\varphi}]\psi & [\vec{\varphi}]H_i\psi & \leftrightarrow \big(\varphi_i \to K_i(\varphi_i \to [\vec{\varphi}]\psi)\big) \\
[\vec{\varphi}](\psi\wedge\xi) & \leftrightarrow [\vec{\varphi}]\psi \wedge [\vec{\varphi}]\xi & [\vec{\varphi}][\vec{\chi}]\psi & \leftrightarrow \big[[\vec{\varphi}]\chi_1, \ldots, [\vec{\varphi}]\chi_n\big]\psi
\end{array}$$

where $\vec{\varphi} = (\varphi_1, \ldots, \varphi_n) \in (\mathcal{L}_{KH}^{pub})^n$, $\vec{\chi} = (\chi_1, \ldots, \chi_n) \in (\mathcal{L}_{KH}^{pub})^n$, $\psi, \xi \in \mathcal{L}_{KH}^{pub}$, $p \in \mathsf{Prop}$, and $i \in \mathcal{A}$.

Theorem 8 (Soundness). *For all $\varphi \in \mathcal{L}_{KH}^{pub}$, $\mathscr{KH}^{pub} \vdash \varphi$ implies $\mathcal{KH} \models \varphi$.*

Proof. Out of all additional axioms, we only show the most interesting case of hope being updated: we show the validity of $[\vec{\varphi}]H_i\psi \leftrightarrow \big(\varphi_i \to K_i(\varphi_i \to [\vec{\varphi}]\psi)\big)$:
$M, w \models [\vec{\varphi}]H_i\psi$ iff
$M^{\vec{\varphi}}, w \models H_i\psi$ iff
$(\forall v \in \mathcal{H}_i^{\varphi_i}(w))\ M^{\vec{\varphi}}, v \models \psi$ iff

$$
\begin{array}{l}
(\forall v \in W)\big(v \in \mathcal{K}_i(w) \;\&\; M, w \models \varphi_i \;\&\; M, v \models \varphi_i \quad\Longrightarrow\quad M^{\vec{\varphi}}, v \models \psi\big) \;\text{ iff}\\
M, w \models \varphi_i \quad\Longrightarrow\quad (\forall v \in W)\big(v \in \mathcal{K}_i(w) \;\&\; M, v \models \varphi_i \quad\Longrightarrow\quad M^{\vec{\varphi}}, v \models \psi\big) \;\text{ iff}\\
M, w \models \varphi_i \quad\Longrightarrow\quad (\forall v \in \mathcal{K}_i(w))(M, v \models \varphi_i \quad\Longrightarrow\quad M^{\vec{\varphi}}, v \models \psi) \;\text{ iff}\\
M, w \models \varphi_i \quad\Longrightarrow\quad (\forall v \in \mathcal{K}_i(w))(M, v \models \varphi_i \quad\Longrightarrow\quad M, v \models [\vec{\varphi}]\psi) \;\text{ iff}\\
M, w \models \varphi_i \quad\Longrightarrow\quad (\forall v \in \mathcal{K}_i(w))\; M, v \models \varphi_i \to [\vec{\varphi}]\psi \;\text{ iff}\\
M, w \models \varphi_i \quad\Longrightarrow\quad M, w \models K_i(\varphi_i \to [\vec{\varphi}]\psi) \;\text{ iff}\\
M, w \models \varphi_i \to K_i(\varphi_i \to [\vec{\varphi}]\psi).
\end{array}
$$

□

Every formula in $\mathcal{L}_{KH}^{pub}$ is provably equivalent to a formula in $\mathcal{L}_{KH}$ (Lemma 13). To prove this, we first define the *weight* or *complexity* of a given formula (Definition 9) and show a number of inequalities comparing the left-hand side to the right-hand side of the reduction axioms in axiomatization $\mathscr{KH}^{pub}$ (Lemma 10). Subsequently, we define a translation from $\mathcal{L}_{KH}^{pub}$ to $\mathcal{L}_{KH}$ (Definition 11) and finally show that the translation is a terminating rewrite procedure (Proposition 12).

Definition 9. *The* complexity $c : \mathcal{L}_{KH}^{pub} \to \mathbb{N}$ *of* $\mathcal{L}_{KH}^{pub}$*-formulas is defined recursively, where* $p \in \mathsf{Prop}$, $i \in \mathcal{A}$, *and* $c(\vec{\varphi}) := \max\{c(\varphi_i) \mid 1 \leq i \leq n\}$*:*

$$
\begin{array}{llll}
c(p) & := 1 & c(K_i\varphi) & := c(\varphi) + 1\\
c(\neg\varphi) & := c(\varphi) + 1 & c(H_i\varphi) & := c(\varphi) + 4\\
c(\varphi \wedge \xi) & := \max\{c(\varphi), c(\xi)\} + 1 & c([\vec{\varphi}]\xi) & := \big(c(\vec{\varphi}) + 1\big) \cdot c(\xi)
\end{array}
$$

Lemma 10. *For each axiom* $\theta_l \leftrightarrow \theta_r$ *from Definition 7,* $c(\theta_l) > c(\theta_r)$*.*

Definition 11. *The* translation $t : \mathcal{L}_{KH}^{pub} \to \mathcal{L}_{KH}$ *is defined recursively, where* $p \in \mathsf{Prop}$, $i \in \mathcal{A}$, *and the i-th formula of* $\vec{\varphi}$ *is* φ_i*:*

$$
\begin{array}{llll}
t(p) & := p & t([\vec{\varphi}]p) & := p\\
t(\neg\varphi) & := \neg t(\varphi) & t([\vec{\varphi}]\neg\xi) & := \neg t([\vec{\varphi}]\xi)\\
t(\varphi \wedge \xi) & := t(\varphi) \wedge t(\xi) & t([\vec{\varphi}](\xi \wedge \chi)) & := t([\vec{\varphi}]\xi \wedge [\vec{\varphi}]\chi)\\
t(K_i\varphi) & := K_i t(\varphi) & t([\vec{\varphi}]K_i\xi) & := t(K_i[\vec{\varphi}]\xi)\\
t(H_i\varphi) & := H_i t(\varphi) & t([\vec{\varphi}]H_i\xi) & := t(\varphi_i \to K_i(\varphi_i \to [\vec{\varphi}]\xi))\\
 & & t([\vec{\varphi}][\chi_1, \dots, \chi_n]\xi) & := t([[\vec{\varphi}]\chi_1, \dots, [\vec{\varphi}]\chi_n]\xi)
\end{array}
$$

Proposition 12 (Termination). *For all* $\varphi \in \mathcal{L}_{KH}^{pub}$, $t(\varphi) \in \mathcal{L}_{KH}$*.*

Proof This follows by induction on $c(\varphi)$. □

Lemma 13 (Equiexpressivity). *Language* $\mathcal{L}_{KH}^{pub}$ *is equiexpressive with* $\mathcal{L}_{KH}$*.*

Proof. It follows by induction on $c(\varphi)$ that $\mathscr{KH}^{pub} \vdash \varphi \leftrightarrow t(\varphi)$ for all $\varphi \in \mathcal{L}_{KH}^{pub}$, where, by Proposition 12, $t(\varphi) \in \mathcal{L}_{KH}$. □

Theorem 14 (Soundness and completeness). *For all* $\varphi \in \mathcal{L}_{KH}^{pub}$*,*

$$\mathscr{KH}^{pub} \vdash \varphi \quad\Longleftrightarrow\quad \mathcal{KH} \models \varphi.$$

Proof. Soundness was proven in Theorem 8. To prove completeness, assume $\mathcal{KH} \models \varphi$. According to Lemma 13, we have $\mathscr{KH}^{pub} \vdash \varphi \leftrightarrow t(\varphi)$. Therefore, by Theorem 8, $\mathcal{KH} \models \varphi \leftrightarrow t(\varphi)$ follows. Since $\mathcal{KH} \models \varphi$ (by assumption), we obtain $\mathcal{KH} \models t(\varphi)$. By applying Theorem 1, $\mathscr{KH} \vdash t(\varphi)$ further follows. Consequently, $\mathscr{KH}^{pub} \vdash t(\varphi)$. Finally, since $\mathscr{KH}^{pub} \vdash \varphi \leftrightarrow t(\varphi)$, $\mathscr{KH}^{pub} \vdash \varphi$. □

Corollary 15 (Necessitation for public hope updates).

$$\mathscr{KH}^{pub} \vdash \psi \qquad \Longrightarrow \qquad \mathscr{KH}^{pub} \vdash [\vec{\varphi}]\psi.$$

4 Private Hope Update

In the case of the public hope update mechanism introduced in Sect. 3, after the update there is no uncertainty about what happened. In some distributed FDIR schemes, including self-correction, however, the hope update at an agent occurs in a less public way. To increase the application coverage of our logic, we therefore provide the alternative of private hope updates. For that, we use structures inspired by action models. Strictly speaking, such updates are known as *semi-private* (or *semi-public*) updates, as the agents are aware of their uncertainty and know what they are uncertain about, whereas in fully private update the agent does not know that the action took place [5] and may, in fact, believe that nothing happened. The resulting language can be viewed as a generalization of $\mathcal{L}_{KH}^{pub}$, where the latter now becomes a special case.

4.1 Syntax and Semantics

Definition 16 (Hope update model). *A* hope update model *for a logical language $\mathcal{L}$ is a tuple $U = (E, \vartheta, \mathcal{K}^U)$, where E is a non-empty set of* actions, *$\vartheta : E \to (\mathcal{A} \to \mathcal{L})$ is a* hope update function, *and $\mathcal{K}^U : \mathcal{A} \to \mathcal{P}(E \times E)$ such that all $\mathcal{K}_i^U$ are equivalence relations. For $\vartheta(e)(i)$ we write $\vartheta_i(e)$. As before, formulas $\vartheta_i(e) \in \mathcal{L}$ are* hope update formulas. *A* pointed hope update model *is a pair (U, e) where $e \in E$.*

Definition 17 (Language $\mathcal{L}_{KH}^{priv}$). *We obtain language $\mathcal{L}_{KH}^{priv}$ by adding the construct $[U, e]\varphi$ to BNF (1), where (U, e) is a pointed hope update model.*

Definition 17 is given by mutual recursion as usual: all hope update models U are for the language $\mathcal{L}_{KH}^{priv}$.

Definition 18 (Semantics of private hope update). *Let $U = (E, \vartheta, \mathcal{K}^U)$ be a hope update model, $M = (W, \pi, \mathcal{K}, \mathcal{H}) \in \mathcal{KH}$, $w \in W$, and $e \in E$. Then:*

$$M, w \models [U, e]\varphi \quad \textit{iff} \quad M \times U, (w, e) \models \varphi,$$

where $M \times U = (W^\times, \pi^\times, \mathcal{K}^\times, \mathcal{H}^\times)$ is such that:

$$\begin{array}{lll}
W^\times & := & W \times E \\
(w, e) \in \pi^\times(p) & \textit{iff} & w \in \pi(p) \\
(w, e)\mathcal{K}_i^\times(v, f) & \textit{iff} & w\mathcal{K}_i v \textit{ and } e\mathcal{K}_i^U f \\
(w, e)\mathcal{H}_i^\times(v, f) & \textit{iff} & (w, e)\mathcal{K}_i^\times(v, f), M, w \models \vartheta_i(e), \textit{ and } M, v \models \vartheta_i(f)
\end{array}$$

Public hope updates can be viewed as singleton hope update models. Given formulas $\vec{\varphi} \in (\mathcal{L}_{KH}^{pub})^n$, define $pub := (\{e\}, \vartheta, \mathcal{K}^{pub})$, where $\vartheta_i(e) := \varphi_i$ and $\mathcal{K}^{pub} := \{(e, e)\}$.

Difference with Action Models. Although our hope update models look like action models, they are not really action models in the sense of [2]. Our actions do not have executability preconditions, such that the updated model is not a restricted modal product but rather the full product. Another difference is that, by analogy with Kripke models for knowledge and hope, we would then have expected a hope relation in the update models. But there is none in our approach.

Proposition 19. *$M \times U \in \mathcal{KH}$ for any hope update model U and $M \in \mathcal{KH}$.*

Proof. The proof is somewhat similar to that of Proposition 4. It is obvious that all $\mathcal{K}_i^\times$ are equivalence relations. Let us show now that for all $i \in \mathcal{A}$ relations $\mathcal{H}_i^\times$ are shift-serial and that they satisfy the properties $\mathcal{H}$in$\mathcal{K}$ and one$\mathcal{H}$.

- **$\mathcal{H}_i^\times$ is shift-serial:** Let $(w, e) \in W^\times$. Assume $(w, e)\mathcal{H}_i^\times(v, f)$, that is, $(w, e)\mathcal{K}_i^\times(v, f)$, and $M, w \models \vartheta_i(e)$, and $M, v \models \vartheta_i(f)$. $(v, f)\mathcal{K}_i^\times(w, e)$ follows by symmetry of $\mathcal{K}_i^\times$. Therefore, $\mathcal{H}_i^\times((v, f)) \neq \varnothing$ since $(w, e) \in \mathcal{H}_i^\times((v, f))$.
- **$\mathcal{H}_i^\times$ satisfies $\mathcal{H}$in$\mathcal{K}$:** This follows by definition.
- **$\mathcal{H}_i^\times$ satisfies one$\mathcal{H}$:** Let $(w, e), (v, f) \in W^\times$. Assume that $\mathcal{H}_i^\times((w, e)) \neq \varnothing$, $\mathcal{H}_i^\times((v, f)) \neq \varnothing$, and $(w, e)\mathcal{K}_i^\times(v, f)$. As $\mathcal{H}_i^\times((w, e)) \neq \varnothing$, $M, w \models \vartheta_i(e)$. As $\mathcal{H}_i^\times((v, f)) \neq \varnothing$, $M, v \models \vartheta_i(f)$. Therefore, $(w, e)\mathcal{H}_i^\times(v, f)$. □

Definition 20. *Let $U = (E, \vartheta, \mathcal{K}^U)$ and $U' = (E', \vartheta', \mathcal{K}^{U'})$ be hope update models. The* composition *$(U; U')$ is $(E'', \vartheta'', \mathcal{K}^{U;U'})$ such that:*

$$
\begin{array}{lcl}
E'' & := & E \times E' \\
(e, e')\mathcal{K}_i^{U;U'}(f, f') & \textit{iff} & e\mathcal{K}_i^U f \textit{ and } e'\mathcal{K}_i^{U'} f' \\
\vartheta''(e, e') & := & [U, e]\vartheta'(e')
\end{array}
$$

Since $\mathcal{K}_i^U$ and $\mathcal{K}_i^{U'}$ are equivalence relations, $\mathcal{K}_i^{U;U'}$ is also an equivalence relation, so that $(U; U')$ is a hope update model.

4.2 Applications

The arguably most important usage of private updates in distributed FDIR is to express the uncertainty of agents about whether an update affects other agents.

Example 21 (Private correction). We reconsider the example from Sect. 1, only this time we privately correct agent a based on p_b such that agent b is uncertain whether the hope update happens. This can be modeled by two hope update formulas for agent a: $\neg H_a\bot \vee p_b$ and $\neg H_a\bot$. With $\neg H_a\bot \vee p_b$ we associate an event c_{p_b} where the correction takes place based on the additional constraint p_b, and with $\neg H_a \bot$ we associate an event *noc* where correction does not take place. Writing $\vartheta(e) = \big((\vartheta_a(e), \vartheta_b(e)\big)$, we get $U := (E, \vartheta, \mathcal{K}^U)$, where:

$$
\begin{array}{llll}
E & := \{c_{p_b}, noc\} & \mathcal{K}^U_a & := \text{the identity relation } \{(e,e) \mid e \in E\} \\
\vartheta(c_{p_b}) & := (\neg H_a \bot \vee p_b, \neg H_b \bot) & \mathcal{K}^U_b & := \text{the universal relation } E \times E \\
\vartheta(noc) & := (\neg H_a \bot, \neg H_b \bot) & &
\end{array}
$$

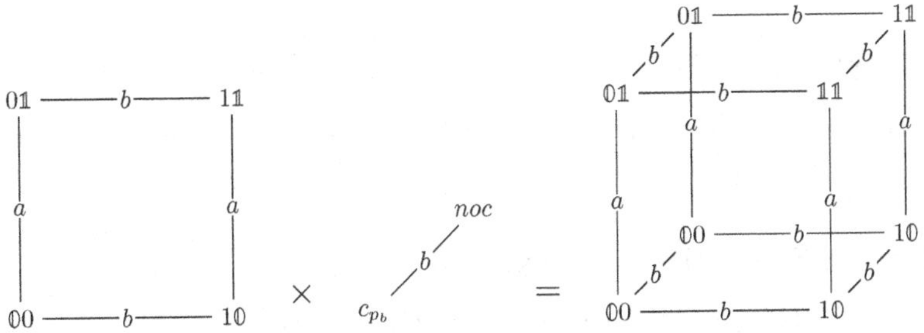

When naming worlds, we have abstracted away from the event being executed in a world. Having the same name therefore does not mean being the same world. For example, the world 11 at the front of the cube 'really' is the pair $(11, c_{p_b})$ with $H_a\big((11, c_{p_b})\big) \neq \varnothing$ and $H_b\big((11, c_{p_b})\big) \neq \varnothing$. We now have for example that:

$$
\begin{array}{ll}
M, 01 \models H_a \bot \wedge [U, c_{p_b}](\neg H_a \bot \wedge K_a \neg H_a \bot) & a \text{ knows it became correct} \\
M, 01 \models [U, c_{p_b}] \neg K_b K_a \neg H_a \bot & \ldots \text{ but } b \text{ doesn't know that} \\
M, 01 \models K_b H_a \bot \wedge [U, c_{p_b}] \neg (K_b H_a \bot \vee K_b \neg H_a \bot) & b \text{ is ignorant of } a\text{'s fault}
\end{array}
$$

4.3 Axiomatization

Definition 22 (Axiomatization $\mathscr{KH}^{priv}$). *$\mathscr{KH}^{priv}$ consists of $\mathscr{KH}$ and*

$$
\begin{array}{ll}
[U,e]p & \leftrightarrow p \\
[U,e]\neg\varphi & \leftrightarrow \neg [U,e]\varphi \\
[U,e](\varphi \wedge \psi) & \leftrightarrow [U,e]\varphi \wedge [U,e]\psi \\
[U,e]K_i\varphi & \leftrightarrow \bigwedge_{e\mathcal{K}^U_i f} K_i [U,f]\varphi \\
[U,e]H_i\varphi & \leftrightarrow \Big(\vartheta_i(e) \rightarrow \bigwedge_{e\mathcal{K}^U_i f} K_i\big(\vartheta_i(f) \rightarrow [U,f]\varphi\big)\Big) \\
[U,e][U',e']\varphi & \leftrightarrow \big[(U;U'),(e,e')\big]\varphi
\end{array}
$$

Theorem 23 (Soundness). *For all $\varphi \in \mathcal{L}^{priv}_{KH}$, $\mathscr{KH}^{priv} \vdash \varphi$ implies $\mathcal{KH} \models \varphi$.*

Similarly to the previous section, one can show that every formula in $\mathcal{L}^{priv}_{KH}$ is provably equivalent to a formula in $\mathcal{L}_{KH}$, by defining $\mathcal{L}^{priv}_{KH}$-formulas complexity, showing complexity inequalities concerning the reduction axioms in axiomatization $\mathscr{KH}^{priv}$, defining a translation from $\mathcal{L}^{priv}_{KH}$ to $\mathcal{L}_{KH}$, and observing that this translation is a terminating rewrite procedure. We thus obtain:

Proposition 24 (Termination). *For all $\varphi \in \mathcal{L}^{priv}_{KH}$, $t(\varphi) \in \mathcal{L}_{KH}$.*

Lemma 25 (Equiexpressivity). *Language $\mathcal{L}^{priv}_{KH}$ is equiexpressive with $\mathcal{L}_{KH}$, i.e., for all $\varphi \in \mathcal{L}^{priv}_{KH}$, $\mathscr{KH}^{priv} \vdash \varphi \leftrightarrow t(\varphi)$.*

Theorem 26 (Soundness and completeness). *For all $\varphi \in \mathcal{L}^{priv}_{KH}$,*

$$\mathscr{KH}^{priv} \vdash \varphi \quad \iff \quad \mathcal{KH} \models \varphi.$$

Necessitation for private hope update is an admissible inference rule in $\mathscr{KH}^{priv}$.

5 Factual Change

In this section, we provide a way to add factual change to our model updates. This is going along well-trodden paths in dynamic epistemic logic [3,8,9].

5.1 Syntax, Semantics, and Axiomatization

Definition 27 (Hope update model with factual change). *To obtain a hope update model with factual change $U = (E, \vartheta, \sigma, \mathcal{K}^U)$ from a hope update model $(E, \vartheta, \mathcal{K}^U)$ for a language $\mathcal{L}$ we add parameter $\sigma : E \to (\mathsf{Prop} \to \mathcal{L})$. We require that each $\sigma(e)$ is only finitely different from the identity function.*

The finitary requirement is needed in order to keep the language well-defined. In this section, by hope update models we mean hope update models with factual change.

Definition 28 (Language $\mathcal{L}^f_{KH}$). *Language $\mathcal{L}^f_{KH}$ is obtained by adding the construct $[U, e]\varphi$ to the BNF of the language $\mathcal{L}_{KH}$, where (U, e) is a pointed hope update model with factual change for the language $\mathcal{L}^f_{KH}$.*

As in the previous section, Definition 28 is given by mutual recursion and from here on all hope update models are for language $\mathcal{L}^f_{KH}$.

Definition 29 (Semantics). *Let $U = (E, \vartheta, \sigma, \mathcal{K}^U)$, $M = (W, \pi, \mathcal{K}, \mathcal{H}) \in \mathcal{KH}$, $w \in W$, and $e \in E$. Then, as in Definition 18, $M, w \models [U, e]\varphi$ iff $M \times U, (w, e) \models \varphi$, only now $M \times U = (W^\times, \pi^\times, \mathcal{K}^\times, \mathcal{H}^\times)$ is such that:*

$$W^\times := W \times E; \qquad (w, e) \in \pi^\times(p) \iff M, w \models \sigma(e)(p);$$
$$(w, e)\mathcal{K}^\times_i(v, f) \iff w\mathcal{K}_i v \text{ and } e\mathcal{K}^U_i f;$$
$$(w, e)\mathcal{H}^\times_i(v, f) \iff (w, e)\mathcal{K}^\times_i(v, f), M, w \models \vartheta_i(e), \text{ and } M, v \models \vartheta_i(f).$$

The only difference between Definitions 18 and 29 is that the clause for the valuation of the former is: $(w, e) \in \pi^\times(p)$ iff $w \in \pi(p)$. In other words, then the valuation of facts does not change, and the valuation in the world w is carried forward to that in the updated worlds (w, e). It is easy to see that $\mathcal{KH} \models [U, e]p \leftrightarrow \sigma(e)(p)$, as we immediately obtain that: $M, w \models [U, e]p$ iff $M \times U, (w, e) \models p$ iff $(w, e) \in \pi^\times(p)$ iff $M, w \models \sigma(e)(p)$. This turns out to be the only difference:

Definition 30 (Axiomatization $\mathscr{KH}^f$). *Axiom system $\mathscr{KH}^f$ is obtained from $\mathscr{KH}^{priv}$ by replacing the first equivalence in Definition 22 with $[U, e]p \leftrightarrow \sigma(e)(p)$.*

Theorem 31 (Soundness). *For all $\varphi \in \mathcal{L}^f_{KH}$, $\mathscr{KH}^f \vdash \varphi$ implies $\mathcal{KH} \models \varphi$.*

In itself it is quite remarkable that the required changes are fairly minimal, given the enormously enhanced flexibility in specifying distributed system behavior. With techniques quite similar to those employed for the hope update model logic without factual change, we can also get completeness for the hope update logic with factual change. Lacking space did not allow us to include many of the details; the interested reader is referred to the extended version [7] of this paper.

Lemma 32 (Equiexpressivity). *Language $\mathcal{L}^f_{KH}$ is equiexpressive with $\mathcal{L}_{KH}$.*

Theorem 33 (Soundness and completeness). *For all $\varphi \in \mathcal{L}^f_{KH}$,*

$$\mathscr{KH}^f \vdash \varphi \qquad \Longleftrightarrow \qquad \mathcal{KH} \models \varphi.$$

5.2 Applications

The importance of adding factual change to our framework comes from the fact that, in practical protocols implementing FDIR mechanisms, agents usually take decisions based on what they recorded in their local states. We demonstrate the essentials of combined hope updates and state recovery in Example 34, which combines the variant of self-correction introduced in Example 6 with state recovery needs that would arise in the alternating bit protocol [19].

Example 34 (Private self-correction with state recovery). The alternating bit protocol (ABP) for transmitting an arbitrarily generated stream of consecutive data packets from a sender to a receiver over an unreliable communication channel uses messages that additionally contain a sequence number consisting of 1 bit only. The latter switches from one message to the next, by alternating atomic propositions q_s and q_r containing the next sequence number to be used for the next message generated by the sender resp. receiver side of the channel. In addition, the ABP maintains atomic propositions p_s and p_r holding the last sequence number used by sender resp. receiver side. In more detail, the sending of data packet d_n, starting from $(q_s, q_r) = (0, 0)$ and $(p_s, p_r) = (1, 1)$, is completed in three phases ([19]): (i) if $q_s \neq p_s$, sender s sets $p_s := q_s = 0$ and generates a message (d_n, p_s) to be repeatedly sent; (ii) when receiver r receives (d_n, q_r) (with $q_r = 0$ here), it records d_n, sets $p_r := q_r = 0$, generates a message (ack, p_r) to be repeatedly sent back to s, and switches to the next sequence number $q_r := 1$; (iii) if sender s receives (ack, p_s) (with $p_s = 0$ here), it switches to the next sequence number $q_s := \neg p_s = 1$. Note that the next sequence numbers (q_s, q_r) have moved from $(0, 0)$ via $(0, 1)$ to $(1, 1)$, whereas the last sequence numbers (p_s, p_r) moved from $(1, 1)$ to $(0, 1)$ to $(0, 0)$. From here, the above phases are just repeated (with all sequence numbers flipped) for sending d_{n+1}. Thus, during a correct run of the ABP, (q_s, q_r) continuously cycles through $(0,0)$, $(0,1)$, $(1,1)$, $(1,0)$, $(0,0)$, ...

If, however, a transient fault would flip the value of either q_s or q_r, the ABP deadlocks and therefore requires correction. Due to the asymmetry of the ABP regarding sender and receiver, the need for a correction of the receiver can be conveniently determined by checking the equality of p_r and q_r, and can be performed by just setting $q_r := \neg p_r$.

We model agent r successfully self-correcting and recovering its state from $p_r = q_r$, that is, based on $p_r \leftrightarrow q_r$. At the same time, s is uncertain whether r has corrected itself (event $scr_{p_r=q_r}$) or not (event $noscr$). Again writing $\vartheta(e)$ as $((\vartheta_a(e), \vartheta_b(e))$, this is encoded in the hope update model $U := (E, \vartheta, \sigma, \mathcal{K}^U)$, where:

$$
\begin{array}{ll|ll}
E & := \{scr_{p_r=q_r}, noscr\} & \sigma(scr_{p_r=q_r})(q_r) := \neg p_r & \\
\vartheta(scr_{p_r=q_r}) & := (\neg H_s\bot, p_r \leftrightarrow q_r) & \mathcal{K}^U_s & := E \times E \\
\vartheta(noscr) & := (\neg H_s\bot, \neg H_r\bot) & \mathcal{K}^U_r & := \{(e,e) \mid e \in E\}
\end{array}
$$

Note that $H_r\bot$ is equivalent to $p_r \leftrightarrow q_r$, making $H_r\bot$ locally detectable by r and resulting in $\vartheta(scr_{p_r=q_r}) = (\neg H_s\bot, H_r\bot)$. All atoms for $noscr$ and all atoms other than q_r for $scr_{p_r=q_r}$ remain unchanged. Coding the atoms in each state as $p_s q_s.p_r q_r$, the resulting update is:

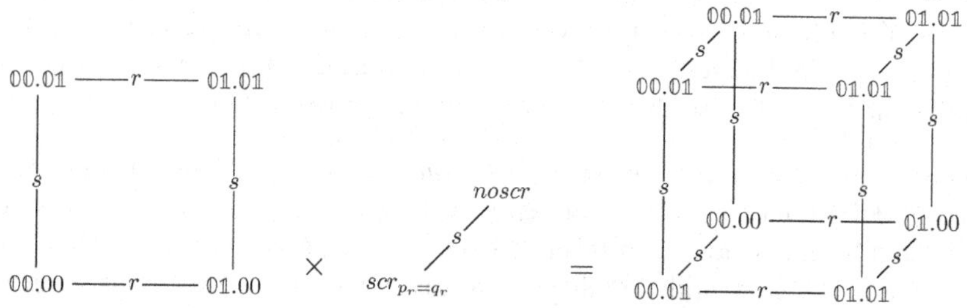

The only change happens in global states 00.00 and 01.00 where $p_r \leftrightarrow q_r$ causes the hope update and q_r is set to be the opposite of p_r. After the update, we get:

$$
\begin{array}{ll}
M, 00.00 \models [U, scr_{p_r=q_r}](\neg H_r\bot \wedge K_r q_r) & r \text{ is correct and learned } q_r \\
M, 00.00 \models [U, scr_{p_r=q_r}]K_r\neg H_r\bot & r \text{ is now sure she is correct} \\
M, 00.00 \models [U, scr_{p_r=q_r}](\neg K_r q_s \wedge \neg K_r \neg q_s) & r \text{ remains unsure regarding } q_s \\
M, 00.00 \models [U, scr_{p_r=q_r}]\widehat{K}_s H_r\bot & s \text{ consid. possible } r \text{ is faulty}
\end{array}
$$

6 Conclusions and Further Research

We gave various dynamic epistemic semantics for the modeling and analysis of byzantine fault-tolerant multi-agent systems, expanding a known logic containing knowledge and hope modalities. We provided complete axiomatizations for our logics and applied them to fault-detection, isolation, and recovery (FDIR) in distributed computing. For future research we envision alternative dynamic epistemic update mechanisms, as well as embedding our logic into the (temporal epistemic) runs-and-systems approach.

Acknowledgments. We thank the anonymous reviewers for the suggestions on how to improve the paper. We are grateful for multiple fruitful discussions with and enthusiastic support from Giorgio Cignarale, Stephan Felber, Rojo Randrianomentsoa, Hugo Rincón Galeana, and Thomas Schlögl.

References

1. Adams, J.C., Ramarao, K.V.S.: Distributed diagnosis of byzantine processors and links. In: Proceedings, The 9th International Conference on Distributed Computing Systems: Newport Beach, California, 5–9 June 1989, pp. 562–569. IEEE (1989). https://doi.org/10.1109/ICDCS.1989.37989
2. Baltag, A., Moss, L.S., Solecki, S.: The logic of public announcements, common knowledge, and private suspicions. In: Gilboa, I. (ed.) Theoretical Aspects of Rationality and Knowledge: Proceedings of the Seventh Conference (TARK 1998), pp. 43–56. Morgan Kaufmann (1998). http://tark.org/proceedings/tark_jul22_98/p43-baltag.pdf
3. van Benthem, J., van Eijck, J., Kooi, B.: Logics of communication and change. Inf. Comput. **204**(11), 1620–1662 (2006). https://doi.org/10.1016/j.ic.2006.04.006
4. van Benthem, J., Liu, F.: Dynamic logic of preference upgrade. J. Appl. Non-Classical Logics **17**(2), 157–182 (2007). https://doi.org/10.3166/jancl.17.157-182
5. van Ditmarsch, H.: Description of game actions. J. Logic Lang. Inform. **11**(3), 349–365 (2002). https://doi.org/10.1023/A:1015590229647
6. van Ditmarsch, H., Fruzsa, K., Kuznets, R.: A new hope. In: Fernández-Duque, D., Palmigiano, A., Pinchinat, S. (eds.) Advances in Modal Logic, vol. 14, pp. 349–369. College Publications (2022). http://www.aiml.net/volumes/volume14/22-vanDitmarsch-Fruzsa-Kuznets.pdf
7. van Ditmarsch, H., Fruzsa, K., Kuznets, R., Schmid, U.: A logic for repair and state recovery in byzantine fault-tolerant multi-agent systems. Eprint 2401.06451, arXiv (2024). https://doi.org/10.48550/arXiv.2401.06451
8. van Ditmarsch, H., van der Hoek, W., Kooi, B.: Dynamic epistemic logic with assignment. In: AAMAS 2005: Proceedings of the Fourth International Joint Conference on Autonomous Agents and Multiagent Systems, pp. 141–148. Association for Computing Machinery (2005). https://doi.org/10.1145/1082473.1082495
9. van Ditmarsch, H., Kooi, B.: Semantic results for ontic and epistemic change. In: Bonanno, G., van der Hoek, W., Wooldridge, M. (eds.) Logic and the Foundations of Game and Decision Theory (LOFT 7). Texts in Logic and Games, vol. 3, pp. 87–118. Amsterdam University Press (2008). https://www.jstor.org/stable/j.ctt46mz4h.6
10. Dolev, D., Függer, M., Posch, M., Schmid, U., Steininger, A., Lenzen, C.: Rigorously modeling self-stabilizing fault-tolerant circuits: an ultra-robust clocking scheme for systems-on-chip. J. Comput. Syst. Sci. **80**(4), 860–900 (2014). https://doi.org/10.1016/j.jcss.2014.01.001

11. van Eijck, J.: DEMO—a demo of epistemic modelling. In: van Benthem, J., Gabbay, D., Löwe, B. (eds.) Interactive Logic: Selected Papers from the 7th Augustus de Morgan Workshop, London. Texts in Logic and Games, vol. 1, pp. 303–362. Amsterdam University Press (2007). https://www.jstor.org/stable/j.ctt45kdbf.15
12. Elnozahy, E.N.M., Alvisi, L., Wang, Y.-M., Johnson, D.B.: A survey of rollback-recovery protocols in message-passing systems. ACM Comput. Surv. **34**(3), 375–408 (2002). https://doi.org/10.1145/568522.568525
13. Fagin, R., Halpern, J.Y., Moses, Y., Vardi, M.Y.: Reasoning About Knowledge. MIT Press, Cambridge (1995). https://doi.org/10.7551/mitpress/5803.001.0001
14. Fruzsa, K.: Hope for epistemic reasoning with faulty agents! In: Pavlova, A., Pedersen, M.Y., Bernardi, R. (eds.) ESSLLI 2019. LNCS, vol. 14354, pp. 93–108. Springer, Cham (2023). https://doi.org/10.1007/978-3-031-50628-4_6
15. Fruzsa, K., Kuznets, R., Schmid, U.: Fire! In: Halpern, J., Perea, A. (eds.) Proceedings of the Eighteenth Conference on Theoretical Aspects of Rationality and Knowledge, Beijing, China, 25–27 June 2021. Electronic Proceedings in Theoretical Computer Science, vol. 335, pp. 139–153. Open Publishing Association (2021). https://doi.org/10.4204/EPTCS.335.13
16. Függer, M., Schmid, U.: Reconciling fault-tolerant distributed computing and systems-on-chip. Distrib. Comput. **24**(6), 323–355 (2012). https://doi.org/10.1007/s00446-011-0151-7
17. Gammie, P., van der Meyden, R.: MCK: model checking the logic of knowledge. In: Alur, R., Peled, D.A. (eds.) CAV 2004. LNCS, vol. 3114, pp. 479–483. Springer, Heidelberg (2004). https://doi.org/10.1007/978-3-540-27813-9_41
18. Halpern, J.Y., Moses, Y.: Knowledge and common knowledge in a distributed environment. J. ACM **37**(3), 549–587 (1990). https://doi.org/10.1145/79147.79161
19. Halpern, J.Y., Zuck, L.D.: A little knowledge goes a long way: knowledge-based derivations and correctness proofs for a family of protocols. J. ACM **39**(3), 449–478 (1992). https://doi.org/10.1145/146637.146638
20. Heuerding, A., Jäger, G., Schwendimann, S., Seyfried, M.: A Logics Workbench. AI Commun. **9**(2), 53–58 (1996). https://doi.org/10.3233/AIC-1996-9203
21. Kieckhafer, R.M., Walter, C.J., Finn, A.M., Thambidurai, P.M.: The MAFT architecture for distributed fault tolerance. IEEE Trans. Comput. **37**(4), 398–404 (1988). https://doi.org/10.1109/12.2183
22. Kuznets, R., Prosperi, L., Schmid, U., Fruzsa, K.: Causality and epistemic reasoning in byzantine multi-agent systems. In: Moss, L.S. (ed.) Proceedings of the Seventeenth Conference on Theoretical Aspects of Rationality and Knowledge, Toulouse, France, 17–19 July 2019. Electronic Proceedings in Theoretical Computer Science, vol. 297, pp. 293–312. Open Publishing Association (2019). https://doi.org/10.4204/EPTCS.297.19
23. Kuznets, R., Prosperi, L., Schmid, U., Fruzsa, K.: Epistemic reasoning with byzantine-faulty agents. In: Herzig, A., Popescu, A. (eds.) FroCoS 2019. LNCS (LNAI), vol. 11715, pp. 259–276. Springer, Cham (2019). https://doi.org/10.1007/978-3-030-29007-8_15
24. Kuznets, R., Prosperi, L., Schmid, U., Fruzsa, K., Gréaux, L.: Knowledge in Byzantine message-passing systems I: Framework and the causal cone. Technical Report TUW-260549, TU Wien (2019). https://publik.tuwien.ac.at/files/publik_260549.pdf
25. Lamport, L., Shostak, R., Pease, M.: The Byzantine Generals Problem. ACM Trans. Program. Lang. Syst. **4**(3), 382–401 (1982). https://doi.org/10.1145/357172.357176

26. Mendes, H., Tasson, C., Herlihy, M.: Distributed computability in Byzantine asynchronous systems. In: STOC 2014, 46th Annual Symposium on the Theory of Computing: 31 May–3 June 2014, New York, New York, USA, pp. 704–713. Association for Computing Machinery (2014). https://doi.org/10.1145/2591796.2591853
27. Mitchell, J.C., Moggi, E.: Kripke-style models for typed lambda calculus. Ann. Pure Appl. Logic **51**(1–2), 99–124 (1991). https://doi.org/10.1016/0168-0072(91)90067-V
28. Moses, Y.: Relating knowledge and coordinated action: the Knowledge of Preconditions principle. In: Ramanujam, R. (ed.) Proceedings Fifteenth Conference on Theoretical Aspects of Rationality and Knowledge, Carnegie Mellon University, Pittsburgh, USA, 4–6 June 2015. Electronic Proceedings in Theoretical Computer Science, vol. 215, pp. 231–245. Open Publishing Association (2016). https://doi.org/10.4204/EPTCS.215.17
29. Pessin, A., Goldberg, S.: The Twin Earth Chronicles: Twenty Years of Reflection on Hilary Putnam's "The Meaning of 'Meaning'". M. E. Sharpe (1995). https://doi.org/10.4324/9781315284811
30. Powell, D., et al.: GUARDS: a generic upgradable architecture for real-time dependable systems. IEEE Trans. Parallel Distrib. Syst. **10**(6), 580–599 (1999). https://doi.org/10.1109/71.774908
31. Robinson, P., Schmid, U.: The Asynchronous Bounded-Cycle model. Theoret. Comput. Sci. **412**(40), 5580–5601 (2011). https://doi.org/10.1016/j.tcs.2010.08.001
32. Rushby, J.: Reconfiguration and transient recovery in state machine architectures. In: Proceedings of the Twenty-Sixth International Symposium on Fault-Tolerant Computing: 25–27 June 1996, Sendai, Japan, pp. 6–15. IEEE (1996). https://doi.org/10.1109/FTCS.1996.534589
33. Schlögl, T., Schmid, U.: A sufficient condition for gaining belief in byzantine fault-tolerant distributed systems. In: Verbrugge, R. (ed.) Proceedings of the Nineteenth conference on Theoretical Aspects of Rationality and Knowledge, Oxford, United Kingdom, 28–30th June 2023. Electronic Proceedings in Theoretical Computer Science, vol. 379, pp. 487–497. Open Publishing Association (2023). https://doi.org/10.4204/EPTCS.379.37
34. Schlögl, T., Schmid, U., Kuznets, R.: The persistence of false memory: brain in a vat despite perfect clocks. In: Uchiya, T., Bai, Q., Marsá Maestre, I. (eds.) PRIMA 2020. LNCS, vol. 12568, pp. 403–411. Springer, Cham (2021). https://doi.org/10.1007/978-3-030-69322-0_30
35. Schneider, F.B.: Implementing fault-tolerant services using the state machine approach: a tutorial. ACM Comput. Surv. **22**(4), 299–319 (1990). https://doi.org/10.1145/98163.98167
36. Srikanth, T.K., Toueg, S.: Optimal clock synchronization. J. ACM **34**(3), 626–645 (1987). https://doi.org/10.1145/28869.28876
37. Srikanth, T.K., Toueg, S.: Simulating authenticated broadcasts to derive simple fault-tolerant algorithms. Distrib. Comput. **2**(2), 80–94 (1987). https://doi.org/10.1007/BF01667080
38. Walter, C.J., Lincoln, P., Suri, N.: Formally verified on-line diagnosis. IEEE Trans. Software Eng. **23**(11), 684–721 (1997). https://doi.org/10.1109/32.637385
39. Widder, J., Schmid, U.: The Theta-Model: achieving synchrony without clocks. Distrib. Comput. **22**(1), 29–47 (2009). https://doi.org/10.1007/s00446-009-0080-x

Calculi, Proof Theory and Decision Procedures

A Decision Method for First-Order Stream Logic

Harald Ruess(✉)

Entalus Computer Science Lab,
2071 Gulf of Mexico Drive, Longboat Key,
FL 34228, USA
harald.ruess@entalus.com

Abstract. Our main result is a doubly exponential decision procedure for the first-order equality theory of streams with addition, convolution, and control-oriented stream operations. This stream logic is shown to be expressive for solving basic problems in stream calculus.

Keywords: Decision Procedures · First-Order Logic · Stream Calculus · Formal Power Series · Real-Closed Rings · Quantifier Elimination

1 Introduction

Quantified stream constraints are often used in the principled design of reactive computing systems [7,8,10,25,26]. However, automated solutions to these constraints can be challenging, as quantifying over streams effectively is second-order.

Quantifying over sets of natural numbers, for instance, encodes quantifying over streams in the monadic second-order logic $MSO(\omega)$ [19] of ω-infinite words over a finite alphabet.[1] This logic is decidable, but only non-elementarily so, based on the well-known characterization of the set of models of any $MSO(\omega)$ formula in terms of a finite-state machine [9]. Equivalently, the logic-automaton connection yields a non-elementary decision procedure for a first-order equality theory of streams [34].

Here we study a first-order stream logic that is not limited to finite alphabets, and which includes an expressive combination of nonlinear arithmetic stream operators, such as convolution, with control-oriented stream operators, such as shifting. Compared to $MSO(\omega)$, however, this stream logic is restrictive in that it only supports quantifying over streams, not over positions in streams.

Our main result is that the validity of first-order stream formulas (in the language of ordered rings) in the structure of real-valued streams is decided in doubly exponential time. In contrast to automata-based procedures for monadic second-order logics, our decision procedure is not limited to streams over a finite

[1] For example, the set of even numbers represents the Boolean-valued stream $(1, 0, 1, 0, 1, \ldots)$, since the i-th position, for $i \in \mathbb{N}$, is 'on' if and only if i is even.

C. Benzmüller et al. (Eds.): IJCAR 2024, LNAI 14740, pp. 137–156, 2024.
https://doi.org/10.1007/978-3-031-63501-4_8

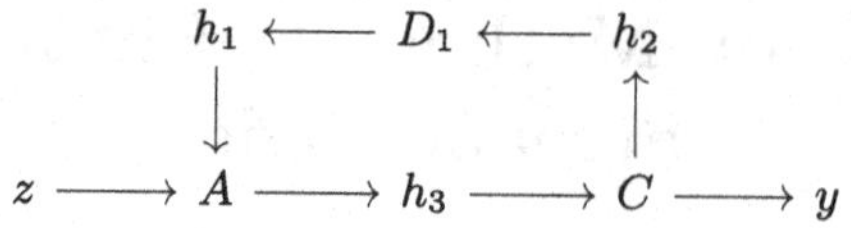

Fig. 1. Stream circuit.

alphabet, and the time complexity of our procedure is doubly exponential instead of non-elementary as in [34]. Definitional extensions demonstrate the expressive power of this stream logic in solving a number of fundamental problems in the coalgebraic *stream calculus* [38].

The structure of the developments is as follows. Section 2 motivates quantified stream logic with typical examples from *stream calculus* [38], and Sect. 3 summarizes, with the intention of making the exposition largely self-contained, essential properties of streams. Since we are targeting stream calculus, we restrict ourselves to streams with real-numbered elements only. However, the results in this paper clearly generalize to streams with elements from either a totally ordered commutative integral ring or a totally ordered field. Streams are identified with *formal power series* [32] and the superset of streams with finite history prefixes is identified with *formal Laurent series*. Based on this identification of streams with their generating function it is straightforward to establish that streams are orderable and also Cauchy complete for the prefix distance.

Based on these developments it is shown in Sect. 4 that streams are a *real closed valuation ring* and their extension with finite histories are a *real closed field*. The main technical hurdle is the derivation of an *intermediate value property* (IVP) for streams. As an ordered and complete non-Archimedean domain, streams lack the *least upper bound* property. The usual dichotomic procedure for proving IVP therefore does not apply. Ordered streams admit quantifier elimination as a consequence of real closedness.

The results in Sect. 5 therefore are direct consequences of the quantifier elimination procedures for real closed valuation rings [12] and for real closed ordered fields [44] together with the doubly exponential bound obtained by cylindrical algebraic decomposition [18] in the case of real closed ordered fields. In Sect. 6, the language of decidable stream logic is conservatively extended by shift operators, constants for rational and automatic streams, and stream projections. Section 7 concludes with some remarks.

2 Examples

We motivate the rôle of quantified stream logic for encoding some typical problems from stream calculus.

Observational Equivalence. Two stream processors T_1, T_2 are *observationally equivalent* if the first-order formula in Example 1 holds.

Example 1 (Observational Equivalence).

$$(\forall z, y_1, y_2)\, T_1(z, y_1) \,\wedge\, T_2(z, y_2) \;\Rightarrow\; y_1 = y_2$$

The logical variables z, y_1, and y_2 are interpreted over discrete and real-valued streams, and $T_i(z, y_i)$, for $i = 1, 2$, are binary predicates for defining the possible output streams y_i of processor T_i on input stream z.

In *stream calculus* [38], the relations $T_i(z, y_i)$ are typically of the form $y_i = f_i \cdot z$, where the *transfer function* f_i is a stream, and the output stream y_i is obtained by stream convolution of f_i with the input stream z. These algebraic specifications are expressive for the set of all stream circuits [40].

Functionality. A stream processor T is *functional* if the first-order stream formula in Example 2 with one quantifier alternation holds.

Example 2 (Functionality).

$$(\forall z)(\exists y)\, T(z, y) \,\wedge\, (\forall u)\, u \neq y \;\Rightarrow\; \neg T(z, u)$$

Non-Interference. We now consider streams of system output that are divided into a *low* and a *high* security part. In such an environment, a stream processor T is said to be *non-interfering* [22,29,30] if executing T always results in indistinguishable low outputs at every step.

Example 3 (Non-Interference).

$$(\forall z, y_1, y_2)\, T(z, y_1) \,\wedge\, T(z, y_2) \;\Rightarrow\; hd(y_1) =_L hd(y_2) \;\Rightarrow\; y_1 =_L y_2,$$

where $hd(y_i)$, for $i = 1, 2$, denote initial values, and $hd(y_1) =_L hd(y_2)$ is assumed to hold if and only if the *low* parts of the two head elements $hd(y_1)$ and $hd(y_1)$ are equal. Similarly, the (overloaded) relation $y_1 =_L y_2$ on streams is assumed to hold if all the respective projections to the low parts are equal. These non-interference properties are prominent examples of a larger class of *hyper-properties* [14] for comparing two or more traces. Quantifier alternation between existential and universal quantifiers is required for the formalization of more general hyper-properties.

Stream Circuits. We take into consideration some typical design steps for the stream circuit in Fig. 1. At moment 0 this circuit inputs the first value z_0. The initial value 0 of the register D_1 is added to this by A, and the result $y_0 = z_0 + 0 = z_0$ is the first value to be output. At the same time, this value z_0 is copied by C, and stored as the new value of the register D_1. The next step is to input the value z_1, add the current value z_0 of the register to it, and output the resulting value $y_1 = z_0 + z_1$. Simultaneously, this value is copied and saved as the new value of the register. In the next step, the input is z_2 and the output is the value $y_2 = z_0 + z_1 + z_2$. In general, the output y_k, for $k \in \mathbb{N}$, of the circuit in Fig. 1 is determined by the sum $\sum_{i=0}^{k} z_i$ of the finite history $z_0 \ldots z_k$ of inputs. In other words, $y = (1, 1, 1, \ldots) \cdot z$, where '$\cdot$' denotes stream convolution. This input-output behavior of the stream circuit in Fig. 1 can be verified by showing that the stream logic formula in Example 4 is valid.

Example 4 (Analysis).

$$\begin{aligned}&(\forall z, y, h_1, h_2, h_3)\\ &\quad h_1 = D_1(h_2) \wedge h_3 = A(z, h_1) \wedge h_2 = C(h_3) \wedge y = C(h_3)\\ &\qquad \Rightarrow y = (1, 1, 1, \ldots) \cdot z\end{aligned}$$

The stream $(1, 1, \ldots)$ is considered to be an interpreted constant symbol in the logic, and D_1, A, and C are interpreted function symbols.

Finally, the formula in Example 5 with one quantifier alternation allows to synthesize the transfer function by constructing explicit witnesses for existentially quantified variables in an underlying proof procedure.

Example 5 (Synthesis).

$$\begin{aligned}&(\forall z, y, h_1, h_2, h_3)\\ &\quad h_1 = D_1(h_2) \wedge h_3 = A(z, h_1) \wedge h_2 = C(h_3) \wedge y = C(h_3)\\ &\qquad \Rightarrow (\exists u)\, y = u \cdot z\end{aligned}$$

3 On Streams

A *real-valued stream* is an infinite sequence $(a_i)_{i \in \mathbb{N}}$ with $a_i \in \mathcal{R}$, where $\mathcal{R}$ denotes the real numbers. Depending on the context, streams are also referred to as real-valued discrete streams or signals, ω-streams, ω-sequences, or ω-words. The *generating function* [11] of a stream is a *formal power series*

$$\sum_{i \in \mathbb{N}} a_i X^i \tag{1}$$

in the *indefinite* X. These power series are *formal* because the symbol X is not instantiated and there is no notion of convergence. The element $a_i \in \mathcal{R}$ is the *coefficient* of X^i, and the set of formal power series with coefficients in $\mathcal{R}$ is denoted by $\mathcal{R}[\![X]\!]$. We also write f_i for the coefficient of X^i in the formal power series. Now, a *polynomial* in $\mathcal{R}[X]$ of degree $n \in \mathbb{N}$ is a formal power series f with $f_n \neq 0$ and $f_i = 0$ for all $i > n$. We use the terms streams and formal power series interchangeably for their one-to-one correspondence.

Addition of streams $f, g \in \mathcal{R}[\![X]\!]$ is pointwise, and streams are multiplied by convolution.

$$f + g := \sum_{i \in \mathbb{N}} (f_i + g_i) X^i \tag{2}$$

$$f \cdot g := \sum_{i \in \mathbb{N}} \Big(\sum_{j=0}^{i} f_j g_{i-j}\Big) X^i \tag{3}$$

With these operations $(\mathcal{R}[\![X]\!], +, \cdot, 0, 1)$ becomes a *commutative integral ring* with additive unit $0 := (0, 0, \ldots)$ and multiplicative unit $1 := (1, 0, 0, \ldots)$. The real number line $\mathcal{R}$ is embedded in the polynomial ring $\mathcal{R}[X]$, which itself is embedded in $\mathcal{R}[\![X]\!]$. Moreover, the *rational functions* $\mathcal{R}(X)$ are defined as the fraction field of the polynomials $\mathcal{R}[X]$. $\mathcal{R}[\![X]\!]$ and $\mathcal{R}(X)$ are incomparable in that neither $\mathcal{R}[\![X]\!]$ nor $\mathcal{R}(X)$ contains the other.

Proposition 1. *For $f \in \mathcal{R}[\![X]\!]$, the* multiplicative inverse *$f^{-1} \in \mathcal{R}[\![X]\!]$ exists if only if $f_0 \neq 0$.*

Proof. Let $f, g \in \mathcal{R}[\![X]\!]$. The identity $f \cdot g = 1$ holds, by the defining identity (3) for convolution, if and only if $f_0 g_0 = 1$ and $\sum_{i=0}^{k} f_i g_{k-i} = 0$ for all $k \geq 1$. The latter equality is rewritten as $f_0 g_k = -\sum_{i=1}^{k} f_i g_{k-i}$. Now, $f_0 g_0 = 1$ can be solved for g_0 if and only if $f_0 \neq 0$. In this case, $g_0 = {}^{1}/_{f_0}$ and $g_k = -g_0 \sum_{i=1}^{k} f_i g_{k-i}$, for $k \geq 1$, yielding a solution for g, which gives the multiplicative inverse of f.

We also write the quotient ${}^{f}/_{g}$ instead of $f \cdot g^{-1}$, whenever g^{-1} exists.

Example 6.

$$
\begin{aligned}
{}^{1}/_{(1-X)} &= (1, 1, 1, 1, \ldots) \\
{}^{1}/_{(1-X)^2} &= (1, 2, 3, 4, \ldots) \\
{}^{1}/_{(1-rX)} &= (1, r, r^2, r^3, \ldots) && \text{for } r \in \mathcal{R}
\end{aligned}
$$

These identities are easily verified by the defining identities for convolution (3) and for the multiplicative inverse. The first stream identity, for instance, is verified by the identity $(1, -1, 0, \ldots) \cdot (1, 1, 1, \ldots) = (1, 0, 0, \ldots)$, since $1 - X$ is identified with $(1, -1, 0, \ldots)$.

A stream in $\mathcal{R}[\![X]\!]$ is *rational* if it is expressible as a quotient ${}^{p}/_{q}$ of polynomials $p, q \in \mathcal{R}[X]$ such that $q_0 \neq 0$ [40]. Rational streams, as a subring of the formal power series $\mathcal{R}[\![X]\!]$, are central to *stream calculus* because of their close correspondence to stream circuits [40].

Example 7 ([37]). Let f, g be rational streams with real-valued coefficients. Using the defining equations

$$
\begin{aligned}
D_1(f) &:= X \cdot f \\
A(f, g) &:= f + g \\
C(f) &:= f
\end{aligned}
$$

for the unit delay register D_1, addition A of two streams, and copying C of a stream, we obtain from the stream circuit in Fig. 1 a system of defining equations $h_1 = X \cdot h_2$, $h_3 = z + h_1$, $h_2 = h_3$, $y = h_3$. Back substitution for the intermediate streams h_3, h_1, and h_2, in this order, yields an equational constraint $y = z + (X \cdot y)$, which is equivalent to $y = {}^{1}/_{(1-X)} \cdot z$. Now, $y = (\sum_{i=0}^{k} z_i)_{k \in \mathbb{N}}$ as a result of the identity for ${}^{1}/_{(1-X)}$ in Example 6.

Remark 1. Rational streams substantially differ from the *rational functions*. The inverse ${}^{1}/_{X}$, for example, is not a rational stream, and it is not even a formal power series. But it is in $\mathcal{R}(X)$.

$$\begin{array}{ccc} \mathcal{R}[X] & \xrightarrow{\ /\ } & \mathcal{R}(X) \\ \downarrow * & & \downarrow * \\ \mathcal{R}[\![X]\!] & \xrightarrow{\ /\ } & \mathcal{R}(\!(X)\!) \end{array}$$

Fig. 2. Commuting stream embeddings ('$*$' denotes completion for valuation $|.|$, and '/' the fraction field construction.

The field $\mathcal{R}(\!(X)\!)$ of *formal Laurent series* is the fraction field of the formal power series $\mathcal{R}[\![X]\!]$. Elements of $\mathcal{R}(\!(X)\!)$ therefore are of the form

$$\sum_{i=-n}^{\infty} a_i X^i, \tag{4}$$

for $n \in \mathbb{N}$ and $a_i \in \mathcal{R}$. They can therefore be thought of as streams that are preceded by a finite, and possibly empty, history, which are used for "rewinding computations". In fact, every formal Laurent series is of the form $X^{-n} \cdot f$, for some $n \in \mathbb{N}$ and for $f \in \mathcal{R}[\![X]\!]$ a formal power series.

The valuation $v : \mathcal{R}(\!(X)\!) \to \mathbb{Z} \cup \{\infty\}$ with $v(0) := \infty$ and $v(f)$, for $f \neq 0$, is the minimal index $k \in \mathbb{Z}$ with $f_k \neq 0$. In the latter case, f_k is also said to be the *lead coefficient* of f. Now, the set $\mathcal{R}(\!(X)\!)$ of formal Laurent series is *orderable* (see Appendix A) by the *positive cone* $\mathcal{R}(\!(X)\!)_+$ of formal Laurent series with positive lead coefficient. This set determines a strict ordering $f < g$, for $f, g \in \mathcal{R}(\!(X)\!)$, which is defined to hold if and only if $g - f \in \mathcal{R}(\!(X)\!)_+$, and a total ordering $f \leq g$, which holds if and only if $f < g$ or $f = g$. The restriction of $\leq$ to the formal power series in $\mathcal{R}[\![X]\!]$ is also a total order.

Proposition 2.

1. $(\mathcal{R}[\![X]\!]; +, \cdot, 0, 1; \leq)$ *is a totally ordered commutative integral ring.*
2. $(\mathcal{R}(\!(X)\!); +, \cdot, 0, 1; \leq)$ *is a totally ordered field.*

As a consequence of Proposition 2.2, $\mathcal{R}(\!(X)\!)$ is *formally real* (-1 can not be written as a sum of nonzero squares in $\mathcal{R}(\!(X)\!)$), $\mathcal{R}(\!(X)\!)$ is not algebraically closed (for example, the polynomial X^2+1 has no root), and $\mathcal{R}(\!(X)\!)$ is of characteristic 0 (0 can not be written as a sum of 1s). Moreover, the Archimedean property (see [41]) fails to hold for $\mathcal{R}(\!(X)\!)$, because $X \not< 1 + 1 + \ldots + 1$, no matter how many 1's we add together.

From the (normalized) valuation v one obtains, with the convention $2^{-\infty} := 0$, the absolute value function $|.| : \mathcal{R}(\!(X)\!) \to \mathcal{R}^{\geq 0}$ by setting

$$|f| := 2^{-v(f)}. \tag{5}$$

By construction, $|.|$ is the *non-Archimedean absolute value* on $\mathcal{R}(\!(X)\!)$ corresponding to the valuation v [31]. Now, the induced metric $d : \mathcal{R}(\!(X)\!) \times \mathcal{R}(\!(X)\!) \to \mathcal{R}^{\geq 0}$ with

$$d(f, g) := |f - g| \tag{6}$$

measures the distance between f and g in terms of the longest common prefix. Again, by construction, the *strong triangle inequality*

$$d(f,h) \leq \max(d(f,g), d(g,h)). \tag{7}$$

holds for all $f, g, h \in \mathcal{R}((X))$, and therefore d is ultrametric.

Proposition 3. *$(\mathcal{R}((X)), d)$ is an ultrametric space.*

Example 8. The scaled identity function $I_f(x) := f \cdot x$, for $f \neq 0$, is uniformly continuous in the topology induced by the metric d.[2] For given $\varepsilon > 0$, let $\delta := \varepsilon/|f|$. Now, $d(x,y) < \delta$ implies $d(f \cdot x, f \cdot y) = |f|\, d(x,y) < |f|\,\delta = \varepsilon$ for all $x, y \in \mathcal{R}((X))$.

Proposition 4. *Both addition and multiplication of formal Laurent series in $\mathcal{R}((X))$ are continuous in the topology induced by the prefix metric d.*

The notions of Cauchy sequences and convergence in the metric space $(\mathcal{R}((X)), d)$ are defined as usual. For example, $\lim_{n\to\infty} X^n = 0$ and $\lim_{n\to\infty} \sum_{k=0}^{n} X^k = 1/(1-X)$. For a given sequence $(f_k)_{k\in\mathbb{N}}$ of formal Laurent series, (1) the sequence $(f_k)_{k\in\mathbb{N}}$ is *Cauchy* iff $\lim_{k\to\infty} d(f_{k+1}, f_k) = 0$, (2) the series $\sum_{k=0}^{\infty} f_k := \lim_{n\to\infty} \sum_{k=0}^{n} f_k$ converges iff $\lim_{k\to\infty} f_k = 0$, and (3) suppose that $\lim_{k\to\infty} f_k = f \neq 0$, then there exists an integer $N > 0$ such that for all $m \geq N$, $|f_m| = |f_N| = |f|$. These properties follow directly from the fact that $|.|$ is a non-Archimedean absolute value.

Proposition 5. *$(\mathcal{R}((X)), d)$ is Cauchy complete.*

Proof. Let $(f_k)_{k\in\mathbb{N}}$ be a Cauchy sequence with $f_k \in \mathcal{R}((X))$. Then, for all $c \in \mathbb{N}$ there is $N_c \in \mathbb{N}$ such that $d(f_n, f_m) < |X^c|$ for all $n, m \geq N_c$. But this means that $f_n - f_m \in X^c \cdot \mathcal{R}((X))$. Since f_k are Laurent series, there are $M_k \in \mathbb{Z}$ and $a_{k,i} \in \mathcal{R}$ such that $f_k = \sum_{i \geq M_k} a_{k,i} X^i$. Consequently, $(a_{k,i})_{k\in\mathbb{N}}$ is constant for k large enough. Now, there exists $J \in \mathbb{Z}$ such that

$$\lim_{k\to\infty} f_k = \sum_{i\geq J} (\lim_{k\to\infty} a_{k,i}) X^i \in \mathcal{R}((X)),$$

and therefore $\mathcal{R}((X))$ is Cauchy complete.

Indeed, $\mathcal{R}((X))$ can be shown to be the Cauchy completion of $\mathcal{R}(X)$, and the stream embeddings discussed so far commute as displayed in Fig. 2.[3] Finally, as a non-Archimedean, Cauchy complete, and totally ordered field, $\mathcal{R}((X))$ lacks the *least upper bound property*, that is, there exists a non-empty subset of $\mathcal{R}((X))$ with an upper bound and no least upper bound in $\mathcal{R}((X))$.

---

[2] The topology induced by the order $\leq$ on streams is identical to the topology induced by the prefix metric d.

[3] This story continues, as $\mathcal{R}((X))$ is a subfield of the real closed Levi-Civita field, which itself is the Cauchy completion of the Newton-Puiseux series $\cup_{l=1}^{\infty} \mathcal{R}((X^{1/l}))$ over the reals, which can also be shown to be real closed.

4 Real Closedness

$\mathcal{R}((X))$ is a totally ordered field by Proposition 2. To show that $\mathcal{R}((X))$ is *real closed*, we therefore still need to demonstrate the existence of a square root for streams and the existence of roots for all odd degree polynomials in $\mathcal{R}((X))[Y]$, where Y is a single indeterminate (cmp. Appendix B). General results on the preservation of real-closedness ([1], §6.23, (1)-(2); [42], p. 221) are not applicable for demonstrating real-closedness of $\mathcal{R}((X))$.

The main step for showing real-closedness of $\mathcal{R}((X))$ is an intermediate value property (IVP) for streams. It should be recalled that the standard proof of the IVP for a continuous function over the field of real numbers essentially uses the fact that intervals and connected subsets coincide in the real number field and that continuous functions preserve connectedness. When working with the non-Archimedean, complete, and ordered field $\mathcal{R}((X))$, however, such an argument is no longer applicable, as it lacks the least upper bound property and therefore also the dichotomic procedure for proving IVP. In this case, not only do the Archimedean proofs of the IVP not work, but the IVP does not hold in general. It nevertheless holds for special cases [6].

Lemma 1 (IVP). *For a polynomial* $P(Y) \in \mathcal{R}[\![X]\!][Y]$ *and* $\alpha, \beta \in \mathcal{R}[\![X]\!]$ *such that* $P(\alpha) < 0 < P(\beta)$*, there exists* $\gamma \in \mathcal{R}[\![X]\!] \cap (\alpha, \beta)$ *with* $P(\gamma) = 0$.

Proof. Since $\mathcal{R}[\![X]\!]$ is the Cauchy completion of $\mathcal{R}[X]$, there are sequences $(a_n)_{n \in \mathbb{N}}$ and $(b_n)_{n \in \mathbb{N}}$ of polynomials $a_n, b_n \in \mathcal{R}[X]$ such that $\lim_{n \to \infty} a_n = \alpha$ and $\lim_{n \to \infty} b_n = \beta$. From the assumptions $P(\alpha) < 0 < P(\beta)$ and continuity of the polynomial P in the topology induced by the prefix metric d, one can therefore find $a, b \in \mathcal{R}[\![X]\!]$ in the sequences (a_n) and (b_n) with $\alpha \leq a < b \leq \beta$ and $P(a) < 0 < P(b)$. For continuity of P, $P(\alpha) = P(\lim_{n \to \infty} a_n) = \lim_{n \to \infty} P(a_n)$. Now, for $0 < \varepsilon := {}^{|P(\alpha)|}/_{2}$, there exists $N \in \mathbb{N}$ such that for $d(P(a_n), P(\alpha)) < \varepsilon$ for all $n \geq N$. Therefore, $P(a) < 0$ for $a := a_N$. The construction for b is similar.

The proof proceeds along two cases. If there is $\gamma \in \mathcal{R}[\![X]\!] \cap (a, b)$ such that $P(\gamma) = 0$ we are finished. Otherwise, $f(\gamma) \neq 0$ for all $\gamma \in \mathcal{R}[\![X]\!] \cap (a, b)$. We define $\alpha_0 := a$, $\beta_0 := b$, and, for $m \in \mathbb{N}$,

$$[\alpha_{m+1}, \beta_{m+1}] = \begin{cases} [\alpha_m, \delta_m] : & \text{if } f(\delta_m) > 0 \\ [\delta_m, \beta_m] : & \text{if } f(\delta_m) < 0 \end{cases},$$

where $\delta_m := {}^{1}/_{2}(\alpha_m + \beta_m) \in \mathcal{R}[\![X]\!]$. By assumption, $P(\delta_m) \neq 0$, and, by construction, $(\alpha_m)_{m \in \mathbb{N}}$ is a non-decreasing and $(\beta_m)_{m \in \mathbb{N}}$ a non-increasing sequence in $\mathcal{R}[X]$ such that, for all $m \in \mathbb{N}$, $\alpha_m < \beta_m$, $d(\alpha_m, \beta_m) \leq 2^{-m}$, $T(\alpha_m) < 0$, and $T(\beta_m) > 0$. Therefore, both $(\alpha_m)_{m \in \mathbb{N}}$ and $(\beta_m)_{m \in \mathbb{N}}$ are Cauchy, $(\alpha_m)_{m \in \mathbb{N}}$ converges from below, and $(\beta_m)_{m \in \mathbb{N}}$ converges from above to a point γ. Now, $\gamma \in \mathcal{R}[\![X]\!]$, since $\mathcal{R}[\![X]\!]$ is the Cauchy completion of $\mathcal{R}[X]$. Since P is continuous we obtain

$$\lim_{m \to \infty} \underbrace{P(\alpha_m)}_{<0} = P(\lim_{m \to \infty} \alpha_m) = P(\gamma) = P(\lim_{m \to \infty} \beta_m) = \lim_{m \to \infty} \underbrace{P(\beta_m)}_{>0},$$

and therefore $P(\gamma) = 0$. This establishes the claim.

A *real closed ring* is an ordered domain which has the intermediate value property for polynomials in one variable. From the IVP for formal power series in Lemma 1 we immediately obtain the following three properties that characterize *real closed rings* [12].

Proposition 6.

1. *f divides g for all $f, g \in \mathcal{R}[\![X]\!]$ with $0 < g < f$;*
2. *Every positive element in $\mathcal{R}[\![X]\!]$ has a square root in $\mathcal{R}[\![X]\!]$;*
3. *Every monic polynomial in $\mathcal{R}[\![X]\!][Y]$ of odd degree has a root in $\mathcal{R}[\![X]\!]$.*

Proof. In each of the three cases a certain polynomial changes sign, and hence has a root. The relevant polynomials in $\mathcal{R}[\![X]\!][Y]$ are:

1. $f \cdot Y + g$ on $[0, 1]$;
2. $Y^2 - f$ on $[0, \max(f, 1)]$;
3. $Y^n + f_{n-1} \cdot Y^{n-1} + \ldots + f_1 \cdot Y + f_0$ on $[-N, N]$, where $n \in \mathbb{N}$ is odd and $N := 1 + |f_{n-1}| + \ldots + |f_0|$.

Example 9. $\sqrt{(1, 2, 3, \ldots)} = (1, 1, 1, \ldots)$, since, using the identities in Example 6, $(1, 1, 1, \ldots)^2 = ({}^1/_{(1-X)})^2 = {}^1/_{(1-X)^2} = (1, 2, 3, \ldots)$.

Alternatively, square roots of streams are constructed as unique solutions of corecursive identities.

Remark 2 (Corecursive definition of square root [39]*).* Assume $f \in \mathcal{R}[\![X]\!]$ with head coefficient $f_0 > 0$ and tail $f' \in \mathcal{R}[\![X]\!]$. Then, $\sqrt{f} \in \mathcal{R}[\![X]\!]$ is the unique solution (for the unknown g) of the corecursive identity $g' = {}^{f'}/_{(\sqrt{f_0}+g)}$, for the tail g' of g, and the initial condition $g_0 = \sqrt{f_0}$ for the head g_0 of g. Now, for all $f, g \in \mathcal{R}[\![X]\!]$ with $f' > 0$, if $g \cdot g = f$ then either $g = \sqrt{f}$ or $g = -\sqrt{f}$, depending on whether the head g_0 is positive or negative ([39], Theorem 7.1).

It is an immediate consequence of property (1) of Proposition 6 that the formal power series $\mathcal{R}[\![X]\!]$ is a proper *valuation ring* of its fraction field $\mathcal{R}(\!(X)\!)$; that is, f or f^{-1} lies in $\mathcal{R}[\![X]\!]$ for each nonzero $f \in \mathcal{R}(\!(X)\!)$. Since $\mathcal{R}[\![X]\!]$ also satisfies the IVP (Lemma 1) we obtain:

Corollary 1. *$(\mathcal{R}[\![X]\!]; +, \cdot, 0, 1; \leq)$ is a* real closed ordered valuation ring.

Formal Laurent series, as the fraction field of formal power series, inherit the properties (2) and (3) in Proposition 6.

Proposition 7.

1. *Every positive stream in $\mathcal{R}(\!(X)\!)$ has a square root in $\mathcal{R}(\!(X)\!)$.*
2. *Every monic polynomial in $\mathcal{R}(\!(X)\!)[Y]$ of odd degree has a root in $\mathcal{R}(\!(X)\!)$.*

Proof. Assume $0 < {}^{f}/_{g} \in \mathcal{R}((X))$. Then $0 < f \cdot g \in \mathcal{R}[\![X]\!]$, and $\sqrt{f \cdot g}/g$ is the square root of f/g. For establishing (2), assume $P(Y) \in \mathcal{R}((X))[Y]$ be a polynomial of odd degree n. Choose $0 \neq h \in \mathcal{R}((X))$ such that $h \cdot P(Y) \in \mathcal{R}[\![X]\!][Y]$. Now, $Q(Y) := h^n \cdot P(Y/h)$ is a monic polynomial in $\mathcal{R}[\![X]\!][Y]$ of odd degree. Applying Proposition (6.2) to $q(Y)$ we see that $p(Y)$ has a root in $\mathcal{R}((X))$.

Formal Laurent series are real closed (see Appendix B) as an immediate consequence of Proposition 7.

Corollary 2. $(\mathcal{R}((X)); +, \cdot, 0, 1; \leq)$ *is a real closed ordered field.*

Therefore the ordering $\leq$ on $\mathcal{R}((X))$ is unique.

5 Decision Method

The first-order theory $\mathcal{T}_{\text{rcf}}$ of ordered, real closed fields (see Appendix B) admits quantifier elimination [16, 44]. That is, for every formula ϕ in the language $\mathcal{L}_{or}$ (cmp. Appendix B) of ordered rings/fields there exists a quantifier free formula ψ in this language with $FV(\psi) \subseteq FV(\phi)$[4] such that $\mathcal{T}_{\text{rcf}} \models (\phi \iff \psi)$. Thus, Corollary 2 implies quantifier elimination for the streams in $\mathcal{R}((X))$.

Theorem 1. *Let φ be a first-order formula in the language $\mathcal{L}_{or}$ of ordered fields; then there is a computable function for deciding whether φ holds in the $\mathcal{L}_{or}$-structure $(\mathcal{R}((X)); +, \cdot, 0, 1; \leq)$ of streams.*

As an immediate consequence of the quantifier elimination property for $\mathcal{R}((X))$, the structure of formal Laurent series with real-valued coefficients is *elementarily equivalent* to the real numbers in that they satisfy the same first-order $\mathcal{L}_{or}$-sentences. Notice that decidability of $\mathcal{R}((X))$ already follows from the developments in ([4], Corollary), since the field $\mathcal{R}$ is of characteristic 0. This observation, however, does not yield quantifier elimination.

There is an explicit quantifier elimination procedure for real closed valuation rings, which uses quantifier elimination on its fraction field as a subprocedure ([12], Section 2). Therefore, by Corollary 1, we obtain a decision procedure for first-order formulas and streams in $\mathcal{R}[\![X]\!]$, which has quantifier elimination for $\mathcal{R}((X))$ as a subprocedure.

Theorem 2. *Let φ be a first-order formula in the language $\mathcal{L}_{or} \cup \{|\}$ of ordered rings extended with divisibility; then there is a computable function for deciding whether φ holds in the $\mathcal{L}_{or} \cup \{|\}$-structure $(\mathcal{R}[\![X]\!]; +, \cdot, 0, 1; |, \leq)$ of streams.*

Tarski's original algorithm for quantifier elimination has non-elementary computational complexity [44], but cylindrical algebraic decomposition provides a decision procedure of complexity $d^{2^{O(n)}}$ [18], where n is the total number of variables (free and bound), and d is the product of the degrees of the polynomials occurring in the formula.

[4] $FV(.)$ denotes the set of free variables in a formula.

Theorem 3. *Let φ be a first-order formula in the language $\mathcal{L}_{or}$ of ordered fields. Then the validity of φ in the structure $\mathcal{R}((X))$ of streams is decided with complexity $d^{2^{O(n)}}$, where n is the total number of variables (free and bound), and d is the product of the degrees of the polynomials occurring in φ.*

This worst-case complexity is nearly optimal for quantifier elimination for real closed fields [20]. For existentially quantified conjunctions of literals of the form $(\exists x_1, \ldots, x_k) \wedge_{i=1}^{n} p_i(x_1, \ldots, x_k) \bowtie 0$, where $\bowtie$ stands for either $<$, $=$, or $>$ the worst-case complexity is $n^{k+1} \cdot d^{O(k)}$ arithmetic operations and polynomial space [5]. Various implementations of decision procedures for real closed fields use virtual term substitution [46] or conflict-driven clause learning [24].

6 Definitional Extensions

We consider definitional extensions of the first-order theory $\mathcal{T}_{\text{rcf}}$ of ordered real closed fields for encoding some fundamental concepts of stream calculus. The transfer function in Example 7 of the stream circuit in Fig. 1, for example, is encoded as a first-order formula in the language $\mathcal{L}_{or}$ of (ordered) rings extended with constant symbols $\overline{X}$ and $\overline{1/(1-X)}$.

Example 10.

$$(\forall z, y, h_1)\,(h_1 = \overline{X} \cdot y \wedge y = z + h_1) \Rightarrow y = \overline{1/(1-X)} \cdot z,$$

where the logical variables z, y, h_1 are interpreted over streams in $\mathcal{R}[\![X]\!]$. To obtain a decision procedure for these kinds of formula, we therefore

- Relativize quantification in $\mathcal{T}_{\text{rcf}}$ to formal power series;
- Define constant symbols $\overline{f}$ for rational streams f (including $\overline{X}$).

Relativization. There is a monadic formula with an $\exists\forall\exists\forall$ quantifier prefix and no parameters for uniformly defining the formal power series $\mathcal{R}[\![X]\!]$ in $\mathcal{R}((X))$, as a direct consequence of Ax's construction [4].[5] Moreover, $\mathcal{R}[\![X]\!]$ is $\forall\exists$-definable in $\mathcal{R}((X))$ by ([35], Theorem 2 together with footnote 2), since the valuation ring $\mathcal{R}[\![X]\!]$ is Henselian. The model-theoretic developments in [35], however, do not provide an explicit definitional formula. But explicit definitions of valuation rings in valued fields are studied in [3,15,21].

From these considerations we obtain an explicit definition in $\mathcal{R}((X))$ of the monadic predicate $\overline{S}(x)$ for characterizing the set of streams in $\mathcal{R}[\![X]\!]$. By relativization of quantifiers with respect to this predicate $\overline{S}$ we therefore assume from now on that all logical variables are interpreted over the streams in $\mathcal{R}[\![X]\!]$. In addition, we are assuming definitions $\overline{R}(x)$ for given, and possibly finite, subsets R of real number embeddings. For example, the algebraic definition

$$(\forall x)\,\overline{\mathbb{F}_2}(x) \iff x = x^2 \tag{8}$$

defines the binary set $\{0, 1\}$ of streams.

[5] This observation holds for any field of coefficients.

Shifting Streams. The *fundamental theorem of stream calculus* [38] states that for every $f \in \mathcal{R}[\![X]\!]$ there exist unique $r \in \mathcal{R}$ and $f' \in \mathcal{R}[\![X]\!]$ with $f = [r] + X \cdot f'$. In this case, r is the *head* coefficient, $[r]$ is the embedding of the real number r as a stream in $\mathcal{R}[\![X]\!]$, and f' is the *tail* of the stream f. Therefore, the definition

$$(\forall z)\, \overline{X} = z \iff (\forall y)\, (\exists^1 y_0, y')\, \overline{R}(y_0) \wedge y = y_0 + z \cdot y', \tag{9}$$

for $\overline{X}$ a fresh constant symbol, yields a conservative extension $\mathcal{T}_{\mathrm{rcf}}[\overline{S}, \overline{R}, \overline{X}]$ of the theory $\mathcal{T}_{\mathrm{rcf}}$, with X, as an element of $\mathcal{R}[\![X]\!]$, the only possible interpretation for the constant symbol $\overline{X}$. Notice that the definitional formula (9) for $\overline{X}$ requires $\forall\exists\forall$ quantifier alternation due to the $\exists^1$ quantifier involved.

Example 11. The basic stream constructors of stream circuits for addition A, multiplication M_q by a rational $q \in \mathbb{Q}$, and unit delay D_1 are defined by (the universal closures of)

$$\begin{aligned} \overline{A}(x_1, x_2) = y &\iff y = x_1 + x_2 \\ \overline{M_{n/m}}(x) = y &\iff my = nx \\ \overline{D_1}(x) = y &\iff y = \overline{X} \cdot x, \end{aligned}$$

where $\overline{D_1}$, $\overline{A}$, and $\overline{M_{n/m}}$ for $n, m \in \mathbb{N}$ with $m \neq 0$, are new function symbols, and the variables are interpreted over $\mathcal{R}(\!(X)\!)$. Synchronous composition of two stream circuits, say $S(x, y)$ and $T(y, z)$, is specified in terms of the quantified conjunction $(\exists y)\, S(x, y) \wedge T(y, z)$, where existential quantification is used for *hiding* the intermediate y stream [43].

Rational Streams. We are now extending the language of ordered rings with constant symbols for rational streams (with rational coefficients). This extended language is expressive, for example, for encoding *equivalence* of rational stream transformers. We are considering rational streams $f = {}^{p(X)}/_{q(X)}$ with rational coefficients. In this case, the head for $q(X)$ is nonzero and $f \in \mathcal{R}[\![X]\!]$. Multiplication by $q(X)$ and by the least common multiple of the denominators of all rational coefficients in $p(X)$ and $q(X)$ yields an equality constraint in the language $\mathcal{L}_{or}[\overline{S}, \overline{R}, \overline{X}]$. More precisely, let $\overline{\mathcal{R}_{\mathbb{Q}}}$ be a set of fresh constant symbols for all rational streams (except for X) and $\mathcal{T}_{\mathrm{rcf}}[\overline{S}, \overline{R}, \overline{X}, \overline{\mathcal{R}_{\mathbb{Q}}}]$ the extension of $\mathcal{T}_{\mathrm{rcf}}$ by the definitions

$$(\forall y)\, \overline{f} = y \iff \tilde{p}(\overline{X}) \cdot y = \tilde{q}(\overline{X}) \tag{10}$$

for each (but X) rational stream f, $\tilde{p}(x) := c\,p(x)$, and $\tilde{q}(x) := c\,q(x)$, for $c \in \mathbb{N}$ the least common multiple of the denominators of coefficients of $p(x)$ and $q(x)$; then: $\mathcal{T}_{\mathrm{rcf}}[\overline{S}, \overline{R}, \overline{X}, \overline{\mathcal{R}_{\mathbb{Q}}}]$ is a conservative extension of $\mathcal{T}_{\mathrm{rcf}}$, and all the symbols $\overline{f} \in \overline{\mathcal{R}_{\mathbb{Q}}}$ have the rational stream interpretation f.

Remark 3. Alternatively, a rational stream f (with rational coefficients) can be finitely represented in terms of linear transformations $H : \mathbb{Q}^d \to \mathbb{Q}$ and $G : \mathbb{Q}^d \to \mathbb{Q}^d$, where d is the finite dimension of the linear span of the iterated tails of f [40]. Constraints for the finite number d of linear independent iterated tails are obtained from the anamorphism $[\![H, G]\!]$, which is the unique homomorphism from the coalgebra $\langle H, G\rangle \in \mathbb{Q}^d \to \mathbb{Q} \times \mathbb{Q}^d$ to the corresponding final stream coalgebra.

Automatic Streams. We exemplify the encoding of a certain class of regular streams as (semi-)algebraic constraints in stream logic. Consider the *Prouhet-Thue-Morse* [2] stream $ptm \in \mathbb{F}_2[\![X]\!]$, for $\mathbb{F}_2$ the finite field of characteristic 2. The nth-coefficient of this stream is 1 if and only if the number of 1's in the 2-adic representation $[n]_2$ of n is even. In other words, the nth-coefficient is 1 if and only if $[n]_2$ is in $0^*(10^*10^*)^*$. This regular expression yields an equivalent deterministic finite automaton with two states, namely "odd number of 1s" and "even number of 1s". Such a stream is also said to be *automatic* [2].

Christol's characterization [13] of algebraic (over the rational functions with coefficients from a finite field) power series in terms of deterministic finite automata (with outputs) implies that the stream *ptm* is algebraic over $\mathbb{F}_2[X]$. For instance, the stream *ptm* can be shown to be a root of the polynomial $X + (1 + X^2) \cdot Y + (1 + X)^3 \cdot Y^2$ of degree 2 and coefficients in $\mathbb{F}_2[X]$. A semi-algebraic constraint for ruling out other than the intended solution can be read-off, say, from a Sturm chain.

In this way, Christol's theorem supports the logical definition in stream logic of all kinds of analytic functions (sin, cos, ...) over finite fields. But not over the reals, as otherwise we could define the natural numbers using expressions such as $\sin(\pi x) = 0$. And we could therefore encode undecidable identity problems over certain classes of analytic functions [36], even without using π [28].

Heads and Tails. On the basis of the *fundamental law of the stream calculus* for formal power series, we define operators for stream projection and consing. Now, the theory $\mathcal{T}_{\text{rcf}}[\overline{S}, \overline{R}, \overline{X}, \overline{hd}, \overline{tl}, \overline{cons}]$ with the new (compared with $\mathcal{T}_{\text{rcf}}[\overline{S}, \overline{R}, \overline{X}]$) definitional axioms

$$(\forall x, x')\, \overline{tl}(x) = x' \iff (\exists x_0)\, \overline{R}(x_0) \wedge x = x_0 + \overline{X} \cdot x' \tag{11}$$

$$(\forall x, x_0)\, \overline{hd}(x) = x_0 \iff \overline{R}(x_0) \wedge (\exists x')\, x = x_0 + \overline{X} \cdot x' \tag{12}$$

$$(\forall x_0, x', y)\, \overline{cons}(x_0, x') = y \iff \overline{R}(x_0) \wedge y = x_0 + \overline{X} \cdot x' \tag{13}$$

is a conservative extension of $\mathcal{T}_{\text{rcf}}$. Moreover, $\overline{hd}(x) = y$ ($\overline{tl}(x) = y$) holds in the structure $\mathcal{R}[\![X]\!]$ if and only if y is interpreted by the head (tail) of the interpretation of x; similarly for consing.

With these definitions we may now also express corecursive identities in a decidable first-order equality theory. The following example codifies the Fibonacci recurrence (see Example 6) in our (extended) decidable logic.

Example 12.

$$\overline{hd}(x) = 0$$
$$\overline{hd}(\overline{tl}(x)) = 1$$
$$\overline{tl}^2(x) - \overline{tl}(x) - x = 0.$$

These kinds of *behavioral stream identities* are ubiquitous in stream calculus [38], for example, for specifying filter circuits.

Example 13 (3-2-filter). A 3-2-filter with input stream x and output y is specified in stream logic by three initial conditions and the difference equation

$$\overline{hd}(y) = \overline{hd}(\overline{tl}(y)) = \overline{hd}(\overline{tl}^2(y)) = 0$$
$$\overline{tl}^3(y) = c_0 x + c_1 \overline{tl}(x) + \overline{tl}^3(x) + c_2 c_3 \overline{tl}^2(y) + c_4 \overline{tl}(y),$$

for constants $c_0, \ldots, c_4 \in \mathbb{Z}$.

Example 14 (Timing Diagrams). The rising edge stream is specified in Scade-like [17] programming notation using the combined equation

$$y = 0 \rightarrow x \wedge \neg pre(x).$$

That is, the head of y is 0 and the tail of y is specified by the expression to the right of the arrow. Notice that the Scade notation $pre(x)$ is similar to the shift operation in that $pre(x) = (\bot, x_0, x_1, \ldots)$, where $\bot$ indicates that the head element is undefined. The rising edge stream E is specified corecursively in stream logic by

$$(\forall x, y)\, \overline{E}(x) = y \iff (\overline{hd}(y) = 0 \ \wedge\ \overline{tl}(y) = \overline{and}(x, \overline{not}(\overline{tl}(x)))),$$

for an arithmetic encoding of the logical stream operators $\overline{and}$ and $\overline{not}$.

The decision procedure for stream logic may also be used in *coinductive* proofs for deciding whether or not a given binary stream relation is a bisimulation.

Example 15 (Bisimulation). A binary relation B on streams, expressed as a formula in stream logic with two free variables, is a *bisimulation* [38] if and only if the $\mathcal{L}_{or}[\overline{S}, \overline{R}, \overline{X}, \overline{hd}, \overline{tl}]$ formula

$$(\forall x, y)\, B(x, y) \Rightarrow \overline{hd}(x) = \overline{hd}(y) \ \wedge\ B(\overline{tl}(x), \overline{tl}(y))$$

holds in the structure of streams.

Finally, we exemplify how corecursively defined stream functions are defined in a conservative extension of $\mathcal{T}_{\text{rcf}}$.

Example 16 (Stream Zip). The function Z for zipping the coefficients of two streams is defined by the corecursive identities

$$(\forall x, y)\ \overline{hd}(\overline{Z}(x, y)) = \overline{hd}(x)\ \wedge\ \overline{tl}(\overline{Z}(x, y)) = \overline{Z}(y, \overline{tl}(x)).$$

Since there is a unique[6] interpretation in $\mathcal{R}[\![X]\!]$ satisfying these identities, the function symbol $\overline{Z}$ is defined implicitly in the theory $\mathcal{T}_{\mathrm{rcf}}[\overline{S}, \overline{R}, \overline{X}, \overline{hd}, \overline{tl}, \overline{Z}]$. Now, by Beth's definability theorem [23], $\overline{Z}$ is also explicitly definable, say, on the basis of Craig interpolation.

Example 17. Assuming definitions $\overline{E}(x)$ and $\overline{O}(x)$ for sampling its stream argument x at even and at odd positions, respectively, we may now prompt our verification procedure to establish stream equalities such as

$$(\forall x)\, x = \overline{Z}(\overline{E}(x), \overline{O}(x)),$$

without using the bisimulation principle and without the need for constructing an explicit bisimulation relation.

The developments in Examples 16 and 17 generalize to all *stream differential equations* ([38], Chapter 11).

7 Conclusions

First-order stream logic is expressive for encoding problems of stream calculus. It is decidable in doubly exponential time, and its decision procedure is based on quantifier elimination for the theory of real closed ordered fields. Some of the proposed encodings for the relativization of quantifiers, however, lead to additional quantifier alternations (and variables and constraints) in problem formulations, which significantly increases the computational effort required to solve these constraints. Thus, it remains to be seen whether and how exactly a decision procedure for stream logic based on quantifier elimination for real closed fields makes practical progress compared to mature implementations of the non-elementary logic-automaton connection [27,33].

Alternatively, the decision procedure for first-order stream logic can be based directly, that is, without relativizing the stream quantifiers, on a quantifier elimination procedure for real closed valuation rings [12]. But these algorithms have not been studied and explored nearly as much as quantifier elimination for real closed fields, and the author is not aware of a reasonable computer implementation.

[6] See ([38], Theorem 252) for constructing unique solutions of corecursive identities based on the uniqueness of anamorphisms into the final stream coalgebra.

A Orderable Fields

A field $\mathcal{K}$ is *orderable* if there exists a non-empty $\mathcal{K}_+ \subset \mathcal{K}$ such that

1. $0 \notin \mathcal{K}_+$
2. $(x+y), xy \in \mathcal{K}_+$ for all $x, y \in \mathcal{K}_+$
3. Either $x \in \mathcal{K}_+$ or $-x \in \mathcal{K}_+$ for all $x \in \mathcal{K} \setminus \{0\}$

Provided that $\mathcal{K}$ is orderable we can generate a strict order on $\mathcal{K}$ by $x < y$ if and only if $(y-x) \in \mathcal{K}_+$. Furthermore, a total ordering $\leq$ on $\mathcal{K}$ is defined by $x \leq y$ if and only if $x < y$ or $x = y$, and $(\mathcal{K}, \leq)$ is said to be a *(totally) ordered field.* Now, the *absolute value* of $x \in \mathcal{K}$ is defined by $|x| := \max(-x, x)$. The *triangle inequality*

$$|x+y| \leq |x| + |y| \tag{14}$$

holds for ordered fields. As $-|x|-|y| \leq x+y \leq |x|+|y|$, we have $|x+y| \leq |x|+|y|$, because $x+y \leq |x|+|y|$ and $-(x+y) \leq |x|+|y|$.

Let $\mathcal{K}$ be an ordered field and $a \in \mathcal{K} \setminus \{0\}$ fixed. The scaled identity function $I_a(x) := ax$ is uniformly continuous in the order topology of $\mathcal{K}$. For given $\varepsilon \in \mathcal{K}_+$, let $\delta := \varepsilon/|a|$. Indeed, for all $x, y \in \mathcal{K}$, $|x-y| < \delta$ implies $|ax - ay| = |a|\,|x-y| < |a|\delta = \varepsilon$. Consequently, every polynomial in $\mathcal{K}$ is continuous.

A field $\mathcal{K}$ is orderable iff it is *formally real* (see [45], Chapter 11), that is, -1 is not the sum of squares, or alternatively, the equation $x_0^2 + \ldots + x_n^2 = 0$ has only trivial (that is, $x_k = 0$ for each k) solutions in $\mathcal{K}$.

B Real Closed Fields

A field $\mathcal{K}$ is a *real closed field* if it satisfies the following.

1. $\mathcal{K}$ is formally real (or orderable).
2. For all $x \in \mathcal{K}$ there exists $y \in \mathcal{K}$ such that $x = y^2$ or $x = -y^2$.
3. For all polynomial $P \in \mathcal{K}[t]$ (over the single indeterminate t) with odd degree there exists $x \in \mathcal{K}$ such that $P(x) = 0$.

Alternatively, a field $\mathcal{K}$ is *real closed* if $\mathcal{K}$ is formally real, but has no formally real proper algebraic extension field.

Let $\mathcal{K}$ be a real closed totally ordered field and $x \in \mathcal{K}$. Then $x > 0$ iff $x = y^2$ for some $y \in \mathcal{K}$. Suppose $x > 0$, then, by definition of real closedness, there exists $y \in \mathcal{K}$ such that $x = y^2$. Conversely, suppose $x = y^2$ for some $y \in \mathcal{K}$, then, by the definition of $\mathcal{K}_+$, we have $y^2 \in \mathcal{K}_+$ for all $y \in \mathcal{K}$, and therefore $x > 0$. Thus every real closed field is ordered in a unique way.

Artin and Schreier's theorem gives us two equivalent conditions for a field $\mathcal{K}$ to be real closed: for a field $\mathcal{K}$, the following are equivalent

1. $\mathcal{K}$ is real closed.
2. $\mathcal{K}^2$ is a positive cone of $\mathcal{K}$ and every polynomial of odd degree has a root in $\mathcal{K}$.

3. $\mathcal{K}(i)$ is algebraically closed and $\mathcal{K} \neq \mathcal{K}(i)$ (where i denotes $\sqrt{-1}$).

This characterization provides the basis (see axioms 16) and 17 below) for a first-order axiomatization of (ordered) real closed fields. The language of ordered rings (and fields), $\mathcal{L}_{or}$ consists of a binary relation symbols $\leq$, two binary operator symbols, $+$, $\cdot$, one unary operator symbol $-$, and two constant symbols 0, 1. Now, the first-order theory $\mathcal{T}_{\text{rcf}}$ of ordered real closed fields consists of all $\mathcal{L}_{or}$-structures M satisfying the following set of axioms.

Field Axioms.

1. $(\forall x, y, z)\, x \cdot (y + z) = x \cdot y + x \cdot z$
2. $(\forall x, y, z)\, x + (y + z) = (x + y) + z$
3. $(\forall x, y, z)\, x \cdot (y \cdot z) = (x \cdot y) \cdot z$
4. $(\forall x, y)\, x + y = y + x$
5. $(\forall x, y)\, x \cdot y = y \cdot x$
6. $(\forall x)\, x + 0 = x$
7. $(\forall x)\, x + (-x) = 0$
8. $(\forall x)\, x \cdot 1 = x$
9. $(\forall x)\, x \neq 0 \Rightarrow (\exists y)\, x \cdot y = 1$

Total Ordering Axioms.

10. $(\forall x)\, x \leq x$
11. $(\forall x, y, z)\, x \leq y \land y \leq z \Rightarrow x \leq z$
12. $(\forall x, y)\, x \leq y \land y \leq x \Rightarrow x = y$
13. $(\forall x, y)\, x \leq y \lor y \leq x$
14. $(\forall x, y, z)\, x \leq y \Rightarrow x + z \leq y + z$
15. $(\forall x, y)\, 0 \leq x \land 0 \leq y \Rightarrow 0 \leq x \cdot y$

Existence of Square Root.

16. $(\forall x)(\exists y)\, y \cdot y = x \lor y \cdot y = -x$

Every polynomial of odd degree has a root.

17. $(\forall a_0, \ldots, a_n)\, a_n \neq 0 \Rightarrow (\exists x)\, a_0 + a_1 \cdot x + \ldots + a_n \cdot x^n = 0$ for odd $n \in \mathbb{N}$

If an $\mathcal{L}_{or}$-structure M satisfies the axioms for ordered real closed fields above, then M is called a *model* of $\mathcal{T}_{\text{rcf}}$. Any model of $\mathcal{T}_{\text{rcf}}$ is *elementarily equivalent* to the real numbers. In other words, it has the same first-order properties as the field of ordered reals.

References

1. Alling, N.L.: Foundations of Analysis Over Surreal Number Fields. Elsevier, Amsterdam (1987)
2. Allouche, J.P., Shallit, J.: Automatic Sequences: Theory, Applications, Generalizations. Cambridge University Press, Cambridge (2003)
3. Anscombe, W., Koenigsmann, J.: An existential ∅-definition of $F_q[[t]]$ in $F_q((t))$. J. Symb. Log. **79**(4), 1336–1343 (2014)
4. Ax, J.: On the undecidability of power series fields. In: Proceedings of the American Mathematical Society, vol. 16, no. 846, p. 4 (1965)
5. Basu, S., Pollack, R., Roy, M.F.: On the combinatorial and algebraic complexity of quantifier elimination. J. ACM (JACM) **43**(6), 1002–1045 (1996)
6. Bourbaki, N.: Eléments de Mathématiques, vol. Livre II, Algèbre, chap. 6, Groupes et corps ordonnés. Hermann, Paris (1964)
7. Broy, M.: Specification and verification of concurrent systems by causality and realizability. Theoret. Comput. Sci. **974**(114106), 1–61 (2023)
8. Broy, M., Stølen, K.: Specification and Development of Interactive Systems: Focus on Streams, Interfaces, and Refinement. Springer, New York (2012). https://doi.org/10.1007/978-1-4613-0091-5
9. Buchi, J.R., Landweber, L.H.: Definability in the monadic second-order theory of successor. J. Symb. Log. **34**(2), 166–170 (1969)
10. Burge, W.H.: Stream processing functions. IBM J. Res. Dev. **19**(1), 12–25 (1975)
11. Charalambides, C.A.: Enumerative Combinatorics. Chapman and Hall/CRC, Boca Raton (2018)
12. Cherlin, G., Dickmann, M.A.: Real closed rings II. Model theory. Ann. Pure Appl. Logic **25**(3), 213–231 (1983)
13. Christol, G., Kamae, T., Mendès France, M., Rauzy, G.: Suites algébriques, automates et substitutions. Bull. Soc. Math. France **108**, 401–419 (1980)
14. Clarkson, M.R., Schneider, F.B.: Hyperproperties. J. Comput. Secur. **18**(6), 1157–1210 (2010)
15. Cluckers, R., Derakhshan, J., Leenknegt, E., Macintyre, A.: Uniformly defining valuation rings in henselian valued fields with finite or pseudo-finite residue fields. Ann. Pure Appl. Logic **164**(12), 1236–1246 (2013)
16. Cohen, P.J.: Decision procedures for real and p-adic fields. Commun. Pure Appl. Math. **22**(2), 131–151 (1969)
17. Colaço, J.L., Pagano, B., Pouzet, M.: Scade 6: a formal language for embedded critical software development. In: 2017 International Symposium on Theoretical Aspects of Software Engineering (TASE), pp. 1–11. IEEE (2017)
18. Collins, G.E.: Quantifier elimination for real closed fields by cylindrical algebraic decompostion. In: Brakhage, H. (ed.) GI-Fachtagung 1975. LNCS, vol. 33, pp. 134–183. Springer, Heidelberg (1975). https://doi.org/10.1007/3-540-07407-4_17
19. Courcelle, B., Engelfriet, J.: Graph Structure and Monadic Second-order Logic: A Language-Theoretic Approach, vol. 138. Cambridge University Press, Cambridge (2012)
20. Davenport, J.H., Heintz, J.: Real quantifier elimination is doubly exponential. J. Symb. Comput. **5**(1–2), 29–35 (1988)
21. Fehm, A.: Existential ∅-definability of henselian valuation rings. J. Symb. Log. **80**(1), 301–307 (2015)
22. Goguen, J.A., Meseguer, J.: Security policies and security models. In: 1982 IEEE Symposium on Security and Privacy, p. 11. IEEE (1982)

23. Hodges, W.: A Shorter Model Theory. Cambridge University Press, Cambridge (1997)
24. Jovanović, D., De Moura, L.: Solving non-linear arithmetic. ACM Commun. Comput. Algebra **46**(3/4), 104–105 (2013)
25. Kahn, G.: The semantics of a simple language for parallel programming. Inf. Process. **74**, 471–475 (1974)
26. Kahn, G., MacQueen, D.: Coroutines and networks of parallel processes. Research Report INRIA-00306565 (1976)
27. Klarlund, N., Møller, A., Schwartzbach, M.I.: Mona implementation secrets. Int. J. Found. Comput. Sci. **13**(04), 571–586 (2002)
28. Laczkovich, M.: The removal of π from some undecidable problems involving elementary functions. Proc. Am. Math. Soc. **131**(7), 2235–2240 (2003)
29. McCullough, D.: Noninterference and the composability of security properties. In: Proceedings 1988 IEEE Symposium on Security and Privacy, p. 177. IEEE Computer Society (1988)
30. McLean, J.: A general theory of composition for trace sets closed under selective interleaving functions. In: Proceedings of 1994 IEEE Computer Society Symposium on Research in Security and Privacy, pp. 79–93. IEEE (1994)
31. Neukirch, J.: Algebraic Number Theory, vol. 322. Springer, Heidelberg (2013). https://doi.org/10.1007/978-3-662-03983-0
32. Niven, I.: Formal power series. Am. Math. Mon. **76**(8), 871–889 (1969)
33. Owre, S., Rueß, H.: Integrating WS1S with PVS. In: Emerson, E.A., Sistla, A.P. (eds.) CAV 2000. LNCS, vol. 1855, pp. 548–551. Springer, Heidelberg (2000). https://doi.org/10.1007/10722167_42
34. Pradic, P.: Some proof-theoretical approaches to Monadic Second-Order logic. Ph.D. thesis, Université de Lyon; Uniwersytet Warszawski. Wydział Matematyki, Informatyki (2020)
35. Prestel, A.: Definable henselian valuation rings. J. Symb. Log. **80**(4), 1260–1267 (2015)
36. Richardson, D., Fitch, J.: The identity problem for elementary functions and constants. In: Proceedings of the International Symposium on Symbolic and Algebraic Computation, pp. 285–290 (1994)
37. Rutten, J.: On streams and coinduction. Technical report, CWI (2002)
38. Rutten, J.: The Method of Coalgebra: exercises in coinduction, vol. ISBN 978-90-6196-568-8. CWI, Amsterdam (2019)
39. Rutten, J.J.: Elements of stream calculus: an extensive exercise in coinduction. Electron. Notes Theor. Comput. Sci. **45**, 358–423 (2001)
40. Rutten, J.J.: Rational streams coalgebraically. Log. Methods Comput. Sci. **4** (2008)
41. Schechter, E.: Handbook of Analysis and Its Foundations. Academic Press, Cambridge (1996)
42. Shamseddine, K., Comicheo, A.B.: On non-archimedean valued fields: a survey of algebraic, topological and metric structures, analysis and applications. In: Advances in Non-Archimedean Analysis and Applications: The p-adic Methodology in STEAM-H, pp. 209–254 (2021)
43. Srivas, M., Rueß, H., Cyrluk, D.: Hardware verification using PVS. In: Kropf, T. (ed.) Formal Hardware Verification. LNCS, vol. 1287, pp. 156–205. Springer, Heidelberg (1997). https://doi.org/10.1007/3-540-63475-4_4
44. Tarski, A.: A Decision Method for Elementary Algebra and Geometry. Springer, Heidelberg (1998)
45. van der Waerden, B.: Algebra (1966)

46. Weispfenning, V.: Quantifier elimination for real algebra-the quadratic case and beyond. Appl. Algebra Eng. Commun. Comput. **8**, 85–101 (1997)

What Is Decidable in Separation Logic Beyond Progress, Connectivity and Establishment?

Tanguy Bozec[1], Nicolas Peltier[1], Quentin Petitjean[2](✉), and Mihaela Sighireanu[2]

[1] Univ. Grenoble Alpes, CNRS, LIG, 38000 Grenoble, France
[2] Univ. Paris-Saclay, CNRS, ENS Paris-Saclay, Laboratoire Méthodes Formelles, 91190 Gif-sur-Yvette, France
quentin.petitjean@ens-paris-saclay.fr

Abstract. The predicate definitions in Separation Logic (SL) play an important role: they capture a large spectrum of unbounded heap shapes due to their inductiveness. This expressiveness power comes with a limitation: the entailment problem is undecidable if predicates have general inductive definitions (ID). Iosif et al. [8] proposed syntactic and semantic conditions, called PCE, on the ID of predicates to ensure the decidability of the entailment problem. We provide a (possibly nonterminating) algorithm to transform arbitrary ID into equivalent PCE definitions when possible. We show that the existence of an equivalent PCE definition for a given ID is undecidable, but we identify necessary conditions that are decidable. The algorithm has been implemented, and experimental results are reported on a benchmark, including significant examples from SL-COMP.

Keywords: Separation logic · Inductive definitions · Bounded treewidth fragment · PCE fragment · Symbolic heaps · Decision procedures

1 Introduction

Separation logic (SL) [9,11] is widely used in verification to reason about programs manipulating dynamically allocated memory. Formulas in SL are defined from atoms of the form $x \to (y_1, \ldots, y_k)$, stating that at location (i.e., a memory address), x is allocated a memory block containing the tuple built from values of $y_1, \ldots, y_k$, and emp, stating that the heap is empty, i.e., that there are no allocated locations. SL includes the standard logical connectives and quantifiers, together with a special connective $\varphi_1 \star \varphi_2$, called separating conjunction, asserting that formulas φ_1 and φ_2 are satisfied on disjoint parts of the heap. This particular feature of the logic ensures the scalability of program analyses by enabling *local reasoning*: the properties of a program may be asserted and established by referring only to the part of the heap that is affected by the program. To specify recursive data structures, the SL formulas include predicate atoms defined by inductive rules with a fixpoint semantics. For instance, list segments from x to y may be defined by the following rules:

This work has been partially funded by the French National Research Agency project ANR-21-CE48-0011.

C. Benzmüller et al. (Eds.): IJCAR 2024, LNAI 14740, pp. 157–175, 2024.
https://doi.org/10.1007/978-3-031-63501-4_9

$$\mathtt{ls}(x,y) \Leftarrow \mathtt{emp} \star x \approx y\,, \qquad \mathtt{ls}(x,y) \Leftarrow \exists z.\,(x \to (z) \star \mathtt{ls}(z,y))\,. \tag{1}$$

Many problems in verification boil down to checking the validity of entailments between formulas in SL. In general, unsurprisingly, entailment is undecidable. However, several fragments have been identified for which the entailment problem is decidable. Among these fragments, the so-called *PCE fragment* is one of the most expressive ones [8]. Decidability was initially established by reduction to monadic second-order logic on graphs with bounded treewidth. Later, more efficient algorithms were proposed [4,10], and the problem turned out to be 2-EXPTIME-complete [3]. The PCE fragment is defined by restricting the syntax and the semantics of the inductive rules defining the predicates. Each rule is required to satisfy three properties (formally defined later): (P)rogress, (C)onnectivity and (E)stablishment. Informally, the conditions respectively assert that: (P) every rule allocates *exactly* one location; (C) the allocated locations have a tree-shaped structure which mimics the call tree of the predicates, and (E) every location not associated with a free variable is (eventually) allocated. A PCE formula is a formula in which all predicates are defined by PCE rules. Most usual data structures in programming can be defined using PCE rules. However, the PCE conditions impose rigid constraints on the rules' syntax, which are not necessarily satisfied in practice by user-provided rules. For instance, the above rules of ls (Eq. (1)) are *not PCE* (because the first rule of ls allocates no location), while the following ones, although specifying non-empty list segments, are PCE:

$$\mathtt{ls}^{+}(x,y) \Leftarrow x \to (y)\,, \qquad \mathtt{ls}^{+}(x,y) \Leftarrow \exists z.\,(x \to (z) \star \mathtt{ls}^{+}(z,y))\,. \tag{2}$$

The non-PCE formula $\mathtt{ls}(x,y)$ can then be written as a PCE formula $(\mathtt{emp} \star x \approx y) \vee \mathtt{ls}^{+}(x,y)$. Other, rather natural, definitions of $\mathtt{ls}^{+}$ can be given, which are not PCE (the second rule of $\mathtt{ls}^{m}$ allocates no location, and the second rule of $\mathtt{ls}^{e}$ is not connected):

$$\mathtt{ls}^{m}(x,y) \Leftarrow x \to (y)\,, \qquad \mathtt{ls}^{m}(x,y) \Leftarrow \exists z.\,(\mathtt{ls}^{m}(x,z) \star \mathtt{ls}^{m}(z,y))\,, \tag{3}$$

$$\mathtt{ls}^{e}(x,y) \Leftarrow x \to (y)\,, \qquad \mathtt{ls}^{e}(x,y) \Leftarrow \exists z.\,(\mathtt{ls}^{e}(x,z) \star z \to (y))\,. \tag{4}$$

Similarly, the following definition of lists of odd length is not PCE:

$$\mathtt{ls}^{1}(x,y) \Leftarrow x \to (y)\,, \qquad \mathtt{ls}^{1}(x,y) \Leftarrow \exists z_1, z_2.\,(x \to (z_1) \star z_1 \to (z_2) \star \mathtt{ls}^{1}(z_2,y))\,, \tag{5}$$

but it is clear that it can be transformed into a PCE definition by replacing the inductive rule (at right) with the following ones:

$$\mathtt{ls}^{1}(x,y) \Leftarrow \exists z_1.\,(x \to (z_1) \star \mathtt{ls}^{2}(z_1,y))\,, \qquad \mathtt{ls}^{2}(z_1,y) \Leftarrow \exists z_2.\,(z_1 \to (z_2) \star \mathtt{ls}^{1}(z_2,y))\,. \tag{6}$$

A natural question thus arises, which has not been investigated so far: can algorithms be provided to identify whether a formula can be rewritten into an equivalent PCE formula and to effectively compute such a formula (and the associated inductive rules) if possible? The present paper aims to address these issues.

Contributions. We first observe that the PCE problem — i.e., the problem of testing whether a given formula admits an equivalent PCE formula — is undecidable. The result follows from the undecidability of testing whether context-free grammar is regular. Then, we provide a procedure for transforming some formulas that do not satisfy the PCE conditions into equivalent PCE formulas. Equivalence is guaranteed in all cases, but the procedure does not always terminate. We also identify cases for which the formulas cannot possibly admit any equivalent PCE formula. More precisely, we identify a property called *PCE-compatibility*, which is strictly weaker than PCE, in the sense that any formula that is equivalent to a PCE formula is PCE-compatible, but the converse does not hold, and we prove that this property is decidable. To sum up, given a formula φ, the procedure may either terminate with a negative answer (if φ is not PCE-compatible) or may terminate with a positive answer and output a PCE formula equivalent to φ or may diverge (if φ is PCE-compatible, but no equivalent PCE formula can be obtained).

To our knowledge, there is no published work on this topic. In [7], the authors proposed inductive definitions (ID, termed "recursive definitions" in [8]) with syntactic restrictions incomparable to PCE since they require linearity and compositionality of the ID to obtain decidability of the entailment problem. This class of ID (disregarding data constraints) may be translated by our procedure into PCE form, i.e., they are PCE-compatible. In [5], other decidable fragments of entailment problems are considered, which do not fulfil the PCE conditions but can be reduced to PCE entailment. Unlike the present approach, the reduction proposed in [5] does not preserve the equivalence of formulas. In [4], the establishment condition is replaced by a condition on the equalities occurring in the problem.

2 Separation Logic with Inductive Definitions

We recall the definition of the syntax and semantics of SL with inductive definitions. Missing definitions, further explanations and examples can be found in [8]. We briefly review standard notations: $\mathrm{card}(A)$ denotes the cardinality of set A, and $A \uplus B$ denotes the disjoint union of sets A and B. The set $\{x \in \mathbb{Z} \mid i \leq x \leq j\}$ is denoted by $[\![i, j]\!]$. The domain of a function f is written $\mathrm{dom}(f)$. The equivalence class of an element x w.r.t. some equivalence relation $\bowtie$ is written $[x]_{\bowtie}$, and the set $\{[x]_{\bowtie} \mid x \in S\}$ is written $\overline{S}_{\bowtie}$. The relation $\bowtie$ will sometimes be omitted if it is clear from the context. We often identify an equivalence relation $\bowtie$ with the set of its equivalence classes. For any binary relation $\rightarrow$, we denote by $\rightarrow^*$ its reflexive and transitive closure. A set R is a set of *roots* for $\rightarrow$ if for all elements x, y such that $x \rightarrow y$, there exists $r \in R$ such that $r \rightarrow^* x$. It is *minimal* if, moreover, there is no set of roots R' such that $R' \subset R$ (where $\subset$ denotes strict inclusion).

Definition 1 (SL formulas). *Let $\mathcal{V}$ be a countably infinite set of* variables, *and let $\mathcal{P}$ be a set of* spatial predicate symbols, *where each symbol $p \in \mathcal{P}$ is associated with a unique arity $\#(p)$ (with countably infinite sets of predicate symbols of each arity). The set of* SL-formulas *(or simply formulas) φ is inductively defined as follows:*

$$\varphi := \mathtt{emp} \mid x \rightarrow (y_1, \ldots, y_k) \mid x \approx y \mid x \not\approx y \mid \varphi_1 \vee \varphi_2 \mid \varphi_1 \star \varphi_2 \mid p(x_1, \ldots, x_{\#(p)}) \mid \exists x.\, \varphi_1$$

where φ_1, φ_2 are formulas, $p \in \mathcal{P}$, $k \in \mathbb{N}$ and $x, y, x_1, \ldots, x_{\#(p)}, y_1, \ldots, y_k \in \mathcal{V}$.

Note that negations are not supported. The considered fragment is similar to that of [4] (with disjunctions added), with the slight difference that points-to atoms $x \to (y_1, \ldots, y_k)$ contain tuples of arbitrary length $k \geq 0$. Let $fv(\varphi)$ be the set of free variables in φ. A *substitution* σ is a function from variables to variables; its domain $\mathrm{dom}(\sigma)$ is the set of variables x such that $\sigma(x) \neq x$, and its image $\mathrm{img}(\sigma) = \sigma(\mathrm{dom}(\sigma))$. For any expression (variable, tuple or set of variables, or formula) e, we denote by $e\sigma$ the expression obtained from e by replacing every free occurrence of a variable x by $\sigma(x)$. A *symbolic heap* is a formula containing no occurrence of $\vee$. By distributivity of $\star$ and $\exists$ over $\vee$, any formula φ can be reduced to an equivalent disjunction of symbolic heaps, denoted by $dnf(\varphi)$. An *inductive rule associated with the predicate* p has the form $p(x_1, \ldots, x_n) \Leftarrow \varphi$, where $x_1, \ldots, x_n$ are pairwise distinct variables, $n = \#(p)$, and φ is a formula with $fv(\varphi) \subseteq \{x_1, \ldots, x_n\}$. If φ is not a symbolic heap, then $p(x_1, \ldots, x_n) \Leftarrow \varphi$ may be replaced by the rules $\{p(x_1, \ldots, x_n) \Leftarrow \varphi_i \mid i \in [\![1, m]\!]\}$, where $\varphi_1, \ldots, \varphi_m$ are symbolic heaps such that $\bigvee_{i=1}^{m} \varphi_i$ is $dnf(\varphi)$. We assume in the following that this transformation is applied eagerly to every rule. A *set of inductive definitions* (SID) $\mathcal{R}$ is a set of inductive rules such that, for all predicates p, $\mathcal{R}$ contains finitely many rules associated with p. We write $p(y_1, \ldots, y_n) \Leftarrow_{\mathcal{R}} \psi$ if $\mathcal{R}$ contains a rule $p(x_1, \ldots, x_n) \Leftarrow \varphi$, with $\psi = \varphi\{x_i \mapsto y_i \mid i \in [\![1, n]\!]\}$.

Definition 2 (SL structure). *Let $\mathcal{L}$ be a countably infinite set of so-called* locations. *An SL-structure is a pair $(\mathfrak{s}, \mathfrak{h})$ where $\mathfrak{s}$ is a* store, *i.e., a partial function from $\mathcal{V}$ to $\mathcal{L}$, and $\mathfrak{h}$ is a* heap, *i.e., a partial finite function from $\mathcal{L}$ to $\mathcal{L}^*$, which can be written as a relation: $\mathfrak{h}(\ell) = (\ell_1, \ldots, \ell_k)$ iff $(\ell, \ell_1, \ldots, \ell_k) \in \mathfrak{h}$, $k \in \mathbb{N}$.*

For any heap $\mathfrak{h}$, we let $ref(\mathfrak{h}) = \{\ell \mid \ell_0 \in \mathrm{dom}(\mathfrak{h}), \ell \text{ occurs in } \mathfrak{h}(\ell_0)\}$, $loc(\mathfrak{h}) = ref(\mathfrak{h}) \cup \mathrm{dom}(\mathfrak{h})$ and $dgl(\mathfrak{h}) = loc(\mathfrak{h}) \setminus \mathrm{dom}(\mathfrak{h})$ (for "dangling pointers"). Locations in $\mathrm{dom}(\mathfrak{h})$ and variables x such that $\mathfrak{s}(x) \in \mathrm{dom}(\mathfrak{h})$ are *allocated.* We write $\ell \to_{\mathfrak{h}} \ell'$ iff $\ell \in \mathrm{dom}(\mathfrak{h})$, and ℓ' occurs in $\mathfrak{h}(\ell)$.

Definition 3 (SL semantics). *Given a formula φ, a SID $\mathcal{R}$ and a structure $(\mathfrak{s}, \mathfrak{h})$ with $fv(\varphi) \subseteq \mathrm{dom}(\mathfrak{s})$, the satisfaction relation $\models_{\mathcal{R}}$ is inductively defined as the least relation such that $(\mathfrak{s}, \mathfrak{h}) \models_{\mathcal{R}} \varphi$ iff one of the following conditions holds:*

- $\varphi = \mathtt{emp}$ *and* $\mathfrak{h} = \emptyset$*; or* $\varphi = (x \to (y_1, \ldots, y_k))$ *and* $\mathfrak{h} = \{(\mathfrak{s}(x), \mathfrak{s}(y_1), \ldots, \mathfrak{s}(y_k))\}$*;*
- $\varphi = (x \approx y)$, $\mathfrak{s}(x) = \mathfrak{s}(y)$ *and* $\mathfrak{h} = \emptyset$*; or* $\varphi = (x \not\approx y)$, $\mathfrak{s}(x) \neq \mathfrak{s}(y)$ *and* $\mathfrak{h} = \emptyset$*;*
- $\varphi = \varphi_1 \vee \varphi_2$ *and* $(\mathfrak{s}, \mathfrak{h}) \models_{\mathcal{R}} \varphi_i$*, for some* $i \in \{1, 2\}$*; or* $\varphi = \varphi_1 \star \varphi_2$ *and there exist disjoint domain heaps* $\mathfrak{h}_1, \mathfrak{h}_2$ *such that* $\mathfrak{h} = \mathfrak{h}_1 \uplus \mathfrak{h}_2$ *and* $(\mathfrak{s}, \mathfrak{h}_i) \models_{\mathcal{R}} \varphi_i$*, for all* $i \in \{1, 2\}$*;*
- $\varphi = \exists x. \psi$ *and* $(\mathfrak{s}', \mathfrak{h}) \models_{\mathcal{R}} \psi$*, for some* $\mathfrak{s}'$ *matching* $\mathfrak{s}$ *on all variables distinct from* x*;*
- $\varphi = p(x_1, \ldots, x_{\#(p)})$, $p \in \mathcal{P}$ *and* $(\mathfrak{s}, \mathfrak{h}) \models_{\mathcal{R}} \psi$ *for some* ψ *such that* $\varphi \Leftarrow_{\mathcal{R}} \psi$.

We write $\varphi \models_{\mathcal{R}} \psi$ if for every structure $(\mathfrak{s}, \mathfrak{h})$ we have $(\mathfrak{s}, \mathfrak{h}) \models_{\mathcal{R}} \varphi \implies (\mathfrak{s}, \mathfrak{h}) \models_{\mathcal{R}} \psi$. If both $\varphi \models_{\mathcal{R}} \psi$ and $\psi \models_{\mathcal{R}} \varphi$ hold, then we write $\varphi \equiv_{\mathcal{R}} \psi$.

Definition 4 (SL model). *An $\mathcal{R}$-*model *of φ is a structure $(\mathfrak{s}, \mathfrak{h})$ such that $(\mathfrak{s}, \mathfrak{h}) \models_{\mathcal{R}} \varphi$. Given two pairs $(\varphi, \mathcal{R})$ and $(\varphi', \mathcal{R}')$, where φ, φ' are formulas and $\mathcal{R}, \mathcal{R}'$ are SID, we write $(\varphi, \mathcal{R}) \equiv (\varphi', \mathcal{R}')$ iff $(\mathfrak{s}, \mathfrak{h}) \models_{\mathcal{R}} \varphi \iff (\mathfrak{s}, \mathfrak{h}) \models_{\mathcal{R}'} \varphi'$ holds for all structures $(\mathfrak{s}, \mathfrak{h})$.*

We emphasize that the atoms $x \approx y$ or $x \not\approx y$ only hold for empty heaps (this convention simplifies notations as it avoids the use of standard conjunction). Formulas are taken modulo the usual properties of SL connectives: associativity and commutativity of $\star$ and $\vee$, neutrality of $\mathtt{emp}$ for $\star$, commutativity of $\approx, \not\approx$, and also modulo prenex form and α-renaming. We also assume that bound variables are renamed to avoid any name collision. Rules are defined up to a renaming of free variables.

3 The PCE Problem

We now recall the conditions from [8], ensuring the decidability of the entailment problem.

Definition 5 (PCE rule and SID). *Let r be a function mapping every spatial predicate $p \in \mathcal{P}$ to an element of $[\![1, \#(p)]\!]$. For any atom $p(x_1, \ldots, x_n)$, the variable $x_{r(p)}$ is the* root *of $p(x_1, \ldots, x_n)$, and the root of an atom $x \to (y_1, \ldots, y_k)$ is x. A rule $p(x_1, \ldots, x_n) \Leftarrow \varphi$ is PCE w.r.t. some SID $\mathcal{R}$ if it is:*

- progressing, *i.e., φ is of the form $\exists u_1, \ldots, u_m. (x_i \to (y_1, \ldots, y_k) \star \psi)$, where $m \geq 0$, ψ is a formula with no occurrence of $\to, \exists, \vee$, and $i = r(p)$;*
- connected, *i.e., moreover, all spatial predicate atoms occurring in ψ are of the form $q(z_1, \ldots, z_{\#(q)})$ with $z_{r(q)} \in \{y_1, \ldots, y_k\}$;*
- established, *i.e., moreover, for all $i \in [\![1, m]\!]$, and for all structures $(\mathfrak{s}, \mathfrak{h})$ such that $(\mathfrak{s}, \mathfrak{h}) \models_{\mathcal{R}} \psi$, either $\mathfrak{s}(u_i) \in \mathrm{dom}(\mathfrak{h})$ or $\mathfrak{s}(u_i) \in \{\mathfrak{s}(x_j) \mid j \in [\![1, n]\!]\}$.*

A SID $\mathcal{R}$ is PCE if every rule is PCE w.r.t. $\mathcal{R}$. A formula φ is PCE if every predicate used in φ is defined by PCE rules.

The problem we are investigating in the present paper is the following:

Definition 6 (PCE problem). *Given a pair $(\varphi, \mathcal{R})$, the* PCE problem *lies in deciding whether there exists a formula φ' and a PCE SID $\mathcal{R}'$ such that $(\varphi, \mathcal{R}) \equiv (\varphi', \mathcal{R}')$.*

Assuming that φ is atomic is sufficient (complex formulas may be introduced by inductive rules), but the possibility that φ' is non-atomic allows for greater expressiveness. If one restricts oneself to list-shaped structures denoting words, then the PCE conditions essentially state that the set of denoted words is regular. This entails the following result, obtained by reduction from the regularity of context-free languages:

Theorem 1. *The PCE problem is undecidable.*

It may be observed that the structures $(\mathfrak{s}, \mathfrak{h})$ satisfying PCE pairs $(\varphi, \mathcal{R})$ necessarily satisfy two essential properties. First, due to the connectivity condition, these structures necessarily admit a bounded number of roots, which correspond to locations assigned by $\mathfrak{s}$ to (possibly quantified) variables occurring inside φ (at some root position in a predicate or points-to atom, as defined in Definition 5).

Structures with multiple roots are permitted (e.g., doubly linked lists), but due to the connectivity condition, if x is the root of an atom φ, then, for every model $(\mathfrak{s}, \mathfrak{h})$ of φ, the singleton $\{\mathfrak{s}(x)\}$ is a set of roots for $\to_{\mathfrak{h}}$ (i.e., all locations in $loc(\mathfrak{h})$ must be accessible from $\mathfrak{s}(x)$). Disjoint structures built in parallel (such as two lists with the same length) are not allowed[1]. Second, these structures also admit a bounded number of "dangling pointers" (i.e., elements of $dgl(\mathfrak{h})$), which again correspond (by $\mathfrak{s}$) to variables occurring in φ, since all the variables introduced by unfolding rules must be allocated due to the establishment property. The latter property turned out to be essential for decidability [6]. This yields the definition of a property called *PCE-compatibility*:

Definition 7 (PCE-compatibility). *Let $k \in \mathbb{N}$. A structure $(\mathfrak{s}, \mathfrak{h})$ is* k-PCE-compatible *if (i)* $\text{card}(dgl(\mathfrak{h})) \leq k$ *and (ii) there exists a set of roots R for $\rightarrow_{\mathfrak{h}}$ with* $\text{card}(R) \leq k$. *A pair $(\varphi, \mathcal{R})$ is* k-PCE-compatible *if every $\mathcal{R}$-model of φ is k-PCE-compatible.*

Proposition 1. *Let φ be a formula, and $\mathcal{R}$ be a PCE SID. Every $\mathcal{R}$-model $(\mathfrak{s}, \mathfrak{h})$ of φ is k-PCE-compatible, where k is the number of (free or bound) variables in φ.*

Example 1. Let us consider the formula $\varphi = p(x, y)$ and the SID $\mathcal{R}_1$ below. For readability, we employ the same variable names in predicate definitions and predicate calls to avoid introducing the renaming of variables:

$$\begin{array}{ll} p(x,y) \Leftarrow \exists z.\, z \rightarrow (x,y)\,, & q(y) \Leftarrow \exists z,u,t.\, (y \rightarrow (z,t) \star r(z,u,t))\,, \\ p(x,y) \Leftarrow x \rightarrow (y) \star q(y)\,, & r(z,u,t) \Leftarrow u \not\approx t \star z \rightarrow (u) \star t \rightarrow (t)\,. \end{array} \tag{7}$$

The SID $\mathcal{R}_1$, and thus $(\varphi, \mathcal{R}_1)$, are not PCE. In the first rule for p, z is root but not a free variable, the rule defining q is not established for the existential variable u and the rule defining r does not respect the progress condition as it has two points-to atoms.

4 Overview of Our Procedure

The (nonterminating) algorithm for transforming a pair $(\Phi, \mathcal{R})$ into an equivalent PCE pair is divided into four main steps (from now on, we denote the target formula by Φ, whereas the meta-variable φ is reserved for formulas occurring in inductive rules).

Step 1: We compute abstractions of the models of Φ (and of all relevant predicate atoms). The aim is to extract relevant information about the constraints satisfied by these models concerning (dis)equalities, heap reachability and allocated locations. The abstractions are constructed over a set of variables that includes the variables freely occurring in the formulas, together with some additional variables — the so-called *invisible variables* — that correspond to existential variables that either occur in Φ or are introduced by unfolding inductive rules. The usefulness of invisible variables will be demonstrated later. The computation does not terminate in general, as the set of abstractions is infinite (due to the presence of invisible variables). However, we prove that the computation terminates exactly when the considered formula is k-PCE-compatible (for some $k \in \mathbb{N}$). Furthermore, we introduce a technique — the so-called *ISIV* condition — to detect when the formula is not k-PCE-compatible during the computation of the abstractions. This ensures termination in all cases and also proves that the problem of

[1] Indeed, to satisfy the connectivity condition the two lists must be defined in distinct atoms (as they are not connected). But then it is impossible to ensure that they have the same number of elements.

deciding whether a given pair is k-PCE-compatible, for some k, is decidable. This step is detailed in Sect. 5.

Step 2: We transform the set of rules in order to ensure that every predicate is associated with a unique abstraction, in which all invisible variables are replaced by visible ones. This step always terminates. It adds some combinatorial explosion that could be reduced by a smart transformation, but it greatly simplifies the technical developments. This step is detailed in Sect. 6.

Step 3: We apply some transformations on the SID to ensure that every abstraction admits exactly one root. This step may fail in the case where the structures described by the rules do not have this property. See Sect. 7.

Step 4: We recursively transform any rule $p(\overrightarrow{x}) \Leftarrow \varphi$ into a PCE rule by decomposing φ into a separating conjunction $y \rightarrow (z_1, \ldots, z_k) \star \varphi_1 \star \cdots \star \varphi_k$ where y is the root of the structure and every φ_i encodes a structure of root z_i. Each of these formulas φ_i may then be associated with fresh predicate atoms if needed. The process is repeated until one gets a fixpoint. Equivalence is always preserved, but termination is not guaranteed. This step is detailed in Sect. 8.

Before describing all these steps, we wish to convey some general explanations about the difficulties that arise when one tries to enforce each condition in Definition 5.

The progress condition can often be enforced by introducing additional predicates to ensure that each rule allocates exactly one location. For instance, the definition of lists of odd length in Eq. (5) is not PCE, but it can be transformed into a PCE definition by replacing the inductive rule (at right) with the two inductive rules given in Eq. (6) (introducing a new predicate $\mathtt{ls}^2(x, y)$). The key point is that the root of the structure must be associated with a parameter of the predicate, which sometimes requires the addition of new existential variables in the formula. For instance, the formula $p(x)$ with $p(x) \Leftarrow \exists y. y \rightarrow (x)$ will be written: $\exists y. p'(x, y)$ with $p'(x, y) \Leftarrow y \rightarrow (x)$. The set of roots is computed in Step 1 above, and invisible roots (like y in the above example) are made visible during Step 2. Note that this technique is applicable only if the number of such roots is bounded; the ISIV condition will ensure that this constraint is satisfied.

The connectivity condition is enforced by using the abstract reachability relation computed during Step 1 to identify the predicate atoms that do not satisfy this condition and by modifying the rules to delay the call to these predicates until the connectivity condition is satisfied. For instance, the first rule below is modified into the second one:

$$q(x) \Leftarrow \exists y_1, y_2, y_3. (x \rightarrow (y_1, y_2) \star \mathtt{ls}^+(y_1, y_3) \star \mathtt{ls}^+(y_3, y_3) \star \mathtt{ls}^+(y_2, y_2)), \quad (8)$$

$$q(x) \Leftarrow \exists y_1, y_2, y_3. (x \rightarrow (y_1, y_2) \star q'(y_1, y_3) \star \mathtt{ls}^+(y_2, y_2)), \quad (9)$$

where $q'(y_1, y_3)$ is defined similarly to $\mathtt{ls}^+(y_1, y_3)$ in Eq. (2) except the first rule:

$$q'(y_1, y_3) \Leftarrow y_1 \rightarrow (y_3) \star \mathtt{ls}^+(y_3, y_3), \qquad q'(y_1, y_3) \Leftarrow \exists z. (y_1 \rightarrow (z) \star q'(z, y_3)). \quad (10)$$

The establishment condition may be enforced in two ways. If the considered existential variable only occurs in pure atoms (disequalities or equalities), then it can be eliminated using usual quantifier elimination techniques. For instance, the predicate $r(x) \Leftarrow \exists y. x \rightarrow () \star x \not\approx y$ can be reduced into $r(x) \Leftarrow x \rightarrow ()$ since a location y distinct from x always exists (recall that the equational atom $x \not\approx y$ only holds for empty heaps).

Otherwise, one must collect the set of all variables that are reachable but not allocated and associate them with new existential variables in φ (and parameters of predicates). For instance, the formula $r'(x)$ with $r'(x) \Leftarrow \exists y.\, x \to (y)$ is transformed into $\exists y.\, r''(x, y)$ with $r''(x, y) \Leftarrow x \to (y)$. These variables correspond to invisible variables computed during Step 1 and transformed into visible variables in Step 2. Again, the ISIV condition ensures that the number of such variables is bounded.

5 Abstracting Models and Formulas

We formalize the notion of abstraction that summarizes the main features (locations defined and allocated, reachability, etc.) of models and SL-formulas. Then, we define two relations between abstractions and SL-structures. Finally, we define the abstraction process for a formula, i.e., how we attach a set of abstractions to an SL-formula.

Definition 8 (Abstraction). *An* abstraction *is a tuple* $A = \langle V, \backsim, \neq, V_v, \overline{V}_a, h, \rightsquigarrow \rangle$ *where: (i)* V *is a set of variables and* $\backsim$ *is an equivalence relation on* V*; (ii)* $\neq$ *(disequality relation) is a symmetric and irreflexive binary relation on* $\overline{V}$*; (iii)* $V_v \subseteq V$ *is a finite set of variables called* visible variables*; (iv)* $\overline{V}_a \subseteq \overline{V}$ *is a subset of classes of variables called* allocated variables*; (v)* $h : \overline{V}_a \longrightarrow \overline{V}^*$ *is a partial* heap mapping *which associates a tuple of classes of variables of arbitrary size to some class of allocated variables; (vi)* $\rightsquigarrow \subseteq \overline{V} \times \overline{V}$ *is a* reachability relation *which is a relation such that* $\forall [x] \in \overline{V}_a$ *and* $\forall [y] \in h([x])$, $([x], [y]) \in \rightsquigarrow$*. The set of all abstractions is denoted by* $\mathcal{A}$*. We designate the components of an abstraction* A *using the dotted notation by* $A.V$, $A.V_v$*, etc. The set of* invisible variables *of* A *is* $A.V_{inv} \triangleq A.V \setminus A.V_v$.

Abstractions are taken modulo renaming of invisible variables: two abstractions, A_1 and A_2, are considered equal, denoted $A_1 = A_2$, if there exists a renaming σ of invisible variables such that $A_1 = A_2\sigma$.

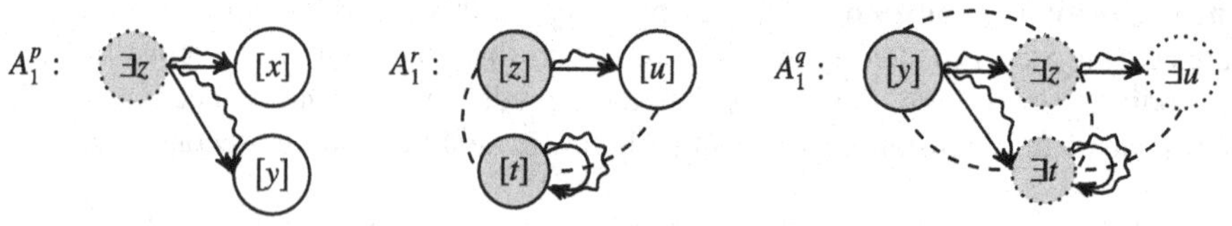

Fig. 1. Examples of abstractions.

Example 2. Figure 1 graphically represents three abstractions denoted A_1^p, A_1^r and A_1^q. Equivalence classes are represented by circles and are labelled by variable names. Allocated classes are filled grey; invisible variables are prefixed with ∃, and [ ] are omitted. Disequalities are represented with dashed lines, while heap and reachability relations are represented with tick resp. snaked arrows.

An SL-structure is a model of an abstraction if its store is *coherent* with the abstraction (i.e., it maps equal variables to the same location and disequal variables to different locations) and its heap contains at least all the reachability relations of the abstraction. However, the model may contain more allocated locations and paths between locations. On the other hand, an abstraction of an SL-structure captures *exactly* the visibility of variables in the store, the equivalence between variables and the reachability of locations in the heap; it abstracts the paths between locations labelled by (visible or invisible) variables and going through locations not labelled by some variable.

Definition 9 (Model and Abstraction). *A structure* $(\mathfrak{s}, \mathfrak{h})$ *is a* model *of an abstraction* A*, denoted by* $(\mathfrak{s}, \mathfrak{h}) \models A$*, if there exists a functional extension* $\dot{\mathfrak{s}}$ *of* $\mathfrak{s}$ *satisfying the following conditions: (i)* $\mathrm{dom}(\dot{\mathfrak{s}}) = A.V$ *and* $\mathrm{dom}(\mathfrak{s}) = A.V_v$*; (ii) If* $(x, y) \in A.\backsim$ *then* $\dot{\mathfrak{s}}(x) = \dot{\mathfrak{s}}(y)$*; (iii) If* $([x], [y]) \in A.\not\backsim$ *then* $\dot{\mathfrak{s}}(x) \neq \dot{\mathfrak{s}}(y)$*; (iv) For all* $x \in A.V$*, if* $[x] \in A.\overline{V}_a$ *then* $\dot{\mathfrak{s}}(x) \in \mathrm{dom}(\mathfrak{h})$*; (v) For all* $[x] \in A.\overline{V}_a$ *if* $A.h([x]) = ([y_1], \ldots, [y_k])$ *then* $\mathfrak{h}(\dot{\mathfrak{s}}(x)) = (\dot{\mathfrak{s}}(y_1), \ldots, \dot{\mathfrak{s}}(y_k))$*; (vi) For all* $x, y \in V$*, if* $([x], [y]) \in A.\rightsquigarrow$ *then there exists a path* $\ell_0 \to_{\mathfrak{h}} \cdots \to_{\mathfrak{h}} \ell_n$ *in* $\mathfrak{h}$ *such that* $\ell_0 = \dot{\mathfrak{s}}(x)$*,* $\ell_n = \dot{\mathfrak{s}}(y)$ *and* $\{\ell_1, \ldots, \ell_{n-1}\} \cap \mathrm{img}(\dot{\mathfrak{s}}) = \emptyset$*. If* $(\mathfrak{s}, \mathfrak{h}) \models A$ *and the converses of Items (ii), (iii) and (vi) hold, then* A is an abstraction of $(\mathfrak{s}, \mathfrak{h})$*. The set of all abstractions of* $(\mathfrak{s}, \mathfrak{h})$ *is denoted by* $\mathfrak{abs}(\mathfrak{s}, \mathfrak{h})$*.*

Example 3. Consider the structure $(\mathfrak{s}_1, \mathfrak{h}_1)$ defined over the set of variables $\{x, y\}$ with $\mathfrak{s}_1(x) = \ell_1$, $\mathfrak{s}_1(y) = \ell_2 \neq \ell_1$, $\mathfrak{h}_1(\ell_0) = (\ell_1, \ell_2)$. A_1^P from Fig. 1 is an abstraction of $(\mathfrak{s}_1, \mathfrak{h}_1)$ for $\dot{\mathfrak{s}}_1(z) = \ell_0$. Moreover, A_1^P has as model $(\mathfrak{s}_2, \mathfrak{h}_2)$ with $\mathfrak{s}_1(x) = \mathfrak{s}_1(y) = \ell_1$, $\mathfrak{h}_1(\ell_0) = (\ell_1, \ell_1)$.

The following operations on abstractions are used in our abstraction process.

Definition 10 (Pure abstractions). *The* empty abstraction*, denoted* A_{emp}*, has all its components empty sets. Let* V_0 *be a set of variables. The* abstraction of equalities *over* V_0*, denoted* $A_{\approx}(V_0)$*, is* $\langle V_0, \{V_0\}, \emptyset, V_0, \emptyset, \emptyset, \emptyset\rangle$*, i.e., all variables are visible and in the same equivalence class. The* abstraction of disequalities *over* V_0 *is* $A_{\not\approx}(V_0) = \langle V_0, \mathtt{Id}_{V_0}, V_0^2 \setminus \mathtt{Id}_{V_0}, V_0, \emptyset, \emptyset, \emptyset\rangle$*, i.e., all variables are visible and pairwise distinct, and none is allocated.*

Note that we identify equivalence relations with the set of their equivalence classes so that $\{V_0\}$ denotes the relation $\{(x, y) \mid x, y \in V_0\}$.

Definition 11 (Quantified abstractions). *Let* $V_0 \subseteq A.V$ *be a set of variables. The* hiding of V_0 in A*, denoted by* $A_{\exists(V_0)}$*, is the abstraction having the same components as* A *except the set of visible variables, i.e.,* $A_{\exists(V_0)}.V_v = A.V_v \setminus V_0$*.*

Definition 12 (Separated abstractions). *Let* A_1 *and* A_2 *be two abstractions; w.l.o.g., we consider that* $A_1.V_{inv} \cap A_2.V_{inv} = \emptyset$*, i.e., the sets of invisible variables are disjoint (modulo renaming). Let* $V^\star = A_1.V \cup A_2.V$ *and the equivalence relation* $\backsim_\star$ *over* $V^\star$ *defined by the transitive closure of* $A_1.\backsim \cup A_2.\backsim$*. Consider now the relation* $\not\backsim_\star$ *over* $\overline{V^\star}_{\backsim_\star}$ *(the set of equivalence classes of* $\backsim_\star$*) defined by the symmetric closure of the relation:* $\{([x]_{\backsim_\star}, [y]_{\backsim_\star}) \mid x, y \in V^\star, ([x]_{A_i.\backsim}, [y]_{A_i.\backsim}) \in A_i.\not\backsim, i \in \{1, 2\}\} \cup \{([x_1]_{\backsim_\star}, [x_2]_{\backsim_\star}) \mid x_i \in V^\star, [x_i]_{A_i.\backsim} \in A_i.\overline{V}_a, i \in \{1, 2\}\}$*. If* $\not\backsim_\star$ *is irreflexive, then* A_1 *and* A_2 *are* separated*.*

Definition 13 (Separating abstractions). *The* separating composition $A_1 \star A_2$ *of two separated abstractions* A_1 *and* A_2 *is the abstraction* $A_\star$ *such that:*

- $A_\star{\bullet}V = V^\star$; $A_\star{\bullet}\backsim\, = \backsim_\star$; $A_\star{\bullet}\neq\, = \neq_\star$;
- $A_\star{\bullet}V_v = A_1{\bullet}V_v \cup A_2{\bullet}V_v$;
- $A_\star{\bullet}\overline{V}_a = \{[x]_{A_\star{\bullet}\backsim} \mid [x]_{A_i{\bullet}\backsim} \in A_i{\bullet}\overline{V}_a, i \in \{1,2\}\}$;
- $A_\star{\bullet}h = [[x]_{A_\star{\bullet}\backsim} \mapsto ([y_1]_{A_\star{\bullet}\backsim}, \ldots, [y_n]_{A_\star{\bullet}\backsim}) \mid A_i{\bullet}h([x]_{A_i{\bullet}\backsim}) = ([y_1]_{A_i{\bullet}\backsim}, \ldots, [y_n]_{A_i{\bullet}\backsim}), i \in \{1,2\}]$;
- $A_\star{\bullet}\rightsquigarrow\, = \{([x]_{A_\star{\bullet}\backsim}, [y]_{A_\star{\bullet}\backsim}) \mid ([x]_{A_i{\bullet}\backsim}, [y]_{A_i{\bullet}\backsim}) \in A_i{\bullet}\rightsquigarrow, i \in \{1,2\}\}$.

The following definitions are used to build the reachability relation in abstractions by replacing chains $[x_0] \mapsto [x_1] \mapsto \ldots \mapsto [x_{n-1}] \mapsto [x_n]$ related by $A{\bullet}h$ with the tuple $([x_0], [x_n])$ in $A{\bullet}\rightsquigarrow$ if the variables x_i with $i \in [1, n-1]$ are not "special" for A.

Definition 14 (Roots). *The* roots of an abstraction A, root(A), *is the set of minimal sets of roots of* $A{\bullet}\rightsquigarrow$. *We denote by* $x \in_\forall$ root(A) *or* $[x] \in_\forall$ root(A) *that* $[x]$ *belongs to all sets in* root(A) *and by* $x \in_\exists$ root(A) *or* $[x] \in_\exists$ root(A) *that* $[x]$ *belongs to at least one set in* root(A).

As $A{\bullet}\rightsquigarrow$ may contain cycles, roots are not uniquely defined. However, the algorithm for computing abstractions will ensure that root(A) is always non-empty.

Definition 15 (Special and persistent variables). *A variable* $x \in A{\bullet}V_{inv}$ *is* special *if its equivalence class is a singleton and it satisfies one of the following conditions: (i)* $x \in_\forall$ root(A), *i.e., x occurs in all sets of roots of A; (ii)* $[x] \notin A{\bullet}\overline{V}_a$, *i.e., x is not allocated, and there exists* $[y] \in A{\bullet}\overline{V}_a$ *such that* $([y], [x]) \in A{\bullet}\rightsquigarrow$, *i.e., x is reachable from an allocated variable; (iii) there exists* $y \in A{\bullet}V_v$ *such that* $y \in_\exists$ root(A) *and* $[x] \in A{\bullet}h([y])$, *i.e., x is pointed to by a possible root that is visible; (iv) there exists* $[y] \in A{\bullet}\overline{V}_a$ *such that* $[y] \in_\forall$ root(A) *and* $[x] \in A{\bullet}h([y])$, *i.e., x is pointed to by a necessary root that is visible or invisible. An invisible variable is* persistent *if it satisfies one of the items (i) or (ii) above. The set of persistent variables is denoted by* $A{\bullet}V_{per}$.

Example 4. Abstractions A_1^p and A_1^q in Fig. 1 have a singleton set of roots built from one class: root(A_1^p) = $\{\{[z]\}\}$ and root(A_1^q) = $\{\{[y]\}\}$, while A_1^r has a unique set of roots but containing two classes root(A_1^r) = $\{\{[z], [t]\}\}$. The variable z is not visible in A_1^p, but it is special and persistent since it fulfils the condition (i) of Definition 15. All the variables in A_1^q are special, but only y and u are persistent.

Definition 16 (Disconnected variable). *A variable* $x \in A{\bullet}V_v$ *is disconnected if it satisfies the following two conditions: (1)* $[x] \notin A{\bullet}\overline{V}_a$, *i.e., x is not allocated; and (2) for all* $[y] \in A{\bullet}\overline{V}_a, ([y], [x]) \notin A{\bullet}\rightsquigarrow$, *i.e., x is not pointed by an allocated variable.*

If a variable is disconnected, any variable in its equivalence class is also disconnected. Moreover, a disconnected variable cannot be special. For any equivalence relation $\bowtie$, we denote by $\bowtie \setminus x$ the restriction of $\bowtie$ to the elements distinct from x. Similarly, $\overline{S} \setminus x$ denotes the set $\{[y] \mid y \in S, y \neq x\}$, and for any relation $\rightarrow$ on equivalence classes of $\bowtie$, $\rightarrow \setminus x$ is the corresponding relation on equivalence classes of $\bowtie \setminus x$.

Definition 17 (Deletion of variables not special). *Let A be an abstraction and $x \in A.V_{inv}$ a variable that is not special. We define* rem(A, x), *the abstraction obtained by deleting x from A as follows: $A_{\text{rem}} = \langle A.V \setminus \{x\}, A.\backsim \setminus x, A.\neq \setminus x, A.V_v, A.\overline{V}_a \setminus x, A.h \setminus x, \rightsquigarrow' \setminus x\rangle$ with $\rightsquigarrow' = \{([y],[z]) \mid [y],[z] \in A.\overline{V} \wedge ([y],[x]) \in A.\rightsquigarrow \wedge ([x],[z]) \in A.\rightsquigarrow\} \cup A.\rightsquigarrow$. We denote by* rem$(A)$ *the abstraction obtained by removing all variables not special in A.*

Definition 18 (Set of abstractions of a symbolic heap). *Let φ be a symbolic heap formula of SL. The set of abstractions of a formula φ, denoted* abs(φ), *is inductively constructed using the rules in Tab. 1.*

Example 5. Consider the pair $(\varphi, \mathcal{R})$ introduced by Example 1. The abstractions of φ are built by firstly building the abstractions of the predicates $r(z, u, t)$ and then $q(y)$ — that calls r — defined by the rules in Eq. (7). Then $\varphi = p(x, y)$ has two abstractions. The first is A_1^p from Fig. 1, obtained from the non-recursive rule of p. The second is A_2^p in Fig. 2, obtained from A_2 by removing variables z and t using the procedure in Definition 17 because they are not special. The abstraction A_2 is obtained by applying the rule [Sep] on A_1^q in Fig. 1, which is an abstraction of $q(y)$, and the abstraction obtained by the rule [Pto] for $x \rightarrow (y)$.

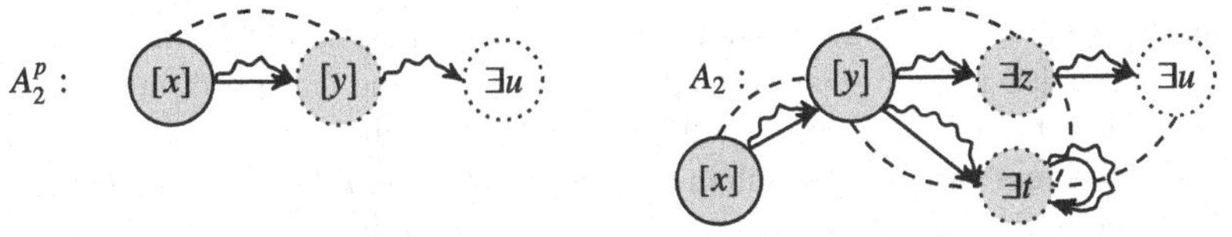

Fig. 2. Abstraction A_2

Given $A \in$ abs(φ), we consider the implicit tree of construction of A using rules in Definition 18: every node of this tree is an abstraction created by one of the rules [Ex], [Pred] and [Sep], and every leaf is an abstraction of an atomic formula. Therefore, every node of this tree is associated with a formula, which is a sub-formula of an unfolding of φ.

Table 1. Computing Abstractions of a Symbolic Heap Formula

$$\textsc{Emp}\ \frac{}{\mathrm{abs}(\mathtt{emp}) \ni A_{\mathtt{emp}}} \qquad \textsc{Eq}\ \frac{}{\mathrm{abs}(x \approx y) \ni A_{\approx}(\{x, y\})} \qquad \textsc{NEq}\ \frac{}{\mathrm{abs}(x \not\approx y) \ni A_{\not\approx}(\{x, y\})}$$

$$\textsc{Pto}\ \frac{\begin{array}{c} A.V = A.V_v = \{x, y_1, \ldots, y_n\} \qquad A.\backsim = \mathtt{Id} \qquad A.\not\approx = \emptyset \\ A.\overline{V}_a = \{[x]\} \qquad A.h = [[x] \mapsto ([y_1], \ldots, [y_n])] \qquad A.\rightsquigarrow = \{([x], [y_i]) \mid i \in [\![1, n]\!]\} \end{array}}{\mathrm{abs}(x \rightarrow (y_1, \ldots, y_n)) \ni A}$$

$$\textsc{Sep}\ \frac{\mathrm{abs}(\psi_1) \ni A_1 \qquad \mathrm{abs}(\psi_2) \ni A_2 \qquad A_1, A_2 \text{ are separated} \qquad A = \mathrm{rem}(A_1 \star A_2)}{\mathrm{abs}(\psi_1 \star \psi_2) \ni A}$$

$$\textsc{Ex}\ \frac{\mathrm{abs}(\psi) \ni A' \qquad A = \mathrm{rem}(A'_{\exists(\{x\})})}{\mathrm{abs}(\exists x.\, \psi) \ni A}$$

$$\textsc{Pred}\ \frac{\mathrm{abs}(\exists y_1, \ldots, y_n.\, (y_1 \approx x_1 \star \cdots \star y_n \approx x_n \star \psi)) \ni A \qquad p(y_1, \ldots, y_n) \Leftarrow \psi \in \mathcal{R}}{\mathrm{abs}(p(x_1, \ldots, x_n)) \ni A}$$

Definition 19 (Condition "Infinite Set of Invisible Variables" (ISIV)). *The abstraction $A \in \mathrm{abs}(p(x_1, \ldots, x_n))$ satisfies the condition ISIV if there exists an abstraction A' in the construction tree of A such that:*

1. *A' is associated with a renaming $p(y_1, \ldots, y_n)$ of $p(x_1, \ldots, x_n)$;*
2. *A has strictly more persistent variables than A': $\mathrm{card}(A'.V_{per}) < \mathrm{card}(A.V_{per})$;*
3. *the projections of abstractions A and A' on their visible variables are equal (modulo a renaming of the arguments $x_i \leftarrow y_i$).*

Intuitively, the condition asserts that a "loop" exists in the unfolding tree of p, where persistent variables are introduced inside the loop. As one can go through the loop an arbitrary number of times, this entails that some branch exists with an unbounded number of persistent variables, which in turn entails that non-k-PCE-compatible models exist. If this condition is satisfied by one abstraction built during this step, the algorithm fails. The following theorem states that the algorithm is correct and complete:

Theorem 2. *Let φ be a formula and let $\mathcal{R}$ be an SID. We suppose that the construction of abstractions terminates without failing. If $A \in \mathrm{abs}(\varphi)$, then there exists a model $(\mathfrak{s}, \mathfrak{h})$ of φ such that A is an abstraction of $(\mathfrak{s}, \mathfrak{h})$. Moreover, if φ admits a model $(\mathfrak{s}, \mathfrak{h})$, then there exists an abstraction A of φ such that $(\mathfrak{s}, \mathfrak{h}) \models A$.*

We also show that the algorithm terminates, provided the ISIV condition is used to dismiss pairs $(\varphi, \mathcal{R})$ that are not k-PCE-compatible (thus that cannot admit any equivalent PCE pair, by Proposition 1):

Theorem 3. *Let φ be a formula and let $\mathcal{R}$ be an SID. If there exists $k \in \mathbb{N}$ such that $(\varphi, \mathcal{R})$ is k-PCE-compatible, then the computation of $\mathrm{abs}(\varphi)$ terminates without failure (hence the ISIV condition is never fulfilled). Otherwise, the ISIV condition eventually applies during the computation of $\mathrm{abs}(\varphi)$. Consequently, the problem of testing whether $(\varphi, \mathcal{R})$ is k-PCE-compatible for some $k \in \mathbb{N}$ is decidable.*

6 Predicates with Exactly One Abstraction

We describe an algorithm reducing any pair $(\Phi, \mathcal{R})$ into an equivalent pair $(\Phi^\dagger, \mathcal{R}^\dagger)$ such that every predicate atom admits exactly one abstraction with no invisible variables. We also get rid of some existential variables when possible. The eventual goal is to ensure that the rules that were obtained are established (in the sense of Definition 5). We need to introduce some definitions and notations. A *disconnected set* for an n-ary predicate p and an abstraction $A \in \text{abs}(p(x_1, \dots, x_n))$ is any subset I of $\{1, \dots, n\}$ such that all variables x_i for $i \in I$ are disconnected in A. Let $\mathcal{R}$ be an SID. Let $x_1, \dots, x_n, \dots$ be an infinite sequence of pairwise distinct variables, which will be used to denote the formal parameters of the predicates. For each n-ary predicate p occurring in $\mathcal{R}$, for each abstraction $A \in \text{abs}(p(x_1, \dots, x_n))$ and for all disconnected sets I for p, A, we introduce a fresh predicate p_I^A, of arity $n + m - \text{card}(I)$, where $m = \text{card}(A.V_{inv})$. Intuitively, p_I^A will denote some "projection" of the structures corresponding to the abstraction A. The additional arguments will denote the invisible variables. The removed arguments correspond to disconnected variables.

Example 6. The predicate p, defined by rules on the left in Example 1, has two abstractions (one by rule), A_1^p and A_2^p, where all roots are connected. In the same example, predicates q and r also have only one abstraction. For all these predicates, the sets I are always $\emptyset$.

The rules associated with p_I^A are obtained from those associated with p as follows. For every formula φ such that $p(x_1, \dots, x_n) \Leftarrow_{\mathcal{R}} \varphi$, where φ is of the form $\exists \vec{y}. (q_1(\vec{u}_1) \star \dots \star q_k(\vec{u}_k) \star \varphi')$ and φ' contains no predicate symbol, and for all abstractions $A_i \in \text{abs}(q_i(x_1, \dots, x_{\#(q_i)}))$ (for $i \in [\![1, k]\!]$), we add the rule:

$$p_I^A(\vec{s}, x'_1, \dots, x'_m) \Leftarrow \exists \vec{z}. (q_1{}_{J_1}^{A_1}(\vec{t}_1, \vec{v}_1) \star \dots \star q_k{}_{J_k}^{A_k}(\vec{t}_k, \vec{v}_k) \star \varphi'')\sigma \qquad (11)$$

if all the following conditions hold:

- A is the abstraction computed from φ as explained in Definition 18, selecting A_i for the abstraction of $q_i(x_1, \dots, x_{\#(q_i)})$, i.e., $A = \text{rem}(A'_{\exists(\vec{z})})$, where $\{A''\} = \text{abs}(\varphi')$ (since φ' contains no predicate) and $A' = A_1 \star \dots \star A_k \star A''$ is the abstraction computed from the matrix $(q_1(\vec{u}_1) \star \dots \star q_k(\vec{u}_k) \star \varphi')$ of φ.
- $\vec{s}$ (resp. $\vec{t}_i$) is the subsequence of $x_1, \dots, x_n$ (resp. of $\vec{u}_i$) obtained by removing all components of rank $j \in I$ (resp. $j \in J_i$). Intuitively, I and J_i denote the parameters that are removed from the arguments of p and q_i, respectively.
- J_i is a subset of $\{1, \dots, \#(q_i)\}$, and for all variables z occurring as the j-th component of $\vec{u}_i$, the following equivalence holds: $j \in J_i$ iff $z \in \vec{z} \cup \{x_i \mid i \in I\}$ and z is disconnected in A'. Note that the last condition entails that the j-th component of $\vec{u}_i$ is also disconnected in A_i; hence the predicate $q_i{}_{J_i}^{A_i}$ exists. Intuitively, a variable is removed if it is disconnected, and either it is existentially quantified in the rule, or it is a free variable that was removed from the argument of p.
- $(x'_1, \dots, x'_m)$ and $\vec{v}_i$ are the sequences of invisible variables in A and A_i, respectively (the order is irrelevant and can be chosen arbitrarily). We assume by renaming that the $A_i.V_{inv}$ are pairwise disjoint.

– σ is any substitution with $\text{dom}(\sigma) \subseteq \vec{y}$ and $\text{img}(\sigma) \subseteq \vec{y} \cup \vec{s}$ such that for all $y \in \vec{y}$ and for all $y' \in \vec{y} \cup \vec{s}$: $\sigma(y) = \sigma(y') \iff (y, y') \in A'.\sim$. Intuitively, σ is applied to get rid of superfluous existential variables by instantiating them when it is possible, i.e., when the variable is known to be equal to a free variable or another existential variable[2].
– φ'' is obtained from φ' by removing all pure atoms containing a variable that is disconnected in A' and does not occur in $\vec{s}$.
– $\vec{z}$ is the sequence of variables occurring either in the formula φ'' or in the sequences $\vec{t}_i$ or $\vec{v}_i$ (for some $i \in [\![1, k]\!]$) but not in $\{x_1, \dots, x_n, x'_1, \dots, x'_m\} \cup \text{dom}(\sigma)$ (again, the order is irrelevant). These variables correspond to variables from $\vec{y}$ or $\vec{v}_i$ that can be eliminated during the computation of A using the rule introduced in Definition 17.

The obtained set of rules is denoted by $\mathcal{R}^\dagger$. It is clear that $\mathcal{R}^\dagger$ is finite (up to α-renaming) if $\mathcal{R}$ is finite and $\text{abs}(p(x_1, \dots, x_n))$ is finite for all n-ary predicates p in $\mathcal{R}$.

Example 7. The new rules for p, q, and r defined in the SID $\mathcal{R}_1$ in Ex. 1 are given below:

$$\begin{aligned} p_\emptyset^{A_1^p}(x, y, z) &\Leftarrow z \to (x, y)\,, & q_\emptyset^{A_1^q}(y, z, t, u) &\Leftarrow y \to (z, t) \star r(z, t, u)\,, \\ p_\emptyset^{A_2^p}(x, y, u) &\Leftarrow \exists z, t.\, (x \to (y) \star & r_\emptyset^{A_1^r}(z, t, u) &\Leftarrow u \not\approx t \star z \to (u) \star t \to (t)\,. \\ & \quad q_\emptyset^{A_1^q}(y, z, t, u))\,, \end{aligned} \tag{12}$$

The arity of predicates $p_\emptyset^{A_2^p}$ and $q_\emptyset^{A_1^q}$ has been changed to include the invisible but special variable u, and the predicate $p_\emptyset^{A_1^p}$ now does not have an invisible root any more.

Example 8. In this example, we show how disconnected variables may be eliminated. Let p, q be predicates defined by the rules: $p(x, y) \Leftarrow \exists z.\, (x \to (y) \star q(x, z))$, $q(x, y) \Leftarrow x \not\approx y$. $p(x_1, x_2)$ and $q(x_1, x_2)$ both admit one abstraction, A_p and A_q, respectively, defined by:

$$A_p = (\{x_1, x_2\}, \{\{x_1\}, \{x_2\}\}, \emptyset, \{x_1, x_2\}, \{[x_1]\}\{[x_1] \mapsto [x_2]\}, \emptyset)\,, \tag{13}$$
$$A_q = (\{x_1, x_2\}, \{\{x_1\}, \{x_2\}\}, \{([x_1], [x_2])\}, \{x_1, x_2\}, \emptyset, \emptyset, \emptyset)\,. \tag{14}$$

The above transformation produces the rules: $p_\emptyset^{A_p}(x, y) \Leftarrow (x \to (y) \star q_{\{2\}}^{A_q}(x))$ and $q_{\{2\}}^{A_r}(x) \Leftarrow \texttt{emp}$. The variable z is eliminated, as it is disconnected in the abstraction corresponding to $x \to (y) \star q(x, z)$. This yields the introduction of a predicate $q_{\{2\}}^{A_r}$ in which the second argument of q is dismissed.

The above transformation may be applied to the formulas Φ occurring in pairs $(\Phi, \mathcal{R})$. Since the establishment condition applies only to the variables occurring in the rule and not to the existential variables of Φ, there is no need to eliminate any predicate argument in this case; thus, we may simply take $I = \emptyset$ for the predicates

[2] In the latter case several substitutions exist, one of them can be chosen arbitrarily (the resulting rules are identical up to α-renaming, e.g., $\exists x \exists y (x \approx y \star q(x, y))$ can be written $\exists x (x \approx y \star q(x, y))\{y \leftarrow x\}$ or $\exists y (x \approx y \star q(x, y))\{x \leftarrow y\}$).

p_I^A such that p appears in Φ. Predicates of the form q_I^B with $I \neq \emptyset$ will never appear at the root level in Φ, but they may appear in the rules of the predicates $p_\emptyset^A$ (in practice, such rules will be computed on demand). More precisely, we denote by $\Phi^\dagger$ the formula obtained from Φ by replacing every atom $p(y_1, \ldots, y_n)$ in Φ by the formula $\bigvee_{A \in \mathrm{abs}(p(x_1,\ldots,x_n))} \exists \vec{y}_A .\, p_\emptyset^A(y_1, \ldots, y_n, \vec{y}_A)$, where $\vec{y}_A$ is the sequence of variables in $A.V_{inv}$ (with arbitrary order). Note that in the case where $\mathrm{abs}(p(x_1, \ldots, x_n)) = \emptyset$, $p(y_1, \ldots, y_n)$ is replaced by an empty disjunction, i.e., by false. The properties of this transformation are stated by the following result:

Theorem 4. $(\Phi, \mathcal{R}) \equiv (\Phi^\dagger, \mathcal{R}^\dagger)$. *Moreover, for all predicates* p_I^A *defined in* $\mathcal{R}^\dagger$, *the set* $\mathrm{abs}(p_I^A(\vec{y}, x'_1, \ldots, x'_m))$ *contains exactly one abstraction.*

7 Abstractions with Exactly One Root

We introduce an algorithm that transforms the considered SID by introducing and removing predicates such that the abstraction of each predicate p defined by the new $\mathcal{R}$ has only one root. This transformation is done in two steps: first, change predicates with an abstraction without roots, and then change predicates with an abstraction with more than one root. The transformation may fail if the structures corresponding to a given recursive predicate have multiple roots, as such structures cannot be defined by PCE rules (e.g., two parallel lists of the same length).

Removal of Abstractions Without Root: Let us consider every predicate p such that its abstraction $A_p \in \mathrm{abs}(p(\vec{x}))$ satisfies $\mathrm{root}(A_p) = \emptyset$. Because the abstraction of p has no root, the associated structure has no allocated locations, and the predicate can only be unfolded into formulas that do not contain points-to. Thus, for each unfolding of p of abstraction A, which cannot be unfolded any more, it only contains equalities and disequalities that are abstracted in A by $A.\backsim$ and $A.\not\approx$. As a consequence, we can create a formula $\varphi_A = (\bigstar_{i,j \in I_\approx} a_i \approx a_j) \star (\bigstar_{i,j \in I_{\not\approx}} b_i \not\approx b_j)$ with $\{a_i \approx a_j \mid i, j \in I_\approx\} = A.\backsim$ and $\{b_i \not\approx b_j \mid i, j \in I_{\not\approx}\} = A.\not\approx$. We can then replace every occurrence of p with φ_A.

Removal of Abstractions With Several Roots: We suppose now that for all predicates p, the abstraction $A_p \in \mathrm{abs}(p(\vec{x}))$ verifies $\mathrm{root}(A_p) \neq \emptyset$. Now let us consider every predicate p such that its abstraction $A_p \in \mathrm{abs}(p(\vec{x}))$ has at least two roots, i.e., for all $R \in \mathrm{root}(A_p)$, $\mathrm{card}(R) \geq 2$. If p does not call itself, we unfold p by replacing each occurrence of p with its definition using the rules in SID. Otherwise, the transformation is considered impossible, and it fails.

At this point, if the transformation does not fail, we obtain:

Proposition 2 (Every abstraction has a single root). *After applying the transformation in this section, for all predicates p, for all abstractions* $A \in \mathrm{abs}(p(\vec{x}))$, *there exists a set* $R \in \mathrm{root}(A)$ *such that* $\mathrm{card}(R) = 1$.

Remark 1. We wish to emphasize that the failure of the above operation does not imply that the transformation is unfeasible. For instance, one could, in principle, define two lists of arbitrary (possibly distinct) lengths using one single inductive predicate, adding elements in one of the lists in a non-deterministic way, although such a definition is very unlikely to occur in practice. Then, our algorithm would fail (as it will detect that the structure has two roots), although a PCE presentation exists. Extending the algorithm to cover such cases is part of future work.

8 Transformation into PCE Rules

The last step of the transformation is a procedure reducing any pair $(\Phi^{\dagger}, \mathcal{R}^{\dagger})$ into an equivalent pair $(\Phi^{\ddagger}, \mathcal{R}^{\ddagger})$ such that $\Phi^{\ddagger}$ and $\mathcal{R}^{\ddagger}$ are PCE formula resp. SID.

To this aim, we first introduce so-called *derived predicates* (adapted and extended from [4]), the rules of which can be computed from the rules defining predicate symbols. The aim is to extract from the call tree of a spatial atom the part that corresponds to another atom. Given a SID $\mathcal{R}$ and two spatial atoms γ and λ, we denote by $\gamma \multimap \lambda$ the atom defined by the following rules:

$$\begin{aligned} &\gamma \multimap \lambda \Leftarrow \exists \vec{x}.\,(\varphi \star (\gamma \multimap \lambda')), && \text{for all } \varphi, \lambda' \text{ with } \lambda \Leftarrow_{\mathcal{R}} \exists \vec{x}.\,(\varphi \star \lambda') \text{ (up to AC of } \star), \\ &\gamma \multimap \lambda \Leftarrow x_1 \approx y_1 \star \cdots \star x_n \approx y_n, && \text{if } \gamma = p(x_1, \ldots, x_n) \text{ and } \lambda = p(y_1, \ldots, y_n), \text{ or} \\ & && \gamma = x_1 \to (x_2, \ldots, x_n) \text{ and } \lambda = y_1 \to (y_2, \ldots, y_n). \end{aligned} \tag{15}$$

We assume that all such rules occur in $\mathcal{R}$. Intuitively, $\gamma \multimap \lambda$ encodes a structure defined as the atom λ but in which a call to γ is removed. It is easy to see that $\gamma \multimap \lambda$ is unsatisfiable if λ is a points-to atom and γ is a predicate atom. By definition, $(x_1 \to (x_2, \ldots, x_n)) \multimap (y_1 \to (y_2, \ldots, y_m))$ is equivalent to $x_1 \approx y_1 \star \cdots \star x_n \approx y_n$ if $m = n$ and unsatisfiable otherwise. These remarks can be used to simplify the rules above (e.g., by removing rules with unsatisfiable bodies).

For instance, given the rules $p(x) \Leftarrow \exists y.\,(x \to (y) \star p(y))$ and $p(x) \Leftarrow x \to ()$, the derived atoms $p(x') \multimap p(x)$ and $(x' \to ()) \multimap p(x)$ both denote a list segment from x to x', whereas $(x' \to (x'')) \multimap p(x)$ denotes a list with a "hole" at x'. The corresponding rules are, after simplification:

$$p(x') \multimap p(x) \Leftarrow \exists y.\,(x \to (y) \star (p(x') \multimap p(y))), \qquad p(x') \multimap p(x) \Leftarrow x \approx x', \tag{16}$$

$$x' \to () \multimap p(x) \Leftarrow \exists y.\,(x \to (y) \star (x' \to () \multimap p(y))), \qquad x' \to () \multimap p(x) \Leftarrow x \approx x', \tag{17}$$

$$(x' \to (x'')) \multimap p(x) \Leftarrow \exists y.\,(x \to (y) \star (x' \to (x'') \multimap p(y))), \tag{18}$$

$$(x' \to (x'')) \multimap p(x) \Leftarrow x \approx x' \star p(x''). \tag{19}$$

The operator $\multimap$ can be nested, for instance $(x_1 \to (x_1')) \multimap (p(x_2) \multimap p(x))$ denotes a list segment from x to x_2 with a hole at x_1.

Consider a rule $\rho = p(x_1, \ldots, x_n) \Leftarrow \varphi$, where φ' denotes the quantifier-free formula such that $\varphi = \exists \vec{z}.\varphi'$. By Theorem 4, the formulas φ and φ' have unique abstractions A_φ and $A_{\varphi'}$, respectively (in what follows the notations $[x]$ and $\rightsquigarrow$ always refer to abstraction $A_{\varphi'}$). Recall that, at this point, establishment is ensured, and all roots are visible. As φ only has a unique abstraction, there is a unique $k \in [\![1, n]\!]$ such that $[x_k]$ is the root of A_φ and the tuple pointed to by the location associated with x_k contains only locations associated with variables $y_1, \ldots, y_m$ that are visible or special in A_φ, with $A_\varphi.h([x_k]) = ([y_1], \ldots, [y_m])$. To make the rule ρ PCE, it must be rewritten to have the form $p(x_1, \ldots, x_n) \Leftarrow \exists \vec{z}.\,x_k \to (y_1, \ldots, y_m) \star q_1(\vec{w_1}) \star \cdots \star q_l(\vec{w_l}) \star \psi$, where ψ is a pure formula, and the root of each atom $q_i(\vec{w_i})$ is in $\{y_1, \ldots, y_m\}$. There are two cases:

Case 1: Assume that φ contains a points-to atom $x'_k \to (y'_1, \ldots, y'_l)$, with $\left[x'_k\right] = [x_k]$ and $\left[y'_i\right] = [y_i]$ for all $i \in [\![1, l]\!]$. The formula φ' is of the form $x'_k \to (y'_1, \ldots, y'_m) \star \psi \star \psi'$, where ψ contains only points-to and predicate atoms and ψ' is a pure formula. The formula ψ may be decomposed into $\varphi_1 \star \cdots \star \varphi_{l'}$, where each formula φ_i allocates only variables z such that $\left[y_{j_i}\right] \leadsto^* [z]$, where $y_{j_1}, \ldots, y_{j_{l'}}$ are variables in $\{y_1, \ldots, y_l\}$ such that the $\left[y_{j_i}\right]$ are pairwise distinct. Such a decomposition necessarily exists[3] since $[x_k]$ is the root of $\leadsto$, and every class reachable from $[x_k]$ must be reachable from one of the $[y_i]$. For $i \in [\![1, l']\!]$, if φ_i is not a predicate atom, then we create a fresh predicate q_i whose arguments are all the variables $\vec{w_i}$ that appear in φ_i, we create the rule $q_i(\vec{w_i}) \Leftarrow \varphi_i$, and we replace in φ the formula φ_i by $q_i(\vec{w_i})$. We get a rule ρ' that is now PCE.

Case 2: Now assume that φ contains no such points-to atom $x'_k \to (y'_1, \ldots, y'_l)$. We have to extract this points-to from some rule that, when unfolded, creates it and add it to a new rule equivalent to ρ. Because A_φ is unique and because every predicate also has a unique abstraction, only one atom can allocate x_k, and this atom must be a predicate atom (because of case 1). Thus φ' is of the form $q(\vec{w}) \star \varphi''$, where x_k is allocated in every model of $q(\vec{w})$. By the previous construction, the atom $q(\vec{w})$ may be replaced by $x_k \to (y_1, \ldots, y_l) \star (x_k \to (y_1, \ldots, y_l) \multimap q(\vec{w}))$. We get a new rule $\rho' = p(x_1, \ldots, x_n) \Leftarrow \exists \vec{z} . x_k \to (y_1, \ldots, y_l) \star (x_k \to (y_1, \ldots, y_l) \multimap q(\vec{w})) \star \varphi''$ which fulfils the previous condition, and we may apply the transformation described in the previous item to ρ'. The new rules associated with $x_k \to (y_1, \ldots, y_l) \multimap p'_1(\vec{x'_1})$ are added to the set of rules.

The above transformations are applied until all rules are PCE. Note that termination is not guaranteed (indeed, not all k-PCE-compatible pairs $(\Phi, \mathcal{R})$ admit an equivalent PCE pair, and the existence of such a pair is undecidable by Theorem 1). To enforce termination in some cases, a form of memoization may be used: the predicates introduced above may be reused if the corresponding formulas are equivalent. As logical equivalence is hard to test (undecidable in general), we only check that the rules associated with both predicates are identical up to a renaming of existential variables and spatial predicates. In practice, termination may be ensured by imposing limitations on the number of rules or predicates. We show that if the transformation terminates, we obtain the desired result.

Theorem 5. *Let $(\Phi^\dagger, \mathcal{R}^\dagger)$ be any pair obtained by applying the transformations in Secs. 6 and 7. If the computation of $(\Phi^\ddagger, \mathcal{R}^\ddagger)$ terminates, then $(\Phi^\dagger, \mathcal{R}^\dagger) \equiv (\Phi^\ddagger, \mathcal{R}^\ddagger)$. Also, the SID $\mathcal{R}^\ddagger$, and thus $\Phi^\ddagger$, are PCE.*

9 Experimental Evaluation and Conclusion

We devised an algorithm to construct PCE rules for a given formula (if possible). The existence of such a presentation is undecidable, but we identify a property called PCE-compatibility, which is decidable and weaker. Our algorithm helps to relax the rigid conditions on the PCE presentations. It is also able to construct PCE rules in some more complex cases by performing deep, global transformations on the rules. We have

[3] If several decompositions exist, then one of them is chosen arbitrarily.

implemented an initial version of the algorithm in OCaml using the Cyclist [2] framework and applied it to benchmarks taken from this framework and SL-COMP [1]. The program comprises approximately 3000 lines of code. To ensure efficiency, the implemented procedure is somewhat simplified compared to the algorithm described in this paper: in Step Sect. 8, we avoid the use of derived predicates and instead employ a fixed-depth unfolding of predicate atoms (the other sections strictly adhere to the theoretical definitions). All tests are performed with a timeout of 30 seconds. The running time is low in most examples. In the 145 tested examples, 105 are successfully transformed into equivalent PCE-formulas, 20 trigger the ISIV condition (the structures are not k-PCE-compatible), 3 examples fail at Step Sect. 7 (recursive structures with multiple roots) and 17 other timeout. The program and input data are available at https://hal.science/hal-04549937. We find the results highly encouraging, as about 86% of the tested examples are successfully managed. Therefore, this tool may be used to provide a measure of the difficulty of the examples in the SL-COMP benchmark.

We end the paper by identifying some lines of future work. For efficiency, we first plan to refine the transformation by avoiding the systematic reduction to one-abstraction predicates given in Sect. 6. Indeed, this transformation is very convenient from a theoretical point of view but introduces some additional computational blow-up, which could be avoided in some cases. We wish to strengthen the definition of k-PCE-compatible ID in order to capture additional properties of PCE definitions. Notice that the semi-decidability of the PCE problem is an open question. Finally, it could also be interesting to extend the transformation to E-restricted IDs, a fragment of non-established IDs introduced in [4], for which the entailment is decidable.

References

1. SL-COMP website. https://sl-comp.github.io/
2. Brotherston, J., Gorogiannis, N., Petersen, R.L.: A generic cyclic theorem prover. In: Jhala, R., Igarashi, A. (eds.) APLAS 2012. LNCS, vol. 7705, pp. 350–367. Springer, Heidelberg (2012). https://doi.org/10.1007/978-3-642-35182-2_25
3. Echenim, M., Iosif, R., Peltier, N.: Entailment checking in separation logic with inductive definitions is 2-EXPTIME hard. In: Albert, E., Kovacs, L. (eds.) LPAR23. LPAR-23: 23rd International Conference on Logic for Programming, Artificial Intelligence and Reasoning, vol. 73. EPiC Series in Computing, pp. 191–211. EasyChair, May 2020. ISSN: 2398-7340. https://easychair.org/publications/paper/DdNg, https://doi.org/10.29007/f5wh
4. Echenim, M., Iosif, R., Peltier., N.: Decidable entailments in separation logic with inductive definitions: beyond establishment. In: Baier, C., Goubault-Larrecq, J. (eds.) 29th EACSL Annual Conference on Computer Science Logic (CSL 2021), vol. 183. Leibniz International Proceedings in Informatics (LIPIcs), pp. 20:1–20:18, Dagstuhl, Germany, 2021. Schloss Dagstuhl - Leibniz-Zentrum für Informatik. https://drops.dagstuhl.de/entities/document/10.4230/LIPIcs.CSL.2021.20, https://doi.org/10.4230/LIPIcs.CSL.2021.20
5. Echenim, M., Iosif, R., Peltier, N.: Unifying decidable entailments in separation logic with inductive definitions. In: Platzer, A., Sutcliffe, G. (eds.) CADE 2021. LNCS (LNAI), vol. 12699, pp. 183–199. Springer, Cham (2021). https://doi.org/10.1007/978-3-030-79876-5_11
6. Echenim, M., Iosif, R., Peltier, N.: Entailment is Undecidable for Symbolic Heap Separation Logic Formulæ with Non-Established Inductive Rules. Inf. Process. Lett. 173:106169, January 2022. https://www.sciencedirect.com/science/article/pii/S0020019021000843, https://doi.org/10.1016/j.ipl.2021.106169

7. Gu, X., Chen, T., Wu, Z.: A complete decision procedure for linearly compositional separation logic with data constraints. In: Olivetti, N., Tiwari, A. (eds.) IJCAR 2016. LNCS (LNAI), vol. 9706, pp. 532–549. Springer, Cham (2016). https://doi.org/10.1007/978-3-319-40229-1_36
8. Iosif, R., Rogalewicz, A., Simacek, J.: The tree width of separation logic with recursive definitions. In: Bonacina, M.P. (ed.) CADE 2013. LNCS (LNAI), vol. 7898, pp. 21–38. Springer, Heidelberg (2013). https://doi.org/10.1007/978-3-642-38574-2_2
9. Ishtiaq, S.S., O'Hearn, P.W.: BI as an assertion language for mutable data structures. In: Proceedings of the 28th ACM SIGPLAN-SIGACT Symposium on Principles of Programming Languages, POPL 2001, pp. 14–26. Association for Computing Machinery, New York, January 2001. https://doi.org/10.1145/360204.375719
10. Matheja, C., Pagel, J., Zuleger, F.: A decision procedure for guarded separation logic complete entailment checking for separation logic with inductive definitions. ACM Trans. Comput. Logic **24**(1), 1:1–1:76 (2023). https://doi.org/10.1145/3534927
11. Reynolds, J.C.: Separation logic: a logic for shared mutable data structures. In: Proceedings 17th Annual IEEE Symposium on Logic in Computer Science, pp. 55–74, Copenhagen, Denmark, July 2002. ISSN: 1043-6871. https://ieeexplore.ieee.org/document/1029817, https://doi.org/10.1109/LICS.2002.1029817

Sequents vs Hypersequents for Åqvist Systems

Agata Ciabattoni and Matteo Tesi(✉)

Institute of Logic and Computation,
Vienna University of Technology, Vienna, Austria
agata@logic.at, matteo.tesi@tuwien.ac.at

Abstract. Enhancing cut-free expressiveness through minimal structural additions to sequent calculus is a natural step. We focus on Åqvist's system **F** with cautious monotonicity (**CM**), a deontic logic extension of **S5**, for which we define a sequent calculus employing (semi) analytic cuts.The transition to hypersequents is key to develop modular and cut-free calculi for **F** + (**CM**) and **G**, also supporting countermodel construction.

1 Introduction

Normative reasoning is crucial across various fields, including law and artificial intelligence. It is effectively formalized by deontic logic, the branch of logic that deals with obligations and related concepts. Numerous deontic logics have emerged, and they can be broadly classified into *preference-based* and *norm-based systems* [11]. The latter analyse deontic modalities with reference to a set of explicit norms, while the former employ possible world semantics. Preference-based systems are particularly useful to model contrary to duty obligations (i.e., obligations that come into force when some other obligation is violated) and defeasible deontic conditionals. Åqvist's landmark systems [1] **E**, **F**, and **G**, fall into this category. Semantically, they are characterized by preference models using relations to represent the betterness of states. They extend the modal logic **S5** with a dyadic obligation $\bigcirc(B/A)$ ("B is obligatory, given A") which is true when the best A-worlds are all B-worlds. A more recent addition to the family [27] is **F** with the addition of cautious monotonicity (CM) from the non-monotonic literature [12,18]. **E**, **F**, **F** + (**CM**), and **G** are modular systems with increasing deductive strength w.r.t. the sets of theorems they derive. The last two systems correspond to well-known conditional logics: **G** is **VTA** [13], one of Lewis' logics, while **F** + (**CM**) corresponds to Preferential Conditional Logic **PCL** [6] supplemented with the absoluteness axiom, that reflects the fact that the ranking is not world-relative. **PCL** contains as a fragment the **KLM** preferential logic **P** [18] for default reasoning.

Reasoning necessitates (finding) derivations and countermodels. The exploration of the proof theory for these logics has only recently become a focal point.

C. Benzmüller et al. (Eds.): IJCAR 2024, LNAI 14740, pp. 176–195, 2024.
https://doi.org/10.1007/978-3-031-63501-4_10

Prior to that, the only available calculi for them were Hilbert systems, which are unsuitable for the mentioned tasks. Since Gentzen's introduction in 1935, sequent calculi in which the cut rule is admissible (or eliminable) have been employed for these purposes. Although crucial to simulate modus ponens, the cut rule poses a hindrance to proof search. Cut-free sequent systems are not available for Åqvist's systems insofar as they contain an **S5** modality which impedes their formulation[1]. Many sequent calculus generalizations, like hypersequents, nested, and labelled sequents, have been introduced to capture logics without cut-free formulations. Notably, hypersequents are characterized by less complex objects and expressiveness compared to nested sequents, which, in turn, are less complex and expressive than labelled sequents, see e.g. [22]. Using hypersequents, modular cut-free calculi have been introduced for **E** and **F** in [8,9]. The situation for **G** and **F** + (**CM**) is less clear. Although **G** semantically arises by imposing to **F** + (**CM**) totality on frames, this is not reflected in their calculi: (forms of) labelled sequents [20,24] have been employed for **PCL**, and a hypersequent calculus with blocks (incorporating a shallow form of nesting) [14] for **G**.

This leaves open the question whether *modular* and *cut-free* calculi, using a *simpler framework*, can be defined for **F** + (**CM**) and **G**. Simplicity in the proof formalism is advantageous for proving meta-logical results and streamlining the proof search space. Indeed the introduction of additional structure in the basic objects manipulated by the formalism often poses obstacles in these endeavors.

Our positive answer to the question relies on the use of an alternative semantics (w.r.t. preference models) [28]. We first introduce a *sequent* calculus **SFcm** for **F** + (**CM**). Like the calculus in [25] for **S5**, **SFcm** lacks completeness without cuts. Nevertheless, we show that a restricted form of cuts, we call them semi-analytic, suffices. We present a syntactic procedure, akin to cut-elimination, to transform **SFcm** proofs with arbitrary cuts into proofs with semi-analytic cuts, simplifying the method in [7]. Extending **SFcm** to encompass **G** would be hard, if possible at all. Sequent calculi, are indeed known to be inadequate for capturing modal logics with linear frames (Ch.9 in [15]). To achieve modular and cut-free calculi for **F** + (**CM**) and **G**, we shift from the sequent to the hypersequent framework. The use of hypersequents (which are sequents working in parallel) enables the definition of structural rules operating across multiple sequents. In particular, adapting the peculiar hypersequent rule for **S5** from [4] simplifies the rules for **SFcm**, resulting in a cut-free hypersequent calculus for **F** + (**CM**). A calculus for **G** is obtained by adding (a version of) the communication rule from [3], designed to capture Gödel logic [10]. We prove cut-elimination for both calculi and modify them into proof-search oriented calculi, providing proofs of decidability and countermodel construction from failed derivations.

Similarly to the calculi for **E** and **F** in [8,9] we encode maximality by a (**S4**-type) modal operator. $\bigcirc(B/A)$ can be indirectly defined as $\Box(A \to \neg \mathcal{B}et \neg(A \wedge$

[1] The standard sequent calculus [25] for **S5** is not cut-free but it is complete with analytic cuts [30] (i.e. cuts whose cut-formula is a subformula of the conclusion [29]).

$\mathcal{B}et(A \to B)))$. $\mathcal{B}et$ is not part of the language of $\mathbf{F} + (\mathbf{CM})$ and $\mathbf{G}$, but is used at the meta-level in the calculi to define rules for the dyadic obligation.

2 F + (CM) and G in a Nutshell

We present the logics $\mathbf{F} + (\mathbf{CM})$ and $\mathbf{G}$ both syntactically and semantically. Let PropVar be a countable set of atomic formulas. Their language is defined by the following BNF:

$$A ::= p \in \text{PropVar} \mid \neg A \mid A \to A \mid \Box A \mid \bigcirc(A/A)$$

$\Box A$ is read as "A is settled as true", and $\bigcirc(B/A)$ as "B is obligatory, given A". The Boolean connectives other than $\neg$ and $\to$ are defined as usual.

Definition 1. $\mathbf{F}$ *consists of any Hilbert system for S5 augmented with:*

$\bigcirc(B \to C/A) \to (\bigcirc(B/A) \to \bigcirc(C/A))$	(COK)	$\bigcirc(A/A)$	(Id)
$\bigcirc(C/A \wedge B) \to \bigcirc(B \to C/A)$	(Sh)	$\Box A \to \bigcirc(A/B)$	(O-Nec)
$\bigcirc(B/A) \to \Box\bigcirc(B/A)$	(Abs)	$\Diamond A \to \neg\bigcirc(\bot/A)$	(D*)
$\Box(A \leftrightarrow B) \to (\bigcirc(C/A) \leftrightarrow \bigcirc(C/B))$	(Ext)		

$\mathbf{F} + (\mathbf{CM})$ *and* $\mathbf{G}$ *extend* $\mathbf{F}$ *with axioms (CM) and (RM) respectively:*

$$\bigcirc(B/A) \wedge \bigcirc(C/A) \to \bigcirc(C/A \wedge B) \qquad \text{(CM)}$$

$$\neg\bigcirc(\neg B/A) \wedge \bigcirc(C/A) \to \bigcirc(C/A \wedge B) \qquad \text{(RM)}$$

(COK) is the analogue of axiom $\mathbf{K}$, (Sh) expresses a "half" of deduction theorem (or residuation property). The absoluteness axiom (Abs) of [21] corresponds to the removal of world-relative accessibility relations. (O-Nec) is the deontic counterpart of the necessitation rule. (Ext) enables the substitution of necessarily equivalent sentences in the antecedent of deontic conditionals. (Id) is the deontic analogue of the identity principle. These axioms define the logic $\mathbf{E}$.

$\mathbf{F}$ extends $\mathbf{E}$ with (D*) that rules out conflicts between obligations for possible antecedents. (CM) and (RM) are cautious and rational monotony from the non-monotonic literature [18]. Introduced in [12] (CM) expresses a weakened form of strengthening of the antecedent, while (RM) a stronger form: if B is permitted given A, and C is obligatory given A, then C is obligatory given $A \wedge B$.

Semantics for the logics $\mathbf{E}$, $\mathbf{F}$, $\mathbf{F} + (\mathbf{CM})$ and $\mathbf{G}$ can be given in terms of preference models, see [28]. This semantics was used in [8,9] to define cut-free hypersequent calculi for $\mathbf{E}$ and $\mathbf{F}$. With preference models, structures are easily described, but they come with complex model theoretic conditions on the valuation function. In this paper we adopt a different semantics. This semantics has a more complex truth condition for the deontic operator, involving a $\forall\exists\forall$ nesting of quantifiers [28], but simpler frame and valuation conditions.

The original language does not include the modality $\mathcal{B}et$, but we add it to the semantic explanation of connectives for clarity.

Definition 2. *A preference model for* $\mathbf{F} + (\mathbf{CM})$ *is a triple* $\langle W, \leq, v\rangle$, *where* $\leq$ *is a reflexive and transitive order on* W *and* $v : PropVar \to \mathcal{P}(W)$ *a valuation function. The truth conditions for a formula in a world are defined as:*

- $x \Vdash P$ *if and only if* $x \in v(P)$.
- $x \Vdash \neg A$ *if and only if* $x \nVdash A$.
- $x \Vdash A \to B$ *if and only if* $x \nVdash A$ *or* $x \Vdash B$.
- $x \Vdash \mathcal{B}etA$ *if and only if* $\forall y(x \leq y \Rightarrow y \Vdash A)$.
- $x \Vdash \Box A$ *if and only if* $\forall y(y \Vdash A)$.
- $x \Vdash \bigcirc(B/A)$ *if and only if* $\forall y(y \Vdash A \Rightarrow \exists z(y \leq z \,\&\, z \Vdash A \,\&\, \forall u(z \leq u \Rightarrow u \Vdash A \to B)))$.

Models for **G** *are obtained by imposing totality, i.e.,* $\forall x \forall y(x \leq y \vee y \leq x)$.

Theorem 1 ([28]). **F** + **(CM)** *(resp.* **G***) is sound and complete with respect to the semantics of (resp. total) preference models.*

Note that the truth condition for the operator $\bigcirc(B/A)$ can be rewritten, using the conditions for $\Box, \to, \neg$ and $\mathcal{B}et$, as:

$$x \Vdash \bigcirc(B/A) \quad \text{iff} \quad x \Vdash \Box(A \to \neg\mathcal{B}et\neg(A \wedge \mathcal{B}et(A \to B)))$$

3 A Sequent Calculus for F + (CM)

We introduce a sequent calculus **SFcm** for **F** + **(CM)**, whose completeness relies on the use of cuts of a restricted form.

SFcm is obtained by adding the rules for the deontic modality and for the betterness operator to a (slightly modified[2] version of) the sequent calculus in [25] for **S5**. The cuts required in **SFcm** are a generalization of analytic cuts (arising from the calculus for **S5** [30]), due to the shape of the rules for the deontic modality[3]. We use $\Gamma, \Delta, \Pi, ...$ as metavariables for multisets of formulas.

Definition 3. *The sequent calculus* **SFcm** *consists of a variant of Gentzen's calculus LK for classical logic, with axioms* $\Gamma, p \Rightarrow p, \Delta$, *extended with the rules below*

$$\frac{\Gamma^{\Box\bigcirc} \Rightarrow A, \Delta^{\Box\bigcirc}}{\Gamma \Rightarrow \Box A, \Delta} R\Box \qquad \frac{A, \Gamma \Rightarrow \Delta}{\Box A, \Gamma \Rightarrow \Delta} L\Box \qquad \frac{\Gamma^{\Box\bigcirc}, \Gamma^{b} \Rightarrow A, \Delta^{\Box\bigcirc}}{\Gamma \Rightarrow \Delta, \mathcal{B}etA} R\mathcal{B}et \qquad \frac{A, \Gamma \Rightarrow \Delta}{\mathcal{B}etA, \Gamma \Rightarrow \Delta} L\mathcal{B}et$$

$$\frac{\Gamma^{\Box\bigcirc}, A, \mathcal{B}et\neg(A \wedge \mathcal{B}et(A \to B)) \Rightarrow \Delta^{\Box\bigcirc}}{\Gamma \Rightarrow \bigcirc(B/A), \Delta} R\bigcirc \qquad \frac{\Gamma \Rightarrow \Delta, A \qquad \Gamma \Rightarrow \Delta, \mathcal{B}et\neg(A \wedge \mathcal{B}et(A \to B))}{\bigcirc(B/A), \Gamma \Rightarrow \Delta} L\bigcirc$$

where $\Gamma^{b} = \{\mathcal{B}etA \mid \mathcal{B}etA \in \Gamma\}$ *and* $\Gamma^{\Box\bigcirc} = \{\Box A \mid \Box A \in \Gamma\} \cup \{\bigcirc(B/A) \mid \bigcirc(B/A) \in \Gamma\}$.

---

[2] Our $R\Box$ rule derives the absoluteness axiom.

[3] $\bigcirc(B/A)$ could have been introduced as a defined operator. However, since our main concern is the investigation of dyadic deontic logics we preferred to retain the obligation connective as a primitive element, and generalize the notion of analytic cut.

The notion of derivation, principal formulas and *height* of a derivation are as usual. The derived rules for conjunction and disjunction are as in Genten's LK and the generalization of initial sequents to arbitrary formulas is provable. A rule is (height-preserving) admissible if, whenever the premises are derivable, so is the conclusion (with at most the same height). In **SFcm** the weakening rules ($\dfrac{\Gamma \Rightarrow \Delta}{A, \Gamma \Rightarrow \Delta}\,\text{LW}$ and $\dfrac{\Gamma \Rightarrow \Delta}{\Gamma \Rightarrow \Delta, A}\,\text{RW}$) are height-preserving admissible. The rules of contraction ($\dfrac{A, A, \Gamma \Rightarrow \Delta}{A, \Gamma \Rightarrow \Delta}\,\text{LC}$ and $\dfrac{\Gamma \Rightarrow \Delta, A, A}{\Gamma \Rightarrow \Delta, A}\,\text{RC}$) are explicitly present.

Theorem 2 (Soundness). SFcm *is sound for* $\mathbf{F} + (\mathbf{CM})$.

Proof. By induction on the height of the **SFcm** derivation distinguishing cases according to the last rule applied. Initial sequents are clearly sound. We discuss only the cases of the right rules for the modal operator $\mathcal{B}et$ and $\bigcirc(A/B)$.

R$\mathcal{B}et$: Let us assume that the sequent $\Gamma^{\Box\bigcirc}, \Gamma^{b} \Rightarrow \Delta^{\Box\bigcirc}, A$ is valid. Let x, y be worlds such that $x \leq y$ and we assume that $x \Vdash \bigwedge \Gamma$. Hence we get $y \Vdash \bigwedge \Gamma^{\Box\bigcirc} \wedge \bigwedge \Gamma^{b}$ (by transitivity of $\leq$) which yields (i) $y \Vdash \bigvee \Delta^{\Box\bigcirc}$ or (ii) $y \Vdash A$. In (i), we get $x \Vdash \bigvee \Delta$, in (ii) $x \Vdash \mathcal{B}et A$, giving the desired conclusion.

R$\bigcirc$: Assume that $\Gamma^{\Box\bigcirc}, A, \mathcal{B}et\neg(A \wedge \mathcal{B}et(A \to B)) \Rightarrow \Delta^{\Box\bigcirc}$ is valid. We argue by contradiction assuming that the conclusion $\Gamma \Rightarrow \Delta, \bigcirc(B/A)$ is not valid. Hence there is a world x which satisfies every formula in Γ and falsifies every formula in Δ and $\bigcirc(B/A)$. By definition there is y s.t.: $y \Vdash A$ and there is not a world z such that $y \leq z$ and $z \Vdash A$ and $z \Vdash \mathcal{B}et(A \to B)$. Since $x \Vdash \bigwedge \Gamma^{\Box\bigcirc}$, we get that $y \Vdash \bigwedge \Gamma^{\Box\bigcirc}$. We also have $y \Vdash A$ and $y \Vdash \mathcal{B}et\neg(A \wedge \mathcal{B}et(A \to B))$. As a consequence of the validity of $\Gamma^{\Box\bigcirc}, A, \mathcal{B}et\neg(A \wedge \mathcal{B}et(A \to B)) \Rightarrow \Delta^{\Box\bigcirc}$, we get that $y \Vdash \bigvee \Delta^{\Box\bigcirc}$, which entails $x \Vdash \bigvee \Delta^{\Box\bigcirc}$, a contradiction.

Theorem 3 (Completeness with cut). *Each theorem of* $\mathbf{F} + (\mathbf{CM})$ *has a proof in* **SFcm** *with the addition of the cut rule.*

Proof. It suffices to show that all the axioms of $\mathbf{F} + (\mathbf{CM})$ are provable in **SFcm**. Modus Ponens corresponds to the provability of $A, A \to B \Rightarrow B$ and two applications of cut. The necessity rule is a particular case of $R\Box$. The axioms of classical logic are clearly derivable. In what follows, we omit to write trivially derivable premises to increase the readability of the derivations.

- A derivation of (CM) is as follow (omitting trivially derivable premises)

$$\begin{array}{cl}
A, \mathcal{B}et(A \to C), A \to B \Rightarrow A \wedge B \wedge \mathcal{B}et(A \to C) & \\ \hline
A, \mathcal{B}et(A \to C), A \to B, \mathcal{B}et\neg(A \wedge B \wedge \mathcal{B}et(A \wedge B \to C)) \Rightarrow & \text{L}\mathcal{B}et,\ \text{L}\neg \\ \hline
A, \mathcal{B}et(A \to C), \mathcal{B}et(A \to B), \mathcal{B}et\neg(A \wedge B \wedge \mathcal{B}et(A \wedge B \to C)) \Rightarrow & \text{L}\mathcal{B}et \\ \hline
A \wedge \mathcal{B}et(A \to C), \mathcal{B}et(A \to B), \mathcal{B}et\neg(A \wedge B \wedge \mathcal{B}et(A \wedge B \to C)) \Rightarrow & \text{L}\wedge \\ \hline
A, \mathcal{B}et(A \to B), \mathcal{B}et\neg(A \wedge B \wedge \mathcal{B}et(A \wedge B \to C)) \Rightarrow \mathcal{B}et\neg(A \wedge \mathcal{B}et(A \to C)) & \text{R}\mathcal{B}et,\ \text{L}\neg \\ \hline
\bigcirc(C/A), A, \mathcal{B}et(A \to B), \mathcal{B}et\neg(A \wedge B \wedge \mathcal{B}et(A \wedge B \to C)) \Rightarrow & \text{L}\bigcirc \\ \hline
\bigcirc(C/A), A \wedge \mathcal{B}et(A \to B), \mathcal{B}et\neg(A \wedge B \wedge \mathcal{B}et(A \wedge B \to C)) \Rightarrow & \text{L}\wedge \\ \hline
\bigcirc(C/A), A, B, \mathcal{B}et\neg(A \wedge B \wedge \mathcal{B}et(A \wedge B \to C)) \Rightarrow \mathcal{B}et\neg(A \wedge \mathcal{B}et(A \to B)) & \text{R}\mathcal{B}et,\ \text{L}\neg \\ \hline
\bigcirc(C/A), \bigcirc(B/A), A, B, \mathcal{B}et\neg(A \wedge B \wedge \mathcal{B}et(A \wedge B \to C)) \Rightarrow & \text{L}\bigcirc \\ \hline
\bigcirc(C/A), \bigcirc(B/A), A \wedge B, \mathcal{B}et\neg(A \wedge B \wedge \mathcal{B}et(A \wedge B \to C)) \Rightarrow & \text{L}\wedge \\ \hline
\bigcirc(C/A), \bigcirc(B/A) \Rightarrow \bigcirc(C/A \wedge B) & \text{R}\bigcirc
\end{array}$$

- The **S4** axioms are trivially derivable. The characteristic axiom of **S5** is derivable using analytic cuts, as follows

$$\dfrac{\dfrac{\dfrac{\dfrac{A \Rightarrow A}{A, \neg A \Rightarrow}\,\mathrm{L}\neg}{A, \Box\neg A \Rightarrow}\,\mathrm{L}\Box}{A \Rightarrow \neg\Box\neg A}\,\mathrm{R}\neg \qquad \dfrac{\dfrac{\dfrac{\Box\neg A \Rightarrow \Box\neg A}{\Rightarrow \neg\Box\neg A, \Box\neg A}\,\mathrm{R}\neg}{\Rightarrow \Box\neg\Box\neg A, \Box\neg A}\,\mathrm{R}\Box}{\neg\Box\neg A \Rightarrow \Box\neg\Box\neg A}\,\mathrm{L}\neg}{A \Rightarrow \Box\neg\Box\neg A}\,\mathrm{Cut}$$

  The cut on $\neg\Box\neg A$ is analytic because it is a subformula of $\Box\neg\Box\neg A$.
- The axiom (D*) $\bigcirc(\bot/A) \to \Box\neg A$ is derivable in **SFcm** as follow

$$\dfrac{\dfrac{\dfrac{A \Rightarrow A \qquad \dfrac{\dfrac{\dfrac{\bigcirc(\bot/A), A, A \to \bot, \mathcal{B}et(A \to \bot) \Rightarrow}{\bigcirc(\bot/A), A, \mathcal{B}et(A \to \bot) \Rightarrow}\,\mathrm{L}\mathcal{B}et}{\bigcirc(\bot/A), A \wedge \mathcal{B}et(A \to \bot) \Rightarrow}\,\mathrm{L}\wedge}{\bigcirc(\bot/A), A \Rightarrow \mathcal{B}et\neg(A \wedge \mathcal{B}et(A \to \bot))}\,\mathrm{R}\mathcal{B}et,\mathrm{R}\neg}{\bigcirc(\bot/A), A \Rightarrow}\,\mathrm{L}\bigcirc}{\bigcirc(\bot/A) \Rightarrow \neg A}\,\mathrm{R}\neg}{\bigcirc(\bot/A) \Rightarrow \Box\neg A}\,\mathrm{R}\Box$$

  item The axiom (Sh) $\bigcirc(C/A \wedge B) \Rightarrow \bigcirc(B \to C/A)$ is derivable in **SFcm**. We construct the following derivation (the topmost sequent is clearly derivable).

$$\dfrac{\dfrac{\dfrac{\dfrac{\dfrac{\dfrac{\dfrac{A \wedge B \wedge \mathcal{B}et(A \wedge B \to C), \mathcal{B}et\neg(A \wedge \mathcal{B}et(A \to (B \to C))) \Rightarrow}{A, B, \mathcal{B}et\neg(A \wedge \mathcal{B}et(A \to (B \to C))) \Rightarrow C, \mathcal{B}et\neg(A \wedge B \wedge \mathcal{B}et(A \wedge B \to C)))}\,\mathrm{R}\mathcal{B}et,\mathrm{R}\neg}{\bigcirc(C/A \wedge B), A, B, \mathcal{B}et\neg(A \wedge \mathcal{B}et(A \to (B \to C))) \Rightarrow C}\,\mathrm{L}\bigcirc}{\bigcirc(C/A \wedge B), A, \mathcal{B}et\neg(A \wedge \mathcal{B}et(A \to (B \to C))) \Rightarrow \mathcal{B}et(A \to (B \to C))}\,\mathrm{R}\mathcal{B}et,\ \mathrm{R}{\to}\ \text{(twice)}}{\bigcirc(C/A \wedge B), A, \mathcal{B}et\neg(A \wedge \mathcal{B}et(A \to (B \to C)) \Rightarrow A \wedge \mathcal{B}et(A \to (B \to C))}\,\mathrm{R}\wedge}{\bigcirc(C/A \wedge B), A, \mathcal{B}et\neg(A \wedge \mathcal{B}et(A \to (B \to C))), \mathcal{B}et\neg(A \wedge \mathcal{B}et(A \to (B \to C))) \Rightarrow}\,\mathrm{L}\mathcal{B}et,\mathrm{L}\neg}{\bigcirc(C/A \wedge B), A, \mathcal{B}et\neg(A \wedge \mathcal{B}et(A \to (B \to C))) \Rightarrow}\,\mathrm{LC}}{\bigcirc(C/A \wedge B) \Rightarrow \bigcirc(B \to C/A)}\,\mathrm{R}\bigcirc$$

- The axiom (COK) $\bigcirc(B \to C/A), \bigcirc(B/A) \Rightarrow \bigcirc(C/A)$ is derivable in **SFcm**. We construct the following derivation.

$$\dfrac{\dfrac{\dfrac{\dfrac{\dfrac{A, \mathcal{B}et(A \to (B \to C)), \mathcal{B}et(A \to B), \mathcal{B}et\neg(A \wedge \mathcal{B}et(A \to C)) \Rightarrow}{A, \mathcal{B}et(A \to B), \mathcal{B}et\neg(A \wedge \mathcal{B}et(A \to C)) \Rightarrow \mathcal{B}et\neg(A \wedge \mathcal{B}et(A \to (B \to C)))}\,\mathrm{R}\mathcal{B}et,\ \mathrm{R}\neg,\ \mathrm{L}\wedge}{\bigcirc(B \to C/A), A, \mathcal{B}et(A \to B), \mathcal{B}et\neg(A \wedge \mathcal{B}et(A \to C)) \Rightarrow}\,\mathrm{L}\bigcirc}{\bigcirc(B \to C/A), A, \mathcal{B}et\neg(A \wedge \mathcal{B}et(A \to C)) \Rightarrow \mathcal{B}et\neg(A \wedge \mathcal{B}et(A \to B))}\,\mathrm{R}\mathcal{B}et,\ \mathrm{R}\neg,\ \mathrm{L}\wedge}{\bigcirc(B \to C/A), \bigcirc(B/A), A, \mathcal{B}et\neg(A \wedge \mathcal{B}et(A \to C)) \Rightarrow}\,\mathrm{L}\bigcirc}{\bigcirc(B \to C/A), \bigcirc(B/A) \Rightarrow \bigcirc(C/A)}\,\mathrm{R}\bigcirc,\ \mathrm{L}\wedge$$

  The topmost sequent is clearly derivable.

The derivations in **SFcm** of axioms (Id) $\bigcirc(A/A)$ and (Abs) $\bigcirc(B/A) \to \Box\bigcirc(B/A)$ are evident. Also the extensionality axiom $\Box(A \leftrightarrow B) \to (\bigcirc(C/A) \leftrightarrow \bigcirc(C/B))$ is easy to derive.

3.1 From Cuts to Semi-analytic Cuts

We provide a syntactic procedure to restrict cuts in **SFcm** to semi-analytic cuts, where an instance of the cut rule

$$\frac{\Gamma \Rightarrow C, \Delta \quad \Sigma, C \Rightarrow \Pi}{\Gamma, \Sigma \Rightarrow \Delta, \Pi}\ cut$$

is *semi-analytic* if C is a generalized subformula of the conclusion, i.e. $C \in \mathsf{SUB}(\Gamma \cup \Sigma \cup \Delta \cup \Pi)$, where for any formula A, $\mathsf{SUB}(A)$ is inductively defined as

- $A \in \mathsf{SUB}(A)$; If $B \to C \in \mathsf{SUB}(A)$, then $B, C \in \mathsf{SUB}(A)$
- If $\Box B, \neg B, \mathcal{B}et B \in \mathsf{SUB}(A)$, then $B \in \mathsf{SUB}(A)$
- $\bigcirc(C/B) \in \mathsf{SUB}(A)$, then $\mathcal{B}et\neg(B \wedge \mathcal{B}et(B \to C)) \in \mathsf{SUB}(A)$

The notion of generalized subformula naturally extends to multisets of formulas.

To restrict the use of cuts to semi-analytic cuts we reformulate, simplify and also broaden the applicability of the method in [7] to apply to rules more general than so-called simple rules. Specifically, the inherent (almost) local structure of the proof below could seamlessly accommodate rules having more than one principal formula, as well as rules that do not obey the subformula property. Prior to [7], proofs of restriction of cuts to analytic cuts, e.g., [17,26,30,31] were all logic-tailored and, with the exception of [30], relied on semantic arguments.

Proof Idea: We start considering an uppermost non semi-analytic cut (semi-analytic cuts are left in the derivation). Cuts on boolean connectives are handled using rule invertibilities (and reduced in the usual way). Non semi-analytic cuts with cut-formulas $\Box A$, $\mathcal{B}et\ A$ and $\bigcirc(B/A)$ need a different approach as their rules are not invertible; we shift them upwards until their cut formulas are principal (and then reduced). Notice that the rules R$\mathcal{B}et$, R$\Box$ and R$\bigcirc$ do not allow to shift *any* cut upwards; however they permit to permute upward any cut in which (∗) the other premise is a right rule introducing the cut formula $\mathcal{B}et A$, $\Box A$ or $\bigcirc(B/A)$ (because of the "good" contexts of these rules). To reach the scenario (∗) we need to bring the considered cut beyond the rules that do not allow the permutation, jumping directly to the point where the cut-formula is introduced. We do that by tracing (bottom up) all the ancestors[4] of the cut formulas on the right hand side (RHS), and replacing the cut (actually we consider mix) by new semi-analytic cuts. Following [7], the premises of these new semi-analytic cuts are obtained by replacing the cut-formulas in the original derivation with the contexts of the right rules introducing the cut-formulas (switching their side of the sequent), taking care that the resulting proof is still a correct derivation.

Smaller cuts are cuts of lesser degrees, according to the following definition.

Definition 4. *The degree of a formula A, $\mathsf{dg}(A)$ is inductively defined:*

- $\mathsf{dg}(p) = 0$ *if* $A = p$ *atomic;* $\mathsf{dg}(B \to C) = \mathsf{dg}(B) + \mathsf{dg}(C) + 1$
- $\mathsf{dg}(\neg B) = \mathsf{dg}(\Box B) = \mathsf{dg}(BetB) = \mathsf{dg}(B) + 1$

[4] This is the familiar parametric ancestor relation of [5].

– $\mathtt{dg}(\bigcirc(C/B)) = 3 \cdot \mathtt{dg}(B) + \mathtt{dg}(C) + 7$

Definition 5. *The non-analytic cut rank $\sigma(\mathfrak{D})$ of a proof is the maximal degree +1 of non-semi analytic cut formulas in $\mathfrak{D}$. The cut rank of a proof $\rho(\mathfrak{D})$ is the maximal degree +1 of cut formulas in $\mathfrak{D}$.*

By A^n we denote n-repetitions of the formula A. As here we focus on the elimination of cuts that are non semi-analytic, we use the non-analytic cut rank.

Lemma 1. *The rules for $\rightarrow$ and $\neg$ are height and (non-analytic) rank-preserving invertible.*

Lemma 2. *Given derivations $\mathfrak{D}_1$ and $\mathfrak{D}_2$ of $\Gamma \Rightarrow \Delta, X$ and $X, \Pi \Rightarrow \Sigma$ with $\sigma(\mathfrak{D}_1), \sigma(\mathfrak{D}_2) \leq \mathtt{dg}(X)$ and with X principal in the last rule applied in $\mathfrak{D}_1$ and $\mathfrak{D}_2$, there is a derivation $\mathfrak{D}$ of $\Gamma, \Pi \Rightarrow \Delta, \Sigma$ with $\sigma(\mathfrak{D}) \leq \mathtt{dg}(X)$.*

Proof. Easy in case of the propositional connectives, $\mathfrak{Bet}$, and $\Box$.

If the cut formula is principal in applications of the rule for $\bigcirc$, we have:

$$\dfrac{\dfrac{\Gamma^{\Box\bigcirc}, A, \mathfrak{Bet}\neg(A \wedge \mathfrak{Bet}(A \rightarrow B)) \Rightarrow \Delta^{\Box\bigcirc}}{\Gamma \Rightarrow \Delta, \bigcirc(B/A)}\,\mathrm{R}\bigcirc \qquad \dfrac{\Pi \Rightarrow \Sigma, A \qquad \Pi \Rightarrow \Sigma, \mathfrak{Bet}\neg(A \wedge \mathfrak{Bet}(A \rightarrow B))}{\bigcirc(B/A), \Pi \Rightarrow \Sigma}\,\mathrm{L}\bigcirc}{\Gamma, \Pi \Rightarrow \Delta, \Sigma}\,\mathrm{Cut}$$

We construct the following derivation:

$$\dfrac{\dfrac{\Pi \Rightarrow \Sigma, \mathfrak{Bet}\neg(A \wedge \mathfrak{Bet}(A \rightarrow B)) \qquad \dfrac{\Pi \Rightarrow \Sigma, A \qquad \Gamma^{\Box\bigcirc}, A, \mathfrak{Bet}\neg(A \wedge \mathfrak{Bet}(A \rightarrow B)) \Rightarrow \Delta^{\Box\bigcirc}}{\Gamma^{\Box\bigcirc}, \Pi, \mathfrak{Bet}\neg(A \wedge \mathfrak{Bet}(A \rightarrow B)) \Rightarrow \Sigma, \Delta^{\Box\bigcirc}}\,\mathrm{Cut}}{\Gamma^{\Box\bigcirc}, \Pi^2 \Rightarrow \Delta^{\Box\bigcirc}, \Sigma^2}\,\mathrm{Cut}}{\Gamma, \Pi \Rightarrow \Delta, \Sigma}\,\mathrm{LC,RC,\ LW,RW}$$

The modified version of the rules $R\Box$, $R\bigcirc$ and $R\mathfrak{Bet}$ in the lemma below will be used to simplify the presentation of case (**B**) in the proof of Theorem 4: when shifting upward a non semi-analytic cut over the right rules for $\Box$, $\mathfrak{Bet}$ or $\bigcirc$.

Lemma 3. *The versions $R'\Box$, $R'\bigcirc$ and $R'\mathfrak{Bet}$ of the rules $R\Box$, $R\bigcirc$ and $R\mathfrak{Bet}$ with $\bigvee \Sigma_1^{\Box\bigcirc}, \ldots, \bigvee \Sigma_m^{\Box\bigcirc}$ (resp. $\bigwedge \Pi_1^{\Box\bigcirc}, \ldots, \bigwedge \Pi_n^{\Box\bigcirc}$) in their antecedent (resp. consequent) are admissible.*

Proof. ($R'\Box$): Given $\bigvee \Sigma_1^{\Box\bigcirc}, \ldots, \bigvee \Sigma_m^{\Box\bigcirc}, \Gamma^{\Box\bigcirc} \Rightarrow \Delta^{\Box\bigcirc}, \bigwedge \Pi_1^{\Box\bigcirc}, \ldots, \bigwedge \Pi_n^{\Box\bigcirc}, B$, we first apply the invertibility of the derived rules for $\bigwedge$ and $\bigvee$ (Lemma 1). The $R'\Box$ conclusion $\bigvee \Sigma_1^{\Box\bigcirc}, \ldots, \bigvee \Sigma_m^{\Box\bigcirc}, \Gamma^{\Box\bigcirc} \Rightarrow \Delta^{\Box\bigcirc}, \bigwedge \Pi_1^{\Box\bigcirc}, \ldots, \bigwedge \Pi_n^{\Box\bigcirc}, \Box B$ is obtained by multiple applications of $R\Box$, and of the logical rules. The proof for $R'\bigcirc$ and $R'\mathfrak{Bet}$ is analogous.

Theorem 4. *Given the derivations $\mathfrak{D}_1$ of $\Gamma \Rightarrow \Delta, X^m$ and $\mathfrak{D}_2$ of $X^n, \Pi \Rightarrow \Sigma$ containing only semi-analytic cuts, there is a derivation $\mathfrak{D}$ of $\Gamma, \Pi \Rightarrow \Delta, \Sigma$ with $\sigma(\mathfrak{D}) \leq \mathtt{dg}(X)$.*

Proof. We first replace all (analytic) cuts on X in $\mathcal{D}_1$ and $\mathcal{D}_2$, by applications of contraction. The theorem's claim is proved by induction on the sum of the height of the derivations $\mathcal{D}_1$ and $\mathcal{D}_2$. If the cut-formula is a connective of classical logic the claim follows by Lemmas 1 and 2. We consider $\mathcal{D}_1$ and distinguish two cases: the cut formula is principal in the last rule applied or it is not.

(A) The cut formula is principal in the last rule applied in $\mathcal{D}_1$. We consider cases according to the last rule (r) applied in $\mathcal{D}_2$:

- (r)**is an initial sequent**, hence the cut is analytic.
- (r)**is a rule introducing the cut formula**. We use Lemma 2 (with obvious adjustments given by the use of mix).
- (r)**is any rule different from R$\bigcirc$, R$\Box$, and R$\mathcal{B}et$.** The cut can be permuted upwards.
- (r)**is R$\mathcal{B}et$, R$\Box$or R$\bigcirc$.** Note that these rules' contexts permit moving the cut upward in $\mathcal{D}_2$. As an example, consider the case in which the cut formula is of the shape $\mathcal{B}etB$ and the last rule applied in $\mathcal{D}_2$ is R$\mathcal{B}et$, as in:

$$\dfrac{\dfrac{\Gamma^b, \Gamma^{\Box\bigcirc} \Rightarrow \Delta^{\Box\bigcirc}, B}{\Gamma \Rightarrow \Delta, \mathcal{B}etB^n}\,\text{R}\mathcal{B}et \qquad \dfrac{\mathcal{B}etB^m, \Pi^b, \Pi^{\Box\bigcirc} \Rightarrow \Sigma^{\Box\bigcirc}, C}{\mathcal{B}etB^m, \Pi \Rightarrow \Sigma, \mathcal{B}etC}\,\text{R}\mathcal{B}et}{\Gamma, \Pi \Rightarrow \Delta, \Sigma, \mathcal{B}etC}\,\text{Cut}$$

We proceed as follows:

$$\dfrac{\dfrac{\dfrac{\Gamma^b, \Gamma^{\Box\bigcirc} \Rightarrow \Delta^{\Box\bigcirc}, B}{\Gamma^b, \Gamma^{\Box\bigcirc} \Rightarrow \Delta^{\Box\bigcirc}, \mathcal{B}etB}\,\text{R}\mathcal{B}et \qquad \mathcal{B}etB^m, \Pi^b, \Pi^{\Box\bigcirc} \Rightarrow \Sigma^{\Box\bigcirc}, C}{\Gamma^b, \Gamma^{\Box\bigcirc}, \Pi^b, \Pi^{\Box\bigcirc} \Rightarrow \Delta^{\Box\bigcirc}, \Sigma^{\Box\bigcirc}, C}\,\text{Cut}}{\Gamma, \Pi \Rightarrow \Delta, \Sigma, \mathcal{B}etC}\,\text{R}\mathcal{B}et$$

(B) The cut formula is not principal in the last rule applied in $\mathcal{D}_1$. We distinguish sub-cases according to the last rule (r) applied in $\mathcal{D}_1$.

- (r)**is an initial sequent**, then the required derivation follows by weakening.
- (r)**is any rule different from R$\bigcirc$, R$\Box$, and R$\mathcal{B}et$**, then we simply permute the cut upwards.
- (r)**is R$\bigcirc$, R$\Box$, or R$\mathcal{B}et$.** This is the key case, which requires peculiar proof transformations and the introduction of new semi-analytic cuts. We focus on cases where the cut formula is $\Box A$ or $\bigcirc(B/A)$, as other cases are trivial due to the removal of formulas from the RHS with different shapes by the application of (r). We detail the case $\Box A$ (the case with cut formula $\bigcirc(B/A)$ is analogous), assuming, for illustration purposes, that the last applied rule is R$\mathcal{B}et$. We trace the cut formula in $\mathcal{D}_1$, till it is introduced a first time (in each branch), as in

$$\cdots \qquad \dfrac{\Theta_i^{\Box\bigcirc} \Rightarrow \Lambda_i^{\Box\bigcirc}, \Box A^{l-1}, A}{\Theta_i \Rightarrow \Lambda_i, \Box A^{l_i}}\,\text{R}\Box \qquad \cdots$$

$$\vdots$$

$$\dfrac{\dfrac{\Gamma^b, \Gamma^{\Box\bigcirc} \Rightarrow \Delta^{\Box\bigcirc}, \Box A^n, B}{\Gamma \Rightarrow \Delta, \Box A^n, \mathcal{B}etB}\,\text{R}\mathcal{B}et \qquad \Box A^m, \Pi \Rightarrow \Sigma}{\Gamma, \Pi \Rightarrow \Delta, \Sigma, \mathcal{B}etB}\,\text{Cut}$$

For the sake of simplicity we first consider the case in which the cut formula is principal only in *one* branch of $\mathcal{D}_1$ (w.l.o.g. the one displayed above); the general case is handled in the same way with an additional combinatorial argument. The cut is replaced by ($\Theta_i^{\Box\bigcirc} \Rightarrow \bigwedge \Theta_i^{\Box\bigcirc}$ and $\bigvee \Lambda_i^{\Box\bigcirc} \Rightarrow \Lambda_i^{\Box\bigcirc}$ are clearly derivable):

$$
\dfrac{
\dfrac{\begin{array}{c}\dfrac{\Theta_i^{\Box\bigcirc} \Rightarrow \bigwedge\Theta_i^{\Box\bigcirc}}{\Theta_i \Rightarrow \Lambda_i, \bigwedge\Theta_i^{\Box\bigcirc}}\,\text{LW,RW}\\ \vdots \\ \Gamma^b, \Gamma^{\Box\bigcirc} \Rightarrow \Delta^{\Box\bigcirc}, B, \bigwedge\Theta_i^{\Box\bigcirc}\end{array}}{\Gamma \Rightarrow \Delta, \mathcal{B}etB, \bigwedge\Theta_i^{\Box\bigcirc}}\,\text{R}'\mathcal{B}\text{et}
\quad
\dfrac{\begin{array}{c}\dfrac{\bigvee\Lambda_i^{\Box\bigcirc} \Rightarrow \Lambda_i^{\Box\bigcirc}}{\bigvee\Lambda_i^{\Box\bigcirc}, \Theta_i \Rightarrow \Lambda_i}\,\text{LW,RW}\\ \vdots \\ \bigvee\Lambda_i^{\Box\bigcirc}, \Gamma^b, \Gamma^{\Box\bigcirc} \Rightarrow \Delta^{\Box\bigcirc}, B\end{array}}{\bigvee\Lambda_i^{\Box\bigcirc}, \Gamma \Rightarrow \Delta, \mathcal{B}etB}\,\text{R}'\mathcal{B}\text{et}
\quad
\dfrac{\dfrac{\dfrac{\dfrac{\Theta_i^{\Box\bigcirc} \Rightarrow \Lambda_i^{\Box\bigcirc}, \Box A^{l_i-1}, A}{\Theta_i^{\Box\bigcirc} \Rightarrow \Lambda_i^{\Box\bigcirc}, \Box A^{l_i}}\,\text{R}\Box \qquad \Box A^m, \Pi \Rightarrow \Sigma}{\Theta_i^{\Box\bigcirc}, \Pi \Rightarrow \Lambda_i^{\Box\bigcirc}, \Sigma}\,\text{Cut}}{\bigwedge\Theta_i^{\Box\bigcirc}, \Pi \Rightarrow \bigvee\Lambda_i^{\Box\bigcirc}, \Sigma}\,\text{L}\wedge,\text{R}\vee
}{
\dfrac{\Gamma, \Gamma, \Pi \Rightarrow \Delta, \Delta, \Sigma, \mathcal{B}etB}{\Gamma, \Pi \Rightarrow \Delta, \Sigma, \mathcal{B}etB}\,\text{LC,RC}
}\,\text{Cut}^*
$$

The first derivation above, say $\mathcal{D}_1'$ is obtained from $\mathcal{D}_1$ by substituting *all* occurrences of the cut formulas with $\bigwedge \Theta_i^{\Box\bigcirc}$, and the second derivation $\mathcal{D}_1''$ by removing the cut formula from the RHS and adding $\bigvee \Lambda_i^{\Box\bigcirc}$ to the LHS. The correctness of the application of the rules in these sub-derivations is guaranteed by Lemma 3. The cut between $\Theta_i^{\Box\bigcirc} \Rightarrow \Lambda_i^{\Box\bigcirc}, \Box A^{l_i}$ and $\Box A^m, \Pi \Rightarrow \Sigma$ is handled by induction hypothesis. The rule Cut* can be replaced by new semi-analytic cuts (see Lemma 4 below, in the particular case $n = 1$). The argument which ensures the semi-analyticity of the new cuts is at the end of the proof.

In the general case, there may be k branches in which the cut formula is principal, with the following conclusions of $R\Box$ rules introducing $\Box A$'s:

$$\{\Theta_j^{\Box\bigcirc} \Rightarrow \Lambda_j^{\Box\bigcirc}, \Box A^{l_j} \mid j \in \{1, \ldots, k\}\}.$$

We now need to construct - following the pattern detailed for $\mathcal{D}_1'$ and $\mathcal{D}_1''$ - derivations with all the possible combinations of length k of the contexts $\bigwedge \Theta_{k_1}^{\Box\bigcirc}$ and $\bigvee \Lambda_{k_2}^{\Box\bigcirc}$, with $k_1 \neq k_2$ and $k_1, k_2 \in \{1, \ldots, k\}$, inverting their polarities, i.e. their position w.r.t. the sequent arrow. To witness a concrete example, if $k = 2$, we construct the derivations of the sequents: $\bigvee \Lambda_1^{\Box\bigcirc}, \bigvee \Lambda_2^{\Box\bigcirc}, \Gamma \Rightarrow \Delta, \mathcal{B}etB$; $\bigvee \Lambda_1^{\Box\bigcirc}, \Gamma \Rightarrow \Delta, \mathcal{B}etB, \bigwedge \Theta_2^{\Box\bigcirc}$; $\bigvee \Lambda_2^{\Box\bigcirc}, \Gamma \Rightarrow \Delta, \mathcal{B}etB, \bigwedge \Theta_1^{\Box\bigcirc}$ and $\Gamma \Rightarrow \Delta, \mathcal{B}etB, \bigwedge \Theta_1^{\Box\bigcirc}, \bigwedge \Theta_2^{\Box\bigcirc}$.

In general, by suitably replacing all the occurrences of the cut formulas in $\mathcal{D}_1$ we obtain 2^k derivations of $\Upsilon, \Gamma \Rightarrow \Delta, \mathcal{B}etB, \Xi$, for any multiset Υ and Ξ s.t. $C_j \in \Upsilon$ if and only if $C_j = \bigvee \Lambda_j^{\Box\bigcirc}$ and $C_j \in \Xi$ if and only if $C_j = \bigwedge \Theta_j^{\Box\bigcirc}$ for some j, $|\Upsilon \cup \Xi| = k$ and if $C_j, C_l \in \Upsilon \cup \Xi$, then $j \neq l$. The correctness of the resulting derivations follows again by Lemma 3. The desired sequent $\Gamma, \Pi \Rightarrow \Delta, \mathcal{B}etB, \Sigma$ is obtained by using the derived rule Cut* (Lemma 4 below) also with the k derivations of $\Theta_j^{\Box\bigcirc}, \Pi \Rightarrow \Lambda_j^{\Box\bigcirc}, \Sigma$ obtained by the induction hypothesis. It remains to show that all cut-formulas of the newly introduced cuts are generalized subformulas, i.e. that $E \in \mathsf{SUB}(\Gamma, \Delta)$ for every $E \in \Theta_j^{\Box\bigcirc} \cup \Lambda_j^{\Box\bigcirc}$, and hence that the newly introduced cuts are semi-analytic (by Lemma 4). Indeed, by assumption every formula in $\mathcal{D}_1$ is in $\mathsf{SUB}(\Gamma, \Delta, X)$. Therefore the only case to be excluded is that E is $\Box A$. Assume by contradiction that this is the case. The $\Box A$ cannot change side of the sequent, and is not in $\mathsf{SUB}(\Gamma, \Delta)$ by hypothesis. As there is no cut on $\Box A$ in $\mathcal{D}_1$ (being all these cuts replaced by contractions), the only remaining possibility is that $\Box A$ has been removed by a cut on a formula containing $\Box A$ as a subformula, but this cannot be the case by hypothesis.

The lemma below shows that cuts on conjunctions and disjunctions of generalized subformulas can be simulated by semi-analytic cuts.

Lemma 4. *Let $\Theta = A_1, ..., A_n, \Lambda = B_1, ..., B_n$ be conjunctions and disjunctions of formulas in $\mathsf{SUB}(\Gamma, \Pi, \Delta, \Sigma)$, the rule, with $\Lambda_j \subseteq \Lambda$, $\Theta_j \subseteq \Theta$, $|\Lambda_j \cup \Theta_j| = n$:*

$$\frac{\{\Lambda_j, \Pi \Rightarrow \Sigma, \Theta_j \mid \textit{for all } C_l, C_t \in \Lambda_j \cup \Theta_j (l \neq t)\} \qquad \{A_i, \Gamma \Rightarrow \Delta, B_i\}_{i=1,\dots,n}}{\Pi, \Gamma \Rightarrow \Delta, \Sigma}\ \mathit{Cut}^*$$

is admissible in **SFcm** *without using non semi-analytic cuts.*

Proof. We first show that the rule Cut* is admissible using arbitrary cuts on the formulas A_i, B_is and the contraction rules. The proof is by induction on n.

- If $n = 1$, then the proof follows applying twice the cut rule:

$$\dfrac{\dfrac{\dfrac{\Pi \Rightarrow \Sigma, A_1 \qquad A_1, \Gamma \Rightarrow \Delta, B_1}{\Pi, \Gamma \Rightarrow \Delta, \Sigma, B_1}\ \text{Cut} \qquad B_1, \Pi \Rightarrow \Sigma}{\Pi, \Pi, \Gamma \Rightarrow \Delta, \Sigma, \Sigma}\ \text{Cut}}{\Pi, \Gamma \Rightarrow \Delta, \Sigma}\ \text{LC,RC}$$

- Let $n = k + 1$ and assume that the claim holds for k. We have $\Theta = A_1, ..., A_k, A_{k+1}, \Lambda = B_1, ..., B_k, B_{k+1}$ and the 2^{k+1} left premises of the rule can be rewritten as:

$$\{\Lambda_j, \Pi \Rightarrow \Sigma, \Theta_j, A_{k+1} \mid \textit{for all } C_l, C_t \in \Lambda_j \cup \Theta_j (l \neq t)\} \cup$$
$$\{B_{k+1}, \Lambda_j, \Pi \Rightarrow \Sigma, \Theta_j \mid \textit{for all } C_l, C_t \in \Lambda_j \cup \Theta_j (l \neq t)\}$$

  with $\Theta_j \subseteq \{A_1, \dots, A_k\}$ and $\Lambda_j \subseteq \{A_1, \dots, A_k\}$. Hence we proceed as follows:

$$\frac{\{\Lambda_j, \Pi \Rightarrow \Sigma, \Theta_j, A_{k+1} \mid \textit{for all } C_l, C_t \in \Lambda_j \cup \Theta_j (l \neq t)\} \qquad \{A_i, \Gamma \Rightarrow \Delta, B_i\}_{i=1,\dots,k}}{\Pi, \Gamma \Rightarrow \Delta, \Sigma, A_{k+1}}\ \text{Cut}^*$$

  the application of Cut* is admissible by induction hypothesis.
  Analogously, we construct a derivation of $B_{k+1}, \Pi, \Gamma \Rightarrow \Delta, \Sigma$:

$$\frac{\{B_{k+1}, \Lambda_j, \Pi \Rightarrow \Sigma, \Theta_j \mid \textit{for all } C_l, C_t \in \Lambda_j \cup \Theta_j (l \neq t)\} \qquad \{A_i, \Gamma \Rightarrow \Delta, B_i\}_{i=1,\dots,k}}{B_{k+1}, \Pi, \Gamma \Rightarrow \Delta, \Sigma}\ \text{Cut}^*$$

  applying the induction hypothesis.
  The conclusion now follows from two applications of the cut rule with the sequent $A_{k+1}, \Pi \Rightarrow \Sigma, B_{k+1}$ followed by contraction.

The claim of the lemma is now obtained observing that cuts on A_i and B_i can be transformed into semi-analytic cuts by exploiting the invertibility of the derived rules for $\wedge$ and $\vee$, because by hypothesis $A_i, B_j \in \mathsf{SUB}(\Gamma, \Pi, \Delta, \Sigma)$.

Theorem 5. *Any* **SFcm** *proof with cuts can be transformed into a proof of the same sequent that only uses semi-analytic cuts.*

Proof. Let $\mathfrak{D}$ be an **SFcm** proof with $\sigma(\mathfrak{D}) > 0$. We proceed by a double induction on $\langle \sigma(\mathfrak{D}), n\sigma(\mathfrak{D}) \rangle$, where $n\sigma(\mathfrak{D})$ is the number of applications of cut in $\mathfrak{D}$ with non-analytic cut rank $\sigma(\mathfrak{D})$. Consider an uppermost application of non-analytic (*cut*) in $\mathfrak{D}$ with rank $\sigma(\mathfrak{D})$. By applying Theorem 4 to its premises either $\sigma(\mathfrak{D})$ or $n\sigma(\mathfrak{D})$ decreases.

Remark 1. The above result can be adapted to define sequent calculi with restricted cuts for the sequent calculus version of the calculi for **E** and **F** in [8,9]. These calculi would be obtained by replacing in **SFcm** the rules for $\mathcal{B}et$ and $\bigcirc(B/A)$ with the corresponding sequent rules for **E** and **F**.

4 A Hypersequent Calculus for F + (CM) and G

The calculus **SFcm** uses semi-analytic cuts, and is not easily extendable to capture **G**[5]. Additionally, it would be challenging, if possible at all, to adapt it into a proof-search-oriented calculus for **F** + (**CM**). Inspired by the transition in [4,19,23] from sequent calculus with analytic cuts [25] for the logic **S5** to a cut-free hypersequent calculus, we shift from the sequent to the hypersequent framework. Hypersequents are arguably the easiest generalization of sequents [2–4], consisting of multisets of sequents (called *components*) working in parallel and separated by the symbol "|". We introduce a cut-free hypersequent calculus **HFcm** for **F** + (**CM**). **HFcm** incorporates the sequent calculus for the logic **S4** as a sub-calculus and adds an additional layer of information by considering a single sequent to live in the context of hypersequents. Axioms and rules (including cut) of **HFcm** are obtained by adding to each sequent in **SFcm** a context G or H, standing for a (possibly empty) hypersequent, and simplifying the right rules for $\Box$, $\mathcal{B}et$ and $\bigcirc$, as follows (with explicit weakening rules):

$$\frac{G \mid \Gamma^{\Box\bigcirc} \Rightarrow A}{G \mid \Gamma^{\Box\bigcirc} \Rightarrow \Box A} \qquad \frac{G \mid \Gamma^{\Box\bigcirc}, \Gamma^{b} \Rightarrow A}{G \mid \Gamma^{\Box\bigcirc}, \Gamma^{b} \Rightarrow \mathcal{B}et A} \qquad \frac{G \mid \Gamma^{\Box\bigcirc}, A, \mathcal{B}et \neg(A \wedge \mathcal{B}et(A \to B)) \Rightarrow}{G \mid \Gamma^{\Box\bigcirc} \Rightarrow \bigcirc(B/A)}$$

To manipulate the additional structure w.r.t. sequents, any hypersequent calculus contains *external structural rules* that operate on whole sequents. Standard rules are ext. weakening (ew) and ext. contraction (ec) (see below), which behave like weakening and contraction over whole sequents. The hypersequent structure opens the possibility to define new rules that allow the "exchange of information" between different components. These rules increase the expressive power of hypersequent calculi compared to sequent calculi, enabling the definition of cut-free calculi for logics that escape a cut-free sequent formulation; in the case of **S5** this is done using the rule $(s5')$ below (the $\bigcirc$ is added to deal with **F** + (**CM**))

$$\frac{G}{G \mid \Gamma \Rightarrow \Pi}\,(\mathrm{ew}) \qquad \frac{G \mid \Gamma \Rightarrow \Pi \mid \Gamma \Rightarrow \Pi}{G \mid \Gamma \Rightarrow \Pi}\,(\mathrm{ec}) \qquad \frac{G \mid \Gamma^{\Box\bigcirc}, \Gamma' \Rightarrow \Pi'}{G \mid \Gamma \Rightarrow \mid \Gamma' \Rightarrow \Pi'}\,(s5')$$

[5] The totality conditions, is the same as for Gödel logic [4] and S4.3 [16].

Hence the crucial difference w.r.t. the calculus **SFcm** is that, due to the structural rules (ec) and $(s5')$, we can now restrict to single-succedent modal right rules without impairing cut-free completeness.

Remark 2. A cut-free hypersequent calculus for **F** was introduced in [9] by adding one rule to the calculus for **E** [8]. While $\mathbf{F} + (\mathbf{CM})$ extends **F** (and **E**), our calculus is not a modular extension of these two. Indeed **HFcm** stems from an *alternative semantics* definition. Note that the premise $A, \mathcal{B}et\neg A \Rightarrow B$ of the right rule for $\bigcirc$ in these calculi would be trivially derivable in **HFcm**.

Given a hypersequent $\Gamma_1 \Rightarrow \Delta_1 \mid \dots \mid \Gamma_n \Rightarrow \Delta_n$, its interpretation ι is defined: $(\Gamma_1 \Rightarrow \Delta_1 \mid \dots \mid \Gamma_n \Rightarrow \Delta_n)^\iota := \Box(\bigwedge \Gamma_1 \to \bigvee \Delta_1) \vee \dots \vee \Box(\bigwedge \Gamma_n \to \bigvee \Delta_n)$

Theorem 6. **HFcm** *is sound and complete with cuts w.r.t.* $\mathbf{F} + (\mathbf{CM})$.

Proof. The soundness proof follows the pattern detailed for **SFcm**. Completeness is ensured by the derivation of (CM).

A calculus for **G** is obtained in a modular way by adding an external structural rule to the calculus **HFcm** for $\mathbf{F} + (\mathbf{CM})$. The additional rule is a slightly modified version of the well known communication rule, introduced by Avron [3] for capturing Gödel logic, and used in [16] for the modal logic **S4.3**:

$$\frac{G \mid \Pi^{\Box\bigcirc}, \Pi^{b}, \Gamma \Rightarrow \Delta \qquad G \mid \Gamma^{\Box\bigcirc}, \Gamma^{b}, \Pi \Rightarrow \Sigma}{G \mid \Gamma \Rightarrow \Delta \mid \Pi \Rightarrow \Sigma}\ com$$

Theorem 7. **HG** *is sound and complete in presence of cuts w.r.t.* **G**

Proof. Soundness: By induction on the height of the derivation. We only consider the case of the rule *com*. If the conclusion is not valid, then there are worlds x and y where x (y) forces every formula in Γ (Π) and x (y) falsifies every formula in Δ (Σ). By totality $x \leq y$ or $y \leq x$. If $x \leq y$, then y forces all the $\Box$, $\bigcirc$ and $\mathcal{B}et$ formulas in Γ and thus, by the validity of the premise $G \mid \Gamma^{\Box\bigcirc}, \Gamma^{b}, \Pi \Rightarrow \Sigma$, we get an immediate contradiction. The other case is symmetrical.

Completeness in Presence of Cuts: follows by the derivability of axiom (RM) (the topmost sequent is derivable).

$$\begin{array}{cl}
A, B, \mathcal{B}et\neg(A \wedge \mathcal{B}et(A \to \neg B)), \mathcal{B}et\neg(A \wedge B \wedge \mathcal{B}et(A \wedge B \to C)), \mathcal{B}et(A \to C) \Rightarrow \mathcal{B}et(A \wedge B \to C) & \\ \hline
A, B, \mathcal{B}et\neg(A \wedge \mathcal{B}et(A \to \neg B)), \mathcal{B}et\neg(A \wedge B \wedge \mathcal{B}et(A \wedge B \to C)), \mathcal{B}et(A \to C) \Rightarrow A \wedge B \wedge \mathcal{B}et(A \wedge B \to C) & \mathrm{R}\wedge \\ \hline
A, B, \mathcal{B}et\neg(A \wedge \mathcal{B}et(A \to \neg B)), \mathcal{B}et\neg(A \wedge B \wedge \mathcal{B}et(A \wedge B \to C)), \mathcal{B}et(A \to C) \Rightarrow & \mathrm{L}\mathcal{B}et, \mathrm{L}\neg \\ \hline
A, \mathcal{B}et\neg(A \wedge \mathcal{B}et(A \to \neg B)), \mathcal{B}et\neg(A \wedge B \wedge \mathcal{B}et(A \wedge B \to C)), A, \mathcal{B}et(A \to C) \Rightarrow A \wedge \mathcal{B}et(A \to \neg B) & \mathrm{R}\wedge, \mathrm{R}\mathcal{B}et, \mathrm{R}\neg \\ \hline
A, \mathcal{B}et\neg(A \wedge \mathcal{B}et(A \to \neg B)), \mathcal{B}et\neg(A \wedge B \wedge \mathcal{B}et(A \wedge B \to C)), A, \mathcal{B}et(A \to C) \Rightarrow & \mathrm{L}\mathcal{B}et, \mathrm{L}\neg \\ \hline
A, \mathcal{B}et\neg(A \wedge \mathcal{B}et(A \to \neg B)), \mathcal{B}et\neg(A \wedge B \wedge \mathcal{B}et(A \wedge B \to C)) \Rightarrow \mathcal{B}et\neg(A \wedge \mathcal{B}et(A \to C)) & \mathrm{R}\mathcal{B}et, \mathrm{R}\neg, \mathrm{L}\wedge \\ \hline
\bigcirc(C/A), A, \mathcal{B}et\neg(A \wedge \mathcal{B}et(A \to \neg B)), \mathcal{B}et\neg(A \wedge B \wedge \mathcal{B}et(A \wedge B \to C)) \Rightarrow & \mathrm{L}\bigcirc \\ \hline
\bigcirc(C/A), A, \mathcal{B}et\neg(A \wedge \mathcal{B}et(A \to \neg B)) \Rightarrow \mid \bigcirc(C/A), A \wedge B, \mathcal{B}et\neg(A \wedge B \wedge \mathcal{B}et(A \wedge B \to C)) \Rightarrow & com \\ \hline
\bigcirc(C/A) \Rightarrow \bigcirc(C/A \wedge B), \bigcirc(\neg B/A) \mid \bigcirc(C/A) \Rightarrow \bigcirc(C/A \wedge B), \bigcirc(\neg B/A) & \mathrm{R}\bigcirc\ \text{(twice)} \\ \hline
\bigcirc(C/A) \Rightarrow \bigcirc(C/A \wedge B), \bigcirc(\neg B/A) & EC \\ \hline
\neg\bigcirc(\neg B/A), \bigcirc(C/A) \Rightarrow \bigcirc(C/A \wedge B) & \mathrm{L}\neg
\end{array}$$

one premise of the rule *com* is omitted for space reasons.

5 Cut-Elimination for HFcm and HG

We prove that the calculus **HG** (and hence **HFcm**) admits cut-elimination. The strategy is the same as for the hypersequent calculus for **E** in [8].

Proof idea: As for the cut-reduction proof of **SFcm**, cuts on a formula of the form $\neg A$ or $A \to B$ are reduced using invertibility. In contrast with **SFcm**, we can shift cuts with cut-formulas of the form $\Box A$, $\mathcal{B}et\ A$ and $\bigcirc(B/A)$ upwards until the cut formula is principal, using a specific order. First over the premise containing the cut formula on the right hand side (Lemma 6), due to the change made w.r.t. **SFcm** to the right rules of $\mathcal{B}et$, $\Box$, and $\bigcirc$. Afterwards, over the other premise (Lemma 7). Note that when a rule introducing the cut formula on the right hand side is reached, the context has a shape that matches with the other premise of the cut and allows us to permute the cut upwards, similarly to case (**A**) from Theorem 4. When the cut formula becomes principal also on the left hand side, it can be replaced by cuts on smaller formulas.

Henceforth we use the same inductive measure of the *degree* of formulas as in Sect. 3, while the rank of a derivation $\mathcal{D}$ is now $\rho(\mathcal{D})$ (Definition 5). The following lemmas refer to derivations in **HG** (and hence in **HFcm**).

The invertibility of the hypersequent version of the rules for $\to$ and $\neg$ (Lemma 1) also holds in **HG** and is rank-preserving.

Lemma 5. *Given derivations* $\mathcal{D}_1$ *of* $G \mid \Gamma \Rightarrow \Delta, X$ *and* $\mathcal{D}_2$ *of* $H \mid X, \Pi \Rightarrow \Sigma$ *with* X *principal in a logical, modal or deontic rule in both premises and* $\rho(\mathcal{D}_i) \leq \mathsf{dg}(X)$, *there is a derivation* $\mathcal{D}$ *of* $G \mid H \mid \Gamma, \Pi \Rightarrow \Delta, \Sigma$ *with* $\rho(\mathcal{D}) \leq \mathsf{dg}(X)$.

Proof. As in Lemma 2 (the hypersequent structure plays no role).

The following lemmas are formulated in order to prove the admissibility of cuts on multiple occurrences of formulas taking into account the presence of explicit rules for contraction, both internal and external.

Lemma 6 (Right shift). *Given* $\mathcal{D}_1$ *of* $H \mid \Pi_1 \Rightarrow \Sigma_1, X^{n_1} \mid \ldots \mid \Pi_m \Rightarrow \Sigma_m, X^{n_m}$ *in* **HG**(**HFcm**) *and* $\mathcal{D}_2$ *of* $G \mid X, \Gamma \Rightarrow \Delta$ *with* $\rho(\mathcal{D}_1), \rho(\mathcal{D}_2) \leq \mathsf{dg}(X)$, *there is a derivation* $\mathcal{D}$, *with* $\rho(\mathcal{D}) \leq \mathsf{dg}(X)$, *of*

$$G \mid H \mid \Gamma^{n_1}, \Pi_1 \Rightarrow \Sigma_1, \Delta^{n_1} \mid \ldots \mid \Gamma^{n_m}, \Pi_m \Rightarrow \Sigma_m, \Delta^{n_m}$$

Proof. By induction on the height of $\mathcal{D}_1$. If it is an initial sequent or the last applied rule acts on sequents in H, the proof is trivial. If the cut formula is principal in a logical (modal, deontic) rule, then we use Lemma 7. Assume that the cut formula is not principal. If the rule is R$\bigcirc$, R$\mathcal{B}et$ and R$\Box$, then the claim follows by internal and external weakening (because such rules permit a single formula in the RHS). Otherwise, the cut is permuted and removed by induction hypothesis (note that the RHS of the rules ($s5'$) and (*com*), if present, remains unchanged in the premises, along with the associated context on the LHS).

Once we have reached the right rule introducing the cut formula $\mathcal{B}et A$, $\bigcirc(A/B)$, or $\Box A$, we can shift the cut upward over the other premise of the cut, as shown in the next lemma.

Lemma 7 (Left shift). *Given* $\mathcal{D}_2$ *of* $G\mid X^{n_1},\Gamma_1 \Rightarrow \Delta_1\mid \ldots \mid X^{n_m},\Gamma_m \Rightarrow \Delta_m$ *and* $\mathcal{D}_1$ *of* $H\mid \Pi \Rightarrow \Sigma, X$ *where* X *is principal in the last rule applied in* $\mathcal{D}_1$ *with* $\rho(\mathcal{D}_1), \rho(\mathcal{D}_2) \leq \mathtt{dg}(X)$, *there is a derivation* $\mathcal{D}$ *with* $\rho(\mathcal{D}) \leq \mathtt{dg}(X)$ *of*

$$G\mid H\mid \Pi^{n_1},\Gamma_1 \Rightarrow \Delta_1,\Sigma^{n_1}\mid \ldots \mid \Pi^{n_m},\Gamma_m \Rightarrow \Delta_m,\Sigma^{n_m}$$

Proof. By induction on the height of the derivation $\mathcal{D}_2$. The proof is similar to case **(A)** in Theorem 4. The hypersequent structure does not alter the proof, the only additional cases to consider are those involving hypersequent structural rules. See, e.g. [8] for $(s5')$. We consider the case of (com) where the cut formula moves from a component to another. W.l.o.g. we show a case in which we have two components in $\mathcal{D}_2$, as in:

$$\dfrac{\dfrac{G\mid \Pi^{\Box\bigcirc},\Pi^b \Rightarrow B}{G\mid \Pi \Rightarrow \Sigma,\mathcal{B}etB}\,\mathrm{R}\mathcal{B}\mathrm{et} \qquad \dfrac{\Gamma_1,\mathcal{B}etB^{n_2},\Gamma_2^b \Rightarrow \Delta_1 \qquad \mathcal{B}etB^{n_2},\Gamma_2,\Gamma_1^b \Rightarrow \Delta_2}{\Gamma_1 \Rightarrow \Delta_1\mid \mathcal{B}etB^{n_2},\Gamma_2 \Rightarrow \Delta_2}\,\mathrm{com}}{G\mid \Gamma_1 \Rightarrow \Delta_1\mid \Pi^{n_2},\Gamma_2 \Rightarrow \Delta_2,\Sigma^{n_2}}\,\mathrm{Cut}$$

assuming that one of the active components does not contain the cut formula (the other case is analogous). We construct the following derivation:

$$\dfrac{\dfrac{\dfrac{\dfrac{\dfrac{\dfrac{\dfrac{\dfrac{G\mid \Pi^{\Box\bigcirc},\Pi^b \Rightarrow B}{G\mid \Pi^{\Box\bigcirc},\Pi^b \Rightarrow \mathcal{B}etB}\,\mathrm{R}\mathcal{B}\mathrm{et} \qquad \Gamma_1,\mathcal{B}etB^{n_2},\Gamma_2^b \Rightarrow \Delta_1}{G\mid \Gamma_1,(\Pi^{\Box\bigcirc},\Pi^b)^{n_2},\Gamma_2^b \Rightarrow \Delta_1}\,\mathrm{Cut}}{G\mid \Gamma_1,\Pi^{\Box\bigcirc},\Pi^b,\Gamma_2^b \Rightarrow \Delta_1}\,\mathrm{LC} \qquad \dfrac{\dfrac{\dfrac{\dfrac{G\mid \Pi^{\Box\bigcirc},\Pi^b \Rightarrow B}{G\mid \Pi^{\Box\bigcirc},\Pi^b \Rightarrow \mathcal{B}etB}\,\mathrm{R}\mathcal{B}\mathrm{et} \qquad G\mid \mathcal{B}etB^{n_2},\Gamma_2,\Gamma_1^b \Rightarrow \Delta_2}{G\mid (\Pi^{\Box\bigcirc},\Pi^b)^{n_2},\Gamma_2,\Gamma_1^b \Rightarrow \Delta_2}\,\mathrm{Cut}}{G\mid \Pi^{\Box\bigcirc},\Pi^b,\Gamma_2,\Gamma_1^b \Rightarrow \Delta_2}\,\mathrm{LC}}{G\mid \Pi^{\Box\bigcirc},\Gamma_1 \Rightarrow \Delta_1\mid \Pi^{\Box\bigcirc},\Pi^b,\Gamma_2 \Rightarrow \Delta_2}\,\mathrm{com}}{G\mid \Pi^{\Box\bigcirc},\Gamma_1 \Rightarrow \Delta_1\mid \Pi^{n_2},\Gamma_2 \Rightarrow \Delta_2,\Sigma^{n_2}}\,\mathrm{LW,RW}}{G\mid \Pi^{\Box\bigcirc} \Rightarrow \mid \Gamma_1 \Rightarrow \Delta_1\mid \Pi^{n_2},\Gamma_2 \Rightarrow \Delta_2,\Sigma^{n_2}}\,\mathrm{s5'}}{G\mid \Pi^{n_2},\Gamma_2 \Rightarrow \Delta_2,\Sigma^{n_2}\mid \Gamma_1 \Rightarrow \Delta_1\mid \Pi^{n_2},\Gamma_2 \Rightarrow \Delta_2,\Sigma^{n_2}}\,\mathrm{LW,RW}}{G\mid \Gamma_1 \Rightarrow \Delta_1\mid \Pi^{n_2},\Gamma_2 \Rightarrow \Delta_2,\Sigma^{n_2}}\,\mathrm{EC}$$

where cuts are removed by induction hypothesis on the height of the derivation.

Theorem 8. *Any* **HFcm** (**HG**) *proof with cuts can be transformed into a proof of the same hypersequent that does not use cuts.*

Corollary 1. **HFcm** *and* **HG** *are cut-free complete w.r.t.* $\mathbf{F} + (\mathbf{CM})$ *and* **G**.

6 Proof Search Oriented Calculi for $\mathbf{F} + (\mathbf{CM})$ and $\mathbf{G}$

We transform the hypersequent calculi **HFcm** and **HG** into proof-search oriented calculi. The resulting systems feature reversible rules, with structural rules absorbed into logical ones, allowing for the construction of countermodels. This process follows the pattern established, e.g., for system **E** in [8].

Definition 6. *The* $\mathbf{HFcm}^{ps}$ *calculus consists of the initial hypersequents of the shape* $G\mid \Gamma,p \Rightarrow \Delta,p$, *the (usual) rules for the propositional connectives that repeat the introduced formulas in the premises, together with:*

$$\dfrac{G\mid \Gamma \Rightarrow \Delta,\bigcirc(B/A)\mid A,\mathcal{B}et\neg(A\wedge \mathcal{B}et(A\to B)) \Rightarrow}{G\mid \Gamma \Rightarrow \Delta,\bigcirc(B/A)}\,\mathrm{R}\bigcirc \qquad \dfrac{G\mid \bigcirc(B/A),\Gamma \Rightarrow \Delta,A \qquad G\mid \bigcirc(B/A),\Gamma \Rightarrow \Delta,\mathcal{B}et\neg(A\wedge \mathcal{B}et(A\to B))}{G\mid \bigcirc(B/A),\Gamma \Rightarrow \Delta}\,\mathrm{L}\bigcirc_1$$

$$\dfrac{G\mid \bigcirc(B/A),\Gamma \Rightarrow \Delta\mid \Pi \Rightarrow \Sigma,A \qquad G\mid \bigcirc(B/A),\Gamma \Rightarrow \Delta\mid \Pi \Rightarrow \Sigma,\mathcal{B}et\neg(A\wedge \mathcal{B}et(A\to B))}{G\mid \bigcirc(B/A),\Gamma \Rightarrow \Delta\mid \Pi \Rightarrow \Sigma}\,\mathrm{L}\bigcirc_2$$

- $\dfrac{G \mid \Gamma \Rightarrow \Delta, \mathcal{B}etA \mid \Gamma^b \Rightarrow A}{G \mid \Gamma \Rightarrow \Delta, \mathcal{B}etA}\ R\mathcal{B}et \quad \dfrac{G \mid A, \mathcal{B}etA, \Gamma \Rightarrow \Delta}{G \mid \mathcal{B}etA, \Gamma \Rightarrow \Delta}\ L\mathcal{B}et$

- $\dfrac{G \mid \Gamma \Rightarrow \Box A, \Delta \mid \Rightarrow A}{G \mid \Gamma \Rightarrow \Box A, \Delta}\ R\Box \quad \dfrac{G \mid \Box A, A, \Gamma \Rightarrow \Delta}{G \mid \Box A, \Gamma \Rightarrow \Delta}\ L\Box_1 \quad \dfrac{G \mid \Box A, \Gamma \Rightarrow \Delta \mid A, \Pi \Rightarrow \Sigma}{G \mid \Box A, \Gamma \Rightarrow \Delta \mid \Pi \Rightarrow \Sigma}\ L\Box_2$

The proof search oriented calculus $\mathbf{HG}^{ps}$ *for* **G** *extends* $\mathbf{HFcm}^{ps}$ *with the rule:*

$$\frac{G \mid \Gamma_1, \Gamma_2^b \Rightarrow \Delta_1 \mid \Gamma_2 \Rightarrow \Delta_2 \qquad G \mid \Gamma_1 \Rightarrow \Delta_1 \mid \Gamma_2, \Gamma_1^b \Rightarrow \Delta_2}{G \mid \Gamma_1 \Rightarrow \Delta_1 \mid \Gamma_2 \Rightarrow \Delta_2}\ com$$

Notice the peculiar shape of the rules $L\bigcirc_2$ and $L\Box_2$, designed to absorb the hypersequent structural rule ($s5'$). The rule *com* acts only on $\mathcal{B}et$ formulas. This depends on the fact that $\bigcirc$ and $\Box$ are governed by rules which introduce bottom-up formulas in every component.

Lemma 8. *The rules of (internal and external weakening) and contraction are height-preserving admissible in* $\mathbf{HFcm}^{ps}$. *Every rule of the calculus is height-preserving invertible in* $\mathbf{HFcm}^{ps}$.

Proof. The height-preserving admissibility of internal and external weakening follows from a straightforward induction on the height of the derivation. Invertibility follows from weakening. The contraction rules are admissible due to the repetition of every formula and component in each premise.

Theorem 9 (Soundness of $\mathbf{HFcm}^{ps}$ ($\mathbf{HG}^{ps}$)). *If a hypersequent G is derivable in* $\mathbf{HFcm}^{ps}$ ($\mathbf{HG}^{ps}$), *then so is in* **HFcm** (**HG**).

Proof. Follows from the structural rules of **HFcm**.

6.1 Decidability and Countermodel Construction

We define a proof search procedure which terminates for every sequent. If the proof search fails, we show how to extract a countermodel out of it.

Definition 7. *A hypersequent H is saturated w.r.t. the system* $\mathbf{HFcm}^{ps}$ *if it is not an initial sequent and for every component $\Gamma \Rightarrow \Delta$ in H, whenever $\Gamma \Rightarrow \Delta$ contains the principal formulas in the conclusion of a rule (r), then H also contains the formulas introduced by one of the premisses of (r) for every rule (r). For example, in the case of $\mathcal{B}et$, we have:*

- *($L\mathcal{B}et$). If $\Gamma, \mathcal{B}etA \Rightarrow \Delta \in H$, then $A \in \Gamma$.*
- *($R\mathcal{B}et$). If $\Gamma \Rightarrow \Delta, \mathcal{B}etA \in H$, then $\Pi, \Gamma^b \Rightarrow \Sigma, A \in H$ for some Π, Σ.*

The saturation condition w.r.t. $\mathbf{HG}^{ps}$ *is defined adding the condition:*

- *(com). If $\Gamma \Rightarrow \Delta \in H$ and $\Pi \Rightarrow \Sigma \in H$ then either Π^b in Γ or Γ^b in Π.*

Theorem 10. *Given $\Rightarrow A$ there is a derivation or a saturated hypersequent.*

Proof. We start showing that the number of hypersequent components can be bounded in any derivation $\mathcal{D}$ of $\Rightarrow A$. Indeed, the rules which introduce new components are R$\Box$, R$\bigcirc$ and R$\mathcal{B}et$. Consider first R$\Box$: we show that this rule is applied exactly once to each formula (say $\Box B$), occurring in the consequent of a component and creates only one new component, no matter if $\Box B$ appears in the consequent of many components. To illustrate the situation, consider, e.g.,

$$\begin{array}{c}
\dfrac{H \mid \Gamma_i \Rightarrow \Delta_i, \Box B \mid \Theta \Rightarrow B, \Lambda \mid \dots \mid \Pi, \Gamma_j \Rightarrow \Delta_j, \Sigma, \Box B \mid \Rightarrow B}{H \mid \Gamma_i \Rightarrow \Delta_i, \Box B \mid \Theta \Rightarrow B, \Lambda \mid \dots \mid \Pi, \Gamma_j \Rightarrow \Delta_j, \Sigma, \Box B}\,\mathrm{R}\Box \\
\vdots \mathcal{D} \\
\dfrac{H \mid \Gamma_i \Rightarrow \Delta_i, \Box B \mid \Rightarrow B \mid \dots \mid \Gamma_j \Rightarrow \Delta_j, \Box B}{H \mid \Gamma_i \Rightarrow \Delta_i, \Box B \mid \dots \mid \Gamma_j \Rightarrow \Delta_j, \Box B}\,\mathrm{R}\Box
\end{array}
\quad\rightsquigarrow\quad
\begin{array}{c}
\dfrac{\dfrac{H \mid \Gamma_i \Rightarrow \Delta_i, \Box B \mid \Theta \Rightarrow B, \Lambda \mid \dots \mid \Pi, \Gamma_j \Rightarrow \Delta_j, \Sigma, \Box B \mid \Rightarrow B}{H \mid \Gamma_i \Rightarrow \Delta_i, \Box B \mid \Theta \Rightarrow B, \Lambda \mid \dots \mid \Pi, \Gamma_j \Rightarrow \Delta_j, \Sigma, \Box B \mid \Theta \Rightarrow B, \Lambda}\,\mathrm{LW,RW}}{H \mid \Gamma_i \Rightarrow \Delta_i, \Box B \mid \Theta \Rightarrow B, \Lambda \mid \dots \mid \Pi, \Gamma_j \Rightarrow \Delta_j, \Sigma, \Box B}\,\mathrm{EC} \\
\vdots \mathcal{D} \\
\dfrac{H \mid \Gamma_i \Rightarrow \Delta_i, \Box B \mid \Rightarrow B \mid \dots \mid \Gamma_j \Rightarrow \Delta_j, \Box B}{H \mid \Gamma_i \Rightarrow \Delta_i, \Box B \mid \dots \mid \Gamma_j \Rightarrow \Delta_j, \Box B}\,\mathrm{R}\Box
\end{array}$$

Hence the number of components created by R$\Box$ is bounded by the number of boxed subformulas of A, whence it is O(n). The situation for R$\bigcirc$ is similar.

R$\mathcal{B}et$ requires more care, being $\mathcal{B}et$ an **S4** modality. In this case, having bounded the number of applications of R$\Box$ and R$\bigcirc$, we assume that if there is an infinite introduction bottom-up of components these are introduced by the rule R$\mathcal{B}et$. Hence, since the number of possible sequents is finite (in particular $2^{|2^{|\mathsf{SUB}(A)|}|}$), there has to be a repetition. In this case, we have met the saturation condition for the rule R$\mathcal{B}et$. Thus the number of components is finite. Since we can rule out rule applications for which the saturation condition has already been met (due to the admissibility of contraction), every rule introduces bottom-up a new component or new formulas in the components, hence the length of every branch of a putative derivation of A is bounded and the derivation is finite.

The next theorem ensures the completeness of our calculi and show how to extract countermodels out of a failed proof search.

Theorem 11. *If A is valid in* $\mathbf{F} + (\mathbf{CM})$ *(*$\mathbf{G}$*), is derivable in* $\mathbf{HFcm}^{ps}$ *(*$\mathbf{HG}^{ps}$*).*

Proof. By contraposition. If A is not derivable, by Theorem 10 there is a saturated hypersequent: $\Gamma_1 \Rightarrow \Delta_1 \mid \dots \mid \Gamma_n \Rightarrow \Delta_n$. We assign labels to the components $i : \Gamma_i \Rightarrow \Delta_i$ $(i \in \{1, \dots, n\})$ and consider the model: $\mathcal{M} = \langle \{1, \dots, n\}, \leq, v \rangle$ with $i \leq j$ if and only if $\Gamma_i^b \subseteq \Gamma_j$ and $i \in v(p)$ if and only if $p \in \Gamma_i$.

We have to check that the model is reflexive and transitive in the case of $\mathbf{HFcm}^{ps}$ and total in the case of $\mathbf{HG}^{ps}$. The relation $\leq$ is reflexive and transitive, because set inclusion is reflexive and transitive. As regards totality, we observe that the saturation condition for (*com*) ensures that for every i and j, $\Gamma_i^b \subseteq \Gamma_j$ or $\Gamma_j^b \subseteq \Gamma_i$ which gives by definition $i \leq j$ or $j \leq i$.

We now show that for every i in the model $\mathcal{M}$ we have $i \Vdash B$ if $B \in \Gamma_i$ and $i \nVdash B$ if $B \in \Delta_i$. We argue by induction on the degree of the formulas.

- If B is atomic, the claim stems from the definition of the valuation function and by the saturation condition.
- If B is a compound formula, the proof follows from the use of the induction hypothesis and saturation. We deal with the case in which B is $\mathcal{B}etC$; the other cases are handled similarly. If $\mathcal{B}etC \in \Gamma_i$, suppose $i \leq j$, then $\Gamma_i^b \subseteq \Gamma_j$. By the saturation condition for L$\mathcal{B}et$, we get $C \in \Gamma_j$ and by induction

hypothesis we have $j \Vdash C$, hence the desired conclusion. If $\mathcal{B}etC \in \Delta_i$, then by definition of saturation there is $\Gamma_j \Rightarrow \Delta_j, C$ with $\Gamma_i^b \subseteq \Gamma_j$ so $i \leq j$, and by induction hypothesis $i \nVdash C$, so the desired conclusion follows.

Remark 3. The above countermodel construction can be adapted[6] to define a proof-search-oriented calculus for Gödel-Dummett logic [10].

Concluding Remark: we demonstrated that for $\mathbf{F} + (\mathbf{CM})$ (and Åqvist systems **E** and **F**), while it is possible to define sequent calculi that use semi-analytic cuts, the hypersequent framework provides a modular and cut-free approach, enabling the capture of $\mathbf{F} + (\mathbf{CM})$ and **G**, and supporting countermodel construction.

Acknowledgements. Work supported by the FWF project I 6372-N.

References

1. Åqvist, L.: Deontic logic. In: Gabbay, D., Guenthner, F. (eds.) Handbook of Philosophical Logic. Synthese Library, vol. 165, pp. 605–714. Springer, Dordrecht (1984). https://doi.org/10.1007/978-94-009-6259-0_11
2. Avron, A.: A constructive analysis of RM. J. Symb. Logic **52**(4), 939–951 (1987)
3. Avron, A.: Hypersequents, logical consequence and intermediate logics for concurrency. Ann. Math. Artif. Intell. **4**, 225–248 (1991)
4. Avron, A.: The method of hypersequents in the proof theory of propositional non-classical logics. In: Logic: From Foundations to Applications, pp. 1–32. OUP, New York (1996)
5. Belnap, N.D., Jr.: Display logic. J. Philos. Logic **11**(4), 375–417 (1982)
6. Burgess, J.: Quick completeness proofs for some logics of conditionals. Notre Dame J. Formal Logic **22**(3), 76–84 (1981)
7. Ciabattoni, A., Lang, T., Ramanayake, R.: Cut-restriction: from cuts to analytic cuts. In: LICS, pp. 1–13 (2023)
8. Ciabattoni, A., Olivetti, N., Parent, X.: Dyadic obligations: proofs and countermodels via hypersequents. In: Aydoğan, R., Criado, N., Lang, J., Sanchez-Anguix, V., Serramia, M. (eds.) PRIMA 2022. LNCS, vol. 13753, pp. 54–71. Springer, Cham (2022). https://doi.org/10.1007/978-3-031-21203-1_4
9. Ciabattoni, A., Olivetti, N., Parent, X., Ramanayake, R., Rozplokhas, D.: Analytic proof theory for Aqvist's system F. In: Maranhão, J., Peterson, C., Straßer, C., van der Torre, L. (eds.) DEON 2023, pp. 79–98 (2023)
10. Dummett, M.: A propositional logic with denumerable matrix. J. Symb. Log. **24**, 96–107 (1959)
11. Gabbay, D., Horty, J., Parent, X., van der Torre, L., van der Meyden, R. (eds.) Handbook of Deontic Logic and Normative Systems, vol. 2. College Publications, London (2021)

[6] Using the multiple conclusion version of calculus in [3] (whose rule *com* moves any multiset of formulas) in which the rules for $\rightarrow$ are replaced by:

$$\frac{G \mid \Gamma \Rightarrow \Delta, A \rightarrow B \mid \Gamma, A \Rightarrow B}{G \mid \Gamma \Rightarrow \Delta, A \rightarrow B}\ \mathrm{R}\!\rightarrow \qquad \frac{G \mid A \rightarrow B, \Gamma \Rightarrow \Delta, A \qquad G \mid B, A \rightarrow B, \Gamma \Rightarrow \Delta}{G \mid A \rightarrow B, \Gamma \Rightarrow \Delta}\ \mathrm{L}\!\rightarrow .$$

12. Gabbay, D.M.: Theoretical foundations for non-monotonic reasoning in expert systems. In: Apt, K.R. (ed.) Logics and Models of Concurrent Systems. NATO ASI Series, vol. 13, pp. 439–457. Springer, Heidelberg (1985). https://doi.org/10.1007/978-3-642-82453-1_15
13. Giordano, L., Gliozzi, V., Olivetti, N., Pozzato, G.L.: Analytic tableaux calculi for KLM logics of nonmonotonic reasoning. ACM Trans. Comput. Log. **10**(3), 18:1–18:47 (2009)
14. Girlando, M., Lellmann, B., Olivetti, N., Pozzato, G.L.: Hypersequent calculi for Lewis' conditional logics with uniformity and reflexivity. In: Proceedings of Tableaux (2017)
15. Indrzejczak, A.: Natural Deduction, Hybrid Systems and Modal Logics. Springer, Dordrecht (2010). https://doi.org/10.1007/978-90-481-8785-0
16. Indrzejczak, A.: Cut-free hypersequent calculus for S4.3. Bull. Sect. Logic Univ. Łódź **41**(1–2), 89–104 (2012)
17. Kowalski, T., Ono, H.: Analytic cut and interpolation for bi-intuitionistic logic. Rev. Symb. Log. **10**(2), 259–283 (2017)
18. Kraus, S., Lehmann, D., Magidor, M.: Nonmonotonic reasoning, preferential models and cumulative logics. Artif. Intell. **44**(1–2), 167–207 (1990)
19. Kurokawa, H.: Hypersequent calculi for modal logics extending S4. In: Nakano, Y., Satoh, K., Bekki, D. (eds.) JSAI-isAI 2013. LNCS (LNAI), vol. 8417, pp. 51–68. Springer, Cham (2014). https://doi.org/10.1007/978-3-319-10061-6_4
20. Schröder, L., Pattinson, D., Hausmann, D.: Optimal tableaux for conditional logics with cautious monotonicity. In: Wooldridge, M. Coelho, H., Studer, R. (eds.) Proceedings of the 2010 conference on ECAI 2010: 19th European Conference on Artificial Intelligence, pp. 707–712. IOS Press, Amsterdam (2010)
21. Lewis, D.: Counterfactuals. Blackwell, Oxford (1973)
22. Lyon, T.S., et al.: Internal and external calculi: ordering the jungle without being lost in translations. CoRR, abs/2312.03426 (2023)
23. Minc, G.: Some calculi of modal logic. Trudy Mat. Inst. Steklov **98**, 88–111 (1968)
24. Negri, S., Olivetti, N.: A sequent calculus for preferential conditional logic based on neighbourhood semantics. In: Proceedings of Tableaux, vol. 9323, pp. 115–134 (2015)
25. Ohnishi, M., Matsumoto, K.: Gentzen method in modal calculi. Osaka Math. J. **9**, 113–130 (1957)
26. Ono, H., Sano, K.: Analytic cut and Mints' symmetric interpolation method for Bi-intuitionistic tense logic. In: Advances in Modal Logic, pp. 601–624. College Publications (2022)
27. Parent, X.: Maximality vs. optimality in dyadic deontic logic. J. Philos. Log. **43**(6), 1101–1128 (2014)
28. Parent, X.: Preference semantics for Hansson-type dyadic deontic logic: a survey of results. In: Gabbay, et al. [11], pp. 7–70
29. Smullyan, R.M.: Analytic cut. J. Symb. Log. **33**, 560–564 (1968)
30. Takano, M.: Subformula property as a substitute for cut-elimination in modal propositional logics. Math. Japon. **37**, 1129–1145 (1992)
31. Takano, M.: New modification of the subformula property for a modal logic. Bull. Sect. Log. **49**, 08 (2020)

Uniform Substitution for Differential Refinement Logic

Enguerrand Prebet and André Platzer(✉)

Karlsruhe Institute of Technology, Karlsruhe, Germany
{enguerrand.prebet,platzer}@kit.edu

Abstract. This paper introduces a uniform substitution calculus for differential refinement logic dRL. The logic dRL extends the differential dynamic logic dL such that one can simultaneously reason about properties of and relations between hybrid systems. Refinements are useful e.g. for simplifying proofs by relating a concrete hybrid system to an abstract one from which the property can be proved more easily. Uniform substitution is the key to parsimonious prover microkernels. It enables the verbatim use of single axiom formulas instead of axiom schemata with soundness-critical side conditions scattered across the proof calculus. The uniform substitution rule can then be used to instantiate all axioms soundly. Access to differential variables in dRL enables more control over the notion of refinement, which is shown to be decidable on a fragment of hybrid programs.

Keywords: Uniform substitution · Differential dynamic logic · Refinement · Hybrid systems

1 Introduction

Hybrid systems modeled by joint discrete dynamics and continuous dynamics are important and subtle systems in need of sound proofs [26] on account of their important applications [15,16,20,22,32]. Since such systems are important to get right, hybrid systems verification techniques themselves should be sound. Uniform substitution [24,25,27,28], originally phrased by Church for first-order logic [10, §35,40], has been identified as the key technique reducing the soundness-critical core to a prover microkernel and is behind the KeYmaera X prover [14].

This paper designs a corresponding uniform substitution proof calculus for differential refinement logic (dRL) [19]. The logic dRL is unique in its capabilities of proving simultaneous hybrid systems properties and hybrid systems refinement relations. This ability of dRL has been shown to be beneficial for establishing refinement relations of system implementations to verification abstractions and for relating time-triggered implementation models to event-triggered

Funding has been provided by an Alexander von Humboldt Professorship and the pilot program Core Informatics (KiKIT) of the Helmholtz Association (HGF).

C. Benzmüller et al. (Eds.): IJCAR 2024, LNAI 14740, pp. 196–215, 2024.
https://doi.org/10.1007/978-3-031-63501-4_11

verification models [18]. The latter relation overcomes a stark divide in embedded system design principles while combining ease of verification with ease of implementation in ways that neither design paradigm alone supports. But such proving power only helps practical system verification if the theoretical proof calculi are implemented in a sound way and, in fact, dRL has not yet been implemented at all. Such an implementation is significantly simplified and significantly easier to get sound by identifying a uniform substitution calculus, which has no axiom schemata with their usual side conditions (and the algorithms implementing them) but merely a finite list of concrete dRL formulas as axioms. Reasoning directly with these concrete formulas also makes the proofs easier as the conditions are checked only when uniform substitution is used. This means that a direct consequence of the axioms could have more admissible substitution instances than the axioms themselves, whereas with schemata, the side conditions would pile up and not generalize as well. Other beneficial side effects include the fact that dRL now acquires a Hilbert-style proof calculus that is significantly more flexible and also more modular than dRL's previous sequent calculus.

Challenges include the fact that uniform substitution calculi for hybrid systems give a differential-form semantics to differentials and differential symbols [25], which is critical to obtain logic-based decision procedures for differential equation invariants [30], but also renders some sequent calculus proof rules of dRL unsound due to the resulting finer-grained view on differential equations. The flip side is that this finer view distinguishes widely different classes of differential equations better, thereby making it easier to tell apart different differential equations that merely coincide on the overall reachable set while having different temporal behavior. This difference is exploited here to obtain a decidability result for refinement for a fragment of hybrid systems. Other challenges to overcome are the unexpected definition of free variables of refinements, which are required for soundness. The core of the resulting calculus has been implemented in KeYmaera X[1], extending the prover microkernel in 4 h of work with about 300 lines of code, mostly spent on writing down all the new axioms.

2 Related Work

Hybrid programs in dRL form a Kleene algebra with tests [17]. Program equivalence for Kleene algebra with tests is known to be decidable for abstract atomic programs. Refinement $\alpha \leq \beta$ can be recovered and defined as $\alpha \cup \beta = \beta$, but that duplicates reasoning about β. Certain classes of hypotheses can be added to the theory, e.g. Hoare-like triples $?p; \alpha; ?\neg q = ?\mathit{false}$, without breaking the decidability [11]. This however does not extend when limited commutativity is allowed, which arises even in the discrete fragment: $(x := 2; y := 3) = (y := 3; x := 2)$ but $(x := 2; x := 3) \neq (x := 3; x := 2)$. KAT with only discrete assignments has been studied as Schematic KAT [4]. dRL can derive the axioms of Schematic KAT, but also allows reasoning with continuous dynamics and differential equations.

[1] https://github.com/LS-Lab/KeYmaeraX-release/tree/dRL.

The Event-B method [1] is a formalism for reasoning about discrete models where the primary mechanism is refinement to check the conformance between abstract models and more detailed ones. Multiple different formalisms have been proposed. Hybrid Event-B [2,5,6] is an extension with tool support [8] for hybrid systems with events corresponding to discrete and continuous evolutions. These continuous steps are however abstracted by the invariants they are assumed to satisfy. Event-B can also be extended with theories [9]. By adding some axioms about differential equations, it allows refinement reasoning with some continuous dynamics [3,12]. In contrast, dRL captures the continuous dynamics directly and proves the invariants as a consequence of the continuous dynamics.

Uniform substitution was proposed by Alonzo Church for first-order logic to capture axioms instead of axiom schemata [10, §35,40]. Modern uniform substitution originated for dL to support hybrid systems theorem proving in simple ways [25], extended to hybrid games in differential game logic dGL [27], and to communicating parallel programs dL_{CHP} [7]. This work is complementing the approach by adding refinement reasoning in a uniform substitution calculus for hybrid systems. Developing uniform substitution calculi are key to the design of small soundness-critical prover microkernels such as KeYmaera X [14].

3 Differential Refinement Logic dRL

Differential refinement logic dRL [19] extends the differential dynamic logic dL for hybrid systems [23] with a first-class refinement operator $\leq$ on hybrid systems. This section presents *differential-form* dRL, which prepares dRL for the features needed for dL's uniform substitution axiomatization, most notably the inclusion of differential terms alongside function symbols, predicate symbols, and program constant symbols, but also the requisite inclusion of differential variable symbols. Differential terms $(\theta)'$ are the fundamental logical device with which to enable sound [25] and complete [29,30] reasoning about differential equations.

3.1 Syntax

This section defines the syntax of the differential refinement logic dRL. The set of all variables is $\mathcal{V}$. To each variable $x \in \mathcal{V}$ is associated a *differential symbol* x' which is also in $\mathcal{V}$. Its purpose is to use x' to refer to the time-derivative of variable x during a differential equation, but also to cleverly relay that information to surrounding formulas in a sound way [25]. It is this (crucial) presence of differential symbols, that gives differential-form dRL a refined notion of refinement, especially of differential equations, compared to its sequent calculus predecessor [19].

Definition 1 (Terms). Terms *are defined by the grammar below where* $x \in \mathcal{V}$ *is a variable,* f *is a function symbol of arity* n *and* $\theta, \eta, \theta_1, \ldots, \theta_n$ *are terms:*

$$\theta, \eta ::= x \mid f(\theta_1, \ldots, \theta_n) \mid \theta + \eta \mid \theta \cdot \eta \mid (\theta)'$$

Terms have the usual arithmetic operations and function symbols. They also have differentials of terms $(\theta)'$ which describe how the value of θ changes locally depending on the values of the differential symbols associated to the variables of θ.

Definition 2 (Formulas). Formulas *are defined by the grammar below where* $\theta, \eta, \theta_1, \ldots, \theta_n$ *are terms,* p *is a predicate symbol of arity* n, ϕ, ψ *are formulas and* α, β *are hybrid programs (Definition 3):*

$$\phi, \psi ::= \theta \leq \eta \mid p(\theta_1, \ldots, \theta_n) \mid \neg\phi \mid \phi \wedge \psi \mid \forall x\, \phi \mid [\alpha]\phi \mid \alpha \leq \beta$$

In addition to the operators of first-order logic of real arithmetic, formulas also contain the dL modality $[\alpha]\phi$ which expresses that the formula ϕ holds after all possible runs of the hybrid program α. dRL extends dL with the refinement operator $\alpha \leq \beta$ which expresses that α refines β as β has more behaviors than α: it is true in a state ν if all states reachable by hybrid program α from ν can be reached by hybrid program β. The program equivalence $\alpha = \beta$ is shorthand for $\alpha \leq \beta \wedge \beta \leq \alpha$. This will be made explicit by axiom (=) in Sect. 5.

Note the fundamental difference between dRL modal formula $[\alpha]\phi$, which expresses that all runs of hybrid program α satisfy dRL formula ϕ, compared to the dRL refinement formula $\alpha \leq \beta$, which expresses that all runs of hybrid program α are also runs of hybrid program β. Both dRL formulas refer to the runs of a hybrid program α, but only the former states a property of the (final) states reached, while only the latter relates the overall transition behavior of hybrid program α to that of another program. Just like $[\alpha]\phi$, formula $\alpha \leq \beta$ is a dRL formula and not just a judgment, so it can be true in some states and false in others. This makes it possible to easily express conditional refinement as $\phi \rightarrow \alpha \leq \beta$ meaning that if ϕ is true initially, then α refines β. The logic dRL is closed under all operators. For example the dRL formula $[\alpha]\beta \leq \gamma$ expresses that after all runs of α it is the case that all runs of β are also runs of γ. Just like in an ordinary implication, $\phi \rightarrow \alpha \leq \beta$ says nothing about what happens when the initial state does not satisfy ϕ. Just like ordinary dynamic logic modalities, $[\alpha]\beta \leq \gamma$ says nothing about what happens before program α ran. Indeed, this extended capabilities that dRL is closed under all operators will add to its expressibility and the eloquence of its uniform substitution proof calculus.

Definition 3 (Hybrid Programs). Hybrid programs *are defined by the grammar below where* x *is a variable,* θ *is a term,* a *is a program constant,* ψ *is a differential-free formula and* α, β *are hybrid programs:*

$$\alpha, \beta ::= a \mid ?\psi \mid x := \theta \mid x := * \mid x' = \theta \,\&\, \psi \mid \alpha \cup \beta \mid \alpha; \beta \mid \alpha^*$$

The *test* $?\psi$ behaves like a skip if the formula ψ is true in the current state and blocks the system otherwise. The *assignment* $x := \theta$ instantaneously updates the value of the variable x to the value of the term θ. The *nondeterministic assignment* $x := *$ updates the value of the variable x to an arbitrary value.

The *differential equation* $x' = \theta \,\&\, \psi$ behaves like a continuous evolution where both the differential equation $x' = \theta$ and the evolution domain ψ holds. The *nondeterministic choice* $\alpha \cup \beta$ can behave like either α or β. The *sequence* $\alpha; \beta$ behaves like α followed by β. The *nondeterministic repetition* α^* behaves like α repeated an arbitrary natural number of times.

Example 1 (Modelling safe breaking). Let us consider a car that needs to stop before a wall at distance m. It starts from a safe position and can accelerate with acceleration A if some safety condition $\text{safe}_T(x)$ is true or brake with braking force B. The controller is run at most every T seconds. Proving its safety can be achieved by proving the following dRL formula:

$$A \geq 0 \wedge B > 0 \wedge x + v^2/2B \leq m \rightarrow [car_T]x \leq m$$
$$car_T ::= (a := -B \cup ?\text{safe}_T(x); a := A); t_0 := t; x' = v, v' = a, t' = 1 \,\&\, t - t_0 \leq T$$

Such system, called *time-triggered*, can be refined to a *event-triggered* system where the controller is sure to run before a critical event, leaving the domain $E(x)$, occurs. Event-triggered systems are easier to verify but less realistic. With dRL and the axiom ([≤]) below, the time-triggered system can be proved safe by proving the safety of the event-triggered system and the refinement between the two systems:

$$A \geq 0 \wedge B \geq 0 \wedge x + v^2/2B \leq m \rightarrow car_T \leq car_E \wedge [car_E]x \leq m$$

$$car_E ::= (a := -B \cup ?\text{safe}_E(x); a := A); t_0 := t; x' = v, v' = a, t' = 1 \,\&\, E(x)$$

3.2 Semantics

A state ν is a mapping $\mathcal{V} \rightarrow \mathbb{R}$. The state ν_x^r agrees with the state ν except for the variable x whose value is $r \in \mathbb{R}$. State ω is a *U-variation* of ν if ω and ν are equal on the complement $U^{\complement}$ of that set of variables U. For instance, ν_x^r is an $\{x\}$-variation of ν. The set of all states is $\mathcal{S}$. The interpretation of a function symbol of arity n in *interpretation* I is a smooth function $I(f) : \mathbb{R}^n \rightarrow \mathbb{R}$.

Definition 4 (Term semantics). *The* semantics of a term θ *in interpretation* I *and state* ν *is its value* $I\nu[\![\theta]\!] \in \mathbb{R}$ *and is defined as follows:*

1. $I\nu[\![x]\!] = \nu(x)$
2. $I\nu[\![f(\theta_1, \ldots, \theta_n)]\!] = I(f)(I\nu[\![\theta_1]\!], \ldots, I\nu[\![\theta_n]\!])$
3. $I\nu[\![\theta + \eta]\!] = I\nu[\![\theta]\!] + I\nu[\![\eta]\!]$
4. $I\nu[\![\theta \cdot \eta]\!] = I\nu[\![\theta]\!] \cdot I\nu[\![\eta]\!]$
5. $I\nu[\![(\theta)']\!] = \sum_{x \in \mathcal{V}} \nu(x') \frac{\partial I[\![\theta]\!]}{\partial x}(\nu) = \sum_{x \in \mathcal{V}} \nu(x') \frac{\partial I\nu[\![\theta]\!]}{\partial x}$

The partial derivative $\frac{\partial I\nu[\![\theta]\!]}{\partial x}$ corresponds to the derivative of the one-dimensional function $X \mapsto I\nu_x^X[\![\theta]\!]$ at $X = \nu(x)$. Since $I\nu[\![\theta]\!]$ denotes a smooth function, the derivative always exists.

Since hybrid programs appear in formulas and vice versa, the interpretation of hybrid programs and formulas is defined by simultaneous induction. The interpretation of a predicate symbol of arity n in interpretation I is an n-ary relation $I(p) \subseteq \mathbb{R}^n$. The interpretation of a program constant symbol a in interpretation I is a state-transition relation $I(a) \subseteq \mathcal{S} \times \mathcal{S}$ where $(\nu, \omega) \in I[\![a]\!]$ iff the program constant a can reach the state ω starting from the state ν.

Definition 5 (dRL semantics). *The* semantics of a formula ϕ *for an interpretation* I *is the subset* $I[\![\phi]\!] \subseteq \mathcal{S}$ *of states in which* ϕ *is true and defined as:*

1. $\nu \in I[\![\theta \leq \eta]\!]$ *iff* $I\nu[\![\theta]\!] \leq I\nu[\![\eta]\!]$
2. $\nu \in I[\![p(\theta_1, \dots, \theta_n)]\!]$ *iff* $(I\nu[\![\theta_1]\!], \dots, I\nu[\![\theta_n]\!]) \in I(p)$
3. $\nu \in I[\![\neg\phi]\!]$ *iff* $\nu \notin I[\![\phi]\!]$
4. $\nu \in I[\![\phi \wedge \psi]\!]$ *iff* $\nu \in I[\![\phi]\!]$ *and* $\nu \in I[\![\psi]\!]$
5. $\nu \in I[\![\forall x\, \phi]\!]$ *iff* $\nu_x^r \in I[\![\phi]\!]$ *for all* $r \in \mathbb{R}$
6. $\nu \in I[\![[\alpha]\phi]\!]$ *iff* $\omega \in I[\![\phi]\!]$ *for all* $(\nu, \omega) \in I[\![\alpha]\!]$
7. $\nu \in I[\![\alpha \leq \beta]\!]$ *iff* $(\nu, \omega) \in I[\![\beta]\!]$ *for all* $(\nu, \omega) \in I[\![\alpha]\!]$

A formula ϕ is *valid in* I if $I[\![\phi]\!] = \mathcal{S}$. A formula ϕ is *valid* if it is valid in all interpretations.

Definition 6 (Transition semantics of programs). *The* semantics of a hybrid program α *for an interpretation* I *is the transition relation* $I[\![\alpha]\!] \subseteq \mathcal{S} \times \mathcal{S}$ *and is defined as follows:*

1. $I[\![a]\!] = I(a)$
2. $I[\![?\psi]\!] = \{(\nu, \nu) \; : \; \nu \in I[\![\psi]\!]\}$
3. $I[\![x := *]\!] = \{(\nu, \nu_x^r) \; : \; \textit{for all } r \in \mathbb{R}\}$
4. $I[\![x := \theta]\!] = \{(\nu, \nu_x^r) \; : \; r = I\nu[\![\theta]\!]\}$
5. $I[\![x' = \theta \,\&\, \psi]\!] = \{(\nu, \omega) \; : \; \varphi(0)$ *is a* $\{x'\}$*-variation of* ν *and* $\omega = \varphi(r)$*for some function* $\varphi \; : \; [0, r] \rightarrow \mathcal{S}$ *where* $\varphi(t)$ *is a* $\{x, x'\}$*-variation of* ν*, satisfies*$\varphi(t) \in I[\![x' = \theta \wedge \psi]\!]$ *and* $\frac{\mathrm{d}I\varphi(t)[\![x]\!]}{\mathrm{d}t} = I\varphi(t)[\![\theta]\!]$ *for all* $t \in [0, r]\}$
6. $I[\![\alpha \cup \beta]\!] = I[\![\alpha]\!] \cup I[\![\beta]\!]$
7. $I[\![\alpha; \beta]\!] = I[\![\alpha]\!] \circ I[\![\beta]\!] = \{(\nu, \omega) : (\nu, \mu) \in I[\![\alpha]\!], (\mu, \omega) \in I[\![\beta]\!]$ *for some* $\mu \in \mathcal{S}\}$
8. $I[\![\alpha^*]\!] = \bigcup_{n \in \mathbb{N}} I[\![\alpha^n]\!]$

Most importantly, $\alpha \leq \beta$ is true in a state ν iff all states ω reachable from ν by running program α are also reachable by running β from ν.

The transition for a differential equation $x' = \theta \,\&\, \psi$ synchronizes the differential symbol x' with the current time-derivative of x, i.e. θ, and then evolves the system continuously along the solution φ of the differential equation $x' = \theta$ within the domain ψ. Differential equations are the only hybrid programs that intrinsically relate variables with their associated differential symbol.

As differential equations effectively *change* the value of differential symbols, this is taken into account in the semantics of refinements. The differential equations $x' = 1$ and $x' = 2$ are *not* equivalent: although both can reach the same values for x, their respective end states will always have a different value for x'.

This behavior differs from the original semantics of dRL [19]. Intuitively, this notion of refinement corresponds to assuming that differential equations evolve with a global time $t' = 1$. Other extensions of dL like $\mathsf{dL}_{\mathrm{CHP}}$ [7] already assume the presence of such global time. This property allows to express refinements of differential equations as a dL formula as shown in the axiom (ODE) below.

3.3 Static Semantics

Uniform substitution relies on the notions of free and bound variables to prevent any unsound substitution attempts. Static semantics gives a definition for free and bound variables of terms, formulas and hybrid programs based on their (dynamic) semantics, which can be defined as in dL [25]:

Definition 7 (Static semantics). *The* static semantics *defines the free variables* $\mathsf{FV}(\theta)$*,* $\mathsf{FV}(\phi)$ *and* $\mathsf{FV}(\alpha)$*, which are the variables whose values the expression depends on, and the bound variables* $\mathsf{BV}(\alpha)$*, which are the variables whose values may change during the execution of* α*. They are defined formally as follows:*

$$\begin{aligned}
\mathsf{FV}(\theta) &= \{x \in \mathcal{V} \ : \ \exists I, \nu, \tilde{\nu} \, a \ \{x\}\text{-variation of } \nu \text{ such that } I\nu[\![\theta]\!] \neq I\tilde{\nu}[\![\theta]\!]\} \\
\mathsf{FV}(\theta) &= \{x \in \mathcal{V} \ : \ \exists I, \nu, \tilde{\nu} \, a \ \{x\}\text{-variation of } \nu \text{ such that } \nu \in I[\![\phi]\!] \not\ni \tilde{\nu}\} \\
\mathsf{FV}(\alpha) &= \{x \in \mathcal{V} \ : \ \exists I, \nu, \omega, \tilde{\nu} \, a \ \{x\}\text{-variation of } \nu \text{ such that } (\nu, \omega) \in I[\![\alpha]\!] \\
& \qquad\qquad\quad \text{and } \forall \tilde{\omega} \{x\}\text{-variation of } \omega \text{ such that } (\tilde{\nu}, \tilde{\omega}) \notin I[\![\alpha]\!]\} \\
\mathsf{BV}(\alpha) &= \{x \in \mathcal{V} \ : \ \exists I, \nu, \omega \text{such that } (\nu, \omega) \in I[\![\alpha]\!] \text{ and } \nu(x) \neq \omega(x)\}
\end{aligned}$$

Free and bounds variables are the only information needed about the logic to ensure that the result of uniform substitution is only defined when sound. The coincidence lemmas [25] show that the truth-values of formulas only depend on their free variables and the interpretation of the symbols appearing in them (similarly for terms and hybrid programs). The set of function, predicate, and program symbols appearing in a formula, term or hybrid program is denoted $\Sigma(\cdot)$.

Lemma 1 (Coincidence for terms [25]). *The set* $\mathsf{FV}(\theta)$ *is the smallest set with the coincidence property for* θ*: If* $\nu = \tilde{\nu}$ *on* $V \supseteq \mathsf{FV}(\theta)$ *and* $I = J$ *on* $\Sigma(\theta)$*, then* $I\nu[\![\theta]\!] = J\tilde{\nu}[\![\theta]\!]$*.*

Lemma 2 (Coincidence for formulas [25]). *The set* $\mathsf{FV}(\phi)$ *is the smallest set with the coincidence property for* ϕ*: If* $\nu = \tilde{\nu}$ *on* $V \supseteq \mathsf{FV}(\phi)$ *and* $I = J$ *on* $\Sigma(\phi)$*, then* $\nu \in I[\![\phi]\!]$ *iff* $\tilde{\nu} \in J[\![\phi]\!]$*.*

Lemma 3 (Coincidence for hybrid programs [25]). *The set* $\mathsf{FV}(\alpha)$ *is the smallest set with the coincidence property for* α*: If* $\nu = \tilde{\nu}$ *on* $V \supseteq \mathsf{FV}(\alpha)$ *and* $I = J$ *on* $\Sigma(\alpha)$*, then* $(\nu, \omega) \in I[\![\alpha]\!]$ *implies* $(\tilde{\nu}, \tilde{\omega}) \in J[\![\alpha]\!]$ *for some* $\tilde{\omega}$ *with* $\omega = \tilde{\omega}$ *on* V*.*

The proof [25] requires a mutual induction on the structure of the formula and hybrid program to show that $I[\![\phi]\!] = J[\![\phi]\!]$ and $I[\![\alpha]\!] = J[\![\alpha]\!]$ which extends to the refinement case. The rest is done by induction on the set of variables S where the states ν and $\tilde{\nu}$ can differ.

Lemma 4 (Bound effect [25]**).** *The set* $\mathsf{BV}(\alpha)$ *is the smallest set with the bound effect property for* α*: If* $(\nu, \omega) \in I[\![\alpha]\!]$*, then* $\nu = \omega$ *on* $\mathsf{BV}(\alpha)^{\complement}$*.*

These sets are the smallest sets with the coincidence property, which means that all conservative extensions of these sets can also be used soundly. We define $\mathrm{FV}(\theta), \mathrm{FV}(\phi), \mathrm{FV}(\alpha)$ and $\mathrm{BV}(\alpha)$ as such overapproximations that can be computed syntactically. Computing the free variables for a formula $[\alpha]\phi$ requires the *must-bound variables* of the hybrid program α, written $\mathrm{MBV}(\alpha)$. They represent the variables that will be written in all executions of α. These sets are given in [31] and are constructed in a standard way [25], except for the new refinement operator.

Since the behavior of hybrid program α and β only depends on their respective free variables (Lemma 3), it would be tempting to define $\mathrm{FV}(\alpha \leq \beta) = \mathrm{FV}(\alpha) \cup \mathrm{FV}(\beta)$ stating that the refinement depends on the variables for which either program depends on. Somewhat surprisingly, this would be unsound for reasons that truly touch on the nature of refinement. Take the refinement formula $?true \leq x := 1$ and a state ν with $\nu(x) = 0$. Then $\nu \notin I[\![?true \leq x := 1]\!]$. However if the initial value of x is 1, then the refinement holds: $\nu_x^1 \in I[\![?true \leq x := 1]\!]$, because the assignment $x := 1$ has no effect. In fact $\mathsf{FV}(?true \leq x := 1) = \{x\}$ even though $\mathsf{FV}(?true) = \mathsf{FV}(x := 1) = \emptyset$. To obtain a sound definition of $\mathrm{FV}(\alpha \leq \beta)$, one needs to take into account the variables that may be written in one program, $\mathrm{BV}(\alpha) \cup \mathrm{BV}(\beta)$, but that can also remain unmodified (which makes them depend on their initial values), so not in $\mathrm{MBV}(\alpha) \cap \mathrm{MBV}(\beta)$. Hence, the (syntactic) free variables of a refinement are defined as follows:

$$\mathrm{FV}(\alpha \leq \beta) = \mathrm{FV}(\alpha) \cup \mathrm{FV}(\beta) \cup ((\mathrm{BV}(\alpha) \cup \mathrm{BV}(\beta)) \setminus (\mathrm{MBV}(\alpha) \cap \mathrm{MBV}(\beta)))$$

With this definition for refinements as the only but notable outlier to an otherwise standard definition of the syntatic computations for a static semantics [25], the static semantics $\mathrm{FV}(\phi)$ etc. can be proved to be sound overapproximations of the static semantics $\mathsf{FV}(\phi)$ from Definition 7 and thereby enjoy the coincidence Lemmas 1–3 and the bound effect Lemma 4, respectively.

Lemma 5 (Soundness of static semantics). *For all terms* θ*, formulas* ϕ *and hybrid programs* α*:*

$$FV(\theta) \supseteq \mathsf{FV}(\theta) \quad FV(\phi) \supseteq \mathsf{FV}(\phi) \quad FV(\alpha) \supseteq \mathsf{FV}(\alpha) \quad BV(\alpha) \supseteq \mathsf{BV}(\alpha)$$

The proof of $\mathrm{FV}(\cdot) \supseteq \mathsf{FV}(\cdot)$ for formulas and hybrid programs is the only case affected by the addition of refinement operators compared to prior proofs [25, Lem. 17]. It is proved by induction on the structure of the formulas and hybrid programs. For hybrid programs, the property shown for $\mathrm{FV}(\alpha)$ is stronger than the coincidence property from Lemma 3, enforcing $\omega = \tilde{\omega}$ on $V \cup \mathrm{MBV}(\alpha)$ rather than V.

For the case of the refinement operator $\alpha \leq \beta$, the main insight is visible when proving that $\tilde{\nu} \in J[\![\alpha \leq \beta]\!]$ implies $\nu \in I[\![\alpha \leq \beta]\!]$ with $\nu = \tilde{\nu}$ on V and $I = J$ on $\Sigma(\alpha \leq \beta)$. For any $(\nu, \omega) \in I[\![\alpha]\!]$, we have $(\tilde{\nu}, \tilde{\omega}) \in J[\![\alpha]\!]$, $(\tilde{\nu}, \tilde{\omega}) \in J[\![\beta]\!]$ and $(\nu, \mu) \in I[\![\beta]\!]$ for some states $\tilde{\omega}, \mu$ by repeated use of the induction hypothesis and the definition of refinement. Both the induction hypothesis and Lemma 4 give us information on $\tilde{\omega}$ and μ. As $V \supseteq \mathrm{FV}(\alpha \leq \beta)$, the definition of $\mathrm{FV}(\alpha \leq \beta)$ is crucial for ensuring that this knowledge is enough to fully determine $\tilde{\omega}$ and μ from ν, ω and $\tilde{\nu}$, and then that $\omega = \mu$.

4 Uniform Substitution

A *uniform substitution* σ is a mapping from terms of the form $f(\cdot)$ to terms $\sigma(f(\cdot))$, from formulas of the form $p(\cdot)$ to formulas $\sigma(p(\cdot))$, and from program constants a to hybrid programs $\sigma(a)$. The reserved 0-ary function symbol $\cdot$ marks

$$
\begin{aligned}
\sigma^U(x) &= \sigma(x) && \text{for } x \in \mathcal{V} \\
\sigma^U(f(\theta)) &= \{\cdot \mapsto \sigma^U\theta\}^{\emptyset}\sigma(f(\cdot)) && \text{if } \mathrm{FV}(\sigma(f(\cdot))) \cap U = \emptyset \\
\sigma^U(\theta + \eta) &= \sigma^U\theta + \sigma^U\eta \\
\sigma^U(\theta \cdot \eta) &= \sigma^U\theta \cdot \sigma^U\eta \\
\sigma^U((\theta)') &= (\sigma^{\mathcal{V}}\theta)' \\
\hline
\sigma^U(p(\theta)) &= \{\cdot \mapsto \sigma^U\theta\}^{\emptyset}\sigma(p(\cdot)) && \text{if } \mathrm{FV}(\sigma(p(\cdot))) \cap U = \emptyset \\
\sigma^U(\neg\phi) &= \neg\sigma^U\phi \\
\sigma^U(\phi \wedge \psi) &= \sigma^U\phi \wedge \sigma^U\psi \\
\sigma^U(\forall x\, \phi) &= \forall x\, \sigma^{U \cup \{x\}}\phi \\
\sigma^U([\alpha]\phi) &= [\sigma^U_V\alpha]\sigma^V\phi \\
\sigma^U(\alpha \leq \beta) &= \sigma^U_V\alpha \leq \sigma^U_W\beta \\
\hline
\sigma^U_{U \cup \mathrm{BV}(\sigma(a))}(a) &= \sigma(a) \\
\sigma^U_U(?\phi) &= ?\sigma^U\phi \\
\sigma^U_{U \cup \{x\}}(x := \theta) &= x := \sigma^U\theta \\
\sigma^U_{U \cup \{x\}}(x := *) &= x := * \\
\sigma^U_{U \cup \{x, x'\}}(x' = \theta \,\&\, \phi) &= x' = \sigma^{U \cup \{x, x'\}}\theta \,\&\, \sigma^{U \cup \{x, x'\}}\phi \\
\sigma^U_{V \cup W}(\alpha \cup \beta) &= \sigma^U_V\alpha \cup \sigma^U_W\beta \\
\sigma^U_W(\alpha; \beta) &= \sigma^U_V\alpha; \sigma^V_W\beta \\
\sigma^U_V(\alpha^*) &= (\sigma^V_V\alpha)^* && \text{where } \sigma^U_V\alpha \text{ is defined}
\end{aligned}
$$

Fig. 1. Recursive application of uniform substitution with input taboos $U \subseteq \mathcal{V}$

the position where the argument, e.g. θ in $p(\theta)$, will be substituted in the resulting expression. Soundness of such substitutions requires that the substitution does not introduce new free variables in a context where they are bound [10].

Figure 1 defines the result $\sigma^U\phi$ of applying a uniform substitution σ with taboo set $U \subseteq \mathcal{V}$ to a formula ϕ (or term θ, or hybrid programs α respectively) [28]. For hybrid programs α, the substitution result $\sigma^U_V\alpha$ for input taboo $U \subseteq \mathcal{V}$ also outputs a taboo set $V \subseteq \mathcal{V}$, written in subscript notation, that will be tabooed after program α. Taboos U, V are sets of variables that cannot be substituted in free during the application of the substitution, because they have been bound within the context and, thus, potentially changed their meaning compared to the original substitution σ. The difference is that the input U is already taboo when the substitution σ is applied to α while V is the new output taboo after α. Finally, $\sigma(\phi)$ is short for $\sigma^\emptyset\phi$ started without initial taboos. The key advantage to working with uniform substitution applications with taboo passing is that they enable an efficient one-pass substitution [28] compared to the classical Church-style uniform substitution application mechanism that checks admissibility at every binding operator along the way [25]. One-pass uniform substitution postpones admissibility checks till the actual substitutions of function and predicate symbols according to explicit taboos carried around.

Despite the surprising definition of the free variables of a refinement, defining uniform substitution for the refinement case is standard, the input taboo U is given to both programs except that their output taboos V, W are discarded:

$$\sigma^U(\alpha \leq \beta) = \sigma^U_V\alpha \leq \sigma^U_W\beta$$

The reason is two-fold:

1. Unlike quantifiers and modalities, refinements do not subsequently bind any variables.
2. The free variables of a refinement introduced by a substitution can only be introduced free in the programs, and thus checking these against the input taboo set U is sufficient.

This last statement is a consequence of $\mathrm{BV}(\sigma\alpha) \subseteq \mathrm{BV}(\alpha)$ and $\mathrm{MBV}(\sigma\alpha) \supseteq \mathrm{MBV}(\alpha)$, which is proved by a direct induction.

4.1 Uniform Substitutions and Adjoint Interpretations

The proof of the soundness of uniform substitution follows the same structure as the proof of the uniform substitution lemma for dGL [28] but adapted to hybrid programs instead of hybrid games and generalized to the presence of refinements. The output taboo V of a uniform substitution $\sigma^U_V\alpha$ will include the original taboo set U and all variables bound in the program α.

Lemma 6 (Taboo set computation [28]**).** *If $\sigma^U_V\alpha$ is defined, then $V \supseteq U \cup \mathsf{BV}(\sigma^U_V\alpha)$.*

Whereas uniform substitutions are syntactic transformations on expressions, their semantic counterparts are semantic transformations on interpretations. The two are related by Lemmas 7 and 8. Let $I^d_\cdot$ denote the interpretation that agrees with interpretation I except for the constant function symbol $\cdot$ which is interpreted as the constant $d \in \mathbb{R}$.

Definition 8 (Adjoint interpretation). *For an interpretation I and a state ω, the* adjoint interpretation *$\sigma^*_\omega I$ modifies the interpretation of each function symbol $f \in \sigma$, predicate symbol $p \in \sigma$ and program constant $a \in \sigma$ as follows:*

$$\sigma^*_\omega I(f) : \mathbb{R} \to \mathbb{R}; d \mapsto I^d_\cdot\omega[\![\sigma f(\cdot)]\!]$$
$$\sigma^*_\omega I(p) = \{d \in \mathbb{R} \; : \; \omega \in I^d_\cdot[\![\sigma p(\cdot)]\!]\}$$
$$\sigma^*_\omega I(a) = I[\![\sigma a]\!]$$

Lemma 7 (Uniform substitution for terms [28]). *The uniform substitution σ for taboo $U \subseteq \mathcal{V}$ and its adjoint interpretation $\sigma^*_\omega I$ for I, ω have the same semantics on U-variations ν of ω for all* terms *θ:*

$$I\nu[\![\sigma^U \theta]\!] = \sigma^*_\omega I\nu[\![\theta]\!]$$

Lemma 8 (Uniform substitution for formulas, programs). *Uniform substitution σ for taboo $U \subseteq \mathcal{V}$ and its adjoint interpretation $\sigma^*_\omega I$ for I, ω have the same semantics on U-variations ν of ω for all* formulas *ϕ and* hybrid programs *α:*

$$\text{for all } U\text{-variations } \nu \text{ of } \omega : \nu \in I[\![\sigma^U \phi]\!] \text{ iff } \nu \in \sigma^*_\omega I[\![\phi]\!]$$
$$\text{for all states } \mu \text{ and all } U\text{-variations } \nu \text{ of } \omega : (\nu, \mu) \in I[\![\sigma^U_V \alpha]\!] \text{ iff } (\nu, \mu) \in \sigma^*_\omega I[\![\alpha]\!]$$

The proof is done by simultaneous induction on the structure of σ, α and ϕ for all U, ν, ω and μ [31]. The use of U-variations is critical when the induction hypothesis needs to be used in a state other than ν, e.g. for quantifiers and modalities. Without considering the extension of the refinement operator, this result was previously proved in a weaker form ($U = \emptyset$) for dL [25] or for more complex semantics like hybrid games [28].

4.2 Soundness of Uniform Substitution

Lemma 8 is essentially all that is required to ensure the sound application of uniform substitution. First, uniform substitution can be used to have a sound instantiation of the axioms, using the uniform substitution rule (US). A proof rule is *sound* if the validity of the premises implies the validity of the conclusion.

Theorem 1 (Soundness of uniform substitution [28]). *The proof rule* (US) *is sound.*

$$(\text{US})\frac{\phi}{\sigma(\phi)}$$

Uniform substitution can also be used on rules or whole inferences, as long as they are *locally sound*, i.e. the conclusion is valid in any interpretation where the premises are valid. Locally sound inferences are also sound.

Theorem 2 (Soundness of uniform substitution for rules [28]**).** *All locally sound inferences remain locally sound when substituted with a uniform substitution σ with taboo set $\mathcal{V}$.*

$$\frac{\phi_1 \quad \dots \quad \phi_n}{\psi} \text{ locally sound implies } \frac{\sigma^{\mathcal{V}}\phi_1 \quad \dots \quad \sigma^{\mathcal{V}}\phi_n}{\sigma^{\mathcal{V}}\psi} \text{ locally sound.}$$

5 Proof Calculus

Most notably, uniform substitution makes it possible to use concrete dRL formulas as axioms instead of axiom schemata that accept infinitely many formulas as axioms. Axioms are finite syntactic objects, and are thus easy to implement, while axiom schemata are ultimately algorithms accepting certain formulas as input while rejecting others [25]. Figure 2 lists the axioms of dRL. dRL also satisfies the axioms of KAT [17], Schematic KAT [4] and the axioms of dL [31]. Some axioms use the reverse implication $\phi \leftarrow \psi$ instead of $\psi \rightarrow \phi$ for emphasis.

In the axiom ([≤]), $\bar{x}$ stands for the (finite) vector of all relevant variables (alternative treatments [25,28] of $p(\bar{x})$ use quantifier symbols or additional program constants instead, but are not necessary for this paper). This characteristic axiom of dRL expresses that if formula $p(\bar{x})$ holds after all runs of hybrid program b, then it also holds after any refinement a. Thus, as long as a proof of the refinement is given, it is possible to replace hybrid programs inside modalities. In general, axioms are meant to be applied to the axiom key (marked blue).

Refinement is transitive ($\leq_t$), allowing the introduction of intermediate refinements c similar to the role that cuts play in first-order logic.

Axioms ($\cup_l$) and ($\cup_r$) decompose the choice operator using logical connectives. As the choice $a \cup b$ can behave like either subprograms, whenever it refines a program c, both a and b must refine c. Axiom ($\cup_r$) is not an equivalence though. $a \leq b \vee a \leq c$ says that for each initial state, one of the two refinement holds. However, when a is nondeterministic, and so can have multiple end states for one initial state, it may not be the case despite the left-hand side being true.

Axiom (;) helps proving a refinement between two sequences of programs ($a; b \leq c; d$) by proving the refinement of the first programs ($a \leq c$) and the refinement of the second programs, but only after all executions of a ($[a]b \leq d$). Axioms ($?_{\text{det}}$) and ($:=_{\text{det}}$) are particular cases of the axiom (;) where the implication can be strengthened to an equivalence. As such, the implication from right to left is not required for both axioms [31].

Axioms (loop_l), (loop_r) and (unloop) are used to prove refinements of loops. The first two state that if adding a program before or after only leads to less executions, then adding an unbounded number of executions, i.e. a loop, will also lead to less executions. The axiom (unloop) is useful for comparing two loops, as it allows to reduce the problem to comparing the loop bodies. Both axioms (loop_l) and (unloop) need a box modality when proving the refinement of the

$$(\leq_t)\ a \leq b \leftarrow a \leq c \wedge c \leq b$$

$$(\cup_l)\ a \cup b \leq c \leftrightarrow a \leq c \wedge b \leq c$$

$$(=)\ a = b \leftrightarrow a \leq b \wedge b \leq a$$

$$(\cup_r)\ a \leq b \cup c \leftarrow a \leq b \vee a \leq c$$

$$([\leq])\ a \leq b \rightarrow ([a]p(\bar{x}) \leftarrow [b]p(\bar{x}))$$

$$(;)\ a; b \leq c; d \leftarrow a \leq c \wedge [a]b \leq d$$

$$(?)\ (?p \leq ?q) \leftrightarrow (p \rightarrow q)$$

$$(\text{loop}_l)\ a^*; b \leq b \leftarrow [a^*]a; b \leq b$$

$$(:=)\ x := f \ = \ x := *; ?x = f$$

$$(\text{loop}_r)\ a; b^* \leq a \leftarrow a; b \leq a$$

$$(?_{\text{det}})\ ?p; a \leq ?p; b \leftrightarrow [?p]a \leq b$$

$$(\text{unloop})\ a^* \leq b^* \leftarrow [a^*](a \leq b)$$

$$(\text{stutter})\ x := x \ = \ ?true$$

$$(:=_{\text{det}})\ x := f; a \leq x := f; b \leftrightarrow [x := f]a \leq b$$

$$(:*_{\text{merge}})\ x := *; ?p(x); x := * \ = \ x := *; ?\exists y\, p(y)$$

$$(:=*_{\text{merge}})\ x := *; ?p(x); x := f(x) \ = \ x := *; ?\exists y\, (p(y) \wedge x = f(y))$$

$$(\text{ODE})\ x' = f(x)\,\&\,p(x) \leq x' = g(x)\,\&\,q(x) \leftrightarrow [x' = f(x)\,\&\,p(x)](x' = g(x) \wedge q(x))$$

$$(\text{DW}_=)\ x' = f(x)\,\&\,p(x) \ = \ ?p(x); x' = f(x)\,\&\,p(x); ?p(x)$$

$$(\text{DE}_=)\ x' = f(x)\,\&\,p(x) \ = \ x' = f(x)\,\&\,p(x); x' := f(x)$$

$$(\text{DX})\ x' := f(x); ?p(x) \ \leq \ x' = f(x)\,\&\,p(x)$$

$$(\text{ODE}_{\text{idemp}})\ x' = f(x)\,\&\,p(x); x' = f(x)\,\&\,p(x) \ = \ x' = f(x)\,\&\,p(x)$$

Fig. 2. Axioms of dRL

loop body, as the refinement must be proved after any number of iterations of a.

The axiom (ODE) describes how to prove refinements between differential equations. A refinement $x' = f(x)\,\&\,p(x) \leq x' = g(x)\,\&\,q(x)$ is true iff throughout the execution of the former ODE, it always satisfies the latter differential equation and evolution domain. Along with the axioms ($\text{DW}_=$) and ($\text{DE}_=$), these axioms subsume differential cut (DC), differential weakening (DW) and differential effect (DE) from dL [31]. The equivalence in the axiom (ODE) effectively means that refinements of differential equations can *always* be reduced to standard dL formulas, which is essential to our decidability result.

The axiom (DX) states that a differential equation always has a solution for the interval $[0, 0]$. In that case, the execution succeeds only if the domain holds, and the correct value $f(x)$ is assigned to the differential variable x'. The axiom ($\text{ODE}_{\text{idemp}}$) states that following the same differential equation twice in a row is equivalent to following it only once, because the concatenation of solutions of the same differential equation is still a solution of the same differential equation.

Compared to the original sequent calculus for dRL [19], the proof rule schemata matching infinitely many instances are now replaced by a *finite* number of axioms that are concrete dRL formulas rather than standing for infinitely many instances. The infinitely many possible instances can then be recovered soundly using the uniform substitution rule (US). Because of this two-step mechanism, reasoning with the axioms can be done without considering the possible instantiations. Take for instance the sound equivalence $x := f; x := * = x := *$. The proof can be done by transitivity ($\leq_t$) with $x := *; ?x = f; x := *$ as intermediate step [31]. But the same proof cannot be done by replacing f by any term θ: the intermediate program is not always equivalent to the other two (e.g. for $\theta = x + 1$). On the other hand, by proving the equivalence for f and then using rule (US), the equivalence can be proved for all terms θ.

The dRL axioms are also more modular than its cast-in-stone sequent calculus rules. For instance, with rule (G) and axiom (K), any implication $\phi \rightarrow \psi$, e.g. ($\cup_r$), can be used to prove $[a]\phi \rightarrow [a]\psi$. This would not fit the shape of the corresponding sequent rule, which requires ψ at the top level. The lack of differential symbols in the original sequent calculus [19] changes the soundness of some rules: the match direction field rule (MDF) would allow rescaling the right-hand side of a differential equation, which is unsound here as it would change the resulting differential symbols. Conversely, only the reverse implication of the axiom (ODE) would be sound in the original calculus, again for lack of differential symbols. The dRL axioms are proved sound [31]:

Theorem 3 (Soundness of dRL axioms). *All axioms of dRL are sound.*

6 Decidability of Refinement for a Fragment of dRL

This section identifies a subset of hybrid programs for which the refinement problem is decidable. It is focused on concrete programs, i.e. programs without function symbols, predicate symbols or program constants. They have the following high-level structure: $(ctrl; plant)^*$ where a discrete, loop-free program $ctrl$, modelling a controller that sets some parameters $\bar{u}$, then a continuous program $plant$ that describes the dynamics of the variables $\bar{y}$ according to the choice of the parameters $\bar{u}$. These steps are then repeated nondeterministically. The continuous variables $\bar{y}$ (and by extension $\bar{y}'$) are expected to be distinct from the discrete variables $\bar{u}$ and also contain a global clock t which follows the differential equation $t' = 1$. The presence of the clock t is not needed for comparing the differential equations, but to distinguish between discrete executions and hybrid executions.

For two such programs, $(ctrl_a; plant_a)^*$ and $(ctrl_b; plant_b)^*$, a canonical proof of the refinement has the following shape (omitting uses of MP for brevity):

$$\text{unloop}\,\dfrac{\text{G}\,\dfrac{;\,\dfrac{\dfrac{\cdots}{ctrl_a \leq ctrl_b} \quad \dfrac{\cdots}{[ctrl_a](plant_a \leq plant_b)}}{ctrl_a; plant_a \leq ctrl_b; plant_b}}{[(ctrl_a; plant_a)^*](ctrl_a; plant_a \leq ctrl_b; plant_b)}}{(ctrl_a; plant_a)^* \leq (ctrl_b; plant_b)^*}$$

This means that proving the refinement of the whole programs is reduced to proving the refinement of the controllers, $ctrl_a \leq ctrl_b$ and the refinement of the plants after all $ctrl_a$ executions, $[ctrl_a](plant_a \leq plant_b)$. With our restrictions on the controllers, the first refinement is always decidable.

Lemma 9. *For concrete, discrete and loop-free controllers $ctrl_a$ and $ctrl_b$, the validity of $ctrl_a \leq ctrl_b$ is decidable by dRL proof.*

Given a controller $ctrl_a$, it is possible to synthesize a first-order formula $\phi_a(x, x^+)$ that characterizes the behavior of $ctrl_a$, where x (resp. x^+) corresponds to the variables after (resp. before) the controller [21]. Using the dRL axioms, $ctrl_a \leq ctrl_b$ is provable from $\phi_a(x, x^+) \rightarrow \phi_b(x, x^+)$. The validity of the latter is decidable as it is first-order real arithmetic [33]. The full proof is in [31].

The second refinement, $[ctrl_a](plant_a \leq plant_b)$, is more complex. Let us write the two plants as $plant_a \equiv \bar{y}' = p(\bar{y}, \bar{u}) \,\&\, Q$ and $plant_b \equiv \bar{y}' = q(\bar{y}, \bar{u}) \,\&\, R$ for some polynomials $p(\bar{y}, \bar{u}), q(\bar{y}, \bar{u})$ and formulas Q, R. The axiom ODE entails that we must prove $[ctrl_a][plant_a](p(\bar{y}, \bar{u}) = q(\bar{y}, \bar{u}) \wedge R)$, which no longer contains any refinement. For the decidability result (Theorem 4) to hold, we require that the validity of this formula is decidable.

There are two cases which always ensure this. First, if the differential equation $plant_a$ admits a solution expressible in dRL (e.g. a polynomial), then using standard dL reasoning, the formula can be reduced to a first-order formula and thus its validity can be decided. The differential equation from Example 1, $x' = v, v' = a$, is such a case.

The second case is when domain R is algebraic, i.e. of the form $\bigwedge_i \bigvee_j p_{ij}(x) = 0$ for some polynomial p_{ij} and Q, the domain of $plant_a$, is a semialgebraic set [30].

The remaining question is now to show that the approach presented above is complete, meaning it always succeeds when the refinement holds. The only additional constraint we require is that the controller $ctrl_b$ is idempotent.

Definition 9. (Idempotent controller). *A controller $ctrl$ is* idempotent *if it satisfies $ctrl; ctrl = ctrl$.*

An idempotent controller cannot reach more states by executing multiple times without any continuous dynamics happening. Pure reactive controllers, i.e. controllers for which the parameters' values only depend on the values of the continuous variables, are always idempotent. This is the case for the controllers in Example 1: $x := -B \cup ?\text{safe}_T(x); x := A$. On the other hand, counting the number of times the controller has been executed would not be idempotent.

Lemma 10. *This derived rule is invertible, if $ctrl_b$ is idempotent.*

$$\frac{ctrl_a; plant_a \leq ctrl_b; plant_b}{(ctrl_a; plant_a)^* \leq (ctrl_b; plant_b)^*}$$

The derivation of the rule is given in the canonical proof. The converse, that the conclusion implies the premise, is more involved [31]. Proving $ctrl_a; plant_a \leq (ctrl_b; plant_b)^*$ from $(ctrl_a; plant_a)^* \leq (ctrl_b; plant_b)^*$ is done by unfolding the loop on the left. To get rid of the loop on the right, we use the fact that $ctrl_b$

is idempotent. It means that if the global time is not modified, then we can assume without loss of generality that the controller (and thus also the plant) is executed only once. The case when the global time is modified additionally considers the value of the derivative to ensure that there is an execution of the right program that does not require looping.

With the above lemma, we can now state the decidability result.

Theorem 4 (Decidability of refinement for idempotent controllers). *For concrete hybrid programs* $ctrl_a; plant_a$ *and* $ctrl_b; plant_b$ *discrete loop-free* $ctrl_a, ctrl_b$ *and with* $plant_a \equiv \bar{y}' = p(\bar{y}, \bar{u})\,\&\,Q$ *and* $plant_b \equiv \bar{y}' = q(\bar{y}, \bar{u})\,\&\,R$, *if* $ctrl_b$ *is idempotent, and the validity of* $[ctrl_a][plant_a](p(\bar{y}, \bar{u}) = q(\bar{y}, \bar{u}) \wedge R)$ *is decidable, then the validity of* $(ctrl_a; plant_a)^* \leq (ctrl_b; plant_b)^*$ *is also decidable.*

In particular, the theorem applies to the event-triggered model and the time-triggered model templates used to show how to prove that the latter refines the former [19]. Indeed, their controller template is loop-free and idempotent and the differential equation are assumed to be solvable. Theorem 4 strengthens their result by showing the completeness of the approach.

7 Conclusion

This paper introduced a uniform substitution proof calculus for differential refinement logic dRL. This yields a parsimonious prover microkernel for hybrid systems verification that simultaneously works for properties of and relations between hybrid systems. The handling of refinement relations between hybrid systems is subtle even only in its static semantics, which makes the correctness proofs of this paper particularly interesting. The uniform substitution is one-pass [28] giving it respectable performance advantages compared to Church-style uniform substitutions. While the joint presence of differential equations reasoning and refinement reasoning causes challenges, a resulting benefit besides soundness is that a finer notion of differential equation refinement is obtained with logical decidability properties on a fragment of hybrid systems refinements.

Future work involves improving the implementation of the uniform substitution calculus in KeYmaera X. Although the prover microkernel was straightforward following the uniform substitution process and list of dRL's uniform substitution axioms, the prover would benefit from quality of life features, e.g. using the axioms to rewrite on subprograms, and an implementation of the refinement decision algorithm for the decidable fragment. Another axis of research is to combine refinements with hybrid games, with a proper semantics and adapt the new axioms of dRL to games, some of which would not be sound as is.

A Additional dRL Axioms

Axioms of dL also include the differential axioms, e.g. $(x)' = x'$ [25], to reason on terms, which are omitted as it is not the main focus of this paper. Axioms preceded by a star can be derived from other axioms [31].

$$([?])\ [?q]p \leftrightarrow (q \to p)$$

$$([:=])\ [x := f]p(x) \leftrightarrow p(f)$$

$$([:*])\ [x := *]p(x) \leftrightarrow \forall x\, p(x)$$

$$([\cup])\ [a \cup b]p(\bar{x}) \leftrightarrow [a]p(\bar{x}) \wedge [b]p(\bar{x})$$

$$*([^*])\ [a^*]p(\bar{x}) \leftrightarrow p(\bar{x}) \wedge [a][a^*]p(\bar{x})$$

$$(\mathrm{K})\ [a](p(\bar{x}) \to q(\bar{x})) \to ([a]p(\bar{x}) \to [a]q(\bar{x}))$$

$$(\mathrm{I})\ [a^*]p(\bar{x}) \leftrightarrow p(\bar{x}) \wedge [a^*](p(\bar{x}) \to [a]p(\bar{x}))$$

$$([;])\ [a;b]p(\bar{x}) \leftrightarrow [a][b]p(\bar{x})$$

$$(\mathrm{V})\ p \to [a]p$$

$$(\mathrm{G})\ \frac{p(\bar{x})}{[a]p(\bar{x})}$$

$$(\forall)\ \frac{p(x)}{\forall x\, p(x)}$$

$$(\mathrm{MP})\ \frac{p \to q \quad p}{q}$$

$$*(\mathrm{DE})\ [x' = f(x)\,\&\,q(x)]p(\bar{x}) \leftrightarrow [x' = f(x)\,\&\,q(x)][x' := f(x)]p(\bar{x})$$

$$*(\mathrm{DW})\ [x' = f(x)\,\&\,q(x)]p(x) \leftrightarrow [x' = f(x)\,\&\,q(x)](q(x) \to p(x))$$

$$(\mathrm{DI})\ \big([x' = f(x)\,\&\,q(x)]p(x) \leftrightarrow [?q(x)]p(x)\big) \leftarrow (q(x) \to [x' = f(x)\,\&\,q(x)](p(x))')$$

$$*(\mathrm{DC})\ \big([x' = f(x)\,\&\,q(x)]p(x) \leftrightarrow [x' = f(x)\,\&\,q(x) \wedge r(x)]p(x)\big) \leftarrow [x' = f(x)\,\&\,q(x)]r(x)$$

$$(\mathrm{DG})\ [x' = f(x)\,\&\,q(x)]p(x) \leftrightarrow \exists y\, [x' = f(x), y' = a(x) \cdot y + b(x)\,\&\,q(x)]p(x)$$

$$(\mathrm{DS})\ [x' = f\,\&\,q(x)]p(x) \leftrightarrow \forall t{\geq}0\, \big((\forall 0{\leq}s{\leq}t\, q(x + fs)) \to [x := x + ft]p(x)\big)$$

(a) Axioms of dL

$$(\leq_{\mathrm{refl}})\ a \leq a$$

$$(;_{\mathrm{id\text{-}l}})\ ?true; a = a$$

$$(\mathrm{dist\text{-}l})\ (a;b) \cup (a;c) = a;(b \cup c)$$

$$(\mathrm{annih\text{-}l})\ ?false; a = ?false$$

$$(\mathrm{unfold\text{-}l})\ ?true \cup (a;a^*) = a^*$$

$$(\cup_{\mathrm{id}})\ a \cup ?false = a$$

$$(;_{\mathrm{assoc}})\ a;(b;c) = (a;b);c$$

$$(;_{\mathrm{id\text{-}r}})\ a; ?true = a$$

$$(\mathrm{annih\text{-}r})\ a; ?false = ?false$$

$$(\mathrm{unfold\text{-}r})\ ?true \cup (a^*;a) = a^*$$

(b) Axioms of KAT

$$(:*_{\mathrm{comm}})\ x := *; y := * = y := *; x := *$$

$$(:*_{\mathrm{test}})\ x := *; ?p = ?p; x := *$$

(c) Axioms of SKAT with nondeterministic assignment

Fig. 3. Additional axioms of dRL

References

1. Abrial, J.: Modeling in Event-B - System and Software Engineering. Cambridge University Press, Cambridge (2010). https://doi.org/10.1017/CBO9781139195881
2. Abrial, J.-R., Su, W., Zhu, H.: Formalizing hybrid systems with Event-B. In: Derrick, J., et al. (eds.) ABZ 2012. LNCS, vol. 7316, pp. 178–193. Springer, Heidelberg (2012). https://doi.org/10.1007/978-3-642-30885-7_13
3. Afendi, M., Laleau, R., Mammar, A.: Modelling hybrid programs with Event-B. In: Raschke, A., Méry, D., Houdek, F. (eds.) ABZ 2020. LNCS, vol. 12071, pp. 139–154. Springer, Cham (2020). https://doi.org/10.1007/978-3-030-48077-6_10

4. Angus, A., Kozen, D.: Kleene algebra with tests and program schematology. Technical report TR2001-1844, Cornell University, USA (2001). https://ecommons.cornell.edu/items/b376f0d0-ca43-4896-b8b3-4c8a31e24ab1
5. Banach, R., Butler, M.J., Qin, S., Verma, N., Zhu, H.: Core hybrid Event-B I: single hybrid Event-B machines. Sci. Comput. Program. **105**, 92–123 (2015). https://doi.org/10.1016/J.SCICO.2015.02.003
6. Banach, R., Zhu, H., Su, W., Huang, R.: Continuous KAOS, ASM, and formal control system design across the continuous/discrete modeling interface: a simple train stopping application. Formal Aspects Comput. **26**(2), 319–366 (2014). https://doi.org/10.1007/S00165-012-0263-2
7. Brieger, M., Mitsch, S., Platzer, A.: Uniform substitution for dynamic logic with communicating hybrid programs. In: Pientka, B., Tinelli, C. (eds.) CADE 2023. LNCS, vol. 14132, pp. 96–115. Springer, Cham (2023). https://doi.org/10.1007/978-3-031-38499-8_6
8. Butler, M.J., Abrial, J., Banach, R.: Modelling and refining hybrid systems in Event-B and Rodin. In: Petre, L., Sekerinski, E. (eds.) From Action Systems to Distributed Systems - The Refinement Approach, pp. 29–42. Chapman and Hall/CRC (2016). https://doi.org/10.1201/B20053-5
9. Butler, M., Maamria, I.: Practical theory extension in Event-B. In: Liu, Z., Woodcock, J., Zhu, H. (eds.) Theories of Programming and Formal Methods. LNCS, vol. 8051, pp. 67–81. Springer, Heidelberg (2013). https://doi.org/10.1007/978-3-642-39698-4_5
10. Church, A.: Introduction to Mathematical Logic. Princeton University Press, Princeton (1956)
11. Doumane, A., Kuperberg, D., Pous, D., Pradic, P.: Kleene algebra with hypotheses. In: Bojańczyk, M., Simpson, A. (eds.) FoSSaCS 2019. LNCS, vol. 11425, pp. 207–223. Springer, Cham (2019). https://doi.org/10.1007/978-3-030-17127-8_12
12. Dupont, G.: Correct-by-Construction Design of Hybrid Systems Based on Refinement and Proof. (Conception correcte par construction de systèmes hybrides basée sur le raffinement et la preuve). Ph.D. thesis, National Polytechnic Institute of Toulouse, France (2021). https://tel.archives-ouvertes.fr/tel-04165215
13. Felty, A., Middeldorp, A. (eds.): Automated Deduction, CADE-25. LNCS, vol. 9195. Springer, Cham (2015). https://doi.org/10.1007/978-3-319-21401-6
14. Fulton, N., Mitsch, S., Quesel, J.D., Völp, M., Platzer, A.: KeYmaera X: an axiomatic tactical theorem prover for hybrid systems. In: Felty and Middeldorp [13], pp. 527–538. https://doi.org/10.1007/978-3-319-21401-6_36
15. Jeannin, J., et al.: A formally verified hybrid system for safe advisories in the next-generation airborne collision avoidance system. STTT **19**(6), 717–741 (2017). https://doi.org/10.1007/s10009-016-0434-1
16. Kabra, A., Mitsch, S., Platzer, A.: Verified train controllers for the Federal Railroad Administration train kinematics model: balancing competing brake and track forces. IEEE Trans. Comput. Aided Des. Integr. Circuits Syst. **41**(11), 4409–4420 (2022). https://doi.org/10.1109/TCAD.2022.3197690
17. Kozen, D.: Kleene algebra with tests. ACM Trans. Program. Lang. Syst. **19**(3), 427–443 (1997). https://doi.org/10.1145/256167.256195
18. Loos, S.M.: Differential refinement logic. Ph.D. thesis, Computer Science Department, School of Computer Science, Carnegie Mellon University (2016). http://reports-archive.adm.cs.cmu.edu/anon/2015/CMU-CS-15-144.pdf
19. Loos, S.M., Platzer, A.: Differential refinement logic. In: Grohe, M., Koskinen, E., Shankar, N. (eds.) LICS, pp. 505–514. ACM, New York (2016). https://doi.org/10.1145/2933575.2934555

20. Mitsch, S., Ghorbal, K., Vogelbacher, D., Platzer, A.: Formal verification of obstacle avoidance and navigation of ground robots. I. J. Robot. Res. **36**(12), 1312–1340 (2017). https://doi.org/10.1177/0278364917733549
21. Mitsch, S., Platzer, A.: ModelPlex: verified runtime validation of verified cyber-physical system models. Form. Methods Syst. Des. **49**(1-2), 33–74 (2016). https://doi.org/10.1007/s10703-016-0241-z. Special issue of selected papers from RV'14
22. Pereira, A., Baumann, M., Gerstner, J., Althoff, M.: Improving efficiency of human-robot coexistence while guaranteeing safety: theory and user study. IEEE Trans. Autom. Sci. Eng. **20**(4), 2706–2719 (2023)
23. Platzer, A.: Differential dynamic logic for hybrid systems. J. Autom. Reas. **41**(2), 143–189 (2008). https://doi.org/10.1007/s10817-008-9103-8
24. Platzer, A.: A uniform substitution calculus for differential dynamic logic. In: Felty and Middeldorp [13], pp. 467–481. https://doi.org/10.1007/978-3-319-21401-6_32
25. Platzer, A.: A complete uniform substitution calculus for differential dynamic logic. J. Autom. Reas. **59**(2), 219–265 (2017). https://doi.org/10.1007/s10817-016-9385-1
26. Platzer, A.: Logical Foundations of Cyber-Physical Systems. Springer, Cham (2018). https://doi.org/10.1007/978-3-319-63588-0
27. Platzer, A.: Uniform substitution for differential game logic. In: Galmiche, D., Schulz, S., Sebastiani, R. (eds.) IJCAR 2018. LNCS (LNAI), vol. 10900, pp. 211–227. Springer, Cham (2018). https://doi.org/10.1007/978-3-319-94205-6_15
28. Platzer, A.: Uniform substitution at one fell swoop. In: Fontaine, P. (ed.) CADE 2019. LNCS (LNAI), vol. 11716, pp. 425–441. Springer, Cham (2019). https://doi.org/10.1007/978-3-030-29436-6_25
29. Platzer, A., Tan, Y.K.: Differential equation axiomatization: the impressive power of differential ghosts. In: Dawar, A., Grädel, E. (eds.) LICS, pp. 819–828. ACM, New York (2018). https://doi.org/10.1145/3209108.3209147
30. Platzer, A., Tan, Y.K.: Differential equation invariance axiomatization. J. ACM **67**(1), 6:1–6:66 (2020). https://doi.org/10.1145/3380825
31. Prebet, E., Platzer, A.: Uniform substitution for differential refinement logic (2024). https://doi.org/10.48550/arXiv.2404.16734
32. Stauner, T., Müller, O., Fuchs, M.: Using HyTech to verify an automotive control system. In: Maler, O. (ed.) HART 1997. LNCS, vol. 1201, pp. 139–153. Springer, Heidelberg (1997). https://doi.org/10.1007/BFb0014722
33. Tarski, A., McKinsey, J.C.C.: A Decision Method for Elementary Algebra and Geometry. University of California Press, Berkeley (1951). https://doi.org/10.1525/9780520348097

Sequent Systems on Undirected Graphs

Matteo Acclavio(✉)

University of Sussex, Brighton, UK
m.acclavio@sussex.ac.uk

Abstract. In this paper we explore the design of sequent calculi operating on graphs. For this purpose, we introduce logical connectives allowing us to extend the well-known correspondence between classical propositional formulas and cographs. We define sequent systems operating on formulas containing such connectives, and we prove, using an analyticity argument based on cut-elimination, that our systems provide conservative extensions of multiplicative linear logic (without and with mix) and classical propositional logic. We conclude by showing that one of our systems captures graph isomorphism as logical equivalence and that it is sound and complete for the graphical logic GS.

Keywords: Sequent Calculus · Graph Modular Decomposition · Analyticity

1 Introduction

In theoretical computer science, *formulas* play a crucial role in describing complex abstract objects. At the syntactical level, the formulas of a logic describe complex structures by means of unary and binary operators, usually thought of as *connectives* and *modalities* respectively. On the other hand, graph-based syntaxes are often favored in formal representation, as they provide an intuitive and canonical description of properties, relations and systems. By means of example, consider the two graphs below:

$$a \longleftarrow b \longrightarrow c \longleftarrow d \qquad \text{or} \qquad a \longrightarrow b \longrightarrow c \longrightarrow d$$

It follows from results in [21,62] that describing any of the above graphs by means of formulas only employing binary connectives would require repeating at least one vertex. As a consequence, formulas describing complex graphs are usually long and convoluted, and specific *encodings* are needed to standardize such formulas.

Since graphs are ubiquitous in theoretical computer science and its applications, a natural question to ask is whether it is possible to define formalisms having graphs, instead of formulas, as first-class terms of the syntax. Such a paradigm shift would allow the design of efficient automated tools, reducing the need to handle the bureaucracy introduced in order to deal with the encoding required to represent graphs. At the same time, a graphical syntax would provide a useful tool for investigations such as the ones in [36] or [25,27], where the authors restrain their framework to sequential-parallel orders, as these can be represented by means of formulas with at most binary connectives.

Two recent lines of work have generalized proof theoretical methodologies to graphs, extending the correspondence between classical propositional formulas and

C. Benzmüller et al. (Eds.): IJCAR 2024, LNAI 14740, pp. 216–236, 2024.
https://doi.org/10.1007/978-3-031-63501-4_12

cographs. In these works, systems operating on graphs are defined via local and context-free rewriting rules, similar to the approach in *deep inference* systems [8,33,34]. The first line of research, carried out by Calk, Das, Rice and Waring in various works, explores the use of maximal stable sets/cliques-preserving homomorphisms to define notions of entailment[1], and study the resulting proof theory [16,17,23,24,63]. Here, the use of a deep inference formalism is natural, since the rules of the calculus are local rewritings. The second line of research, investigated by the author, Horne, Mauw and Straßburger in several contributions [3–5], studies the (sub-)structural proof theory of arbitrary graphs, with an approach inspired by linear logic [29] and deep inference [33]. The main goal of this line of research, partially achieved with the system $\mathsf{GV}^{\mathsf{sl}}$ operating on mixed graphs [3], is to obtain a generalization of the completeness result of the logic BV with respect to pomset inclusion. The logic BV contains a non-commutative binary connective $\lhd$ allowing to represent series-parallel partial order multisets as formulas in the syntax (as in Retoré's Pomset logic [57]), and to capture order inclusion as logical implication. However, as shown in [60], no cut-free sequent system for BV can exist – therefore neither for Pomset logic, which strictly contains it [53,54]. For this reason, the aforementioned line of work focused on deep inference systems, and the question about the existence of a cut-free sequent calculus for GS (the restriction of $\mathsf{GV}^{\mathsf{sl}}$ on undirected graphs originally defined in [4]) was left open.

In this paper, we focus on the definition of sequent calculi for *graphical logics*, and we positively answer the above question by providing, among other results, a cut-free sound and complete sequent calculus for GS. By using standard techniques in sequent calculus, we thus obtain a proof of analyticity for this logic which is simpler and more concise with respect to the one in [5].

To achieve these results, we introduce *graphical connectives*, which are operators that can be naturally interpreted as graphs. We then define the sequent calculi MGL, MGL° and KGL, containing rules to handle these connectives. After showing that cut-elimination holds for these systems, we prove that MGL, MGL° and KGL define conservative extensions of *multiplicative linear logic*, *multiplicative linear logic with mix* and *classical propositional logic* respectively. We then prove that formulas interpreted as the same graph are logically equivalent, thus justifying the fact that we consider these systems as operating on graphs rather than formulas. We conclude by showing that MGL° is sound and complete with respect to the logic GS, thus providing a simple sequent calculus for the logic.

The paper is structured as follows. In Sect. 2 we show how to use the notion of *modular decomposition* for graphs from [28,41] to define graphical connectives. In this way, we extend to general graphs the well-known correspondence between classical propositional formulas and *cographs* [21,28,41]. Then, in Sect. 3, we introduce the proof systems MGL, MGL° and KGL, and we prove their cut-elimination and analyticity. This section also discusses the conservativity results. In Sect. 4 we show that formulas representing isomorphic graphs are logically equivalent in these logics. Finally, in Sect. 5 we prove that MGL° is sound and complete with respect to the graphical logic GS. We conclude with Sect. 6, by discussing future research directions and applications. Due to space limitations, details of certain proofs have been omitted from this manuscript However, detailed proofs can be found in [2].

---

[1] A similar approach was proposed in [56] for studying pomsets.

2 From Graphs to Formulas

In this section we first recall standard results from the literature on graphs, the notion of *modular decomposition* and the one of *cographs*, which are graphs whose modular decomposition only contains two prime graphs which can be naturally interpreted as (binary) conjunction and disjunction. We then introduce the notion of *graphical connectives*, allowing us to extend the correspondence between cographs and propositional formulas to general graphs, allowing us to represent graphs via formulas constructed using graphical connectives.

2.1 Graphs and Modules

In this work are interested in using *(labeled) graphs* to represent patterns of interactions by means of the binary relations (edges) between their components (vertices). We recall the standard notion of identity on labeled graphs (i.e., *isomorphism*) and define the rougher notion of *similarity* (isomorphism up-to vertex labels).

Definition 1. *A* ***$\mathcal{L}$-labeled graph*** *(or simply* ***graph****)* $G = \langle V_G, \ell_G, \overset{G}{\frown}\rangle$ *is given by a finite set of* ***vertices*** V_G*, a partial* ***labeling function*** $\ell_G\colon V_G \to \mathcal{L}$ *associating a label* $\ell(v)$ *from a given set of labels* $\mathcal{L}$ *to each vertex* $v \in V_G$ *(we may represent* ℓ_G *as a set of equations of the form* $\ell(v) = \ell_v$ *and denote by* $\varnothing$ *the empty function), and a non-reflexive symmetric edge relation* $\overset{G}{\frown} \subset V_G \times V_G$ *whose elements, called* ***edges****, may be denoted* vw *instead of* (v, w)*. The* ***empty*** *graph* $\langle\varnothing, \varnothing, \varnothing\rangle$ *is denoted* $\varnothing$ *and we define the edge relation* $\overset{G}{\not\frown} := \left\{(v, w) \mid v \neq w \text{ and } vw \notin \overset{G}{\frown}\right\}$.

A ***similarity*** *between two graphs* G *and* G' *is a bijection* $f\colon V_G \to V_{G'}$ *such that* $x \overset{G}{\frown} y$ *iff* $f(x) \overset{G'}{\frown} f(y)$ *for any* $x, y \in V_G$*. A* ***symmetry*** *is a similarity of a graph with itself. An* ***isomorphism*** *is a similarity* f *such that* $\ell(v) = \ell(f(v))$ *for any* $v \in V_G$*. Two graphs* G *and* G' *are* ***similar*** *(denoted* $G \sim G'$*) if there is a similarity between* G *and* G'*. They are* ***isomorphic*** *(denoted* $G = G'$*) if there is an isomorphism between* G *and* G'*. From now on, we consider two isomorphic graphs to be* ***the same*** *graph.*

Two vertices v *and* w *in* G *are* ***connected*** *if there is a sequence* $v = u_0, \ldots, u_n = w$ *of vertices in* G *(called* ***path****) such that* $u_{i-1} \overset{G}{\frown} u_i$ *for all* $i \in \{1, \ldots, n\}$*. A* ***connected component*** *of* G *is a maximal set of connected vertices in* G*. A graph* G *is a* ***clique*** *(resp. a* ***stable set****) iff* $\overset{G}{\not\frown} = \varnothing$ *(resp.* $\overset{G}{\frown} = \varnothing$*).*

Note 1. When drawing a graph or an unlabeled graph we draw v—w whenever $v \frown w$, we draw no edge at all whenever $v \not\frown w$. We may represent a vertex by using its label instead of its name. For example, the single-vertex graph $G = \langle\{v\}, \ell_G, \varnothing\rangle$ may be represented either by the vertex (name) v or by the vertex label $\ell_G(v)$ (in this case we may write $\bullet$ if $\ell_G(v)$ is not defined).

Example 1. Consider the following graphs:

$$\begin{array}{l}
F = \langle \{u_1, u_2, u_3, u_4\}, \{\ell(u_1) = a, \ell(u_2) = b, \ell(u_3) = c, \ell(u_4) = d\}, \{u_1u_2, u_2u_3, u_3u_4\} \rangle \\
G = \langle \{v_1, v_2, v_3, v_4\}, \{\ell(v_1) = b, \ell(v_2) = a, \ell(v_3) = c, \ell(v_4) = d\}, \{v_1v_2, v_1v_3, v_3v_4\} \rangle \\
H = \langle \{w_1, w_2, w_3, w_4\}, \{\ell(w_1) = a, \ell(w_2) = b, \ell(w_3) = c, \ell(w_4) = d\}, \{w_1w_2, w_1w_3, w_3w_4\} \rangle
\end{array} \tag{1}$$

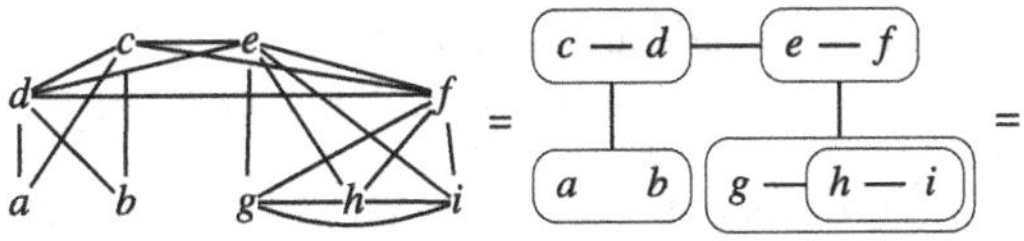

$$\mathsf{P}_4(\!|\parr(\!|a,b|\!),\otimes(\!|c,d|\!),\otimes(\!|e,f|\!),\otimes(\!|g,\otimes(\!|h,i|\!)|\!)|\!)$$
or
$$\mathsf{P}_4(\!|a \parr b, c\otimes d, e\otimes f, g\otimes(h\otimes i)|\!)$$

Fig. 1. A graph and one of its modular and the corresponding formula-like representations.

We have $F \sim G \sim H$ and $G = F = a—b—c—d \neq b—a—c—d = H.$.

Note 2. Whenever we say that two graphs are the same, we assume they share the same set of vertices and labeling function, therefore implicitly assuming the isomorphism f to be given. This allows us to verify whether two graphs are isomorphic (i.e., the same) in polynomial time on the number of vertices.

We recall the notion of *module* [26,28,35,41,45,48], allowing us to represent a graph using a tree-like syntax. A module is a subset of vertices of a graph having the same edge-relation with any vertex outside the subset, generalizing what can usually be observed in formulas, where, in the formula tree, each literal in a subformula has the same least common ancestor with a given literal not belonging to the subformula itself.

Definition 2. *Let $G = \langle V_G, \ell_G, E_G\rangle$ be a graph and $W \subseteq V_G$. The **graph induced** by W is the graph $G|_W := \left\langle W, \ell_G|_W, \overset{G}{\frown} \cap (W \times W)\right\rangle$ where $\ell_G|_W(v) := \ell_G(v)$ for all $v \in W$.*

*A **module** of a graph G is a subset M of V_G such that $x \frown z$ iff $y \frown z$ for any $x, y \in M$, $z \in V_G \setminus M$. A module M is **trivial** if $M = \emptyset$, $M = V_G$, or $M = \{x\}$ for some $x \in V_G$. From now on, we identify a module M of a graph G with the induced subgraph $G|_M$.*

Remark 1. A connected component of a graph G is a module of G.

Note 3. We may optimize graph representations by bordering vertices of a same module by a closed line. An edge connected to such a closed line denotes the existence of an edge to each vertex inside it (see Fig. 1). By means of example, consider the following graph and its more compact modular representation.

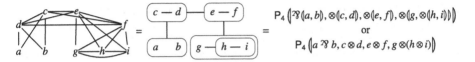

(2)

The notion of module is related to a notion of context, which can be intuitively formulated as a graph with a "hole".

Definition 3. *A **context** $C[\square]$ is a (non-empty) graph containing a single occurrence of a special vertex $\square$ (with $\ell(\square)$ undefined). It is **trivial** if $C[\square] = \square$. If $C[\square]$ is a context and G a graph, we define $C[G]$ as the graph obtained by replacing $\square$ by G. Formally,*

$$C[G] := \left\langle \begin{array}{l} (V_{C[\square]} \setminus \{\square\}) \uplus V_G\ , \\ \ell_C \cup \ell_G\ , \\ \left\{vw \mid v, w \in V_{C[\square]} \setminus \{\square\}, v \overset{C[\square]}{\frown} w\right\} \cup \left\{vw \mid v \in V_{C[\square]} \setminus \{\square\}, w \in V_G, v \overset{C[\square]}{\frown} \square\right\} \end{array} \right\rangle$$

Remark 2. The notion of context and the one of module are interdefinable. In fact, a set of vertices M is a module of a graph G iff there is a context $C[\square]$ such that $G = C[M]$.

Note that M is a module of a graph G iff there is a context $C[\square]$ such that $G = C[M]$. We generalize this idea of replacing a vertex of a graph with a module by defining the operations of *composition-via* a graph, where all vertices of a graph are replaced in a "modular way" by modules.

Definition 4. *Let G be a graph with* $V_G = \{v_1, \dots, v_n\}$ *and let* $H_1, \dots, H_n$ *be graphs. We define the* **composition of** $H_1, \dots, H_n$ **via** *G as the graph* $G(\!|H_1, \dots, H_n|\!)$ *obtained by replacing each vertex* v_i *of G with a module* H_i *for all* $i \in \{1, \dots, n\}$*. Formally,*

$$G(\!|H_1, \dots, H_n|\!) = \left\langle \biguplus_{i=1}^{n} V_{H_i} \,,\, \bigcup_{i=1}^{n} \ell_{H_i} \,,\, \left(\bigcup_{i=1}^{n} \overset{H_i}{\frown} \right) \cup \left\{ (x, y) \middle| x \in V_{H_i}, y \in V_{H_j}, v_i \overset{G}{\frown} v_j \right\} \right\rangle \quad (3)$$

The subgraphs $H_1, \dots, H_n$ *are called* ***factors*** *of* $G(\!|H_1, \dots, H_n|\!)$ *and, by definition, are (possibly not maximal) modules of* $G(\!|H_1, \dots, H_n|\!)$*.*

Remark 3. The operation of composition-via G forgets the information carried by the labeling function ℓ_G. Moreover, if σ is a similitude between two graphs G and G', then $G(\!|H_1, \dots, H_n|\!) = G'(\!|H_{\sigma(1)}, \dots, H_{\sigma(n)}|\!)$.

In order to establish a connection between graphs and formulas, from now on we only consider graphs whose set of labels belong to the set $\mathcal{L} = \{a, a^\perp \mid a \in \mathcal{A}\}$ where $\mathcal{A}$ is a fixed set of propositional variables. We then define the *dual* of a graph.

Definition 5. *Let* $G = \langle V_G, \ell_G, E_G \rangle$ *be a graph. We define the* **dual** *graph of G as the graph* $G^\perp := \left\langle V_G, \overset{G}{\not\frown}, \ell_{G^\perp} \right\rangle$ *with* $\ell_{G^\perp}(v) = (\ell_G(v))^\perp$ *(assuming* $a^{\perp\perp} = a$ *for all* $a \in \mathcal{A}$*).*

2.2 Classical Propositional Formulas as Cographs

The set of ***classical (propositional) formulas*** is generated from a set of propositional variable $\mathcal{A}$ using the ***negation*** $(\cdot)^\perp$, the ***disjunction*** $\vee$ and the ***conjunction*** $\wedge$ using the following grammar:

$$\phi, \psi := a \mid \phi \vee \psi \mid \phi \wedge \psi \mid \phi^\perp \qquad \text{with } a \in \mathcal{A}. \quad (4)$$

We define a map from literals to single-vertex graphs, which extends to formulas via the composition-via the unlabeled two-vertices stable set and two-vertices clique.

Definition 6. *Let* ϕ *be a classical formula, and let* $\mathsf{S}_2 = \langle \{v_1, v_2\}, \varnothing, \varnothing \rangle$ *and* $\mathsf{K}_2 = \langle \{v_1, v_2\}, \varnothing, \{v_1 v_2\} \rangle$*. We define the graph* $[\![\phi]\!]$ *as follows:*

$$[\![a]\!] = a \quad \left[\!\left[\phi^\perp\right]\!\right] = [\![\phi]\!]^\perp \quad [\![\phi \vee \psi]\!] = \mathsf{S}_2\left(\!\left|[\![\phi]\!], [\![\psi]\!]\right|\!\right) \quad [\![\phi \wedge \psi]\!] = \mathsf{K}_2\left(\!\left|[\![\phi]\!], [\![\psi]\!]\right|\!\right)$$

where we denote by a the single-vertex graph, whose vertex is labeled by a. A ***cograph*** *is a graph G such that there is a classical formula* ϕ *such that* $G = [\![\phi]\!]$*.*

Example 2. Let ϕ and ψ classical formulas containing occurrences of atoms $\{a_1, \ldots, a_n\}$ and $\{b_1, \ldots b_m\}$ respectively. Then the graph $[\![\phi \wedge \psi]\!]$ can be represented as follows:

$$[\![\phi \wedge \psi]\!] = \begin{pmatrix} a_1 & b_1 \\ \vdots & \bowtie & \vdots \\ a_n & b_m \end{pmatrix} = \begin{pmatrix} a_1 \\ \vdots \\ a_n \end{pmatrix} - \begin{pmatrix} b_1 \\ \vdots \\ b_m \end{pmatrix} = \left(\begin{pmatrix} a_1 \\ \vdots \\ a_n \end{pmatrix}^{\perp} \begin{pmatrix} b_1 \\ \vdots \\ b_m \end{pmatrix}^{\perp} \right)^{\perp} = ([\![\phi^{\perp} \vee \psi^{\perp}]\!])^{\perp}$$

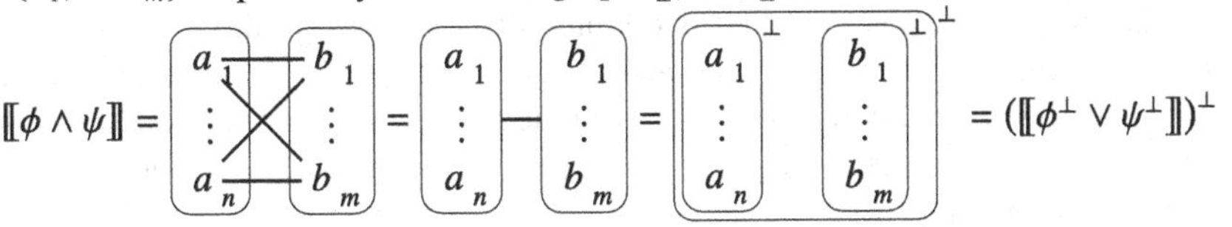

Note that an equivalent definition of cographs can be given using only the graph S_2 (or K_2) and duality.

We can easily observe that the map $[\![\cdot]\!]$ well-behaves with respect to the equivalence over formulas generated by the associativity and commutativity of connectives and the de Morgan laws below.

$$\textbf{Equivalence laws} \begin{cases} \phi \vee \psi \equiv \psi \vee \phi & \phi \vee (\psi \vee \chi) \equiv (\phi \vee \psi) \vee \chi \\ \phi \wedge \psi \equiv \psi \wedge \phi & \phi \wedge (\psi \wedge \chi) \equiv (\phi \wedge \psi) \wedge \chi \end{cases} \quad (5)$$

$$\textbf{De-Morgan laws} \begin{cases} (\phi^{\perp})^{\perp} \equiv \phi & (\phi \wedge \psi)^{\perp} \equiv \phi^{\perp} \vee \psi^{\perp} \end{cases}$$

Proposition 1. *Let ϕ and ψ be classical formulas. Then $\phi \equiv \psi$ iff $[\![\phi]\!] = [\![\psi]\!]$.*

We finally recall an alternative definition of cographs as graphs containing no induced subgraph of a specific shape, and we recall the theorem establishing the relation between

Definition 7. *A graph G is P_4-free if there it contains no four vertices v_1, v_2, v_3, v_4 such that the induced subgraph $G|_{\{v_1,v_2,v_3,v_4\}}$ is similar to the graph a—b—c—d .*

Theorem 1 ([28]). *Let G be a graph. Then G is a cograph iff G is P_4-free.*

2.3   Modular Decomposition of Graphs

We recall the notion of *prime graph*, allowing us to provide canonical representatives of graphs via modular decomposition. (see e.g., [26, 28, 35, 41, 45, 48]).

Definition 8. *A graph G is **prime** if $|V_G| > 1$ and all its modules are trivial.*

We recall the following standard result from the literature.

Theorem 2 ([41]). *Let G be a graph with at least two vertices. Then there are non-empty modules $M_1, \ldots, M_n$ of G and a prime graph P such that $G = P(\!(M_1, \ldots, M_n)\!)$.*

This result allows us to describe graphs using its *modular decomposition*, that is, using single-vertex graphs and operations of composition-via prime graphs only.

Definition 9. *Let G be a non-empty graph. A **modular decomposition** of G is a way to write G using single-vertex graphs and the operation of composition-via prime graphs:*

- *if G is a graph with a single vertex x labeled by a, then $G = a$;*
- *if $H_1, \ldots, H_n$ are maximal modules of G such that $V_G = \uplus_{i=1}^{n} V_{H_i}$, then there is a unique prime graph P such that $G = P(\!(H_1, \ldots, H_n)\!)$.*

Ambiguity arises in modular decomposition due to the presence of cliques or stable sets with more than three vertices, graph symmetries, and the presence of symmetric but non-isomorphic graphs. The first two ambiguities are akin to the one observed in propositional logic, where conjunction and disjunction are considered associative and commutative. These are addressed similarly in the framework we discuss in this paper. However, to reduce the latter source of ambiguity, we introduce the notion of *basis of graphical connectives*.

Definition 10. *A* ***graphical connective*** $C = \langle V_C, \overset{C}{\frown} \rangle$ *(with* ***arity*** $n = |V_C|$*) is given by a finite list of vertices* $V_C = \langle v_1, \ldots, v_n \rangle$ *and a non-reflexive symmetric edge relation* $\overset{C}{\frown}$ *over the set of vertices occurring in* V_C*. We denote by* G_C *the graph corresponding to* C*, that is, the graph* $G_C = \langle \{v \mid v \text{ in } V_C\}, \emptyset, \overset{C}{\frown} \rangle$*. The* ***composition-via*** *a graphical connective is defined as the composition-via the graph* G_C*. A graphical connective is* ***prime*** *if* G_C *is a prime graph. A set* $\mathcal{P}$ *of prime graphical connectives is a* ***basis*** *if for each prime graph* P *there is a unique connective* $C \in \mathcal{P}$ *such that* $P \sim G_C$*.*

Given an n-ary connective C*, we define the* ***group***[2] ***of symmetries of*** C *(*$\mathfrak{S}(C)$*) and the* ***set of dualizing symmetries of*** C *(*$\mathfrak{S}^\perp(C)$*) as the following sets of permutations over the set* $\{1, \ldots, n\}$*:*

$$\left.\begin{array}{l} \mathfrak{S}(C) := \{ \sigma \mid C(\!|H_1, \ldots, H_n|\!) = C(\!|H_{\sigma(1)}, \ldots, H_{\sigma(n)}|\!) \} \\ \mathfrak{S}^\perp(C) := \left\{ \sigma \mid (C(\!|H_1, \ldots, H_n|\!))^\perp = C(\!|H^\perp_{\sigma(1)}, \ldots, H^\perp_{\sigma(n)}|\!) \right\} \end{array}\right. \text{(for any } H_1, \ldots, H_n\text{)}. \tag{6}$$

We introduce the following graphical connectives:

$$\begin{array}{ll} \parr(\!|v_1, v_2|\!) := \langle\langle v_1, v_2\rangle, \emptyset\rangle = \boxed{v_1 \quad v_2} & \otimes(\!|v_1, v_2|\!) := \langle\langle v_1, v_2\rangle, \{v_1v_2\}\rangle = \boxed{v_1 - v_2} \\ \mathsf{P}_n(\!|v_1, \ldots, v_n|\!) := \langle\langle v_1, \ldots, v_n\rangle, \{v_iv_{i+1} \mid i \in \{1, \ldots, n-1\}\}\rangle & = \boxed{v_1 - v_2 - \cdots - v_n} \\ \mathsf{Bull}(\!|v_1, \ldots, v_5|\!) := \langle\langle v_1, \ldots, v_5\rangle, \{(v_1v_2, v_2v_3, v_3v_4, v_5v_2, v_5v_3)\}\rangle = & \boxed{\begin{array}{c} v_1 - v_2 - v_3 - v_4 \\ \diagdown \; \diagup \\ v_5 \end{array}} \end{array} \tag{7}$$

We can reformulate the standard result on modular decomposition as follows.

Theorem 3. *Let* G *be a non-empty graph and* $\mathcal{P}$ *a basis. Then there is a unique way (up to symmetries of graphical connectives and associativity of* $\parr$ *and* $\otimes$*) to write* G *using single-vertex graphs and the graphical connectives in* $\mathcal{P}$*.*

Corollary 1. *Two graphs are isomorphic iff they admit a same modular decomposition.*

2.4 Graphs as Formulas

In order to represent graphs as formulas, we define new connectives beyond conjunction and disjunction to represent graphical connectives in a basis $\mathcal{P}$. From now on, we assume to be fixed a basis $\mathcal{P}$ containing the graphical connectives in Eq. (7).

---

[2] It can be easily shown that $\mathfrak{S}_n$ contains the identity permutation (denoted id) and is a subgroup of the group of permutations over the set $\{1, \ldots, n\}$.

Definition 11. *The set of* ***formulas*** *is generated by the set of propositional atoms* $\mathcal{A}$, *a* ***unit*** $\circ$, *and a basis of graphical connective* $\mathcal{P}$ *using the following syntax:*

$$\phi_1, \dots, \phi_n := \circ \mid a \mid a^\perp \mid \kappa_P(\!|\phi_1, \dots, \phi_{n_P}|\!) \qquad \text{with } a \in \mathcal{A} \text{ and } P \in \mathcal{P} \tag{8}$$

We simply denote $\parr$ *(resp.* $\otimes$*) the binary connective* $\kappa_\parr$ *(resp.* $\kappa_\otimes$*) and we write* $\phi \parr \psi$ *instead of* $\kappa_\parr(\!|\phi, \psi|\!)$ *(resp.* $\phi \otimes \psi$ *instead of* $\kappa_\otimes(\!|\phi, \psi|\!)$*). The* ***arity*** *of the connective* κ_P *is the arity* n_P *of* P*. A* ***literal*** *is a formula of the form* a *or* $a^\perp$ *for an atom* $a \in \mathcal{A}$*. The set of literals is denoted* $\mathcal{L}$*. A formula is* ***unit-free*** *if it contains no occurrences of* $\circ$ *and* ***vacuous*** *if it contains no atoms. A formula is* ***pure*** *if non-vacuous and such that its vacuous subformulas are* $\circ$*. A* **MLL*-formula*** *is a formula containing only occurrences of connectives* $\parr$ *and* $\otimes$*. A* ***context formula*** *(or simply* ***context****)* $\zeta[\square]$ *is a formula containing an* ***hole*** $\square$ *taking the place of an atom. Given a context* $\zeta[\square]$*, the formula* $\zeta[\phi]$ *is defined by simply replacing the atom* $\square$ *with the formula* ϕ*. For example, if* $\zeta[\square] = \psi \parr (\square \otimes \chi)$*, then* $\zeta[\phi] = \psi \parr (\phi \otimes \chi)$*.*

For each ϕ *formula (or context), the graph* $[\![\phi]\!]$ *is defined as follows:*

$$[\![\square]\!] = \square \quad [\![\circ]\!] = \emptyset \quad [\![a]\!] = a \quad [\![a^\perp]\!] = a^\perp \quad [\![\kappa_P(\!|\phi_1, \dots, \phi_n|\!)]\!] = P\left(\!\left|[\![\phi_1]\!], \dots, [\![\phi_n]\!]\right|\!\right) \tag{9}$$

Note 4. We may consider a formula ϕ over the set of occurrences of literals $\{x_1, \dots, x_n\}$ as a ***synthetic connective*** ϕ with arity n. That is, we may denote by $\phi(\!|\psi_1, \dots, \psi_n|\!)$ the formula obtained by replacing each literal x_i (with $i \in \{1, \dots, n\}$) with a formula ψ_i. The set of ***symmetries*** of ϕ (denoted $\mathfrak{S}(\phi)$) is the set of permutations σ over $\{1, \dots, n\}$ such that $[\![\phi(\!|x_1, \dots, x_n|\!)]\!] = [\![\phi(\!|x_{\sigma(1)}, \dots, x_{\sigma(n)}|\!)]\!]$.

Definition 12. *The equivalence relation* $\equiv$ *over formulas is generated by the following:*

$$\textbf{\textit{Equivalence laws}} \begin{cases} \kappa_P(\!|\phi_1, \dots, \phi_{n_P}|\!) \equiv \kappa_P(\!|\phi_{\sigma(1)}, \dots, \phi_{\sigma(n_P)}|\!) \\ \phi \otimes (\psi \otimes \chi) \equiv (\phi \otimes \psi) \otimes \chi \\ \phi \parr (\psi \parr \chi) \equiv (\phi \parr \psi) \parr \chi \end{cases}$$

$$\textbf{\textit{De-Morgan laws}} \begin{cases} \circ^\perp \equiv \circ \qquad \phi^{\perp\perp} \equiv \phi \\ \text{only if } \mathfrak{S}^\perp(P) = \emptyset: \quad (\kappa_P(\!|\phi_1, \dots \phi_{n_P}|\!))^\perp \equiv \kappa_{P^\perp}(\!|\phi^\perp_{\sigma(1)}, \dots, \phi^\perp_{\sigma(n_P)}|\!) \\ \text{only if } \mathfrak{S}^\perp(P) \neq \emptyset: \quad (\kappa_P(\!|\phi_1, \dots \phi_{n_P}|\!))^\perp \equiv \kappa_P(\!|\phi^\perp_{\rho(1)}, \dots, \phi^\perp_{\rho(n_P)}|\!) \end{cases}$$

for each $P \in \mathcal{P}$ *(with arity* $n_P = |V_P|$*), and for each* $\sigma \in \mathfrak{S}(P)$ *and* $\rho \in \mathfrak{S}^\perp(P)$*.*

The ***(linear) negation*** *over formulas is defined by letting*

$$\circ^\perp = \circ \qquad \text{and} \qquad \phi^{\perp\perp} = \phi \qquad \text{and} \qquad (\kappa_P(\!|\phi_1, \dots, \phi_{n_P}|\!))^\perp = \kappa_Q(\!|\phi^\perp_{\sigma(1)}, \dots, \phi^\perp_{\sigma(n_P)}|\!)$$

where Q *is the (unique) prime connective in* $\mathcal{P}$ *such that we have* $[\![\kappa_P(\!|a_1, \dots, a_n|\!)]\!] = Q(\!|a^\perp_{\sigma(1)}, \dots, a^\perp_{\sigma(n)}|\!)$ *for a permutation* σ *over the set* $\{1, \dots, n\}$*.* [3]

The ***linear implication*** $\phi \multimap \psi$ *is defined as* $\phi^\perp \parr \psi$*, while the* ***logical equivalence*** $\phi \multimapboth \psi$ *is defined as* $(\phi \multimap \psi) \otimes (\psi \multimap \phi)$*.*

---

[3] Note that the permutation σ may be not unique. If we consider formulas up-to the equivalence relation $\equiv$, this is irrelevant. Otherwise, in the definition of the linear negation we should also provide a specific permutation σ_P for each prime connective $P \in \mathcal{P}$.

Remark 4. As explained in [5] (Sect. 9), the graphical connectives we discuss in this paper are *multiplicative connectives* (in the sense of [6,22,32,47]) but they are not the same as the *connectives-as-partitions* discussed in these works. In fact, there is a unique 4-ary graphical connective P_4, which has the symmetry group $\{\mathsf{id}, (1,4)(2,3)\}$, while, as shown in [6,47], there is a unique pair of dual *non-decomposable* (i.e., which cannot be described using smaller connectives) 4-ary multiplicative connectives-as-partitions G_4 and $\mathsf{G}_4^\perp$, and $\mathfrak{S}(\mathsf{P}_4) \subsetneq \mathfrak{S}(\mathsf{G}_4) = \mathfrak{S}(\mathsf{G}_4^\perp)$.

The following result is a consequence of Theorem 2.

Proposition 2. *Let ϕ and ψ be formulas. If $\phi \equiv \psi$, then $[\![\phi]\!] = [\![\psi]\!]$. Moreover, if ϕ and ψ are unit-free, then $\phi \equiv \psi$ iff $[\![\phi]\!] = [\![\psi]\!]$.*

For an example of why the equivalence result does not hold in the presence of units, consider the (non-equivalent) formulas $\circ \otimes \circ$ and $\circ \parr \circ$.

3 Sequent Calculi over Graphs-as-Formulas

We assume the reader to be familiar with the definition of sequent calculus derivations as trees of sequents (see, e.g., [61]) but we recall here some definitions.

Definition 13. *A* ***sequent*** *is a set of occurrences of formulas. A* ***sequent system*** S *is a set of* ***sequent rules*** *as the ones in Fig. 2. A* ***derivation*** *(resp.* ***open derivation****) over* S *is a tree of sequents such that each node (resp. each node except some leaves, called* ***open premises****) is the conclusion of a rule with premises its children. In a sequent rule* r*, we say that a formula is* ***active*** *(resp.* ***principal****) if it occurs in one of its premises (resp. in its conclusion) but not in its conclusion (resp. but in none of its premises) A* ***proof*** *of a sequent Γ is a derivation with root Γ denoted $\overset{\pi}{}\!\!\underset{\Gamma}{\rVert}\mathsf{S}$. We denote by $\begin{array}{c}\Gamma'\\ \pi' \,\|\, \mathsf{S}\\ \Gamma\end{array}$ an* ***open derivation*** *with conclusion Γ and a single open premise Γ'. A rule is* ***admissible*** *in* S *if there is a derivation of the conclusion of the rule whenever all premises of the rule are derivable. A rule is* ***derivable*** *in* S*, if there is a derivation in* S *from the premises to the conclusion of the rule.*

Definition 14. *We define the following sequent systems using the rules* ***axiom*** *(*ax*),* ***par*** *(*$\parr$*),* ***tensor*** *(*$\otimes$*),* ***weakening*** *(*w*),* ***contraction*** *(*c*),* ***mix*** *(*mix*),* ***dual connectives*** *(*d-κ*)* ***unitor*** *(*u_κ*), and* ***weak-distributivity*** *(*$\mathsf{wd}_\otimes$*) in Fig. 2.*

$$
\begin{array}{lll}
\textit{\textbf{Multiplicative Graphical Logic}}: & \mathsf{MGL} & = \{\mathsf{ax}, \parr, \otimes, \mathsf{d}\text{-}P \mid P \in \mathcal{P}\} \\
\textit{\textbf{Multiplicative Graphical Logic with mix}}: & \mathsf{MGL}^\circ & = \mathsf{MGL} \cup \{\mathsf{mix}, \mathsf{wd}_\otimes, \mathsf{u}_\kappa\} \\
\textit{\textbf{Classical Graphical Logic}} & \mathsf{KGL} & = \mathsf{MGL} \cup \{\mathsf{w}, \mathsf{c}\}
\end{array}
\tag{10}
$$

Remark 5. Rules ***axiom*** (ax), ***par*** ($\parr$), ***tensor*** ($\otimes$), ***cut*** (cut), and ***mix*** (mix) are the standard as in multiplicative linear logic with mix. Note that ax is restricted to atomic formulas. The rule d-κ handles a pair of dual connectives at the same time, as it may be done by rules in focused proof systems (see, e.g. [9,50,51]) or rules for modalities

$$\mathsf{ax}\,\frac{}{\vdash a, a^{\perp}}\; a \in \mathcal{A} \qquad ⅋\,\frac{\vdash \Gamma, \phi, \psi}{\vdash \Gamma, \phi ⅋ \psi} \qquad \otimes\,\frac{\vdash \Gamma, \phi \quad \vdash \psi, \Delta}{\vdash \Gamma, \phi \otimes \psi, \Delta} \qquad \Big| \qquad \mathsf{w}\,\frac{\vdash \Gamma}{\vdash \Gamma, \phi}$$

$$\mathsf{d}\text{-}\kappa\,\frac{\vdash \Gamma_1, \phi_{\sigma(1)}, \psi_{\tau(1)} \quad \cdots \quad \vdash \Gamma_n, \phi_{\sigma(n)}, \psi_{\tau(n)}}{\vdash \Gamma_1, \ldots, \Gamma_n, \kappa(\!|\phi_1, \ldots, \phi_n|\!), \kappa^{\perp}(\!|\psi_1, \ldots \psi_n|\!)} \begin{cases} \sigma \in \mathfrak{S}(\kappa) \\ \tau \in \mathfrak{S}(\kappa^{\perp}) \end{cases} \qquad \Big| \qquad \mathsf{c}\,\frac{\vdash \Gamma, \phi, \phi}{\vdash \Gamma, \phi}$$

$$\mathsf{mix}\,\frac{\vdash \Gamma_1 \quad \vdash \Gamma_2}{\vdash \Gamma_1, \Gamma_2} \qquad \mathsf{wd}_{\otimes}\,\frac{\vdash \Gamma, \phi_k \quad \vdash \Delta, \kappa(\!|\phi_1, \ldots, \phi_{k-1}, \circ, \phi_{k+1}, \ldots, \phi_n|\!)}{\vdash \Gamma, \Delta, \kappa(\!|\phi_1, \ldots, \phi_n|\!)}$$

$$\mathsf{u}_{\kappa}\,\frac{\vdash \Gamma, \chi(\!|\phi_{\sigma(1)}, \ldots, \phi_{\sigma(n)}|\!)}{\vdash \Gamma, \kappa(\!|\phi_1, \ldots, \phi_k, \circ, \phi_{k+1}, \ldots, \phi_n|\!)} \begin{cases} \sigma \in \mathfrak{S}(\chi) \\ [\![\kappa(\!|\phi_1, \ldots, \phi_k, \circ, \phi_{k+1}, \ldots, \phi_n|\!)]\!] = [\![\chi(\!|\phi_{\sigma(1)}, \ldots, \phi_{\sigma(n)}|\!)]\!] \neq \varnothing \end{cases}$$

Fig. 2. Sequent rules.

in modal logic and linear logic (see, e.g., [12, 14, 31, 44]). Intuitively, while in standard two-sided sequent calculi the right-conjunction rule ($\wedge_R$ below) internalizes a meta-conjunction between the premises of the rule, that is,

$$\wedge_R\,\frac{\boxed{\Gamma_1, \phi_1 \vdash \psi_1, \Delta_1} \quad \text{“and”} \quad \boxed{\Gamma_2, \phi_2 \vdash \psi_2, \Delta_2}}{\Gamma_1, \Gamma_2, \phi_1, \phi_2 \vdash \psi_1 \wedge \psi_2, \Delta_1, \Delta_2} \tag{11}$$

the rule $\mathsf{d}\text{-}\kappa$ internalizes a meta-κ-connective between the premises by introducing the same connective on both sides of the sequent, as shown below in the case $\kappa = \mathsf{P}_4$.

$$\frac{\mathsf{P}_4\Big(\!\Big|\boxed{\Gamma_1, \phi_1 \vdash \psi_1, \Delta_1}, \boxed{\Gamma_2, \phi_2 \vdash \psi_2, \Delta_2}, \boxed{\Gamma_3, \phi_3 \vdash \psi_3, \Delta_3}, \boxed{\Gamma_4, \phi_4 \vdash \psi_4, \Delta_4}\Big|\!\Big)}{\Gamma_1, \Gamma_2, \Gamma_3, \Gamma_4, \kappa_{\mathsf{P}_4}(\!|\phi_1, \phi_2, \phi_3, \phi_4|\!) \vdash \kappa_{\mathsf{P}_4}(\!|\psi_1, \psi_2, \psi_3, \psi_4|\!), \Delta_1, \Delta_2, \Delta_3, \Delta_4} \tag{12}$$

Note that in the rule $\wedge_R$ in Eq. (11) only a single occurrence of the connective $\wedge$ occurs in the conclusion, on the right-hand side of $\vdash$. This because the absence of the conjunction $\wedge$ on the left-hand side is irrelevant since a two-sided sequent $\Gamma \vdash \Delta$ is interpreted as the formula $\left(\bigwedge_{\phi \in \Gamma} \phi^{\perp}\right) \vee \left(\bigvee_{\psi \in \Delta} \psi\right)$.

The names of the rules *unitor* (u_{κ}) and *weak-distributivity* ($\mathsf{wd}_{\otimes}$) are inspired by the literature of *monoidal categories* [46] and *weakly distributive categories* [19, 20, 59]. The rule u_{κ} internalizes the fact that the unit $\circ$ is the neutral element for all connectives (its side condition prevents the creation of non-pure formulas). Under the assumption of the existence of a $\circ$ which is the unit of both $\otimes$ and ⅋, the rule $\mathsf{wd}_{\otimes}$ generalizes the *weak-distributive law* of the $\otimes$ over the ⅋, that is,

$$\phi \otimes (\psi ⅋ \chi) \longrightarrow (\phi \otimes \psi) ⅋ \chi \tag{13}$$

to the weak-distributive law of $\otimes$ over any connective (see below on the top)

$$\begin{array}{lcl} \chi \otimes \kappa(\!|\phi_1, \ldots, \phi_k, \psi, \phi_{k+1}, \ldots, \phi_n|\!) & \longrightarrow & \kappa(\!|\phi_1, \ldots, \phi_k, \psi \otimes \chi, \phi_{k+1}, \ldots, \phi_n|\!) \\ \kappa(\!|\phi_1, \ldots, \phi_k, \psi ⅋ \chi, \phi_{k+1}, \ldots, \phi_n|\!) & \longrightarrow & \kappa(\!|\phi_1, \ldots, \phi_k, \psi, \phi_{k+1}, \ldots, \phi_n|\!) ⅋ \chi \end{array} \tag{14}$$

Note that an additional law is required to formalize the weak-distributive law of all connectives over ⅋ (see the bottom of Eq. (14)). This law corresponds to the rule $\mathsf{wd}_{⅋}$ in Fig. 3.

$$\mathsf{AX}\,\frac{}{\vdash \phi, \phi^{\perp}}\ \phi \text{ pure} \qquad \mathsf{cut}\,\frac{\vdash \Gamma_1, \phi \quad \vdash \Gamma_2, \phi^{\perp}}{\vdash \Gamma_1, \Gamma_2} \qquad \mathsf{wd}_{\invamp}\,\frac{\vdash \Gamma, \kappa(\!|\phi, \psi_1, \ldots, \psi_n|\!)}{\vdash \Gamma, \kappa(\!|\circ, \psi_1, \ldots, \psi_n|\!), \phi}\ \phi \neq \circ$$

$$\mathsf{deep}\,\frac{\vdash \Gamma, \phi \quad \vdash \Delta, \psi}{\vdash \Gamma, \Delta, \zeta[\phi]}\ [\![\zeta[\circ]]\!] = [\![\psi]\!] \qquad \mathsf{d}\text{-}\chi\,\frac{\vdash \Gamma_1, \phi_{\sigma(1)}, \psi_{\tau(1)} \quad \cdots \quad \vdash \Gamma_n, \phi_{\sigma(n)}, \psi_{\tau(n)}}{\vdash \Gamma_1, \ldots, \Gamma_n, \chi(\!|\phi_1, \ldots, \phi_n|\!), \chi^{\perp}(\!|\psi_1, \ldots \psi_n|\!)}\ \begin{cases} \sigma \in \mathfrak{S}(\chi) \\ \tau \in \mathfrak{S}(\chi^{\perp}) \end{cases}$$

Fig. 3. Admissible rules in MGL°.

3.1 Properties of the Sequent Systems

We start by observing that these systems are *initial coherent* [10,50], that is, we can derive the implication $\phi \multimap \phi$ for any pure formula ϕ only using atomic axioms. To prove this result we observe that the generalized version of $\mathsf{d}\text{-}\kappa$ (that is, the rule $\mathsf{d}\text{-}\chi$) is derivable by induction on the structure of χ using the rule $\mathsf{d}\text{-}\kappa$

Lemma 1. *Let χ be a pure formula. Then rule $\mathsf{d}\text{-}\chi$ is derivable.*

Corollary 2. *The rule* AX *is derivable in* MGL *and in* MGL°.

Theorem 4. MGL, MGL°, *and* KGL *are initial coherent w.r.t. pure formulas.*

The admissibility of cut is proven via *cut-elimination.*

Theorem 5. *Let* $\mathsf{X} \in \{\mathsf{MGL}, \mathsf{MGL}^{\circ}, \mathsf{KGL}\}$. *The rule* cut *is admissible in* X.

Proof. We define the *size* of a formula as the sum of the number of $\circ$, connectives and twice the number of literals in it. The *size* of a derivation is the sum of the sizes of the active formulas in all cut-rules. In Fig. 4 we only provide the less standard cut-elimination steps: the ones for ax, w, c, and $\otimes$-*vs*-$\invamp$ are the standard ones, while $\mathsf{d}\text{-}\kappa$-*vs*-$\mathsf{d}\text{-}\kappa$ and u_{κ}-*vs*-u_{κ} (where both u_{κ} rules introduce a $\circ$ in the same "position") are as expected, that is, by cutting each of the corresponding premises of the rules. The result for MGL and MGL° follows by the fact that each *cut-elimination step* applied to any cut-rule reduces the size of a derivation, while for KGL we have to consider also weak-normalization result via a cut-elimination strategy prioritizing the elimination of top-most cut-rules.

Note that to ensure that both active formulas of a cut-rule are principal with respect to the rule immediately above it, we also need to consider among the standard *commutative* cut-elimination steps (independent rule permutations) and the special step in Fig. 5. The treatment of these steps, as well as the definition of a size taking into account them, is not covered in detail here because it is standard in the literature.

Corollary 3. *Let* $\mathsf{X} \in \{\mathsf{MGL}, \mathsf{MGL}^{\circ}, \mathsf{KGL}\}$. *If* $\vdash_{\mathsf{X}} \phi \multimap \psi$ *and* $\vdash_{\mathsf{X}} \psi \multimap \chi$, *then* $\vdash_{\mathsf{X}} \phi \multimap \chi$.

The admissibility of the cut-rule implies analyticity of MGL and KGL via the standard *sub-formula property*, that is, all formulas occurring in a premise of a rule are subformulas of the ones in the conclusion. However, as already observed in [3–5], the same result does not hold for MGL° because the rule u_{κ} and more-than-binary connectives introduce the possibility of having *sub-connectives*, that is, connectives with smaller arity behaving as if certain entries of the connective are fixed to be units.

$$\dfrac{\dfrac{\vdash \Gamma_1, \phi_1 \quad \vdash \Gamma_2, \kappa_P(\!|\circ, \phi_2, \ldots, \phi_n|\!)}{\vdash \Gamma_1, \Gamma_2, \kappa_P(\!|\phi_1, \ldots, \phi_n|\!)}\,\mathsf{wd}_\otimes \qquad \dfrac{\vdash \Delta_1, \phi_1^\perp \quad \vdash \Delta_2, \kappa_{P^\perp}(\!|\circ, \phi_2^\perp, \ldots, \phi_n^\perp|\!)}{\vdash \Delta, \kappa_{P^\perp}(\!|\phi_1^\perp, \ldots, \phi_n^\perp|\!)}\,\mathsf{wd}_\otimes}{\vdash \Gamma_1, \Gamma_2, \Delta_1, \Delta_2}\,\mathsf{cut}$$

$$\rightsquigarrow$$

$$\dfrac{\dfrac{\vdash \Gamma_1, \phi_1 \quad \vdash \Delta_1, \phi_1^\perp}{\vdash \Gamma_1, \Delta_1}\,\mathsf{cut} \qquad \dfrac{\vdash, \Gamma_2, \kappa_P(\!|\circ, \phi_2, \ldots \phi_n|\!) \quad \vdash \Delta_2, \kappa_{P^\perp}(\!|\circ, \phi_2^\perp, \ldots \phi_n^\perp|\!)}{\vdash \Gamma_2, \Delta_2}\,\mathsf{cut}}{\vdash \Gamma_1, \Gamma_2, \Delta_1, \Delta_2}\,\mathsf{mix}$$

$$\dfrac{\dfrac{\vdash \Gamma_1, \phi_1, \psi_1 \quad \cdots \quad \vdash \Gamma_n, \phi_n, \psi_n}{\vdash \Gamma_1, \ldots, \Gamma_n, \kappa_P(\!|\phi_1, \ldots, \phi_n|\!), \kappa_{P^\perp}(\!|\psi_1, \ldots, \psi_n|\!)}\,\mathsf{d}\text{-}\kappa \qquad \dfrac{\vdash \Delta, \psi_1^\perp \quad \vdash \Sigma, \kappa_P(\!|\circ, \psi_2^\perp, \ldots, \psi_n^\perp|\!)}{\vdash \Delta, \Sigma, \kappa_P(\!|\psi_1^\perp, \ldots, \psi_n^\perp|\!)}\,\mathsf{wd}_\otimes}{\vdash \Gamma_1, \ldots, \Gamma_n, \Delta, \Sigma, \kappa_P(\!|\phi_1, \ldots, \phi_n|\!)}\,\mathsf{cut}$$

$$\rightsquigarrow$$

$$\dfrac{\dfrac{\vdash \Gamma_1, \phi_1, \psi_1 \quad \vdash \Delta, \psi_1^\perp}{\vdash \Gamma_1, \Delta, \phi_1}\,\mathsf{cut} \qquad \dfrac{\dfrac{\dfrac{\vdash \Gamma_2, \phi_2, \psi_2 \quad \cdots \quad \vdash \Gamma_n, \phi_n, \psi_n}{\vdash \Gamma_2, \ldots, \Gamma_n, \kappa_\chi(\!|\phi_1, \ldots, \phi_n|\!), \kappa_\chi^\perp(\!|\psi_1, \ldots, \psi_n|\!)}\,\mathsf{d}\text{-}\chi}{\vdash \Gamma_2, \ldots, \Gamma_n, \kappa_P(\!|\circ, \phi_1, \ldots, \phi_n|\!), \kappa_{P^\perp}(\!|\circ, \psi_1, \ldots, \psi_n|\!)}\,2{\times}\mathsf{u}_\kappa \quad \vdash \Sigma, \kappa_P(\!|\circ, \psi_2^\perp, \ldots, \psi_n^\perp|\!)}{\vdash \Gamma_2, \ldots, \Gamma_n, \Sigma, \kappa_P(\!|\circ, \phi_2, \ldots, \phi_n|\!)}\,\mathsf{cut}}{\vdash \Gamma_1, \ldots, \Gamma_n, \Delta, \Sigma, \kappa_P(\!|\phi_1, \ldots, \phi_n|\!)}\,\mathsf{wd}_\otimes$$

Fig. 4. The cut-elimination steps for the structural rules.

$$\dfrac{\dfrac{\vdash \Gamma, \chi(\!|\phi_1, \ldots, \phi_{i-1}, \phi_{i+1}, \ldots, \phi_{j-1}, \phi_{j+1}, \ldots, \phi_n|\!)}{\vdash \Gamma, \kappa_P(\!|\phi_1, \ldots, \phi_{i-1}, \circ, \phi_{i+1}, \ldots, \phi_{j-1}, \phi_{j+1}, \ldots, \phi_n|\!)}\,\mathsf{u}_\kappa}{\vdash \Gamma \kappa_P(\!|\phi_1, \ldots, \phi_{i-1}, \circ, \phi_{i+1}, \ldots, \phi_{j-1}, \circ, \phi_{j+1}, \ldots, \phi_n|\!)}\,\mathsf{u}_\kappa \quad \rightsquigarrow \quad \dfrac{\dfrac{\vdash \Gamma, \chi(\!|\phi_1, \ldots, \phi_{i-1}, \phi_{i+1}, \ldots, \phi_{j-1}, \phi_{j+1}, \ldots, \phi_n|\!)}{\vdash \Gamma, \kappa_{P'}(\!|\phi_1, \ldots, \phi_{i-1}, \phi_{i+1}, \ldots, \phi_{j-1}, \circ, \phi_{j+1}, \ldots, \phi_n|\!)}\,\mathsf{u}_\kappa}{\vdash \Gamma, \kappa_P(\!|\phi_1, \ldots, \phi_{i-1}, \circ, \phi_{i+1}, \ldots, \phi_{j-1}, \circ, \phi_{j+1}, \ldots, \phi_n|\!)}\,\mathsf{u}_\kappa$$

Fig. 5. Special commutative cut-elimination step for u_κ.

Definition 15. *Let P and Q be prime graphs and let $i_1 < \ldots < i_k$ be integers in $\{1, \ldots, |P|\}$. If $P(\!|\circ, \ldots, \circ, v_{i_1}, \circ, \ldots, \circ, v_{i_k}, \circ, \ldots, \circ|\!) \sim Q(\!|v_1, \ldots, v_n|\!)$ for (any) single-vertex graphs $v_1, \ldots, v_n$, then we say that the connective κ_Q is a* ***sub-connective*** *of κ_P and we may write $\kappa_{P|_{i_1,\ldots,i_k}} = \kappa_Q$. A* ***quasi-subformula*** *of a formula $\phi = \kappa_P(\!|\psi_1, \ldots, \psi_n|\!)$ is a formula of the form $\kappa_{P'|_{i_1,\ldots,i_k}}(\!|\psi'_{i_1}, \ldots, \psi'_{i_k}|\!)$ with ψ'_{i_j} a quasi-subformula of ψ_{i_j} for all $i_j \in \{i_1, \ldots, i_k\}$.*

Corollary 4 (Conservativity). MGL *is a conservative extension of* $\mathsf{MLL} = \{\mathsf{ax}, ⅋, \otimes\}$. MGL° *is a conservative extension of* $\mathsf{MLL}^\circ = \{\mathsf{ax}, ⅋, \otimes, \mathsf{mix}\}$. KGL *is a conservative extension of* $\mathsf{LK} = \mathsf{MLL} \cup \{\mathsf{w}, \mathsf{c}\}$.

Proof. The results for MGL and KGL follow from the fact that these systems satisfy the standard sub-formula property for cut-free derivations, therefore no connective other than ⅋ and ⊗ can be introduced during proof search. The result for MGL° follows from the fact that it satisfies the *quasi-subformula property* (i.e., every formula in the premise of a rule is a quasi-subformula a formula in its conclusion), and that ⅋ and ⊗ have no sub-connectives.

For both MGL and MGL° we have the following *splitting* result, ensuring that it is always possible, during proof search, to apply a rule removing a connective after having applied certain rules in the context. Note that, in the literature of linear logic, the

$$\dfrac{\dfrac{\vdash \Gamma,\phi,\psi}{\vdash \Gamma,\phi \parr \psi}\,\parr}{\vdash \Gamma,\phi,\circ \parr \psi}\,\mathsf{wd}_{\parr} \rightsquigarrow \dfrac{\vdash \Gamma,\phi,\psi}{\vdash \Gamma,\phi,\circ \parr \psi}\,\mathsf{u}_{\kappa} \qquad \dfrac{\dfrac{\vdash \Gamma,\phi \quad \vdash \Delta,\psi}{\vdash \Gamma,\Delta,\phi \otimes \psi}\,\otimes}{\vdash \Gamma,\Delta,\phi,\circ \otimes \psi}\,\mathsf{wd}_{\otimes} \rightsquigarrow \dfrac{\dfrac{\vdash \Gamma,\phi \quad \vdash \Delta,\psi}{\vdash \Gamma,\Delta,\phi,\psi}\,\mathsf{mix}}{\vdash \Gamma,\Delta,\phi,\circ \otimes \psi}\,\mathsf{u}_{\kappa}$$

$$\dfrac{\dfrac{\vdash \Gamma,\chi\llparenthesis\phi,\psi_2,\ldots,\psi_{n-1}\rrparenthesis}{\vdash \Gamma,\kappa\llparenthesis\phi,\psi_2,\ldots,\psi_{n-1},\circ\rrparenthesis}\,\mathsf{u}_{\kappa}}{\vdash \Gamma,\kappa\llparenthesis\circ,\psi_2,\ldots,\psi_{n-1},\circ\rrparenthesis,\phi}\,\mathsf{wd}_{\parr} \rightsquigarrow \dfrac{\dfrac{\vdash \Gamma,\chi\llparenthesis\phi,\psi_2,\ldots,\psi_{n-1}\rrparenthesis}{\vdash \Gamma,\chi\llparenthesis\circ,\psi_2,\ldots,\psi_{n-1}\rrparenthesis,\phi}\,\mathsf{wd}_{\parr}}{\vdash \Gamma,\kappa\llparenthesis\circ,\psi_2,\ldots,\psi_{n-1},\circ\rrparenthesis,\phi}\,\mathsf{u}_{\kappa}$$

$$\dfrac{\dfrac{\vdash \Gamma_1,\psi_k \quad \vdash \Gamma_2,\kappa\llparenthesis\phi,\psi_2,\ldots,\psi_{k-1},\circ,\psi_{k+1},\ldots,\psi_n\rrparenthesis}{\vdash \Gamma_1,\Gamma_2,\kappa\llparenthesis\phi,\psi_2,\ldots,\psi_n\rrparenthesis}\,\mathsf{wd}_{\otimes}}{\vdash \Gamma_1,\Gamma_2,\kappa\llparenthesis\circ,\psi_2,\ldots,\psi_n\rrparenthesis,\phi}\,\mathsf{wd}_{\parr}$$

$$\rightsquigarrow$$

$$\dfrac{\vdash \Gamma_1,\psi' \qquad \dfrac{\vdash \Gamma_2,\kappa\llparenthesis\phi,\psi_2,\ldots,\psi_{k-1},\circ,\psi_{k+1},\ldots,\psi_n\rrparenthesis}{\vdash \Gamma_2,\kappa\llparenthesis\circ,\psi_2,\ldots,\psi_{k-1},\circ,\psi_{k+1},\ldots,\psi_n\rrparenthesis,\phi}\,\mathsf{wd}_{\parr}}{\vdash \Gamma,\kappa\llparenthesis\circ,\psi_2,\ldots,\psi_k,\psi',\psi_{k+1},\ldots,\psi_n\rrparenthesis,\phi}\,\mathsf{wd}_{\otimes}$$

$$\dfrac{\dfrac{\vdash \Gamma_1,\phi,\psi_1 \quad \vdash \Gamma_2,\phi_2,\psi_2 \quad \cdots \quad \vdash \Gamma_n,\phi_n,\psi_n}{\vdash \Gamma_1,\ldots,\Gamma_n,\kappa^{\perp}\llparenthesis\psi_1,\ldots,\psi_n\rrparenthesis,\kappa\llparenthesis\phi,\phi_2,\ldots,\phi_n\rrparenthesis}\,\mathsf{d}\text{-}\kappa}{\vdash \Gamma_1,\ldots,\Gamma_n,\kappa^{\perp}\llparenthesis\psi_1,\ldots,\psi_n\rrparenthesis,\kappa\llparenthesis\circ,\phi_2,\ldots,\phi_n\rrparenthesis,\phi}\,\mathsf{wd}_{\parr}$$

$$\rightsquigarrow$$

$$\dfrac{\vdash \Gamma_1,\phi,\psi_1 \qquad \dfrac{\dfrac{\vdash \Gamma_2,\psi_2,\chi_2 \quad \cdots \quad \vdash \Gamma_n,\psi_n,\chi_n}{\vdash \Gamma_2,\ldots,\Gamma_n,\chi^{\perp}\llparenthesis\psi_2,\ldots,\psi_n\rrparenthesis,\chi\llparenthesis\phi_2,\ldots,\phi_n\rrparenthesis}\,\mathsf{d}\text{-}\chi}{\vdash \Gamma_2,\ldots,\Gamma_n,\kappa^{\perp}\llparenthesis\circ,\psi_1,\ldots,\psi_n\rrparenthesis,\kappa\llparenthesis\circ,\phi_2,\ldots,\phi_n\rrparenthesis}\,2{\times}\mathsf{u}_{\kappa}}{\vdash \Gamma_1,\ldots,\Gamma_n,\kappa^{\perp}\llparenthesis\psi_1,\ldots,\psi_n\rrparenthesis,\kappa\llparenthesis\circ,\phi_2,\ldots,\phi_n\rrparenthesis,\phi}\,\mathsf{wd}_{\otimes}$$

Fig. 6. Steps to eliminate $\mathsf{wd}_{\parr}$ rules.

splitting lemma is usually formulated as a special case of the next lemma, ensuring that an occurrence of the connective ⊗ can be removed (by applying a ⊗-rule), but without requiring the possibility of the need of applying rules to the context.

Lemma 2 (Splitting). *Let $\Gamma,\kappa\llparenthesis\phi_1,\ldots,\phi_n\rrparenthesis$ be a sequent and let* $\mathsf{X} \in \{\mathsf{MGL},\mathsf{MGL}^{\circ}\}$*. If* $\vdash_{\mathsf{X}} \Gamma,\kappa\llparenthesis\phi_1,\ldots,\phi_n\rrparenthesis$*, then there is a derivation of the following shape*

$$\begin{array}{c}\pi_1\\ \dfrac{\vdash \Gamma',\chi\llparenthesis\phi_1,\ldots,\phi_{k-1},\phi_{k+1},\phi_n\rrparenthesis}{\vdash \Gamma',\kappa\llparenthesis\phi_1,\ldots,\phi_{k-1},\circ,\phi_{k+1},\phi_n\rrparenthesis}\,\mathsf{u}_{\kappa}\\ \pi_0\,\Vert\\ \vdash \Gamma,\kappa\llparenthesis\phi_1,\ldots,\phi_{k-1},\circ,\phi_{k+1},\phi_n\rrparenthesis\end{array} \quad \textit{or} \quad \begin{array}{c}\pi_1 \qquad\qquad \pi_n\\ \dfrac{\vdash \Delta_1,\phi_1 \quad \cdots \quad \vdash \Delta_n,\phi_n}{\vdash \Gamma',\kappa\llparenthesis\phi_1,\ldots,\phi_n\rrparenthesis}\,\mathsf{r}\\ \pi_0\,\Vert\\ \vdash \Gamma,\kappa\llparenthesis\phi_1,\ldots,\phi_n\rrparenthesis\end{array} \quad \textit{with } \mathsf{r} \in \{\parr,\otimes,\mathsf{d}\text{-}\kappa\}.$$

Proof. By case analysis of the last rule occurring in a proof π of $\Gamma,\kappa\llparenthesis\phi_1,\ldots,\phi_n\rrparenthesis$.

We conclude this section by proving the admissibility of rules $\mathsf{wd}_{\parr}$ and deep.

Lemma 3. *The rule* $\mathsf{wd}_{\parr}$ *is admissible in* MGL°.

$$\mathsf{w}\!\downarrow \frac{\vdash \Gamma, \zeta[\psi]}{\vdash \Gamma, \zeta[\psi \parr \phi]} \quad \mathsf{c}\!\downarrow \frac{\vdash \Gamma, \zeta[\phi \parr \phi]}{\vdash \Gamma, \zeta[\phi]} \quad \Big| \quad \mathsf{ac}\!\downarrow \frac{\vdash \Gamma, \zeta[a \parr a]}{\vdash \Gamma, \zeta[a]} \quad \mathsf{m} \frac{\vdash \Gamma, \zeta[P(\!|\phi_1, \ldots, \phi_n|\!) \parr P(\!|\psi_1, \ldots, \psi_n|\!)]}{\vdash \Gamma, \zeta[P(\!|\phi_1 \parr \psi_1, \ldots, \phi_n \parr \psi_n|\!)]} \parr \neq P \text{ prime}$$

Fig. 7. Deep inference structural rules, the atomic contraction and the generalized medial rule.

Proof. In Fig. 6 we provide a procedure to remove (top-down) all occurrences of $\mathsf{wd}_{\parr}$. Similar to cut-elimination, this procedure requires the use the commutative steps to ensure that the active formula of a $\mathsf{wd}_{\parr}$ we aim at removing is principal with respect to the rule immediately above it.

Lemma 4. *The rule* deep *is admissible in* MGL°.

Proof. By induction on the structure of $\zeta[\square]$. The case with $\zeta[\square] = \square$ is an application of $\mathsf{wd}_\otimes$, otherwise we conclude using Lemma 2.

3.2 A Decomposition Result for KGL

We can extend the decomposition result for deep inference systems in the context of classical logic [13, 15] to KGL using the deep inference (structural) rules from Fig. 7, including the ***generalized medial*** rule proposed in [17].

Theorem 6 (Decomposition). *Let Γ be a sequent. If $\vdash_{\mathsf{KGL}} \Gamma$, then:*

1. *there is a sequent Γ' such that $\vdash_{\mathsf{MGL}} \Gamma' \vdash_{\{\mathsf{w}\downarrow,\mathsf{c}\downarrow\}} \Gamma$*
2. *there are sequent Γ', Δ', and Δ such that $\vdash_{\mathsf{MGL}} \Gamma' \vdash_{\{\mathsf{m}\}} \Delta' \vdash_{\{\mathsf{ac}\downarrow\}} \Delta \vdash_{\{\mathsf{w}\downarrow\}} \Gamma$*

Proof. The proof of Item 1 is immediate by replacing structural rules with deep ones, and applying rule permutations. Item 2 is a consequence of the previous point after showing (by induction) that each instance of c↓-rule can be replaced by a derivation containing m and ac↓ only, and conclude by applying rule permutations to push ac-rules below m-rules, and w↓ to the bottom of a derivation. For a reference, see [7].

4 Graph Isomorphism as Logical Equivalence

In this section we show that two pure formulas ϕ and ψ are interpreted by the same graph (i.e., $[\![\phi]\!] = [\![\psi]\!]$) iff they are logically equivalent (i.e., $\phi \multimapboth \psi$).

Theorem 7. *Let ϕ and ψ be formulas.*

1. *If ϕ and ψ are unit-free, then $[\![\phi]\!] = [\![\psi]\!]$ iff $\vdash_{\mathsf{MGL}} \phi \multimapboth \psi$.*
2. *If ϕ and ψ are pure, then $[\![\phi]\!] = [\![\psi]\!]$ iff $\vdash_{\mathsf{MGL}^\circ} \phi \multimapboth \psi$.*

Proof. After Proposition 2, to prove Item 1 it suffices to show that each De Morgan law $\phi \equiv \psi$ in Definition 12 (with ϕ and ψ unit-free) corresponds to a logical equivalence $\phi \multimapboth \psi$ which is derivable in MGL. We then conclude by Corollary 3. To prove Item 2, we first show that we can find unit-free formulas ϕ' and ψ' such that $\phi \multimapboth \phi'$ and $\psi \multimapboth \psi'$ are derivable in MGL° (using AX, d-κ, and u_κ only), and we then conclude using the previous point.

$$\mathsf{ai}\!\downarrow \frac{\varnothing}{a^\perp \parr a} \qquad \mathsf{p}\!\downarrow \frac{(M_1 \parr N_1)\otimes\cdots\otimes(M_n \parr M'_n)}{P^\perp(\!|M_1,\ldots,M_n|\!) \parr P(\!|M'_1,\ldots,M'_n|\!)}$$

$$\mathsf{s}_{\parr} \frac{P(\!|M_1,\ldots,M_{i-1},M_i \parr N, M_{i+1},\ldots M_n|\!)}{M_i \parr P(\!|M_1,\ldots,M_{i-1},N,M_{i+1},\ldots,M_n|\!)} \qquad \mathsf{s}_{\otimes} \frac{M_i \otimes P(\!|M_1,\ldots,M_{i-1},N,M_{i+1},\ldots,M_n|\!)}{P(\!|M_1,\ldots,M_{i-1},M_i\otimes N,M_{i+1},\ldots,M_n|\!)}$$

Fig. 8. Inference rules in GS, with P any prime graph and $M_i \neq \varnothing \neq M'_i$ for all $i \in \{1,\ldots,n\}$.

5 Soundness and Completeness of MGL° with Respect to GS

In this section, we show that the graphical logic GS from [4,5], defined by a deep inference system operating on graphs, is the set of graphs corresponding to formulas that are provable in MGL°. Note that we here consider the system GS = $\{\mathsf{ai}\!\downarrow, \mathsf{s}_{\parr}, \mathsf{s}_{\otimes}, \mathsf{p}\!\downarrow\}$ defined by the rules in Fig. 8, which have a slightly different formulation with respect to [4,5]: we consider p-rules with a stronger side condition which is balanced by the presence of $\mathsf{s}_{\otimes}$ in the system.[4]

To prove the main result of this section, we use the admissibility of $\mathsf{wd}_{\parr}$ and deep (Lemmas 3 and 4) to prove that if H and G are graphs such that there is an application of a rule $\mathsf{s}_{\parr}$, $\mathsf{s}_{\otimes}$, or $\mathsf{p}\!\downarrow$ (even deep in a context) with premise H and conclusion G, then there are formulas ϕ and ψ, with $[\![\phi]\!] = H$ and $[\![\psi]\!] = G$, such that $\psi \multimap \phi$.

Lemma 5. *Let* $\mathsf{r} \in \{\mathsf{s}_{\parr}, \mathsf{s}_{\otimes}, \mathsf{p}\!\downarrow\}$. *If* $\mathsf{r}\frac{H}{G}$, *then there are formulas* ϕ *and* ψ *with* $[\![\phi]\!] = G$ *and* $[\![\psi]\!] = H$ *such that* $\vdash_{\mathsf{MGL}^\circ} \psi^\perp, \phi$.

Proof. If $C[\square] = \square$, then the following implications trivially hold in MGL°:

$$\kappa(\!|\mu_1,\ldots,\mu_{i-1},\mu_i \parr \nu,\mu_{i+1},\ldots\mu_n|\!) \multimap \mu_i \parr \kappa(\!|\mu_1,\ldots,\mu_{i-1},\circ \parr \nu,\mu_{i+1},\ldots\mu_n|\!)$$
$$\mu_i \otimes \kappa(\!|\mu_1,\ldots,\mu_{i-1},\circ \otimes \nu,\mu_{i+1},\ldots\mu_n|\!) \multimap \kappa(\!|\mu_1,\ldots,\mu_{i-1},\mu_i \otimes \nu,\mu_{i+1},\ldots\mu_n|\!)$$
$$(\mu_1 \parr \nu_1)\otimes\cdots\otimes(\mu_n \parr \nu_n) \multimap \kappa_{P^\perp}(\!|\mu_1,\ldots,\mu_n|\!) \parr \kappa_P(\!|\nu_1,\ldots,\nu_n|\!)$$

If $C[\square] = \kappa_P(\!|C'[\square], M_1,\ldots,M_n|\!) \neq \square$, then we assume w.l.o.g., there is a context formula $\zeta[\square] = \kappa_P(\!|\zeta'[\square],\mu_1,\ldots,\mu_n|\!)$ such that $[\![\zeta[\square]]\!] = C[\square]$ and $[\![\zeta'[\square]]\!] = C'[\square]$. We conclude since, by inductive hypothesis on $C[\square]$, there is a derivation as follows:

$$\mathsf{d}\text{-}\kappa \frac{\dfrac{\Pi\,\mathsf{IH}}{\vdash (\zeta'[\psi'])^\perp, \zeta'[\phi']} \quad \mathsf{AX}\dfrac{}{\vdash \mu_1^\perp,\mu_1} \quad \cdots \quad \mathsf{AX}\dfrac{}{\vdash \mu_n^\perp,\mu_n}}{\vdash \kappa_{P^\perp}\left(\!\left|(\zeta'[\psi'])^\perp,\mu_1^\perp,\ldots,\mu_n^\perp\right|\!\right), \kappa_P\left(\!\left|\zeta'[\phi'],\mu_1,\ldots,\mu_n\right|\!\right)} \quad .$$

We are now able to prove the main result of this section, that is, establishing a correspondence between graphs provable in GS and graphs which are the image via $[\![\cdot]\!]$ of formulas provable in MGL°.

Theorem 8. *Let* ϕ *a pure formula and let* $G = [\![\phi]\!] \neq \varnothing$. *Then* $\vdash_{\mathsf{GS}} G$ *iff* $\vdash_{\mathsf{MGL}^\circ} \phi$.

[4] The proof that the formulation we consider in this paper, where all factors M_i and N_i are required to be non-empty is equivalent to the ones in the literature, where is either asked that only all factors M_i (as in [5]) or $M_i \parr N_i$ (as in [4]) are non-empty, is provided in [2].

Proof. If there is a derivation π of Γ in MGL°, then we define a derivation $[\![\pi]\!]$ of $[\![\Gamma]\!]$ in GS by induction by induction on the last rule r in π. The translation translates a ax into an instance of $\mathsf{ai}\!\downarrow$, a $⅋$, mix and u_κ into no rule (using properties of the open deduction formalism, and the fact premise and conclusion sequents correspond to the same graph), $\otimes$ and $\mathsf{d}\text{-}\kappa$ into an instance of $\mathsf{p}\!\downarrow$, and $\mathsf{wd}_\otimes$ into an instance of $\mathsf{p}\!\downarrow$.

Conversely, if $\mathcal{D}$ is a proof of $G \neq \varnothing$ in GS, then we define a proof $\pi_{\mathcal{D}}$ of ϕ by induction on the number n of rules in $\mathcal{D}$, where $n \neq 0$ because we are assuming $G \neq \varnothing$.

– If $n = 1$, then $G = a ⅋ a^\perp$ and $\pi_{\mathcal{D}} = \dfrac{\dfrac{}{\vdash a, a^\perp}\,\mathsf{ax}}{\vdash a ⅋ a^\perp}\,⅋$.

– If $n > 1$, then the derivation $\mathcal{D}$ is of the form $\mathcal{D} = \dfrac{\overset{\mathcal{D}'\,\Vert}{H}}{G}\,\mathsf{r}$ and by inductive hypothesis we have a proof $\pi_{\mathcal{D}'}$ of a formula ψ such that $[\![\psi]\!] = H$. If $\mathsf{r} \in \{\mathsf{s}_⅋, \mathsf{s}_\otimes, \mathsf{p}\!\downarrow\}$, then by Lemma 5 we have a derivation with cut as the one below on the left of a formula ϕ such that $[\![\phi]\!] = G$. Thus we conclude by Theorem 5.

$$\mathsf{cut}\,\dfrac{\overset{\Vert\,\mathsf{IH}}{\psi} \qquad \overset{\Vert\,\text{Lemma 5}}{\vdash \psi^\perp, \phi}}{\vdash \phi} \quad \overset{\text{Theorem5}}{\rightsquigarrow^*} \quad \overset{\Vert\,\mathsf{MGL}^\circ}{\phi} \qquad\Bigg|\qquad \dfrac{\dfrac{\dfrac{}{\vdash a, a^\perp}\,\mathsf{ax}}{\vdash a ⅋ a^\perp}\,⅋ \qquad \overset{\pi_{\mathcal{D}'}\,\Vert\,\mathsf{IH}}{\psi}}{\dfrac{\vdash \zeta[a ⅋ a^\perp]}{\vdash \phi}\,=}\,\mathsf{deep}$$

Otherwise $\mathsf{r} = \mathsf{ai}\!\downarrow$, then it must have been applied deep inside a context $C[\square] = [\![\zeta[\square]]\!] \neq \square$ such that $C[\varnothing] = H = [\![\psi]\!]$. Therefore $\phi = \zeta[a ⅋ a^\perp]$. We conclude by applying Lemma 4 to the derivation above on the right.

Remark 6. In a different line of work [17] the authors define the ***boolean graphical logic*** (or GBL), as a graphical logic conservatively extending LK defined by maximal-clique-preserving graph morphisms. As a consequence of Corollary 4 and theorem 8, we conclude that KGL and GBL are not the same since the following counterexample from [5] (for GS) is in GBL but not in KGL 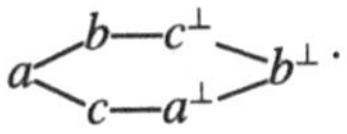

.

6 Conclusion and Future Works

In this paper we have provided foundations for the design of proof systems operating on graphs by defining *graphical connectives*, a class of logical operators generalizing the classical conjunction and disjunction, and whose semantics is solely defined by their interpretation as prime graphs. We introduced cut-free sequent calculi operating on formulas containing graphical connectives, where graph isomorphism can be captured by logical equivalence. We also discussed the relationship of these systems with graphical logics studied in the literature [4,5,17].

We illustrate below a number of future research directions originating from this work different from the suggestions of the respective authors of using the graphical logic GS to extend the works in [11,18,49], where the authors suggest the possibility of extending their current results by generalizing their methods based on "classical" formulas to graphs.

Categorical Semantics. Unit-free *star-autonomous* and *IsoMix* categories [19,20] provide categorical models of MLL and MLL° respectively. We conjecture that categorical models for MGL and MGL° can be defined by enriching such structures with additional n-ary monoidal products and natural transformations, reflecting the symmetries observed in the symmetry groups of prime graphs.

Digraphs, Games and Event Structures. In this work we have extended the correspondence between classical propositional and cographs from [21] to the case of general (undirected) graphs using graphical connectives, and the same idea can be found in [3] where mixed graphs generalize *relation webs* used to encode BV-formulas [33]. Similarly, we foresee the definition of proof systems operating on directed graphs as conservative extensions of intuitionistic propositional logic beyond *arenas* – directed graphs used in Hyland-Ong *game semantics* [40] to encode propositional intuitionistic formulas, which are characterized by the absence of induced subgraphs of a specific shape. This would provide new insights on the proof theory connected to concurrent games [1,58,64], and could be used to define automated tools operating on event structures [55].

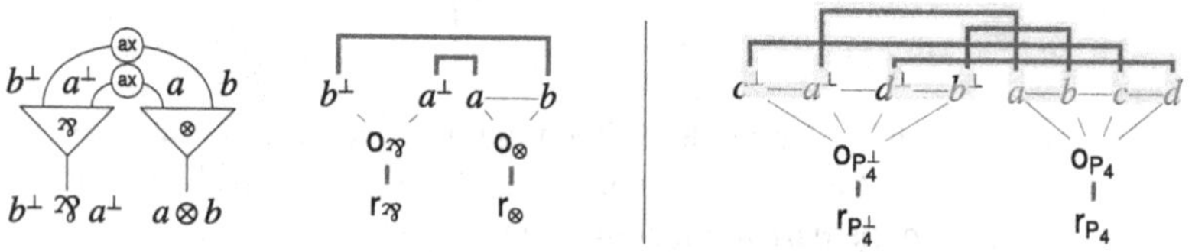

Fig. 9. On the left: the same proof net in the original Girard's syntax and Retoré's one. On the right: an RB-proof net of $\kappa_{P_4}(\!|a,b,c,d|\!) \multimap \kappa_{P_4}(\!|a,b,c,d|\!)$ containing the chorded æ-cycle $a \cdot b \cdot b^\perp \cdot d^\perp \cdot d \cdot c \cdot c^\perp \cdot a^\perp$.

Proof Nets and Automated Proof Search. We plan to design proof nets [22,29,30] for MGL and MGL°, as well as combinatorial proofs [38,39] for KGL. For this purpose, we envisage extending Retoré's *handsome proof net* syntax, where proof nets are represented by two-colored graphs (see the left of Fig. 9). In Retoré's syntax, the graph induced by the vertices corresponding to the inputs of a $\parr$-gate (or a $\otimes$-gate) is similar to the corresponding prime graph $\parr$ (resp. $\otimes$). Thus, gates for graphical connectives could be easily defined by extending this correspondence (see the proof net on the right of Fig. 9). The standard correctness condition defined via *acyclicity* fails for these proof nets, as shown in the right-hand side of Fig. 9: the (correct) proof-net of the sequent $\mathsf{P}_4(\!|a,b,c,d|\!) \multimap \mathsf{P}_4(\!|a,b,c,d|\!)$ contains a cycle. We foresee the possibility of using results on the *primeval* decomposition of graphs [37,42] to isolate those cycles witnessing unsoundness, as proposed in [52]. This may provide a methodology to develop machine-learning guided automated theorem provers using the methods in [43].

Acknowledgments. The author thanks the anonymous reviewers for the feedback which helped improve the final version of this manuscript.

References

1. Abramsky, S., Mellies, P.A.: Concurrent games and full completeness. In: Proceedings. 14th Symposium on Logic in Computer Science (Cat. No. PR00158), pp. 431–442. IEEE (1999)
2. Acclavio, M.: Graphical proof theory I: sequent systems on undirected graphs (2023)
3. Acclavio, M., Horne, R., Mauw, S., Straßburger, L.: A graphical proof theory of logical time. In: Felty, A.P. (ed.) 7th International Conference on Formal Structures for Computation and Deduction (FSCD 2022). Leibniz International Proceedings in Informatics (LIPIcs), vol. 228, pp. 22:1–22:25. Schloss Dagstuhl – Leibniz-Zentrum für Informatik, Dagstuhl, Germany (2022). https://doi.org/10.4230/LIPIcs.FSCD.2022.22, https://drops.dagstuhl.de/opus/volltexte/2022/16303
4. Acclavio, M., Horne, R., Straßburger, L.: Logic beyond formulas: a proof system on graphs. In: Proceedings of the 35th Annual ACM/IEEE Symposium on Logic in Computer Science. LICS '20, pp. 38–52. Association for Computing Machinery, New York, NY, USA (2020). https://doi.org/10.1145/3373718.3394763
5. Acclavio, M., Horne, R., Straßburger, L.: An analytic propositional proof system on graphs. Logical Methods Comput. Sci. **18**(4) (2022). https://doi.org/10.46298/lmcs-18(4:1)2022, https://lmcs.episciences.org/10186
6. Acclavio, M., Maieli, R.: Generalized connectives for multiplicative linear logic. In: Fernández, M., Muscholl, A. (eds.) 28th EACSL Annual Conference on Computer Science Logic (CSL 2020). LIPIcs, vol. 152, pp. 6:1–6:16. Schloss Dagstuhl–Leibniz-Zentrum fuer Informatik, Dagstuhl, Germany (2020). https://doi.org/10.4230/LIPIcs.CSL.2020.6, https://drops.dagstuhl.de/opus/volltexte/2020/11649
7. Acclavio, M., Straßburger, L.: From syntactic proofs to combinatorial proofs. In: Galmiche, D., Schulz, S., Sebastiani, R. (eds.) IJCAR 2018. LNCS (LNAI), vol. 10900, pp. 481–497. Springer, Cham (2018). https://doi.org/10.1007/978-3-319-94205-6_32
8. Aler Tubella, A., Straßburger, L.: Introduction to Deep Inference, August 2019. https://hal.inria.fr/hal-02390267, lecture
9. Andreoli, J.M.: Logic programming with focusing proofs in linear logic. J. Log. Comput. **2**(3), 297–347 (1992)
10. Avron, A., Lev, I.: Canonical propositional Gentzen-type systems. In: Goré, R., Leitsch, A., Nipkow, T. (eds.) IJCAR 2001. LNCS, vol. 2083, pp. 529–544. Springer, Heidelberg (2001). https://doi.org/10.1007/3-540-45744-5_45
11. Bellandi, V., Frati, F., Siccardi, S., Zuccotti, F.: Management of uncertain data in event graphs. In: Ciucci, D., et al. (eds.) IPMU 2022. CCIS, vol. 1601, pp. 568–580. Springer, Cham (2022). https://doi.org/10.1007/978-3-031-08971-8_47
12. Blackburn, P., De Rijke, M., Venema, Y.: Modal logic: graph. Darst, vol. 53. Cambridge University Press (2001)
13. Brünnler, K.: Locality for classical logic. Notre Dame J. Formal Logic **47**(4), 557–580 (2006). http://www.iam.unibe.ch/~kai/Papers/LocalityClassical.pdf
14. Brünnler, K., Straßburger, L.: Modular sequent systems for modal logic. In: Giese, M., Waaler, A. (eds.) TABLEAUX 2009. LNCS (LNAI), vol. 5607, pp. 152–166. Springer, Heidelberg (2009). https://doi.org/10.1007/978-3-642-02716-1_12
15. Bruscoli, P., Straßburger, L.: On the length of medial-switch-mix derivations. In: Kennedy, J., de Queiroz, R.J.G.B. (eds.) WoLLIC 2017. LNCS, vol. 10388, pp. 68–79. Springer, Heidelberg (2017). https://doi.org/10.1007/978-3-662-55386-2_5

16. Calk, C.: A graph theoretical extension of Boolean logic. Bachelor's thesis (2016). http://www.anupamdas.com/graph-bool.pdf
17. Calk, C., Das, A., Waring, T.: Beyond formulas-as-cographs: an extension of Boolean logic to arbitrary graphs (2020)
18. Chaudhuri, K., Donato, P., Massacci, L., Werner, B.: Certifying proof-by-linking. In: Working Paper or Preprint, September 2022. https://inria.hal.science/hal-04317972
19. Cockett, J., Seely, R.: Proof theory for full intuitionistic linear logic, bilinear logic, and mix categories. Theory Appl. Categories **3**(5), 85–131 (1997)
20. Cockett, J., Seely, R.: Weakly distributive categories. J. Pure Appl. Algebra **114**, 133–173 (1997)
21. Corneil, D., Lerchs, H., Burlingham, L.: Complement reducible graphs. Discrete Appl. Math. **3**(3), 163–174 (1981). https://doi.org/10.1016/0166-218X(81)90013-5, https://www.sciencedirect.com/science/article/pii/0166218X81900135
22. Danos, V., Regnier, L.: The structure of multiplicatives. Arch. Math. Logic **28**(3), 181–203 (1989). https://doi.org/10.1007/BF01622878
23. Das, A.: Complexity of evaluation and entailment in Boolean graph logic (2019, preprint). http://www.anupamdas.com/complexity-graph-bool-note.pdf
24. Das, A., Rice, A.A.: New minimal linear inferences in Boolean logic independent of switch and medial. In: Kobayashi, N. (ed.) 6th International Conference on Formal Structures for Computation and Deduction. FSCD 2021, 17–24 July 2021, Buenos Aires, Argentina (Virtual Conference). LIPIcs, vol. 195, pp. 14:1–14:19. Schloss Dagstuhl - Leibniz-Zentrum für Informatik (2021). https://doi.org/10.4230/LIPIcs.FSCD.2021.14
25. Deniélou, P.-M., Yoshida, N.: Buffered communication analysis in distributed multiparty sessions. In: Gastin, P., Laroussinie, F. (eds.) CONCUR 2010. LNCS, vol. 6269, pp. 343–357. Springer, Heidelberg (2010). https://doi.org/10.1007/978-3-642-15375-4_24
26. Ehrenfeucht, A., Harju, T., Rozenberg, G.: The Theory of 2-Structures a Framework for Decomposition and Transformation of Graphs. World Scientific, Singapore (1999). https://doi.org/10.1142/4197
27. Fu, X., Bultan, T., Su, J.: Analysis of interacting BPEL web services. In: Proceedings of the 13th International Conference on World Wide Web, pp. 621–630. ACM (2004)
28. Gallai, T.: Transitiv orientierbare Graphen. Acta Mathematica Academiae Scientiarum Hungarica **18**(1–2), 25–66 (1967)
29. Girard, J.Y.: Linear logic. Theor. Comput. Sci. **50**, 1–102 (1987). https://doi.org/10.1016/0304-3975(87)90045-4
30. Girard, J.Y.: Proof-nets: the parallel syntax for proof-theory. In: Ursini, A., Agliano, P. (eds.) Logic and Algebra. Marcel Dekker, New York (1996)
31. Girard, J.Y.: Light linear logic. Inf. Comput. **143**, 175–204 (1998)
32. Girard, J.Y.: On the meaning of logical rules II: multiplicatives and additives. NATO ASI Seri. F: Comput. Syst. Sci. **175**, 183–212 (2000)
33. Guglielmi, A.: A system of interaction and structure. ACM Trans. Comput. Log. **8**(1), 1–64 (2007). https://doi.org/10.1145/1182613.1182614
34. Guglielmi, A., Gundersen, T., Parigot, M.: A proof calculus which reduces syntactic bureaucracy. In: Lynch, C. (ed.) Proceedings of the 21st International Conference on Rewriting Techniques and Applications. LIPIcs, vol. 6, pp. 135–150. Schloss Dagstuhl–Leibniz-Zentrum fuer Informatik, Dagstuhl, Germany (2010). https://doi.org/10.4230/LIPIcs.RTA.2010.135, http://drops.dagstuhl.de/opus/volltexte/2010/2649
35. Habib, M., Paul, C.: A survey of the algorithmic aspects of modular decomposition. Comput. Sci. Rev. **4**(1), 41–59 (2010). https://doi.org/10.1016/j.cosrev.2010.01.001, https://www.sciencedirect.com/science/article/pii/S157401371000002X

36. van Heerdt, G., Kappé, T., Rot, J., Silva, A.: Learning Pomset Automata. In: FOSSACS 2021. LNCS, vol. 12650, pp. 510–530. Springer, Cham (2021). https://doi.org/10.1007/978-3-030-71995-1_26
37. Hougardy, S.: On the P4-structure of perfect graphs. Citeseer (1996)
38. Hughes, D.: Proofs without syntax. Ann. Math. **164**(3), 1065–1076 (2006). https://doi.org/10.4007/annals.2006.164.1065
39. Hughes, D.: Towards Hilbert's 24th problem: combinatorial proof invariants: (preliminary version). Electr. Notes Theor. Comput. Sci. **165**, 37–63 (2006)
40. Hyland, J.M.E., Ong, C.H.L.: On full abstraction for PCF: I. Models, observables and the full abstraction problem, II. Dialogue games and innocent strategies, III. A fully abstract and universal game model. Inf. Comput. **163**, 285–408 (2000)
41. James, L.O., Stanton, R.G., Cowan, D.D.: Graph decomposition for undirected graphs. In: Proceedings of the Third Southeastern Conference on Combinatorics, Graph Theory, and Computing (Florida Atlantic Univ., Boca Raton, Fla., 1972). pp. 281–290 (1972)
42. Jamison, B., Olariu, S.: P-components and the homogeneous decomposition of graphs. SIAM J. Discret. Math. **8**(3), 448–463 (1995)
43. Kogkalidis, K., Moortgat, M., Moot, R.: Neural proof nets. In: Fernández, R., Linzen, T. (eds.) Proceedings of the 24th Conference on Computational Natural Language Learning, pp. 26–40. Association for Computational Linguistics, Online (2020). https://doi.org/10.18653/v1/2020.conll-1.3, https://aclanthology.org/2020.conll-1.3
44. Lellmann, B., Pimentel, E.: Modularisation of sequent calculi for normal and non-normal modalities. ACM Trans. Comput. Logic **20**(2) (2019). https://doi.org/10.1145/3288757
45. Lovász, L., Plummer, M.D.: Matching Theory, vol. 367. American Mathematical Society, Providence (2009)
46. Mac Lane, S.: Categories for the Working Mathematician. Graduate Texts in Mathematics, vol. 5. Springer, New York (1971). https://doi.org/10.1007/978-1-4757-4721-8
47. Maieli, R.: Non decomposable connectives of linear logic. Ann. Pure Appl. Logic **170**(11), 102709 (2019). https://doi.org/10.1016/j.apal.2019.05.006, http://www.sciencedirect.com/science/article/pii/S0168007219300600
48. McConnell, R.M., Spinrad, J.P.: Linear-time modular decomposition and efficient transitive orientation of comparability graphs. In: Proceedings of the Fifth Annual ACM-SIAM Symposium on Discrete Algorithms. SODA '94, pp. 536–545. Society for Industrial and Applied Mathematics, USA (1994)
49. Mell, S., Bastani, O., Zdancewic, S.: Ideograph: a language for expressing and manipulating structured data. In: Grabmayer, C. (ed.) Proceedings Twelfth International Workshop on Computing with Terms and Graphs, TERMGRAPH@FSCD 2022, Technion, Haifa, Israel, 1st August 2022. EPTCS, vol. 377, pp. 65–84 (2022). https://doi.org/10.4204/EPTCS.377.4
50. Miller, D., Pimentel, E.: A formal framework for specifying sequent calculus proof systems. Theor. Comput. Sci. **474**, 98–116 (2013)
51. Miller, D., Saurin, A.: From proofs to focused proofs: a modular proof of focalization in linear logic. In: Duparc, J., Henzinger, T.A. (eds.) CSL 2007. LNCS, vol. 4646, pp. 405–419. Springer, Heidelberg (2007). https://doi.org/10.1007/978-3-540-74915-8_31
52. Nguyên, L.T.D., Seiller, T.: Coherent interaction graphs: a non-deterministic geometry of interaction for MLL (2019)
53. Nguyên, L.T.D., Straßburger, L.: A system of interaction and structure III: the complexity of BV and Pomset logic. In: Working Paper or Preprint (2022). https://hal.inria.fr/hal-03909547
54. Nguyên, L.T.D., Straßburger, L.: BV and Pomset logic are not the same. In: Manea, F., Simpson, A. (eds.) 30th EACSL Annual Conference on Computer Science Logic (CSL 2022). Leibniz International Proceedings in Informatics (LIPIcs), vol. 216, pp. 3:1–3:17. Schloss Dagstuhl – Leibniz-Zentrum für Informatik, Dagstuhl, Germany (2022). https://doi.org/10.4230/LIPIcs.CSL.2022.3, https://drops.dagstuhl.de/opus/volltexte/2022/15723

55. Nielsen, M., Plotkin, G., Winskel, G.: Petri nets, event structures and domains, part I. Theor. Comput. Sci. **13**(1), 85–108 (1981)
56. Pratt, V.: Modeling concurrency with partial orders. Int. J. Parallel Prog. **15**, 33–71 (1986)
57. Retoré, C.: Pomset logic: the other approach to noncommutativity in logic. In: Joachim Lambek: The Interplay of Mathematics, Logic, and Linguistics, pp. 299–345 (2021)
58. Rideau, S., Winskel, G.: Concurrent strategies. In: 2011 IEEE 26th Annual Symposium on Logic in Computer Science, pp. 409–418. IEEE (2011)
59. Seely, R.: Linear logic, *-autonomous categories and cofree coalgebras. Contemp. Math. **92** (1989)
60. Tiu, A.F.: A system of interaction and structure II: the need for deep inference. Logic. Methods Comput. Sci. **2**(2), 1–24 (2006). https://doi.org/10.2168/LMCS-2(2:4)2006
61. Troelstra, A.S., Schwichtenberg, H.: Basic Proof Theory, 2nd edn. Cambridge University Press, Cambridge (2000)
62. Valdes, J., Tarjan, R.E., Lawler, E.L.: The recognition of series parallel digraphs. In: Proceedings of the Eleventh Annual ACM Symposium on Theory of Computing, pp. 1–12. ACM (1979)
63. Waring, T.: A graph theoretic extension of Boolean logic. Master's thesis (2019). http://anupamdas.com/thesis_tim-waring.pdf
64. Winskel, G., Rideau, S., Clairambault, P., Castellan, S.: Games and strategies as event structures. Logic. Methods Comput. Sci. **13** (2017)

A Proof Theory of (ω-)Context-Free Languages, via Non-wellfounded Proofs

Anupam Das and Abhishek De(✉)

School of Computer Science, University of Birmingham, Birmingham, UK
{a.das,a.de}@bham.ac.uk

Abstract. We investigate the proof theory of regular expressions with fixed points, construed as a notation for (ω-)context-free grammars. Starting with a hypersequential system for regular expressions due to Das and Pous [15], we define its extension by least fixed points and prove the soundness and completeness of its non-wellfounded proofs for the standard language model. From here we apply proof-theoretic techniques to recover an infinitary axiomatisation of the resulting equational theory, complete for inclusions of context-free languages. Finally, we extend our syntax by greatest fixed points, now computing ω-context-free languages. We show the soundness and completeness of the corresponding system using a mixture of proof-theoretic and game-theoretic techniques.

Keywords: Proof theory · Context-free languages · Omega-languages · Games · Chomsky algebra · Non-wellfounded proofs

1 Introduction

The characterisation of context-free languages (CFLs) as the least solutions of algebraic inequalities, sometimes known as the *ALGOL-like theorem*, is a folklore result attributed to several luminaries of formal language theory including Ginsburg and Rice [21], Schutzenberger [52], and Gruska [23]. This induces a syntax for CFLs by adding least fixed point operators to regular expressions, as first noted by Salomaa [51]. Leiß [38] called these constructs "μ-expressions" and defined an algebraic theory over them by appropriately extending Kleene algebras, which work over regular expressions. Notable recent developments include a generalisation of Antimirov's partial derivatives to μ-expressions [54] and criteria for identifying μ-expressions that can be parsed unambiguously [34].

Establishing axiomatisations and proof systems for classes of formal languages has been a difficult challenge. Many *theories* of regular expressions, such as Kleene algebras (KA) were proposed in the late 20th century (see, e.g., [6,28,29]). The completeness of KA for the (equational) theory of regular languages, due to Kozen [29] and Krob [35] independently, is a celebrated result that has led to several extensions and refinements, e.g. [7,31–33]. More recently the proof theory of KA has been studied via *infinitary* systems. On one hand, [49] proposed an ω-*branching* sequent calculus and on the other hand [12,15,25] have studied *cyclic* 'hypersequential' calculi.

C. Benzmüller et al. (Eds.): IJCAR 2024, LNAI 14740, pp. 237–256, 2024.
https://doi.org/10.1007/978-3-031-63501-4_13

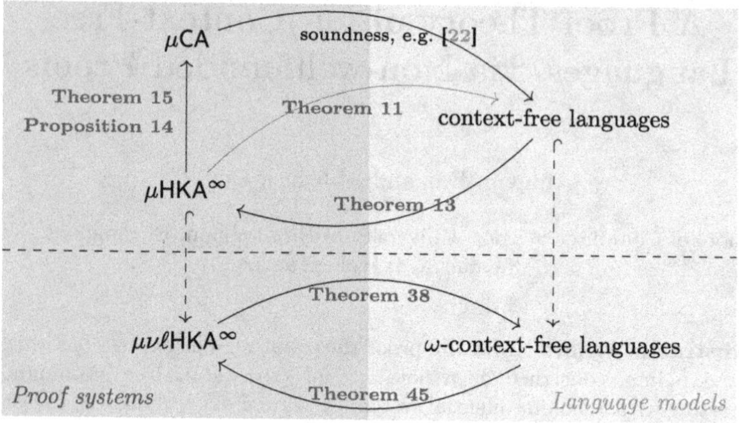

Fig. 1. Summary of our main contributions. Each arrow → denotes an inclusion of equational theories, over an appropriate language of μ-expressions. The gray arrow, Theorem 11, is also a consequence of the remaining black ones. (Color figure online)

Inclusion of CFLs is Π_1^0-complete, so any recursive (hence also cyclic) axiomatisation must necessarily be incomplete. Nonetheless various theories of μ-expressions have been extensively studied, in particular *Chomsky algebras* and *μ-semirings* [17,18,39,40], giving rise to a rich algebraic theory. Indeed Grathwohl, Henglein, and Kozen [22] have given a complete (but infinitary) axiomatisation of the equational theory of μ-expressions, by extending these algebraic theories with a *continuity* principle for least fixed points.

Contributions. In this paper, we propose a *non-wellfounded* system $\mu\mathsf{HKA}^\infty$ for μ-expressions. It can be seen as an extension of the cyclic system of [15] for regular expressions. Our first main contribution is the adequacy of this system for CFLs: $\mu\mathsf{HKA}^\infty$ proves $e = f$ just if the CFLs computed by e and f, $\mathcal{L}(e)$ and $\mathcal{L}(f)$ respectively, are the same. We use this result to obtain an alternative proof of completeness of the infinitary axiomatisation $\mu\mathsf{CA}$ of [22], comprising our second main result. Our method is inspired by previous techniques in non-wellfounded proof theory, namely [11,53], employing 'projections' to translate non-wellfounded proofs to wellfounded ones. Our result is actually somewhat stronger than that of [22], since our wellfounded proofs are furthermore *cut-free*.

Finally we develop an extension $\mu\nu\ell\mathsf{HKA}$ of (leftmost) $\mu\mathsf{HKA}$ by adding *greatest* fixed points, ν, for which $\mathcal{L}(\cdot)$ extends to a model of *ω-context-free languages*. Our third main contribution is the soundness and completeness of $\mu\nu\ell\mathsf{HKA}$ for $\mathcal{L}(\cdot)$. Compared to $\mu\mathsf{HKA}$, the difficulty for metalogical reasoning here is to control interleavings of μ and ν, both for soundness argument and in controlling proof search for completeness. To this end, we employ *game theoretic* techniques to characterise word membership and control proof search.

All our main results are summarised in Fig. 1. Due to space constraints many proofs and auxiliary material are omitted, but may be found in a full version [9].

2 A Syntax for Context-Free Grammars

Throughout this work we make use of a finite set $\mathcal{A}$ (the **alphabet**) of **letters**, written $a, b, \ldots$, and a countable set $\mathcal{V}$ of **variables**, written $X, Y, \ldots$. When speaking about context-free grammars (CFGs), we always assume non-terminals are from $\mathcal{V}$ and the terminals are from $\mathcal{A}$.

We define **(μ-)expressions**, written e, f, etc., by:

$$e, f, \ldots \quad ::= 0 \mid 1 \mid X \mid a \mid e + f \mid e \cdot f \mid \mu X e \tag{1}$$

We usually simply write ef instead of $e \cdot f$. μ is considered a variable binder, with the *free variables* $\mathrm{FV}(e)$ of an expression e defined as expected. We sometimes refer to expressions as *formulas*, and write $\sqsubseteq$ for the subformula relation.

μ-expressions compute languages of finite words in the expected way:

Definition 1 (Language Semantics). *Let us temporarily expand the syntax of expressions to include each language $A \subseteq \mathcal{A}^*$ as a constant symbol. We interpret each closed expression (of this expanded language) as a subset of $\mathcal{A}^*$ as follows:*

- $\mathcal{L}(0) := \varnothing$
- $\mathcal{L}(1) := \{\varepsilon\}$
- $\mathcal{L}(a) := \{a\}$
- $\mathcal{L}(A) := A$
- $\mathcal{L}(e + f) := \mathcal{L}(e) \cup \mathcal{L}(f)$
- $\mathcal{L}(ef) := \{vw : v \in \mathcal{L}(e), w \in \mathcal{L}(f)\}$
- $\mathcal{L}(\mu X e(X)) := \bigcap\{A \supseteq \mathcal{L}(e(A))\}$

Note that all the operators of our syntax correspond to monotone operations on $\mathcal{P}(\mathcal{A}^*)$, with respect to $\subseteq$. Thus $\mathcal{L}(\mu X e(X))$ is just the least fixed point of the operation $A \mapsto \mathcal{L}(e(A))$, by the Knaster-Tarski fixed point theorem.

The **productive** expressions, written p, q etc. are generated by:

$$p, q, \ldots \quad ::= \quad a \quad \mid \quad p + q \quad \mid \quad p \cdot e \quad \mid \quad e \cdot p \quad \mid \quad \mu X p \tag{2}$$

We say that an expression is **guarded** if each variable occurrence occurs free in a productive subexpression. **Left-productive** and **left-guarded** are defined in the same way, only omitting the clause $e \cdot p$ in the grammar above. For convenience of exposition we shall employ the following convention throughout:

Convention 2. *Henceforth we assume all expressions are guarded.*

Example 3. (Empty language). In the semantics above, note that the empty language $\varnothing$ is computed by several expressions, not only 0 but also $\mu X X$ and $\mu X(aX)$. Note that whle the former is unguarded the latter is (left-)guarded. In this sense the inclusion of 0 is somewhat 'syntactic sugar', but it will facilitate some of our later development.

Example 4. (Kleene star and universal language). For any expression e we can compute its Kleene star $e^* := \mu X(1+eX)$ or $e^* := \mu X(1+Xe)$. These definitions are guarded just when e is productive. Now, note that we also have not included a symbol $\top$ for the universal language $\mathcal{A}^*$. We can compute this by the expression $(\sum \mathcal{A})^*$, which is guarded as $\sum \mathcal{A}$ is productive.

Non-logical rules:

$$\text{init}\ \frac{}{\rightarrow []} \qquad \text{w-}r\ \frac{\Gamma \rightarrow S}{\Gamma \rightarrow S, [\Delta]} \qquad \mathsf{k}^l_a\ \frac{\Gamma \rightarrow S}{a, \Gamma \rightarrow aS} \qquad \mathsf{k}^r_a\ \frac{\Gamma \rightarrow S}{\Gamma, a \rightarrow Sa}$$

Left logical rules:

$$0\text{-}l\ \frac{}{\Gamma, 0, \Gamma' \rightarrow S} \qquad 1\text{-}l\ \frac{\Gamma, \Gamma' \rightarrow S}{\Gamma, 1, \Gamma' \rightarrow S} \qquad \cdot\text{-}l\ \frac{\Gamma, e, f, \Gamma' \rightarrow S}{\Gamma, ef, \Gamma' \rightarrow S}$$

$$+\text{-}l\ \frac{\Gamma, e, \Gamma' \rightarrow S \quad \Gamma, f, \Gamma' \rightarrow S}{\Gamma, e+f, \Gamma' \rightarrow S} \qquad \mu\text{-}l\ \frac{\Gamma, e(\mu X e(X)), \Gamma' \rightarrow S}{\Gamma, \mu X e(X), \Gamma' \rightarrow S}$$

Right logical rules:

$$0\text{-}r\ \frac{\Gamma \rightarrow S}{\Gamma \rightarrow S, [\Delta, 0, \Delta']} \qquad 1\text{-}r\ \frac{\Gamma \rightarrow S, [\Delta, \Delta']}{\Gamma \rightarrow S, [\Delta, 1, \Delta']} \qquad \cdot\text{-}r\ \frac{\Gamma \rightarrow S, [\Delta, e, f, \Delta]}{\Gamma \rightarrow S, [\Delta, ef, \Delta']}$$

$$+\text{-}r\ \frac{\Gamma \rightarrow S, [\Delta, e, \Delta'], [\Delta, f, \Delta']}{\Gamma \rightarrow S, [\Delta, e+f, \Delta']} \qquad \mu\text{-}r\ \frac{\Gamma \rightarrow S, [\Delta, e(\mu X e(X)), \Delta']}{\Gamma \rightarrow S, [\Delta, \mu X e(X), \Delta']}$$

Fig. 2. Rules of the system $\mu\mathsf{HKA}$.

It is well-known that μ-expressions compute just the context-free (CF) languages [21,23,52]. In fact this holds even under the restriction to left-guarded expressions, by simulating the *Greibach normal form*:

Theorem 5. (Adequacy, see, e.g., [17,18]). *L is context-free (and $\varepsilon \notin L$) $\iff$ $L = \mathcal{L}(e)$ for some e left-guarded (and left-productive, respectively).*

Example 6. Consider the left-guarded expressions $\text{Dyck}_1 := \mu X(1 + \langle X \rangle X)$ and $\{a^n b^n\}_n := \mu X(1 + aXb)$. As suggested, Dyck_1 indeed computes the language of well-bracketed words over alphabet $\{\langle, \rangle\}$, whereas $\{a^n b^n\}_n$ computes the set of words $\boldsymbol{ab}$ with $|\boldsymbol{a}| = |\boldsymbol{b}|$. We can also write $(a^* b^*) := \mu X(1 + aX + Xb)$, which is guarded but not left-guarded. However, if we define Kleene $*$ as in Example 4, then we can write a^* and b^* as left-guarded expressions and then take their product for an alternative representation of $(a^* b^*)$. Note that the empty language $\varnothing$ is computed by the left-guarded expression $\mu X(aX)$, cf. Example 3.

3 A Non-wellfounded Proof System

In this section we extend a calculus HKA from [15] for regular expressions to all μ-expressions, and prove soundness and completeness of its non-wellfounded proofs for the language model $\mathcal{L}(\cdot)$. We shall apply this result in the next section to deduce completeness of an infinitary axiomatisation for $\mathcal{L}(\cdot)$, before considering the extension to *greatest* fixed points later.

A **hypersequent** has the form $\Gamma \rightarrow S$ where Γ (the LHS) is a list of expressions (a **cedent**) and S (the RHS) is a set of such lists. We interpret lists by the product of their elements, and sets by the sum of their elements. Thus we extend our notation for language semantics by $\mathcal{L}(\Gamma) := \mathcal{L}(\prod \Gamma)$ and $\mathcal{L}(S) := \bigcup_{\Gamma \in S} \mathcal{L}(\Gamma)$.

The system $\mu\mathsf{HKA}$ is given by the rules in Fig. 2. Here we use commas to delimit elements of a list or set and square brackets $[,]$ to delimit lists in a set. In the k rules, we write $aS := \{[a, \Gamma] : \Gamma \in S\}$ and $Sa := \{[\Gamma, a] : \Gamma \in S\}$.

For each inference step, as typeset in Fig. 2, the **principal** formula is the distinguished magenta formula occurrence in the lower sequent, while any distinguished magenta formula occurrences in upper sequents are **auxiliary**. (Other colours may be safely ignored for now).

Our system differs from the original presentation of HKA in [15] as (a) we have general fixed point rules, not just for the Kleene $*$; and (b) we have included both left and right versions of the k rule, for symmetry. We extend the corresponding notions of non-wellfounded proof appropriately:

Definition 7 (Non-wellfounded Proofs). *A* ***preproof*** *(of μHKA) is generated* coinductively *from the rules of μHKA i.e. it is a possibly infinite tree of sequents (of height $\leq \omega$) generated by the rules of μHKA. A preproof is* ***regular*** *or* ***cyclic*** *if it has only finitely many distinct subproofs. An infinite branch of a preproof is* ***progressing*** *if it has infinitely many μ-l steps. A preproof is progressing, or a* ***∞-proof****, if all its infinite branches are progressing. We write $\mu\mathsf{HKA} \vdash^{\infty} \Gamma \rightarrow S$ if $\Gamma \rightarrow S$ has a ∞-proof in μHKA, and sometimes write $\mu\mathsf{HKA}^{\infty}$ for the class of ∞-proofs of μHKA.*

Note that our progress condition on preproofs is equivalent to simply checking that every infinite branch has infinitely many left-logical or k steps, as μ-l is the only rule among these that does not decrease the size of the LHS. This is simpler than usual conditions from non-wellfounded proof theory, as we do not have any alternations between the least and greatest fixed points. Indeed we shall require a more complex criterion later when dealing with ω-languages. Note that, as regular preproofs may be written naturally as finite graphs, checking progressiveness for them is efficiently decidable (even in **NL**, see e.g. [8,15]).

The need for such a complex hypersequential line structure is justified in [15] by the desideratum of *regular* completeness for the theory of regular expressions: intuitionistic 'Lambek-like' systems, cf. e.g. [16,26,49] are incomplete (wrt regular cut-free proofs). The complexity of the RHS of sequents in HKA is justified by consideration of proof search for, say, $a^* \rightarrow (aa)^* + a(aa)^*$ and $(a+b)^* \rightarrow a^*(ba^*)^*$, requiring reasoning under sums and products, respectively.

In our extended system, we gain *more* regular proofs of inclusions between context-free languages. For instance:

Example 8. Recall the guarded expressions $\{a^n b^n\}_n$ and (a^*b^*) from Example 6. We have the regular ∞-proof R in Fig. 3 of $\{a^n b^n\}_n \rightarrow [(a^*b^*)]$, where $\bullet$ marks roots of identical subproofs. Note that indeed the only infinite branch, looping on $\bullet$, has infinitely many μ-l steps.

Remark 9 (Impossibility of General Regular Completeness). At this juncture let us make an important point: it is impossible to have any (sound) recursively enumerable system, let alone regular cut-free proofs, complete for context-free inclusions, since this problem is Π^0_1-complete (see e.g. [27]). In this sense examples of regular proofs are somewhat coincidental.

It is not hard to see that each rule of μHKA is sound for language semantics:

$$
\cfrac{
  \cfrac{
    \cfrac{
      \cfrac{
        \cfrac{
          \cfrac{
            \cfrac{
              \cfrac{\vdots}{\{a^n b^n\}_n \to (a^*b^*)}\; \bullet
            }{\{a^n b^n\}_n, b \to [(a^*b^*), b]}\; k_b^r
          }{\{a^n b^n\}_n b \to [(a^*b^*)b]}\; {\cdot}\text{-}l,{\cdot}\text{-}r
        }{\{a^n b^n\}_n b \to [(a^*b^*)]}\; \mu\text{-}r,{+}\text{-}r,w\text{-}r
      }{a, \{a^n b^n\}_n b \to [a, (a^*b^*)]}\; k_a^l
    }{a\{a^n b^n\}_n b \to [a(a^*b^*)]}\; {\cdot}\text{-}l,{\cdot}\text{-}r
  }{a\{a^n b^n\}_n b \to [1 + a(a^*b^*) + (a^*b^*)b]}\; w\text{-}r,{+}\text{-}r
}{\;}
$$

$$
\cfrac{\;}{\;}
$$

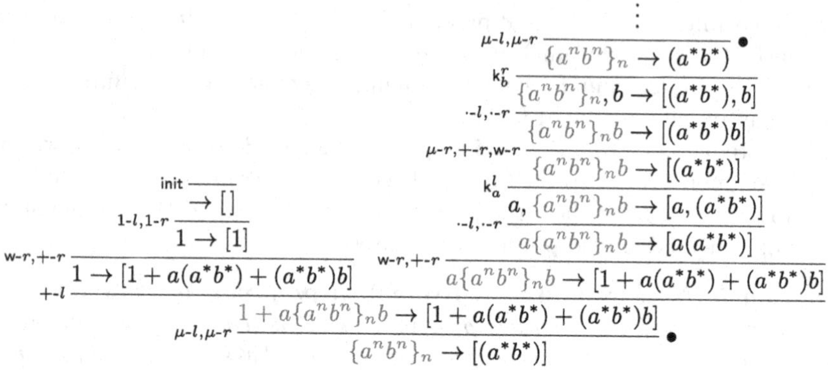

Fig. 3. A regular ∞-proof R of $\{a^n b^n\}_n \to [(a^*b^*)]$.

Lemma 10 (Local Soundness). *For each inference step,*

$$
r\,\frac{\Gamma_0 \to S_0 \quad \cdots \quad \Gamma_{k-1} \to S_{k-1}}{\Gamma \to S} \tag{3}
$$

for some $k \leq 2$, we have: $\forall i < k\, \mathcal{L}(\Gamma_i) \subseteq \mathcal{L}(S_i) \implies \mathcal{L}(\Gamma) \subseteq \mathcal{L}(S)$.

Consequently wellfounded μHKA proofs are also sound for $\mathcal{L}(\cdot)$, by induction on their structure. For non-wellfounded proofs, we must employ a less constructive argument, typical of non-wellfounded proof theory:

Theorem 11 (Soundness). μHKA $\vdash^\infty \Gamma \to S \implies \mathcal{L}(\Gamma) \subseteq \mathcal{L}(S)$.

Proof (Sketch). For contradiction, we use (the contrapositive of) Lemma 10 to construct an infinite 'invalid' branch B, along with an associated sequence of words $(w_i)_{i<\omega}$ of non-increasing length separating the LHS from the RHS. Now, either B has infinitely many k steps, meaning $(|w_i|)_{i<\omega}$ has no least element, or there are only finitely many k steps, in which case $|w_i|$ is eventually dominated by the number of productive expressions in the sequent, by guardedness.

By inspection of the rules of μHKA we have:

Lemma 12 (Invertibility). *Let r be a logical step as in (3).* $\mathcal{L}(\Gamma) \subseteq \mathcal{L}(S) \implies \mathcal{L}(\Gamma_i) \subseteq \mathcal{L}(S_i)$, *for each $i < k$.*

Theorem 13 (Completeness). $\mathcal{L}(\Gamma) \subseteq \mathcal{L}(S) \Rightarrow \mu$HKA $\vdash^\infty \Gamma \to S$.

In fact, we can obtain a stronger result for left-guarded sequents, namely the 'leftmost completeness' as we will see later in Sect. 5. There leftmostness is necessary for soundness, but here completeness is rather straightforward.

Proof (Sketch). We describe a bottom-up proof search strategy:

1. Apply left logical rules maximally, preserving validity by Lemma 12. Any infinite branch is necessarily progressing.
2. This can only terminate at a sequent of the form $a_1, \ldots, a_n \to S$ with $a \in \mathcal{L}(S)$, whence we mimic a 'leftmost' parsing derivation for a wrt S.

4 Completeness of an Infinitary Cut-Free Axiomatisation

While our completeness result above was relatively simple to establish we can use it, along with proof theoretic techniques, to deduce completeness of an infinitary axiomatisation of the theory of μ-expressions. In fact we obtain an alternative proof of the result of [22], strengthening it to a 'cut-free' calculus $\mu\mathsf{HKA}_\omega$.

Write $\mu\mathsf{CA}$ for the set of axioms consisting of:

- $(0, 1, +, \cdot)$ forms an idempotent semiring (aka a *dioid*).
- **(μ-continuity)** $e\mu X f(X) g = \sum_{n<\omega} e f^n(0) g$.

We are using the notation $f^n(0)$ defined by $f^0(0) := 0$ and $f^{n+1}(0) := f(f^n(0))$. We also write $e \leq f$ for the natural order given by $e + f = f$. Now define $\mu\mathsf{HKA}_\omega$ to be the extension of $\mu\mathsf{HKA}$ by the 'ω-rule':

$$\omega \frac{\{\Gamma, e^n(0), \Gamma' \to S\}_{n<\omega}}{\Gamma, \mu X e(X), \Gamma' \to S}$$

By inspection of the rules we have soundness of $\mu\mathsf{HKA}_\omega$ for $\mu\mathsf{CA}$:

Proposition 14. $\mu\mathsf{HKA}_\omega \vdash \Gamma \to S \implies \mu\mathsf{CA} \vdash \prod \Gamma \leq \sum_{\Delta \in S} \prod \Delta$.

Here the soundness of the ω-rule above is immediate from μ-continuity in $\mu\mathsf{CA}$. Note, in particular, that $\mu\mathsf{CA}$ already proves that $\mu X e(X)$ is indeed a fixed point of $e(\cdot)$, i.e. $e(\mu X e(X)) = \mu X e(X)$ [22]. The main result of this section is:

Theorem 15. $\mu\mathsf{HKA} \vdash^\infty e \to f \implies \mu\mathsf{HKA}_\omega \vdash e \leq f$

Note that, immediately from Theorem 13 and Proposition 14, we obtain:

Corollary 16. $\mathcal{L}(e) \subseteq \mathcal{L}(f) \implies \mu\mathsf{HKA}_\omega \vdash e \leq f \implies \mu\mathsf{CA} \vdash e \leq f$

To prove Theorem 15 we employ similar techniques to those used for an extension of *linear logic* with least and greatest fixed points [11], only specialised to the current setting.

Lemma 17 (Projection). *For each ∞-proof P of $\Gamma, \mu X e(X), \Gamma' \to S$ there are ∞-proofs $P(n)$ of $\Gamma, e^n(0), \Gamma' \to S$, for each $n < \omega$.*

The definition of $P(n)$ is somewhat subtle, relying on a form of 'signature' common in fixed point logics, restricted to ω. See [11, Definition 15, Proposition 18] for a formal definition and proof of the analogous result. We shall thus use the notation $P(n)$ etc. freely in the sequel.

From here it is simple to provide a translation from $\mu\mathsf{HKA}$ ∞-proofs to $\mu\mathsf{HKA}_\omega$ preproofs, as in Definition 22 shortly. However, to prove the image of the translation is *wellfounded*, we shall need some structural proof theoretic machinery, which will also serve later use when dealing with greatest fixed points in Sects. 5 and 6.

4.1 Intermezzo: Ancestry and Threads

Given an inference step r, as typeset in Fig. 2, we say a formula occurrence f in an upper sequent is an **immediate ancestor** of a formula occurrence e in the lower sequent if they have the same colour; furthermore if e and f are occur in a cedent $\Gamma, \Gamma', \Delta, \Delta'$, they must be the matching occurrences of the same formula (i.e. at the same position in the cedent); similarly if e and f occur in the RHS context S, they must be matching occurrences in matching lists.

Construing immediate ancestry as a directed graph allows us to characterise progress by consideration of its paths:

Definition 18 ((Progressing) Threads). *Fix a preproof P. A **thread** is a maximal path in the graph of immediate ancestry. An infinite thread on the LHS is **progressing** if it is infinitely often principal (i.o.p.) for a μ-l step.*

Our overloading of terminology is suggestive:

Proposition 19. *P is progressing $\Leftrightarrow$ each branch of P has a progressing thread.*

This has a somewhat subtle proof, relying on König's lemma on the ancestry graph of a progressing branch in order to recover a progressing thread.

Example 20. Recall the ∞-proof in Example 8. The only infinite branch, looping on $\bullet$, has a progressing thread indicated in magenta.

Fact 21 (See, e.g., [30,36]) *Any i.o.p. thread has a unique smallest i.o.p. formula, under the subformula relation. This formula must be a fixed point formula.*

4.2 Translation to ω-Branching System

We are now ready to give a translation from $\mu\mathsf{HKA}^\infty$ to $\mu\mathsf{HKA}_\omega$.

Definition 22 (ω-Translation). *For preproofs P define P^ω by coinduction:*

- $\cdot^\omega$ *commutes with any step not a μ-l.*
- $$\left(\mu\text{-}l\,\frac{\begin{array}{c} \vdots\, P \\ \Gamma, e(\mu X e(X)), \Gamma' \rightarrow S \end{array}}{\Gamma, \mu X e(X), \Gamma' \rightarrow S} \right)^\omega := \omega\,\frac{\left\{ \begin{array}{c} \vdots\, P(n)^\omega \\ \Gamma, e^n(0), \Gamma' \rightarrow S \end{array} \right\}_{n<\omega}}{\Gamma, \mu X e(X), \Gamma' \rightarrow S}$$

Theorem 15 now follows immediately from the following result, obtained by analysis of progressing threads in the image of the ω-translation:

Lemma 23. *P is progressing $\implies$ P^ω is wellfounded.*

The proof of Lemma 23 follows the same argument as for the analogous result in [11, Lemma 23].

Example 24. Recalling Example 8, let us see the ω-translation of R in 3. First, let us (suggestively) write $\{a^kb^k\}_{k<n}$ for the nth approximant of $\{a^nb^n\}_n$, i.e. $\{a^kb^k\}_{k<0} := 0$ and $\{a^kb^k\}_{k<n+1} := 1 + a\{a^kb^k\}_{k<n}b$. Now R^ω is given below, left, where recursively $R(0) := \text{0-}l\,\dfrac{}{0 \to (a^*b^*)}$ and $R(n+1)$ is given below, right:

$$\omega,\mu\text{-}r\ \dfrac{\left\{ \begin{matrix} R(n) \\ \{a^kb^k\}_{k<n} \to [(a^*b^*)] \end{matrix} \right\}_{n<\omega}}{\{a^nb^n\}_n \to [(a^*b^*)]} \quad ; \quad \text{+-}l\ \dfrac{\dfrac{\text{1-}l,\text{1-}r\ \dfrac{\text{init}\ \dfrac{}{\to []}}{1 \to [1]}}{1 \to [(a^*b^*)]} \qquad \dfrac{\cdot\text{-}l,\cdot\text{-}r\ \dfrac{\mathsf{k}_a^l\ \dfrac{\mu\text{-}r,\text{+-}r,\text{w-}r\ \dfrac{\cdot\text{-}l,\cdot\text{-}r\ \dfrac{\mathsf{k}_b^r\ \dfrac{\dfrac{R(n)}{\{a^kb^k\}_{k<n} \to (a^*b^*)}}{\{a^kb^k\}_{k<n}, b \to [(a^*b^*), b]}}{\{a^kb^k\}_{k<n}b \to [(a^*b^*)b]}}{\{a^kb^k\}_{k<n}b \to [(a^*b^*)]}}{a, \{a^kb^k\}_{k<n}b \to [a, (a^*b^*)]}}{a\{a^kb^k\}_{k<n}b \to [a(a^*b^*)]}}{a\{a^kb^k\}_{k<n}b \to [(a^*b^*)]}}{1 + a\{a^kb^k\}_{k<n}b \to [(a^*b^*)]}$$

5 Greatest Fixed Points and ω-Languages

We extend the grammar of expressions from (1) by:

$$e, f \ldots \quad ::= \quad \ldots \quad | \quad \nu X e(X)$$

We call such expressions *$\mu\nu$-expressions* when we need to distinguish them from ones without ν. The notions of a *(left-)productive* and *(left-)guarded* expression are defined in the same way, extending the grammar of (2) by the clause $\nu X p$.

As expected $\mu\nu$-expressions denote languages of finite and infinite words:

Definition 25 (Intended Semantics of $\mu\nu$-Expressions). *We extend the notation vw to all $v, w \in \mathcal{A}^{\leq\omega}$ by setting $vw = v$ when $|v| = \omega$. We extend the definition of $\mathcal{L}(\cdot)$ from Definition 1 to all $\mu\nu$-expressions by setting $\mathcal{L}(\nu X e(X)) := \bigcup\{A \subseteq \mathcal{L}(e(A))\}$ where now A varies over subsets of $\mathcal{A}^{\leq\omega}$.*

Again, since all the operations are monotone, $\mathcal{L}(\nu X e(X))$ is indeed the greatest fixed point of the operation $A \mapsto \mathcal{L}(e(A))$, by the Knaster-Tarski theorem. In fact (ω-)languages computed by $\mu\nu$-expressions are just the 'ω-context-free languages' (ω-CFLs), cf. [5,42], defined as the 'Kleene closure' of CFLs:

Definition 26 (ω-Context-Free Languages). *For $A \subseteq \mathcal{A}^+$ we write $A^\omega := \{w_0w_1w_2\cdots : \forall i < \omega\, w_i \in A\}$. The class of ω-**CFLs** (CF^ω) is defined by:*

$$\mathsf{CF}^\omega := \left\{ \bigcup_{i<n} A_i B_i^\omega \ : \ n < \omega;\ A_i, B_i \text{ context-free and } \varepsilon \notin A_i, B_i,\ \forall i < n \right\}$$

It is not hard to see that each ω-CFL is computed by a $\mu\nu$-expression, by noting that $\mathcal{L}(e)^\omega = \mathcal{L}(\nu X(eX))$:

Proposition 27. *$L \in \mathsf{CF}^\omega \implies L = \mathcal{L}(e)$ for some left-productive e.*

We shall address the converse of this result later. First let us present our system for $\mu\nu$-expressions, a natural extension of μHKA earlier:

Definition 28 (System). *The system $\mu\nu$HKA extends μHKA by the rules:*

$$\nu\text{-}l \frac{\Gamma, e(\nu X e(X)), \Gamma' \to S}{\Gamma, \nu X e(X), \Gamma' \to S} \qquad \nu\text{-}r \frac{\Gamma \to S, [\Delta, e(\nu X e(X), \Delta']}{\Gamma \to S, [\Delta, \nu X e(X), \Delta']} \tag{4}$$

Preproofs *for this system are defined just as for μHKA before. The definitions of* immediate ancestor *and* thread *for $\mu\nu$HKA extends that of μHKA from Definition 18 according to the colouring above in* (4).

However we must be more nuanced in defining progress, requiring a definition at the level of threads as in Sect. 4. Noting that Fact 21 holds for our extended language with νs as well as μs, we call an i.o.p. thread a **μ-thread** (or **ν-thread**) if its smallest i.o.p. formula is a μ-formula (or ν-formula, respectively).

Definition 29 (Progress). *Fix a preproof P. We say that an infinite thread τ along a (infinite) branch B of P is* **progressing** *if it is i.o.p. and it is a μ-thread on the LHS or it is a ν-thread on the RHS. B is* **progressing** *if it has a progressing thread. P is a* **∞-proof** *of $\mu\nu$HKA if each of its infinite branches has a progressing thread.*

Example 30. Write $e := \nu Z(abZ)$ and $f := \mu Y(b + \nu X(aYX))$. The sequent $e \to [f]$ has a preproof given in Fig. 4. This preproof has just one infinite branch, looping on $\bullet$, which indeed has a progressing thread following the magenta formulas. The only fixed point infinitely often principal along this thread is $\nu X(afX)$, which is principal at each $\bullet$. Thus this preproof is a proof and $e \to [f]$ is a theorem of $\mu\ell\mathsf{HKA}^\infty$.

Note that, even though this preproof is progressing, the infinite branch's smallest i.o.p. formula on the RHS is *not* a ν-formula, e.g. given by the magenta thread, as f is also i.o.p. Let us point out that (a) the progressiveness condition only requires *existence* of a progressing thread, even if other threads are not progressing (like the unique LHS thread above).

Some Necessary Conventions: Left-Guarded and Leftmost

Crucially, due to the asymmetry in the definition of the product of infinite words, we must employ further conventions to ensure soundness and completeness of ∞-proofs for $\mathcal{L}(\cdot)$. Our choice of conventions is inspired by the usual 'leftmost' semantics of 'ω-CFGs', which we shall see in the next section.

First, we shall henceforth work with a *lefmost* restriction of $\mu\nu$HKA in order to maintain soundness for $\mathcal{L}(\cdot)$:

$$
\begin{array}{rc}
 & \vdots \\ \hline
\nu\text{-}r & e \to [\nu X(afX)] \quad \bullet \\ \hline
\mathsf{k}_b & b, e \to [b, \nu X(afX)] \\ \hline
\mathsf{w}\text{-}r & b, e \to [b, \nu X(afX)], [\nu X(aYX), \nu X(afX)] \\ \hline
+\text{-}r & b, e \to [b + \nu X(aYX), \nu X(afX)] \\ \hline
\mu\text{-}r & b, e \to [f, \nu X(afX)] \\ \hline
\mathsf{k}_a & a, b, e \to [a, f, \nu X(afX)] \\ \hline\hline
\cdot\text{-}l, \cdot\text{-}r & abe \to [af\nu X(afX)] \\ \hline
\nu\text{-}r & e \to [\nu X(afX)] \quad \bullet \\ \hline
\mathsf{w}\text{-}r & e \to [b], [\nu X(afX)] \\ \hline
+\text{-}r & e \to [b + \nu X(afX)] \\ \hline
\mu\text{-}r & e \to [f]
\end{array}
$$

Fig. 4. A $\mu\nu\ell\mathsf{HKA}$ ∞-preproof of $e \to [f]$, where $e := \nu Z(abZ)$ and $f := \mu Y(b + \nu X(aYX))$.

Definition 31. *A $\mu\nu\mathsf{HKA}$ preproof is* ***leftmost*** *if each logical step has principal formula the leftmost formula of its cedent, and there are no k^r-steps. Write $\mu\nu\ell\mathsf{HKA}$ for the restriction of $\mu\nu\mathsf{HKA}$ to only leftmost steps and $\mu\nu\ell\mathsf{HKA}^\infty$ for the class of ∞-proofs of $\mu\nu\ell\mathsf{HKA}$.*

We must also restrict ourselves to left-guarded expressios in the sequel:

Convention 32 *Henceforth, all expressions are assumed to be left-guarded.*

Let us justify both of these restrictions via some examples.

Remark 33 (Unsound for Non-leftmost). Unlike the μ-only setting it turns out that $\mu\nu\mathsf{HKA}^\infty$ is unsound without the leftmost restriction, regardless of left-guardedness. For instance consider the preproof,

$$
\begin{array}{rc}
 & \vdots \\ \hline
\nu\text{-}r & \to [a, \nu X(aX)] \quad a, \bullet \\ \hline
\cdot\text{-}r & \to [a\nu X(aX)] \\ \hline
\nu\text{-}r & \to [\nu X(aX)] \quad \bullet
\end{array}
$$

where $a, \bullet$ roots the same subproof as $\bullet$, but for an extra a on the left of every RHS. Of course the endsequent is not valid, as the LHS denotes $\{\varepsilon\}$ while the RHS denotes $\{a^\omega\}$. Note also that, while it is progressing thanks to the thread in magenta, it is not leftmost due to the topmost displayed ν-r step.

Remark 34 (Incomplete for Unguarded). On the other hand, without the left-guardedness restriction, $\mu\nu\ell\mathsf{HKA}^\infty$ is not complete. For instance the sequent $\nu XX \to [\,], \{[a, \nu XX]\}_{a\in\mathcal{A}}$ is indeed valid as both sides compute all of $\mathcal{P}(\mathcal{A}^{\leq\omega})$:

Position	Available move(s)
$(aw, [a, \Delta])$	(w, Δ)
$(w, [1, \Delta])$	(w, Δ)
$(w, [e + f, \Delta])$	$(w, [e, \Delta]), (w, [f, \Delta])$
$(w, [ef, \Delta])$	$(w, [e, f, \Delta])$
$(w, [\mu X f(X), \Delta])$	$(w, [f(\mu X f(X)), \Delta])$
$(w, [\nu X f(X), \Delta])$	$(w, [f(\nu X f(X)), \Delta])$

Fig. 5. Rules of the evaluation puzzle.

any word is either empty or begins with a letter. However the only available (leftmost) rule application, bottom-up, is ν-l, which is a fixed point of leftmost proof search, obviously not yielding a progressing preproof.

6 Metalogical Results: A Game-Theoretic Approach

Now we return to addressing the expressiveness of both the syntax of $\mu\nu$-expressions and our system $\mu\nu\ell\mathsf{HKA}^\infty$, employing game-theoretic methods.

6.1 Evaluation Puzzle and Soundness

As an engine for our main metalogical results about $\mu\nu\ell\mathsf{HKA}$, and for a converse to Proposition 27, we first characterise membership via games:

Definition 35. *The* ***evaluation puzzle*** *is a puzzle (i.e. one-player game) whose positions are pairs* (w, Γ) *where* $w \in \mathcal{A}^{\leq\omega}$ *and* Γ *is a cedent, i.e. a list of* $\mu\nu$*-expressions. A* ***play*** *of the puzzle runs according to the rules in Fig. 5: puzzle-play is deterministic at each state except when the expression is a sum, in which case a choice must be made. During a play of the evaluation puzzle, formula ancestry and threads are defined as for* $\mu\nu\ell\mathsf{HKA}$ *preproofs, by associating each move with the LHS of a left logical rule. A play is* ***winning*** *if:*

- *it terminates at the winning state* $(\varepsilon, [\,])$*; or,*
- *it is infinite and has a* ν*-thread (along its right components).*

Example 36. Define $d := \mu X(\langle\rangle + \langle X\rangle X)$, the set of non-empty well-bracketed words. Let $d^\omega := \nu Y dY$. Let us look at a play from $(\langle^\omega, [d^\omega])$.

$$\longrightarrow (\langle^\omega, [d^\omega]) \longrightarrow (\langle^\omega, [dd^\omega]) \longrightarrow (\langle^\omega, [d, d^\omega]) \longrightarrow (\langle^\omega, [\langle\rangle + \langle d\rangle d, d^\omega]) \longrightarrow (\langle^\omega, [\langle d\rangle d, d^\omega])$$
$$\downarrow$$
$$\dots \longleftarrow (\langle^\omega, [d, \rangle d, d^\omega]) \longleftarrow (\langle^\omega, [d\rangle d, d^\omega]) \longleftarrow (\langle^\omega, [\langle, d\rangle d, d^\omega])$$

The play continues without d^ω ever being principal (essentially, going into deeper and deeper nesting to match a $\langle$ with a $\rangle$). Since even the first match is never made there is no hope of progress. The play (and, in fact, any play) is thus losing. On the other hand the following play from $(u, [d^\omega])$, where $u = (\langle\rangle)^\omega$ is indeed winning, with progressing ν-thread indicated in magenta.

$$\to (u,[d^\omega]) \xrightarrow{3} (u,[d,d^\omega]) \to (u,[\langle\rangle + \langle d\rangle d, d^\omega]) \to (u,[\langle\rangle, d^\omega]) \to (u,[\langle,\rangle, d^\omega]) \to ()u,[\rangle, d^\omega])$$

Theorem 37 (Evaluation). *$w \in \mathcal{L}(\Gamma) \Leftrightarrow$ there is a winning play from (w, Γ).*

The proof is rather involved, employing the method of 'signatures' common in fixed point logics, cf. e.g. [48], which serve as 'least witnesses' to word membership via carefully managing *ordinal approximants* for fixed points. Here we must be somewhat more careful in the argument because positions of our puzzle include *cedents*, not single formulas: we must crucially assign signatures to *each* formula of a cedent. Working with cedents rather than formulas allows the evaluation puzzle to remain strictly single player. This is critical for expressivity: *alternating* context-free grammars and pushdown automata compute more than just CFLs [4,45].

We can now prove the soundness of $\mu\nu\ell\mathsf{HKA}^\infty$ by reduction to Theorem 37:

Theorem 38 (Soundness). $\mu\nu\ell\mathsf{HKA} \vdash^\infty \Gamma \to S \implies \mathcal{L}(\Gamma) \subseteq \mathcal{L}(S)$.

Proof (Sketch). Let P be a ∞-proof of $\Gamma \to S$ and $w \in \mathcal{L}(\Gamma)$. We show $w \in \mathcal{L}(S)$. First, since $w \in \mathcal{L}(\Gamma)$ there is a winning play π from (w, Γ) by Theorem 37, which induces a unique (maximal) branch B_π of P which must have a progressing thread τ. Now, since π is a *winning* play from (w, e), τ cannot be on the LHS, so it is an RHS ν-thread following, say, a sequence of cedents $[\Gamma_i]_{i<\omega}$. By construction $[\Gamma_i]_{i<\omega}$ has an infinite subsequence, namely whenever it is principal, that forms (the right components of) a winning play from (w, Γ_0), with $\Gamma_0 \in S$. Thus indeed $w \in \mathcal{L}(S)$ by Theorem 37.

6.2 ω-Context-Freeness via Muller Grammars

We can now use the adequacy of the evaluation puzzle to recover a converse of Proposition 27. For this, we need to recall a grammar-formulation of CF^ω, due to Cohen and Gold [5] and independently Nivat [46,47].

A **Muller (ω-)CFG** (MCFG) is a CFG $\mathcal{G}$, equipped with a set $F \subseteq \mathcal{P}(\mathcal{V})$ of **accepting** sets of productions. We define a rewrite relation $\to_\mathcal{G} \subseteq (\mathcal{V} \cup \mathcal{A})^* \times (\mathcal{V} \cup \mathcal{A})^*$, **leftmost reduction**, by $\boldsymbol{a}Xv \to_\mathcal{G} \boldsymbol{a}uv$ whenever $\boldsymbol{a} \in \mathcal{A}^*$, $X \to u$ is a production of $\mathcal{G}$ and $v \in (\mathcal{V} \cup \mathcal{A})^*$. A **leftmost derivation** is just a maximal (possibly infinite) sequence along $\to_\mathcal{G}$. We say $\mathcal{G}$ **accepts** $w \in \mathcal{A}^{\leq\omega}$ if there is a leftmost derivation δ such that δ converges to w and the set of infinitely often occurring states that are LHSs of productions along δ is in F. We write $\mathcal{L}(\mathcal{G})$ for the set of words $\mathcal{G}$ accepts.

Theorem 39 ([5,46,47]). *Let $L \subseteq \mathcal{A}^\omega$. $L \in \mathsf{CF}^\omega \Leftrightarrow L = \mathcal{L}(\mathcal{G})$ for a MCFG $\mathcal{G}$.*

Now we have a converse of Proposition 27 by:

Proposition 40. *For each expression e there is a MCFG $\mathcal{G}$ s.t. $\mathcal{L}(e) = \mathcal{L}(\mathcal{G})$.*

Proof (sketch). Given a $\mu\nu$-expression e, we construct a grammar just like in the proof of Theorem 5, but with extra clause $X_{\nu X f(X)} \to X_{f(\nu X f(X))}$. We maintain two copies of each non-terminal, one magenta and one normal so that a derivation also 'guesses' a ν-thread 'on the fly'. Now set F, the set of acceptable sets, to include all sets extending some $\{X_f : f \in E\}$, for E with the smallest expression a ν-formula, by normal non-terminals. Now any accepting leftmost derivation of a word w from X_e describes a winning play of the evaluation puzzle from (w, e) and vice-versa.

6.3 Proof Search Game and Completeness

In order to prove completeness of $\mu\nu\ell\mathsf{HKA}^\infty$, we need to introduce a game-theoretic mechanism for organising proof search, in particular so that we can rely on *determinacy* principles thereof.

Definition 41 (Proof Search Game). *The* proof search game *(for $\mu\nu\ell\mathsf{HKA}$) is a two-player game played between Prover* (**P**)*, whose positions are inference steps of $\mu\nu\ell\mathsf{HKA}$, and Denier* (**D**)*, whose positions are sequents of $\mu\nu\ell\mathsf{HKA}$. A* ***play*** *of the game starts from a particular sequent: at each turn,* **P** *chooses an inference step with the current sequent as conclusion, and* **D** *chooses a premiss of that step; the process repeats from this sequent as long as possible.*

An infinite play of the game is ***won*** *by* **P** *(aka* ***lost*** *by* **D***) if the branch constructed has a progressing thread; otherwise it is won by* **D** *(aka lost by* **P***). In the case of deadlock, the player with no valid move loses.*

Proposition 42 (Determinacy ($\exists 0\#$)). *The proof search game is determined, i.e. from any sequent $\Gamma \to S$, either* **P** *or* **D** *has a winning strategy.*

Note that the winning condition of the proof search game is (lightface) analytic, i.e. Σ^1_1: "there *exists* a progressing thread". Lightface analytic determinacy lies beyond ZFC, as indicated equivalent to the existence of 0# [24]. Further consideration of our metatheory is beyond the scope of this work.

It is not hard to see that **P**-winning-strategies are 'just' ∞-proofs. Our goal is to show a similar result for **D**, a sort of 'countermodel construction'.

Lemma 43. **D** *has a winning strategy from $\Gamma \to S \implies \mathcal{L}(\Gamma) \setminus \mathcal{L}(S) \neq \varnothing$.*

Before proving this, let us point out that Lemma 12 applies equally to the system $\mu\nu\mathsf{HKA}$. We also have the useful observation:

Proposition 44 (Modal). $\mathcal{L}(a\Gamma) \subseteq \{\varepsilon\} \cup \bigcup_{a \in \mathcal{A}} \mathcal{L}(aS_a) \implies \mathcal{L}(\Gamma) \subseteq \mathcal{L}(S_a)$.

This follows directly from the definition of $\mathcal{L}(\cdot)$. Now we can carry out our 'countermodel construction' from **D**-winning-strategies:

Proof (Sketch, of Lemma 43). Construct a **P**-strategy $\mathfrak{p}$ that is deadlock-free by always preserving validity, relying on Lemma 12 and Proposition 44. Now, suppose $\mathfrak{d}$ is a **D**-winning-strategy and play $\mathfrak{p}$ against it to construct a play $B = (\mathcal{S}_i)_{i<\omega} = (\Gamma_i \to S_i)_{i<\omega}$. Note that indeed this play must be infinite since

(a) $\mathfrak{p}$ is deadlock-free; and (b) $\mathfrak{d}$ is **D**-winning. Now, let $w = \prod_{\mathsf{k}_a^l \in B} a$ be the product of labels of k steps along B, in the order they appear bottom-up. We claim $w \in \mathcal{L}(\Gamma) \setminus \mathcal{L}(S)$:

- $w \in \mathcal{L}(\Gamma)$. By construction $[\Gamma_i]_i$ has a subsequence forming an infinite play π of the evaluation puzzle from (w, Γ). Since the play B is won by **D**, B cannot have a μ-thread so it must have a ν-thread (since it is i.o.p.), and so π is winning. Thus $w \in \mathcal{L}(\Gamma)$ by Theorem 37.
- $w \notin \mathcal{L}(S)$. Take an arbitrary play π of the evaluation puzzle from some (w, Δ) with $\Delta \in S$. This again induces an infinite sequence of cedents $[\Delta_i]_{i<\omega}$ along the RHSs of B. Now, $[\Delta_i]_{i<\omega}$ cannot have a ν-thread by assumption that B is winning for **D**, and so π is not a winning play of the evaluation puzzle from (w, Δ). Since the choices of $\Delta \in S$ and play π were arbitrary, indeed we have $w \notin \mathcal{L}(S)$ by Theorem 37.

Now from Proposition 42 and Lemma 43, observing that **P**-winning-strategies are just ∞-proofs, we conclude:

Theorem 45 (Completeness). $\mathcal{L}(\Gamma) \subseteq \mathcal{L}(S) \implies \mu\nu\ell\mathsf{HKA} \vdash^\infty \Gamma \to S$.

7 Complexity Matters and Further Perspectives

In this section we make further comments, in particular regarding the complexity of our systems, at the level of arithmetical and analytical hierarchies. These concepts are well-surveyed in standard textbooks, e.g. [44,50], as well as various online resources.

Complexity and Irregularity for Finite Words. The equational theory of μ-expressions in $\mathcal{L}(\cdot)$ is Π^0_1-complete, i.e. co-recursively-enumerable, due to the same complexity of universality of context-free grammars (see, e.g., [27]). In this sense there is no hope of attaining a finitely presentable (e.g. cyclic, inductive) system for the equational theory of μ-expressions in $\mathcal{L}(\cdot)$. However it is not hard to see that our wellfounded system $\mu\mathsf{HKA}_\omega$ enjoys optimal Π^0_1 proof search, thanks to invertibility and termination of the rules, along with decidability of membership checking. Indeed a similar argument is used by Palka in [49] for the theory of '$*$-continuous action lattices'. Furthermore let us point out that our non-wellfounded system also enjoys optimal proof search: $\mu\mathsf{HKA} \vdash^\infty \Gamma \to S$ is equivalent, by invertibility, to checking that *every* sequent $\boldsymbol{a} \to S$ reachable by only left rules in bottom-up proof search has a polynomial-size proof (bound induced by length of leftmost derivations). This is a Π^0_1 property.

Complexity and Inaxiomatisability for Infinite Words. It would be natural to wonder whether a similar argument to Sect. 4 gives rise to some infinitary axiomatisation of the equational theory of $\mu\nu$-expressions in $\mathcal{L}(\cdot)$. In fact, it turns out this is impossible: the equational theory of ω-CFLs is Π^1_2-complete [19], so there is no hope of a Π^0_1 (or even Σ^1_2) axiomatisation. In particular, the projection argument of Sect. 4 cannot be scaled to the full system $\mu\nu\ell\mathsf{HKA}$ because $\cdot$ does not distribute over $\bigcap$ in $\mathcal{L}(\cdot)$, for the corresponding putative 'right ω steps' for ν. For instance $0 = ((aa)^* \cap a(aa)^*)a^* \neq (aa)^*a^* \cap a(aa)^*a^* = aa^*$. Indeed let us point out that here it is crucial to use our hypersequential system HKA as a base rather than, say, the intuitionistic systems of other proof theoretic works for regular expressions (and friends) [16,49]: the appropriate extension of those systems by μs and νs should indeed enjoy an ω-translation, due to only one formula on the right, rendering them incomplete.

Again let us point out that ∞-provability in $\mu\nu\ell$HKA, in a sense, enjoys optimal complexity. By determinacy of the proof search game, $\mu\nu\ell\mathsf{HKA} \vdash^\infty \Gamma \rightarrow S$ if and only if there is *no* **D**-winning-strategy from $\Gamma \rightarrow S$. The latter is indeed a Π^1_2 statement: "*for every* **D**-strategy, *there exists* a play along which *there exists* a progressing thread".

Comparison to [22]. Our method for showing completeness of $\mu\mathsf{HKA}_\omega$ is quite different from the analogous result of [22] which uses the notion of 'rank' for μ-formulas, cf. [1]. Our result is somewhat stronger, giving *cut-free* completeness, but it could be possible to use ranks directly to obtain such a result too. More interestingly, the notion of projections and ω-translation should be well-defined (for LHS μ formulas) even in the presence of νs, cf. [11], whereas the rank method apparently breaks down in such extensions. This means that our method should also scale to $\mu\nu$HKA ∞-proofs where, say, each infinite branch has a LHS μ-thread. It would be interesting to see if this method can be used to axiomatise some natural fragments of ω-context-free inclusions.

Note that, strictly speaking, our completeness result for μCA was only given for the guarded fragment. However it is known that μCA (and even weaker theories) already proves the equivalence of each expression to one that is even left-guarded, by formalising conversion to Greibach normal form [18].

8 Conclusions

In this work we investigated of the proof theory of context-free languages (CFLs) over a syntax of μ-expressions. We defined a non-wellfounded proof system $\mu\mathsf{HKA}^\infty$ and showed its soundness and completeness for the model $\mathcal{L}(\cdot)$ of context-free languages. We used this completeness result to recover the same for a cut-free ω-branching system $\mu\mathsf{HKA}_\omega$ via proof-theoretic techniques. This gave an alternative proof of the completeness for the theory of μ-continuous Chomsky algebras from [22]. We extended μ-expressions by *greatest* fixed points to obtain a syntax for ω-context-free languages. We studied an extension by *greatest* fixed points, $\mu\nu\ell\mathsf{HKA}^\infty$ and showed its soundness and completeness for the model $\mathcal{L}(\cdot)$ of context-free languages, employing game theoretic techniques.

Since inclusion of CFLs is Π^0_1-complete, no recursively enumerable (r.e.) system can be sound and complete for their equational theory. However, by restricting products to a letter on the left one can obtain a syntax for *right-linear grammars*. Indeed, for such a restriction complete cyclic systems can be duly obtained [10]. It would be interesting to investigate systems for related decidable or r.e. inclusion problems, e.g. inclusions of context-free languages in regular languages, and inclusions of *visibly pushdown* languages [2,3].

The positions of our evaluation puzzle for $\mu\nu$-expressions use cedents to decompose products, similar to the stack of a pushdown automaton, rather than requiring an additional player. Previous works have similarly proposed model-checking games for (fragments/variations of) context-free expressions, cf. [37,43], where more complex winning conditions seem to be required. It would be interesting to compare our evaluation puzzle to those games in more detail.

Note that our completeness result, via determinacy of the proof search game, depends on the assumption of (lightface) analytic determinacy. It is natural to ask whether this is necessary, but this consideration is beyond the scope of this work. Let us point out, however, that even ω-context-free determinacy exceeds the capacity of ZFC [20,41].

Finally, it would be interesting to study the *structural* proof theory arising from systems $\mu\mathsf{HKA}^\infty$ and $\mu\nu\mathsf{HKA}^\infty$, cf. [16]. It would also be interesting to see if the restriction to leftmost ∞-proofs can be replaced by stronger progress conditions, such as the 'alternating threads' from [13,14], in a similar hypersequential system for predicate logic. Note that the same leftmost constraint was employed in [25] for an extension of HKA to *ω-regular languages.*

Acknowledgments. This work was supported by a UKRI Future Leaders Fellowship, 'Structure vs Invariants in Proofs', project reference MR/S035540/1. The authors are grateful to anonymous reviewers for their helpful comments (in particular, leading to Example 30) and for pointing us to relevant literature such as [37,43,45].

References

1. Alberucci, L., Krähenbühl, J., Studer, T.: Justifying induction on modal μ-formulae. Logic J. IGPL **22**(6), 805–817 (2014). https://doi.org/10.1093/jigpal/jzu001
2. Alur, R., Madhusudan, P.: Visibly pushdown languages. In: Proceedings of the Thirty-Sixth Annual ACM Symposium on Theory of Computing (STOC 2004), pp. 202–211. Association for Computing Machinery, New York (2004). https://doi.org/10.1145/1007352.1007390
3. Alur, R., Madhusudan, P.: Adding nesting structure to words. J. ACM **56**(3) (2009). https://doi.org/10.1145/1516512.1516518
4. Chandra, A.K., Kozen, D.C., Stockmeyer, L.J.: Alternation. J. ACM **28**(1), 114–133 (1981). https://doi.org/10.1145/322234.322243
5. Cohen, R.S., Gold, A.Y.: Theory of ω-languagesi, II: characterizations of ω-context-free languages. J. Comput. Syst. Sci. **15**(2), 169–208 (1977)
6. Conway, J.H.: Regular Algebra and Finite Machines. Chapman and Hall Mathematics Series. Chapman and Hall (1971)
7. Cranch, J., Laurence, M.R., Struth, G.: Completeness results for omega-regular algebras. J. Logic. Algeb. Methods Program. **84**(3), 402–425 (2015). https://doi.org/10.1016/j.jlamp.2014.10.002. 13th International Conference on Relational and Algebraic Methods in Computer Science (RAMiCS 2012)
8. Curzi, G., Das, A.: Cyclic implicit complexity. In: Baier, C., Fisman, D. (eds.) 37th Annual ACM/IEEE Symposium on Logic in Computer Science, 2–5 August 2022 (LICS 2022), pp. 19:1–19:13. ACM, Haifa (2022). https://doi.org/10.1145/3531130.3533340

9. Das, A., De, A.: A proof theory of (omega-)context-free languages, via non-wellfounded proofs (2024). https://doi.org/10.48550/arXiv.2404.16231
10. Das, A., De, A.: A proof theory of right-linear (omega-)grammars via cyclic proofs. arXiv preprint arXiv:2401.13382 (2024). https://doi.org/10.48550/ARXIV.2401.13382
11. Das, A., De, A., Saurin, A.: Comparing infinitary systems for linear logic with fixed points. In: Bouyer, P., Srinivasan, S. (eds.) 43rd IARCS Annual Conference on Foundations of Software Technology and Theoretical Computer Science (FSTTCS 2023). Leibniz International Proceedings in Informatics (LIPIcs), vol. 284, pp. 40:1–40:17. Schloss Dagstuhl – Leibniz-Zentrum für Informatik, Dagstuhl (2023). https://doi.org/10.4230/LIPIcs.FSTTCS.2023.40
12. Das, A., Doumane, A., Pous, D.: Left-handed completeness for kleene algebra, via cyclic proofs. In: Barthe, G., Sutcliffe, G., Veanes, M. (eds.) 22nd International Conference on Logic for Programming, Artificial Intelligence and Reasoning (LPAR-22). EPiC Series in Computing, vol. 57, pp. 271–289. EasyChair (2018). https://doi.org/10.29007/hzq3
13. Das, A., Girlando, M.: Cyclic proofs, hypersequents, and transitive closure logic. In: Blanchette, J., Kovács, L., Pattinson, D. (eds.) Automated Reasoning (IJCAR 2022). LNCS, vol. 13385, pp. 509–528. Springer, Cham (2022). https://doi.org/10.1007/978-3-031-10769-6_30
14. Das, A., Girlando, M.: Cyclic hypersequent system for transitive closure logic. J. Autom. Reason. **67**(3), 27 (2023). https://doi.org/10.1007/S10817-023-09675-1
15. Das, A., Pous, D.: A cut-free cyclic proof system for Kleene algebra. In: Schmidt, R.A., Nalon, C. (eds.) Automated Reasoning with Analytic Tableaux and Related Methods (TABLEAUX 2017). LNCS, vol. 10501, pp. 261–277. Springer, Cham (2017). https://doi.org/10.1007/978-3-319-66902-1_16
16. Das, A., Pous, D.: Non-wellfounded proof theory for (Kleene+Action) (Algebras+Lattices). In: Ghica, D.R., Jung, A. (eds.) 27th EACSL Annual Conference on Computer Science Logic (CSL 2018). Leibniz International Proceedings in Informatics (LIPIcs), vol. 119, pp. 19:1–19:18. Schloss Dagstuhl – Leibniz-Zentrum für Informatik, Dagstuhl (2018). https://doi.org/10.4230/LIPIcs.CSL.2018.19
17. Ésik, Z., Lei, H.: Greibach normal form in algebraically complete semirings. In: Bradfield, J. (ed.) CSL 2002. LNCS, vol. 2471, pp. 135–150. Springer, Heidelberg (2002). https://doi.org/10.1007/3-540-45793-3_10
18. Ésik, Z., Leiß, H.: Algebraically complete semirings and greibach normal form. Annal. Pure Appl. Logic **133**(1), 173–203 (2005). https://doi.org/10.1016/j.apal.2004.10.008. Festschrift on the occasion of Helmut Schwichtenberg's 60th birthday
19. Finkel, O.: Highly undecidable problems for infinite computations. RAIRO - Theor. Inf. Appl. **43**(2), 339–364 (2009). https://doi.org/10.1051/ita/2009001
20. Finkel, O.: The determinacy of context-free games. J. Symbol. Logic **78**(4), 1115–1134 (2013). http://www.jstor.org/stable/43303700
21. Ginsburg, S., Rice, H.G.: Two families of languages related to algol. J. ACM **9**(3), 350–371 (1962)
22. Grathwohl, N.B.B., Henglein, F., Kozen, D.: Infinitary axiomatization of the equational theory of context-free languages. Electron. Proc. Theor. Comput. Sci. **126**, 44–55 (2013). https://doi.org/10.4204/eptcs.126.4
23. Gruska, J.: A characterization of context-free languages. J. Comput. Syst. Sci. **5**(4), 353–364 (1971). https://doi.org/10.1016/S0022-0000(71)80023-5
24. Harrington, L.: Analytic determinacy and 0#. J. Symb. Log. **43**(4), 685–693 (1978). https://doi.org/10.2307/2273508

25. Hazard, E., Kuperberg, D.: Cyclic proofs for transfinite expressions. In: Manea, F., Simpson, A. (eds.) 30th EACSL Annual Conference on Computer Science Logic (CSL 2022), 14–19 February 2022, Göttingen (Virtual Conference). LIPIcs, vol. 216, pp. 23:1–23:18. Schloss Dagstuhl - Leibniz-Zentrum für Informatik (2022). https://doi.org/10.4230/LIPICS.CSL.2022.23
26. Jipsen, P.: From semirings to residuated kleene lattices. Stud. Logica **76**, 291–303 (2004). https://doi.org/10.1023/B:STUD.0000032089.54776.63
27. Hopcroft, J.E., Rajeev Motwani, J.D.U.: Introduction to Automata Theory, Languages, and Computation, 2nd edn. Addison-Wesley (2001)
28. Kleene, S.C.: Representation of Events in Nerve Nets and Finite Automata, pp. 3–42. Princeton University Press, Princeton (1956). https://doi.org/10.1515/9781400882618-002
29. Kozen, D.: A completeness theorem for Kleene algebras and the algebra of regular events. Inf. Comput. **110**(2), 366–390 (1994). https://doi.org/10.1006/inco.1994.1037
30. Kozen, D.: Results on the propositional μ-calculus. Theor. Comput. Sci. **27**(3), 333–354 (1983). https://doi.org/10.1016/0304-3975(82)90125-6. Special Issue Ninth International Colloquium on Automata, Languages and Programming (ICALP) Aarhus, Summer 1982
31. Kozen, D., Silva, A.: Left-handed completeness. In: Kahl, W., Griffin, T.G. (eds.) RAMICS 2012. LNCS, vol. 7560, pp. 162–178. Springer, Heidelberg (2012). https://doi.org/10.1007/978-3-642-33314-9_11
32. Kozen, D., Silva, A.: Left-handed completeness. Theor. Comput. Sci. **807**, 220–233 (2020). https://doi.org/10.1016/j.tcs.2019.10.040. In memory of Maurice Nivat, a founding father of Theoretical Computer Science - Part II
33. Kozen, D., Smith, F.: Kleene algebra with tests: completeness and decidability. In: van Dalen, D., Bezem, M. (eds.) CSL 1996. LNCS, vol. 1258, pp. 244–259. Springer, Heidelberg (1997). https://doi.org/10.1007/3-540-63172-0_43
34. Krishnaswami, N.R., Yallop, J.: A typed, algebraic approach to parsing. In: PLDI (PLDI 2019), pp. 379–393. Association for Computing Machinery, New York (2019). https://doi.org/10.1145/3314221.3314625
35. Krob, D.: A complete system of B-rational identities. In: Paterson, M.S. (ed.) ICALP 1990. LNCS, vol. 443, pp. 60–73. Springer, Heidelberg (1990). https://doi.org/10.1007/BFb0032022
36. Kupke, C., Marti, J., Venema, Y.: Succinct graph representations of μ-calculus formulas. In: Manea, F., Simpson, A. (eds.) 30th EACSL Annual Conference on Computer Science Logic (CSL 2022). Leibniz International Proceedings in Informatics (LIPIcs), vol. 216, pp. 29:1–29:18. Schloss Dagstuhl – Leibniz-Zentrum für Informatik, Dagstuhl (2022). https://doi.org/10.4230/LIPIcs.CSL.2022.29
37. Lange, M.: Local model checking games for fixed point logic with chop. In: Brim, L., Jancar, P., Kretínský, M., Kucera, A. (eds.) Concurrency Theory. CONCUR 2002. LNCS, vol. 2421, pp. 240–254. Springer, Heidelberg (2002). https://doi.org/10.1007/3-540-45694-5_17
38. Leiß, H.: Towards Kleene algebra with recursion. In: Börger, E., Jäger, G., Kleine Büning, H., Richter, M.M. (eds.) CSL 1991. LNCS, vol. 626, pp. 242–256. Springer, Heidelberg (1992). https://doi.org/10.1007/BFb0023771
39. Leiss, H.: The matrix ring of a mu-continuous chomsky algebra is mu-continuous. In: Talbot, J.M., Regnier, L. (eds.) 25th EACSL Annual Conference on Computer Science Logic (CSL 2016). Leibniz International Proceedings in Informatics (LIPIcs), vol. 62, pp. 6:1–6:15. Schloss Dagstuhl – Leibniz-Zentrum für Informatik, Dagstuhl (2016). https://doi.org/10.4230/LIPIcs.CSL.2016.6

40. Leiß, H., Hopkins, M.: C-Dioids and μ-continuous chomsky-algebras. In: Desharnais, J., Guttmann, W., Joosten, S. (eds.) RAMiCS 2018. LNCS, vol. 11194, pp. 21–36. Springer, Cham (2018). https://doi.org/10.1007/978-3-030-02149-8_2
41. Li, W., Tanaka, K.: The determinacy strength of pushdown ω-languages. RAIRO-Theor. Inf. Appl. **51**(1), 29–50 (2017). https://doi.org/10.1051/ita/2017006
42. Linna, M.: On ω-sets associated with context-free languages. Inf. Control **31**(3), 272–293 (1976)
43. Löding, C., Madhusudan, P., Serre, O.: Visibly pushdown games. In: Lodaya, K., Mahajan, M. (eds.) FSTTCS 2004. LNCS, vol. 3328, pp. 408–420. Springer, Heidelberg (2004). https://doi.org/10.1007/978-3-540-30538-5_34
44. Mansfield, R., Weitkamp, G.: Recursive aspects of descriptive set theory. In: Oxford Logic Guides, Oxford University Press (1985). https://books.google.co.uk/books?id=jPzuAAAAMAAJ
45. Moriya, E., Hofbauer, D., Huber, M., Otto, F.: On state-alternating context-free grammars. Theoret. Comput. Sci. **337**(1–3), 183–216 (2005)
46. Nivat, M.: Mots infinis engendrés par une grammaire algébrique. RAIRO - Theor. Inf. Appl. Inf. Théor. Appl. **11**(4), 311–327 (1977). http://eudml.org/doc/92059
47. Nivat, M.: Sur les ensembles de mots infinis engendrés par une grammaire algébrique. RAIRO - Theor. Inf. Appl. Inf. Théor. Appl. **12**(3), 259–278 (1978). http://eudml.org/doc/92080
48. Niwiński, D., Walukiewicz, I.: Games for the μ-calculus. Theoret. Comput. Sci. **163**(1), 99–116 (1996) https://doi.org/10.1016/0304-3975(95)00136-0
49. Palka, E.: An infinitary sequent system for the equational theory of *-continuous action lattices. Fund. Inform. **78**(2), 295–309 (2007)
50. Sacks, G.E.: Higher Recursion Theory. Perspectives in Logic. Cambridge University Press (2017). https://doi.org/10.1017/9781316717301
51. Salomaa, A.: Formal Languages. ACM Monograph Series. Academic Press (1973)
52. Schützenberger, M.: On context-free languages and push-down automata. Inf. Control **6**(3), 246–264 (1963). https://doi.org/10.1016/S0019-9958(63)90306-1
53. Studer, T.: On the proof theory of the modal mu-calculus. Stud. Logica. **89**(3), 343–363 (2008). https://doi.org/10.1007/S11225-008-9133-6
54. Thiemann, P.: Partial derivatives for context-free languages. In: Esparza, J., Murawski, A.S. (eds.) FoSSaCS 2017. LNCS, vol. 10203, pp. 248–264. Springer, Heidelberg (2017). https://doi.org/10.1007/978-3-662-54458-7_15

A Cyclic Proof System for Guarded Kleene Algebra with Tests

Jan Rooduijn[1(✉)], Dexter Kozen[2], and Alexandra Silva[2]

[1] Institute of Logic, Language and Computation, University of Amsterdam, Amsterdam, The Netherlands
janrooduijn@gmail.com
[2] Cornell University, Ithaca, NY, USA

Abstract. Guarded Kleene Algebra with Tests (GKAT for short) is an efficient fragment of Kleene Algebra with Tests, suitable for reasoning about simple imperative while-programs. Following earlier work by Das and Pous on Kleene Algebra, we study GKAT from a proof-theoretical perspective. The deterministic nature of GKAT allows for a non-well-founded sequent system whose set of regular proofs is complete with respect to the guarded language model. This is unlike the situation with Kleene Algebra, where hypersequents are required. Moreover, the decision procedure induced by proof search runs in NLOGSPACE, whereas that of Kleene Algebra is in PSPACE.

Keywords: Kleene Algebra · Guarded Kleene Algebra with Tests · Cyclic proofs

1 Introduction

Guarded Kleene Algebra with Test (GKAT) is the fragment of Kleene Algebra with Tests (KAT) comprised of the deterministic while programs. Those are the programs built up from sequential composition ($e \cdot f$), conditional branching (`if`-b-`then`-e-`else`-f) and loops (`while` b `do` e). For an introduction to KAT we refer the reader to [10]. The first papers focusing on the fragment of KAT that is nowadays called GKAT are Kozen's [11] and Kozen & Tseng's [12], where it is used to study the relative power of several programming constructs.

As GKAT is a fragment of KAT, it directly inherits a rich theory. It admits a language semantics in the form of *guarded strings* and for every expression there is a corresponding KAT-automaton. Already in [12] it was argued that GKAT expressions are more closely related to so-called *strictly deterministic automata*, where every state transition executes a primitive program. Smolka et al. significantly advanced the theory of GKAT in [22], by studying various additional semantics, identifying the precise class of strictly deterministic automata corresponding

The research of Jan Rooduijn has been made possible by a grant from the Dutch Research Council NWO, project number 617.001.857.

C. Benzmüller et al. (Eds.): IJCAR 2024, LNAI 14740, pp. 257–275, 2024.
https://doi.org/10.1007/978-3-031-63501-4_14

to GKAT-expressions (proving a *Kleene theorem*), giving a nearly linear decision procedure of the equivalence of GKAT-expressions, and studying its equational axiomatisation. Since then GKAT has received considerable further attention, *e.g.* in [17,20,21,24].

One of the most challenging and intriguing aspects of GKAT is its proof theory. The standard equational axiomatisation of KAT from [10] does not simply restrict to GKAT, since a derivation of an expression that lies within the GKAT-fragment might very well contain expressions that lie outside of it. Moreover, the axiomatisation of KAT contains a least fixed point rule that relies on the equational definability of inclusion, which does not seem to be available in GKAT.

In [22], this problem is circumvented by introducing a custom equational axiomatisation for GKAT that uses a *unique* fixed point rule. While a notable result, this solution is still not entirely satisfactory. First, completeness is only proven under the inclusion of a variant of the unique fixed point rule that operates on entire systems of equations (this problem was recently addressed for the so-called *skip-free* fragment of GKAT in [21]). Moreover, even the ordinary, single-equation, unique fixed point rule contains a non-algebraic side-condition, analogous to the empty word property in Salomaa's axiomatisation of Kleene Algebra [18]. Because of this, a proper definition of 'a GKAT' is still lacking.

In recent years the proof theory of logics with fixed point operators (such as while-b-do-e) has seen increasing interest in *non-well-founded* proofs. In such proofs, branches need not to be closed by axioms, but may alternatively be infinitely deep. To preserve soundness, a progress condition is often imposed on each infinite branch, facilitating a soundness proof by infinite descent. In some cases non-well-founded proofs can be represented by finite trees with back-edges, which are then called *cyclic proofs*. See *e.g.* [2,4,5,8,13] for a variety of such approaches. Often, the non-well-founded proof theory of some logic is closely related to its corresponding automata theory. Taking the proof-theoretical perspective, however, can be advantageous because it is more fine-grained and provides a natural setting for establishing results such as interpolation [3,14], cut elimination [1,19], and completeness by proof transformation [6,23].

In [7], Das & Pous study the non-well-founded proof theory of Kleene Algebra, a close relative of GKAT (for background on Kleene Algebra we refer the reader to [9]). They show that a natural non-well-founded sequent system for Kleene Algebra is not complete when restricting to the subset of cyclic proofs. To remedy this, they introduce a *hypersequent* calculus, whose cyclic proofs *are* complete. They give a proof-search procedure for this calculus and show that it runs in PSPACE. Since deciding Kleene Algebra expressions is PSPACE-complete, their proof-search procedure induces an optimal decision procedure for this problem. In a follow-up paper together with Doumane, left-handed completeness of Kleene Algebra is proven by translating cyclic proofs in the hypersequent calculus to well-founded proofs in left-handed Kleene Algebra [6].

The goal of the present paper is to study the non-well-founded proof theory of GKAT. This is interesting in its own right, for instance because, as we will see, it has some striking differences with Kleene Algebra. Moreover, we hope it opens up new avenues for exploring the completeness of algebraic proof systems for GKAT, through the translation of our cyclic proofs.

Outline. Our paper is structured as follows.

- In Sect. 2 we introduce preliminary material: the syntax of GKAT and its language semantics.
- Sect. 3 introduces our non-well-founded proof system SGKAT for GKAT.
- In Sect. 4 we show that (possibly infinitary) proofs in SGKAT are sound. That is, the interpretation of each derivable sequent - a GKAT-*inequality* - is true in the language model (which means that a certain *inclusion* of languages holds).
- In Sect. 5 we show that proofs are *finite-state*: each proof contains only finitely many distinct sequents. More precisely, by employing a more fine-grained analysis than in [7], we give a quadratic bound on the number of distinct sequents occurring in a proof, in terms of the size of its endsequent. It follows that the subset of cyclic proofs proves exactly the same sequents as the set of all non-well-founded proofs.
- Sect. 6 deals with completeness and complexity. We first use a proof-search procedure to show that SGKAT is complete: every sequent whose interpretation is valid in the language model, can be derived. We then show that this proof-search procedure runs in coNLOGSPACE. This gives an NLOGSPACE upper bound on the complexity of the language inclusion problem for GKAT-expressions.

Our Contributions. Our paper closely follows the treatment of Kleene Algebra in [7]. Nevertheless, we make the following original contributions:

- Structure of sequents: we devise a form of sequents bespoke to GKAT, by labelling the sequents by sets of atoms. This is similar to how the appropriate automata for GKAT are not simply KAT-automata. In contrast to Kleene Algebra, it turns out that we do not need to extend our sequents to hypersequents in order to obtain completeness for the fragment of cyclic proofs.
- Soundness argument: our modest contribution here is the notion of priority of rules and the fact that our rules are all invertible when they have priority. The soundness argument for finite proofs is, of course, slightly different, because our rules are different. (The step from the soundness of finite proofs, towards the soundness of infinite proofs, is completely analogous to that of [7].)
- Regularity: this concerns showing that every proof contains only finitely many distinct sequents. As in [7], our argument views each expression in a proof as a subexpression of an expression in the proof's root. A modest contribution is that our argument is made more formal by considering these expressions as nodes in a syntax tree. More importantly, the bound on the number of distinct cedents we obtain is sharper: where in [7] it is exponential in the size of the syntax tree, our bound is linear (yielding a quadratic bound on the number of sequents).

- Completeness: the structure of the argument is identical to that in [7], but the details differ due to the different rules and different type of sequents. This for instance shows in our proof of Lemma 9 (which is analogous to Lemma 20 in [7]), where we make crucial use of the set of atoms annotating a sequent.
- Complexity: our complexity argument is necessarily different because it applies to a different system and is designed to give a different upper bound.

Due to space limitations several proofs are only sketched or omitted entirely. Full versions of these proofs can be found in the extended version of this paper [15].

2 Preliminaries

2.1 Syntax

The language of GKAT has two sorts, namely *programs* and a subset thereof consisting of *tests*. It is built from a finite and non-empty set T of *primitive tests* and a non-empty set Σ of *primitive programs*, where T and Σ are disjoint. For the rest of this paper we fix such sets T and Σ. We reserve the letters t and p to refer, respectively, to arbitrary primitive tests and primitive programs. The first of the following grammars defines the *tests*, and the second the *expressions*.

$$b, c ::= 0 \mid 1 \mid t \mid \overline{b} \mid b \vee c \mid b \cdot c \qquad e, f ::= b \mid p \mid e \cdot f \mid e +_b f \mid e^{(b)},$$

where $t \in T$ and $p \in \Sigma$. Intuitively, the operator $+_b$ stands for the `if-then-else` construct, and the operator $(-)^{(b)}$ stands for the `while` loop. Note that the tests are simply propositional formulas. It is convention to use $\cdot$ instead of $\wedge$ for conjunction. As usual, we often omit $\cdot$ for syntactical convenience, *e.g.* by writing pq instead of $p \cdot q$.

Example 1. The idea of GKAT is to model imperative programs. For instance, the expression $(p +_b q)^{(a)}$ represents the following imperative program:

```
while a do (if b then p else q)
```

Remark 1. As mentioned in the introduction, GKAT is a fragment of Kleene Algebra with Tests, or KAT [10]. The syntax of KAT is the same as that of GKAT, but with unrestricted union $+$ instead of guarded union $+_b$, and unrestricted iteration $(-)^*$ instead of the while loop operator $(-)^{(b)}$. The embedding φ of GKAT into KAT acts on guarded union and guarded iteration as follows, and commutes with all other operators: $\varphi(e +_b f) = b \cdot \varphi(e) + \overline{b} \cdot \varphi(f)$, and $\varphi(e^{(b)}) = (b \cdot \varphi(e))^* \cdot \overline{b}$.

2.2 Semantics

There are several kinds of semantics for GKAT. In [22], a *language* semantics, a *relational* semantics, and a *probabilistic* semantics are given. In this paper we are only concerned with the language semantics, which we shall now describe.

We denote by At the set of *atoms* of the free Boolean algebra generated by $T = \{t_1, \ldots t_n\}$. That is, At consists of all tests of the form $c_1 \cdots c_n$, where $c_i \in \{t_i, \overline{t_i}\}$ for each $1 \leq i \leq n$. Lowercase Greek letters $(\alpha, \beta, \gamma, \ldots)$ will be used to denote elements of At. A *guarded string* is an element of the regular set $\mathsf{At} \cdot (\Sigma \cdot \mathsf{At})^*$. That is, a string of the form $\alpha_1 p_1 \alpha_2 p_2 \cdots \alpha_n p_n \alpha_{n+1}$. We will interpret expressions as languages (formally just sets) of guarded strings. The sequential composition operator $\cdot$ is interpreted by the *fusion product* $\diamond$, given by $L \diamond K := \{x\alpha y \mid x\alpha \in L \text{ and } \alpha y \in K\}$. For the interpretation of $+_b$, we define for every set of atoms $B \subseteq \mathsf{At}$ the following operation of *guarded union* on languages: $L +_B K := (B \diamond L) \cup (\overline{B} \diamond K)$, where $\overline{B}$ is $\mathsf{At} \setminus B$. For the interpretation of $(-)^{(b)}$, we stipulate:

$$L^0 := \mathsf{At} \qquad L^{n+1} := L^n \diamond L \qquad L^B := \bigcup_{n \geq 0} (B \diamond L)^n \diamond \overline{B}$$

Finally, the semantics of GKAT is inductively defined as follows:

$$[\![b]\!] := \{\alpha \in \mathsf{At} : \alpha \leq b\} \qquad [\![p]\!] := \{\alpha p \beta : \alpha, \beta \in \mathsf{At}\} \qquad [\![e \cdot f]\!] := [\![e]\!] \diamond [\![f]\!]$$

$$[\![e +_b f]\!] := [\![e]\!] +_{[\![b]\!]} [\![f]\!] \qquad [\![e^{(b)}]\!] := [\![e]\!]^{[\![b]\!]}$$

Note that the interpretation of $\cdot$ between tests is the same whether they are regarded as tests or as programs, *i.e.* $[\![b]\!] \cap [\![c]\!] = [\![b]\!] \diamond [\![c]\!]$.

Remark 2. While the semantics of expressions is explicitly defined, the semantics of tests is derived implicitly through the free Boolean algebra generated by T. It is standard in the GKAT literature to address the Boolean content in this manner.

Example 2. In a guarded string, atoms can be thought of as states of a machine, and programs as executions. For instance, in case of the guarded string $\alpha p \beta$, the machine starts in state α, then executes program p, and ends in state β. Let us briefly check which guarded strings of, say, the form $\alpha p \beta q \gamma$ belong to the interpretation $[\![(p +_b q)^{(a)}]\!]$ of the program of Example 1. First, we must have $\alpha \leq a$, for otherwise we would not enter the loop. Moreover, we have $\alpha \leq b$, for otherwise q rather than p would be executed. Similarly, we find that $\beta \leq a, \overline{b}$. Since the loop is exited after two iterations, we must have $\gamma \leq \overline{a}$. Hence, we find

$$\alpha p \beta q \gamma \in [\![(p +_b q)^{(a)}]\!] \Leftrightarrow \alpha \leq a, b \text{ and } \beta \leq a, \overline{b} \text{ and } \gamma \leq \overline{a}.$$

We state two simple facts that will be useful later on.

Lemma 1. *For any two languages L, K of guarded strings, and primitive program p, we have:*
(i) $L^{n+1} = L \diamond L^n$; *(ii)* $[\![p]\!] \diamond L = [\![p]\!] \diamond K$ *implies* $L = K$.

Remark 3. The fact that GKAT models deterministic programs is reflected in the fact that sets of guarded strings arising as interpretations of GKAT-expressions satisfy a certain *determinacy property*. Namely, for every $x\alpha y$ and $x\alpha z$ in L, either y and z are both empty, or both begin with the same primitive program. We refer the reader to [22] for more details.

Remark 4. The language semantics of GKAT is the same as that of KAT (see [10]), in the sense that $\llbracket e \rrbracket = \llbracket \varphi(e) \rrbracket$, where φ is the embedding from Remark 1, the semantic brackets on the right-hand side denote the standard interpretation in KAT, and e is any GKAT-expression.

3 The Non-well-founded Proof System SGKAT$^\infty$

In this section we commence our proof-theoretical study of GKAT. We will present a cyclic sequent system for GKAT, inspired by the cyclic sequent system for Kleene Algebra presented in [7]. In passing, we will compare our system to the latter.

Definition 1 (Sequent). *A* sequent *is a triple* (Γ, A, Δ), *written* $\Gamma \Rightarrow_A \Delta$, *where* $A \subseteq \mathsf{At}$ *and* Γ *and* Δ *are (possibly empty) lists of* GKAT*-expressions.*

The list on the left-hand side of a sequent is called its *antecedent*, and the list on the right-hand side its *succedent*. In general we refer to lists of expressions as *cedents*. The symbol ϵ refers to the empty cedent.

Remark 5. As the system in [7] only deals with Kleene Algebra, it does not include tests. We choose the deal with the tests present in GKAT by augmenting each sequent by a set of atoms. This tucks away the Boolean content, as is usual in the GKAT literature, allowing us to omit propositional rules.

Definition 2 (Validity). *We say that a sequent* $e_1, \ldots, e_n \Rightarrow_A f_1, \ldots, f_m$ *is* valid *whenever* $A \diamond \llbracket e_1 \cdots e_n \rrbracket \subseteq \llbracket f_1 \cdots f_n \rrbracket$.

We often abuse notation writing $\llbracket \Gamma \rrbracket$ instead of $\llbracket e_1 \cdots e_n \rrbracket$, where $\Gamma = e_1, \ldots, e_n$.

Example 3. An example of a valid sequent is given by $(cp)^{(b)} \Rightarrow_{\mathsf{At}} (p(cp +_b 1))^{(b)}$. The antecedent denotes guarded strings $\alpha_1 p \alpha_2 p \cdots \alpha_n p \alpha_{n+1}$ where $\alpha_i \leq b, c$ for each $1 \leq i \leq n$, and $\alpha_{n+1} \leq \bar{b}$. The succedent denotes such strings where $\alpha_i \leq c$ is only required for those $1 \leq i \leq n$ where i is even.

Remark 6. Like the sequents for Kleene Algebra in [7], our sequents express language *inclusion*, rather than language equivalence. For Kleene Algebra this difference is insignificant, as the two notions are interdefinable using unrestricted union: $\llbracket e \rrbracket \subseteq \llbracket f \rrbracket \Leftrightarrow \llbracket e + f \rrbracket = \llbracket f \rrbracket$. For GKAT, however, it is not clear how to define language inclusion in terms of language equivalence. As a result, an advantage of axiomatising language inclusion rather than language equivalence, is that the while-operator can be axiomatised as a *least* fixed point, eliminating the need for a *strict productivity* requirement as is present in the axiomatisation in [22].

Given a set of atoms A and a test b, we write $A \restriction b$ for $A \diamond \llbracket b \rrbracket$, *i.e.* the set of atoms $\{\alpha \in A : \alpha \leq b\}$. The rules of SGKAT are given in Fig. 1. Importantly, the rules are always applied to the leftmost expression in a cedent. As a result, we have the following lemma, that later will be used in the completeness proof.

Lemma 2. *Let* $\Gamma \Rightarrow_A \Delta$ *be a sequent, and let* r *be any rule of* SGKAT. *Then there is at most one rule instance of* r *with conclusion* $\Gamma \Rightarrow_A \Delta$.

Left logical rules

$$\frac{\Gamma \Rightarrow_{A\restriction b} \Delta}{b, \Gamma \Rightarrow_A \Delta}\ b\text{-}l \qquad \frac{e, \Gamma \Rightarrow_{A\restriction b} \Delta \qquad f, \Gamma \Rightarrow_{A\restriction \bar{b}} \Delta}{e +_b f, \Gamma \Rightarrow_A \Delta}\ +_b\text{-}l$$

$$\frac{e, g, \Gamma \Rightarrow_A \Delta}{e \cdot g, \Gamma \Rightarrow_A \Delta}\ \cdot\text{-}l \qquad \frac{e, e^{(b)}, \Gamma \Rightarrow_{A\restriction b} \Delta \qquad \Gamma \Rightarrow_{A\restriction \bar{b}} \Delta}{e^{(b)}, \Gamma \Rightarrow_A \Delta}\ (b)\text{-}l$$

Right logical rules

$$(\dagger)\ \frac{\Gamma \Rightarrow_A \Delta}{\Gamma \Rightarrow_A b, \Delta}\ b\text{-}r \qquad \frac{\Gamma \Rightarrow_{A\restriction b} e, \Delta \qquad \Gamma \Rightarrow_{A\restriction \bar{b}} f, \Delta}{\Gamma \Rightarrow_A e +_b f, \Delta}\ +_b\text{-}r$$

$$\frac{\Gamma \Rightarrow_A e, f, \Delta}{\Gamma \Rightarrow_A e \cdot f, \Delta}\ \cdot\text{-}r \qquad \frac{\Gamma \Rightarrow_{A\restriction b} e, e^{(b)}, \Delta \qquad \Gamma \Rightarrow_{A\restriction \bar{b}} \Delta}{\Gamma \Rightarrow_A e^{(b)}, \Delta}\ (b)\text{-}r$$

Axioms and modal rules

$$\frac{}{\epsilon \Rightarrow_A \epsilon}\ \mathsf{id} \qquad \frac{}{\Gamma \Rightarrow_\emptyset \Delta}\ \bot \qquad \frac{\Gamma \Rightarrow_{\mathsf{At}} \Delta}{p, \Gamma \Rightarrow_A p, \Delta}\ \mathsf{k} \qquad \frac{\Gamma \Rightarrow_{\mathsf{At}} 0}{p, \Gamma \Rightarrow_A \Delta}\ \mathsf{k}_0$$

Fig. 1. The rules of SGKAT. The side condition (†) requires that $A \restriction b = A$.

Remark 7. Following [7], we call k a 'modal' rule. The reason is simply that it looks like the rule k (sometimes called K or □) in the standard sequent calculus for basic modal logic. Our system also features a second modal rule, called k_0. Like k, this rule adds a primitive program p to the antecedent of the sequent. Since the premiss of k_0 entails that $[\![\Gamma]\!] = [\![0]\!]$, the antecedent of its conclusion will denote the empty language, and is therefore included in any succedent Δ.

Remark 8. Note that the rules of SGKAT are highly symmetric. Indeed, the only rules that behave differently on the left than on the right, are the b-rules and k_0. Note that b-l changes the set of atoms, while b-r uses a side condition. The asymmetry of k_0 is clear: the succedent of the premiss has a 0, whereas the antecedent does not. A third asymmetry will be introduced in Definition 3, with a condition on infinite branches that is sensitive to (b)-l but not to (b)-r.

Remark 9. The authors of [20] study a variant of GKAT that omits the so-called *early termination axiom*, which equates all programs that eventually fail. They give a denotational model of this variant in the form of certain kinds of trees. We conjecture that omitting the rule k_0 from our system will make it sound and complete with respect to this denotational model.

$$
\dfrac{\dfrac{\dfrac{p \Rightarrow_{\mathsf{At}\restriction b} 1, 1^{(b)}, p \;(\bullet) \qquad \dfrac{}{p \Rightarrow_{\emptyset} p}\,\bot}{p \Rightarrow_{\mathsf{At}\restriction b} 1^{(b)}, p}\,(b)\text{-}r}{p \Rightarrow_{\mathsf{At}\restriction b} 1, 1^{(b)}, p \;(\bullet)}\,1\text{-}r \qquad \dfrac{\dfrac{}{\epsilon \Rightarrow_{\mathsf{At}} \epsilon}\,\mathsf{id}}{p \Rightarrow_{\mathsf{At}\restriction \bar{b}} p}\,\mathsf{k}}{\dfrac{p \Rightarrow_{\mathsf{At}} 1^{(b)}, p}{p \Rightarrow_{\mathsf{At}} 1^{(b)} \cdot p}\,\cdot\text{-}r}\,(b)\text{-}r
$$

Fig. 2. An SGKAT$^\infty$-derivation that is not a proof.

An SGKAT$^\infty$-*derivation* is a (possibly infinite) tree generated by the rules of SGKAT. Such a derivation is said to be *closed* if every leaf is an axiom.

Definition 3 (Proof). *A closed* SGKAT$^\infty$*-derivation is said to be an* SGKAT$^\infty$-proof *if every infinite branch is* fair *for* (b)-l, i.e. *contains infinitely many applications of the rule* (b)-l.

We write SGKAT $\vdash^\infty \Gamma \Rightarrow_A \Delta$ if there is an SGKAT$^\infty$-proof of $\Gamma \Rightarrow_A \Delta$.

Example 4. Not every SGKAT$^\infty$-derivation is a proof. Consider for instance the following derivation, where $(\bullet)$ indicates that the derivation repeat itself (Fig. 2).

Example 5. Let $\Delta_1 := (p(cp +_b 1))^{(b)}$ and $\Delta_2 := cp +_b 1, \Delta_1$. The following proof Π_1 is an example SGKAT$^\infty$-proof of the sequent of Example 3. We again use $(\bullet)$ to indicate that the proof repeats itself at this leaf and, for the sake of readability, omit branches that can be closed immediately by an application of $\bot$ (Fig. 3).

To illustrate the omission of branches that can be immediately closed by an application of $\bot$, let us write out the two applications of $+_b$-r in Π_1.

$$
\dfrac{\epsilon \Rightarrow_{\mathsf{At}\restriction bc} cp, \Delta_1 \qquad \dfrac{}{\epsilon \Rightarrow_{\emptyset} 1, \Delta_1}\,\bot}{\epsilon \Rightarrow_{\mathsf{At}\restriction bc} \Delta_2}\,+_b\text{-}r
\qquad
\dfrac{\bot\,\dfrac{}{\epsilon \Rightarrow_{\emptyset} cp, \Delta_1} \qquad \epsilon \Rightarrow_{\mathsf{At}\restriction \bar{b}} 1, \Delta_1}{\epsilon \Rightarrow_{\mathsf{At}\restriction \bar{b}} \Delta_2}\,+_b\text{-}r
$$

It can also be helpful to think of the set of atoms as *selecting* one of the premisses.

We close this section with a useful definition and a lemma.

Definition 4 (Exposure). *A list* Γ *of expressions is said to be* exposed *if it is either empty or begins with a primitive program.*

Recall that the sets of primitive tests and primitive programs are disjoint. Hence an exposed list Γ cannot start with a test. The following easy lemma will be useful later on.

Lemma 3. *Let* Γ *and* Δ *be exposed lists of expressions. Then:*

(i) $\alpha x \in [\![\Gamma]\!] \Leftrightarrow \beta x \in [\![\Gamma]\!]$ *for all* $\alpha, \beta \in \mathsf{At}$
(ii) $\Gamma \Rightarrow_{\mathsf{At}} \Delta$ *is valid if and only if* $\Gamma \Rightarrow_A \Delta$ *is valid for some* $A \neq \emptyset$.

$$
\begin{array}{l}
\mathsf{k} \dfrac{(cp)^{(b)} \Rightarrow_{\mathsf{At}} \Delta_1 \quad (\bullet)}{}\\[2pt]
\text{c-r} \dfrac{p, (cp)^{(b)} \Rightarrow_{\mathsf{At}\upharpoonright bc} p, \Delta_1}{}\\[2pt]
\text{$\cdot$-r} \dfrac{p, (cp)^{(b)} \Rightarrow_{\mathsf{At}\upharpoonright bc} c, p, \Delta_1}{}\\[2pt]
\text{$+_b$-r} \dfrac{p, (cp)^{(b)} \Rightarrow_{\mathsf{At}\upharpoonright bc} cp, \Delta_1}{} \qquad\qquad \text{id} \dfrac{\epsilon \Rightarrow_{\mathsf{At}\upharpoonright\bar{b}} \epsilon}{}\\[2pt]
\text{c-l} \dfrac{p, (cp)^{(b)} \Rightarrow_{\mathsf{At}\upharpoonright bc} \Delta_2}{} \qquad\qquad\quad (b)\text{-}r \dfrac{\epsilon \Rightarrow_{\mathsf{At}\upharpoonright\bar{b}} \Delta_1}{}\\[2pt]
\text{$\cdot$-l} \dfrac{c, p, (cp)^{(b)} \Rightarrow_{\mathsf{At}\upharpoonright b} \Delta_2}{} \qquad\qquad\quad 1\text{-}r \dfrac{\epsilon \Rightarrow_{\mathsf{At}\upharpoonright\bar{b}} 1, \Delta_1}{}\\[2pt]
\dfrac{cp, (cp)^{(b)} \Rightarrow_{\mathsf{At}\upharpoonright b} \Delta_2}{} \qquad\qquad\qquad +_b\text{-}r \dfrac{\epsilon \Rightarrow_{\mathsf{At}\upharpoonright\bar{b}} \Delta_2}{}\\[2pt]
\qquad\qquad\qquad\qquad\qquad\qquad\qquad (b)\text{-}l\\[2pt]
\mathsf{k} \dfrac{(cp)^{(b)} \Rightarrow_{\mathsf{At}} \Delta_2}{}\\[2pt]
\text{$\cdot$-r} \dfrac{p, (cp)^{(b)} \Rightarrow_{\mathsf{At}\upharpoonright bc} p, (cp+_b 1), \Delta_1}{}\\[2pt]
(b)\text{-}r \dfrac{p, (cp)^{(b)} \Rightarrow_{\mathsf{At}\upharpoonright bc} p(cp+_b 1), \Delta_1}{}\\[2pt]
\text{c-l} \dfrac{p, (cp)^{(b)} \Rightarrow_{\mathsf{At}\upharpoonright bc} \Delta_1}{}\\[2pt]
\text{$\cdot$-l} \dfrac{c, p, (cp)^{(b)} \Rightarrow_{\mathsf{At}\upharpoonright b} \Delta_1}{} \qquad\qquad\qquad \text{id} \dfrac{\epsilon \Rightarrow_{\mathsf{At}\upharpoonright\bar{b}} \epsilon}{}\\[2pt]
\dfrac{cp, (cp)^{(b)} \Rightarrow_{\mathsf{At}\upharpoonright b} \Delta_1}{} \qquad\qquad\qquad (b)\text{-}r \dfrac{\epsilon \Rightarrow_{\mathsf{At}\upharpoonright\bar{b}} \Delta_1}{}\\[2pt]
\qquad\qquad\qquad\qquad\qquad\qquad\qquad\qquad (b)\text{-}l\\[2pt]
\qquad\qquad (cp)^{(b)} \Rightarrow_{\mathsf{At}} \Delta_1 \quad (\bullet)
\end{array}
$$

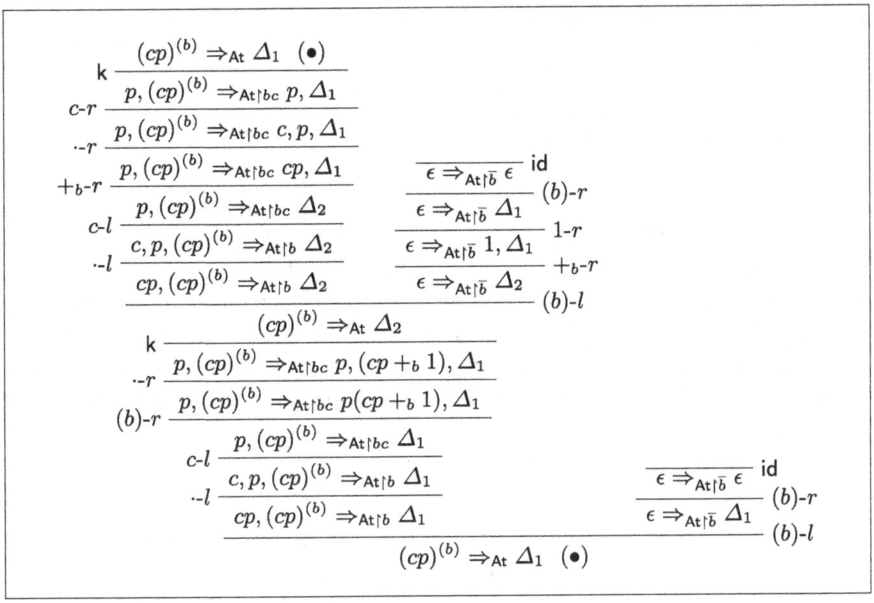

Fig. 3. The SGKAT^∞-proof Π_1.

4   Soundness

In this section we prove that SGKAT^∞ is sound. We will first prove that *well-founded* (that is, finite) SGKAT^∞-proofs are sound. The following straightforward facts will be useful in the soundness proof.

Lemma 4. *For any set A of atoms, test b, and cedent Θ, we have:*

(i) $\llbracket e +_b f, \Theta \rrbracket = (\llbracket b \rrbracket \diamond \llbracket e, \Theta \rrbracket) \cup (\llbracket \bar{b} \rrbracket \diamond \llbracket f, \Theta \rrbracket)$;
(ii) $\llbracket e^{(b)}, \Theta \rrbracket = (\llbracket b \rrbracket \diamond \llbracket e, e^{(b)}, \Theta \rrbracket) \cup (\llbracket \bar{b} \rrbracket \diamond \llbracket \Theta \rrbracket)$.

We prioritise the rules of SGKAT in order of occurrence in Fig. 1, reading left-to-right, top-to-bottom. Hence, each left logical rule is of higher priority than each right logical rule, which is of higher priority than each axiom or modal rule. Recall that a rule is *sound* if the validity of all its premises implies the validity of its conclusion. Conversely, a rule is *invertible* if the validity of its conclusion implies the validity of all of its premises.

We say that a rule application *has priority* of there is no higher-priority rule with the same conclusion. Conveniently, the following proposition entails that every rule instance which has priority is invertible. This will aid our proof search procedure in Sect. 6.

Proposition 1. *Every rule of SGKAT is sound. Moreover, every rule is invertible except for k and k_0, which are invertible whenever they have priority.*

Proof (sketch). We treat two illustrative cases. For the rule $+_b$-r, we find

$$\begin{aligned} &A \diamond [\![\Gamma]\!] \subseteq [\![e +_b f]\!] \diamond [\![\Delta]\!] \\ &\Leftrightarrow A \diamond [\![\Gamma]\!] \subseteq ([\![b]\!] \diamond [\![e, \Delta]\!]) \cup ([\![\bar{b}]\!] \diamond [\![f, \Delta]\!]) \\ &\Leftrightarrow A \restriction b \diamond [\![\Gamma]\!] \subseteq [\![e, \Delta]\!] \text{ or } A \restriction \bar{b} \subseteq [\![f, \Delta]\!], \end{aligned}$$

where the first equivalence holds due to Lemma 4.(ii), and the second due to $A \diamond [\![\Gamma]\!] = ([\![b]\!] \diamond A \diamond [\![\Gamma]\!]) \cup ([\![\bar{b}]\!] \diamond A \diamond [\![\Gamma]\!])$ and Lemma 4.(i).

The other rule we will treat is k. Suppose first that some application of k does *not* have priority. The only rule of higher priority than k which can have a conclusion of the form $p, \Gamma \Rightarrow_A p, \Delta$ is $\bot$. In this case $A = \emptyset$, which means that the conclusion must be valid. Hence any application of k that does not have priority is vacuously sound. It need, however, not be invertible, as the following rule instance demonstrates

$$\mathsf{k}\,\frac{1 \Rightarrow_{\mathsf{At}} 0}{p, 1 \Rightarrow_{\emptyset} p, 0}$$

Next, suppose that some application of k does have priority. This means that the set A of atoms in the conclusion $p, \Gamma \Rightarrow_A p, \Delta$ is *not* empty. We will show that under this restriction the rule is both sound and invertible. Let $\alpha \in A$. We have

$$\begin{aligned} A \diamond [\![p, \Gamma]\!] \subseteq [\![p, \Delta]\!] &\Leftrightarrow A \diamond [\![p]\!] \diamond [\![\Gamma]\!] \subseteq [\![p]\!] \diamond [\![\Delta]\!] && \text{(seq. int.)} \\ &\Leftrightarrow \alpha \diamond [\![p]\!] \diamond [\![\Gamma]\!] \subseteq [\![p]\!] \diamond [\![\Delta]\!] && (\alpha \in A, \text{Lem.3}) \\ &\Leftrightarrow [\![p]\!] \diamond [\![\Gamma]\!] \subseteq [\![p]\!] \diamond [\![\Delta]\!] && \text{(Lem. 3)} \\ &\Leftrightarrow [\![\Gamma]\!] \subseteq [\![\Delta]\!], && (\dagger) \end{aligned}$$

as required. The step marked by † is the following property of guarded languages: $[\![p]\!] \diamond L = [\![p]\!] \diamond K$ implies $L = K$.

Proposition 1 entails that all finite proofs are sound. We will now extend this result to non-well-founded proofs, closely following the treatment in [7]. We first recursively define a syntactic abbreviation: $[e^{(b)}]^0 := \bar{b}$ and $[e^{(b)}]^{n+1} := be[e^{(b)}]^n$.

Lemma 5. *For every $n \in \mathbb{N}$: if we have $\mathsf{SGKAT} \vdash^\infty e^{(b)}, \Gamma \Rightarrow_A \Delta$, then we also have $\mathsf{SGKAT} \vdash^\infty [e^{(b)}]^n, \Gamma \Rightarrow_A \Delta$.*

We let the *while-height* $\mathsf{wh}(e)$ be the maximal nesting of while loops in a given expression e. Formally,

- $\mathsf{wh}(b) = \mathsf{wh}(p) = 0$;
- $\mathsf{wh}(e \cdot f) = \mathsf{wh}(e +_b f) = \max\{\mathsf{wh}(e), \mathsf{wh}(f)\}$;
- $\mathsf{wh}(e^{(b)}) = \mathsf{wh}(e) + 1$.

Given a list Γ, the *weighted while-height* $\mathsf{wwh}(\Gamma)$ of Γ is defined to be the multiset $[\mathsf{wh}(e) : e \in \Gamma]$. We order such multisets using the Dershowitz-Manna ordering (for linear orders): we say that $N < M$ if and only if $N \neq M$ and for the greatest n such that $N(n) \neq M(n)$, it holds that $N(n) < M(n)$.

Note that in any SGKAT-derivation the weighted while-height of the antecedent does not increase when reading bottom-up. Moreover, we have:

Lemma 6. $\mathsf{wwh}([e^{(b)}]^n, \Gamma) < \mathsf{wwh}(e^{(b)}, \Gamma)$ *for every* $n \in \mathbb{N}$.

Finally, we can prove the soundness theorem using induction on $\mathsf{wwh}(\Gamma)$.

Theorem 1 (Soundness). *If* $\mathsf{SGKAT} \vdash^{\infty} \Gamma \Rightarrow_A \Delta$, *then* $A \diamond [\![\Gamma]\!] \subseteq [\![\Delta]\!]$.

Proof. We prove this by induction on $\mathsf{wwh}(\Gamma)$. Given a proof π of $\Gamma \Rightarrow_A \Delta$, let $\mathcal{B}$ contain for each infinite branch of π the node of least depth to which a rule (b)-l is applied. Note that $\mathcal{B}$ must be finite, for otherwise, by Kőnig's Lemma, the proof π cut off along $\mathcal{B}$ would have an infinite branch that does not satisfy the fairness condition.

Note that Proposition 1 entails that of every finite derivation with valid leaves the conclusion is valid. Hence, it suffices to show that each of the nodes in $\mathcal{B}$ is valid. To that end, consider an arbitrary such node labelled $e^{(b)}, \Gamma' \Rightarrow_{A'} \Delta'$ and the subproof π' it generates. By Lemma 5, we have that $[e^{(b)}]^n, \Gamma' \Rightarrow_{A'} \Delta'$ is provable for every n. Lemma 6 gives $\mathsf{wwh}([e^{(b)}]^n, \Gamma') < \mathsf{wwh}(e^{(b)}, \Gamma') \leq \mathsf{wwh}(\Gamma)$, and thus we may apply the induction hypothesis to obtain

$$A' \diamond [\![[e^{(b)}]^n]\!] \diamond [\![\Gamma]\!] \subseteq [\![\Delta]\!]$$

for every $n \in \mathbb{N}$. Then by

$$\bigcup_n (A' \diamond [\![[e^{(b)}]^n]\!] \diamond [\![\Gamma]\!]) = A' \diamond \bigcup_n ([\![[e^{(b)}]^n]\!]) \diamond [\![\Gamma]\!] = A' \diamond [\![e]\!]^{[\![b]\!]} \diamond [\![\Gamma]\!],$$

we obtain that $e^{(b)}, \Gamma' \Rightarrow_{A'} \Delta'$ is valid, as required.

5 Regularity

Before we show that SGKAT^{∞} is not only sound, but also complete, we will first show that every SGKAT^{∞}-proof is *finite-state*, *i.e.* that it contains at most finitely many distinct sequents.

The results of this section crucially depend on the fact that we are only applying rules to the leftmost expressions of cedents. Indeed, otherwise one could easily create infinitely many distinct sequents by simply unravelling the same while loop $e^{(b)}$ infinitely often.

Our treatment differs from that in [7] in two major ways. First, we formalise the notion of (sub)occurrence using the standard notion of a *syntax tree*. Secondly, and more importantly, we obtain a quadratic bound on the number of distinct sequents occurring in a proof, rather than an exponential one. In fact, we will show that the number of distinct antecedents (succedents) is *linear* in the size of the syntax tree of the antecedent (succedent) of the root. We will do this by showing that each leftmost expression of a cedent in the proof (given as node of the syntax tree of a root cedent) can only occur in the proof as the leftmost expression of that *unique* cedent.

Definition 5. *The* syntax tree (T_e, l_e) *of an expression* e *is a well-founded, labelled and ordered tree, defined by the following induction on* e.

- *If* e *is a test or primitive program, its syntax tree only has a root node* ρ, *with label* $l_e(\rho) := e$.
- *If* $e = f_1 \circ f_2$ *where* $\circ = \cdot$ *or* $\circ = +_b$, *its syntax tree again has a root node* ρ *with label* $l_e(\rho) = e$, *and with two outgoing edges. The first edge connects* ρ *to* (T_{f_1}, l_{f_1}), *the second edge connects it to* (T_{f_2}, l_{f_2}).
- *If* $e = f^{(b)}$, *its syntax tree again has a root node* ρ *with label* $l_e(\rho) = e$, *but now with just one outgoing edge. This edge connects* ρ *to* (T_f, l_f).

Definition 6. *An* e-cedent *is a list of nodes in the syntax tree of* e. *The* realisation *of an e-cedent* $u_1, \ldots, u_n$ *is the cedent* $l_e(u_1), \ldots, l_e(u_n)$.

Given the leftmost expression of a cedent, we will now explicitly define the cedent that it must be the leftmost expression of.

Definition 7. *Let* u *be a node in the syntax tree of* e. *We define the e-cedent* $\mathsf{tail}(u)$ *inductively as follows:*

- *For the root* ρ *of* T_e, *we set* $\mathsf{tail}(\rho)$ *to be the empty list* ϵ.
- *For every node* u *of* T_e, *we define* tail *on its children by a case distinction on the main connective* mc *of* u:
  - *if* $\mathsf{mc} = \cdot$, *let* u_1 *and* u_2 *be, respectively, the first and second child of* u. *We set* $\mathsf{tail}(u_1) := u_2, \mathsf{tail}(u)$ *and* $\mathsf{tail}(u_2) := \mathsf{tail}(u)$.
  - *if* $\mathsf{mc} = +_b$, *let* u_1 *and* u_2 *again be its first and second child. We set* $\mathsf{tail}(u_1) := \mathsf{tail}(u_2) := \mathsf{tail}(u)$.
  - *if* $\mathsf{mc} = (-)^{(b)}$, *let* v *be the single child of* u. *We set* $\mathsf{tail}(v) := u, \mathsf{tail}(u)$.

An e-cedent is called tail-generated *if it is empty or of the form* $u, \mathsf{tail}(u)$ *for some node* u *in the syntax tree of* e.

Example 6. Below is the syntax tree of $(p(p +_b 1))^{(b)}$ and a calculation of $\mathsf{tail}(u_3)$.

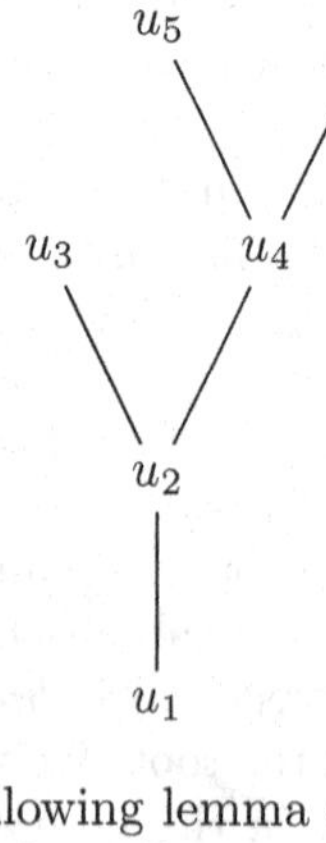

$$
\begin{aligned}
l(u_1) &= (p(p +_b 1))^{(b)} \\
l(u_2) &= p(p +_b 1) \\
l(u_3) &= p \\
l(u_4) &= p +_b 1 \\
l(u_5) &= p \\
l(u_6) &= 1
\end{aligned}
\qquad
\begin{aligned}
\mathsf{tail}(u_3) &= u_4, \mathsf{tail}(u_2) \\
&= u_4, u_1, \mathsf{tail}(u_1) \\
&= u_4, u_1
\end{aligned}
$$

The following lemma embodies the key idea for the main result of this section: every leftmost expression is the leftmost expression of a unique cedent.

Lemma 7. *Let* π *be an* SGKAT^∞*-derivation of a sequent of the form* $e \Rightarrow_A f$. *Then every antecedent in* π *is the realisation of a* tail*-generated e-sequent, and every succedent is the realisation of a* tail*-generated* f*-sequent or* 0*-sequent.*

Proof. We first prove the following claim.

Let e be an expression and let u be a node in its syntax tree. Then $\mathsf{tail}(u)$ is a tail-generated e-sequent.

We prove this by induction on the syntax tree of e. For the root ρ, we have $\mathsf{tail}(\rho) = \epsilon$, which is tail-generated by definition. Now suppose that the thesis holds for some arbitrary node u in the syntax tree of e. We will show that the thesis holds for the children of u by a case distinction on the main connective mc of u.

- $\mathsf{mc} = \cdot$. Let u_1 and u_2 be the first and second child of u, respectively. We have $\mathsf{tail}(u_1) = u_2, \mathsf{tail}(u) = u_2, \mathsf{tail}(u_2)$, which is tail-generated by definition. Moreover, we have that $\mathsf{tail}(u_2) = \mathsf{tail}(u)$ is tail-generated by the induction hypothesis.
- $\mathsf{mc} = +_b$. Then for each child v of u, we have $\mathsf{tail}(v) = \mathsf{tail}(u)$ and thus we can again invoke the induction hypothesis.
- $\mathsf{mc} = (-)^{(b)}$. Then for the single child v of u, it holds that $\mathsf{tail}(v) = u, \mathsf{tail}(u)$, which is tail-generated by definition.

Using this claim, the lemma follows by bottom-up induction on π. For the base case, note that e and f are realisations of the roots of their respective syntax trees. Such a root ρ is tail-generated, since $\rho = \rho, \epsilon = \rho, \mathsf{tail}(\rho)$. The induction step follows by direct inspection of the rules of SGKAT.

The number of realisations of tail-generated e-sequents is clearly linear in the size of the syntax tree of e, for every expression e. Hence we obtain:

Corollary 1. *The number of distinct sequents in an* SGKAT^∞*-proof of* $e \Rightarrow_A f$ *is quadratic in* $|T_e| + |T_f|$.

Note that the above lemma and corollary can easily be generalised to arbitrary (rather than singleton) cedents, by rewriting each cedent $e_1, \ldots, e_n$ as $e_1 \cdots e_n$.

Recall that a non-well-founded tree is *regular* if it contains only finitely many pairwise non-isomorphic subtrees. The following corollary follows by a standard argument in the literature (see *e.g* [16, Corollary I.2.23]).

Corollary 2. *If* $\Gamma \Rightarrow_A \Delta$ *has an* SGKAT^∞*-proof, then it has a regular one.*

We define a *cyclic* SGKAT*-proof* as a regular SGKAT^∞-proof. Cyclic proofs can be equivalently described using finite trees with back edges, but this is not needed for the purposes of the present paper.

6 Completeness and Complexity

In this section we prove the completeness of SGKAT^∞. Our argument uses a proof search procedure, which we will show to induce a $\mathsf{NLOGSPACE}$ decision procedure for the language inclusion problem of GKAT expressions. The material in this section is again inspired by [7], but requires several modifications to treat the tests present in GKAT.

First note the following fact.

Lemma 8. *Any valid sequent is the conclusion of some rule application.*

Note that in the following lemma A and B may be distinct.

Lemma 9. *Let π be a derivation using only right logical rules and containing a branch of the form:*

$$\dfrac{\begin{array}{c}\Gamma \Rightarrow_B e^{(b)}, \Delta \\ \vdots\end{array}}{\Gamma \Rightarrow_A e^{(b)}, \Delta}\ (b)\text{-}r \qquad (*)$$

such that (1) $\Gamma \Rightarrow_A e^{(b)}, \Delta$ is valid, and (2) every succedent on the branch has $e^{(b)}, \Delta$ as a final segment. Then $\Gamma \Rightarrow_B 0$ is valid.

Proof. We claim that $e^{(b)} \Rightarrow_B 0$ is provable. We will show this by exploiting the symmetry of the left and right logical rules of SGKAT (cf. Remark 8). Since on the branch (*) every rule is a right logical rule, and $e^{(b)}, \Delta$ is preserved throughout, we can construct a derivation π' of $e^{(b)} \Rightarrow_B 0$ from π by applying the analogous left logical rules to $e^{(b)}$. Note that the set of atoms B precisely determines the branch (*), in the sense that for every leaf $\Gamma \Rightarrow_C \Theta$ of π it holds that $C \cap B = \emptyset$. Hence, as the root of π' is $e^{(b)} \Rightarrow_B 0$, every branch of π' except for the one corresponding to (*) can be closed directly by an application of $\perp$. The branch corresponding to (*) is of the form

$$\dfrac{\begin{array}{c}e^{(b)} \Rightarrow_B 0 \\ \vdots\end{array}}{e^{(b)} \Rightarrow_B 0}\ (b)\text{-}l \qquad (*)$$

and can thus be closed by a back edge. The resulting finite tree with back edges clearly represents an SGKAT$^\infty$-proof.

Now by soundness, we have $B \diamond [\![e^{(b)}]\!] = \emptyset$. Moreover, by the invertibility of the right logical rules and hypothesis (1), we get

$$B \diamond [\![\Gamma]\!] \subseteq B \diamond [\![e^{(b)}]\!] \diamond [\![\Delta]\!] = \emptyset,$$

as required.

Lemma 10. *Let $(\Gamma_n \Rightarrow_{A_n} \Delta_n)_{n \in \omega}$ be an infinite branch of some SGKAT$^\infty$-derivation on which the rule (b)-r is applied infinitely often. Then there are n, m with $n < m$ such that the following hold:*

(i) the sequents $\Gamma_n \Rightarrow_{A_n} \Delta_n$ and $\Gamma_m \Rightarrow_{A_m} \Delta_m$ are equal;
(ii) the sequent $\Gamma_n \Rightarrow_{A_n} \Delta_n$ is the conclusion of (b)-r in π;
(iii) for every $i \in [n, m)$ it holds that Δ_n is a final segment of Δ_i.

Proof. First note that $\mathsf{k_0}$ is not applied on this branch, because if it were then there could not be infinitely many applications of (b)-r.

Since the proof is finite-state (cf. Corollary 1), there must be a $k \geq 0$ be such that every Δ_i with $i \geq k$ occurs infinitely often on the branch above. Denote by

$|\Delta|$ the length of a given list Δ and let l be minimum of $\{|\Delta_i| : i \geq k\}$. In other words, l is the minimal length of the Δ_i with $i \geq k$.

To prove the lemma, we first claim that there is an $n \geq k$ such that $|\Delta_n| = l$ and the leftmost expression in Δ_n is of the form $e^{(b)}$ for some e. Suppose, towards a contradiction, that this is not the case. Then there must be a $u \geq k$ such that $|\Delta_u| = l$ and the leftmost expression in Δ_u is *not* of the form $e^{(b)}$ for any e. Note that (b)-r is the only rule apart from k_0 that can increase the length of the succedent (when read bottom-up). It follows that for no $w \geq u$ the leftmost expression in Δ_w is of the form $e^{(b)}$, contradicting the fact that (b)-r is applied infinitely often.

Now let $n \geq k$ be such that $|\Delta_n| = l$ and the leftmost expression of Δ_n is $e^{(b)}$. Since the rule (b)-r must at some point after Δ_n be applied to $e^{(b)}$, we may assume without loss of generality that $\Gamma_n \Rightarrow_{A_n} \Delta_n$ is the conclusion of an application of (b)-r. By the pigeonhole principle, there must be an $m > n$ such that $\Gamma_n \Rightarrow_{A_n} \Delta_n$ and $\Gamma_m \Rightarrow_{A_m} \Delta_m$ are the same sequents. We claim that these sequents satisfy the three properties above. Properties (i) and (ii) directly hold by construction. Property (iii) follows from the fact that Δ_n is of minimal length and has $e^{(b)}$ as leftmost expression.

With the above lemmas in place, we are ready for the completeness proof.

Theorem 2 (Completeness). *Every valid sequent is provable in* SGKAT^∞.

Proof. Given a valid sequent, we do a bottom-up proof search with the following strategy. Throughout the procedure all leaves remain valid, in most cases by an appeal to invertibility.

1. Apply left logical rules as long as possible. If this stage terminates, it will be at a leaf of the form $\Gamma \Rightarrow_A \Delta$, where Γ is exposed. We then go to stage (2). If left logical rules remain applicable, we stay in this stage (1) forever and create an infinite branch.
2. Apply right logical rules until one of the following happens:
   (a) We reach a leaf at which no right logical rule can be applied. This means that the leaf must be a valid sequent of the form $\Gamma \Rightarrow_A \Delta$ such that Γ is exposed, and Δ is either exposed or begins with a test b such $A \upharpoonright b \neq A$. We go to stage (4).
   (b) If (a) does not happen, then at some point we must reach a valid sequent of the $\Gamma \Rightarrow_A e^{(b)}, \Delta$ which together with an ancestor satisfies properties (i) - (iii) of Lemma 10. In this case Lemma 9 is applicable. Hence we must be at a leaf of the form $\Gamma \Rightarrow_A e^{(b)}, \Delta$ such that $e^{(b)} \Rightarrow_A 0$ is valid. We then go to stage (3).

   Since at some point either (a) or (b) must be the case, stage (2) always terminates.
3. We are at a valid leaf of the form $\Gamma \Rightarrow_A e^{(b)}, \Delta$, where Γ is exposed. If $A = \emptyset$, we apply $\perp$. Otherwise, if $A \neq \emptyset$, we use the validity of $\Gamma \Rightarrow_A e^{(b)}, \Delta$ and $e^{(b)} \Rightarrow_A 0$ to find:

$$A \diamond [\![\Gamma]\!] \subseteq A \diamond [\![e^{(b)}]\!] \diamond [\![\Delta]\!] = \emptyset.$$

We claim that $[\![\Gamma]\!] = \emptyset$. Indeed, suppose towards a contradiction that $\alpha x \in [\![\Gamma]\!]$. By the exposedness of Γ and item (i) of Lemma 3, we would have $\beta x \in [\![\Gamma]\!]$ for some $\beta \in A$, contradicting the statement above. Therefore, the sequent $\Gamma \Rightarrow_{\mathsf{At}} 0$ is valid. We apply the rule $\mathsf{k_0}$ and loop back to stage (1).
Stage (3) only comprises a single step and thus always terminates.

4. Let $\Gamma \Rightarrow_A \Delta$ be the current leaf. By construction $\Gamma \Rightarrow_A \Delta$ is valid, Γ is exposed, and Δ is either exposed or begins with a test b such that $A \upharpoonright b \neq A$. Note that only rules id, $\bot$, k, and $\mathsf{k_0}$ can be applicable. By Lemma 8, at least one of them must be applicable. If id is applicable, apply id. If $\bot$ is applicable, apply $\bot$. If k is applicable, apply k and loop back to stage (1). Note that this application of k will have priority and is therefore invertible.
Finally, suppose that only $\mathsf{k_0}$ is applicable. We claim that, by validity, the list Γ is not ϵ. Indeed, since A is non-empty, and Δ either begins with a primitive program p or a test b such that $A \upharpoonright b \neq A$, the sequent

$$\epsilon \Rightarrow_A \Delta$$

must be invalid. Hence Γ must be of the form p, Θ. We apply $\mathsf{k_0}$, which has priority and thus is invertible, and loop back to stage (1).
Similarly to stage (3), stage (4) only comprises a single step and thus always terminates.

We claim that the constructed derivation is fair for (b)-l. Indeed, every stage except stage (1) terminates. Therefore, every infinite branch must either eventually remain in stage (1), or pass through stages (3) or (4) infinitely often. Since k and $\mathsf{k_0}$ shorten the antecedent, and no left logical rule other than (b)-l lengthens it, such branches must be fair.

By Corollary 2 we obtain that the subset of cyclic SGKAT-proofs is also complete.

Corollary 3. *Every valid sequent has a regular* SGKAT^∞*-proof.*

Proposition 2. *The proof search procedure of Theorem 2 runs in* coNLOGSPACE. *Hence proof search, and thus also the language inclusion problem for* GKAT*-expressions, is in* NLOGSPACE.

Proof (sketch). Assume without loss of generality that the initial sequent is of the form $e \Rightarrow_A f$. We non-deterministically search for a failing branch, at each iteration storing only the last sequent. By Lemma 7 this can be done by storing two pointers to, respectively, the syntax trees T_e and T_f, together with a set of atoms. The loop check of stage (2) can be replaced by a counter. Indeed, stage (2) must always hit a repetition after $|\mathsf{At}| \cdot |T_f|$ steps, where m is the number of nodes in the syntax tree. After this repetition there must be a continuation that reaches a repetition to which Lemma 9 applies before this stage has taken $2 \cdot |\mathsf{At}| \cdot |T_f|$ steps in total. Finally, a global counter can be used to limit the depth of the search. Indeed, a failing branch needs at most one repetition (in stage (2), to which $\mathsf{k_0}$ is applied) and all other repetitions can be cut out. Hence if there is a failing branch, there must be one of size at most $4 \cdot |T_e| \cdot |\mathsf{At}| \cdot |T_f|$.

7 Conclusion and Future Work

In this paper we have presented a non-well-founded proof system SGKAT^{∞} for GKAT. We have shown that the system is sound and complete with respect to the language model. In fact, the fragment of *regular* proofs is already complete, which means one can view SGKAT as a cyclic proof system. Our system is similar to the system for Kleene Algebra in [7], but the deterministic nature of GKAT allows us to use ordinary sequents rather than hypersequents. To deal with the tests of GKAT every sequent is annotated by a set of atoms. Like in [7], our completeness argument makes use of a proof search procedure. Here again the relative simplicity of GKAT pays off: the proof search procedure induces an NLOGSPACE decision procedure, whereas that of Kleene Algebra is in PSPACE.

The most natural question for future work is whether our system could be used to prove the completeness of some (ordered)-algebraic axiomatisation of GKAT. We envision using the original GKAT axioms (see [22, Figure 1]), but basing it on *inequational* logic rather than equational logic. This would allow one to use a *least* fixed point rule of the form

$$\frac{eg +_b f \leq g}{e^{(b)} f \leq g}$$

eliminating the need for a Salomaa-style side condition. We hope to be able to prove the completeness of such an inequational system by translating cyclic SGKAT-proofs into well-founded proofs in the inequational system. This is inspired by the paper [6], where a similar strategy is used to give an alternative proof of the left-handed completeness of Kleene Algebra.

Another relevant question is the exact complexity of the language inclusion problem for GKAT-expressions. We have obtained an upper bound of NLOGSPACE, but do not know whether it is optimal.

Finally, it would be interesting to verify the conjecture in Remark 9 above.

Acknowledgments. Jan Rooduijn thanks Anupam Das, Tobias Kappé, Johannes Marti and Yde Venema for insightful discussions on the topic of this paper. Alexandra Silva wants to acknowledge Sonia Marin, who some years ago proposed a similar master project at UCL. We moreover thank the reviewers for their helpful comments, in particular for pointing out that our complexity result could be sharpened. Lastly, Jan Rooduijn is grateful for the inspiring four-week research visit at the Computer Science department of Cornell in the summer of 2022.

References

1. Acclavio, M., Curzi, G., Guerrieri, G.: Infinitary cut-elimination via finite approximations. In: 32nd Annual Conference on Computer Science Logic, CSL. LIPIcs, vol. 288, pp. 8:1–8:19. Schloss Dagstuhl (2024)
2. Afshari, B., Enqvist, S., Leigh, G.E.: Cyclic proofs for the first-order μ-calculus. Log. J. IGPL **32**(1), 1–34 (2022)

3. Afshari, B., Leigh, G.E., Menéndez Turata, G.: Uniform interpolation from cyclic proofs: the case of modal mu-calculus. In: Das, A., Negri, S. (eds.) TABLEAUX 2021. LNCS (LNAI), vol. 12842, pp. 335–353. Springer, Cham (2021). https://doi.org/10.1007/978-3-030-86059-2_20
4. Afshari, B., Wehr, D.: Abstract cyclic proofs. In: Ciabattoni, A., Pimentel, E., de Queiroz, R.J.G.B. (eds.) WoLLIC 2022. LNCS, vol. 13468, pp. 309–325. Springer, Cham (2022). https://doi.org/10.1007/978-3-031-15298-6_20
5. Brotherston, J.: Cyclic proofs for first-order logic with inductive definitions. In: Beckert, B. (ed.) TABLEAUX 2005. LNCS (LNAI), vol. 3702, pp. 78–92. Springer, Heidelberg (2005). https://doi.org/10.1007/11554554_8
6. Das, A., Doumane, A., Pous, D.: Left-handed completeness for Kleene algebra, via cyclic proofs. In: 22nd International Conference on Logic for Programming, Artificial Intelligence and Reasoning, LPAR. EPiC Series in Computing, vol. 57, pp. 271–289 (2018)
7. Das, A., Pous, D.: A cut-free cyclic proof system for Kleene algebra. In: Schmidt, R.A., Nalon, C. (eds.) TABLEAUX 2017. LNCS (LNAI), vol. 10501, pp. 261–277. Springer, Cham (2017). https://doi.org/10.1007/978-3-319-66902-1_16
8. Dekker, M., Kloibhofer, J., Marti, J., Venema, Y.: Proof systems for the modal μ-calculus obtained by determinizing automata. In: Ramanayake, R., Urban, J. (eds.) TABLEAUX 2023. LNCS, vol. 14278, pp. 242–259. Springer, Cham (2023). https://doi.org/10.1007/978-3-031-43513-3_14
9. Kozen, D.: A completeness theorem for Kleene algebras and the algebra of regular events. Inf. Comput. **110**(2), 366–390 (1994)
10. Kozen, D.: Kleene algebra with tests. ACM Trans. Program. Lang. Syst. **19**(3), 427–443 (1997)
11. Kozen, D.: Nonlocal flow of control and Kleene algebra with tests. In: 23rd Annual Symposium on Logic in Computer Science, LICS, pp. 105–117. IEEE (2008)
12. Kozen, D., Tseng, W.-L.D.: The Böhm–Jacopini theorem is false, propositionally. In: Audebaud, P., Paulin-Mohring, C. (eds.) MPC 2008. LNCS, vol. 5133, pp. 177–192. Springer, Heidelberg (2008). https://doi.org/10.1007/978-3-540-70594-9_11
13. Kuperberg, D., Pinault, L., Pous, D.: Cyclic proofs, system T, and the power of contraction. In: 48th Annual Symposium on Principles of Programming Languages, POPL, pp. 1–28 (2021)
14. Marti, J., Venema, Y.: Focus-style proof systems and interpolation for the alternation-free μ-calculus, arXiv preprint arXiv:2103.01671 (2021)
15. Rooduijn, J., Kozen, D., Silva, A.: A cyclic proof system for Guarded Kleene Algebra with Tests (full version) (2024). https://arxiv.org/abs/2405.07505
16. Rooduijn, J.: Fragments & Frame Classes. Ph.D. thesis, University of Amsterdam (2024)
17. Rozowski, W., Kappé, T., Kozen, D., Schmid, T., Silva, A.: Probabilistic guarded KAT modulo bisimilarity: completeness and complexity. In: 50th International Colloquium on Automata, Languages, and Programming, ICALP. LIPIcs, vol. 261, pp. 136:1–136:20. Schloss Dagstuhl (2023)
18. Salomaa, A.: Two complete axiom systems for the algebra of regular events. J. ACM **13**(1), 158–169 (1966)
19. Savateev, Y., Shamkanov, D.: Cut-elimination for the modal Grzegorczyk logic via non-well-founded proofs. In: Kennedy, J., de Queiroz, R.J.G.B. (eds.) WoLLIC 2017. LNCS, vol. 10388, pp. 321–335. Springer, Heidelberg (2017). https://doi.org/10.1007/978-3-662-55386-2_23

20. Schmid, T., Kappé, T., Kozen, D., Silva, A.: Guarded Kleene algebra with tests: coequations, coinduction, and completeness. In: 48th International Colloquium on Automata, Languages, and Programming, ICALP. LIPIcs, vol. 198, pp. 142:1–142:14. Schloss Dagstuhl (2021)
21. Schmid, T., Kappé, T., Silva, A.: A complete inference system for skip-free guarded Kleene algebra with tests. In: Wies, T. (ed.) ESOP 2023. LNCS, vol. 13990, pp. 309–336. Springer, Cham (2023). https://doi.org/10.1007/978-3-031-30044-8_12
22. Smolka, S., Foster, N., Hsu, J., Kappé, T., Kozen, D., Silva, A.: Guarded Kleene algebra with tests: verification of uninterpreted programs in nearly linear time. In: 47th Annual Symposium on Principles of Programming Languages, POPL, pp. 61:1–61:28 (2020)
23. Sprenger, C., Dam, M.: On the structure of inductive reasoning: circular and tree-shaped proofs in the μ-calculus. In: Gordon, A.D. (ed.) FoSSaCS 2003. LNCS, vol. 2620, pp. 425–440. Springer, Heidelberg (2003). https://doi.org/10.1007/3-540-36576-1_27
24. Zetzsche, S., Silva, A., Sammartino, M.: Guarded Kleene algebra with tests: automata learning. In: Proceedings of the 38th Conference on the Mathematical Foundations of Programming Semantics, MFPS. EPTICS, vol. 1. EpiSciences (2022)

Unification, Rewriting and Computational Models

Unification in the Description Logic $\mathcal{ELH}_{\mathcal{R}^+}$ Without the Top Concept Modulo Cycle-Restricted Ontologies

Franz Baader[1,2] and Oliver Fernández Gil[1,2(✉)]

[1] Institute of Theoretical Computer Science, TU Dresden, Dresden, Germany
{franz.baader,oliver.fernandez}@tu-dresden.de
[2] Center for Scalable Data Analytics and Artificial Intelligence (ScaDS.AI), Dresden/Leipzig, Germany

Abstract. Unification has been introduced in Description Logic (DL) as a means to detect redundancies in ontologies. In particular, it was shown that testing unifiability in the DL $\mathcal{EL}$ is an NP-complete problem, and this result has been extended in several directions. Surprisingly, it turned out that the complexity increases to PSpace if one disallows the use of the top concept in concept descriptions. Motivated by features of the medical ontology SNOMED CT, we extend this result to a setting where the top concept is disallowed, but there is a background ontology consisting of restricted forms of concept and role inclusion axioms. We are able to show that the presence of such axioms does not increase the complexity of unification without top, i.e., testing for unifiability remains a PSpace-complete problem.

Keywords: Unification · Description Logics · Complexity

1 Introduction

Description Logics (DLs) [10] are a prominent family of logic-based knowledge representation languages, which offer their users a good compromise between expressiveness and complexity of reasoning, and constitute the formal and algorithmic foundation of the standard Web Ontology Language OWL 2.[1] The DL $\mathcal{EL}$, which provides the concept constructors conjunction ($\sqcap$), existential restriction ($\exists r.C$), and top concept ($\top$), is a rather inexpressive, but nevertheless very useful member of this family. On the one hand, the important reasoning problems, such as the subsumption and the equivalence problem, in $\mathcal{EL}$ and some of its extensions are decidable in polynomial time [8,22]. On the other hand, $\mathcal{EL}$ and its tractable extensions are frequently used to define biomedical ontologies, such as the large medical ontology SNOMED CT.[2] To illustrate the use of the top concept, whose absence plays an important rôle in this paper, consider the

[1] https://www.w3.org/TR/owl2-overview/.
[2] https://www.ihtsdo.org/snomed-ct/.

C. Benzmüller et al. (Eds.): IJCAR 2024, LNAI 14740, pp. 279–297, 2024.
https://doi.org/10.1007/978-3-031-63501-4_15

$\mathcal{EL}$ concept descriptions $Man \sqcap \exists child.\top$ and $Man \sqcap \exists child.Female$ of the concepts *Father* and *Father of a daughter*, respectively. In the former description, the top concept is used since no further properties of the child are to be required.

Unification in DLs has been introduced in [17] as a new inference service, motivated by the need for detecting redundancies in ontologies, in a setting where different ontology engineers (OEs) constructing the ontology may model the same concepts on different levels of granularity. For example, assume that (using the style of SNOMED CT definitions) one OE models the concept of a *viral infection of the lung* as

$$ViralInfection \sqcap \exists findingSite.LungStructure,$$

whereas another one models it as

$$LungInfection \sqcap \exists causativeAgent.Virus.$$

Here *ViralInfection* and *LungInfection* are used as atomic concepts without further defining them, i.e., the two OEs made different decisions when to stop the modelling process. The resulting concept descriptions are not equivalent, but they are nevertheless meant to represent the same concept. They can be made equivalent by treating the concept names *ViralInfection* and *LungInfection* as variables, and then substituting the first one by $Infection \sqcap \exists causativeAgent.Virus$ and the second one by $Infection \sqcap \exists findingSite.LungStructure$. In this case, we say that the descriptions are unifiable, and call the substitution that makes them equivalent a *unifier*. Intuitively, such a unifier proposes definitions for the concept names that are used as variables. In [7], unification and its extension to disunification are used to construct new medical concepts from SNOMED CT.

Unification in $\mathcal{EL}$ was first investigated in [14], where it was proved that deciding unifiability is an NP-complete problem. The NP upper bound was shown in that paper using a brute-force "guess and then test" NP algorithm. More practical algorithms for solving this problem and for computing unifiers were presented in [16] and [15], where the former describes a goal-oriented transformation-based algorithm and the latter is based on a translation to SAT. Implementations of these two algorithms are provided by the system UEL[3] [13], which is also available as a plug-in for the ontology editor Protégé. At the time these algorithms were developed, SNOMED CT was an $\mathcal{EL}$ ontology consisting of acyclic concept definitions. Since such definitions can be encoded into the unification problem (see Sect. 2.3 in [16]), algorithms for unification of $\mathcal{EL}$ concept descriptions (without background ontology) could be applied to SNOMED CT.

There was, however, one problem with employing these algorithms in the context of SNOMED CT: the top concept is not used in SNOMED CT, but the concepts generated by $\mathcal{EL}$ unification might contain $\top$, even if applied to concept descriptions not containing $\top$. Thus, the concept descriptions produced by the

[3] https://sourceforge.net/projects/uel/.

unifier are not necessarily in the style of SNOMED CT. For example, assume that we are looking for a unifier satisfying the two subsumption constraints[4]

$$\exists \mathit{findingSite}.\mathit{LungStructure} \sqsubseteq^? \exists \mathit{findingSite}.X,$$

$$\exists \mathit{findingSite}.\mathit{HeartStructure} \sqsubseteq^? \exists \mathit{findingSite}.X.$$

It is easy to see that there is only one unifier of these two constraints, which replaces X with $\top$. Unification in $\mathcal{EL}^{-\top}$, i.e., the fragment of $\mathcal{EL}$ in which the top constructor is disallowed, was investigated in [1,18]. Surprisingly, it turned out that the absence of $\top$ makes unification considerably harder, both from a conceptual and a computational complexity point of view. In fact, the complexity of deciding unifiability increases from NP-complete for $\mathcal{EL}$ to PSpace-complete for $\mathcal{EL}^{-\top}$. The unification algorithm for $\mathcal{EL}^{-\top}$ introduced in [1,18] basically proceeds as follows. It first applies the unification algorithm for $\mathcal{EL}$ to compute so-called local unifiers. If none of them is an $\mathcal{EL}^{-\top}$-unifier, then it tries to augment the images of the variables by conjoining concept descriptions called particles. The task of finding appropriate particles is reduced to solving certain systems of linear language inclusions, which can be realized in PSpace using an automata-based approach.

The current version of SNOMED CT consists not only of acyclic concept definitions, but also contains more general concept inclusions (GCIs). In addition, properties of the part-of relation are no longer encoded using the so-called SEP-triplet encoding [27], but are directly expressed via role axioms [29], which can, for instance, be used to state that the part-of relation is transitive and that proper-part-of is a subrole of part-of. Decidability of unification in $\mathcal{EL}$ w.r.t. a background ontology consisting of GCIs is still an open problem. In [2], it is shown that the problem remains in NP if the ontology is cycle-restricted, which is a condition that the current version of SNOMED CT satisfies. Extensions of this result to the DL $\mathcal{ELH}_{\mathcal{R}^+}$, which additionally allows for transitive roles and role inclusion axioms, were presented in [3,5], where the former introduces a SAT-based algorithm and the latter a transformation-based one. However, in all these algorithms, unifiers may introduce concept descriptions containing $\top$. In our example with the different finding site, however, the presence of the GCIs *LungStructure* $\sqsubseteq$ *UpperBodyStructure* and *HeartStructure* $\sqsubseteq$ *UpperBodyStructure* would yield a unifier not using $\top$, namely the one that replaces X with *UpperBodyStructure*.

The purpose of this paper is to combine the approach for unification in $\mathcal{EL}^{-\top}$ [1,18] with the one for unification in $\mathcal{ELH}_{\mathcal{R}^+}$ w.r.t. cycle-restricted ontologies [2,3,5], to obtain a unification algorithm for $\mathcal{ELH}_{\mathcal{R}^+}^{-\top}$ w.r.t. cycle-restricted ontologies. This algorithm follows the line of the one for $\mathcal{EL}^{-\top}$ in that it basically first generates $\mathcal{ELH}_{\mathcal{R}^+}$-unifiers, which it then tries to augment with particles.

[4] Instead of equivalence constraints, as in our above example and in early work on unification in DLs, we consider here a set of subsumption constraints as unification problem. It is easy to see that these two kinds of unification problems can be reduced to each other [2].

Appropriate particles are found as solutions of certain linear language inclusions. However, due to the presence of GCIs and role axioms, quite a number of non-trivial changes and additions are required. In particular, the solutions of the systems of linear language inclusions as constructed in [1, 18] cannot capture particles that are appropriate due to the presence of an ontology. For instance, in our example, *UpperBodyStructure* would be such a particle. To repair this problem, we first need to show that, in $\mathcal{ELH}_{\mathcal{R}+}^{-\top}$, unifiability w.r.t. a cycle-restricted ontology can be characterized by the existence of a special type of unifiers. Afterwards, we exploit the properties of this kind of unifiers to define more sophisticated systems of language inclusions, which encode the semantics of GCIs and role axioms occurring in a background ontology. The solutions of such systems then yield also particles that are appropriate only due to the presence of this ontology.

While the unification problem investigated in this paper is motivated by an application in ontology engineering, it is also of interest for unification theory [19], which is concerned with unification-related properties of equational theories. In fact, unification in DLs can be seen as a special case of unification modulo equational theories, where the respective equational theory axiomatizes equivalence in the DL under consideration. For $\mathcal{EL}$ and $\mathcal{ELH}_{\mathcal{R}+}$, the corresponding equational theories can be found in [28]. The ones for the case without top can be obtained from them by removing the constant 1 from the signature, and all identities containing it from the axiomatization. The results in [1, 18] and in the present paper show that the seemingly harmless removal of a constant from the equational theory may increase the complexity of the unification problem considerably. Considering unification w.r.t. a background ontology corresponds to adding a finite set of ground identities to the corresponding equational theory. For the word problem, it was shown that decidability is stable under adding finite sets of ground identities to theories such as commutativity or associativity-commutativity [11, 20, 24, 25]. For unification, it was shown in [12] that adding finite sets of ground identities to the theory *ACUI* of an associativity-commutativity-idempotent symbol with a unit leaves the unification problem decidable. The results in [2, 3, 5] can be seen as such transfer results, but they require a restriction on the ground identities corresponding to cycle-restrictedness.

Due to space constraints, we cannot give detailed proof of our results here. They can be found in [9].

2 Subsumption and Unification in $\mathcal{ELH}_{\mathcal{R}+}$ and $\mathcal{ELH}_{\mathcal{R}+}^{-\top}$

First, we briefly introduce syntax and semantics of the DLs investigated in this paper. Then, we recall a useful characterization of subsumption for these logics, and finally define the unification problem.

2.1 The DLs $\mathcal{ELH}_{\mathcal{R}^+}$ and $\mathcal{ELH}_{\mathcal{R}^+}^{-\top}$

Starting with countably infinite sets $\mathsf{N_C}$ and $\mathsf{N_R}$ of concept names and role names, $\mathcal{ELH}_{\mathcal{R}^+}$*-concept descriptions* (for short, *concepts*) are built using the concept constructors *conjunction* ($\sqcap$), *existential restriction* ($\exists r.C$), and *top* ($\top$). When building $\mathcal{ELH}_{\mathcal{R}^+}^{-\top}$-concepts, the constructor $\top$ is not available. An $\mathcal{ELH}_{\mathcal{R}^+}$-ontology $\mathcal{O}$ is a finite set of *general concept inclusions (GCIs)* $C \sqsubseteq D$, *role hierarchy axioms* $r \sqsubseteq s$, and *transitivity axioms* $r \circ r \sqsubseteq r$, where C, D are $\mathcal{ELH}_{\mathcal{R}^+}$-concepts and r, s are role names. In an $\mathcal{ELH}_{\mathcal{R}^+}^{-\top}$-ontology, the concepts occurring in GCIs must be $\mathcal{ELH}_{\mathcal{R}^+}^{-\top}$-concepts.

The following two notions will play an important rôle in our unification algorithm. An *atom* is either a concept name or an existential restriction, and a *particle* is an atom of the form $\exists r_1.\exists r_2.\cdots\exists r_n.A$ for a concept name A, which we write as $\exists w.A$, where $w = r_1 \dots r_n$ is viewed as a word over the alphabet $\mathsf{N_R}$. Every $\mathcal{ELH}_{\mathcal{R}^+}$-concept C is a conjunction of atoms, where the empty conjunction represents $\top$. These atoms are called the *top-level atoms* of C. The set $\mathit{Ats}(C)$ consists of all atoms (not just top-level ones) occurring in C, and $\mathit{Ats}(\mathcal{O})$ for an ontology $\mathcal{O}$ consists of the atoms of all concepts occurring in $\mathcal{O}$. The set of particles of an $\mathcal{ELH}_{\mathcal{R}^+}^{-\top}$-concept is defined inductively: $\mathit{Part}(A) := \{A\}$ for each concept name A, $\mathit{Part}(\exists r.C) := \{\exists r.P \mid P \in \mathit{Part}(C)\}$, and $\mathit{Part}(C \sqcap D) := \mathit{Part}(C) \cup \mathit{Part}(D)$. For example, if $C = \exists r.(\exists s.A \sqcap \exists r.B)$, then $\mathit{Part}(C) = \{\exists rs.A, \exists rr.B\}$ and $\mathit{Ats}(C) = \{C, \exists s.A, \exists r.B, A, B\}$, where C is the only top-level atom.

The *semantics* of $\mathcal{ELH}_{\mathcal{R}^+}$-concepts and ontologies is defined using the notion of an *interpretation* $\mathcal{I} = (\Delta^\mathcal{I}, \cdot^\mathcal{I})$, which has a set $\Delta^\mathcal{I} \neq \emptyset$ as interpretation domain, and assigns a subset $A^\mathcal{I} \subseteq \Delta^\mathcal{I}$ to each concept name A and a binary relation $r^\mathcal{I} \subseteq \Delta^\mathcal{I} \times \Delta^\mathcal{I}$ to each role name r. The interpretation function $\cdot^\mathcal{I}$ is extended to $\mathcal{ELH}_{\mathcal{R}^+}$-concepts as usual: $\top^\mathcal{I} := \Delta^\mathcal{I}$, $(C \sqcap D)^\mathcal{I} := C^\mathcal{I} \cap D^\mathcal{I}$, and $(\exists r.C)^\mathcal{I} := \{d \in \Delta^\mathcal{I} \mid \exists e.((d,e) \in r^\mathcal{I} \wedge e \in C^\mathcal{I})\}$. The interpretation $\mathcal{I}$ is a *model* of the $\mathcal{ELH}_{\mathcal{R}^+}$-ontology $\mathcal{O}$ if $C \sqsubseteq D \in \mathcal{O}$ implies $C^\mathcal{I} \subseteq D^\mathcal{I}$, $r \sqsubseteq s \in \mathcal{O}$ implies $r^\mathcal{I} \subseteq s^\mathcal{I}$, and $r \circ r \sqsubseteq r \in \mathcal{O}$ implies that $r^\mathcal{I}$ is transitive.

2.2 Subsumption in $\mathcal{ELH}_{\mathcal{R}^+}$ and $\mathcal{ELH}_{\mathcal{R}^+}^{-\top}$

Given an $\mathcal{ELH}_{\mathcal{R}^+}$-ontology $\mathcal{O}$ and $\mathcal{ELH}_{\mathcal{R}^+}$-concepts C, D, we say that C is *subsumed* by D w.r.t. $\mathcal{O}$ (written $C \sqsubseteq_\mathcal{O} D$) if $C^\mathcal{I} \subseteq D^\mathcal{I}$ for all models $\mathcal{I}$ of $\mathcal{O}$. They are *equivalent* w.r.t. $\mathcal{O}$ (written $C \equiv_\mathcal{O} D$) if $C \sqsubseteq_\mathcal{O} D$ and $D \sqsubseteq_\mathcal{O} C$.

Subsumption (and thus also equivalence) between $\mathcal{ELH}_{\mathcal{R}^+}$-concepts w.r.t. arbitrary $\mathcal{ELH}_{\mathcal{R}^+}$-ontologies can be decided in polynomial time [8]. In the context of unification, a recursive characterization of subsumption turns out to be useful, which for $\mathcal{ELH}_{\mathcal{R}^+}$ was first given in [5], and later reformulated in [3]. In this paper we use the one given in [3], but before we can formulate this characterization, we must introduce the *role hierarchy* induced by an $\mathcal{ELH}_{\mathcal{R}^+}$-ontology $\mathcal{O}$: given role names r, s, we say that r is a *subrole* of s (written $r \trianglelefteq_\mathcal{O} s$) if $r^\mathcal{I} \subseteq s^\mathcal{I}$ holds for all models $\mathcal{I}$ of $\mathcal{O}$. It is easy to see that the relation $\trianglelefteq_\mathcal{O}$ is the reflexive-transitive closure of the explicitly stated subrole relationships $\{(r,s) \mid r \sqsubseteq s \in \mathcal{O}\}$. We call a role name r *transitive* if $r \circ r \sqsubseteq r \in \mathcal{O}$.

The characterization of subsumption in [3] uses the notion of *structural subsumption*: given atoms C, D, we say that C *is structurally subsumed by* D w.r.t. an $\mathcal{ELH}_{\mathcal{R}^+}$-ontology $\mathcal{O}$ (written $C \sqsubseteq^s_{\mathcal{O}} D$) if one of the following cases applies:

1. $C = D$ is a concept name.
2. $C = \exists r.C'$, $D = \exists s.D'$, $r \trianglelefteq_{\mathcal{O}} s$, and $C' \sqsubseteq_{\mathcal{O}} D'$.
3. $C = \exists r.C'$, $D = \exists s.D'$, and $C' \sqsubseteq_{\mathcal{O}} \exists t.D'$ for some transitive role name t satisfying $r \trianglelefteq_{\mathcal{O}} t \trianglelefteq_{\mathcal{O}} s$.

Lemma 1 [3]. *Let $\mathcal{O}$ be an $\mathcal{ELH}_{\mathcal{R}^+}$-ontology and $C_1, \ldots, C_n, D_1, \ldots, D_m$ atoms. Then, $C_1 \sqcap \cdots \sqcap C_n \sqsubseteq_{\mathcal{O}} D_1 \sqcap \cdots \sqcap D_m$ iff for every $j \in \{1, \ldots, m\}$:*

1. *there is an index $i \in \{1, \ldots, n\}$ such that $C_i \sqsubseteq^s_{\mathcal{O}} D_j$, or*
2. *there are atoms $At_1, \ldots, At_k, At'$ of $\mathcal{O}$ $(k \geq 0)$ such that:*
   (a) $At_1 \sqcap \cdots \sqcap At_k \sqsubseteq_{\mathcal{O}} At'$,
   (b) for every $\ell \in \{1, \ldots, k\}$ there exists $i \in \{1, \ldots, n\}$ with $C_i \sqsubseteq^s_{\mathcal{O}} At_\ell$, and
   (c) $At' \sqsubseteq^s_{\mathcal{O}} D_j$.

If $\mathcal{O}$ is empty, then the second case in the definition of structural subsumption can be modified to require that $r = s$ and $C' \sqsubseteq_{\emptyset} D'$, whereas the third case in the same definition as well as the second case in Lemma 1 can be removed. This then yields the characterization of subsumption in $\mathcal{EL}$ of [16]. Since $\mathcal{ELH}^{-\top}_{\mathcal{R}^+}$ is a fragment of $\mathcal{ELH}_{\mathcal{R}^+}$, this characterization also applies to subsumption between $\mathcal{ELH}^{-\top}_{\mathcal{R}^+}$-concepts w.r.t. $\mathcal{ELH}^{-\top}_{\mathcal{R}^+}$-ontologies. However, in this setting, the case $k = 0$ in 2. cannot occur. This is a direct consequence of the following result.

Lemma 2. *If $\mathcal{O}$ is an $\mathcal{ELH}^{-\top}_{\mathcal{R}^+}$-ontology and At an atom of $\mathcal{O}$, then $\top \not\sqsubseteq_{\mathcal{O}} At$.*

2.3 Unification in $\mathcal{ELH}_{\mathcal{R}^+}$ and $\mathcal{ELH}^{-\top}_{\mathcal{R}^+}$

When defining unification, we assume that the set of concept names is partitioned into a set $\mathsf{N_C}$ of concept constants and a set $\mathsf{N_V}$ of concept variables. Given a DL $\mathcal{L} \in \{\mathcal{ELH}_{\mathcal{R}^+}, \mathcal{ELH}^{-\top}_{\mathcal{R}^+}\}$, an $\mathcal{L}$-*substitution* σ is a mapping from a finite subset of $\mathsf{N_V}$ to the set of $\mathcal{L}$-concepts. The application of σ to an arbitrary $\mathcal{L}$-concept is defined inductively in the usual way. A concept (ontology) is *ground* if it does not contain variables. A substitution σ is ground if $\sigma(X)$ is ground for all variables X that have an image under σ.

Definition 1. *Let $\mathcal{O}$ be a ground ontology. An $\mathcal{L}$-*unification problem *w.r.t. $\mathcal{O}$ is of the form $\Gamma = \{C_1 \sqsubseteq^? D_1, \ldots, C_n \sqsubseteq^? D_n\}$, where $C_1, D_1, \ldots, C_n, D_n$ are $\mathcal{L}$-concepts. An $\mathcal{L}$-substitution σ is an $\mathcal{L}$-*unifier *of Γ w.r.t. $\mathcal{O}$ if $\sigma(C_i) \sqsubseteq_{\mathcal{O}} \sigma(D_i)$ for all $i \in \{1, \ldots, n\}$. The unification problem Γ is called $\mathcal{L}$-*unifiable *w.r.t. $\mathcal{O}$ if it has an $\mathcal{L}$-unifier w.r.t. $\mathcal{O}$.*

The following example illustrates that unifiability of a given unification problem may depend on the considered DL $\mathcal{L}$ and on the presence of a non-empty ontology.

Example 1. Let $\mathcal{O} = \emptyset$ and consider the following unification problem:

$$\Gamma_1 := \{\exists r.A \sqsubseteq^? X,\ \ \exists u.B \sqsubseteq^? Y,\ \ \exists s.X \sqcap A \sqsubseteq^? Y\}.$$

Viewed as an $\mathcal{ELH}_{\mathcal{R}^+}$-unification problem, it has the unifier σ with $\sigma(X) = \sigma(Y) = \top$. However, Γ_1 does not have an $\mathcal{ELH}^{-\top}_{\mathcal{R}^+}$-unifier w.r.t. $\mathcal{O} = \emptyset$. To see this, suppose that δ is such a unifier. Using Lemma 1 for the special case of an empty ontology, we can deduce from $\exists u.B \sqsubseteq_\emptyset \delta(Y)$ that every top-level atom of $\delta(Y)$ is an existential restriction for the role u. However, we can also deduce from $\exists s.\delta(X) \sqcap A \sqsubseteq_\emptyset \delta(Y)$ that every top-level atom of $\delta(Y)$ is either A or an existential restriction for the role s. Since not both is possible, $\delta(Y)$ cannot have any top-level atoms, and thus must be $\top$, contradicting our assumption that δ is an $\mathcal{ELH}^{-\top}_{\mathcal{R}^+}$-unifier. If we define $\mathcal{O}' := \{B \sqsubseteq \exists r.A,\ u \sqsubseteq s\}$, then the $\mathcal{ELH}^{-\top}_{\mathcal{R}^+}$-unifiability status of Γ_1 changes to unifiable since δ with $\delta(X) = \exists r.A$ and $\delta(Y) = \exists s.\exists r.A$ is an $\mathcal{ELH}^{-\top}_{\mathcal{R}^+}$-unifier of Γ_1 w.r.t. $\mathcal{O}'$.

In the next section we will show how to decide unifiability of an $\mathcal{ELH}^{-\top}_{\mathcal{R}^+}$-unification problem w.r.t. a cycle-restricted $\mathcal{ELH}^{-\top}_{\mathcal{R}^+}$-ontology.

Definition 2. *An $\mathcal{ELH}_{\mathcal{R}^+}$-ontology $\mathcal{O}$ is called* cycle-restricted *if there is no sequence of $n > 0$ role names $r_1, \ldots, r_n \in \mathsf{N_R}$ and $\mathcal{ELH}_{\mathcal{R}^+}$-concept C such that $C \sqsubseteq_\mathcal{O} \exists r_1.\exists r_2.\cdots\exists r_n.C$.*

As stated in [5] (and proved in [6]), one can test in polynomial time whether a given $\mathcal{ELH}_{\mathcal{R}^+}$-ontology is cycle-restricted or not.

According to [5,18], we can without loss of generality assume that the given ontology and the unification problem are *flat.* An $\mathcal{ELH}^{-\top}_{\mathcal{R}^+}$-atom is flat if it is a concept name or of the form $\exists r.A$ for a concept name A. A GCI $C_1 \sqcap\cdots\sqcap C_n \sqsubseteq D$ or subsumption constraint $C_1 \sqcap\cdots\sqcap C_n \sqsubseteq^? D$ is flat if $C_1, \ldots, C_n$ and D are flat $\mathcal{ELH}^{-\top}_{\mathcal{R}^+}$-atoms. Finally, an $\mathcal{ELH}^{-\top}_{\mathcal{R}^+}$-ontology or $\mathcal{ELH}^{-\top}_{\mathcal{R}^+}$-unification problem is flat if all it elements are flat.

The following result for flat, cycle-restricted $\mathcal{ELH}_{\mathcal{R}^+}$-ontologies will turn out to be quite useful in the next section. It basically follows from the proof of Lemma 8 in [4].

Lemma 3. *Let $\mathcal{O}$ be a flat, cycle-restricted $\mathcal{ELH}_{\mathcal{R}^+}$-ontology, $A \in \mathsf{N_C}$ and $\exists r.C$ an $\mathcal{ELH}_{\mathcal{R}^+}$-atom. Then, $A \sqsubseteq_\mathcal{O} \exists r.C$ iff there exists $\exists u.B \in Ats(\mathcal{O})$ such that $B \sqsubseteq_\mathcal{O} C$, and*

- *$A \sqsubseteq_\mathcal{O} \exists u.B$ and $u \trianglelefteq_\mathcal{O} r$, or*
- *$A \sqsubseteq_\mathcal{O} \exists t.B$ for a transitive role t with $u \trianglelefteq_\mathcal{O} t \trianglelefteq_\mathcal{O} r$.*

3 The Unification Algorithm for $\mathcal{ELH}^{-\top}_{\mathcal{R}^+}$

In the following, we assume that $\mathcal{O}$ is a flat and cycle-restricted $\mathcal{ELH}^{-\top}_{\mathcal{R}^+}$-ontology and Γ is a flat $\mathcal{ELH}^{-\top}_{\mathcal{R}^+}$-unification problem. We introduce an algorithm that can test whether Γ has an $\mathcal{ELH}_{\mathcal{R}+}^{-\top}$-unifier and needs only polynomial space for this task. This algorithm follows the approach developed in [18] for unification in $\mathcal{EL}^{-\top}$, but must take the ontology into account, which means that it must deal with a considerably more complex characterization of subsumption (see Lemma 1 and our remarks on how the characterization can be simplified if $\mathcal{O} = \emptyset$).

Before presenting our new approach, we briefly sketch the one employed in [18]. The original NP procedure for unification in $\mathcal{EL}$ [16] is based on the (non-trivial) observation that an $\mathcal{EL}$-unification problem Γ has a unifier iff it has a *local unifier*, i.e., one that is built using only atoms occurring in the unification problem. The procedure guesses an appropriate representation of a local substitution, and then checks by $\mathcal{EL}$ reasoning whether it really is a unifier. Basically, to guess a local substitution σ, one must guess for every variable X and non-variable atom C of Γ whether $\sigma(X) \sqsubseteq_\emptyset \sigma(C)$ is supposed to hold. A *subsumption mapping* τ describing a local unifier σ more generally guesses for every pair C, D of atoms whether $\sigma(C) \sqsubseteq_\emptyset \sigma(D)$ is supposed to hold. The restrictions imposed on such subsumption mappings ensure that the local substitution induced by such a mapping is indeed an $\mathcal{EL}$-unifier of Γ [18], i.e., the subsequent $\mathcal{EL}$ reasoning testing this can be dispensed with. The local unifier obtained from a subsumption mapping τ need not be an $\mathcal{EL}^{-\top}$-unifier. To test for the existence of an $\mathcal{EL}^{-\top}$-unifier related to τ, the subsumption mapping τ together with the original unification problem Γ is then used to construct a new unification problem $\Delta_{\Gamma,\tau}$, in which only variables can occur on the right-hand side of subsumption constraints. Existence of an $\mathcal{EL}^{-\top}$-unifier of $\Delta_{\Gamma,\tau}$ that is compatible with τ is then reduced in [18] to the existence of an admissible solution of a corresponding set $\mathfrak{I}_{\Gamma,\tau}$ of linear language inclusions. The latter problem can in turn be reduced in polynomial time to checking emptiness of alternating finite automata with ε-transitions [18], which is a PSpace-complete problem [23].

In this section we show how this approach can be extended from $\mathcal{EL}^{-\top}$ to $\mathcal{ELH}_{\mathcal{R}+}^{-\top}$ w.r.t. cycle-restricted ontologies. We start by introducing subsumption mappings and the induced unification problems of the form $\Delta_{\Gamma,\tau}$.

3.1 The Subsumption Mapping

Let $Ats(\Gamma, \mathcal{O})$ be the set of atoms occurring in Γ or $\mathcal{O}$. Due to the third case in the definition of structural subsumption, we also need to consider certain atoms that are not explicitly present in the input:

$$Ats_{tr}(\Gamma, \mathcal{O}) := Ats(\Gamma, \mathcal{O}) \cup \{\exists t.C \mid \exists s.C \in Ats(\Gamma, \mathcal{O}),\ t \trianglelefteq_{\mathcal{O}} s,\ t \text{ is transitive}\}.$$

A *non-variable atom* is an atom in $Ats_{tr}(\Gamma, \mathcal{O})$ that is not a variable. We denote the set of all such atoms as $At_{nv}(\Gamma, \mathcal{O})$. A mapping of the form $\tau : Ats_{tr}(\Gamma, \mathcal{O}) \times Ats_{tr}(\Gamma, \mathcal{O}) \to \{0, 1\}$ induces an assignment S^τ that maps variables in Γ to sets of non-variable atoms in $Ats_{tr}(\Gamma, \mathcal{O})$:

$$S^\tau(X) := \{D \in At_{nv}(\Gamma, \mathcal{O}) \mid \tau(X, D) = 1\}.$$

This assignment induces the relation

$$>_{S^\tau} := \{(X,Y) \in \mathit{Vars}(\Gamma) \times \mathit{Vars}(\Gamma) \mid Y \text{ occurs in an atom of } S^\tau(X)\}.$$

We say that S^τ is *acyclic* if the transitive closure of $>_{S^\tau}$ is irreflexive, and thus a strict partial order, which we denote as $>_\tau$. If S^τ is acyclic, then it induces a substitution σ_τ, defined by induction on $>_\tau$:

- If X is minimal w.r.t. $>_\tau$, then $\sigma_\tau(X) := \bigsqcap_{D \in S^\tau(X)} D$.
- Otherwise, assuming that $\sigma_\tau(Y)$ has already been defined for all Y such that $X >_\tau Y$, one defines $\sigma_\tau(X) := \bigsqcap_{D \in S^\tau(X)} \sigma_\tau(D)$.

The conditions imposed on a subsumption mapping τ ensure that the induced substitution σ_τ is an $\mathcal{ELH}_{\mathcal{R}^+}$-unifier of Γ. In order to simplify the definition of these conditions, we introduce the following notation (for atoms $\exists r.C, \exists s.D$):

$$\mathcal{F}(\exists r.C, \exists s.D) := \{D \mid \text{if } r \trianglelefteq_{\mathcal{O}} s\} \cup \{\exists t.D \mid r \trianglelefteq_{\mathcal{O}} t \trianglelefteq_{\mathcal{O}} s,\ t \text{ transitive}\}.$$

Basically, this set collects all concepts F such that $C \sqsubseteq_{\mathcal{O}} F$ implies $\exists r.C \sqsubseteq^s_{\mathcal{O}} \exists s.D$ (see the second and third case in the definition of $\sqsubseteq^s_{\mathcal{O}}$).

Definition 3. *The mapping* $\tau : \mathit{Ats}_{tr}(\Gamma, \mathcal{O}) \times \mathit{Ats}_{tr}(\Gamma, \mathcal{O}) \to \{0,1\}$ *is called a* subsumption mapping *for* Γ w.r.t. $\mathcal{O}$ *if it satisfies the following conditions:*

1. *It respects the properties of subsumption w.r.t.* $\mathcal{O}$*:*
   (a) $\tau(D,D) = 1$*, for each* $D \in \mathit{Ats}_{tr}(\Gamma, \mathcal{O})$.
   (b) *For all* $D_1, D_2, D_3 \in \mathit{Ats}_{tr}(\Gamma, \mathcal{O})$*, if* $\tau(D_1, D_2) = \tau(D_2, D_3) = 1$ *then* $\tau(D_1, D_3) = 1$.
   (c) $\tau(C,D) = 1$ *iff* $C \sqsubseteq_{\mathcal{O}} D$*, for all ground atoms* $C, D \in \mathit{Ats}_{tr}(\Gamma, \mathcal{O})$.
   (d) *For each concept constant* $A \in \mathit{Ats}(\Gamma, \mathcal{O})$*, role name* r*, and variable* X *with* $\exists r.X \in \mathit{Ats}_{tr}(\Gamma)$*:*
      i. $\tau(A, \exists r.X) = 1$ *iff*[5] *there is an atom* $\exists u.B$ *of* $\mathcal{O}$ *such that* $\tau(B, X) = 1$*, and*
         - $A \sqsubseteq_{\mathcal{O}} \exists u.B$ *and* $u \trianglelefteq_{\mathcal{O}} r$*, or*
         - $A \sqsubseteq_{\mathcal{O}} \exists t.B$ *for a transitive role* t *with* $u \trianglelefteq_{\mathcal{O}} t \trianglelefteq_{\mathcal{O}} r$.
      ii. $\tau(\exists r.X, A) = 1$ *iff*
         - *there are atoms* $\exists r_1.A_1, \dots, \exists r_k.A_k$ *of* $\mathcal{O}$ $(k \geq 0)$ *and atoms* $F_\ell \in \mathcal{F}(\exists r.X, \exists r_\ell.A_\ell)$ $(1 \leq \ell \leq k)$ *such that:* $\tau(X, F_\ell) = 1$ $(1 \leq \ell \leq k)$ *and* $\exists r_1.A_1 \sqcap \cdots \sqcap \exists r_k.A_k \sqsubseteq_{\mathcal{O}} A$.
   (e) *For all role names* $r, s \in \mathsf{N_R}$*, variables* X*, and atoms* $\exists r.C, \exists s.D \in \mathit{Ats}_{tr}(\Gamma)$ *with* $C = X$ *or* $D = X$*:* $\tau(\exists r.C, \exists s.D) = 1$ *iff*
      - *there exists* $F \in \mathcal{F}(\exists r.C, \exists s.D)$ *such that* $\tau(C, F) = 1$*, or*
      - *there are atoms* $\exists r_1.A_1, \dots, \exists r_k.A_k, \exists u.B$ *of* $\mathcal{O}$ $(k \geq 0)$*, atoms* $F_\ell \in \mathcal{F}(\exists r.C, \exists r_\ell.A_\ell)$ $(1 \leq \ell \leq k)$*, and an atom* $F \in \mathcal{F}(\exists u.B, \exists s.D)$*, such that:* $\tau(C, F_\ell) = 1$ $(1 \leq \ell \leq k)$*,* $\exists r_1.A_1 \sqcap \cdots \sqcap \exists r_k.A_k \sqsubseteq_{\mathcal{O}} \exists u.B$*,* $\tau(B, F) = 1$.

[5] This condition is justified by Lemma 3.

2. *The assignment S^τ is acyclic. Note that this means that τ induces the $\mathcal{ELH}_{\mathcal{R}^+}$-substitution σ^τ.*
3. *The substitution σ^τ is an $\mathcal{ELH}_{\mathcal{R}^+}$-unifier of Γ w.r.t. $\mathcal{O}$. In combination with the conditions already introduced, this is expressed by the following conditions for each subsumption constraint $C_1 \sqcap \cdots \sqcap C_n \sqsubseteq^? D \in \Gamma$:*
   (a) If D is a non-variable atom, then either $\tau(C_i, D) = 1$ for some $i \in \{1, \ldots, n\}$, or there are atoms $At_1, \ldots, At_k, At'$ of $\mathcal{O}$ ($k \geq 0$) such that:
      - *$At_1 \sqcap \cdots \sqcap At_k \sqsubseteq_{\mathcal{O}} At'$,*
      - *for each $\ell \in \{1, \ldots, k\}$ there is $i \in \{1, \ldots, n\}$ s.t. $\tau(C_i, At_\ell) = 1$, and*
      - *$\tau(At', D) = 1$.*

   (b) If D is a variable and $\tau(D, C) = 1$ for a non-variable atom $C \in At_{nv}(\Gamma, \mathcal{O})$, then $C_1 \sqcap \cdots \sqcap C_n \sqsubseteq^? C$ must satisfy the previous case.

By using the close relationship between this definition and the characterization of subsumption in Lemma 1, one can show that Γ has an $\mathcal{ELH}_{\mathcal{R}^+}$-unifier w.r.t. $\mathcal{O}$ iff there is a subsumption mapping for Γ w.r.t. $\mathcal{O}$. In the proof of the if-direction, one shows that the substitution induced by the subsumption mapping is indeed a unifier. For the other direction, one takes a unifier σ and shows that the mapping τ satisfying $\tau(C, D) = 1$ iff $\sigma(C) \sqsubseteq_{\mathcal{O}} \sigma(D)$ is a subsumption mapping for Γ w.r.t. $\mathcal{O}$.

However, using subsumption mappings to characterize unifiability in $\mathcal{ELH}^{-\top}_{\mathcal{R}^+}$ requires more effort. Together with the unification problem Γ, a subsumption mapping τ yields a simpler unification problem $\Delta_{\Gamma,\tau} := \Delta_\Gamma \cup \Delta_\tau$, where

$$\Delta_\Gamma := \{C_1 \sqcap \cdots \sqcap C_n \sqsubseteq^? X \in \Gamma \mid X \in \mathsf{N_V}\} \quad \text{and} \quad \Delta_\tau := \{C \sqsubseteq^? X \mid \tau(C, X) = 1\}.$$

In addition, any substitution σ induces an assignment S^σ of the form:

$$S^\sigma(X) := \{D \in At_{nv}(\Gamma, \mathcal{O}) \mid \sigma(X) \sqsubseteq_{\mathcal{O}} \sigma(D)\}.$$

We write $S^\tau \leq S^\sigma$ if $S^\tau(X) \subseteq S^\sigma(X)$ holds for all variables X. In this case we say that σ is *compatible* with τ.

The following result gives a characterization of the existence of an $\mathcal{ELH}^{-\top}_{\mathcal{R}^+}$-unifier w.r.t. an $\mathcal{ELH}^{-\top}_{\mathcal{R}^+}$-ontology.

Proposition 1. *Let $\mathcal{O}$ be a flat and cycle-restricted $\mathcal{ELH}^{-\top}_{\mathcal{R}^+}$-ontology and Γ a flat $\mathcal{ELH}^{-\top}_{\mathcal{R}^+}$-unification problem. Then, Γ has an $\mathcal{ELH}^{-\top}_{\mathcal{R}^+}$-unifier w.r.t. $\mathcal{O}$ iff there exists a subsumption mapping τ for Γ w.r.t. $\mathcal{O}$ such that $\Delta_{\Gamma,\tau}$ has an $\mathcal{ELH}^{-\top}_{\mathcal{R}^+}$-unifier γ w.r.t. $\mathcal{O}$ that is compatible with τ.*

Example 2. Let $\mathcal{O} = \emptyset$ and consider the following unification problem:

$$\Gamma_2 := \{\exists r.B \sqsubseteq^? \exists r.Y, \;\; \exists s.X \sqcap \exists r.A \sqsubseteq^? Y\}.$$

Due to Condition 3 in Definition 3 and the fact that $\mathcal{O}$ is empty, any subsumption mapping τ must satisfy $\tau(\exists r.B, \exists r.Y) = 1$. Condition 1e then implies that $\tau(B, Y) = 1$ must hold as well. We can conclude that, for any subsumption mapping τ, the set $\Delta_{\Gamma_2,\tau}$ contains at least the subsumption constraints $B \sqsubseteq^? Y$ and

$\exists s.X \sqcap \exists r.A \sqsubseteq^? Y$. Using an argument similar to the one employed in Example 1, one can show that such a set $\Delta_{\Gamma_2,\tau}$ cannot have an $\mathcal{ELH}_{\mathcal{R}^+}^{-\top}$-unifier w.r.t. $\emptyset$.

Definition 3 also tells us that Condition 3b does not apply to the constraints $B \sqsubseteq^? Y$ and $\exists s.X \sqcap \exists r.A \sqsubseteq^? Y$ as long as there is no non-variable atom C with $\tau(Y, C) = 1$. Hence, it is easy to see that there also is a subsumption mapping τ that has only these two constraints in $\Delta_{\Gamma_2,\tau}$ since the only other mandatory values 1 are the ones required by 1a. For the ontology $\mathcal{O}'' = \{B \sqsubseteq \exists r.A\}$, the set $\Delta_{\Gamma_2,\tau}$ then has an $\mathcal{ELH}_{\mathcal{R}^+}^{-\top}$-unifier w.r.t. $\mathcal{O}''$, which maps Y to $\exists r.A$. This unifier is compatible with τ since the subsumption mapping τ that yields value 1 only if required satisfies $S^\tau(X) = S^\tau(Y) = \emptyset$. Thus, by Lemma 1, Γ_2 has an $\mathcal{ELH}_{\mathcal{R}^+}^{-\top}$-unifier w.r.t. $\mathcal{O}''$. Note that this unifier is not σ_τ since σ_τ in this case assigns $\top$ to X and Y.

3.2 Translation into Language Inclusions

Linear language inclusions are a special case of the linear language equations considered in [17] in the context of unification in the DL $\mathcal{FL}_0$. In contrast to the general case, where solvability is an ExpTime-complete problem [17], the linear language inclusions introduced in [18] in the context of unification in $\mathcal{EL}^{-\top}$ have a PSpace-complete solvability problem [18].

Definition 4. *Let $X_1, \ldots, X_n$ be a finite set of* indeterminates. *A* linear language inclusion *over this set of indeterminates and the alphabet* $\mathsf{N_R}$ *is an expression of the form*

$$X_i \subseteq L_0 \cup L_1 X_1 \cup \cdots \cup L_n X_n,$$

where $i \in \{1, \ldots, n\}$ and each $L_j \subseteq \{\varepsilon\} \cup \mathsf{N_R}$ $(0 \le j \le n)$. As usual, the symbol ε denotes the empty word. A solution θ of such an inclusion assigns sets of words $\theta(X_i) \subseteq \mathsf{N_R}^*$ to each indeterminate X_i such that $\theta(X_i) \subseteq L_0 \cup L_1 \cdot \theta(X_1) \cup \cdots \cup L_n \cdot \theta(X_n)$, where "$\cdot$" denotes concatenation of languages. The solution θ is finite *if $\theta(X_i)$ is a finite set for all $i \in \{1, \ldots, n\}$.*

Checking whether $\Delta_{\Gamma,\tau}$ has an $\mathcal{ELH}_{\mathcal{R}^+}^{-\top}$-unifier w.r.t. $\mathcal{O}$ that is compatible with a given subsumption mapping τ can be reduced to solving a system $\mathfrak{I}_{\Gamma,\tau}^{\mathcal{O}}$ of such linear language inclusion. The basic idea is that, for each concept variable X and concept constant A, we introduce an indeterminate X_A. Intuitively, the system $\mathfrak{I}_{\Gamma,\tau}^{\mathcal{O}}$ is constructed such that the following holds:

- if γ is an $\mathcal{ELH}_{\mathcal{R}^+}^{-\top}$-unifier of $\Delta_{\Gamma,\tau}$ compatible with τ, then there is an assignment θ_γ satisfying $\theta_\gamma(X_A) = \{w \mid \exists w.A \in \mathit{Part}(\gamma(X))\}$ that is a finite solution of the system $\mathfrak{I}_{\Gamma,\tau}^{\mathcal{O}}$.

Since γ is an $\mathcal{ELH}_{\mathcal{R}^+}^{-\top}$-unifier, of which we can assume without loss of generality that it is ground [19], the solution θ_γ satisfies an additional property: for every variable X there is a concept constant A such that $\theta_\gamma(X_A) \neq \emptyset$. We call a solution of $\mathfrak{I}_{\Gamma,\tau}^{\mathcal{O}}$ satisfying this property *admissible*. Conversely, finite, admissible solutions of $\mathfrak{I}_{\Gamma,\tau}^{\mathcal{O}}$ yield an appropriate unifier of $\Delta_{\Gamma,\tau}$:

– if $\mathfrak{I}^{\mathcal{O}}_{\Gamma,\tau}$ has a finite, admissible solution, then it has such a solution θ that yields an $\mathcal{ELH}^{-\top}_{\mathcal{R}^+}$-unifier γ_θ of $\Delta_{\Gamma,\tau}$ that is compatible with τ. This unifier is defined similarly to σ_τ, but using particles provided by θ for padding:
  - if X is minimal w.r.t. $>_\tau$, then

$$\gamma_\theta(X) := \bigsqcap_{D \in S^\tau(X)} D \sqcap \bigsqcap_{A \in \mathsf{N_C}} \bigsqcap_{w \in \theta(X_A)} \exists w.A,$$

  - if $\gamma_\theta(Y)$ has already been defined for all Y such that $X >_\tau Y$, then

$$\gamma_\theta(X) := \bigsqcap_{D \in S^\tau(X)} \gamma_\theta(D) \sqcap \bigsqcap_{A \in \mathsf{N_C}} \bigsqcap_{w \in \theta(X_A)} \exists w.A.$$

Basically, to define the linear language inclusions in $\mathfrak{I}^{\mathcal{O}}_{\Gamma,\tau}$, we consider the following situation: given a particle $\exists w.A \in Part(\gamma(X))$ and a constraint $C_1 \sqcap \cdots \sqcap C_n \sqsubseteq^? X \in \Delta_{\Gamma,\tau}$, we know (by Lemma 2 in [18]) that $\gamma(C_1)\sqcap\cdots\sqcap\gamma(C_n) \sqsubseteq_{\mathcal{O}} \exists w.A$ holds. Hence, the idea is to encode, within the inclusions in $\mathfrak{I}^{\mathcal{O}}_{\Gamma,\tau}$, whether a conjunction of atoms and a particle satisfy the characterization of subsumption in Lemma 1.

For the case of an empty ontology, the construction of the system $\mathfrak{I}^{\emptyset}_{\Gamma,\tau}$ is relatively straightforward since the characterization of subsumption is quite simple in this case. As described in [18], for each concept constant $A \in \mathsf{N_C}$ and each subsumption constraint $\mathfrak{s} = C_1 \sqcap \cdots \sqcap C_n \sqsubseteq^? X$ in $\Delta_{\Gamma,\tau}$, a linear inclusion $\mathfrak{i}_A(\mathfrak{s})$ of the following form is added to $\mathfrak{I}^{\emptyset}_{\Gamma,\tau}$:

$$X_A \subseteq f_A(C_1) \cup \cdots \cup f_A(C_n), \quad \text{where } f_A(C) := \begin{cases} \{r\} f_A(C') & \text{if } C = \exists r.C', \\ Y_A & \text{if } C = Y \in \mathsf{N_V}, \\ \{\varepsilon\} & \text{if } C = A, \\ \emptyset & \text{if } C \in \mathsf{N_C} \setminus \{A\}. \end{cases}$$

Example 3. Consider the system $\Delta_{\Gamma_2,\tau} = \{B \sqsubseteq^? Y, \exists s.X \sqcap \exists r.A \sqsubseteq^? Y, \ldots\}$ from Example 2. The first subsumption constraint yields the language inclusions $Y_A \subseteq \emptyset$ and $Y_B \subseteq \{\varepsilon\}$, and the second yields $Y_A \subseteq \{s\}X_A \cup \{r\}\{\varepsilon\}$ and $Y_B \subseteq \{s\}X_B \cup \{r\}\emptyset$. There are no language inclusions constraining X_A or X_B. Any solution θ of $\mathfrak{I}^{\emptyset}_{\Gamma_2,\tau}$ thus must satisfy $\theta(Y_A) = \emptyset$. If θ is admissible, then $\theta(Y_B)$ must be non-empty. The first inclusion for Y_B says that $\theta(Y_B)$ consists of the empty word, whereas the second says that every element of $\theta(Y_B)$ must start with the letter s. Thus, $\mathfrak{I}^{\emptyset}_{\Gamma_2,\tau}$ cannot have an admissible solution.

To take a non-empty ontology into account, the right-hand sides of the language inclusions must be extended. Our new translation yields linear language inclusions $\mathfrak{i}^*_A(\mathfrak{s})$ of the form

$$X_A \subseteq f^*_A(C_1) \cup \cdots \cup f^*_A(C_n) \cup \mathcal{U}_A(\mathfrak{s}), \tag{1}$$

where $f^*_A(C)$ differs from $f_A(C)$ in the way existential restrictions are treated:

$$f^*_A(\exists r.C') := L_r f_A(C') \text{ where } L_r := \{s \in \mathsf{N_R} \mid r \trianglelefteq_{\mathcal{O}} s\}.$$

This modification of f_A to f_A^* takes care of the role hierarchy.

Example 4. For instance, if in the system of Example 3 we replace $B \sqsubseteq^? Y$ with $\exists u.X \sqsubseteq^? Y$, then the language inclusions corresponding to this constraint are $Y_A \subseteq \{u\}X_A$ and $Y_B \subseteq \{u\}X_B$. The new system again does not have an admissible solution. However, if we consider an ontology $\mathcal{O}$ containing $u \sqsubseteq s$, then the new translation yields the language inclusions $Y_A \subseteq \{u, s\}X_A$ and $Y_B \subseteq \{u, s\}X_B$ for this constraint. Consequently, the new system of language inclusions has a finite, admissible solution, which reflects the fact that the system of subsumption constraints has an $\mathcal{ELH}_{\mathcal{R}+}^{-\top}$-unifier w.r.t. $\mathcal{O}$.

The GCIs and transitivity axioms of the ontology are taken care of by the additional term $\mathcal{U}_A(\mathfrak{s})$ in (1). This term uses additional types of indeterminates whose meaning is encoded using additional language inclusions. Indeterminates of the form $Z_{B\to A}$, where A, B are concept constants occurring in Γ or $\mathcal{O}$, are supposed to represent languages containing only words w such that $B \sqsubseteq_{\mathcal{O}} \exists w.A$. This intuition is formalized by the set of linear inclusions $\mathfrak{I}_{\mathcal{O}}$, which consists of one language inclusion for each indeterminate $Z_{B\to A}$ having the following form:

$$Z_{B\to A} \subseteq L \cup \bigcup_{(r,B')\in I(B)} \{r\}Z_{B'\to A}, \tag{2}$$

where $I(B) := \{(r, B') \in \mathsf{N_R} \times (Ats(\mathcal{O}) \cap \mathsf{N_C}) \mid B \sqsubseteq_{\mathcal{O}} \exists r.B'\}$ and $L := \{\varepsilon\}$ if $B \sqsubseteq_{\mathcal{O}} A$, and $L := \emptyset$ otherwise. The set of linear inclusions $\mathfrak{I}_{\mathcal{O}}$ captures subsumptions of the form $B \sqsubseteq_{\mathcal{O}} \exists w.A$ in the following sense.

Lemma 4. *Let $\mathcal{O}$ be a flat, cycle-restricted $\mathcal{ELH}_{\mathcal{R}+}$-ontology.*

1. *If θ is a solution of $\mathfrak{I}_{\mathcal{O}}$, then $w \in \theta(Z_{B\to A})$ implies $B \sqsubseteq_{\mathcal{O}} \exists w.A$.*
2. *If we define $\theta(Z_{B\to A}) := \{w \in \mathsf{N_R}^* \mid B \sqsubseteq_{\mathcal{O}} \exists w.A\}$, then θ is a* finite *solution of $\mathfrak{I}_{\mathcal{O}}$.*

Example 5. Consider again the system $\Delta_{\Gamma_2,\mathcal{T}}$ of Example 3, but replace $B \sqsubseteq^? Y$ with $\exists r.B \sqsubseteq^? Y$. The language inclusions corresponding to this constraint are $Y_A \subseteq \{r\}\emptyset$ and $Y_B \subseteq \{r\}\{\varepsilon\}$. The new system again does not have an admissible solution. However, if we consider the ontology $\mathcal{O} = \{B \sqsubseteq A\}$, then there are solutions θ of $\mathfrak{I}_{\mathcal{O}}$ that satisfy $\varepsilon \in \theta(Z_{B\to A})$. Thus, if we extend the inclusion $Y_A \subseteq \{r\}\emptyset$ obtained from $\exists r.B \sqsubseteq^? Y$ to $Y_A \subseteq \{r\}\emptyset \cup \{r\}Z_{B\to A}$, then the new system has a solution θ such that $r \in \theta(Y_A)$ since the other inclusion for Y_A is $Y_A \subseteq \{s\}X_A \cup \{r\}\{\varepsilon\}$. This implies that there is an admissible solution since there are no language inclusions constraining X_A or X_B.

To deal with transitivity axioms, we introduce additional indeterminates of the form $X_{A,t}$, which are constrained by the following linear language inclusions: $\mathfrak{i}_{A,t}(\mathfrak{s}) = X_{A,t} \subseteq f_{A,t}(C_1) \cup \cdots \cup f_{A,t}(C_n) \cup \mathcal{U}_{A,t}(\mathfrak{s})$ where

$$f_{A,t}(C) := \begin{cases} f_A(C') & \text{if } C = \exists r.C' \wedge r \trianglelefteq_{\mathcal{O}} t, \\ Y_{A,t} & \text{if } C = Y \in \mathsf{N_V}, \\ \emptyset & \text{otherwise.} \end{cases}$$

Intuitively, the difference between $\mathfrak{i}^*_A(\mathfrak{s})$ and $\mathfrak{i}_{A,t}(\mathfrak{s})$ is that, given a particle $\exists t.\exists w.A$ satisfying $\sigma(C_1)\sqcap\cdots\sqcap\sigma(C_n) \sqsubseteq_{\mathcal{O}} \exists t.\exists w.A$, the right-hand side of $\mathfrak{i}_{A,t}(\mathfrak{s})$ is designed to recognize w instead of tw.

Example 6. Assume that

$$\Delta_{\Gamma,\tau} = \{\exists r.B \sqsubseteq^? Y, \exists s.X \sqcap \exists r.A \sqsubseteq^? Y, \exists t.B \sqsubseteq^? X\}.$$

In addition, consider the ontology $\mathcal{O} = \{s \sqsubseteq t, t \sqsubseteq r\}$. Since $\exists r.B \sqsubseteq^? Y$ yields the language inclusion $Y_A \subseteq \{r\}\emptyset$, any solution θ of $\mathfrak{I}^{\mathcal{O}}_{\Gamma,\tau}$ must satisfy $\theta(Y_A) = \emptyset$. Hence, if θ is admissible, then $\theta(Y_B) \neq \emptyset$. In the presence of $\mathcal{O}$, the new translation also yields the inclusions:

$$Y_B \subseteq \{r\}\{\varepsilon\},\ Y_B \subseteq \{s,t,r\}X_B \cup \{r\}\emptyset \text{ and } X_B \subseteq \{t,r\}\{\varepsilon\}.$$

Together with $\theta(Y_B) \neq \emptyset$, the first of these inclusions yields $\theta(Y_B) = \{r\}$. Thus, the second inclusion implies that $\varepsilon \in \theta(X_B)$, and thus θ does not solve the third inclusion. Thus, $\mathfrak{I}^{\mathcal{O}}_{\Gamma,\tau}$ cannot have an admissible solution, corresponding to the fact that $\Delta_{\Gamma,\tau}$ does not have an $\mathcal{ELH}^{-\top}_{\mathcal{R}+}$-unifier w.r.t. $\mathcal{O}$.

However, if we add the transitivity axiom $t \circ t \sqsubseteq t$ to $\mathcal{O}$, then $\Delta_{\Gamma,\tau}$ has an $\mathcal{ELH}^{-\top}_{\mathcal{R}+}$-unifier γ with $\gamma(X) = \exists t.B$ and $\gamma(Y) = \exists r.B$ w.r.t. this ontology. The inclusion $\mathfrak{i}_{B,t}(\mathfrak{s}) = X_{B,t} \subseteq \{\varepsilon\}$, obtained from $\mathfrak{s} = \exists t.B \sqsubseteq^? X$, admits solutions θ with $\theta(X_{B,t}) = \{\varepsilon\}$. Hence, if we extend the language inclusion $Y_B \subseteq \{s,t,r\}X_B \cup \{r\}\emptyset$ to the new one

$$Y_B \subseteq \{s,t,r\}X_B \cup \{r\}\emptyset \cup \{r\}X_{B,t}$$

that takes transitivity of t into account, then the new system of language inclusions has an admissible solution with $\theta(Y_B) = \{r\}$ and $\theta(X_B) = \{t\}$, which corresponds to the unifier γ.

Since the definitions of the terms $\mathcal{U}_A(\mathfrak{s})$ and $\mathcal{U}_{A,t}(\mathfrak{s})$ are quite long and technical, we refer to [9] for exact definitions and detailed explanations motivating them. Let $\mathfrak{I}^{\mathcal{O}}_{\Gamma,\tau}$ be the system of linear language inclusions consisting of $\mathfrak{I}_{\mathcal{O}}$ and the inclusions $\mathfrak{i}^*_A(\mathfrak{s})$ and $\mathfrak{i}_{A,t}(\mathfrak{s})$ for every subsumption constraint $\mathfrak{s}$ in $\Delta_{\Gamma,\tau}$. Note that the definition of these language inclusions does not only depend on $\Delta_{\Gamma,\tau}$, but also on τ itself (see Definition 4.17 in [9] for the exact definition).

Proposition 2. *Let τ be a subsumption mapping for Γ w.r.t. $\mathcal{O}$. The unification problem $\Delta_{\Gamma,\tau}$ has an $\mathcal{ELH}^{-\top}_{\mathcal{R}+}$-unifier γ w.r.t. $\mathcal{O}$ that is compatible with τ iff the system of linear language inclusions $\mathfrak{I}^{\mathcal{O}}_{\Gamma,\tau}$ has a finite, admissible solution.*

The proof of the only-if direction of this proposition makes use of the fact that we can assume without loss of generality that γ is a simple unifier. In fact, this is already taken into account in the definition of $\mathfrak{I}^{\mathcal{O}}_{\Gamma,\tau}$ (see [9]).

Definition 5. *The $\mathcal{ELH}^{-\top}_{\mathcal{R}+}$-unifier γ of $\Delta_{\Gamma,\tau}$ w.r.t. $\mathcal{O}$ is called* simple *if, for all $C_1 \sqcap\cdots\sqcap C_n \sqsubseteq^? X \in \Delta_{\Gamma,\tau}$ and $\exists w.A \in Part(\gamma(X))$, the following holds:*

1. *there exists* $i, 1 \leq i \leq n$ *such that*
   (a) C_i *is a ground atom and* $C_i \sqsubseteq^s_{\mathcal{O}} \exists w.A$, *or*
   (b) $C_i = Y$ *is a variable and* $\exists w.A \in Part(\gamma(C_i))$, *or*
   (c) $C_i = \exists r.Y$ *for a variable* Y, $w = sw'$ *for some* $s \in \mathsf{N_R}$ *and* $w' \in \mathsf{N_R}^*$, *and*
      - $\exists w'.A \in Part(\gamma(Y))$ *and* $r \trianglelefteq_{\mathcal{O}} s$, *or*
      - $\exists t.\exists w'.A \in Part(\gamma(Y))$ *for a transitive role* t *s.t.* $r \trianglelefteq_{\mathcal{O}} t \trianglelefteq_{\mathcal{O}} s$; *or*
2. *There are atoms* $At_1, \ldots, At_k, At'$ *of* $\mathcal{O}$ $(k \geq 0)$ *such that:*
   (a) $At_1 \sqcap \cdots \sqcap At_k \sqsubseteq_{\mathcal{O}} At'$,
   (b) *for all* $\ell \in \{1, \ldots, k\}$, *there exists* $i \in \{1, \ldots, n\}$ *s.t.* $\tau(C_i, At_\ell) = 1$, *and*
   (c) $At' \sqsubseteq^s_{\mathcal{O}} \exists w.A$.

Lemma 5. *If* Γ *is an* $\mathcal{ELH}^{-\top}_{\mathcal{R}^+}$*-unification problem that is unifiable w.r.t.* $\mathcal{O}$, *then there exists a subsumption mapping* τ *for* Γ *w.r.t.* $\mathcal{O}$ *such that* $\Delta_{\Gamma,\tau}$ *has a* simple $\mathcal{ELH}^{-\top}_{\mathcal{R}^+}$*-unifier* σ *w.r.t.* $\mathcal{O}$ *that is compatible with* τ.

3.3 The PSpace Algorithm

Using the results described in the previous two subsections, we can construct an NPSpace decision procedure for unification in $\mathcal{ELH}^{-\top}_{\mathcal{R}^+}$ w.r.t. cycle-restricted $\mathcal{ELH}^{-\top}_{\mathcal{R}^+}$-ontologies. Due to Savitch's theorem [26], this implies that the problem is also in PSpace.

Given an input consisting of an $\mathcal{ELH}^{-\top}_{\mathcal{R}^+}$-unification problem and a cycle-restricted $\mathcal{ELH}^{-\top}_{\mathcal{R}^+}$-ontology, the algorithm transforms the ontology and the unification problem into flat ones, which we denote as Γ and $\mathcal{O}$. It then proceeds as follows:

1. It guesses a subsumption mapping τ for Γ w.r.t. $\mathcal{O}$. If no such mapping exists, then it fails.
2. It transforms Γ into $\Delta_{\Gamma,\tau}$, and then translates the latter into the set of linear language inclusions $\mathfrak{I}^{\mathcal{O}}_{\Gamma,\tau}$.
3. Finally, the algorithm answers "yes" iff $\mathfrak{I}^{\mathcal{O}}_{\Gamma,\tau}$ has a finite, admissible solution.

Flattening can be done in polynomial time and preserves unifiability [5,18]. A mapping $\tau : Ats_{tr}(\Gamma, \mathcal{O}) \times Ats_{tr}(\Gamma, \mathcal{O}) \rightarrow \{0, 1\}$ can be guessed in non-deterministic polynomial time, and checking whether it satisfies the properties of a subsumption mapping (see Definition 3) can clearly also be realized within polynomial space, as can the translations into $\Delta_{\Gamma,\tau}$ and $\mathfrak{I}^{\mathcal{O}}_{\Gamma,\tau}$. Finally, as shown in [18], testing for the existence of a finite, admissible solution of $\mathfrak{I}^{\mathcal{O}}_{\Gamma,\tau}$ can be reduced in polynomial time to checking emptiness of alternating finite automata with ε-transitions, which is a PSpace-complete problem [23]. This shows that the introduced algorithm really is an NPSpace algorithm. Its correctness is an immediate consequence of Propositions 1 and 2. Since PSpace-hardness already holds for the special case of an empty ontology, we thus have shown the following main result of this paper.

Theorem 1. *Deciding unifiability of* $\mathcal{ELH}^{-\top}_{\mathcal{R}^+}$*-unification problems w.r.t. cycle-restricted* $\mathcal{ELH}^{-\top}_{\mathcal{R}^+}$*-ontologies is PSpace-complete.*

4 Conclusion

We have shown that the approach for obtaining a PSpace decision procedure for $\mathcal{EL}^{-\top}$-unification without a background ontology [18] can be extended to unification w.r.t. a cycle-restricted $\mathcal{ELH}_{\mathcal{R}^+}$-ontology, i.e., an ontology that may contain general concept inclusions (GCIs) formulated in $\mathcal{EL}^{-\top}$ as well as role inclusion and transitivity axioms, but does not entail a cyclic subsumption of the form $C \sqsubseteq_{\mathcal{O}} \exists r_1.\exists r_2.\cdots\exists r_n.C$ $(n \geq 1)$. As explained in the introduction, both considering concept descriptions not containing the top concept $\top$ and considering GCIs and role axioms is motivated by the expressivity employed in the medical ontology SNOMED CT. Dealing with such a background ontology not only makes the approach more complicated due to the more involved characterization of subsumption (see Lemma 1 and Definition 3, compared to the much simpler versions in [18]). It also requires the development of new notions, such as simple unifiers and the extension of the system of linear language inclusions with new indeterminates and corresponding inclusions.

With SNOMED CT in mind, it would be interesting to see whether results on unification (with or without top) can be further extended to ontologies additionally containing so-called right-identity rules, i.e., role axioms of the form $r \circ s \sqsubseteq r$, since they are also needed to get rid of the SEP-triplet encoding mentioned in the introduction. However, extending the characterization of subsumption to this setting is probably a non-trivial problem. From a theoretical point of view, the big open problem is whether one can dispense with the requirement that the ontology must be cycle-restricted. Even for pure $\mathcal{EL}$, decidability of unification w.r.t. unrestricted ontologies is an open problem.

From a practical point of view, the next step is to develop an algorithm that replaces non-deterministic guessing by a more intelligent search procedure. Since the unification problem is PSpace-complete, a polynomial translation of the whole problem into SAT is not possible (unless NP = PSpace). However, one could try to delegate the search for a subsumption mapping to a SAT solver, which interacts with a solver for the additional condition on such a mapping (existence of a finite, admissible solution of $\mathfrak{I}^{\mathcal{O}}_{\Gamma,\tau}$) in an SMT-like fashion [21].

Acknowledgments. This work was partially supported by the German Federal Ministry of Education and Research (BMBF, SCADS22B) and the Saxon State Ministry for Science, Culture and Tourism (SMWK) by funding the competence center for Big Data and AI "ScaDS.AI Dresden/Leipzig". The authors would like to thank Stefan Borgwardt and Francesco Kriegel for helpful discussions on the form of the definitions and axioms used in the current version of SNOMED CT.

References

1. Baader, F., Binh, N.T., Borgwardt, S., Morawska, B.: Unification in the description logic $\mathcal{EL}$ without the top concept. In: Bjørner, N., Sofronie-Stokkermans, V. (eds.) CADE 2011. LNCS (LNAI), vol. 6803, pp. 70–84. Springer, Heidelberg (2011). https://doi.org/10.1007/978-3-642-22438-6_8

2. Baader, F., Borgwardt, S., Morawska, B.: Extending unification in $\mathcal{EL}$ towards general tboxes. In: Principles of Knowledge Representation and Reasoning: Proceedings of the Thirteenth International Conference (KR 2012), Rome, 10–14 June 2012. AAAI Press (2012)
3. Baader, F., Borgwardt, S., Morawska, B.: A goal-oriented algorithm for unification in $\mathcal{ELH}_{R^+}$ w.r.t. cycle-restricted ontologies. In: Thielscher, M., Zhang, D. (eds.) AI 2012. LNCS (LNAI), vol. 7691, pp. 493–504. Springer, Heidelberg (2012). https://doi.org/10.1007/978-3-642-35101-3_42
4. Baader, F., Borgwardt, S., Morawska, B.: A goal-oriented algorithm for unification in $\mathcal{ELH}_{R^+}$ w.r.t. cycle-restricted ontologies. LTCS-Report 12-05, Chair for Automata Theory, Institute for Theoretical Computer Science, Technische Universität Dresden, Dresden (2012). https://doi.org/10.25368/2022.189
5. Baader, F., Borgwardt, S., Morawska, B.: SAT encoding of unification in $\mathcal{ELH}_{R^+}$ w.r.t. cycle-restricted ontologies. In: Gramlich, B., Miller, D., Sattler, U. (eds.) IJCAR 2012. LNCS (LNAI), vol. 7364, pp. 30–44. Springer, Heidelberg (2012). https://doi.org/10.1007/978-3-642-31365-3_5
6. Baader, F., Borgwardt, S., Morawska, B.: SAT encoding of unification in $\mathcal{ELH}_{R^+}$ w.r.t. cycle-restricted ontologies. LTCS-Report 12-02, Chair for Automata Theory, Institute for Theoretical Computer Science, Technische Universität Dresden, Dresden (2012). https://doi.org/10.25368/2022.186
7. Baader, F., Borgwardt, S., Morawska, B.: Constructing SNOMED CT concepts via disunification. LTCS-Report 17-07, Chair for Automata Theory, Institute for Theoretical Computer Science, Technische Universität Dresden, Dresden (2017). https://doi.org/10.25368/2022.237
8. Baader, F., Brandt, S., Lutz, C.: Pushing the $\mathcal{EL}$ envelope. In: Kaelbling, L.P., Saffiotti, A. (eds.) Proceedings of the Nineteenth International Joint Conference on Artificial Intelligence (IJCAI 2005), Edinburgh, 30 July–5 August 2005, pp. 364–369. Professional Book Center (2005)
9. Baader, F., Fernández Gil, O.: Unification in the description logic $\mathcal{ELH}_{\mathcal{R}^+}$ without the top concept modulo cycle-restricted ontologies (extended version). In: LTCS-Report 24-01, Chair for Automata Theory, Institute of Theoretical Computer Science, Technische Universität Dresden, Dresden (2024). https://doi.org/10.25368/2024.34
10. Baader, F., Horrocks, I., Lutz, C., Sattler, U.: An Introduction to Description Logic. Cambridge University Press (2017)
11. Baader, F., Kapur, D.: Deciding the word problem for ground identities with commutative and extensional symbols. In: Peltier, N., Sofronie-Stokkermans, V. (eds.) IJCAR 2020. LNCS (LNAI), vol. 12166, pp. 163–180. Springer, Cham (2020). https://doi.org/10.1007/978-3-030-51074-9_10
12. Baader, F., Marantidis, P., Mottet, A., Okhotin, A.: Extensions of unification modulo ACUI. Math. Struct. Comput. Sci. **30**(6), 597–626 (2020). https://doi.org/10.1017/S0960129519000185
13. Baader, F., Mendez, J., Morawska, B.: UEL: unification solver for the description logic $\mathcal{EL}$—system description. In: Gramlich, B., Miller, D., Sattler, U. (eds.) IJCAR 2012. LNCS (LNAI), vol. 7364, pp. 45–51. Springer, Heidelberg (2012). https://doi.org/10.1007/978-3-642-31365-3_6
14. Baader, F., Morawska, B.: Unification in the description logic $\mathcal{EL}$. In: Treinen, R. (ed.) RTA 2009. LNCS, vol. 5595, pp. 350–364. Springer, Heidelberg (2009). https://doi.org/10.1007/978-3-642-02348-4_25

15. Baader, F., Morawska, B.: SAT encoding of unification in $\mathcal{EL}$. In: Fermüller, C.G., Voronkov, A. (eds.) LPAR 2010. LNCS, vol. 6397, pp. 97–111. Springer, Heidelberg (2010). https://doi.org/10.1007/978-3-642-16242-8_8
16. Baader, F., Morawska, B.: Unification in the description logic $\mathcal{EL}$. Log. Methods Comput. Sci. **6**(3) (2010)
17. Baader, F., Narendran, P.: Unification of concept terms in description logics. J. Symb. Comput. **31**(3), 277–305 (2001)
18. Baader, F., Nguyen, T.B., Borgwardt, S., Morawska, B.: Deciding unifiability and computing local unifiers in the description logic $\mathcal{EL}$ without top constructor. Notre Dame J. Formal Log. **57**(4), 443–476 (2016)
19. Baader, F., Snyder, W.: Unification theory. In: Robinson, J.A., Voronkov, A. (eds.) Handbook of Automated Reasoning (in 2 volumes), pp. 445–532. Elsevier and MIT Press (2001)
20. Bachmair, L., Ramakrishnan, I.V., Tiwari, A., Vigneron, L.: Congruence closure modulo associativity and commutativity. In: Kirchner, H., Ringeissen, C. (eds.) FroCoS 2000. LNCS (LNAI), vol. 1794, pp. 245–259. Springer, Heidelberg (2000). https://doi.org/10.1007/10720084_16
21. Barrett, C.W., Sebastiani, R., Seshia, S.A., Tinelli, C.: Satisfiability modulo theories. In: Biere, A., Heule, M., van Maaren, H., Walsh, T. (eds.) Handbook of Satisfiability - Second Edition, Frontiers in Artificial Intelligence and Applications, vol. 336, pp. 1267–1329. IOS Press (2021). https://doi.org/10.3233/FAIA201017
22. Brandt, S.: Polynomial time reasoning in a description logic with existential restrictions, GCI axioms, and - what else? In: Proceedings of the 16th European Conference on Artificial Intelligence (ECAI 2004), Including Prestigious Applicants of Intelligent Systems, PAIS 2004, Valencia, 22–27 August 2004, pp. 298–302. IOS Press (2004)
23. Jiang, T., Ravikumar, B.: A note on the space complexity of some decision problems for finite automata. Inf. Process. Lett. **40**(1), 25–31 (1991)
24. Kapur, D.: Modularity and combination of associative commutative congruence closure algorithms enriched with semantic properties. Log. Methods Comput. Sci. **19**(1) (2023)
25. Narendran, P., Rusinowitch, M.: Any ground associative-commutative theory has a finite canonical system. J. Autom. Reason. **17**(1), 131–143 (1996)
26. Savitch, W.J.: Relationships between nondeterministic and deterministic tape complexities. J. Comput. Syst. Sci. **4**(2), 177–192 (1970). https://doi.org/10.1016/S0022-0000(70)80006-X
27. Schulz, S., Romacker, M., Hahn, U.: Part-whole reasoning in medical ontologies revisited—introducing SEP triplets into classification-based description logics. In: AMIA 1998, American Medical Informatics Association Annual Symposium. AMIA (1998)
28. Sofronie-Stokkermans, V.: Locality and subsumption testing in $\mathcal{EL}$ and some of its extensions. In: Advances in Modal Logic 7, papers from the Seventh Conference on Advances in Modal Logic, pp. 315–339. College Publications (2008)
29. Suntisrivaraporn, B., Baader, F., Schulz, S., Spackman, K.: Replacing SEP-triplets in SNOMED CT using tractable description logic operators. In: Bellazzi, R., Abu-Hanna, A., Hunter, J. (eds.) AIME 2007. LNCS (LNAI), vol. 4594, pp. 287–291. Springer, Heidelberg (2007). https://doi.org/10.1007/978-3-540-73599-1_38

Confluence of Logically Constrained Rewrite Systems Revisited

Jonas Schöpf(✉), Fabian Mitterwallner, and Aart Middeldorp

Department of Computer Science, University of Innsbruck, Innsbruck, Austria
{jonas.schoepf,fabian.mitterwallner,aart.middeldorp}@uibk.ac.at

Abstract. We show that (local) confluence of terminating logically constrained rewrite systems is undecidable, even when the underlying theory is decidable. Several confluence criteria for logically constrained rewrite systems are known. These were obtained by replaying existing proofs for plain term rewrite systems in a constrained setting, involving a non-trivial effort. We present a simple transformation from logically constrained rewrite systems to term rewrite systems such that critical pairs of the latter correspond to constrained critical pairs of the former. The usefulness of the transformation is illustrated by lifting the advanced confluence results based on (almost) development closed critical pairs as well as on parallel critical pairs to the constrained setting.

1 Introduction

Logically constrained rewrite systems (LCTRSs) [12] are a natural extension of plain term rewrite systems (TRSs) with native support for constraints that are handled by SMT solvers. The latter makes LCTRSs suitable for program analysis [3–5,22]. In this paper we are concerned with confluence techniques for LCTRSs. Numerous techniques exist to (dis)prove confluence of TRSs. For LCTRSs much less is known. Kop and Nishida [12] established (weak) orthogonality as sufficient confluence criteria for LCTRSs. Joinability of critical pairs for terminating systems is implicit in [22]. Very recently, strong closedness for linear LCTRSs and (almost) parallel closedness for left-linear LCTRSs were established [17]. The proofs of these results were obtained by *replaying* existing proofs for TRSs in a constrained setting, involving a non-trivial effort. For more advanced confluence criteria, this is not feasible.

In particular, the conclusion in [12] that LCTRSs "are *flexible*: common analysis techniques for term rewriting extend to LCTRSs without much effort" is not accurate. On the contrary, in Sect. 3 we show that (local) confluence of terminating LCTRSs is undecidable, even for a decidable fragment of the theory of integers.

In Sect. 4 we present a simple transformation from LCTRSs to TRSs which allows us to relate results for the latter to the former. We use the transformation to extend two advanced confluence criteria based on (parallel) critical

This research is funded by the Austrian Science Fund (FWF) project I5943.

C. Benzmüller et al. (Eds.): IJCAR 2024, LNAI 14740, pp. 298–316, 2024.
https://doi.org/10.1007/978-3-031-63501-4_16

pairs from TRSs to LCTRSs: In Sect. 5 we prove that (almost) development closed left-linear LCTRSs are confluent by *reusing* the corresponding result for TRSs obtained by van Oostrom [15] and in Sect. 6 we lift the result of Toyama [20] based on parallel critical pairs from TRSs to LCTRSs. Both results are employed in state-of-the-art confluence provers for TRSs (ACP [2], CSI [14], Hakusan [19]) and have only recently been formally verified in the Isabelle proof assistant [7,10,11].

For the LCTRS extension of the result of Toyama [20] we observed a subtle problem in the definition of the equivalence relation on constrained terms, which goes back to [12] and has been used in subsequent work on LCTRSs [5,17,22]. We briefly discuss the issue at the end of the next section, after recalling basic notions for LCTRSs. For space reasons some of the more technical proofs are only available in an extended version of this paper [18]. The results in Sect. 4 and Sect. 5 were first announced in [13].

2 Preliminaries

We assume familiarity with the basic notions of term rewriting. In this section we recall a few key notions for LCTRSs. For more background information we refer to [12,17,22]. We assume a many-sorted signature $\mathcal{F} = \mathcal{F}_{\mathsf{te}} \cup \mathcal{F}_{\mathsf{th}}$ with a term and theory part. For every sort ι in $\mathcal{F}_{\mathsf{th}}$ we have a non-empty set $\mathcal{V}\mathsf{al}_\iota \subseteq \mathcal{F}_{\mathsf{th}}$ of value symbols, such that all $c \in \mathcal{V}\mathsf{al}_\iota$ are constants of sort ι. We demand $\mathcal{F}_{\mathsf{te}} \cap \mathcal{F}_{\mathsf{th}} \subseteq \mathcal{V}\mathsf{al}$ where $\mathcal{V}\mathsf{al} = \bigcup_\iota \mathcal{V}\mathsf{al}_\iota$. In the case of integers this results in an infinite signature with $\mathbb{Z} \subseteq \mathcal{V}\mathsf{al} \subseteq \mathcal{F}_{\mathsf{th}}$. A term in $\mathcal{T}(\mathcal{F}_{\mathsf{th}}, \mathcal{V})$ is called a *logical* term. Ground logical terms are mapped to values by an interpretation $\mathcal{J}$: $[\![f(t_1, \ldots, t_n)]\!] = f_{\mathcal{J}}([\![t_1]\!], \ldots, [\![t_n]\!])$. We assume a bijection between value symbols and elements in the domain of $\mathcal{J}$, e.g., for integers: $[\![\mathsf{0}]\!] = 0$, $[\![-1]\!] = -1$, $[\![1]\!] = 1$ and so on. Logical terms of sort bool are called *constraints*. A constraint φ is *valid* if $[\![\varphi\gamma]\!] = \top$ for all substitutions γ such that $\gamma(x) \in \mathcal{V}\mathsf{al}$ for all $x \in \mathcal{V}\mathsf{ar}(\varphi)$. A *constrained rewrite rule* is a triple $\ell \to r\ [\varphi]$ where $\ell, r \in \mathcal{T}(\mathcal{F}, \mathcal{V})$ are terms of the same sort such that $\mathsf{root}(\ell) \in \mathcal{F}_{\mathsf{te}} \setminus \mathcal{F}_{\mathsf{th}}$ and φ is a constraint. We denote the set $\mathcal{V}\mathsf{ar}(\varphi) \cup (\mathcal{V}\mathsf{ar}(r) \setminus \mathcal{V}\mathsf{ar}(\ell))$ of *logical* variables in $\ell \to r\ [\varphi]$ by $\mathcal{LV}\mathsf{ar}(\ell \to r\ [\varphi])$. A constrained rewrite rule is left-linear (right-linear) if non-logical variables in the left-hand side (right-hand side) occur at most once. If a rule is left-linear and right-linear then it is called linear. An LCTRS is a set of constrained rewrite rules.

A substitution σ is said to *respect* a rule $\ell \to r\ [\varphi]$, denoted by $\sigma \vDash \ell \to r\ [\varphi]$, if $\mathcal{D}\mathsf{om}(\sigma) \subseteq \mathcal{V}\mathsf{ar}(\ell) \cup \mathcal{V}\mathsf{ar}(r) \cup \mathcal{V}\mathsf{ar}(\varphi)$, $\sigma(x) \in \mathcal{V}\mathsf{al}$ for all $x \in \mathcal{LV}\mathsf{ar}(\ell \to r\ [\varphi])$, and $[\![\varphi\sigma]\!] = \top$. Moreover, a constraint φ is respected by σ, denoted by $\sigma \vDash \varphi$, if $\sigma(x) \in \mathcal{V}\mathsf{al}$ for all $x \in \mathcal{V}\mathsf{ar}(\varphi)$ and $[\![\varphi\sigma]\!] = \top$. We call $f(x_1, \ldots, x_n) \to y\ [y = f(x_1, \ldots, x_n)]$ with a fresh variable y and $f \in \mathcal{F}_{\mathsf{th}} \setminus \mathcal{V}\mathsf{al}$ a *calculation rule*. Calculation rules are not part of the rules of an LCTRS $\mathcal{R}$. The set of all calculation rules induced by the signature $\mathcal{F}_{\mathsf{th}}$ of an LCTRS $\mathcal{R}$ is denoted by $\mathcal{R}_{\mathsf{ca}}$ and we abbreviate $\mathcal{R} \cup \mathcal{R}_{\mathsf{ca}}$ to $\mathcal{R}_{\mathsf{rc}}$. An LCTRS is called linear (left-linear, right-linear) if all its rules in $\mathcal{R}$ are linear (left-linear, right-linear). A rewrite step

$s \to_{\mathcal{R}} t$ satisfies $s|_p = \ell\sigma$ and $t = s[r\sigma]_p$ for some position p, constrained rewrite rule $\ell \to r\ [\varphi]$ in $\mathcal{R}_{\mathsf{rc}}$, and substitution σ such that $\sigma \vDash \ell \to r\ [\varphi]$. We drop the subscript $\mathcal{R}$ from $\to_{\mathcal{R}}$ when no confusion arises. An LCTRS $\mathcal{R}$ is confluent if there exists a term v with $t \to^* v\ {}^*\!\leftarrow u$ whenever $t\ {}^*\!\leftarrow s \to^* u$, for all terms s, t and u. For confluence analysis we need to rewrite constrained terms.

A *constrained term* is a pair $s\ [\varphi]$ consisting of a term s and a constraint φ. Two constrained terms $s\ [\varphi]$ and $t\ [\psi]$ are *equivalent*, denoted by $s\ [\varphi] \sim t\ [\psi]$, if for every substitution $\gamma \vDash \varphi$ with $\mathcal{D}\mathsf{om}(\gamma) = \mathcal{V}\mathsf{ar}(\varphi)$ there is some substitution $\delta \vDash \psi$ with $\mathcal{D}\mathsf{om}(\delta) = \mathcal{V}\mathsf{ar}(\psi)$ such that $s\gamma = t\delta$, and vice versa. Let $s\ [\varphi]$ be a constrained term. If $s|_p = \ell\sigma$ for some constrained rewrite rule $\rho\colon \ell \to r\ [\psi] \in \mathcal{R}_{\mathsf{rc}}$, position p, and substitution σ such that $\sigma(x) \in \mathcal{V}\mathsf{al} \cup \mathcal{V}\mathsf{ar}(\varphi)$ for all $x \in \mathcal{LV}\mathsf{ar}(\rho)$, φ is satisfiable and $\varphi \Rightarrow \psi\sigma$ is valid then $s\ [\varphi] \to_{\mathcal{R}} s[r\sigma]_p\ [\varphi]$. The rewrite relation $\xrightarrow{\sim}_{\mathcal{R}}$ on constrained terms is defined as $\sim \cdot \to_{\mathcal{R}} \cdot \sim$ and $s\ [\varphi] \xrightarrow{\sim}_p t\ [\psi]$ indicates that the rewrite step in $\xrightarrow{\sim}_{\mathcal{R}}$ takes place at position p. Similarly, we write $s\ [\varphi] \xrightarrow{\sim}_{\geqslant p} t\ [\psi]$ if the position in the rewrite step is below position p. Note that in our definition of $\to_{\mathcal{R}}$ the constraint is not modified. This equals [5, Definition 2.15], but is different from [12,17] where calculation steps $s[f(v_1,\dots,v_n)]_p\ [\varphi] \to s[v]_p\ [\varphi \wedge v = f(v_1,\dots,v_n)]$ modify the constraint. However, the relation $\xrightarrow{\sim}$ can simulate the relation $\to_{\mathcal{R}}$ from [12,17] as exemplified below.

Example 1. Consider the constrained term $x + 1\ [x > 3]$. Calculation steps as defined in [12,17] permit $x + 1\ [x > 3] \to z\ [z = x + 1 \wedge x > 3]$. In our setting, an initial equivalence step is required to introduce the fresh variable z and the corresponding assignment needed to perform a calculation: $x + 1\ [x > 3] \sim x + 1\ [z = x + 1 \wedge x > 3] \to z\ [z = x + 1 \wedge x > 3]$.

Our treatment allows for a much simpler definition of parallel and multi-step rewriting since we do not have to merge different constraints.

Equivalence on Constrained Terms

The equivalence on constrained terms $\sim$ used in this paper also differs from the equivalence relation used in [12,17], which we will denote by $\sim'$. In $\sim'$ the domain of substitutions is not restricted, i.e., $s\ [\varphi] \sim' t\ [\psi]$ if and only if for all substitutions $\gamma \vDash \varphi$ there exists a substitution δ where $\delta \vDash \psi$ and $s\gamma = t\delta$. Intuitively, constrained terms are equivalent with respect to $\sim'$ if their sets of "allowed" instances are equivalent, while for $\sim$ we only instantiate variables appearing in the constraints and therefore representing some value. We have $\sim \subsetneq \sim'$. This can be seen as follows. First of all, any substitution γ with $\gamma \vDash \varphi$ can be split into γ_1 and γ_2 such that $\gamma = \gamma_1 \cup \gamma_2 = \gamma_1\gamma_2$ with $\mathcal{D}\mathsf{om}(\gamma_1) = \mathcal{V}\mathsf{ar}(\varphi)$ and $\gamma_1 \vDash \varphi$. From $s\ [\varphi] \sim t\ [\psi]$ we obtain a substitution δ_1 where $\mathcal{D}\mathsf{om}(\delta_1) = \mathcal{V}\mathsf{ar}(\psi)$, $\delta_1 \vDash \psi$ and $s\gamma_1 = t\delta_1$. Hence also $s\gamma = s\gamma_1\gamma_2 = t\delta_1\gamma_2 = t\delta$ for $\delta = \delta_1\gamma_2$, which implies $s\ [\varphi] \sim' t\ [\psi]$. However, $\sim' \subseteq \sim$ does not hold since $x\ [\mathsf{true}] \sim' y\ [\mathsf{true}]$ and $x\ [\mathsf{true}] \not\sim y\ [\mathsf{true}]$.

The change is necessary, since we have to differentiate (non-logical) variables in constrained terms from one another, to keep track of them through rewrite sequences. Take the (LC)TRS $\mathcal{R}$ consisting of the rule $\mathsf{f}(x,y) \to x$. When rewriting unconstrained terms we have $\mathsf{f}(x,y) \to_{\mathcal{R}} x$ and $\mathsf{f}(x,y) \not\to_{\mathcal{R}} y$. When rewriting on constrained terms with respect to $\sim'$, however, we have $\mathsf{f}(x,y)\ [\mathsf{true}] \sim' \cdot \to \cdot \sim' x\ [\mathsf{true}]$ and $\mathsf{f}(x,y)\ [\mathsf{true}] \sim' \cdot \to \cdot \sim' y\ [\mathsf{true}]$, losing any information connecting the resulting variable to the initial term. This is especially problematic in our analysis of parallel critical pairs in Sect. 6, where keeping track of variables through rewrite sequences is essential. Note that $\mathsf{f}(x,y)\ [\mathsf{true}] \stackrel{\sim}{\to} x\ [\mathsf{true}]$ but not $\mathsf{f}(x,y)\ [\mathsf{true}] \stackrel{\sim}{\to} y\ [\mathsf{true}]$.

3 Undecidability

Confluence is a decidable property of finite terminating TRSs, a celebrated result of Knuth and Bendix [9] which forms the basis of completion. For LCTRSs matters are more complicated.

Theorem 1. *Local confluence is undecidable for terminating* LCTRS*s.*

Proof. We use a reduction from PCP [16]. Let $P = \{(\alpha_1,\beta_1),\dots,(\alpha_N,\beta_N)\}$ with $\alpha_1,\dots,\alpha_N,\beta_1,\dots,\beta_N \in \{0,1\}^+$ be an instance of PCP, where we assume that $\alpha_i \neq \beta_i$ for at least one $i \in \{1,\dots,N\}$. This entails no loss of generality, since instances that violate this assumption are trivially solvable. We encode candidate strings over $\{1,\dots,N\}$ as natural numbers where the empty string ϵ is represented by $[\epsilon] = 0$, and a non-empty string $i_0 i_1 \cdots i_k$ is represented by $[i_0 i_1 \cdots i_k] = N \cdot [i_1 \cdots i_k] + i_0$. So $[i_0 i_1 \cdots i_k] = i_0 + i_1 \cdot N + \cdots + i_k \cdot N^k$. For instance, assuming $N = 3$, the number 102 encodes the candidate string $\underline{3313}$ since $102 = 3 \cdot 33 + \underline{3}$, $33 = 3 \cdot 10 + \underline{3}$, $10 = 3 \cdot 3 + \underline{1}$ and $3 = 3 \cdot 0 + \underline{3}$. Conversely, the candidate string $\underline{112}$ is mapped to $22 = \underline{1} + \underline{1} \cdot 3^1 + \underline{2} \cdot 3^2$. It is not difficult to see that this results in a bijection between $\mathbb{N}$ and candidate strings, for each $N > 0$.

The LCTRS $\mathcal{R}_P$ that we construct is defined over the theory Ints, with theory symbols $\mathcal{F}_{\mathsf{th}} = \{>,+,\cdot,=,\wedge\} \cup \mathcal{V}\mathsf{al}$ and values $\mathcal{V}\mathsf{al} = \mathbb{B} \cup \mathbb{Z}$, with the additional sorts PCP and String and the following term signature:

$$\begin{aligned} &\mathsf{e} : \mathsf{String} && \mathsf{0},\mathsf{1} : \mathsf{String} \to \mathsf{String} \\ &\mathsf{start}, \top, \bot : \mathsf{PCP} && \mathsf{test} : \mathsf{String} \times \mathsf{String} \to \mathsf{PCP} \\ &\mathsf{alpha}, \mathsf{beta} : \mathsf{Int} \to \mathsf{String} \end{aligned}$$

The LCTRS $\mathcal{R}_P$ consists of the following rules:

$$\begin{aligned} \mathsf{start} &\to \mathsf{test}(\mathsf{alpha}(n), \mathsf{beta}(n)) \quad [n > 0] \\ \mathsf{test}(\mathsf{e},\mathsf{e}) &\to \top \\ \mathsf{test}(\mathsf{0}(x),\mathsf{0}(y)) &\to \mathsf{test}(x,y) & \mathsf{test}(\mathsf{0}(x),\mathsf{1}(y)) &\to \bot \\ \mathsf{test}(\mathsf{1}(x),\mathsf{1}(y)) &\to \mathsf{test}(x,y) & \mathsf{test}(\mathsf{1}(x),\mathsf{0}(y)) &\to \bot \\ \mathsf{test}(\mathsf{0}(x),\mathsf{e}) &\to \bot & \mathsf{test}(\mathsf{e},\mathsf{0}(y)) &\to \bot \\ \mathsf{test}(\mathsf{1}(x),\mathsf{e}) &\to \bot & \mathsf{test}(\mathsf{e},\mathsf{1}(y)) &\to \bot \end{aligned}$$

$$\mathsf{alpha}(0) \to \mathsf{e} \qquad\qquad \mathsf{beta}(0) \to \mathsf{e}$$

and, for all $i \in \{1, \ldots, N\}$,

$$\begin{aligned} \mathsf{alpha}(n) &\to \alpha_i(\mathsf{alpha}(m)) \quad [N \cdot m + i = n \wedge n > 0] \\ \mathsf{beta}(n) &\to \beta_i(\mathsf{beta}(m)) \quad [N \cdot m + i = n \wedge n > 0] \end{aligned}$$

Here, for a string $\gamma \in \{0,1\}^*$ and a term $t : \mathsf{String}$, $\gamma(t) : \mathsf{String}$ is defined as

$$\gamma(t) = \begin{cases} t & \text{if } \gamma = \epsilon \\ \mathsf{0}(\gamma'(t)) & \text{if } \gamma = 0\gamma' \\ \mathsf{1}(\gamma'(t)) & \text{if } \gamma = 1\gamma' \end{cases}$$

Note that in the constraints n and m are variables, while N and i are values. Hence all constraints are in the decidable fragment of linear integer arithmetic and the rewrite relation $\to_{\mathcal{R}_P}$ is computable.

We claim that $\mathcal{R}_P$ is locally confluent if and only if P has no solution. The LCTRS $\mathcal{R}_P$ admits the constrained critical pair

$$\mathsf{test}(\mathsf{alpha}(n), \mathsf{beta}(n)) \approx \mathsf{test}(\mathsf{alpha}(m), \mathsf{beta}(m)) \quad [n > 0 \wedge m > 0]$$

with $n \neq m$. The rules with left-hand sides $\mathsf{alpha}(n)$ and $\mathsf{beta}(n)$ give rise to further constrained critical pairs but these are harmless since for all $n, N > 0$ there are unique numbers i and m satisfying the constraint $[N \cdot m + i = n \wedge n > 0]$.

By construction of the rules for test, $\mathsf{test}(\mathsf{alpha}(n), \mathsf{beta}(n)) \to^* \top$ if n represents a solution of P and $\mathsf{test}(\mathsf{alpha}(n), \mathsf{beta}(n)) \to^* \bot$ if n does not represent a solution of P. Since we assume that P is non-trivial, the latter happens for some $n > 0$. Hence all instances of the constrained critical pairs can only be joined if $\mathsf{test}(\mathsf{alpha}(n), \mathsf{beta}(n)) \to^* \bot$ for all $n > 0$. Hence $\mathcal{R}_P$ is locally confluent if and only if P has no solution.

The LCTRS $\mathcal{R}_P$ is terminating by the recursive path order [12] with the precedence $\mathsf{start} > \mathsf{test} > \mathsf{alpha} > \mathsf{beta} > \mathsf{1} > \mathsf{0} > \mathsf{e} > \top > \bot$ and the well-founded order $\sqsupset_{\mathsf{Int}}$ on integers where $x \sqsupset_{\mathsf{Int}} y$ if and only if $x > y$ and $x \geqslant 0$. The key observation is that the constraint $[N \cdot m + i = n \wedge n > 0]$ in the recursive rules for alpha and beta ensure $n > m$ since $N > 0$ and $i \geqslant 1$. □

A key difference between TRSs and LCTRSs leading to this undecidability result can be seen in the first rule: $\mathsf{start} \to \mathsf{test}(\mathsf{alpha}(n), \mathsf{beta}(n))\ [n > 0]$. Plain TRSs usually do not allow variables appearing only in the right-hand side of a rule, as is the case for n here, because then termination never holds. However, in LCTRSs such variables are useful, since they can be used to model computations on arbitrary values which are often used to represent user input in program analysis. For $\mathcal{R}_P$ this leads to infinitely many possible steps starting from the term start and in turn to infinitely many critical pairs, breaking decidability.

4 Transformation

In this section we present a simple transformation from LCTRSs to possibly infinite TRSs, which exactly corresponds to the intuition behind LCTRSs. This allows us to lift results on TRSs more easily to LCTRSs than previously possible.

Definition 1. *Given an* LCTRS $\mathcal{R}$, *the* TRS $\overline{\mathcal{R}}$ *consists of the following rules:* $\ell\tau \to r\tau$ *for all* $\rho\colon \ell \to r\ [\varphi] \in \mathcal{R}_{\mathsf{rc}}$ *with* $\tau \vDash \rho$ *and* $\mathcal{D}\mathsf{om}(\tau) = \mathcal{LV}\mathsf{ar}(\rho)$.

Note that $\overline{\mathcal{R}}$ typically consists of infinitely many rules.

Lemma 1. *The rewrite relations of* $\mathcal{R}$ *and* $\overline{\mathcal{R}}$ *are the same. Moreover* $\to_{p,\mathcal{R}} = \to_{p,\overline{\mathcal{R}}}$ *for all positions* p.

Proof. We first show $\to_{p,\mathcal{R}} \subseteq \to_{p,\overline{\mathcal{R}}}$. Assume $s \to_{p,\mathcal{R}} t$. We have $s = s[\ell\sigma]_p \to s[r\sigma]_p = t$ for some $\rho\colon \ell \to r\ [\varphi] \in \mathcal{R}_{\mathsf{rc}}$ and $\sigma \vDash \rho$. We split σ into two substitutions $\tau = \{x \mapsto \sigma(x) \mid x \in \mathcal{LV}\mathsf{ar}(\rho)\}$ and $\delta = \{x \mapsto \sigma(x) \mid x \in \mathcal{V}\mathsf{ar}(\ell) \setminus \mathcal{LV}\mathsf{ar}(\rho)\}$. From $\sigma \vDash \rho$ we infer $\tau \vDash \rho$ and thus $\tau(x) \in \mathcal{V}\mathsf{al}$ for all $x \in \mathcal{LV}\mathsf{ar}(\rho)$. Hence $\sigma = \tau \cup \delta = \tau\delta$. We have $\ell\tau \to r\tau \in \overline{\mathcal{R}}$. Hence $s = s[\ell\tau\delta]_p \to_{p,\overline{\mathcal{R}}} s[r\tau\delta]_p = t$ as desired. To show the reverse inclusion $\to_{p,\overline{\mathcal{R}}} \subseteq \to_{p,\mathcal{R}}$ we assume $s \to_{p,\overline{\mathcal{R}}} t$. Otherwise $s = s[\ell\mu\nu]_p \to_{p,\overline{\mathcal{R}}} s[r\mu\nu]_p$ for some rule $\rho\colon \ell \to r\ [\varphi] \in \mathcal{R}$ with $\mu \vDash \rho$. Let $\sigma = \mu\nu$. Since $\mu(x) \in \mathcal{V}\mathsf{al}$ for all $x \in \mathcal{LV}\mathsf{ar}(\rho)$, we have $x\sigma = x\mu$ for all $x \in \mathcal{LV}\mathsf{ar}(\rho)$. Hence $\sigma \vDash \rho$ and thus $s = s[\ell\sigma]_p \to_{p,\mathcal{R}} s[r\sigma]_p = t$. $\square$

Since $\to_{\mathcal{R}}$ and $\to_{\overline{\mathcal{R}}}$ coincide, we drop the subscript in the sequel. We write $\mathcal{EV}\mathsf{ar}(\ell \to r\ [\varphi])$ for the set $\mathcal{V}\mathsf{ar}(r) \setminus (\mathcal{V}\mathsf{ar}(\ell) \cup \mathcal{V}\mathsf{ar}(\varphi))$ of extra variables of a rule. In the computation of constrained critical pairs these variables of the overlapping rules would lose the property of being a logical variable without adding trivial constraints. Given a constrained rewrite rule ρ, we write $\mathcal{EC}_\rho$ for $\bigwedge\{x = x \mid x \in \mathcal{EV}\mathsf{ar}(\rho)\}$. The set of positions in a term s is denoted by $\mathcal{P}\mathsf{os}(s)$. We write ϵ for the root position and $\mathcal{P}\mathsf{os}_{\mathcal{F}}(s)$ for the set of positions of function symbols in s.

Definition 2. *An* overlap *of an* LCTRS $\mathcal{R}$ *is a triple* $\langle \rho_1, p, \rho_2\rangle$ *with rules* $\rho_1\colon \ell_1 \to r_1\ [\varphi_1]$ *and* $\rho_2\colon \ell_2 \to r_2\ [\varphi_2]$, *satisfying the following conditions: (1)* ρ_1 *and* ρ_2 *are variable-disjoint variants of rewrite rules in* $\mathcal{R}_{\mathsf{rc}}$, *(2)* $p \in \mathcal{P}\mathsf{os}_{\mathcal{F}}(\ell_2)$, *(3)* ℓ_1 *and* $\ell_2|_p$ *unify with mgu* σ *such that* $\sigma(x) \in \mathcal{V}\mathsf{al} \cup \mathcal{V}$ *for all* $x \in \mathcal{LV}\mathsf{ar}(\rho_1) \cup \mathcal{LV}\mathsf{ar}(\rho_2)$, *(4)* $\varphi_1\sigma \wedge \varphi_2\sigma$ *is satisfiable, and (5) if* $p = \epsilon$ *then* ρ_1 *and* ρ_2 *are not variants, or* $\mathcal{V}\mathsf{ar}(r_1) \nsubseteq \mathcal{V}\mathsf{ar}(\ell_1)$. *In this case we call* $\ell_2\sigma[r_1\sigma]_p \approx r_2\sigma\ [\varphi_1\sigma \wedge \varphi_2\sigma \wedge \psi\sigma]$ *a* constrained critical pair *obtained from the overlap* $\langle \rho_1, p, \rho_2\rangle$. *Here* $\psi = \mathcal{EC}_{\rho_1} \wedge \mathcal{EC}_{\rho_2}$. *The peak* $\ell_2\sigma[r_1\sigma]_p\ [\Phi] \leftarrow \ell_2\sigma\ [\Phi] \to_\epsilon r_2\sigma\ [\Phi]$ *with* $\Phi = (\varphi_1 \wedge \varphi_2 \wedge \psi)\sigma$, *from which the constrained critical pair originates, is called a* constrained critical peak. *The set of all constrained critical pairs of* $\mathcal{R}$ *is denoted by* $\mathsf{CCP}(\mathcal{R})$. *A constrained critical pair* $s \approx t\ [\varphi]$ *is* trivial *if* $s\sigma = t\sigma$ *for every substitution* σ *with* $\sigma \vDash \varphi$.

A key ingredient of our approach is to relate critical pairs of the transformed TRS to constrained critical pairs of the original LCTRS.

Theorem 2. *For every critical pair $s \approx t$ of $\overline{\mathcal{R}}$ there exists a constrained critical pair $s' \approx t'$ $[\varphi']$ of $\mathcal{R}$ and a substitution γ such that $s = s'\gamma$, $t = t'\gamma$ and $\gamma \vDash \varphi'$.*

Proof. Let $s \approx t$ be a critical pair of $\overline{\mathcal{R}}$, originating from the critical peak $\ell_2\mu\sigma[r_1\nu\sigma]_p \leftarrow \ell_2\mu\sigma = \ell_2\mu\sigma[\ell_1\nu\sigma]_p \rightarrow r_2\mu\sigma$ with variants $\rho_1\colon \ell_1 \rightarrow r_1$ $[\varphi_1]$ and $\rho_2\colon \ell_2 \rightarrow r_2$ $[\varphi_2]$ of rules in $\mathcal{R}_{\mathsf{rc}}$ without shared variables. Let $\psi_i = \mathcal{EC}_{\rho_i}$ for $i \in \{1,2\}$. Furthermore we have $\mathcal{D}\mathsf{om}(\nu) = \mathcal{LV}\mathsf{ar}(\rho_1)$, $\mathcal{D}\mathsf{om}(\mu) = \mathcal{LV}\mathsf{ar}(\rho_2)$, $\nu \vDash \varphi_1 \wedge \psi_1$, $\mu \vDash \varphi_2 \wedge \psi_2$, $p \in \mathcal{P}\mathsf{os}_{\mathcal{F}}(\ell_2\mu)$, and σ is an mgu of $\ell_2\mu|_p$ and $\ell_1\nu$. Moreover, if $p = \epsilon$ then $\ell_1\nu \rightarrow r_1\nu$ and $\ell_2\mu \rightarrow r_2\mu$ are not variants. Define $\tau = \nu \uplus \mu$. We have $\mathcal{D}\mathsf{om}(\tau) = \mathcal{LV}\mathsf{ar}(\rho_1) \cup \mathcal{LV}\mathsf{ar}(\rho_2)$. Let $\varphi = \varphi_1 \wedge \varphi_2 \wedge \psi_1 \wedge \psi_2$. Clearly, $\ell_1\tau = \ell_1\nu$, $r_1\tau = r_1\nu$, $\ell_2\tau = \ell_2\mu$, $r_2\tau = r_2\mu$ and $\tau \vDash \varphi$. Hence the given peak can be written as $\ell_2\tau\sigma[r_1\tau\sigma]_p \leftarrow \ell_2\tau\sigma = \ell_2\tau\sigma[\ell_1\tau\sigma]_p \rightarrow r_2\tau\sigma$ and $\tau \vDash \varphi$. Since $\ell_2|_p\tau\sigma = \ell_1\tau\sigma$ there exists an mgu δ of $\ell_2|_p$ and ℓ_1, and a substitution γ such that $\delta\gamma = \tau\sigma$. Let $s' = \ell_2\delta[r_1\delta]_p$ and $t' = r_2\delta$. We claim that $\langle \rho_1, p, \rho_2 \rangle$ is an overlap of $\mathcal{R}$, resulting in the constrained critical pair $s' \approx t'$ $[\varphi\delta]$. Condition (1) of Definition 2 is trivially satisfied. For condition (2) we need to show $p \in \mathcal{P}\mathsf{os}_{\mathcal{F}}(\ell_2)$. This follows from $p \in \mathcal{P}\mathsf{os}_{\mathcal{F}}(\ell_2\mu)$, $\mu(x) \in \mathcal{V}\mathsf{al}$ for every $x \in \mathcal{D}\mathsf{om}(\mu)$, and $\mathsf{root}(\ell_2\mu|_p) = \mathsf{root}(\ell_1\nu) \in \mathcal{F} \setminus \mathcal{V}\mathsf{al}$. For condition (3) it remains to show that $\delta(x) \in \mathcal{V}\mathsf{al} \cup \mathcal{V}$ for all $x \in \mathcal{LV}\mathsf{ar}(\rho_1) \cup \mathcal{LV}\mathsf{ar}(\rho_2)$. Suppose to the contrary that $\mathsf{root}(\delta(x)) \in \mathcal{F} \setminus \mathcal{V}\mathsf{al}$ for some $x \in \mathcal{LV}\mathsf{ar}(\rho_1) \cup \mathcal{LV}\mathsf{ar}(\rho_2)$. Then $\mathsf{root}(\delta(x)) = \mathsf{root}(\gamma(\delta(x))) = \mathsf{root}(\sigma(\tau(x))) \in \mathcal{F} \setminus \mathcal{V}\mathsf{al}$, which contradicts $\tau \vDash \varphi$. Condition (4) follows from the identity $\delta\gamma = \tau\sigma$ together with $\tau \vDash \varphi$ which imply $\delta\gamma \vDash \varphi$ and thus $\varphi\delta$ is satisfiable. Hence also $\varphi_1\delta \wedge \varphi_2\delta$ is satisfiable. It remains to show condition (5), so let $p = \epsilon$ and further assume that ρ_1 and ρ_2 are variants. So there exists a variable renaming π such that $\rho_1\pi = \rho_2$. In particular, $\ell_1\pi = \ell_2$ and $r_1\pi = r_2$. Let $x \in \mathcal{V}\mathsf{ar}(\ell_1)$. If $x \in \mathcal{LV}\mathsf{ar}(\rho_1) = \mathcal{D}\mathsf{om}(\nu)$ then $\tau(x) = \nu(x) \in \mathcal{V}\mathsf{al}$. Moreover, $\pi(x) \in \mathcal{LV}\mathsf{ar}(\rho_2) = \mathcal{D}\mathsf{om}(\mu)$ and thus $\tau(\pi(x)) = \mu(\pi(x)) \in \mathcal{V}\mathsf{al}$. Since $\ell_1\tau$ and $\ell_2\tau$ are unifiable, $\pi(\tau(x)) = \tau(x) = \tau(\pi(x))$. If $x \notin \mathcal{LV}\mathsf{ar}(\rho_1)$ then $\tau(x) = x$, $\pi(x) \notin \mathcal{LV}\mathsf{ar}(\rho_2)$ and similarly $\tau(\pi(x)) = \pi(x) = \pi(\tau(x))$. All in all, $\ell_1\tau\pi = \ell_1\pi\tau = \ell_2\tau$. Now, if $\mathcal{V}\mathsf{ar}(r_1) \subseteq \mathcal{V}\mathsf{ar}(\ell_1)$ then we obtain $r_1\tau\pi = r_1\pi\tau = r_2\tau$, contradicting the fact that $\ell_1\nu \rightarrow r_1\nu$ and $\ell_2\mu \rightarrow r_2\mu$ are not variants. We conclude that $s' \approx t'$ $[\varphi\delta]$ is a constrained critical pair of $\mathcal{R}$. So we can take $\varphi' = \varphi\delta$. Clearly, $s = s'\gamma$ and $t = t'\gamma$. Moreover, $\gamma \vDash \varphi'$ since $\varphi'\gamma = \varphi\tau\sigma = \varphi\tau$ and $\tau \vDash \varphi$. □

The converse does not hold in general.

Example 2. Consider the LCTRS $\mathcal{R}$ consisting of the single rule $\mathsf{a} \rightarrow x$ $[x = 0]$ where the variable x ranges over the integers. Since x appears on the right-hand side but not the left, we obtain a constrained critical pair $x \approx x'$ $[x = 0 \wedge x' = 0]$. Since the constraint uniquely determines the values of x and x', the TRS $\overline{\mathcal{R}}$ consists of the single rule $\mathsf{a} \rightarrow 0$. Obviously $\overline{\mathcal{R}}$ has no critical pairs.

The above example also shows that orthogonality of $\overline{\mathcal{R}}$ does not imply orthogonality of $\mathcal{R}$. However, the counterexample relies somewhat on a technicality in condition (5) of Definition 2. It only occurs when the two rules $\ell_1 \rightarrow r_1$ $[\varphi_1]$ and $\ell_2 \rightarrow r_2$ $[\varphi_2]$ involved in the critical pair overlap at the root and have instances

$\ell_1\tau_1 \to r_1\tau_1$ and $\ell_2\tau_2 \to r_2\tau_2$ in $\overline{\mathcal{R}}$ which are variants of each other. By dealing with such cases separately we can prove the following theorem.

Theorem 3. *For every constrained critical pair $s \approx t$ $[\varphi]$ of $\mathcal{R}$ and every substitution σ with $\sigma \vDash \varphi$, (1) $s\sigma = t\sigma$ or (2) there exist a critical pair $u \approx v$ of $\overline{\mathcal{R}}$ and a substitution δ such that $s\sigma = u\delta$ and $t\sigma = v\delta$.*

Proof. Let $s \approx t$ $[\varphi]$ be a constrained critical pair of $\mathcal{R}$ originating from the critical peak $s = \ell_2\theta[r_1\theta]_p \leftarrow \ell_2\theta[\ell_1\theta]_p \to r_2\theta = t$ with variants $\rho_1 \colon \ell_1 \to r_1$ $[\varphi_1]$ and $\rho_2 \colon \ell_2 \to r_2$ $[\varphi_2]$ of rules in $\mathcal{R}_{\mathsf{rc}}$, and an mgu θ of $\ell_2|_p$ and ℓ_1 where $p \in \mathcal{P}\mathsf{os}_{\mathcal{F}}(\ell_2)$. Moreover $\theta(x) \in \mathcal{V}\mathsf{al} \cup \mathcal{V}$ for all $x \in \mathcal{LV}\mathsf{ar}(\rho_1) \cup \mathcal{LV}\mathsf{ar}(\rho_2)$, and $\varphi = \varphi_1\theta \wedge \varphi_2\theta \wedge \psi\theta$ with $\psi = \mathcal{EC}_{\rho_1} \wedge \mathcal{EC}_{\rho_2}$. Let σ be a substitution with $\sigma \vDash \varphi$. Hence $\theta\sigma \vDash \varphi_1 \wedge \varphi_2 \wedge \psi$ and further $\sigma(\theta(x)) \in \mathcal{V}\mathsf{al}$ for all $x \in \mathcal{LV}\mathsf{ar}(\rho_1) \cup \mathcal{LV}\mathsf{ar}(\rho_2)$. We split $\theta\sigma$ into substitutions τ_1, τ_2 and π as follows: $\tau_i(x) = x\theta\sigma$ if $x \in \mathcal{LV}\mathsf{ar}(\rho_i)$ and $\tau_i(x) = x$ otherwise, for $i \in \{1,2\}$, and $\pi(x) = x\theta\sigma$ if $x \in \mathcal{D}\mathsf{om}(\theta\sigma) \setminus (\mathcal{LV}\mathsf{ar}(\rho_1) \cup \mathcal{LV}\mathsf{ar}(\rho_2))$ and $\pi(x) = x$ otherwise. From $\theta\sigma \vDash \varphi_1 \wedge \varphi_2 \wedge \psi$ and $\mathcal{V}\mathsf{ar}(\varphi_i) \subseteq \mathcal{LV}\mathsf{ar}(\rho_i)$ we infer $\tau_i \vDash \varphi_i$ for $i \in \{1,2\}$. Since $\mathcal{D}\mathsf{om}(\tau_i) = \mathcal{LV}\mathsf{ar}(\rho_i)$, $\ell_i\tau_i \to r_i\tau_i \in \overline{\mathcal{R}}$ for $i \in \{1,2\}$. Furthermore, $\tau_i\pi = \tau_i \cup \pi$ for $i \in \{1,2\}$. Hence $\ell_2|_p\tau_2\pi = \ell_2|_p\theta\sigma = \ell_1\theta\sigma = \ell_1\tau_1\pi$, implying that $\ell_2|_p\tau_2$ and $\ell_1\tau_1$ are unifiable. Let γ be an mgu of these two terms. There exists a substitution δ such that $\gamma\delta = \pi$. Clearly $p \in \mathcal{P}\mathsf{os}_{\mathcal{F}}(\ell_2\tau_2)$. If $p \neq \epsilon$ or $\ell_1\tau_1 \to r_1\tau_1$ and $\ell_2\tau_2 \to r_2\tau_2$ are not variants, then $u \approx v$ with $u = \ell_2\tau_2\gamma[r_1\tau_1\gamma]_p$ and $v = r_2\tau_2\gamma$ is a critical pair of $\overline{\mathcal{R}}$. Moreover $t\sigma = r_2\theta\sigma = r_2\tau_2\pi = r_2\tau_2\gamma\delta = v\delta$, and similarly $s\sigma = u\delta$. Thus option (2) is satisfied. If $p = \epsilon$ and $\ell_1\tau_1 \to r_1\tau_1$ and $\ell_2\tau_2 \to r_2\tau_2$ are variants then $s\sigma = r_1\tau_1\gamma\delta = r_2\tau_2\gamma\delta = t\sigma$, fulfilling (1). □

A TRS (LCTRS) is weakly orthogonal if it is left-linear and all its (constrained) critical pairs are trivial. Since $\overline{\mathcal{R}}$ is left-linear if and only if $\mathcal{R}$ is left-linear, a direct consequence of Theorem 3 is that weak orthogonality of $\overline{\mathcal{R}}$ implies weak orthogonality of $\mathcal{R}$.

Our transformation is not only useful for confluence analysis.

Example 3. For the LCTRS $\mathcal{R}_P$ in the proof of Theorem 1 the TRS $\overline{\mathcal{R}_P}$ consists of all unconstrained rules of $\mathcal{R}_P$ together with $f(v_1,\ldots,v_n) \to [\![f(v_1,\ldots,v_n)]\!]$ for all $f \in \mathcal{F}_{\mathsf{th}} \setminus \mathcal{V}\mathsf{al}$ and $v_1,\ldots,v_n \in \mathcal{V}\mathsf{al}$, $\mathsf{start} \to \mathsf{test}(\mathsf{alpha}(n),\mathsf{beta}(n))$ for all $n > 0$, $\mathsf{alpha}(n) \to \alpha_i(\mathsf{alpha}(m))$ and $\mathsf{beta}(n) \to \beta_i(\mathsf{beta}(m))$ for all $i \in \{1,\ldots,N\}$, $n > 0$ and $m \geqslant 0$ such that $N \cdot m + i = n$. Termination of the infinite TRS $\overline{\mathcal{R}_P}$ is easily shown by LPO or dependency pairs.

5 Development Closed Critical Pairs

Using Theorem 2 we can easily transfer confluence criteria for TRSs to LCTRSs. Rather than reproving the confluence results reported in [12,17,22], in this section we illustrate this by extending the result of van Oostrom [15] concerning (almost) development closed critical pairs from TRSs to LCTRSs. This result subsumes most critical-pair based confluence criteria, as can be seen in Fig. 2 in the concluding section.

Definition 3. *Let $\mathcal{R}$ be an* LCTRS. *The multi-step relation $\multimap\!\!\!\rightarrow$ on terms is defined inductively as follows: (1) $x \multimap\!\!\!\rightarrow x$ for all variables x, (2) $f(s_1,\ldots,s_n) \multimap\!\!\!\rightarrow f(t_1,\ldots,t_n)$ if $s_i \multimap\!\!\!\rightarrow t_i$ with $1 \leqslant i \leqslant n$, (3) $\ell\sigma \multimap\!\!\!\rightarrow r\tau$ if $\ell \rightarrow r\ [\varphi] \in \mathcal{R}_{\mathsf{rc}}$, $\sigma \vDash \ell \rightarrow r\ [\varphi]$ and $\sigma \multimap\!\!\!\rightarrow \tau$, where $\sigma \multimap\!\!\!\rightarrow \tau$ denotes $\sigma(x) \multimap\!\!\!\rightarrow \tau(x)$ for all variables $x \in \mathcal{D}\mathsf{om}(\sigma)$.*

Definition 4. *A critical pair $s \approx t$ is* development closed *if $s \multimap\!\!\!\rightarrow t$. It is* almost development closed *if it is not an overlay and development closed, or it is an overlay and $s \multimap\!\!\!\rightarrow \cdot\ {}^*\!\!\leftarrow t$. A* TRS *is called (almost) development closed if all its critical pairs are (almost) development closed.*

The following result from [15] has recently been formalized in Isabelle [10,11].

Theorem 4. *Left-linear almost development closed* TRSs *are confluent.* □

We define multi-step rewriting on constrained terms.

Definition 5. *Let $\mathcal{R}$ be an* LCTRS. *The multi-step relation $\multimap\!\!\!\rightarrow$ on constrained terms is defined inductively as follows:*

1. *$x\ [\varphi] \multimap\!\!\!\rightarrow x\ [\varphi]$ for all variables x,*
2. *$f(s_1,\ldots,s_n)\ [\varphi] \multimap\!\!\!\rightarrow f(t_1,\ldots,t_n)\ [\varphi]$ if $s_i\ [\varphi] \multimap\!\!\!\rightarrow t_i\ [\varphi]$ for $1 \leqslant i \leqslant n$,*
3. *$\ell\sigma\ [\varphi] \multimap\!\!\!\rightarrow r\tau\ [\varphi]$ if $\rho\colon \ell \rightarrow r\ [\psi] \in \mathcal{R}_{\mathsf{rc}}$, $\sigma(x) \in \mathcal{V}\mathsf{al} \cup \mathcal{V}\mathsf{ar}(\varphi)$ for all $x \in \mathcal{LV}\mathsf{ar}(\rho)$, φ is satisfiable, $\varphi \Rightarrow \psi\sigma$ is valid, and $\sigma\ [\varphi] \multimap\!\!\!\rightarrow \tau\ [\varphi]$.*

Here $\sigma\ [\varphi] \multimap\!\!\!\rightarrow \tau\ [\varphi]$ denotes $\sigma(x)\ [\varphi] \multimap\!\!\!\rightarrow \tau(x)\ [\varphi]$ for all variables $x \in \mathcal{D}\mathsf{om}(\sigma)$. The relation $\tilde{\multimap\!\!\!\rightarrow}$ on constrained terms is defined as $\sim \cdot \multimap\!\!\!\rightarrow \cdot \sim$.

Example 4. Consider the following LCTRS $\mathcal{R}$ over the theory Ints with the rules:

$$\mathsf{max}(x,y) \rightarrow x\ [x \geqslant y] \qquad\qquad \mathsf{max}(x,y) \rightarrow y\ [y \geqslant x]$$

Rewriting the term $\mathsf{max}(1+2,3+2)$ to its normal form $\mathsf{5}$ requires three single steps. These steps can be combined into a single multi-step $\mathsf{max}(1+2,3+2) \multimap\!\!\!\rightarrow \mathsf{5}$.

The constrained term $\mathsf{max}(1+x,3+y)\ [x > 3 \wedge y = 1]$ rewrites in a single multi-step to its normal form $z\ [z = 1 + x \wedge x > 3]$. This involves the following parts of Definition 5. Let φ be $x > 3 \wedge y = 1 \wedge z = 1 + x \wedge z' = 3 + y$. Case (3) gives $1 + x\ [\varphi] \multimap\!\!\!\rightarrow z\ [\varphi]$ and $3 + y\ [\varphi] \multimap\!\!\!\rightarrow z'\ [\varphi]$. Using this we obtain $\mathsf{max}(1+x,3+y)\ [\varphi] \multimap\!\!\!\rightarrow \mathsf{max}(z,z')\ [\varphi]$ by case (2). A final application of case (3) yields $\mathsf{max}(z,z')\ [\varphi] \multimap\!\!\!\rightarrow z\ [\varphi]$. Together with the equivalences

$$\begin{aligned}\mathsf{max}(1+x,3+y)\ [x > 3 \wedge y = 1] &\sim \mathsf{max}(1+x,3+y)\ [\varphi]\\ z\ [\varphi] &\sim z\ [z = 1 + x \wedge x > 3]\end{aligned}$$

we obtain $\mathsf{max}(1+x,3+y)\ [x > 3 \wedge y = 1] \tilde{\multimap\!\!\!\rightarrow} z\ [z = 1 + x \wedge x > 3]$.

Definition 4 is extended to LCTRSs as follows.

Definition 6. *A constrained critical pair* $s \approx t\ [\varphi]$ *is* development closed *if* $s \approx t\ [\varphi] \mathrel{\widetilde{\circ\!\!\!\!\rightarrow}}_{\geqslant 1} u \approx v\ [\psi]$ *for some trivial* $u \approx v\ [\psi]$*. A constrained critical pair is* almost development closed *if it is not an overlay and development closed, or it is an overlay and* $s \approx t\ [\varphi] \mathrel{\widetilde{\circ\!\!\!\!\rightarrow}}_{\geqslant 1} \cdot \mathrel{\tilde{\rightarrow}}^*_{\geqslant 2} u \approx v\ [\psi]$ *for some trivial* $u \approx v\ [\psi]$*. An* LCTRS *is called (almost) development closed if all its constrained critical pairs are (almost) development closed.*

Similar to [17,22], the symbol $\approx$ is treated as a fresh binary function symbol, resulting in constrained equations whose positions are addressed in the usual way. Therefore positions below 1 in $s \approx t\ [\varphi]$ refer to subterms of s.

Figure 1 conveys the idea how the main result (Theorem 5) in this section is obtained. For every critical pair in the transformed TRS $\overline{\mathcal{R}}$ there exists a corresponding constrained critical pair in the original LCTRS $\mathcal{R}$ (Theorem 2). Almost development closure of the constrained critical pair implies almost development closure of the critical pair (Lemma 4). Since the rewrite relations of $\mathcal{R}$ and $\overline{\mathcal{R}}$ coincide (Lemma 1), we obtain the confluence of almost development closed left-linear LCTRSs from the corresponding result in [15].

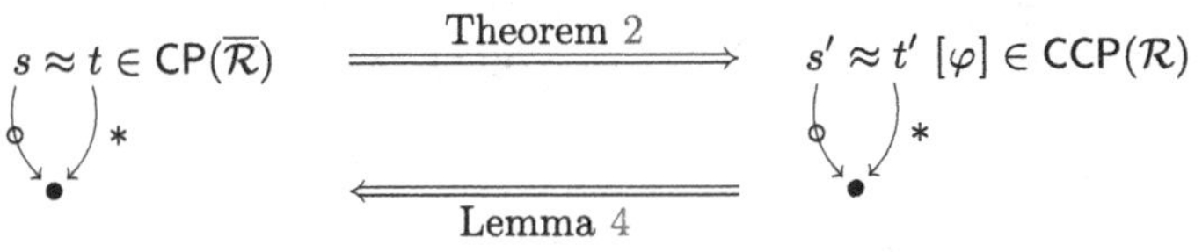

Fig. 1. Proof idea for Theorem 5.

We now present a few technical results that relate rewrite sequences and multi-steps on (constrained) terms. These prepare for the use of Theorem 2 to obtain the confluence of (almost) development closed LCTRSs. The proofs of the following two lemmata can be found in [18].

Lemma 2. *Suppose* $s \approx t\ [\varphi] \mathrel{\tilde{\rightarrow}}^*_{\geqslant p} u \approx v\ [\psi]$ *with* $\gamma \vDash \varphi$ *and position* p*. If* $p = 1q$ *for a position* q *then* $s\gamma \rightarrow^*_{\geqslant q} u\delta$ *and* $t\gamma = v\delta$ *for some substitution* δ *with* $\delta \vDash \psi$*. If* $p = 2q$ *for a position* q *then* $s\gamma = u\delta$ *and* $t\gamma \mathrel{\tilde{\rightarrow}}^*_{\geqslant q} v\delta$ *for some substitution* δ *with* $\delta \vDash \psi$*.* □

Lemma 3. *If* $s \approx t\ [\varphi] \mathrel{\widetilde{\circ\!\!\!\!\rightarrow}}_{\geqslant 1} u \approx v\ [\psi]$ *then for all substitutions* $\sigma \vDash \varphi$ *there exists* $\delta \vDash \psi$ *such that* $s\sigma \mathrel{\circ\!\!\!\!\rightarrow} u\delta$ *and* $t\sigma = v\delta$*.* □

Lemma 4. *If a constrained critical pair* $s \approx t\ [\varphi]$ *is almost development closed then for all substitutions* σ *with* $\sigma \vDash \varphi$ *we have* $s\sigma \mathrel{\circ\!\!\!\!\rightarrow} \cdot\ {}^*\!\!\leftarrow t\sigma$*.*

Proof. Let $s \approx t\ [\varphi]$ be an almost development closed constrained critical pair, and $\sigma \vDash \varphi$ some substitution. From Definition 6 we obtain

$$s \approx t\ [\varphi] \mathrel{\widetilde{\circ\!\!\!\!\rightarrow}}_{\geqslant 1} u' \approx v'\ [\psi'] \mathrel{\tilde{\rightarrow}}^*_{\geqslant 2} u \approx v\ [\psi] \tag{1}$$

where $u\tau = v\tau$ for all $\tau \vDash \psi$ for some constrained term $u' \approx v'$ $[\psi']$. We apply Lemma 3 to the first step in (1). This yields a substitution δ where $s\sigma \twoheadrightarrow\!\!\!\!\!\!\!\ominus\; u'\delta$, $t\sigma = v'\delta$ and $\delta \vDash \psi'$. For the second part of (1) we use Lemma 2 and obtain $v'\delta \to^* v\gamma$, $u'\delta = u\gamma$ for some $\gamma \vDash \psi$. Moreover we have $u\gamma = v\gamma$. Hence $s\sigma \twoheadrightarrow\!\!\!\!\!\!\!\ominus\; u'\delta = u\gamma = v\gamma\ {}^*\!\!\leftarrow v'\delta = t\sigma$. □

Theorem 5. *If an LCTRS $\mathcal{R}$ is almost development closed then so is $\overline{\mathcal{R}}$.*

Proof. Take any critical pair $s \approx t$ from $\overline{\mathcal{R}}$. From Theorem 2 we know that there exists a constrained critical pair $s' \approx t'$ $[\varphi]$ in $\mathcal{R}$ where $s'\sigma = s$ and $t'\sigma = t$ for some $\sigma \vDash \varphi$. Since the constrained critical pair must be almost development closed, Lemma 4 yields $s = s'\sigma \twoheadrightarrow\!\!\!\!\!\!\!\ominus\; \cdot\ {}^*\!\!\leftarrow t'\sigma = t$ if it is an overlay and $s = s'\sigma \twoheadrightarrow\!\!\!\!\!\!\!\ominus\; t'\sigma = t$ otherwise. This proves that $\overline{\mathcal{R}}$ is almost development closed. □

Interestingly, the converse does not hold, as seen in the following example.

Example 5. Consider the LCTRS $\mathcal{R}$ over the theory Ints with the rules

$$\mathsf{f}(x) \to \mathsf{g}(x) \qquad\qquad \mathsf{g}(x) \to \mathsf{h}(2)\ [x = 2z]$$
$$\mathsf{f}(x) \to \mathsf{h}(x)\ [1 \leqslant x \leqslant 2] \qquad\qquad \mathsf{g}(x) \to \mathsf{h}(1)\ [x = 2z + 1]$$

The TRS $\overline{\mathcal{R}}$ consists of the rules

$$\mathsf{f}(x) \to \mathsf{g}(x) \qquad \mathsf{f}(1) \to \mathsf{h}(1) \qquad \mathsf{g}(n) \to \mathsf{h}(1) \quad \text{for all odd } n \in \mathbb{Z}$$
$$\mathsf{f}(2) \to \mathsf{h}(2) \qquad \mathsf{g}(n) \to \mathsf{h}(2) \quad \text{for all even } n \in \mathbb{Z}$$

and has two (modulo symmetry) critical pairs $\mathsf{g}(1) \approx \mathsf{h}(1)$ and $\mathsf{g}(2) \approx \mathsf{h}(2)$. Since $\mathsf{g}(1) \twoheadrightarrow\!\!\!\!\!\!\!\ominus\; \mathsf{h}(1)$ and $\mathsf{g}(2) \twoheadrightarrow\!\!\!\!\!\!\!\ominus\; \mathsf{h}(2)$, $\overline{\mathcal{R}}$ is almost development closed. The constrained critical pair $\mathsf{g}(x) \approx \mathsf{h}(x)$ $[1 \leqslant x \leqslant 2]$ is not almost development closed, since it is a normal form with respect to the rewrite relation on constrained terms.

This also makes intuitive sense, since a rewrite step $s \approx t$ $[\varphi] \xrightarrow{\sim} u \approx v$ $[\psi]$ implies that the same step can be taken on all instances $s\sigma \approx t\sigma$ where $\sigma \vDash \varphi$. However it may be the case, like in the above example, that different instances of the constrained critical pair require different steps to obtain a closing sequence, which cannot directly be modeled using rewriting on constrained terms.

Since left-linearity of $\overline{\mathcal{R}}$ is preserved, the following corollary is obtained from Theorems 4 and 5. In fact $\mathcal{R}$ only has to be linear in the variables $x \notin \mathcal{LV}\mathsf{ar}$, since that is sufficient for $\overline{\mathcal{R}}$ to be linear.

Corollary 1. *Left-linear almost development closed* LCTRSs *are confluent.* □

Example 6. The LCTRS $\mathcal{R}$ over the theory Ints with the rules

$$\mathsf{f}(x, y) \to \mathsf{h}(\mathsf{g}(y, 2 \cdot 2))\ [x \leqslant y \land y = 2] \qquad \mathsf{g}(x, y) \to \mathsf{g}(y, x) \qquad \mathsf{h}(x) \to x$$
$$\mathsf{f}(x, y) \to \mathsf{c}(4, x)\ [y \leqslant x] \qquad \mathsf{c}(x, y) \to \mathsf{g}(4, 2)\ [x \neq y]$$

admits the two constrained critical pairs (with simplified constraints)

$$\mathsf{h}(\mathsf{g}(y, 2 \cdot 2)) \approx \mathsf{c}(4, x)\ [\varphi] \qquad \mathsf{c}(4, x) \approx \mathsf{h}(\mathsf{g}(y, 2 \cdot 2))\ [\varphi]$$

Both are almost development closed:

$$\begin{array}{ll} & \mathsf{h}(\mathsf{g}(y, 2 \cdot 2)) \approx \mathsf{c}(4, x)\ [\varphi] \\ \tilde{\multimap}_{\geqslant 1} & \mathsf{g}(4, 2) \approx \mathsf{c}(4, x)\ [x = 2] \\ \tilde{\to}_{\geqslant 2} & \mathsf{g}(4, 2) \approx \mathsf{g}(4, 2)\ [\mathsf{true}] \end{array} \qquad \begin{array}{ll} & \mathsf{c}(4, x) \approx \mathsf{h}(\mathsf{g}(y, 2 \cdot 2))\ [\varphi] \\ \tilde{\multimap}_{\geqslant 1} & \mathsf{g}(4, 2) \approx \mathsf{h}(\mathsf{g}(y, 2 \cdot 2))\ [y = 2] \\ \tilde{\to}^{*}_{\geqslant 2} & \mathsf{g}(4, 2) \approx \mathsf{g}(4, 2)\ [\mathsf{true}] \end{array}$$

Here φ is the constraint $x = y \wedge y = 2$. Hence $\mathcal{R}$ is almost development closed. Since $\mathcal{R}$ is left-linear, confluence follows by Corollary 1.

6 Parallel Critical Pairs

In this section we extend the confluence result by Toyama [20] based on parallel critical pairs to LCTRSs. Recently there is a renewed interest in this result; Shintani and Hirokawa proved in [19] that it subsumes Toyama's later confluence result in [21]. The latter was already lifted to LCTRSs in [17] and is also subsumed by Corollary 1. The result of Toyama [20] is a proper extension of the confluence criterion on parallel critical pairs by Gramlich [6]. In the sequel we mainly follow the notions from [19].

Definition 7. *Let $\mathcal{R}$ be an* LCTRS. *The parallel rewrite relation $\mathrel{+\!\!\!\!\!\!\to}$ on terms is defined inductively as follows:*

1. $x \mathrel{+\!\!\!\!\!\!\to} x$ *for all variables* x,
2. $f(s_1, \dots, s_n) \mathrel{+\!\!\!\!\!\!\to} f(t_1, \dots, t_n)$ *if* $s_i \mathrel{+\!\!\!\!\!\!\to} t_i$ *for* $1 \leqslant i \leqslant n$,
3. $\ell\sigma \mathrel{+\!\!\!\!\!\!\to} r\sigma$ *if* $\ell \to r\ [\varphi] \in \mathcal{R}_{\mathsf{rc}}$ *and* $\sigma \vDash \ell \to r\ [\varphi]$

We extend $\mathrel{+\!\!\!\!\!\!\to}$ to constrained terms inductively as follows:

1. $x\ [\varphi] \mathrel{+\!\!\!\!\!\!\to} x\ [\varphi]$ *for all variables* x,
2. $f(s_1, \dots, s_n)\ [\varphi] \mathrel{+\!\!\!\!\!\!\to} f(t_1, \dots, t_n)\ [\varphi]$ *if* $s_i\ [\varphi] \mathrel{+\!\!\!\!\!\!\to} t_i\ [\varphi]$ *for* $1 \leqslant i \leqslant n$,
3. $\ell\sigma\ [\varphi] \mathrel{+\!\!\!\!\!\!\to} r\sigma\ [\varphi]$ *if* $\rho\colon \ell \to r\ [\psi] \in \mathcal{R}_{\mathsf{rc}}$, $\sigma(x) \in \mathcal{V}\mathsf{al} \cup \mathcal{V}\mathsf{ar}(\varphi)$ *for all* $x \in \mathcal{LV}\mathsf{ar}(\rho)$, *$\varphi$ is satisfiable and $\varphi \Rightarrow \psi\sigma$ is valid.*

The parallel rewrite relation $\tilde{\mathrel{+\!\!\!\!\!\!\to}}$ on constrained terms is defined as $\sim \cdot \mathrel{+\!\!\!\!\!\!\to} \cdot \sim$.

Let s be a term and $P \subseteq \mathcal{P}\mathsf{os}(s)$ be a set of parallel positions. Given terms t_p for $p \in P$, we denote by $s[t_p]_{p \in P}$ the simultaneous replacement of the terms at position $p \in P$ in s by t_p. We recall the definition of parallel critical pairs for TRSs.

Definition 8. *Let $\mathcal{R}$ be a* TRS, *$\rho\colon \ell \to r$ a rule in $\mathcal{R}$, and $P \subseteq \mathcal{P}\mathsf{os}_{\mathcal{F}}(\ell)$ a non-empty set of parallel positions. For every $p \in P$ let $\rho_p\colon \ell_p \to r_p$ be a variant of a rule in $\mathcal{R}$. The peak $\ell\sigma[r_p\sigma]_{p \in P} \mathrel{\leftarrow\!\!\!\!\!\!+} \ell\sigma \to_{\epsilon,\mathcal{R}} r\sigma$ forms a* parallel critical pair *$\ell\sigma[r_p\sigma]_{p \in P} \approx r\sigma$ if the following conditions are satisfied:*

1. $\mathcal{V}\mathsf{ar}(\rho_1) \cap \mathcal{V}\mathsf{ar}(\rho_2) = \varnothing$ *for different rules* ρ_1 *and* ρ_2 *in* $\{\rho\} \cup \{\rho_p \mid p \in P\}$,
2. σ *is an mgu of* $\{\ell_p \approx \ell|_p \mid p \in P\}$,
3. *if* $P = \{\epsilon\}$ *then* ρ_ϵ *is not a variant of* ρ.

The set of all constrained parallel critical pairs of $\mathcal{R}$ *is denoted by* $\mathsf{PCP}(\mathcal{R})$.

We lift this notion to the constrained setting and define it for LCTRSs.

Definition 9. *Let* $\mathcal{R}$ *be an* LCTRS, $\rho\colon \ell \to r\ [\varphi]$ *a rule in* $\mathcal{R}_{\mathsf{rc}}$, *and* $P \subseteq \mathcal{P}\mathsf{os}_{\mathcal{F}}(\ell)$ *a non-empty set of parallel positions. For every* $p \in P$ *let* $\rho_p\colon \ell_p \to r_p\ [\varphi_p]$ *be a variant of a rule in* $\mathcal{R}_{\mathsf{rc}}$. *Let* $\psi = \mathcal{EC}_\rho \wedge \bigwedge_{p \in P} \mathcal{EC}_{\rho_p}$ *and* $\Phi = \varphi\sigma \wedge \psi\sigma \wedge \bigwedge_{p \in P} \varphi_p\sigma$. *The peak* $\ell\sigma[r_p\sigma]_{p \in P}\ [\Phi] \mathrel{{+}\!\!\!\!{\leftarrow}\!\!\!\!{+}} \ell\sigma\ [\Phi] \to_{\epsilon,\mathcal{R}} r\sigma\ [\Phi]$ *forms a* constrained parallel critical pair $\ell\sigma[r_p\sigma]_{p \in P} \approx r\sigma\ [\Phi]$ *if the following conditions are satisfied:*

1. $\mathcal{V}\mathsf{ar}(\rho_1) \cap \mathcal{V}\mathsf{ar}(\rho_2) = \varnothing$ *for different rules* ρ_1 *and* ρ_2 *in* $\{\rho\} \cup \{\rho_p \mid p \in P\}$,
2. σ *is an mgu of* $\{\ell_p = \ell|_p \mid p \in P\}$ *such that* $\sigma(x) \in \mathcal{V}\mathsf{al} \cup \mathcal{V}$ *for all* $x \in \mathcal{LV}\mathsf{ar}(\rho) \cup \bigcup_{p \in P} \mathcal{LV}\mathsf{ar}(\rho_p)$,
3. $\varphi\sigma \wedge \bigwedge_{p \in P} \varphi_p\sigma$ *is satisfiable,*
4. *if* $P = \{\epsilon\}$ *then* ρ_ϵ *is not a variant of* ρ *or* $\mathcal{V}\mathsf{ar}(r) \nsubseteq \mathcal{V}\mathsf{ar}(\ell)$.

A constrained peak forming a constrained parallel critical pair is called a constrained parallel critical peak. *The set of all constrained parallel critical pairs of* $\mathcal{R}$ *is denoted by* $\mathsf{CPCP}(\mathcal{R})$.

For a term t and a set of parallel positions P in t, we write $\mathcal{V}\mathsf{ar}(t, P)$ to denote $\bigcup_{p \in P} \mathcal{V}\mathsf{ar}(t|_p)$. For a set of parallel positions P we denote by $\mathrel{+\!\!\!\!\!\to}^P$ that each rewrite step obtained in case (3) of Definition 7 is performed at a position $p \in P$ and no two steps share a position. Moreover, for a set of parallel positions P and a position q we denote by $\mathrel{+\!\!\!\!\!\to}^P_{\geqslant q}$ that $p \geqslant q$ for all $p \in P$.

Definition 10. *A critical pair* $s \approx t$ *is* 1-parallel closed *if* $s \mathrel{+\!\!\!\!\!\to} \cdot\ {}^*\!\!\leftarrow t$. *A* TRS *is 1-parallel closed if all its critical pairs are 1-parallel closed. A parallel critical pair* $\ell\sigma[r_p\sigma]_{p \in P} \approx r\sigma$ *originating from the peak* $\ell\sigma[r_p\sigma]_{p \in P} \mathrel{\leftarrow\!\!\!\!\!+} \ell\sigma \to_\epsilon r\sigma$ *is* 2-parallel closed *if there exists a term* v *and a set of parallel positions* Q *such that* $\ell\sigma[r_p\sigma]_{p \in P} \to^* v\ {}^Q\!\!\mathrel{\leftarrow\!\!\!\!\!+} r\sigma$ *with* $\mathcal{V}\mathsf{ar}(v, Q) \subseteq \mathcal{V}\mathsf{ar}(\ell\sigma, P)$. *A* TRS *is 2-parallel closed if all its parallel critical pairs are 2-parallel closed. A* TRS *is parallel closed if it is 1-parallel closed and 2-parallel closed.*

The following result from [20] has recently been formalized in Isabelle [7].

Theorem 6. *Left-linear parallel closed* TRSs *are confluent.* □

In the remainder of this section we extend this result to LCTRSs. To this end we introduce the notion $\mathcal{TV}\mathsf{ar}(t, \varphi) = \mathcal{V}\mathsf{ar}(t) \setminus \mathcal{V}\mathsf{ar}(\varphi)$ denoting the set of non-logical variables in term t with respect to the logical constraint φ. We restrict this to non-logical variables in subterms below a set of parallel positions P in t: $\mathcal{TV}\mathsf{ar}(t, \varphi, P) = \bigcup_{p \in P} \mathcal{TV}\mathsf{ar}(t|_p, \varphi)$.

Definition 11. *A constrained critical pair* $s \approx t\ [\varphi]$ *is* 1-parallel closed *if* $s \approx t\ [\varphi] \nrightarrow_{\geqslant 1} \cdot \overset{\sim}{\rightarrow}^*_{\geqslant 2} u \approx v\ [\psi]$ *for some trivial* $u \approx v\ [\psi]$*. An* LCTRS *is 1-parallel closed if all its constrained critical pairs are 1-parallel closed. A constrained parallel critical pair* $\ell\sigma[r_p\sigma]_{p \in P} \approx r\sigma\ [\varphi]$ *is* 2-parallel closed *if there exists a set of parallel positions* Q *such that*

$$\ell\sigma[r_p\sigma]_{p\in P} \approx r\sigma\ [\varphi] \nrightarrow^{Q}_{\geqslant 2} \cdot \overset{\sim}{\rightarrow}^*_{\geqslant 1} u \approx v\ [\psi]$$

for some trivial $u \approx v\ [\psi]$ *and* $\mathcal{TV}\mathsf{ar}(v, \psi, Q) \subseteq \mathcal{TV}\mathsf{ar}(\ell\sigma, \varphi, P)$*. An* LCTRS *is 2-parallel closed if all its constrained parallel critical pairs are 2-parallel closed. An* LCTRS *is parallel closed if it is 1-parallel closed and 2-parallel closed.*

Recall from Sect. 2 that our definition of $\sim$ differs from the equivalence relation $\sim'$ defined in [12,17]. The change is necessary for the variable condition of 2-parallel closedness to make sense, as illustrated in the following example.

Example 7. Consider the (LC)TRS consisting of the rules

$$\mathsf{f}(\mathsf{g}(x), y) \rightarrow \mathsf{f}(\mathsf{b}, y) \qquad \mathsf{g}(x) \rightarrow \mathsf{a} \qquad \mathsf{f}(\mathsf{a}, x) \rightarrow x \qquad \mathsf{f}(\mathsf{b}, x) \rightarrow x$$

The peak $\mathsf{f}(\mathsf{a}, y)\ [\mathsf{true}]\ {}^{\{1\}}\!\nleftarrow \mathsf{f}(\mathsf{g}(x), y)\ [\mathsf{true}] \rightarrow \mathsf{f}(\mathsf{b}, y)\ [\mathsf{true}]$ gives rise to the (constrained) parallel critical pair $\mathsf{f}(\mathsf{a}, y) \approx \mathsf{f}(\mathsf{b}, y)\ [\mathsf{true}]$. Using $\sim'$ we have

$$\mathsf{f}(\mathsf{a}, y) \approx \mathsf{f}(\mathsf{b}, y)\ [\mathsf{true}] \nrightarrow^{\{\epsilon\}}_{\geqslant 2} \cdot \rightarrow^*_{\geqslant 1} y \approx y\ [\mathsf{true}] \sim' x \approx x\ [\mathsf{true}]$$

and the variable condition $\mathcal{TV}\mathsf{ar}(x, \mathsf{true}, \{\epsilon\}) \subseteq \mathcal{TV}\mathsf{ar}(\mathsf{f}(\mathsf{g}(x), y), \mathsf{true}, \{1\})$ holds. Since the system has no logical constraints it can also be analyzed in the TRS setting. Following Definition 10 we would have to check the variable condition $\mathcal{V}\mathsf{ar}(y, \{\epsilon\}) \subseteq \mathcal{V}\mathsf{ar}(\mathsf{f}(\mathsf{g}(x), y), \{1\})$, which does not hold. Using $\sim$ resolves this difference, since $y \approx y\ [\mathsf{true}] \not\sim x \approx x\ [\mathsf{true}]$. So the conditions in Definition 11 reduce to the ones in Definition 10 for TRSs.

In Theorem 2 in Sect. 4 we related critical pairs of the transformed TRS to constrained critical pairs of the originating LCTRS. The following theorem does the same for parallel critical pairs.

Theorem 7. *For every parallel critical pair* $s \approx t$ *of* $\overline{\mathcal{R}}$ *there exists a constrained parallel critical pair* $s' \approx t'\ [\varphi']$ *of* $\mathcal{R}$ *and a substitution* γ *such that* $s = s'\gamma$*,* $t = t'\gamma$ *and* $\gamma \vDash \varphi'$*.*

Proof. Let $s \approx t$ be a parallel critical pair of $\overline{\mathcal{R}}$, originating from the parallel critical peak $\ell\mu\sigma[r_p\nu_p\sigma]_{p\in P} \nleftarrow \ell\mu\sigma = \ell\mu\sigma[\ell_p\nu_p\sigma]_{p\in P} \rightarrow_\epsilon r\mu\sigma$ with variants $\rho\colon \ell \rightarrow r\ [\varphi]$ and $\rho_p\colon \ell_p \rightarrow r_p\ [\varphi_p]$ for $p \in P$ of rules in $\mathcal{R}_{\mathsf{rc}}$ without shared variables, $\psi = \mathcal{EC}_\rho$ and $\psi_p = \mathcal{EC}_{\rho_p}$ for $p \in P$. Furthermore, $\mathcal{D}\mathsf{om}(\nu_p) = \mathcal{LV}\mathsf{ar}(\rho_p)$ for $p \in P$, $\mathcal{D}\mathsf{om}(\mu) = \mathcal{LV}\mathsf{ar}(\rho)$, $\nu_p \vDash \varphi_p \wedge \psi_p$ for $p \in P$, $\mu \vDash \varphi \wedge \psi$, $p \in \mathcal{P}\mathsf{os}_\mathcal{F}(\ell\mu)$, and σ is an mgu of $\{\ell\mu|_p \approx \ell_p\nu_p \mid p \in P\}$. Moreover, if $P = \{\epsilon\}$ then $\ell_\epsilon\nu_\epsilon \rightarrow r_\epsilon\nu_\epsilon\ [\varphi_\epsilon\nu_\epsilon]$ and $\ell\mu \rightarrow r\mu\ [\varphi\mu]$ are not variants. Define the substitution τ as $\bigcup\{\nu_p \mid p \in P\} \uplus \mu$. Clearly, $\ell_p\tau = \ell_p\nu_p$ and $r_p\tau = r_p\nu_p$ for $p \in P$, $\ell\tau = \ell\mu$,

$r\tau = r\mu$, $\tau \vDash \varphi \wedge \psi$ and $\tau \vDash \varphi_p \wedge \psi_p$ for all $p \in P$. Hence the given peak can be written as $\ell\tau\sigma[r_p\tau\sigma]_{p\in P} \nleftarrow\!\!\!\!\!\!\leftarrow \ell\tau\sigma = \ell\tau\sigma[\ell_p\tau\sigma]_{p\in P} \to_\epsilon r\tau\sigma$ with $\tau \vDash \varphi''$ where

$$\varphi'' = \varphi \wedge \mathcal{EC}_\rho \wedge \bigwedge_{p\in P} (\varphi_p \wedge \mathcal{EC}_{\rho_p})$$

Since $\ell|_p\tau\sigma = \ell_p\tau\sigma$ for all $p \in P$ there exists an mgu δ of $\{\ell|_p = \ell_p \mid p \in P\}$ and a substitution γ such that $\delta\gamma = \tau\sigma$. Let $s' = \ell\delta[r_p\delta]_{p\in P}$ and $t' = r\delta$. We claim that this results in the constrained parallel critical pair $s' \approx t'$ $[\varphi''\delta]$. Condition (1) of Definition 9 is trivially satisfied. We obtain $P \subseteq \mathcal{P}\mathsf{os}_\mathcal{F}(\ell)$ because $P \subseteq \mathcal{P}\mathsf{os}_\mathcal{F}(\ell\mu)$, $\mu(x) \in \mathcal{V}\mathsf{al}$ for every $x \in \mathcal{D}\mathsf{om}(\mu)$, and $\mathsf{root}(\ell\mu|_p) = \mathsf{root}(\ell_p\nu) \in \mathcal{F} \setminus \mathcal{V}\mathsf{al}$ for all $p \in P$. For condition (2) it remains to show that $\delta(x) \in \mathcal{V}\mathsf{al} \cup \mathcal{V}$ for all $x \in \mathcal{LV}\mathsf{ar}(\rho) \cup \bigcup_{p\in P} \mathcal{LV}\mathsf{ar}(\rho_p)$. Suppose to the contrary that $\mathsf{root}(\delta(x)) \in \mathcal{F} \setminus \mathcal{V}\mathsf{al}$ for some $x \in \mathcal{LV}\mathsf{ar}(\rho) \cup \bigcup_{p\in P} \mathcal{LV}\mathsf{ar}(\rho_p)$. Then $\mathsf{root}(\delta(x)) = \mathsf{root}(\gamma(\delta(x))) = \mathsf{root}(\sigma(\tau(x))) \in \mathcal{F} \setminus \mathcal{V}\mathsf{al}$, which contradicts $\tau \vDash \varphi''$. Condition (3) follows from the identity $\delta\gamma = \tau\sigma$ together with $\tau \vDash \varphi''$ which imply $\delta\gamma \vDash \varphi''$ and thus $\varphi''\delta$ is satisfiable. Hence also $\varphi\delta \wedge \bigwedge_{p\in P} \varphi_p\delta$ is satisfiable. It remains to show condition (4), so let $P = \{\epsilon\}$ and further assume that ρ_ϵ and ρ are variants. So there exists a variable renaming π such that $\rho_\epsilon\pi = \rho$. In particular, $\ell_\epsilon\pi = \ell$ and $r_\epsilon\pi = r$. We show $\tau(\pi(x)) = \pi(\tau(x))$ for all $x \in \mathcal{V}\mathsf{ar}(\ell_\epsilon)$. Let $x \in \mathcal{V}\mathsf{ar}(\ell_\epsilon)$. If $x \in \mathcal{LV}\mathsf{ar}(\rho_\epsilon) = \mathcal{D}\mathsf{om}(\nu)$ then $\tau(x) = \nu(x) \in \mathcal{V}\mathsf{al}$. Moreover, $\pi(x) \in \mathcal{LV}\mathsf{ar}(\rho) = \mathcal{D}\mathsf{om}(\mu)$ and thus $\tau(\pi(x)) = \mu(\pi(x)) \in \mathcal{V}\mathsf{al}$. Since $\ell_\epsilon\tau$ and $\ell\tau$ are unifiable, $\pi(\tau(x)) = \tau(x) = \tau(\pi(x))$. If $x \notin \mathcal{LV}\mathsf{ar}(\rho_\epsilon)$ then $\tau(x) = x$, $\pi(x) \notin \mathcal{LV}\mathsf{ar}(\rho)$ and similarly $\tau(\pi(x)) = \pi(x) = \pi(\tau(x))$. All in all, $\ell_\epsilon\tau\pi = \ell_\epsilon\pi\tau = \ell\tau$. Now, if $\mathcal{V}\mathsf{ar}(r_\epsilon) \subseteq \mathcal{V}\mathsf{ar}(\ell_\epsilon)$ then we obtain $r_\epsilon\tau\pi = r_\epsilon\pi\tau = r\tau$, contradicting the fact that $\ell_\epsilon\nu \to r_\epsilon\nu$ and $\ell\mu \to r\mu$ are not variants. We conclude that $s' \approx t'$ $[\varphi''\delta]$ is a constrained parallel critical pair of $\mathcal{R}$. So we can take $\varphi' = \varphi''\delta$. Clearly, $s = s'\gamma$ and $t = t'\gamma$. Moreover, $\gamma \vDash \varphi'$ since $\varphi'\gamma = \varphi''\tau\sigma = \varphi''\tau$ and $\tau \vDash \varphi''$. □

The proofs of the following lemmata are given in [18].

Lemma 5. *If $s \approx t$ $[\varphi]$ $\nrightarrow\!\!\!\!\!\!\rightarrow^P_{\geqslant 1}$ $u \approx v$ $[\psi]$ then for all substitutions $\sigma \vDash \varphi$ there exists a substitution δ such that $\delta \vDash \psi$, $s\sigma \nrightarrow\!\!\!\!\!\!\rightarrow^P u\delta$ and $t\sigma = v\delta$.* □

Lemma 6. *If a constrained critical pair $s \approx t$ $[\varphi]$ is 1-parallel closed then $s\sigma \nrightarrow\!\!\!\!\!\!\rightarrow \cdot {}^*\!\!\leftarrow t\sigma$ for all substitutions σ with $\sigma \vDash \varphi$.* □

Lemma 7. *If a constrained parallel critical pair $s = \ell\sigma'[r_p\sigma']_{p\in P} \approx r\sigma' = t$ $[\varphi]$ is 2-parallel closed then there exist a term v and a set Q of parallel positions such that $s\sigma \to^* v \;{}^Q\!\!\nleftarrow\!\!\!\!\!\!\leftarrow t\sigma$ and $\mathcal{V}\mathsf{ar}(v, Q) \subseteq \mathcal{V}\mathsf{ar}(\ell\sigma'\sigma, P)$ for all substitutions σ with $\sigma \vDash \varphi$.* □

Theorem 8. *If an* LCTRS *$\mathcal{R}$ is parallel closed then $\overline{\mathcal{R}}$ is parallel closed.*

Proof. Let $\mathcal{R}$ be a parallel closed LCTRS. First consider an arbitrary critical pair $s \approx t \in \mathsf{CP}(\overline{\mathcal{R}})$. From Theorem 2 we know that there exist a constrained critical pair $s' \approx t'$ $[\varphi] \in \mathsf{CCP}(\mathcal{R})$ and a substitution σ such that $s'\sigma = s$, $t'\sigma = t$

and $\sigma \vDash \varphi$. Since the constrained critical pair is 1-parallel closed, Lemma 6 yields $s \twoheadrightarrow\!\!\!\!\!\!\| \cdot {}^*\!\!\leftarrow t$. Hence $\overline{\mathcal{R}}$ is 1-parallel closed.

Next consider an arbitrary parallel critical pair $s \approx t \in \mathsf{PCP}(\overline{\mathcal{R}})$. Theorem 7 yields a constrained parallel critical pair $s' = \ell\sigma'[r_p\sigma']_{p\in P} \approx r\sigma' = t'$ $[\varphi]$ in $\mathsf{CPCP}(\mathcal{R})$ and a substitution σ such that $s'\sigma = s$, $t'\sigma = t$ and $\sigma \vDash \varphi$. Since the constrained parallel critical pair is 2-parallel closed, by Lemma 7 there exist a term v and a set of parallel positions Q such that $s \to^* v \;{}^{Q}\!\!\leftarrow\!\!\!\!\!\!\| \; t$ and $\mathcal{V}\mathsf{ar}(v, Q) \subseteq \mathcal{V}\mathsf{ar}(\ell\sigma'\sigma, P)$. Hence $\overline{\mathcal{R}}$ is 2-parallel closed. □

Since left-linearity of $\mathcal{R}$ is preserved in $\overline{\mathcal{R}}$ and left-linear, parallel closed TRSs are confluent by Theorem 6, we obtain the following corollary via Theorems 7 and 8. Again, $\mathcal{R}$ only has to be left-linear in the variables $x \notin \mathcal{L}\mathcal{V}\mathsf{ar}$, since that is sufficient for $\overline{\mathcal{R}}$ to be left-linear.

Corollary 2. *Every left-linear parallel closed* LCTRS *is confluent.* □

We illustrate the corollary on a concrete example.

Example 8. Consider the LCTRS $\mathcal{R}$ over the theory Ints with the rules

$$\mathsf{f}(\mathsf{a}) \to \mathsf{g}(4,4) \qquad \mathsf{a} \to \mathsf{g}(1+1, 3+1) \qquad \mathsf{g}(x,y) \to \mathsf{f}(\mathsf{g}(z,y))\ [z = x - 2]$$

The constrained (parallel) critical pair $\mathsf{f}(\mathsf{g}(1+1,3+1)) \approx \mathsf{g}(4,4)$ $[\mathsf{true}]$ originating from the peak $\mathsf{f}(\mathsf{g}(1+1,3+1))$ $[\mathsf{true}]$ ${}^{\{1\}}\!\!\leftarrow\!\!\!\!\!\!\|\ \mathsf{f}(\mathsf{a})$ $[\mathsf{true}] \to_\epsilon \mathsf{g}(4,4)$ $[\mathsf{true}]$ is 2-parallel closed:

$$\begin{aligned}\mathsf{f}(\mathsf{g}(1+1,3+1)) \approx \mathsf{g}(4,4)\ [\mathsf{true}] &\twoheadrightarrow\!\!\!\!\!\!\!\|\;_{\geqslant 1}\ \mathsf{f}(\mathsf{g}(2,4)) \approx \mathsf{g}(4,4)\ [\mathsf{true}] \\ &\twoheadrightarrow\!\!\!\!\!\!\!\|\;^{\{2\}}_{\geqslant 2}\ \mathsf{f}(\mathsf{g}(2,4)) \approx \mathsf{f}(\mathsf{g}(2,4))\ [\mathsf{true}]\end{aligned}$$

Note that the condition $\mathcal{TV}\mathsf{ar}(\mathsf{f}(\mathsf{g}(2,4)), \mathsf{true}, \{2\}) \subseteq \mathcal{TV}\mathsf{ar}(\mathsf{f}(\mathsf{a}), \mathsf{true}, \{1\})$ is trivially satisfied. One easily checks that the corresponding constrained critical pair is 1-parallel closed. Since the only other remaining constrained critical pair is trivial, we conclude confluence by Corollary 2.

7 Conclusion

We presented a left-linearity preserving transformation from LCTRSs to TRSs such that (parallel) critical pairs in the latter correspond to constrained (parallel) critical pairs in the former. As a consequence, confluence results for TRSs based on restricted joinability conditions easily carry over to LCTRSs. This was illustrated by generalizing the advanced confluence results of van Oostrom [15] and Toyama [20] from TRSs to LCTRSs. We also proved that (local) confluence of terminating LCTRSs over a decidable theory is undecidable in general.

Figure 2 relates the confluence criteria in this paper to the earlier ones from [12,17]. The acronyms stand for weak orthogonality (WO, [12, Theorem 4]),

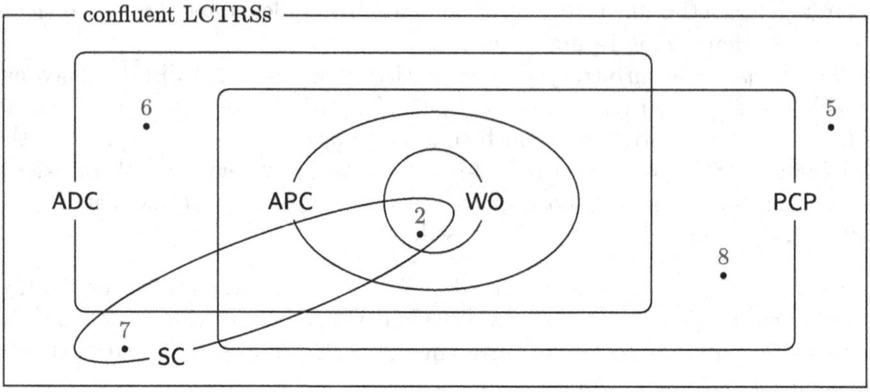

Fig. 2. Relating confluence criteria for LCTRSs.

strong closedness (SC, [17, Theorem 2]), almost parallel closedness (APC, [17, Theorem 4]), almost development closedness (ADC, Corollary 1), and parallel closedness of (parallel) critical pairs (PCP, Corollary 2). All areas are inhabited and the numbers refer to examples in this paper.

The confluence results of [12,17] have been implemented in crest.[1] The tool is currently under heavy development, not only to incorporate the results in this paper but also termination and completion techniques. Confluence of LCTRSs is a new category in the upcoming edition of the Confluence Competition[2] and we expect to present experimental results obtained with crest at the conference.

For TRSs numerous other confluence techniques, not based on restricted joinability conditions of critical pairs, as well as sufficient conditions for non-confluence are known [1,8,19,23]. We plan to investigate which techniques generalize to LCTRSs with our transformation. The transformation also makes the formal verification of confluence criteria for LCTRSs in a proof assistant a more realistic goal.

Acknowledgments. The detailed feedback of the reviewers improved the presentation.

Disclosure of Interests. The authors have no competing interests to declare that are relevant to the content of this article.

[1] http://cl-informatik.uibk.ac.at/software/crest/.
[2] https://project-coco.uibk.ac.at/2024/.

References

1. Aoto, T.: Disproving confluence of term rewriting systems by interpretation and ordering. In: Fontaine, P., Ringeissen, C., Schmidt, R.A. (eds.) FroCoS 2013. LNCS (LNAI), vol. 8152, pp. 311–326. Springer, Heidelberg (2013). https://doi.org/10.1007/978-3-642-40885-4_22
2. Aoto, T., Yoshida, J., Toyama, Y.: Proving confluence of term rewriting systems automatically. In: Treinen, R. (ed.) RTA 2009. LNCS, vol. 5595, pp. 93–102. Springer, Heidelberg (2009). https://doi.org/10.1007/978-3-642-02348-4_7
3. Ciobâcă, S., Lucanu, D., Buruiană, A.S.: Operationally-based program equivalence proofs using LCTRSs. J. Log. Algebr. Methods Program. **135**, 100894 (2023). https://doi.org/10.1016/j.jlamp.2023.100894
4. Ciobâcă, Ş, Lucanu, D.: A coinductive approach to proving reachability properties in logically constrained term rewriting systems. In: Galmiche, D., Schulz, S., Sebastiani, R. (eds.) IJCAR 2018. LNCS (LNAI), vol. 10900, pp. 295–311. Springer, Cham (2018). https://doi.org/10.1007/978-3-319-94205-6_20
5. Fuhs, C., Kop, C., Nishida, N.: Verifying procedural programs via constrained rewriting induction. ACM Trans. Comput. Log. **18**(2), 14:1–14:50 (2017). https://doi.org/10.1145/3060143
6. Gramlich, B.: Confluence without termination via parallel critical pairs. In: Kirchner, H. (ed.) CAAP 1996. LNCS, vol. 1059, pp. 211–225. Springer, Heidelberg (1996). https://doi.org/10.1007/3-540-61064-2_39
7. Hirokawa, N., Kim, D., Shintani, K., Thiemann, R.: Certification of confluence- and commutation-proofs via parallel critical pairs. In: Timany, A., Traytel, D., Pientka, B., Blazy, S. (eds.) Proceedings of 13th ACM SIGPLAN International Conference on Certified Programs and Proofs, pp. 147–161. ACM (2024). https://doi.org/10.1145/3636501.3636949
8. Hirokawa, N., Nagele, J., van Oostrom, V., Oyamaguchi, M.: Confluence by critical pair analysis revisited. In: Fontaine, P. (ed.) CADE 2019. LNCS (LNAI), vol. 11716, pp. 319–336. Springer, Cham (2019). https://doi.org/10.1007/978-3-030-29436-6_19
9. Knuth, D.E., Bendix, P.B.: Simple word problems in universal algebras. In: Leech, J. (ed.) Computational Problems in Abstract Algebra, pp. 263–297. Pergamon Press, Oxford (1970). https://doi.org/10.1016/B978-0-08-012975-4.50028-X
10. Kohl, C., Middeldorp, A.: A formalization of the development closedness criterion for left-linear term rewrite systems. In: Krebbers, R., Traytel, D., Pientka, B., Zdancewic, S. (eds.) Proceedings of 12th ACM SIGPLAN International Conference on Certified Programs and Proofs, pp. 197–210 (2023). https://doi.org/10.1145/3573105.3575667
11. Kohl, C., Middeldorp, A.: Formalizing almost development closed critical pairs. In: Naumowicz, A., Thiemann, R. (eds.) Proceedings of 14th International Conference on Interactive Theorem Proving. Leibniz International Proceedings in Informatics, vol. 268, pp. 38:1–38:8 (2023). https://doi.org/10.4230/LIPIcs.ITP.2023.38
12. Kop, C., Nishida, N.: Term rewriting with logical constraints. In: Fontaine, P., Ringeissen, C., Schmidt, R.A. (eds.) FroCoS 2013. LNCS (LNAI), vol. 8152, pp. 343–358. Springer, Heidelberg (2013). https://doi.org/10.1007/978-3-642-40885-4_24
13. Mitterwallner, F., Schöpf, J., Middeldorp, A.: Reducing confluence of LCTRSs to confluence of TRSs. In: Proceedings of 12th International Workshop on Confluence, pp. 3–8 (2023)

14. Nagele, J., Felgenhauer, B., Middeldorp, A.: CSI: new evidence – a progress report. In: de Moura, L. (ed.) CADE 2017. LNCS (LNAI), vol. 10395, pp. 385–397. Springer, Cham (2017). https://doi.org/10.1007/978-3-319-63046-5_24
15. van Oostrom, V.: Developing developments. Theor. Comput. Sci. **175**(1), 159–181 (1997). https://doi.org/10.1016/S0304-3975(96)00173-9
16. Post, E.L.: A variant of a recursively unsolvable problem. Bull. Am. Math. Soc. **52**, 264–268 (1946). https://doi.org/10.1090/S0002-9904-1946-08555-9
17. Schöpf, J., Middeldorp, A.: Confluence criteria for logically constrained rewrite systems. In: Pientka, B., Tinelli, C. (eds.) CADE 2023. LNCS, vol. 14132, pp. 474–490. Springer, Cham (2023). https://doi.org/10.1007/978-3-031-38499-8_27
18. Schöpf, J., Mitterwallner, F., Middeldorp, A.: Confluence of logically constrained rewrite systems revisited. CoRR abs/2402.13552 (2024). https://doi.org/10.48550/ARXIV.2402.13552
19. Shintani, K., Hirokawa, N.: Compositional confluence criteria. In: Felty, A.P. (ed.) Proceedings of 7th International Conference on Formal Structures for Computation and Deduction. Leibniz International Proceedings in Informatics, vol. 228, pp. 28:1–28:19 (2022). https://doi.org/10.4230/LIPICS.FSCD.2022.28
20. Toyama, Y.: On the Church–Rosser property of term rewriting systems. NTT ECL Technical report 17672, NTT ECL (1981). (in Japanese)
21. Toyama, Y.: Commutativity of term rewriting systems. In: Programming of Future Generation Computers II, pp. 393–407. North-Holland (1988)
22. Winkler, S., Middeldorp, A.: Completion for logically constrained rewriting. In: Kirchner, H. (ed.) Proceedings of 3rd International Conference on Formal Structures for Computation and Deduction. Leibniz International Proceedings in Informatics, vol. 108, pp. 30:1–30:18 (2018). https://doi.org/10.4230/LIPIcs.FSCD.2018.30
23. Zankl, H., Felgenhauer, B., Middeldorp, A.: Labelings for decreasing diagrams. J. Autom. Reason. **54**(2), 101–133 (2015). https://doi.org/10.1007/s10817-014-9316-y

Equational Anti-unification over Absorption Theories

Mauricio Ayala-Rincón[1], David M. Cerna[2(✉)], Andrés Felipe González Barragán[1], and Temur Kutsia[3]

[1] Universidade de Brasília, Brasília, Brazil
ayala@unb.br, andres.felipe@aluno.unb.br
[2] Czech Academy of Sciences Institute of Computer Science, Prague, Czechia
dcerna@cs.cas.cz
[3] Research Institute for Symbolic Computation, Johannes Kepler University, Linz, Austria
kutsia@risc.jku.at

Abstract. Interest in anti-unification, the dual problem of unification, is rising due to various new applications. For example, anti-unification-based techniques have been used recently in software analysis and related areas such as clone detection and automatic program repair. While syntactic forms of anti-unification have found many interesting uses, some aspects of modern applications are more appropriately modeled by reasoning modulo an equational theory. Thus, extending existing anti-unification methods to deal with important equational theories is the natural step forward. This paper considers anti-unification modulo pure absorption theories, i.e., where some function symbols are associated with a special constant satisfying the axiom $f(x, \varepsilon_f) \approx f(\varepsilon_f, x) \approx \varepsilon_f$. We provide a sound and complete rule-based algorithm for such theories. Furthermore, we show that anti-unification modulo absorption is infinitary. Despite this, our algorithm terminates and produces a finitary algorithmic representation of the minimal complete set of solutions.

Keywords: Anti-unification · Generalization · Equational Theories

1 Introduction

Anti-unification (AU) is a fundamental operation for reasoning about generalizations of formal objects. It is the dual operation to unification. The seminal works of Plotkin and Reynolds, introducing the area, were published more than fifty years ago [27,28]. Recent applications renewed the interest in this technique. This current tendency is mainly due to the significance of generalization operations within frameworks crucial for software analysis and related areas [19].

In contrast to unification, where identifying the equivalence classes induced by a set of expressions is the main objective, AU methods search for the least general commonalities induced by a set of expressions. Investigations have exploited

C. Benzmüller et al. (Eds.): IJCAR 2024, LNAI 14740, pp. 317–337, 2024.
https://doi.org/10.1007/978-3-031-63501-4_17

AU methods for various applications such as the implementation of efficient parallel compilers [8], plagiarism detection and code cloning [33,35,36], automated bug detection and fixing [7,24,32,34], and indexing/compression/library learning [15,26], just to name a few. Anti-unification has been studied for several mathematical and computational structures such as term-graphs [13], higher-order terms [12,20,25], unranked (variadic) languages [10,21], nominal terms [11,29,30], modulo approximations [5,22,23] and background (first-order) equational theories, which is also the subject of this paper. Some of these algorithms have been implemented and can be accessed online [2,9].

Syntactic AU algorithms [27,28] compute the *least general generalizations* (*lgg*). In the equational case, the given terms do not necessarily have a single *lgg*. Problems are instead characterized by their *minimal complete sets of generalizations* (*mcsg*), which leads to the classification of theories depending on the existence and cardinality of such sets: If the *mcsg* does not exist for some problem in the given theory, then the theory has the nullary AU type. Otherwise, theories may have unitary (all problems have a singleton *mcsg*, i.e., a single *lgg*), finitary (all problems have a finite *mcsg*, at least one of which is not a singleton), or infinitary (there is a problem with the infinite *mcsg*) AU type.

There have been quite a few developments concerned with AU modulo equational theories. For example, Burghardt [14] considered AU modulo an arbitrary equational theory using grammars. Most other authors studied AU over fundamental algebraic properties and their combinations, e.g., associative (A), commutative (C), AC, idempotent (I) operators, or operators with unit (U) elements. An early work by Baader [6] studied AU over so-called "commutative theories", covering commutative monoids (ACU), commutative idempotent monoids ($ACUI$), and Abelian groups. In a restricted setting, he showed that AU in such theories is unitary. Alpuente et al. [1,3] studied AU over combinations of A, C, and U operators in an order-sorted setting, providing complete AU algorithms, and proving that all studied problems are finitary. Cerna and Kutsia [18] showed that some results depend on the number of symbols that satisfy the associated equational axioms. For instance, they proved the nullarity of theories containing more than one equational symbol: $U^{>1}$, $(AU)^{>1}(CU)^{>1}$, $(ACU)^1$, and $(AU)(CU)$. They also show that I, AI, CI are infinitary [17], and Cerna proved that $(UI)^{>1}, (AUI)^{>1}, (CUI)^{>1}, (ACUI)^{>1}$, and semirings are nullary [16].

This paper extends the state-of-the-art on equational anti-unification by providing an algorithm to solve first-order AU problems in which collapsing symbols may occur. These are symbols that are associated with an *absorption constant* such that $f(\varepsilon_f, x) \approx \varepsilon_f \approx f(x, \varepsilon_f)$. Such properties often appear in syntactic, logical, and algebraic frameworks (e.g., $0 \times x \approx 0$, false $\wedge\, p \approx$ false). They are an instance of the *subterm-collapsing* property. Concerning applications, one could consider such operations as modeling exception handling and other methods of flagging errors in software development, where much of the context is discarded when the error handling code is triggered. In such cases, like absorption theories, the state before triggering the error handling code is not precisely captured by the resulting context and, in a sense, can be abstracted away.

In this paper, we provide a detailed study of anti-unification in absorption theories: investigating its type (which turns out to be infinitary), coming up with a finitary algorithmic representation of the potentially infinite *mcsg*, developing an algorithm that computes such a representation, and studying its properties. Moreover, our work opens a way toward characterizing anti-unification for a bigger class of subterm-collapsing equational theories, where techniques introduced in this paper can be useful. We leave this as a future work.

Plan of the Paper. After defining the notions (Sect. 2), we introduce an algorithm for anti-unification over absorption theories (Sect. 3), prove its soundness and completeness (Sect. 4), show that anti-unification over absorption theories is of type infinitary and provide a brief complexity analysis (Sect. 5). Some proofs and explanatory examples can be found in [4].

2 Preliminaries

Let $\mathcal{V}$ be a countable set of variables and $\mathcal{F}$ a set of function symbols with a fixed arity. Additionally, we assume $\mathcal{F}$ contains a special constant $\star$, referred to as the *wild card*. The set of terms derived from $\mathcal{F}$ and $\mathcal{V}$ is denoted by $\mathcal{T}(\mathcal{F},\mathcal{V})$, whose members are constructed using the grammar $t ::= x \mid f(t_1,\dots,t_n)$, where $x \in \mathcal{V}$ and $f \in \mathcal{F}$ with arity $n \geq 0$. When $n = 0$, f is called a *constant*. Constant and function symbols, terms, and variables are denoted by lower-case letters of the first, second, third, and fourth quarter of the alphabet ($a, b, \dots$; $f, g, \dots$; $r, s, \dots$; $x, y, \dots$). The set of variables occurring in t is denoted by $var(t)$. The *size* of a term is defined inductively as: $size(x) = 1$, and $size(f(t_1,\dots,t_n)) = 1 + \sum_{i=1}^{n} size(t_i)$. The *depth* of a term t is defined inductively as $dep(x) = 1$ for variables and $dep(f(t_1,\dots,t_n)) = max\{dep(t_1),\dots,dep(t_n)\} + 1$ otherwise.

The set of *positions* of a term t, denoted by $pos(t)$, is a set of strings of positive integers, defined as $pos(f(t_1,\dots,t_n)) = \{\epsilon\} \cup \bigcup_{i=1}^{n}\{i.p \mid p \in pos(t_i)\}$, where $f \in \mathcal{F}$, $t_1,\dots,t_n$ are terms, and ϵ denotes the empty string. For example, the term at position 1.2 of $g(f(x,a))$ is a. Given a term t and $p \in pos(t)$, then $t|_p$ denotes the subterm of t at position p. Given a term t and $p, q \in pos(t)$, we write $p \sqsubseteq q$ if $q = p.q'$ and $p \sqsubset q$ if $p \sqsubseteq q$ and $p \neq q$. The *set of subterms of a term* t is defined as $sub(t) = \{t|_p \mid p \in pos(t)\}$. The *head* of a term t is defined as $head(x) = x$ and $head(f(t_1,\dots,t_n)) = f$, for $n \geq 0$.

A *substitution* is a function $\sigma : \mathcal{V} \to \mathcal{T}(\mathcal{F},\mathcal{V})$ such that $\sigma(x) \neq x$ for only finitely many variables. The set of the variables that are not mapped to themselves is called the *domain* of σ, denoted as $dom(\sigma)$. The *range* of σ, denoted $ran(\sigma)$, is the set of terms $\{\sigma(x) \mid x \in dom(\sigma)\}$. We refer to a *ground* term t if $var(t) = \emptyset$ and a ground substitution σ if for all $t \in ran(\sigma)$, t is ground. Substitutions are extended to terms in the usual manner. We use the postfix notation for substitution application to terms and write $t\sigma$ instead of $\sigma(t)$.

Substitutions can be described as sets of *bindings* of variables in their domains into terms in their ranges, e.g., we represent a substitution σ as the set $\{x \mapsto x\sigma \mid x \in dom(\sigma)\}$. Lowercase Greek letters denote substitutions except for the identity substitution that we denote by *id*. The set of variables occurring in the terms of $ran(\sigma)$ is denoted as $rvar(\sigma)$. The *composition* of substitutions σ and ρ is written $\sigma\rho$ and is defined by $(\sigma\rho)(x) = (x\sigma)\rho$ for each $x \in \mathcal{V}$. The *restriction of a substitution* σ to a set of variables V, denoted by $\sigma|_V$, is a substitution defined as $\sigma|_V(x) = \sigma(x)$ for all $x \in V$ and $\sigma|_V(x) = x$ otherwise.

In this work, we focus on equational anti-unification. Thus, we refrain from presenting syntactic variants of the concepts discussed below. For such details, we refer to the recent survey on the topic [19].

Definition 1 (Equational theory [31]**).** *An equational theory T_E is a class of algebraic structures that hold a set of equational axioms E over $\mathcal{T}(\mathcal{F},\mathcal{V})$.*

The relation $\{(s,t) \in \mathcal{T}(\mathcal{F},\mathcal{V}) \times \mathcal{T}(\mathcal{F},\mathcal{V}) \mid E \models (s,t)\}$ induced by a set of equalities E gives the set of equalities satisfied by all structures in the theory of E. We will use the notation $s \approx_E t$ for (s,t) belonging to this set. Also, we will identify T_E with the set of axioms E. Groups, monoids, and semirings are examples of equational theories.

Definition 2 (E-generalization, $\preceq_E$). *The generalization relation of the theory induced by E holds for terms $r, s \in \mathcal{T}(\mathcal{F},\mathcal{V})$, written $r \preceq_E s$, if there exists a substitution σ such that $r\sigma \approx_E$. In this case, we say that r is more general than s modulo E. If $r \preceq_E s$ and $r \preceq_E t$, we say that r is an E-generalization of s and t. The set of all E-generalizations of s and t is denoted as $\mathcal{G}_E(s,t)$. By $\prec_E$ and $\simeq_E$, we denote the strict and equivalence relations induced by $\preceq_E$, respectively.*

Example 1. Consider the equational theory $\mathtt{Abs} = \{f(\varepsilon_f, x) \approx \varepsilon_f, f(x, \varepsilon_f) \approx \varepsilon_f\}$, and the terms $s = \varepsilon_f$ and $t = f(f(b,c),a)$. Then $f(f(b,x),a)$ is an Abs-generalization of s and t. Indeed, $\sigma = \{x \mapsto \varepsilon_f\}$ and $\rho = \{x \mapsto c\}$ satisfy $f(f(b,x),a)\sigma = f(f(b,\varepsilon_f),a) \approx_{\mathtt{Abs}} \varepsilon_f$ and $f(f(b,x),a)\rho = f(f(b,c),a)$.

Definition 3 (Minimal complete set of E-generalizations). *The* minimal complete set of E-generalizations *of the terms s and t, denoted as $mcsg_E(s,t)$, is a subset of $\mathcal{G}_E(s,t)$ satisfying:*

1. *For each $r \in \mathcal{G}_E(s,t)$ there exists $r' \in mcsg_E(s,t)$ such that $r \preceq_E r'$.*
2. *If $r, r' \in mcsg_E(s,t)$ and $r \preceq_E r'$, then $r = r'$ (minimality).*

Example 2. For Example 1, the minimal complete set of Abs-generalizations is $mcsg_{\mathtt{Abs}}(\varepsilon_f, f(f(b,c),a)) = \{f(f(x,c),a), f(f(b,x),a), f(f(b,c),x)\}$.

Definition 4 (Anti-unification type). *The anti-unification type of an equational theory E may have one of the following forms:*

- *Unitary: $mcsg_E(s,t)$ exists for all $s,t \in \mathcal{T}(\mathcal{F},\mathcal{V})$ and is always singleton.*
- *Finitary: $mcsg_E(s,t)$ exists and is finite for all $s,t \in \mathcal{T}(\mathcal{F},\mathcal{V})$, and there exist $s',t' \in \mathcal{T}(\mathcal{F},\mathcal{V})$ for which $1 < |mcsg_E(s',t')| < \infty$.*
- *Infinitary: $mcsg_E(s,t)$ exists for all $s,t \in \mathcal{T}(\mathcal{F},\mathcal{V})$, and there exist $s',t' \in \mathcal{T}(\mathcal{F},\mathcal{V})$ such that $mcsg_E(s',t')$ is infinite.*

– *Nullary: for some* $s, t \in \mathcal{T}(\mathcal{F}, \mathcal{V})$, $mcsg_E(s,t)$ *does not exist.*

Example 3. From the introduction: Syntactic AU is *unitary* [27,28], AU over associative (A) and commutative (C) theories is *finitary* [1], AU over idempotent theories is *infinitary* [16], and AU with multiple unital equations is *nullary* [18].

3 Anti-unification in Absorption Theories

Absorption is one of the fundamental properties used in various algebraic structures. For example, in semirings, rings, and Boolean algebras, the additive identity is the absorption constant for multiplication. Concrete examples are the product operation and 0 in number fields and the intersection operation and $\varnothing$ in set theory. So far, investigations on anti-unification over absorption theories have only considered equational theories defining more elaborate algebraic structures (*semirings* [16]). In this work, we study pure absorption theories as part of a general study on the anti-unification of subterm-collapsing theories.

Remark 1. We only consider anti-unification of ground terms. Given that the generalization of two distinct variables is a fresh variable and the generalization of a variable with itself is the same variable, we can treat variables in the input problem as constants.

For a binary function symbol $f \in \mathcal{F}$ and a constant $\varepsilon_f \in \mathcal{F}$, the absorption property $\mathtt{Abs}(f, \varepsilon_f)$ is given by the axioms $\{f(x, \varepsilon_f) \approx \varepsilon_f, f(\varepsilon_f, x) \approx \varepsilon_f\}$. An absorption theory is induced by a finite union of absorption axiom sets $\mathtt{Abs}(f_1, \varepsilon_{f_1}) \cup \cdots \cup \mathtt{Abs}(f_n, \varepsilon_{f_n})$, $n \geq 1$, such for all $1 \leq i \neq j \leq n$, $f_i \neq f_j$ and $\varepsilon_{f_i} \neq \varepsilon_{f_j}$. Each pair f_i, ε_{f_i} is called a pair of *related absorption symbols*. When the concrete symbols are not relevant or if they are clear from the context, we refer to an absorption theory simply as Abs.

An *anti-unification triple* (AUT) is a triple of the form $s \triangleq_x t$, where $x \in \mathcal{V}$, called the *label of the AUT*, and $s, t \in \mathcal{T}(\mathcal{F}, \mathcal{V})$. Given a set A of AUTs, $labels(A) = \{x \mid s \triangleq_x t \in A\}$ and $size(A) = \sum_{s \triangleq_x t \in A} (size(s) + size(t))$. A set of AUTs is *valid* if its labels are pairwise disjoint. An AUT is referred to as *wild* if either the left or right side is the wild card.

Definition 5 (Solved AUT). *An AUT* $s \triangleq_x t$ *is* solved *over an absorption theory* Abs *if* $head(s) \neq head(t)$, $head(s)$ *and* $head(t)$ *are not related absorption symbols, and* $s \triangleq_x t$ *is not wild.*

Intuitively, *solved* means the label of the AUT is the lgg of the two terms.

3.1 Generalization Procedure for Abs Theories

We present a set of inference rules (Table 1), which, when applied exhaustively (AUNIF procedure), return a set of objects from which Abs-generalizations of the input AUTs may be derived. The inference rules of the AUNIF procedure work on *configurations*, defined below.

Definition 6 (Configuration). *A configuration is a quadruple of the form* $\langle A; S; D; \theta \rangle$, *where:*

- A *is a valid set of AUTs (*active set*);*
- S *is a valid set of solved AUTs (*store*);*
- D *is a valid set of* wild *AUTs (*delayed set*);*
- θ *is a* substitution *such that* $rvar(\theta) = labels(A) \cup labels(S) \cup labels(D)$ *(*anti-unifier*);*
- $labels(A), labels(S), labels(D)$, *and* $dom(\theta)$ *are pairwise disjoint.*

All terms occurring in a configuration are in their Abs*-normal forms: an absorption constant does not occur as the argument to its absorption symbol.*

The rules in the Table 1 will be referred to as follows: Decompose ($\stackrel{Dec}{\Longrightarrow}$), Solve ($\stackrel{Sol}{\Longrightarrow}$), Expansions for Left Absorption, ($\stackrel{ExpLA1}{\Longrightarrow}$ and $\stackrel{ExpLA2}{\Longrightarrow}$), Expansions for Right Absorption ($\stackrel{ExpRA1}{\Longrightarrow}$ and $\stackrel{ExpRA2}{\Longrightarrow}$), Expansion Absorption in Both sides ($\stackrel{ExpBA1}{\Longrightarrow}$) and ($\stackrel{ExpBA2}{\Longrightarrow}$), and Merge ($\stackrel{Mer}{\Longrightarrow}$). By $\mathcal{C} \Longrightarrow \mathcal{C}'$ we denote the application of some inference rule of Table 1 to $\mathcal{C}$ resulting in $\mathcal{C}'$. By $\mathcal{C} \Longrightarrow^* \mathcal{C}'$ we denote a finite sequence of inference rule applications starting at $\mathcal{C}$ and ending with $\mathcal{C}'$. In both cases we say $\mathcal{C}'$ is *derived* from $\mathcal{C}$. An initial configuration is a configuration of the form $\langle A; \varnothing; \varnothing; \iota \rangle$, where $\iota = \{\mathsf{f}_A(x) \mapsto x \mid x \in labels(A)\}$ with $\mathsf{f}_A : \mathcal{V} \to (\mathcal{V} \setminus labels(A))$ being a bijection. A configuration $\mathcal{C}$ is referred to as *final* if no inference rule is applicable to $\mathcal{C}$. We denote the set of final configurations finitely derived from an initial configuration $\mathcal{C}$ by $\textsc{AUnif}(\mathcal{C})$.

Lemma 1 (Preservation). *If* $\mathcal{C}$ *is a configuration and* $\mathcal{C} \Longrightarrow \mathcal{C}'$, *then* $\mathcal{C}'$ *is a configuration.*

Proof. According to the rules in Table 1, we can have the following two cases:

- A rule removes an AUT $s \triangleq_x t$ from the active set of $\mathcal{C}$. Then either $s \triangleq_x t$ occurs in the store of $\mathcal{C}'$, or the anti-unifier component of $\mathcal{C}'$ is the composition of the anti-unifier component of $\mathcal{C}$ with $\{x \mapsto r\}$, where $var(r)$ are fresh variables labeling newly added AUTs in the active and delayed sets of $\mathcal{C}'$.
- A rule removes an AUT $s \triangleq_x t$ from the store of $\mathcal{C}$. Then the store of $\mathcal{C}'$ is a subset of the store of $\mathcal{C}$ and the anti-unifier component of $\mathcal{C}'$ is the composition of the anti-unifier component of $\mathcal{C}$ with $\{x \mapsto y\}$, where y is a label of an AUT in the store of $\mathcal{C}$ such that $x \neq y$.

In both cases, the properties of a configuration are preserved. □

Remark 2. For the rest of the paper, we will only consider configurations derived from initial configurations.

Theorem 1 (Termination). *Let* $\mathcal{C}$ *be a configuration. Then* $\textsc{AUnif}(\mathcal{C})$ *is computable in a finite number of steps.*

Table 1. Inference rules for the AUNIF procedure for Abs theory.

$$(\overset{Dec}{\Longrightarrow})\quad \frac{\langle\{f(s_1,\ldots,s_n) \triangleq_x f(t_1,\ldots,t_n)\} \uplus A; S; D; \theta\rangle}{\langle\{s_1 \triangleq_{y_1} t_1,\ldots,s_n \triangleq_{y_n} t_n\} \cup A; S; D; \theta\{x \mapsto f(y_1,\ldots,y_n)\}\rangle}$$

where f is an n-ary symbol, $n \geq 0$, and $y_1,\ldots,y_n$ are fresh variables.

$$(\overset{Sol}{\Longrightarrow})\quad \frac{\langle\{s \triangleq_x t\} \uplus A; S; D; \theta\rangle}{\langle A; \{s \triangleq_x t\} \cup S; D; \theta\rangle}$$

where $head(s) \not\approx head(t)$ and they are not related absorption symbols.

$$(\overset{Mer}{\Longrightarrow})\quad \frac{\langle\varnothing; \{s \triangleq_x t, s \triangleq_y t\} \cup S; D; \theta\rangle}{\langle\varnothing; \{s \triangleq_y t\} \cup S; D; \theta\{x \mapsto y\}\rangle}$$

In the following rules, f is an absorption symbol and y_1, y_2 are fresh variables:

$$(\overset{ExpLA1}{\Longrightarrow})\quad \frac{\langle\{\varepsilon_f \triangleq_x f(t_1,t_2)\} \uplus A; S; D; \theta\rangle}{\langle\{\varepsilon_f \triangleq_{y_1} t_1\} \cup A; S; \{\star \triangleq_{y_2} t_2\} \cup D; \theta\{x \mapsto f(y_1,y_2)\}\rangle}$$

$$(\overset{ExpLA2}{\Longrightarrow})\quad \frac{\langle\{\varepsilon_f \triangleq_x f(t_1,t_2)\} \uplus A; S; D; \theta\rangle}{\langle\{\varepsilon_f \triangleq_{y_2} t_2\} \cup A; S; \{\star \triangleq_{y_1} t_1\} \cup D; \theta\{x \mapsto f(y_1,y_2)\}\rangle}$$

$$(\overset{ExpRA1}{\Longrightarrow})\quad \frac{\langle\{f(s_1,s_2) \triangleq_x \varepsilon_f\} \uplus A; S; D; \theta\rangle}{\langle\{s_1 \triangleq_{y_1} \varepsilon_f\} \cup A; S; \{s_2 \triangleq_{y_2} \star\} \cup D; \theta\{x \mapsto f(y_1,y_2)\}\rangle}$$

$$(\overset{ExpRA2}{\Longrightarrow})\quad \frac{\langle\{f(s_1,s_2) \triangleq_x \varepsilon_f\} \uplus A; S; D; \theta\rangle}{\langle\{s_2 \triangleq_{y_2} \varepsilon_f\} \cup A; S; \{s_1 \triangleq_{y_1} \star\} \cup D; \theta\{x \mapsto f(y_1,y_2)\}\rangle}$$

$$(\overset{ExpBA1}{\Longrightarrow})\quad \frac{\langle\{\varepsilon_f \triangleq_x \varepsilon_f\} \uplus A; S; D; \theta\rangle}{\langle A; S; \{\varepsilon_f \triangleq_{y_1} \star, \star \triangleq_{y_2} \varepsilon_f\} \cup D; \theta\{x \mapsto f(y_1,y_2)\}\rangle}$$

$$(\overset{ExpBA2}{\Longrightarrow})\quad \frac{\langle\{\varepsilon_f \triangleq_x \varepsilon_f\} \uplus A; S; D; \theta\rangle}{\langle A; S; \{\star \triangleq_{y_1} \varepsilon_f, \varepsilon_f \triangleq_{y_2} \star\} \cup D; \theta\{x \mapsto f(y_1,y_2))\}\rangle}$$

Proof. Let $\mathcal{C} = \langle A; S; D; \theta\rangle$. We define $size(\mathcal{C}) := (size(A), size(S))$ and compare these pairs lexicographically. This ordering is well-founded since the size of a set of AUTs is a natural number. Observe that if $\mathcal{C} \Longrightarrow \mathcal{C}'$ then $size(\mathcal{C}) > size(\mathcal{C}')$. Thus, every sequence of rule applications terminates. Furthermore, any configuration can be transformed by rules from Table 1 in finitely many ways. Thus, by König's Lemma, AUNIF($\mathcal{C}$) is finite and finitely computable. □

Let $\langle\varnothing, S, D, \theta\rangle \in$ AUNIF($\langle A; \varnothing; \varnothing; \iota\rangle$), where $\langle A; \varnothing; \varnothing; \iota\rangle$ is an initial configuration. We will show that for any AUT $s \triangleq_x t \in A$, $x\theta \in \mathcal{G}_{\mathsf{Abs}}(s,t)$. Moreover, we can construct additional generalizations by considering the AUTs in the delayed sets. We discuss this process in the next section.

3.2 Abstraction Set and Substitutions

We construct the *abstraction set* and *abstraction substitutions* from the store and delayed sets of the final configurations derived using AUNIF procedure. Let $\langle\{s \triangleq_x t\}; \varnothing; \varnothing; \iota\rangle$ be an initial configuration and $\langle\varnothing; S; D; \theta\rangle \in$ AUNIF($\langle\{s \triangleq_x t\}; \varnothing; \varnothing; \iota\rangle$). While $x\theta$ may be more specific than the syntactic generalization of s and t, any use of the absorption theory while computing $x\theta$ is completely dependent on the presence of absorption symbols and constants within s and t. Absorption theories allow the introduction of additional structure beyond what is present in the initial AUTs. For example, AUNIF computes the generalization $f(x,y)$ for the terms ε_f and $f(h(\varepsilon_f), h(h(\varepsilon_f)))$, yet Abs allows a more specific generalization, $f(x, h(x))$. In more extreme cases, infinitely many more specific generalizations may exist.

Definition 7 (Abstraction set). *Let t be a ground term in Abs-normal form, and σ be a substitution whose range is in Abs-normal form. The abstraction set of t with respect to σ is the set*

$$\uparrow(t,\sigma) := \{r \mid r\sigma \approx_{\texttt{Abs}} t,\ r \textit{ is in } \texttt{Abs}\textit{-normal form, and } var(r) \subseteq dom(\sigma)\}.$$

Observe that $t \in \uparrow(t,\sigma)$ since $var(t) = \varnothing \subseteq dom(\sigma)$ and $t\sigma = t$. To obtain an $r \in \uparrow(t,\sigma)$, we abstract some occurrences of some $x\sigma$'s in t by x, where $x \in dom(\sigma)$; this is the origin of the term "abstraction set".

Example 4. Let $t = g(\varepsilon_f, f(h(a), b))$ and $\sigma = \{x \mapsto a, y \mapsto f(h(a), b), z \mapsto b\}$. Then the abstraction set of t with respect to σ is

$$\uparrow(t,\sigma) = \{t,\ g(\varepsilon_f, y),\ g(\varepsilon_f, f(h(x), b)),\ g(\varepsilon_f, f(h(a), z)),\ g(\varepsilon_f, f(h(x), z))\}.$$

Now, consider $t = h(\varepsilon_f)$ and $\sigma = \{y \mapsto a, v \mapsto \varepsilon_f\}$. Then $\uparrow(t,\sigma)$ is infinite:

$$\begin{aligned}\uparrow(t,\sigma) = \{h(\varepsilon_f),\ h(v)\} &\cup \{h(f(v,s)) \mid s \in \mathcal{T}(\mathcal{F},\{y,v\})\} \cup \\ &\{h(f(s,v)) \mid s \in \mathcal{T}(\mathcal{F},\{y,v\})\} \cup \\ &\{h(f(f(v,s),r)) \mid s,r \in \mathcal{T}(\mathcal{F},\{y,v\})\} \cup \cdots\end{aligned}$$

Let us consider a particular configuration $\mathcal{C}$. Observe that all AUTs occurring in the delayed set of $\mathcal{C}$ are *wild*, i.e., of the form $\star \triangleq_x t$ or $t \triangleq_x \star$ where t is ground and $\star$ is a constant, indicating that the particular term occurring in the AUT at this position is irrelevant. We produce more specific generalizations by composing *abstraction substitutions* with the anti-unifier of $\mathcal{C}$. Essentially, *abstraction substitutions* are anti-unifiers of AUTs in the delayed set of $\mathcal{C}$ constructed from an interpretation of the *wild cards* as particular terms. The variables occurring in the range of an *abstraction substitution* are restricted to labels of the store of $\mathcal{C}$. In Sect. 4, we show that this restriction does not influence completeness.

Definition 8 (Abstraction substitutions). *Let $\mathcal{C} = \langle A; S; D; \theta\rangle$ be a configuration such that $D \neq \varnothing$. A substitution τ is called an* abstraction substitution *of $\mathcal{C}$ if $dom(\tau) = labels(D)$, and for each $y \in dom(\tau)$ we have $y\tau \in \uparrow_y(D,S)$, where*

$$\uparrow_y(D,S) := \begin{cases} \uparrow(t, \{x \mapsto r \mid l \triangleq_x r \in S, \textit{ for some } l\}) & \textit{if } \star \triangleq_y t \in D, \\ \uparrow(s, \{x \mapsto l \mid l \triangleq_x r \in S, \textit{ for some } r\}) & \textit{if } s \triangleq_y \star \in D. \end{cases}$$

The set of abstraction substitutions of $\mathcal{C}$ is denoted by $\Psi(D,S)$.

Corollary 1. *Let $\langle A; S; D; \theta\rangle$ be a configuration such that $D \neq \varnothing$. Then for any $y \in labels(D)$ and $\tau \in \Psi(D,S)$, $var(y\tau) \subseteq labels(S)$.*

The following example illustrates the computation of final configurations using AUNIF and the construction of the abstraction sets.

Example 5. Applying AUNIF to $g(\varepsilon_f, f(a, h(\varepsilon_f))) \triangleq_x g(f(h(\varepsilon_f), a), \varepsilon_f)$, we get the following four derivations that lead to four final configurations:

Derivation 1 :

$$\langle \{g(\varepsilon_f, f(a, h(\varepsilon_f))) \triangleq_x g(f(h(\varepsilon_f), a), \varepsilon_f)\}; \varnothing; \varnothing; \iota\rangle \overset{Dec}{\Longrightarrow}$$
$$\langle \{\varepsilon_f \triangleq_{w_1} f(h(\varepsilon_f), a), f(a, h(\varepsilon_f)) \triangleq_{w_2} \varepsilon_f\}; \varnothing; \varnothing; \{x \mapsto g(w_1, w_2), \ldots\}\rangle \overset{ExpLA1}{\Longrightarrow}$$
$$\langle \{\varepsilon_f \triangleq_{u_1} h(\varepsilon_f), f(a, h(\varepsilon_f)) \triangleq_{w_2} \varepsilon_f\}; \varnothing; \{\star \triangleq_{v_1} a\}; \{x \mapsto g(f(u_1, v_1), w_2), \ldots\}\rangle \overset{ExpRA1}{\Longrightarrow}$$
$$\langle \{\varepsilon_f \triangleq_{u_1} h(\varepsilon_f), a \triangleq_{u_2} \varepsilon_f\}; \varnothing; \{\star \triangleq_{v_1} a, h(\varepsilon_f) \triangleq_{v_2} \star\};$$
$$\{x \mapsto g(f(u_1, v_1), f(u_2, v_2)), \ldots\}\rangle \overset{Sol\times 2}{\Longrightarrow}$$
$$\langle \varnothing; \{\varepsilon_f \triangleq_{u_1} h(\varepsilon_f), a \triangleq_{u_2} \varepsilon_f\}; \{\star \triangleq_{v_1} a, h(\varepsilon_f) \triangleq_{v_2} \star\};$$
$$\{x \mapsto g(f(u_1, v_1), f(u_2, v_2)), \ldots\}\rangle.$$

Then $D = \{\star \triangleq_{v_1} a, h(\varepsilon_f) \triangleq_{v_2} \star\}$ and $S = \{\varepsilon_f \triangleq_{u_1} h(\varepsilon_f), a \triangleq_{u_2} \varepsilon_f\}$. For the variable v_1, $\uparrow_{v_1}(D, S) = \uparrow(a, \{u_1 \mapsto h(\varepsilon_f), u_2 \mapsto \varepsilon_f\}) = \{a\}$. For the variable v_2, $\uparrow_{v_2}(D, S) = \uparrow(h(\varepsilon_f), \{u_1 \mapsto \varepsilon_f, u_2 \mapsto a\})$ is an infinite set

$$\begin{aligned}\{h(\varepsilon_f),\ h(u_1)\} &\cup \{h(f(u_1, s)) \mid s \in \mathcal{T}(\mathcal{F}, \{u_1, u_2\})\}\\ &\cup \{h(f(s, u_1)) \mid s \in \mathcal{T}(\mathcal{F}, \{u_1, u_2\})\}\\ &\cup \{h(f(f(u_1, s), t)) \mid s, t \in \mathcal{T}(\mathcal{F}, \{u_1, u_2\})\} \cup \cdots\end{aligned}$$

The set of abstraction substitutions $\Psi(D, S)$ is an infinite set including $\{\{v_1 \mapsto a, v_2 \mapsto h(\varepsilon_f)\}, \{v_1 \mapsto a, v_2 \mapsto h(u_1)\}, \{v_1 \mapsto a, v_2 \mapsto h(f(u_1, a))\}, \ldots\}$. From the final configuration, we get an infinite set Abs-generalizations of the initial AUT, including, e.g., $g(f(u_1, a), f(u_2, h(\varepsilon_f)))$, $g(f(u_1, a), f(u_2, h(u_1)))$, $g(f(u_1, a), f(u_2, h(f(u_1, a))))$, etc.

Derivation 2 :

$$\langle \{g(\varepsilon_f, f(a, h(\varepsilon_f))) \triangleq_x g(f(h(\varepsilon_f), a), \varepsilon_f)\}; \varnothing; \varnothing; \iota\rangle \overset{Dec}{\Longrightarrow}$$
$$\langle \{\varepsilon_f \triangleq_{w_1} f(h(\varepsilon_f), a), f(a, h(\varepsilon_f)) \triangleq_{w_2} \varepsilon_f\}; \varnothing; \varnothing; \{x \mapsto g(w_1, w_2), \ldots\}\rangle \overset{ExpLA1}{\Longrightarrow}$$
$$\langle \{\varepsilon_f \triangleq_{u_1} h(\varepsilon_f), f(a, h(\varepsilon_f)) \triangleq_{w_2} \varepsilon_f\}; \varnothing; \{\star \triangleq_{v_1} a\}; \{x \mapsto g(f(u_1, v_1), w_2), \ldots\}\rangle \overset{ExpRA2}{\Longrightarrow}$$
$$\langle \{\varepsilon_f \triangleq_{u_1} h(\varepsilon_f), h(\varepsilon_f) \triangleq_{v_2} \varepsilon_f\}; \varnothing; \{\star \triangleq_{v_1} a, a \triangleq_{u_2} \star\};$$
$$\{x \mapsto g(f(u_1, v_1), f(u_2, v_2)), \ldots\}\rangle \overset{Sol\times 2}{\Longrightarrow}$$
$$\langle \varnothing; \{\varepsilon_f \triangleq_{u_1} h(\varepsilon_f), h(\varepsilon_f) \triangleq_{v_2} \varepsilon_f\}; \{\star \triangleq_{v_1} a, a \triangleq_{u_2} \star\};$$
$$\{x \mapsto g(f(u_1, v_1), f(u_2, v_2)), \ldots\}\rangle.$$

Then $D = \{\star \triangleq_{v_1} a, a \triangleq_{u_2} \star\}$ and $S = \{\varepsilon_f \triangleq_{u_1} h(\varepsilon_f), h(\varepsilon_f) \triangleq_{v_2} \varepsilon_f\}$. Thus, $\uparrow_{v_1}(D, S) = \uparrow(a, \{u_1 \mapsto h(\varepsilon_f), v_2 \mapsto \varepsilon_f\}) = \{a\}$, and $\uparrow_{u_2}(D, S) = \uparrow(a, \{u_1 \mapsto \varepsilon_f, v_2 \mapsto h(\varepsilon_f)\}) = \{a\}$. This leads to the generalization $g(f(u_1, a), f(a, v_2))$.

Derivation 3 : $\langle\{g(\varepsilon_f, f(a, h(\varepsilon_f))) \triangleq_x g(f(h(\varepsilon_f), a), \varepsilon_f)\}; \varnothing; \varnothing; \iota\rangle \overset{Dec}{\Longrightarrow}$

$\langle\{\varepsilon_f \triangleq_{w_1} f(h(\varepsilon_f), a), f(a, h(\varepsilon_f)) \triangleq_{w_2} \varepsilon_f\}; \varnothing; \varnothing; \{x \mapsto g(w_1, w_2), \dots\}\rangle \overset{ExpLA2}{\Longrightarrow}$

$\langle\{\varepsilon_f \triangleq_{v_1} a, f(a, h(\varepsilon_f)) \triangleq_{w_2} \varepsilon_f\}; \varnothing; \{\star \triangleq_{u_1} h(\varepsilon_f)\};$

$\{x \mapsto g(f(u_1, v_1), w_2), \dots\}\rangle \overset{ExpRA1}{\Longrightarrow}$

$\langle\{\varepsilon_f \triangleq_{v_1} a, a \triangleq_{u_2} \varepsilon_f\}; \varnothing; \{\star \triangleq_{u_1} h(\varepsilon_f), h(\varepsilon_f) \triangleq_{v_2} \star\};$

$\{x \mapsto g(f(u_1, v_1), f(u_2, v_2)), \dots\}\rangle \overset{Sol\times 2}{\Longrightarrow}$

$\langle\varnothing; \{\varepsilon_f \triangleq_{v_1} a, a \triangleq_{u_2} \varepsilon_f\}; \{\star \triangleq_{u_1} h(\varepsilon_f), h(\varepsilon_f) \triangleq_{v_2} \star\};$

$\{x \mapsto g(f(u_1, v_1), f(u_2, v_2)), \dots\}\rangle.$

Then $D = \{\star \triangleq_{u_1} h(\varepsilon_f), h(\varepsilon_f) \triangleq_{v_2} \star\}$ and $S = \{\varepsilon_f \triangleq_{v_1} a, a \triangleq_{u_2} \varepsilon_f\}$. Thus, we get

$$\begin{aligned}
\uparrow_{u_1}(D, S) &= \uparrow(h(\varepsilon_f), \{v_1 \mapsto a,\ u_2 \mapsto \varepsilon_f\}) = \\
&\{h(\varepsilon_f),\ h(u_2)\} \cup \{h(f(u_2, s)) \mid s \in \mathcal{T}(\mathcal{F}, \{v_1, u_2\})\} \cup \cdots, \text{ and} \\
\uparrow_{v_2}(D, S) &= \uparrow(h(\varepsilon_f), \{v_1 \mapsto \varepsilon_f,\ u_2 \mapsto a\}) = \\
&\{h(\varepsilon_f),\ h(v_1)\} \cup \{h(f(v_1, s)) \mid s \in \mathcal{T}(\mathcal{F}, \{v_1, u_2\})\} \cup \cdots
\end{aligned}$$

Then $\Psi(D, S)$ is infinite, it contains, e.g., the substitutions $\{u_1 \mapsto h(\varepsilon_f), v_2 \mapsto h(\varepsilon_f)\}$, $\{u_1 \mapsto h(\varepsilon_f), v_2 \mapsto h(v_1)\}$, $\{u_1 \mapsto h(u_2), v_2 \mapsto h(\varepsilon_f)\}$, etc. This leads to infinitely many generalizations of the initial AUT, including, e.g., $g(f(h(\varepsilon_f), v_1), f(u_2, h(\varepsilon_f)))$, $g(f(h(\varepsilon_f), v_1), f(u_2, h(v_1)))$, etc.

Derivation 4 : $\langle\{g(\varepsilon_f, f(a, h(\varepsilon_f))) \triangleq_x g(f(h(\varepsilon_f), a), \varepsilon_f)\}; \varnothing; \varnothing; \iota\rangle \overset{Dec}{\Longrightarrow}$

$\langle\{\varepsilon_f \triangleq_{w_1} f(h(\varepsilon_f), a), f(a, h(\varepsilon_f)) \triangleq_{w_2} \varepsilon_f\}; \varnothing; \varnothing; \{x \mapsto g(w_1, w_2)\}\rangle \overset{ExpLA2}{\Longrightarrow}$

$\langle\{\varepsilon_f \triangleq_{v_1} a, f(a, h(\varepsilon_f)) \triangleq_{w_2} \varepsilon_f\}; \varnothing; \{\star \triangleq_{u_1} h(\varepsilon_f)\}; \{x \mapsto g(f(u_1, v_1), w_2), \dots\}\rangle \overset{ExpRA2}{\Longrightarrow}$

$\langle\{\varepsilon_f \triangleq_{v_1} a, h(\varepsilon_f) \triangleq_{v_2} \varepsilon_f\}; \varnothing; \{\star \triangleq_{u_1} h(\varepsilon_f), a \triangleq_{u_2} \star\};$

$\{x \mapsto g(f(u_1, v_1), f(u_2, v_2)), \dots\}\rangle \overset{Sol\times 2}{\Longrightarrow}$

$\langle\varnothing; \{\varepsilon_f \triangleq_{v_1} a, h(\varepsilon_f) \triangleq_{v_2} \varepsilon_f\}; \{\star \triangleq_{u_1} h(\varepsilon_f), a \triangleq_{u_2} \star\};$

$\{x \mapsto g(f(u_1, v_1), f(u_2, v_2)), \dots\}\rangle.$

Then $D = \{\star \triangleq_{u_1} h(\varepsilon_f), a \triangleq_{u_2} \star\}$ and $S = \{\varepsilon_f \triangleq_{v_1} a, h(\varepsilon_f) \triangleq_{v_2} \varepsilon_f\}$. This leads to infinitely many generalizations f the initial AUT, including, e.g., $g(f(h(\varepsilon_f), v_1), f(a, v_2))$, $g(f(h(v_2), v_1), f(a, v_2))$, $g(f(h(f(v_2, a)), v_1), f(a, v_2))$, etc., since

$$\begin{aligned}
\uparrow_{u_1}(D, S) &= \uparrow(h(\varepsilon_f), \{v_1 \mapsto a, v_2 \mapsto \varepsilon_f\}) = \\
&\{h(\varepsilon_f), h(v_2)\} \cup \{h(f(v_2, s)) \mid s \in \mathcal{T}(\mathcal{F}, \{v_1, v_2\})\} \cup \cdots \text{ and} \\
\uparrow_{u_2}(D, S) &= \uparrow(a, \{v_1 \mapsto \varepsilon_f, v_2 \mapsto h(\varepsilon_f)\}) = \{a\}.
\end{aligned}$$

Example 6. To generalize $g(\varepsilon_f, \varepsilon_f, a)$ and $g(\varepsilon_f, b, \varepsilon_f)$, the AUNIF procedure generates two derivations, which differ from each other only in the last step:

$$\textbf{Derivation 1}: \quad \langle \{g(\varepsilon_f, \varepsilon_f, a) \triangleq_x g(\varepsilon_f, b, \varepsilon_f)\}; \varnothing; \varnothing; \iota \rangle \overset{Dec}{\Longrightarrow}$$
$$\langle \{\varepsilon_f \triangleq_{y_1} \varepsilon_f, \varepsilon_f \triangleq_{y_2} b, a \triangleq_{y_3} \varepsilon_f\}; \varnothing; \varnothing; \{x \mapsto g(y_1, y_2, y_3), \ldots\} \rangle \overset{Sol\times 2}{\Longrightarrow}$$
$$\langle \{\varepsilon_f \triangleq_{y_1} \varepsilon_f\}; \{\varepsilon_f \triangleq_{y_2} b, a \triangleq_{y_3} \varepsilon_f\}; \varnothing; \{x \mapsto g(y_1, y_2, y_3), \ldots\} \rangle \overset{ExpBA1}{\Longrightarrow}$$
$$\langle \varnothing; \{\varepsilon_f \triangleq_{y_2} b, a \triangleq_{y_3} \varepsilon_f\}; \{\star \triangleq_{u_1} \varepsilon_f, \varepsilon_f \triangleq_{u_2} \star\}; \{x \mapsto g(f(u_1, u_2), y_2, y_3), \ldots\} \rangle.$$

Here, for the store S and the delayed set D in the last configuration, we get

$$\begin{aligned}
\uparrow_{u_1}(D, S) &= \uparrow(\varepsilon_f, \{y_2 \mapsto b, y_3 \mapsto \varepsilon_f\}) = \\
&\{\varepsilon_f, y_3\} \cup \{f(y_3, s) \mid s \in \mathcal{T}(\mathcal{F}, \{y_2, y_3\})\} \cup \{f(s, y_3) \mid s \in \mathcal{T}(\mathcal{F}, \{y_2, y_3\}) \cup \\
&\{f(f(y_3, s), t) \mid s, t \in \mathcal{T}(\mathcal{F}, \{y_2, y_3\})\} \cup \cdots \\
\uparrow_{u_2}(D, S) &= \uparrow(\varepsilon_f, \{y_2 \mapsto \varepsilon_f, y_3 \mapsto a\}) = \\
&\{\varepsilon_f, y_2\} \cup \{f(y_2, s) \mid s \in \mathcal{T}(\mathcal{F}, \{y_2, y_3\})\} \cup \{f(s, y_2) \mid s \in \mathcal{T}(\mathcal{F}, \{y_2, y_3\}) \cup \\
&\{f(f(y_2, s), t) \mid s, t \in \mathcal{T}(\mathcal{F}, \{y_2, y_3\})\} \cup \cdots
\end{aligned}$$

From these, we get an infinite set of generalizations that includes, among others, e.g., $g(\varepsilon_f, y_2, y_3)$, $g(f(y_3, y_2), y_2, y_3)$, $g(f(f(y_3, y_3), y_2), y_2, y_3)$, etc.

$$\textbf{Derivation 2}: \quad \langle \{g(\varepsilon_f, \varepsilon_f, a) \triangleq_x g(\varepsilon_f, b, \varepsilon_f)\}; \varnothing; \varnothing; \iota \rangle \overset{Dec}{\Longrightarrow}$$
$$\langle \{\varepsilon_f \triangleq_{y_1} \varepsilon_f, \varepsilon_f \triangleq_{y_2} b, a \triangleq_{y_3} \varepsilon_f\}; \varnothing; \varnothing; \{x \mapsto g(y_1, y_2, y_3)\} \rangle \overset{Sol\times 2}{\Longrightarrow}$$
$$\langle \{\varepsilon_f \triangleq_{y_1} \varepsilon_f\}; \{\varepsilon_f \triangleq_{y_2} b, a \triangleq_{y_3} \varepsilon_f\}; \varnothing; \{x \mapsto g(y_1, y_2, y_3)\} \rangle \overset{ExpBA2}{\Longrightarrow}$$
$$\langle \varnothing; \{\varepsilon_f \triangleq_{y_2} b, a \triangleq_{y_3} \varepsilon_f\}; \{\varepsilon_f \triangleq_{v_1} \star, \star \triangleq_{v_2} \varepsilon_f\}; \{x \mapsto g(f(v_1, v_2), y_2, y_3), \ldots\} \rangle.$$

Again, taking S and D from the last configuration, we get

$$\begin{aligned}
\uparrow_{v_1}(D, S) &= \uparrow(\varepsilon_f, \{y_2 \mapsto \varepsilon_f, y_3 \mapsto a\}) = \\
&\{\varepsilon_f, y_2\} \cup \{f(y_2, s) \mid s \in \mathcal{T}(\mathcal{F}, \{y_2, y_3\})\} \cup \{f(s, y_2) \mid s \in \mathcal{T}(\mathcal{F}, \{y_2, y_3\}) \cup \\
&\{f(f(y_2, s), t) \mid s, t \in \mathcal{T}(\mathcal{F}, \{y_2, y_3\})\} \cup \cdots \\
\uparrow_{v_2}(D, S) &= \uparrow(\varepsilon_f, \{y_2 \mapsto b, y_3 \mapsto \varepsilon_f\}) \\
&\{\varepsilon_f, y_3\} \cup \{f(y_3, s) \mid s \in \mathcal{T}(\mathcal{F}, \{y_2, y_3\})\} \cup \{f(s, y_3) \mid s \in \mathcal{T}(\mathcal{F}, \{y_2, y_3\}) \cup \\
&\{f(f(y_3, s), t) \mid s, t \in \mathcal{T}(\mathcal{F}, \{y_2, y_3\})\} \cup \cdots
\end{aligned}$$

From these, we get an infinite set of generalizations that includes, among others, e.g., $g(\varepsilon_f, y_2, y_3)$, $g(f(y_2, y_3), y_2, y_3)$, $g(f(f(y_2, y_2), y_3), y_2, y_3)$, etc.

4 Soundness and Completeness

Preserving the stated properties of configurations (Definition 6) is essential to both the soundness and completeness proofs as these properties enforce consistency with respect to the use of the labels.

Theorem 2 (Soundness). *Consider* $\langle A_0; S_0; D_0; \theta_0\rangle \Longrightarrow^* \langle \varnothing; S_n; D_n; \theta_n\rangle$*, a derivation to a final configuration. Then for all* $s \triangleq_x t \in A_0 \cup S_0$*,* $x\theta_n \in \mathcal{G}_{\mathsf{Abs}}(s,t)$*.*

Proof. We proceed by induction over the derivation length.
Basecase. If the derivation has length 0, then it starts with a final configuration implying that $A_0 = \varnothing$ and for all $s \triangleq_x t \in S_0$, $x\theta_0 = x \in \mathcal{G}_{\mathsf{Abs}}(s,t)$.
Stepcase. Now consider a derivation having the following form:

$$\langle A_0; S_0; D_0; \theta_0\rangle \Longrightarrow \langle A_1; S_1; D_1; \theta_1\rangle \Longrightarrow^n \langle \varnothing; S_{n+1}; D_{n+1}; \theta_{n+1}\rangle \quad (1)$$

We assume for the induction hypothesis (IH) that for derivations of the form

$$\langle A_1; S_1; D_1; \theta_1\rangle \Longrightarrow^n \langle \varnothing; S_{n+1}; D_{n+1}; \theta_{n+1}\rangle,$$

the theorem holds and show that the theorem holds for derivations of the form presented in Derivation 1. We continue the proof considering the various options for the transition from $\langle A_0; S_0; D_0; \theta_0\rangle$ to $\langle A_1; S_1; D_1; \theta_1\rangle$.

1. **(Dec)**. Assume that the derivation is of the form:

$$\langle\{f(s_1,\dots,s_m) \triangleq_y f(t_1,\dots,t_m)\} \uplus A'; S_0; D_0; \theta_0\rangle \overset{Dec}{\Longrightarrow}$$
$$\langle\{s_1 \triangleq_{x_1} t_1,\dots,s_m \triangleq_{x_m} t_m\} \cup A'; S_1; D_1; \theta_1\rangle \Longrightarrow^n \langle \varnothing; S_{n+1}; D_{n+1}; \theta_{n+1}\rangle$$

where $\theta_1 = \theta_0\{y \mapsto f(x_1,\dots,x_m)\}$. By the IH, we know that for all $1 \le i \le m$, $x_i\theta_{n+1} \in \mathcal{G}_{\mathsf{Abs}}(s_i,t_i)$ implying that

$$f(x_1,\dots,x_m)\theta_{n+1} \in \mathcal{G}_{\mathsf{Abs}}(f(s_1,\dots,s_m), f(t_1,\dots,t_m)).$$

2. **(Sol)**. Assume that the derivation is of the form:

$$\langle\{s \triangleq_y t\} \uplus A'; S_0; D_0; \theta_0\rangle \overset{Sol}{\Longrightarrow} \langle A'; S_1; D_0; \theta_0\rangle \Longrightarrow^n \langle \varnothing; S_{n+1}; D_{n+1}; \theta_{n+1}\rangle,$$

where $S_1 = \{s \triangleq_y t\} \cup S_0$. By IH, θ_{n+1} generalizes all the AUTs with labels in S_1. Thus, $y\theta_{n+1} \in \mathcal{G}_{\mathsf{Abs}}(s,t)$.
3. **(ExpLA1)**. Assume that the derivation is of the form:

$$\langle\{\varepsilon_f \triangleq_y f(s,t)\} \uplus A'; S_0; D_0; \theta_0\rangle \overset{ExpLA1}{\Longrightarrow}$$
$$\langle\{\varepsilon_f \triangleq_{x_1} s\} \cup A'; S_1; D_1; \theta_1\rangle \Longrightarrow^n \langle \varnothing; S_{n+1}; D_{n+1}; \theta_{n+1}\rangle$$

where $D_1 = \{\star \triangleq_{x_2} t\} \cup D_0$ and $\theta_1 = \theta_0\{y \mapsto f(x_1,x_2)\}$. By the IH, all the AUTs in $\{\varepsilon_f \triangleq_{x_1} s\} \cup A'$ are generalized by the substitution θ_{n+1}, thus, $x_1\theta_{n+1} \in \mathcal{G}_{\mathsf{Abs}}(\varepsilon_f, s)$. Furthermore, since $x_2 \in$ *labels*(D) then $x_2\theta_{n+1} = x_2$ and $x_2 \preceq_{\mathsf{Abs}} t$. We can build the generalization $y\theta_{n+1} = f(x_1\theta_{n+1}, x_2\theta_{n+1})$. Observe that $f(x_1\theta_{n+1}, x_2\theta_{n+1}) = f(x_1\theta_{n+1}, x_2) \in \mathcal{G}_{\mathsf{Abs}}(f(\varepsilon_f, t), f(s,t))$ and since $f(\varepsilon_f, t) \approx_{\mathsf{Abs}} \varepsilon_f$, we get that $y\theta_{n+1}$ belongs to $\mathcal{G}_{\mathsf{Abs}}(\varepsilon_f, f(s,t))$.
4. The analysis of other one-side expansion rules is analogous to the previous one.

5. **(ExpBA1)**. Assume that the derivation is of the form:

$$\langle\{\varepsilon_f \triangleq_y \varepsilon_f\} \cup A'; S_0; D_0; \theta_0\rangle \overset{ExpBA1}{\Longrightarrow}$$
$$\langle A'; S_1; D_1; \theta_1\rangle \Longrightarrow^n \langle\varnothing; S_{n+1}; D_{n+1}; \theta_{n+1}\rangle$$

where $D_1 = \{\varepsilon_f \triangleq_{x_1} \star, \star \triangleq_{x_2} \varepsilon_f\} \cup D_0$ and $\theta_1 = \theta_0\{y \mapsto f(x_1, x_2)\}$. Notice, $x_i\theta_{n+1} = x_i$ and $x_i \preceq_{\mathsf{Abs}} \varepsilon_f$, for $i \in \{1,2\}$. This implies that $y\theta_{n+1} = f(x_1\theta_{n+1}, x_2\theta_{n+1}) = f(x_1, x_2) \in \mathcal{G}_{\mathsf{Abs}}(\varepsilon_f, \varepsilon_f)$. The case **(ExpBA2)** is analogous.
6. **(Mer)** Assume that the derivation is of the form:

$$\langle\varnothing; \{s \triangleq_y t, s \triangleq_z t\} \cup S'; D_0; \theta_0\rangle \overset{Mer}{\Longrightarrow}$$
$$\langle\varnothing; \{s \triangleq_z t\} \cup S'; D_1; \theta_1\rangle \Longrightarrow^n \langle\varnothing; S_{n+1}; D_{n+1}; \theta_{n+1}\rangle.$$

Notice that $\theta_1 = \theta_0\{y \mapsto z\}$, where z is the label of the AUT $\{s \triangleq_z t\} \in S_0$. By IH, $z\theta_{n+1} \in \mathcal{G}_{\mathsf{Abs}}(s,t)$ implying that $y\theta_{n+1} = y\{y \mapsto z\}\theta_{n+1} \in \mathcal{G}_{\mathsf{Abs}}(s,t)$. □

While the soundness theorem covers the construction of generalizations of AUTs present in a given configuration, it does not consider the abstraction set or the construction of more specific generalizations when generalizing over an absorption theory. The abstraction set allows us to consider generalizations between a given term and an arbitrary term.

Lemma 2. *Let $\langle A_0; S_0; D_0; \theta_0\rangle \Longrightarrow^* \langle\varnothing; S_n; D_n; \theta_n\rangle$ be a derivation. Then for all $\star \triangleq_u t \in D_n$ (resp. for all $s \triangleq_u \star \in D_n$) and $\tau \in \Psi(D_n, S_n)$, there exists a term r such that $u\tau \in \mathcal{G}_{\mathsf{Abs}}(r,t)$ (resp. $u\tau \in \mathcal{G}_{\mathsf{Abs}}(r,s)$).*

Proof. Let η be a ground substitution with $dom(\eta) = var(u\tau)$. Then $r = u\tau\eta$. □

Intuitively, Lemma 2 formalizes the following observation: if $\star \triangleq_u t \in D_n$, then $u\tau \in \uparrow_u(D_n, S_n)$ implies $u\tau \in \uparrow(t, \{x \mapsto t' \mid s \triangleq_x t' \in S_n \text{ for some } s\})$. From this, we can deduce that $u\tau \preceq_{\mathsf{Abs}} t$. Thus, for every AUT in the set D_n, the wild card can be interpreted as r and $u\tau \preceq_{\mathsf{Abs}} r$. We can now prove the following:

Theorem 3. *Let $\langle A_0; S_0; D_0; \theta_0\rangle \Longrightarrow^* \langle\varnothing; S_n; D_n; \theta_n\rangle$ be a derivation to a final configuration and $s \triangleq_x t \in A_0 \cup S_0$. Then for all $\tau \in \Psi(D_n, S_n)$, $x\theta_n\tau \in \mathcal{G}_{\mathsf{Abs}}(s,t)$.*

Proof. From Theorem 2, $x\theta_n \in \mathcal{G}_{\mathsf{Abs}}(s,t)$. Furthermore, every $u \in labels(D_n)$ is unique, only occurs once in $x\theta_n$, and $u\theta_n\tau = u\tau$. Considering these facts together with Lemma 2 and u being an Abs-generalization of the respective subterms in s and t, we deduce that $x\theta_n\tau \in \mathcal{G}_{\mathsf{Abs}}(s,t)$. □

Theorem 4 (Completeness). *Let $r \in \mathcal{G}_{\mathsf{Abs}}(t_1, t_2)$. Then for all configurations $\langle A; S; D; \theta\rangle$ such that $t_1 \triangleq_x t_2 \in A$ there exist a final configuration $\langle\varnothing; S'; D'; \theta'\rangle \in$ AUNIF$(\langle A; S; D; \theta\rangle)$ and $\tau \in \Psi(D', S')$ such that $r \preceq_{\mathsf{Abs}} x\theta'\tau$.*

Proof. The proof is by structural induction over r.

Basecase

1. Let r be a variable. Then, we must consider the following three cases:
   (a) If $head(t_1) = head(t_2)$, then from $\langle A; S; D; \theta\rangle$ such that $t_1 \triangleq_x t_2 \in A$, we can reach $\langle A'; S; D; \theta'\rangle$ by decomposition so that $head(x\theta') = head(t_1) = head(t_2)$. Thus, for any final configuration $\langle \emptyset; S''; D''; \theta''\rangle \in \text{AUNIF}(\langle A'; S; D; \theta'\rangle)$, $r \preceq_{\mathtt{Abs}} x\theta''$ as θ'' can only be more specific than θ'.
   (b) If $head(t_1) = head(t_2)$ are absorption constants, w.l.o.g, $t_1 = \varepsilon_f$, then from $\langle A; S; D; \theta\rangle$ such that $t_1 \triangleq_x t_2 \in A$, we can reach $\langle A'; S; D; \theta'\rangle$ by (ExpBA1) so that $head(x\theta') = f$. Thus, for any final configuration $\langle \emptyset; S''; D''; \theta''\rangle \in \text{AUNIF}(\langle A'; S; D; \theta'\rangle)$, $r \preceq_{\mathtt{Abs}} x\theta''$ as θ'' can only be more specific than θ'.
   (c) W.l.o.g, if $t_1 = \varepsilon_f$ and $t_2 = f(s_1, s_2)$, then from $\langle A; S; D; \theta\rangle$ such that $t_1 \triangleq_x t_2 \in A$, we can reach $\langle A'; S'; D'; \theta'\rangle$ using *ExpLA1* such that $head(x\theta') = head(t_2)$. Thus, for any final configuration $\langle \emptyset; S''; D''; \theta''\rangle \in \text{AUNIF}(\langle A'; S'; D'; \theta'\rangle)$, $r \preceq_{\mathtt{Abs}} x\theta''$ as θ'' is more specific than θ'.
   (d) Otherwise, if $head(t_1) \neq head(t_2)$, then from $\langle A; S; D; \theta\rangle$ with $t_1 \triangleq_x t_2 \in A$, we reach $\langle A'; S'; D; \theta\rangle$ using *Solve* where $t_1 \triangleq_x t_2 \in S$. Thus, for any final configuration $\langle \emptyset; S''; D''; \theta''\rangle \in \text{AUNIF}(\langle A'; S'; D; \theta\rangle)$, we get $r \approx_{\mathtt{Abs}} x\theta''$.

   In all four cases $r \preceq_{\mathtt{Abs}} x\theta''$ and by Theorem 3 we get $r \preceq_{\mathtt{Abs}} x\theta'\tau$.
2. Let r be a constant. Then $t_1 = t_2 = r$ and from a configuration $\langle A; S; D; \theta\rangle$ where $t_1 \triangleq_x t_2 \in A$, we can reach a configuration $\langle A'; S; D; \theta'\rangle$ using the decomposition rule such that $x\theta' = t_1 = t_2 = r$. Thus, for any final configuration $\langle \emptyset; S''; D''; \theta''\rangle \in \text{AUNIF}(\langle A'; S'; D'; \theta'\rangle)$, $r \preceq_{\mathtt{Abs}} x\theta''\tau$ trivially follows.

Stepcase

1. $r = g(r_1, \ldots, r_n)$, $t_1 = g(t'_1, \ldots, t'_n)$, and $t_2 = g(t''_1, \ldots, t''_n)$; This implies that r_i is a generalization of $t'_i \triangleq_{y_i} t''_i$ for $1 \leq i \leq n$. From $\langle A; S; D; \theta\rangle$ we can reach $\langle A'; S'; D'; \theta'\rangle$, using the decomposition rule, such that $t'_i \triangleq_{y_i} t''_i \in A'$. Note that there may exist $1 \leq i < j \leq n$ such that $var(r_i) \cap var(r_j) \neq \emptyset$. Let $R \subseteq var(r)$ such that for $z \in R$ there exist $1 \leq i < j \leq n$ such that $z \in var(r_i) \cap var(r_j)$. For any $z \in R$, there are two cases to consider:
   (i) There does not exist a position $p \in pos(t_1) \cap pos(t_2)$ such that $s^* \triangleq_z t^*$ where $s^* = t_1|_p$ and $t^* = t_2|_p$. In other words, z generalizes terms which are absorbed during Abs-normalization of $r\sigma$ and $r\rho$, where $r\sigma \approx_{\mathtt{Abs}} t_1$ and $r\rho \approx_{\mathtt{Abs}} t_2$; this implies that replacing occurrences of z by ε_f (for the appropriate absorption symbol f) within r results in a more specific generalization r'. For the remainder of this proof, we can consider r to be the generalization resulting from replacing all such variables in R by the appropriate absorption constant ε_f.
   (ii) There exists a position $p \in pos(t_1) \cap pos(t_2)$ such that $s^* \triangleq_z t^*$ where $s^* = t_1|_p$ and $t^* = t_2|_p$. Notice that z is structurally smaller than r and thus, by the IH, there exists a final configuration $\langle \emptyset; S^*; D^*; \theta^*\rangle \in \text{AUNIF}(\langle \{s^* \triangleq_z t^*\}; \emptyset; \emptyset; \iota\rangle)$ and $\tau^* \in \Psi(D^*, S^*)$ such that $z \leq x'\theta^*\tau^*$. We will use $\theta^*\tau^*$ to guarantee variables occurring in multiple r_i, for $0 \leq i \leq n$, are replaced by the same term in the generalizations resulting from the IH.

By the induction hypothesis, there exists a final configuration $\langle\varnothing; S''; D''; \theta''\rangle \in \text{AUNIF}(\langle A'; S'; D'; \theta'\rangle)$ and $\tau_i \in \Psi(D'', S'')$ such that $r_i \preceq_{\mathsf{Abs}} y_i\theta''\tau_i$ where $1 \le i \le n$. Note, we can choose the same configuration $\langle\varnothing; S''; D''; \theta''\rangle$ for all AUTs $t'_i \triangleq_{y_i} t''_i$ as the procedure produces all combinations of solutions to the subproblems. Furthermore, we can choose $\langle\varnothing; S''; D''; \theta''\rangle$ such that $S^* \subseteq S''$ and $D^* \subseteq D''$ modulo label renaming as s^* and t^* are subterms of t_1 and t_2, respectively, modulo absorption symbol introduction. Now, we define γ_i as the substitution such that $r_i\gamma_i \approx_{\mathsf{Abs}} y_i\theta''\tau_i$. By the above construction, we can safely assume for all $z \in var(r_1) \cap var(r_2)$ such that z has not been replaced by an absorption constant, that $z\gamma_i \approx_{\mathsf{Abs}} z\theta^*\tau^*$ as there exist AUTs corresponding to S^* and D^* in S'' and D'', respectively.
Now let μ be a substitution and r'_i $(1 \le i \le n)$ be terms such that for all $1 \le i \le n$, $r_i = r'_i\mu$ and $g(r'_1, \dots, r'_n) \preceq_{\mathsf{Abs}} g(y_1\theta'', \dots, y_n\theta'')$. If μ is the identity substitution, then we are done. Otherwise, we can use μ to construct a $\tau \in \Psi(D'', S'')$. Additionally, we need to consider the $\tau_i \in \Psi(D'', S'')$ derived above for each r_i, where $1 \le i \le n$, and the corresponding substitutions γ_i. Thus, $r'_i\mu \preceq_{\mathsf{Abs}} y_i\theta''\tau_i$ and $r'_i\mu\gamma_i \approx_{\mathsf{Abs}} y_i\theta''\tau_i$.
Now let μ_i^1 and μ_i^2 be substitutions such that $\mu\gamma_i = (\mu_i^1\mu_i^2)|_{dom(\mu\gamma_i)}$ and $r'_i\mu_i^1 \approx_{\mathsf{Abs}} y_i\theta''$. This is possible given the assumption that $g(r'_1, \dots, r'_n) \preceq_{\mathsf{Abs}} g(y_1\theta'', \cdots, y_n\theta'')$. Note that $r'_i\mu_i^1 \approx_{\mathsf{Abs}} y_i\theta''$ implies that for every $x \in dom(\mu_i^2)$ there exists a $z \in dom(\tau_i)$ such that $z\tau_i \approx_{\mathsf{Abs}} x\mu_i^2$.
We now construct $\tau \in \Psi(D'', S'')$ using the μ_i^2, that is for all $1 \le j \le n$ and $x \in dom(\mu_j^2)$ there exists a $z \in dom(\tau)$ such that $z\tau \approx_{\mathsf{Abs}} x\mu_j^2$. It now follows that $r_i \preceq_{\mathsf{Abs}} y_i\theta''\tau$ holds for all $1 \le i \le n$ and thus we have shown that $g(r_1, \dots, r_n) \preceq_{\mathsf{Abs}} g(y_1, \cdots, y_n)\theta''\tau$.

2. $r = f(r_1, r_2)$, where f is an absorption symbol and, w.l.o.g, $t_1 = \varepsilon_f$ and $t_2 = f(s_1, s_2)$. Then from $\langle A; S; D; \theta\rangle$ we can derive a configuration $\langle A'; S'; D'; \theta'\rangle$ using the *ExpLA1* rule such that $\star \triangleq_{y_2} s_2 \in D'$ and $\varepsilon_f \triangleq_{y_1} s_1 \in A'$. Now let $\langle\varnothing; S''; D''; \theta''\rangle \in \text{AUNIF}(\langle A'; S'; D'; \theta'\rangle)$ be a final configuration.
By the induction hypothesis we know that $r_1 \preceq_{\mathsf{Abs}} y_1\theta''\tau_1$ for some $\tau_1 \in \Psi(S'', D'')$. Let μ' be a substitution such that $r_1\mu' \approx_{\mathsf{Abs}} y_1\theta''\tau_1$ and $R_2 \subseteq var(r)$ such that $R_2 \cap var(r_1) = \varnothing$. Using R_2 we define a bijective renaming ν such that for all $z \in R_2$, $z\nu \notin \in var(r_1\mu') \cup var(r_1)$.
We will now consider the term $r\nu\mu' = f(r_1\mu', r_2\nu\mu')$. Note that for all variables $z \in var(r_1) \cap var(r_2\nu)$, it must be the case that $z\mu' \preceq_{\mathsf{Abs}} z\mu^*$ where $r_1\mu^* \approx_{\mathsf{Abs}} s_1$ and $r_2\mu^* \approx_{\mathsf{Abs}} s_2$. Thus, observe that $r_2\nu\mu' \preceq_{\mathsf{Abs}} s_2$.
Now let γ' be a substitution such that $dom(\gamma') = var(r_2\nu\mu')$, $r_2\nu\mu'\gamma' \approx_{\mathsf{Abs}} s_2$, and $r_1\mu'\gamma' \approx_{\mathsf{Abs}} s_1$. Now consider $R'_2 = \{z \mid z \in dom(\gamma') \wedge z \notin \in var(r_1\mu')\}$ and $\nu' = \{z \mapsto l \mid z \in R'_2 \wedge z\gamma' = l\}$. Note that $r_2\nu\mu'\nu' \preceq_{\mathsf{Abs}} s_2$ and there exists $t^* \in \uparrow_{y_2}(D'', S'')$ such that $r_2\nu\mu'\nu' \approx_{\mathsf{Abs}} t^*$ by the definition of the *abstraction set*. For terms in $\uparrow_{y_2}(D'', S'')$ we know how to build a $\tau_2 \in \Psi(D'', S'')$.
Now let μ'_1 and μ'_2 be substitutions such that $r_1\mu' \approx_{\mathsf{Abs}} r'_1\mu'_1\mu'_2$ and for all $z \in dom(\mu'_2)$ there exists $y \in dom(\tau_1)$ such that $z\mu'_2 \approx_{\mathsf{Abs}} y\tau_1$. Notice we can apply the same rewriting to $r_2\nu\mu'\nu'$ that is $r'_2\mu''_1\mu''_2 \approx_{\mathsf{Abs}} r_2\nu\mu'\nu'$. We are free to choose the $dom(\nu')$ such that it does not compose with the range of μ'. Thus for variables $z \in var(r'_1\mu'_1) \cap var(r'_2\mu''_1)$ such that $z \in dom(\mu''_2)$, there exists

$y \in dom(\tau_2)$ such that $z\mu_2'' \approx_{\mathsf{Abs}} y\tau_2$ and $z\mu_2' \approx_{\mathsf{Abs}} y\tau_1$. We can safely assume that the $dom(\tau_2) \cap var(ran(\tau_1)) = \emptyset$, thus we can choose $\tau \in \Psi(D'', S'')$ such that $\tau = \tau_1\tau_2$ as the required substitution; So, $r \preceq_{\mathsf{Abs}} f(y_1, y_2)\theta''\tau$.

3. $r = f(r_1, r_2)$, where f is an absorption symbol and, $t_1 = \varepsilon_f$ and $t_2 = \varepsilon_f$. Then from $\langle A; S; D; \theta\rangle$ we can derive a configuration $\langle A'; S'; D'; \theta'\rangle$ using, w.l.o.g, the *ExpBA1* rule such that $\varepsilon_f \triangleq_{y_1} \star, \star \triangleq_{y_2} \varepsilon_f \in D'$. Now let $\langle \emptyset; S''; D''; \theta''\rangle \in$ AUNIF($\langle A'; S'; D'; \theta'\rangle$) be a final configuration. Because $y_1, y_2 \in labels(D')$, $y_1\theta' = y_1$ and $y_2\theta' = y_2$. Thus, there exist $t_1 \in \uparrow_{y_1}(D'', S'')$, $t_2 \in \uparrow_{y_2}(D'', S'')$, a renaming ν, and $\tau \in \Psi(D'', S'')$ such that $r_1\nu \approx_{\mathsf{Abs}} y_1\tau$ and $r_2\nu \approx_{\mathsf{Abs}} y_2\tau$; this follows from the abstraction set containing all terms Abs-equivalent to ε_f under the substitution derived from S''. The substitution ν is required to rename variables in r by the appropriate variables in $labels(S'')$. □

Given the complexity of the construction used in this theorem, the extended version contains examples that illustrate it [4]. We also show there that completeness would not hold if the Merge rule were applied to T.

5 Anti-unification Type, Complexity

Here we show that the complete set of generalizations produced by AUNIF is minimal. Merging the set of final configurations and then showing that constructible generalizations are incomparable play an important role in the proof.

Definition 9 (Merged configurations). *Let s and t be terms. We refer to* AUNIF($\langle\{s \triangleq_x t\}; \emptyset; \emptyset; \iota\rangle$) *as* merged *if for all* $\langle \emptyset; S_0; D_0; \theta_0\rangle, \langle \emptyset; S_1; D_1; \theta_1\rangle \in$ AUNIF($\langle\ \{s \triangleq_x t\}; \emptyset; \emptyset; \iota\rangle$) *and* $s' \triangleq_{y_1} t' \in S_0$, $s' \triangleq_{y_2} t' \in S_1$ *iff* $y_1 = y_2$.

A merged set of final configurations can be obtained by an appropriate renaming of the store labels and applying this renaming to the final substitutions.

Lemma 3. *Let s and t be terms and* $\langle \emptyset; S; D; \theta\rangle \in$ AUNIF($\langle\{s \triangleq_x t\}; \emptyset; \emptyset; \iota\rangle$). *Then for all $s' \triangleq_y t' \in S$ and any non-variable term r, $x\theta\{y \mapsto r\} \notin \mathcal{G}_{\mathsf{Abs}}(s, t)$.*

Proof. Given that $s' \triangleq_y t' \in S$, we know that $head(s') \neq head(t')$ and, $head(s')$ and $head(t')$ are not related absorption symbols. In $x\theta\{y \mapsto r\}$, the non-variable term r replaces y which was a generalization of s' and t', but by this replacement, $head(r)$ will clash with $head(s')$, $head(t')$, or both. Hence, it cannot be a generalization of s' and t', which implies $x\theta\{y \mapsto r\} \notin \mathcal{G}_{\mathsf{Abs}}(s, t)$. □

Definition 10. *Let s and t be terms and* AUNIF($\langle\{s \triangleq_x t\}; \emptyset; \emptyset; \iota\rangle$) *merged. We define the set* $\mathcal{C}_{\text{AUNIF}}(s, t)$ *as* $\mathcal{C}_{\text{AUNIF}}(s, t) = \{x\theta\tau \mid \langle \emptyset; S; D; \theta\rangle \in \text{AUNIF}(\langle\{s \triangleq_x t\}; \emptyset; \emptyset; \iota\rangle) \wedge \tau \in \Psi(D, S)\}$.

Lemma 4. *For any s, t, $\mathcal{C}_{\text{AUNIF}}(s, t)$ is their complete set of* Abs*-generalizations.*

Proof. The lemma follows from the completeness of AUNIF (Theorem 4). □

Lemma 5. *For all terms s, t, and $r_0, r_1 \in \mathcal{C}_{\text{AUNIF}}(s,t)$, if $r_0 \neq r_1$ then neither $r_0 \preceq_{\texttt{Abs}} r_1$ nor $r_1 \preceq_{\texttt{Abs}} r_0$ holds.*

Proof. By Corollary 1, $var(r_0) \subseteq labels(S_0)$ and $var(r_1) \subseteq labels(S_1)$ for some final configurations $\langle \varnothing; S_0; D_0; \theta_0\rangle, \langle \varnothing; S_1; D_1; \theta_1\rangle \in \text{AUNIF}(\langle \{s \triangleq_x t\}; \varnothing; \varnothing; \iota\rangle)$ as r_0 and r_1 are derived via the composition of the anti-unifiers of the associated final configurations with an abstraction substitution. By Lemma 3, w.l.o.g., for $x \in labels(S_0)$ we have $r_0\{x \mapsto r\} \notin \mathcal{G}_{\texttt{Abs}}(s,t)$ when r is not a variable. If r is a variable and $r \in labels(S_0) \cup labels(S_1)$, then $r_0\{x \mapsto r\} \notin \mathcal{G}_{\texttt{Abs}}(s,t)$ because labels in $labels(S_0) \cup labels(S_1)$ are assigned to unique AUTs (due to merging of AUNIF) and thus x and r generalize different terms. Thus, $r \notin labels(S_0) \cup labels(S_1)$ implying neither $r_0 \preceq_{\texttt{Abs}} r_1$ nor $r_1 \preceq_{\texttt{Abs}} r_0$ hold. □

Theorem 5. *For all terms s, t, $\mathcal{C}_{\text{AUNIF}}(s,t)$ is actually $mcsg_{\texttt{Abs}}(s,t)$.*

Proof. Lemma 4 shows completeness. Minimality follows from Lemma 5. □

Corollary 2. *Anti-unification modulo* Abs *theories is of type infinitary.*

Proof. By Theorem 5, the set of Abs-generalizations computed in Example 5 is an *mcsg*, which is infinite since **Configuration 1** produces infinitely many.

Theorem 5 shows contrast to idempotent anti-unification [17]: another infinitary anti-unification problem where the algorithm produces a finitely representable complete set of generalizations which should be further minimized to get an *mcsg*. In our case, AUNIF directly gives a finitely represented *mcsg*.

Finally, we briefly comment on the complexity of AUNIF in terms of the number of final configurations produced.

Definition 11 (Absorption positions). *An* absorption position of terms s and t *is a position $p \in pos(s) \cap pos(t)$ such that $\{\varepsilon_f, f\} = \{head(s|_p), head(t|_p)\}$ for some $f \in Abs_f$, and $head(s|_q) = head(t|_q)$ for all $q \sqsubset p$. The set of absorption positions of s and t is denoted as $ap(s,t)$.*

Absorption positions are disjoint from each other. If $s \triangleq_x t$ is an initial AUT and $p \in ap(s,t)$, after finitely many steps the AUNIF algorithm will generate an AUT $s|_p \triangleq_x t|_p$, that is, an AUT whose side heads form an absorption pair. To each such AUT, two inference rules from AUNIF are applicable, i.e., this is a branching point in the algorithm. No other pair of joint positions causes branching. Hence, $\text{AUNIF}(\langle \{s \triangleq_x t\}; \varnothing; \varnothing; \iota\rangle)$ contains more than one final configuration iff $ap(s,t) \neq \varnothing$. Each absorption position may lead to at most $\max\{size(s), size(t)\}$ branches due to nested f's below absorption positions (as, e.g., in $\varepsilon_f \triangleq_x f(f(a,b),c)$); they resurface after applying the expansion rules and create new AUTs between terms whose heads are absorption pairs (ε_f and f). It implies the following:

Theorem 6. *Let s and t be terms and n be the cardinality of $ap(s,t)$. Then the cardinality of $\text{AUNIF}(\langle \{s \triangleq_x t\}; \varnothing; \varnothing; \theta\rangle)$ is bounded by $\max\{size(s), size(t)\}^n$.*

If we fix the number of absorbing positions in the input terms, the set of final configurations has a polynomial size. Moreover, note that computing one final configuration requires a linear number of steps since each rule eliminates at least one pair of symbols from the set of AUTs to be transformed.

6 Conclusion

We introduced a rule-based algorithm that computes generalizations for problems modulo absorption symbols and proved its soundness and completeness. Furthermore, the algorithm finitely computes a finite set of final configurations from which we can extract a minimal complete set of generalizations. This set can be infinite, implying that Abs-anti-unification is of type infinitary.

In contrast to other grammar-based approaches, our algorithm is generalizable to similar subterm-collapsing theories, which would allow a finite representation of the minimal complete set of generalizations. Therefore, studying extensions of our method for such theories would be a natural next step.

For future work, we will consider how to combine our algorithm with algorithms for computing generalizations in other equational theories, similar to [3]. It would also be interesting to see how generalization techniques in such (combined) theories can be used in practice as part of methods for software analysis.

Acknowledgements. This work was supported by the Czech Science Foundation Grant 22-06414L; the Austrian Science Fund (FWF) project P 35530; Cost Action CA20111 EuroProofNet; the Brazilian agency CNPq, Grant Universal 409003/21-2, and RG 313290/21-0; the Brazilian Federal District Research Foundation FAPDF, Grant DE 00193-00001175/2021-11; and the Georgian Rustaveli National Science Foundation, project FR-21-16725. The Brazilian Higher Education Council (CAPES) supported the Brazilian-Austrian cooperation through the program PrInt.

References

1. Alpuente, M., Escobar, S., Espert, J., Meseguer, J.: A modular order-sorted equational generalization algorithm. Inf. Comput. **235**, 98–136 (2014). https://doi.org/10.1016/j.ic.2014.01.006
2. Alpuente, M., Escobar, S., Espert, J., Meseguer, J.: ACUOS^2: A High-Performance System for Modular ACU Generalization with Subtyping and Inheritance. In: European Conference on Logics in Artificial Intelligence, JELIA. LNCS, vol. 11468 LNAI, pp. 171–181. Springer (2019). https://doi.org/10.1007/978-3-030-19570-0_11
3. Alpuente, M., Escobar, S., Espert, J., Meseguer, J.: Order-sorted equational generalization algorithm revisited. Ann. Math. Artif. Intell. **90**(5), 499–522 (2022). https://doi.org/10.1007/s10472-021-09771-1
4. Ayala-Rincón, M., Cerna, D.M., González Barragán, A.F., Kutsia, T.: Equational anti-unification over absorption theories. CoRR **abs/2310.11136** (2023). https://doi.org/10.48550/arXiv.2310.11136

5. Aït-Kaci, H., Pasi, G.: Fuzzy lattice operations on first-order terms over signatures with similar constructors: A constraint-based approach. Fuzzy Sets Syst. **391**, 1–46 (2020). https://doi.org/10.1016/j.fss.2019.03.019
6. Baader, F.: Unification, weak unification, upper bound, lower bound, and generalization problems. In: Int. Conference on Rewriting Techniques and Applications, RTA. LNCS, vol. volume 488, p. 86-97. Springer (1991). https://doi.org/10.1007/3-540-53904-2_88
7. Bader, J., Scott, A., Pradel, M., Chandra, S.: Getafix: learning to fix bugs automatically. Proceedings of the ACM on Programming Languages **3**(OOPSLA) (2019). https://doi.org/10.1145/3360585
8. Barwell, A.D., Brown, C., Hammond, K.: Finding parallel functional pearls: Automatic parallel recursion scheme detection in Haskell functions via anti-unification. Future Gener. Comput. Syst. **79**, 669–686 (2018). https://doi.org/10.1016/j.future.2017.07.024
9. Baumgartner, A., Kutsia, T.: A library of anti-unification algorithms. In: European Conference on Logics in Artificial Intelligence, JELIA. LNCS, vol. 8761, p. 543-557. Springer (2014). https://doi.org/10.1007/978-3-319-11558-0_38
10. Baumgartner, A., Kutsia, T.: Unranked second-order anti-unification. Inf. Comput. **255**, 262–286 (2017). https://doi.org/10.1016/j.ic.2017.01.005
11. Baumgartner, A., Kutsia, T., Levy, J., Villaret, M.: Nominal anti-unification. In: Int. Conference on Rewriting Techniques and Applications, RTA. LIPIcs (2015). https://doi.org/10.4230/LIPIcs.RTA.2015.57
12. Baumgartner, A., Kutsia, T., Levy, J., Villaret, M.: Higher-order pattern anti-unification in linear time. J. Autom. Reason. **58**(2), 293–310 (2017). https://doi.org/10.1007/s10817-016-9383-3
13. Baumgartner, A., Kutsia, T., Levy, J., Villaret, M.: Term-graph anti-unification. In: 3rd International Conference on Formal Structures for Computation and Deduction, FSCD. LIPIcs, vol. 108, pp. 9:1–9:17 (2018). https://doi.org/10.4230/LIPIcs.FSCD.2018.9
14. Burghardt, J.: E-generalization using grammars. Artif. Intell. **165**(1), 1–35 (2005). https://doi.org/10.1016/j.artint.2005.01.008
15. Cao, D., Kunkel, R., Nandi, C., Willsey, M., Tatlock, Z., Polikarpova, N.: babble: Learning better abstractions with e-graphs and anti-unification. Proceedings of the ACM on Programming Languages **7**(POPL), 396–424 (2023). https://doi.org/10.1145/3571207
16. Cerna, D.M.: Anti-unification and the theory of semirings. Theor. Comput. Sci. **848**, 133–139 (2020). https://doi.org/10.1016/j.tcs.2020.10.020
17. Cerna, D.M., Kutsia, T.: Idempotent anti-unification. ACM Trans. Comput. Log. **21**(2), 10:1–10:32 (2020). https://doi.org/10.1145/3359060
18. Cerna, D.M., Kutsia, T.: Unital anti-unification: Type and algorithms. In: 5th Int. Conference on Formal Structures for Computation and Deduction, FSCD. LIPIcs, vol. 167, pp. 26:1–26:20 (2020). https://doi.org/10.4230/LIPICS.FSCD.2020.26
19. Cerna, D.M., Kutsia, T.: Anti-unification and generalization: A survey. In: Proceedings of the 32nd Int. Joint Conference on Artificial Intelligence, IJCAI. pp. 6563–6573. ijcai.org (2023). https://doi.org/10.24963/ijcai.2023/736
20. Krumnack, U., Schwering, A., Gust, H., Kühnberger, K.: Restricted higher-order anti-unification for analogy making. In: 20th Australian Joint Conference on Artificial Intelligence, AI. LNCS, vol. 4830, pp. 273–282. Springer (2007). https://doi.org/10.1007/978-3-540-76928-6_29

21. Kutsia, T., Levy, J., Villaret, M.: Anti-unification for unranked terms and hedges. J. Autom. Reason. **52**(2), 155–190 (2014). https://doi.org/10.1007/s10817-013-9285-6
22. Kutsia, T., Pau, C.: Matching and generalization modulo proximity and tolerance relations. In: Thirteenth International Tbilisi Symposium on Logic, Language and Computation, TbiLLC. LNCS, vol. 13206, p. 323-342. Springer (2019). https://doi.org/10.1007/978-3-030-98479-3_16
23. Kutsia, T., Pau, C.: A framework for approximate generalization in quantitative theories. In: International Joint Conference on Automated Reasoning, IJCAR. LNCS, vol. 13385, p. 578-596. Springer (2022). https://doi.org/10.1007/978-3-031-10769-6_34
24. Mehta, S., Bhagwan, R., Kumar, R., Bansal, C., Maddila, C.S., Ashok, B., Asthana, S., Bird, C., Kumar, A.: Rex: Preventing bugs and misconfiguration in large services using correlated change analysis. In: 17th USENIX Symposium on Networked Systems Design and Implementation, NSDI 2020. pp. 435–448. USENIX Association (2020), https://www.usenix.org/conference/nsdi20/presentation/mehta
25. Pfenning, F.: Unification and anti-unification in the calculus of constructions. In: LICS (1991). https://doi.org/10.1109/LICS.1991.151632
26. Pientka, B.: Higher-order term indexing using substitution trees. ACM Trans. Comput. Log. **11**(1), 6:1–6:40 (2009). https://doi.org/10.1145/1614431.1614437
27. Plotkin, G.D.: A note on inductive generalization. Machine Intell. **5**(1), 153–163 (1970)
28. Reynolds, J.C.: Transformational systems and the algebraic structure of atomic formulas. Machine Intell. **5**(1), 135–151 (1970)
29. Schmidt-Schauß, M., Nantes-Sobrinho, D.: Nominal anti-unification with atom-variables. In: 7th Int. Conference on Formal Structures for Computation and Deduction, FSCD. LIPIcs, vol. 228, pp. 7:1–7:22 (2022). https://doi.org/10.4230/LIPIcs.FSCD.2022.7
30. Schmidt-Schauß, M., Nantes-Sobrinho, D.: Towards fast nominal anti-unification of letrec-expressions. In: Proc. 29th Int. Conference on Automated Deduction, CADE. LNCS, vol. 14132, pp. 456–473. Springer (2023). https://doi.org/10.1007/978-3-031-38499-8_26
31. Siekmann, J.H.: Unification theory. J. Symb. Comput. **7**(3/4), 207–274 (1989). https://doi.org/10.1016/S0747-7171(89)80012-4
32. de Sousa, R.R., Soares, G., Gheyi, R., Barik, T., D'Antoni, L.: Learning quick fixes from code repositories. In: Simpósio Brasileiro de Engenharia de Software, SBES. ACM (2021). https://doi.org/10.1145/3474624.3474650
33. Vanhoof, W., Yernaux, G.: Generalization-driven semantic clone detection in CLP. In: 29th Int. Symposium on Logic-Based Program Synthesis and Transformation, LOPSTR. LNCS, vol. 12042, pp. 228–242 (2019). https://doi.org/10.1007/978-3-030-45260-5_14
34. Winter, E.R., Nowack, V., Bowes, D., Counsell, S., Hall, T., Haraldsson, S.Ó., Woodward, J.R., Kirbas, S., Windels, E., McBello, O., Atakishiyev, A., Kells, K., Pagano, M.W.: Towards developer-centered automatic program repair: findings from Bloomberg. In: Joint European Software Engineering Conference and Symposium on the Foundations of Software Engineering, ESEC/FSE. ACM (2022). https://doi.org/10.1145/3540250.3558953

35. Yernaux, G., Vanhoof, W.: Anti-unification in constraint logic programming. Theory Pract. Logic Program. **19**(5–6), 773–789 (2019). https://doi.org/10.1017/S1471068419000188
36. Yernaux, G., Vanhoof, W.: Anti-unification of unordered goals. In: 30th Annual Conference on Computer Science Logic, CSL. LIPIcs, vol. 216, pp. 37:1–37:17 (2022). https://doi.org/10.4230/LIPIcs.CSL.2022.37

The Benefits of Diligence

Victor Arrial[1(✉)], Giulio Guerrieri[2], and Delia Kesner[1]

[1] Université Paris Cité, CNRS, IRIF, Paris, France
{arrial,kesner}@irif.fr

[2] Department of Informatics, University of Sussex, Brighton, UK
g.guerrieri@sussex.ac.uk

Abstract. This paper studies the strength of embedding Call-by-Name (dCBN) and Call-by-Value (dCBV) into a unifying framework called the Bang Calculus (dBANG). These embeddings enable establishing (static and dynamic) properties of dCBN and dCBV through their respective counterparts in dBANG. While some specific static properties have been already successfully studied in the literature, the dynamic ones are more challenging and have been left unexplored. We accomplish that by using a standard embedding for the (easy) dCBN case, while a novel one must be introduced for the (difficult) dCBV case. Moreover, a key point of our approach is the identification of dBANG diligent reduction sequences, which eases the preservation of dynamic properties from dBANG to dCBN/dCBV. We illustrate our methodology through two concrete applications: confluence/factorization for both dCBN and dCBV are respectively derived from confluence/factorization for dBANG.

1 Introduction

Call-by-Name (CBN) and Call-by-Value (CBV) stand as two foundational evaluation strategies inspiring distinct techniques and models of computation in the theory of programming languages and proof assistants [46]. Notably, most theoretical studies in the λ-calculus still continues to focus on its CBN variant, while CBV, the cornerstone of operational semantics for most programming languages and proof assistants, has been less extensively explored. This is due in particular to the CBV stipulation that an argument can be passed to a function only when it is a *value* (*i.e.* variable or abstraction), making the reasoning notably challenging to grasp. Consequently, some fundamental concepts in the theory of the λ-calculus (e.g. denotational semantics, contextual equivalence, solvability, Böhm trees) make subtle –and not entirely understood– distinctions between CBN and CBV, sometimes resulting in completely ad-hoc scenarios for CBV, not being uniform with the corresponding notion in CBN. This is for example the case of CBV Böhm trees [33] or the notion of substitution in [23].

Unifying Frameworks. Reynolds [47] (quoted by Levy [37]) advocated for a unifying framework for CBN and CBV. This not only minimizes their arbitrariness, but also avoids developing and proving distinct and independent concepts and

C. Benzmüller et al. (Eds.): IJCAR 2024, LNAI 14740, pp. 338–359, 2024.
https://doi.org/10.1007/978-3-031-63501-4_18

properties for them from scratch. Indeed, both paradigms can be encompassed into broader foundational frameworks [1,16,17,21,24,37,38,40,49] that explicitly differentiate values by marking them with a distinguished constructor. While multiple such frameworks exist, our focus lies on the Bang Calculus [18,22,30]. Inspired by Girard's Linear Logic (LL) [28] and Ehrhard's interpretation [21] of Levy's Call-by-Push-Value [37] into LL, the Bang Calculus is obtained by enriching the λ-calculus with two distinguished modalities ! and $\mathtt{der}$. The modality ! plays a twofold role: it marks what can be duplicated or erased during evaluation (*i.e.* copied an arbitrary number of times, including zero), and it freezes the evaluation of subterms (called *thunks*). The modality $\mathtt{der}$ annihilates the effect of !. Embedding CBN or CBV into the Bang Calculus just consists in decorating λ-terms with ! and $\mathtt{der}$, thus forcing one model of computation or the other one. Thanks to these two modalities, the Bang Calculus eases the identification of shared behaviors and properties of CBN and CBV, encompassing both syntactic and semantic aspects of them, within a unifying and simple framework.

Adequate Models of Computation. Both CBN and CBV were originally defined on *closed* terms (without occurrences of free variables), that are enough to model execution of programs. However, evaluation in proof assistants must be performed on possibly *open* terms, that is, with free variables. While open terms are harmless to CBN, the theory of the CBV λ-calculus on open terms turns out to be much more subtle and trickier (see [6–8] for a detailed discussion). In particular, Plotkin's original CBV [46] is not *adequate* for open terms, as there exist terms that may be both *irreducible* and *meaningless/unsolvable*. The non-adequacy problem in Plotkin's CBV calculus can be repaired by introducing a form of sharing implemented by *explicit substitutions (ES)*, together with a notion of *reduction at a distance* [9,10], like in the Value Substitution Calculus [11] (here called $\mathtt{dCBV}$), a CBV variant of Accattoli and Kesner's linear substitution calculus [2,3] (generalizing in turn Milner's calculus [35,41]). Adequacy also fails for the version of the Bang Calculus studied in [25,30], for the same reasons as in CBV. It can be repaired again via ES and distance, resulting in the Distant Bang Calculus $\mathtt{dBANG}$ [18,19]. It is then natural to also integrate ES and distance in the CBN specification: this gives rise to CBN substitution calculi at a distance [9,10], here we call $\mathtt{dCBN}$ the one in [2], which is adequate as the usual CBN. In summary, we focus in this paper on a CBN calculus $\mathtt{dCBN}$, an adequate CBV calculus $\mathtt{dCBV}$, and the adequate unifying Distant Bang Calculus $\mathtt{dBANG}$.

Static and Dynamic. The literature has shown that some *static* properties of CBN and CBV, including normal forms [36], quantitative typing [18], tight typing [19,36], inhabitation [12], and denotational semantics [30], can be inferred from their corresponding counterparts in the (Distant) Bang Calculus by exploiting suitable CBN and CBV encodings. However, retrieving *dynamic* properties from the Bang Calculus into CBN or CBV turns out to be a more intricate task, especially in their *adequate* (distant) variant [18,19,25,30]. Indeed, it is easy to obtain *simulation* (a CBN or CBV reduction sequence is always embedded into a dBANG reduction sequence), *but* the converse, known as *reverse simulation*, fails: a dBANG reduction sequence from a term in the image of the CBN or CBV embedding may not correspond to a valid reduction sequence in CBN or CBV (counterexample in Fig. 1). Up to these days, there are no embeddings in the literature enjoying reverse simulation for an adequate CBV calculus, so that it is impossible to export dynamic properties from dBANG to both dCBN and dCBV.

Contributions. We first revisit and *extend* the existing static and dynamic preservation results relating dCBN and dBANG, including simulation and reverse simulation, exploiting the embedding used in [18,19]. However, our primary and most significant contribution is a new *methodology* to deal with the (adequate) calculus dCBV. Indeed, we define a *novel embedding* from dCBV into dBANG, *refining* the one of [18,19], that finely decorates terms with the modalities ! and der. To avoid redundant decorations, as ! and der annihilate each other, a dedicated d!-reduction step is then applied *on the fly* by the embedding, as in [18,19]. But our new dCBV embedding not only preserves static and dynamic properties, but also satisfies *reverse simulation*, an essential property that was previously lacking. This achievement is realized by the second ingredient of our new methodology, given by the notion of *diligent sequence* in dBANG, a concept standing independently of the embeddings. Indeed, a challenge at this point is to prove that the earlier mentioned d!-reductions have a purely *administrative* nature, and additionally, that they can be treated *diligently*, by executing all of them as soon as possible. We call this method *diligent administration*: we consistently address all administrative steps before proceeding with any other *computational* steps. A further challenge is then to establish that working with administrative diligence does not alter the CBN or CBV nature of evaluation.

As explained above, reverse simulation is crucial to derive properties for dCBN and dCBV from their respective properties in dBANG. We provide two main illustrative *applications* of this by studying the cases of *confluence* and *factorization*. Confluence is a well-known property, and factorization is crucial to prove important results in (or via) rewriting [2,4,5,15,26,27,29,32,42,45,51,53]: we say that a reduction enjoys factorization when every reduction sequence can be rearranged so that some specific external steps (head in dCBN, weak in dCBV, surface in dBANG) are performed first. In the two last sections, we use confluence/factorization for dBANG as a basis to easily deduce confluence/factorization for dCBN and dCBV. This is done by exploiting the CBN and CBV embeddings back and forth, via reduction simulation and reverse simulation. Just one proof is enough for three confluence/factorization results: it's a three-for-one deal! The fact that dCBN and dCBV confluence/factorizations can be *easily* derived from dBANG confluence/factorization in essentially the *same* way is another achievement, attained thanks to having introduced good tools, such as diligence and the new dCBV embedding.

We actually provide a first proof of factorization for dBANG, another major contribution of this paper. Factorizations in dCBN and dCBV were already proved in [2] and [11], respectively, but their proofs are not trivial, even when applying some abstract approach [2]. Deducing from dBANG the same dCBN/dCBV factorizations as in [2,11] shows that our methodology is robust and not ad-hoc.

Road Map. Section 2 recalls dBANG and introduces diligence. The dCBN/dCBV calculi and their embeddings are presented in Sect. 3, together with their corresponding (static and dynamic) preservation results. Sect. 4 derives dCBN/dCBV confluence from that of dBANG. Section 5 proves a factorization result for dBANG, and deduces factorization for dCBN and dCBV by projection. Section 6 discusses future and related work and concludes. Proofs can be found in [13], the long version of this paper.

1.1 Basic Notions Used All Along the Paper

An **abstract rewriting system** (*ARS*) $\mathcal{E}$ is a set E with a binary relation $\to_{\mathcal{E}}$ on E, called **reduction**. We write $u \;{}_{\mathcal{E}}\!\leftarrow t$ if $t \to_{\mathcal{E}} u$, and we denote by $\to_{\mathcal{E}}^{+}$ (resp. $\to_{\mathcal{E}}^{*}$) the transitive (resp. reflexive-transitive) closure of $\to_{\mathcal{E}}$. Given $t \in E$, t is an **$\mathcal{E}$-normal form** ($\mathcal{E}$-NF) if there is no $u \in E$ such that $t \to_{\mathcal{E}} u$; t is **$\mathcal{E}$-terminating** if there is no infinite $\to_{\mathcal{E}}$ reduction sequence starting at t. Reduction $\to_{\mathcal{E}}$ is **terminating** if every $t \in E$ is $\mathcal{E}$-terminating; $\to_{\mathcal{E}}$ is **diamond** if for any $t, u_1, u_2 \in E$ such that $u_1 \;{}_{\mathcal{E}}\!\leftarrow t \to_{\mathcal{E}} u_2$ and $u_1 \neq u_2$, there is $s \in E$ such that $u_1 \to_{\mathcal{E}} s \;{}_{\mathcal{E}}\!\leftarrow u_2$; $\to_{\mathcal{E}}$ is **confluent** if $\to_{\mathcal{E}}^{*}$ is diamond.

All reductions in this paper will be defined by a set of rewrite rules $\mathbb{R}$, closed by a set of contexts $\mathbb{E}$. A term being an instance of the left-hand side of a rewrite rule $\mathcal{R} \in \mathbb{R}$ is called a **$\mathcal{R}$-redex**. Given a rule $\mathcal{R} \in \mathbb{R}$, and a context $\mathtt{E} \in \mathbb{E}$, we use $\to_{\mathtt{E}\langle\mathcal{R}\rangle}$ to denote the reduction of the $\mathcal{R}$-redex under the context $\mathtt{E}$. The reduction $\to_{\mathbb{E}\langle\mathcal{R}\rangle}$ is the union of reductions $\to_{\mathtt{E}\langle\mathcal{R}\rangle}$ over *all* contexts $\mathtt{E} \in \mathbb{E}$. In other words, $\to_{\mathbb{E}\langle\mathcal{R}\rangle}$ is the closure of the rule $\mathcal{R}$ under all the contexts in $\mathbb{E}$.

2 The Distant Bang Calculus dBANG

We introduce the term syntax of dBANG [18]. Given a countably infinite set $\mathcal{X}$ of variables $x, y, z, \ldots$, the set $\Lambda_!$ of terms is defined inductively as follows:

$$\textbf{(Terms)} \qquad t, u, s \;::=\; x \in \mathcal{X} \mid tu \mid \lambda x.t \mid !t \mid \mathsf{der}(t) \mid t[x\backslash u]$$

The set $\Lambda_!$ includes **variables** x, **abstractions** $\lambda x.t$, **applications** tu, **closures** $t[x\backslash u]$ representing a pending **explicit substitution** (*ES*) $[x\backslash u]$ on t, **bangs** $!t$ and **derelictions** $\mathsf{der}(t)$ (their operational meaning is explained below).

Abstractions $\lambda x.t$ and closures $t[x\backslash u]$ bind the variable x in their body t. The set of **free variables** $\mathtt{fv}(t)$ of a term t is defined as expected, in particular $\mathtt{fv}(\lambda x.t) := \mathtt{fv}(t) \setminus \{x\}$ and $\mathtt{fv}(t[x\backslash u]) := \mathtt{fv}(u) \cup (\mathtt{fv}(t) \setminus \{x\})$. The usual notion of α-conversion [15] is extended to the whole set $\Lambda_!$, and terms are identified up to α-conversion, *e.g.* $y[y\backslash \lambda x.x] = z[z\backslash \lambda y.y]$. We denote by $t\{x\backslash u\}$ the usual (capture avoiding) meta-level substitution of u for all free occurrences of x in t.

Full contexts ($\mathtt{F} \in \mathbb{F}$), **surface contexts** ($\mathtt{S} \in \mathbb{S}$) and **list contexts** ($\mathtt{L} \in \mathbb{L}$), which can be seen as terms with exactly one **hole** $\diamond$, are inductively defined by:

$$\begin{array}{rl} \textbf{(Full Contexts)} & \mathtt{F} ::= \diamond \mid \mathtt{F}\,t \mid t\,\mathtt{F} \mid \lambda x.\mathtt{F} \mid !\mathtt{F} \mid \mathsf{der}(\mathtt{F}) \mid \mathtt{F}[x\backslash t] \mid t[x\backslash \mathtt{F}] \\ \textbf{(Surface Contexts)} & \mathtt{S} ::= \diamond \mid \mathtt{S}\,t \mid t\,\mathtt{S} \mid \lambda x.\mathtt{S} \mid \mathsf{der}(\mathtt{S}) \mid \mathtt{S}[x\backslash t] \mid t[x\backslash \mathtt{S}] \\ \textbf{(List Contexts)} & \mathtt{L} ::= \diamond \mid \mathtt{L}[x\backslash t] \end{array}$$

$\mathtt{L}$ and $\mathtt{S}$ are special cases of $\mathtt{F}$: the hole may occur everywhere in $\mathtt{F}$, while in $\mathtt{S}$ it cannot appear under a !. List contexts $\mathtt{L}$ are arbitrary lists of ES, used to implement reduction at a distance [9,10]. We write $\mathtt{F}\langle t\rangle$ for the term obtained by replacing the hole in $\mathtt{F}$ with the term t (possibly capturing the free variables of t).

The following **rewrite rules** are the base components of our reductions.

$$\mathtt{L}\langle \lambda x.t\rangle u \mapsto_{\mathtt{dB}} \mathtt{L}\langle t[x\backslash u]\rangle \qquad t[x\backslash \mathtt{L}\langle !u\rangle] \mapsto_{\mathtt{s!}} \mathtt{L}\langle t\{x\backslash u\}\rangle \qquad \mathsf{der}(\mathtt{L}\langle !t\rangle) \mapsto_{\mathtt{d!}} \mathtt{L}\langle t\rangle$$

Rule $\mathtt{dB}$ (resp. $\mathtt{s!}$) is assumed to be capture-free, so no free variable of u (resp. t) is captured by the context $\mathtt{L}$. The rule $\mathtt{dB}$ fires a β-redex, generating an ES. The rule $\mathtt{s!}$ fires an ES provided that its argument is duplicable, *i.e.* is a bang. The rule d! uses der to erase a !. In all of these rewrite rules, the reduction acts *at a distance* [9,10]: the main constructors involved in the rule can be separated by a finite—possibly empty—list $\mathtt{L}$ of ES. This mechanism unblocks desired computations that otherwise would be stuck, *e.g.* $(\lambda x.x)[y\backslash w]!z \mapsto_{\mathtt{dB}} x[x\backslash !z][y\backslash w]$.

Reductions are defined, as specified in Sect. 1.1, by taking the set of rewrite rules $\{\mathtt{dB}, \mathtt{s!}, \mathtt{d!}\}$ and the sets of contexts $\mathbb{S}$ and $\mathbb{F}$. **Surface reduction** is the relation $\rightarrow_{\mathbb{S}} := \rightarrow_{\mathbb{S}\langle\mathtt{dB}\rangle} \cup \rightarrow_{\mathbb{S}\langle\mathtt{s!}\rangle} \cup \rightarrow_{\mathbb{S}\langle\mathtt{d!}\rangle}$, while **full reduction** is the relation $\rightarrow_{\mathbb{F}} := \rightarrow_{\mathbb{F}\langle\mathtt{dB}\rangle} \cup \rightarrow_{\mathbb{F}\langle\mathtt{s!}\rangle} \cup \rightarrow_{\mathbb{F}\langle\mathtt{d!}\rangle}$. For example, for $\mathtt{S}_1 = \diamond \in \mathbb{S}$ and $\mathtt{F}_1 = !\diamond \in \mathbb{F} \setminus \mathbb{S}$: $(\lambda x.!\mathsf{der}(!x))!y \rightarrow_{\mathtt{S}_1\langle\mathtt{dB}\rangle} (!\mathsf{der}(!x))[x\backslash !y] \rightarrow_{\mathtt{S}_1\langle\mathtt{s!}\rangle} !\mathsf{der}(!y) \rightarrow_{\mathtt{F}_1\langle\mathtt{d!}\rangle} !y$. The first two steps are $\rightarrow_{\mathbb{S}}$- and also $\rightarrow_{\mathbb{F}}$-steps, while the last one is a $\rightarrow_{\mathbb{F}}$-step but not a $\rightarrow_{\mathbb{S}}$-step. More generally, $\rightarrow_{\mathbb{S}} \subsetneq \rightarrow_{\mathbb{F}}$. For instance, $!(\mathsf{der}(!y))$ is a $\mathbb{S}$-NF but not a $\mathbb{F}$-NF since $!(\mathsf{der}(!y)) \rightarrow_{\mathbb{F}} !y$, while $!y$ is a $\mathbb{F}$-NF (and hence a $\mathbb{S}$-NF too).

The ! modality plays a twofold role. First, it marks the only subterms that can be substituted (*i.e.* erased or arbitrarily copied): the $\mathtt{s!}$-rule fires an ES only if there is a ! in its argument (up to a list context). Second, it freezes (surface) evaluation of the term under the scope of !: surface reduction $\rightarrow_{\mathbb{S}}$ does not reduce under !. In full reduction $\rightarrow_{\mathbb{F}}$, the ! modality looses its freezing behavior.

Diligent Administration. While reductions $\rightarrow_{\mathbb{F}\langle\mathtt{dB}\rangle}$ and $\rightarrow_{\mathbb{F}\langle\mathtt{s!}\rangle}$ are actual *computational* steps, reduction $\rightarrow_{\mathbb{F}\langle\mathtt{d!}\rangle}$ is rather *administrative* in nature. As we use dBANG to simulate other calculi, we need to align with the *implicit nature* of these administrative steps: this can be achieved by executing them as soon as possible. We thus introduce a *diligent process* that reorders some reduction steps to ensure that administrative steps are always performed as soon as there is a d!-redex.

To begin, we formally introduce the concept of **diligent administrative** reduction sequence, characterizing sequences where each *computational* step (dB or s!) can be performed only *after* all *administrative* steps (d!) have been executed.

Definition 1 (Diligent Administrative Reduction). *The* diligent administrative surface *(resp.* full*) reduction* $\to_{\mathbb{S}\mathtt{ad}}$ *(resp.* $\to_{\mathbb{F}\mathtt{ad}}$*) is a subset of the surface (resp. full) reduction obtained by restricting* dB- *and* s!*-steps to* $\mathbb{S}\langle\mathtt{d!}\rangle$*-normal forms (resp.* $\mathbb{F}\langle\mathtt{d!}\rangle$*-normal forms). More precisely, it is defined as follows:*

$$\to_{\mathbb{S}\mathtt{ad}} := (\to_{\mathbb{S}\langle\mathtt{dB}\rangle} \cap \mathbb{S}\langle\mathtt{d!}\rangle\text{-}\mathtt{NF} \times \Lambda_!) \cup (\to_{\mathbb{S}\langle\mathtt{s!}\rangle} \cap \mathbb{S}\langle\mathtt{d!}\text{-}\mathtt{NF}\rangle \times \Lambda_!) \cup \to_{\mathbb{S}\langle\mathtt{d!}\rangle}$$

$$\to_{\mathbb{F}\mathtt{ad}} := (\to_{\mathbb{F}\langle\mathtt{dB}\rangle} \cap \mathbb{F}\langle\mathtt{d!}\rangle\text{-}\mathtt{NF} \times \Lambda_!) \cup (\to_{\mathbb{F}\langle\mathtt{s!}\rangle} \cap \mathbb{F}\langle\mathtt{d!}\text{-}\mathtt{NF}\rangle \times \Lambda_!) \cup \to_{\mathbb{F}\langle\mathtt{d!}\rangle}$$

Example 2. Consider the two surface reduction sequences $\mathsf{der}(!x)[x\backslash!y] \to_{\mathbb{S}\langle\mathtt{s!}\rangle} \mathsf{der}(!y) \to_{\mathbb{S}\langle\mathtt{d!}\rangle} y$ and $\mathsf{der}(!x)[x\backslash!y] \to_{\mathbb{S}\langle\mathtt{d!}\rangle} x[x\backslash!y] \to_{\mathbb{S}\langle\mathtt{s!}\rangle} y$. The first one is not diligent administrative, as the step $\to_{\mathbb{S}\langle\mathtt{s!}\rangle}$ is performed in a term that is not $\mathbb{S}\langle\mathtt{d!}\rangle$-NF. But the second one is diligent administrative: $\mathsf{der}(!x)[x\backslash!y] \to_{\mathbb{S}\mathtt{ad}} x[x\backslash!y] \to_{\mathbb{S}\mathtt{ad}} y$.

To show that every reduction sequence can be transformed into a diligent one (Lemma 3), we first observe that it is possible to perform *all* administrative steps from any term: indeed, reductions $\to_{\mathbb{F}\langle\mathtt{d!}\rangle}$ and $\to_{\mathbb{S}\langle\mathtt{d!}\rangle}$ are *terminating*, because each administrative step erase two constructors, der and !, so the term size decreases.

Some reduction sequences can be made diligent, as in Example 2, but this is not the case for all reduction sequences. For instance $\mathsf{der}(!x)[x\backslash!y] \to_{\mathbb{S}} \mathsf{der}(!y)$ but $\mathsf{der}(!x)[x\backslash!y] \not\to_{\mathbb{S}\mathtt{ad}} \mathsf{der}(!y)$. Therefore, we focus solely on reduction sequences reaching terms that are normal for d!. Under these conditions and by commuting computational steps with administrative ones, we obtain the following results:

Lemma 3 (Diligence Process). *Let* $t, u \in \Lambda_!$ *be terms.*

- ***(Surface)*** *If* $t \to_{\mathbb{S}}^* u$ *and* u *is a* $\mathbb{S}\langle\mathtt{d!}\rangle$-NF*, then* $t \to_{\mathbb{S}\mathtt{ad}}^* u$.
- ***(Full)*** *If* $t \to_{\mathbb{F}}^* u$ *and* u *is a* $\mathbb{F}\langle\mathtt{d!}\rangle$-NF*, then* $t \to_{\mathbb{F}\mathtt{ad}}^* u$.

3 Call-by-Name and Call-by-Value Embeddings

In this section we present the call-by-name dCBN (Sect. 3.1) and call-by-value dCBV (Sect. 3.2) calculi, as well as their embeddings into dBANG, which preserve static properties (Corollaries 7.2 and 9.2 for dCBN, 13.2 and 14.2 for dCBV) and dynamic ones (Corollaries 7.3 and 9.3 for dCBN, 13.3 and 14.3 for dCBV).

Both dCBN [2,9,10] and dCBV [11] are specified using ES and action at a distance, as explained in Sect. 1, and they share the same term syntax. The sets Λ of **terms** and Υ of **values** are inductively defined below.

$$\textbf{(Terms)}\ t, u ::= v \mid t\,u \mid t[x\backslash u] \qquad \textbf{(Values)}\ v ::= x \mid \lambda x.t$$

Note that the syntax contains neither der nor !. The distinction between terms and values is irrelevant in dCBN but crucial in dCBV. The two calculi also share the same **full contexts** F and **list contexts** L, which can be seen as terms with exactly one **hole** $\diamond$ and are inductively defined below. The differences between dCBN and dCBV are in the definitions of *surface* contexts and *rewrite rules.*

$$\begin{array}{ll}\textbf{(List Contexts)} & \mathtt{L} ::= \diamond \mid \mathtt{L}[x\backslash t] \\ \textbf{(Full Contexts)} & \mathtt{F} ::= \diamond \mid \mathtt{F}\,t \mid t\,\mathtt{F} \mid \lambda x.\mathtt{F} \mid \mathtt{F}[x\backslash t] \mid t[x\backslash \mathtt{F}]\end{array}$$

3.1 The Call-by-Name Calculus dCBN and Its Embedding to dBANG

In dCBN, **surface contexts** $\mathtt{S_N} \in \mathbb{S}_\mathtt{N}$ are defined below: the hole cannot be in the argument of an application or ES. To align the notations, in dCBN full contexts are denoted by $\mathtt{F_N} \in \mathbb{F}_\mathtt{N}$ and list contexts by $\mathtt{L_N} \in \mathbb{L}_\mathtt{N}$.

$$\text{(dCBN Surface Contexts)} \qquad \mathtt{S_N} ::= \diamond \mid \mathtt{S_N}\, t \mid \lambda x.\mathtt{S_N} \mid \mathtt{S_N}[x\backslash t]$$

As explained in Sect. 1.1, reductions in dCBN are defined by taking the set of rewrite rules $\{\mathtt{dB}, \mathtt{s}\}$ defined below and the sets of contexts $\mathbb{S}_\mathtt{N}$ and $\mathbb{F}_\mathtt{N}$.

$$\mathtt{L_N}\langle \lambda x.t\rangle u \mapsto_{\mathtt{dB}} \mathtt{L_N}\langle t[x\backslash u]\rangle \qquad\qquad t[x\backslash u] \mapsto_{\mathtt{s}} t\{x\backslash u\}$$

Rule dB is capture-free: no free variable of u is captured by the context $\mathtt{L_N}$. The dCBN **surface reduction** is the relation $\to_{\mathbb{S}_\mathtt{N}} := \to_{\mathbb{S}_\mathtt{N}\langle\mathtt{dB}\rangle} \cup \to_{\mathbb{S}_\mathtt{N}\langle\mathtt{s}\rangle}$, while the dCBN **full reduction** is the relation $\to_{\mathbb{F}_\mathtt{N}} := \to_{\mathbb{F}_\mathtt{N}\langle\mathtt{dB}\rangle} \cup \to_{\mathbb{F}_\mathtt{N}\langle\mathtt{s}\rangle}$. *E.g.*, for $\mathtt{F_N} = \lambda z.\diamond$, $t_0 = \lambda z.((\lambda x.yxx)(zz)) \to_{\mathtt{F_N}\langle\mathtt{dB}\rangle} t_1 = \lambda z.((yxx)[x\backslash zz]) \to_{\mathtt{F_N}\langle\mathtt{s}\rangle} t_2 = \lambda z.(y(zz)(zz))$.

The dCBN surface reduction is nothing but (a non-deterministic but diamond variant of) the well-known *head* reduction.

Embedding dCBN *into* dBANG . The dCBN **embedding** $\cdot^{\mathtt{n}}: \Lambda \to \Lambda_!$ from dCBN to dBANG, introduced in [18,19] and presented below, extends Girard's one [22] to ES.

$$x^{\mathtt{n}} := x \qquad (\lambda x.t)^{\mathtt{n}} := \lambda x.t^{\mathtt{n}} \qquad (tu)^{\mathtt{n}} := t^{\mathtt{n}}\,!u^{\mathtt{n}} \qquad (t[x\backslash u])^{\mathtt{n}} := t^{\mathtt{n}}[x\backslash !u^{\mathtt{n}}].$$

As an example, $(yx)[y\backslash z]^{\mathtt{n}} = (y!x)[y\backslash !z]$. Note that $\cdot^{\mathtt{n}}$ never introduces der, hence $t^{\mathtt{n}}$, and every term it reduces to, are always a $\mathbb{F}\langle\mathtt{d!}\rangle$-NF (this does not hold for the dCBV embedding, Sect. 3.2). In every application and ES, $\cdot^{\mathtt{n}}$ puts a ! in front of their argument, which shows the two roles—called *duplicability* and *accessibility*—played by ! in this embedding: dCBN duplicability means that any argument can be duplicated (or erased), dCBN accessibility means that surface reduction cannot take place inside arguments. Indeed, the ! seals all subterms in argument position.

The embedding is trivially extended to dCBN contexts by setting $\diamond^{\mathtt{n}} = \diamond$.

The static properties of this embedding have already been partially discussed in [18,19]. We will revisit and refine them (Corollaries 7, 9 and 23), but our main focus lies in the preservation of the dynamics of dCBN within dBANG. For that, we first extend the embedding to rule names, by defining $\mathtt{dB}^{\mathtt{n}} := \mathtt{dB}$ and $\mathtt{s}^{\mathtt{n}} := \mathtt{s!}$.

The reduction of a dCBN redex can be effectively simulated in dBANG by reducing the corresponding redex occurring at the translated location/context.

Lemma 4 (dCBN One-Step Simulation). *Let $t, u \in \Lambda$ and $\mathtt{F_N} \in \mathbb{F}_\mathtt{N}$ and $\mathcal{R} \in \{\mathtt{dB}, \mathtt{s}\}$. If $t \to_{\mathtt{F_N}\langle\mathcal{R}\rangle} u$ then $t^{\mathtt{n}} \to_{\mathtt{F_N^n}\langle\mathcal{R}^{\mathtt{n}}\rangle} u^{\mathtt{n}}$.*

Example 5. Consider the dCBN reductions $t_0 \to_{\mathtt{F_N}\langle\mathtt{dB}\rangle} t_1$ and $t_1 \to_{\mathtt{F_N}\langle\mathtt{s}\rangle} t_2$ seen above with $\mathtt{F_N} = \lambda z.\diamond$. Since $\mathtt{F_N^n} = \lambda z.\diamond$, we have $t_0^{\mathtt{n}} = \lambda z.((\lambda x.y!x!x)!(z!z)) \to_{\mathtt{F_N^n}\langle\mathcal{R}^{\mathtt{n}}\rangle} \lambda z.((y\,!x!x)[x\backslash !(z!z)]) = t_1^{\mathtt{n}}$ and $t_1^{\mathtt{n}} \to_{\mathtt{F_N^n}\langle\mathtt{s!}\rangle} \lambda z.(y!(z!z)!(z!z)) = t_2^{\mathtt{n}}$.

So, every dCBN reduction step is simulated by the corresponding dBANG reduction step, without the need for any administrative step. Simulation of dCBV (Lemma 11) is instead more involved, requiring some further administrative steps.

The following property, which effectively reverses the simulation process, extends the one holding for the original Bang Calculus (without distance) [30].

Lemma 6 (dCBN One-Step Reverse Simulation). *Let* $t \in \Lambda$, $u' \in \Lambda_!$, $\mathtt{F} \in \mathbb{F}$ *and* $\mathcal{R}' \in \{\mathtt{dB}, \mathtt{s!}, \mathtt{d!}\}$.

$$t^{\mathtt{n}} \to_{\mathtt{F}\langle\mathcal{R}'\rangle} u' \quad \Longrightarrow \quad \left\{ \begin{array}{ll} \exists\, u \in \Lambda, & u^{\mathtt{n}} = u' \\ \exists\, \mathcal{R} \in \{\mathtt{dB}, \mathtt{s}\}, & \mathcal{R}^{\mathtt{n}} = \mathcal{R}' \\ \exists\, \mathtt{F_N} \in \mathbb{F}_{\mathtt{N}}, & \mathtt{F}_{\mathtt{N}}^{\mathtt{n}} = \mathtt{F} \end{array} \right\} \text{ such that } t \to_{\mathtt{F_N}\langle\mathcal{R}\rangle} u.$$

Lemma 6 states that any dBANG step from the image $t^{\mathtt{n}}$ of a dCBN term t (which is necessarily diligent, because $t^{\mathtt{n}}$ is a $\mathtt{F}\langle\mathtt{d!}\rangle$-NF) actually simulates a dCBN step from t. In Example 5, $t_0^{\mathtt{n}}$ dB-reduces in the context $\mathtt{F} = \lambda z.\diamond$ to $\lambda z.((y\,!x!x)[x\backslash!(z!z)])$, which is indeed equal to $t_1^{\mathtt{n}}$, and $t_0 \to_{\mathtt{F_N}\langle\mathtt{dB}\rangle} t_1$ in the context $\mathtt{F_N} = \lambda z.\diamond$ as well, with $\mathtt{F}_{\mathtt{N}}^{\mathtt{n}} = \mathtt{F}$. Note that Lemma 6 is vacuously true for $\mathcal{R} = \mathtt{d!}$, since there is no term t such that der occurs in $t^{\mathtt{n}}$. Lemmas 4 and 6 have some significant consequences:

Corollary 7. *Let* $t, u \in \Lambda$ *and* $s' \in \Lambda_!$.

1. ***(Stability)**: if* $t^{\mathtt{n}} \to_{\mathbb{F}}^{*} s'$ *then there is* $s \in \Lambda$ *such that* $s^{\mathtt{n}} = s'$.
2. ***(Normal Forms)**:* t *is a* $\mathbb{F}_{\mathtt{N}}$-NF *if and only if* $t^{\mathtt{n}}$ *is a* $\mathbb{F}$-NF.
3. ***(Simulations)**:* $t \to_{\mathbb{F}_{\mathtt{N}}}^{*} u$ *if and only if* $t^{\mathtt{n}} \to_{\mathbb{F}}^{*} u^{\mathtt{n}}$. *Moreover, the number of* dB/s*-steps on the left matches the number* dB/s!*-steps on the right.*

These results deserve some comments. Point 1 states that the image of the dCBN embedding is *stable under reduction.* However, it is not stable under expansion. For instance, $\mathsf{der}(!x) \to_S x = x^{\mathtt{n}}$, although $\mathsf{der}(!x)$ does not belong to the embedding's image, which only contains terms without der. Point 2 guarantees the *preservation of normal forms* in both directions. Finally, Point 3 concerns the *preservation of reduction sequences.* It is worth highlighting that this is an equivalence, enabling to inject reduction sequences from dCBN into dBANG and project them back from dBANG into dCBN. This is a key property allowing in particular to infer confluence and factorization for dCBN from that for dBANG.

The reader may wonder whether similar preservation results hold for surface reduction. Since it is a subreduction of full reduction, Corollary 7.1 already implies stability for surface reduction. However, it does not imply preservation of surface normal forms, and only yields back and forth simulation of surface reduction via full reduction, which is not exactly what we want: $t^{\mathtt{n}} \to_{\mathbb{F}}^{*} u^{\mathtt{n}}$ if $t \to_{\mathbb{S}_{\mathtt{N}}}^{*} u$, and $t \to_{\mathbb{F}_{\mathtt{N}}}^{*} u$ if $t^{\mathtt{n}} \to_{\mathbb{S}}^{*} u^{\mathtt{n}}$. So let us come back to analyze the situation for the *one-step* simulation and reverse simulation. Since surface contexts are special cases of full contexts, then $t \to_{\mathtt{S_N}\langle\mathcal{R}\rangle} u$ implies $t^{\mathtt{n}} \to_{\mathtt{S_N^n}\langle\mathcal{R}^n\rangle} u^n$ by Lemma 4. To prove that this simulating step is actually a surface step, we need an additional property: that dCBN surface contexts are translated into dBANG surface contexts (Lemma 8.1). A more subtle analysis will be required for surface reverse simulation: positions of dBANG surface *redexes* are always in the image of dCBN surface contexts:

Lemma 8.

1. (dCBN $\to$ dBANG) *If* $\mathtt{S_N} \in \mathbb{S}_\mathtt{N}$, *then* $\mathtt{S_N^n} \in \mathbb{S}$.
2. (dBANG $\to$ dCBN) *If* $\mathtt{S} \in \mathbb{S}$ *and* $\mathtt{F_N} \in \mathbb{F}_\mathtt{N}$ *such that* $\mathtt{F_N^n} = \mathtt{S}$, *then* $\mathtt{F_N} \in \mathbb{S}_\mathtt{N}$.

Thanks to Lemma 8, one-step simulation and reverse simulation (Lemmas 4 and 6) can be iterated to obtain the following results about *surface* reduction.

Corollary 9. *Let* $t, u \in \Lambda$ *and* $s' \in \Lambda_!$.

1. ***(Stability)****: if* $t^{\mathtt{n}} \to_{\mathbb{S}}^* s'$ *then there is* $s \in \Lambda$ *such that* $s^{\mathtt{n}} = s'$.
2. ***(Normal Forms)****:* t *is a* $\mathbb{S}_\mathtt{N}$-NF *if and only if* $t^{\mathtt{n}}$ *is a* $\mathbb{S}$-NF.
3. ***(Simulations)****:* $t \to_{\mathbb{S}_\mathtt{N}}^* u$ *if and only if* $t^{\mathtt{n}} \to_{\mathbb{S}}^* u^{\mathtt{n}}$. *Moreover, the number of* dB/s*-steps on the left matches the number of* dB/s!*-steps on the right.*

Our results for dCBN notably extend the ones in [18,19], where it was only shown that N-NF translates to $\mathbb{S}$-NF, and that dCBN surface reduction is simulated by dBANG surface reduction: we went further by encompassing their converses.

3.2 The Call-by-Value Calculus dCBV and Its Embedding into dBANG

In dCBV, **surface contexts** $\mathtt{S_V} \in \mathbb{S}_\mathtt{V}$ are defined below: the hole cannot be under an abstraction. To align the notations, in dCBV full contexts are denoted by $\mathtt{F_V} \in \mathbb{F}_\mathtt{V}$ and list contexts by $\mathtt{L_V} \in \mathbb{L}_\mathtt{V}$.

$$\textbf{(dCBV Surface Contexts)} \qquad \mathtt{S_V} ::= \diamond \mid \mathtt{S_V}\, t \mid t\, \mathtt{S_V} \mid \mathtt{S_V}[x\backslash t] \mid t[x\backslash \mathtt{S_V}]$$

As explained in Corollary1.1, reductions in dCBV are defined by taking the set of rewrite rules $\{\mathtt{dB}, \mathtt{sV}\}$ defined below and the sets of contexts $\mathbb{S}_\mathtt{V}$ and $\mathbb{F}_\mathtt{V}$.

$$\mathtt{L_V}\langle \lambda x.t\rangle\, u \mapsto_{\mathtt{dB}} \mathtt{L_V}\langle t[x\backslash u]\rangle \qquad\qquad t[x\backslash \mathtt{L_V}\langle v\rangle] \mapsto_{\mathtt{sV}} \mathtt{L_V}\langle t\{x\backslash v\}\rangle$$

Rule dB (resp. sV) is capture-free: no free variable of u (resp. t) is captured by context $\mathtt{L_V}$. The dCBV **surface reduction** is the relation $\to_{\mathbb{S}_\mathtt{V}} := \to_{\mathbb{S}_\mathtt{V}\langle\mathtt{dB}\rangle} \cup \to_{\mathbb{S}_\mathtt{V}\langle\mathtt{sV}\rangle}$, while the dCBV **full reduction** is the relation $\to_{\mathbb{F}_\mathtt{V}} := \to_{\mathbb{F}_\mathtt{V}\langle\mathtt{dB}\rangle} \cup \to_{\mathbb{F}_\mathtt{V}\langle\mathtt{sV}\rangle}$.

The calculi dCBN and dCBV differ in that dCBN can always fire an ES (rule s), while dCBV only does when the ES argument is a value, possibly wrapped by a finite list of ES (rule sV). So *e.g.*, for $\mathtt{S_V} = (yxx)[x\backslash\diamond]$, we have:

$$\begin{aligned} u_0 = (\lambda x.yxx)((\lambda z.z)y) &\to_{\diamond\langle dB\rangle} u_1 = (yxx)[x\backslash(\lambda z.z)y] \\ &\to_{\mathtt{S_V}\langle\mathtt{dB}\rangle} u_1' = (yxx)[x\backslash z[z\backslash y]] \to_{\mathtt{S_V}\langle\mathtt{sV}\rangle} u_2 = (yxx)[x\backslash y] \to_{\diamond\langle\mathtt{sV}\rangle} u_3 = yyy \end{aligned} \tag{1}$$

Reduction at a distance in dCBV fires redexes that are blocked in Plotkin's CBV [46]. For instance, given $\delta := \lambda z.zz$, the term $t := (\lambda y.\delta)(xx)\delta$ is a normal form in Plotkin's CBV, but is non-terminating in dCBV: $t \to_{\mathbb{S}_\mathtt{V}} \delta[y\backslash xx]\delta \to_{\mathbb{S}_\mathtt{V}} (zz)[z\backslash\delta][y\backslash xx] \to_{\mathbb{S}_\mathtt{V}} (\delta\delta)[y\backslash xx] \to^*_{\mathbb{S}_\mathtt{V}} (\delta\delta)[y\backslash xx]$, as one would expect, since t is observationally equivalent to the diverging term $\delta\delta$ in CBV [6,8,20,44,48].

The dCBV surface reduction is nothing but the well-known *weak* reduction that does not evaluate under abstractions.

Embedding dCBV *into* dBANG. Values (*i.e.*, variables and abstractions) are the erasable and duplicable terms of dCBV. Girard's CBV encoding (used in [22,30], noted $(\cdot)^{\mathtt{v}_1}$ here) is built upon this insight, placing a bang in front of each variable $x^{\mathtt{v}_1} = !x$ and abstraction $(\lambda x.t)^{\mathtt{v}_1} = !\lambda x.t^{\mathtt{v}_1}$. The encoding of an application is $(tu)^{\mathtt{v}_1} = \mathsf{der}(t^{\mathtt{v}_1})u^{\mathtt{v}_1}$, where the der is used to enable a d!-step if t (the left-hand side of the application) is a value, so as to restore its functional role. However, as highlighted in [18,19], such a definition fails normal forms preservation: a dCBV normal form is not necessarily encoded by a dBANG normal form, for example given the normal term $t_0 = xy$ we have $t_0^{\mathtt{v}_1} = \mathsf{der}(!x)\,!y$ which is not normal. Consequently, [18,19] proposed an alternative encoding (noted $(\cdot)^{\mathtt{v}_2}$ here, whose details are omitted for lack of space), based on the same principle, but with an additional *super-development*: all d!-redexes appearing during the encoding on the left of an application are eliminated *on the fly*, so that the embedding $(\cdot)^{\mathtt{v}_2}$ preserves normal forms (*e.g.*, $t_0^{\mathtt{v}_2} = x\,!y$, which is normal in dBANG). But, as shown in Fig. 1, $(\cdot)^{\mathtt{v}_2}$ breaks reverse simulation with respect to surface reduction.

$$
\begin{array}{ccc}
(\lambda x.(\lambda y.y)z)z & \not\to_{\mathbb{S}_\mathtt{V}} & (\lambda x.y[y\backslash z])z \\
\downarrow \cdot^{\mathtt{v}_2} & & \downarrow \cdot^{\mathtt{v}_2} \\
(\lambda x.(\lambda y.!y)!z)!z & \to_{\mathtt{S}} & (\lambda x.(!y)[y\backslash !z])!z
\end{array}
$$

Fig. 1. Counterexample to dCBV reverse simulation using the embedding $\cdot^{\mathtt{v}_2}$

We introduce a *new* dCBV embedding that preserves normal forms and fulfills simulation *and* reverse simulation (this is one of our main contributions).

Definition 10. *The* dCBV ***embedding*** $\cdot^{\mathtt{v}} : \Lambda \to \Lambda_!$ *is defined as follows:*

$$
\begin{array}{rl}
x^{\mathtt{v}} &:= !x \\
(\lambda x.t)^{\mathtt{v}} &:= !\lambda x.!t^{\mathtt{v}} \\
(t[x\backslash u])^{\mathtt{v}} &:= t^{\mathtt{v}}[x\backslash u^{\mathtt{v}}].
\end{array}
\qquad
(tu)^{\mathtt{v}} := \begin{cases} \mathsf{der}(\mathtt{L}\langle s\rangle u^{\mathtt{v}}) & \text{if } t^{\mathtt{v}} = \mathtt{L}\langle !s\rangle \\ \mathsf{der}(\mathsf{der}(t^{\mathtt{v}})\,u^{\mathtt{v}}) & \text{otherwise;} \end{cases}
$$

Note that, thanks to super-development, $t^{\mathtt{v}}$ is always a $\mathbb{F}\langle \mathtt{d!}\rangle$-NF. For instance, $(\lambda z.z)^{\mathtt{v}} = !\lambda z.!!z$ and $(yxx)^{\mathtt{v}} = \mathsf{der}(\mathsf{der}(\mathsf{der}(y!x))!x)$, whereas $((\lambda x.yxx)(II))^{\mathtt{v}} = \mathsf{der}\big((\lambda x.!\mathsf{der}(\mathsf{der}(\mathsf{der}(y!x))!x))\,\mathsf{der}((\lambda z.!!z)!\lambda z.!!z)\big)$ where $I = \lambda z.z$.

As in the dCBN embedding, the modality ! plays a *twofold* role in our new dCBV embedding. First, $\cdot^{\mathtt{v}}$ marks with ! subterms to be considered as values, *i.e.* potentially *erasable* or *duplicable*. This induces the use of super-developments in the case of applications to avoid some administrative steps that would otherwise affect preservation of normal forms. Second, $\cdot^{\mathtt{v}}$ marks the positions where surface reduction must not occur: inside values; thus it introduces a *second* (internal) ! in the encoding of abstractions to encapsulate its body and shield it from surface computation. Additionally, to restore access to the abstraction's body when it is applied, a second (external) der is added to the encoding of applications. These two principles highlights the dual role of ! in dBANG: enabling duplication (and erasure) as well as isolating subterms from surface computation processes.

The dCBV embedding is extended to rule names, by defining $\mathtt{dB}^{\mathtt{v}} := \mathtt{dB}$ and $\mathtt{sV}^{\mathtt{v}} := \mathtt{s!}$. Similarly to dCBN, we have the fundamental simulation result below.

Lemma 11 (dCBV One-Step Simulation). *Let* $t, u \in \Lambda_!$, *and* $\mathcal{R} \in \{\mathtt{dB}, \mathtt{sV}\}$. *If* $t \to_{\mathtt{F}_{\mathtt{V}}\langle\mathcal{R}\rangle} u$ *then there is* $\mathtt{F} \in \mathbb{F}$ *such that* $t^{\mathtt{v}} \to_{\mathtt{F}\langle\mathcal{R}^{\mathtt{v}}\rangle}\to^*_{\mathbb{F}\langle\mathtt{d!}\rangle} u^{\mathtt{v}}$, *where* F *and all contexts used for the steps in* $\to^*_{\mathbb{F}\langle\mathtt{d!}\rangle}$ *can be specified using* $\mathtt{F}_{\mathtt{V}}^{\mathtt{v}}, \mathcal{R}$ *and* t.

Let us see how F and the contexts used in the steps $\to^*_{\mathbb{F}\langle\mathtt{d!}\rangle}$ are constructed: it highlights the difference between Lemma 11 for dCBV and Lemma 4 for dCBN.

- Additional administrative steps ($\to^*_{\mathbb{F}\langle\mathtt{d!}\rangle}$) may be needed at the end. For example, for the dCBV steps $u_0 \to_{\mathbb{F}_{\mathtt{V}}\langle\mathtt{dB}\rangle} u_1$ and $u_2 \to_{\mathbb{F}_{\mathtt{V}}\langle\mathtt{sV}\rangle} u_3$ seen in (1), we have:

$$\begin{aligned} u_0^{\mathtt{v}} &= \mathtt{der}\big((\lambda x.!\mathtt{der}(\mathtt{der}(\mathtt{der}(y!x))\,!x))\,\mathtt{der}((\lambda z.!!z)!y)\big) \\ &\to_{\mathbb{F}\langle\mathtt{dB}\rangle} \mathtt{der}\big(\,!\mathtt{der}(\mathtt{der}(\mathtt{der}(y!x))\,!x)\,[x\backslash\mathtt{der}((\lambda z.!!z)!y)]\,\big) = s' \qquad (2) \\ &\to_{\mathbb{F}\langle\mathtt{d!}\rangle} \mathtt{der}(\mathtt{der}(\mathtt{der}(y!x))\,!x)\,[x\backslash\mathtt{der}((\lambda z.!!z)!y)] = u_1^{\mathtt{v}} \\ u_2^{\mathtt{v}} &= \mathtt{der}\big(\mathtt{der}(\mathtt{der}(y!x))\,!x\big)[x\backslash !y] \to_{\mathbb{F}\langle\mathtt{s!}\rangle} \mathtt{der}\big(\mathtt{der}(\mathtt{der}(y\,!y))\,!y\big) = u_3^{\mathtt{v}} \end{aligned}$$

- In dCBN one-step simulation the rule name and context are independently translated. It is slightly more subtle in dCBV: the rule name translates to the corresponding one in dBANG without any ambiguity, yet the translation of the context $\mathtt{F}_{\mathtt{V}}$ depends not only on the initial context $\mathtt{F}_{\mathtt{V}}$ but also on the rule name $\mathcal{R}$ and the initial term t. Two distinct situations can emerge:
  - dB-steps require to add a dereliction to the translated context: for example, the dB-redex position $\diamond$ in $t = (\lambda x.x)y$ needs to be translated to the redex position $\mathtt{der}(\diamond)$ in $t^{\mathtt{v}} = \mathtt{der}((\lambda x.!x)!y)$.
  - sV-steps may need to remove a dereliction from the translated context: for instance, the sV-redex position $\diamond y$ in $t = (\lambda z.x)[x\backslash y]\,y$ is translated to the redex position $\mathtt{der}(\diamond\,!y)$ in $t^{\mathtt{v}} = \mathtt{der}((\lambda z.!x)[x\backslash !y]\,(!y))$. The context translation anticipates the super-development used in $t^{\mathtt{v}}$.

  Note that both situations can be detected by case-analysis on $\mathcal{R}$ and t, where the target context translation is a slight variation over the original one.

While the dCBV embedding $\cdot^{\mathtt{v}_2}$ used in [18,19] successfully enables the simulation of dCBV into dBANG, it falls short when it comes to reverse simulation, as shown in Fig. 1. Therefore, $\cdot^{\mathtt{v}_2}$ cannot be used to transfer dynamic properties from dBANG back to dCBV, thus failing in particular to derive dCBV factorization from dBANG (Sect. 5). Our new embedding instead satisfies reverse simulation.

Lemma 12 (dCBV One-Step Reverse Simulation). *Let $t \in \Lambda$, $u' \in \Lambda_!$, $\mathtt{F} \in \mathbb{F}$ and $\mathcal{R}' \in \{\mathtt{dB}, \mathtt{s!}, \mathtt{d!}\}$. If u' is a $\mathbb{F}\langle\mathtt{d!}\rangle$-NF, then*

$$t^{\mathtt{v}} \rightarrow_{F\langle\mathcal{R}'\rangle} \rightarrow^*_{\mathbb{F}\langle\mathtt{d!}\rangle} u' \implies \left\{ \begin{array}{ll} \exists\, u \in \Lambda, & u^{\mathtt{v}} = u' \\ \exists\, \mathcal{R} \in \{\mathtt{dB}, \mathtt{sV}\}, & \mathcal{R}^{\mathtt{v}} = \mathcal{R}' \\ \exists\, \mathtt{F_V} \in \mathbb{F}_{\mathtt{V}}, & \end{array} \right\} \text{ such that } t \rightarrow_{\mathtt{F_V}\langle\mathcal{R}\rangle} u.$$

Lemma 12 states that any dBANG diligent step from the image $t^{\mathtt{v}}$ of a dCBV term t actually simulates a dCBV step from t. As expected, the same subtleties encountered in the dCBV one-step simulation (Lemma 11) apply in this last result, in particular regarding the construction of $\mathtt{F_V}$. In the dCBN case, the absence of administrative steps renders all sequences from images of dCBN terms diligent, making stability, normal form preservation and simulations direct consequences of one-step simulation (Lemma 4) and reverse simulation (Lemma 6). This is not the case for dCBV, due to the presence of administrative steps in the simulation process. Indeed, when simulating dCBV reduction within dBANG (Lemma 11), administrative steps are performed as soon as they become available, thus constructing a diligent sequence. Conversely, projecting a reduction step from dBANG to dCBV (Lemma 12) requires a diligent step. However, in the case of sequences, in contrast to one-steps, there is no requirement for administrative steps to be correctly synchronized, and this may lead to deviations from the embedding's image, significantly complicating reverse simulation. Fortunately, the diligence presented in dBANG (Lemma 3) resynchronizes administrative steps yielding sequences that are easy to project.

Corollary 13. *Let $t, u \in \Lambda$ and $s' \in \Lambda_!$.*

1. ***(Stability)**: if $t^{\mathtt{v}} \rightarrow^*_{\mathbb{F}} s'$ and s' is a $\mathbb{F}\langle\mathtt{d!}\rangle$-NF, then $s' = s^{\mathtt{v}}$ for some $s \in \Lambda$.*
2. ***(Normal Forms)**: t is a $\mathbb{F}_{\mathtt{V}}$-NF if and only if $t^{\mathtt{v}}$ is a $\mathbb{F}$-NF.*
3. ***(Simulations)**: $t \rightarrow^*_{\mathbb{F}_{\mathtt{V}}} u$ if and only if $t^{\mathtt{v}} \rightarrow^*_{\mathbb{F}} u^{\mathtt{v}}$. Moreover, the number of dB/sV-steps on the left matches the number dB/s!-steps on the right.*

As in dCBN, we may wonder whether similar preservation results hold for surface reductions. Such results cannot be entirely derived out from Corollary 13 alone. Still, as with dCBN, the dCBV one-step simulation and reverse simulation properties (Lemmas 11 and 12) already encompass the surface case. However, even though surface redexes positions are mutually mapped by the embedding, it does not yet imply surface stability, preservation of normal forms, and simulations. As previously explained, diligence is required to deal with administrative steps. Fortunately, the surface fragment admits a diligence process, as illustrated in Lemma 3, which can then be leveraged to obtain the following results.

Corollary 14. *Let $t, u \in \Lambda$ and $s' \in \Lambda_!$.*

1. ***(Stability)**: if $t^{\mathtt{v}} \rightarrow^*_{\mathbb{S}} s'$ and s' is a $\mathbb{S}\langle\mathtt{d!}\rangle$-NF, then $s' = s^{\mathtt{v}}$ for some $s \in \Lambda$.*
2. ***(Normal Forms)**: t is a $\mathbb{S}_{\mathtt{V}}$-NF if and only if $t^{\mathtt{v}}$ is a $\mathbb{S}$-NF.*
3. ***(Simulations)**: $t \rightarrow^*_{\mathbb{S}_{\mathtt{V}}} u$ if and only if $t^{\mathtt{v}} \rightarrow^*_{\mathbb{S}} u^{\mathtt{v}}$. Moreover, the number of dB/sV-steps on the left matches the number of dB/s!-steps on the right.*

Stability statements in dCBV (Corollary 13.1 and 14.1) require the reached term s' to be normal for d!, otherwise stability does not hold (*e.g.*, s' in (2) before is not in the image of $\cdot^{\mathtt{v}}$), This is not required in the dCBN stability statements (Corollary 7.1 and 9.1) since every term to which $t^{\mathtt{n}}$ reduces is der-free and so normal for d!.

Proving simulation and reverse simulation requires a considerable effort. But this initial investment, made once and for all, lays the groundwork for numerous benefits without extra costs. For example, in Sects. 4 and 5, we demonstrate that typically challenging tasks like proving confluence and factorization in dCBN and dCBV can be easily achieved by deriving them from dBANG through simulation and reverse simulation, essentially for free. This approach not only unifies the proofs but also minimizes the workload for future proofs.

4 Confluence

Confluence is a crucial property in λ-calculi, ensuring that every term can reduce to at most one normal form, regardless of the chosen reduction path. In this section, we examine confluence of different reductions (surface and full) in the three calculi we considered: dCBN, dCBV, and dBANG. We specifically leverage simulation and reverse simulation properties to project these results from dBANG to dCBN and dCBV, providing a comprehensive solution across three frameworks.

Surface confluence is usually proved by showing that surface reduction is diamond, as for example in [18,19]. Full confluence is more complex, since full reduction is not diamond, as one can easily see in dBANG with the term $(xx)[x\backslash!(II)]$ where $I := \lambda z.z$. Alternative techniques [43,52] can establish full reduction's confluence, albeit often requiring numerous commutation diagrams and possibly non-trivial decreasing measures.

Theorem 15 (dBANG **Confluence).**

1. ***(Surface)*** *The reduction* $\to_{\mathbb{S}}$ *is diamond and confluent. Moreover, any two surface reduction paths from a given term to a* $\mathbb{S}$*-normal form have the same length and number of* dB, s! *and* d!*-steps.*
2. ***(Full)*** *The reduction* $\to_{\mathbb{F}}$ *is confluent.*

Proof. **(Surface)** See [18,19]. **(Full)** See [34].

These proofs are typically highly technical, requiring a significant amount of time to write and of cases to verify, and are prone to errors. Therefore, it is extremely beneficial to have a method to streamline them, especially when mechanizing proofs. With the robust preservation of dCBN reductions in the dBANG, we can actually project dCBN confluences directly from those of dBANG.

Corollary 16 (dCBN **Confluence).**

1. ***(Surface)*** *The reduction* $\to_{\mathbb{S}_{\mathtt{N}}}$ *is diamond and confluent. Moreover, any two surface reduction paths from a given term to a* $\mathbb{S}_{\mathtt{N}}$*-normal form have the same length and same number of* dB *and* s*-steps.*

2. ***(Full)*** *The reduction* $\to_{\mathbb{F}_N}$ *is confluent.*

Proof. **(Surface)** See Fig. 2. **(Full)** Following the same reasoning as Fig. 3.

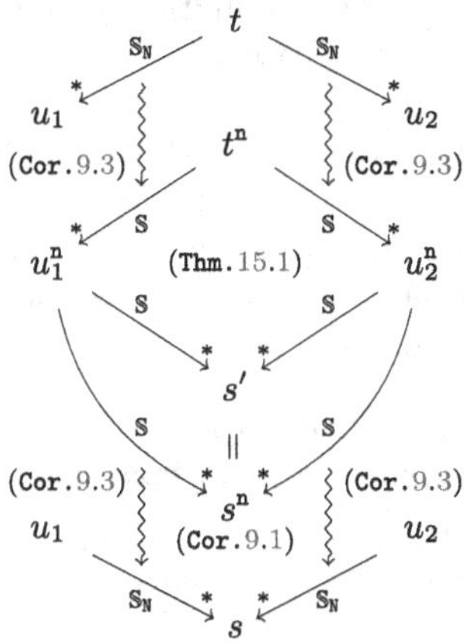

Fig. 2. Schematic proof of Corollary 16.1

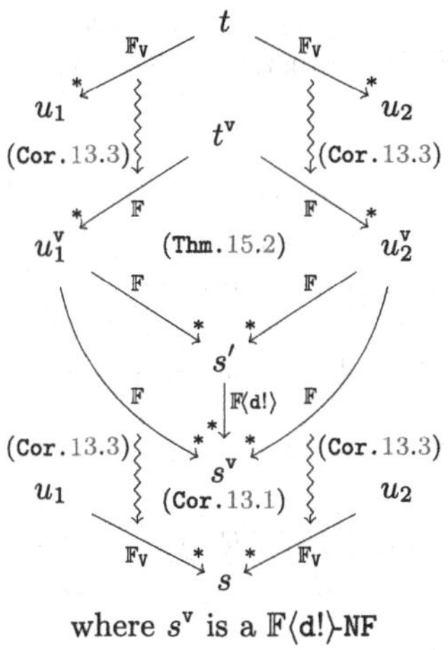

Fig. 3. Schematic proof of Corollary 17.2

The same technique can be used for dCBV, with the additional help of *diligence* (Corollary 13.1 and 14.1). Thus, we get the following results for free.

Corollary 17 (dCBV **Confluence**).

1. ***(Surface)*** *The reduction* $\to_{\mathbb{S}_V}$ *is diamond and confluent. Moreover, any two surface reduction paths from a given term to a* $\mathbb{S}_V$*-normal form have the same length and same number of* dB *and* sV*-steps.*
2. ***(Full)*** *The reduction* $\to_{\mathbb{F}_V}$ *is confluent.*

Proof. **(Surface)** Following the same reasoning as Fig. 2. **(Full)** See Fig. 3.

5 Factorization

In λ-calculi, reduction is a relation, so different reduction steps are possible starting from the same term. Some steps (*e.g.* head steps) are more significant than others, and they may occur in the middle of a reduction sequence. Factorization is the process of disentangling the significant steps from the "superfluous" ones, bringing the former forward and leaving the start and end terms unchanged.

This section is devoted to the factorization property for dBANG, dCBN and dCBV. We start by revisiting an abstract factorization theorem [2]. We first apply this abstract method to dBANG, thus obtaining a new result of factorization not previously appearing in the literature. Then, we use the properties of simulation and reverse simulation proved in Sect. 3 to project the factorization result for dBANG into dCBN and dCBV. Although these two results can be directly derived from the abstract factorization theorem [2], our approach circumvents the numerous commutation properties required by the abstract approach. Also, it provides a tangible illustration of how the simulation and reverse simulation properties discussed in Sects. 3.1 and 3.2 can be applied in concrete cases.

Abstract Factorization. We recall an abstract factorization method from [2] that relies on local rewrite conditions given by the notion of *square factorization system* (SFS). While its original presentation concerns only two subreductions, we (straightforwardly) extend the notion of SFS to a *family* of subreductions, as in dBANG the reduction consists of more than two subreductions.

Definition 18. *Let $\mathcal{R} = (R, \to_{\mathcal{R}})$ be an abstract rewriting system The family $(\to_{\mathcal{R}_k^\circ}, \to_{\mathcal{R}_k^\bullet})_{k \in K}$ of paired reduction relations is a* **square factorization system (SFS)** *for $\mathcal{R}$ if it covers the reduction relation (i.e. $\to_{\mathcal{R}} = \bigcup_{k \in K} \to \mathcal{R}_k$ where $\to \mathcal{R}_k := \to_{\mathcal{R}_k^\circ} \cup \to_{\mathcal{R}_k^\bullet}$) and satisfies the following conditions:*

1. ***Termination:*** *$\forall\, k \in K$, $\to_{\mathcal{R}_k^\circ}$ is terminating.*
2. ***Row-swaps:*** *$\forall\, k \in K$, $\to_{\mathcal{R}_k^\bullet}\to_{\mathcal{R}_k^\circ} \subseteq \to^+_{\mathcal{R}_k^\circ}\to^*_{\mathcal{R}_k^\bullet}$.*
3. ***Diagonal-swaps:*** *$\forall\, k_1, k_2 \in K$, $k_1 \neq k_2$, $\to_{\mathcal{R}_{k_1}^\bullet}\to_{\mathcal{R}_{k_2}^\circ} \subseteq \to_{\mathcal{R}_{k_2}^\circ}\to^*_{\mathcal{R}_{k_1}}$.*

The symbol $\circ$ tags *significant* (also called *external*) steps, while $\bullet$ is used for *irrelevant* (also called *internal*) ones. The commutations required in an SFS are sufficient to achieve factorization, which consists in rearranging a reduction sequence to prioritize significant steps $\to_{\mathcal{R}^\circ}$ over irrelevant steps $\to^\bullet_{\mathcal{R}}$.

Proposition 19 ([2]). *Let $\mathcal{R} = (R, \to_{\mathcal{R}})$ be an abstract rewriting system and $(\to_{\mathcal{R}_k^\circ}, \to_{\mathcal{R}_k^\bullet})_{k \in K}$ be an SFS for $\mathcal{R}$. Then the reduction relation factorizes, that is, $\to^*_{\mathcal{R}} \subseteq \to^*_\circ \to^*_\bullet$ where $\to_\circ := \bigcup_{k \in K} \to_{\mathcal{R}_k^\circ}$ and $\to_\bullet := \bigcup_{k \in K} \to_{\mathcal{R}_k^\bullet}$.*

Factorization in dBANG . In dBANG we claim that surface reduction is the significant part of full reduction, and our goal is to factor it out. To exploit the abstract method, we first formally identify the irrelevant subreduction of full reduction, called here *internal*, as reduction under the scope of a !. **Internal contexts** $\mathtt{I} \in \mathbb{I}$ are full contexts $\mathbb{F}$ for which the hole is placed under a bang. Formally,

$$\textbf{(dBANG Internal Contexts)} \qquad \mathtt{I} ::= !\mathtt{F} \mid \mathtt{S}^*\langle \mathtt{I} \rangle \qquad \text{with } \mathtt{S}^* \in \mathbb{S} \setminus \{\diamond\}$$

Clearly, $\mathbb{I} = \mathbb{F} \setminus \mathbb{S}$. As usual, $\to_{\mathbb{I}\langle\mathcal{R}\rangle}$ is the closure of the rewrite rules $\mathcal{R} \in \{\mathtt{dB}, \mathtt{s!}, \mathtt{d!}\}$ over all contexts $\mathtt{I} \in \mathbb{I}$. The dBANG **internal reduction** is the relation $\to_{\mathbb{I}} := \to_{\mathbb{I}\langle\mathtt{dB}\rangle} \cup \to_{\mathbb{I}\langle\mathtt{s!}\rangle} \cup \to_{\mathbb{I}\langle\mathtt{d!}\rangle}$. For example, $(\lambda x.!\diamond)\, y$ is an internal context while $\diamond$ is not. Thus, $(\lambda x.!(z[z\backslash x]))\, y \to_{\mathbb{I}\langle\mathtt{s!}\rangle} (\lambda x.!x)\, y \not\to_{\mathbb{I}} (!x)[x\backslash y]$. We can now show that surface and internal reductions enjoy the abstract properties of an SFS.

Lemma 20. *The family* $(\rightarrow_{\mathbb{S}\langle\mathcal{R}\rangle}, \rightarrow_{\mathbb{I}\langle\mathcal{R}\rangle})_{\mathcal{R}\in\{\mathtt{dB},\mathtt{s!},\mathtt{d!}\}}$ *is an SFS for* $(\Lambda_!, \rightarrow_F)$.

This immediately gives the following novel factorization result for the Distant Bang Calculus, by applying Proposition 19 and Lemma 20.

Corollary 21 (dBANG Factorization). *We have that* $\rightarrow_{\mathbb{F}}^* = \rightarrow_{\mathbb{S}}^* \rightarrow_{\mathbb{I}}^*$.

Example 22. Take $t = (xy)[y\backslash!(I!!(Iw))]$ where $I = \lambda z.z$. Then, the factorization of the first sequence starting at t below, is given by the second one:

$$t \rightarrow_{\mathbb{F}} (xy)[y\backslash!(z[z\backslash!!(Iw)])] \rightarrow_{\mathbb{S}} x(z[z\backslash!!(Iw)]) \rightarrow_{\mathbb{F}} x(z[z\backslash!!(z[z\backslash w])]) \rightarrow_{\mathbb{S}} x!(z[z\backslash w])$$
$$t \rightarrow_{\mathbb{S}} x(I!!(Iw)) \rightarrow_{\mathbb{S}} x(z[z\backslash!!(Iw)]) \rightarrow_{\mathbb{S}} x!(Iw) \rightarrow_{\mathbb{I}} x!(z[z\backslash w])$$

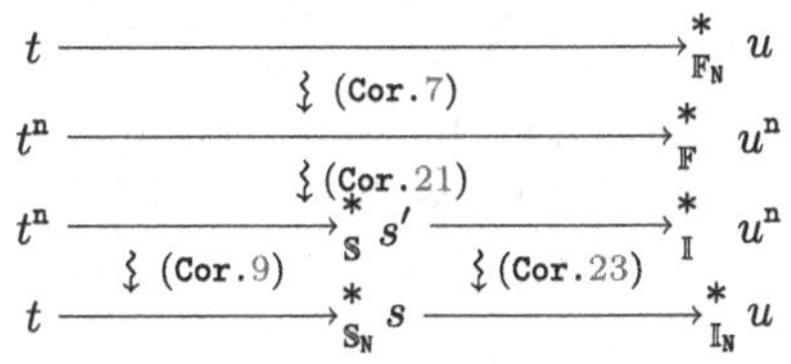

Fig. 4. Schematic proof of Corollary 16.1

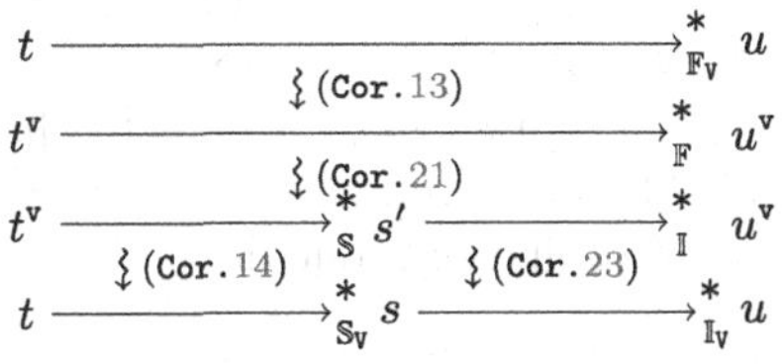

Fig. 5. Schematic proof of Corollary 17.2

Factorizations in dCBN *and* dCBV . To achieve factorization in dCBN and dCBV via the abstract method, we need to establish the existence of an *SFS* in each case. This requires validating multiple commutations. We bypass these lengthy proofs by adopting a simpler projection approach from dBANG.

As in dBANG, we claim that surface reduction is the significant part of full reduction in dCBN/dCBV, and we consequently identify the irrelevant subreduction, called here *internal.* The dCBN (resp. dCBV) internal contexts $\mathtt{I}_\mathtt{N} \in \mathbb{I}_\mathtt{N}$ (resp. $\mathtt{I}_\mathtt{V} \in \mathbb{I}_\mathtt{V}$) are full contexts whose hole is in an argument (resp. under a λ). Formally,

$$\textbf{(dCBN Internal Contexts)} \quad \mathtt{I}_\mathtt{N} ::= t\,\mathtt{F}_\mathtt{N} \mid t[x\backslash\mathtt{F}_\mathtt{N}] \mid \mathtt{N}^*\mathtt{N}\mathtt{I}_\mathtt{N} \quad \text{with } \mathtt{S}_\mathtt{N}^* \in \mathbb{S}_\mathtt{N} \setminus \{\diamond\}$$
$$\textbf{(dCBV Internal Contexts)} \quad \mathtt{I}_\mathtt{V} ::= \lambda x.\mathtt{F}_\mathtt{V} \mid \mathtt{S}_\mathtt{V}^*\langle\mathtt{I}_\mathtt{V}\rangle \quad \text{with } \mathtt{S}_\mathtt{V}^* \in \mathbb{S}_\mathtt{V} \setminus \{\diamond\}$$

The dCBN **(resp.** dCBV**) internal reduction** $\rightarrow_{\mathbb{I}_\mathtt{N}}$ (resp. $\rightarrow_{\mathbb{I}_\mathtt{V}}$) is the closure over all internal contexts $\mathtt{I}_\mathtt{N} \in \mathbb{I}_\mathtt{N}$ (resp. $\mathtt{I}_\mathtt{V} \in \mathbb{I}_\mathtt{V}$) of the rewrite rules dB and s (resp.dB and sV). For example, $(\lambda x.x)\diamond$ is a dCBN internal context, while $\diamond$ is not, thus $(\lambda x.x)((\lambda y.z)t) \rightarrow_{\mathbb{I}_\mathtt{N}} (\lambda x.x)z \not\rightarrow_{\mathbb{I}_\mathtt{N}} z$. And $(\lambda x.\diamond)z$ is a dCBV internal context while $\diamond$ is not, thus $(\lambda x.(\lambda y.y)z)z \rightarrow_{\mathbb{I}_\mathtt{V}} (\lambda x.y[y\backslash z])z \rightarrow_{\mathbb{I}_\mathtt{V}} (\lambda x.z)z \not\rightarrow_{\mathbb{I}_\mathtt{V}} z[x\backslash z]$.

As in the surface case, the one-step simulation and reverse simulation (Lemmas 4 and 6 for dCBN, Lemmas 11 and 12 for dCBV) can be specialized to the internal case. This allows us to show in particular the following property.

Corollary 23. *Let $t, u \in \Lambda$ and $s' \in \Lambda_!$.*

- ***(Stability)**: if $t^{\mathtt{n}} \rightarrow^*_{\mathbb{I}} s'$ (resp. $t^{\mathtt{v}} \rightarrow^*_{\mathbb{I}} s'$ and s' is a $\mathbb{I}\langle \mathtt{d!} \rangle$-NF) then there is $s \in \Lambda$ such that $s^{\mathtt{n}} = s'$ (resp. $s^{\mathtt{v}} = s'$).*
- ***(Normal Forms)**: t is a $\mathbb{I}_{\mathtt{N}}$-NF (resp. $\mathbb{I}_{\mathtt{V}\text{-NF}}$) iff $t^{\mathtt{n}}$ (resp. $t^{\mathtt{v}}$) is a $\mathbb{I}$-NF.*
- ***(Simulations)**: $t \rightarrow^*_{\mathbb{I}_{\mathtt{N}}} u$ (resp. $t \rightarrow^*_{\mathbb{I}_{\mathtt{V}}} u$) iff $t^{\mathtt{n}} \rightarrow^*_{\mathbb{I}} u^{\mathtt{n}}$ (resp. $t^{\mathtt{v}} \rightarrow^*_{\mathbb{I}} u^{\mathtt{v}}$). Moreover, the number of* dB/s*-steps (resp.* dB/sV*-steps) on the left matches the number of* dB/s!*-steps on the right.*

Via Corollaries 9, 14 and 23, we can project factorization from dBANG back to dCBN/dCBV.

Theorem 24 (dCBN/dCBV Factorizations). $\rightarrow^*_{\mathbb{F}_{\mathtt{N}}} = \rightarrow^*_{\mathbb{S}_{\mathtt{N}}} \rightarrow_{\mathbb{I}_{\mathtt{N}}}$ *and* $\rightarrow^*_{\mathbb{F}_{\mathtt{V}}} = \rightarrow^*_{\mathbb{S}_{\mathtt{V}}} \rightarrow^*_{\mathbb{I}_{\mathtt{V}}}$.

Proof. The proof for dCBN is depicted in Fig. 4. In particular, since $t^{\mathtt{n}} \rightarrow^*_{\mathbb{S}} s'$, one deduces using Corollary 9 that there exists $s \in \Lambda$ such that $s^{\mathtt{n}} = s'$.

The proof for dCBV is depicted in Fig. 5. In particular, by construction $u^{\mathtt{v}}$ is a $\mathbb{F}\langle \mathtt{d!} \rangle$-NF and by induction on the length of $s' \rightarrow^*_{\mathbb{I}} u^{\mathtt{V}}$, one has that s' is a $\mathbb{S}\langle \mathtt{d!} \rangle$-NF. Using Corollary 14, one deduces that there exists $s \in \Lambda$ such that $s^{\mathtt{v}} = s'$. □

6 Conclusion and Related Work

Our first contribution is to revisit and extend several properties concerning the encoding of dCBN into dBANG. The second contribution, more significant, consists in introducing a new embedding from dCBV to dBANG, which is conservative with respect to previous results in the literature [18,19], but also (and this is a novelty) allows us to establish the essential reverse simulation property, achieved through the non-trivial concept of diligent sequence. We illustrate the strength of our methodology by means of an example, namely factorization. For that, we first prove a factorization theorem for dBANG, another major contribution of the paper, and we then deduce factorization for dCBN and dCBV by projecting that for dBANG.

In [25], factorization for the (non-distant) Bang Calculus has been proved and from that, factorizations results for standard (non distant) CBN λ-calculus and Plotkin's original CBV λ-calculus has been deduced. But the (non-distant) Bang Calculus and Plotkin's CBV are *not adequate*, in the sense explained in Sect. 1, thus decreasing the significance of those preliminary results.

When taking *adequate* versions of the Bang Calculus, by adding ES and distance, or σ-reduction [22,31], the CBV encodings in the literature [18,19,22,25,30] fail to enjoy reverse simulation, thus preventing one deducing dynamic properties from the Bang Calculus into CBV. Other CBN and CBV encodings into a unifying framework appear in [14], but there is no reverse simulation property, so that no concrete application of the proposed encoding to export properties into CBN and CBV. The same occurs in [24]. The only exceptions are [12,36] —where only *static* properties are obtained—, and [25,30] —where the Bang and CBV calculi are not adequate in the sense explained in Sect. 1.

Sabry and Wadler [50] showed that simulation and reverse simulation between two calculi are for free when their back and forth translations give rise to an adjoint. One of the difficulties to achieve our results is that our CBN and CBV embeddings, as well as the ones used in [18,19,22,25,30], do not form an adjoint. This is basically due to the fact that a CBN/CBV term can be decorated by ! and der so as that administrative steps performed in the (Distant) Bang Calculus do not correspond to anything in CBN or CBV. Our contribution is precisely to achieve simulation and reverse simulation without the need for any adjoint.

As discussed at the end of Sect. 3, proving simulation and reverse simulation requires a considerable effort. But this initial investment lays the groundwork for numerous benefits without extra costs, as we showed in Sects. 4 and 5.

In addition to the tangible contributions presented in this paper, we believe our methodology enhances the understanding of the semantic aspects of CBV, especially concerning untyped and typed approximants. This remains a topic that, while gradually gaining attention in the literature [12,33,39], is yet to be thoroughly explored. Our novel CBV embedding would also suggest a logical counterpart (a new encoding of intuitionistic logic into linear logic), which remains to be investigated. Moreover, we aim to further leverage our technique to explore other crucial dynamic properties of dCBN and dCBV, such as standardization, normalization, genericity as well as some specific deterministic strategies.

References

1. Abramsky, S.: Computational interpretations of linear logic. Theor. Comput. Sci. **111**(1), 3–57 (1993). https://doi.org/10.1016/0304-3975(93)90181-R
2. Accattoli, B.: An abstract factorization theorem for explicit substitutions. In: 23rd International Conference on Rewriting Techniques and Applications (RTA'12). Leibniz International Proceedings in Informatics (LIPIcs), vol. 15, pp. 6–21. Schloss Dagstuhl–Leibniz-Zentrum fuer Informatik (2012). https://doi.org/10.4230/LIPIcs.RTA.2012.6
3. Accattoli, B., Bonelli, E., Kesner, D., Lombardi, C.: A nonstandard standardization theorem. In: Jagannathan, S., Sewell, P. (eds.) The 41st Annual ACM SIGPLAN-SIGACT Symposium on Principles of Programming Languages. POPL '14, pp. 659–670. ACM Press (2014). https://doi.org/10.1145/2535838.2535886
4. Accattoli, B., Faggian, C., Guerrieri, G.: Factorization and normalization, essentially. In: Lin, A.W. (ed.) APLAS 2019. LNCS, vol. 11893, pp. 159–180. Springer, Cham (2019). https://doi.org/10.1007/978-3-030-34175-6_9
5. Accattoli, B., Faggian, C., Guerrieri, G.: Factorize factorization. In: 29th EACSL Annual Conference on Computer Science Logic, CSL 2021. LIPIcs, vol. 183, pp. 6:1–6:25. Schloss Dagstuhl - Leibniz-Zentrum für Informatik (2021). https://doi.org/10.4230/LIPIcs.CSL.2021.6
6. Accattoli, B., Guerrieri, G.: Open call-by-value. In: Igarashi, A. (ed.) APLAS 2016. LNCS, vol. 10017, pp. 206–226. Springer, Cham (2016). https://doi.org/10.1007/978-3-319-47958-3_12
7. Accattoli, B., Guerrieri, G.: Abstract machines for open call-by-value. Sci. Comput. Program. **184** (2019). https://doi.org/10.1016/j.scico.2019.03.002
8. Accattoli, B., Guerrieri, G.: The theory of call-by-value solvability. Proc. ACM Program. Lang. **6**(ICFP), 855–885 (2022). https://doi.org/10.1145/3547652

9. Accattoli, B., Kesner, D.: The structural λ-calculus. In: Dawar, A., Veith, H. (eds.) CSL 2010. LNCS, vol. 6247, pp. 381–395. Springer, Heidelberg (2010). https://doi.org/10.1007/978-3-642-15205-4_30
10. Accattoli, B., Kesner, D.: Preservation of strong normalisation modulo permutations for the structural lambda-calculus. Logic. Methods Comput. Sci. **8**(1) (2012). https://doi.org/10.2168/LMCS-8(1:28)2012
11. Accattoli, B., Paolini, L.: Call-by-value solvability, revisited. In: Schrijvers, T., Thiemann, P. (eds.) FLOPS 2012. LNCS, vol. 7294, pp. 4–16. Springer, Heidelberg (2012). https://doi.org/10.1007/978-3-642-29822-6_4
12. Arrial, V., Guerrieri, G., Kesner, D.: Quantitative inhabitation for different lambda calculi in a unifying framework. Proc. ACM Program. Lang. **7**(POPL), 1483–1513 (2023). https://doi.org/10.1145/3571244
13. Arrial, V., Guerrieri, G., Kesner, D.: The benefits of diligence. CoRR abs/2404.12951 (2024). https://arxiv.org/abs/2404.12951
14. van Bakel, S., Emma Tye, N.W.: A calculus of delayed reductions. In: International Symposium on Principles and Practice of Declarative Programming. PPDP 2023, pp. 1:1–1:13. ACM (2023). https://doi.org/10.1145/3610612.3610613
15. Barendregt, H.P.: The Lambda Calculus: Its Syntax and Semantics. Studies in Logic and the Foundations of Mathematics, vol. 103. North-Holland, Amsterdam (1984)
16. Benton, N., Wadler, P.: Linear logic, monads and the lambda calculus. In: Proceedings 11th Annual IEEE Symposium on Logic in Computer Science (LICS '96), pp. 420–431. IEEE (1996). https://doi.org/10.1109/LICS.1996.561458
17. Benton, N., Bierman, G., de Paiva, V., Hyland, M.: A term calculus for Intuitionistic Linear Logic. In: Bezem, M., Groote, J.F. (eds.) TLCA 1993. LNCS, vol. 664, pp. 75–90. Springer, Heidelberg (1993). https://doi.org/10.1007/BFb0037099
18. Bucciarelli, A., Kesner, D., Ríos, A., Viso, A.: The bang calculus revisited. In: Nakano, K., Sagonas, K. (eds.) FLOPS 2020. LNCS, vol. 12073, pp. 13–32. Springer, Cham (2020). https://doi.org/10.1007/978-3-030-59025-3_2
19. Bucciarelli, A., Kesner, D., Ríos, A., Viso, A.: The bang calculus revisited. Inf. Comput. **293**, 105047 (2023). https://doi.org/10.1016/j.ic.2023.105047
20. Carraro, A., Guerrieri, G.: A semantical and operational account of call-by-value solvability. In: Muscholl, A. (ed.) FoSSaCS 2014. LNCS, vol. 8412, pp. 103–118. Springer, Heidelberg (2014). https://doi.org/10.1007/978-3-642-54830-7_7
21. Ehrhard, T.: Call-by-push-value from a linear logic point of view. In: Thiemann, P. (ed.) ESOP 2016. LNCS, vol. 9632, pp. 202–228. Springer, Heidelberg (2016). https://doi.org/10.1007/978-3-662-49498-1_9
22. Ehrhard, T., Guerrieri, G.: The bang calculus: an untyped lambda-calculus generalizing call-by-name and call-by-value. In: Proceedings of the 18th International Symposium on Principles and Practice of Declarative Programming. PPDP'16, pp. 174–187. ACM (2016). https://doi.org/10.1145/2967973.2968608
23. Espírito Santo, J.: The call-by-value lambda-calculus with generalized applications. In: 28th EACSL Annual Conference on Computer Science Logic. CSL 2020. LIPIcs, vol. 152, pp. 35:1–35:12. Schloss Dagstuhl - Leibniz-Zentrum für Informatik (2020). https://doi.org/10.4230/LIPICS.CSL.2020.35
24. Espírito Santo, J., Pinto, L., Uustalu, T.: Modal embeddings and calling paradigms. In: 4th International Conference on Formal Structures for Computation and Deduction. FSCD 2019. LIPIcs, vol. 131, pp. 18:1–18:20. Schloss Dagstuhl (2019). https://doi.org/10.4230/LIPIcs.FSCD.2019.18

25. Faggian, C., Guerrieri, G.: Factorization in call-by-name and call-by-value calculi via linear logic. In: FOSSACS 2021. LNCS, vol. 12650, pp. 205–225. Springer, Cham (2021). https://doi.org/10.1007/978-3-030-71995-1_11
26. Faggian, C., Guerrieri, G.: Strategies for asymptotic normalization. In: 7th International Conference on Formal Structures for Computation and Deduction. FSCD 2022. LIPIcs, vol. 228, pp. 17:1–17:24. Schloss Dagstuhl - Leibniz-Zentrum für Informatik (2022). https://doi.org/10.4230/LIPICS.FSCD.2022.17
27. Faggian, C., Guerrieri, G., de'Liguoro, U., Treglia, R.: On reduction and normalization in the computational core. Math. Struct. Comput. Sci. **32**(7), 934–981 (2022). https://doi.org/10.1017/S0960129522000433
28. Girard, J.: Linear logic. Theor. Comput. Sci. **50**, 1–102 (1987). https://doi.org/10.1016/0304-3975(87)90045-4
29. Guerrieri, G.: Head reduction and normalization in a call-by-value lambda-calculus. In: 2nd International Workshop on Rewriting Techniques for Program Transformations and Evaluation. WPTE@RDP 2015. OASIcs, vol. 46, pp. 3–17. Schloss Dagstuhl - Leibniz-Zentrum für Informatik (2015). https://doi.org/10.4230/OASICS.WPTE.2015.3
30. Guerrieri, G., Manzonetto, G.: The bang calculus and the two Girard's translations. In: Proceedings Joint International Workshop on Linearity and Trends in Linear Logic and Applications. Linearity-TLLA@FLoC 2018. EPTCS, vol. 292, pp. 15–30 (2018). https://doi.org/10.4204/EPTCS.292.2
31. Guerrieri, G., Olimpieri, F.: Categorifying non-idempotent intersection types. In: 29th EACSL Annual Conference on Computer Science Logic. CSL 2021. LIPIcs, vol. 183, pp. 25:1–25:24. Schloss Dagstuhl - Leibniz-Zentrum für Informatik (2021). https://doi.org/10.4230/LIPIcs.CSL.2021.25
32. Guerrieri, G., Paolini, L., Ronchi Della Rocca, S.: Standardization and conservativity of a refined call-by-value lambda-calculus. Logic. Methods Comput. Sci. **13**(4) (2017). https://doi.org/10.23638/LMCS-13(4:29)2017
33. Kerinec, A., Manzonetto, G., Pagani, M.: Revisiting call-by-value BöHM trees in light of their Taylor expansion. Logic. Methods Comput. Sci. **16**(3) (2020). https://lmcs.episciences.org/6638
34. Kesner, D., Arrial, V., Guerrieri, G.: Meaningfulness and genericity in a subsuming framework. CoRR abs/2404.06361 (2024). https://arxiv.org/abs/2404.06361, submitted to FSCD 2024
35. Kesner, D., Ó Conchúir, S.: Milner's lambda-calculus with partial substitutions. CoRR **abs/2312.13270** (2023). https://doi.org/10.48550/ARXIV.2312.13270
36. Kesner, D., Viso, A.: Encoding tight typing in a unified framework. In: 30th EACSL Annual Conference on Computer Science Logic. CSL 2022. LIPIcs, vol. 216, pp. 27:1–27:20. Schloss Dagstuhl - Leibniz-Zentrum für Informatik (2022). https://doi.org/10.4230/LIPIcs.CSL.2022.27
37. Levy, P.B.: Call-by-push-value: a subsuming paradigm. In: Girard, J.-Y. (ed.) TLCA 1999. LNCS, vol. 1581, pp. 228–243. Springer, Heidelberg (1999). https://doi.org/10.1007/3-540-48959-2_17
38. Lincoln, P., Mitchell, J.C.: Operational aspects of linear lambda calculus. In: Proceedings of the Seventh Annual IEEE Symposium on Logic in Computer Science (LICS '92). pp. 235–246 (1992). https://doi.org/10.1109/LICS.1992.185536
39. Manzonetto, G., Pagani, M., Ronchi Della Rocca, S.: New semantical insights into call-by-value λ-calculus. Fundamenta Informaticae **170**(1–3), 241–265 (2019). https://doi.org/10.3233/FI-2019-1862

40. Maraist, J., Odersky, M., Turner, D.N., Wadler, P.: Call-by-name, call-by-value, call-by-need and the linear lambda calculus. Theor. Comput. Sci. **228**(1–2), 175–210 (1999). https://doi.org/10.1016/S0304-3975(98)00358-2
41. Milner, R.: Local bigraphs and confluence: two conjectures: (extended abstract). In: Proceedings of the 13th International Workshop on Expressiveness in Concurrency. EXPRESS 2006. Electronic Notes in Theoretical Computer Science, vol. 175:3, pp. 65–73. Elsevier (2006). https://doi.org/10.1016/J.ENTCS.2006.07.035
42. Mitschke, G.: The standardization theorem for λ-calculus. Math. Log. Q. **25**(1–2), 29–31 (1979). https://doi.org/10.1002/malq.19790250104
43. Oostrom, V.: Confluence by decreasing diagrams. In: Voronkov, A. (ed.) RTA 2008. LNCS, vol. 5117, pp. 306–320. Springer, Heidelberg (2008). https://doi.org/10.1007/978-3-540-70590-1_21
44. Paolini, L., Ronchi Della Rocca, S.: Call-by-value solvability. RAIRO - Theor. Inform. Appl. **33**(6), 507–534 (1999). https://doi.org/10.1051/ita:1999130
45. Paolini, L., Ronchi Della Rocca, S.: Parametric parameter passing lambda-calculus. Inf. Comput. **189**(1), 87–106 (2004). https://doi.org/10.1016/j.ic.2003.08.003
46. Plotkin, G.D.: Call-by-name, call-by-value and the λ-calculus. Theor. Comput. Sci. **1**(2), 125–159 (1975). https://doi.org/10.1016/0304-3975(75)90017-1
47. Reynolds, J.C.: Where theory and practice meet: Popl past and future (1998). http://www.luca.demon.co.uk/POPL98/InvitedTalks.html, invited talk at POPL '98: The 25th ACM SIGPLAN-SIGACT Symposium on Principles of Programming Languages
48. Ronchi Della Rocca, S., Paolini, L.: The Parametric Lambda Calculus - A Metamodel for Computation. Texts in Theoretical Computer Science. An EATCS Series, Springer, Heidelberg (2004). https://doi.org/10.1007/978-3-662-10394-4
49. Ronchi Della Rocca, S., Roversi, L.: Lambda calculus and intuitionistic linear logic. Stud Logica **59**(3), 417–448 (1997). https://doi.org/10.1023/A:1005092630115
50. Sabry, A., Wadler, P.: A reflection on call-by-value. ACM Trans. Program. Lang. Syst. **19**(6), 916–941 (1997). https://doi.org/10.1145/267959.269968
51. Takahashi, M.: Parallel reductions in lambda-calculus. Inf. Comput. **118**(1), 120–127 (1995). https://doi.org/10.1006/inco.1995.1057
52. Terese: Term Rewriting Systems, Cambridge Tracts in Theoretical Computer Science, vol. 55. Cambridge University Press (2003)
53. Wadsworth, C.P.: The relation between computational and denotational properties for Scott's D_∞-models of the lambda-calculus. SIAM J. Comput. **5**(3), 488–521 (1976). https://doi.org/10.1137/0205036

A Dependency Pair Framework for Relative Termination of Term Rewriting

Jan-Christoph Kassing(✉), Grigory Vartanyan, and Jürgen Giesl

RWTH Aachen University, Aachen, Germany
{kassing,giesl}@cs.rwth-aachen.de, grigory.vartanyan@rwth-aachen.de

Abstract. *Dependency pairs* are one of the most powerful techniques for proving termination of term rewrite systems (TRSs), and they are used in almost all tools for termination analysis of TRSs. Problem #106 of the RTA List of Open Problems asks for an adaption of dependency pairs for *relative termination*. Here, infinite rewrite sequences are allowed, but one wants to prove that a certain subset of the rewrite rules cannot be used infinitely often. Dependency pairs were recently adapted to *annotated dependency pairs (ADPs)* to prove almost-sure termination of probabilistic TRSs. In this paper, we develop a novel adaption of ADPs for relative termination. We implemented our new ADP framework in our tool AProVE and evaluate it in comparison to state-of-the-art tools for relative termination of TRSs.

1 Introduction

Termination is an important topic in program verification. There is a wealth of work on automatic termination analysis of term rewrite systems (TRSs) which can also be used to analyze termination of programs in many other languages. Essentially all current termination tools for TRSs (e.g., AProVE [13], NaTT [36], MU-TERM [15], TTT2 [27], etc.) use *dependency pairs (DPs)* [1,11,12,16,17].

A combination of two TRSs (a *main* TRS $\mathcal{R}$ and a *base* TRS $\mathcal{B}$) is "*relatively terminating*" if there is no rewrite sequence that uses infinitely many steps with rules from $\mathcal{R}$ (whereas rules from $\mathcal{B}$ may be used infinitely often). Relative termination of TRSs has been studied since decades [8], and approaches based on relative rewriting are used for many applications, e.g., in complexity analysis [3,6,7,29,37], for proving confluence [19,25], for certifying confluence proofs [30], for proving termination of narrowing [20,31,34], and for proving liveness [26].

However, while techniques and tools for analyzing ordinary termination of TRSs are very powerful due to the use of DPs, a direct application of standard DPs to analyze relative termination is not possible. Therefore, most existing approaches for automated analysis of relative termination are quite restricted

Funded by the Deutsche Forschungsgemeinschaft (DFG, German Research Foundation) - 235950644 (Project GI 274/6-2) and DFG Research Training Group 2236 UnRAVeL.

C. Benzmüller et al. (Eds.): IJCAR 2024, LNAI 14740, pp. 360–380, 2024.
https://doi.org/10.1007/978-3-031-63501-4_19

in power. Hence, one of the largest open problems regarding DPs is Problem #106 of the RTA List of Open Problems [5]: *Can we use the dependency pair method to prove relative termination?* A first major step towards an answer to this question was presented in [21] by giving criteria for $\mathcal{R}$ and $\mathcal{B}$ that allow the use of ordinary DPs for relative termination.

Recently, we adapted DPs to analyze probabilistic innermost term rewriting, by using so-called *annotated dependency pairs (ADPs)* [23] or *dependency tuples (DTs)* [22] (which were originally proposed for innermost complexity analysis of TRSs [32]).[1] In these adaptions, one considers all *defined* function symbols in the right-hand side of a rule at once, whereas ordinary DPs consider them separately.

In this paper, we show that considering the defined symbols on right-hand sides separately (as for classical DPs) does not suffice for relative termination. On the other hand, we do not need to consider all of them at once either (i.e., we do not have to use the notions of ADPs or DTs from [22,23,32]). Instead, we introduce a new definition of ADPs that is suitable for relative termination and develop a corresponding ADP framework for automated relative termination proofs of TRSs. Moreover, while ADPs and DTs were only applicable for *innermost* rewriting in [22,23,32], we now adapt ADPs to *full* (relative) rewriting, i.e., we do not impose any specific evaluation strategy. So while [21] presented conditions under which the *ordinary classical* DP framework can be used to prove relative termination, in this paper we develop the first *specific* DP framework for relative termination.

Structure: We start with preliminaries on relative rewriting in Sect. 2. In Sect. 3 we recapitulate the core processors of the DP framework and show that classical DPs are unsound for relative termination in general. Moreover, we state the main results of [21] on criteria when ordinary DPs may nevertheless be used for relative termination. Afterwards, we introduce our novel notion of *annotated dependency pairs* for relative termination in Sect. 4 and present a corresponding new ADP framework in Sect. 5. We implemented our framework in the tool AProVE and in Sect. 6, we evaluate our implementation in comparison to other state-of-the-art tools. All proofs can be found in [24].

2 Relative Term Rewriting

We assume familiarity with term rewriting [2] and regard (finite) TRSs over a (finite) signature Σ and a set of variables $\mathcal{V}$.

Example 1. Consider the following TRS $\mathcal{R}_{\mathsf{divL}}$, where $\mathsf{divL}(x, xs)$ computes the number that results from dividing x by each element of the list xs. As usual, natural numbers are represented by the function symbols $\mathsf{0}$ and s, and lists

[1] As shown in [23], using ADPs instead of DTs leads to a more elegant, more powerful, and less complicated framework, and to completeness of the underlying *chain criterion*.

are represented via nil and cons. Then $\mathsf{divL}(\mathsf{s}^{24}(\mathsf{0}), \mathsf{cons}(\mathsf{s}^4(\mathsf{0}), \mathsf{cons}(\mathsf{s}^3(\mathsf{0}), \mathsf{nil})))$ evaluates to $\mathsf{s}^2(\mathsf{0})$, because $(24/4)/3 = 2$. Here, $\mathsf{s}^2(\mathsf{0})$ stands for $\mathsf{s}(\mathsf{s}(\mathsf{0}))$, etc.

$$\mathsf{minus}(x, \mathsf{0}) \to x \quad (1) \qquad \mathsf{div}(\mathsf{s}(x), \mathsf{s}(y)) \to \mathsf{s}(\mathsf{div}(\mathsf{minus}(x, y), \mathsf{s}(y))) \quad (4)$$

$$\mathsf{minus}(\mathsf{s}(x), \mathsf{s}(y)) \to \mathsf{minus}(x, y) \quad (2) \qquad \mathsf{divL}(x, \mathsf{nil}) \to x \quad (5)$$

$$\mathsf{div}(\mathsf{0}, \mathsf{s}(y)) \to \mathsf{0} \quad (3) \qquad \mathsf{divL}(x, \mathsf{cons}(y, xs)) \to \mathsf{divL}(\mathsf{div}(x, y), xs) \quad (6)$$

A TRS $\mathcal{R}$ induces a *rewrite relation* $\to_{\mathcal{R}} \subseteq \mathcal{T}(\Sigma, \mathcal{V}) \times \mathcal{T}(\Sigma, \mathcal{V})$ on terms where $s \to_{\mathcal{R}} t$ holds if there is a $\pi \in \mathrm{Pos}(s)$, a rule $\ell \to r \in \mathcal{R}$, and a substitution σ such that $s|_\pi = \ell\sigma$ and $t = s[r\sigma]_\pi$. For example, $\mathsf{minus}(\mathsf{s}(\mathsf{0}), \mathsf{s}(\mathsf{0})) \to_{\mathcal{R}_{\mathsf{divL}}} \mathsf{minus}(\mathsf{0}, \mathsf{0}) \to_{\mathcal{R}_{\mathsf{divL}}} \mathsf{0}$. We call a TRS $\mathcal{R}$ *terminating* (abbreviated SN, for "strongly normalizing") if $\to_{\mathcal{R}}$ is well founded. Using the DP framework, one can easily prove that $\mathcal{R}_{\mathsf{divL}}$ is SN (see Sect. 3.1). In particular, in each application of the recursive divL-rule (6), the length of the list in divL's second argument is decreased by one.

In the relative setting, one considers two TRSs $\mathcal{R}$ and $\mathcal{B}$. We say that $\mathcal{R}$ is *relatively terminating* w.r.t. $\mathcal{B}$ (i.e., $\mathcal{R}/\mathcal{B}$ is SN) if there is no infinite $(\to_{\mathcal{R}} \cup \to_{\mathcal{B}})$-rewrite sequence that uses an infinite number of $\to_{\mathcal{R}}$-steps. We refer to $\mathcal{R}$ as the *main* and $\mathcal{B}$ as the *base* TRS.

Example 2. Let $\mathcal{R}_{\mathsf{divL}}$ be the *main* TRS. Since the order of the list elements does not affect the termination of $\mathcal{R}_{\mathsf{divL}}$, this algorithm also works for multisets. To abstract lists to multisets, we add the *base* TRS $\mathcal{B}_{\mathsf{mset}} = \{(7)\}$.

$$\mathsf{cons}(x, \mathsf{cons}(y, zs)) \to \mathsf{cons}(y, \mathsf{cons}(x, zs)) \quad (7)$$

$\mathcal{B}_{\mathsf{mset}}$ is non-terminating, since it can switch elements in a list arbitrarily often. However, $\mathcal{R}_{\mathsf{divL}}/\mathcal{B}_{\mathsf{mset}}$ is SN as each application of Rule (6) still reduces the list length. Indeed, termination of $\mathcal{R}_{\mathsf{divL}}/\mathcal{B}_{\mathsf{mset}}$ can also be shown via the approach of [21], because it allows us to apply (standard) DPs in this example, see Example 13.

However, if $\mathcal{B}_{\mathsf{mset}}$ is replaced by the base TRS $\mathcal{B}_{\mathsf{mset2}}$ with the rule

$$\mathsf{divL}(z, \mathsf{cons}(x, \mathsf{cons}(y, zs))) \to \mathsf{divL}(z, \mathsf{cons}(y, \mathsf{cons}(x, zs))), \quad (8)$$

then $\mathcal{R}_{\mathsf{divL}}/\mathcal{B}_{\mathsf{mset2}}$ remains terminating, but the approach of [21] is no longer applicable, see Example 14. In contrast, with our new DP framework in Sects. 4 and 5, termination of such examples can be proved automatically.[2]

We will use the following four examples to illustrate the problems that one has to take into account when analyzing relative termination. So these examples show why a naive adaption of dependency pairs does not work in the relative

[2] To ease the presentation, the rule (8) only switches the first two elements in a list. Our approach also succeeds on a more complicated variant where the elements of lists in divL's second argument can be permuted arbitrarily. We included such an example in the benchmark collection that we used for our evaluation in Sect. 6.

setting and why we need our new notion of *annotated dependency pairs.* The examples represent different types of infinite rewrite sequences that can lead to non-termination in the relative setting: *redex-duplicating, redex-creating* (or "-emitting"), and *ordinary infinite sequences.*

Example 3 (Redex-Duplicating). Consider the TRSs $\mathcal{R}_1 = \{\mathsf{a} \to \mathsf{b}\}$ and $\mathcal{B}_1 = \{\mathsf{f}(x) \to \mathsf{d}(\mathsf{f}(x), x)\}$ from [21, Example 4]. $\mathcal{R}_1/\mathcal{B}_1$ is not SN due to the infinite rewrite sequence $\underline{\mathsf{f}(\mathsf{a})} \to_{\mathcal{B}_1} \mathsf{d}(\mathsf{f}(\mathsf{a}), \underline{\mathsf{a}}) \to_{\mathcal{R}_1} \mathsf{d}(\underline{\mathsf{f}(\mathsf{a})}, \mathsf{b}) \to_{\mathcal{B}_1} \mathsf{d}(\mathsf{d}(\mathsf{f}(\mathsf{a}), \underline{\mathsf{a}}), \mathsf{b}) \to_{\mathcal{R}_1} \mathsf{d}(\mathsf{d}(\mathsf{f}(\mathsf{a}), \mathsf{b}), \mathsf{b}) \to_{\mathcal{B}_1} \ldots$ The reason is that $\mathcal{B}_1$ can be used to duplicate an arbitrary $\mathcal{R}_1$-redex infinitely often.

Example 4 (Redex-Creating on Parallel Position). Next, consider $\mathcal{R}_2 = \{\mathsf{a} \to \mathsf{b}\}$ and $\mathcal{B}_2 = \{\mathsf{f} \to \mathsf{d}(\mathsf{f}, \mathsf{a})\}$. $\mathcal{R}_2/\mathcal{B}_2$ is not SN as we have the infinite rewrite sequence $\underline{\mathsf{f}} \to_{\mathcal{B}_2} \mathsf{d}(\mathsf{f}, \underline{\mathsf{a}}) \to_{\mathcal{R}_2} \mathsf{d}(\underline{\mathsf{f}}, \mathsf{b}) \to_{\mathcal{B}_2} \mathsf{d}(\mathsf{d}(\mathsf{f}, \underline{\mathsf{a}}), \mathsf{b}) \to_{\mathcal{R}_2} \mathsf{d}(\mathsf{d}(\underline{\mathsf{f}}, \mathsf{b}), \mathsf{b}) \to_{\mathcal{B}_2} \ldots$ Here, $\mathcal{B}_2$ can create an $\mathcal{R}_2$-redex infinitely often (where in the right-hand side $\mathsf{d}(\mathsf{f}, \mathsf{a})$ of $\mathcal{B}_2$'s rule, the $\mathcal{B}_2$-redex f and the created $\mathcal{R}_2$-redex a are on parallel positions).

Example 5 (Redex-Creating on Position Above). Let $\mathcal{R}_3 = \{\mathsf{a}(x) \to \mathsf{b}(x)\}$ and $\mathcal{B}_3 = \{\mathsf{f} \to \mathsf{a}(\mathsf{f})\}$. $\mathcal{R}_3/\mathcal{B}_3$ is not SN as we have $\underline{\mathsf{f}} \to_{\mathcal{B}_3} \underline{\mathsf{a}}(\mathsf{f}) \to_{\mathcal{R}_3} \mathsf{b}(\underline{\mathsf{f}}) \to_{\mathcal{B}_3} \mathsf{b}(\underline{\mathsf{a}}(\mathsf{f})) \to_{\mathcal{R}_3} \mathsf{b}(\mathsf{b}(\underline{\mathsf{f}})) \to_{\mathcal{B}_3} \ldots$, i.e., again $\mathcal{B}_3$ can be used to create an $\mathcal{R}_3$-redex infinitely often. In the right-hand side $\mathsf{a}(\mathsf{f})$ of $\mathcal{B}_3$'s rule, the position of the created $\mathcal{R}_3$-redex $\mathsf{a}(\ldots)$ is above the position of the $\mathcal{B}_3$-redex f.

Example 6 (Ordinary Infinite). Finally, consider $\mathcal{R}_4 = \{\mathsf{a} \to \mathsf{b}\}$ and $\mathcal{B}_4 = \{\mathsf{b} \to \mathsf{a}\}$. Here, the base TRS $\mathcal{B}_4$ can neither duplicate nor create an $\mathcal{R}_4$-redex infinitely often, but in combination with the main TRS $\mathcal{R}_4$ we obtain the infinite rewrite sequence $\mathsf{a} \to_{\mathcal{R}_4} \mathsf{b} \to_{\mathcal{B}_4} \mathsf{a} \to_{\mathcal{R}_4} \mathsf{b} \to_{\mathcal{B}_4} \ldots$ Thus, $\mathcal{R}_4/\mathcal{B}_4$ is not SN.

3 DP Framework

We first recapitulate dependency pairs for ordinary (non-relative) rewriting in Sect. 3.1 and summarize existing results on DPs for relative rewriting in Sect. 3.2.

3.1 Dependency Pairs for Ordinary Term Rewriting

We recapitulate DPs and the two most important processors of the DP framework, and refer to, e.g., [1,11,12,16,17] for more details. As an example, we show how to prove termination of $\mathcal{R}_{\mathsf{divL}}$ without the base $\mathcal{B}_{\mathsf{mset}}$. We decompose the signature $\Sigma = \mathcal{C} \uplus \mathcal{D}$ of a TRS $\mathcal{R}$ such that $f \in \mathcal{D}$ if $f = \mathrm{root}(\ell)$ for some rule $\ell \to r \in \mathcal{R}$. The symbols in $\mathcal{C}$ and $\mathcal{D}$ are called *constructors* and *defined symbols* of $\mathcal{R}$, respectively. For every $f \in \mathcal{D}$, we introduce a fresh *annotated* (or "marked") symbol $f^{\#}$ of the same arity. Let $\mathcal{D}^{\#}$ denote the set of all annotated symbols, and let $\Sigma^{\#} = \Sigma \uplus \mathcal{D}^{\#}$. To ease readability, we often use capital letters like F instead of $\mathsf{f}^{\#}$. For any term $t = f(t_1, \ldots, t_n) \in \mathcal{T}(\Sigma, \mathcal{V})$ with $f \in \mathcal{D}$, let $t^{\#} = f^{\#}(t_1, \ldots, t_n)$. For each rule $\ell \to r$ and each subterm t of r with defined root symbol, one obtains a *dependency pair* $\ell^{\#} \to t^{\#}$. Let $\mathcal{DP}(\mathcal{R})$ denote the set of all dependency pairs of the TRS $\mathcal{R}$.

Example 7. For $\mathcal{R}_{\mathsf{divL}}$ from Example 1, we obtain the following five dependency pairs.

$$\mathsf{M}(\mathsf{s}(x),\mathsf{s}(y)) \to \mathsf{M}(x,y) \quad (9) \qquad \mathsf{DL}(x,\mathsf{cons}(y,xs)) \to \mathsf{D}(x,y) \quad (12)$$
$$\mathsf{D}(\mathsf{s}(x),\mathsf{s}(y)) \to \mathsf{M}(x,y) \quad (10) \qquad \mathsf{DL}(x,\mathsf{cons}(y,xs)) \to \mathsf{DL}(\mathsf{div}(x,y),xs) \quad (13)$$
$$\mathsf{D}(\mathsf{s}(x),\mathsf{s}(y)) \to \mathsf{D}(\mathsf{m}(x,y),\mathsf{s}(y)) \quad (11)$$

The DP framework operates on *DP problems* $(\mathcal{P},\mathcal{R})$ where $\mathcal{P}$ is a (finite) set of DPs, and $\mathcal{R}$ is a (finite) TRS. A (possibly infinite) sequence $t_0, t_1, t_2, \ldots$ with $t_i \xrightarrow{\varepsilon}_{\mathcal{P}} \circ \to_{\mathcal{R}}^* t_{i+1}$ for all i is a $(\mathcal{P},\mathcal{R})$*-chain.* Here, $\xrightarrow{\varepsilon}$ are rewrite steps at the root. A chain represents subsequent "function calls" in evaluations. Between two function calls (corresponding to steps with $\mathcal{P}$, called **p**-steps) one can evaluate the arguments using arbitrary many steps with $\mathcal{R}$ (called **r**-steps). So **r**-steps are rewrite steps that are needed in order to enable another **p**-step at a position above later on. Hence, $\mathsf{DL}(\mathsf{s}(0),\mathsf{cons}(\mathsf{s}(0),\mathsf{nil})), \mathsf{DL}(\mathsf{s}(0),\mathsf{nil})$ is a $(\mathcal{DP}(\mathcal{R}_{\mathsf{divL}}),\mathcal{R}_{\mathsf{divL}})$-chain, as $\mathsf{DL}(\mathsf{s}(0),\mathsf{cons}(\mathsf{s}(0),\mathsf{nil})) \xrightarrow{\varepsilon}_{\mathcal{DP}(\mathcal{R}_{\mathsf{divL}})} \mathsf{DL}(\mathsf{div}(\mathsf{s}(0),\mathsf{s}(0)),\mathsf{nil}) \to_{\mathcal{R}_{\mathsf{divL}}}^* \mathsf{DL}(\mathsf{s}(0),\mathsf{nil})$.

A DP problem $(\mathcal{P},\mathcal{R})$ is called *terminating (SN)* if there is no infinite $(\mathcal{P},\mathcal{R})$-chain. The main result on DPs is the *chain criterion* which states that a TRS $\mathcal{R}$ is SN iff $(\mathcal{DP}(\mathcal{R}),\mathcal{R})$ is SN. The key idea of the DP framework is a *divide-and-conquer* approach which applies *DP processors* to transform DP problems into simpler sub-problems. A *DP processor* Proc has the form $\mathrm{Proc}(\mathcal{P},\mathcal{R}) = \{(\mathcal{P}_1,\mathcal{R}_1),\ldots,(\mathcal{P}_n,\mathcal{R}_n)\}$, where $\mathcal{P},\mathcal{P}_1,\ldots,\mathcal{P}_n$ are sets of DPs and $\mathcal{R},\mathcal{R}_1,\ldots,\mathcal{R}_n$ are TRSs. Proc is *sound* if $(\mathcal{P},\mathcal{R})$ is SN whenever $(\mathcal{P}_i,\mathcal{R}_i)$ is SN for all $1 \le i \le n$. It is *complete* if $(\mathcal{P}_i,\mathcal{R}_i)$ is SN for all $1 \le i \le n$ whenever $(\mathcal{P},\mathcal{R})$ is SN.

So for a TRS $\mathcal{R}$, one starts with the initial DP problem $(\mathcal{DP}(\mathcal{R}),\mathcal{R})$ and applies sound (and preferably complete) DP processors until all sub-problems are "solved" (i.e., processors transform them to the empty set). This allows for modular termination proofs, as different techniques can be applied on each sub-problem.

One of the most important processors is the *dependency graph processor*. The $(\mathcal{P},\mathcal{R})$*-dependency graph* indicates which DPs can be used after each other in chains. Its set of nodes is $\mathcal{P}$ and there is an edge from $s_1 \to t_1$ to $s_2 \to t_2$ if there are substitutions σ_1,σ_2 with $t_1\sigma_1 \to_{\mathcal{R}}^* s_2\sigma_2$. Any infinite $(\mathcal{P},\mathcal{R})$-chain corresponds to an infinite path in the dependency graph, and since the graph is finite, this infinite path must end in a strongly connected component (SCC).[3] Hence, it suffices to consider the SCCs of this graph independently.

Theorem 8 (Dep. Graph Processor). *For the SCCs* $\mathcal{P}_1,\ldots,\mathcal{P}_n$ *of the* $(\mathcal{P},\mathcal{R})$*-dependency graph,* $\mathrm{Proc}_{\mathsf{DG}}(\mathcal{P},\mathcal{R}) = \{(\mathcal{P}_1,\mathcal{R}),\ldots,(\mathcal{P}_n,\mathcal{R})\}$ *is sound and complete.*

[3] Here, a set $\mathcal{P}'$ of dependency pairs is an *SCC* if it is a maximal cycle, i.e., it is a maximal set such that for any $s_1 \to t_1$ and $s_2 \to t_2$ in $\mathcal{P}'$ there is a non-empty path from $s_1 \to t_1$ to $s_2 \to t_2$ which only traverses nodes from $\mathcal{P}'$.

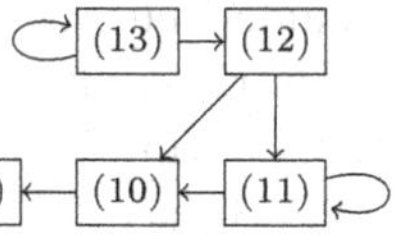

While the exact dependency graph is not computable in general, there are several techniques to over-approximate it automatically [1,12,16]. The $(\mathcal{DP}(\mathcal{R}_{\mathsf{divL}}), \mathcal{R}_{\mathsf{divL}})$-dependency graph for our example is on the right. Here, $\mathrm{Proc}_{\mathsf{DG}}(\mathcal{DP}(\mathcal{R}_{\mathsf{divL}}),\mathcal{R}_{\mathsf{divL}})$ yields $(\{(9)\},\mathcal{R}_{\mathsf{divL}})$, $(\{(11)\},\mathcal{R}_{\mathsf{divL}})$, and $(\{(13)\},\mathcal{R}_{\mathsf{divL}})$.

The second crucial processor adapts classical reduction orders to DP problems. A *reduction pair* $(\succsim, \succ)$ consists of two relations on terms such that $\succsim$ is reflexive, transitive, and closed under contexts and substitutions, and $\succ$ is a well-founded order that is closed under substitutions but does not have to be closed under contexts. Moreover, $\succsim$ and $\succ$ must be compatible, i.e., $\succsim \circ \succ \circ \succsim \;\subseteq\; \succ$. The *reduction pair processor* requires that all rules and dependency pairs are weakly decreasing, and it removes those DPs that are strictly decreasing.

Theorem 9 (Reduction Pair Processor). *Let* $(\succsim, \succ)$ *be a reduction pair such that* $\mathcal{P} \cup \mathcal{R} \subseteq \succsim$. *Then* $\mathrm{Proc}_{\mathsf{RPP}}(\mathcal{P}, \mathcal{R}) = \{(\mathcal{P} \setminus \succ, \mathcal{R})\}$ *is sound and complete.*

For example, one can use reduction pairs based on polynomial interpretations [28]. A *polynomial interpretation* Pol is a $\Sigma^{\#}$-algebra which maps every function symbol $f \in \Sigma^{\#}$ to a polynomial $f_{\mathrm{Pol}} \in \mathbb{N}[\mathcal{V}]$. $\mathrm{Pol}(t)$ denotes the *interpretation* of a term t by the $\Sigma^{\#}$-algebra Pol. Then Pol induces a reduction pair $(\succsim, \succ)$ where $t_1 \succsim t_2$ $(t_1 \succ t_2)$ holds if the inequation $\mathrm{Pol}(t_1) \geq \mathrm{Pol}(t_2)$ $(\mathrm{Pol}(t_1) > \mathrm{Pol}(t_2))$ is true for all instantiations of its variables by natural numbers.

For the three remaining DP problems $(\{(9)\}, \mathcal{R}_{\mathsf{divL}})$, $(\{(11)\}, \mathcal{R}_{\mathsf{divL}})$, and $(\{(13)\}, \mathcal{R}_{\mathsf{divL}})$ in our example, we can apply the reduction pair processor using the polynomial interpretation which maps $\mathsf{0}$ and nil to 0, $\mathsf{s}(x)$ to $x+1$, $\mathsf{cons}(y, xs)$ to $xs + 1$, $\mathsf{DL}(x, xs)$ to xs, and all other symbols to their first arguments. Since (9), (11), and (13) are strictly decreasing, $\mathrm{Proc}_{\mathsf{RPP}}$ transforms all three remaining DP problems into DP problems of the form $(\varnothing, \ldots)$. As $\mathrm{Proc}_{\mathsf{DG}}(\varnothing, \ldots) = \varnothing$ and all processors used are sound, this means that there is no infinite chain for the initial DP problem $(\mathcal{DP}(\mathcal{R}_{\mathsf{divL}}), \mathcal{R}_{\mathsf{divL}})$ and thus, $\mathcal{R}_{\mathsf{divL}}$ is SN.

3.2 Dependency Pairs for Relative Termination

Up to now, we only considered DPs for ordinary termination of TRSs. The easiest idea to use DPs in the relative setting is to start with the DP problem $(\mathcal{DP}(\mathcal{R} \cup \mathcal{B}), \mathcal{R} \cup \mathcal{B})$. This would prove termination of $\mathcal{R} \cup \mathcal{B}$, which implies termination of $\mathcal{R}/\mathcal{B}$, but ignores that the rules in $\mathcal{B}$ do not have to terminate. Since termination of DP problems is already defined via a relative condition (finite chains can only have finitely many $\mathbf{p}$-steps but there may exist rewrite sequences with infinitely many $\mathbf{r}$-steps that are no chains), another idea for proving termination of $\mathcal{R}/\mathcal{B}$ is to start with the DP problem $(\mathcal{DP}(\mathcal{R}), \mathcal{R} \cup \mathcal{B})$, which only considers the DPs of $\mathcal{R}$. However, this is unsound in general.

Example 10. The only defined symbol of $\mathcal{R}_2$ from Example 4 is a. Since the right-hand side of $\mathcal{R}_2$'s rule does not contain defined symbols, we would get the DP problem $(\varnothing, \mathcal{R}_2 \cup \mathcal{B}_2)$, which is SN as it has no DP. Thus, we would falsely conclude that $\mathcal{R}_2/\mathcal{B}_2$ is SN. Similarly, this approach would also falsely "prove" SN for Examples 3 and 5. Thus, the standard notion of DPs is unsound for relative termination.

In [21], it was shown that under certain conditions on $\mathcal{R}$ and $\mathcal{B}$, starting with the DP problem $(\mathcal{DP}(\mathcal{R} \cup \mathcal{B}_a), \mathcal{R} \cup \mathcal{B})$ for a subset $\mathcal{B}_a \subseteq \mathcal{B}$ is sound for relative termination.[4] The two conditions on the TRSs are *dominance* and being *non-duplicating*. We say that $\mathcal{R}$ *dominates* $\mathcal{B}$ if defined symbols of $\mathcal{R}$ do not occur in the right-hand sides of rules of $\mathcal{B}$. A TRS is *non-duplicating* if no variable occurs more often on the right-hand side of a rule than on its left-hand side.

Theorem 11 (First Main Result of [21], Sound and Complete). *Let $\mathcal{R}$ and $\mathcal{B}$ be TRSs such that $\mathcal{B}$ is non-duplicating and $\mathcal{R}$ dominates $\mathcal{B}$. Then the DP problem $(\mathcal{DP}(\mathcal{R}), \mathcal{R} \cup \mathcal{B})$ is SN iff $\mathcal{R}/\mathcal{B}$ is SN.*

Theorem 12 (Second Main Result of [21], only Sound). *Let $\mathcal{R}$ and $\mathcal{B} = \mathcal{B}_a \uplus \mathcal{B}_b$ be TRSs. If $\mathcal{B}_b$ is non-duplicating, $\mathcal{R} \cup \mathcal{B}_a$ dominates $\mathcal{B}_b$, and the DP problem $(\mathcal{DP}(\mathcal{R} \cup \mathcal{B}_a), \mathcal{R} \cup \mathcal{B})$ is SN, then $\mathcal{R}/\mathcal{B}$ is SN.*

Example 13. For the main TRS $\mathcal{R}_{\mathsf{divL}}$ from Example 1 and base TRS $\mathcal{B}_{\mathsf{mset}}$ from Example 2 we can apply Theorem 11 and consider the DP problem $(\mathcal{DP}(\mathcal{R}_{\mathsf{divL}}), \mathcal{R}_{\mathsf{divL}} \cup \mathcal{B}_{\mathsf{mset}})$, since $\mathcal{B}_{\mathsf{mset}}$ is non-duplicating and $\mathcal{R}_{\mathsf{divL}}$ dominates $\mathcal{B}_{\mathsf{mset}}$. As for $(\mathcal{DP}(\mathcal{R}_{\mathsf{divL}}), \mathcal{R}_{\mathsf{divL}})$, the DP framework can prove that $(\mathcal{DP}(\mathcal{R}_{\mathsf{divL}}), \mathcal{R}_{\mathsf{divL}} \cup \mathcal{B}_{\mathsf{mset}})$ is SN. In this way, the tool NaTT which implements the results of [21] proves that $\mathcal{R}_{\mathsf{divL}}/\mathcal{B}_{\mathsf{mset}}$ is SN. Note that sophisticated techniques like DPs are needed to prove SN for $\mathcal{R}_{\mathsf{divL}}/\mathcal{B}_{\mathsf{mset}}$ because classical (simplification) orders already fail to prove termination of $\mathcal{R}_{\mathsf{divL}}$.

Example 14. As mentioned in Example 2, if we consider $\mathcal{B}_{\mathsf{mset2}}$ with the rule

$$\mathsf{divL}(z, \mathsf{cons}(x, \mathsf{cons}(y, zs))) \to \mathsf{divL}(z, \mathsf{cons}(y, \mathsf{cons}(x, zs))) \tag{8}$$

instead of $\mathcal{B}_{\mathsf{mset}}$ as the base TRS, then $\mathcal{R}_{\mathsf{divL}}/\mathcal{B}_{\mathsf{mset2}}$ is still terminating, but we cannot use Theorem 11 since $\mathcal{R}_{\mathsf{divL}}$ does not dominate $\mathcal{B}_{\mathsf{mset2}}$. If we try to split $\mathcal{B}_{\mathsf{mset2}}$ as in Theorem 12, then $\varnothing \neq \mathcal{B}_a \subseteq \mathcal{B}_{\mathsf{mset2}}$ implies $\mathcal{B}_a = \mathcal{B}_{\mathsf{mset2}}$, but $\mathcal{B}_{\mathsf{mset2}}$ is non-terminating. Therefore, all previous tools for relative termination fail in proving that $\mathcal{R}_{\mathsf{divL}}/\mathcal{B}_{\mathsf{mset2}}$ is SN. In Sect. 4 we will present our novel DP framework which can prove relative termination of relative TRSs like $\mathcal{R}_{\mathsf{divL}}/\mathcal{B}_{\mathsf{mset2}}$.

As remarked in [21], Theorems 11 and 12 are unsound if one only considers *minimal* chains, i.e., if for a DP problem $(\mathcal{P}, \mathcal{R})$ one only considers chains $t_0, t_1, \ldots$, where all t_i are $\mathcal{R}$-terminating. In the DP framework for ordinary rewriting, the restriction to minimal chains allows the use of further processors, e.g., based on *usable rules* [12,17] or the *subterm criterion* [17]. As shown in [21], usable rules and the subterm criterion can nevertheless be applied if $\mathcal{B}$ is *quasi-terminating* [4], i.e., $\{t \mid s \to_{\mathcal{B}}^* t\}$ is finite for every term s. This restriction would also be needed to integrate processors that rely on minimality into our new framework in Sect. 4.

[4] As before, for the construction of $\mathcal{DP}(\mathcal{R} \cup \mathcal{B}_a)$, only the root symbols of left-hand sides of $\mathcal{R} \cup \mathcal{B}_a$ are considered to be "defined".

4 Annotated Dependency Pairs for Relative Termination

As shown in Sect. 3.2, up to now there only exist criteria [21] that state when it is sound to apply *ordinary* DPs for proving relative termination, but there is no *specific* DP-based technique to analyze relative termination directly. For ordinary termination, we create a separate DP for each occurrence of a defined symbol in the right-hand side of a rule (and no DP is created for rules without defined symbols in their right-hand sides). This would work to detect *ordinary infinite* sequences like the one in Example 6 in the relative setting, i.e., such an infinite sequence would give rise to an infinite chain. However, as shown in Example 10, this would not suffice to detect infinite redex-creating sequences as in Examples 4 and 5. Thus, ordinary DPs are unsound for analyzing relative termination.

To solve this problem, we now adapt the concept of *annotated dependency pairs* (ADPs) for relative termination. ADPs were introduced in [23] to prove innermost almost-sure termination of probabilistic term rewriting. In the relative setting, we can use similar dependency pairs as in the probabilistic setting, but with a different rewrite relation $\hookrightarrow$ to deal with non-innermost steps. Compared to [21], we (a) remove the requirement of dominance, which will be handled by the dependency graph processor, and (b) allow for ADP processors that are specifically designed for the relative setting before possibly moving to ordinary DPs.

The requirement that $\mathcal{B}$ must be non-duplicating remains, since relative non-termination because of duplicating rules is not necessarily due to the relation between the left-hand side and the subterms with defined root symbols in the right-hand side of a rule. Therefore, this cannot be captured by (A)DPs, i.e., DPs do not help in analyzing redex-duplicating sequences as in Example 3, where the crucial redex a is not generated from a "function call" in the right-hand side of a rule, but it just corresponds to a duplicated variable. To handle TRSs $\mathcal{R}/\mathcal{B}$ where $\mathcal{B}_{dup} \subseteq \mathcal{B}$ is duplicating, one can move the duplicating rules to the main TRS $\mathcal{R}$ and try to prove relative termination of $(\mathcal{R} \cup \mathcal{B}_{dup})/(\mathcal{B} \setminus \mathcal{B}_{dup})$ instead, or one can try to find a reduction pair $(\succsim, \succ)$ where $\succ$ is closed under contexts such that $\mathcal{R} \cup \mathcal{B} \subseteq \succsim$ and $\mathcal{B}_{dup} \subseteq \succ$. Then it suffices to prove relative termination of $(\mathcal{R} \setminus \succ)/(\mathcal{B} \setminus \succ)$ instead.

We will now define a notion of DPs that can detect infinite redex-creating sequences as in Example 4 with $\mathcal{R}_2 = \{\mathsf{a} \to \mathsf{b}\}$ and $\mathcal{B}_2 = \{\mathsf{f} \to \mathsf{d}(\mathsf{f}, \mathsf{a})\}$: $\underline{\mathsf{f}} \to_{\mathcal{B}_2} \mathsf{d}(\mathsf{f}, \underline{\mathsf{a}}) \to_{\mathcal{R}_2} \mathsf{d}(\underline{\mathsf{f}}, \mathsf{b}) \to_{\mathcal{B}_2} \mathsf{d}(\mathsf{d}(\mathsf{f}, \underline{\mathsf{a}}), \mathsf{b}) \to_{\mathcal{R}_2} \dots$ To this end, (1) we need a DP for the rule $\mathsf{a} \to \mathsf{b}$ to track the reduction of the created $\mathcal{R}_2$-redex a, although b is a constructor. Moreover, (2) both defined symbols f and a in the right-hand side of the rule $\mathsf{f} \to \mathsf{d}(\mathsf{f}, \mathsf{a})$ have to be considered simultaneously: We need f to create an infinite number of $\mathcal{R}_2$-redexes, and we need a since it is the created $\mathcal{R}_2$-redex. Hence, for rules from the base TRS $\mathcal{B}_2$, we have to consider all possible pairs of defined symbols in their right-hand sides simultaneously.[5] This is not needed for

[5] For relative termination, it suffices to consider *pairs* of defined symbols. The reason is that to "track" a non-terminating reduction, one only has to consider a single

the main TRS $\mathcal{R}_2$, i.e., if the f-rule were in the main TRS, then the f in the right-hand side could be considered separately from the a that it generates. Therefore, we distinguish between *main* and *base ADPs* (that are generated from the main and the base TRS, respectively).

As in [23], we now annotate defined symbols directly in the original rewrite rule instead of extracting annotated subterms from its right-hand side. In this way, we may have terms containing several annotated symbols, which allows us to consider pairs of defined symbols in right-hand sides simultaneously. At the same time, an ADP maintains the information on the positions of the subterms in the original right-hand side. (This information will be needed for the "completeness" of the chain criterion in Theorem 23, i.e., it allows us to obtain an *equivalent* characterization of relative termination via chains of ADPs.[6])

Definition 15 (Annotations). *For* $t \in \mathcal{T}(\Sigma^{\#}, \mathcal{V})$ *and* $\mathcal{X} \subseteq \Sigma^{\#} \cup \mathcal{V}$, *let* $\mathrm{Pos}_{\mathcal{X}}(t)$ *be the set of all positions of* t *with symbols or variables from* $\mathcal{X}$. *For* $\Phi \subseteq \mathrm{Pos}_{\mathcal{D} \cup \mathcal{D}^{\#}}(t)$, $\#_{\Phi}(t)$ *is the variant of* t *where the symbols at positions from* Φ *are annotated and all other annotations are removed. Thus,* $\mathrm{Pos}_{\mathcal{D}^{\#}}(\#_{\Phi}(t)) = \Phi$, *and* $\#_{\varnothing}(t)$ *removes all annotations from* t, *where we often write* $\flat(t)$ *instead of* $\#_{\varnothing}(t)$. *Moreover, for a singleton* $\{\pi\}$, *we often write* $\#_{\pi}$ *instead of* $\#_{\{\pi\}}$. *We write* $t \trianglelefteq_{\#}^{\pi} s$ *if* $\pi \in \mathrm{Pos}_{\mathcal{D}^{\#}}(s)$ *and* $t = \flat(s|_{\pi})$ *(i.e.,* t *results from a subterm of* s *with annotated root symbol by removing its annotations). We also write* $\trianglelefteq_{\#}$ *instead of* $\trianglelefteq_{\#}^{\pi}$ *if* π *is irrelevant.*

Example 16. If $\mathsf{f} \in \mathcal{D}$, then we have $\#_1(\mathsf{f}(\mathsf{f}(x))) = \#_1(\mathsf{F}(\mathsf{F}(x))) = \mathsf{f}(\mathsf{F}(x))$ and $\flat(\mathsf{F}(\mathsf{F}(x))) = \mathsf{f}(\mathsf{f}(x))$. Moreover, we have $\mathsf{f}(x) \trianglelefteq_{\#}^{1} \mathsf{f}(\mathsf{F}(x))$.

While in [23] all defined symbols on the right-hand sides of rules were annotated, we now define our novel variant of *annotated dependency pairs* for relative rewriting. As explained before Definition 15, we have to track (at most) two redexes for base ADPs and only one redex for main ADPs.

Definition 17 (Annotated Dependency Pair). *A rule* $\ell \to r$ *with* $\ell \in \mathcal{T}(\Sigma, \mathcal{V}) \setminus \mathcal{V}$, $r \in \mathcal{T}(\Sigma^{\#}, \mathcal{V})$, *and* $\mathcal{V}(r) \subseteq \mathcal{V}(\ell)$ *is called an* annotated dependency pair (ADP). *Let* $\mathcal{D}$ *be the defined symbols of* $\mathcal{R} \cup \mathcal{B}$, *and for* $n \in \mathbb{N}$, *let* $\mathcal{A}_n(\ell \to r) = \{\ell \to \#_{\Phi}(r) \mid \Phi \subseteq \mathrm{Pos}_{\mathcal{D}}(r), |\Phi| = \min(n, |\mathrm{Pos}_{\mathcal{D}}(r)|)\}$. *The* canonical main ADPs *for* $\mathcal{R}$ *are* $\mathcal{A}_1(\mathcal{R}) = \bigcup_{\ell \to r \in \mathcal{R}} \mathcal{A}_1(\ell \to r)$ *and the* canonical base ADPs *for* $\mathcal{B}$ *are* $\mathcal{A}_2(\mathcal{B}) = \bigcup_{\ell \to r \in \mathcal{B}} \mathcal{A}_2(\ell \to r)$.

So the left-hand side of an ADP is just the left-hand side of the original rule. The right-hand side results from the right-hand side of the original rule by replacing certain defined symbols f with $f^{\#}$.

redex plus possibly another redex of the base TRS which may later create a redex of the main TRS again.

[6] This is the main advantage of ADPs over related formalisms like *dependency tuples* [22,32] where this information on the positions is lost. Therefore, as shown in [23] for almost-sure termination analysis of probabilistic term rewriting, using ADPs instead of DTs leads to a more elegant, more powerful, and less complicated framework.

Example 18. The canonical ADPs of Example 4 are $\mathcal{A}_1(\mathcal{R}_2) = \{\mathsf{a} \to \mathsf{b}\}$ and $\mathcal{A}_2(\mathcal{B}_2) = \{\mathsf{f} \to \mathsf{d}(\mathsf{F}, \mathsf{A})\}$ and for Example 5 we get $\mathcal{A}_1(\mathcal{R}_3) = \{\mathsf{a}(x) \to \mathsf{b}(x)\}$ and $\mathcal{A}_2(\mathcal{B}_3) = \{\mathsf{f} \to \mathsf{A}(\mathsf{F})\}$. For $\mathcal{R}_{\mathsf{divL}}/\mathcal{B}_{\mathsf{mset2}}$ from Examples 1 and 14, the ADPs $\mathcal{A}_1(\mathcal{R}_{\mathsf{divL}})$ are

$$\mathsf{minus}(x, \mathsf{0}) \to x \quad (14) \qquad \mathsf{div}(\mathsf{s}(x), \mathsf{s}(y)) \to \mathsf{s}(\mathsf{D}(\mathsf{minus}(x, y), \mathsf{s}(y))) \quad (18)$$

$$\mathsf{minus}(\mathsf{s}(x), \mathsf{s}(y)) \to \mathsf{M}(x, y) \quad (15) \qquad \mathsf{div}(\mathsf{s}(x), \mathsf{s}(y)) \to \mathsf{s}(\mathsf{div}(\mathsf{M}(x, y), \mathsf{s}(y))) \quad (19)$$

$$\mathsf{div}(\mathsf{0}, \mathsf{s}(y)) \to \mathsf{0} \quad (16) \qquad \mathsf{divL}(x, \mathsf{cons}(y, xs)) \to \mathsf{DL}(\mathsf{div}(x, y), xs) \quad (20)$$

$$\mathsf{divL}(x, \mathsf{nil}) \to x \quad (17) \qquad \mathsf{divL}(x, \mathsf{cons}(y, xs)) \to \mathsf{divL}(\mathsf{D}(x, y), xs) \quad (21)$$

and $\mathcal{A}_2(\mathcal{B}_{\mathsf{mset2}})$ contains $\mathsf{divL}(z, \mathsf{cons}(x, \mathsf{cons}(y, zs))) \to \mathsf{DL}(z, \mathsf{cons}(y, \mathsf{cons}(x, zs)))$ (22)

In [23], ADPs were only used for innermost rewriting. We now modify their rewrite relation and define what happens with annotations inside the substitutions during a rewrite step. To simulate redex-creating sequences as in Example 5 with ADPs (where the position of the created redex $\mathsf{a}(\dots)$ is above the position of the creating redex f), ADPs should be able to rewrite above annotated arguments without removing their annotation (we will demonstrate that in Example 25). Thus, for an ADP $\ell \to r$ with a variable $\ell|_\pi = x$, we use a *variable reposition function (VRF)* to indicate which occurrence of x in r should keep the annotations if one rewrites an instance of ℓ where the subterm at position π is annotated. So a VRF maps positions of variables in the left-hand side of a rule to positions of the same variable in the right-hand side.

Definition 19 (Variable Reposition Function). *Let $\ell \to r$ be an ADP. A function $\varphi : \mathrm{Pos}_{\mathcal{V}}(\ell) \to \mathrm{Pos}_{\mathcal{V}}(r) \uplus \{\bot\}$ is called a* variable reposition function (VRF) *for $\ell \to r$ iff $\ell|_\pi = r|_{\varphi(\pi)}$ whenever $\varphi(\pi) \neq \bot$.*

Example 20. For the ADP $\mathsf{a}(x) \to \mathsf{b}(x)$ for $\mathcal{R}_3$ from Example 5, if x on position 1 of the left-hand side is instantiated by F, then the VRF $\varphi(1) = 1$ indicates that this ADP rewrites $\mathsf{A}(\mathsf{F})$ to $\mathsf{b}(\mathsf{F})$, while $\varphi(1) = \bot$ means that it rewrites $\mathsf{A}(\mathsf{F})$ to $\mathsf{b}(\mathsf{f})$.

With VRFs we can define the rewrite relation for ADPs w.r.t. full rewriting.

Definition 21 ($\hookrightarrow_{\mathcal{P}}$). *Let $\mathcal{P}$ be a set of ADPs. A term $s \in \mathcal{T}(\Sigma^\#, \mathcal{V})$ rewrites to t using $\mathcal{P}$ (denoted $s \hookrightarrow_{\mathcal{P}} t$) if there are an ADP $\ell \to r \in \mathcal{P}$, a substitution σ, a position $\pi \in \mathrm{Pos}_{\mathcal{D} \cup \mathcal{D}^\#}(s)$ such that $\flat(s|_\pi) = \ell\sigma$, a VRF φ for $\ell \to r$, and*[7]

$$t = s[\#_\Phi(r\sigma)]_\pi \quad \text{if } \pi \in \mathrm{Pos}_{\mathcal{D}^\#}(s) \qquad (\mathbf{pr})$$
$$t = s[\#_\Psi(r\sigma)]_\pi \quad \text{if } \pi \in \mathrm{Pos}_{\mathcal{D}}(s) \qquad (\mathbf{r})$$

7 In [23] there were two additional cases in the definition of the corresponding rewrite relation. One of them was needed for processors that restrict the rules applicable for **r**-steps (e.g., based on usable rules), and the other case was needed to ensure that the innermost evaluation strategy is not affected by the application of ADP processors. This is unnecessary here since we consider full rewriting. On the other hand, VRFs are new compared to [23], since they are not needed for innermost rewriting.

with $\Psi = \{\varphi(\rho).\tau \mid \rho \in \mathrm{Pos}_{\mathcal{V}}(\ell),\ \varphi(\rho) \neq \bot,\ \rho.\tau \in \mathrm{Pos}_{\mathcal{D}^\#}(s|_\pi)\}$ *and* $\Phi = \mathrm{Pos}_{\mathcal{D}^\#}(r) \cup \Psi$*.*

So Ψ considers all positions of annotated symbols in $s|_\pi$ that are below positions ρ of variables in ℓ. If the VRF maps ρ to a variable position ρ' in r, then the annotations below $\pi.\rho$ in s are kept in the resulting subterm at position $\pi.\rho'$ after the rewriting.

Rewriting with $\mathcal{P}$ is like ordinary term rewriting, while considering and modifying annotations. Note that we represent a DP resulting from a rule as well as the original rule by just one ADP. So the ADP $\mathsf{div}(\mathsf{s}(x), \mathsf{s}(y)) \to \mathsf{s}(\mathsf{D}(\mathsf{minus}(x, y), \mathsf{s}(y)))$ represents both the DP resulting from div in the right-hand side of the rule (4), and the rule (4) itself (by simply disregarding all annotations of the ADP).

Similar to the classical DP framework, our goal is to track specific reduction sequences. As before, there are **p**-steps where a DP is applied at the position of an annotated symbol. These steps may introduce new annotations. Moreover, between two **p**-steps there can be several **r**-steps.

A step of the form (**pr**) at position π in Definition 21 represents a **p**- or an **r**-step (or both), where an **r**-step is only possible if one later rewrites an annotated symbol at a position above π. All annotations are kept during this step except for annotations of subterms that correspond to variables of the applied rule. Here, the used VRF φ determines which of these annotations are kept and which are removed. As an example, with the canonical ADP $\mathsf{a}(x) \to \mathsf{b}(x)$ from $\mathcal{A}_1(\mathcal{R}_3)$ we can rewrite $\mathsf{A}(\mathsf{F}) \hookrightarrow_{\mathcal{A}_1(\mathcal{R}_3)} \mathsf{b}(\mathsf{F})$ as in Example 20. Here, we have $\pi = \varepsilon$, $\flat(s|_\varepsilon) = \mathsf{a}(\mathsf{f}) = \ell\sigma$, $r = \mathsf{b}(x)$, and the VRF φ with $\varphi(1) = 1$ such that the annotation of F in A's argument is kept in the argument of b.

A step of the form (**r**) rewrites at the position of a non-annotated defined symbol, and represents just an **r**-step. Hence, we remove all annotations from the right-hand side r of the ADP. However, we may have to keep the annotations inside the substitution, hence we move them according to the VRF. For example, we obtain the rewrite step $\mathsf{s}(\mathsf{D}(\underline{\mathsf{minus}(\mathsf{s}(0), \mathsf{s}(0))}, \mathsf{s}(0))) \hookrightarrow_{\mathcal{A}_1(\mathcal{R}_{\mathsf{divL}})} \mathsf{s}(\mathsf{D}(\mathsf{minus}(0, 0), \mathsf{s}(0)))$ using the ADP $\mathsf{minus}(\mathsf{s}(x), \mathsf{s}(y)) \to \mathsf{M}(x, y)$ (15) and any VRF.

A *(relative) ADP problem* has the form $(\mathcal{P}, \mathcal{S})$, where $\mathcal{P}$ and $\mathcal{S}$ are finite sets of ADPs. $\mathcal{P}$ is the set of all main ADPs and $\mathcal{S}$ is the set of all base ADPs. Now we can define chains in the relative setting.

Definition 22 (Chains and Terminating ADP Problems). *Let* $(\mathcal{P}, \mathcal{S})$ *be an ADP problem. A sequence of terms* $t_0, t_1, \ldots$ *with* $t_i \in \mathcal{T}(\Sigma^\#, \mathcal{V})$ *is a* $(\mathcal{P}, \mathcal{S})$*-*chain *if we have* $t_i \hookrightarrow_{\mathcal{P} \cup \mathcal{S}} t_{i+1}$ *for all* $i \in \mathbb{N}$*. The chain is called* infinite *if infinitely many of these rewrite steps use* $\hookrightarrow_{\mathcal{P}}$ *with Case* (**pr**)*. We say that an ADP problem* $(\mathcal{P}, \mathcal{S})$ *is* terminating (SN) *if there is no infinite* $(\mathcal{P}, \mathcal{S})$*-chain.*

Note the two different forms of relativity in Definition 22: In a finite chain, we may not only use infinitely many steps with $\mathcal{S}$ but also infinitely many steps with $\mathcal{P}$ where Case (**r**) applies. Thus, an ADP problem $(\mathcal{P}, \mathcal{S})$ without annotated symbols or without any main ADPs (i.e., where $\mathcal{P} = \varnothing$) is obviously SN. Finally, we obtain our desired chain criterion.

Theorem 23 (Chain Criterion for Relative Rewriting). *Let $\mathcal{R}$ and $\mathcal{B}$ be TRSs such that $\mathcal{B}$ is non-duplicating. Then $\mathcal{R}/\mathcal{B}$ is SN iff the ADP problem $(\mathcal{A}_1(\mathcal{R}), \mathcal{A}_2(\mathcal{B}))$ is SN.*

Example 24. The infinite rewrite sequence of Example 4 can be simulated by the following infinite chain using $\mathcal{A}_1(\mathcal{R}_2) = \{\mathsf{a} \to \mathsf{b}\}$ and $\mathcal{A}_2(\mathcal{B}_2) = \{\mathsf{f} \to \mathsf{d}(\mathsf{F}, \mathsf{A})\}$.

$$\underline{\mathsf{F}} \hookrightarrow_{\mathcal{A}_2(\mathcal{B}_2)} \mathsf{d}(\mathsf{F}, \underline{\mathsf{A}}) \hookrightarrow_{\mathcal{A}_1(\mathcal{R}_2)} \mathsf{d}(\underline{\mathsf{F}}, \mathsf{b}) \hookrightarrow_{\mathcal{A}_2(\mathcal{B}_2)} \mathsf{d}(\mathsf{d}(\mathsf{F}, \underline{\mathsf{A}}), \mathsf{b}) \hookrightarrow_{\mathcal{A}_1(\mathcal{R}_2)} \cdots$$

The steps with $\hookrightarrow_{\mathcal{A}_2(\mathcal{B}_2)}$ use Case (**pr**) at the position of the annotated symbol F and the steps with $\hookrightarrow_{\mathcal{A}_1(\mathcal{R}_2)}$ use (**pr**) as well. For this infinite chain, we indeed need two annotated symbols in the right-hand side of the base ADP: If A were not annotated (i.e., if we had the ADP $\mathsf{f} \to \mathsf{d}(\mathsf{F}, \mathsf{a})$), then the step with $\hookrightarrow_{\mathcal{A}_1(\mathcal{R}_2)}$ would just use Case (**r**) and the chain would not be considered "infinite". If F were not annotated (i.e., if we had the ADP $\mathsf{f} \to \mathsf{d}(\mathsf{f}, \mathsf{A})$), then we would have the step $\mathsf{f} \hookrightarrow_{\mathcal{A}_2(\mathcal{B}_2)} \mathsf{d}(\mathsf{f}, \mathsf{a})$ which uses Case (**r**) and removes all annotations from the right-hand side. Hence, again the chain would not be considered "infinite".

Example 25. The infinite rewrite sequence of Example 5 is simulated by the following chain with $\mathcal{A}_1(\mathcal{R}_3) = \{\mathsf{a}(x) \to \mathsf{b}(x)\}$ and $\mathcal{A}_2(\mathcal{B}_3) = \{\mathsf{f} \to \mathsf{A}(\mathsf{F})\}$.

$$\underline{\mathsf{F}} \hookrightarrow_{\mathcal{A}_2(\mathcal{B}_3)} \underline{\mathsf{A}}(\mathsf{F}) \hookrightarrow_{\mathcal{A}_1(\mathcal{R}_3)} \mathsf{b}(\underline{\mathsf{F}}) \hookrightarrow_{\mathcal{A}_2(\mathcal{B}_3)} \mathsf{b}(\underline{\mathsf{A}}(\mathsf{F})) \hookrightarrow_{\mathcal{A}_1(\mathcal{R}_3)} \mathsf{b}(\mathsf{b}(\underline{\mathsf{F}})) \hookrightarrow_{\mathcal{A}_2(\mathcal{B}_3)} \cdots$$

Here, it is important to use the VRF $\varphi(1) = 1$ for $\mathsf{a}(x) \to \mathsf{b}(x)$ which keeps the annotation of A's argument F when rewriting with $\mathcal{A}_1(\mathcal{R}_3)$, i.e., these steps must yield $\mathsf{b}(\mathsf{F})$ instead of $\mathsf{b}(\mathsf{f})$ to generate further subterms $\mathsf{A}(\ldots)$ afterwards.

5 The Relative ADP Framework

Now we present processors for our novel relative ADP framework. An *ADP processor* Proc has the form $\mathrm{Proc}(\mathcal{P}, \mathcal{S}) = \{(\mathcal{P}_1, \mathcal{S}_1), \ldots, (\mathcal{P}_n, \mathcal{S}_n)\}$, where $\mathcal{P}, \mathcal{P}_1, \ldots, \mathcal{P}_n, \mathcal{S}_1, \ldots, \mathcal{S}_n$ are sets of ADPs. Proc is *sound* if $(\mathcal{P}, \mathcal{S})$ is SN whenever $(\mathcal{P}_i, \mathcal{S}_i)$ is SN for all $1 \leq i \leq n$. It is *complete* if $(\mathcal{P}_i, \mathcal{S}_i)$ is SN for all $1 \leq i \leq n$ whenever $(\mathcal{P}, \mathcal{S})$ is SN. To prove relative termination of $\mathcal{R}/\mathcal{B}$, we start with the canonical ADP problem $(\mathcal{A}_1(\mathcal{R}), \mathcal{A}_2(\mathcal{B}))$ and apply sound (and preferably complete) ADP processors until all sub-problems are transformed to the empty set.

In Sect. 5.1, we present two processors to remove (base) ADPs, and in Sects. 5.2 and 5.3, we adapt the main processors of the classical DP framework from Sect. 3.1 to the relative setting. As mentioned, the soundness and completeness proofs for our processors and the chain criterion (Theorem 23) can be found in [24].

5.1 Derelatifying Processors

The following two *derelatifying* processors can be used to switch from ADPs to ordinary DPs, similar to Theorems 11 and 12. We extend $\flat$ to ADPs and sets of ADPs $\mathcal{S}$ by defining $\flat(\ell \to r) = \ell \to \flat(r)$ and $\flat(\mathcal{S}) = \{\ell \to \flat(r) \mid \ell \to r \in \mathcal{S}\}$.

If the ADPs in $\mathcal{S}$ contain no annotations anymore, then it suffices to use ordinary DPs. The corresponding set of DPs for a set of ADPs $\mathcal{P}$ is defined as $\text{dp}(\mathcal{P}) = \{\ell^\# \to t^\# \mid \ell \to r \in \mathcal{P}, t \trianglelefteq_\# r\}$.

Theorem 26 (Derelatifying Processor (1)). *Let* $(\mathcal{P}, \mathcal{S})$ *be an ADP problem such that* $\flat(\mathcal{S}) = \mathcal{S}$*. Then* $\text{Proc}_{\mathtt{DRP1}}(\mathcal{P}, \mathcal{S}) = \varnothing$ *is sound and complete iff the ordinary DP problem* $(\text{dp}(\mathcal{P}), \flat(\mathcal{P} \cup \mathcal{S}))$ *is SN.*

Furthermore, similar to Theorem 12, we can always move ADPs from $\mathcal{S}$ to $\mathcal{P}$, but such a processor is only sound and not complete. However, it may help to satisfy the requirements of Theorem 26 by moving ADPs with annotations from $\mathcal{S}$ to $\mathcal{P}$ such that the ordinary DP framework can be used afterwards.

Theorem 27 (Derelatifying Processor (2)). *Let* $(\mathcal{P}, \mathcal{S})$ *be an ADP problem, and let* $\mathcal{S} = \mathcal{S}_a \uplus \mathcal{S}_b$*. Then* $\text{Proc}_{\mathtt{DRP2}}(\mathcal{P}, \mathcal{S}) = \{(\mathcal{P} \cup \mathtt{split}(\mathcal{S}_a), \mathcal{S}_b)\}$ *is sound. Here,* $\mathtt{split}(\mathcal{S}_a) = \{\ell \to \#_\pi(r) \mid \ell \to r \in \mathcal{S}_a, \pi \in \text{pos}_{\mathcal{D}^\#}(r)\}$.

So if $\mathcal{S}_a$ contains an ADP with two annotations, then we split it into two ADPs, where each only contains a single annotation.

Example 28. There are also redex-creating examples that are terminating, e.g., $\mathcal{R}_2 = \{\mathsf{a} \to \mathsf{b}\}$ and the base TRS $\mathcal{B}_2' = \{\mathsf{f}(\mathsf{s}(y)) \to \mathsf{d}(\mathsf{f}(y), \mathsf{a})\}$. Relative (and full) termination of this example can easily be shown by using the second derelatifying processor from Theorem 27 to replace the base ADP $\mathsf{f}(\mathsf{s}(y)) \to \mathsf{d}(\mathsf{F}(y), \mathsf{A})$ by the main ADPs $\mathsf{f}(\mathsf{s}(y)) \to \mathsf{d}(\mathsf{F}(y), \mathsf{a})$ and $\mathsf{f}(\mathsf{s}(y)) \to \mathsf{d}(\mathsf{f}(y), \mathsf{A})$. Then the processor of Theorem 26 is used to switch to the ordinary DPs $\mathsf{F}(\mathsf{s}(y)) \to \mathsf{F}(y)$ and $\mathsf{F}(\mathsf{s}(y)) \to \mathsf{A}$.

5.2 Relative Dependency Graph Processor

Next, we develop a dependency graph processor in the relative setting. The definition of the dependency graph is analogous to the one in the standard setting and thus, the same techniques can be used to over-approximate it automatically.

Definition 29 (Relative Dependency Graph). *Let* $(\mathcal{P}, \mathcal{S})$ *be an ADP problem. The* $(\mathcal{P}, \mathcal{S})$*-dependency graph has the set of nodes* $\mathcal{P} \cup \mathcal{S}$ *and there is an edge from* $\ell_1 \to r_1$ *to* $\ell_2 \to r_2$ *if there exist substitutions* σ_1, σ_2 *and a term* $t \trianglelefteq_\# r_1$ *such that* $t^\# \sigma_1 \to^*_{\flat(\mathcal{P} \cup \mathcal{S})} \ell_2^\# \sigma_2$.

So similar to the standard dependency graph, there is an edge from an ADP $\ell_1 \to r_1$ to $\ell_2 \to r_2$ if the rules of $\flat(\mathcal{P} \cup \mathcal{S})$ (without annotations) can reduce an instance of a subterm t of r_1 to an instance of ℓ_2, if one only annotates the roots of t and ℓ_2 (i.e., then the rules can only be applied below the root).

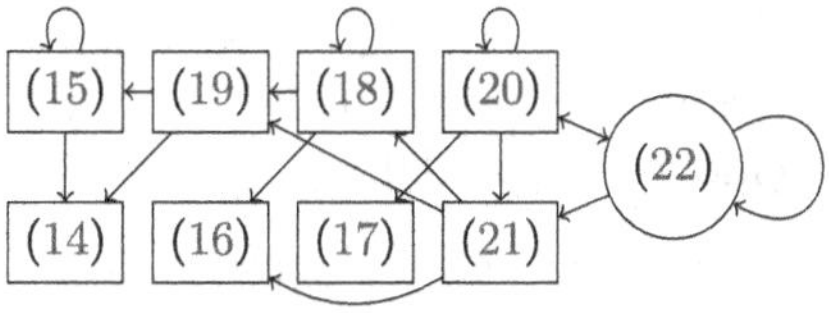

Fig. 1. $(\mathcal{A}_1(\mathcal{R}_{\mathsf{divL}}), \mathcal{A}_2(\mathcal{B}_{\mathsf{mset2}}))$-Dep. Graph

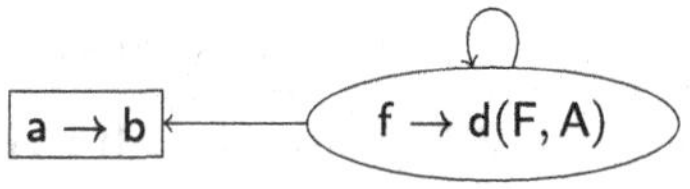

Fig. 2. $(\mathcal{A}_1(\mathcal{R}_2), \mathcal{A}_2(\mathcal{B}_2))$-Dep. Graph

Example 30. The dependency graph for the ADP problem $(\mathcal{A}_1(\mathcal{R}_{\mathsf{divL}}), \mathcal{A}_2(\mathcal{B}_{\mathsf{mset2}}))$ from Example 18 is shown in Fig. 1. Here, nodes from $\mathcal{A}_1(\mathcal{R}_{\mathsf{divL}})$ are denoted by rectangles and the node from $\mathcal{A}_2(\mathcal{B}_{\mathsf{mset2}})$ is a circle.

To detect possible ordinary infinite rewrite sequences as in Example 6, we again have to regard SCCs of the dependency graph, where we only need to consider SCCs that contain a node from $\mathcal{P}$, because otherwise, all steps in the SCC are relative (base) steps. However, in the relative ADP framework, non-termination can also be due to chains representing redex-creating sequences. Here, it does not suffice to look at SCCs. Thus, the relative dependency graph processor differs substantially from the corresponding processor for ordinary rewriting (and also from the corresponding processor for the probabilistic ADP framework in [23]).

Example 31 (Dependency Graph for Redex-Creating TRSs). For $\mathcal{R}_2$ and $\mathcal{B}_2$ from Example 4, the dependency graph for $(\mathcal{A}_1(\mathcal{R}_2), \mathcal{A}_2(\mathcal{B}_2))$ from Example 24 is in Fig. 2. Here, we cannot regard the SCC $\{\mathsf{f} \to \mathsf{d}(\mathsf{F}, \mathsf{A})\}$ separately, as we need $\mathcal{A}_1(\mathcal{R}_2)$'s rule $\mathsf{a} \to \mathsf{b}$ to reduce the created redex. To find the ADPs that can reduce the created redexes, we have to regard the outgoing paths from the SCCs of $\mathcal{S}$ to ADPs of $\mathcal{P}$.

The structure that we are looking for in the redex-creating case is a path from an SCC to a node from $\mathcal{P}$ (i.e., a form of a *lasso*), which is *minimal* in the sense that if we reach a node from $\mathcal{P}$, then we stop and do not move further along the edges of the graph. Moreover, the SCC needs to contain an ADP with more than one annotated symbol, as otherwise the generation of the infinitely many $\mathcal{P}$-redexes would not be possible. Here, it suffices to look at SCCs in the graph restricted to only $\mathcal{S}$-nodes (i.e., in the $(\flat(\mathcal{P}), \mathcal{S})$-dependency graph). The reason is that if the SCC contains a node from $\mathcal{P}$, then as mentioned above, we have to prove anyway that the SCC does not give rise to infinite chains.

Definition 32 ($\mathtt{SCC}_{\mathcal{P}'}^{(\mathcal{P},\mathcal{S})}$, $\mathtt{Lasso}$)**.** *Let $(\mathcal{P}, \mathcal{S})$ be an ADP problem. For any $\mathcal{P}' \subseteq \mathcal{P} \cup \mathcal{S}$, let $\mathtt{SCC}_{\mathcal{P}'}^{(\mathcal{P},\mathcal{S})}$ denote the set of all SCCs of the $(\mathcal{P}, \mathcal{S})$-dependency graph that contain an ADP from $\mathcal{P}'$. Moreover, let $\mathcal{S}_{>1} \subseteq \mathcal{S}$ denote the set of all ADPs from $\mathcal{S}$ with more than one annotation. Then the set of all* minimal lassos *is defined as $\mathtt{Lasso} = \{\mathcal{Q} \cup \{n_1, \ldots, n_k\} \mid \mathcal{Q} \in \mathtt{SCC}_{\mathcal{S}_{>1}}^{(\flat(\mathcal{P}),\mathcal{S})},\ n_1, \ldots, n_k$ is a path in the $(\flat(\mathcal{P}), \mathcal{S})$-dependency graph such that $n_1 \in \mathcal{Q}$ and $n_k \in \flat(\mathcal{P})\}$.*

We remove the annotations of ADPs which do not have to be considered anymore for **p**-steps due to the dependency graph, but we keep the ADPs for possible **r**-steps and thus, consider them as relative (base) ADPs.

Theorem 33 (Dep. Graph Processor). *Let* $(\mathcal{P}, \mathcal{S})$ *be an ADP problem. Then*

$$\mathrm{Proc}_{\mathtt{DG}}(\mathcal{P}, \mathcal{S}) = \{(\mathcal{P} \cap \mathcal{Q},\ (\mathcal{S} \cap \mathcal{Q}) \cup \flat(\,(\mathcal{P} \cup \mathcal{S}) \setminus \mathcal{Q})) \mid \mathcal{Q} \in \mathtt{SCC}_{\mathcal{P}}^{(\mathcal{P},\mathcal{S})} \cup \mathtt{Lasso}\}$$

is sound and complete.

Example 34. For $(\mathcal{A}_1(\mathcal{R}_{\mathsf{divL}}), \mathcal{A}_2(\mathcal{B}_{\mathsf{mset2}}))$ from Example 30 we have three SCCs $\{(15)\}$, $\{(18)\}$, and $\{(20), (22)\}$ containing nodes from $\mathcal{A}_1(\mathcal{R}_{\mathsf{divL}})$. The set $\{(22)\}$ is the only SCC of $(\flat(\mathcal{A}_1(\mathcal{R}_{\mathsf{divL}})), \mathcal{A}_2(\mathcal{B}_{\mathsf{mset2}}))$ and there are paths from that SCC to the ADPs (20) and (21) of $\mathcal{P}$. However, they are not in $\mathtt{Lasso}$, because the SCC $\{(22)\}$ does not contain an ADP with more than one annotation. Hence, we result in the three new ADP problems $(\{(15)\}, \{\flat(22)\} \cup \flat(\mathcal{A}_1(\mathcal{R}_{\mathsf{divL}}) \setminus \{(15)\}))$, $(\{(18)\}, \{\flat(22)\} \cup \flat(\mathcal{A}_1(\mathcal{R}_{\mathsf{divL}}) \setminus \{(18)\}))$, and $(\{(20)\}, \{(22)\} \cup \flat(\mathcal{A}_1(\mathcal{R}_{\mathsf{divL}}) \setminus \{(20)\}))$. For the first two of these new ADP problems, we can use the derelatifying processor of Theorem 26 and prove SN via ordinary DPs, since their base ADPs do not contain any annotated symbols anymore.

The dependency graph processor in combination with the derelatifying processors of Theorems 26 and 27 already subsumes the techniques of Theorems 11 and 12. The reason is that if $\mathcal{R}$ dominates $\mathcal{B}$, then there is no edge from an ADP of $\mathcal{A}_2(\mathcal{B})$ to any ADP of $\mathcal{A}_1(\mathcal{R})$ in the $(\mathcal{A}_1(\mathcal{R}), \mathcal{A}_2(\mathcal{B}))$-dependency graph. Hence, there are no minimal lassos and the dependency graph processor just creates ADP problems from the SCCs of $\mathcal{A}_1(\mathcal{R})$ where the base ADPs do not have any annotations anymore. Then Theorem 26 allows us to switch to ordinary DPs. For example, if we consider $\mathcal{B}_{\mathsf{mset}}$ instead of $\mathcal{B}_{\mathsf{mset2}}$, then the dependency graph processor yields the three sub-problems for the SCCs $\{(15)\}$, $\{(18)\}$, and $\{(20)\}$, where the base ADPs do not contain annotations anymore. Then, we can move to ordinary DPs via Theorem 26.

Compared to Theorems 11 and 12, the dependency graph allows for more precise over-approximations than just "dominance" to detect when the base ADPs do not depend on the main ADPs. Moreover, the derelatifying processors of Theorems 26 and 27 allow us to switch to the ordinary DP framework also for sub-problems which result from the application of other processors of our relative ADP framework. In other words, Theorems 26 and 27 allow us to apply this switch in a modular way, even if their prerequisites do not hold for the initial canonical ADP problem (i.e., even if the prerequisites of Theorems 11 and 12 do not hold for the whole TRSs).

5.3 Relative Reduction Pair Processor

Next, we adapt the reduction pair processor to ADPs for relative rewriting. While the reduction pair processor for ADPs in the probabilistic setting [23] was restricted to polynomial interpretations, we now allow arbitrary reduction pairs using a similar idea as in [18] for complexity analysis via DPs.

To find out which ADPs cannot be used for infinitely many **p**-steps, the idea is not to compare the annotated left-hand side with the whole right-hand side, but just with the set of its annotated subterms. To combine these subterms in the case of ADPs with two or no annotated symbols, we extend the signature by two fresh *compound* symbols c_0 and c_2 of arity 0 and 2, respectively. Similar to [18], we have to use c-*monotonic* and c-*invariant* reduction pairs.

Definition 35 (c-Monotonic, c-Invariant). *For $r \in \mathcal{T}(\Sigma^\#, \mathcal{V})$, we define* $\mathrm{ann}(r) = \mathsf{c}_0$ *if r does not contain any annotation,* $\mathrm{ann}(r) = t^\#$ *if $t \trianglelefteq_\# r$ and r only contains one annotated symbol, and* $\mathrm{ann}(r) = \mathsf{c}_2(r_1^\#, r_2^\#)$ *if $r_1 \trianglelefteq_\#^{\pi_1} r$, $r_2 \trianglelefteq_\#^{\pi_2} r$, and $\pi_1 <_{lex} \pi_2$ where $<_{lex}$ is the (total) lexicographic order on positions.*

A reduction pair $(\succsim, \succ)$ is called c-monotonic *if $\mathsf{c}_2(s_1, t) \succ \mathsf{c}_2(s_2, t)$ and $\mathsf{c}_2(t, s_1) \succ \mathsf{c}_2(t, s_2)$ for all $s_1, s_2, t \in \mathcal{T}(\Sigma^\#, \mathcal{V})$ with $s_1 \succ s_2$. Moreover, it is* c-invariant *if $\mathsf{c}_2(s_1, s_2) \sim \mathsf{c}_2(s_2, s_1)$ and $\mathsf{c}_2(s_1, \mathsf{c}_2(s_2, s_3)) \sim \mathsf{c}_2(\mathsf{c}_2(s_1, s_2), s_3)$ for $\sim = \succsim \cap \precsim$ and all $s_1, s_2, s_3 \in \mathcal{T}(\Sigma^\#, \mathcal{V})$.*

So for example, reduction pairs based on polynomial interpretations are c-monotonic and c-invariant if $\mathsf{c}_2(x, y)$ is interpreted by $x + y$.

For an ADP problem $(\mathcal{P}, \mathcal{S})$, now the reduction pair processor has to orient the non-annotated rules $\flat(\mathcal{P} \cup \mathcal{S})$ weakly and for all ADPs $\ell \to r$, it compares the annotated left-hand side $\ell^\#$ with $\mathrm{ann}(r)$. In strictly decreasing ADPs, one can then remove all annotations and consider them as relative (base) ADPs again.

Theorem 36 (Reduction Pair Processor). *Let $(\mathcal{P}, \mathcal{S})$ be an ADP problem and let $(\succsim, \succ)$ be a* c*-monotonic and* c*-invariant reduction pair such that $\flat(\mathcal{P} \cup \mathcal{S}) \subseteq \succsim$ and $\ell^\# \succsim \mathrm{ann}(r)$ for all $\ell \to r \in \mathcal{P} \cup \mathcal{S}$. Moreover, let $\mathcal{P}_\succ \subseteq \mathcal{P} \cup \mathcal{S}$ such that $\ell^\# \succ \mathrm{ann}(r)$ for all $\ell \to r \in \mathcal{P}_\succ$. Then $\mathrm{Proc}_{\mathsf{RPP}}(\mathcal{P}, \mathcal{S}) = \{(\mathcal{P} \setminus \mathcal{P}_\succ, (\mathcal{S} \setminus \mathcal{P}_\succ) \cup \flat(\mathcal{P}_\succ))\}$ is sound and complete.*

Example 37. For the remaining ADP problem $(\{(20)\}, \{(22)\} \cup \flat(\mathcal{A}_1(\mathcal{R}_{\mathsf{divL}}) \setminus \{(20)\}))$ from Example 34, we can apply the reduction pair processor using the polynomial interpretation from the end of Sect. 3.1 which maps $\mathsf{0}$ and nil to 0, $\mathsf{s}(x)$ to $x + 1$, $\mathsf{cons}(y, xs)$ to $xs + 1$, $\mathsf{DL}(x, xs)$ to xs, and all other symbols to their first arguments. Then, (20) is oriented strictly (i.e., it is in $\mathcal{P}_\succ$), and (22) and all other base ADPs are oriented weakly. Hence, we remove the annotation from (20) and move it to the base ADPs. Now there is no main ADP anymore, and thus the dependency graph processor returns $\varnothing$. This proves SN for $(\mathcal{A}_1(\mathcal{R}_{\mathsf{divL}}), \mathcal{A}_2(\mathcal{B}_{\mathsf{mset2}}))$, hence $\mathcal{R}_{\mathsf{divL}}/\mathcal{B}_{\mathsf{mset2}}$ is also SN.

Example 38. Regard the ADPs $\mathsf{a} \to \mathsf{b}$ and $\mathsf{f} \to \mathsf{d}(\mathsf{F}, \mathsf{A})$ for the redex-creating Example 4 again. When using a polynomial interpretation Pol that maps c_0 to 0 and $\mathsf{c}_2(x, y)$ to $x + y$, then for the reduction pair processor one has to satisfy $\mathrm{Pol}(\mathsf{A}) \geq 0$ and $\mathrm{Pol}(\mathsf{F}) \geq \mathrm{Pol}(\mathsf{F}) + \mathrm{Pol}(\mathsf{A})$, i.e., one cannot make any of the ADPs strictly decreasing.

In contrast, for the variant with the terminating base rule $\mathsf{f}(\mathsf{s}(y)) \to \mathsf{d}(\mathsf{f}(y), \mathsf{a})$ from Example 28, we have the ADPs $\mathsf{a} \to \mathsf{b}$ and $\mathsf{f}(\mathsf{s}(y)) \to \mathsf{d}(\mathsf{F}(y), \mathsf{A})$. Here, the second constraint is $\mathrm{Pol}(\mathsf{F}(\mathsf{s}(y))) \geq \mathrm{Pol}(\mathsf{F}(y)) + \mathrm{Pol}(\mathsf{A})$. To make one of the ADPs strictly decreasing, one can set $\text{Pol}(\mathsf{F}(x)) = x$, $\text{Pol}(\mathsf{s}(x)) = x + 1$, and $\text{Pol}(\mathsf{A}) = 1$ or $\text{Pol}(\mathsf{A}) = 0$. Then the reduction pair processor removes the annotations from the strictly decreasing ADP and the dependency graph processor proves SN.

6 Evaluation and Conclusion

In this paper, we introduced the first notion of (annotated) dependency pairs and the first DP framework for relative termination, which also features suitable dependency graph and reduction pair processors for relative ADPs. Of course, further classical DP processors can be adapted to our relative ADP framework as well. For example, in our implementation of the novel ADP framework in our tool AProVE [13], we also included a straightforward adaption of the classical *rule removal processor* [11], see [24].[8] While the soundness proofs for the processors in the new relative ADP framework are more involved than in the standard DP framework, the new processors themselves are quite analogous to their original counterparts and thus, adapting an existing implementation of the ordinary DP framework to the relative ADP framework does not require much effort. In future work, we will investigate how to use our new form of ADPs for full (instead of innermost) rewriting also in the probabilistic setting and for complexity analysis.

To evaluate the new relative ADP framework, we compared its implementation in "*new* AProVE" to all tools that participated in the most recent *termination competition (TermComp 2023)* [14] on relative rewriting, i.e., NaTT [36], $\mathsf{T_TT_2}$ [27], MultumNonMulta [9], and "*old* AProVE" which did not yet contain the contributions of the current paper. In *TermComp 2023*, 98 benchmarks were used for relative termination. However, these benchmarks only consist of examples where the main TRS $\mathcal{R}$ dominates the base TRS $\mathcal{B}$ (i.e., which can be handled by Theorem 11 from [21]) or which can already be solved via simplification orders directly.

Therefore, we extended the collection by 32 new "typical" examples for relative rewriting, including both $\mathcal{R}_{\mathsf{divL}}/\mathcal{B}_{\mathsf{mset}}$ from Examples 1 and 2, and our leading example $\mathcal{R}_{\mathsf{divL}}/\mathcal{B}_{\mathsf{mset2}}$ from Examples 2 and 14 (where only *new* AProVE can prove SN). Except for $\mathcal{R}_{\mathsf{divL}}/\mathcal{B}_{\mathsf{mset}}$, in these examples $\mathcal{R}$ does not dominate $\mathcal{B}$. Most of these examples adapt well-known classical TRSs from the *Termination Problem Data Base* [33] used at *TermComp* to the relative setting. Moreover, 5 of our new examples illustrate the application of relative termination for proving confluence, i.e., in these examples one can prove confluence with the approach of [19] via our new technique for relative termination proofs.

In the following table, the number in the "YES" ("NO") row indicates for how many of the 130 examples the respective tool could prove (disprove) relative termination and "MAYBE" refers to the benchmarks where the tool could not

---

[8] This processor works analogously to the preprocessing at the beginning of Sect. 4 which can be used to remove duplicating rules: For an ADP problem $(\mathcal{P}, \mathcal{S})$, it tries to find a reduction pair $(\succsim, \succ)$ where $\succ$ is closed under contexts such that $\flat(\mathcal{P} \cup \mathcal{S}) \subseteq \succsim$. Then for $\mathcal{P}_{\succ} \subseteq \mathcal{P} \cup \mathcal{S}$ with $\flat(\mathcal{P}_{\succ}) \subseteq \succ$, the processor replaces the ADP by $(\mathcal{P} \setminus \mathcal{P}_{\succ}, \mathcal{S} \setminus \mathcal{P}_{\succ})$.

solve the problem within the timeout of 300 s per example. The numbers in brackets are the respective results when only considering our new 32 examples. "AVG(s)" gives the average runtime of the tool on solved examples in seconds.

	new AProVE	NaTT	*old* AProVE	$\mathsf{T_TT_2}$	MultumNonMulta
YES	91 (32)	68 (10)	48 (5)	39 (3)	0 (0)
NO	13 (0)	5 (0)	13 (0)	7 (0)	13 (0)
MAYBE	26 (0)	57 (22)	69 (27)	84 (29)	117 (32)
AVG(s)	5.11	0.41	4.02	1.67	1.60

The table clearly shows that while *old* AProVE was already the second most powerful tool for relative termination, the integration of the ADP framework in *new* AProVE yields a substantial advance in power (i.e., it only fails on 26 of the examples, compared to 57 and 69 failures of NaTT and *old* AProVE, respectively). In particular, previous tools (including *old* AProVE) often have problems with relative TRSs where the main TRS does not dominate the base TRS, whereas the ADP framework can handle such examples.

A special form of relative TRSs are *relative string rewrite systems (SRSs)*, where all function symbols have arity 1. Due to the base ADPs with two annotated symbols on the right-hand side, here the ADP framework is less powerful than dedicated techniques for string rewriting. For the 403 relative SRSs at *TermComp 2023*, the ADP framework only finds 71 proofs, mostly due to the dependency graph and the rule removal processor, while termination analysis via AProVE's standard strategy for relative SRSs succeeds on 209 examples, and the two most powerful tools for relative SRSs at *TermComp 2023* (MultumNonMulta and Matchbox [35]) succeed on 274 and 269 examples, respectively.

Another special form of relative rewriting is *equational rewriting*, where one has a set of equations E which correspond to relative rules that can be applied in both directions. In [10], DPs were adapted to equational rewriting. However, this approach requires E-unification to be decidable and finitary (i.e., for (certain) pairs of terms, it has to compute finite complete sets of E-unifiers). This works well if E are AC- or C-axioms, and for this special case, dedicated techniques like [10] are more powerful than our new ADP framework for relative termination. For example, on the 76 AC- and C-benchmarks for equational rewriting at *TermComp 2023*, the relative ADP framework finds 36 proofs, while dedicated tools for AC-rewriting like AProVE's equational strategy or MU-TERM [15] succeed on 66 and 64 examples, respectively. However, in general, the requirement of a finitary E-unification algorithm is a hard restriction. In contrast to existing tools for equational rewriting, our new ADP framework can be used for arbitrary (non-duplicating) relative rules.

For details on our experiments, our collection of examples, and for instructions on how to run our implementation in AProVE via its *web interface* or locally, see: https://aprove-developers.github.io/RelativeDTFramework/.

References

1. Arts, T., Giesl, J.: Termination of term rewriting using dependency pairs. Theor. Comput. Sci. **236**(1–2), 133–178 (2000). https://doi.org/10.1016/S0304-3975(99)00207-8
2. Baader, F., Nipkow, T.: Term Rewriting and All That. Cambridge University Press (1998). https://doi.org/10.1017/CBO9781139172752
3. Baudon, T., Fuhs, C., Gonnord, L.: Analysing parallel complexity of term rewriting. In: Villanueva, A. (ed.), LOPSTR 2022, LNCS, vol. 13474, pp. 3–23. Springer, Cham (2022). https://doi.org/10.1007/978-3-031-16767-6_1
4. Dershowitz, N.: Termination of rewriting. J. Symbol. Comput **3**(1), 69–115 (1987). https://doi.org/10.1016/S0747-7171(87)80022-6
5. Dershowitz, N.: The RTA List of Open Problems. https://www.cs.tau.ac.il/~nachum/rtaloop/
6. Frohn, F., Giesl, J., Hensel, J., Aschermann, C., Ströder, T.: Lower bounds for runtime complexity of term rewriting. J. Automat. Reason. **59**(1), 121–163 (2017). https://doi.org/10.1007/S10817-016-9397-X
7. Fuhs, C.: Transforming derivational complexity of term rewriting to runtime complexity. In: Herzig, A., Popescu, A. (eds.) FroCoS 2019. LNCS (LNAI), vol. 11715, pp. 348–364. Springer, Cham (2019). https://doi.org/10.1007/978-3-030-29007-8_20
8. Geser, A.: Relative Termination. PhD thesis. University of Passau (1990). https://www.uni-ulm.de/fileadmin/websiteuniulm/iui/UlmerInformatikBerichte/1991/UIB-1991-03.pdf
9. Geser, A., Hofbauer, D., Waldmann, J.: Sparse tiling through overlap closures for termination of string rewriting. In: Geuvers, H. (ed.), FSCD 2019. LIPIcs, vol. 131, pp. 21:1–21:21 (2019). https://doi.org/10.4230/LIPICS.FSCD.2019.21
10. Giesl, J., Kapur, D.: Dependency Pairs for equational rewriting. In: Middeldorp, A. (ed.) RTA 2001. LNCS, vol. 2051, pp. 93–107. Springer, Heidelberg (2001). https://doi.org/10.1007/3-540-45127-7_9
11. Giesl, J., Thiemann, R., Schneider-Kamp, P.: The dependency pair framework: combining techniques for automated termination proofs. In: Baader, F., Voronkov, A. (eds.) LPAR 2005. LNCS (LNAI), vol. 3452, pp. 301–331. Springer, Heidelberg (2005). https://doi.org/10.1007/978-3-540-32275-7_21
12. Giesl, J., Thiemann, R., Schneider-Kamp, P., Falke, S.: Mechanizing and improving dependency pairs. In: J. Automat. Reason. **37**(3), 155–203 (2006). https://doi.org/10.1007/s10817-006-9057-7
13. Giesl, J., et al.: Analyzing program termination and complexity automatically with AProVE. In: J. Automat. Reason. **58**(1), 3–31 (2017). https://doi.org/10.1007/s10817-016-9388-y
14. Giesl, J., Rubio, A., Sternagel, C., Waldmann, J., Yamada, A.: The termination and complexity competition. In: Beyer, D., Huisman, M., Kordon, F., Steffen, B. (eds.) TACAS 2019. LNCS, vol. 11429, pp. 156–166. Springer, Cham (2019). https://doi.org/10.1007/978-3-030-17502-3_10
15. Gutiérrez, R., Lucas, S.: MU-TERM: verify termination properties automatically (system description). In: Peltier, N., Sofronie-Stokkermans, V. (eds.) IJCAR 2020. LNCS (LNAI), vol. 12167, pp. 436–447. Springer, Cham (2020). https://doi.org/10.1007/978-3-030-51054-1_28
16. Hirokawa, N., Middeldorp, A.: Automating the dependency pair method. Inf. Computat. **199**(1–2), 172–199 (2005). https://doi.org/10.1016/j.ic.2004.10.004

17. Hirokawa, N., Middeldorp, A.: Tyrolean termination tool: techniques and features. Inf. Comput. **205**(4), 474–511 (2007). https://doi.org/10.1016/J.IC.2006.08.010
18. Hirokawa, N., Moser, G.: Automated complexity analysis based on the dependency pair method. In: Armando, A., Baumgartner, P., Dowek, G. (eds.) IJCAR 2008. LNCS (LNAI), vol. 5195, pp. 364–379. Springer, Heidelberg (2008). https://doi.org/10.1007/978-3-540-71070-7_32
19. Hirokawa, N., Middeldorp, A.: Decreasing diagrams and relative termination. J. Automat. Reason. **47**(4), 481–501 (2011). https://doi.org/10.1007/S10817-011-9238-X
20. Iborra, J., Nishida, N., Vidal, G.: Goal-directed and relative dependency pairs for proving the termination of narrowing. In: De Schreye, D. (ed.) LOPSTR 2009. LNCS, vol. 6037, pp. 52–66. Springer, Heidelberg (2010). https://doi.org/10.1007/978-3-642-12592-8_5
21. Iborra, J., Nishida, N., Vidal, G., Yamada, A.: Relative termination via dependency pairs. J. Automat. Reason. **58**(3), 391–411 (2017). https://doi.org/10.1007/S10817-016-9373-5
22. Kassing, J.-C., Giesl, J.: Proving almost-sure innermost termination of probabilistic term rewriting using dependency pairs. In: Pientka, B., Tinelli, C. (eds.) CADE 2023. LNCS, vol. 14132, pp. 344–364. Springer, Cham (2023). https://doi.org/10.1007/978-3-031-38499-8_20
23. Kassing, J.-C., Dollase, S., Giesl, J.: A complete dependency pair framework for almost-sure innermost termination of probabilistic term rewriting. In: Gibbons, J., Miller, D. (eds.) FLOPS 2024. LNCS, vol. 14659, pp. 62–80. Springer, Cham (2024). https://doi.org/10.1007/978-981-97-2300-3_4
24. Kassing, J.-C., Vartanyan, G., Giesl, J.: A dependency pair framework for relative termination of term rewriting. arXiv preprint arXiv:2404.15248 (2024). https://doi.org/10.48550/arXiv.2404.15248
25. Klein, D., Hirokawa, N.: Confluence of non-left-linear TRSs via relative termination. In: Bjørner, N., Voronkov, A. (eds.) LPAR 2012. LNCS, vol. 7180, pp. 258–273. Springer, Heidelberg (2012). https://doi.org/10.1007/978-3-642-28717-6_21
26. Koprowski, A., Zantema, H.: Proving liveness with fairness using rewriting. In: Gramlich, B. (ed.) FroCoS 2005. LNCS (LNAI), vol. 3717, pp. 232–247. Springer, Heidelberg (2005). https://doi.org/10.1007/11559306_13
27. Korp, M., Sternagel, C., Zankl, H., Middeldorp, A.: Tyrolean termination tool 2. In: Treinen, R. (ed.) RTA 2009. LNCS, vol. 5595, pp. 295–304. Springer, Heidelberg (2009). https://doi.org/10.1007/978-3-642-02348-4_21
28. Lankford, D.S.: n Proving Term Rewriting Systems are Noetherian. Memo MTP-3, Math. Dept., Louisiana Technical University, Ruston (1979). https://www.ens-lyon.fr/LIP/REWRITING/TERMINATION/LankfordPolyTerm.pdf
29. Naaf, M., Frohn, F., Brockschmidt, M., Fuhs, C., Giesl, J.: Complexity analysis for term rewriting by integer transition systems. In: Dixon, C., Finger, M. (eds.) FroCoS 2017. LNCS (LNAI), vol. 10483, pp. 132–150. Springer, Cham (2017). https://doi.org/10.1007/978-3-319-66167-4_8
30. Nagele, J., Felgenhauer, B., Zankl, H.: Certifying confluence proofs via relative termination and rule labeling. Logic. Methods Comput. Sci. **13**(2) (2017). https://doi.org/10.23638/LMCS-13(2:4)2017
31. Nishida, N., Vidal, G.: Termination of narrowing via termination of rewriting. Appl. Algebra Eng. Commun. Comput. **21**(3), 177–225 (2010). https://doi.org/10.1007/S00200-010-0122-4

32. Noschinski, L., Emmes, F., Giesl, J.: Analyzing innermost runtime complexity of term rewriting by dependency pairs. J. Autom. Reason. **51**, 27–56 (2013). https://doi.org/10.1007/978-3-642-22438-6_32
33. TPDB (Termination Problem Data Base). https://github.com/TermCOMP/TPDB
34. Vidal, G.: Termination of narrowing in left-linear constructor systems. In: Garrigue, J., Hermenegildo, M.V. (eds.) FLOPS 2008. LNCS, vol. 4989, pp. 113–129. Springer, Heidelberg (2008). https://doi.org/10.1007/978-3-540-78969-7_10
35. Waldmann, J.: Matchbox: A tool for match-bounded string rewriting. In: van Oostrom, V. (ed.) RTA 2004. LNCS, vol. 3091, pp. 85–94. Springer, Heidelberg (2004). https://doi.org/10.1007/978-3-540-25979-4_6
36. Yamada, A., Kusakari, K., Sakabe, T.: Nagoya termination tool. In: Dowek, G. (ed.) RTA 2014. LNCS, vol. 8560, pp. 466–475. Springer, Cham (2014). https://doi.org/10.1007/978-3-319-08918-8_32
37. Zankl, H., Korp, M.: Modular complexity analysis for term rewriting. Logic. Methods Comput. Sci. **10**(1) (2014). https://doi.org/10.2168/LMCS-10(1:19)2014

Solving Quantitative Equations

Georg Ehling(✉) and Temur Kutsia

RISC, Johannes Kepler University Linz, Linz, Austria
{gehling,kutsia}@risc.jku.at

Abstract. Quantitative equational reasoning provides a framework that extends equality to an abstract notion of proximity by endowing equations with an element of a quantale. In this paper, we discuss the unification problem for a special class of shallow subterm-collapse-free quantitative equational theories. We outline rule-based algorithms for solving such equational unification problems over generic as well as idempotent Lawvereian quantales and study their properties.

Keywords: Quantitative equational reasoning · Lawvereian quantales · Equational unification

1 Introduction

Extending the equality predicate to a notion that expresses similarity or proximity is a task that has been addressed in various ways. While fuzzy reasoning [8,23] approaches this endeavor by equipping equations with real numbers between 0 and 1 to express the degree to which they hold true, quantitative algebraic reasoning [4,17] follows a more proximity-oriented approach, attempting to establish a notion of distance between two terms.

Recently, Gavazzo and Di Florio [12] introduced a framework of metric and quantitative equational reasoning that generalizes these approaches (with a slight modification). It is based on the idea of modeling abstract quantities in quantales [22], following Lawvere's fundamental work [16]. In this framework, equations between terms are endowed with an element of a Lawvereian quantale that expresses, in one sense or another, the degree to which they hold true. The exact meaning of this degree depends on the choice of the quantale; for instance, it could correspond to the distance of two terms in a metric space, or to the probability that the terms are equal. This approach is quite general and includes various known quantitative theories as special cases.

In recent years, quantitative and approximate techniques have become increasingly popular due to various applications. In these applications, e.g., in those related to reasoning about probabilistic computations [5], reasoning about privacy and security of systems [1,21], reasoning about resource consumption during computation [7], approximate program transformations [13], etc. equalities are replaced with their quantitative approximations to model distances between programs, processes, or systems, resulting in metric-based approximate

C. Benzmüller et al. (Eds.): IJCAR 2024, LNAI 14740, pp. 381–400, 2024.
https://doi.org/10.1007/978-3-031-63501-4_20

relations. Various techniques have been used to model such metric reasoning principles, among them quantitative equational logic, discussed in [3,4,17,18].

In this paper, we address one of the central problems in equational reasoning: unification (or solving equations). We approach this problem in the framework as described in [12], studying a generalization of classical unification to solving equations in a quantitative equational theory in Lawvereian quantales.

The theories we consider in this paper are induced by shallow subterm-collapse-free equations of a special form, between terms whose arguments are the same sequence of variables, e.g. $f(x_1, \ldots, x_n)$ and $g(x_1, \ldots, x_n)$. This is a natural first step toward investigating quantitative equational unification since such quantitative equations generalize the principle of "extending proximity between function symbols to proximity between terms" of unification in the fuzzy quantale to unification in an arbitrary Lawvereian quantale. Despite their simple form, such theories still pose several challenges (originating from, e.g., tensor-based transitivity or extending proximity between arguments to whole terms), which affect the notions of completeness and minimality of unifier sets. We redefine these notions and show that unification (modulo the abovementioned theories) in arbitrary Lawvereian quantale is finitary, while for idempotent Lawvereian quantales, it becomes unitary. We develop the corresponding unification algorithms and study their properties. Due to space limitations, we refer to the more detailed technical report [10] for some of the proofs.

2 Preliminaries

We start by introducing the basic notions and fixing the terminology.

Quantales. For the notions in this part, we follow [11,12].

Definition 1 (Quantale). *A (unital)* quantale $\mathfrak{Q} = (\Omega, \precsim, \otimes, \kappa)$ *consists of a monoid* $(\Omega, k, \otimes)$ *and a complete lattice* $(\Omega, \precsim)$ *(with join* $\vee$ *and meet* $\wedge$*) satisfying the following distributivity laws:* $\delta \otimes \left(\bigvee_{i \in I} \varepsilon_i\right) = \bigvee_{i \in I}(\delta \otimes \varepsilon_i)$ *and* $\left(\bigvee_{i \in I} \varepsilon_i\right) \otimes \delta = \bigvee_{i \in I}(\varepsilon_i \otimes \delta)$.

The element κ is called the *unit* of the quantale, and $\otimes$ is called its *tensor* (or multiplication). Besides κ, we use Greek letters $\varepsilon, \delta, \eta, \zeta, \iota$, and ω to denote elements of Ω. The *top* and *bottom* elements of a quantale are denoted by $\top$ and $\bot$, respectively. Quantales in which the unit κ coincides with $\top$ are called *integral quantales.* A quantale is *commutative* if its underlying monoid is. It is *non-trivial* if $\kappa \neq \bot$. It is *cointegral* if $\varepsilon \otimes \delta = \bot$ implies either $\varepsilon = \bot$ or $\delta = \bot$.

We assume our quantales are commutative, integral, cointegral, and nontrivial. Such quantales are called *Lawvereian.* (Note that the fuzzy quantale $\mathbb{I}$ is Lawvereian for the Gödel and product T-norms, but not for the Łukasiewicz T-norm.)

Tensors in quantales always have left and right *adjoints*. For commutative quantales, these adjoints are the same, defined as $\varepsilon \multimap \delta := \bigvee\{\eta \mid \varepsilon \otimes \eta \precsim \delta\}$.

Table 1. Correspondence between quantales Ω (generic), 2 (Boolean), $\mathbb{L}$ (Lawvere), $\mathbb{L}^{\max}$ (strong Lawvere), and $\mathbb{I}$ (fuzzy).

	Ω	2	$\mathbb{L}$	$\mathbb{L}^{\max}$	$\mathbb{I}$
Carrier	Ω	$\{0,1\}$	$[0,\infty]$	$[0,\infty]$	$[0,1]$
Order	$\precsim$	$\leqslant$	$\geqslant$	$\geqslant$	$\leqslant$
Join	$\bigvee$	$\exists$	inf	inf	sup
Meet	$\bigwedge$	$\forall$	sup	sup	inf
Tensor	$\otimes$	$\wedge$	$+$	max	left-continuous T-norm
Unit	κ	1	0	0	1

An element $\iota \in \Omega$ is an *idempotent element* (or simply an *idempotent*) of a quantale Ω if it satisfies $\iota \otimes \iota = \iota$. A quantale is called *idempotent* if every element is idempotent. Among the quantales in Table 1, the idempotent ones are 2, $\mathbb{L}^{\max}$, and $\mathbb{I}$ for the minimum (Gödel) T-norm.

In any Lawvereian quantale, (i) $\otimes$ is monotonous: $\alpha \precsim \beta \Rightarrow \alpha \otimes \gamma \precsim \beta \otimes \gamma$ (using distributivity: $(\alpha \otimes \gamma) \vee (\beta \otimes \gamma) = (\alpha \vee \beta) \otimes \gamma = \beta \otimes \gamma$); (ii) $\alpha \otimes \beta \precsim \alpha \wedge \beta$ (using monotonicity and integrality: $\alpha \otimes \beta \precsim \alpha \otimes \top = \alpha$).

Given a quantale Ω and $\varepsilon, \delta \in \Omega$, the *way-below relation* $\ll$ is defined as $\delta \ll \varepsilon$ iff for every $\Psi \subseteq \Omega$, if $\varepsilon \precsim \bigvee \Psi$ then there exists a finite subset $\Psi_0 \subseteq \Psi$ such that $\delta \precsim \bigvee \Psi_0$. A quantale Ω is called *continuous* if $\varepsilon = \bigvee_{\delta \ll \varepsilon} \delta$ for all $\varepsilon \in \Omega$.

Definition 2 (Ω-relations, Ω-ternary relations). *An* Ω-relation *R between sets A and B is a function $R\colon A \times B \to \Omega$. For any set A, the identity Ω-relation $\Delta_A\colon A \times A \to \Omega$ maps the diagonal elements (a,a) to κ, and all other elements to $\bot$. The composition $(R;S)\colon A \times C \to \Omega$ of two Ω-relations $R\colon A \times B \to \Omega$ and $S\colon B \times C \to \Omega$ is defined as $(R;S)(a,c) := \bigvee_{b \in B} \big(R(a,b) \otimes S(b,c)\big)$.*

An Ω-ternary relation *over $A \times B$ is a ternary relation $R \subseteq A \times \Omega \times B$ such that $R(a,\varepsilon,b)$ implies $R(a,\delta,b)$ for any $\delta \precsim \varepsilon$.*

Any Ω-ternary relation R induces an Ω-relation $R^{\bullet}(a,b) := \bigvee_{R(a,\varepsilon,b)} \varepsilon$, and any Ω-relation R induces an Ω-ternary relation $R^{\circ}(a,\varepsilon,b) :\Longleftrightarrow \varepsilon \precsim R(a,b)$. Moreover, we have $R^{\bullet\circ} = R^{\circ\bullet} = R$, and we can freely switch between Ω-ternary relations and Ω-relations.

The complete lattice structure of Ω lifts to Ω-relations pointwise, and we can say that an Ω-relation R on $A \times A$ is reflexive if $\Delta_A \precsim R$; transitive if $(R;R) \precsim R$; symmetric if $R^{-} \precsim R$ (where R^{-} is defined as $R^{-}(b,a) := R(a,b)$). Thus, we get the notions of a preorder (i.e., reflexive and transitive) and equivalence (i.e., reflexive, transitive, and symmetric) Ω-relation.

Terms and Substitutions. We assume that the reader is familiar with the standard notions of unification theory, see, e.g., [2]. A *signature* $\mathcal{F}$ is a set of function symbols, each equipped with a fixed nonnegative arity. The set of *terms* over a signature $\mathcal{F}$ and a set of variables $\mathcal{V}$ is denoted by $T(\mathcal{F},\mathcal{V})$. Given a term

$t \in T(\mathcal{F}, \mathcal{V})$, we denote by $\mathcal{V}(t)$ the set of variables appearing in t. A term is *ground* if it contains no variables. The notion of a *position* in a term is defined in the standard way.

The set of *leaves* of a term is defined as $\ell(e) := \{e\}$, if e is a constant symbol or a variable, and $\ell(f(t_1, \dots, t_n)) := \bigcup_{i=1}^{n} \ell(t_i)$. (The leaves of a term t correspond to the leaves of the tree representing t.) If s is a subterm of t, then the *depth of s in t* as the minimal length of a position at which s occurs in t.

A *substitution* is a map $\sigma\colon \mathcal{V} \to T(\mathcal{F}, \mathcal{V})$ which maps all but finitely many variables to themselves. Greek letters $\sigma, \varphi, \vartheta, \tau$ are used for them, while *Id* denotes the identity substitution. The set of substitutions is denoted by *Sub*. We use the set notation for substitutions, writing σ explicitly as a finite set $\{x \mapsto \sigma(x) \mid x \neq \sigma(x)\}$. The *domain* of σ is defined as $dom(\sigma) := \{x \mid x \neq \sigma(x)\}$. A substitution σ extends naturally to an endomorphism on $T(\mathcal{F}, \mathcal{V})$. The image of a term t under this endomorphism is denoted $t\sigma$.

3 Quantitative Equational Theories

We now fix a signature $\mathcal{F}$, a set of variables $\mathcal{V}$, and a Lawvereian quantale Ω.

Let $\approx_E$ be an Ω-ternary relation, assumed to be induced from a given set E of triples (t, ε, s), which we write as $\varepsilon \Vdash t \approx_E s$ (called Ω-equalities). A *quantitative equational theory* (or *Ω-equational theory*) $=_E$ is an Ω-ternary relation generated from $\approx_E$ by the rules in Fig. 1. We call E a *presentation* of $=_E$. Informally, we read $\varepsilon \Vdash t =_E s$ as "t and s are at most ε-apart modulo E" or "t and s are equal modulo E with degree ε".

$$\textsf{(Ax)}\ \frac{\varepsilon \Vdash t \approx_E s}{\varepsilon \Vdash t =_E s} \qquad \textsf{(Refl)}\ \frac{}{\kappa \Vdash t =_E t} \qquad \textsf{(Sym)}\ \frac{\varepsilon \Vdash t =_E s}{\varepsilon \Vdash s =_E t} \qquad \textsf{(Trans)}\ \frac{\varepsilon \Vdash t =_E s \quad \delta \Vdash s =_E r}{\varepsilon \otimes \delta \Vdash t =_E r}$$

$$\textsf{(NExp)}\ \frac{\varepsilon_1 \Vdash t_1 =_E s_1 \quad \cdots \quad \varepsilon_n \Vdash t_n =_E s_n}{\varepsilon_1 \otimes \cdots \otimes \varepsilon_n \Vdash f(t_1, \dots, t_n) =_E f(s_1, \dots, s_n)} \qquad \textsf{(Subst)}\ \frac{\varepsilon \Vdash t =_E s}{\varepsilon \Vdash t\sigma =_E s\sigma}$$

$$\textsf{(Ord)}\ \frac{\varepsilon \Vdash t =_E s \quad \delta \precsim \varepsilon}{\delta \Vdash t =_E s} \qquad \textsf{(Join)}\ \frac{\varepsilon_1 \Vdash t =_E s \quad \cdots \quad \varepsilon_n \Vdash t =_E s}{\varepsilon_1 \vee \cdots \vee \varepsilon_n \Vdash t =_E s}$$

$$\textsf{(Arch)}\ \frac{\forall \delta \ll \varepsilon .\, \delta \Vdash t =_E s}{\varepsilon \Vdash t =_E s}$$

Fig. 1. Quantitative equational theory

Observe that the Ω-relation $=_E^{\bullet}$ induced from $=_E$ (i.e., $t =_E^{\bullet} s := \bigvee_{\varepsilon \Vdash t =_E s} \varepsilon$) is a reflexive, symmetric, transitive quantitative relation that contains $\approx_E^{\bullet}$ and where function symbols and substitutions behave in a non-expansive way:

$$\left(t_1 =^{\bullet}_{E} s_1 \otimes \cdots \otimes t_n =^{\bullet}_{E} s_n\right) \precsim \left(f(t_1,\ldots,t_n) =^{\bullet}_{E} f(s_1,\ldots,s_n)\right),$$
$$\left(t =^{\bullet}_{E} s\right) \precsim \left(t\sigma =^{\bullet}_{E} s\sigma\right).$$

We will often slightly abuse terminology by calling both $=^{\bullet}_{E}$ and a presentation E a quantitative equational theory.

The rules in Fig. 1 were introduced in [11] with the aim of generalizing previous approaches to quantitative reasoning [4,17]. This generalization is achieved up to a slight modification of the (NExp) rule, whose analogue in [17] would feature the join of $\varepsilon_1, \ldots, \varepsilon_n$ rather than their tensor product.[1]

It should further be remarked that the (Join) rule also applies to an empty hypothesis, whence $\bot \Vdash t =_E s$ holds for any t and s. The infinitary (Arch) rule is needed to guarantee the semantic completeness of the deduction system in [17], but has no effect on $=_E$ whenever the presentation E is finite, whence it can be safely ignored in that case.

Analogous to classical equational theories, an Ω-equation $\varepsilon \Vdash t = s$, where s is a proper subterm of t, is called a *subterm-collapse equation.* A quantitative equational theory E is said to be *simple* (or *subterm-collapse-free*) if whenever $\varepsilon \Vdash t =_E s$ with $\varepsilon \neq \bot$ holds, the equation $\varepsilon \Vdash t = s$ is not subterm-collapsing. An equation $\varepsilon \Vdash t = s$ is called *shallow* [6] if the depth of each variable occurrence in t or in s is at most 1. An equational theory is called shallow if each equation in its presentation is shallow.

Definition 3. *Let E be an Ω-equational theory and $\mathcal{X}$ be a set of variables. A ternary relation $\lessapprox_{E,\mathcal{X}} \subseteq Sub \times \Omega \times Sub$ is defined as*

$\lessapprox_{E,\mathcal{X}} (\sigma, \varepsilon, \vartheta)$ iff there exists a φ such that $\varepsilon \Vdash x\sigma\varphi =_E x\vartheta$ for all $x \in \mathcal{X}$.

In this case, we say that the substitution σ is more general than *ϑ* modulo *E* on *$\mathcal{X}$* up to *ε. We shortly write $\sigma \lessapprox_{E,\mathcal{X},\varepsilon} \vartheta$ and call ϑ an $(E, \mathcal{X}, \varepsilon)$*-instance *of σ (or an $(E, \mathcal{X})$-instance with degree ε).*

It is not hard to see that $\lessapprox_{E,\mathcal{X}}$ is an Ω-ternary relation over $Sub \times Sub$. To show this, we need to prove that $\sigma \lessapprox_{E,\mathcal{X},\varepsilon} \vartheta$ implies $\sigma \lessapprox_{E,\mathcal{X},\delta} \vartheta$ for any $\delta \precsim \varepsilon$, which follows from the definition of $=_E$.

Lemma 1. *If $\sigma \lessapprox_{E,\mathcal{X},\varepsilon} \vartheta$ and $\vartheta \lessapprox_{E,\mathcal{Y},\delta} \psi$, then $\sigma \lessapprox_{E,\mathcal{X}\cap\mathcal{Y},\varepsilon\otimes\delta} \psi$.*

Proof. By definition of $\lessapprox_{E,\mathcal{X}}$ and $\lessapprox_{E,\mathcal{Y}}$, we have $\varepsilon \Vdash x\sigma\varphi_1 =_E x\vartheta$ for all $x \in \mathcal{X}$, and $\delta \Vdash y\vartheta\varphi_2 =_E y\psi$ for all $y \in \mathcal{Y}$. From these equalities, for all $z \in \mathcal{X} \cap \mathcal{Y}$ by the Subst rule we get $\varepsilon \Vdash z\sigma\varphi_1\varphi_2 =_E z\vartheta\varphi_2$ and $\delta \Vdash z\vartheta\varphi_2 =_E z\psi$. Therefore, by $\otimes$-transitivity (the Trans rule) we obtain $\varepsilon\otimes\delta \Vdash z\sigma\varphi_1\varphi_2 =_E z\psi$ for all $z \in \mathcal{X}\cap\mathcal{Y}$, which, by definition of $\lessapprox_{E,\mathcal{X}\cap\mathcal{Y}}$, gives $\sigma \lessapprox_{E,\mathcal{X}\cap\mathcal{Y},\varepsilon\otimes\delta} \psi$. □

[1] The reason for this modification in [11] is that (NExp) should be compatible with (Trans), which is based on the tensor rather than the join. Without it, one would obtain a system where performing various transformation steps one after the other would lead to a different distance than performing the same steps in parallel.

Corollary 1. *If* $\sigma \lessapprox_{E,\mathcal{X},\varepsilon} \vartheta$ *and* $\vartheta \lessapprox_{E,\mathcal{X},\delta} \psi$*, then* $\sigma \lessapprox_{E,\mathcal{X},\varepsilon\otimes\delta} \psi$.

Theorem 1. *Given a set of* Ω*-equalities* E *and a set of variables* $\mathcal{X}$*, the* Ω*-relation* $\lessapprox^{\bullet}_{E,\mathcal{X}}$ *induced by* $\lessapprox_{E,\mathcal{X}}$ *is a preorder on Sub.*

Proof. We should show that $\lessapprox^{\bullet}_{E,\mathcal{X}}$ is reflexive and transitive.

- Reflexivity: We need to show $\kappa \precsim \sigma \lessapprox^{\bullet}_{E,\mathcal{X}} \sigma$ for all σ, which follows directly from the definitions of $\lessapprox_{E,\mathcal{X}}$ and $=_E$.
- Transitivity: We should prove $(\sigma \lessapprox^{\bullet}_{E,\mathcal{X}} \vartheta \otimes \vartheta \lessapprox^{\bullet}_{E,\mathcal{X}} \psi) \precsim (\sigma \lessapprox^{\bullet}_{E,\mathcal{X}} \psi)$ for all σ, ϑ, and ψ. This statement can be inferred from Corollary 1. □

The equivalence relation on substitutions induced by $\lessapprox_{E,\mathcal{X}}$ is denoted by $\cong_{E,\mathcal{X}}$. It is an Ω-ternary relation. We write $\sigma \cong_{E,\mathcal{X},\varepsilon} \vartheta$ if $\varepsilon \precsim (\sigma \cong^{\bullet}_{E,\mathcal{X}} \vartheta)$.

Example 1. Let Ω be the Lawvere quantale $\mathbb{L} = ([0,\infty], \geqslant, +, 0)$ and consider $E = \{1 \Vdash a \approx b, 1 \Vdash b \approx c\}$, $\varepsilon = 2$ and $\mathcal{X} = \{x\}$. Let $\sigma = \{x \mapsto a\}$, $\vartheta = \{x \mapsto b\}$, and $\varphi = \{x \mapsto c\}$. Then we have:

- $\sigma \lessapprox_{E,\mathcal{X},\varepsilon} \vartheta$, because $x\sigma Id = a$, $x\vartheta = b$, and $1 \Vdash a =_E b$;
- $\vartheta \lessapprox_{E,\mathcal{X},\varepsilon} \varphi$, because $x\vartheta Id = b$, $x\varphi = c$, and $1 \Vdash b =_E c$;
- $\varphi \lessapprox_{E,\mathcal{X},\varepsilon} \sigma$, because $x\varphi Id = c$, $x\sigma = a$, and $2 \Vdash c =_E a$.

Hence, $\sigma \cong_{E,\mathcal{X},\varepsilon} \vartheta$, $\vartheta \cong_{E,\mathcal{X},\varepsilon} \varphi$, and $\sigma \cong_{E,\mathcal{X},\varepsilon} \varphi$. ■

Theorem 2. *Given* E, $\mathcal{X}$, t, *and* s *such that* $\mathcal{V}(t) \cup \mathcal{V}(s) \subseteq \mathcal{X}$*, let* R *denote* $=^{\bullet}_E$ *and* S *denote* $\lessapprox^{\bullet}_{E,\mathcal{X}}$*. Assume* σ *and* ϑ *are substitutions such that* $R(t\sigma, s\sigma) = \varepsilon$ *and* $S(\sigma, \vartheta) = \delta$*. Then* $\varepsilon \otimes \bigotimes_{i=1}^{n+m} \delta \precsim R(t\vartheta, s\vartheta)$*, where* n *and* m *are the number of occurrences of variables from* $\mathcal{X}$ *in* t *and* s*, respectively.*

Proof. From $S(\sigma, \vartheta) = \delta$ we know that there exists φ such that $\delta \precsim R(x\sigma\varphi, x\vartheta)$ holds for all $x \in \mathcal{X}$. From this, by structural induction over terms, we can prove $\bigotimes_{i=1}^{n} \delta \precsim R(t\sigma\varphi, t\vartheta)$ and $\bigotimes_{i=1}^{m} \delta \precsim R(s\sigma\varphi, s\vartheta)$. From $R(t\sigma, s\sigma) = \varepsilon$ we get $\varepsilon \precsim R(t\sigma\varphi, s\sigma\varphi)$. Applying transitivity twice we get $\varepsilon \otimes \bigotimes_{i=1}^{n+m} \delta \precsim R(t\vartheta, s\vartheta)$. □

Example 2. In the Boolean quantale 2, this theorem implies the well-known fact that if σ is a unifier of t and s and ϑ is an instance of σ, then ϑ is also a unifier of t and s. (In that case, $\varepsilon = \delta = 1$.)

Consider the fuzzy quantale $\mathbb{I}$ with the minimum T-norm, $E = \{0.5 \Vdash a \approx b, 0.7 \Vdash b \approx c\}$, $t = f(x, x, y)$, $s = f(y, b, c)$, $\mathcal{X} = \{x, y\}$, $\sigma = \{x \mapsto b, y \mapsto b\}$, and $\vartheta = \{x \mapsto a, y \mapsto c\}$. Then $0.5 \Vdash a =_E c$ and

$t\sigma = f(b, b, b)$, $s\sigma = f(b, b, c)$, $\varepsilon = 0.7$, $0.7 \Vdash t\sigma =_E s\sigma$;

$\delta = 0.5$, $\sigma \lessapprox_{E,\{x,y\},0.5} \vartheta$ (actually, $\sigma \cong_{E,\{x,y\},0.5} \vartheta$);

$t\vartheta = f(a, a, c)$, $s\vartheta = f(c, b, c)$;

Variables of $\mathcal{X}$ occur in t and s in total 4 times;

$\min(0.7, 0.5, 0.5, 0.5, 0.5) = 0.5$; $0.5 \Vdash t\vartheta =_E s\vartheta$.

Now consider the Lawvere quantale $\mathbb{L}$ with $E = \{1 \Vdash a \approx b, 1 \Vdash b \approx c, 1 \Vdash c \approx d, 1 \Vdash f(x) \approx g(x)\}$, $t = x$, $s = f(y)$, $\mathcal{X} = \{x, y\}$, $\sigma = \{x \mapsto g(y)\}$, and $\vartheta = \{x \mapsto g(a), y \mapsto d\}$. Besides, $\precsim = \geqslant$ and we have

$t\sigma = g(y), \quad s\sigma = f(y), \quad \varepsilon = 1, \quad 1 \Vdash t\sigma =_E s\sigma;$

$\delta = 2, \qquad \sigma \lesssim_{E,\{x,y\},2} \vartheta;$

$t\vartheta = g(a), \quad s\vartheta = f(d);$

Variables of $\mathcal{X}$ occur in t and s in total twice;

$\varepsilon + 2\delta = 5;$

$5 \Vdash t\vartheta =_E s\vartheta$. (In fact, $=_E^\bullet (t\vartheta, s\vartheta) = 1 + 3 = 4$ and $5 \precsim 4$.) ■

Theorem 2 implies that if δ is an idempotent element of the quantale and it can be absorbed by ε (i.e., $\varepsilon \otimes \delta = \varepsilon$), then $\varepsilon \Vdash t\vartheta =_E s\vartheta$. Obviously, this will be fulfilled if $\delta = \kappa$. In idempotent quantales, it will also hold when $\varepsilon \precsim \delta$. For idempotent elements, a stronger version of transitivity holds. Namely, if ι is an idempotent element of a quantale, then we have for all $E, t, s, r, \mathcal{X}, \sigma, \vartheta, \varphi$:

- $\iota \Vdash t =_E s$ and $\iota \Vdash s =_E r$ imply $\iota \Vdash t =_E r$,
- $\sigma \lesssim_{E,\mathcal{X},\iota} \vartheta$ and $\vartheta \lesssim_{E,\mathcal{X},\iota} \varphi$ imply $\sigma \lesssim_{E,\mathcal{X},\iota} \varphi$.

4 Quantitative Equational Unification

Definition 4 (Quantitative equational unification). *A quantitative equational unification problem is formulated as follows:*

Given: *A quantale $\mathfrak{Q}$, $\varepsilon \in \Omega$ (called the threshold) with $\varepsilon \neq \bot$, a set of $\mathfrak{Q}$-equalities E (a presentation of an equational theory), and two terms t and s.*

Find: *A substitution σ such that $\varepsilon \Vdash t\sigma =_E s\sigma$.*

*We call this problem (E, ε)-*unification problem *over $\mathfrak{Q}$. The quantale name is usually skipped when it does not cause confusion. For unification problems, we use the notation $\varepsilon \Vdash t =_E^? s$, called a* unification equation, *where the question mark indicates that the equation is supposed to be solved. For simplicity, we write the problem as $t =_{E,\varepsilon}^? s$, and further skip E if it is clear from the context.*

*The substitution σ, if it exists, is called an (E, ε)-*unifier *of t and s (alternatively, a unifier or a solution of $t =_{E,\varepsilon}^? s$) over $\mathfrak{Q}$. In such a case we say that the given unification problem is* solvable, *or that the terms t and s are (E, ε)-*unifiable *over $\mathfrak{Q}$. The set of all unifiers of $t =_{E,\varepsilon}^? s$ is denoted by $\mathfrak{U}_{E,\varepsilon}(t, s)$.*

For a given presentation E, a function symbol from $\mathcal{F}$ is called *free* if it does not appear in E. If $\mathcal{F}$ contains a free m-ary function symbol for some $m > 1$, the unification problem formulated above is equivalent to a problem of finding a solution of a system of unification equations (instead of a single equation) formulated as a constrained problem:

Given: A quantale $\mathfrak{Q}$, the threshold value $\varepsilon \in \Omega$ with $\varepsilon \neq \bot$, a set of $\mathfrak{Q}$-equalities E (a presentation of an equational theory), and a set of term-pairs t_i, s_i, $1 \leq i \leq n$.

Find: A substitution σ such that $\delta_i \Vdash t_i\sigma =_E s_i\sigma$, $1 \leq i \leq n$, for some δ_i with $\varepsilon \precsim \delta_1 \otimes \cdots \otimes \delta_n$.

In such a case we can write the unification problem as a pair of a set of unification equations and a $\precsim$-constraint: $\{t_1 =^?_{E,\boldsymbol{\alpha}_1} s_1, \dots, t_n =^?_{E,\boldsymbol{\alpha}_n} s_n\}; \varepsilon \precsim \boldsymbol{\alpha}_1 \otimes \cdots \otimes \boldsymbol{\alpha}_n$, where $\boldsymbol{\alpha}_i$ are new metavariables whose values are also to be found alongside with variables that appear in the given t's and s's. This problem can be transformed to a single-equation problem. For instance, the constrained problem $\{t_1 =^?_{E,\boldsymbol{\alpha}_1} s_1, t_2 =^?_{E,\boldsymbol{\alpha}_2} s_2, t_3 =^?_{E,\boldsymbol{\alpha}_3} s_3\}; \varepsilon \precsim \boldsymbol{\alpha}_1 \otimes \boldsymbol{\alpha}_2 \otimes \boldsymbol{\alpha}_3$ can be transformed to $f(f(t_1,t_2),t_3) =^?_{E,\varepsilon} f(f(s_1,s_2),s_3)$, where f is a free binary function symbol. The two problems are equivalent in the sense that they have exactly the same set of (E,ε)-unifiers.If the arity of f is bigger than the number of equations, the missing arguments will be filled in by fresh variables. For instance, for a quaternary f, the problem above can be encoded as $f(t_1,t_2,t_3,x) =^?_{E,\varepsilon} f(s_1,s_2,s_3,x)$, where x is fresh.

In classical unification, an important property of the instantiation relation is that any substitution that is less general than a given unifier of two terms will still be a unifier. In the quantitative case, we should take into account the approximation, which complicates things. First, we have the following fact as a consequence of Theorem 2:

Fact 1. *If σ is an (E,ε)-unifier of t and s and $\sigma \lessapprox_{E,\mathcal{V}(t,s),\delta} \vartheta$ for some δ, then ϑ is an $(E,\varepsilon \otimes \delta^k)$-unifier of t and s, where k is the total number of occurrences of variables in t and s.*

Some results become simpler for idempotent elements:

Lemma 2. *Let ι be an idempotent element of $\mathfrak{Q}$, and σ and ϑ be substitutions.*

(i) If $\iota \Vdash y\sigma =_E y\vartheta$ holds for every $y \in \mathcal{Y} \subseteq \mathcal{V}$, then $\iota \Vdash r\sigma =_E r\vartheta$ holds for every term $r \in T(\mathcal{F},\mathcal{Y})$.

(ii) Suppose that $\varepsilon \in \Omega$ satisfies $\varepsilon \otimes \iota = \varepsilon$. If $\sigma \lessapprox_{E,\mathcal{V}(t,s),\iota} \vartheta$ and σ is an (E,ε)-unifier of the terms t and s, then so is ϑ.

Proof. Part (i) is proved by structural induction, using idempotence. For (ii), as $\sigma \lessapprox_{E,\mathcal{V}(t,s),\iota} \vartheta$, there exists a substitution φ such that $\iota \Vdash x\sigma\varphi =_E x\vartheta$ holds for every variable $x \in \mathcal{V}(t,s)$. Thus, $\iota \Vdash r\sigma\varphi =_E r\vartheta$ holds for any term $r \in T(\mathcal{F},\mathcal{V}(t,s))$ by (i). Hence, we have $\iota \Vdash s\vartheta =_E s\sigma\varphi$, $\varepsilon \Vdash s\sigma\varphi =_E t\sigma\varphi$, and $\iota \Vdash t\sigma\varphi =_E t\vartheta$. From these equalities, using $\varepsilon \otimes \iota = \varepsilon$, we get $\varepsilon \Vdash s\vartheta =_E t\vartheta$. □

This lemma implies that $(E,\mathcal{V}(t,s),\kappa)$-instances of (E,ε)-unifiers of t and s are still their (E,ε)-unifiers. Besides, it has the following corollary:

Corollary 2. *Let Ω be an idempotent quantale, in which σ is an (E,ε)-unifier of t and s, $\sigma \lesssim_{E,\mathcal{V}(t,s),\delta} \vartheta$, and $\varepsilon \precsim \delta$. Then ϑ is an (E,ε)-unifier of t and s in Ω.*

These results motivate a specialized version of the notion of a minimal complete set of unifiers that we use in this paper:

Definition 5 (Minimal ι-complete set of unifiers). *Let P be an (E,ε)-unification problem over a quantale Ω and signature $\mathcal{F}$. Let $\mathcal{X} = \mathcal{V}(P)$ be the set of all variables of P, and let ι be an idempotent element of Ω such that $\varepsilon \otimes \iota = \varepsilon$. An* ι-complete set of (E,ε)-unifiers *of P is a set $\mathcal{C}$ of substitutions such that*

1) $\mathcal{C} \subseteq \mathfrak{U}_{E,\varepsilon}(P)$, i.e., each element of $\mathcal{C}$ is an (E,ε)-unifier of P,
2) for each $\vartheta \in \mathfrak{U}_{E,\varepsilon}(P)$ there exists $\sigma \in \mathcal{C}$ such that $\sigma \lesssim_{E,\mathcal{X},\iota} \vartheta$.

The set $\mathcal{C}$ is a minimal ι-complete set of (E,ε)-unifiers *of P iff it is an ι-complete set that satisfies the following minimality property:*

3) for all $\sigma,\sigma' \in \mathcal{C}$, if $\sigma \lesssim_{E,\mathcal{X},\iota} \sigma'$, then $\sigma = \sigma'$.

We denote a minimal ι-complete set of (E,ε)-unifiers of P by $mcsu_{E,\varepsilon,\iota}(P)$.

Given a unification problem with threshold ε, in order to make use of this definition, one first needs to find an idempotent element ι such that $\varepsilon \otimes \iota = \varepsilon$. In an arbitrary quantale, we can always take $\iota = \kappa$. If ε is idempotent itself, then we can also choose $\iota = \varepsilon$.[2]

Let P be an (E,ε)-unification problem. If it is unsolvable, then for any idempotent ι with $\varepsilon \otimes \iota = \varepsilon$ we have $mcsu_{E,\varepsilon,\iota}(t,s) = \emptyset$. Depending on E, ε, and ι, minimal ι-complete sets of (E,ε)-unifiers may not always exist. Even if they do, they may be infinite. When they exist, they are unique modulo the instantiation equivalence relation $\cong_{E,\mathcal{X},\iota}$.[3]

Example 3. Let Ω be the Lawvere quantale $\mathbb{L}$, E be the set of equations $E = \{1 \Vdash a \approx b, 1 \Vdash b \approx c, 1 \Vdash c \approx d\}$, $\varepsilon = 1$, $t = f(x,b)$, and $s = f(c,x)$.

The substitutions $\sigma = \{x \mapsto b\}$, $\vartheta = \{x \mapsto c\}$ are (E,ε)-unifiers of t and s:

- $t\sigma = f(b,b)$, $s\sigma = f(c,b)$ and $1 \Vdash f(b,b) =_E f(c,b)$,
- $t\vartheta = f(c,b)$, $s\vartheta = f(c,c)$ and $1 \Vdash f(c,b) =_E f(c,c)$.

In fact, $\{\sigma,\vartheta\} = mcsu_{E,\varepsilon,0}(t,s)$. Note that we have $\sigma \cong_{E,\mathcal{X},1} \vartheta$, but also $\sigma \cong_{E,\mathcal{X},1} \{x \mapsto a\}$ and $\vartheta \cong_{E,\mathcal{X},1} \{x \mapsto d\}$. However, neither $\{x \mapsto a\}$ nor $\{x \mapsto d\}$ is an (E,ε)-unifier of t and s (but they are $(E,3)$-unifiers of t and s). ∎

The notion of an *occurrence cycle* will be needed later on.

Definition 6 (Occurrence cycle). *A set of unification equations $\{x_1 \approx^?_{\varepsilon_1} t_1, \ldots, x_n \approx^?_{\varepsilon_n} t_n\}$ constitutes an* occurrence cycle *if t_i is a non-variable term for at least one i, $x_i \in \mathcal{V}(t_{i-1})$ for $1 < i \leqslant n$ and $x_1 \in \mathcal{V}(t_n)$.*

[2] This is how it is done, e.g., for fuzzy proximity/similarity relations [9,14,15,19,20,23].

[3] $\cong_{E,\mathcal{X},\iota}$ is a standard binary relation on *Sub* induced by the Ω-ternary relation $\cong_{E,\mathcal{X}}$ for a fixed ι.

4.1 Unification: Simple Shallow Theories (Special Form)

In this section, we will consider Ω-equational theories that admit a presentation consisting of a finite number of equations of the form $\gamma \Vdash f(x_1,\ldots,x_n) \approx g(x_1,\ldots,x_n)$, where $n \geqslant 0$, $f \neq g$, and all x's are pairwise distinct. Also, the γ's in different equations can be different. This is the very basic form of quantitative axioms. The quantale Ω, as said above, is an arbitrary Lawvereian quantale. In the next subsection we consider the special case of idempotent Lawvereian quantales.

The presentation is shallow. One can easily show that the theory generated from such a presentation is simple. Hence, we consider simple shallow quantitative equational theories (of a special form). We will refer to such theories by E_{ssh}. In them, it makes sense to speak about the *approximation degree of two function symbols*, which is defined as $\eth_{E_{\mathsf{ssh}}}(f,g) := \big(f(x_1,\ldots,x_n) \stackrel{\bullet}{=}_{E_{\mathsf{ssh}}} g(x_1,\ldots,x_m)\big)$ for an n-ary f and m-ary g. (Obviously, $\eth_{E_{\mathsf{ssh}}}(f,g) = \bot$ if $n \neq m$.) We say that f and g are $(E_{\mathsf{ssh}},\varepsilon)$-proximal, if $\varepsilon \precsim \eth_{E_{\mathsf{ssh}}}(f,g)$.

Remark 1. Since the equational theories we consider here are finitely presented, the degree of two function symbols of the same arity can be effectively computed as $\eth_{E_{\mathsf{ssh}}}(f,g) = \bigvee\{\gamma \mid \gamma \Vdash f(x_1,\ldots,x_n) = g(x_1,\ldots,x_n) \in C\}$, where C is the closure of the presentation of E_{ssh} under the (Trans) and (Sym) rules.

Theorem 3. *E_{ssh}-unification is finitary in a Lawvereian quantale Ω in the sense that for any $\varepsilon \in \Omega$, every $(E_{\mathsf{ssh}},\varepsilon)$-unification problem $t =^?_{E_{\mathsf{ssh}},\varepsilon} s$ has a finite minimal κ-complete set of unifiers.*

Proof (Sketch). Let $N_{E_{\mathsf{ssh}},\varepsilon}(r)$ denote an ε-neighborhood of a term r with respect to E_{ssh}, defined as the set of all terms obtained from r by replacing some function symbols by their $(E_{\mathsf{ssh}},\varepsilon)$-proximal ones. Then $mcsu_{E_{\mathsf{ssh}},\varepsilon,\kappa}(t,s) \subseteq \bigcup_{t'\in T, s'\in S}\{mgu(t' =^? s')\}$, where $T = N_{E_{\mathsf{ssh}},\varepsilon}(t)$, $S = N_{E_{\mathsf{ssh}},\varepsilon}(s)$, and $mgu(t' =^? s')$ is a most general unifier of the syntactic unification problem $t' =^? s'$. Since the presentation of theories of the form E_{ssh} is finite, the set $N_{E_{\mathsf{ssh}},\varepsilon}(r)$ is finite for $\varepsilon \neq \bot$ for any r. Hence, the set $\bigcup_{t'\in T, s'\in S}\{mgu(t' =^? s')\}$ is finite, which implies that $mcsu_{E_{\mathsf{ssh}},\varepsilon,\kappa}(t,s)$ is finite as well. □

Remark 2. In principle, the above proof already outlines an E_{ssh}-unification algorithm. However, there are several reasons for not using it: first, it would be a brute-force approach blindly replacing symbols with all their proximal ones in all possible ways. Second, it would not be sound because non-unifier answers would be returned and we would have to clean the computed set afterwards. Third, we want to keep our approach flexible, leaving equations between variables as a part of the output instead of forcing them to have only a syntactic solution.

In the following, we use bold-face upright Greek letters $\boldsymbol{\alpha}, \boldsymbol{\beta}, \boldsymbol{\gamma}$ for metavariables that range over the domain of the quantale. The rules constituting our unification method operate on configurations whose form is stated below.

Definition 7 (Configuration). *A* configuration *is either a special symbol* $\boldsymbol{F}$ *or a quadruple* $P; C; \delta; \sigma$*, where*

- *P is a set of unification equations of the form $t =^?_{\boldsymbol{\alpha}} s$, where $\boldsymbol{\alpha}$ is a metavariable (intuitively, P is the remaining problem to be solved),*
- *C is a constraint of the form $\varepsilon \precsim \boldsymbol{\alpha}_1 \otimes \cdots \otimes \boldsymbol{\alpha}_n$, where $\boldsymbol{\alpha}_1, \ldots, \boldsymbol{\alpha}_n$ are metavariables and $\varepsilon \in \Omega$,*
- *δ is an element of the quantale domain (the current approximation degree),*
- *σ is a substitution (part of the unifier computed so far).*

In C, we also allow for the case where $n = 0$, in which the empty product on the right-hand side is κ by convention.

The solving rules for a theory E_{ssh} are given below. They operate on configurations and are formulated modulo associativity and commutativity of $\otimes$. We use f and g to denote (not necessarily distinct) n-ary function symbols, t, t_i and s_i for terms and x to denote a variable symbol. The symbol Δ denotes the tensor product of finitely many metavariables.

Tri: **Trivial**

$$\{t =^?_{\boldsymbol{\alpha}} t\} \uplus P; \zeta \precsim \boldsymbol{\alpha} \otimes \Delta; \delta; \sigma \Longrightarrow P; \zeta \precsim \Delta; \delta; \sigma.$$

Dec: **Decompose**

$$\{f(t_1, \ldots, t_n) =^?_{\boldsymbol{\alpha}} g(s_1, \ldots, s_n)\} \uplus P; \zeta \precsim \boldsymbol{\alpha} \otimes \Delta; \delta; \sigma \Longrightarrow$$
$$\{t_1 =^?_{\boldsymbol{\beta}_1} s_1, \ldots, t_n =^?_{\boldsymbol{\beta}_n} s_n\} \cup P;$$
$$\eth_{E_{\mathsf{ssh}}}(f, g) \multimap \zeta \precsim \boldsymbol{\beta}_1 \otimes \cdots \otimes \boldsymbol{\beta}_n \otimes \Delta; \delta \otimes \eth_{E_{\mathsf{ssh}}}(f, g); \sigma,$$

where $\boldsymbol{\beta}_1, \ldots, \boldsymbol{\beta}_n$ are new metavariables and $\zeta \precsim \eth_{E_{\mathsf{ssh}}}(f, g)$.

Cla: **Clash**

$$\{f(t_1, \ldots, t_n) =^?_{\boldsymbol{\alpha}} g(s_1, \ldots, s_m)\} \uplus P; \zeta \precsim \boldsymbol{\alpha} \otimes \Delta; \delta; \sigma \Longrightarrow \mathbf{F}, \text{ if } \zeta \not\precsim \eth_{E_{\mathsf{ssh}}}(f, g).$$

L-Sub: **Substitute (lazy)**

$$\{x =^?_{\boldsymbol{\alpha}} f(s_1, \ldots, s_n)\} \uplus P; \zeta \precsim \boldsymbol{\alpha} \otimes \Delta; \delta; \sigma \Longrightarrow$$
$$\{x_1 =^?_{\boldsymbol{\beta}_1} s_1, \ldots, x_n =^?_{\boldsymbol{\beta}_n} s_n\} \cup P\rho;$$
$$\eth_{E_{\mathsf{ssh}}}(f, g) \multimap \zeta \precsim \boldsymbol{\beta}_1 \otimes \cdots \otimes \boldsymbol{\beta}_n \otimes \Delta; \delta \otimes \eth_{E_{\mathsf{ssh}}}(f, g); \sigma\rho,$$

where x does not appear in an occurrence cycle in $\{x =^?_{\boldsymbol{\alpha}} f(s_1, \ldots, s_n)\} \cup P$, and $\rho = \{x \mapsto g(x_1, \ldots, x_n)\}$ with $x_1, \ldots, x_n$ being fresh variables and $\zeta \precsim \eth_{E_{\mathsf{ssh}}}(f, g)$.

CCh: **Cycle check**

$$\{x =^?_{\boldsymbol{\alpha}} t\} \uplus P; C; \delta; \sigma \Longrightarrow \mathbf{F},$$

if x appears in an occurrence cycle in $\{x =^?_{\boldsymbol{\alpha}} t\} \uplus P$.

Ori: **Orient**

$$\{t =^?_{\boldsymbol{\alpha}} x\} \uplus P; C; \delta; \sigma \Longrightarrow P \cup \{x =^?_{\boldsymbol{\alpha}} t\}; C; \delta; \sigma, \text{ where } t \notin \mathcal{V}.$$

To solve an $(E_{\mathsf{ssh}}, \varepsilon)$-unification problem between terms t and s, we create the initial configuration $\{t =^?_{\boldsymbol{\alpha}} s\}; \varepsilon \precsim \boldsymbol{\alpha}; \kappa; Id$ and start applying the rules as long as possible. The equation to be transformed is chosen arbitrarily ("don't care nondeterminism"). We call the obtained algorithm QUNIF.

Note that a configuration $P; C; \sigma$ obtained from an $(E_{\mathsf{ssh}}, \varepsilon)$-unification problem satisfies the following properties:

- Any metavariable occurring in P also occurs in C and vice versa.
- No metavariable appears more than once in P or C.
- The domain of σ is disjoint from the set of variables occurring in P.

We will refer to such configurations as *admissible*.

To prove termination of QUNIF, we introduce some terminology.

Definition 8. *Let P be a set of quantitative equations and let P_{st} be the set of standard equations obtained from P by ignoring the indices: $P_{\mathsf{st}} := \{t = s \mid \varepsilon \Vdash t = s \in P\}$. Then $\mathsf{DecNF}_{E_{\mathsf{ssh}}}(P)$ denotes the decomposition normal form of P with respect to E_{ssh}, which is the set of standard equations obtained from P_{st} by applying the following version of the decomposition rule as long as possible:*

$$\{f(t_1, \ldots, t_n) = g(s_1, \ldots, s_n)\} \uplus S \Longrightarrow \{t_1 = s_1, \ldots, t_n = s_n\} \cup S,$$

where $\eth_{E_{\mathsf{ssh}}}(f, g) \neq \bot$.

It is easy to see that every equation in $\mathsf{DecNF}_{E_{\mathsf{ssh}}}(P)$ is of the form $x = s$ where s is an arbitrary term, or $t = x$ where t is not a variable.

For a set of (quantitative) equations P, the *variable dependency graph* $\Gamma(P)$ is constructed as follows:

- For each variable x appearing in P, add a node with label x to $\Gamma(P)$.
- Add a node with label G (the "ground node").
- For every equation $x = y \in \mathsf{DecNF}(P)$ between variables x and y, merge the nodes corresponding to x and y.
- In order to construct the set of edges of $\Gamma(P)$, we consider all equations of the form $x = t$ (or $t = x$) in $\mathsf{DecNF}(P)$, where t is a non-variable term. For such an equation, we consider the set of leaves of t. For each element $l \in \ell(t)$, if d is the depth in which l appears in t, we add an weighted edge to $\Gamma(P)$:
  - If l is a constant, then we add an edge $x \rightarrow_{d+1} G$ (with weight $d + 1$).
  - If l is a variable y, then we add an edge $x \rightarrow_d y$ (with weight d).

In this way, we obtain a directed, weighted graph $\Gamma(P)$, which is acyclic (hence, a *dag*) if and only if P does not contain any occurrence cycles.

For any variable x occurring in P, we define now the level $lev_P(x)$ of x with respect to P as the maximal weight of a walk in $\Gamma(P)$ starting in x. Here, the weight of a walk is defined as the sum of the weights of its edges. Note that lev_P may take the value ∞ if P contains occurrence cycles.

We now consider the multiset $\lambda(P) := \{lev_P(x) \mid x \in \mathcal{V}(P)\}$. (It will be used as a component of a termination measure below.) We compare such multisets via the multiset extension $>_m$ of the standard order on $\mathbb{N} \cup \{\infty\}$, which is well-founded. The following lemma is the main ingredient for the termination proof. Its proof can be found in [10].

Lemma 3. *Let $\mathfrak{C} = P; C; \delta; \sigma$ be a configuration.*

(i) If $P'; C'; \delta'; \sigma'$ is obtained from $\mathfrak{C}$ by L-Sub*, then $\lambda(P) >_m \lambda(P')$.*
(ii) If $P'; C'; \delta'; \sigma'$ is obtained from $\mathfrak{C}$ by Tri, Dec, *or* Ori*, then $\lambda(P) \geqslant_m \lambda(P')$.*

Theorem 4 (Termination of QUNIF). *For a given $(E_{\mathsf{ssh}}, \varepsilon)$-unification problem, the algorithm* QUNIF *terminates either with the configuration* $\boldsymbol{F}$ *(indicating failure) or with a configuration of the form $V; C; \delta; \sigma$ (indicating success), where V is a set of unification equations between variables.*

Proof. A simple analysis of the rules of QUNIF shows that all terminal configurations are of the form described above. In order to prove that the algorithm terminates, first note that the Cla and CCh rules terminate the derivation immediately, so it suffices to show that the remaining rules cannot yield an infinite derivation. For this purpose, we consider the measures λ, n_2 and n_3, where n_2 is the size of P and n_3 is the number of equations of the form $t =^?_{\boldsymbol{\alpha}} x$ in P such that t is a non-variable term. By Lemma 3, L-Sub decreases λ while all other rules do not increase it; Dec and Tri decrease n_2, and Ori decreases n_3 while leaving n_2 invariant. Hence, the lexicographical combination of λ with n_2 and n_3 yields a measure that strictly decreases upon each of the aforementioned rules with respect to a well-founded order, thus proving termination. □

Proceeding now to the soundness and completeness proofs for QUNIF, we fix a notion of solution of a configuration.

Definition 9 (Solution of a configuration). *A substitution τ is a* solution *of the configuration $P; \zeta \precsim \boldsymbol{\alpha}_1 \otimes \boldsymbol{\alpha}_2 \otimes \cdots \otimes \boldsymbol{\alpha}_n; \delta; \sigma$ if there exists a function μ mapping metavariables to elements of Ω such that*

(S1) $\zeta \precsim \mu(\boldsymbol{\alpha}_1) \otimes \mu(\boldsymbol{\alpha}_2) \otimes \cdots \otimes \mu(\boldsymbol{\alpha}_n)$ is valid,
(S2) $\mu(\boldsymbol{\beta}) \Vdash s\tau =_E t\tau$ holds for every equation $s =^?_{\boldsymbol{\beta}} t$ in P.
(S3) $x\tau = x\sigma\tau$ (syntactic equality) holds for every variable $x \in dom(\sigma)$.

The configuration $\boldsymbol{F}$ *has no solutions.*

This definition is compatible with Definition 4 in the following sense:

Lemma 4. *Let $\varepsilon \in \Omega$. A substitution τ is an (E, ε)-unifier of t and s if and only if τ is a solution for the corresponding initial configuration $\{t =^?_{\boldsymbol{\alpha}} s\}; \varepsilon \precsim \boldsymbol{\alpha}; \kappa; Id$.*

Proof. By definition, τ solves $\{t =^?_{\boldsymbol{\alpha}} s\}; \varepsilon \precsim \boldsymbol{\alpha}; \kappa; Id$ iff there exists μ such that $\varepsilon \precsim \mu(\boldsymbol{\alpha})$ and $\mu(\boldsymbol{\alpha}) \Vdash t\tau =_E s\tau$, which is equivalent to $\varepsilon \Vdash t\tau =_E s\tau$. □

The lemma below is needed to show soundness and completeness of QUNIF. Its proof can be found in [10].

Lemma 5. *Let $\mathfrak{C}$ be an admissible configuration.*

(i) If $\mathfrak{C} \Longrightarrow \mathfrak{C}'$ and τ solves $\mathfrak{C}'$, then τ solves $\mathfrak{C}$.
(ii) If τ solves $\mathfrak{C}$, then either $\mathfrak{C}$ is terminal, or there exist a configuration $\mathfrak{C}'$ and a substitution τ' such that $\mathfrak{C} \Longrightarrow \mathfrak{C}'$, $\tau'|_{dom(\tau)} = \tau$ and τ' solves $\mathfrak{C}'$.

Theorem 5 (Soundness and completeness of QUNIF). *Consider an $(E_{\mathsf{ssh}}, \varepsilon)$-unification problem between terms t and s.*

Soundness: *If* QUNIF *terminates in a configuration $V; C; \delta; \sigma$ starting from the initial configuration $\{t =^?_{\alpha} s\}; \varepsilon \precsim \boldsymbol{\alpha}; \kappa; Id$, then any solution of $V; C; \delta; \sigma$ is an $(E_{\mathsf{ssh}}, \varepsilon)$-unifier of t and s.*

Completeness: *If τ is an (E, ε)-unifier of t and s, then there is a run of* QUNIF *starting from the initial configuration $\{t =^?_{\alpha} s\}; \varepsilon \precsim \boldsymbol{\alpha}; \kappa; Id$ that terminates in a configuration $\{x_1 =_{\boldsymbol{\alpha}_1} y_1, \ldots, x_n =_{\boldsymbol{\alpha}_n} y_n\}; \zeta \precsim \boldsymbol{\alpha}_1 \otimes \cdots \otimes \boldsymbol{\alpha}_n; \delta; \sigma$ such that there exist a substitution φ and a map μ satisfying the following conditions:*
(i) $\zeta \precsim \mu(\boldsymbol{\alpha}_1) \otimes \cdots \otimes \mu(\boldsymbol{\alpha}_n)$;
(ii) $\mu(\boldsymbol{\alpha}_i) \Vdash x_i\varphi =_{E_{\mathsf{ssh}}} y_i\varphi$ for all $1 \leqslant i \leqslant n$;
(iii) $x\sigma\varphi = x\tau$ for all $x \in \mathcal{V}(s, t)$.

Proof. For soundness, suppose that QUNIF produces a derivation $\mathfrak{C}_0 \Longrightarrow \ldots \Longrightarrow \mathfrak{C}_m$, where $\mathfrak{C}_0$ is the initial configuration $\{t =^?_{\alpha} s\}; \varepsilon \precsim \boldsymbol{\alpha}; \kappa; Id$ and $\mathfrak{C}_m$ is a terminal configuration given by $V; S; \delta; \sigma$. If τ is a solution of $\mathfrak{C}_m$ then τ is also a solution of $\mathfrak{C}_0$ (by Lemma 5(i)), and therefore, τ is an $(E_{\mathsf{ssh}}, \varepsilon)$-unifier of t and s (by Lemma 4).

For completeness, suppose that τ is an (E, ε)-unifier of t and s. Then τ solves the corresponding initial configuration $\mathfrak{C}_0$ (by Lemma 4). If $\mathfrak{C}_0$ is not terminal, then there exists a rule application $\mathfrak{C}_0 \Longrightarrow \mathfrak{C}_1$ and a substitution τ_1 such that $\tau_1|_{dom(\tau)} = \tau$ and τ_1 solves $\mathfrak{C}_1$ (by Lemma 5(ii)). Iterating this argument, we obtain a derivation $\mathfrak{C}_0 \Longrightarrow \mathfrak{C}_1 \Longrightarrow \ldots$ and a sequence of substitutions $\tau, \tau_1, \ldots$. After a finite number of steps, this derivation reaches a terminal configuration $\mathfrak{C}_m$ by Theorem 4, and with it, we obtain a solution τ_m such that $\tau_m|_{\mathcal{V}(s,t)} = \tau$. Since τ_m solves $\mathfrak{C}_m$, there exist φ and μ satisfying (i) and (ii), as well as $x\sigma\varphi = x\tau_m$ for all $x \in \mathcal{V}(\mathfrak{C}_m)$, yielding (iii). □

Remark 3. In particular, a κ-complete set of solutions for the problem $t =^?_{\varepsilon} s$ can be obtained by determining for every terminal configuration obtained via QUNIF the set of substitutions that meet conditions (i)–(iii) above. If one is just interested in finding some solution, it suffices to compute a terminal configuration $V; \zeta \precsim \Delta; \delta; \sigma$ and compose σ with a substitution that maps all variables in V to a fresh variable. The value of δ corresponds to the "degree" to which such a solution τ solves the unification problem, i.e. $\delta = (t\tau \overset{\bullet}{=}_{E_{\mathsf{ssh}}} s\tau)$.

Example 4. Consider the unification problem $f(y, g(x, x)) =^?_{E,\varepsilon} g(f(c, a), y)$, where $\mathfrak{Q} = \mathbb{L}$, $E = \{1 \Vdash a \approx b, 1 \Vdash b \approx c, 1 \Vdash f(x_1, x_2) \approx g(x_1, x_2)\}$ and

$\varepsilon = 5$. The following derivation can be obtained by QUNIF:

$$\{f(y, g(x,x)) =^?_{\alpha} g(f(c,a), y)\};\ 5 \geqslant \alpha;\ 0;\ Id$$
$$\Longrightarrow_{\mathsf{Dec}} \{y =^?_{\beta_1} f(c,a),\ g(x,x) =^?_{\beta_2} y\};\ 4 \geqslant \beta_1 + \beta_2;\ 1;\ Id$$
$$\Longrightarrow^{y \mapsto f(z_1,z_2)}_{\mathsf{L\text{-}Sub}} \{z_1 =^?_{\gamma_1} c,\ z_2 =^?_{\gamma_2} a,\ g(x,x) =^?_{\beta_2} f(z_1,z_2)\};$$
$$4 \geqslant \gamma_1 + \gamma_2 + \beta_2;\ 1;\ \{y \mapsto f(z_1,z_2)\}$$
$$\Longrightarrow^{z_1 \mapsto b}_{\mathsf{L\text{-}Sub}} \{z_2 =^?_{\gamma_2} a,\ g(x,x) =^?_{\beta_2} f(b,z_2)\};$$
$$3 \geqslant \gamma_2 + \beta_2;\ 2;\ \{y \mapsto f(b,z_2), z_1 \mapsto b\}$$
$$\Longrightarrow_{\mathsf{Dec}} \{z_2 =^?_{\gamma_2} a,\ x =^?_{\delta_1} b,\ x =^?_{\delta_2} z_2\};$$
$$2 \geqslant \gamma_2 + \delta_1 + \delta_2;\ 3;\ \{y \mapsto f(b,z_2), z_1 \mapsto b\}$$
$$\Longrightarrow^{z_2 \mapsto a}_{\mathsf{L\text{-}Sub}} \{x =^?_{\delta_1} b,\ x =^?_{\delta_2} a\};\ 2 \geqslant \delta_1 + \delta_2;\ 3;\ \{y \mapsto f(b,a), z_1 \mapsto b, z_2 \mapsto a\}$$
$$\Longrightarrow^{x \mapsto a}_{\mathsf{L\text{-}Sub}} \{a =^?_{\delta_2} a\};\ 1 \geqslant \delta_2;\ 4;\ \{y \mapsto f(b,a), z_1 \mapsto b, z_2 \mapsto a, x \mapsto a\}$$
$$\Longrightarrow_{\mathsf{Tri}} \emptyset;\ 1 \geqslant 0;\ 4;\ \{y \mapsto f(b,a), z_1 \mapsto b, z_2 \mapsto a, x \mapsto a\}$$

This leads to the solution $\{y \mapsto f(b,a), x \mapsto a\}$ (with degree 4). Further solutions can be obtained via different choices in the Subst steps. ■

Example 5. Consider $\Omega = \mathbb{L}$, $E = \{1 \Vdash f(x,y) \approx g(x,y)\}$, and the E-unification problem $g(a,x) =^?_3 f(y, g(b,z))$. A derivation of QUNIF is given below.

$$\{g(a,x) =^?_{\alpha} f(y, g(b,z))\};\ 3 \geqslant \alpha;\ 0;\ Id$$
$$\Longrightarrow_{\mathsf{Dec}} \{a =^?_{\beta_1} y,\ x =^?_{\beta_2} g(b,z)\};\ 2 \geqslant \beta_1 + \beta_2;\ 1;\ Id$$
$$\Longrightarrow_{\mathsf{Ori}} \{y =^?_{\beta_1} a,\ x =^?_{\beta_2} g(b,z)\};\ 2 \geqslant \beta_1 + \beta_2;\ 1;\ Id$$
$$\Longrightarrow^{y \mapsto a}_{\mathsf{L\text{-}Sub}} \{x =^?_{\beta_2} g(b,z)\};\ 2 \geqslant \beta_2;\ 1;\ \{y \mapsto a\}$$
$$\Longrightarrow^{x \mapsto f(x_1,x_2)}_{\mathsf{L\text{-}Sub}} \{x_1 =^?_{\gamma_1} b,\ x_2 =^?_{\gamma_2} z\};\ 1 \geqslant \gamma_1 + \gamma_2;\ 2;\ \{y \mapsto a, x \mapsto f(x_1,x_2)\}$$
$$\Longrightarrow^{x_1 \mapsto b}_{\mathsf{L\text{-}Sub}} \{x_2 =^?_{\gamma_2} z\};\ 1 \geqslant \gamma_2;\ 2;\ \{y \mapsto a, x \mapsto f(b,x_2), x_1 \mapsto b\}$$

The computed terminal configuration still contains equations between variables. For any ψ such that $1 \Vdash x_2\psi =_E z\psi$, the substitution $\{y \mapsto a, x \mapsto f(b,x_2)\}\psi$ is an (E,ε)-unifier of the given terms. In particular, unifiers that can be obtained from this configuration include, e.g., $\{y \mapsto a, x \mapsto f(b,u), z \mapsto u\}$, where u is a fresh variable (with degree 2), and also $\{y \mapsto a, x \mapsto f(b, f(a,a)), z \mapsto g(a,a)\}$ (with degree 3). ■

4.2 Idempotent Quantales

Now we consider the case where Ω is idempotent. Under this hypothesis, we can strengthen our results and show that – with the right definitions – the unification problem is unitary, and that a simplified version of QUNIF computes a most general unifier of two given terms. For the fuzzy quantale $\Omega = \mathbb{I}_{\min} = ([0,1], \leqslant, \min)$, our algorithm coincides with Sessa's weak unification algorithm [23].

Note that in any integral idempotent quantale, meet and tensor coincide. As a consequence, in an idempotent quantale, $\alpha \precsim \beta$ implies $\beta \multimap \alpha = \alpha$.

Definition 10 (Weak mgu). *A substitution σ is a* weak most general (E,ε)-unifier *of t and s, denoted $wmgu_{E,\varepsilon}(t,s)$, if $\mathfrak{U}_{E,\varepsilon}(t,s) = \{\tau \mid \sigma \lessapprox_{E,\mathcal{V}(t,s),\varepsilon} \tau\}$.*

By Lemma 2 (ii), $\sigma = wmgu_{E,\varepsilon}(t,s)$ iff $\sigma \in \mathfrak{U}_{E,\varepsilon}(t,s)$ and $\sigma \lessapprox_{E,\mathcal{V}(t,s),\varepsilon} \tau$ holds for every $\tau \in \mathfrak{U}_{E,\varepsilon}(t,s)$; that is, iff $\{\sigma\} = mcsu_{E,\varepsilon,\varepsilon}(t,s)$.

In the idempotent setting, the rules L-Sub and CCh from QUNIF can be replaced by simpler versions:

E-Sub: **Substitute (eager)**

$$\{x =^?_{\boldsymbol{\alpha}} s\} \uplus P; \zeta \precsim \boldsymbol{\alpha} \otimes \Delta; \delta; \sigma \Longrightarrow P\{x \mapsto s\}; \zeta \precsim \Delta; \delta; \sigma\{x \mapsto s\}, \text{ if } x \notin \mathcal{V}(s).$$

OCh: **Occurrence check**

$$\{x =^?_{\boldsymbol{\alpha}} s\} \uplus P; C; \delta; \sigma \Longrightarrow \mathbf{F}, \quad \text{if } x \in \mathcal{V}(s) \text{ and } s \neq x.$$

Note that both of these rules constitute steps that could also be achieved by the rules from QUNIF: E-Sub can be viewed as a composition of L-Sub and Dec steps, and OCh is just a restricted version of CCh. As before, we use these rules to transform the initial configuration corresponding to a given $(E_{\mathsf{ssh}}, \iota)$-unification problem. As an output, we return Failure if $\mathbf{F}$ has been obtained, or σ if a terminal configuration $P; C; \delta; \sigma$ has been reached. We denote the resulting algorithm by QUNIF-ID.

In order to obtain a stronger completeness theorem than in the general case, we refine the notion of a solution of a configuration.

Definition 11 (ι-solution of a configuration). *Let $\iota \in \Omega$ be idempotent. A substitution τ is an ι-*solution *of the configuration $P; \zeta \precsim \boldsymbol{\alpha}_1 \otimes \boldsymbol{\alpha}_2 \otimes \cdots \otimes \boldsymbol{\alpha}_n; \delta; \sigma$ if there exists a function μ mapping metavariables to elements of Ω such that*

(ι1) $\zeta \precsim \mu(\boldsymbol{\alpha}_1) \otimes \mu(\boldsymbol{\alpha}_2) \otimes \cdots \otimes \mu(\boldsymbol{\alpha}_n)$ is valid,
(ι2) $\mu(\boldsymbol{\beta}) \Vdash t\tau =_E s\tau$ holds for every equation $t =^?_{\boldsymbol{\beta}} s$ in P.
(ι3) $\iota \Vdash x\tau =_E x\sigma\tau$ holds for every variable $x \in dom(\sigma)$.

The configuration $\mathbf{F}$ has no solutions.

Note that the only difference in comparison with Definition 9 is that (ι3) features a quantitative equality over E_{ssh}, whereas in (S3) we have a syntactic equality.

The lemmas below are needed in the proof of soundness and completeness of QUNIF-ID (see [10] for their proofs).

Lemma 6. *Let Ω be a (not necessarily idempotent) quantale, $\iota \in \Omega$ be an idempotent element of Ω, τ be a substitution, and t and s be terms.*

(i) τ is an (E,ι)-unifier of t and s iff τ is an ι-solution for the corresponding initial configuration $\{t =^?_{\boldsymbol{\alpha}} s\}; \iota \precsim \boldsymbol{\alpha}; \kappa; Id$.
(ii) τ is an ι-solution for an admissible configuration of the form $\emptyset; C; \delta; \sigma$ iff $\sigma \lessapprox_{E,dom(\sigma),\iota} \tau$.

Lemma 7. *Let $\mathfrak{Q}$ be an idempotent quantale, $\iota \in \Omega$, and $\mathfrak{C}$ be a configuration obtained from an $(E_{\mathsf{ssh}}, \iota)$-unification problem in $\mathfrak{Q}$ by applying rules from* QUNIF-ID. *If $\mathfrak{C}'$ is obtained from $\mathfrak{C}$ by a rule from* QUNIF-ID, *then a substitution τ is an ι-solution of $\mathfrak{C}$ iff it is an ι-solution of $\mathfrak{C}'$.*

Theorem 6 (Soundness and completeness of QUNIF-ID**).** *Consider an $(E_{\mathsf{ssh}}, \iota)$-unification problem between terms t and s in an idempotent quantale $\mathfrak{Q}$, where $\iota \in \Omega$. Any run of* QUNIF-ID *starting from $\{t =^?_{\boldsymbol{\alpha}} s\}; \boldsymbol{\alpha} \precsim \iota; \kappa; Id$ terminates and returns $wmgu_{E_{\mathsf{ssh}},\iota}(t, s)$ if it exists, or fails otherwise.*

Proof. Termination follows from termination of QUNIF (Theorem 4). For soundness and completeness, by Lemma 6(i), a substitution τ is an $(E_{\mathsf{ssh}}, \iota)$-unifier of t and s iff it is an ι-solution of the initial configuration $\mathfrak{C}_0$. By Lemma 7, the latter holds iff τ is an ι-solution for any terminal configuration $\emptyset; C; \delta; \sigma$, or equivalently, iff $\sigma \lessapprox_{E_{\mathsf{ssh}}, \mathcal{V}(t,s), \iota} \tau$ (by Lemma 6(ii)), concluding the proof. □

Example 6. We demonstrate algorithm QUNIF-ID for the problem $f(x, c) =^?_{\mathbb{I},0.4,E} h(a, x)$ in the (idempotent) fuzzy quantale $\mathbb{I}$ with the min T-norm modulo $E = \{0.5 \Vdash a \approx b,\ 0.5 \Vdash b \approx c,\ 0.6 \Vdash f(x_1, x_2) \approx g(x_1, x_2),\ 0.7 \Vdash g(x_1, x_2) \approx h(x_1, x_2)\}$.

A derivation of QUNIF-ID is shown below:

$$
\begin{aligned}
&\{f(x, c) =^?_{\boldsymbol{\alpha}} h(a, x)\}; 0.4 \leqslant \boldsymbol{\alpha}; 1; Id\\
&\Longrightarrow_{\mathsf{Dec}} \{x =^?_{\boldsymbol{\beta}_1} a,\ c =^?_{\boldsymbol{\beta}_2} x\}; 0.4 \leqslant \min(\boldsymbol{\beta}_1, \boldsymbol{\beta}_2); 0.6; Id\\
&\Longrightarrow^{x \mapsto a}_{\mathsf{L\text{-}Sub}} \{c =^?_{\boldsymbol{\beta}_2} a\}; 0.4 \leqslant \boldsymbol{\beta}_2; 0.6; \{x \mapsto a\}\\
&\Longrightarrow_{\mathsf{Dec}} \emptyset; 0.4 \leqslant 1; 0.5; \{x \mapsto a\}.
\end{aligned}
$$

Choosing the other equation in the L-Sub step would lead to a different unifier $\{x \mapsto c\}$ with the same degree 0.5. The solution $\{x \mapsto b\}$ (with degree 0.5) is not computed. All three solutions are 0.5-equivalent. ■

5 Conclusion

In the quantitative setting, equality is replaced by its quantitative counterpart modeling the abstract notion of proximity between terms. A quantitative unification problem asks for finding a substitution that brings the given terms close to each other within a predefined range (with respect to this abstract proximity). However, unlike the standard unification, here it is not guaranteed that an instance of a unifier is still a unifier. The reason is that the instantiation is also quantitative, and it might move the more specific substitution "too far away" from a unifier of the given problem.

In studying quantitative unification, one has to address such and related challenges. We investigated the quantitative equational unification problem in Lawvereian quantales modulo theories presented by axioms of the form $\gamma \Vdash f(x_1, \ldots, x_n) \approx g(x_1, \ldots, x_n)$. Our notion of a minimal complete set of unifiers takes into account two (abstract) distances: between terms to be unified and between substitutions via instantiation. We showed that our unification problems in arbitrary Lawvereian quantales are finitary, while for idempotent Lawvereian quantales, they are unitary. The corresponding algorithms were developed and their properties were studied.

The equational theories that we considered here are a special case of simple shallow theories. An interesting future work would be to extend this work to a larger class of shallow theories (which have some desirable properties in the standard case [6]). Further, the related problem of disunification in Lawvereian quantales is worth investigating.

Acknowledgments. Supported by the Austrian Science Fund (FWF) under project P 35530 (SQUEE).

Disclosure of Interests. The authors have no competing interests to declare that are relevant to the content of this article.

References

1. de Amorim, A.A., Gaboardi, M., Hsu, J., Katsumata, S., Cherigui, I.: A semantic account of metric preservation. In: Castagna, G., Gordon, A.D. (eds.) Proceedings of the 44th ACM SIGPLAN Symposium on Principles of Programming Languages, POPL 2017, Paris, France, 18–20 January 2017, pp. 545–556. ACM (2017). https://doi.org/10.1145/3009837.3009890
2. Baader, F., Snyder, W.: Unification theory. In: Robinson, A., Voronkov, A. (eds.) Handbook of Automated Reasoning, pp. 445–533. North-Holland, Amsterdam (2001). https://doi.org/10.1016/B978-044450813-3/50010-2
3. Bacci, G., Mardare, R., Panangaden, P., Plotkin, G.D.: An algebraic theory of Markov processes. In: Dawar, A., Grädel, E. (eds.) Proceedings of the 33rd Annual ACM/IEEE Symposium on Logic in Computer Science, LICS 2018, Oxford, UK, 09–12 July 2018, pp. 679–688. ACM (2018). https://doi.org/10.1145/3209108.3209177
4. Bacci, G., Mardare, R., Panangaden, P., Plotkin, G.D.: Quantitative equational reasoning. In: Barthe, G., Katoen, J.P., Silva, A. (eds.) Foundations of Probabilistic Programming, pp. 333–360. Cambridge University Press, Cambridge (2020). https://doi.org/10.1017/9781108770750.011
5. Barthe, G., Katoen, J.P., Silva, A. (eds.): Foundations of Probabilistic Programming. Cambridge University Press, Cambridge (2020). https://doi.org/10.1017/9781108770750
6. Comon, H., Haberstrau, M., Jouannaud, J.P.: Syntacticness, cycle-syntacticness, and shallow theories. Inf. Comput. **111**(1), 154–191 (1994). https://doi.org/10.1006/INCO.1994.1043
7. Dal Lago, U., Gavazzo, F.: A relational theory of effects and coeffects. Proc. ACM Program. Lang. **6**(POPL), 1–28 (2022). https://doi.org/10.1145/3498692
8. Dubois, D., Prade, H.: Fuzzy Sets and Systems: Theory and Applications. Mathematics in Science and Engineering, vol. 144. Academic Press (1980). https://www.worldcat.org/oclc/05726778

9. Dundua, B., Kutsia, T., Marin, M., Pau, I.: Constraint solving over multiple similarity relations. In: Ariola, Z.M. (ed.) 5th International Conference on Formal Structures for Computation and Deduction, FSCD 2020, 29 June–6 July 2020, Paris, France (Virtual Conference). LIPIcs, vol. 167, pp. 30:1–30:19. Schloss Dagstuhl - Leibniz-Zentrum für Informatik (2020). https://doi.org/10.4230/LIPICS.FSCD.2020.30
10. Ehling, G., Kutsia, T.: Solving quantitative equations. Technical report, RISC, JKU Linz (2024). https://doi.org/10.35011/risc.24-03
11. Gavazzo, F., Di Florio, C.: Quantitative and metric rewriting: abstract, non-expansive, and graded systems. CoRR abs/2206.13610 (2022). https://doi.org/10.48550/ARXIV.2206.13610
12. Gavazzo, F., Di Florio, C.: Elements of quantitative rewriting. Proc. ACM Program. Lang. **7**(POPL), 1832–1863 (2023). https://doi.org/10.1145/3571256
13. Geoffroy, G., Pistone, P.: A partial metric semantics of higher-order types and approximate program transformations. In: Baier, C., Goubault-Larrecq, J. (eds.) 29th EACSL Annual Conference on Computer Science Logic, CSL 2021, 25–28 January 2021, Ljubljana, Slovenia (Virtual Conference). LIPIcs, vol. 183, pp. 23:1–23:18. Schloss Dagstuhl - Leibniz-Zentrum für Informatik (2021). https://doi.org/10.4230/LIPICS.CSL.2021.23
14. Julián-Iranzo, P., Rubio-Manzano, C.: Proximity-based unification theory. Fuzzy Sets Syst. **262**, 21–43 (2015). https://doi.org/10.1016/j.fss.2014.07.006
15. Kutsia, T., Pau, C.: A framework for approximate generalization in quantitative theories. In: Blanchette, J., Kovács, L., Pattinson, D. (eds.) IJCAR 2022. LNCS, vol. 13385, pp. 578–596. Springer, Cham (2022). https://doi.org/10.1007/978-3-031-10769-6_34
16. Lawvere, F.W.: Metric spaces, generalized logic, and closed categories. Rendiconti del Seminario Matematico e Fisico di Milano **43**, 135–166 (1973)
17. Mardare, R., Panangaden, P., Plotkin, G.D.: Quantitative algebraic reasoning. In: Proceedings of the 31st Annual ACM/IEEE Symposium on Logic in Computer Science, LICS 2016, pp. 700–709. Association for Computing Machinery, New York (2016). https://doi.org/10.1145/2933575.2934518
18. Mardare, R., Panangaden, P., Plotkin, G.D.: On the axiomatizability of quantitative algebras. In: 32nd Annual ACM/IEEE Symposium on Logic in Computer Science, LICS 2017, Reykjavik, Iceland, 20–23 June 2017, pp. 1–12. IEEE Computer Society (2017). https://doi.org/10.1109/LICS.2017.8005102
19. Pau, C.: Symbolic techniques for approximate reasoning. Ph.D. thesis, RISC, Johannes Kepler University Linz (2022)
20. Pau, C., Kutsia, T.: Proximity-based unification and matching for fully fuzzy signatures. In: 30th IEEE International Conference on Fuzzy Systems, FUZZ-IEEE 2021, Luxembourg, 11–14 July 2021, pp. 1–6. IEEE (2021). https://doi.org/10.1109/FUZZ45933.2021.9494438
21. Reed, J., Pierce, B.C.: Distance makes the types grow stronger: a calculus for differential privacy. In: Hudak, P., Weirich, S. (eds.) Proceeding of the 15th ACM SIGPLAN International Conference on Functional Programming, ICFP 2010, Baltimore, Maryland, USA, 27–29 September 2010, pp. 157–168. ACM (2010). https://doi.org/10.1145/1863543.1863568
22. Rosenthal, K.I.: Quantales and Their Applications. Pitman Research Notes in Mathematics, Longman Scientific & Technical (1990)
23. Sessa, M.I.: Approximate reasoning by similarity-based SLD resolution. Theor. Comput. Sci. **275**(1–2), 389–426 (2002). https://doi.org/10.1016/S0304-3975(01)00188-8

Equivalence Checking of Quantum Circuits by Model Counting

Jingyi Mei(✉), Tim Coopmans, Marcello Bonsangue, and Alfons Laarman

Leiden University, Leiden, The Netherlands
{j.mei,t.j.coopmans,m.m.bonsangue,a.w.laarman}@liacs.leidenuniv.nl

Abstract. Verifying equivalence between two quantum circuits is a hard problem, that is nonetheless crucial in compiling and optimizing quantum algorithms for real-world devices. This paper gives a Turing reduction of the (universal) quantum circuits equivalence problem to weighted model counting (WMC). Our starting point is a folklore theorem showing that equivalence checking of quantum circuits can be done in the so-called Pauli-basis. We combine this insight with a WMC encoding of quantum circuit simulation, which we extend with support for the Toffoli gate. Finally, we prove that the weights computed by the model counter indeed realize the reduction. With an open-source implementation, we demonstrate that this novel approach can outperform a state-of-the-art equivalence-checking tool based on ZX calculus and decision diagrams.

Keywords: Quantum computing · Circuit equivalence · Satisfiability · #SAT · Weighted model counting · Pauli basis

1 Introduction

Physicists and chemists regularly deal with 'quantum NP'-hard problems, for example when finding the ground state (energy) of a physical system [30] or assessing the consistency of local density matrices (the quantum analog of deciding the consistency of marginal probability distributions) [32]. Quantum computing not only holds the potential to provide a matching computational resource for tackling these challenges but also serves as a bridge to incorporate classical reasoning techniques for tackling nature's hardest problems. Quantum circuits, in particular, offer a precise view into these problems, because the quantum circuit equivalence checking problem is also 'quantum NP'-hard.

Circuit equivalence [2,4,8,22,23,52,55,56,61] also has many important applications. Since quantum computers are highly affected by noise, it is necessary to optimize the circuits to maximize the performance when running them on a real device. Furthermore, many devices can only handle shallow-depth circuits and are subject to various constraints such as connectivity, topology, and native gate sets. An essential aspect of designing and optimizing quantum circuits isverifying whether two quantum circuits implement the same quantum operation.

C. Benzmüller et al. (Eds.): IJCAR 2024, LNAI 14740, pp. 401–421, 2024.
https://doi.org/10.1007/978-3-031-63501-4_21

Equivalence checking for so-called Clifford circuits is tractable [52], which is surprising considering their wide applicability, e.g. in quantum error correction [9,48,49]. Extending the Clifford gate set with any non-Clifford gate, however, e.g. with a T or Toffoli gate, makes the problem immediately 'quantum NP'-hard, that is: NQP-hard to compute exactly [51] and QMA-hard to approximate [24], even for constant-depth circuits [25].[1] The exact formulation of equivalence checking allows its discretization [29], exposing the underlying combinatorial problem that classical reasoning methods excel in. Indeed, exact reasoning methods based on decision diagrams are even used to compute the approximate version of the problem (see e.g. [23,57]).

Our aim is to use reasoning tools based on satisfiability (SAT) for *exact* equivalence checking of *universal* quantum circuits. Like SAT solvers [7,16], model counters, or #SAT solvers, can handle complex constraints from industrial-scale applications [40,47], despite the #P-completeness of the underlying problem.

We propose a new equivalence-checking algorithm based on weighted model counting (WMC). To do so, we generalize the WMC encoding of quantum circuit simulation from [34], showing that it essentially only relies on expressing quantum information in the so-called Pauli basis [18], thus obviating the need for the arguably more complex stabilizer theory [20,63]. In addition, we extend the encoding with support for the (non-Clifford) Toffoli gate, allowing more efficient encodings for many circuits. We then prove that a folklore theorem on quantum circuit equivalence checking [52] enables the reduction of the problem to a sequence of weighted Boolean formulas that can be solved using existing weighted model counters (provided they support negative weights [34]).

We show how the WMC encoding satisfies the conditions of the theorem from [52] and implement the proposed equivalence checking algorithm in the open-source tool `ECMC`, which uses the weighted model-counting tool GPMC [50].[2] To assess the scalability and practicality of `ECMC`, we conduct experimental evaluations using random Clifford+T circuits which closely resemble quantum chemistry applications [59] and various quantum algorithms from the MQT benchmark [43], which includes important quantum algorithms such as QAOA, W-state, and VQE among others. We compare the results of our method against that of the state-of-the-art circuit equivalence checker QCEC [8], showing that in several cases the WMC approach used by our `ECMC` tool is competitive.

In summary, this paper provides a many-to-many reduction of (universal) quantum circuit equivalence to weighted model counting (WMC). As a consequence, we contribute additional new benchmarks for the WMC competition: basically, each pair of universal quantum circuits can be reduced to a sequence of weighted CNF encodings that need to be solved to (dis)prove equivalence. This opens up numerous possibilities and challenges to better adapt model counters for this new application area in quantum computing.

---

[1] A similar "jump" in hardness was noted for quantum circuit simulation in [54].

[2] While the theorem presented in [52] already supported universal circuits, the provided tool implementation in [52] is limited to (non-universal) Clifford circuits.

2 General Background

We only provide the necessary background. For a more complete description see the full version of this paper [35].

Quantum Computing. We fix n as the number of qubits in the circuit(s) under consideration and write $[m]$ for the set $\{1,\dots,m\}$. Qubits are numbered as $[n]$. We represent an n-qubit quantum state $|\varphi\rangle \in \mathbb{C}^{2^n}$ as its *density matrix* $|\varphi\rangle\langle\varphi| \in \mathbb{C}^{2^n} \times \mathbb{C}^{2^n}$, where $\langle\varphi|$ represents the conjugate transpose $|\varphi\rangle^\dagger$ of $|\varphi\rangle$ [38].

A quantum gate G on n qubits can be expressed by a $2^n \times 2^n$ complex matrix U_G which is unitary, i.e. U_G is invertible and satisfies $U_G^\dagger = U_G^{-1}$. If a quantum state is represented by a density matrix $|\varphi\rangle\langle\varphi|$, then the density matrix after applying G is given by *conjugation* of $|\varphi\rangle\langle\varphi|$, i.e. $U_G\,|\varphi\rangle\langle\varphi|\,U_G^\dagger$. For an n-qubit quantum system, applying a single-qubit gate U on the j-th qubit is represented by

$$U_j = I^{\otimes j-1} \otimes U \otimes I^{\otimes n-j}, \tag{1}$$

where I is the single-qubit identity matrix and $\otimes$ denotes the Kronecker product. A circuit in our text is simply a list of n-qubit unitaries, i.e., $C = (G^0,\dots,G^{m-1})$ where C can in turn be understood as unitary itself $U_C = U_{G^{m-1}} \cdot U_{G^{m-2}} \cdots U_{G^0}$. We will sometimes refer to a gate or circuit as its unitary, and vice versa, because it is clear from context which is meant.

The gates

$$H = \frac{1}{\sqrt{2}}\begin{bmatrix}1 & 1\\ 1 & -1\end{bmatrix}, \quad S = \begin{bmatrix}1 & 0\\ 0 & i\end{bmatrix}, \quad CZ = \begin{bmatrix}1&0&0&0\\0&1&0&0\\0&0&1&0\\0&0&0&-1\end{bmatrix}$$

form the so-called Clifford (generating) set.

Though non-universal and classically simulatable [1], Clifford circuits, i.e., circuits composed of Clifford gates only, are expressive enough to describe entanglement, teleportation and superdense coding, and are used in quantum error-correcting codes [9,48,49] and in measurement-based quantum computation [46]. Nonetheless, even equivalence checking of Clifford circuits is in P [52]. By extending the Clifford gate set with any non-Clifford gate, such as the $T = \sqrt{S}$, Toffoli or arbitrary rotation gates R_X, R_Y, R_Y, we immediately obtain a universal gate set, in the sense that arbitrary unitaries can be approximated [14,30,31].

In this work, we express matrices not in the standard basis but in the Pauli basis. We define the 2×2 *Pauli matrices* X, Y, Z, together with identity, as:

$$\sigma[00] \equiv I \equiv \left[\begin{smallmatrix}1&0\\0&1\end{smallmatrix}\right],\ \sigma[01] \equiv Z \equiv \left[\begin{smallmatrix}1&0\\0&-1\end{smallmatrix}\right],\ \sigma[10] \equiv X \equiv \left[\begin{smallmatrix}0&1\\1&0\end{smallmatrix}\right],\ \sigma[11] \equiv Y \equiv \left[\begin{smallmatrix}0&-i\\i&0\end{smallmatrix}\right]$$

For n qubits, we define the set of "Pauli strings" $\hat{\mathcal{P}}_n \triangleq \{P_1 \otimes P_2 \otimes \ldots \otimes P_n \mid P_j \in \{I, X, Y, Z\}\}$. Inheriting the properties of Pauli matrices, Pauli strings are unitary, involutory and Hermitian. It is well-known that the scaled Pauli strings $\{\frac{1}{\sqrt{2^n}} \cdot P \mid P \in \hat{\mathcal{P}}_n\}$ form an orthonormal basis for $2^n \times 2^n$ complex matrices [27]. Hence, we can decompose any $2^n \times 2^n$ complex matrix M as $M = \sum_{P \in \hat{\mathcal{P}}_n} \gamma_P \cdot P$ where the *Pauli coefficient* $\gamma_P = \frac{1}{2^n}\mathrm{Tr}(P^\dagger \cdot M)$.

In general, the coefficients γ_P are complex numbers, but for Hermitian matrices, they are real [18,35].

Example 1. The matrix $M = \begin{bmatrix} 1 & 4+i \\ 4-i & -5 \end{bmatrix}$ is Hermitian. We calculate the coefficients:

$$\tfrac{1}{2^1}\operatorname{Tr}(I^\dagger M) = -2, \quad \tfrac{1}{2^1}\operatorname{Tr}(Z^\dagger M) = 3, \quad \tfrac{1}{2^1}\operatorname{Tr}(X^\dagger M) = 4, \quad \tfrac{1}{2^1}\operatorname{Tr}(Y^\dagger M) = -1$$

It is straightforward to verify that these are M's Pauli *real* coefficients:

$$-2I + 4X - 1Y + 3Z = -2 \cdot \begin{bmatrix} 1 & 0 \\ 0 & 1 \end{bmatrix} + 4 \cdot \begin{bmatrix} 0 & 1 \\ 1 & 0 \end{bmatrix} - 1 \cdot \begin{bmatrix} 0 & -i \\ i & 0 \end{bmatrix} + 3 \cdot \begin{bmatrix} 1 & 0 \\ 0 & -1 \end{bmatrix} = \begin{bmatrix} 1 & 4+i \\ 4-i & -5 \end{bmatrix}.$$

□

Weighted Model Counting (WMC). In this work, we will encode the Pauli coefficients of specific matrices as weighted model counting: a sum of weights over all satisfying assignments of a boolean formula. We here formally describe WMC.

For boolean variables $x, y \in \mathbb{B} = \{0, 1\}$, we define a literal as e.g. x and $\overline{x}$ and write conjunctions of literals (cubes) as products, e.g., $x\overline{y} = x \wedge \overline{y}$. A clause is a disjunction of literals, e.g., $\overline{x} \vee y$. A formula in conjunctive normal form (CNF) is a conjunction of clauses.

Let $F\colon \mathbb{B}^{\vec{x}} \to \mathbb{B}$ be a propositional formula over boolean variables $\vec{x} \in \mathbb{B}^n$. We assign weights to literals using a weight function $W\colon \{\overline{x}, x \mid x \in \vec{x}\} \to \mathbb{R}$. Given an assignment $\alpha \in \mathbb{B}^{\vec{x}}$, let $W(\alpha) = \prod_{x \in \vec{x}} W(x = \alpha(x))$. We define *weighted model counting* [7,10,19,21] as follows.

$$MC_W(F) \triangleq \sum_{\alpha \in \mathbb{B}^{\vec{x}}} F(\alpha) \cdot W(\alpha)$$

Example 2. An example, consider a formula $F = b \wedge c$ over $\vec{x} = (a, b, c)$. There exist two satisfying assignments: $\alpha_1 = abc$ and $\alpha_2 = \overline{a}bc$. Suppose a weight function W is defined as follows: $W(a) = -2$, $W(\overline{a}) = 3$, $W(b) = 1/2$, $W(\overline{b}) = 2$, while c remains unbiased, i.e., $W(c) = W(\overline{c}) = 1$. The weighted model counting for F with respect to W is computed as follows. $MC_W(F) = F(abc) \cdot W(abc) + F(\overline{a}bc) \cdot W(\overline{a}bc) = (-2 \cdot \frac{1}{2} \cdot 1) + (3 \cdot \frac{1}{2} \cdot 1) = \frac{1}{2}$. □

3 Equivalence Checking Circuits in the Pauli Basis

In this section, we introduce (exact) equivalence checking [2,4,8,22,52,55,56,61] in Definition 1, the task we set out to solve. In this work, we will only consider circuits which consist of gates, and do not contain measurements (this is without loss of generality since measurements be deferred to the end of the circuit [38]).

Definition 1. *Given two n-qubit circuits U and V where $n \in \mathbb{N}^+$, U is equivalent to V, written $U \equiv V$, if there exists a complex number c (the global phase [38]) such that for all input states $|\psi\rangle$, we have $U|\psi\rangle = cV|\psi\rangle$.*

At first sight, one might think that Definition 1 requires iterating over all quantum states. However, although the n-qubit quantum state space is continuous, it is a complex vector space of dimension 2^n, so it suffices to only consider 2^n basis vectors for proving U and V equivalent. In fact, the novice approach to equivalence checking is to decompose U and V in the standard basis; that is, to find U and V each by writing each of their individual gates in the standard basis and determining the full unitaries U and V by matrix multiplication, and finally checking whether the matrix entries of U equal those of V, modulo a uniform constant c. One could also perform such an approach when the individual gates in U and V are specified in a different basis, such as the Pauli basis (see Sect. 2), but this would have no a priori advantage over the use of the standard basis. Instead, we will use the following folklore result (for proof see e.g. [52]).

Theorem 1. *Let U, V be two circuits on $n \in \mathbb{N}^+$ qubits. Then U is equivalent to V if and only if the following condition holds (for notation P_j see Eq. 1): For all $j \in [n]$ and $P \in \{X, Z\}$, we have $UP_jU^\dagger = VP_jV^\dagger$.*

The main advantage of using Theorem 1 instead of directly computing the (matrix entries of the) unitaries U and V is that for Clifford gates G, G' it is computationally easy to update the Pauli coefficients of $GP_jG^\dagger$ to those of $(GG')P_j(GG')^\dagger = G\left(G'P_jG'^\dagger\right)G^\dagger$. This feature forms the basis for efficient simulation of Clifford circuits and has lead to efficient Clifford circuit equivalence checking [52]. Here, we will include T gates, Toffoli, and Pauli rotation gates, enabling equivalence checking of universal quantum computing (lifting the hardness of equivalence checking to quantum analogs of NP, see Sect. 1). Another advantage of Theorem 1 is that, since U is a unitary, $UP_jU^\dagger$ is Hermitian, so that its Pauli coefficients are real numbers as noted in Sect. 2, relieving us from the need to use complex numbers.

Example 3. Choose $V = S_1$ and $U = T_1T_1$. In order to determine whether $U \equiv V$, we compute the Pauli coefficients of $UXU^\dagger, UZU^\dagger, VXV^\dagger$ and $VZV^\dagger$ as follows using Table 1. By Theorem 1, this implies that U and V are equivalent, which we verify by writing their unitaries in the standard basis as follows.

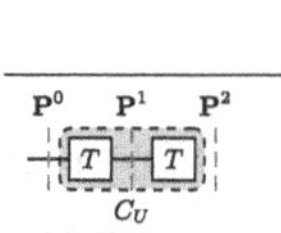

	$\mathbf{P}^0$	$\mathbf{P}^1 = T\mathbf{P}^0T^\dagger$	$\mathbf{P}^2 = T\mathbf{P}^1T^\dagger$
$UXU^\dagger$	X	$\frac{1}{\sqrt{2}}(X+Y)$	$\frac{1}{2}(X+Y+Y-X) = Y$
$UZU^\dagger$	Z	Z	Z

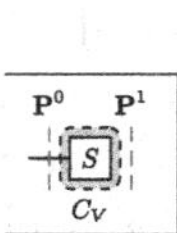

	$\mathbf{P}^0$	$\mathbf{P}^1 = S\mathbf{P}^0S^\dagger$
$VXV^\dagger$	X	Y
$VZV^\dagger$	Z	Z

$$U = S = \begin{bmatrix} 1 & 0 \\ 0 & i \end{bmatrix}, \quad V = T \cdot T = \begin{bmatrix} 1 & 0 \\ 0 & \sqrt{i} \end{bmatrix} \cdot \begin{bmatrix} 1 & 0 \\ 0 & \sqrt{i} \end{bmatrix} = \begin{bmatrix} 1 & 0 \\ 0 & i \end{bmatrix}$$

Finally, we remark that $UXU^\dagger = \frac{1}{2}(\cancel{X} + Y + Y - \cancel{X}) = Y$ represents both constructive (Y terms add up) as well as destructive interference (X terms cancel).

We will finish this section by explaining the intuition behind Theorem 1, by rephrasing its proof from [52]. The first step in the proof is to realize that Definition 1 is equivalent to the following in density matrix representation.

Lemma 1. *Given two n-qubit circuits U and V where* $n \in \mathbb{N}^+$, *U is equivalent to V iff for all n-qubit quantum states* $|\varphi\rangle$, *we have* $U|\varphi\rangle\langle\varphi|U^\dagger = V|\varphi\rangle\langle\varphi|V^\dagger$.

Recall that for any unitary U, with $|\psi\rangle = U|\varphi\rangle$, the corresponding operation on the density matrix $|\varphi\rangle\langle\varphi|$ is conjugation, i.e., $|\psi\rangle\langle\psi| = U|\varphi\rangle\langle\varphi|U^\dagger$. Density matrices are $2^n \times 2^n$ Hermitian matrices and can thus be expressed as a (real-weighted) linear combination of Pauli strings. For this reason, we observe that if $UPU^\dagger = VPV^\dagger$ for each Pauli string P, i.e. U and V coincide on all Pauli strings by conjugation, then U and V must also coincide on all density matrices by conjugation, and thus they are equivalent by Lemma 1.

The final step in proving Theorem 1 is to realize that for a unitary matrix, the conjugation action is completely determined by fixing its conjugation action on only all X_j and Z_j for $j \in [n]$. This insight relies on two parts: First, each Pauli string can be written as the product of X_j and Z_j modulo a factor $\in\{\pm 1, \pm i\}$. Second, for a unitary M, we have $M^\dagger M = I$, which implies that instead of first multiplying X_js and Z_js to construct a Pauli string, followed by conjugation, one can first conjugate and subsequently multiply to arrive at the same result.[3] For example, $MX_jM^\dagger \cdot MZ_jM^\dagger = MX_jIZ_jM^\dagger = MX_jZ_jM^\dagger$.

We observe that in Table 1, the last two non-Clifford gates yield a linear combination of Pauli strings [34] for each Pauli string (matrix). This potentially causes an explosion of the number of Pauli strings when conjugating multiple non-Clifford gates. To handle this, we will exploit the strength of model counters in Sect. 4 by representing Pauli strings $\hat{P}$ as satisfying assignments which are weighted by the coefficient $\gamma_{\hat{P}}$, as explained next in Sect. 4.

4 Encoding Quantum Circuit Equivalence in SAT

The previous section Sect. 3, centered around Theorem 1, explained that equivalence checking can be done by conjugating Pauli strings with unitaries, and that the required calculations for this approach are the same as in simulation of quantum circuits using a density matrix representation of the quantum state. In this section, we show how we reduce equivalence checking of universal quantum circuits to weighted model counting, which is formalized in Corollary 1 below. Our approach is based on the $\mathcal{O}(n+m)$-length encoding for quantum circuit simulation provided in [34]. Finally, our encoding in this work extends [34] with Toffoli gates. For the rest of the paper, we use P for an unweighted Pauli string and we use $\mathbf{P}$ for a summation of weighted Pauli strings, e.g. $\frac{1}{\sqrt{2}}X + \frac{1}{\sqrt{2}}Y$.

[3] The conjugation map $P \mapsto UPU^\dagger$ is a group isomorphism.

Table 1. Lookup table for conjugating Pauli gates by Clifford+T+R_X gates. The subscripts "c" and "t" stand for "control" and "target". Adapted from [34].

Gate	In	Out	Gate	In	Out	Gate	In	Out
H	X	Z	CZ	$I_c \otimes X_t$	$Z_c \otimes X_t$		X	$\frac{1}{\sqrt{2}}(X+Y)$
	Y	$-Y$		$X_c \otimes I_t$	$X_c \otimes Z_t$	T	Y	$\frac{1}{\sqrt{2}}(Y-X)$
	Z	X		$I_c \otimes Y_t$	$Z_c \otimes Y_t$		Z	Z
S	X	Y		$Y_c \otimes I_t$	$Y_c \otimes Z_t$		X	X
	Y	$-X$		$I_c \otimes Z_t$	$I_c \otimes Z_t$	$R_X(\theta)$	Y	$\cos(\theta)Y + \sin(\theta)Z$
	Z	Z		$Z_c \otimes I_t$	$Z_c \otimes I_t$		Z	$\cos(\theta)Z - \sin(\theta)Y$

To simplify notation, we will solve a rephrased version of the equivalence checking problem from Definition 1 in Sect. 3: to check whether a unitary A is equivalent to the identity unitary I, which leaves every input unchanged. By choosing $A \triangleq V^\dagger U$, we see that $U \equiv V$ precisely if $A \equiv I$. If U and V consist of gates $U = (U_0, U_1, \ldots, U_{m-1})$ and $V = (V_0, V_1, \ldots, V_{\ell-1})$ for $m, \ell \in \mathbb{N}^+$, then a circuit for A is given as the $m+\ell$ gates $A = (U_0, U_1, \ldots, U_{m-1}, V^\dagger_{\ell-1}, V^\dagger_{\ell-2}, \cdots, V^\dagger_0)$. Following Theorem 1, our task will be as follows: Given a circuit $A = (G^0, \ldots, G^{m-1}) \in \{H_j, S_j, CZ_{jk}, T_j, \text{Toffoli}_{jkl}, R_X(\theta)_j, \cdots \mid j,k,l \in [n]\}^m$, we need to obtain $\mathbf{P}^m = A\mathbf{P}^0 A^\dagger$ from an initial $\mathbf{P}^0 \in \{+X_i, +Z_i \mid i \in [n]\}$, showing that $\mathbf{P}^m = \mathbf{P}^0$. Since $\mathbf{P}^0$ is a Pauli string and thus Hermitian, so is $\mathbf{P}^m$. Our approach is to construct a boolean formula whose weighted model counts represent the terms in the Pauli decomposition of $\mathbf{P}^m$.

4.1 Encoding Pauli Coefficients as Weighted Model Counts

We first explain the encoding for circuit simulation from [34], where we encode the real-weighted sum of Pauli operators $\mathbf{P}$ and the update rules of the circuit A as weighted boolean formulas. We start with the simplest case—a Pauli string, then consider how to encode a single summand, i.e., a single weighted Pauli operator, and in the end extend this to a weighted sum of Pauli operators.

Given a Pauli string $P = \bigotimes_{i\in[n]} \sigma[a_i, b_i]$ with $a_i, b_i \in \{0,1\}$, the corresponding encoding is denoted as F_P, which is the boolean formula which only has $\{x_1 \leftarrow a_1, \cdots, x_n \leftarrow a_n, z_1 \leftarrow b_1, \cdots, z_n \leftarrow b_n\}$ as satisfying assignment, for example $F_{Z\otimes X} = F_{\sigma[01]\otimes\sigma[10]} = \overline{x}_1 x_2 z_1 \overline{z}_2$. When it comes to weighted Pauli string, although the weights are never imaginary in case of a Hermitian matrix, they can still have a $\pm$ sign. A weighted Pauli operator can be therefore encoded by $2n+1$ boolean variables: two bits x_i, z_i for each of the n Pauli matrices and one sign bit r, such that $\mathbf{P} = (-1)^r \sigma[x_1, z_1] \otimes \ldots \otimes \sigma[x_n, z_n]$. For example, consider boolean formula $F_\mathbf{P} = r\overline{x}_1 z_1 x_2 z_2$ where $\mathbf{P} = -Z \otimes Y$. Its one satisfying assignment is $\{r \leftarrow 1, x_1 \leftarrow 0, z_1 \leftarrow 1, x_2 \leftarrow 1, z_2 \leftarrow 1\} \equiv -Z \otimes Y$. We later introduce weights $W(r) = -1$ and $W(\overline{r}) = 1$ to interpret the sign. So for a formula $F(x_1, z_1, \ldots, x_n, z_n, r)$, we let the satisfying assignment represent a set (linear combination) of Pauli strings. The base case is the formula $F_{\mathbf{P}^0} = F_P$ for a Pauli string $P \in \{X_j, Z_j \mid j \in [n]\}$.

Next, we need to encode how sums of Pauli operators evolve when conjugating with the gates of the circuit, one by one. For this, our encoding duplicates the variables for all m gates (each time step) as follows (which is similar to encodings for bounded model checking [6]).

$$\vec{w}^t = \{x_j^t, z_j^t, r^t \mid j \in [n]\} \text{ for } t \in \{0,1,\ldots,m\} \text{ and } \vec{v}^t = \bigcup_{i \in [t] \cup \{0\}} \vec{w}^i. \tag{2}$$

For example, $\mathbf{P}^0 = X_1$ is encoded as $\overline{r}^0 x_1^0 \overline{z}_1^0 x_2^0 \overline{z}_2^0 \ldots x_n^0 \overline{z}_n^0$. Also, the satisfying assignments of a boolean formula $F_A(\vec{v}^m)$ projected to variables $\vec{w}^t$ represent the sum of Pauli operators after conjugating the initial t gates $G_0, G_1, \ldots, G_{t-1}$ of the circuit A, written:

$$F_A(\vec{v}^m)[\vec{w}^t] = \sum_{\alpha \in \{0,1\}^{\vec{v}^m}} F_A(\alpha) \cdot (-1)^{\alpha(r^t)} \cdot \bigotimes_{j \in [n]} \sigma[\alpha(x_j^t), \alpha(z_j^t)]$$

The next question is how to encode gate semantics, i.e., define a constraint to get $\mathbf{P}^1$ by conjugating gate G^0 to $\mathbf{P}^0$, etc. Note that since $\mathbf{P}^0 \in \{X_j, Z_j \mid j \in [n]\}$ consists of a sum of only one Pauli operator. For Clifford circuits C, there will only be a single satisfying assignment α for all time steps $t \in [m]$, since e.g. $HXH^\dagger = Z$ (and not e.g. $Z + Y$). Non-Clifford gates, like T or Toffoli, will add satisfying assignments representing summands with different weights (e.g. sums of accumulated weights of $1/\sqrt{2}$ for the T gate as discussed above). To encode these weights, we introduce new variables u^t, but only at time steps t with a T gate (i.e., $G^t = T$).

When a gate T_j is performed and there is a satisfying assignment with $x_j^t = 1$, it means that we are conjugating a T gate on the j-th qubit set to $\pm X$ or $\pm Y$ and the result should be either $TXT^\dagger = \frac{1}{\sqrt{2}}(X+Y)$ or $TYT^\dagger = \frac{1}{\sqrt{2}}(Y-X)$ (modulo sign). To achieve this the encoding should let z^{t+1} unconstrained and set $u^t \Leftrightarrow x_j^t$. Accordingly, we set the weights $W(u^t) = \frac{1}{\sqrt{2}}$ and $W(\overline{u}^t) = 1$. Table 2 illustrates how the boolean variables $\vec{w}^t$ and $\vec{w}^{t+1}$ relate for a T gate (derived by computing $TPT^\dagger$ for Pauli gate P).

The encoding of gate semantics can be derived similarly. For example the boolean constraint for H_j^t follows from Table 1 and is given by

$$F_{H_j^t}(\vec{w}^t, \vec{w}^{t+1}) \triangleq r^{t+1} \Leftrightarrow r^t \oplus x_j^t z_j^t \wedge z_j^{t+1} \Leftrightarrow x_j^t \wedge x_j^{t+1} \Leftrightarrow z_j^t$$

Here we omit additional constraints $a^{t+1} \Leftrightarrow a^t$ for all unconstrained time-step-$t+1$ variables a, i.e., for $a = x_l^{t+1}, z_l^{t+1}$ with $l \not= j$. Similarly, by abbreviating $F_{G^t}(\vec{w}^t, \vec{w}^{t+1})$ as G^t, the encoding for other Clifford+T gates are as follows:

$$\begin{aligned}
S_j^t &\triangleq r^{t+1} \Leftrightarrow r^t \oplus x_j^t z_j^t \wedge z_j^{t+1} \Leftrightarrow x_j^t \oplus z_j^t, \\
T_j^t &\triangleq r^{t+1} \Leftrightarrow r^t \oplus x_j^t z_j^t \neg z_j^{t+1} \wedge x_j^{t+1} \Longleftrightarrow x_j^t \wedge x_j^t \vee (z_j^{t+1} \Leftrightarrow z_j^t) \wedge u^t \Leftrightarrow x_j^t, \\
CZ_{jk}^t &\triangleq r^{t+1} \Leftrightarrow r^t \oplus x_j^t x_k^t (z_k^t \oplus z_j^t) \wedge z_k^{t+1} \Leftrightarrow z_j^t \oplus x_k^t \wedge z_j^{t+1} \Leftrightarrow z_k^t \oplus x_j^t.
\end{aligned}$$

Table 2. Boolean variables under the action of conjugating one T gate. Here we omit the sign $(-1)^{r^t}$ for all P and sign $(-1)^{r^{t+1}}$ for all $TPT^\dagger$.

P	$x^t z^t r^t$	$TPT^\dagger$	x^{t+1}	z^{t+1}	r^{t+1}	u^t
I	$00\ r^t$	I	0	z^t	r^t	0
Z	$01\ r^t$	Z				
X	$10\ r^t$	$\frac{1}{\sqrt{2}}(X+Y)$	1	{0,1}	r^t	1
Y	$11\ r^t$	$\frac{1}{\sqrt{2}}(Y-X)$			$r^t \oplus \neg z^{t+1}$	

To this end, we can inductively define boolean constraints for each time step as $F_{\mathbf{P}^t}(\vec{v}^t) = F_{\mathbf{P}^0}(\vec{w}^0) \wedge \bigwedge_{i\in[t-1]\cup\{0\}} G^i(\vec{w}^i, \vec{w}^{i+1})$ for $t \sqcap 1$, where G_i denotes the gate at time step i and $F_{\mathbf{P}^0}(\vec{v}^0)$ encodes $\mathbf{P}^0$.

Example 4. Reconsider the circuit $U{=}T{\cdot}T$ from Example 3. Starting with $\mathbf{P}^0{=}X$, the formulas are $F_{\mathbf{P}^0} = x_1^0\overline{z_1^0}\,\overline{r^0}$, $F_{\mathbf{P}^1} = F_{\mathbf{P}^0} \wedge F_{T_1^0}$, i.e.

$$F_{\mathbf{P}^0} \wedge F_{T_1^0} = x_1^0\overline{z_1^0}\,\overline{r^0} \ \wedge\ x_1^1 \Leftrightarrow x_1^0 \ \wedge\ x_1^0 \vee (z_1^1 \Leftrightarrow z_1^0) \ \wedge \\ r^1 \Leftrightarrow r^0 \oplus x_1^0 z_1^0 \neg z_1^1 \ \wedge\ u^0 \Leftrightarrow x_1^0,$$

and similarly $F_{\mathbf{P}^2} = F_{\mathbf{P}^1} \wedge F_{T_1^1}$. □

Formalizing the explanation above as induction over the gates proves Proposition 1, relating weighted model counting the Pauli coefficients (see Sect. 2).

Proposition 1 (WMC computes the Pauli coefficients). *Let $C_A = (G^0, \ldots, G^{m-1})$ be an n-qubit circuit, $A = G^0 \cdots G^{m-1}$ the corresponding unitary and $\mathbf{P}^0$ a Pauli string, so that the encoding of $\mathbf{P}^m \triangleq A\mathbf{P}^0 A^\dagger$ is given by $F_{\mathbf{P}^m} \triangleq F_{\mathbf{P}^0} \wedge \bigwedge_{i=0}^{m-1} F_{G^i}$ with according weight function W. For any $\mathbf{P}^0 \in \{+X_j, +Z_j \mid j \in [n]\}$ and $P \in \hat{\mathcal{P}}_n$, the weighted model count of $F_{\mathbf{P}^m} \wedge F_P$ equals the Pauli coefficient γ_P of $\mathbf{P}^m$. That is, $MC_W(F_{\mathbf{P}^m} \wedge F_P) = \frac{1}{2^n} \cdot \mathrm{Tr}(P^\dagger \cdot A\mathbf{P}^0 A^\dagger)$ for all $P \in \hat{\mathcal{P}}_n$.*

We emphasize the necessity for using negative weights. For example, in Example 3, we have $\mathbf{P}^2 = U\mathbf{P}^0U^\dagger = \frac{1}{2}(\cancel{X} + Y + Y - \cancel{X}) = Y$ for $\mathbf{P}^0 = X$, where the terms X and $-X$ cancel each other out, while the Y terms add up. *This is why weighted model counting with negative weights is required; to reason about such constructive and destructive interference, ubiquitous to quantum computing.*

Example 5. Following Example 4, we have the satisfying assignments for $F_{\mathbf{P}^0}$, $F_{\mathbf{P}^1}$ and $F_{\mathbf{P}^2}$ as:

$$\begin{aligned} SAT(F_{\mathbf{P}^0}) &= \{x_1^0\overline{z_1^0}\,\overline{r_1^0}\}, \\ SAT(F_{\mathbf{P}^1}) &= \{x_1^0\overline{z_1^0}\,\overline{r_1^0}\ x_1^1\overline{z_1^1}\,\overline{r_1^1}\ u^0,\ x_1^0\overline{z_1^0}\,\overline{r_1^0}\ x_1^1 z_1^1\overline{r_1^1}\ u^0\}, \\ SAT(F_{\mathbf{P}^2}) &= \{x_1^0\overline{z_1^0}\,\overline{r_1^0}\ x_1^1\overline{z_1^1}\,\overline{r_1^1}\ x_1^2\overline{z_1^2}\,\overline{r_1^2}\ u^0u^1,\ x_1^0\overline{z_1^0}\,\overline{r_1^0}\ x_1^1\overline{z_1^1}\,\overline{r_1^1}\ x_1^2 z_1^2\overline{r_1^2}\ u^0u^1, \\ &\quad\ x_1^0\overline{z_1^0}\,\overline{r_1^0}\ x_1^1 z_1^1\overline{r_1^1}\ x_1^2 z_1^2\overline{r_1^2}\ u^0u^1,\ x_1^0\overline{z_1^0}\,\overline{r_1^0}\ x_1^1 z_1^1\overline{r_1^1}\ x_1^2\overline{z_1^2} r_1^2\ u^0u^1\}, \end{aligned}$$

with the weight function $W(r_1^2)=-1$, $W(\overline{r_1^2})=1$, $W(u^0)=W(u^1)=\frac{1}{\sqrt{2}}$ and $W(\overline{u^0})=W(\overline{u^1})=1$. Each of the satisfying assignments corresponds to a term in the Pauli decomposition of $\mathbf{P}^2$, which we recall from Example 3 to be

$$\mathbf{P}^2 = \tfrac{1}{2}X + \tfrac{1}{2}Y + \tfrac{1}{2}Y - \tfrac{1}{2}X = (\tfrac{1}{2} - \tfrac{1}{2})X + (\tfrac{1}{2} + \tfrac{1}{2})Y = Y. \tag{3}$$

For example, the term $-\frac{1}{2}X$ is encoded by $x_1^0\overline{z_1^0 r_1^0}\ x_1^1 z_1^1 \overline{r_1^1}\ x_1^2\overline{z_1^2} r_1^2\ u^0 u^1$ because it contains $x_1^2\overline{z_1^2}$ (corresponding to X) and its weight is $W(r_1^2)\cdot W(u^0)\cdot W(u^1) = (-1)\cdot\frac{1}{\sqrt{2}}\cdot\frac{1}{\sqrt{2}} = -\frac{1}{2}$. We verify that the constructive interference of the Y terms in (3) (i.e. they add up) results in an aggregate Pauli coefficient γ_Y of $\mathbf{P}^2$ of 1:

$$MC_W(F_{\mathbf{P}^2} \wedge F_Y) = \tfrac{1}{\sqrt{2}}\cdot\tfrac{1}{\sqrt{2}} + \tfrac{1}{\sqrt{2}}\cdot\tfrac{1}{\sqrt{2}} = 1 = \tfrac{1}{2}\mathrm{Tr}(Y\cdot\mathbf{P}^2).$$

Similarly, we verify that destructive interference of the X terms in (3) (i.e. they cancel) results in the coefficient γ_X being 0:

$$MC_W(F_{\mathbf{P}^2} \wedge F_X) = \tfrac{1}{\sqrt{2}}\cdot\tfrac{1}{\sqrt{2}} - \tfrac{1}{\sqrt{2}}\cdot\tfrac{1}{\sqrt{2}} = 0 = \tfrac{1}{2}\mathrm{Tr}(X\cdot\mathbf{P}^2).$$ □

Toffoli Gate. Similar to the way gate encodings of other non-Clifford gates were derived, we can encode the Toffoli gate. To this end, we brute forced the Toffoli gate behavior in the Pauli domain. To keep things readable, we will only present a lookup table in the Pauli basis in Table 3, like Table 1. The corresponding boolean constraint can easily be derived. To subsequently obtain a minimal (weighted) CNF formula, we applied the Quine-McCluskey algorithm [33,44].

Table 3. An partial lookup table for the Toffoli gate for in/output Pauli operators P and Q. The extended version of this paper [35] includes the full table.

$P \in \mathcal{P}_3$	$Q = \text{Toffoli}\cdot P\cdot\text{Toffoli}^\dagger$ with $Q \in \frac{1}{2}\sum_{i\in[4]}\mathcal{P}_3$ or $Q \in \mathcal{P}_3$
$I\otimes I\otimes Z$	$(I\otimes I\otimes Z + I\otimes Z\otimes Z + Z\otimes I\otimes Z - Z\otimes Z\otimes Z)/2$
$I\otimes I\otimes X$	$I\otimes I\otimes X$
$I\otimes Z\otimes I$	$I\otimes Z\otimes I$
$I\otimes X\otimes I$	$(I\otimes X\otimes I + I\otimes X\otimes X + Z\otimes X\otimes I - Z\otimes X\otimes X)/2$
$Z\otimes I\otimes I$	$Z\otimes I\otimes I$
$X\otimes I\otimes I$	$(X\otimes I\otimes I + X\otimes I\otimes X + X\otimes Z\otimes I - X\otimes Z\otimes X)/2$
$X\otimes X\otimes Z$	$(X\otimes X\otimes Z + Y\otimes Y\otimes Z - X\otimes Y\otimes Y - Y\otimes X\otimes Y)/2$
$Y\otimes Y\otimes Y$	$(X\otimes X\otimes Y + Y\otimes Y\otimes Y - X\otimes Y\otimes Z - Y\otimes X\otimes Z)/2$

4.2 WMC-Based Algorithm for Equivalence Checking

The previous subsection explains how to encode the Pauli coefficients of $APA^\dagger$, where A is a unitary and P a Pauli string, in a boolean formula together with a weight function. We here connect this encoding to Theorem 1, which expresses that determining whether a unitary A is equivalent to the identity circuit can be done by checking if $APA^\dagger \stackrel{?}{=} P$ for Pauli strings $P \in \{X_j, Z_j \mid j \in [n]\}$. We use the following lemma, which expresses that for any unitary A and Pauli string P, the P-Pauli coefficient of $APA^\dagger$ can only become 1 if $APA^\dagger$ equals P.

Lemma 2. *Let A be a unitary and $P \in \hat{\mathcal{P}}_n$ be a Pauli string. Then $APA^\dagger = P$ if and only if $\frac{1}{2^n}\mathrm{Tr}(APA^\dagger \cdot P) = 1$.*

Proof. If $AP_jA^\dagger = P_j$, then $\mathrm{Tr}(AP_jA^\dagger \cdot P_j) = \mathrm{Tr}(P_j \cdot P_j) = \mathrm{Tr}(I^{\otimes n}) = 2^n$. For the converse direction, we observe that $\mathrm{Tr}(AP_jA^\dagger \cdot P_j)$ is the Frobenius inner product $\langle U, V\rangle \triangleq \mathrm{Tr}(U^\dagger V)$ for $U \triangleq AP_jA^\dagger$ and $V \triangleq P_j$. It now follows from the Cauchy-Schwarz inequality $|\langle U, V\rangle|^2 \sqcup \langle U, U\rangle \cdot \langle V, V\rangle$ that

$$\begin{aligned}
|\mathrm{Tr}(AP_jA^\dagger \cdot P_j)|^2 &\sqcup \mathrm{Tr}((AP_jA^\dagger)^\dagger \cdot AP_jA^\dagger) \cdot \mathrm{Tr}(P_j^\dagger \cdot P_j) \\
&= \mathrm{Tr}(AP_jA^\dagger \cdot AP_jA^\dagger) \cdot \mathrm{Tr}(P_j^\dagger \cdot P_j) \\
&= \mathrm{Tr}(AP_j \cdot P_jA^\dagger) \cdot \mathrm{Tr}(I^{\otimes n}) && (\ A \text{ and } P_j \text{ are unitary}) \\
&= \mathrm{Tr}(AA^\dagger) \cdot \mathrm{Tr}(I^{\otimes n}) && (\ P^2 = I \text{ for all } P \in \hat{\mathcal{P}}_n\ ) \\
&= \mathrm{Tr}(I^{\otimes n}) \cdot \mathrm{Tr}(I^{\otimes n}) = 2^n \cdot 2^n = 4^n && (\ A \text{ is unitary})
\end{aligned}$$

and therefore $|\mathrm{Tr}(AP_jA^\dagger \cdot P_j)| \sqcup 2^n$. Since $\mathrm{Tr}(AP_jA^\dagger \cdot P_j) = 2^n$ by assumption, the Cauchy-Schwarz inequality is tight, which only happens if $U = AP_jA^\dagger$ and $V = P_j$ are linearly dependent. Thus, there exists a complex number λ such that $AP_jA^\dagger = \lambda P_j$. Substituting this expression in $\mathrm{Tr}(AP_jA^\dagger \cdot P_j)$ yields $\mathrm{Tr}(\lambda P_j \cdot P_j) = \lambda \cdot \mathrm{Tr}(I^{\otimes n}) = \lambda 2^n$, hence $\lambda = 1$ and $AP_jA^\dagger = P_j$. □

Combining Lemma 2 and Proposition 1 with Theorem 1 yields Corollary 1 below, which in turn implies correctness of Algorithm 1 which reduces equivalence checking to WMC.

Corollary 1. *Let A be an n-qubit circuit with m gates and $P \in \{X_j, Z_j \mid j \in [n]\}$, which are encoded by F_A and F_P respectively, with according weight function W. We have $A \equiv I$ if and only if $MC_W(F_P(\vec{w}^0) \wedge F_A(\vec{v}^t) \wedge F_P(\vec{w}^m)) = 1$ for all $P \in \{X_j, Z_j \mid j \in [n]\}$, where $\vec{w}^{t+1}$ are boolean variables encoding the quantum state in circuit A after the t-th gate of A $(0 \sqcup t \sqcup m-1)$ and $\vec{v}^t = \bigcup_{t \in [m] \cup \{0\}} \vec{w}^t$ as defined in Eq. (2).*

Example 6. Consider $A = V^\dagger U$ where $=U = (T, T)$ and $V = (S)$ as in Example 3. We show how to reduce the equivalence check $A \stackrel{?}{\equiv} I$ to weighted model counting. First, we encode the check $AXA^\dagger \stackrel{?}{=} X$ using $F_1 \triangleq F_{AXA^\dagger} \wedge F_X$:

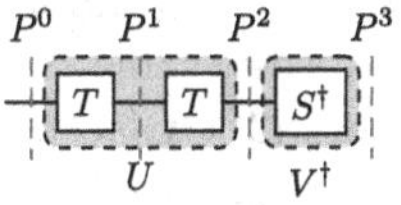

$$F_1 = \underbrace{x_1^0 \overline{z_1^0} \overline{r^0} \wedge T_1^0 \wedge T_1^1 \wedge S_1^{\dagger,2}}_{F_{AXA^\dagger}} \wedge \underbrace{x_1^3 \overline{z_1^3}}_{F_X}$$

Algorithm 1. Quantum circuit equivalence checking algorithm based on WMC. Given an n-qubit circuit $A = (G^0, G^1, \ldots, G^{m-1})$, the algorithm decides whether A is equivalent to the identity circuit.

```
for P ∈ {X, Z} do
    for j ∈ {1, 2, ..., n} do
        P⁰ ← +P_j
        F_M ← F_{P⁰}(w⃗⁰)
        for k ranging from 0 to m − 1 do
            F_M ← F_M ∧ F_{G^k}(w⃗^k ∪ w⃗^{k+1})
        if MC_W(F_M ∧ F_{P_j}(w⃗^m)) ≠ 1 then        ▷ Following Corollary 1
            return 'not equivalent'
return 'equivalent'
```

The satisfying assignments of F_1 are

$$SAT(F_1) = \{x_1^1\overline{z_1^1}\,\overline{r_1^1}\ x_1^2\overline{z_1^2}\,\overline{r_1^2}\ x_1^3\overline{z_1^3}\,\overline{r_1^3}\ u^0u^1,\ x_1^1\overline{z_1^1}\,\overline{r_1^1}\ x_1^2\overline{z_1^2}\,\overline{r_1^2}\ x_1^3\overline{z_1^3}\,\overline{r_1^3}\ u^0u^1\}.$$

so $MC_W(F_1) = \sum_{\sigma \in SAT(F_1)} W(\sigma(r_1^3))W(\sigma(u^0))W(\sigma(u^1)) = \frac{1}{\sqrt{2}} \cdot \frac{1}{\sqrt{2}} + \frac{1}{\sqrt{2}} \cdot \frac{1}{\sqrt{2}} = 1$.

Now we turn to the check $AZA^\dagger \stackrel{?}{=} Z$, obtaining the formula $F_2 \triangleq F_{AZA^\dagger} \wedge F_Z$, where $F_{AZA^\dagger}$ is the same formula from F_1 and $F_Z = \overline{x_1^3} z_1^3$. The satisfying assignments of F_2 are $SAT(F_2) = \{\overline{x_1^0} z_1^0 \overline{r_1^0}\,\overline{x_1^1} z_1^1 \overline{r_1^1}\,\overline{x_1^2} z_1^2 \overline{r_1^2}\,\overline{x_1^3} z_1^3 \overline{r_1^3}\,\overline{u^0}\,\overline{u^1}\}$, and $MC_W(F_2) = W(\overline{r_1^3})W(\overline{u^0})W(\overline{u^1}) = 1$. Since both weighted model counts evaluate to 1, we conclude that $A \equiv I$. □

5 Implementation: The ECMC Tool

We implemented our method in an open-source tool called ECMC, available at https://github.com/System-Verification-Lab/Quokka-Sharp. ECMC takes two quantum circuits in QASM format [13] as input. It encodes these circuits to a sequence of $2n$ weighted conjunctive normal form (CNF) formulas as explained in Sect. 4, and then uses the weighted model counter GPMC [50] to solve these constraints in parallel, terminating as soon as one returns a negative result. Here we set the number of parallel cores to be 16 as it is shown to be the optimal number of cores for our task.

We choose GPMC as it supports the negative weights in our encoding and performs the best among solvers with that capability in the model counting competition 2023 [21]. To demonstrate the effectiveness of our method, we conducted a set of broad experiments as discussed in the following.

We performed equivalence checking of quantum circuits comparing our method against the state-of-the-art tool QCEC [8], which runs different algorithms and heuristics based on ZX calculus and decision diagrams (shorted as DD) in portfolio with 16 parallel threads [60]. Similar to ECMC, QCEC also terminates earlier when one thread returns "non-equivalent". Since the ZX-calculus based method is still incomplete for universal quantum circuits, in the sense

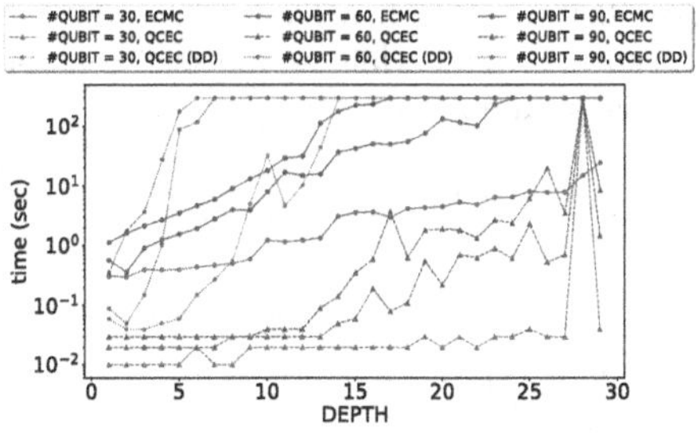

Fig. 1: Growing circuit depth

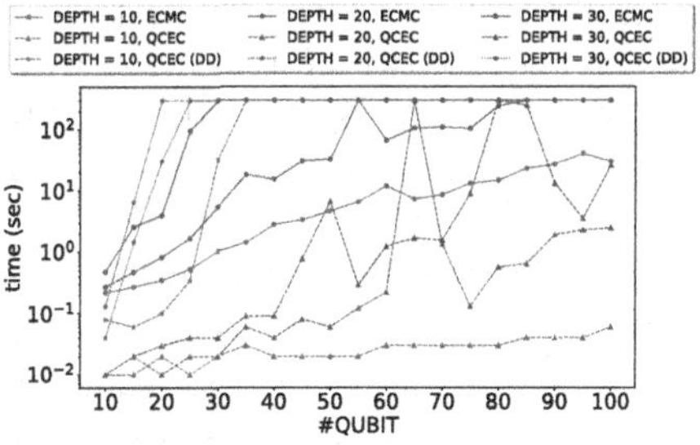

Fig. 2: Growing qubit counts

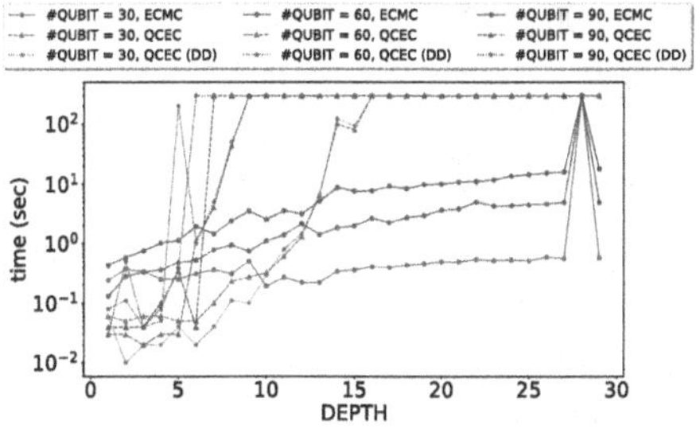

Fig. 3: Growing circuit depth

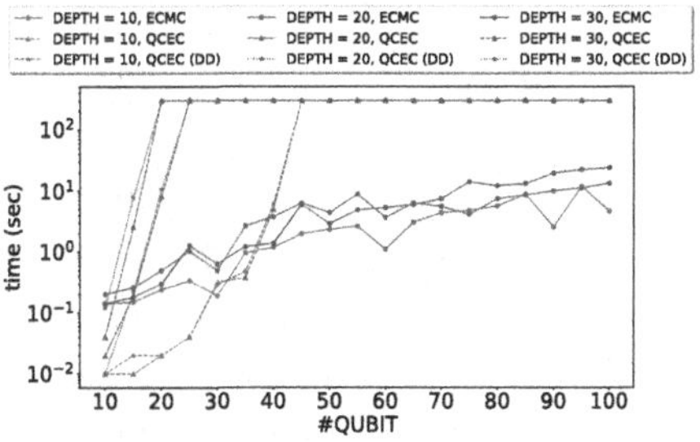

Fig. 4: Growing qubit counts

Fig. 1. Equivalence check of typical random Clifford+T circuits against their optimized circuits (equivalent cases, Fig 1 & Fig 2) and optimized circuits with one random gate missing (non-equivalent cases, Fig 3 & Fig 4). (Both vertical axes are on a logarithmic scale.)

that it is only capable of proving equivalence, we use this tool under two settings: one is the default setting which uses DD and ZX calculus in portfolio; the other is to exclusively enable DD [8]. We use two families of circuits: (i) random Clifford+T circuits, which mimic hard problems arising in quantum chemistry [59] and quantum many-body physics [17]; (ii) all benchmarks from the public benchmark suite MQT Bench [43], which includes many important quantum algorithms like QAOA, VQE, QNN, Grover, etc. All experiments have been conducted on a 3.5 GHz M2 Machine with MacOS 13 and 16 GB RAM. We set the time limit to be 5 min (300 s) and include the time to read a QASM file, construct the weighted CNF and perform the model counting in all reported runtimes.

Results. First, to show the scalability of both methods on checking equivalence, we consider random circuits that resemble typical oracle implementations—random quantum circuits with varying qubits and depths, which comprise the CX, H, S, and T gates with appearing ratio 10%, 35%, 35%, 20% [41]. We use a ZX-calculus tool PyZX [28] to generate optimized circuits, to construct equivalent, yet very different, counterparts. To construct non-equivalent instances, we inject an error by removing one random gate from the corresponding optimized circuits. So by

Table 4. Results of verifying equivalence of circuits from MQT bench against optimized circuits. For cases within time limit, we give runtime (sec), while > 300 represents a timeout (5 min) and × means that the result was 'unknown'.

Algorithm	n	$\lvert G\rvert$	G'	ECMC	QCEC (DD)	QCEC
graphstate	16	160	32	0.41	0.11	0.01
	32	320	64	1.67	0.1	0.01
	64	640	128	8.11	24.37	0.02
grover (noancilla)	5	499	629	> 300	0.12	0.04
	6	1568	1870	> 300	6.04	×
	7	3751	5783	> 300	> 300	1.97
qaoa	7	133	117	0.48	0.02	0.01
	9	171	296	1.44	0.11	×
	11	209	359	1.56	0.28	0.01
qnn	2	43	36	0.06	0.01	0.01
	8	319	494	> 300	0.24	×
	16	1023	2002	> 300	> 300	×
qft	2	14	14	0.02	0.01	0.01
	8	176	228	36.56	0.07	0.02
	16	672	814	> 300	18.28	×
qpe (inexact)	16	712	848	> 300	> 300	×
	32	2712	3179	> 300	> 300	> 300
	64	10552	9695	> 300	> 300	> 300
vqe	5	83	83	1.07	0.01	0.01
	10	168	221	> 300	0.04	0.02
	15	253	349	> 300	0.12	0.05
wstate	16	271	242	1.74	23.68	×
	32	559	498	9.52	> 300	×
	64	1135	1010	70.51	> 300	> 300

construction, we know the correct answer for all equivalence checking instances in advance. The resulting runtimes can be seen in Fig. 1.

In addition to random circuits, to test structural quantum circuits, we empirically evaluated our method on the MQTBench benchmark set [43]. We also generate the optimized circuits of the circuits from MQT-bench using PyZX [28]. To generate non-equivalent instances, three kinds of errors are injected into the optimized circuits: one with a random gate removed, one where a random CNOT gate is flipped, switching control and target qubits, and one where the phase of the angle of a random rotation gate is shifted. For the last error, since many optimizations on rotation gates involve phase shifts in the rotation angles, we consider two sizes of phase shift: one with the angle of a random rotation gate

Table 5. Results of verifying non-equivalence of circuits from MQT bench against optimized circuits with flipped CNOT gate (Flipped) and one missing gate (1 Gate Missing). For cases within time limit, we give runtime (sec), while > 300 represents a timeout (5 min).

Algorithm	n	$\|G\|$	$\|G'\|$	Flipped			1 Gate Missing		
				`ECMC`	QCEC (DD)	QCEC	`ECMC`	QCEC (DD)	QCEC
grover (noancilla)	5	499	629	> 300	0.04	0.02	1.26	0.05	0.02
	6	1568	1870	> 300	0.14	0.06	> 300	0.13	0.05
	7	3751	5783	> 300	1.41	0.46	24.27	5.05	0.35
qaoa	7	133	117	0.36	0.03	0.01	0.39	0.03	0.01
	9	171	296	0.77	0.06	0.03	0.8	0.07	0.02
	11	209	359	3.32	0.53	0.23	2.28	0.87	0.09
qft	2	14	14	0.05	0.02	0.01	0.1	0.04	0.01
	8	176	228	1.53	0.05	0.01	1.89	0.04	0.01
	16	672	814	2.7	12.47	5.47	6.68	75.73	1.33
qnn	2	43	36	0.24	0.07	0.01	0.22	0.1	0.01
	8	319	494	> 300	0.59	0.05	> 300	0.61	0.05
	16	1023	2002	> 300	> 300	97.22	> 300	> 300	90.58
qpe (inexact)	16	712	848	19.97	1.72	4.98	19.59	186.29	1.12
	32	2712	3179	13.28	> 300	> 300	22.0	> 300	> 300
	64	10552	9695	> 300	> 300	> 300	75.46	> 300	> 300
vqe	5	83	83	0.81	0.05	0.01	0.37	0.22	0.01
	10	168	221	55.06	0.58	0.18	3.98	3.9	0.03
	15	253	349	4.08	0.94	81.03	5.09	> 300	0.05
wstate	16	271	242	6.47	0.41	0.03	1.46	0.37	0.02
	32	559	498	13.65	2.0	> 300	2.28	> 300	59.07
	64	1135	1010	13.32	> 300	> 300	6.48	> 300	> 300

added by 10^{-4}, one with the angle added by 10^{-7}. We note that this experimental setup is stronger than the one used in [41], where only two errors are considered: bit flip and phase shift without giving the shifting scale. We present a representative subset of equivalence checking results in Table 4. The complete results can be found in the extended version of this paper [35]. The first three columns list the number of qubits n and gates $|G|$ in original circuits, and the number of gates $|G'|$ in optimized circuits. Then we give the runtime of the weighted model counting tool `ECMC`, the decision diagram-based QCEC (DD) and the default setting of QCEC respectively. For the non-equivalent cases, we show the flipped-CNOT and one-gate-missing error in Table 5. The first three columns are the same as Table 4 and then the performance of all three tools on CNOT flipped error and one-gate-missing error respectively. Finally, Table 6 shows the performance of phase shift errors, where Shift-10^{-4} (resp. Shift-10^{-4}) denotes adding 10^{-4} (resp. 10^{-7}) to the phase of a random rotation gate.

Table 6. Results of verifying non-equivalence of circuits from MQT bench against optimized circuits with 10^{-4} size and 10^{-7} size phase shift in one random rotation gate. For cases within time limit, we give runtime (sec), while > 300 represents a timeout (5 min), "wrong" a wrong result and × that the results was 'unknown'.

Algorithm	n	$\|G\|$	$\|G'\|$	Shift-10^{-4}			Shift-10^{-7}		
				ECMC	QCEC (DD)	QCEC	ECMC	QCEC (DD)	QCEC
groundstate	4	180	36	0.26	Wrong	Wrong	Wrong	Wrong	Wrong
	12	1212	164	> 300	Wrong	Wrong	> 300	Wrong	Wrong
	14	1610	206	> 300	Wrong	Wrong	> 300	Wrong	Wrong
qaoa	7	133	117	0.15	0.03	×	0.15	> 300	×
	9	171	296	0.29	Wrong	×	0.32	> 300	×
	11	209	359	0.33	0.12	0.1	0.32	> 300	Wrong
qft	2	14	14	0.02	0.01	0.01	0.02	0.01	0.01å
	8	176	228	0.2	Wrong	×	0.21	> 300	×
	16	672	814	0.79	Wrong	×	0.92	> 300	×
qnn	2	43	36	0.04	Wrong	Wrong	0.04	Wrong	Wrong
	8	319	494	> 300	0.24	Wrong	> 300	56.55	×
	16	1023	2002	> 300	> 300	×	> 300	> 300	×
qpeinexact	16	712	848	8.59	> 300	×	11.9	> 300	×
	32	2712	3179	> 300	> 300	> 300	> 300	> 300	> 300
	64	10552	9695	> 300	> 300	> 300	> 300	> 300	> 300
routing	2	43	29	0.06	Wrong	Wrong	0.05	> 300	Wrong
	6	135	142	0.33	0.02	0.01	2.49	0.03	0.01
	12	273	409	144.3	0.05	0.03	> 300	0.09	0.04
wstate	16	271	242	0.33	12.85	×	0.23	11.67	×
	32	559	498	1.55	> 300	×	1.28	> 300	×
	64	1135	1010	5.4	> 300	> 300	5.24	> 300	> 300

Discussion. For random circuits, Fig. 1 shows that the runtime of ECMC exhibits a clear correlation with the size of the circuits. While QCEC and QCEC (DD) are very fast for small size circuits, for non-equivalent cases, both of them are less scalable and reach time limit much earlier than ECMC. For the equivalent cases, QCEC benefits from ZX calculus and outperforms the other two methods. We suspect that QCEC (DD) shows poor performance when solving random circuits because these circuits don't contain the structure found in quantum algorithms, which decision diagrams can typically exploit.

When considering structural quantum circuits, the results vary between equivalent and non-equivalent instances. For equivalent instances, QCEC (DD) significantly surpasses ECMC on Grover, QFT and QNN, primarily due to the decision diagram-based method's proficiency in handling circuits featuring repeated structures and oracles. While for those circuits featuring a large number of rotation gates with various rotation angles, like graphstate and wstate, ECMC demonstrates clear advantages. Moreover, the default QCEC is much faster than QCEC

(DD) on all cases while it reports "no information" for many cases as ZX calculus method and decision diagram method give different answers.

For non-equivalent instances, since ECMC can terminate when a single out of $2n$ WMC calls returns a negative result, it shows better performance than checking equivalence. For example, in the case of QPE, where both tools face time constraints when checking equivalent instances, ECMC can efficiently demonstrate non-equivalence and resolve the majority of cases within the time limit, while both QCEC and QCEC (DD) still get timeout in most instances.

In all instances, ECMC outperforms both QCEC and QCEC (DD) on graph state and wstate, each featuring many rotation gates. When dealing with rotation gates, decision diagrams might suffer from numerical instability [39,41], as can be clearly observed in Table 6 for the instances with errors in the phase shift, where both QCEC and QCEC (DD) get wrong results for many benchmarks. In contrast, the WMC approach—also numerical in nature—iteratively computes a sum of products, which we think avoids numerical instability. Table 6 also demonstrates this point as ECMC yields the correct answer for most benchmarks with 10^{-4} and 10^{-7}-size error. In contrast, the default QCEC gives no answer for a large amount of cases.

6 Related Work

Bauer et al. [3] verify quantum programs by encoding the verification problem in SMT, using an undecidable theory of nonlinear real arithmetic with trigonometric expressions. An SMT theory for quantum computing was proposed in [11]. Berent et al. [4] realize a Clifford circuit simulator and equivalence checker based on a SAT encoding. The equivalence checker was superseded by the deterministic polynomial-time algorithm proposed and implemented in [52]. Using weighted model counting, universal quantum circuit simulation is realized in [34], which we extend by providing encodings for the CZ and Toffoli gates and which we apply to circuit equivalence checking according to the approach of [52]. Amy [2] uses path integrals to check equivalence of circuits, which is complete for Clifford circuits and can prove equivalence of Clifford+T and Clifford+R circuits.

Yu and Palsberg [62] use an abstract interpretation to simulate quantum circuits. Abstraqt [5] improves upon this by using the stabilizer basis. SAT solvers have proven successful in quantum compilation [53], e.g., for reversible simulation of circuits [58] and optimizing space requirements of quantum circuits [36,45].

The ZX calculus [12] offers a diagrammatic approach to manipulate and analyze quantum circuits. A circuit is almost trivially expressible as a diagram, but the diagram language is more powerful and circuit extraction is consequently #P-complete [15]. It has proven enormously successful in applications from equivalence checking [41,42], to circuit optimization [28] and simulation [29].

Decision diagrams [37] have been used for simulating quantum circuits, checking their equivalence [8] and synthesis [64]. Jimenez et al. use bisimulation for circuit reduction, reducing simulation time compared to DDs in some cases [26].

7 Conclusions

We have shown circuit equivalence checking reduces to weighted model counting by considering quantum states in the Pauli basis, which allows for an efficient reduction of the equivalence checking problem to weighted model counting. We extended a linear-length encoding with the three-qubit Toffoli gate, so that most common non-Clifford gates are supported (previously the T, phase shift and rotation gates were already supported).

Given two n-qubit quantum circuits, their equivalence (up to global phase) can be decided by $2n$ calls to a weighted model counter, each with an encoding that is linear in the circuit size. Our open source implementation demonstrates that this technique is competitive to state-of-the-art methods based on a combination of decision diagrams and ZX calculus. This result demonstrates the strength of classical reasoning tools can transfer to the realm of quantum computing, despite the general 'quantum-hardness' of these problems. In future work, we plan to extract diagnostics for non-equivalent circuits from the satisfying assignments of the model counter.

References

1. Aaronson, S., Gottesman, D.: Improved simulation of stabilizer circuits. Phys. Rev. A **70**(5), 052328 (2004)
2. Amy, M.: Towards large-scale functional verification of universal quantum circuits. arXiv:1805.06908 (2018)
3. Bauer-Marquart, F., Leue, S., Schilling, C.: symQV: automated symbolic verification of quantum programs. In: Chechik, M., Katoen, J.-P., Leucker, M. (eds.) FM 2023. LNCS, vol. 14000, pp. 181–198. Springer, Cham (2023). https://doi.org/10.1007/978-3-031-27481-7_12
4. Berent, L., Burgholzer, L., Wille, R.: Towards a SAT encoding for quantum circuits: a journey from classical circuits to clifford circuits and beyond. In: SAT 2022. Schloss Dagstuhl - Leibniz-Zentrum für Informatik (2022)
5. Bichsel, B., Paradis, A., Baader, M., Vechev, M.: Abstraqt: analysis of quantum circuits via abstract stabilizer simulation. Quantum **7**, 1185 (2023)
6. Biere, A., Cimatti, A., Clarke, E.M., Strichman, O., Zhu, Y.: Bounded model checking. In: Handbook of Satisfiability, vol. 185, no. 99, pp. 457–481 (2009)
7. Biere, A., Heule, M., van Maaren, H., Walsh, T. (eds.) Handbook of Satisfiability. Frontiers in Artificial Intelligence and Applications, vol. 185. IOS Press (2009)
8. Burgholzer, L., Wille, R.: Advanced equivalence checking for quantum circuits. IEEE Trans. Comput. Aided Des. Integr. Circuits Syst. **40**(9), 1810–1824 (2021)
9. Calderbank, A.R., Shor, P.W.: Good quantum error-correcting codes exist. Phys. Rev. A **54**, 1098–1105 (1996)
10. Chavira, M., Darwiche, A.: On probabilistic inference by weighted model counting. Artif. Intell. **172**(6), 772–799 (2008)
11. Chen, Y.-F., Rümmer, P., Tsai, W.-L.: A theory of cartesian arrays (with applications in quantum circuit verification). In: Pientka, B., Tinelli, C. (eds.) CADE 2023. LNCS, pp. 170–189. Springer, Cham (2023). https://doi.org/10.1007/978-3-031-38499-8_10

12. Coecke, B., Duncan, R.: Interacting quantum observables: categorical algebra and diagrammatics. New J. Phys. **13**(4), 043016 (2011)
13. Cross, A., et al.: OpenQASM3: a broader and deeper quantum assembly language. ACM Trans. Quantum Comput. **3**(3), 1–50 (2022)
14. Dawson, C.M., Nielsen, M.A.: The Solovay-Kitaev algorithm. Quantum Inf. Comput. **6**(1), 81–95 (2006)
15. de Beaudrap, N., Kissinger, A., van de Wetering, J.: Circuit extraction for ZX-diagrams can be #P-hard. In: ICALP 2022. Schloss Dagstuhl - Leibniz-Zentrum für Informatik (2022)
16. Feng, N., Marsso, L., Sabetzadeh, M., Chechik, M.: Early verification of legal compliance via bounded satisfiability checking. In: Enea, C., Lal, A. (eds.) CAV 2023. LNCS, vol. 13966, pp. 374–396. Springer, Cham (2023). https://doi.org/10.1007/978-3-031-37709-9_18
17. Fisher, M.P.A., Khemani, V., Nahum, A., Vijay, S.: Random quantum circuits. Annu. Rev. Condens. Matter Phys. **14**(1), 335–379 (2023)
18. Gay, S.J.: Stabilizer states as a basis for density matrices. CoRR, abs/1112.2156 (2011)
19. Gomes, C.P., Sabharwal, A., Selman, B.: Model counting. In: Handbook of Satisfiability, pp. 993–1014. IOS Press (2021)
20. Gottesman, D.: Stabilizer codes and quantum error correction. Ph.D. thesis, California Institute of Technology (1997)
21. Hecher, M., Fichte, J.K.: Model counting competition 2023. https://mccompetition.org/. Accessed 07 Jan 2024
22. Hong, X., Feng, Y., Li, S., Ying, M.: Equivalence checking of dynamic quantum circuits. In: Proceedings of the 41st IEEE/ACM International Conference on Computer-Aided Design, ICCAD 2022. Association for Computing Machinery, New York (2022)
23. Hong, X., Ying, M., Feng, Y., Zhou, X., Li, S.: Approximate equivalence checking of noisy quantum circuits. In: 2021 58th ACM/IEEE Design Automation Conference (DAC), pp. 637–642 (2021)
24. Janzing, D., Wocjan, P., Beth, T.: "Non-identity-check" is QMA-complete. Int. J. Quantum Inf. **3**(03), 463–473 (2005)
25. Ji, Z., Wu, X.: Non-identity check remains QMA-complete for short circuits. arXiv:0906.5416 (2009)
26. Jiménez-Pastor, A., Larsen, K.G., Tribastone, M., Tschaikowski, M.: Forward and backward constrained bisimulations for quantum circuits (2024)
27. Jones, T.: Decomposing dense matrices into dense Pauli tensors. arXiv:2401.16378 (2024)
28. Kissinger, A., van de Wetering, J.: PyZX: large scale automated diagrammatic reasoning. In: QPL (2019)
29. Kissinger, A., van de Wetering, J.: Simulating quantum circuits with ZX-calculus reduced stabiliser decompositions. Quantum Sci. Technol. **7**(4), 044001 (2022). arXiv:2109.01076 [quant-ph]
30. Kitaev, A.Y.: Quantum computations: algorithms and error correction. Russ. Math. Surv. **52**(6), 1191 (1997)
31. Kitaev, A.Y., Shen, A., Vyalyi, M.N.: Classical and quantum computation. American Mathematical Society (2002)
32. Liu, Y.-K.: Consistency of local density matrices is QMA-complete. In: Díaz, J., Jansen, K., Rolim, J.D.P., Zwick, U. (eds.) APPROX/RANDOM -2006. LNCS, vol. 4110, pp. 438–449. Springer, Heidelberg (2006). https://doi.org/10.1007/11830924_40

33. McCluskey, E.J.: Minimization of boolean functions. Bell Syst. Tech. J. **35**(6), 1417–1444 (1956)
34. Mei, J., Bonsangue, M., Laarman, A.: Simulating quantum circuits by model counting. In: CAV 2024. Springer, Cham (2024, accepted for publication). Pre-print available at arXiv:2403.07197
35. Mei, J., Coopmans, T., Bonsangue, M., Laarman, A.: Equivalence checking of quantum circuits by model counting. arXiv preprint arXiv:2403.18813 (2024)
36. Meuli, G., Soeken, M., De Micheli, G.: SAT-based CNOT, T quantum circuit synthesis. In: Kari, J., Ulidowski, I. (eds.) RC 2018. LNCS, vol. 11106, pp. 175–188. Springer, Cham (2018). https://doi.org/10.1007/978-3-319-99498-7_12
37. Miller, D.M., Thornton, M.A.: QMDD: a decision diagram structure for reversible and quantum circuits. In: 36th International Symposium on Multiple-Valued Logic (ISMVL 2006), pp. 30–30 (2006)
38. Nielsen, M.A., Chuang, I.L.: Quantum Information and Quantum Computation, vol. 2, no. 8, p. 23. Cambridge University Press, Cambridge (2000)
39. Niemann, P., Zulehner, A., Drechsler, R., Wille, R.: Overcoming the tradeoff between accuracy and compactness in decision diagrams for quantum computation. IEEE Trans. Comput. Aided Des. Integr. Circuits Syst. **39**(12), 4657–4668 (2020)
40. Oztok, U., Darwiche, A.: A top-down compiler for sentential decision diagrams. In: SEA 2020, IJCAI 2015, pp. 3141–3148. AAAI Press (2015)
41. Peham, T., Burgholzer, L., Wille, R.: Equivalence checking of quantum circuits with the ZX-calculus. IEEE J. Emerg. Sel. Top. Circ. Syst. **12**(3), 662–675 (2022)
42. Peham, T., Burgholzer, L., Wille, R.: Equivalence checking of parameterized quantum circuits: verifying the compilation of variational quantum algorithms. In: 2023 28th Asia and South Pacific Design Automation Conference (ASP-DAC), pp. 702–708 (2023)
43. Quetschlich, N., Burgholzer, L., Wille, R.: MQT bench: benchmarking software and design automation tools for quantum computing. Quantum **7**, 1062 (2023)
44. Quine, W.V.: The problem of simplifying truth functions. Am. Math. Mon. **59**(8), 521–531 (1952)
45. Quist, A.-J., Laarman, A.: Optimizing quantum space using spooky pebble games. In: Kutrib, M., Meyer, U. (eds.) RC 2023. LNCS, vol. 13960, pp. 134–149. Springer, Cham (2023). https://doi.org/10.1007/978-3-031-38100-3_10
46. Raussendorf, R., Briegel, H.J.: A one-way quantum computer. Phys. Rev. Lett. **86**, 5188–5191 (2001)
47. Sang, T., Bacchus, F., Beame, P., Kautz, H.A., Pitassi, T.: Combining component caching and clause learning for effective model counting. In: International Conference on Theory and Applications of Satisfiability Testing (2004)
48. Shor, P.W.: Scheme for reducing decoherence in quantum computer memory. Phys. Rev. A **52**(4), R2493 (1995)
49. Steane, A.M.: Error correcting codes in quantum theory. Phys. Rev. Lett. **77**(5), 793 (1996)
50. Suzuki, R., Hashimoto, K., Sakai, M.: Improvement of projected model-counting solver with component decomposition using SAT solving in components. Technical report, JSAI Technical Report, SIG-FPAI-103-B506 (2017). (in Japanese)
51. Tanaka, Yu.: Exact non-identity check is NQP-complete. Int. J. Quantum Inf. **8**(05), 807–819 (2010)
52. Thanos, D., Coopmans, T., Laarman, A.: Fast equivalence checking of quantum circuits of Clifford gates. In: André, É., Sun, J. (eds.) ATVA 2023. LNCS, vol.

14216, pp. 199–216. Springer, Cham (2023). https://doi.org/10.1007/978-3-031-45332-8_10
53. Thanos, D., et al.: Automated reasoning in quantum circuit compilation. In: Model Checking Software (SPIN) 2024. Springer, Cham (2024, accepted for publication)
54. van den Nest, M.: Classical simulation of quantum computation, the gottesman-knill theorem, and slightly beyond. Quantum Inf. Comput. **10**(3), 258–271 (2010)
55. Viamontes, G.F., Markov, I.L., Hayes, J.P.: Checking equivalence of quantum circuits and states. In: 2007 IEEE/ACM International Conference on Computer-Aided Design, pp. 69–74 (2007)
56. Wang, S.-A., Lu, C.-Y., Tsai, I.-M., Kuo, S.-Y.: An XQDD-based verification method for quantum circuits. IEICE Trans. Fundam. Electron. Commun. Comput. Sci. **91**(2), 584–594 (2008)
57. Wei, C.-Y., Tsai, Y.-H., Jhang, C.-S., Jiang, J.-H.R.: Accurate BDD-based unitary operator manipulation for scalable and robust quantum circuit verification. In: Proceedings of the 59th ACM/IEEE Design Automation Conference, pp. 523–528 (2022)
58. Wille, R., Zhang, H., Drechsler, R.: ATPG for reversible circuits using simulation, Boolean satisfiability, and pseudo Boolean optimization. In: 2011 IEEE Computer Society Annual Symposium on VLSI, pp. 120–125 (2011)
59. Wright, J., et al.: Numerical simulations of noisy quantum circuits for computational chemistry. Mater. Theory **6**(1), 18 (2022)
60. Lin, X., Hutter, F., Hoos, H., Leyton-Brown, K.: SATzilla2009: an automatic algorithm portfolio for SAT. SAT **4**, 53–55 (2009)
61. Yamashita, S., Markov, I.L.: Fast equivalence-checking for quantum circuits. In: 2010 IEEE/ACM International Symposium on Nanoscale Architectures, pp. 23–28. IEEE (2010)
62. Yu, N., Palsberg, J.: Quantum abstract interpretation. In: Proceedings of the 42nd ACM SIGPLAN International Conference on Programming Language Design and Implementation, pp. 542–558 (2021)
63. Zhang, Y., Tang, Y., Zhou, Y., Ma, X.: Efficient entanglement generation and detection of generalized stabilizer states. Phys. Rev. A **103**, 052426 (2021)
64. Zulehner, A., Wille, R.: Improving synthesis of reversible circuits: exploiting redundancies in paths and nodes of QMDDs. In: Phillips, I., Rahaman, H. (eds.) RC 2017. LNCS, vol. 10301, pp. 232–247. Springer, Cham (2017). https://doi.org/10.1007/978-3-319-59936-6_18

Author Index

C. Benzmüller et al. (Eds.): IJCAR 2024, LNAI 14740, pp. 423–424, 2024.
https://doi.org/10.1007/978-3-031-63501-4

Printed in the United States
by Baker & Taylor Publisher Services